SEXUAL DEVIANCE

SEXUAL DEVIANCE

Theory, Assessment, and Treatment

SECOND EDITION

Edited by
D. RICHARD LAWS
WILLIAM T. O'DONOHUE

THE GUILFORD PRESS
New York   London

© 2008 The Guilford Press
A Division of Guilford Publications, Inc.
72 Spring Street, New York, NY 10012
www.guilford.com

Printed in the United States of America

This book is printed on acid-free paper.

Last digit is print number: 9 8 7 6 5 4 3 2 1

The authors have checked with sources believed to be reliable in their efforts to provide
information that is complete and generally in accord with the standards of practice that
are accepted at the time of publication. However, in view of the possibility of human
error or changes in medical sciences, neither the authors, nor the editor and publisher,
nor any other party who has been involved in the preparation or publication of this
work warrants that the information contained herein is in every respect accurate or
complete, and they are not responsible for any errors or omissions or the results obtained from the use of such information. Readers are encouraged to confirm the information contained in this book with other sources.

Library of Congress Cataloging-in-Publication Data

Sexual deviance : theory, assessment, and treatment / edited by D.
Richard Laws, William T. O'Donohue. — 2nd ed.
       p. ; cm.
   Includes bibliographical references and index.
   ISBN-13: 978-1-59385-605-2 (hardcover : alk. paper)
   ISBN-10: 1-59385-605-9 (hardcover : alk. paper)
   1. Sexual deviation. 2. Sex therapy. I. Laws, D. Richard. II. O'Donohue, William T.
   [DNLM: 1. Paraphilias—therapy. WM 610 S5155 2008]   `
   RC556.S4765 2008
   616.85′8306—dc22

                                                                    2007026806

ABOUT THE EDITORS

D. Richard Laws, PhD, received his doctorate from Southern Illinois University–Carbondale in 1969. He was the director of the Sexual Behavior Laboratory at Atascadero State Hospital in California from 1970 to 1985; project director at the Florida Mental Health Institute, Tampa, from 1985 to 1989; manager of forensic psychology at Alberta Hospital, Edmonton, Alberta, from 1989 to 1994; and a psychologist with Adult Forensic Psychiatric Community Services in Victoria, British Columbia, from 1994 until his retirement in 1999. He is presently the codirector of the Pacific Psychological Assessment Corporation and the director of Pacific Design Research in Victoria, British Columbia; an adjunct faculty member at Simon Fraser University, Burnaby, British Columbia; and Honourary Professor at the University of Birmingham, United Kingdom. Dr. Laws is past president of the Association for the Treatment of Sexual Abusers. He is known in the field of sexual deviance for his development of assessment procedures, program development, and evaluation. He is the author of numerous articles and book chapters in this area; serves on the editorial boards of several journals; and is the editor of *Relapse Prevention with Sex Offenders* (1989), coeditor with W. L. Marshall and H. E. Barbaree of *Handbook of Sexual Assault* (1990), coeditor with W. T. O'Donohue of the first edition of *Sexual Deviance* (1997), coeditor with S. M. Hudson and T. Ward of *Remaking Relapse Prevention with Sex Offenders* (2000), coeditor with T. Ward and S. M. Hudson of *Sexual Deviance: Issues and Controversies* (2003), and coeditor with D. Thornton of *Cognitive Approaches to the Assessment of Sexual Interest in Sexual Offenders* (2008).

William T. O'Donohue, PhD, received a doctorate in psychology from the State University of New York at Stony Brook and a master's degree in philosophy from Indiana University. He is a licensed clinical psychologist in Nevada, and since 1999 he has been a full Professor of Clinical Psychology at the University of Nevada, Reno. Dr. O'Donohue is a member of the Association for Behavioral and Cognitive Therapies and has served on the board of directors for this organization. Since 1996, he has received over $1.5 million in federal grant monies from sources including the National Institute of Mental Health and the National Institute of Justice. He has edited over 30 books, coauthored three books, and published more than 100 articles in scholarly journals.

CONTRIBUTORS

Fiona Ainsworth, MSc, Offending Behavior Programmes Unit, Her Majesty's Prison Service, London, United Kingdom

Zainab Al-Attar, PhD, Her Majesty's Prison Wymott, Preston, United Kingdom

Howard E. Barbaree, PhD, Department of Psychiatry, University of Toronto, Toronto, Ontario, Canada

Anthony R. Beech, DPhil, School of Psychology, University of Birmingham, Birmingham, United Kingdom

Ray Blanchard, PhD, Law and Mental Health Program, Centre for Addiction and Mental Health, Toronto, Ontario, Canada

Joseph A. Camilleri, MA, Department of Psychology, Queen's University, Kingston, Ontario, Canada

Rachael M. Collie, MA, School of Psychology, Victoria University of Wellington, Wellington, New Zealand

Franca Cortoni, PhD, School of Criminology, University of Montreal, Montreal, Quebec, Canada

Julie L. Crouch, PhD, Center for the Study of Family Violence and Sexual Assault, Northern Illinois University, DeKalb, Illinois

Shauna Darcangelo, PhD, Forensic Psychiatric Services Commission, Victoria Regional Program, Victoria, British Columbia, Canada

Margaret Davies, MSc, Her Majesty's Prison Usk and Prescoed, Usk, United Kingdom

David L. Delmonico, PhD, School of Education, Duquesne University, Pittsburgh, Pennsylvania

Cynthia A. Dopke, PhD, Department of Psychiatry and Behavioral Sciences, Feinberg School of Medicine, Northwestern University, Chicago, Illinois

Crissa Draper, BA, Department of Psychology, University of Nevada, Reno, Nevada

Hannah Ford, PsyD, School of Clinical Psychology, University of Birmingham, Birmingham, United Kingdom

Theresa A. Gannon, DPhil, Department of Psychology, University of Kent, Canterbury, United Kingdom

Elizabeth J. Griffin, MA, Internet Behavior Consulting, Eden Prairie, Minnesota

Don Grubin, MD, Department of Forensic Psychiatry, Newcastle University/
Northumberland Tyne and Wear NHS Trust, Newcastle upon Tyne, United Kingdom

Stephen D. Hart, PhD, Department of Psychology, Simon Fraser University, Burnaby,
British Columbia, Canada

Peggy Heil, MSW, Clinical Services Department, Colorado Department of Corrections,
Colorado Springs, Colorado

Alana Hollings, PsyD, Community Psychological Resources, Norfolk, Virginia

Stephen J. Hucker, MD, Law and Mental Health Program, Department of Psychiatry,
University of Toronto, Toronto, Ontario, Canada

Martin P. Kafka, MD, Department of Psychiatry, McLean Hospital, Harvard Medical
School, Belmont, Massachusetts

Meg S. Kaplan, PhD, Department of Psychiatry, College of Physicians and Surgeons,
Columbia University, New York, New York

Drew A. Kingston, BA, Department of Clinical Psychology, University of Ottawa, Ottawa,
Ontario, Canada

P. Randall Kropp, PhD, Forensic Psychiatric Services Commission, Vancouver,
British Columbia, Canada

Richard B. Krueger, MD, Department of Psychiatry, College of Physicians and Surgeons,
Columbia University, New York, New York

Michael Lavin, PhD, private practice, Washington, DC

D. Richard Laws, PhD, Pacific Psychological Assessment Corporation, Victoria,
British Columbia, Canada

Jill S. Levenson, PhD, LCSW, Department of Human Services, Lynn University,
Boca Raton, Florida

Caroline Logan, DPhil, Secure Psychological Services, Mersey Care NHS Trust, Ashworth
Hospital, Liverpool, United Kingdom

Patrick Lussier, PhD, School of Criminology, Simon Fraser University, Burnaby,
British Columbia, Canada

Ruth E. Mann, PhD, Offending Behavior Programmes Unit, Her Majesty's Prison Service,
London, United Kingdom

Joel S. Milner, PhD, Center for the Study of Family Violence and Sexual Assault,
Department of Psychology, Northern Illinois University, DeKalb, Illinois

John W. Morin, PhD, Center for Offender Rehabilitation and Education, Fort Lauderdale,
Florida

William D. Murphy, PhD, Department of Psychiatry, University of Tennessee Health
Sciences Center, Memphis, Tennessee

Kirk A. B. Newring, PhD, Nebraska Department of Correctional Services, Lincoln,
Nebraska

William T. O'Donohue, PhD, Department of Psychology, University of Nevada, Reno,
Nevada

I. Jacqueline Page, PsyD, Department of Psychiatry, University of Tennessee, Memphis,
Tennessee

Gabrielle Paladino, MD, Atascadero State Hospital, Atascadero, California; private
practice, Fresno, California

Tamara M. Penix, PhD, Department of Psychology, Eastern Michigan University, Ypsilanti,
Michigan

Lyne Piché, PhD, Correctional Service of Canada, Abbotsford, British Columbia, Canada

Ethel Quayle, PsychD, Department of Applied Psychology, University College Cork, Cork, Ireland

Vernon L. Quinsey, PhD, Department of Psychology, Queen's University, Kingston, Ontario, Canada

Michael C. Seto, PhD, Department of Psychiatry and Centre of Criminology, University of Toronto, Toronto, Ontario, Canada

Dominique Simons, MA, Colorado Department of Corrections, Canon City, Colorado

Jo Thakker, PhD, Department of Psychology, University of Waikato, Hamilton, New Zealand

Tony Ward, PhD, Department of Psychology, Victoria University of Wellington, Wellington, New Zealand

Jennifer Wheeler, PhD, private practice, Seattle, Washington

Pamela M. Yates, PhD, Cabot Consulting and Research Services, Ottawa, Ontario, Canada

CONTENTS

Contents

CHAPTER 1

INTRODUCTION

D. RICHARD LAWS
WILLIAM T. O'DONOHUE

The professional approach to sexual deviance involves the scientific study of the paraphilias and related sexual misbehaviors (e.g., rape), as well as the clinical assessment and treatment of these domains. In this chapter we briefly overview the major issues involved in the scientific study and clinical treatment of sexual deviance.

DEFINITIONAL ISSUES

Problems with Defining Sexual Deviance as Mental Disorder

There are continuing controversies about what constitutes "sexual deviance." The present book generally follows the *Diagnostic and Statistical Manual of Mental Disorders*, fourth edition, text revision (DSM-IV-TR; American Psychiatric Association, 2000), although admittedly this is ultimately an institutional rather than a scientific resolution to the definitional problem. That is, the American Psychiatric Association—by working committee, and ultimately by a vote of its membership—decides both what kinds of sexual behaviors are considered mental disorders, and the specific criteria to be used in attempting to define these demarcations. This is in stark distinction to the chemists' periodic table of elements, which is a taxonomy that carves nature at its joints. There are no votes by the American Chemical Association to determine whether oxygen or hydrogen is inside or outside this taxonomy. Committees, of course, are not carving nature at its joints. They instead are subject to political, personal, and other extrascientific considerations. Various editions of the DSM have included as paraphilias different entities (such as homosexuality), and have used different diagnostic criteria. In addition, controversies continue. For example, there is no explicit paraphilia that directly covers rape; some who commit rape may meet the current diagnostic criteria for sexual sadism, but many do not. Whether this is a gap is debatable.

The DSM-IV-TR offers a general definition of "mental disorder," which presumably all paraphilic diagnoses must meet:

A clinically significant behavioral or psychological syndrome or pattern that occurs in an individual and that is associated with present distress (e.g., a painful symptom) or disability (i.e., impairment in one of more important areas of functioning) or with a significantly increased risk of suffering death, pain, disability, or an important loss of freedom. In addition, this syndrome or pattern must not be merely an expectable and culturally sanctioned response to a particular event, for example, the death of a loved one. Whatever its original cause, it must currently be considered a manifestation of a behavioral, psychological, or biological dysfunction in the individual. Neither deviant behavior (e.g., political, religious, *or sexual*) nor conflicts that are primarily between the individual and society are mental disorders unless the deviance or conflict is a symptom of a dysfunction in the individual, as described above. (American Psychiatric Association, 2000, p. xxxi; emphasis added)

This definition raises the question of whether deviant sexual behavior "is a symptom of a dysfunction in the individual, as described above." Apparently, the American Psychiatric Association thinks so, as it includes in the DSM-IV-TR a number of paraphilias. However, nowhere does it explicitly state exactly how the included categories meet this standard, or why some categories such as rape or homosexuality do not. Thus the principles used to make decisions regarding what should be included and what should be excluded are unclear. This is unfortunate, because if they were explicated not only would the taxonomy seem more open and reasoned, but it could be criticized and thus potentially improved.

Value Judgments and Sexual Liberation Movements

We also need to recognize that a somewhat complex issue involves value judgments that a type of sexual behavior is disordered or deviant. Certain value judgments have at times flown and continue to fly in the face of various "sexual liberation" movements that have been prominent in the past century. To some extent, these have probably been inspired by what happened with the diagnostic category of homosexuality. In some earlier editions of the DSM, homosexuality was regarded as sexual deviance, but after some effective political campaigning (and some rather weak scientific study) it was removed. In the first edition of this book, the authors of one chapter took issue with the view of sexual masochism as deviant (Baumeister & Butler, 1997).

One of the best-known current sexual liberation movements is the pedophilic one. It has previously received endorsements from such prominent sex researchers as Alfred Kinsey and John Money. For example, Kinsey, Pomeroy, Martin, and Gebhard (1953) stated:

When children are constantly warned by parents and teachers against contacts with adults, and when they receive no explanation of the exact nature of the contacts, they are ready to become hysterical as soon as any older person approaches, or stops and speaks to them in the street, or fondles them, or proposes to do something for them, even though the adult may have had no sexual objective in mind. Some of the more experienced students of juvenile problems have come to believe that the emotional reactions of the parents, police officers, and other adults who discover that the child has had such a contact, may disturb the child more seriously than the sexual contacts themselves. The current hysteria over sex offenders may very well have serious effects on the ability of many of these children to work out sexual adjustments some years later. . . . (p. 122)

John Money (1991), the prominent Johns Hopkins sex therapist (although see Colapinto, 2000), said:

> If I were to see the case of a boy aged ten or eleven who's intensely erotically attracted toward a man in his twenties or thirties, if the relationship is totally mutual, and the bonding is genuinely totally mutual . . . then I would not call it pathological in any way. (p. 3)

Groups such as the North American Man/Boy Love Association (NAMBLA) and the René Guyon Society describe themselves as representing the most recent wave of sexual liberation. Typically they assert that the first wave of sexual liberation was women's sexual liberation, that the second was liberation associated with the acceptance of premarital sex, and that the third was gay liberation. For example, a speech posted first on the NAMBLA website and then elsewhere on the Internet asserts the following regarding "cross-generational love":

> The issue of love between men and boys has intersected the gay movement since the late nineteenth century, with the rise of the first gay rights movement in Germany. In the United States, as the gay movement has retreated from its vision of sexual liberation, in favor of integration and assimilation into existing social and political structures, it has increasingly sought to marginalize even demonize cross-generational love. Pederasty—that is, love between a man and a youth of 12 to 18 years of age—say middle-class homosexuals, lesbians, and feminists, has nothing to do with gay liberation. Some go so far as to claim, absurdly, that it is a heterosexual phenomenon, or even "sexual abuse." What a travesty! (Thorstad, 1998)

Mary DeYoung (1989) has analyzed the literature produced by pedophile organizations, and has found the use of the following persuasion strategies:

1. Adoption of value-neutral terminology.
2. Redefining the term "child sexual abuse" (to terms such as "adult–child sex" or even "intergenerational intimacy").
3. Promoting the idea that children can consent to sex with adults.
4. Questioning the assumption of harm.
5. Promoting "objective" research (as opposed to the research produced by "biased" researchers).
6. Declassification of pedophilia as mental illness.

This sort of thinking has also received some agreement from a few current researchers, such as Theo Sandfort of the Netherlands. Sandfort was one of the editors of the Dutch journal *Paidika: The Journal of Paedophilia*, which advocated adult–child sexual contact. Sandfort (1982) has stated that when he gave a screening questionnaire to a small group of boys who reported sexual contact with adults, "the question was whether a sexual contact with an adult could be a positive experience for a child. To the extent to which this research material can give a definite answer, the question must be answered in the affirmative" (p. 84). O'Donohue (1992) has criticized Sandfort's research and conclusions, on the grounds that both the psychometrics of the clinical screening scales he used and his reasoning are problematic. Sandfort's research is based on utilitarian ethics: One has to show harm to render a negative moral evaluation. Sandfort seems oblivious to duty-based ethics or voluntariness-based ethics. O'Donohue has argued that (1) Sandfort's methodology is insufficient to detect all possible harm; (2) children do not by definition have the cognitive capacity to enter into negotiations with adults regarding sexual contact; and (3) adults have the duty to protect and not to harm children, and sexual contact can be harmful to children in a variety of ways. Based on these three considerations, O'Donohue has argued that there is no "sexual liberation" associated with pedophilia, but rather just a problematic argument that has the potential to do much harm. Nevertheless, in 2003 Sandfort was elected president of the International Academy of Sex Research.

In conclusion, professionals in this field need to be aware of these "liberation" movements and these debates, as their arguments and evidence at first blush can seem to have some merit. There is certainly no consensus regarding such definitional issues. However, much is at stake concerning these issues, and open consideration and clarity are important.

Problems with the Current Diagnostic Criteria

O'Donohue, Regev, and Hagstrom (2000) criticized the 1994 DSM-IV diagnostic criteria for pedophilia—and, by extension, the criteria for all the paraphilias, because of their similar structure—on a number of grounds. In DSM-IV, Criterion B for all paraphilias was "The behavior, sexual urges, or fantasies cause clinically significant distress or impairment in social, occupational, or other important areas of functioning" (American Psychiatric Association, 1994, p. 523). O'Donohue and colleagues suggested that this would allow the contented pedophile who has not acted on his urges[1] to avoid the diagnoses. Although the DSM-IV-TR was supposed to make no changes in diagnostic criteria, the editors *have* changed the diagnostic criteria for pedophilia and all the other paraphilias that involve a nonconsenting person, so that acting on the urges alone currently meets Criterion B. Although this change is a significant improvement, many problems still remain:

1. The interdiagnostician reliability of all the paraphilic diagnoses is still unknown.
2. There is still much vagueness in the criteria (e.g., what is meant by "recurrent" and "intense" in Criterion A for these diagnoses?).
3. There is significant arbitrariness in the Criterion A specification that the person must experience a paraphilia for 6 months before a diagnosis is made. What is the argument or evidence that this time frame is reasonable?

MEASUREMENT ISSUES

Measurement is a fundamental process and skill in both research and clinical endeavors. The task of accurate measurement is not easily achieved in any domain, but it may be particularly difficult with regard to sexual deviance.

Sensitivity and Specificity

Scientists rely on measurement for several basic goals. First, scientists want to be able to accurately detect the presence or absence of something (e.g., does this person experience violent fantasies?). An accurate instrument is characterized by both "sensitivity" and "specificity." Sensitivity is a quality metric that addresses the question "If X is present, to what extent will the measurement operation detect X?" Another way to look at sensitivity is that it is an index of false negatives. Specificity is the converse; it addresses the question "If X is *not* present, to what extent will the measurement process indicate that it is not present?" Specificity is a measure of false positives. We want our measurements to detect as accurately as possible—that is, with no false negatives and no false positives. Often, although not always, there is a tradeoff between these two attributes. When we make our measure more sensitive, we also "buy" more false positives.

Detection of phenomena related to sexual deviance may be difficult because the target may be covert (e.g., fantasies), and/or because a person may have an interest in providing distorted information (as is usually the case when a person has been arrested for a sexual offense). In our field, we need to know through careful scientific psychometric studies the specificity and sensitivity of our measures, as much can ride on false positives or false negatives. In too many cases, this information is missing; despite this important gap, such instruments are often still used.

Quantification

In addition to presence or absence, some phenomena allow for quantification. Height is not simply present in people; it can be quantified. Thus another measurement task is to accurately measure quantity. Sometimes, though, it can be difficult to discern what the underlying scale would be. Sex drive seems to be not simply present or absent; it seems to have magnitude. But what scale is to be used? This is a complex question (e.g., would men and women use the same scale, or are their sex drives so different in some basic way as to require separate scales?). Quantification is important because many of the questions we are interested in depend on it. Clinically, we are often interested in reducing (or eliminating) some phenomena and thus are interested in quantity.

Evidence-Based Assessment

It is axiomatic in psychometrics that all measures contain error. The keys are to try to estimate or understand the size of the error term, and to consider this in all inferences and decisions based on the assessment. These are among the aims of a recent movement called "evidence-based assessment." Hunsley and Mash (2005) define this movement as follows:

> First, research findings and scientifically viable theories on both psychopathology and normal human development should be used to guide the selection of constructs to be assessed and the assessment process.
>
> Second, as much as possible, psychometrically strong measures should be used to assess the constructs targeted in the assessment. Specifically, these measures should have replicated evidence of reliability, validity, and, ideally, clinical utility. Given the range of purposes for which assessment instruments can be used (e.g., screening, diagnosis, treatment monitoring) and the fact that psychometric evidence is always conditional (based on sample characteristics and assessment purpose), supporting psychometric evidence must be available for each purpose for which an instrument or assessment strategy is used. Psychometrically strong measures must also possess appropriate norms for norm-referenced interpretation and/or replicated supporting evidence for the accuracy (i.e.,

sensitivity, specificity, predictive power, etc) of cut-scores for criterion-referenced inter-pretation.

Third, although at present little evidence bears on the issue, it is critical that the entire process of assessment (i.e., selection, use and interpretation of an instrument, and integration of multiple sources of assessment data) be empirically evaluated. In other words, a critical distinction must be made between evidence-based assessment methods and tools, on the one hand, and evidence-based assessment processes, on the other. (p. 251)

The question then arises: How do these general principles apply to measurement instruments used for the paraphilias? The chapters that follow can help in the first task: identifying key constructs to be measured. However, the reader will see that there are no well-corroborated accounts of the psychopathology involved in the paraphilias. In addition, too little is known about "normal" sexuality and sexual development. Thus, again, there are gaps in what constructs ought to be measured. The reader will also see key gaps in the second defining characteristic of evidence-based assessment: Much psychometric information regarding accuracy is missing for our existing measures, and in particular the clinical utility and incremental validity of measures are missing. Finally, there are few guidelines or studies showing how multiple pieces of assessment data ought to be integrated and interpreted. Much work needs to be done regarding this, but we strongly recommend that the field embrace the value of moving toward evidence-based assessment and begin to do so.

A Diagnostic Example of Measurement Difficulties

The diagnostic criteria for exhibitionism are as follows (American Psychiatric Association, 2000, p. 569):

> A. Over a period of at least 6 months, recurrent, intense sexually arousing fantasies, sexual urges, or behaviors involving the exposure of one's genitals to an unsuspecting stranger.
> B. The person has acted on these sexual urges, or the sexual urges or fantasies cause marked distress or interpersonal difficulty.

Note all the constructs that must be measured with accuracy just to make this diagnosis:

1. Incidence during a 6-month period.
2. Recurrence (of "sexually arousing fantasies, sexual urges, or behaviors . . . ").
3. Intensity (of "sexually arousing fantasies, sexual urges, or behaviors . . . ").
4. Fantasies.
5. Sexual urges.
6. Sexual behaviors.
7. Exposure of one's genitals.
8. Unsuspectingness of the stranger.
9. "Stranger" status.
10. Whether the person has acted on these urges.
11. Marked distress (including causal nexus).
12. Interpersonal difficulty (including causal nexus).

The reader is referred to the relevant chapter in this volume (see Morin & Levenson, Chapter 5), but one can already perceive that even the diagnostic task (let alone the assessment tasks involved with treatment or comorbidity) is difficult, given the present psychometric status of our assessment instruments.

TREATMENT STATUS

Continuing Problems

We would very much like to be optimistic about the future of diagnosing and treating sexual deviance. As a basis for some such optimism, we believe that this volume is in many ways a considerable improvement over the first edition. However, many of the deficiencies we noted in 1997 remain. As editors of a popular book that will be widely read and frequently consulted, it is our duty to point some of these out.

If we examine the results of treatment outcome research (such as it is), we find that there are three outstanding problem areas. First and foremost, there are what we term "orphaned treatment problems." These are problems in outcome that result from the fact that there is simply not enough information to make a judgment about what does and does not work. Outcome research in this field can be very tough to conduct. Obtaining an adequate sample size can be difficult, as can training therapists and ensuring treatment fidelity. Following up patients for several years (5 is good) also contrives to make this quite difficult. But, most of all, many paraphilias are orphaned because there is little federal or private money to conduct this research. At times there is a conflict between the apparent societal importance of overcoming these problems, and the actual amount of funding available to accomplish this goal. It might be useful for an influential organization such as the Association for the Treatment of Sexual Abusers (ATSA) to publish total dollars available for this type of research and where it is going. Advocacy, in which we clearly inform decision makers about this issue is critical. If this is not done, and done effectively, then 10 years from now when the third edition of this volume comes out, we will find the same orphans.

Second, there are far from enough positive findings regarding treatment outcome that are encouraging. The most optimistic of these findings come from meta-analytic studies (e.g., Hanson & Harris, 2001; Hanson et al., 2002; Lösel & Schmucker, 2005), although specific information on various treatment interventions is available (e.g., Marshall, Anderson, & Fernandez, 1999; Marshall, Fernandez, Marshall, & Serran, 2006; Ward et al., 2004; Ward, Yates, & Long, 2006). However, much information is still missing. Paul (1967) posed the great question: "What treatment, by whom, is most effective for this individual, with that specific problem, under which set of circumstances, and how does it come about?" We can identify several gaps in our knowledge base:

1. What treatments have sufficient evidence even to be viable candidates for "evidence-based practice"? (This admittedly presupposes the question of what standards of evidence ought to be employed.)
2. What therapist variables are critical? Is a graduate degree necessary? Is competence in some circumscribed skill set required? Are the "nonspecifics" important, and if so, how important? Does therapist competence "drift" or degrade over time? What do we know about efficacy trials versus effectiveness trials?
3. What about individual differences and treatment prescriptiveness? Is comorbidity a particular problem? What do good case formulation and treatment planning re-

quire when there are other problems present (e.g., substance abuse, depression, anger, attention-deficit/hyperactivity disorder [ADHD], social skill deficits)?

4. What other circumstances are relevant (legal status, social support, prison vs. out-patient treatment, etc.)?

5. What exactly are the key active ingredients in our treatment successes? We are still at the stage of too little outcome research, and we have virtually no process research.

In addition, there are important pragmatic questions. First, what is the financial case for treatment? Can we show that it is the most economical alternative? How much exactly does successful treatment cost? We want someone (usually a third party such as the government) to pay the bill, but we have been none too clear about what the bill is, or what value the payer receives. Finally, there is an important question of access: How many competent treatment programs are there now, and how can we disseminate these so more (or all) sex offenders have access to competent treatment? This is a very tough problem.

Third, there are also some very important negative findings about treatment outcome (e.g., Berliner, 2002; Marques, Nelson, Wiederanders, & Day, 2002; Marques, Wiederanders, Day, Nelson, & van Ommeren, 2005; Schweitzer & Dwyer, 2003), and these have had a major impact upon the field. The long-term implications of these findings have, at this writing, been largely ignored or too quickly explained away. Science must weigh negative findings with positive findings (see, e.g., Karl Popper's work on falsification; Popper, 1959). Science is, in essence, an attempt to mitigate our confirmation biases. When well-controlled negative research such as that of Marques and colleagues (2005) is published, it must be scrutinized honestly. This very elegantly designed research gives rise to this question: Is relapse prevention still to be considered an empirically supported treatment?

Examination of the clinical chapters in this volume subtitled "Psychopathology and Theory" shows that the etiology of most paraphilias remains informative but largely speculative. Examination of the chapters subtitled "Assessment and Treatment" tells the tale of where we stand today in these areas. Anyone who has worked in this business for a number of years knows that most clinical attention in sexual deviance treatment is devoted to the three (supposedly) major forms of sexual deviance: pedophilia, rape, and exhibitionism. The remaining paraphilias that we have chosen to include in this volume are the ones that we term "orphans": fetishism, frotteurism, sadism, masochism (considered by some not to be a paraphilia, as noted earlier; see Baumeister & Butler, 1997), transvestism, voyeurism, and the catch-all category of paraphilia not otherwise specified. This was essentially the state of affairs in 1997 when the first edition of this volume appeared, and not much has changed in the ensuing years.

How Should Outcome Research Be Guided?

The problems described above can be solved, although not easily, and probably not in the very near term. If we were to attack the problem of not knowing enough about how to treat either the major or minor paraphilias across the board, we would have to resort to a structure such as the Chambless and Hollon (1998) criteria for "empirically supported therapies" (ESTs). The criteria were described by their authors as "a scheme . . . for determining when a psychological treatment for a specific problem or disorder may be considered to be established in efficacy or to be possibly efficacious" (p. 7). Treatments so established are referred to as ESTs and are defined by Chambless and Hollon (1998, p. 7) as "clearly specified psychological treatments shown to be efficacious in controlled research with a delineated population." These criteria were designed for application to more common clinical syndromes (e.g., anxiety, depression, phobia) than sexual deviance, and might have to be slightly modified to be made applicable to the paraphilias. Nevertheless, it is worth summarizing these criteria at some length.[2] The Chambless and Hollon criteria consider the evaluation of treatment outcome research in terms of two major characteristics: (1) "treatment efficacy" (can the treatment be shown to work in controlled research?) and (2) "treatment effectiveness" (does it work in actual clinical practice?).

Efficacy

1. *Overall research design.* Treatment efficacy must be demonstrated in controlled research where we can conclude that the benefits observed are due to the treatment and not to chance or confounding factors. This is best accomplished in randomized clinical trials or carefully controlled single-case design experiments. Replication is critical, particularly by an independent research team. If the treatment is found to be efficacious in at least two studies by independent research terms its efficacy is said to be established. If efficacy is supported by only one study, the findings are considered to be promising.

2. *Comparisons with no treatment.* A treatment is compared with a type of minimal or no-treatment condition (waiting list or assessment only control). If two or more studies conducted by independent research teams show that the treatment is more beneficial than no treatment (and these findings are not contradicted by others) the treatment is considered to be efficacious. Evidence of specificity of effect is typically not required.

3. *Comparisons with other treatments or placebo.* Treatments found to be superior to conditions that control for nonspecific processes (e.g., attention) or to another treatment are said to be efficacious and specific in their mechanism of action.

4. *Combination treatments.* A typical study of combination treatments might involve comparison of a multiple component treatment and one or more of its individual parts.

5. *Sample description.* If outcome research is to be informative, it is essential that researchers clearly define the population for which the treatment was designed and tested. The question here is not just whether the treatment is efficacious, but whether it is efficacious for a specific problem or population.

6. *Outcome assessment selection of instruments.* These tools must evaluate significant dimensions of the problem. They must have demonstrated validity and reliability in previous research. Reliance solely on self-report should be avoided. Some indices lack psychometric properties but have high face validity (e.g., number of arrests, days in jail). It would be desirable if instruments could go beyond merely the effects of treatment and examine more general measures of functioning and quality of life.

7. *Follow-up.* Information on the long-term effects of treatment is rarely found. It is important to know if different treatments differ with respect to their stability over time. It is not clear how long follow-ups should be maintained.

8. *Clinical significance.* It is not enough that treatment effects be shown to be statistically significant. They must be large enough to be clinically useful and meaningful.

9. *Treatment implementation/Treatment manuals.* Outcome research is not informative if clinicians do not know what treatment was tested. Undefined treatment interventions cannot be replicated. At minimum, manuals should clearly and explicitly

describe the kinds of techniques and strategies that constitute the intervention. These may be highly detailed or provide general but clear guidelines.

10. *Therapist training and monitoring.* A particular treatment may fail to impress not because it lacked efficacy but because it was poorly implemented as a result of inadequate training or supervision. When there are specific interventions to learn, training matters. Measurement of the *quality* of implementation is not an area that is well understood.

11. *Investigator allegiance.* Any given therapy will tend to do better in comparison with other interventions when it is conducted by people who are expert in its use. For comparison purposes, allegiances cannot be eliminated but they can be balanced.

12. *Single-case experiments.* The principles listed above all apply to single-case designs. However, there are some special issues applying only to these approaches.

   a. *Establishing a stable baseline.* The baseline serves as the comparison condition that controls for the effects of assessment and the passage of time and that, depending on the nature of the baseline (no intervention vs. control intervention), may control for expectancy, attention, and the like.

   b. *Acceptable designs.* There are two.
      i. *ABAB design.* A is the baseline, B is the treatment.
      ii. *Multiple baseline.* Variations include multiple baselines across behaviors, settings, and participants.

   c. *Efficacy in single-case experiments.* Treatment is considered to be efficacious if it has proved beneficial to at least three participants in research by a single group. Multiple replications (a least three each) by two or more independent research groups would be needed to consider the efficacy of the treatment to be established.

   d. *Interpretation of results.* Data are usually interpreted visually because effects are often so striking that they are readily convincing to the naked eye.

   e. *Conflicting results.* If a group of well-designed studies point to one conclusion and poorly designed studies point to another, the former will be chosen. In a group of studies with roughly comparable methodological rigor, the question is whether the preponderance of the studies point to efficacy. Meta-analyses are useful but they can obscure qualitative differences. Therefore it is necessary to know something about the standards for the quality of studies included in the analysis.

Effectiveness

1. *Generalizability across populations.* Can the results of randomized controlled trials really be trusted? It is widely believed that participants in stringently controlled outcome research are less complex and easier to treat because they have been selected to have specific characteristics and do not resemble the ordinary client seen in typical clinical settings.

2. *Generalizability across therapists and settings.* Therapists working in controlled trials may have received a level of training and supervision not typically available to the average practitioner. Another problem is that the act of controlling treatment alters its nature and threatens the practical utility of the obtained results. Those studies that, as closely as possible, reproduce the conditions found in actual clinical practice are most likely to produce findings that generalize to those settings. Efficacy is one thing; whether it works in a naturalistic setting is another.

3. *Patient acceptance and compliance.* When treatment options are offered, clients may be expected to choose the easier, less demanding option rather than the more effec-

tive but arduous intervention. Many clients do not benefit from treatment because they are unable or unwilling to stick to the required regimen.

4. *Ease of dissemination*. Treatments that are straightforward and easy to learn are more likely to be disseminated to the larger practice community.
5. *Cost effectiveness*. Those treatments that cost the least are likely to be preferred if there is no great difference in outcome.

We have presented the Chambless and Hollon (1998) criteria in some detail for a very good reason: The status of treatment outcome research in the field of sexual deviance, with very few exceptions, is quite discouraging. Almost none of the studies published would begin to meet these quite reasonable criteria.

Positive Outcome Research Findings

There are unquestionably numerous reports in the literature that show positive effects for the psychological treatment of sex offenders—far too many to attempt to summarize here. What can be said about them is that they typically are not large-scale investigations and rarely are able to show that a specific intervention is effective with a specific population.

For decades, reports have been appearing piecemeal that describe the success (as well as the indifferent performance) of sex offender treatment programs. These typically take the form of comprehensive reviews (e.g., Craig, Browne, & Stringer, 2003; Furby, Weinrott, & Blackshaw, 1989), reports on single programs (Marshall et al., 1999; McGrath, Cumming, Livingston, & Hoke, 2003; Pithers, Martin, & Cumming, 1989), or reports on multisite programs (Friendship, Mann, & Beech, 2003). Craig and colleagues (2003) make two essential points regarding evaluation of sex offender treatment:

1. Methodological differences in treatment and recidivism research make it difficult to assess treatment efficacy, ultimately affecting predictive accuracy of recidivism.
2. There is a small but increasing number of treatment and meta-analytic studies using robust methodologies that demonstrate positive treatment effects.

Craig and colleagues are referring to a meta-analysis performed by Hanson and colleagues (2000; Hanson & Harris, 2001). The Hanson and colleagues analysis evaluated a combined sample of rapists and pedophiles (*N* = 9,454). Average follow-up time was 4–5 years. According to Hanson and colleagues (2002), treatments provided prior to 1980 were not shown to be effective. Current treatments were associated with a significant reduction in sexual recidivism (from 17% to 20%). Cognitive-behavioral treatments (undefined) proved to be the most effective with adult offenders. Programs delivered in institutions were as effective as community programs. Hanson (2002) listed the policy implications of this meta-analysis:

1. Treatment programs contribute to public safety by reducing the risk of sexual recidivism.
2. Not all treatment programs are effective. Before deciding that an offender's risk has been reduced by treatment, evaluators need to consider the nature and quality of the treatment provided.
3. Training and supervision efforts should focus on those treatments that have the strongest evidence for effectiveness (i.e., cognitive-behavioral).

4. No treatment program can guarantee a complete cessation of offending. They are simply one element in a comprehensive risk management strategy.

More recently, Lösel and Schmucker (2005) examined 69 studies ($N > 22,000$). They used a broad definition of "recidivism," ranging from incarceration to lapses in behavior. Their analysis revealed a 11% recidivism rate for treated offenders and a 17.5% rate in comparison groups. They concluded that treatment had a substantial effect upon sexual recidivism. As in the earlier Hanson and colleagues (2002) meta-analysis, Lösel and Schmucker found that cognitive-behavioral interventions produced the greatest impact.

Negative Outcome Research Findings

Despite the positive findings noted above, many researchers are quite pessimistic regarding the efficacy of sexual offender treatment. They argue that there is simply no good evidence that treatment of any sort is effective with sex offenders, and in particular that the effectiveness of psychological treatment for sex offenders remains to be demonstrated (see, e.g., Camilleri & Quinsey, Chapter 11, this volume; Rice & Harris, 2003).

There is certainly evidence that might discourage the most optimistic among clinicians and researchers.[3] Perhaps the outstanding example is the Sex Offender Treatment and Evaluation Project (SOTEP) (Marques, Day, Nelson, & Miner, 1989; Marques, Nelson, Alarcon, & Day, 2000), funded by the state of California from 1985 to 1995. This was thought by many to be the gold standard of sex offender treatment. Using a relapse prevention model (see Laws, 1989, 2003), this was a major attempt at empirical validation. SOTEP followed treatment completers, dropouts, and nonparticipants for nearly a decade after the program terminated. By 1999 a treatment effect had not yet emerged. Marques and colleagues (2000, 2002) continued to report this fact; they termed it "unanticipated." By 2005 it was all over. Marques and colleagues (2005), in a final report, stated that no significant differences were found among the three groups in their rates of sexual or violent offending over an 8-year follow-up period. The researchers found this null result for both rapists and child molesters, using time to reoffense as the outcome and controlling for static risk differences across the groups. The best face that could be put on these disappointing results was that those offenders who had closely adhered to the program's relapse prevention model had lower reoffense rates than those who did not.

Over the past 20 years, SOTEP has been imprinted upon the literature. Rice and Harris (2003, p. 443) stated that SOTEP was "the most well-designed and executed study the sex offender field has ever seen or is likely to see for some time." Berliner (2002) wrote the epitaph for SOTEP and perhaps for the classical model of relapse prevention as well:

> It should not be overlooked that the most well designed and executed study, the California . . . study that used random assignment, that included volunteers and nonvolunteers, that implemented a state of the art intervention program, that had a follow-up treatment component, and that calculated recidivism in the most comprehensive way found no significant effects for treatment. (pp. 196–197)

Given these appalling results, it is difficult not to conclude that something is very wrong here. The most stringent experimental design—the vaunted randomized controlled group comparison that is repeatedly recommended—proved unable to demonstrate a treatment effect over a period now exceeding 10 years.

This is not a one-off, unexplainable event. In 2003 Schweitzer and Dwyer reported a very similar outcome evaluation in Australia. The design was very like that of SOTEP; it contained the typical cognitive-behavioral components, including relapse prevention. The Australian study examined outcome for three groups: completers, dropouts, and nonparticipants. As in SOTEP, no differences in recidivism were found over an average at-risk period of 5 years.

When it became apparent that SOTEP was going to fail, one of us (D. Richard Laws) contacted R. Karl Hanson and simply asked him whether he really believed that sex offender treatment was effective. He replied in so many words that there was evidence that treatment was effective, but that the evidence was not strong. Laws contacted Hanson again in late 2006 and asked the same question. Hanson replied (personal communication, October 10, 2006):

> My reading of the literature is that certain forms of psychological intervention can be effective in reducing the sexual and general recidivism rate of sexual offenders. The evidence is stronger now than it was five years ago but it is still not strong. Reasonable people can read the literature and come to different conclusions. I think they are mistaken, but I don't think they are irrational.

And, of course, another question can be asked: What is the magnitude of the effect? We want the effects of therapies not just to be statistically significant (i.e., reliably different from those of some comparison treatment), but to exhibit a large magnitude of difference. This issue has been dealt with mainly in the terms of the harm reduction model. Although it is true that if the offense rate at baseline is 10 per year and if at some subsequent point of time it is 8 per year, harm has been reduced, most would also agree that the intervention is relatively weak and could be substantially improved. O'Donohue and Fisher (2006) have suggested that treatments should have benchmarks (what is the standard amount of improvement?), and that transparent quality improvement processes should be used consistently in efforts to meet or exceed these benchmarks.

In explaining away negative or unpromising results, we often hear senior clinicians state, "This is a young field." This is absolute nonsense. Marshall and Laws (2003) and Marshall and colleagues (1999) have noted that Eysenck's (1952) evaluation of traditional psychotherapy was the event that set off the behavior therapy revolution, first in the United Kingdom and later in the United States. These procedures eventually filtered into sex offender treatment and formed the initial foundation for many of the treatments used today. We now have a 50-year history of such treatments, and it is entirely reasonable to ask: What have we got to show for it? The answer, sadly, is very little. If other sciences had proceeded as glacially as ours, the 21st century would indeed be in a bad way. Saying that ours is a soft, social science is no excuse. We *can* do better, and we must. The small amount of progress in the years since the first edition of this book was published appeared points to the fact that we are not doing better. Again, we ought to look at a macro-organizational level and plan strategies (as opposed to letting this remain a *laissez-faire* process) so that in the coming years more progress will be made. Closing the books and abandoning sex offender treatment do not constitute a likely option; nor should it be based on the negative outcome of two major studies, even given their eerily similar outcomes. What *is* an option is starting to look for other ways to perform these interventions, or perhaps looking at options other than treatment.

New Interventions

The Self-Regulation Model

The Ward and Hudson self-regulation model is the obvious candidate to replace relapse prevention (Laws, 2003; Laws, Hudson, & Ward, 2000; Ward & Hudson, 2000; Ward et al., 2004, 2006). This model (admittedly a work in progress) postulates four possible pathways to relapse and interventions for responding to each. It has now been formalized in two manuals (Ward et al., 2004, 2006) and comes very close to meeting the Chambless and Hollon (1998) criteria. It has been adopted as a major feature of the nationwide sex offender treatment program operated by Correctional Service Canada (P. M. Yates, personal communication, March 17, 2003; see also Yates et al., 2000).

The Good-Lives Model

The good-lives model is gradually being incorporated into the self-regulation model. In the Chambless and Hollon (1998) criteria is the statement that beyond the assessment of changes in symptoms, outcome evaluations should ideally focus on more general issues of human functioning and quality of life. Ward and Stewart (2003) argue that beyond attempts to control recidivism, sex offender treatment must also focus on positive enhancement of an offender's life—the pursuit of what they call "primary human goods" (states of affairs, states of mind, personal characteristics, activities or experiences sought for their own sake), which are likely to promote psychological well-being. These are the things that most of us take for granted and consider our due. It is our belief (and hope) that the good-lives model is going to achieve a paramount place in treatment.

Desistance

The desistance literature comes to us from sociology, criminology, and various writings on probation-related subjects (Farrall & Calverley, 2006; Laub & Sampson, 2001; Maruna, 2001; Maruna & Immarigeon, 2004). Although interest in it is developing, desistance has not yet found a place in the management of sex offenders.

Numerous sociological/criminological theories have been advanced to account for desistance from crime. Many of these theories agree that a series of rather ordinary human events—what Ward and Stewart (2003) would call the pursuit of primary human goods—can often account for desistance. These include getting married; having children; renewing bonds with close family and friends; obtaining stable and rewarding employment; redefining oneself as a worthy, noncriminal person; feeling in control of one's life; or just getting tired of a criminal career. Maruna (2001) argues that to really understand offenders, we must examine their life course narratives and must listen to the stories that they tell, because in this process lies the capacity to transform the self and desist from crime. Lest this sound overly simplistic, Maruna describes the transformative process as a rough one. A more familiar perspective would be to see it as the process of preventing relapse originally proposed by Marlatt and Gordon (1985): a process of starts and stops, replete with relapses and recoveries, until the final desired state is achieved.

No one at present knows the extent to which this model applies to sex offenders. Surely there are offenders who, over time, gradually achieve a state of desistance. And surely there are those who do not. This is entirely consistent with the criminological description of persisters and desisters. Although this approach is certainly not antithetical to treatment, it does not make treatment a centerpiece, but rather one of the building blocks. It is tantalizing to speculate that the treatment effect about which we hear so much may serve not so much to instruct people on the errors of their ways as to awaken new possibilities for growth. R. E. Mann (personal communication, June 2006) has speculated that a good place to begin, and an approach that might prove sufficient in itself, would be the use of motivational interviewing (Ginsburg, Mann, Rotgers, & Weekes, 2002; Miller & Rollnick, 2002). It is certainly striking how much Maruna's findings agree with the propositions of the good-lives model of rehabilitation (Ward & Stewart, 2003), described above. Since the good-lives approach is already being incorporated into the Ward and colleagues (2006) self-regulation model, perhaps this is the initial path to take in dealing with desistance from sexual crime.

Information on Best Practices

Finally, the field also needs to be concerned with the issue of dissemination of best practices. Many have realized that simply discovering that a treatment is efficacious is not sufficient to ensure that it is widely adopted and competently practiced. The Substance Abuse and Mental Health Services Administration, and the Agency for Healthcare Research and Quality, are two U.S. government organizations that attempt to sponsor research and provide support for those struggling with this problem. We know that there are disparities not only around the world but within a single country in health care quality (e.g., Elko, Nevada, has fewer good-quality alternatives than does San Francisco, California). The question for our field is not only what best practices are, but how these best practices can be disseminated across all treatment settings. This is a complex problem. The problem involves agreeing on what best practices are, finding the right managers and clinicians, training them, maintaining their competencies, keeping up with innovations, and supporting managers and clinicians in a variety of ways. There are certainly centers of excellence in our field, but the question of how the other treatment facilities can be brought up to these standards remains. Thus dissemination research and a dissemination agenda also need to be part of the focus of this field.

FORENSIC ISSUES

The use of risk assessment instruments has proliferated enormously in the past decade. These are typically of two varieties. Actuarial risk assessments use complex algorithms based on static risk factors to make rather precise predictions of reoffense at specific time intervals (usually 5, 10, or 15 years). These are exemplified by the Static-99 (Hanson & Thornton, 1999) and by the Violence Risk Appraisal Guide (VRAG) and Sex Offender Risk Appraisal Guide (SORAG) (Quinsey, Rice, Harris, & Cormier, 1998). Because of their apparent predictive power, these instruments have become extremely popular and are widely used in forensic evaluations (see Doren, 2002). Although we acknowledge their scientific basis and obvious statistical power, the problem with these instruments is that they tell one very little. Clinicians are not very interested in an unspecified event that might or might not happen in 5 or 10 years. They want to know what might happen to-morrow, next week, or 3–6 months from now. Actuarial instruments are unable to provide this information.

The second type of risk assessment instrument is a structured professional guidelines assessment, exemplified by the Sexual Violence Risk–20 (SVR-20; Boer, Hart, Kropp, & Webster, 1997) and the Risk for Sexual Violence Protocol (RSVP; Hart et al., 2003). These instruments evaluate static as well as dynamic risk factors. Detailed descriptors instruct the user on how to rate the items. As a summary, there is no total score or probability statement, but rather an evaluation of whether the individual presents a low, moderate, or high risk of reoffending. The most recent of these instruments, the RSVP (Hart et al., 2003), provides considerable information beyond the simple evaluation of low, medium, or high risk. Possible scenarios for reoffense are constructed, and evaluations of how to deal with any potential threat(s) are described in detail. This approach (explained more fully by Hart & Kropp, Chapter 29, this volume) most closely meets the need for immediate information and suggestions that clinicians require.

PREVENTION ISSUES

Virtually all of this volume is devoted to traditional ways of thinking about the psychopathology, assessment, and treatment of sexual deviance. We have added a final chapter (Chapter 32) that describes how we might approach sexual deviance through a public health model of prevention. Briefly, there are three levels of prevention in public health: (1) "primary," preventing an undesired event from ever occurring; (2) "secondary," quickly intervening in a problem when it shows its early stages; and (3) "tertiary," containing a well-established problem and keeping it from happening again. Chapter 32 argues that most of our efforts have been devoted to the secondary and tertiary levels of prevention, because this is where we find most of the clients with whom we work. The chapter presents a detailed example of a community prevention program that gives strong emphasis to the primary level but actually works at all three. Public health approaches have been shown to work successfully against smallpox, tuberculosis, and polio, but less successfully against drunk driving or smoking. It has not worked against sexual deviance because it has not been tried.

STRUCTURE OF THIS BOOK

The first edition of this book (Laws & O'Donohue, 1997) proved successful beyond our expectations. As nearly as we can tell, it is considered a solid piece of work that is widely consulted and cited. When we were approached by the publisher to compile a second edition, we were at first reluctant to undertake the task. Both of us have long experience in the field, and we are painfully aware of how slowly things change in the sexual deviance business. However, new areas of study have emerged in the past decade, and we decided to prepare the work.

Readers will notice similarities and differences between the two editions. We have retained the structure we used previously for dealing with the major clinical syndromes (present Chapters 4–23). Each is again addressed in two chapters: one dealing with psychopathology and theory, and one dealing with assessment and treatment. To avoid overlap between the two chapters in each pair, we have provided authors with detailed guidelines for structuring their chapters.

Much in the present volume is new. We have added a chapter on the etiology of sexual deviance (Chapter 2). Since there is a forensic concern regarding the decrease of risk with age, we have included a chapter on sexual deviance across the lifespan (Chapter 3). New areas of interest include online sexual offending (Chapters 24 and 25), sexual deviance in females (Chapters 26 and 27), multiple paraphilias (Chapter 28), legal issues with sexual offenders (Chapter 29), and the public health approach (Chapter 32).

We are pleased with the new structure and believe that it substantially broadens the reach of the book. It is our hope that we have preserved what was best in the first edition and extended that information. The inclusion of the new material should increase interest in this field. Overall, we feel that this volume clearly shows that we are moving ahead in dealing with the problems presented by sexual deviance in our society.

NOTES

1. Both in the O'Donohue and colleagues (2000) paper and in most of the first edition of the present volume (except for the chapter on female sexual deviance), only masculine generic pronouns—"he," "his," and "him"—were used, because most individuals with paraphilias are males. The same will be done in this edition of this book, except for the two chapters on female sexual deviance (Chapters 26 and 27).
2. The criteria are from Chambless and Hollon (1998, pp. 7–16).
3. Some of what follows is a revision of Laws and Ward (2006).

REFERENCES

American Psychiatric Association. (1994). *Diagnostic and statistical manual of mental disorders* (4th ed.). Washington, DC: Author.

American Psychiatric Association. (2000). *Diagnostic and statistical manual of mental disorders* (4th ed., text rev.). Washington, DC: Author.

Baumeister, R. F., & Butler, J. L. (1997). Sexual masochism: Deviance without pathology. In D. R. Laws & W. O'Donohue (Eds.), *Sexual deviance: Theory, assessment, and treatment* (pp. 225-239). New York: Guilford Press.

Berliner, L. (2002). Commentary. *Sexual Abuse: A Journal of Research and Treatment, 14,* 195–197.

Boer, D. P., Hart, S. D., Kropp, P. R., & Webster, C. D. (1997). *Manual for the Sexual Violence Risk–20.* Vancouver: British Columbia Institute Against Family Violence.

Chambless, D. L., & Hollon, S. D. (1998). Defining empirically supported therapies. *Journal of Consulting and Clinical Psychology, 66*(1), 7–18.

Colapinto, J. (2000). *As nature made him: The boy who was raised a girl.* New York: HarperCollins.

Craig, L. A., Browne, K. D., & Stringer, I. (2003). Treatment and sexual offence recidivism. *Trauma, Violence and Abuse, 4,* 70–89.

DeYoung, M. (1989). The world according to NAMBLA: Accounting for deviance. *Journal of Sociology and Social Welfare, 16*(1), 111–126.

Doren, D. M. (2002). *Evaluating sex offenders: A manual for civil commitment and beyond.* Thousand Oaks, CA: Sage.

Eysenck, H. J. (1952). The effects of psychotherapy: An evaluation. *Journal of Consulting Psychology, 16,* 319–324.

Farrall, S., & Calverley, A. (2006). *Understanding desistance from crime: Theoretical directions in re-settlement and rehabilitation*. Maidenhead, UK: Open University Press.

Friendship, C., Mann, R. E., & Beech, A. R. (2003). Evaluation of a national prison-based program for sexual offenders in England and Wales. *Journal of Interpersonal Violence, 18*, 744–759.

Furby, L., Weinrott, M. R., & Blackshaw, L. (1989). Sex offender recidivism: A review. *Psychological Bulletin, 105*, 3–30.

Ginsburg, J. I. D., Mann, R. E., Rotgers, F., & Weekes, J. R. (2002). Motivational interviewing with criminal justice populations. In W. R. Miller & S. Rollnick (Eds.), *Motivational interviewing* (2nd ed.): *Preparing people for change* (pp. 333–346). New York: Guilford Press.

Hanson, R. K. (2002, July). *The effectiveness of treatment for sexual offenders* (Research summary, Vol. 7, No. 4). Ottawa: Public Safety Canada.

Hanson, R. K., Gordon, A., Harris, A. J. R., Marques, J. K., Murphy, W., Quinsey, V. L., et al. (2000). *The effectiveness of treatment for sexual offenders: Report of the Association for the Treatment of Sexual Abusers Collaborative Research Committee*. Plenary presentation at the meeting of the Association for the Treatment of Sexual Abusers, San Diego, CA.

Hanson, R. K., Gordon, A., Harris, A. J. R., Marques, J. K., Murphy, W., Quinsey, V. L., et al. (2002). First report of the Collaborative Outcome Data Project on the effectiveness of psychological treatment for sex offenders. *Sexual Abuse: A Journal of Research and Treatment, 14*, 169–197.

Hanson, R. K., & Harris, A. J. R. (2001). A structured approach to evaluating change among sexual offenders. *Sexual Abuse: A Journal of Research and Treatment, 13*(2), 105–122.

Hanson, R. K., & Thornton, D. (1999). *Static-99: Improving actuarial risk assessment for sexual offenders* (User Report No. 1999-02). Ottawa: Department of the Solicitor General of Canada.

Hart, S. D., Kropp, P. R., Laws, D. R., Klaver, J., Long, C., & Watt, K. A. (2003). *The Risk for Sexual Violence Protocol (RSVP): Structured professional guidelines for assessing risk of sexual violence*. Burnaby, BC, Canada: Simon Fraser University, Mental Health Law and Policy Institute.

Hunsley, J., & Mash, E. J. (2005). Introduction to the special section on developing guidelines for the evidence-based assessment (EBA) of adult disorders. *Psychological Assessment, 17*(3), 251–255.

Kinsey, A. C., Pomeroy, W. B., Martin, C. E., & Gebhard, P. (1953). *Sexual behavior in the human female*. Philadelphia: Saunders.

Laub, J. H., & Sampson, R. J. (2001). Understanding desistance from crime. In M. H. Tonry & N. Norris (Eds.), *Crime and justice: An annual review of research* (pp. 1–78). Chicago: University of Chicago Press.

Laws, D. R. (Ed.). (1989). *Relapse prevention with sex offenders*. New York: Guilford Press.

Laws, D. R. (2003). The rise and fall of relapse prevention. *Australian Psychologist, 38*, 22–30.

Laws, D. R., Hudson, S. M., & Ward, T. (2000). *Remaking relapse prevention with sex offenders: A sourcebook*. Thousand Oaks, CA: Sage.

Laws, D. R., & O'Donohue, W. (Eds.). (1997). *Sexual deviance: Theory, assessment, and treatment*. New York: Guilford Press.

Laws, D. R., & Ward, T. (2006). When one size doesn't fit all: The reformulation of relapse prevention. In W. L. Marshall, Y. M. Fernandez, L. E. Marshall, & G. A. Serran (Eds.), *Sexual offender treatment: Controversial issues* (pp. 241–254). Chichester, UK: Wiley.

Lösel, F., & Schmucker, M. (2005). The effectiveness of treatment for sexual offenders: A comprehensive meta-analysis. *Journal of Experimental Criminology, 1*, 117–146.

Marlatt, G. A., & Gordon, J. R. (Eds.). (1985). *Relapse prevention: Maintenance strategies in the treatment of addictive behaviors*. New York: Guilford Press.

Marques, J. K., Day, D. M., Nelson, C., & Miner, M. H. (1989). The Sex Offender Treatment and Evaluation Project: California's relapse prevention program. In D. R. Laws (Ed.), *Relapse prevention with sex offenders* (pp. 247–267). New York: Guilford Press.

Marques, J. K., Nelson, C., Alarcon, J.-M., & Day, D. M. (2000). Preventing relapse in sex offenders: What we learned from SOTEP's experimental treatment program. In D. R. Laws, S. M. Hudson, & T. Ward (Eds.), *Remaking relapse prevention with sex offenders: A sourcebook* (pp. 321–340). Thousand Oaks, CA: Sage.

Marques, J. K., Nelson, C., Wiederanders, M., & Day, D. M. (Chairs). (2002, October). *Main effects and beyond: New findings from California's Sex Offender Treatment and Evaluation Project (SOTEP)*. Symposium presented at the meeting of the Association for the Treatment of Sexual Abusers, Montreal [Abstract].

Marques, J. K., Wiederanders, M., Day, D. M., Nelson, C., & van Ommeren, A. (2005). Effects of a relapse prevention program on sexual recidivism: Final results from California's Sex Offender Treatment and Evaluation Project (SOTEP). *Sexual Abuse: A Journal of Research and Treatment, 17*, 79–107.

Marshall, W. L., Anderson, D., & Fernandez, Y. (1999). *Cognitive behavioural treatment of sexual offenders*. Chichester, UK: Wiley.

Marshall, W. L., Fernandez, Y. M., Marshall, L. E., & Serran, G. A. (Eds.). (2006). *Sexual offender treatment: Controversial issues*. Chichester, UK: Wiley.

Marshall, W. L., & Laws, D. R. (2003). A brief history of behavioral and cognitive behavioral approaches to sexual offender treatment: Part 2. The modern era. *Sexual Abuse: A Journal of Research and Treatment, 15*, 93–120.

Maruna, S. (2001). *Making good: How ex-convicts reform and rebuild their lives*. Washington, DC: American Psychological Association.

Maruna, S., & Immarigeon, R. (2004) *After crime and punishment: Pathways to offender reintegration*. Cullompton, UK: Willan.

McGrath, R. J., Cumming, G., Livingston, J. A., & Hoke, S. E. (2003). Outcome of a treatment program for adult sex offenders: From prison to community. *Journal of Interpersonal Violence, 18*, 3–17.

Miller, W. R., & Rollnick, S. (Eds.). (2002). *Motivational interviewing* (2nd ed.).: *Preparing people for change*. New York: Guilford Press.

Money, J. (1991). Interview. *Paidika: The Journal of Paedophilia, 2*(3), 5.

O'Donohue, W. T. (1992). Definitional and ethical issues in child sexual abuse. In W. T. O'Donohue & J. H. Geer (Eds.), *Sexual abuse of children: Theory and research* (Vol. 1, pp. 14–37). Hillsdale, NJ: Erlbaum.

O'Donohue, W. T., & Fisher, J. E. (2006). Introduction. In J. E. Fisher & W. T. O'Donohue (Eds.), *Practitioner's guide to evidence-based psychotherapy* (pp. 1–23). New York: Springer.

O'Donohue, W. T., Regev, L., & Hagstrom, A. (2000). Problems with the DSM-IV diagnosis of pedophilia. *Sexual Abuse: A Journal of Research and Treatment, 12*(2), 95–105.

Paul, G. (1967). Strategy of outcome research in psychotherapy. *Journal of Consulting and Clinical Psychology, 31*, 109–118.

Pithers, W. D., Martin, G. R., & Cumming, G. F. (1989). Vermont Treatment Program for Sexual Aggressors. In D. R. Laws (Ed.), *Relapse prevention with sex offenders* (pp. 292–310). New York: Guilford Press.

Popper, K. R. (1959). *The logic of scientific discovery*. New York: Basic Books.

Quinsey, V. L., Harris, G. T., Rice, M. E., & Cormier, C. A. (1998). *Violent offenders: Appraising and managing risk*. Washington, DC: American Psychological Association.

Rice, M. E., & Harris, G. T. (2003). The size and sign of treatment effects in sex offender therapy. *Annals of the New York Academy of Sciences, 989*, 428–440.

Sandfort, T. (1982). *The sexual aspect of paedophile relations: The experience of twenty-five boys*. Amsterdam: Pan/Spartacus.

Schweitzer, R., & Dwyer, J. (2003). Sex crime recidivism: Evaluation of a sexual offender treatment program. *Journal of Interpersonal Violence, 18*, 1292–1310.

Thorstad, D. (1998, June 26). *Pederasty and homosexuality*. Speech presented to the Semana Cultural Lesbica-Gay, Mexico City. Retrieved from *www.phxnews.com/fullstory.php?article=20703*

Ward, T., Bickley, J., Webster, S. D., Fisher, D., Beech, A. R., & Eldridge, H. (2004). *The self-regulation model of the offense and relapse process: Vol. 1. Assessment*. Victoria, BC, Canada: Pacific Psychological Assessment Corporation.

Ward, T., & Hudson, S. M. (2000). A self-regulation model of relapse prevention. In D. R. Laws, S. M.

Hudson, & T. Ward (Eds.), *Remaking relapse prevention with sex offenders: A sourcebook* (pp. 79–101). Thousand Oaks, CA: Sage.

Ward, T., & Stewart, C. A. (2003). The treatment of sex offenders: Risk management and good lives. *Professional Psychology: Research and Practice, 34,* 353–360.

Ward, T., Yates, P. M., & Long, C. A. (2006). *The self-regulation model of the offense and relapse process: Vol. 2. Treatment.* Victoria, BC, Canada: Pacific Psychological Assessment Corporation.

Yates, P. M., Goguen, B. C., Nicholaichuk, T. P., Williams, S. M., Long, C. A., Jeglic, E., et al. (2000). *National sex offender programs (moderate, low, and maintenance intensity levels).* Ottawa: Correctional Service Canada.

CHAPTER 2

AN INTEGRATED THEORY
OF SEXUAL OFFENDING

TONY WARD
ANTHONY R. BEECH

The empirical and theoretical achievements in the sexual offending field have been considerable, and researchers have formulated a number of rich and insightful accounts of sexual offending (Ward, Polaschek, & Beech, 2006). The foci of these theories have been broad and have included biological, psychological, and social/cultural levels of analysis. An important implication of this theoretical work is that a satisfactory explanation of sexual abuse is likely to be multifactorial in nature, and to allow for a diversity of etiological pathways leading to the onset and maintenance of sexual offending. The types of causes canvassed in the research literature include genetic predispositions (Siegert & Ward, 2003); adverse developmental experiences (e.g., abuse, rejection, attachment difficulties—Beech & Ward, 2004); psychological dispositions/trait factors, such as empathy deficits, attitudes supportive of sexual assault, deviant sexual preferences, emotional skill deficits, and interpersonal problems (Thornton, 2002); social and cultural structures and processes (Cossins, 2000); and contextual factors, such as intoxication and severe stress (Hanson & Harris, 2000, 2001).

In the spirit of advancing theory construction, we propose that it is timely to present a comprehensive etiological framework that is capable of encompassing the clinical phenomena evident in sexual offenders, as well as all the causal mechanisms asserted by leading theorists. Our aim is to knit together a number of areas said to be causally implicated in the occurrence of sexual abuse into an integrated theory of sexual offending (ITSO). It is a broad etiological framework that arguably has the capacity to inform the construction of more specific theories of particular types of sexual offending (e.g., rape, child sexual abuse).

In brief, according to the ITSO, sexual abuse occurs as a consequence of a network of causal factors: biological factors (evolution, genetic variations, and neurobiology); ecological variables (social and cultural environment, personal circumstances, physical environment); and core neuropsychological systems. The ITSO, we will argue, is able to explain how clinical phenomena observed in sexual offenders arise from the interaction between these diverse sets of factors. It also has the ability to absorb competing theories of sexual offending and to generate new and exciting lines of research.

DESCRIPTION OF THE THEORY

The ITSO has both horizontal and vertical depth, and therefore is able to provide a comprehensive etiological framework for explaining sexual crimes. "Horizontal depth" refers to the ecological and multisystemic nature of the theory, while "vertical depth" denotes the ability of the ITSO to provide a multilevel analysis of sexual offending. According to our approach (which follows that of Pennington, 2002), a neuroscientific account of human behavior/psychopathology requires consideration of four levels of analysis:

1. An *etiological* level, concerned with the influence of genetic and environmental factors in causing psychopathology.
2. A level of *brain mechanisms*, concerned with the effects of etiological factors on the development of the brain and its subsequent functioning (e.g., prolonged abuse—Sapolsky, 1997).
3. A *neuropsychological* level, concerned with the brain-based psychological systems generating human behavior (e.g., spatial perception and language production). This third level of neuropsychological functioning is particularly important from an explanatory perspective, as it directly informs researchers of the possible psychological mechanisms generating offenders' psychological symptoms and problems.
4. A *symptom* level of analysis, concerned with the clinical phenomena thought to characterize the various forms of psychopathology under investigation (e.g., deviant sexual arousal, mood disturbances, hallucinations).

Following Pennington, we propose that all four of these levels are mutually constraining, and that theories at the different levels need to be consistent with each other.

We now systematically outline the ITSO, which is shown in schematic form in Figure 2.1. We propose that three sets of factors converge to cause sexual offending and its associated problems: *biological* factors (influenced by genetic inheritance and brain development); *ecological niche* factors (i.e., social, cultural, and personal circumstances and learning); and *neuropsychological* factors. According to the ITSO, sexual offending occurs through the ongoing confluence of distal and proximal variables that interact in a dynamic way. Genetic predispositions and social learning have a significant impact upon brain development and result in the establishment of three interlocking neuropsychological systems (described by Pennington, 2002), each associated with distinct functions and brain structures: *motivation/emotion*; *perception and memory*; and *action selection and control* (from Luria, 1966).

We would further argue that genes, social learning, and neuropsychological systems work together to generate the clinical problems evident in offenders (i.e., deviant arousal, offense related thoughts and fantasies, negative or positive emotional states, and social difficulties). These state factors, as shown in Figure 2.1, directly result in sexually abusive actions. The consequences of these actions in turn function to maintain a positive feed-

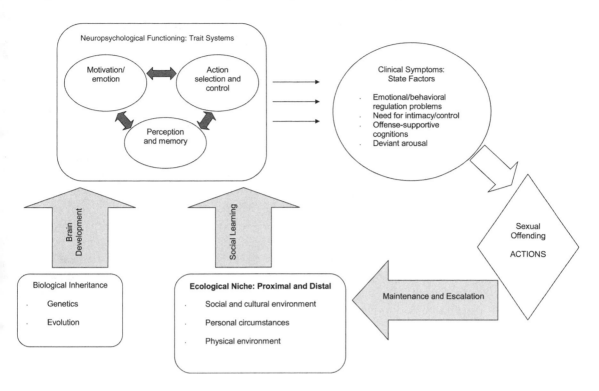

FIGURE 2.1. The integrated theory of sexual offending (ITSO). From Ward and Beech (2006). Copyright 2006 by Elsevier Science. Adapted by permission.

back loop that entrenches the offender's vulnerabilities through their impact on the environment and on psychological functioning. That is, the consequences of sexual offending will function to maintain and/or escalate further sexually deviant actions, via the modification of environmental factors and the reduction or enhancement of the individual's psychological functioning (e.g., mood, sexual arousal and satisfaction, feelings of powerlessness, etc.). For example, reducing negative mood states is likely to negatively reinforce the maladaptive emotional regulation strategies utilized, while an improvement in mood will function as a positive reinforcer.

Therefore, in our theory brain development (influenced by biological inheritance and genetics) and social learning interact to establish an individual's level of psychological functioning. This functioning may be compromised in some way by poor genetic inheritance, biological damage, or developmental adversity to make it difficult for the individual concerned to function in an adaptive manner; this will lead to problematic psychological functioning and subsequent clinical symptomatology. We now examine each of these areas in more detail.

Brain Development

The first source for offense-related vulnerabilities is brain development. It is clear that many different biological variables are associated with abnormal brain development, including the existence of biologically inherited mating strategies that malfunction (i.e., the acquisition of aggressive or problematic strategies—Buss, 1999); the modulation of sexual behavior by hormonal activity in normal and abnormal contexts; and, for example, the biological processes associated with attachment (Nelson & Panksepp, 1998).

The Role of Evolution in Brain Development

The fundamental idea in evolutionary theory is that organisms slowly evolve over time, and through a process of natural selection, either adapt to environmental challenges or become extinct. The process of change is gradual, comprising small, incremental modifications in existing organs or characteristics, which can lead to the emergence of new characteristics or even a new species. Through the processes of natural selection and sexual selection, animals that are the winners in the evolutionary struggle develop specific physical and psychological adaptations that enable them to meet these challenges.

There are three fundamental elements in Darwin's (1859/1998) theory of natural selection. First, individual members of a species vary with respect to their physical and psychological traits. Second, some members of a species will demonstrate variations that make them better able to survive or adapt to changing environmental conditions. Third, those individuals who are better equipped to survive will be more likely to breed, and in doing so will pass on these characteristics to their progeny. Consequently, these inherited characteristics will become more common within that species. In addition to natural selection, Darwin also discerned one other important process in evolution: *sexual selection*. This is the idea that male and female members of a particular species will demonstrate distinct preferences in their choice of mates, based on the physical or behavioral characteristics of such organisms. Some of these genetically based predispositions may be linked to the sex of the individual, and in this sense may create gender-linked vulnerabilities—for example, the tendency for males to engage in impersonal sex (Brennan & Shaver, 1995) or for males to rape if they cannot attract a sexual partner (Thornhill & Palmer, 2000).

Genetic Determinants of Brain Development

An evolutionary approach to human behavior that is able to incorporate the plasticity of human beings and their capacity for culture is gene–culture coevolution theory (Odling-Smee, Laland, & Feldman, 2003). This is a flexible evolutionary model claiming that genetic, individual learning, and cultural processes all propel the evolution of human beings. Because of this, the explanation of human traits is likely to involve these three sets of processes (Odling-Smee et al., 2003). *Genetic factors* may result in a predisposition to seek certain types of basic goods (e.g., relationships, sexual satisfaction, autonomy, mastery), while *learning events*, within a particular cultural context, provide *socially constructed* ways of achieving these valued experiences, activities, and outcomes. For our ITSO, this means that the causes of sexually aggressive behavior are likely to have a naturalistic basis, and that motivational and cognitive biases lead individuals to seek basic human needs in socially unacceptable ways. An important aspect of this idea is the powerful influence of genetic and cultural processes; neither dominates the other, giving both biology-oriented and social-learning-oriented researchers an important role in accounting for sexually abusive behavior.

Neurobiological Functioning

The neurobiological level of analysis is concerned with the nature of the physical processes associated with the functioning of the brain, such as types and levels of neurotransmitters, the existence of neural pathways, and the integrity of neural structures. There are at least two ways such brain processes affect the neuropsychological systems underpinning human actions: (1) Functional systems may be *disrupted* by brain-based abnormalities, and (2) the *calibration* of the systems may be directly influenced by physical processes. An example of the first possibility occurs when high levels of stress hormones such as cortisol compromise the operation of the action selection and control system; for instance, an individual behaves impulsively (Bremner et al., 1997; Sapolsky, 1997). An example of the second type of relationship occurs when persistently high levels of sex hormones increase the salience and availability of sexual goals and strengthen their influence in the life of an individual; for instance, a person becomes preoccupied with sexual goals and needs.

Thus neurobiological research reveals that structural brain damage and/or neurotransmitter malfunction can have an adverse impact upon sexual behavior. For example, we suggest that for some individuals the motivational/emotional system can be compromised by dysfunctional neurotransmitter mechanisms. This may lower the threshold for sexually aggressive behavior by increasing the strength, salience, and duration of sexual goals, and desires, and additionally by weakening the action selection and control system. Put simply, the presence of extremely intense sexual feelings might override an individual's ability to control his sexual behavior.

Ecological Niche: Proximal and Distal Factors

A second source for offense-related vulnerabilities is an individual's *ecological niche*, which in certain circumstances may cause the person to commit a sexual offense in the absence of any significant psychological deficits or vulnerabilities. We have used the term "ecological niche" to refer to the set of potentially adverse social and cultural circumstances, personal circumstances, and physical environments confronting each person in the course of development throughout life.

The content and functional integrity of a person's psychological system is determined by a combination of biological inheritance and social learning. Once acquired, psychological vulnerabilities are thought to function as a diathesis, making it more probable that an individual will struggle to meet specific environmental challenges effectively, and therefore making it likely that the individual will commit a sexual offense at some future time. These circumstances can be regarded as a more *distal* dimension of risk. An individual's current ecology or physical environment is also an important contributor to the etiology of sexual offending through making available potential victims, and by creating the specific circumstances that trigger the psychological deficits involved; this is a *proximal* or current dimension of risk. For example, the experience of fighting in a war (Henry, Ward, & Hirshberg, 2004), being subject to such social circumstances as the erosion of one culture by another, or losing a partner to death or divorce may sometimes lead to individuals' deciding to commit a sexual offense. In these kinds of extreme circumstances, individuals can behave in ways they would not normally consider, and may even engage in actions that they would view as utterly reprehensible in their normal environments.

In other words, sometimes the major causal factors resulting in sexual offending reside in the ecological niche rather than within the person. The offending may be quite opportunistic, or the consequence of circumstances that effectively erode an individual's capacity to behave in an ethical, and typical, manner (see Marshall & Barbaree, 1990). Consideration of these factors leads us to an understanding that sexual offending emerges from a network of relationships between individuals and their local niches, and is not simply the consequence of individual psychopathology. Furthermore, an individual's unique circumstances are hypothesized to influence the person's psychological and social development by virtue of their influence on core functional systems. For example, Watkins and Bentovim (1992) report evidence that the long-term effects of childhood sexual victimization are psychological disorder, with marked risk for the development of alcohol and drug misuse. In a similar vein, Beitchman and colleagues (1992) state that the long-term effects of childhood sexual victimization include disturbed adult sexual functioning, poor social adjustment, confusion over sexual identity, inappropriate attempts to reassert masculinity and recapitulation of the abuse. Each of these problems is associated with impaired psychological skills and competencies.

Neuropsychological Functioning

Both biological inheritance and social learning can have a significant impact on individuals' developing brains, and particularly upon the three interlocking neuropsychological systems—*motivation/emotion*, *perception and memory*, and *action selection and control* (Luria, 1966; Pennington, 2002)—that arguably underpin psychological functioning. Although the systems may be differentially compromised in some ways, it is likely that problems in any of the systems will adversely affect the others in some respects. We now examine each of these systems, and consider how they can be involved in specific aspects of dysfunction, in more detail.

The Motivational/Emotional System

The motivational/emotional system is associated with cortical, limbic, and brainstem brain structures. According to Pennington (2002), a major function of this system is "to allow goals and values to influence both perception and action selection rapidly and to adjust motivational state to fit changing environmental circumstances" (p. 79). Problems in an individual's genetic inheritance or cultural upbringing, or negative individual experiences, may lead to defects in the motivational/emotional system. For example, someone who was brought up in an emotionally impoverished environment may find it difficult to identify his emotions in an accurate manner, and may also become confused when confronted with emotionally charged interpersonal situations. Such an individual may become angry and act in an antisocial manner on occasions. Another type of problem could be related to the range of needs or goals sought by a person. Because of poor early learning, an individual may lack the skills necessary (internal conditions) to establish strong interpersonal relationships; this could result in social isolation and in further psychological and social deficits that could lead to sexual offending, such as intimacy problems (Marshall, 1989) or attachment problems (Baker & Beech, 2004; Ward, Hudson, & Marshall, 1996). These deficits in interpersonal functioning are exactly the kinds of problems that Thornton (2002) and Hanson and Harris (2001) regard as a particular type of stable dynamic risk factor for sexual offending—that is, causal psychological risk factors

(Beech & Ward, 2004; Ward & Beech, 2004). Our point here is that the psychological vulnerabilities that have been previously described in the sexual offending literature as a stable dynamic risk domain can be reconceptualized as disturbances in the motivational/emotional system.

The Action Selection and Control System

The action selection and control system is associated with the frontal cortex, the basal ganglia, and parts of the thalamus. A major function of this system is to help the organism to plan, implement, and evaluate action plans, and to control behavior, thoughts, and emotions in the service of higher-level goals. The action selection and control system is concerned with the formation and implementation of action plans designed to achieve individuals' goals. It draws heavily upon the motivational/emotional system for the goals that effectively energize behavior, and upon the perception and memory system for procedural and declarative knowledge (i.e., knowledge about how to do certain things, and relevant facts and information pertaining to a given situation). Problems that may arise from malfunctions in the action control and selection system essentially span such self-regulation problems as impulsivity, failure to inhibit negative emotions, inability to adjust plans to changing circumstances, and poor problem-solving skills.

Again, these deficits in self-management/general self-regulation are exactly the kinds of problems that in the sexual offending literature have been described as a stable dynamic risk factor (Hanson & Harris, 2000, 2001; Thornton, 2002). As we have argued above, it is possible to view these "vulnerability factors" as essentially disturbances in the action selection and control system—in conjunction with input from the other two neuropsychological systems included in the ITSO. In other words, the "self-control" theoretical constructs involved in many theories/descriptions of sexual offending (e.g., Ward & Hudson, 1998) can be reformulated in terms of the interlocking neuropsychological systems. Thus we are not simply *relabeling* clinical phenomena, but rather are showing how these factors can be produced by the casual mechanisms involved in the ITSO.

The Perception and Memory System

The perception and memory system is associated primarily with the hippocampal formation and the posterior neocortex. A major function of this system is to process incoming sensory information and to construct representations of objects and events, and make them available to the other two systems. Problems in the perceptual and memory system can lead to maladaptive beliefs, attitudes, and problematic interpretations of social encounters. The presence of maladaptive beliefs that are chronically activated (i.e., frequently available to guide information processing) is likely to cause the subsequent activation of problematic goals and emotions, which in turn make it difficult for a person to control his sexual behavior effectively. We hypothesize that these cognitive structures can function as preattentive filters biasing the processing of social information and resulting in a variety of personal and social difficulties.

These problems may underlie the kinds of offense-supportive cognitions that Thornton (2002) and Hanson and Harris (2000, 2001) regard as another particular type of stable dynamic risk factor for sexual offending. What have been termed "cognitive distortions" (Abel et al., 1989) are arguably caused by entrenched beliefs and subsequent biased information processing originating in the perception and memory system. An intriguing aspect of the ITSO is that different types of cognitive distortions are predicted to have their origins in different neuropsychological systems.

Clinical Phenomena

Problems in any of the three neuropsychological systems outlined above will compromise a person's adaptive functioning in any number of ways, depending on the specific dysfunction in question. For instance, if there are problems in the action selection and control system, these will make adequate mood regulation more difficult for an individual. Exposure to antisocial models is also likely to teach an individual maladaptive ways of solving personal and interpersonal problems and to result in problematic values and attitudes, which will have an impact upon the perception and memory system. The three functional systems are hypothesized as always interacting to cause a sexual offense, but the motives and particular issues related to a person's offense pathway will vary, depending on the specific types of problems with these systems. In addition, numerous types of problems can occur within the three systems that might result in different clinical presentations and treatment needs. The fact that the three functional systems can either individually or collectively create offense-related vulnerabilities means that different types of deficits in these systems will be associated with different offense variables. That is to say, individuals will commit sexual crimes for quite different reasons and therefore present with varied clinical problems.

According to the ITSO, deficits in neuropsychological functioning interrelate with individuals' current ecology (proximal dimension) to cause the emergence of four groups of symptoms or clinical phenomena that are directly associated with sexual offending. These clinical phenomena can be usefully viewed as acute risk factors (Hanson & Harris, 2000, 2001), or as the *acute state* of Thornton's (2002) four stable dynamic risk domains: self-management problems, socioaffective functioning problems, distorted attitudes, and deviant sexual interests. Once these clinical phenomena are expressed in state forms—that is, as powerful emotional/behavioral expression, need for intimacy/control, offense-supportive cognitions (deviant thoughts and fantasies), and deviant sexual arousal—they are likely to lead the individual concerned to commit a sexual offense, depending of course on the availability and accessibility of a potential victim (an ecological variable). We now examine each of these clinical phenomena in more detail.

Emotional/Behavioral Regulation Problems

The first set of clinical symptoms/problems includes the commission of impulsive acts, poor emotional control (tendency to explosive outbursts), or other behavioral expressions of emotional impulses. These phenomena may arise from problems in two different neuropsychological systems. For example, problems in an individual's motivational/emotional system may manifest at a psychological functioning level as mood problems, while problems in the action selection and control system will present as impulsive behaviors. Therefore, we would argue that what Thornton describes as problems in self-management (Domain 4 problems) have their roots in more than one neuropsychological system.

We would suggest that these problems originate in exposure to sexual activities such as compulsive masturbation during early adolescence, and in the absence of alternative means of increasing self-esteem or mood; this combination can create a profound link between sex and emotional well-being (Cortoni & Marshall, 2001). Emotional competency deficits are likely to produce powerful negative emotional states—for example, following an argument with a partner or a stressful life event such as losing a job—especially if an individual lacks the ability to dampen down, or communicate, emotions in a "healthy" way. Such an inability to manage mood states efficiently may result in a loss of control, which, in conjunction with sexual desire, can lead an individual either to become disinhibited or else opportunistically to use sex as a soothing strategy for meeting emotional and sexual needs. This may be especially likely when the individual is confronted with triggering risk factors (Beech & Ward, 2004; Ward & Beech, 2004), such as substance abuse, anger/hostility, or emotional collapse.

Need for Intimacy and Control

The second set of clinical symptoms revolves around social difficulties and includes emotional loneliness, inadequacy, low self-esteem, passive victim stance, and suspiciousness. Problems in this area are arguably reflections of dysfunction in the motivational/emotional system and can be viewed in terms of attachment insecurity, leading to problems in establishing appropriate adult intimate relationships (Ward et al., 1996). Attachment style is a relatively enduring set of characteristics for making sense of one's life experiences (Young, Klosko, & Weishaar, 2003); it determines whether one has a positive or negative view of self and others. Beech and Mitchell (2005) have outlined how distal ecological factors (such as adverse childhood experiences) are highly significant for neurological systems (especially events such as abuse, stress, and rejection), which can produce biochemical changes in the neuropsychological systems that underlie and modulate attachment behaviors (Kraemer, 1992).

Several different kinds of attachment styles have been identified in sexual offenders, each reflecting different types of motivational/emotional system dysfunction. Ward and colleagues (1996) have argued that the three insecure attachment styles in the four-category model may be related to different types of sexual offending, given the particular environmental triggers. For example, *dismissive* individuals may be more likely to demonstrate hostility to others, making them likely to offend violently against adult women; *preoccupied* individuals may tend to seek approval from others and sexualize attachment relationships, leading them to engage in sexual contact with children. Furthering these ideas, Burk and Burkhart (2003) note that individuals with a *disorganized* style of attachment are likely to use sexual offending as one of several possible strategies of externally based control, in response to the intense negative emotional states that are the sequelae of such an attachment style. In regard to intrafamilial abuse, Smallbone and Dadds (1998, 2000) suggest that if an individual has some level of disorganized attachment, distress (which normally activates the attachment system) may in fact activate the sexual system, such that the individual may employ sex in the service of nonsexual needs. Taken together, these ideas suggest that the relative levels of need for intimacy and control will vary, depending on the type of attachment style an individual has.

Offense-Supportive Cognitions

The third set of clinical symptoms associated with committing sexual offenses in child molesters and rapists consists of offense-supportive cognitions (i.e., cognitive distortions). The types of cognitive distortions that child abusers typically report reflect the views that children are sexual beings and that sex does not cause harm to children (Ward & Keenan, 1999). The kinds of offense-supportive cognitions evident in rapists include the beliefs that heterosexual encounters are inherently adversarial, that women seek to deceive men about what they really want, and that women are constantly sexually receptive to men's needs (Polaschek & Ward, 2002). Ward and Keenan (1999) proposed that underlying these surface-level cognitions are sets of schemas that are utilized by individuals to explain, predict, and interpret interpersonal phenomena. These schemas can be regarded as "implicit theories," in that they are part of the process by which offenders explain and interpret the actions of others. Implicit theories are likely to have been formed during offenders' early lives and therefore exert their effects through the filtering of perceptual information. In other words, implicit theories are located in the perception and memory system.

Sexual Interests

It is commonly thought that child molesters sexually abuse children because they have a deviant sexual interest in children, and that rapists prefer forced sexual contact with women to consensual sex. In other words, the expression of deviant sexual behaviors is thought to be the direct product of deviant sexual preferences. These deviant sexual preferences (or "paraphilias") are thought by many to have become entrenched prior to the initial deviant acts (Abel et al., 1987; Marshall, Barbaree, & Eccles, 1991). Paraphilias have been defined as "recurrent, intense sexually arousing fantasies, sexual urges, or behaviors generally involving 1) nonhuman objects, 2) the suffering or humiliation of oneself or one's partner, or 3) children or other nonconsenting persons that occur over a period of at least 6 months" (American Psychiatric Association, 2000, p. 566).

More recently, those who have described the acquisition of deviant sexual preferences have suggested more sophisticated views of how paraphilias are acquired. Here, fantasy is seen as being important in the maintenance of deviant interests. Leitenberg and Henning (1995) define "sexual fantasy" as almost any mental imagery that is sexually arousing or erotic to the individual. Sexual fantasies do not have to be accompanied by masturbation, although they often are. The role of sexual fantasy in the etiology of sexual offending was described by Abel and colleagues (1987), who reported that in a sample of 400 outpatient sexual offenders, 58% stated that prior to the age of 18, they had experienced sexual arousal to deviant ideas that were later translated into deviant acts. Marshall and Eccles (1991) reported that 41% of men who had molested extrafamilial male children had experienced deviant fantasy prior to the age of 20. Hence it is hypothesized that deviant fantasies precede deviant arousal, which in turn leads to sexual offending.

We would suggest these problems arise through an interaction among the three dysfunctional neuropsychological systems discussed above. That is, the inability to manage attachment issues and mood problems effectively (problems in the motivational/emotional system), in the presence of dysfunctional schemas/implicit theories (problems in the perception and memory system), may lead to the occurrence of deviant sexual fantasies and sexual preoccupation. These problems, coupled with a failure to regulate sexual desire (a basic physiological drive—motivational/emotional system), might lead an individual to use sex to meet emotional and sexual needs. Specifically, if an individual has problems with sexual control (problems in the action selection and control system), in conjunction with high levels of sexual arousal driven by deviant interests, this would mean that deviant sexual arousal could easily occur in particular situations—given certain triggering factors, such as anger/hostility or the presence of a potential victim. In these situations, due to personal circumstances and/or the nature of the physical environment, the individual would become deviantly aroused to children or to the thought of coercive sex with a woman. We now describe how such deviant arousal, and the other three types of clinical problems, are maintained and can escalate.

Maintenance and Escalation of Clinical Factors

The ITSO accounts for the maintenance and escalation of sexual offending by virtue of its impact on the ecology and psychological functioning of the offender. The sexual abuse of a child might result in a person's becoming even further isolated from normal social supports, and lessen still further his chances of forming appropriate intimate relationships. If an individual in this situation also has problems with mood, then sex with a child may become an increasingly powerful way of regulating problematic emotional states. In other words, the consequences of sexually abusive actions can modify, entrench, or worsen the personal circumstances of an offender, and in this way can increase or maintain the offending behavior.

From the perspective of the ITSO, cultural factors interact with biological and individual learning to create situations that support or discourage sexual offending. An example of a relevant cultural process might be the portrayal of females as essentially sexual objects and of males as entitled to have sex with whomever and whenever they want (Polaschek & Ward, 2002). For some males, a weak genetic predisposition toward sexual promiscuity may interact with a learning environment where females are routinely ridiculed and presented as inferior, and with a culture where females are not valued and are underrepresented in positions of power and influence. In this situation, it is probable that males will grow up with pro-rape attitudes and beliefs. Furthermore, continued exposure to a social environment characterized by sexist and hostile attitudes to women, and by dysfunctional sexual norms, can help to maintain and even escalate sexual offending.

RELATIONSHIP TO OTHER THEORIES OF SEXUAL OFFENDING

We propose that the ITSO has the theoretical resources to unify other prominent theories of sexual offending. We do not have the space in this chapter to demonstrate this for every theory, so we have chosen what we see as two of the most promising etiological theories in order to illustrate how this can be done. The theories we have selected are Finkelhor's (1984) precondition theory and Marshall and Barbaree's (1990) integrated theory. We limit ourselves to a brief description of each theory and a few comments about how it can be incorporated within the ITSO.

Finkelhor's Precondition Theory

Finkelhor (1984) has suggested that four underlying factors have typically been used to explain the occurrence of child sexual abuse, usually in the form of single-factor theories. These theories are based on the following claims: Sex with children is emotionally satisfying to the offenders (emotional congruence); men who offend are sexually aroused by a child (sexual arousal); men have sex with children because they are unable to meet their sexual needs in socially appropriate ways (blockage); and, finally, these men become disinhibited and behave in ways contrary to their normal behavior (disinhibition). He argues that the first three factors explain why some individuals develop sexual interest in children, and the fourth why this interest manifests itself as sexual deviance.

In Finkelhor's theory, these four factors are grouped into four preconditions that must be satisfied before the sexual abuse of a child occurs. The first precondition implies that the offender must be motivated to sexually abuse a child, and encompasses three of the four factors (i.e., emotional congruence, sexual arousal, and blockage). The second precondition involves means of overcoming internal inhibitions (e.g., alcohol use, impulse disorder, senility, psychosis, severe stress, socially entrenched patriarchal attitudes, or social tolerance of sexual interest in children) and is related to the disinhibition factor. The third precondition involves means of overcoming external inhibitions, or conditions that increase the possibility of offending (e.g., maternal absence or illness, lack of maternal closeness, social isolation of family, lack of parental supervision, unusual sleeping conditions, or paternal domination or abuse of mother). The final precondition states that the offender must overcome a child's resistance to the abuse (e.g., giving gifts, desensitizing the child to sex, establishing emotional dependence, using threats or violence). The two remaining preconditions are associated with the "how" of the offense process and do not relate to the four causal factors. Finkelhor hypothesizes that the preconditions occur in a temporal sequence, with each being necessary for the next to occur.

The four factors or motives in Finkelhor's theory can be subsumed within the three neuropsychological systems outlined earlier: motivation/emotion, perception and memory, and action selection and control. Emotional congruence and sexual arousal are motivational constructs with affective aspects; in the ITSO, they can both be incorporated within the motivational/emotional system. The constructs of blockage and disinhibition can be seen as reflecting faulty planning or self-regulation and can be viewed as parts of the action and control system. The preconditions of overcoming both external inhibitions and a child's resistance can also be viewed as reflecting control strategies, and as additionally involving the retrieval of information from the perception and memory system.

Marshall and Barbaree's Integrated Theory

Marshall and Barbaree's (1990) integrated theory proposes that the sexual abuse of children occurs as a consequence of several interacting distal and proximal factors. Specifically, this theory states that individuals experiencing developmentally adverse events (e.g., poor parenting, inconsistent and harsh discipline, physical and sexual abuse) are likely to exhibit distorted internal working models of relationships, particularly with respect to sex and aggression, resulting in poor social and self-regulation skills from an early age.

For these individuals, the transition into adolescence is a particularly critical period. It is at this stage that individuals are most receptive to acquiring enduring sexual scripts, preferences, interests, and attitudes. Furthermore, the massive increase of sex hormones during this period increases the salience and potency of these sexual cues. According to Marshall and Barbaree, sex and aggression originate from the same neural substrates (e.g., the hypothalamus, amygdala, septum, etc.) and are thought to cause qualitatively similar experiences. If an individual comes from an adverse background and therefore is already predisposed to behaving in an antisocial manner, the pubertal release of hormones may serve to fuse sex and aggression, and to consolidate or enhance already acquired sexually abusive tendencies.

When this individual becomes a young adult, the lack of effective social and self-regulation skills makes it more probable that relationships (or attempted relationships) with women will be met by rejection, and that such rejection will result in lowered self-esteem, anger, and negative attitudes toward females. These powerful negative emotions may fuel the intensity of sexual desires and the development of deviant sexual fantasies. Masturbation to these fantasies will increase their strength and will also function as a form of mental rehearsal in which future sexual offenses are planned. Young children may be viewed as more inherently trustworthy and as constituting a "safe haven" for the individual. The individual may therefore see deviant sex or fantasies as meeting a multitude of needs—including releasing sexual tension, as well as increasing personal effectiveness and control, interpersonal closeness, self-esteem, and masculinity.

According to the integrated theory, the vulnerability factors described above interact with more transient situational elements—such as stress, intoxication, strong negative affect, sexual stimuli, and the presence of a potential victim—to impair the individual's ability to control behaviors, resulting in a sexual offense. The reinforcing effects of deviant sexual activity and the development of cognitive distortions maintain offending. This reinforcement may be positive (e.g., sexual arousal, sense of power) or negative (e.g., reduction of low mood) in nature.

Marshall and Barbaree's integrated theory is a very sophisticated and powerful theory, and its accommodation within the ITSO requires considerable thought. In order to ease the task, we simply take each of the three systems constituting the trait factors of the ITSO and consider its relationship to key ideas in the integrated theory. With respect to the trait or vulnerability factors, the following analysis is feasible: (1) The motivational/emotional system can incorporate the sexual attachment, intimacy, emotional, and needs constructs of the Marshall and Barbaree theory; (2) the action selection and control system of the ITSO can absorb the impulsivity, social skills, and self-regulation components of the integrated theory; and (3) the perception and memory system is able to integrate the entrenched beliefs, strategies, identity, and values referred to in the integrated theory. Many of the other variables included in this elegant theory, such as the emphases on ecological, social learning, circumstantial, and biological factors, are easily dealt with. For example, early learning events are viewed as part of the developing offender's social ecology. One of the virtues of the integrated theory is that it explicitly addresses the role of biological and hormonal variables in the genesis of sexual abuse. With its strong neurobiological orientation, the ITSO is also able to take these factors into account without neglecting the important role of psychological agency and identity.

SUMMARY AND FUTURE DIRECTIONS

In this chapter, we have sketched out a possible framework for integrating many of the factors identified in research and theory as determinants of sexual offending. In our view, the ITSO shows considerable potential for bringing together theories from different levels, including the major multifactorial theories of sexual abuse (strong unifying power). It incorporates the insight from the comprehensive etiological theories that sexual offending has multiple trajectories. It also provides a useful way of incorporating single-factor theories in terms of the three neuropsychological systems outlined earlier. Individually and collectively, the three systems can be utilized to explain specific problems evident in sexual offenders, such as emotional loneliness or deviant sexual arousal. It is also possible to create a unified or integrated account such as the one sketched out in this chapter. Finally, theories of the offense and relapse process are easily accommodated by virtue of the ITSO's stress on self-regulatory capacities and the role of ecological factors in facilitating sexual crime. Cultural factors are considered to be both developmental resources and also aspects of the offender's current ecology.

Furthermore, the ITSO provides a clinically useful framework for the assessment and treatment of sexual offenders. Its ability to account for multiple offense trajectories and varying clinical presentations means that it will help clinicians to focus on offenders' unique problems. The multisystemic nature of the ITSO prompts therapists to take into account a range of causal variables when formulating a case; to think dynamically with respect to their interaction; and to appreciate the role of ecological (i.e., social, cultural, circumstantial) variables in both creating the conditions for abuse and in shaping offender vulnerabilities. In our view, the use of the ITSO by clinicians will facilitate the construction of tailored treatment programs and avoid the mistakes inherent in a one-size-fits-all perspective.

Finally, the ITSO is really an abstract framework for thinking systematically about sexual offending and its constituent causal variables. It is necessary for researchers to unpack its assumptions in greater detail and apply it to different types of sexual crimes, such as rape, exhibitionism, or child molestation (i.e., to achieve greater explanatory depth, and to improve upon its existing heuristic value). The abstract nature of the ITSO allows for variety in the types of goals, strategies, contexts, beliefs, emotions, and biological mechanisms involved in different sexual crimes. In other words, the ITSO possesses both horizontal and vertical depth—the former by virtue of its strong ecological orientation, and the latter because it assumes that human beings are embodied beings whose actions are conjointly influenced by a network of causal influences. Like all of us, sexual offenders are both psychological agents who seek to realize their personal goals, and animals whose evolved capacities allow them the possibility of changing their lives.

ACKNOWLEDGMENT

We would like to thank Elsevier Science for giving us permission to adapt about 50% of the material previously published in Ward and Beech (2006). Copyright 2006 by Elsevier Science.

REFERENCES

Abel, G. G., Becker, J. V., Cunningham-Rathner, J., Mittelman, M. S., Murphy, W. D., & Rouleau, J. L. (1987). Self-reported sex crimes of nonincarcerated paraphiliacs. *Journal of Interpersonal Violence, 2,* 3–25.

Abel, G. G., Gore, D. K., Holland, C. L., Camp, N., Becker, J., & Rathner, J. (1989). The measurement of the cognitive distortions of child molesters. *Annals of Sex Research, 2,* 135–153.

American Psychiatric Association. (2000). *Diagnostic and statistical manual of mental disorders* (4th ed., text rev.). Washington, DC: Author.

Baker, E., & Beech, A. R. (2004). Dissociation and variability of adult attachment dimensions and early maladaptive schemas in sexual and violent offenders. *Journal of Interpersonal Violence, 19,* 1119–1136.

Beech, A. R., & Mitchell, I. J. (2005). A neurobiological perspective on attachment problems in sexual offenders and the role of selective serotonin re-uptake inhibitors in treatment of such problems. *Clinical Psychology Review, 25,* 153–182.

Beech, A. R., & Ward, T. (2004). The integration of etiology and risk in sex offenders: A theoretical model. *Aggression and Violent Behavior, 10*, 31–63.

Beitchman, J., Zucker, K., Hood, J., DaCosta, G., Akman, D., & Cassavia, E. (1992). A review of the long-term effects of child sexual abuse. *Child Abuse and Neglect, 16*, 101–118.

Bremner, J. D., Licinio, J., Darnell, A., Krystal, J. H., Owens, M. J., Southwick, S. M., et al. (1997). Elevated corticotropin-releasing factor concentrations in posttraumatic stress disorder. *American Journal of Psychiatry, 154*, 624–629.

Brennan, K. A., & Shaver, P. R. (1995). Dimensions of adult attachment: An integrative overview. In J. A. Simpson & W. S. Rholes (Eds.), *Attachment theory and close relationships* (pp. 46–76). New York: Guilford Press.

Burk, L. R., & Burkhart, B. R. (2003). Disorganized attachment as a diathesis for sexual deviance developmental experience and the motivation for sexual offending. *Aggression and Violent Behavior, 8*, 487–511.

Buss, D. M. (1999). *Evolutionary psychology: The new science of the mind.* Boston: Allyn & Bacon.

Cortoni, F., & Marshall, W. L. (2001). Sex as a coping strategy and its relationship to juvenile sexual history and intimacy in sexual offenders. *Sexual Abuse: A Journal of Research and Treatment, 13*, 27–43.

Cossins, A. (2000). *Masculinities, sexualities and child sexual abuse.* The Hague, Netherlands: Kluwer Law International.

Darwin, C. (1998). *The origin of species.* Ware, UK: Wordsworth Editions. (Original work published 1859)

Finkelhor, D. (1984). *Child sexual abuse: New theory and research.* New York: Free Press.

Hanson, R. K., & Harris, A. J. R. (2000). Where should we intervene?: Dynamic predictors of sexual offence recidivism. *Criminal Justice and Behavior, 27*, 6–35.

Hanson, R. K., & Harris, A. J. R. (2001). *The Sex Offender Need Assessment Rating (SONAR): A method for measuring change in risk levels.* Retrieved from *www.sgc.gc.ca/epub/corr/e200001a/ e200001b/e200001b.htm* (please note that this is an older version of SONAR and should not be used).

Henry, N. M., Ward, T., & Hirshberg, M. (2004). Why soldiers rape: An integrated model. *Aggression and Violent Behavior, 9*, 535–562.

Kraemer, G. W. (1992). A psychobiological theory of attachment. *Behavioral and Brain Sciences, 15*, 493–541.

Leitenberg, H., & Henning, K. (1995). Sexual fantasy. *Psychological Bulletin, 117*, 469–496.

Luria, A. (1966). *Higher cortical functions in man.* New York: Basic Books.

Marshall, W. L. (1989). Invited essay: Intimacy, loneliness and sexual offenders. *Behaviour Research and Therapy, 27*, 491–503.

Marshall, W. L., & Barbaree, H. E. (1990). An integrated theory of the etiology of sexual offending. In W. L. Marshall, D. R. Laws, & H. E. Barbaree (Eds.), *Handbook of sexual assault: Issues, theories, and treatment of the offender* (pp. 257–275). New York: Plenum Press.

Marshall, W. L., Barbaree, H. E., & Eccles, A. (1991). Early onset and deviant sexuality in child molesters. *Journal of Interpersonal Violence, 6*, 323–336.

Marshall, W. L., & Eccles, A. (1991). Issues in clinical practice with sex offenders. *Journal of Interpersonal Violence, 6*, 68–93.

Nelson, E. E., & Panksepp. J. (1998). Brain substrates of infant–mother attachment, contributions of opioids, oxytocin, and norepinephrine. *Neuroscience and Biobehavioral Reviews, 22*, 437–452.

Odling-Smee, F. J., Laland, K. N., & Feldman, M. W. (2003). *Niche construction: The neglected process in evolution.* Princeton, NJ: Princeton University Press.

Pennington, B. F. (2002). *The development of psychopathology: Nature and nurture.* New York: Guilford Press.

Polaschek, D. L. L., & Ward, T. (2002). The implicit theories of potential rapists: What our questionnaires tell us. *Aggression and Violent Behavior, 7*, 385–406.

Sapolsky, R. M. (1997). Stress and glucocorticoid response. *Science, 275*, 1662–1663.

Siegert, R. J., & Ward, T. (2003). Back to the future: Evolutionary explanations of rape. In T. Ward, D. R. Laws, & S. M. Hudson (Eds.), *Sexual deviance: Issues and controversies* (pp. 45–64). Thousand Oaks, CA: Sage.

Smallbone, S. W., & Dadds, M. R. (1998). Childhood attachment and adult attachment in incarcerated adult male sex offenders. *Journal of Interpersonal Violence, 13,* 555–573.

Smallbone, S. W., & Dadds, M. R. (2000). Attachment and coercive behavior. *Sexual Abuse: A Journal of Research and Treatment, 12,* 3–15.

Thornhill, R., & Palmer, C. T. (2000). *A natural history of rape: Biological bases of sexual coercion.* Cambridge, MA: MIT Press.

Thornton, D. (2002) Constructing and testing a framework for dynamic risk assessment. *Sexual Abuse: A Journal of Research and Treatment, 14,* 139–154.

Ward, T., & Beech, A. R. (2004). The etiology of risk: A preliminary model. *Sexual Abuse: A Journal of Research and Treatment, 16,* 271–284.

Ward, T., & Beech, A. R. (2006). An integrated theory of sexual offending. *Aggression and Violent Behavior, 11,* 44–63.

Ward, T., & Hudson, S. M. (1998). The construction and development of theory in the sexual offending area: A meta-theoretical framework. *Sexual Abuse: A Journal of Research and Treatment, 10,* 47–63.

Ward, T., Hudson, S. M., & Marshall, W. L. (1996). Attachment style in sex offenders: A preliminary study. *Journal of Sex Research, 33,* 17–26.

Ward, T., & Keenan, T. (1999). Child molesters' implicit theories. *Journal of Interpersonal Violence, 14*(8), 821–838.

Ward, T., Polaschek, D., & Beech, A. R. (2006). *Theories of sexual offending.* Chichester, UK: Wiley.

Watkins, B., & Bentovim, A. (1992). The sexual abuse of male children and adolescents: A review of current research. *Journal of Child Psychology and Psychiatry, 33,* 197–248.

Young, J. E., Klosko, J. S., & Weishaar, M. E. (2003). *Schema therapy: A practitioner's guide.* New York: Guilford Press.

CHAPTER 3

SEXUAL DEVIANCE OVER THE LIFESPAN

Reductions in Deviant Sexual Behavior in the Aging Sex Offender

HOWARD E. BARBAREE
RAY BLANCHARD

This chapter reviews evidence for reductions in sexually deviant behavior in the aging sex offender. Predominant sentiments in the field and current theoretical accounts hold that sexual deviance is a lifelong individual trait, and that the expression of sexually deviant behavior continues throughout the lifespan. The current chapter considers an alternative view. We argue that although some individual traits and predispositions underlying sexual deviance, such as sexual preferences or antisocial traits, may persist to the end of life, the expression or performance of sexually deviant behavior decreases with age. The chapter is founded on the proposition that the performance of sexual behavior in the human male is determined in large part by blood levels of the male sex hormone testosterone, and that these blood levels decrease with age. In support of this proposition, the present chapter reviews (1) what is known about the male sex hormone testosterone and its relation to sexual drive and behavior, (2) the effects of aging on blood levels of testosterone, (3) the effects of aging on male sexual behavior, (4) the effects of aging on the strength of sexual arousal in sex offenders, and (5) the effects of aging on sexual recidivism in sex offenders released from custody. The chapter also discusses the challenge to the effects of age on recidivism by the proponents of actuarial assessment. Finally, the chapter discusses the implications of age-related decreases in sexually deviant behavior for policy, legislation, and professional practices relating to the assessment, treatment, and management of the aging sex offender.

STRONG BELIEF IN LIFELONG SEXUAL DEVIANCE

There is a strong belief in the field that sexual deviance persists unabated into old age. Three sources of empirical evidence seem to have been most influential in supporting this view: a highly influential meta-analytic study of recidivism in sex offenders, studies of long-term recidivism in sex offenders, and the development of actuarial instruments that have been demonstrably predictive of recidivism in sex offenders.

In their meta-analytic review of 61 data sets, representing over 23,000 sex offenders, Hanson and Bussière (1998) found that indicators of antisocial behavior and deviant sexual interests were strong predictors of sexual recidivism. Age was identified as only a moderate predictor ($r = -.13$), with younger offenders reoffending at a higher rate. Although the correlation is supportive of the notion that aging leads to reductions in deviant sexual behavior, aging was not identified by the authors as a strong determinant of recidivism in sex offenders.

Two notable studies of recidivism in sex offenders examined recidivism rates 25 years or more after release from custody (Hanson, Steffy, & Gauthier, 1993; Prentky, Lee, Knight, & Cerce, 1997). Although long-term recidivism rates were not found to be high, the mere fact that offenders were still offending so long after release seems to support the notion that sexual deviance persists into the later years. If one considers that the average sex offender is released sometime after age 35, recidivism 25 years later would indicate persistence of sexual deviance to age 60, at least.

Finally, perhaps the most significant advance in the assessment of the sex offender during the past 20 years has been the development and promulgation of actuarial instruments that are demonstrably predictive of recidivism among adult male sexual offenders (Doren, 2002; Hanson, 1997; Quinsey, Harris, Rice, & Cormier, 1998). Hanson and Morton-Bourgon (2004) identified the five most commonly used actuarial instruments as the Violence Risk Appraisal Guide (VRAG; Quinsey et al., 1998), the Sex Offender Risk Appraisal Guide (SORAG; Quinsey et al., 1998), the Rapid Risk Assessment of Sexual Offense Recidivism (RRASOR; Hanson, 1997), the Static-99 (Hanson & Thornton, 1999), and the Minnesota Sex Offender Screening Tool—Revised (MnSOST-R; Epperson et al., 1998). These actuarial instruments consist primarily of items that code "static" or unchanging features of the offender being assessed, reinforcing the idea that offenders cannot or do not change in recidivism risk over time. Three of these instruments code age at assessment as a specific risk factor. For example, on the RRASOR and Static-99, the age of the offender is coded as being younger or older than 25 years of age, with the younger age signifying higher risk. A similar item in the MnSOST-R codes high risk as younger than age 30. These item codings imply that risk for sexual recidivism does not change after the ages of 25–30. The VRAG and SORAG code age at index offense. This is a static age item, since this item response will not change with maturity. In the manuals describing the proper use of these actuarial instruments, there is no advice given concerning adjustments in risk for an older offender. Therefore, from the actuarial perspective, recidivism risk in sex offenders does not decrease due to the aging of the sex offender.

The strong belief in the persistence of sexual deviance into old age is supported by theoretical accounts that posit long-term sexual deviance. Harris and Rice (2003) have articulated this position clearly by stating that "the preponderance of scientific evidence supports the idea that the majority of variance in violent criminal conduct (including sexual aggression) can be attributed to genetically and physiologically based enduring traits that, once initiated, exhibit lifelong persistence under conditions so far observed" (p. 208).

Despite this evidence and these arguments, there are good reasons to question the notion that sexually motivated behaviors of any type—paraphilic or conventional—will continue unabated throughout a man's middle years and into old age. Such an expectation is at variance with the known facts of human endocrinology and male sexuality.

THE ROLE OF THE MALE SEX HORMONE TESTOSTERONE

Mammalian gonads and adrenals secrete several male sex hormones called "androgens." All are steroid hormones produced primarily in the Leydig cells in the male testes, although some small amounts of these hormones are produced in the adrenals in both males and females. Testosterone is the most potent and abundant androgen (Seidman, 2005). Close to 98% of testosterone molecules are protein-bound, with approximately one-third of these weakly bound to albumin and the remainder strongly bound to sex-hormone-binding globulin (SHBG). Because the testosterone molecules that are bound with SHBG cannot bind with receptor cells, this component of testosterone has no behavioral effect. Only the non-SHBG-bound testosterone is biologically active ("bioavailable"), including free testosterone and testosterone that is loosely bound to albumin (Seidman, 2005). Free testosterone diffuses into target cells, where it is converted to dihydrotestosterone and estradiol. Testosterone and dihydrotestosterone bind to androgen receptor cells mediating the effects on sexual behavior (Seidman, 2005).

The male sex hormone testosterone plays a critical role in the production of male sexual behavior—a role first identified by the pioneering work of behavioral endocrinologist Frank Beach (1948). When males are castrated, blood levels of testosterone decline rapidly (Coyotupa, Parlow, & Kovacic, 1973). Sexual behavior also declines, but more gradually—sometimes over weeks and months (Beach, 1970). These effects of castration are seen in birds (Hutchinson, 1974), subprimate mammals including rats and guinea pigs (Beach, 1971), nonhuman primates (Phoenix, 1978), and humans (Heim & Hursch, 1979). In the human male (Heim & Hursch, 1979), the majority of castrates show an immediate decline in sexual behavior, while most of the remainder show a gradual decline over weeks or months. A small percentage of human castrates, approximately 10%, show no decline in sexual behavior (Heim & Hursch, 1979).

When men exhibit low levels of total testosterone in their blood (below 300 ng/dl) due to the malfunctioning of their hypothalamic–pituitary–gonadal axis, they are referred to as "hypogonadal." Hypogonadism is characterized by a loss of libido and a loss of both sleep-associated and spontaneous erections (Anderson, Bancroft, & Wu, 1992). Davidson, Kwan, and Greenleaf (1982) utilized a within-subject design to study the effects of injected doses of exogenous testosterone on sexual behavior in six hypogonadal men. These patients received (1) 100 mg of testosterone, (2) 400 mg of testosterone, or (3) placebo. Each patient received each treatment with a gap of 6 weeks between treatments, and the order of treatment was varied among patients to control for treatment order effects. Results indicated that injections of testosterone increased plasma testosterone levels. The effect was temporary (with peak effects 7 days after injection) and dose-dependent (with larger doses producing larger increases in blood levels). The hypogonadal men kept daily diaries of their sexual behavior and penile erections. The largest behavioral effects of testosterone injections were reported 1 week after injection, corresponding to the time of peak effect on plasma testosterone level. Dose-dependent effects of testosterone injections were observed for total erections, nocturnal erections, coital attempts, masturbation, and orgasm, with larger doses producing larger increases in sexual behavior (Davidson et al., 1982).

Testosterone is necessary or at least important in maintaining libido. Increasing plasma androgens at puberty is correlated with the onset of nocturnal emissions, masturbation, dating, and infatuation (Kemper, 1990). The level of bioavailable testosterone is correlated with sexual thoughts (Meston & Frohlich, 2000). Males with an early onset of androgen secretion develop an early interest in sexuality and erotic fantasies (Feder, 1984). A significant relationship between serum testosterone levels and libido has been found in the following populations: normal men (Anderson et al., 1992; Bagatell, Heiman, Rivier, & Bremner, 1994), normal adolescent boys (Udry, Billy, Morris, Groff, & Raj, 1985), men in or past middle age (Davidson et al., 1983; Tsitouras, Martin, & Harman, 1982), men complaining of loss of sexual interest (O'Carroll & Bancroft, 1984), men with erectile dysfunction (Schiavi, White, Mandeli, & Levine, 1997), and hypogonadal men (Davidson, Camargo, & Smith, 1979; Kwan, Greenleaf, Mann, Crapo, & Davidson, 1983; Luisi & Franchi, 1980; O'Carroll, Shapiro, & Bancroft, 1985). This relationship between blood levels of testosterone and libido will come as no surprise to professionals working in the area of sexual deviance. Medical and pharmacotherapeutic interventions designed to manage sexually deviant behavior have largely employed antiandrogenic medications designed to reduce blood levels of testosterone, libido, and ultimately (of course) sexually deviant behavior (e.g., Bradford & Fedoroff, 2006).

THE EFFECTS OF AGING ON TESTOSTERONE AND SEXUAL BEHAVIOR

Older men do not experience a sudden cessation of gonadal function and hormone secretion, as occurs in women during menopause. Instead, there is a progressive reduction in male hypothalamic–pituitary–gonadal axis function with age. Testosterone levels decline through both central (pituitary) and peripheral (testicular) mechanisms, and there is an age-related loss of circadian rhythm (Seidman, 2005; Swerdloff & Wang, 1993). Numerous studies have established that levels of both total and bioavailable testosterone peak in early adulthood and thereafter decrease with age through the remainder of the lifespan (e.g., Baker et al., 1976; Denti et al., 2000; Harman, Metter, Tobin, Pearson, & Blackman, 2001; Jankowska, Rogucka, Medras, & Welon, 2000; Ooi et al., 1998; Vermeulen, Goemaere, & Kaufman, 1999).

Gray, Berlin, McKinlay, and Longcope (1991) conducted a meta-analysis of 88 published studies examining the effects of aging on testosterone, and the studies reported conflicting results. In cross-study comparisons, certain research design characteristics (e.g., time of day of blood sampling) and various sample characteristics (e.g., volunteers vs. patients as subjects) were related to both mean testosterone level and the slope of the age–testosterone function. Blood levels of testosterone exhibited a circadian rhythm, with higher levels being recorded in the morning. Studies that did not record blood levels specifically in the morning produced lower blood levels. For subgroups of subjects that did not exclude men with significant illness, the mean testosterone levels were low and did not decline with age. In contrast, studies that recorded blood levels in the morning using subgroups that included only healthy subjects had higher overall testosterone levels and showed a decline of testosterone with age. Therefore, when study methodology has employed appropriate controls for extraneous factors, the relationship between aging and testosterone blood levels indicate a significant effect of age.

In the Baltimore Longitudinal Study of Aging (Harman et al., 2001)—a study employing both a longitudinal design (the same subjects were measured at different ages) and a cross-sectional design (different cohorts were tested at different ages)—levels of both total and bioavailable testosterone were seen to decrease in a linear function from age 30 to age 90. Figure 3.1 presents the longitudinal effects of aging on total testosterone and free testosterone (free T index). As can be seen, blood levels of testosterone decrease in a linear fashion from young adulthood to old age.

In the same study, significant numbers of older men could be diagnosed as hypogonadal, in the sense that their blood levels of testosterone had declined below the diagnostic criteria (Harman et al., 2001). Figure 3.2 presents the proportion of different-age samples who met diagnostic criteria for hypogonadism, based on both total and bioavailable testosterone (free T index). As can be seen, the proportion increased significantly with age. Testosterone deficiency in elderly men could be considered a normal aging phenomenon. However, somewhat arbitrarily, age-adjusted norms were not used, and modern medicine regards this state as pathological. This condition in older men has been referred to as "andropause," and it is considered to be the male equivalent of menopause in women.

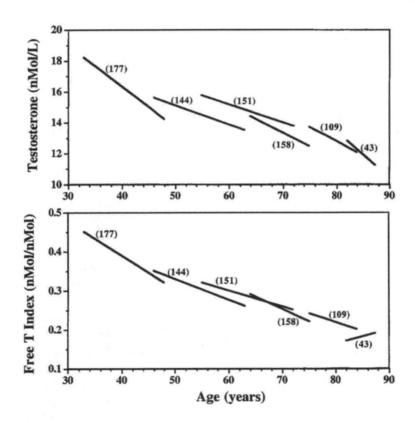

FIGURE 3.1. Longitudinal effects of aging on total testosterone and free testosterone. Linear segment plots are shown for men on at least two visits. Each linear segment has a slope equal to the mean of the individual longitudinal slopes and is centered over the medial age for each cohort of men. Numbers in parentheses represent the number of men in each cohort. Segments show significant downward progression at every age, with no significant change in slopes over the entire age range. From Harman, Metter, Tobin, Pearson, and Blackman (2001, p. 727). Copyright 2001 by the Endocrine Society. Reprinted by permission.

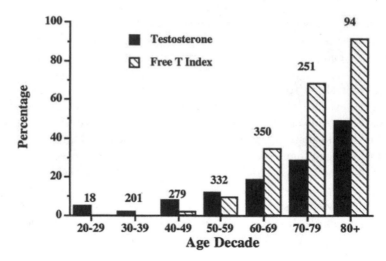

FIGURE 3.2. Hypogonadism in aging men. Bar height indicates the percentage of men in each 10-year interval with at least one testosterone value in the hypogonadal range: total T < 300 ng/dl (shaded bars) or T/SHGB (free T index) < 5.74 (striped bars). The numbers above each pair of bars indicate the number of men studied in the corresponding decade. The percentage of men with hypogonadism increases progressively from the 20s to the 80s by either criterion. More men have hypogonadism by free T index than by total T after age 50, and there is a progressively greater difference with increasing age between the two criteria. From Harman, Metter, Tobin, Pearson, and Blackman (2001, p. 727). Copyright 2001 by the Endocrine Society. Reprinted by permission.

As menopause does, andropause comprises a constellation of sexual and nonsexual health effects. Age-related reduction in the production of androgens is associated with numerous nonsexual physiological changes, including osteoporosis, decreases in muscle mass, decreases in muscle strength, increases in body fat, and psychological effects including depression and irritability (Seidman, 2005). It might be argued that these nonsexual health effects are simply the effects of aging and are unrelated to deficiencies in the functioning of the hypothalamic–pituitary–gonadal axis. However, these same physiological abnormalities are seen in younger men with hypogonadism, and they can be ameliorated somewhat with hormone (exogenous testosterone) replacement therapy in men of all ages (Harman, 2003). Therefore, these age-related symptoms of ill health are seen to be part of the andropause syndrome.

Based on the well-established relationship described above between testosterone and libido, one would therefore expect that the normal decline in testosterone levels with age would be accompanied by a concomitant decrease in libido. The mechanism whereby the decline in testosterone with age influences sexual behavior is not well understood. Although age-related reductions in testosterone availability have been well established, less is known about the effects of age on testosterone utilization. A few authors have suggested that testosterone receptor sites may become less sensitive with age, so that the threshold concentration of testosterone necessary to maintain libido may increase with age (e.g., Baker & Hudson, 1983; Schiavi, 1999, pp. 52–53; Tsitouras et al., 1982). Nevertheless, either or both processes would imply a trend toward decreasing sexual interest or arousability in older men.

Not surprisingly, studies of human sexuality and aging indicate a general decline in the frequency of male sexual behavior and an increase in the number of problems associated with sexual relations with age, including a reduction in the number and quality of erections (Kaiser et al., 1988; Morley et al., 2000). For example, Feldman, Goldstein, Hatzichristou, Krane, and McKinlay (1994) studied erectile function over different age cohorts and reported that while the prevalence of minimal erectile difficulties remained constant (< 20%) from age 40 to age 80, the prevalence of moderate and complete erectile dysfunction increased so that by age 60, the majority of research participants reported at least minimal erectile dysfunction. These results are presented in Figure 3.3.

The Global Study of Sexual Attitudes and Behaviors (Laumann et al., 2005) was an international survey of various aspects of sex and relationships among adults ages 40–80 years. This survey contacted 13,882 women and 13,618 men worldwide and achieved a response rate of almost 20%. Data were collected through a combination of telephone interview and self-report questionnaire. The authors note that the estimated prevalence of sexual problems reported in this survey was comparable to previously published rates. Several factors were found to be consistently related to the likelihood of sexual problems. In men, lack of interest in sex, erectile difficulties, and inability to achieve orgasm were more prevalent in older men; the older the respondents, the more prevalent these problems became. The survey concluded that sexual problems tend to be more closely associated with physical health and aging among men than among women.

Rowland, Greenleaf, Dorfman, and Davidson (1993) examined the sexual arousal and behavior of 39 healthy sexually functional men ranging in age from 21 to 82. These authors recorded erectile responses to visual erotic stimulation. Figures 3.4 and 3.5 present mean magnitude of erectile responses (Figure 3.4) and mean latency to maximum response (Figure 3.5) for four age cohorts. As can be seen, the magnitude of erectile responses decreased and their latency increased with advanced age. These authors also collected data on self-reported sexual activity and functioning in these same subjects. Results

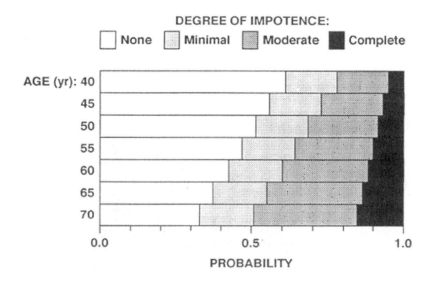

FIGURE 3.3. Prevalence in percentage of men of various ages from 40 to 79 years reporting minimal, moderate, or complete erectile dysfunction. Prevalence of minimal erectile dysfunction remains constant across the age spectrum, whereas prevalence of moderate and complete erectile dysfunction increases progressively with age. From Feldman, Goldstein, Hatzichristou, Krane, and McKinlay (1994, p. 56). Copyright 1994 by Lippincott Williams & Wilkins. Reprinted by permission.

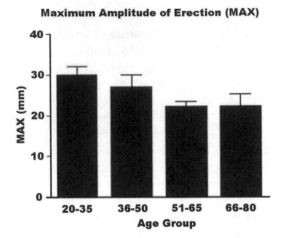

FIGURE 3.4. Mean maximum amplitude (mm) of erectile responses recorded via circumferential penile plethysmography in response to presentations of erotic stimulation. Means are plotted for four age cohorts. Standard deviations are indicated by the hatch marks. From Rowland, Greenleaf, Dorfman, and Davidson (1993, p. 552). Copyright 1993 by Kluwer Academic/Plenum Publishers. Reprinted by permission.

indicated significant age-related decreases in the frequency of sexual activity, including intercourse, orgasm, and masturbation. Perhaps surprisingly, participants in this study reported no reduction in sexual satisfaction with age.

It might be argued that these reductions in sexual arousability with age are due to psychological effects. Perhaps the erotic stimuli are found to be less attractive or stimulating among older participants. However, Karacan, Salis, Thornby, and Williams (1976) re-

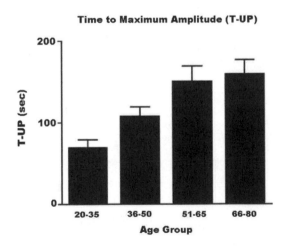

FIGURE 3.5. Mean latency to maximum amplitude (in seconds) of erectile responses recorded via circumferential penile plethysmography in response to presentations of erotic stimulation. Means are plotted for four age cohorts. Standard deviations are indicated by the hatch marks. From Rowland, Greenleaf, Dorfman, and Davidson (1993, p. 552). Copyright 1993 by Kluwer Academic/Plenum Publishers. Reprinted by permission.

corded nocturnal penile tumescence in the course of a study of sleep. Plotting the frequency, duration, and rigidity of nocturnal erections over the age of the research participants, these authors reported that the participants' nocturnal erections peaked at age 13 and declined slowly with age. These data would suggest that the observed aging effects on sexual arousal are due to biological, not psychological, mechanisms.

THE EFFECTS OF AGING ON SEXUAL AROUSAL IN THE SEX OFFENDER

The current literature supports the notion that sexual arousal decreases with age in sex offenders. Hall (1992) examined the relationship between age and erectile responses measured by circumferential penile plethysmography in 169 inpatient adult male sex offenders ranging from 20 to 66 years of age. Age accounted for a significant proportion of the variance in arousal, and arousability was inversely related to age. This reduction in sex offender arousability seems to begin at an early age. Kaemingk, Koselka, Becker, and Kaplan (1995) examined the relationship between age and erectile responses measured by circumferential penile plethysmography in 104 adolescent sex offenders ranging in age from 13 to 17 years. Somewhat surprisingly (given the restricted age range), age accounted for a significant proportion of the variance in arousal, with the younger adolescents showing erectile responses to a greater number of stimulus presentations, and demonstrating a greater mean percentage of full erection scores across stimulus presentations.

Using volumetric penile plethysmography, we (Blanchard & Barbaree, 2005) examined the strength of arousal as a function of age among more than 1,400 sex offenders referred for phallometric testing to the Kurt Freund Phallometric Laboratory. The dependent measure of penile response was a standard quantity in the laboratory, the "output index" or OI (Freund, 1967). This is the average of the three greatest responses to any stimulus category except "neutral," where penile response is expressed in cubic centimeters (cc) of blood volume increase from the start of a trial. As measured by our laboratory equipment, full erection for the average patient corresponds to a blood volume increase of 20–25 cc. Figure 3.6 shows the relation between penile response and age. The bars represent the mean observed blood volume increase for patients of every age from 13 to 79. The amplitude of penile response declined steeply from almost full erection in adolescence to lower levels at about age 30; it continued to decline after that, but at a lower rate. It is clear from the observed data that the decrease would be better described by a curved than by a straight line. The line of best fit was plotted as the reciprocal of age.

THE EFFECTS OF AGING ON SEXUAL RECIDIVISM IN SEX OFFENDERS

Castration was evaluated as a treatment for sex offenders in studies conducted in Europe in the 1960s and 1970s. These studies were quite consistent in their finding that castration of adult sex offenders causes a substantial reduction in the rate of recidivism (Freund, 1980; Heim & Hirsch, 1979). The mechanism for this decrease in sexual recidivism is thought to be reductions in the male sex hormone testosterone brought about by castration (Freund, 1980). Therefore, given the reductions in blood levels of testosterone that occur with age, we would predict that recidivism should decrease in sex offenders with aging.

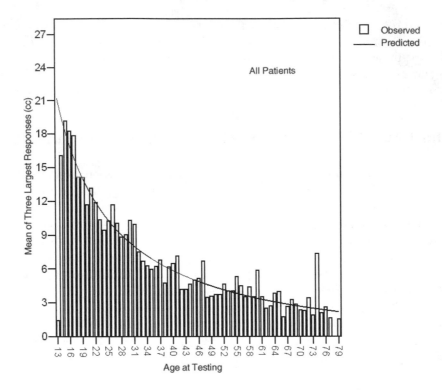

FIGURE 3.6. Phallometric response of all patients as a function of age. The bars represent the mean observed blood volume increase (i.e., mean OI) for patients of every age. The curved line is the predicted blood volume increase for patients of every age, as computed by linear regression. From Blanchard and Barbaree (2005, p. 448). Copyright 2005 by Kluwer Academic/Plenum Publishers. Reprinted by permission.

Hanson (2002) has examined the effects of age at release on rates of sexual recidivism in a large sample of sex offenders. The results indicated that these sex offenders' risk for recidivism decreased with age at release. According to Hanson's description, the patterns of decline differed among rapists, child molesters, and incest offenders. In incest offenders, from an initial peak at ages 18–24, there was a rapid decline to below 10% at ages 25–29, with a continuing gradual decline to age 60, after which there were no incidents of reoffense in these samples. In nonfamilial child molesters, the rate of recidivism peaked when offenders were released at ages 25–29, then gradually declined to release at age 50, at which time the rate of decline increased markedly to release at age 70. Rapists showed a gradual decline in rates of recidivism from 18 years to 60 years. Recidivism rates are plotted for the different age cohorts in Figure 3.7.

When we examine the plotted rates of recidivism over age at release, there are two issues that require mention and clarification—one minor, the other more important. The minor issue is that the age intervals on the abscissa are unequal, and therefore the plots in Figure 3.7 are distorted somewhat. The more important issue concerns the fact that the statistically significant differences between groups in pattern of decline identified by Hanson (2002) are entirely due to performance in the youngest age group (18–24 years) of extrafamilial child molesters. Although only linear trends were evident in the rapists and incest offenders, logistic regression identified a significant curvilinear component to

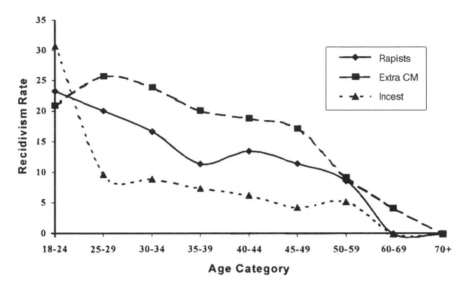

FIGURE 3.7. Recidivism rates (%) plotted for nine age cohorts from 18 to 70+ years of age. Separate plots are provided for three separate offender groups: incest offenders, extrafamiliar child molesters, and rapists. From Hanson (2002, p. 1054). Copyright 2002 by Sage Publications. Reprinted by permission.

the trend of recidivism over age at release in extrafamilial child molesters (Hanson, 2002). Examination of Figure 3.7 indicates that recidivism rates increased from the youngest (18–24) to the next youngest (24–29) age group in these offenders. Thereafter, from age 25 on, rates of recidivism among the extrafamilial child molesters decreased in an approximately linear fashion. Our focus in the present chapter is on changes in behavior that occur with aging. For these reasons, and for the sake of simplicity, our discussion of the Hanson data will exclude consideration of the youngest (18–24 years) age group.

In a previous paper, we (Barbaree, Blanchard, & Langton, 2003) replotted the Hanson (2002) data for offenders released between the ages of 25 and 70+ (see Figure 3.8). The recidivism rate for each offender subgroup (child molesters, rapists, incest offenders) was plotted over the midpoint of the appropriate age interval. For each group, a regression equation was calculated, and a regression line was plotted. Also, we calculated correlations between observed and predicted rates of recidivism and found that all correlations were above .97, indicating that the regression lines were good fits to the observed data. A number of aspects of these data become very clear from this replotting. In the Hanson data set, (1) recidivism in sex offenders declined from the late 20s; (2) the decline can be best characterized as a linear decline over age at release in all offender subgroups; (3) the decline ended at age 70, and at that age the estimated recidivism rate was zero for all subgroups; and (4) in their youth, sex offender subgroups differed in the rate at which they recidivated, with child molesters showing the highest rate and incest offenders showing the lowest rate.

We (Barbaree et al., 2003) then examined sexual recidivism in a sample of sex offenders (N = 477) released from a Canadian federal penitentiary and followed for an average of almost 5 years. It was hypothesized that sexual recidivism would decrease in a linear fashion as a function of age at release. The regression constants derived from Hanson (2002) as described above provided a basis for making a precise prediction of the

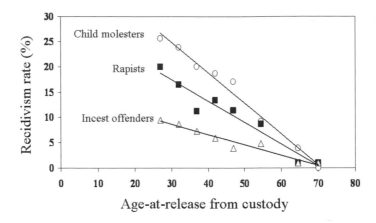

FIGURE 3.8. Recidivism rates (%) replotted as a function of age at release from custody in child molesters, rapists, and incest offenders age 25 and older. From Barbaree, Blanchard, and Langton (2003, p. 64). Copyright 2003 by the New York Academy of Sciences. Reprinted by permission.

values of the regression constants in our study. We divided our sample into age cohorts (21–30; 31–40; 41–50; 51+) and calculated a failure (recidivism) rate for each age cohort. Calculating a regression equation describing the reductions in recidivism over age for our data yielded almost exactly the same slope and intercept (regression constants) as we had derived from the data reported by Hanson.

Between the publication of our 2003 paper and the time of our writing this chapter, three additional studies of the relations between recidivism and age in sex offenders have been published. Fazel, Sjöstedt, Långström, and Grann (2006) followed all adult male sex offenders released from prison in Sweden between 1993 and 1997 (N = 1,303) and recorded criminal convictions for an average of 8.9 years. They divided their sample into age cohorts (< 25; 25–39; 40–54; 55+). Recidivism rates decreased significantly in older cohorts.[1] Thornton (2006) followed a large nationally representative sample (N = 752) of sex offenders for a period of 10 years after their release from prison in the United Kingdom. Dividing his sample by age cohort (< 18; 18–24; 25–39; 40–59; 60+), he found that the rate of sexual recidivism declined generally with age. Finally, Hanson (2006) followed a very large sample (N = 3,425, compiled over eight separate samples) of sex offenders released from prison in North America and the United Kingdom. Hanson calculated 5-year recidivism rates for different age cohorts (18–24; 25–39; 40–49; 50–59; 60+).

In order to compare the results of these five studies (Barbaree et al., 2003; Fazel et al., 2006;[1] Hanson, 2002, 2006; Thornton, 2006) and to highlight similarities among the studies' findings, we plotted their results in a comparable format on one graph. Since the focus in this chapter is on declines in sexual behavior after the peak in testosterone levels in the mid-20s, we eliminated data for age groups below age 25. Since these studies used age cohorts with different class intervals, we calculated a regression equation separately for each study. To estimate the goodness of fit of the obtained straight line, we calculated a correlation between the expected and observed values obtained in each study. Since each of these studies used a different follow-up period, we adjusted the recidivism rates proportionally to correct to a 5-year follow-up period. We then plotted the adjusted regression lines for these five studies in one figure, presented here as Figure 3.9. These regression equations were all good representations of the data obtained from each study,

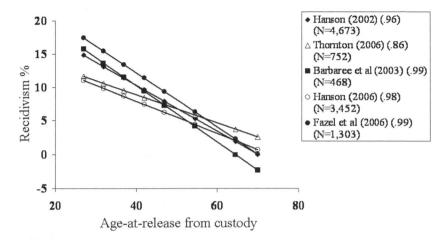

FIGURE 3.9. Replotted recidivism as a function of age at release from custody corrected to 5 years' time at risk (data from Barbaree et al., 2003; Fazel et al., 2006; Hanson, 2002, 2006; Thornton, 2006) (total N = 8,879). Correlations indicate goodness of fit of the regression line to observed recidivism over age in these studies.

with correlations ranging from .86 to .99. These studies showed a very consistent effect of age at release across studies—namely, a linear decline in recidivism from age 25 to age 70.

Based on the data reviewed above, it would be reasonable to conclude that when sex offenders are released from custody at different ages, they show age-related decreases in recidivism. The best description of the age function is a gradual linear decrease in recidivism rates from age 25 to age 70, at which point the estimated recidivism rate is near zero. This age function is similar to that described earlier in this chapter for blood levels of testosterone, for sexual arousal in normal men, and for sexual arousal in sex offenders. Additionally, these reductions in sexual recidivism are very similar to reductions in nonsexual recidivism (both violent and nonviolent) among nonsexual criminals (Hirschi & Gottfredson, 1983; Sampson & Laub, 2003, 2005).

With the support of these empirical data, the present chapter proposes the addition of a new category of risk factor for sexual recidivism—namely, maturation. In the current discussion of risk factors, static risk factors are those characteristics of offenders related to recidivism that do not change over time. Dynamic risk factors are those that may change over time. In contrast to both of these factors, maturation is a risk factor that exhibits changes over time; however, unlike dynamic risk, the change is predictable and inexorable, and once maturational changes occur, they are not reversed under normal circumstances.

THE ACTUARIAL CHALLENGE TO THE EFFECTS OF AGE ON RECIDIVISM

Despite the wealth of data presented above indicating changes in recidivism risk with age, there is no general or widespread acceptance of maturation as an important risk factor among the proponents or developers of actuarial risk instruments. Specifically, there is no acceptance of the necessity for adjustments to estimates of risk in the older sex offender.

Hanson (2006) has suggested that adjustments in actuarial risk estimates might be appropriate after age 60, but discourages any adjustments before that age. Other proponents and developers of actuarial instruments argue against any adjustments being made for older sex offenders. Their argument is based on their challenge to the validity of age-related decreases in recidivism (Harris & Rice, 2007).

The proponents of actuarial assessment argue that the apparent effects of age on sexual recidivism are actually due to actuarial risk. Their argument has a number of interrelated components.[2] First, they argue that the evidence for the age effect is based on cross-sectional rather than longitudinal data. They point out that age at release is confounded with actuarial risk. Offenders who arc released at an older age are also lower in actuarial risk. Second, they argue that age at first offense (a static age variable) is a more powerfully predictive age variable than age at release (a maturational age variable). They postulate that high-risk offenders will, on a probabilistic basis, offend earlier in life, and that these same high-risk offenders will persist in offending into old age. Finally, the proponents of actuarial assessment argue that once the effects of actuarial risk (scores on the actuarial instrument and age at first offense) have been taken into account, age at release adds nothing to the prediction equation. They argue that because age at release does not enter the prediction equation, there is no significant aging effect to be recognized, and therefore no adjustments to risk estimates for the older sex offender. We deal with each of these arguments below.

THE CONFOUND BETWEEN AGE AT RELEASE AND ACTUARIAL RISK

In our data set (see Barbaree, Langton, & Peacock, 2006), age at release was correlated with total actuarial scores on the VRAG, SORAG, Static-99, and MnSOST-R, r's (309) = −.498, −.380, −.233, and −.159, respectively, all p's < .01. Therefore, the proponents of actuarial assessment are correct in saying that age at release and actuarial risk are confounded. Offenders who are older at release have lower actuarial scores. However, the problem with confounds is that they can be legitimately argued either way. If lower actuarial scores among older offenders can be used to explain lower recidivism among older offenders, then older age at release can be used to explain lower rates of recidivism among offenders with lower actuarial scores.

In an effort to illustrate how age at release might be used to explain actuarial risk, we (Barbaree, Langton, & Blanchard, 2007) compared mean age at release between and among subgroups of sex offenders who were assigned different scores on items contained in the VRAG and SORAG. We found 9 items out of the 12 and 14 items on the VRAG and SORAG, respectively, for which mean age at release was significantly different between or among groups with different item responses, and where the older age group(s) were assigned the lower risk score. These items were as follows: lived with both biological parents to age 16, elementary school maladjustment, alcohol problems, marital status, criminal history score nonviolent, sex offenses only against girls < 14 years of age, failure on prior conditional release, age at index offense, and Psychopathy Checklist—Revised score.

It is not clear why these offender subgroups defined by their item responses would have different mean ages at release. A possible explanation is based on the actuarial method itself—the statistical method used in the development of actuarial instruments. In pure actuarial risk assessment, the items have no meaning. They are selected and weighted based on their empirical relationship with outcome. If the studies we reviewed above are correct in concluding that recidivism decreases with age at release, we should not be surprised that the VRAG/SORAG item responses showed a statistical relationship with age at release. In other words, age at release, actuarial item responses, and recidivism are intercorrelated. Age at release is imbedded in the actuarial instruments—not just in items whose nominal meaning has some bearing on some measure of age, but also in items whose meaning has no obvious conceptual relationship to age.

Since these nine items constitute the majority of actuarial items on the VRAG and SORAG, it would be expected that the combination of these items in a total score would reflect an important relationship with age at release. Figures 3.10 and 3.11 present box plots (SPSS version 14) for the VRAG and SORAG actuarial bin scores, respectively, with actuarial bin scores plotted over age-at-release cohorts (21–30; 31–40; 41–50; 51+). For both the VRAG and SORAG, mean actuarial bin scores decreased over age in a linear fashion. For the youngest cohort, the median actuarial bin was at or near the 6th bin, whereas for the oldest cohort, the median actuarial bin was at or near the 4th and 3rd bins for the VRAG and SORAG, respectively. Analyses of trend (using an unweighted means correction for unequal N) indicated that for both the VRAG, F_{linear} (1, 307) = 92.666, $p < .001$), and the SORAG, F_{linear} (1, 307) = 53.539, $p < .001$, the linear function of actuarial bin over age at release was highly significant. Tests of the deviations from linearity were not significant (both F's < 1.00). If recidivism decreases with age, as indicated

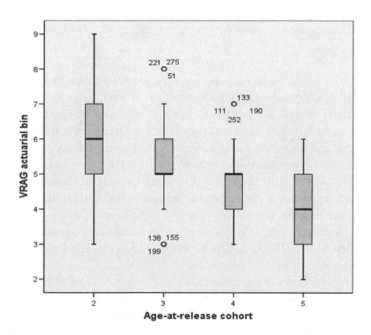

FIGURE 3.10. Box plots of the mean VRAG bin scores plotted as a function of age-at-release cohort. The box depicts scores from the 25th to the 75th percentiles, and the horizontal line through the box represents the median score. The "whiskers" represent the range of values in the sample from lowest to highest. Outliers are excluded from the box plot but indicated on the figure. Age-at-release cohorts 2 through 5 were released from custody at 21–30, 31–40, 41–50, and 51+ years of age, respectively.

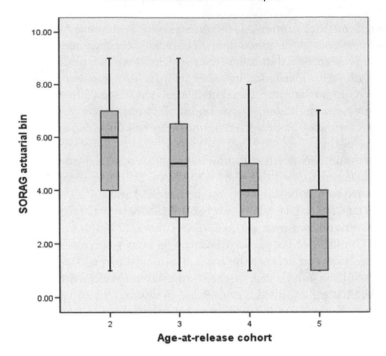

FIGURE 3.11. Box plots of the mean SORAG bin scores plotted as a function of age-at-release cohort. The box depicts scores from the 25th to the 75th percentiles, and the horizontal line through the box represents the median score. The "whiskers" represent the range of values in the sample from lowest to highest. Outliers are excluded from the box plot but indicated on the figure. Age-at-release cohorts 2 through 5 were released from custody at 21–30, 31–40, 41–50, and 51+ years of age, respectively.

in the review above, lower recidivism among offenders who obtain a low actuarial score may be due to their older age at release, not their actuarial risk.

To examine the role of age at release in the prediction of recidivism by the VRAG and SORAG, we (Barbaree et al., 2007) regressed item scores and actuarial bin scores over age at release and saved the residual scores as "age-corrected" actuarial scores. The residual scores had no correlation with age at release. We then compared the age-corrected actuarial scores with the original actuarial scores in their ability to predict recidivism via receiver operating characteristic analysis. For both actuarial items and actuarial bin scores, the original scores were significantly superior in predictive ability to the comparable age-corrected scores. These analyses indicated that age at release has contributed to the ability of the VRAG and SORAG to predict recidivism in sex offenders, at least in our data set.

In the empirical process of selecting items for the VRAG and SORAG, the developers of these actuarial instruments have unwittingly selected items that reflect distinctive characteristics of younger offenders. By virtue of the fact that younger offenders are more likely to reoffend sexually, for reasons reviewed above (including higher blood levels of testosterone), the items that identified younger members of the sample are related to recidivism. By selecting numerous such items and combining them in an actuarial instrument, the total score is predictive of recidivism. In this way, the predictive accuracy of an actuarial instrument can be said to borrow some of its predictive power from the relationship between aging and recidivism in the sex offender.

For Harris and Rice (2007) and the anonymous reviewers of our manuscripts, the fact that age at release does not add to the predictive equation after actuarial scores and age at first offense are entered into the equation leads them to the conclusion that there is no effect of aging on recidivism in sex offenders. We disagree and feel that their logic is flawed. As we have demonstrated (Barbaree et al., 2007), the effects of aging are imbedded in their actuarial instruments. When actuarial scores are entered into the equation first, the effects of aging already contribute to the predictive accuracy of their instruments. In this way, the subsequent "test" of age at release is preempted. The variance due to age at release is at least partly used up in the prior test of the actuarial score. Testing the ability of actuarial scores to predict recidivism is not an appropriate or fair statistical method of evaluating the effects of aging on recidivism.

Ultimately, the actuarial argument seems unconvincing to us. By arguing that there is no reduction in recidivism with age, the proponents and developers of the actuarial instruments are arguing that sexual recidivism is the only index of sexual behavior in the human male that does not decrease with age. (As an aside, they are also arguing that it is the only criminal behavior in men that does not decrease with age. Due to space limitations in this chapter, we have not reviewed the substantial literature on the effects of age on criminal recidivism.) While we have to agree that there is a confound between age at release and actuarial risk, we feel that the more convincing interpretation of the data in all its aspects is that sexual recidivism does decrease with age, and that actuarial risk cannot account for all of the decline observed in the published studies.

AGE AT FIRST OFFENSE VERSUS AGE AT RELEASE

Harris and Rice (2007) have investigated the contribution of age at release to prediction of recidivism in the samples of violent offenders that were used in the development of the VRAG and SORAG. They have concluded that although age at release predicted violent recidivism, it did not do so as well as age at first offense and other actuarial variables. They have concluded that age at release provides no useful additional information concerning recidivism risk.

This argument seems unconvincing to us. These two indices of age are entirely and profoundly different. Age at first offense is a static factor. Once an offender has committed a criminal offense, his age at first offense is determined for the remainder of his life. This index of age bears no relationship whatever to the aging processes we have reviewed and described earlier in this chapter. In contrast, age at release is a maturational variable, in that it reflects the level of maturity of the individual when he is released from custody. This variable is determined by many factors, including age at index offense, sentence length or length of incarceration, parole decision making, and so on. But importantly, age at release changes over time, and with it the level of risk posed by the offender.

Their argument is unconvincing to us, partly because we do not understand why the power of age at first offense to predict recidivism takes anything away from the significance of age at release as a predictor. In other words, whether or not age at first offense is a significant predictor of recidivism seems to us to be totally independent of the predictive ability of age at release. Aging can have its effect on recidivism whether or not higher-risk youthful offenders are convicted of crimes at a young age.

The only possible argument we can think of that could be made in respect of this issue is that age at first offense and age at release are correlated in these samples, and therefore, from a statistical perspective, their collinearity requires us to disentangle their effects. This correlation might be the result of a large proportion of sex offender samples consisting of first-time offenders for whom age at release and age at first conviction are separated by sentence length. The actuarial argument might be that the age at release is not an important predictor and is only a statistical predictor due to its correlation with what Harris and Rice regard as the primary static actuarial age predictor, age at first offense.

To investigate the relationship between age at first offense and age at release, we conducted a further supplemental analysis of our data set (Barbaree et al., 2003, 2007). We constructed a scatter plot showing the statistical relationship between these two age variables. It is presented in Figure 3.12. As will be obvious on inspection of this figure, there is no meaningful relationship between these two indices of age, at least in our data set. Although there is a mathematical correlation between the two age variables, $r(466) = .55, p < .001$, the correlation is a statistical artifact. Since it is impossible for offenders to be released at an age younger than the age of their first offense, the scatter plot is empty above the diagonal, forcing a mathematical correlation. Taking this artifact into account while carefully inspecting the scatter plot leads the reasonable observer to the conclusion that there is no meaningful relationship between these variables.

Harris and Rice (2007) have reported that age at first offense predicts recidivism. They argue further that the effects of age at release are insignificant or small when age at release is entered into the equation after age at first offense. These findings are used by these authors to argue for the primacy of the static actuarial age variable. Our counterargument is based on the spurious correlation between the two age variables depicted in

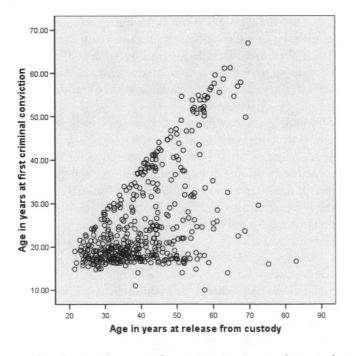

FIGURE 3.12. Scatter plot plotting the age at first conviction in months over the age at release in years in a sample ($N = 468$) of sex offenders. The plot is empty above the diagonal because an offender cannot be released from custody at an age younger than the age of his first conviction.

Figure 3.12. When age at first offense is entered first, it preempts a fair test of age at release. At least some of the variance due to age at release has already been used up in the test of the static age variable. It seems to us that in efforts to make a fair assessment of the aging effect, the relative strength of predictive clout between the two age variables is irrelevant. We would argue that if there is any effect of age at release, after reasonable controls for actuarial risk (i.e., free of the confound with age at release), then we must conclude that aging has a significant effect on recidivism in the sex offender.

THE NEED TO ADJUST ESTIMATES OF RISK IN THE OLDER OFFENDER

Although the actuarial test developers have unwittingly capitalized on the relationship between age at release and recidivism, they deny the effects of aging when applying the instrument score to the evaluation of risk in the individual sex offender. Because actuarial items are predominantly static items, a high actuarial score obtained by a young man will follow him unchanged for the rest of his life, despite repeated scoring by various evaluators. So even while the offender's risk is decreasing as part of the maturational process, the actuarial instrument confirms his static risk for the remainder of his life. Ironically, the validity of the actuarial instrument that asserts his ongoing risk is based partly on the effects of age on recidivism (Barbaree et al., 2007).

In arguing against the need for adjustments in the older offender, the proponents of actuarial assessment state that the existing actuarial instruments weight age more or less appropriately, and that no further adjustments for aging are required. We feel that this represents a significant error in logic. Actuarial items code characteristics of offenders at a particular point in time, usually the date of the assessment as release from custody is imminent (or, in research, the date of the file from which the items are coded). The test of the predictive accuracy of the actuarial test is based on an analysis of relations between the data recorded at the time of the assessment and later recidivism. The maturational variable (age at release) contributes to the prediction equation, either directly or indirectly, through contrasts between different offenders released at different ages. These between-offender contrasts contribute to the predictive power of the actuarial instruments, because offenders released at a younger age recidivate at a higher rate. However, age as a maturational risk factor is a within-offender contrast. Because the instruments were developed without any explicit recognition of maturation as a potential risk factor, and because the resulting items sets do not include any items that reflect changes in risk that occur after the age of 30, the actuarial instruments are not sensitive to the within-offender changes that occur with age. In order to accommodate age as a maturational risk factor, an assessment instrument must make adjustments to estimates of risk as the offender ages.

CONSTRUCTING A PREDICTION EQUATION
THAT IS SENSITIVE TO THE EFFECTS OF AGING

Our method of testing the effects of age controlled for actuarial risk and for the spurious correlation between age at first offense and age at release. Our method recognized that age at release is embedded in actuarial risk scores. We (Barbaree et al., 2005a) used stepwise Cox regression to test the effects of age at release. In the first step, to control for actuarial risk, we entered five actuarial factors that had been calculated in an earlier factor analysis of static actuarial items (Barbaree et al., 2006). These factors were Antisocial Behavior, Persistence, Child Sexual Abuse, Detached Predatory Behavior, and Male Victim(s). These factors were found to be orthogonal (uncorrelated) to a sixth factor, Young and Single, and therefore were thought to be relatively independent of age at release. In the second step, we entered age at first offense. Finally, in the last step, we entered age at release. For both sexual and violent recidivism, we found that age at release was a significant predictor of recidivism, even after controlling for actuarial risk and age at first offense. Hazard ratios derived from the Cox regression indicated that recidivism risk decreased by approximately 5% each year.

SUMMARY AND FUTURE DIRECTIONS

The present chapter has been founded on the premise that the male sex hormone testosterone plays a significant role in the production of sexual behavior in the human male, and that age-related reductions in blood levels of the hormone result in concomitant reductions in numerous indices of male sexual behavior in the aging man. Age-dependent reductions have been observed in libido, coitus, erectile frequency and quality, and frequency of masturbation. Age-dependent increases have been observed in sexual problems in the aging man, including erectile dysfunction and lack of interest in sexual relations. Sex offenders are not immune to these effects of aging. Specific age-related effects have been observed in sex offenders' level or amplitude of sexual arousal and in their recidivism. Both sexual arousal and recidivism decrease in sex offenders with age.

These effects of aging are not widely accepted or recognized in the field. Importantly, current methods of assessment of sex offenders do not account for the effects of aging. In other words, no adjustments or allowances are typically made in estimates of recidivism risk in the current best-practice approaches to assessment. Current assessment methods are based on the development and validation of actuarial instruments. In the studies that have led to percentage estimates of recidivism over 5, 10, and 15 years after release, offenders in the research samples were released from custody in their mid-30s. Currently recommended practice is to apply these percentages to sex offenders at all ages, even elderly offenders. Methods of adjusting these percentages have been recommended. Rich Wollert (2006) has described a method of adjusting estimates of risk for older offenders, based on Hanson's (2002) data. Nevertheless, proponents of actuarial assessment have not recognized or accepted this method of adjustment, and such adjustments are not recommended by them.

Professional standards guiding the use of psychological tests warn against the use of tests if such use may be discriminatory on the basis of age, race, culture, or other factors. If the person being tested is substantially different from the individuals who made up the standardization sample for the test, the test should be applied with extreme caution. The current chapter makes the point that direct application of current actuarial instruments to elderly sex offenders is potentially discriminatory.

The implications of the aging effects reviewed in this chapter are profound. Current policy and legislation in most Western jurisdictions target sex offenders for civil commitment or long-term incapacitation when the offenders are in their middle years. Current practice is to continue the detention of many of these offenders on into old age. Incarceration of these offenders is grossly expensive and seems unjustified if risk is generally lower in the aged sex offender. One solution is the revamping of the current risk assessment methodologies to accommodate reductions in the performance of sexually deviant behavior in the older sex offender.

NOTES

1. The Swedish data showed exceptionally low rates of sexual recidivism, much lower than those reported for the U.K. and North American data here or in previous reports. Allowing for possible differences between Sweden and other jurisdictions in the way sexual crimes are charged, prosecuted, and tried, including possible differences in plea bargaining, we chose to use the Swedish data reflecting "any violent" reconviction—a statistic that included all sexual offenses. These percentages were very similar to those reported in the U.K. and North American data for sexual recidivism.

2. The actuarial position is presented in part in Harris and Rice (2007) and has been articulated by numerous anonymous reviewers of our manuscripts on the effects of aging on sexual recidivism submitted for publication (Barbaree, Langton, & Peacock, 2005a, 2005b), communicated to one of us (Howard E. Barbaree) by Karl Hanson (associate editor of *Sexual Abuse: A Journal of Research and Treatment*). We are unable to identify the individual sources of all these arguments, and we therefore simply refer in this chapter to the general actuarial position or argument.

REFERENCES

Anderson, R. A., Bancroft, J., & Wu, F. C. (1992). The effects of exogenous testosterone on sexuality and mood of normal men. *Journal of Clinical Endocrinology and Metabolism, 75*, 1503–1507.

Bagatell, C. J., Heiman, J. R., Rivier, J. E., & Bremner, W. J. (1994). Effects of endogenous testosterone and estradiol on sexual behavior in normal young men. *Journal of Clinical Endocrinology and Metabolism, 78*, 711–716.

Baker, H. W. G., Burger, H. G., de Kretser, D. M., Hudson, B., O'Connor, S., Wang, C., et al. (1976). Changes in the pituitary–testicular system with age. *Clinical Endocrinology, 5*, 349–372.

Baker, H. W. G., & Hudson, B. (1983). Changes in the pituitary–testicular axis with age. *Monographs on Endocrinology, 25*, 71–83.

Barbaree, H. E., Blanchard, R., & Langton, C. M. (2003). The development of sexual aggression through the life span: The effect of age on sexual arousal and recidivism among sex offenders. *Annals of the New York Academy of Sciences, 989*, 59–71.

Barbaree, H. E., Langton, C. M., & Blanchard, R. (2007). Predicting recidivism in sex offenders using the VRAG and SORAG: The contribution of age-at-release. *International Journal of Forensic Mental Health, 6*, 29–46.

Barbaree, H. E., Langton, C. M., & Peacock, E. J. (2005a). *The effect of age-at-release on recidivism in sex offenders: Making a longitudinal inference on the basis of cross-sectional data.* Unpublished manuscript.

Barbaree, H. E., Langton, C. M., & Peacock, E. J. (2005b). *The effect of age-at-release on recidivism of high-risk sex offenders.* Unpublished manuscript.

Barbaree, H. E., Langton, C. M., & Peacock, E. J. (2006). The factor structure of static actuarial items: Its relation to prediction. *Sexual Abuse: A Journal of Research and Treatment, 18*, 207–228.

Beach, F. A. (1948). *Hormones and behavior.* New York: Hoeber.

Beach, F. A. (1970). Coital behavior in dogs: VI. Long term effects of castration on mating in the male. *Journal of Comparative and Physiological Psychology, 70*, 1–32.

Beach, F. A. (1971). Hormonal factors controlling the differentiation, development and display of copulatory behavior in the ramstergig and related species. In L. Aronson & E. Tobach (Eds.), *Biopsychology of development* (pp. 249–296). New York: Academic Press.

Blanchard, R., & Barbaree, H. E. (2005). The strength of sexual arousal as a function of the age of the sex offender: Comparisons among pedophiles, hebephiles and teliophiles. *Sexual Abuse: A Journal of Research and Treatment, 17*, 441–456.

Bradford, J. M. W., & Fedoroff, P. (2006). Pharmacological treatment of the juvenile sex offender. In H. E. Barbaree & W. L. Marshall (Eds.), *The juvenile sex offender* (2nd ed., pp. 358–382). New York: Guilford Press.

Coyotupa, J., Parlow, A. F., & Kovacic, N. (1973). Serum testosterone and dihydrotestosterone levels following orchiectomy in the adult rat. *Endocrinology, 92*, 1579–1581.

Davidson, J. M., Camargo, C. A., & Smith, E. R. (1979). Effects of androgen on sexual behavior in hypogonadal men. *Journal of Clinical Endocrinology and Metabolism, 48*, 955–958.

Davidson, J. M., Chen, J. J., Crapo, L., Gray, G. D., Greenleaf, W. J., & Catania, J. A. (1983). Hormonal changes and sexual function in aging men. *Journal of Clinical Endocrinology and Metabolism, 57*, 71–77.

Davidson, J. M., Kwan, M., & Greenleaf, W. J. (1982). Hormonal replacement and sexuality. *Clinical Endocrinology and Metabolism, 11*, 599–623.

Denti, L., Pasolini, G., Sanfelici, L., Benedetti, R., Cecchetti, A., Ceda, G. P., et al. (2000). Aging-related decline of gonadal function in healthy men: Correlation with body composition and lipoproteins. *Journal of the American Geriatrics Society, 48*, 51–58.

Doren, D. M. (2002). *Evaluating sex offenders: A manual for civil commitments and beyond.* Thousand Oaks, CA: Sage.

Epperson, D. L., Kaul, J. D., Huot, S. J., Hesselton, D., Alexander, W., & Goldman, R. (1998). *Minnesota Sex Offender Screening Tool—Revised (MnSOST-R).* St. Paul: Minnesota Department of Corrections.

Fazel, S., Sjöstedt, G., Långström, N., & Grann, M. (2006). Risk factors for criminal recidivism in older sexual offenders. *Sexual Abuse: A Journal of Research and Treatment, 18*, 159–167.

Feder, H. H. (1984). Hormones and sexual behavior. *Annual Review of Psychology, 35*, 165–200.

Feldman, H. A., Goldstein, I., Hatzichristou, D. G., Krane, R. J., & McKinlay, J. B. (1994). Impotence and its medical and psychosocial correlates: Results of the Massachusetts male aging study. *Journal of Urology, 151*, 54–61.

Freund, K. (1967). Diagnosing homo- or heterosexuality and erotic age-preference by means of a psychophysiological test. *Behaviour Research and Therapy, 5*, 209–228.

Freund, K. (1980). Therapeutic sex drive reduction. *Acta Psychiatrica Scandinavica, 62*(Suppl. 287), 1–38.

Gray, A., Berlin, J. A., McKinlay, J. B., & Longcope, C. (1991). An examination of research design effects on the association of testosterone and male aging: Results of a meta-analysis. *Journal of Clinical Epidemiology, 44*, 671–684.

Hall, G. N. (1992). Sexual arousal as a function of physiological and cognitive variables in a sexual offender population. *Archives of Sexual Behaviour, 20*, 359–369.

Hanson, R. K. (1997). *The development of a brief actuarial risk scale for sexual offense recidivism* (User Report No. 1997-04). Ottawa: Department of the Solicitor General of Canada.

Hanson, R. K. (2002). Recidivism and age: Follow-up data on 4,673 sexual offenders. *Journal of Interpersonal Violence, 17*, 1046–1062.

Hanson, R. K. (2006). Does Static-99 predict recidivism among older sexual offenders? *Sexual Abuse: A Journal of Research and Treatment, 18*, 343–355.

Hanson, R. K., & Bussière, M. T. (1998). Predicting relapse: A meta-analysis of sexual offender recidivism studies. *Journal of Consulting and Clinical Psychology, 66*, 348–362.

Hanson, R. K., & Morton-Bourgon, K. (2004). *Predictors of sexual recidivism: An updated meta-analysis* (User Report No. 2004-02). Ottawa: Department of the Solicitor General of Canada.

Hanson, R. K., Steffy, R. A., & Gauthier, R. (1993). Long-term recidivism of child molesters. *Journal of Consulting and Clinical Psychology, 61*, 646–652.

Hanson, R. K., & Thornton, D. (1999). *Static-99: Improving actuarial risk assessments for sex offenders* (User Report No. 1999-02). Ottawa: Department of the Solicitor General of Canada.

Harman, S. M. (2003). Testosterone, sexuality, and erectile function in aging men. *Journal of Andrology, 24*(6, Suppl.), S42–S45.

Harman, S. M., Metter, E. J., Tobin, J. D., Pearson, J., & Blackman, M. R. (2001). Longitudinal effects of aging on serum total and free testosterone levels in healthy men. *Journal of Clinical Endocrinology and Metabolism, 86,* 724–731.

Harris, G. T., & Rice, M. E. (2003). Actuarial assessment of risk among sex offenders. *Annals of the New York Academy of Sciences, 989,* 198–210.

Harris, G. T., & Rice, M. E. (2007). Adjusting actuarial violence risk assessments based on aging or the passage of time. *Criminal Justice and Behavior, 34,* 297–313.

Heim, N., & Hursch, C. J. (1979). Castration of sex offenders: Treatment or punishment? A review and critique of recent European literature. *Archives of Sexual Behavior, 8,* 281–304.

Hirschi, T., & Gottfredson, M. (1983). Age and the explanation of crime. *American Journal of Sociology, 89,* 552–584.

Hutchinson, J. B. (1974). Post castration decline in behavioural responsiveness to intra-hypothalamic androgen in doves. *Brain Research, 81,* 169–181.

Jankowska, E. A., Rogucka, E., Medras, M., & Welon, Z. (2000). Relationships between age-related changes of sex steroids, obesity and body fat distribution among healthy Polish males. *Medical Science Monitor, 6,* 1159–1164.

Kaemingk, K. L., Koselka, M., Becker, J. V., & Kaplan, M. S. (1995). Age and adolescent sexual offender arousal. *Sexual Abuse: A Journal of Research and Treatment, 7,* 249–257.

Kaiser, F. E., Viosca, S. P., Morley, J. E., Mooradian, A. D., Davis, S. S., & Korenman, S. G. (1988). Impotence and aging: Clinical and hormonal factors. *Journal of the American Geriatrics Society, 36,* 511–519.

Karacan, I., Salis, P. J., Thornby, J. I., & Williams, R. L. (1976). The ontogeny of nocturnal penile tumescence. *Waking and Sleeping, 1,* 27–44.

Kemper, T. D. (1990). *Social structure and testosterone: Explorations of the socio-bio-social chain.* New Brunswick, NJ: Rutgers University Press.

Kwan, M., Greenleaf, W. J., Mann, J., Crapo, L., & Davidson, J. M. (1983). The nature of androgen action on male sexuality: A combined laboratory–self-report study on hypogonadal men. *Journal of Clinical Endocrinology and Metabolism, 57,* 557–562.

Laumann, E. O., Nicolosi, A., Glasser, D. B., Paik, A., Gingell, C., Moreira, E., et al. (2005). Sexual problems among women and men aged 40–80 y: Prevalence and correlated identified in the Global Study of Sexual Attitudes and Behaviors. *International Journal of Impotence Research, 17,* 39–57.

Luisi, M., & Franchi, F. (1980). Double-blind group comparative study of testosterone undecanoate and mesterolone in hypogonadal male patients. *Journal of Endocrinological Investigation, 3,* 305–308.

Meston, C. M., & Frohlich, P. F. (2000). The neurobiology of sexual function. *Archives of General Psychiatry, 57,* 1012–1030.

Morley, J. E., Charlton, E., Patrick, P., Kaiser, F. E., Cadeau, P., McCready, D., et al. (2000). Validation of a screening questionnaire for androgen deficiency in aging males. *Metabolism, 46,* 1239–1242.

O'Carroll, R., & Bancroft, J. (1984). Testosterone therapy for low sexual interest and erectile dysfunction in men: A controlled study. *British Journal of Psychiatry, 145,* 146–151.

O'Carroll, R., Shapiro, C., & Bancroft, J. (1985). Androgens, behaviour and nocturnal erection in hypogonadal men: The effects of varying the replacement dose. *Clinical Endocrinology, 23,* 527–538.

Ooi, D. S., Innanen, V. T., Wang, D., Chong, G. L., Donnelly, J. G., Arseneault, J. J., et al. (1998). Establishing reference intervals for DPC's free testosterone radioimmunoassay. *Clinical Biochemistry, 31,* 15–21.

Phoenix, C. H. (1978). Steroids and sexual behaviour in castrated male rhesus monkeys. *Hormones and Behavior, 10,* 1–9.

Prentky, R. A., Lee, A. F. S., Knight, R. A., & Cerce, D. (1997). Recidivism rates among child molesters and rapists: A methodological analysis. *Law and Human Behavior, 21,* 635–659.

Quinsey, V. L., Harris, G. T., Rice, M. E., & Cormier, C. A. (1998). *Violent offenders: Appraising and managing risk.* Washington, DC: American Psychological Association.

Rowland, J. M., Greenleaf, L. J., Dorfman, W. J., & Davidson, D. L. (1993). Aging and sexual function in men. *Archives of Sexual Behavior, 22,* 545–557.

Sampson, R. J., & Laub, J. H. (2003). Life course desisters?: Trajectories of crime among delinquent boys followed to age 70. *Criminology, 41,* 301–339.

Sampson, R. J., & Laub, J. H. (2005). A life-course view of the development of crime. *Annals of the American Academy of Political and Social Science, 602,* 12–45.

Seidman, S. N. (2005). Testosterone deficiency, depression and sexual function in aging men. *Psychiatric Times, 22*(11). Retrieved July 24, 2007, from http://psychiatrictimes.com/showArticle.jhtml?articleID=172900880

Schiavi, R. C. (1999). *Aging and male sexuality.* Cambridge, UK: Cambridge University Press.

Schiavi, R. C., White, D., Mandeli, J., & Levine, A. C. (1997). Effect of testosterone administration on sexual behavior and mood in men with erectile dysfunction. *Archives of Sexual Behavior, 26,* 231–241.

Swerdloff, R. S., & Wang, C. (1993). Androgen deficiency and aging in men. *Western Journal of Medicine, 159,* 579–585.

Thornton, D. (2006). Age and sexual recidivism: A variable connection. *Sexual Abuse: A Journal of Research and Treatment, 18,* 123–135.

Tsitouras, P. D., Martin, C. E., & Harman, S. M. (1982). Relationship of serum testosterone to sexual activity in healthy elderly men. *Journal of Gerontology, 37,* 288–293.

Udry, J. R., Billy, J. O. G., Morris, N. M., Groff, T. R., & Raj, M. H. (1985). Serum androgenic hormones motivate sexual behavior in adolescent boys. *Fertility and Sterility, 43,* 90–94.

Vermeulen, A., Goemaere, S., & Kaufman, J. M. (1999). Testosterone, body composition and aging. *Journal of Endocrinological Investigation, 22,* 110–116.

Wollert, R. (2006). Low base rates limit expert certainty when current actuarials are used to identify sexually violent predators. *Psychology, Public Policy and Law, 12,* 56–85.

CHAPTER 4

EXHIBITIONISM
Psychopathology and Theory

WILLIAM D. MURPHY
I. JACQUELINE PAGE

DIAGNOSTIC CRITERIA

The term "exhibitionism" is usually attributed to the French physician Lasègue (cited in Cox, 1980), and it was described in Krafft-Ebing's classic book *Psychopathia Sexualis* (1886/1965). Exhibitionism was, and still is, generally described as a male's exposure of his genitals to other people (primarily females) for sexual pleasure. These early scientists believed that exhibitionism was caused by brain disease and/or mental disorder.

The current nomenclature for the diagnosis of exhibitionism is that of the *Diagnostic and Statistical Manual of Mental Disorders*, fourth edition, text revision (DSM-IV-TR; American Psychiatric Association, 2000) and differs very little from the early descriptions. The DSM-IV-TR criteria are as follows: (1) For at least 6 months, one has recurrent, intense, sexually arousing fantasies or behaviors of exposing one's genitals to unsuspecting strangers; and (2) the fantasies, urges, or behaviors cause clinically significant distress or impairment in social, occupational, or other important areas of functioning.

O'Donohue, Regev, and Hagstrom (2000) have raised concerns about the 1994 DSM-IV diagnosis of pedophilia, noting the lack of research on the reliability and validity of the diagnosis, as well as the use of terms (e.g., "recurrent," "intense," "markedly distressed") that do not have clear behavioral referents. This criticism would also apply to exhibitionism. In addition, the diagnosis provides little information on etiology and treatment needs, and the criteria fail to capture the heterogeneous nature of individuals who expose their genitals for sexual satisfaction.

DESCRIPTION

Exhibitionism appears to be an early-onset disorder, although offenders tend to come into contact with the criminal justice system in their mid-20s (Berah & Myers, 1993; Mohr,

Turner, & Jerry, 1964). Abel and Rouleau (1990) studied 142 exhibitionists in an outpatient clinic who were promised confidentiality and found that 50% of the exhibitionists reported the onset of their sexual interest before the age of 18. Mohr and colleagues (1964), in a study of approximately 54 exhibitionists seen in a forensic clinic, found a bimodal range of onset (midteens or early 20s) in 34 cases. In forensic samples, there appears to be a steady decline of onset after age 40 (Mohr et al., 1964).

Exhibitionism, like most paraphilias, is seen as primarily a male disorder. A literature search through PsycINFO, entering the term "female exhibitionism" for the past 25 years, yielded four case studies of female exhibitionism reporting on a total of 14 female subjects (Fedoroff, Fishell, & Fedoroff, 1999; Grob, 1985; Hugh-Jones, Gough, & Littlewood, 2005; Rhoads & Boekelheide, 1984). However, in a recent study of exhibitionistic and voyeuristic behavior in a Swedish national population survey, Långström and Seto (2006) found fairly high rates of self-reported exhibitionism among females. This study was conducted by the Swedish Public Health Institute; as part of a general sexual health questionnaire, specific questions were asked about exhibitionism and voyeurism. Subjects were randomly selected from the Swedish population and for this study consisted of 1,279 men and 1,171 women between the ages of 18 and 60. Seventy-six respondents answered yes to the following question: "Have you ever exposed your genitals to a stranger and become sexually aroused by this?" Of the 76 subjects who answered yes, 31.6% were female. It is unlikely that all the subjects answering yes to this question would meet diagnostic criteria for exhibitionism in terms of frequency and intensity of the behavior, but it does suggest that in the general population women may engage in acts of self-exposure more frequently than the clinical literature would suggest.

The literature also makes it fairly clear that children and adolescents, as well as women, are frequent targets of exhibitionists. Riordan (1999), in a nonclinical sample of 72 women, found that 49% had been victims of indecent exposure and approximately 57% were below the age of 16 at the time of the first exposure; these findings are similar to those from earlier surveys of women (Cox & MacMahon, 1978; Gittleson, Eacott, & Mehta, 1978). In clinical samples of exhibitionists, MacDonald (1973) found that 20% had victims who were between the ages of 5 and 13, while Mohr and colleagues (1964) reported that 17 of 55 subjects exposed themselves to children only and an additional 6 exposed themselves to adults and children.

EPIDEMIOLOGY

Prevalence and Incidence

The true incidence and prevalence of exhibitionism are unknown. However, criminal justice data, victim surveys, and limited community surveys suggest that exhibitionism occurs frequently. Criminal justice data regarding the frequency of arrest for exhibitionism are available for both the Netherlands and Germany; however, similar data are not available for the United States. In the Netherlands, one-third to one-half of all sex crimes reported to the police between 1980 and 1984 were for exhibitionism, which represents between 24 per 100,000 and 37 per 100,000 of the 12- to 79-year-old Dutch population (Frenken, Gijs, & Van Beek, 1999). Pfäfflin (1999) found that in Germany between 1981 and 1984, there were 8,000 to 12,000 reports of exhibitionism to the police, and 16% of those sentenced for sex crimes were exhibitionists. Reports to the police clearly underestimate the incidence or prevalence, as it has been fairly well established that most victims of exhibitionism do not report these incidents to the police. For example, Riordan (1999) found that only 28.6% of her sample reported the offenses to the police.

Surveys of women also suggest that exhibitionism occurs much more frequently than official police statistics indicate. The results of surveys of women in a number of countries—including samples of college students in the United States (Cox & MacMahon, 1978), Hong Kong (Cox, Tsang, & Lee, 1982), and Germany (Kury, Chouaf, Obergfell-Fuchs, & Woesser, 2004), and two samples of community women in the United Kingdom (Gittelson et al., 1978; Riordan, 1999)—suggest that from 32% to 39% of college women and from 40% to 48% of community samples report experiencing exposure.

One national probability sample, using random digit dialing, has examined the experiences of youth between the ages of 2 and 17 to various forms of abusive experiences, including exhibitionism (Finkelhor, Ormrod, Turner, & Hamby, 2005). The 1-year incidence rate was 7 per 1,000 for exposure by a peer and 3 per 1,000 for exposure by an adult. This data would indicate that 1.6 million youth between the ages of 2 and 17 are exposed to exhibitionism each year.

These data suggest that the act of exhibitionism affects a large number of individuals, but it still does not provide a clear indication of the true number of exhibitionists in the community. Although many women are exposed to exhibitionism, it is also well known that many exhibitionists have multiple victims. Abel and Rouleau (1990) report data on 142 subjects who had exposed themselves. These subjects self-reported a total of 72,974 victims.

Two studies have attempted to sample males in the community. Templeman and Stinnett (1991) found that 1 of 60 (or 2%) of their convenience sample of college males reported exhibitionism. Långström and Seto (2006) found that 3.1% of their national probability sample had exposed their genitals to a stranger for sexual pleasure. The prevalence rate was 4.3% for males and 2.1% for females.

Risk Factors

Our empirical knowledge of factors that place individuals at risk for developing paraphilias in general and exhibitionism in particular is extremely limited. What empirical data do exist are generally based on retrospective reports of individuals identified as sex offenders. In addition, it is not clear that the factors proposed to have etiological significance for the development of sexually offending behavior are actually specific to sexual offending in general or exhibitionism specifically; they may all be factors that are related to general psychological/psychiatric disorders and/or general criminality.

Current theorizing suggests that sexual offending may develop along a number of pathways (Ward, Polaschek, & Beech, 2006; Ward & Siegert, 2002). Ward and colleagues' pathways model suggest that issues such as deviant sexual interest or deviant sexual scripts, intimacy or relationship difficulties, difficulties in general emotional regulation, and antisocial cognitions may all be factors that place individuals at risk for developing sexually offending behavior. Marshall and Marshall (2000), using attachment theory as a basis, propose that poor child–parent bonding increases the child's vulnerability, which may lead to increased risk for sexual abuse and in turn to negative effects on psychosocial/psychosexual development. Both of these theoretical models are described in more detail later.

Data related to family relationships in exhibitionists are quite limited and are somewhat mixed. Early descriptive studies reviewed by Blair and Lanyon (1981) indicated a number of reports of poor relationships with fathers, while Myers and Berah (1983), in a sample of Australian exhibitionists and pedophiles, reported positive family relationships in the exhibitionistic sample. Among adolescents, Saunders, Awad, and White (1986) reported that individuals with so-called "courtship disorders" (see "Theoretical Models," below), which include exhibitionism, had lower rates of family discord than "hands-on" offenders, whereas Saunders and Awad (1991) reported high levels of family discord in a group of exhibitionists. Of the 19 subjects in the 1991 study, 11 had also committed "hands-off" offenses and 50% had histories of antisocial behavior in general, suggesting a somewhat more disturbed sample.

A more recent and better-controlled study by Lee, Jackson, Pattison, and Ward (2002) compared exhibitionists to rapists, pedophiles, a group with multiple paraphilias, and a control group of property offenders on a number of risk factors. Lee and colleagues used a number of validated and reliable instruments, and from these created a composite variable they labeled Childhood Emotional Abuse/Family Dysfunction. Exhibitionists were 3.67 times more likely to have experienced this variable than the control group, but their rate was similar to those for the other paraphilic groups. This variable appears to be a general risk factor for paraphilias and is probably a risk factor for many psychiatric disorders.

There is little evidence that exhibitionists have high rates of physical or sexual abuse. In adolescents, rates of sexual abuse are about 17%, and for physical abuse they are between 9% and 10% (Fehrenbach, Smith, Monastersky, & Deisher, 1986; Saunders & Awad, 1991). The Lee and colleagues (2002) study found that exhibitionists were less likely to be sexually abused than other paraphilic groups and were no different from the control group in this respect. In general, the rates of sexual abuse reported are no different from those expected in the general population (Finkelhor, Hotaling, Lewis, & Smith, 1990).

Deviant sexual interest is a factor that has long been proposed as having etiological significance in the development of sexual offending. However, there is fairly clear evidence that exhibitionists do not have a set deviant sexual arousal pattern; that is, they are not primarily attracted to exposing themselves. Marshall and Fernandez (2003) reviewed 10 studies of penile tumescence measures in exhibitionists, and 9 of the 10 studies found no evidence that exhibitionists had a preference for exposing themselves.

Although there is no evidence that exhibitionists have a preference for exposing, there is some limited evidence that exhibitionists may be generally hypersexual. Kafka and Hennen (1999) reported on a sample of 143 individuals with paraphilias, of whom 37% were exhibitionists. Of these 143 individuals, 123 also reported paraphilia-related disorders, which include compulsive masturbation, protracted heterosexual/homosexual promiscuity, dependence on pornography or telephone sex, and severe sexual desire incompatibility. In a later study, Kafka and Hennen (2003) obtained data on paraphilic subjects (including exhibitionists) that suggested high rates of sexual outlets per week. These findings are somewhat supported by Långström and Seto (2006), who found that those individuals in their community sample who engaged in exhibitionism had more sexual partners, greater sexual arousability, higher frequency of masturbation, higher frequency of pornography use, and greater likelihood of having had a same-sex partner.

In many early descriptive studies (see Blair & Lanyon, 1981, for a review), exhibitionists were described as shy, inhibited, and nonassertive, and these were felt to be risk factors for exhibitionism. However, most of these studies were based on unstructured clinical interviews and did not use standardized instruments. When standardized measures of heterosocial skills and assertiveness have been used, exhibitionists as a group do not appear to differ from controls (Langevin, Paitich, Freeman, Mann, & Handy, 1978; Langevin et al., 1979).

Lee, Pattison, Jackson, and Ward (2001), in a study with the same design as the Lee and colleagues (2002) study, used a number of standardized instruments measuring psychopathology thought to be relevant to paraphilias. Factor analyses of these scales created four composite variables: (1) Anger and Hostility, (2) Sexual Maladjustment and Heterosocial Skills Deficits, (3) Control of Anger and Sexual Thoughts, and (4) Interpersonal Sensitivity. When exhibitionists were compared to the property offenders group, they showed significant differences on the Anger and Hostility variable and the Sexual Maladjustment and Heterosocial Skills Deficits variable, but no differences on the other two variables. When the exhibitionists were contrasted to the other paraphilic groups, no differences were found, suggesting that these are common factors for paraphilias but not specific for exhibitionism.

Krafft-Ebing (1886/1965) proposed that exhibitionism was caused by some type of brain disease or mental disorder that interfered with behavior and control. The data in this area specific to exhibitionists continue to be limited. There have been case reports of exhibitionists with temporal lobe disorders (Hooshmand & Brawley, 1969; Kolarsky, Freund, Machek, & Polak, 1967), and Flor-Henry, Lang, and Frenzel (1988) found left frontal temporal dysfunction on computer-analyzed electroencephalograms during both verbal and nonverbal tests. Currently, the data on neurological deficits in exhibitionists are too limited to establish any role for cortical dysfunction in the etiology of exhibitionism. Future studies may want to focus on functional neuroimaging techniques, which have been shown to be promising in the investigation of aggressive/violent behavior and impulsive behavior (Bufkin & Luttrell, 2005). Also of promise is the role of monoamine neurotransmitters in the regulation of sexual motivation (Kafka, 2003a), which is reviewed by Kafka in Chapter 30 of this volume.

DEGREE OF IMPAIRMENT

Although there are significant data on the impact sexual offending has on its victims, there are few data on how exhibitionism (or any other paraphilia) affects a person with the disorder. Blair and Lanyon (1981), in reviewing data in studies from 1950 to 1980, looked at three social factors (marriage, employment, and educational achievement) that can be affected by psychiatric disorders. Their review found that across studies, 54% and 67% of exhibitionistic subjects were or had been married. In summarizing the clinical data, Blair and Lanyon stated that "marital and sexual adjustment appeared to be somewhat poorer than average, although the data in this area were equivocal" (pp. 463–464). They noted that educational level and vocational interest did not appear to differ from those in the general population.

Långström and Seto (2006), in their community sample, found that those who reported exhibitionistic behavior did not differ in socioeconomic status from those who did not. However, those who reported this behavior reported more psychological problems, lower satisfaction with life, and greater alcohol and drug usage.

From a clinical standpoint, anyone who has worked with an exhibitionist knows that the disorder can have a major impact on the individual and the individual's family. Because the behavior tends to occur frequently, likelihood of arrest is high, leading to possible public stigma and significant stress for the family. In addition, because of the fre-

quency of the behavior, many exhibitionists spend significant time engaging in such behaviors as cruising and looking for victims, which lead to withdrawal from more
prosocial activities.

ASSOCIATED FEATURES

We feel that three factors associated with exhibitionism are important for our theoretical
understanding of paraphilias and for treatment. These are the presence of multiple
paraphilias, the association of paraphilias with general criminality, and the frequency and
presence of comorbid psychiatric disorders.

Multiple Paraphilias

Early psychoanalytic writings (Karpman, 1948) suggested a relationship between exhibitionism and voyeurism, but most early writers considered exhibitionism "harmless."
However, several studies have found that exhibitionists engage in a variety of other
paraphilic behaviors. In a group of 241 exhibitionists, Freund (1990) found that 32% engaged in voyeuristic behavior, 30% in "toucherism" or frottage, and 15% in rape. Abel
and Osborn (1992), in a report of 118 exhibitionists, found that 27% had a secondary
diagnosis of voyeurism, 17% had engaged in frottage, and 14% had committed rape.
Abel and Osborn also found that 39% had a history of molesting children. In an early
study of incarcerated child molesters and rapists, Longo and Groth (1983) found that
31% of the child molesters and 15% of the rapists had histories of exposing themselves
as juveniles. Rooth (1973) suggested that those who expose themselves preferentially to
children may be at risk for pedophilia, hebephilia, or incest. There is no indication in the
Longo and Groth (1983) or the Abel and Osborn (1992) study whether child molesters
had exposed themselves preferentially to children. In a study using polygraphy with parole and probation, English, Jones, Pasini-Hill, Patrick, and Cooley-Towell (2000) found
that prior to polygraphy 22% of a group of primarily hands-on offenders admitted to
hands-off offenses, while after polygraphy 67% reported hands-off offenses. Price,
Kafka, Commons, Gutheil, and Simpson (2002) have also reported in a small sample of
obscene phone callers that 50% also had a history of exhibitionism. Abel and Rouleau
(1990) reported that over 90% of the exhibitionists in their sample had more than one
paraphilic diagnosis, and 73% had over three paraphilic diagnoses.

There also appears to be an overlap between paraphilias and paraphilia-related disorders. As noted above, Kafka and Hennen (1999) reported that 123 (over 86%) of their
143 individuals with paraphilias also had paraphilia-related disorders, although the data
were not broken down specifically by paraphilia type.

In summary, the data indicate that multiple paraphilias seem to be the rule rather
than the exception. However, except for the English and colleagues (2000) sample, the
data come from rather specialized clinics (which may attract more severe cases).

Criminality

The sexual offending field for years treated individuals engaging in paraphilic behavior as
if they were somehow different from individuals engaging in general (violent or nonviolent) criminal behavior. In the general field of criminology, however, there has been sup-

port for a more general theory of crime. Gottfredson and Hirschi's (1990) theory of low self-control suggests that criminality tends to be diverse rather than specialized, and that low self-control is the factor underlying general criminal behavior (through its effects on impulse control and ability to delay gratification). The evidence suggests that this theory applies to exhibitionism. For example, Blair and Lanyon's (1981) review indicated that arrests for previous nonsexual offenses ranged from 17% to 30%. Berah and Myers (1983), in a study of 40 exhibitionists, found that 69% had committed nonsexual offenses. Firestone, Kingston, Wexler, and Bradford (2006), in a 13-year follow-up of over 200 exhibitionists, found that approximately 15% reoffended nonsexually.

Comorbid Psychiatric Disorders

Early studies of exhibitionism reported a variety of psychiatric/psychological disturbances (Blair & Lanyon, 1981; Ellis & Brancale, 1956; Mohr et al., 1964). It is very difficult to draw conclusions from the early studies, however, because they used ill-defined terms based on nonstandardized assessments of psychopathology. For example, Ellis and Brancale (1956) described 72% of their subjects as "neurotic," 10% as "psychotic," and 63% as having "inadequate personality disorders." Researchers using more standardized psychological tests, such as Langevin and colleagues (1978), found little differences between exhibitionists and nonexhibitionistic offenders. In addition, Forgac and Michaels (1982) and Forgac, Cassel, and Michaels (1984) found on the Minnesota Multiphasic Personality Inventory that the most significant psychopathology was in subjects having multiple convictions for nonsexual offenses—that is, those who were generally criminal.

The most extensive study of comorbid psychiatric disorders in paraphilias (all clearly defined according to DSM-IV criteria) is by Kafka and Hennen (2003). They studied 88 individuals with paraphilic diagnoses, including 32 subjects with exhibitionism. In the paraphilia group, 87.5% had at least one DSM-IV nonparaphilic diagnosis, with the average number of diagnoses being 3.4. The most frequent co-occurring diagnoses were mood disorders (71.5%), and within the mood disorders the most frequent diagnoses were dysthymic disorder (69.3%) and major depression (38.6%). Over 38% had an anxiety disorder, 42% had a substance use disorder, and 42% had attention-deficit/hyperactivity disorder (ADHD). This may not have been a representative sample, however: Kafka is one of the few psychiatrists specializing in the treatment of paraphilias, and those referred to his practice may be individuals other clinicians suspect of having psychiatric disorders that need psychopharmacological intervention.

ASSOCIATED JUVENILE FACTORS

As we have already noted, exhibitionism is an early-onset disorder, but there are few clearly identified developmental factors that are specific to exhibitionism. One factor that may have been overlooked is childhood externalizing disorders. Lee and colleagues (2002) found that their exhibitionists scored higher on a measure of childhood behavioral disorders than controls without sexual offenses, but were similar to those with other paraphilias. Kafka and Hennen (2003) also indicated high rates of ADHD, a disorder with a childhood onset, in their general group of individuals with paraphilias (see above). Zolondek, Abel, Northey, and Jordan (2001), in a sample of over 485 young males engaging in a variety of sexually offending behaviors, reported high rates of several childhood conduct problems.

These data suggest that intervening with youth showing general childhood behavioral problems may have an impact on the development of chronic paraphilic behavior. There is an extensive literature on evidence-based approaches for childhood behavioral disorders (Aos, Phipps, Barnoski, & Lieb, 2001).

FORENSIC ISSUES

In most states, exhibitionism is a misdemeanor offense punishable by a fine and usually no more than 11 months, 29 days in jail. Because of this misdemeanor status, the courts are more interested in alternative sanctions such as treatment than necessarily in incarceration, at least in our experience of first and second offenses. The questions directed by courts to mental health professionals are general concerns about progression to more serious offenses, risk of reoffending, and treatment amenability.

Occasionally the question may arise as to whether an individual "fits the profile of an exhibitionist." Murphy and Peters (1992; Peters & Murphy, 1992) have reviewed the evidence related to profiling of child sex offenders, and have concluded that there is no general profile and that such testimony is not appropriate. We feel that this holds both for individuals who have actually engaged in exhibitionistic behavior and for those who are alleged to have engaged in such behavior. As the empirical evidence reviewed in this chapter suggests, there is clearly no one profile for exhibitionists, and they vary on a variety of factors.

The question of whether exhibitionists progress to more serious offending is also one where the data are mixed and may be very dependent on the sampling frame. As we have reviewed above, many studies (Abel & Osborn, 1992; English et al., 2000; Freund, 1990; Freund, Scher, & Hucker, 1983; Longo & Groth, 1983) would suggest that a significant minority of individuals identified as rapists and child molesters may have histories of hands-off offenses—and, conversely, many individuals identified as exhibitionists may report histories of hands-on offenses. Most of the studies cited are retrospective; that is, they are looking at the histories of either known hands-on offenders or known hands-off offenders.

Two prospective studies have looked at exhibitionists' rates of reoffending in the future. The study with the longest follow-up (13.24 years) was Firestone and colleagues (2006). They found an overall sexual reoffense rate of 23.6%, with 38% of the sexual reoffenses being hands-on offenses. Although this was one of the more extensive studies, it was based on patients from a specialized clinic, and the subjects may not have been representative of exhibitionists in general. Sjöstedt, Långström, Sturidsson, and Grann (2004) followed a cohort of all sex offenders released from prison, although the number of noncontact offenders was small (approximately 30), and the number of exhibitionists was not specified. In addition, the overall recidivism rate for this cohort was quite small, with only 6% of the total group reconvicted for at least one sex offense on follow-up. This data suggested that for individuals who had prior arrests for noncontact offenses, future arrests were also for noncontact offenses.

A few studies have specifically looked at risk of reoffending in exhibitionism. Data is quite clear that exhibitionists have one of the highest recidivism rates. An early study by Frisbee and Dondis (1965), in a forensic psychiatric population, found a 40% rate of recidivism; Marshall and Barbaree (1990), in a review of outpatient programs, found recidivism rates ranging from 6% (Maletzky, 1987) to 48% (Marshall & Barbaree, 1988). Of studies of recidivism, Maletzky's (1987) is the only one to report low recidivism rates, with most reporting above 40%. In terms of factors that predict recidivism in exhibitionists, the most extensive study is by Greenberg, Firestone, Bradford, and Greenberg (2002), with a longer-term follow-up of the same cohort by Firestone and colleagues (2006). Firestone and colleagues used a variety of standardized measures, including the Psychopathy Checklist—Revised (PCL-R; Hare, 1991) and measures of deviant sexual interest. They found that those with any sexual reoffending were less educated than nonrecidivists, and that they scored higher on the Michigan Alcohol Screening Test, on the PCL-R, and on a pedophile index. Stepwise discriminant-function analysis indicated that the strongest predictors were the PCL-R and the pedophile index, which correctly classified 70% of the original group. Firestone and colleagues also found that those whose reoffenses were hands-on offenses had more prior violent and criminal charges and/or convictions. The stepwise discriminant function for the hands-on group indicated that only prior violent offenses, which correctly classified 67.3% of subjects, were predictive.

With caution, more general sex offender actuarial risk assessment instruments such as the Static-99 (Hanson & Thornton, 1999) can also be employed with exhibitionists. The caution is that although it appears that there were some exhibitionists in the samples used to develop the Static-99, it is likely that they did not constitute a large percentage of the total sample, because these were primarily residential or prison-based samples and most exhibitionists do not end up in prison. The Static-99 includes two concepts, deviant sexuality and general criminality. It is of interest that the predictors found in the Firestone and colleagues (2006) study also tended to reflect a deviant sexual interest variable (the pedophile index) and a clear marker of criminality (the PCL-R).

Although prediction of risk is a forensic issue, a more important issue may be management of risk. In the general field of sexual offending, there have been increased efforts to develop valid dynamic risk assessment instruments; these have been reviewed by Beech, Fisher, and Thornton (2003) and are supported by meta-analytic literature (Hanson & Morton-Bourgon, 2005). Hanson and Morton-Bourgon's meta-analysis and Beech et al.'s qualitative review suggest that promising treatment targets for sex offenders include such issues as sexual self-regulation and sexual interest, attitudes supportive of offending, management of negative affect, ability to establish intimate relationships, and general behavioral self-regulation and self-management. Although exhibitionists as a group do not show deviant sexual interest, Firestone and colleagues' work suggests that arousal to children may predict recidivism, and Kafka's work indicates that a subset of paraphilic individuals (including exhibitionists) may be hypersexual.

Although there is limited evidence of whether targeting these variables in exhibitionists would reduce recidivism, there are some suggestive data. Marshall, Barbaree, and Eccles (1991) found that expanding their treatment program to include a focus on cognitive and relationship variables resulted in a substantial reduction in recidivism, compared to an earlier program that focused primarily on deviant sexual interest.

In summary, for mental health professionals involved in forensic evaluations of exhibitionists, the major issues are progression to more dangerous behavior, recidivism, and risk management. Forensic evaluation should include actuarial risk assessment instruments, in combination with the findings of such studies as Firestone and colleagues (2006) on specific predictors for exhibitionists. Actuarial scales should guide recommendations on how intensive treatment should be, and the adequate assessment of dynamic risk factors should guide selection of treatment targets that are most likely to reduce risk, as opposed to targets that are unrelated to risk (such as denial, empathy, or history of abuse) (Hanson & Morton-Bourgon, 2005).

THEORETICAL MODELS

Since the publication of the first edition of this book, there has been a significant increase in general theories of sex offending, although most of these have focused on child molestation and rape (Ward et al., 2006). There are a number of what Ward and colleagues (2006) describe as single-factor theories, and we have outlined many of these in the "Risk Factors" section. The data reviewed in this earlier section suggest that the etiology of exhibitionism cannot be explained by a single-factor theory. In the rest of this section, we focus on more comprehensive theories.

Courtship Disorders

The "courtship disorder" model of Freund (Freund, 1990; Freund & Blanchard, 1986; Freund et al., 1983; Freund, Scher, & Hucker, 1984; Freund & Seto, 1998; Freund, Seto, & Kuban, 1997) is one of the only theories specific to exhibitionism. Freund and his colleagues derive their model from the ethological literature (Freund & Seto, 1998), which refers to a sequence of courting behavior in lower species. According to Freund, normal courtship consists of four phases: (1) location of a partner, (2) pretactile interactions, (3) tactile interactions, and (4) genital union. The paraphilia disorders of voyeurism, exhibitionism, and frotteurism/toucherism, and the so-called "preferential rape pattern," can be seen as distortions in each of these courtship phases, respectively. Freund and Watson (1993) also propose that obscene phone calling, which is seen as a variant of exhibitionism, is a disturbance of the second phase of the courtship disorder.

The courtship disorder theory provides an explanation of the overlap in certain paraphilias and ties human research to animal research. Many of the data to support this theory have been presented in the first edition of this book (Freund et al., 1997), and we have already reviewed much of the evidence about the overlap of paraphilias. Freund and colleagues (1997) note significant correlations between the presence of exhibitionism and the presence of toucherism or voyeurism, with the highest correlation being between voyeurism and exhibitionism. The relationship between these paraphilias and between obscene phone calling is also supported by the other literature reviewed earlier in this chapter. In the 1997 summary, however, Freund and colleagues did not find a direct relationship between voyeurism, exhibitionism, or toucherism and rape. However, such overlap has been found by others, such as Abel and Osborn (1992). Freund and colleagues have proposed that correlations between disorders are suppressed because of forensic subjects' reluctance to admit other deviant behavior. They have also proposed that the mixed findings for rape are due to the heterogeneity of rapists, and that only what they have labeled "preferential rape pattern" would be likely to overlap with the other courtship disorders.

On the surface, the data would tend to support Freund's hypothesis, but there are some concerns. First, there has been a finding that at least among exhibitionists, there may be an overlap with other sexually anomalous behaviors. Lang, Langevin, Checkley, and Pugh (1987) found that 41% of their exhibitionists also reported transvestite activity, while Rooth (1973) reported that 6 of their 30 exhibitionists had also engaged in transvestite behavior. Abel and Osborn (1992) also found high rates of victimizing children among their exhibitionistic sample, although, as we have noted, there is no evidence that they excluded subjects who exposed themselves preferentially to children or adolescents. In a fairly complex paper, Freund and Watson (1990) tried to address this issue, but the study still suggested overlap between not only what would be considered courtship disorders but other disorders, such as child molestation, fetishism, and transvestism. Therefore, an alternative hypothesis for the multiple paraphilias might be the general theory of hypersexuality as described by Kafka (2003b).

General Theories of Paraphilia Applied to Exhibitionism

In the first edition of this book, Murphy (1997) reviewed psychoanalytic theories and early cognitive-behavioral theories, especially those relevant to conditioning theories as applied to exhibitionism. Although not specific to exhibitionists, this early literature has been replaced by more complex theories. Ward and colleagues propose multiple pathways to sexual offending (Ward et al., 2006, Ch. 5; Ward & Siegert, 2002). In addition, Marshall and colleagues (Marshall, Anderson, & Fernandez, 1999; Marshall & Barbaree, 1990; Marshall & Marshall, 2000) have introduced attachment concepts into their integrated theory.

In Ward and Siegert's (2002) model of multiple pathways to offending, family environment, learning history, biological factors, and cultural factors can increase an individual's vulnerability, which can lead to common clusters of problems such as deviant sexual scripts and relationship schemas, intimacy deficits, inappropriate emotions, and cognitive distortions. These interact in various ways to create pathways to offending, which will be different for different individuals. This model's value is that it suggests that a search for one pathway to offending is unlikely to be fruitful. In addition, the common clusters of problems are also identified in meta-analytic literature (Hanson & Morton-Bourgon, 2005) as being related to sexual reoffending.

Marshall and colleagues present a vulnerability model that integrates attachment theory with more traditional cognitive-behavioral theory. They propose that poor parent–child attachment bonding creates vulnerability in a child by generating low self-esteem, poor relationship styles, and poor coping strategies, all of which can increase the child's risk of being sexually abused. This may lead to inappropriate juvenile sexual behavior (i.e., the individual may learn to cope by turning to sex), and conditioning processes can increase this tendency, while such factors as cognitive distortions, substance use, and anger can serve as disinhibiting influences. This model integrates a number of theories; although there may be support for some of the components, there is not yet support for the overall model. The model seems most appropriate for those offenders who have experienced childhood abuse, but as we have noted earlier, most exhibitionists do not have a history of sexual abuse.

SUMMARY AND FUTURE DIRECTIONS

There have been few real advances in our understanding of exhibitionism since the first edition of this book. Although exhibitionism is one of the more frequently occurring sex offenses and affects a large number of victims, including children, it receives little research and attention as compared to child molestation or rape.

It is our feeling that the research in this area will not advance until we have a better way of understanding the heterogeneity of this population. As we have pointed out, there are significant overlaps between exhibitionism and other paraphilias, general criminal behavior, and other psychiatric disorders. We also know that some exhibitionists experience child maltreatment and/or poor parental bonds, and some do not. In addition, very few studies separate exhibitionists who expose themselves preferentially to adults from those who expose themselves to children, and these two patterns may be different disorders. We need studies that divide exhibitionists on some of these factors if we are going to identify risk factors for the development of exhibitionism.

REFERENCES

Abel, G. G., & Osborn, C. (1992). Stopping sexual violence. *Psychiatric Annals, 22,* 301–330.

Abel, G. G., & Rouleau, J.-L. (1990). The nature and extent of sexual assault. In W. L. Marshall, D. R. Laws, & H. E. Barbaree (Eds.), *Handbook of sexual assault: Issues, theories, and treatment of the offender* (pp. 9–21). New York: Plenum Press.

American Psychiatric Association. (2000). *Diagnostic and statistical manual of mental disorders* (4th ed., text rev.). Washington, DC: Author.

Aos, S., Phipps, P., Barnoski, R., & Lieb, R. (2001). *The comparative costs and benefits of programs to reduce crime.* Olympia: Washington State Institute for Public Policy. Retrieved from *www.wsipp. wa.gov/pub.asp?docid=01-05-1201*

Beech, A. R., Fisher, D. D., & Thornton, D. (2003). Risk assessment of sex offenders. *Professional Psychology: Research and Practice, 34,* 339–352.

Berah, E. F., & Myers, R. G. (1983). The offense records of a sample of convicted exhibitionists. *Bulletin of the American Academy of Psychiatry and the Law, 11,* 365–369.

Blair, C. D., & Lanyon, R. I. (1981). Exhibitionism: Etiology and treatment. *Psychological Bulletin, 89,* 439–463.

Bufkin, J. L., & Luttrell, V. R. (2005). Neuroimaging studies of aggressive and violent behavior: Current findings and implications for criminology and criminal justice. *Trauma, Violence and Abuse, 6,* 176–191.

Cox, D. J. (1980). Exhibitionism: An overview. In D. J. Cox & R. J. Daitzman (Eds.), *Exhibitionism: Description, assessment and treatment* (pp. 3–10). New York: Garland Press.

Cox, D. J., & MacMahon, B. (1978). Incidence of male exhibitionism in the United States as reported by victimized female college students. *National Journal of Law and Psychiatry, 1,* 453–457.

Cox, D. J., Tsang, K., & Lee, A. (1982). A cross cultural comparison of the incidence and nature of male exhibitionism in college students. *Victimology, 7,* 231–234.

Ellis, A., & Brancale, R. (1956). *The psychology of sex offenders.* Springfield, IL: Thomas.

English, K., Jones, L., Pasini-Hill, D., Patrick, D., & Cooley-Towell, S. (2000). *The value of polygraph testing in sex offender management.* Denver: Office of Research and Statistics, Colorado Department of Public Safety.

Fedoroff, J. P., Fishell, A., & Fedoroff, B. (1999). A case series of women evaluated for paraphilic sexual disorders. *Canadian Journal of Human Sexuality, 8,* 127–140.

Fehrenbach, P. A., Smith, W., Monastersky, C., & Deisher, R. W. (1986). Adolescent sexual offenders: Offender and offense characteristics. *American Journal of Orthopsychiatry, 56,* 225–233.

Finkelhor, D., Hotaling, G., Lewis, I. A., & Smith, C. (1990). Sexual abuse in a national study of adult men and women: Prevalence, characteristics, and risk factors. *Child Abuse and Neglect, 14,* 19–28.

Finkelhor, D., Ormrod, R., Turner, H., & Hamby, S. L. (2005). The victimization of children and youth: A comprehensive, national survey. *Child Maltreatment, 10,* 5–25.

Firestone, P., Kingston, D. A., Wexler, A., & Bradford, J. M. (2006). Long-term follow-up of exhibitionists: Psychological, phallometric, and offense characteristics. *Journal of the American Academy of Psychiatry and the Law, 34*, 349–359.

Flor-Henry, P., Lang, R. A., & Frenzel, R. R. (1988). Quantitative EEG analysis in genital exhibitionism. *Annals of Sex Research, 1*, 49–62.

Forgac, G. E., Cassel, C. A., & Michaels, E. J. (1984). Chronicity of criminal behavior and psychopathology in male exhibitionists. *Journal of Clinical Psychology, 40*, 827–832.

Forgac, G. E., & Michaels, E. J. (1982). Personality characteristics of two types of male exhibitionists. *Journal of Abnormal Psychology, 91*, 287–293.

Frenken, J., Gijs, L., & Van Beek, D. (1999). Sexual offender research and treatment in the Netherlands. *Journal of Interpersonal Violence, 14*, 347–371.

Freund, K. (1990). Courtship disorder. In W. L. Marshall, D. R. Laws, & H. E. Barbaree (Eds.), *Handbook of sexual assault: Issues, theories, and treatment of the offender* (pp. 331–342). New York: Plenum Press.

Freund, K., & Blanchard, R. (1986). The concept of courtship disorder. *Journal of Sex and Marital Therapy, 12*, 79–92.

Freund, K., Scher, H., & Hucker, S. (1983). The courtship disorders. *Archives of Sexual Behavior, 12*, 369–379.

Freund, K., Scher, H., & Hucker, S. (1984). The courtship disorders: A further investigation. *Archives of Sexual Behavior, 13*, 133–139.

Freund, K., & Seto, M. C. (1998). Preferential rape in the theory of courtship disorder. *Archives of Sexual Behavior, 27*, 433–443.

Freund, K., Seto, M. C., & Kuban, M. (1997). Frotteurism: The theory of courtship disorder. In D. R. Laws & W. O'Donohue (Eds.), *Sexual deviance: Theory, assessment, and treatment* (pp. 111–130). New York: Guilford Press.

Freund, K., & Watson, R. (1990). Mapping the boundaries of courtship disorder. *Journal of Sex Research, 27*, 589–606.

Freund, K., & Watson, R. J. (1993). Gender identity disorder and courtship disorder. *Archives of Sexual Behavior, 22*, 13–21.

Frisbee, L. V., & Dondis, E. H. (1965). *Recidivism among treated sex offenders* (California Mental Health Research Monograph No. 5). Sacramento: California Department of Mental Hygiene.

Gittelson, N. L., Eacott, S. E., & Mehta, B. M. (1978). Victims of indecent exposure. *British Journal of Psychiatry, 132*, 61–66.

Gottfredson, M., & Hirschi, T. (1990). *A general theory of crime.* Stanford, CA: Stanford University Press.

Greenberg, S. R., Firestone, P., Bradford, J. M., & Greenberg, D. M. (2002). Prediction of recidivism in exhibitionists: Psychological, phallometric, and offense factors. *Sexual Abuse: A Journal of Research and Treatment, 14*, 329–347.

Grob, C. S. (1985). Female exhibitionism. *Journal of Nervous and Mental Disease, 173*, 253–256.

Hanson, R. K., & Morton-Bourgon, K. E. (2005). The characteristics of persistent sexual offenders: A meta-analysis of recidivism studies. *Journal of Consulting and Clinical Psychology, 73*, 1154–1163.

Hanson, R. K., & Thornton, D. (1999). *Static-99: Improving actuarial risk assessments for sex offenders* (User Report No. 1999-02). Ottawa: Department of the Solicitor General of Canada.

Hare, R. D. (1991). *The Hare Psychopathy Checklist—Revised.* Toronto: Multi-Health Systems.

Hooshmand, H., & Brawley, B. W. (1969). Temporal lobe seizures and exhibitionism. *Neurology, 19*, 1119–1124.

Hugh-Jones, S., Gough, B., & Littlewood, A. (2005). Sexual exhibitionism as "sexuality and individuality": A critique of psycho-medical discourse from the perspectives of women who exhibit. *Sexualities, 8*, 259–281.

Kafka, M. P. (2003a). Hypothesis for the pathophysiology of paraphilic disorders: An update. *Annals of the New York Academy of Sciences, 989*, 86–94.

Kafka, M. P. (2003b). Sex offending and sexual appetite: The clinical and theoretical relevance of hypersexual desire. *International Journal of Offender Therapy and Comparative Criminology*, 47, 439–451.

Kafka, M. P., & Hennen, J. (1999). The paraphilia-related disorders: An empirical investigation of nonparaphilic hypersexuality disorders in outpatient males. *Journal of Sex and Marital Therapy*, 25, 305–319.

Kafka, M. P., & Hennen, J. (2003). Hypersexual desire in males: Are males with paraphilias different from males with paraphilia-related disorders? *Sexual Abuse: A Journal of Research and Treatment*, 4, 307–321.

Karpman, B. (1948). The psychopathology of exhibitionism: Review of the literature. *Clinical Psychopathology*, 9, 179–225.

Kolarsky, A., Freund, K., Machek, J., & Polak, O. (1967). Male sexual deviation: Association with early temporal lobe damage. *Archives of General Psychiatry*, 17, 735–743.

Krafft-Ebing, R. von. (1965). *Psychopathia sexualis*. New York: Bell. (Original work published 1886)

Kury, H., Chouaf, S., Obergfell-Fuchs, J., & Woesser, G. (2004). The scope of sexual victimization in Germany. *Journal of Interpersonal Violence*, 19, 589–602.

Lang, R. A., Langevin, R., Checkley, K. L., & Pugh, G. (1987). Genital exhibitionism: Courtship disorder or narcissism? *Canadian Journal of Behavioural Science*, 19, 216–232.

Langevin, R., Paitich, D., Freeman, R., Mann, K., & Handy, L. (1978). Personality characteristics and sexual anomalies in males. *Canadian Journal of Behavioural Science*, 10, 222–238.

Langevin, R., Paitich, D., Ramsey, G., Anderson, C., Kamrad, J., Pope, S., et al. (1979). Experimental studies of the etiology of genital exhibitionism. *Archives of Sexual Behavior*, 8, 307–331.

Långström, N., & Seto, M. C. (2006). Exhibitionistic and voyeuristic behavior in a Swedish national population survey. *Archives of Sexual Behavior*, 35, 427–435.

Lee, J. K. P., Jackson, H. J., Pattison, P., & Ward, T. (2002). Developmental risk factors for sexual offending. *Child Abuse and Neglect*, 26, 73–92.

Lee, J. K. P., Pattison, P., Jackson, H. J., & Ward, T. (2001). The general, common, and specific features of psychopathology for different types of paraphilias. *Criminal Justice and Behavior*, 28, 227–256.

Longo, R. F., & Groth, A. N. (1983). Juvenile sexual offenses in the histories of adult rapists and child molesters. *International Journal of Offender Therapy and Comparative Criminology*, 27, 150–155.

MacDonald, J. M. (1973). *Indecent exposure*. Springfield, IL: Thomas.

Maletzky, B. M. (1987). *Treating the sexual offender*. Newbury Park, CA: Sage.

Marshall, W. L., Anderson, D., & Fernandez, Y. M. (1999). *Cognitive behavioural treatment for sexual offenders*. Chichester, UK: Wiley.

Marshall, W. L., & Barbaree, H.E. (1988). The long-term evaluation of a behavioural treatment program for child molesters. *Behaviour Research and Therapy*, 26, 499–511.

Marshall, W. L., & Barbaree, H. E. (1990). Outcome of comprehensive cognitive-behavioral treatment programs. In W. L. Marshall, D. R. Laws, & H. E. Barbaree (Eds.), *Handbook of sexual assault: Issues, theories, and treatment of the offender* (pp. 363–385). New York: Plenum Press.

Marshall, W. L., & Barbaree, H. E. (1990). An integrated theory of the etiology of sexual offending. In W. L. Marshall, D. R. Laws, & H. E. Barbaree (Eds.), *Handbook of sexual assault: Issues, theories, and treatment of the offender* (pp. 257–275). New York: Plenum Press.

Marshall, W. L., Barbaree, H. E., & Eccles, A. (1991). Early onset and deviant sexuality in child molesters. *Journal of Interpersonal Violence*, 6, 323–336.

Marshall, W. L., & Fernandez, Y. M. (2003). *Phallometric testing with sexual offenders*. Brandon, VT: Safer Society Press.

Marshall, W. L., & Marshall, L. E. (2000). The origins of sexual offending. *Trauma, Violence and Abuse*, 1, 250–263.

Mohr, J. W., Turner, R. E., & Jerry, M. B. (1964). *Pedophilia and exhibitionism*. Toronto: University of Toronto Press.

Murphy, W. D. (1997). Exhibitionism: Psychopathology and theory. In D. R. Laws & W. T. O'Donohue (Eds.), *Sexual deviance: Theory, assessment, and treatment* (pp. 22–39). New York: Guilford Press.

Murphy, W. D., & Peters, J. M. (1992). Profiling child sexual abusers: Psychological considerations. *Criminal Justice and Behavior, 19*, 24–37.

Myers, R. G., & Berah, E. F. (1983). Some features of Australian exhibitionists compared with pedophiles. *Archives of Sexual Behavior, 12*, 541–547.

O'Donohue, W., Regev, L. G., & Hagstrom, A. (2000). Problems with DSM-IV diagnosis of pedophilia. *Sexual Abuse: A Journal of Research and Treatment, 12*, 95–105.

Peters, J. M., & Murphy, W. D. (1992). Profiling child sexual abusers: Legal considerations. *Criminal Justice and Behavior, 19*, 38–53.

Pfäfflin, F. (1999). Issues, incidence, and treatment of sexual offenders in Germany. *Journal of Interpersonal Violence, 14*, 372–395.

Price, M., Kafka, M., Commons, M. L., Gutheil, T. G., & Simpson, W. (2002). Comorbidity with other paraphilias and paraphilia-related disorders. *International Journal of Law and Psychiatry, 25*, 37–49.

Rhoads, J. M., & Boekelheide, P. D. (1984). Female genital exhibitionism. *Psychiatric Forum, 13*, 1–6.

Riordan, S. (1999). Indecent exposure: The impact upon the victim's fear of sexual crime. *Journal of Forensic Psychiatry, 10*, 309–316.

Rooth, G. (1973). Exhibitionism, sexual violence and paedophilia. *British Journal of Psychiatry, 122*, 705–710.

Saunders, E., Awad, G. A., & White, G. (1986). Male adolescent sex offenders: The offenders and the offense. *Canadian Journal of Psychiatry, 31*, 542–549.

Saunders, E. B., & Awad, G. A. (1991). Male adolescent sexual offenders: Exhibitionism and obscene phone calls. *Child Psychiatry and Human Development, 21*, 169–178.

Sjöstedt, G., Långström, N., Sturidsson, K., & Grann, M. (2004). Stability of modus operandi in sexual offending. *Criminal Justice and Behavior, 31*, 609–623.

Templeman, T. L., & Stinnett, R. D. (1991). Patterns of sexual arousal and history in a "normal" sample of young men. *Archives of Sexual Behavior, 20*, 137–150.

Ward, T., Polaschek, D. L. L., & Beech, A. R. (2006). *Theories of sexual offending.* Chichester, UK: Wiley.

Ward, T., & Siegert, R. J. (2002). Toward a comprehensive theory of child sexual abuse: A theory knitting perspective. *Psychology, Crime, and Law, 9*, 315–351.

Zolondek, S. C., Abel, G. G., Northey, W. F., & Jordan, A. D. (2001). The self-reported behaviors of juvenile sexual offenders. *Journal of Interpersonal Violence, 16*, 73–85.

CHAPTER 5

EXHIBITIONISM

Assessment and Treatment

JOHN W. MORIN
JILL S. LEVENSON

Phil was a 36-year-old truck driver who was angry when he attended his initial evaluation interview. He had no money to pay for the interview, and he didn't think there was going to come a time when he would have money. He had important things to pay for; he was sending his three children to private schools. Treatment wasn't on his list of important things.

Phil had been arrested after he was spotted masturbating in his car in a parking lot by a 15-year-old boy. Phil admitted he was masturbating, but insisted that the boy could not have seen his penis because it was covered by his shirt. In any case, the boy had nothing to do with Phil's offense; Phil was focused on a woman in shorts and a halter top who was putting her groceries into her car. Phil was furious about being charged with lewd exposure simply because the boy had walked by his car and looked in. Phil had no intention of being seen and no desire to be seen. And he bitterly resented being required to attend treatment. He had never been arrested for anything before. There was nothing wrong with what he did, he said. Sometimes he got horny and couldn't wait until he got home to "pleasure himself." He had masturbated in his car "maybe 5 or 10 times."

Phil attended group therapy meetings for over 2 years without ever acknowledging any problem except carelessness. When the treatment program instituted mandatory polygraphy, and all clients were required to take—and pass—full-disclosure examinations, Phil once again developed financial difficulties. After months of resistance, Phil finally went for his exam. He produced a different story for the polygrapher: He had masturbated while driving "at least 200 times." He had been seen "at least 30 times" (and had previously been reported but not arrested), but he continued to insist that he never intended to be seen. He had also date-raped two girls in college. And he had molested 12 children, including a male infant.

Is this man an exhibitionist? Based on his charge, he was. Now consider this individual:

Dale was a 47-year-old married minister who had earned a doctorate in divinity from a correspondence university. He had founded his own church in a storefront, but had to close it when attendance fell off. When a woman who had been in his congregation later contacted him to ask him to christen her baby, he agreed to meet her to plan the event. They met in a parking lot, where the woman got into Dale's car. During the course of the conversation, the woman suddenly noticed that Dale's flaccid penis was out of his pants. When she confronted him, Dale sputtered that he had gone to the bathroom before the meeting and forgotten to zip his fly. The woman reported him to the police.

In his initial assessment interview, Dale explained that the woman had been flirtatious when she called him, and had sparked in him the thought that she was looking for a "relationship." His intention was to let her see his penis, and he would judge from her reaction whether she wanted a "relationship." He denied that he had an erection or derived any sexual excitement from the act. Over time, Dale admitted in his therapy group that years earlier, when he had worked as the manager of a nightclub, he had sometimes taken women into his office and exposed himself in the same way. He also recalled times in college when he had allowed his towel to slip off in mixed company. In all cases, he said, he was attempting to test the sexual availability of the victim. He denied ever having an erection while exposing himself. He denied ever masturbating during or after exposing himself.

Exhibitionism is defined in the *Diagnostic and Statistical Manual of Mental Disorders*, fourth edition, text revision (DSM-IV-TR; American Psychiatric Association, 2000) as a paraphilia characterized by "recurrent, intense sexually arousing fantasies, sexual urges, or behaviors involving the exposure of one's genitals to an unsuspecting stranger" (p. 569); the fantasies, urges, or behaviors must occur over a period of at least 6 months and must cause distress or impairment for the person. By this definition, neither of the cases described above appears to meet diagnostic criteria, even though both of these offenses involved willful exposure of the penis. In fact, although there clearly are "true" exhibitionists as described in the DSM criteria, men who expose their genitals constitute a heterogeneous group displaying a diversity of behaviors and motivations. Should all these men be classified as exhibitionists? If not, should they all be considered paraphilic? Indeed, is there a reliable approach for assessing—or even naming—their condition?

Research on the assessment and treatment of exhibitionism is surprisingly limited, given that this behavior is among the most common of sex offenses (Abel, Becker, Cunningham-Rathner, Mittelman, & Rouleau, 1988; Ahlmeyer, Heil, McKee, & English, 2000; Heil, Ahlmeyer, & Simons, 2003; Maletzky, 1991). Perhaps the paucity of research reflects the assumption that exhibitionism is merely a nuisance behavior that causes little harm to victims, compared with other types of sexual crimes. Evidence exists, however, that many victims of exposure experience traumatizing effects (Cox & Maletzky, 1980). Moreover, exhibitionism is frequently seen in men who engage in an array of sexually deviant acts (Abel & Rouleau, 1990). Although an individual may be convicted for exposing himself and labeled an exhibitionist, exposing may not be his sole, or even primary, paraphilia (Freund, 1990).

ASSESSMENT

Diagnostic Conceptualizations

The first observer to use the word "exhibitionism" was Lasègue in 1877, who noted that the condition involved powerful urges to display one's genitals without making any attempt to form a relationship (cited in Dwyer, 1988). Havelock Ellis (1933) described exhibitionists as shy and timid, and he too noted that they made no approach to their victims. As early as 1939, however, East and Hubert (cited in Taylor, 1947) noted that exhibitionism was not a unitary phenomenon, and they catalogued exhibitionists into discrete groups. The "true exhibitionists," they noted, practiced exposure as their preferred means of sexual relief, replacing normal intercourse. A second group was seen to use exposure as a "prelude" to intercourse; these men were thought to be attempting to incite female victims to sex. A third group, unable to have intercourse or afraid of having intercourse, accepted the pleasure of exposing themselves as a substitute for sexual interactions. A final grouping included "subnormal and defective persons" who were incapable of a normal approach to courtship or mating (Taylor, 1947).

The best-known conceptual model is that of exhibitionism as a "courtship disorder" (Freund, 1990; Freund & Blanchard, 1986). Freund and his associates described a four-step sequence of behaviors that occur within normal courting or mating rituals, and construed exhibitionism as a disturbance in the second phase, "affiliative" or "pretactile" interaction, which normally involves engaging potential partners through smiling, posturing, and conversation. The exhibitionist's exposure of his genitals is thought to represent an anomalous and misguided attempt to initiate interaction before an appropriate partner choice has been made. Noting that normal subjects denied any exposing behaviors (vs. consistent admissions of voyeurism, frottage, and even rape among "normals"), Freund, Seto, and Kuban (1997) called genital exhibitionism "the hub of courtship disorder" (p. 119). However, Freund's model does not appear to account for the "true" exhibitionist, whose exposing is not a prelude to an interaction but a complete sexual act. Moreover, although it is clear that exhibitionists frequently describe their behavior as an invitation to intercourse (Freund, Watson, & Rienzo, 1988), it is not clear that this description is true. Seto (2002) has identified other weaknesses with Freund's theory—namely, that it does not account for the putative mechanism of the disturbance, and that it does not lend itself to empirical testing. Perhaps as a result of these problems, the courtship disorder theory has not generated a significant research base.

More recently, Kafka and his associates (Kafka, 2001a, 2001b; Kafka & Hennen, 2002) have proposed a new diagnostic approach. Kafka (2001a, 2001b) has observed that there is a class of hypersexual individuals, both paraphilic and nonparaphilic, who engage in a host of unconventional sexual behaviors. Focusing on the excessive and maladaptive quality of nondeviant (and legal) sexual behaviors commonly referred to as "compulsive" or "addictive" (i.e., characterized by repetitive volitional impairment and adverse psychosocial consequences), Kafka suggests that all such behaviors, including paraphilic behaviors, share both etiological and curative factors. He has written: "Paraphilic disorders may be the proverbial tip of the iceberg of a broader range of sexual disorders characterized by excessive sexual appetite, sexual preoccupation, and repetitive impulsive enactment of sexual behavior despite adverse consequences" (Kafka, 2001a, p. 236). Indeed, according to Kafka, the commonalities between paraphilic behaviors and hypersexual behaviors are so strong that the latter warrant a new diagnostic category of "paraphilia-related disorders," to include compulsive masturbation, protracted promiscuity, pornography dependence, cybersex dependence, and telephone sex dependence. The primary difference Kafka finds between paraphilias and paraphilia-related disorders is that "paraphilia-related disorders are not socially deviant" (Kafka, 2001a, p. 231). Lending support to this thesis is the finding in a series of studies that hypersexual men, both deviant and nondeviant, are essentially identical in shared comorbidity (Kafka & Hennen, 2002; Kafka & Prentky, 1994, 1998).

The most promising aspect of Kafka's formulation is his consistent finding that hypersexuality, both paraphilic and nonparaphilic, can be ameliorated by psychopharmacological agents that target the comorbid symptoms (Kafka, 1991, 1994; Kafka & Prentky, 1992). (These findings are summarized in the treatment section of this chapter.) Missing from this approach is an explanation for why some hypersexual men are willing to cross the line that separates consenting partners from vulnerable victims and some are not. For present purposes, an important component of assessing exhibitionism is to distinguish between "true exhibitionists" (whose fantasies, urges, and behaviors involve exposing their genitals expressly for the sexual excitement they derive from being seen), "public masturbators" (who masturbate in public places such as cars, allowing for the possibility of being seen but without a clear desire to be observed), and "compulsive masturbators" (those whose hypersexual behavior—no matter how excessive or disruptive to their lives—is kept within the bounds of social acceptability). Kafka (2001a) draws no distinction between "compulsive masturbators" and "compulsive public masturbators," although such a distinction seems important in the identification of exhibitionistic sex offenders.

With regard to the specific offending pattern an exhibitionist displays and the need to tailor treatment accordingly, respondents to a survey of clinicians that we conducted (see below) outlined several approaches for identifying the true motives of exhibitionists and compulsive public masturbators. Using a range of information from interviews, records, and polygraph exams, these clinicians assess the frequency of the behavior, the locations chosen for the behavior, and the thoughts and feelings about the offense in order to specify a client's intentions. There seemed to be a consensus among the clinicians we surveyed that most compulsive masturbators do not risk public exposure and typically masturbate alone, using pornography, Internet interactions, or phone sex. However, it was widely recognized that some of these individuals can be labeled "compulsive public masturbators," and these clinicians seemed to agree that a challenging part of the assessment is determining the intent to be seen. Many, however, said that their treatment is similar for all three types.

Obtaining a History

The assessment and treatment of exhibitionism are complex undertakings that involve differential diagnoses of related symptoms, including comorbid psychopathological conditions, other paraphilias, criminality, and interpersonal deficits. For this reason, the prudent clinician will consider using a variety of assessment approaches.

In preparation for writing this chapter, we surveyed practitioners engaged in clinical practice with exhibitionists in order to determine the most common assessment and treatment strategies in current use. An invitation to participate was sent to 1,639 professionals involved in sex offender treatment and research around the world, via the listserv of the Association for the Treatment of Sexual Abusers (ATSA). ATSA is an international, interdisciplinary professional association whose members specialize in the research and treatment of sexual deviance. The invitation to participate yielded 66 respondents from 29 states within the United States, as well as from Canada, Israel, Australia, and Belgium. The vast majority (74%) reported having over 10 years' experience in treating sex offenders, and 23% reported 5–10 years' experience. The majority of participants (60%) said that exhibitionists or public masturbators constituted 10% or less of their client caseload.

The practitioners surveyed were asked to identify the primary areas they assess when evaluating an exhibitionist. The most common areas identified were offense patterns and victim preferences (98%), frequency of behavior (98%), compulsivity (93%), duration of behavior (92%), motivation and amenability for treatment (85%), and variety of offending behaviors (85%). These clinicians also described other foci of their assessment, including attachment styles, early childhood victimization, symptoms of sexual addiction, and substance abuse. Since virtually all of this information can come only from an offender, it is from a client's clinical presentation that the primary diagnosis, the treatment plan, and the prognosis will be derived (Maletzky, 1997). If a realistic assessment is to be obtained, it will be largely the result of effective interviewing skills combined with a developing therapeutic alliance.

Clinical Interview

Few sex offenders enter treatment voluntarily, and even those who do often minimize and rationalize their deviant behavior out of shame, embarrassment, and/or fear of legal consequences. Most sexual offenders approach the initial evaluation with the goal of convincing the evaluator that they have been falsely accused or that their behaviors were misinterpreted or blown out of proportion (Marshall, Thornton, Marshall, Fernandez, & Mann, 2001; Winn, 1996). Therapists should avoid direct confrontation during assessment. They should instead build rapport by using a positive, empathic approach that encourages and supports client ownership of change. Such an approach may reduce defensiveness and decrease the need for self-protective strategies such as denial (Kear-Colwell & Pollock, 1997). Initial questions regarding an offender's family, educational, social, and work histories are nonthreatening and allow a clinician time to build rapport.

By creating an environment in which a client is allowed to proceed at his own pace, a clinician may be more successful in eliciting and obtaining the important information needed for assessment. Motivational approaches based on empathic understanding, mutual trust, and acceptance help the therapist to understand the client's experience (Kear-Colwell & Pollock, 1997). Ultimately, this type of approach empowers the client to choose to engage in the therapeutic process, rather than have the interventions imposed by the therapist (Birgden & Vincent, 2000).

Structured interviews can be helpful in eliciting specific information about sexual and nonsexual areas of functioning. There should be some flexibility, however, to give clients opportunities to expand on and share information not otherwise generated by the structured interview process. If a client is acknowledging his index offense, a clinician should (1) ask how long he has been engaging in the behavior and how often; (2) accept his admissions, now matter how minimized, as a starting place; (3) ask how he feels both while and after exposing himself; and (4) ask how he feels about the possibility of changing and regaining control of his life. Although exhibitionists are sometimes more self-disclosing than other sex offenders (they are, after all, people who expose themselves), the clinician should not imagine that anything resembling a true picture of the client's sexual issues will be elicited by even the most thorough initial interview(s). The assessment of sex offenders is an ongoing process; as a client engages in the treatment process the true scope of his problems will become more apparent.

Clinicians typically assess psychopathology by using a mental status assessment as part of the clinical interview. This procedure will generally follow standard psychiatric guidelines. Special attention should be given to consideration of those comorbid conditions (noted below) that are commonly associated with paraphilias (e.g., Kafka & Hennen, 2002). In exploring the possibility of a mood disorder, the clinician should be aware that many offenders who have recently been in jail or prison and are now on supervision may demonstrate depression and anxiety about their legal situation. The assessment therefore must elicit reliable information about prearrest functioning to be useful. As the offender describes his thoughts about his index offense and arrest, it will be possible to assess his cognitive functioning and observe the depth of his distorted thinking. Here allowance should be made for the offender's intense emotional investment in his sometimes implausible story. Often offenders' defensive minimizations have served a protective function with family, friends, and lawyers.

Corroboration Interviews

In cases where an exhibitionist is especially guarded and maintains complete denial of his offense, it can sometimes be helpful to solicit the views of partners or relatives. In particular, the parents of a juvenile offender may be highly motivated to ensure that their child receives effective help and may provide a wealth of background information. On the other hand, family members (including parents) can sometimes display denial every bit as entrenched as the offender's, as they contend with their own feelings of shame, guilt, embarrassment, confusion, and anxiety.

Review of Records

Given the typical client's early reluctance to disclose his problems fully or to accept responsibility for them, it is essential to review all available official documents to obtain as much objective information as possible. Police reports, victim statements, presentence investigation reports, criminal records of prior sexual and nonsexual offenses, prior mental health evaluations, and treatment progress assessments can all help the clinician to better understand the offender's behavior, to challenge contradictions between his report and official versions, and to uncover important information that may otherwise remain unrevealed by the client (e.g., information about other mental health or substance abuse problems).

Criminal history and victim characteristics are also important for completing risk assessment instruments such as the Static-99 (Hanson & Thornton, 1999). Exhibitionists are often nonviolent, and about one-third of exhibitionists are law-abiding citizens with the exception of their exposure offenses (Berah & Myers, 1983). However, Berah and Myers also found that 23% of exhibitionists had been convicted of property offenses, 27% had been convicted for assault or indecent assault, and 25% for other offenses. The more often a man has been convicted for exhibitionism, the more likely he is to have convictions in other offense categories (Berah & Myers, 1983). Importantly, researchers have found prior criminal history (both sexual and nonsexual) to be predictive of recidivistic exposure offenses (Greenberg, Firestone, Bradford, & Greenberg, 2002).

Psychological Tests, Rating Scales, and Questionnaires

Assessment of Psychiatric Comorbidity

As noted above, recent research by Kafka and his associates (Kafka & Hennen, 2002; Kafka & Prentky, 1994, 1998) suggests that recognition of psychiatric comorbidity is a key to facilitating maximally effective therapy for hypersexual individuals, whether or not they have paraphilias. The most prevalent Axis I disorders among both groups are mood disorders, especially early-onset dysthymic disorder and major depression. Also prevalent among both groups are anxiety disorders (especially social phobia) and substance abuse (especially alcohol) (Kafka & Hennen, 2002). The one comorbid diagnosis that differentiated the hypersexual groups was attention-deficit/hyperactivity disorder (ADHD), which was associated with paraphilic status among subjects. Also differentiating the groups were developmental variables associated with paraphilic status that included higher incidence of physical (but not sexual) abuse, fewer years of education (and concomitant learning and school behavioral problems), and more psychiatric/substance abuse hospitalizations (Kafka & Hennen, 2002).

The majority of practitioners we surveyed agreed that they commonly observe a range of psychiatric conditions existing concurrently with exhibitionism. Most frequently noted were mood disorders (specifically bipolar spectrum disorders and depression), impulse control disorders including ADHD, obsessive–compulsive features, social anxiety, posttraumatic stress, and personality disorders. Almost half of surveyed practitioners reported that they frequently refer clients to a psychiatrist for evaluation and possible medication management.

Although it has long been known that standard psychological test instruments are inapplicable for diagnosing paraphilias (Marshall & Hall, 1995), personality tests such as the Minnesota Multiphasic Personality Inventory–2 (MMPI-2), the Millon Clinical Multiaxial Inventory–III, and the Beck Depression Inventory–II can be useful in assessing comorbidity. For adolescent offenders, youth versions of several tests (e.g., the Adolescent version of the MMPI, the Millon Adolescent Personality Inventory) are available. Nearly half (40%) of our survey sample used personality tests for this purpose.

Although it is not, strictly speaking, a psychiatric disorder, psychopathy is also routinely assessed by half of our survey sample. Survey respondents did not indicate how often they use the Psychopathy Checklist—Revised (PCL-R; Hare, 1991), the preeminent diagnostic instrument for this purpose. Given that the PCL-R requires both complete records and specialized training for accurate scoring, however, it may not be widely used. When it is practical to administer this instrument, and when an exhibitionistic client displays indicators of psychopathy that warrant a full exploration of this syndrome, the PCL-R is highly recommended. As has been widely noted, psychopathy, in combination with evidence of deviant sexual arousal, yields higher rates of sexual recidivism (e.g., Rice & Harris, 1997).

Assessment of Comorbid Paraphilias

As noted above, it is to be expected that many exposers will have engaged in an assortment of deviant acts (Abel et al., 1987, 1988; Abel & Rouleau, 1990). Various card sorts, questionnaires, and rating scales have been developed to assess the range of deviant fantasies, attitudes, and behaviors engaged in by sex offenders. However, these instruments have rarely been tested for reliability or validity, and when they have, the results have been discouraging (Maletzky, 1997). No recent validation research on any such instrument was uncovered in our literature search, suggesting that these instruments as a class are seeing less usage. In any case, although they give the appearance of objectivity and psychometric sophistication, such instruments represent merely written forms of self-report and are subject to all the limitations of self-report (Maletzky, 1997).

One test that has found wide usage in assessing the depth and scope of deviant sexual interests and attitudes is the Multiphasic Sex Inventory II (MSI II; Nichols & Molinder, 1996). The MSI II is a wide-ranging self-report questionnaire, but unlike other self-report inventories, it was constructed with the expectation that many of its takers would attempt to deny or minimize their sexual deviance. Accordingly, the test is designed to tap into the types of distorted thinking processes that characterize sexual deviance in ways that are not obvious to the test taker. In addition, five scales and indices on the MSI II are used to measure the extent to which a person is willing to be open and disclosing regarding his overall sexuality and behavior. These measures contrast an individual who is being relatively nondefensive about sexual information with a person who is suppressing or "masking" his sexuality. Three scales on the MSI II assess the distorted thinking (denial, rationalizations, justifications) typical of sexual offenders. Two scales, the Molester Comparison and Rapist Comparison scales, have been empirically derived by comparing scores from known child molesters and rapists with scores from known normal subjects. Neither scale appears susceptible to "faking good," and both scales are very stable over time (Nichols & Molinder, 1996). Both scales are useful in assessing the degree of the psychosexual disturbance of the admitting offender. With its focus on distorted cognitions, the MSI II is also useful as a measure of treatment progress.

The MSI II Adult Male Form is a paper-and-pencil test with 560 true–false questions. It takes approximately 90 minutes for a client with at least a seventh-grade reading level. A cassette tape of the test is available for clients who cannot read, and Spanish-language and adolescent forms of the test are also available. The MSI II cannot be hand-scored, but must be sent to Nichols and Molinder Assessments, Inc., for computerized scoring and interpretation.

The authors' website (*www.nicholsandmolinder.com*) indicates that the test has been nationally standardized with approximately 2,000 subjects matched to the 1990 U.S. census on demographic variables, and that psychometric evaluations of the MSI II have produced evidence of reliability and convergent/discriminant validity. Though no cross-validation study of the MSI II has been published in a peer-reviewed journal, the original MSI has been found to have favorable psychometric properties and to be comparable to or better than penile plethysmography (PPG; see below) for identifying deviant sexual preferences (Day, Miner, Sturgeon, & Murphy, 1989; Schlank, 1995). These studies did not investigate the ability of the MSI to discriminate between exhibitionists and other sex offenders.

Risk Assessment

Recidivism base rates for exhibitionists can only be guessed at from the limited and mixed research findings available. A 10-year follow-up of 48 exhibitionists reported a sexual rearrrest rate of 20.5% (Romero & Williams, 1985). Frisbie and Dondis (1965, cited in Marshall, Eccles, & Barbaree, 1991) reported a 40.7% reoffense rate for exhibitionists followed over a 1- to 6-year period. These authors noted, however, that reoffense rates varied widely according to past offense histories: First-offense exhibitionists recidivated at a rate of 9%, whereas 57% of those with past convictions recidivated. Other studies have reported exhibitionist recidivism rates in the 20–41% range (McGrath, 1991). A treatment outcome study that followed 61 exhibitionists for periods of up to 8 years found that treated exhibitionists recidivated at rates of 24–

39%, depending on the treatment administered (Marshall, Eccles, et al., 1991). Of the untreated control subjects, 57% were charged with new sex offenses. However, the authors reported that when they gained access to subjects' police files containing reports of exposures that had not led to official charges, the recidivism rates were 2.3 times higher.

A recent study of 221 Canadian exhibitionists attempted to identify risk factors related to both "hands-off" and "hands-on" sexual recidivism. Over a mean follow-up period of 6.8 years, 12% of those in the sample were charged with a hands-off offense (i.e., any sex offense without physical contact), and 6% were charged with a hands-on (any bodily contact) sex offense (Greenberg et al., 2002). Prior criminal history (sexual and general) differentiated the total recidivist group from the nonrecidivists. In addition, the hands-on recidivists scored significantly higher than the hands-off recidivists on the PCL-R (scored retrospectively), and showed significantly more arousal on PPG to both rape and pedophilic stimuli. For reasons they do not explain, these authors assumed that hands-on offending by exhibitionists evidenced "escalation" (Greenberg et al., 2002). In a Colorado study (Colorado Department of Public Safety, 2004), 130 sex offenders on probation were tracked for 15 months. Fifteen (12%) were rearrested for new sex crimes, all of which were hands-off offenses (peeping/voyeurism or indecent exposure). Thus, although exhibitionism is generally considered to be a highly compulsive and repetitive behavior, this presumption is not consistently reflected in high recidivism rates across studies.

Although actuarial assessment of the risk for reoffending has been applied primarily to child molesters and rapists, it is possible, and important, to assess for recidivism risk among exhibitionists. As noted previously in this chapter, many offenders apprehended for exhibitionistic offenses also have the propensity for hands-on offending. The most commonly used actuarial risk assessment instrument, the Static-99 (Hanson & Thornton, 1999), included a number of hands-off offenders in its development sample, making it applicable for exhibitionists. It is noteworthy, in fact, that one of the Static-99 items is "any conviction for a non-contact offense," which indicates that a history of such behavior increases the likelihood of any future sexual offending. Users of the Static-99 should download updated scoring instructions (Harris, Phenix, Hanson, & Thornton, 2003) from the website of the Solicitor General of Canada (*ww2.psepc-sppcc.gc.ca/publications/ corrections/pdf/Static-99-coding-Rules_e.pdf*).

By itself, the Static-99 provides a long-term recidivism risk estimate with moderate predictive accuracy (Barbaree, Seto, Langton, & Peacock, 2001). In addition, a clinician may wish to consider dynamic risk factors, which can provide information on the imminence of reoffending. Dynamic factors that appear associated with sexual recidivism include access to victims, attitudes that tolerate or condone sexual assault, sexual entitlement, and poor self-management strategies (Hanson & Harris, 1998, 2001). Hanson and Harris (1998) also found that ongoing substance abuse problems were common among recidivists. Because substance use can impair judgment, lower inhibitions, and interfere with impulse control, it may be a particularly important factor to consider when monitoring risk. Consistent with Kafka's (2001a, 2001b) hypersexuality model, sex offenders appear to be at higher risk for reoffending when they show sharp increases in dysphoric moods, particularly anger (Hanson & Harris, 1998). Recidivists failed to acknowledge their recidivism risk even as they increased their involvement in such sexual behaviors as the use of prostitutes, excessive masturbation, and deviant sexual fantasizing (Hanson & Harris, 1998). Dynamic risk factors with the strongest correlations with sex offense recidivism include deviant sexual interest, sexual preoccupations, and self-regulation problems (Hanson & Morton-Bourgon, 2005).

The Sex Offender Need Assessment Rating (SONAR), designed to assess changes in dynamic risk factors among treated offenders (Hanson & Harris, 2001), has shown moderate ability to differentiate recidivists from nonrecidivists (r = .43; receiver operating characteristic = .74) (Hanson & Harris, 2001). Because sexual preoccupation, sexual self-regulation, tolerant attitudes, and dysthymic moods are often salient issues for exhibitionists, the SONAR should be used on a regular basis to assess for changes in the functioning of these clients.

Physiological Assessment

Penile Plethysmography

PPG has long been the standard tool for the assessment and measurement of deviant sexual arousal. This procedure has been described in detail in a number of reports (e.g., Marshall, 2006b) and is not described here. Typically, a PPG protocol exposes a subject to specific types of visual or auditory stimuli to assess the subject's penile responsiveness. The use of this instrument with exhibitionists has been limited, however, by the difficulty in determining appropriate stimuli for creating exhibitionistic arousal. Since the exhibitionist's victim can be of any age, is usually dressed, and is typically in a public place, distilling the erotic essence of the scenario is no small task. Researchers have tried scenes of women walking on a deserted street, but reported only modest arousal in a minority of exhibitionists (Maletzky, 1991). Maletzky reported more consistent arousal among exposing clients when audiotaped scenes were used, and theorized that this type of stimulus presentation allowed an exhibitionist to fill in highly erotic details in his mind's eye. Others (Langevin et al., 1979) have also used audiotaped stimuli, however, and found no differences in responding between exhibitionists and normal control subjects. When audiotaped scenarios of either exposing or consenting sexual intercourse were used to attempt to differentiate 44 exhibitionists from 20 normal subjects, the exhibitionists did respond more to the exposing scenes than the control subjects, but they also responded more to the scenes of consensual sex than to the exposing scenes (Marshall, Payne, Barbaree, & Eccles, 1991).

In sum, attempting to use PPG to assess exhibitionists has produced decidedly mixed results. It does not appear that there has been any significant research in the use of PPG with exhibitionists over the past decade. In fact, it remains unclear what PPG has to offer in the assessment of exhibitionists, or even, for that matter, whether exhibitionists are aroused by the thought of exposing themselves (Marshall, Eccles, et al., 1991; Marshall & Fernandez, 2000). Marshall (2006b) has concluded that there is "little support for the idea that these assessment procedures produce meaningful evidence on these offenders" (p. 18).

PPG is potentially more useful in assessing for additional paraphilias than for exhibitionism itself. For example, it is sometimes unclear what has motivated a man to expose himself to a child. Often what appears to be an exposure is actually an act of "grooming" a child—that is, testing the waters or desensitizing the child to sexualized behavior—and the true intention of the offender is physical molestation. In situations such as this, PPG could help to identify the true pedophilic predilection of the offender. In fact, Greenberg and colleagues (2002) found that in their sample of recidivistic exhibitionists, the hands-on recidivists showed significant arousal on PPG to both rape and pedophilic stimuli. Thus the PPG findings were potentially useful for risk assessment purposes. Moreover, it is obviously relevant for treatment planning to identify offenders whose true interests include rape or child molestation. It is important to note, however, that even among men who have molested children, a sizable percentage do not respond sexually to child stimuli on PPG testing (Barbaree & Seto, 1997). And it is also clear that many rapists do not display deviant arousal upon PPG testing (Baxter, Barbaree, & Marshall, 1986). Thus there is the danger that negative PPG findings regarding rape or child stimuli will create a false impression that a given offender does not harbor a predilection for rape or molestation.

PPG has historically played an important role in the assessment and treatment of paraphilias. As time has gone by, however, it has become more, not less, controversial. In recent years some of its most ardent adherents have questioned its usefulness, due to problems with standardization, susceptibility to faking, reliability, and validity (Laws, Quinsey, Gress, & Konopasky, 2003; Marshall, 2006b). Marshall (2006b) has written: "The evidence on the reliability and validity of phallometrics presently available in the literature certainly offers little support for its use" (p. 20). Despite these limitations, 30% of our survey respondents reported using PPG.

The Abel Assessment for Sexual Interest

The Abel Assessment for Sexual Interest (AASI, also referred to as the Abel Screen) has generated a great deal of interest as a nonintrusive alternative to PPG for the assessment of sexual interest (Fischer, 2000; Hanson, 2002). Conceptually, the AASI is relatively simple: Images of people of various ages and gender are presented on a computer monitor. The subject advances the images by hitting a key on the computer keypad. Unbeknownst to the subject, the length of time it takes him to hit the key for each slide is timed and considered indicative of the subject's attraction to the person pictured in the slide. Although the AASI has obvious advantages over the PPG, it has consistently displayed shortcomings that have precluded its wide application, including concerns about its scoring format, reliability, and validity (Fischer, 2000).

It is unclear what, if any, applicability the AASI has in the diagnosis or treatment planning of exhibitionists. Although the test claims to include a scale that assesses exhibitionism (*www.abelscreen.com*), no information about the psychometric properties of the scale appears to be available for nonsubscribers. Moreover, the limited testing of the instrument that has been published (Abel, Huffman, Warberg, & Holland, 1998; Letourneau, 2002) makes no mention of the exhibitionism scale. Given the difficulties described above in designing appropriate scenarios for PPG assessment of exhibitionism, and given that the AASI uses only static images, it is difficult to imagine an AASI presentation that would effectively elicit specifically exhibitionistic interest.

As with the PPG, the AASI may be useful for assessing other paraphilic interests among exhibitionists. However, as with the PPG, even this limited application appears problematic. The test maker's own research (Abel et al., 1998) has revealed problems with the sensitivity and specificity of the test (e.g., classifying individuals with non-child-related offenses as potential abusers of female children). Independent testing of the AASI (Letourneau, 2002) found the AASI unable to identify either molesters of young girls or rapists of adult women. At this writing, it appears that the AASI needs further refinement before it can be recommended for clinical use.

Neuropsychological Assessment

It has long been suggested that neurological insults, particularly traumatic head injuries, can cause a variety of unusual sexual behaviors, including paraphilias (Langevin, 1990). It is clear, in fact, that head injuries can result in sexual preoccupation and impaired impulse control, and many brain-injured patients demonstrate inappropriate and aggressive sexual behaviors (Graber, Hartmann, & Coffman, 1982; Miller, Cummings, & McIntyre, 1986). A recent study found that among 476 sex offenders, 49% reported suffering a head injury that caused unconsciousness, and 22% sustained significant brain injuries (Langevin, 2006). The most common types of injuries associated with sex offending have been abnormalities in the temporal lobes and the limbic system (Maletzky, 1997). Unusual sexual behaviors have ranged from bizarre preoccupations to violent outbursts to organized paraphilic behaviors (Langevin, 1990).

Early neuropsychological studies appeared to uncover evidence of brain damage in exhibitionists (e.g., Flor-Henry, Koles, Reddon, & Baker, 1986), though others have failed to replicate these findings. For instance, Langevin, Lang, Wortzman, and Frenzel (1989) found that 15 exhibitionists did not differ significantly from controls on neuropsychological testing or computerized tomographic (CT) imaging. Most recently, Langevin (2006) found that sex offenders with head injuries were more likely to offend against adults than children and were more likely to display exhibitionistic and polymorphous sexual behavior. Continuing research on the connection between brain injuries and sex offending has been surprisingly sparse (Langevin, 2006) and available evidence does not allow the drawing of any firm conclusions. In cases of bizarre exposure, offenders should be referred for neuropsychological assessment; in the majority of cases, however, such testing does not currently appear to be justified.

Polygraphy

As controversial as PPG and the AASI has been the use of polygraphy with sex offenders. The major difference in the ongoing debates about these three assessment methods is that the role of polygraphy is clear: Polygraphy yields historical offense information that is important for both diagnostic and treatment purposes, and also allows the offender's current behavior to be monitored (Ahlmeyer et al., 2000; English, Jones, Pasini-Hill, Patrick, & Cooley-Towell, 2000; English, Jones, Patrick, & Pasini-Hill, 2003; Heil et al., 2003). As a result, polygraphy has become the primary physiological assessment tool used by sex offender specialists. The majority (66%) of treatment providers we surveyed said that they utilize polygraph examinations as part of their assessment of exhibitionists.

It has been evident since the 1980s that sex offenders often have many more victims and have committed many more sex crimes than those for which they have been arrested (Abel et al., 1987, 1988; Ahlmeyer et al., 2000; Freeman-Longo, 1985; Heil et al., 2003; Hindman, 1988). Some researchers elicited their subjects' untold stories only by going to extraordinary lengths to protect the subjects' confidentiality (Abel et al., 1987). In the ordinary circumstances that treatment providers encounter, however, little or nothing will initially be known about the scope or duration of an offender's deviant acts beyond what is revealed by official documents. The evaluator and treatment provider are thus left with no reliable history by which to assess offense patterns or develop a treatment plan, or even to make an accurate diagnosis. For instance, Phil (the offender described in the first vignette at the beginning of this chapter) would have been happy to complete treatment without ever mentioning his pedophilia. Usually exhibitionists will minimize their need for treatment by admitting to only a handful of exposing offenses, when in reality they have committed hundreds of such offenses over many years.

The "full-disclosure history" polygraph test requires a client to reveal the full extent of his sexually deviant behavior, including offenses of all types, and including offenses for which he has not been arrested or charged. Truthful offenders provide a wealth of information. Even when such a test results in a deceptive finding, in the great majority of cases the offender reveals important information he would not otherwise have provided (Ahlmeyer et al., 2000; Heil et al., 2003). The test is most effective at eliciting information when treatment providers and probation agents work together as a team, and when the consequences for deceptive results are clear and meaningful to the offender (e.g., loss of privileges, increase in supervision or restrictions) (English et al., 2000, 2003; English, Pullen, & Jones, 1996, 1998; Heil et al., 2003). We have found that effective consequences in an outpatient setting can be as minimal as requiring a deceptive offender to retake the exam at his own expense.

Despite the proven effectiveness of the polygraph in eliciting information vital to assessment and treatment planning for sex offenders, it continues to be regularly assailed as fundamentally flawed (Cross & Saxe, 2001). Saxe (1991a) argued that a major problem with polygraphy is that "the construct allegedly tested is deception, but the construct actually tested is autonomic arousal" (p. 411). Other observers have noted that methodological issues that arise in attempting to test the accuracy of polygraphy preclude any definite conclusions from being derived. In particular, the difficulty in establishing "ground truth" (corroborative evidence that can be compared to the examinee's statements) in polygraph research creates what critics consider to be a lack of construct validity (Fiedler, Schmidt, & Stahl, 2002). Nonetheless, in a recent review of 80 research studies on the validity and reliability of polygraph testing conducted since 1980, 6,380 polygraph examinations were analyzed, and the accuracy of polygraph exams was found to range from 80% to 98% (Forensic Research, 1997).

Critics (e.g., Cross & Saxe, 2001) maintain that this margin of error is unacceptable. In older field studies, correct detection of deception (sensitivity) ranged from 70.6% to 98.6% (mean = 86.3%), and correct detection of truthfulness (specificity) ranged from 12.5% to 94.1% (mean = 76%) (Saxe, Dougherty, & Cross, 1983). Removal of inconclusive results increased detection of deception to 90% accuracy, and truthfulness was detected with 80% accuracy (Raskin, 1988). On the basis of these findings, polygraphy has been castigated as an unreliable tool in the management of sex offenders (Cross & Saxe, 1992, 2001; Iacono & Lykken, 1997; Saxe, 1991b). It should be noted that sexual history tests, because they are less specific than other types of polygraphs, may in fact be less accurate than more limited exams (Kokish, 2003). It has been suggested, however, that advances in computerized polygraph technology have enhanced accuracy since the 1980s (Forensic Research, 1997).

Proponents of polygraph use argue that the way it is used in sex offender treatment renders the psychometrics debate irrelevant. O'Connell (2000) noted that the polygraph is not used in the field to make definitive judgments about truth or falsity (much less guilt or innocence), but only to encourage open disclosures. Indeed, Cross and Saxe (1992) observed that it is more the threat of polygraph testing than the actual test itself that makes the procedure effective, much as the famous "bogus pipeline" was effective in eliciting disclosures.

At the same time, it is interesting that polygraphy appears to evoke resistance disproportionate to its psychometric weaknesses. It is commonly accepted for medical and mental health professionals to use a variety of procedures that have comparable (or inferior) psychometric properties without controversy. By way of illustration, the U.S. Department of Defense compared the accuracy and reliability of the polygraph with other standard screening and diagnostic tools (Crewson, 2000). Data from 198 studies were included, and accuracy estimates were derived from the combined average of sensitivity and specificity measures across all studies in each category. For field diagnostic assessments, the accuracy estimates for polygraph, medical, and psychological tests were .88, .86, and .79, respectively (Crewson, 2000). The average accuracy reported for polygraphy was similar to that reported for magnetic resonance imaging, CT scan, and ultrasound. Polygraphy performed better than the diagnostic accuracy of the MMPI or the DSM-IV. The accuracy of detecting deception by polygraph was similar to the detection of breast cancer by ultrasound (.90) and more accurate than detection of breast cancer by X-ray (.80). The interrater reliability between polygraph examiners (.77) was similar to that of psychologists (.79) and greater than that of physicians (.55) (Crewson, 2000). Polygraphy was more reliable than the diagnosis of depression using the DSM-IV (.67). Obviously, the less than perfect accuracy of medical and psychological tests does not lead us to dismiss or discard them.

Debates about reliability and validity notwithstanding, new research is offering mounting evidence of the utility of polygraph testing to elicit information that offenders are otherwise unlikely to reveal. For instance, in a study of 60 sex offenders in Colorado prison and outpatient settings, the subjects' official records documented an average of five sexual charges involving a mean of two victims (Ahlmeyer et al., 2000). Upon polygraph examination, subjects admitted to an average of 308 offenses and 99 victims. Additional disclosures included sexual assaults, thefts of undergarments, obscene phone calls, voyeurism, exhibitionism, frottage, and production or sale of pornography. Other polygraph studies have also noted markedly increased disclosures of sex crimes and victims (English et al., 2000; Heil et al., 2003; Hindman & Peters, 2000).

Such polygraph tests are especially important with exhibitionists, who frequently hold themselves apart from other offenders and minimize the seriousness of their problem. Exhibitionists are more likely than other offenders to deny other paraphilias, but are more likely than others to have committed other sex crimes and to have large numbers of offenses (Maletzky, 1997). Conversely, offenders arrested for other crimes frequently acknowledge exposing offenses. In a study of 180 convicted sex offenders, it was known by the courts that 14% had committed exhibitionism. After the polygraph testing, that number increased to 47% (English et al., 2003). A similar study concluded:

> The more than ten-fold increase (from 3 percent to 35 percent) in the disclosures of hands-off offenses suggests that information about exhibitionism, voyeurism, and obscene phone calls or Internet use was rarely obtained without the treatment/polygraph process. . . . Obtaining this information is crucial for containment professionals who intend to interrupt the assault pattern and prevent new victimizations by sex offenders they treat and supervise. (English et al., 2000, p. 32)

Notably, in one study researchers asked 99 sex offenders who had been polygraphed how accurate they thought the testing had been (Kokish, Levenson, & Blasingame,

2005). Participants reported that they agreed with the polygraph examiners' conclusions 90% of the time, and a majority opined that polygraph testing was a helpful part of treatment. Although 5% of the tested offenders claimed they had admitted to things they had not actually done in response to an erroneous finding of deception, clearly such statements are most parsimoniously construed as simply another form of denial.

Summary of Assessment

In conclusion, the most crucial components in the assessment of exhibitionists appear to be the differential diagnoses of psychiatric comorbidity, diverse paraphilias, and paraphilia-related disorders. To this end, the most promising tools available appear to be a careful mental status assessment with psychiatric consultation where applicable, the MSI II, and offense history polygraph examination to appraise the extent and diversity of sexually deviant behavior. It is clear that only by obtaining the most thorough psychosocial and offense history possible can an evaluator accurately assess the treatment needs of an exhibitionist. Accurate historical information is also critical in utilizing actuarial risk assessment instruments to estimate the likelihood of sex offense recidivism.

TREATMENT

As noted earlier, the research literature on exhibitionism has been meager over the past decade. Publications specifically addressing the treatment of exhibitionism have been almost nonexistent during this period. At the same time, a lively debate over the effectiveness of sex offender treatment in general has occurred, and the treatment of exhibitionism, as a subset of sex offenses, shares in this discourse. For thorough reviews of the treatment effectiveness debate, see, for example, Laws, Hudson, and Ward (2000). Some recent research has failed to detect differences in recidivism rates between treated and untreated groups of offenders (Hanson, Broom, & Stephenson, 2004; Marques, Miederanders, Day, Nelson, & van Ommeren, 2005). Other meta-analyses, however, have offered evidence that sex offenders who received contemporary cognitive-behavioral treatment reoffended at rates nearly 40% less than those offenders who went untreated (Hanson et al., 2002; Losel & Schmucker, 2005). Noteworthy is that although Marques and colleagues (2005) found no overall differences between treated and untreated groups in a controlled experimental design, the authors observed that sex offenders who successfully completed the goals of the treatment program and demonstrated that they "got it" (p. 97) reoffended less frequently than those who did not. Although the current research is far from unequivocal, there is reason to believe that cognitive-behavioral treatment with a relapse prevention component can be helpful for many sex offenders.

Group and Individual Therapy

Most exhibitionists do not spend much time in prison, even in this era of public outrage. With institutional space limited, exhibitionists are more likely than other sex offenders to be sentenced to probation, community supervision, and treatment. With regard to the type of treatment these offenders receive in the community, a recent survey of sex offender programs indicated that nearly 90% of adult sex offender outpatient programs in the United States provide group treatment, with 83% offering individual therapy as an adjunct to the group sessions (McGrath, Cumming, & Burchard, 2003). Group therapy first emerged as an institutional intervention with sex offenders in the 1950s and it gained popularity in the early 1970s as outpatient therapy became more commonly used to treat sex offenders on parole (Schwartz, 1995). Although empirical studies comparing the effectiveness of group sex offender therapy with individual therapy are virtually nonexistent, group work is generally seen as the modality of choice because of the peer confrontation and peer support it offers (Beech & Fordham, 1997). The group experience can help to reduce denial and minimization, particularly when confrontation is undertaken by peers rather than by authority figures (Clark & Erooga, 1994). Sex offenders often have difficulty with social relationships, intimacy, and coping skills (Marshall, Serran, & Cortoni, 2000), and group therapy also offers clients the opportunity to interact with others and to develop and practice new interpersonal skills (Schwartz, 1995; Yalom, 1995).

Group therapy is a cost-effective treatment modality for clients and clinicians, and can offer an opportunity for exhibitionists to discuss their deviant activities in an atmosphere that models disclosure and accountability (McGrath et al., 2003). Exhibitionism is a highly embarrassing and therefore isolating behavior, so offenders have few opportunities to discuss their behaviors with others. A therapy group provides a safe environment in which to do that, and engagement in group therapy has been associated with treatment progress (Levenson & Macgowan, 2004). Individual treatment alone is not recommended because peer confrontation is especially useful in confronting distorted thinking and reinforcing treatment progress (Beech & Fordham, 1997; Clark & Erooga, 1994). However, individual sessions do provide an opportunity for clients to more fully and deeply discuss interpersonal issues and developmental experiences that contribute to an understanding of their exhibitionistic behavior.

Cognitive-Behavioral Approaches

The vast majority of sex offender treatment programs (85%) describe their theoretical treatment model as cognitive-behavioral or relapse prevention (McGrath et al., 2003). The primary goals of cognitive-behavioral programs are described as offense responsibility, cognitive restructuring, relationship skills, social skills, victim impact/empathy, relapse prevention, arousal control, and family support (McGrath et al., 2003). Our survey revealed that 92% of clinicians utilize cognitive restructuring in their work with exhibitionists, 94% use relapse prevention techniques, and 75% employ empathy training. Empathy training may be particularly important with exhibitionists, as they are less likely than other offenders to recognize the harm their offenses cause. In addition, the vast majority of our survey respondents indicated that they include interventions to enhance social skills (89%) and interpersonal intimacy (83%).

Underlying an exhibitionist's minimization of the impact of his act on victims are distorted beliefs and difficulty in viewing a situation from a victim's perspective. Specifically, the exhibitionist is frequently invested in the idea that because he has not attacked or made physical contact with a victim, little or no trauma has been caused. Emphasizing the fear that a victim often experiences during an indecent exposure can help the offender to more realistically assess the impact he has on the victim. It is important for the exhibitionist to understand that although he knows he has no plans to rape or physically assault a victim, this information is unknown to the victim and she (it is usually a she) may view the exposure as a precursor to stalking, rape, or worse. She may fear that the exposer is "crazy" and has plans for escalating to violence. She may be reluctant to report the crime to police due to concerns that the offender could learn her name or address and return to retaliate against her. Cognitive distortions—particularly the perceptions, assumptions, and beliefs that serve to rationalize, justify, or minimize sexual offending—have been found to be correlated with a lack of victim empathy (Marshall, Hamilton, & Fernandez, 2001). Recognizing and correcting cognitive distortions, and thus assisting the exhibitionist to recognize the impact of his behavior on others, are important treatment goals for these clients (Marshall, Anderson, & Fernandez, 1999).

Relapse Prevention

Relapse prevention, a therapy model adapted from addiction treatment (George & Marlatt, 1989; Laws, 1989), continues to be a popular approach in sex offender programs (for theory and treatment components, see Laws, 1989; Laws et al., 2000). The sexual offense process is seen as a chain or cycle characterized by a recurring pattern of remission and return to the problematic behavior. The path on the return to the sexual behavior problem is predictably paved with a series of decision points, including high-risk situations, internal and external triggers, negative emotional states, and lapses of self-control. The relapse process is conceptualized as a behavioral chain in which events, cognitions, and emotions interact to influence behavior (Marques & Nelson, 1989; Nelson & Jackson, 1989).

For most exposers, the experience of being arrested and adjudicated inspires at least a brief period of abstinence. This remission in the offending cycle can provide a starting point for a therapist to introduce relapse prevention concepts and strategies. Establishing a period of remission one day at a time may serve to decrease the intensity of urges and interrupt the habitual patterns of sexual exposing. The support of the therapist and other group members can be instrumental in helping the client gain this foothold on abstinence. For clients who have an especially difficult time abstaining, medication is indicated.

Exhibitionism is rarely an impulsive act, although it may seem so to offenders at the time. Rather, it typically involves an elaborate plan that is carefully orchestrated. Environmental risk elements for exhibitionists include external or situational variables that influence expectations and motivations toward offending behavior, such as the presence of a potential victim, driving a car, or interpersonal conflict. Lifestyle risk factors, such as isolation from others, can also presage urges to reoffend. Internal triggers such as negative thoughts and emotions may sabotage attempts at self-control.

The primary goal of relapse prevention is improved self-management of deviant urges and impulses. The client must identify the sequences of events, thoughts, and feelings that have occurred prior to exposing himself. Triggering events that have led to dysphoric moods and that activate maladaptive cognitive schemas should be explored (Laws, 1989; Marshall, Anderson, et al., 1999). Alternative ways to cope with a variety of triggering events must be uncovered. Some simple interventions include substitution behaviors, thought stopping, increasing tolerance of uncomfortable affect, and promoting adaptive help seeking (Livesley, 2005). Cognitive reframing involves helping clients to recognize the many types of distorted thinking processes they may be using, such as catastrophizing, all-or-nothing thinking, mind-reading, or overgeneralization (Burns, 1999a, 1999b). Cognitive therapy helps clients to recognize that negative moods are not simply a result of events that are out of their control, and that they can control the way they feel by altering the way they interpret the external environment. This can in turn help them to modify the choices they make regarding how to respond to crises, stress, and conflict (Marshall, Anderson, et al., 1999). Bibliotherapy can be helpful as a supplement to the sex offender treatment program modules; many self-help books can assist individuals in better understanding the relationship between their thoughts, feelings, and behaviors. For instance, books like *The Feeling Good Handbook* (Burns, 1999a) and *Feeling Good: The New Mood Therapy* (Burns, 1999b) are excellent resources.

Relapse prevention strategies for exhibitionists include avoiding high-risk situations and introducing obstacles to the established offense chain. For instance, many exhibitionists expose themselves from their cars while driving. Such an offender may engage in grooming behaviors such as calling an unsuspecting victim over to the window to ask for directions, at which point the victim witnesses the offender exposing himself and masturbating. Such an offender can interfere with this pattern by removing the fuses for the powered windows in his car. Avoiding any unnecessary driving, and avoiding routes that present opportunities for offending, may also be helpful. Offenders can introduce other impediments as well, such as wearing clothes that make it more difficult to disrobe in the car (button-down shirts, long pants, and shoes that tie rather than slip on). Finally, exposers can increase accountability by calling support persons to document their times of departure and arrival while driving; this can diminish the amount of time they spend "cruising" for opportunities to offend.

Relapse prevention should include not only strategies for avoidance, but also opportunities to enhance the development of appropriate peer relationships and other productive activities that give the exhibitionist a sense of satisfaction, meaning, and purpose. Encouraging exhibitionists to reach their potential may result in an increase in self-esteem and the development of coping strategies that allow offenders to meet their needs in healthy, adaptive ways (Morin & Levenson, 2002; Ward & Brown, 2004).

Working with Intimacy Deficits and Boundaries

Researchers have found that sex offenders often display intimacy deficits and dysfunctional styles of attachment (Ward, Hudson, & Marshall, 1995), as well as low self-esteem and difficulties with coping skills (Marshall, Cripps, Anderson, & Cortoni, 1999). Nearly half of the clinicians in our survey identified intimacy deficits as a primary treatment target for exhibitionists, and 44% identified interpersonal skills as an important goal. Although only a minority emphasized boundary issues as a treatment priority, we contend that exhibitionism is often a reflection of poor interpersonal boundaries. That is, interpersonal and intimacy deficits, as well as exposing behaviors, may all be related to a poorly developed ability to properly interpret and respond to social cues in the environment.

In our practice, we have seen a number of exhibitionists with a childhood history not of sexual abuse, but of emotional, physical, or generational boundary violations that appear to have distorted the acquisition of healthy boundaries. For instance, families where privacy is not respected, or where exposure to nudity or pornography is allowed, may confuse children about appropriate physical boundaries. Similarly, parents who inappropriately share personal information with children to meet their own emotional needs can leave children unprepared to negotiate the emotional boundaries that are inherent in all relationships. Enmeshed, intrusive, or overcontrolling parents may deprive a child of an appropriate sense of personal integrity or identity. Such a child may grow into adulthood with an intense need for attention and acknowledgment that manifests itself in a behavior that metaphorically cries, "Look at me!" and "Notice me!" Zechnich (1971) construed this message as "I exist; I have life-space," and "It does make a difference that I have a penis" (p. 75). At the same time, an exhibitionist may feel extremely vulnerable and may avoid truly intimate relationships in an effort to protect himself from emotional harm. Thus exposing himself may be a way to have sexual encounters and be validated in a type of distorted and protected long-distance illusion of intimacy. By establishing and maintaining control over the sexual encounter, the exposer is able to avoid the risks inherent in true emotional intimacy.

Interpersonal boundaries reflect how we all feel about ourselves in relation to others, and how we negotiate the human dilemma of the desire to be close and connected to others while also maintaining our autonomy, identity, and independence (Adams, 2005). Faulty interpersonal boundaries often lead to relationship difficulties in parenting, romantic relationships, friendships, and professional or occupational settings. Boundaries also affect how we cope with intimacy, loneliness, conflict, depression, anxiety, and other personal challenges (Adams, 2005). Marshall (2006a) described his client in a case study as having a history of poor relationship skills, manifested by attempts to secure the affection of his partners by excessively buying gifts and helping with household tasks. This behavior appeared to be driven by an extreme neediness secondary to shame and self-esteem issues stemming from the secret and repetitive nature of exposing himself. Such neediness and solicitousness illustrate how poor boundaries can interfere with successful navigation of intimate adult relationships. Treatment of such boundary deficits involves helping the client to correct his thinking about respecting the rights and personal space of others, issues of entitlement and narcissism, and his role in relationships with others.

Identifying and Meeting Emotional Needs

Assessing the specific emotional needs an individual exhibitionist is attempting to meet through the act of exposing himself will be part of the clinician's task. If the clinician is to help the exposer learn to meet his needs in healthy ways, the starting point will be to understand the reaction he is looking to evoke. This "fantasy reaction" will indicate the emotional need he is trying to meet. It has long been noted (e.g., Taylor, 1947) that there is no single reaction that exhibitionists seek from their victims. Although theorists who see exposing as an act of anger assume that the exhibitionist is invariably looking to shock and frighten his victim (Lee, Pattison, Jackson, & Ward, 2001), in fact exhibitionists seek a range of reactions, from shock to amusement to sexual interest (Freund et al., 1988; Taylor, 1947). The following description by a client illustrates such a range:

> "I have carefully orchestrated the scene in the restroom. I place a wad of paper in the door so it stays open and I can see out. I have a perfect vantage point when I turn the garbage can over so I can stand on it. Looking out, I have a clear view of anyone entering the bathroom. I watch as man after man passes by. I keep myself hard just in case one should decide to come in.
>
> "After a while I see this gorgeous guy coming. Please, please, please, let him be the one! The feeling grips me as I see him approaching. That wonderful, tingling feeling in the pit of my stomach. As he gets closer, it becomes obvious he's coming in, and I begin to get harder. I start to pound it faster in anticipation. I quickly get into position, deciding in a flash whether I want him to actually see me or just hear

the sounds of my moaning. I decide that I want him to see me, so I run to the urinal and pull my pants below my knees.

"My heart begins to race as I imagine the look on his face when he finally sees me. I hear him enter the restroom, his footsteps lightly sounding on the tiled floor. I lean against the urinal and start to moan loudly. I can feel my knees buckling as I hear him get closer and my orgasm rises. I time it so that he rounds the corner just as I spill my juice. My ears are tingling, and I open my eyes to see him staring, wide-eyed in a blend of wonder, amusement, and disbelief. The look in his eyes envelops me like the soft embrace of a lover. I feel wanted. I feel appreciated. I feel that without actually uttering a word, I have been heard. I smile to myself as he regains his composure and enters a stall. I exit quickly, wondering if he will be doing the same thing."

Many exhibitionists claim that they are hoping for a sexual invitation from their victims (Lang, Langevin, Checkley, & Pugh, 1987; Marshall, 2006a), but it seems likely that such statements are frequently geared to create the appearance of a more "normal" motivation. In fact, Jones and Frei (1979, cited in Lang et al., 1987) reported that a majority of their sample of exhibitionists admitted they would be frightened and would flee if a victim approached them. Lang and colleagues (1987), noting that almost half of their sample were cross-dressers and that a sizable number wanted their victims to be impressed by the size of their penises, concluded that the fundamental underlying motivation was a narcissistic need for admiration. As well, some exhibitionists report that an adrenaline "rush" related to the risk-taking aspect of offending adds to their arousal. All of these emotional dimensions of exposing can be addressed in therapy. Zechnich (1971) suggested that there can be therapeutic value in as simple an intervention as encouraging "legitimate showing-off" (p. 74) behavior by the offender, such as demonstrating competence in the arts or disclosing achievements. In other words, the offender should be encouraged to create appropriate opportunities for positive reinforcement and social acceptance.

Behavioral Approaches

Although there is some debate about whether deviant arousal exists in exhibitionists (Marshall, Eccles, et al., 1991; Marshall & Fernandez, 2000), among our survey sample a sizable minority of clinicians reported employing techniques designed to counter such arousal or replace it with appropriate arousal. Most of the behavioral conditioning techniques used have been developed and tested on other types of offenders, but are used with exhibitionists in the expectation that they will be similarly effective. Many such techniques have been proposed and described (for full descriptions, see Maletzky, 1997). Only those techniques showing either significant current usage or recent research attention are described here.

Covert Sensitization

Covert sensitization (Cautela, 1967), an aversive conditioning technique, was the most popular behavioral procedure among our survey sample, with 48% reporting its usage. Although this technique has been criticized as lacking in effectiveness (Quinsey & Marshall, 1983), it is easily conceptualized and administered. The procedure involves having the offender visualize an offense scenario and then imagining, in vivid sensory detail, severe adverse consequences that would potentially follow from the offense (e.g., being arrested). Classical conditioning theory hypothesizes that by repeatedly pairing the arousal scene with its aversive consequences, the offender learns to replace the excitement originally linked to the offense fantasy with the dread linked to the aversive scene. Following the establishment of the new conditioned response, an escape scene is typically added that provides an alternative response to offending. Sample scenarios for exhibitionists are available in Maletzky (1991, 1997). A detailed description of the procedure written for sex offenders is available in Morin and Levenson (2002).

Maletzky (1991, 1997) described a variant of this procedure he called "assisted covert sensitization," designed to boost the power of the exercise by adding a foul odor during the rehearsal of the aversive scene. Maletzky reported a failure rate of only 13.3% with this technique in a sample of 155 patients (cited in Marshall, Eccles, et al., 1991). However, no follow-up research on the procedure is to be found in the literature. Of the practitioners we surveyed, 20% reported using this technique with ammonia as the noxious odor.

Ammonia Aversion

Two studies testing ammonia aversion with exhibitionists were located in our literature search. One procedure required subjects to carry a small bottle of smelling salts with them and take a deep inhalation any time they felt an urge to expose themselves (Marshall, Eccles, et al., 1991). Unfortunately, this technique was included with three other behavioral techniques administered concurrently on the same sample, precluding the possibility of identifying the effects of any one of the techniques. More unfortunately, all the techniques together produced only a limited treatment effect, as 39% of the treated group recidivated.

Recently, Marshall (2006a) reported a case study in which ammonia aversion resulted in complete remission of exhibitionistic behavior by a 35-year-old man who had been exposing himself daily for over 20 years and had been convicted for indecent exposure five times. Marshall had his subject carry a small bottle of smelling salts with him at all times and inhale from the bottle whenever he felt an urge to expose himself. Marshall theorized that the ammonia "effectively removes all current thoughts and feelings" (p. 16), which the subject was then instructed to replace with prosocial thoughts. The subject carried with him cards on which he recorded each urge to expose himself and each actual exposure. Both the urges and the exposures decreased steadily during the treatment phase until, after 6 weeks, the exposures stopped completely. The subject reported one subsequent brief period of relapsing, but at 3-month, 6-month, and 12-month follow-ups he was reportedly offense-free (Marshall, 2006a).

Interestingly, Marshall's client insisted on this unitary treatment approach against Marshall's recommendation for a more comprehensive approach. When the subject, after remission of his deviant behaviors (and a dramatic reduction in the intensity and frequency of urges), reported indirect benefits of improved self-esteem and mood, Marshall theorized: "If a person repeatedly feels unable to control the expression of socially unacceptable urges, [he is] likely to feel depressed and low in self-worth. Gaining control after such a lifelong struggle should produce a general feeling of well-being" (2006a, p. 22). Marshall urged clinicians who use this approach to ensure that their clients continue to keep daily records of their urges and behaviors throughout the treatment period.

Minimal Arousal Conditioning

In contrast to the ammonia aversion technique described by Marshall (2006a), which is construed as punishment in an operant conditioning paradigm, others have described a classical conditioning approach that is also easily applied with exhibitionists (Gray, 1995; Jensen, Laws, & Wolfe, 1994). Offenders are instructed to write the most erotic offense scenarios they can imagine. As they read through the scenario, they are then instructed to inhale ammonia as soon as they encounter the first arousing element of the story. Twenty subsequent repetitions of the ammonia inhalation then dampen any sexual excitation associated with the segment. Although originally Jensen (personal communication, 1998) instructed his clients to read through the full scenario, sniffing ammonia at each stimulating section, he later recognized that enough repetitions of pairing the ammonia with the earliest erotic element of the story would generalize to the complete story. This exercise is described in detail in Morin and Levenson (2002).

Biological Approaches

Hormonal Treatment

The role of testosterone as a factor contributing to sexual violence has been documented by Berlin (1983), who found elevated testosterone levels in very violent sex offenders. Berlin reported a lower recurrence of relapse in men who were treated with antiandrogen medication such as medroxyprogesterone acetate (MPA). Meyer, Collier, and Emory (1992) reported that 18% of their patients reoffended while being treated with MPA, compared to 55% of the untreated control group. However, Berlin has emphasized that sex offending is not totally or even primarily physiologically driven for most men, and that hormonal treatment in the absence of cognitive-behavioral treatment is likely to be ineffective. Research on hormonal therapy for sex offenders has been thoroughly reviewed in a number of publications (Bradford, 1983, 1990; Maletzky, 1991; Prentky, 1997).

Research investigating the effectiveness of hormonal treatment specifically with exhibitionists is almost nonexistent, but one study of this issue reported poor success with MPA (Langevin et al., 1979). Over half of the sample dropped out of this study, and recidivism rates indicated no treatment effect.

Psychopharmacological Treatment

Beginning in the 1980s, accumulating evidence suggested that the neurotransmitter serotonin has an inhibitory effect on male ejaculatory functioning (Greenberg & Bradford, 1997). By the 1990s, when selective serotonin reuptake inhibitors (SSRIs) became widely available, the use of these agents for controlling unwanted sexual arousal began to be explored (Kafka, 1991; Kafka & Prentky, 1992). In a series of studies (summarized in Greenberg & Bradford, 1997) it was found that three different SSRIs—fluoxetine (Prozac), fluvoxamine (Luvox), and sertaline (Zoloft)—were equally effective in reducing deviant sexual fantasies, urges, and contacts and in mitigating sexual impulsivity. Multiple studies, albeit with small samples, also found statistically significant improvement in hypersexual symptoms (e.g., compulsive masturbation) associated with a variety of paraphilias and paraphilia-related behaviors (including exhibitionism) after treatment with SSRIs (Kafka, 1991, 1994; Kafka & Prentky, 1992). Some of the earliest research involved case studies of exhibitionists, but the larger studies typically involved pedophiles or mixed groups of offenders. Thus, as with most of the research reported in this chapter, it is left to the clinician to extrapolate applications from general sex offender research to the exhibitionist clientele.

Although some theorists have suggested that compulsive sexual behaviors (including both paraphilias and paraphilia-like syndromes) manifest themselves similarly to obsessive–compulsive disorder (Bradford, 1988; Prentky, 1997), other observers have reported that the incidence of obsessive–compulsive disorder in nonparaphilic sexuality disorders is only in the range of 10–14% (Kafka, 2001a). Kafka has therefore moved away from a "compulsivity" model toward the "paraphilias and paraphilia-related disorders" schema introduced in an earlier section of this chapter (Kafka, 2001b). According to this model, sexual offending often involves a buildup of tension that is relieved through acting out, and because sexual activity produces endorphins, it may also function as a mood regulator. Kafka emphasized the comorbidity he has found in both paraphilias and paraphilia-related disorders, and implies that mood disorders (especially long-term dysthymia) and anxiety disorders (especially social phobia) underlie conditions involving hypersexuality. Interestingly, several researchers (Bradford, Greenberg, Gojer, Martindale, & Goldberg, 1995; Kafka & Prentky, 1992) have noted that even while SSRIs attenuate deviant and unconventional fantasies, urges, and behaviors, they do not necessarily interfere with conventional sexual performance. These findings suggest that the effects on deviant impulses noted above may not result from the generalized diminution of libido recognized as a common side effect of SSRIs, but from the direct action of these agents on the comorbid conditions. Such findings lend support to Kafka's (2001b) diagnostic scheme.

About three-quarters of the clinicians we surveyed identified sexual compulsivity as a primary treatment target for exhibitionists. An overwhelming majority (70%) reported that they refer exhibitionistic clients for psychiatric consultation and psychotropic medication as supplemental interventions for sexually compulsive masturbation and exposing. Nonetheless, psychopharmacological interventions remain underresearched and underutilized (Greenberg & Bradford, 1997), though they appear to hold much promise for the treatment of exhibitionists.

Other Treatment Considerations

Polygraphy

The role of the sexual history polygraph exam has been discussed earlier in the context of the assessment of exhibitionism. "Monitoring" examinations (sometimes called "maintenance" exams), on the other hand, can be conducted routinely (generally twice per year) to appraise a client's compliance with treatment and probation restrictions (Center for Sex Offender Management, 2002; Kokish, 2003). Although polygraphs are not infallible, when administered properly they provide a good method for monitoring the offender's current behavior and gauging treatment progress. They may reveal dynamic risk factors that an exhibitionist would not otherwise have disclosed, and may also help to uncover ongoing offending or high-risk behaviors while a client is in treatment (English et al., 2000, 2003).

Illustratively, researchers reviewed the maintenance polygraph exams of 122 sex offenders under community supervision in three states (English et al., 2000). Many exams revealed high-risk behaviors that warranted more intensive intervention, and some revealed outright offending. Exhibitionism was one of the most commonly reported behaviors. Specifically, 14 sex offenders admitted to fondling/frottage; 6 reported engaging in exhibitionism; 5 disclosed voyeurism; 1 admitted to bestiality; 2 reported stalking; 2 reported giving alcohol or drugs to victims without their consent; and 1 admitted to sexually abusing a child. Many other offenders admitted using pornography (including child pornography), making obscene phone calls, using the Internet for sexual purposes, or masturbating to deviant fantasies. In addition, one admitted grooming his girlfriend's children. The authors concluded: "Based on the data presented here . . . managing the risk of sex offenders in the community is greatly enhanced by the post-conviction polygraph/treatment process" (English et al., 2000, p. 43).

A client prepares for a monitoring polygraph exam by completing a questionnaire about pertinent behaviors he might have engaged in over the prior 6-month period. After discussing the questions with the therapist and treatment group, and disclosing any inappropriate behavior, the client's declarations are then verified via polygraph examination. Generally, this polygraph examination is coordinated by the offender's treatment provider. Polygraph examiners should be specially trained and certified in sex offender testing according to American Polygraph Association guidelines, and should work collaboratively in a management team with treatment providers, probation officers, and child protection workers (Kokish, 2003). Monitoring polygraphs should not be used in isolation, but as part of a comprehensive treatment and case management package. Informed consent should be obtained regarding the risks and benefits to clients, the limits of confidentiality (particularly with regard to mandatory abuse reporting), and clarification of how admissions of new crimes will be handled. Polygraph results alone should not be used to make parole revocation decisions.

Therapeutic Alliance

Obviously, the empirical testing of treatment effectiveness in large group samples is essential. At the same time, it has been noted that "therapies are entirely dependent on the therapists who practice them" (Ingram, Hayes, & Scott, 2000, p. 49). That is, the outcome of treatment is a result of not only the effectiveness of the intervention, but also the competence of the therapist. Individual variability will lead therapists to practice the same empirically supported therapies in different ways, even when following manualized procedures (Ingram et al., 2000). Relational variables are neglected in many psychotherapy outcome studies (Teyber & McClure, 2000); this is especially true in the study of cognitive-behavioral sex offender treatments, even though these variables can have a profound influence on therapy outcome (Marshall, 2005; Marshall et al., 2002, 2003).

Fundamental principles taught in most counseling programs, such as empathy, validation, collaboration, and flexibility, have been found to facilitate positive outcomes for general psychotherapy clients (Teyber & McClure, 2000). Similarly, it has been found in sex offender treatment that warm, empathic, encouraging, directive, nonconfrontational characteristics of therapists are associated with general treatment benefits, and more specifically with decreased denial and minimization and with improved relationships (Marshall, 2005; Marshall et al., 2002, 2003). It might even be suggested that the therapeutic alliance is a condition that precedes intervention techniques and provides a foundation for the success of any treatment modality.

Conversely, some process variables have been found to create obstacles to successful therapy and to interfere with alliance building and positive outcome. "Negative process" occurs when clinicians fail to respond effectively to hostile, resistant, or critical sentiments expressed by clients (Binder & Strupp, 1997; Teyber & McClure, 2000). Therapists of every theoretical orientation commonly respond to clients' negativity with anger, emotional withdrawal, or subtle rejection (Binder & Strupp, 1997). Therapists who treat sex offenders may be especially vulnerable to negative process, since sex offender clients are usually nonvoluntary and often enter treatment programs with resistance, denial, and lack of motivation for change (Jenkins-Hall, 1994; Jennings & Sawyer, 2003; Marshall, Thornton, et al., 2001; Serran, Fernandez, Marshall, & Mann, 2003; Winn, 1996). Binder and Strupp (1997) further noted that negative process remains largely unaddressed in research, but may account for many treatment failures in every modality.

Teyber and McClure (2000) have asserted that the human element of the therapeutic enterprise may be dismissed by researchers as unscientific, and that the managed care industry has further reinforced the belief that skill-based, standardized procedures are more highly valued. Although manualized treatments may appeal to both researchers and insurance companies because they are more easily studied and appear to be cost-effective, they can interfere with therapist sensitivity and flexibility and can negate the very spirit of psychotherapy (Marshall et al., 2002; Serran et al., 2003).

Sex offender clients often present for therapy with interpersonal problems that stem from long-standing relational deficits and distorted thinking about themselves and others. The interaction between client and therapist is itself a relationship, and therefore allows an immediate opportunity for intervention by exploring relational patterns as they present themselves in the therapeutic relationship. A similar opportunity exists in the group process (Jennings & Sawyer, 2003). Many sex offenders have had few prospects for intimate relationships because of limited interpersonal skills, and their deviant secrets have made intimate sharing even more difficult (Marshall, Cripps, et al., 1999). The sense of belonging and acceptance that results from group members relating with each other can mitigate the loneliness with which many sex offenders struggle prior to disclosure. When offenders first witness this relatedness between other group members and then experience it themselves, a corrective experience is enacted, and the therapeutic climate necessary to engage clients emerges. To foster this area of engagement, therapists should model effective social skills and positively reinforce examples of effective relating in group sessions (Jennings & Sawyer, 2003; Macgowan, 2003; Serran et al., 2003). Relationship skills can be experienced and practiced, rather than taught, in a therapeutic environment that provides an opportunity for true intimacy, trust, and emotional safety. Clients ultimately generalize new relational skills to others in their lives, enhancing both interpersonal experiences and general well-being. According to most theories of sex offending, such growth would be expected to mitigate urges to offend.

Summary of Treatment Options

In this section of the chapter, we have summarized treatment approaches that are in general use and that we believe can reasonably be expected to yield positive treatment gains for exhibitionists. As we have noted, most of the techniques have never been directly proven to be effective with exhibitionists, as exhibitionism in general has commanded little research attention. However, it is not unreasonable to consider exhibitionism as being susceptible to interventions that are effective with other paraphilias; nor is it unreasonable to group exhibitionism with other disorders of hypersexuality.

In some ways, exhibitionism is more difficult to treat than other paraphilias. Exposing is a highly repetitive behavior for a simple reason: Men who engage in it find it enormously exciting. Because exposing is so easily and unobtrusively performed, many exhibitionists have eluded detection for long periods of time in which they have engaged in many hundreds of offenses. Even following arrests, some exhibitionists will not stop exposing themselves long enough to be able to engage meaningfully in treatment. For these men, referrals for psychiatric assessment and SSRI treatment are urgently needed. In addition, conditioning interventions, including both minimal arousal conditioning and ammonia aversion, should be immediately implemented. Over time, exhibitionists must address their relationship and intimacy issues in cognitive therapy, and must learn to meet their needs for attention, affection, control, and approval in socially acceptable ways. In addition, as the true scope of their sexual problems is revealed through polygraphy, they may also need to address other, related sexually deviant interests and behaviors.

Ultimately, we believe that exhibitionism can be successfully treated and controlled. However, it is important for the clinician to keep in mind that virtually all treatment with sex offenders differs from traditional therapy in a fundamental way. Sex offenders do not often choose therapy; therapy is chosen for them. The most skilled therapist, using the most effective techniques, will not change an individual who is not motivated to change. Those therapists with the best chance of engaging clients in the change process are empathic and accepting while providing a directive but nonconfrontational therapeutic approach.

REFERENCES

Abel, G. G., Becker, J. V., Cunningham-Rathner, J., Mittelman, M. S., Murphy, M. S., & Rouleau, J. L. (1987). Self-reported crimes of nonincarcerated paraphiliacs. *Journal of Interpersonal Violence*, 2, 3–25.

Abel, G. G., Becker, J. V., Cunningham-Rathner, J., Mittelman, M. S., & Rouleau, J. L. (1988). Multiple paraphilic diagnoses among sex offenders. *Bulletin of the American Academy of Psychiatry and the Law*, 16(2), 153–168.

Abel, G. G., Huffman, J., Warberg, B., & Holland, C. L. (1998). Visual reaction time and plethysmography as measures of sexual interest in child molesters. *Sexual Abuse: A Journal of Research and Treatment*, 10(2), 81–94.

Abel, G. G., & Rouleau, J. L. (1990). The nature and extent of sexual assault. In W. L. Marshall, D. R. Laws, & H. Barbaree (Eds.), *Handbook of sexual assault: Issues, theories, and treatment of the offender* (pp. 9–21). New York: Plenum Press.

Adams, J. (2005). *Boundary issues*. Hoboken, NJ: Wiley.

Ahlmeyer, S., Heil, P., McKee, B., & English, K. (2000). The impact of polygraphy on admissions of victims and offenses in adult sexual offenders. *Sexual Abuse: A Journal of Research and Treatment*, 12(2), 123–138.

American Psychiatric Association. (2000). *Diagnostic and statistical manual of mental disorders* (4th ed., text rev.). Washington, DC: Author.

Barbaree, H. E., & Seto, M. C. (1997). Pedophilia: Assessment and treatment. In D. R. Laws & W. T. O'Donohue (Eds.), *Sexual deviance: Theory, assessment, and treatment* (pp. 175–193). New York: Guilford Press.

Barbaree, H. E., Seto, M. C., Langton, C. M., & Peacock, E. J. (2001). Evaluating the predictive accuracy of six risk assessment instruments for adult sex offenders. *Criminal Justice and Behavior*, 28(4), 490–521.

Baxter, D. J., Barbaree, H., & Marshall, W. L. (1986). Sexual responses to consenting and forced sex in a large sample of rapists and nonrapists. *Behaviour Research and Therapy, 24*, 513–520.

Beech, A., & Fordham, A. (1997). Therapeutic climate of sexual offender treatment programs. *Sexual Abuse: A Journal of Research and Treatment, 9*(3), 219–238.

Berah, E. F., & Myers, R. G. (1983). The offense records of a sample of convicted exhibitionists. *Bulletin of the American Academy of Psychiatry and the Law, 11*(4), 365–369.

Berlin, F. S. (1983). Sex offenders: A biomedical perspective and a status report on biomedical treatment. In J. G. Greer & I. R. Stuart (Eds.), *The sexual aggressor: Current perspectives on treatment.* New York: Van Nostrand Reinhold.

Binder, J., & Strupp, H. (1997). Negative process: A recurrently discovered and underestimated facet of therapeutic process and outcome in the individual psychotherapy of adults. *Clinical Psychology: Science and Practice, 4*, 121–139.

Birgden, A., & Vincent, J. F. (2000). Maximizing therapeutic effects in treating sexual offenders in an Australian correctional system. *Behavioral Sciences and the Law, 18*, 479–488.

Bradford, J. M. W. (1983). Hormonal treatment of sexual offenders. *Bulletin of the American Academy of Psychiatry and the Law, 11*, 159–169.

Bradford, J. M. W. (1988). Organic treatment for the male sexual offender. *Annals of the New York Academy of Sciences, 258*, 159.

Bradford, J. M. W. (1990). The antiandrogen and hormonal treatment of sex offenders. In W. L. Marshall, D. R. Laws, & H. Barbaree (Eds.), *Handbook of sexual assault: Issues, theories, and treatment of the offender* (pp. 297–310). New York: Plenum Press.

Bradford, J. M. W., Greenberg, D. M., Gojer, J. J., Martindale, J. J., & Goldberg, M. (1995, May). *Sertraline in the treatment of pedophilia: An open labelled study.* Paper presented at the annual meeting of the American Psychiatric Association, Miami, FL.

Burns, D. D. (1999a). *The feeling good handbook* (rev. ed.). New York: Plume.

Burns, D. D. (1999b). *Feeling good: The new mood therapy* (rev. & updated ed.). New York: Avon.

Cautela, J. R. (1967). Covert sensitization. *Psychological Reports, 20*, 459–468.

Center for Sex Offender Management. (2002). *An overview of sex offender management.* Washington, DC: U.S. Department of Justice.

Clark, P., & Erooga, M. (1994). Groupwork with men who sexually abuse children. In T. Morrison, M. Erooga, & R. C. Beckett (Eds.), *Sexual offenders against children: Assessment and treatment of male abusers* (pp. 102–128). London: Routledge.

Colorado Department of Public Safety. (2004). *Report on safety issues raised by living arrangements for and location of sex offenders in the community.* Denver: Author, Sex Offender Management Board.

Cox, D. J., & Maletzky, B. M. (1980). Victims of exhibitionism. In D. J. Cox & R. J. Daitzman (Eds.), *Exhibitionism: Description, assessment, and treatment* (pp. 289–293). New York: Garland Press.

Crewson, P. E. (2000). *A comparative analysis of polygraph with other screening and diagnostic tools* (No. DoDPI01-R-0003). Fort Jackson, SC: U.S. Department of Defense Polygraph Institute.

Cross, T. P., & Saxe, L. (1992). A critique of the validity of polygraph testing in child sexual abuse cases. *Journal of Child Sexual Abuse, 1*(4), 19–33.

Cross, T. P., & Saxe, L. (2001). Polygraph testing and sexual abuse: The lure of the magic lasso. *Child Maltreatment, 6*(3), 195–106.

Day, D. M., Miner, M. H., Sturgeon, V. H., & Murphy, J. (1989). Assessment of sexual arousal by means of physiological and self-report measures. In D. R. Laws (Ed.), *Relapse prevention with sex offenders* (pp. 115–123). New York: Guilford Press.

Dwyer, M. (1988). Exhibitionism/voyeurism. *Journal of Social Work and Human Sexuality, 7*(1), 101–112.

Ellis, H. (1933). *Psychology of sex.* London: William Heinemann.

English, K., Jones, L., Pasini-Hill, D., Patrick, D., & Cooley-Towell, S. (2000). *The value of polygraph testing in sex offender management* (National Institute of Justice Research Report No.

D97LBVX0034). Denver: Colorado Department of Public Safety, Division of Criminal Justice, Office of Research and Statistics.

English, K., Jones, L., Patrick, D., & Pasini-Hill, D. (2003). Sexual offender containment: Use of the postconviction polygraph. *Annals of the New York Academy of Sciences, 989*, 411–427.

English, K., Pullen, S., & Jones, L. (1996). *Managing adult sex offenders: A containment approach.* Lexington, KY: American Probation and Parole Association.

English, K., Pullen, S., & Jones, L. (1998). The containment approach: An aggressive strategy for community management of adult sex offenders. *Psychology, Public Policy, and Law, 4*(1–2), 218–235.

Fiedler, L., Schmidt, J., & Stahl, T. (2002). What is the current truth about polygraph lie detection? *Basic and Applied Social Psychology, 24*(4), 313–324.

Fischer, J. (2000). The Abel Screen. In D. R. Laws, S. M. Hudson, & T. Ward (Eds.), *Remaking relapse prevention with sex offenders: A sourcebook* (pp. 303–318). Thousand Oaks, CA: Sage.

Flor-Henry, P., Koles, Z. J., Reddon, J. R., & Baker, L. (1986). Neurophysiological studies (EEG) of exhibitionism. In C. Shagass, R. C. Josiassen, & R. A. Renner (Eds.), *Brain electrical potentials and psychopathology* (pp. 279–306). Amsterdam: Elsevier.

Forensic Research. (1997). The validity and reliability of polygraph testing. *Polygraph, 26*, 1–25.

Freeman-Longo, R. E. (1985). *Incidence of self-reported sex crimes among incarcerated rapists and child molesters.* Unpublished manuscript.

Freund, K. (1990). Courtship disorder. In W. L. Marshall, D. R. Laws, & H. E. Barbaree (Eds.), *Handbook of sexual assault: Issues, theories, and treatment of the offender* (pp. 331–342). New York: Plenum Press.

Freund, K., & Blanchard, R. (1986). The concept of courtship disorder. *Journal of Sex and Marital Therapy, 12*(2), 80–92.

Freund, K., Seto, M. C., & Kuban, M. (1997). Frotteurism: The theory of courtship disorder. In D. R. Laws & W. T. O'Donahue (Eds.), *Sexual deviance: Theory, assessment, and treatment* (pp. 111–130). New York: Guilford Press.

Freund, K., Watson, R., & Rienzo, D. (1988). The value of self-reports in the study of voyeurism and exhibitionism. *Annals of Sex Research, 1*, 243–262.

George, W. H., & Marlatt, G. A. (1989). Introduction. In D. R. Laws (Ed.), *Relapse prevention with sex offenders* (pp. 1–31). New York: Guilford Press.

Graber, B., Hartmann, K., & Coffman, J. (1982). Brain damage among mentally disordered sex offenders. *Journal of Forensic Science, 27*, 125–134.

Gray, S. R. (1995). A comparison of verbal satiation and minimal arousal conditioning to reduce deviant arousal in the laboratory. *Sexual Abuse: A Journal of Research and Treatment, 7*(2), 143–153.

Greenberg, D. M., & Bradford, J. M. W. (1997). Treatment of the paraphilic disorders: A review of the role of the selective serotonin reuptake inhibitors. *Sexual Abuse: A Journal of Research and Treatment, 9*(4), 349–360.

Greenberg, S. R., Firestone, P., Bradford, J. M., & Greenberg, D. M. (2002). Prediction of recidivism in exhibitionists: Psychological, phallometric, and offense factors. *Sexual Abuse: A Journal of Research and Treatment, 14*(4), 329–348.

Hanson, R. K. (2002). Associate editor's introduction to Dr. Letourneau's paper. *Sexual Abuse: A Journal of Research and Treatment, 14*(3), 205.

Hanson, R. K., Broom, I., & Stephenson, M. (2004). Evaluating community sex offender treatment programs: A 12-year follow-up of 724 offenders. *Canadian Journal of Behavioural Science, 36*(2), 85–94.

Hanson, R. K., Gordon, A., Harris, A. J. R., Marques, J. K., Murphy, W., Quinsey, V. L., et al. (2002). First report of the Collaborative Outcome Data Project on the Effectiveness of Treatment for Sex Offenders. *Sexual Abuse: A Journal of Research and Treatment, 14*(2), 169–194.

Hanson, R. K., & Harris, A. J. R. (1998). *Dynamic predictors of sexual recidivism 1998–01.* Ottawa, ON: Department of the Solicitor General of Canada.

Hanson, R. K., & Harris, A. J. R. (2001). A structured approach to evaluating change among sexual offenders. *Sexual Abuse: A Journal of Research and Treatment, 13*(2), 105–122.

Hanson, R. K., & Morton-Bourgon, K. (2005). The characteristics of persistent sexual offenders: A meta-analysis of recidivism studies. *Journal of Consulting and Clinical Psychology, 73*(6), 1154–1163.

Hanson, R. K., & Thornton, D. (1999). *Static-99: Improving actuarial risk assessments for sex offenders* (User Report No. 1999-02). Ottawa: Department of the Solicitor General of Canada.

Hare, R. D. (1991). *The Hare Psychopathy Checklist—Revised.* Toronto: Multi-Health Systems.

Harris, A. J. R., Phenix, A., Hanson, R. K., & Thornton, D. (2003). *Static-99 Coding Rules.* Ottawa, ON: Solicitor General Canada.

Heil, P., Ahlmeyer, S., & Simons, D. (2003). Crossover sexual offenses. *Sexual Abuse: A Journal of Research and Treatment, 15*(4), 221–236.

Hindman, J. (1988). Research disputes assumptions about child molesters. *National District Attorney's Association Bulletin, 7*(4), 1, 3.

Hindman, J., & Peters, J. M. (2000). How polygraphing adult sex offenders can lead us to better understanding the juvenile sex offender. *Federal Probation, 65*(3), 8–15.

Iacono, W., & Lykken, D. T. (1997). The validity of the lie detector: Two surveys of scientific opinion. *Journal of Applied Psychology, 82*, 426–433.

Ingram, R. E., Hayes, A., & Scott, W. (2000). Empirically supported treatments: A critical analysis. In C. Snyder & R. E. Ingram (Eds.), *Handbook of psychological change: Psychotherapy process and practices for the 21st century* (pp. 40–60). New York: Wiley.

Jenkins-Hall, K. (1994). Outpatient treatment of child molesters: Motivational factors and outcome. In N. J. Pallone (Ed.), *Young victims, young offenders* (pp. 139–150). New York: Haworth Press.

Jennings, J. L., & Sawyer, S. (2003). Principles and techniques for maximizing the effectiveness of group therapy with sex offenders. *Sexual Abuse: A Journal of Research and Treatment, 15*(4), 251–268.

Jensen, S., Laws, D. R., & Wolfe, R. (1994, November). *Reduction of sexual arousal: What to do and not do.* Paper presented at the 13th Annual Research and Treatment Conference of the Association for the Treatment of Sexual Abusers, San Francisco.

Kafka, M. P. (1991). Successful antidepressant treatment of nonparaphilic sexual addictions and paraphilias in men. *Journal of Clinical Psychiatry, 52*(2), 60–65.

Kafka, M. P. (1994). Sertraline pharmacotherapy for paraphilias and paraphilia-related disorders: An open trial. *Annals of Clinical Psychiatry, 6*, 189–195.

Kafka, M. P. (2001a). The paraphilia-related disorders: A proposal for a unified classification of nonparaphilic hypersexuality disorders. *Sexual Addiction and Compulsivity, 8*(3), 227–239.

Kafka, M. P. (2001b). Paraphilias and paraphilia-related disorders. In G. O. Gabbard (Ed.), *Treatments of psychiatric disorders* (3rd ed., pp. 1952–1979). Washington, DC: American Psychiatric Press.

Kafka, M. P., & Hennen, J. (2002). A DSM-IV Axis I comorbidity study of males (*n* = 120) with paraphilias and paraphilia-related disorders. *Sexual Abuse: A Journal of Research and Treatment, 14*(4), 349–366.

Kafka, M. P., & Prentky, R. (1992). Fluoxetine treatment of nonparaphilic sexual addictions and paraphilias in men. *Journal of Clinical Psychiatry, 53*(10), 351–358.

Kafka, M. P., & Prentky, R. A. (1994). Preliminary observations of DSM III-R Axis I comorbidity in men with paraphilias and paraphilia-related disorders. *Journal of Clinical Psychiatry, 55*, 481–487.

Kafka, M. P., & Prentky, R. A. (1998). Attention deficit hyperactivity disorder in males with paraphilias and paraphilia-related disorders: A comorbidity study. *Journal of Clinical Psychiatry, 59*, 388–396.

Kear-Colwell, J., & Pollock, P. (1997). Motivation or confrontation: Which approach to the child sex offender? *Criminal Justice and Behavior, 24*(1), 20–33.

Kokish, R. (2003). The current role of post conviction sex offender polygraph testing in sex offender treatment. *Journal of Child Sexual Abuse, 12*(3–4), 175–194.

Kokish, R., Levenson, J. S., & Blasingame, G. D. (2005). Post conviction sex offender polygraph examination: Client-reported perceptions of utility and accuracy. *Sexual Abuse: A Journal of Research and Treatment, 17*(2), 211–221.

Lang, R. A., Langevin, R., Checkley, K. L., & Pugh, G. (1987). Genital exhibitionism: Courtship disorder or narcissism? *Canadian Journal of Behavioural Science, 19*(2), 216–232.

Langevin, R. (1990). Sexual anomalies and the brain. In W. L. Marshall, D. R. Laws, & H. E. Barbaree (Eds.), *Handbook of sexual assault: Issues, theories, and treatment of the offender* (pp. 103–113). New York: Plenum Press.

Langevin, R. (2006). Sexual offenses and traumatic brain injury. *Brain and Cognition, 60*(2), 206–207.

Langevin, R., Lang, R. A., Wortzman, G., & Frenzel, R. R. (1989). An examination of brain damage and dysfunction in genital exhibitionists. *Annals of Sex Research, 2*(1), 77–87.

Langevin, R., Paitich, D., Ramsey, G., Anderson, C., Kamrad, J., Pope, S., et al. (1979). Experimental studies of the etiology of genital exhibitionism. *Archives of Sexual Behavior, 8*, 307–331.

Laws, D. R. (Ed.). (1989). *Relapse prevention with sex offenders.* New York: Guilford Press.

Laws, D. R., Hudson, S. M., & Ward, T. (Eds.). (2000). *Remaking relapse prevention with sex offenders: A sourcebook.* Thousand Oaks, CA: Sage.

Laws, D. R., Quinsey, V., Gress, C. L., & Konopasky, R. J. (2003, October 10). *The use of viewing time to assess sexual interest: Past, present, future.* Paper presented at the 22nd Annual Research and Treatment Conference of the Association for the Treatment of Sexual Abusers, St. Louis, MO.

Lee, J. K., Pattison, P., Jackson, H. J., & Ward, T. (2001). The general, common, and specific features of psychopathology for different types of paraphilias. *Criminal Justice and Behavior, 28*(2), 227–256.

Letourneau, E. (2002). A comparison of objective measures of sexual arousal and interest: Visual reaction time and penile plethysmography. *Sexual Abuse: A Journal of Research and Treatment, 14*(3), 207–223.

Levenson, J. S., & Macgowan, M. J. (2004). Engagement, denial, and treatment progress among sex offenders in group therapy. *Sexual Abuse: A Journal of Research and Treatment, 16*(1), 49–63.

Livesley, W. J. (2005). Principles and strategies for treating personality disorder. *Canadian Journal of Psychiatry, 50*(8), 442–451.

Losel, F., & Schmucker, M. (2005). The effectiveness of treatment for sexual offenders: A comprehensive meta-analysis. *Journal of Experimental Criminology, 1*, 117–146.

Macgowan, M. J. (2003). Increasing engagement in groups: A measurement based approach. *Social Work with Groups, 26*(1), 5–28.

Maletzky, B. M. (1991). *Treating the sexual offender.* Newbury Park, CA: Sage.

Maletzky, B. M. (1997). Exhibitionism: Assessment and treatment. In D. R. Laws & W. T. O'Donahue (Eds.), *Sexual deviance* (pp. 40–74). New York: Guilford Press.

Marques, J. K., Miederanders, M., Day, D. M., Nelson, C., & van Ommeren, A. (2005). Effects of a relapse prevention program on sexual recidivism: Final results from California's Sex Offender Treatment and Evaluation Project (SOTEP). *Sexual Abuse: A Journal of Research and Treatment, 17*(1), 79–107.

Marques, J. K., & Nelson, C. (1989). Elements of high-risk situations for sex offenders. In D. R. Laws (Ed.), *Relapse prevention with sex offenders* (pp. 35–46). New York: Guilford Press.

Marshall, W. L. (2005). Therapist style in sexual offender treatment: Influence on indices of change. *Sexual Abuse: A Journal of Research and Treatment, 17*(2), 109–116.

Marshall, W. L. (2006a). Ammonia aversion with an exhibitionist: A case study. *Clinical Case Studies, 5*(1), 15–24.

Marshall, W. L. (2006b). Clinical and research limitations in the use of phallometric testing with sexual offenders. *Sex Offender Treatment, 1*(1), 1–32.

Marshall, W. L., Anderson, D., & Fernandez, Y. (1999). *Cognitive behavioural treatment of sexual offenders*. Chichester, UK: Wiley.

Marshall, W. L., Cripps, E., Anderson, D., & Cortoni, F. A. (1999). Self esteem and coping strategies in child molesters. *Journal of Interpersonal Violence, 14*(9), 955–962.

Marshall, W. L., Eccles, A., & Barbaree, H. (1991). The treatment of exhibitionists: A focus on sexual deviance versus cognitive and relationship features. *Behaviour Research and Therapy, 29*(2), 129–135.

Marshall, W. L., & Fernandez, Y. (2000). Phallometric testing with sexual offenders: Limits to its value. *Clinical Psychology Review, 20*, 807–822.

Marshall, W. L., Fernandez, Y. M., Serran, G. A., Mulloy, R., Thornton, D., Mann, R. E., et al. (2003). Process variables in the treatment of sexual offenders: A review of the relevant literature. *Aggression and Violent Behavior, 8*, 205–234.

Marshall , W. L., & Hall, G. C. N. (1995). The value of the MMPI in deciding forensic issues in accused sexual offenders. *Sexual Abuse: A Journal of Research and Treatment, 7*, 205–219.

Marshall, W. L., Hamilton, K., & Fernandez, Y. (2001). Empathy deficits and cognitive distortions in child molesters. *Sexual Abuse: A Journal of Research and Treatment, 13*(2), 123–130.

Marshall , W. L., Payne, K., Barbaree, H., & Eccles, A. (1991). Exhibitionists: Sexual preferences for exposing. *Behaviour Research and Therapy, 29*, 37–40.

Marshall, W. L., Serran, G. A., & Cortoni, F. A. (2000). Childhood attachments, sexual abuse, and their relationship to adult coping in child molesters. *Sexual Abuse: A Journal of Research and Treatment, 12*(1), 17–26.

Marshall, W. L., Serran, G. A., Moulden, H., Mulloy, R., Fernandez, Y. M., Mann, R. E., et al. (2002). Therapist features in sexual offender treatment: Their reliable identification and influence on behavior change. *Clinical Psychology and Psychotherapy, 9*, 395–405.

Marshall, W. L., Thornton, D., Marshall, L. E., Fernandez, Y., & Mann, R. (2001). Treatment of sexual offenders who are in categorical denial: A pilot project. *Sexual Abuse: A Journal of Research and Treatment, 13*(3), 205–215.

McGrath, R. J. (1991). Sex-offender risk assessment and disposition planning: A review of empirical and clinical findings. *International Journal of Offender Therapy and Comparative Criminology, 35*(4), 328–350.

McGrath, R. J., Cumming, G. F., & Burchard, B. L. (2003). *Current practices and trends in sexual abuser management: The Safer Society 2002 Nationwide Survey*. Brandon, VT: Safer Society Foundation.

Meyer, W. J., Collier, C., & Emory, E. (1992). Depo-Provera treatment for sex offending behavior: An evaluation of outcome. *Bulletin of the American Academy of Psychiatry and the Law, 20*(3), 249–259.

Miller, B., Cummings, J., & McIntyre, H. (1986). Hypersexuality or altered sexual preferences following brain injury. *Journal of Neurology, Neurosurgery and Psychiatry, 49*, 867–873.

Morin, J. W., & Levenson, J. S. (2002). *The road to freedom*. Oklahoma City, OK: Authors. (Distributed by Wood & Barnes Publishing).

Nelson, C., & Jackson, P. (1989). High-risk recognition: The cognitive-behavioral chain. In D. R. Laws (Ed.), *Relapse prevention with sex offenders* (pp. 167–177). New York: Guilford Press.

Nichols, H. R., & Molinder, I. (1996). *Multiphasic Sex Inventory II: Clinician's handbook*. Fircrest, WA: Nichols & Molinder Assessments.

O'Connell, M. A. (2000). Polygraphy. In D. R. Laws, S. M. Hudson, & T. Ward (Eds.), *Remaking relapse prevention with sex offenders: A sourcebook* (pp. 285–302). Thousand Oaks, CA: Sage.

Prentky, R. A. (1997). Arousal reduction in sexual offenders: A review of antiandrogen interventions. *Sexual Abuse: A Journal of Research and Treatment, 9*(4), 335–349.

Quinsey, V. L., & Marshall, W. L. (1983). Procedures for reducing inappropriate sexual arousal: An evaluation review. In J. G. Greer & I. R. Stuart (Eds.), *The sexual aggressor: Current perspectives on treatment* (pp. 267–289). New York: Van Nostrand Reinhold.

Raskin, D. C. (1988). Does science support polygraph testing? In A. Gale (Ed.), *The polygraph test: Lies, truth and science* (pp. 96–110). Newbury Park, CA: Sage.

Rice, M. E., & Harris, G. T. (1997). Cross-validation and extension of the Violence Risk Appraisal Guide for child molesters and rapists. *Law and Human Behavior, 21*(2), 231–241.

Romero, J., & Williams, L. (1985). Recidivism among convicted sex offenders: A 10-year follow-up study. *Federal Probation, 49,* 58–64.

Saxe, L. (1991a). Lying: Thought of an applied social psychologist. *American Psychologist, 46*(4), 409–415.

Saxe, L. (1991b). Science and the CQT polygraph: A theoretical critique. *Integrative Physiological and Behavioral Science, 26,* 223–231.

Saxe, L., Dougherty, D., & Cross, T. P. (1983). *Scientific validity of polygraph testing: A research review and evaluation—a technical memorandum* (No. OTA-TM-H-15). Washington, DC: U.S. Congress, Office of Technology Assessment.

Schlank, A. (1995). The utility of the MMPI and the MSI for identifying a sexual offender typology. *Sexual Abuse: A Journal of Research and Treatment, 7*(3), 185–194.

Schwartz, B. (1995). Group therapy. In H. Cellini (Ed.), *The sex offender* (pp. 14.01–14.14). Kingston, NJ: Civic Research Institute.

Serran, G. A., Fernandez, Y., Marshall, W. L., & Mann, R. (2003). Process issues in treatment: Application to sexual offenders. *Professional Psychology: Research and Practice, 34*(4), 368–374.

Seto, M. C. (2002). Courtship disorder. *ATSA Forum, 14*(3), 4–5.

Taylor, F. H. (1947). Observations on some cases of exhibitionism. *Journal of Mental Science, 93,* 631–638.

Teyber, E., & McClure, F. (2000). Therapist variables. In C. Snyder & R. E. Ingram (Eds.), *Handbook of psychological change: Psychotherapy process and practices for the 21st century* (pp. 62–87). New York: Wiley.

Ward, T., & Brown, M. (2004). The good lives model and conceptual issues in offender rehabilitation. *Psychology, Crime and Law, 10*(3), 243–257.

Ward, T., Hudson, S. M., & Marshall, W. L. (1995). Cognitive distortions and affective deficits in sex offenders: A cognitive deconstructionist interpretation. *Sexual Abuse: Journal of Research and Treatment, 7*(1), 67–83.

Winn, M. E. (1996). The strategic and systemic management of denial in the cognitive/behavioral treatment of sexual offenders. *Sexual Abuse: A Journal of Research and Treatment, 8*(1), 25–36.

Yalom, I. (1995). *The theory and practice of group psychotherapy* (4th ed.). New York: Basic Books.

Zechnich, R. (1971). Exhibitionism: Genesis, dynamics and treatment. *Psychiatric Quarterly, 45*(1), 70–75.

CHAPTER 6

FETISHISM

Psychopathology and Theory

SHAUNA DARCANGELO

Fetishism has long held the public's fascination and aroused curiosity. Why do certain objects or certain parts of the body become associated with sexual arousal in some people? Why are attractions to certain objects/body parts (e.g., breasts) considered normal, while attractions to others (e.g., feet or shoes) are viewed as perverse, baffling, and bizarre? These questions have been topics of investigation since sexual functioning became a subject for serious research. Unfortunately, relatively little empirical work has been done, and we are still left with more questions than answers.

DIAGNOSTIC CRITERIA

The 10th revision of the *International Classification of Diseases* (ICD-10; World Health Organization, 1992) and the text revision of the fourth edition of the *Diagnostic and Statistical Manual of Mental Disorders* (DSM-IV-TR; American Psychiatric Association, 2000) both define fetishism in terms of the use of (DSM-IV-TR), or reliance on (ICD-10), nonliving objects for sexual arousal and sexual gratification. Both classification systems also stipulate that fetishism should only be diagnosed if clinically significant distress or impairment is observed. In addition, the ICD-10 indicates that fetishism should only be diagnosed if the fetish is the most important source of sexual stimulation or essential for satisfactory sexual response (World Health Organization, 1992). The DSM-IV-TR does not include a similar criterion.

DESCRIPTIVE FEATURES

Paraphilias in general are believed to originate in childhood or early adolescence (Money, 1990), and to become better defined and elaborated during adolescence and early adulthood (McConaghy, 1993). According to the DSM-IV-TR (American Psychiatric Association, 2000), "elaboration and revision of paraphilic fantasies may continue over the lifetime of the individual. . . . [The fantasies/urges] are recurrent . . . but . . . there are periods of time when the frequency of the fantasies and intensity of the urges vary substantially. . . . [Paraphilic] disorders tend to be chronic and lifelong, but both the fantasies and the behaviors often diminish with advancing age in adults" (p. 568). Various factors can influence the paraphilic behaviors, including psychosocial stressors, other mental disorders, and the environment (e.g., opportunities to engage in fetishism).

As other paraphilias are, fetishism is virtually the exclusive domain of males. In Chalkley and Powell's (1983) review of 48 cases of fetishism, 47 of their subjects were males, and they ranged in age from 12 to 59 years. As well, all races and socioeconomic groups are thought to be represented (Wiederman, 2003). Virtually any object has the potential to serve as a fetish, although certain objects are more likely to be fetishes than others (Steele, 1996). Chalkley and Powell identified clothing (reported by 58.3% of patients) as the most common fetish object, followed by rubber (22.9%), footwear (14.6%), parts of the body (14.6%), leather (10.4%), clothes made of soft material/fabric (8.3%), items made of silk (6.3%), and other soft objects such as handkerchiefs (14.6%). Of the 48 patients, the majority (*n* = 17) reported having only one fetish, although 10 patients reported having four or more fetishes (one patient reported a high of nine fetishes).

To examine fetishism in a nonclinical population, Weinberg, Williams, and Calhan (1994) mailed questionnaires to 500 members of an organization called the "Foot Fraternity." All of the 262 respondents were male (88% homosexual, 12% bisexual), and all expressed a sexual interest in male feet or footwear. The respondents ranged in age from 21 to 65 years (mean age = 38); 81% were employed in white-collar jobs; 69% had a college or graduate degree; and 89% were European American. Twenty percent could not explain their attraction to feet/footwear, while 50% attributed their arousal to the sensual aspects of the fetish object. The remaining 30% emphasized the symbolism of the object (e.g., strength and power). In terms of the strength of the fetish interest, 83% of respondents masturbated at least once a week while fantasizing about feet or footwear. The majority of respondents did not exclude partners from their sex lives, and 72% of respondents indicated that feet and footwear were an important part of their sexual activity with others.

DEGREE OF IMPAIRMENT

By definition, a diagnosis of fetishism requires clinically significant distress or impairment in social, occupational, or other important areas of functioning (American Psychiatric Association, 2000). However, while some individuals experience extreme feelings of guilt, shame, and depression regarding their unusual sexual activity, others report little distress as a result of their behavior, except possibly distress regarding the reactions of others (American Psychiatric Association, 2000). Chalkley and Powell (1983) found that approximately 21% of patients presented initially with problems other than fetishism (perhaps suggesting a lesser degree of impairment). Gosselin and Wilson (1980) reported that 69% of "rubberites" and 66% of "leatherites" had steady partners and could contain their fetishistic activities to forms acceptable to their partners. Unfortunately, this study is marred by several methodological problems, including low response rates.

EPIDEMIOLOGY

Prevalence and Incidence

As is the case with many other sexual disorders, satisfactory epidemiological data for fetishism are lacking. In general, the disorder of fetishism is considered to be rare. Out of a series of 4,000 patients seen in private practice, only 0.1% were identified as having fetishism as the primary problem (Curren, 1954). Chalkley and Powell (1983) estimated that only 0.8% of adult psychiatric cases involved fetishism, while Kafka and Hennen (2002) found that 8.3% of a group of 88 outpatient males with paraphilias were diagnosed with fetishism. Even within a forensic population, fetishism appears to be relatively rare. In a group of 561 nonincarcerated sexual offenders (all diagnosed with paraphilias), only 19 (3.4%) were diagnosed with fetishism (Abel et al., 1988).

In terms of fetishes that do not reach clinical significance, it is virtually impossible to estimate the prevalence of fetishism, due to the secretive nature of the behavior/fantasies/urges. Gosselin and Wilson (1980) reported that 18% of their control sample reported having fetishistic fantasies, while Crepault and Couture (1980) found that 77.7% of males admitted having fantasies in which they imagined part of a female body. Judging by the availability of fetishism sites on the Internet (Wise & Kalyanam, 2000), as well as pornographic magazines catering to specific interests, there appears to be a substantial market.

SEX DIFFERENCES

As mentioned previously, fetishism is considered to be more common in males than in females. However, given the lack of any sound epidemiological evidence, the extent of this difference is unknown. In the previously mentioned study by Chalkley and Powell (1983), the only female identified was a lesbian who had a fetish for breasts. Kinsey, Pomeroy, Martin, and Gebhard (1953) reported only one or two cases of fetishism in their female cohort. Wilson (1987b) investigated the fantasies of 1,862 male and 2,905 female readers of a national newspaper. Content analysis on a subset of these fantasies revealed that 18% ($n = 291$) of men had fetishistic elements in their favorite fantasy (e.g., black stockings and suspenders, sexy underwear, leather, or nurses' uniforms), while only 7% ($n = 409$) of women's fantasies included fetishistic elements.

Several theories have been proposed to account for the difference in sex ratio: (1) Males are more easily conditioned by their sexual experiences and by objects associated with those experiences (Kinsey et al., 1953); (2) females have greater innate sexual preferences and therefore require less learning to establish their sexual preferences, which leads to less "error" (Bancroft, 1989); (3) females are less likely to learn sexual responses to abnormal stimuli, due to the lack of a clear genital signal (i.e., an erect penis; Bancroft, 1989); (4) men's sensitivity to visual stimuli, as well as the strong biofeedback supplied by the penis, increases the likelihood of developing a fetish in males, due to the visual nature of the fetish (Gosselin & Wilson, 1980); (5) males and females exhibit differences in cerebral organization/brain development and in the effects of prenatal hormones (Flor-Henry, 1989; Pitcher, 1990); and (6) males have less erotic plasticity than females, except during a brief developmental window in childhood (Baumeister, 2000).

Baumeister (2000) proposes that in general, the female sex drive is more malleable than the male sex drive in response to sociocultural and situational factors. He suggests that the gender differences in paraphilias can be accounted for by a brief period of plasticity in males during childhood, after which the sexual patterns are reasonably rigid (unlike those of females). Thus, once a fetish is developed during childhood, it will be relatively fixed for males but will be more malleable in females. In support of this premise, Baumeister reviewed a study by Kendrick, Hinton, Atkins, Haupt, and Skinner (1998) in which newborn sheep and goats were exchanged (i.e., sheep were raised by goats, and vice versa). Upon reaching adulthood, they were reunited with their biological species, and their mating preferences were observed. The adult females were willing to mate with either species, while the adult males only mated with their adoptive species (even after living exclusively with their own kind for 3 years). Baumeister suggests that biological intervention for paraphilias in males (i.e., hormone treatments or castration) may be more effective, because male sexuality is less responsive to social and cultural influences during adulthood.

ASSOCIATED FEATURES

Fetishism, transvestic fetishism, and homosexuality have often been linked in the literature, as have fetishism and other paraphilias. Abel and Osborn (1992) investigated the comorbidity rates of various paraphilic behaviors in a group of 859 men diagnosed with a paraphilia. Of the 859 subjects, 12 were diagnosed with fetishism as either a primary or a secondary diagnosis. Forty-one percent ($n = 5$) of subjects with a primary diagnosis of fetishism also had a diagnosis of pedophilia. Thirty-three percent ($n = 4$) had a secondary diagnosis of masochism, 33% of transvestism, 17% ($n = 2$) of sadism, 8% ($n = 1$) of exhibitionism, 8% of voyeurism, and 8% of frotteurism.

Fetishism and other psychiatric disorders have also been linked in the literature. Chalkley and Powell (1983) reported that 33% were diagnosed with an additional psychiatric classification, while 27% were diagnosed with more than one psychiatric classification. Thirteen patients (27%) were diagnosed with personality disorder, 6% with paranoid schizophrenia, 14.5% with depression, 4% with anxiety neurosis, and 18.8% with sexual dysfunction (other than fetishism). Fetishistic behavior has also been linked with kleptomania and "borderline personality organization" (Wise, 1985), obsessive–compulsive personality (Lowenstein, 1997), and attention-deficit/hyperactivity disorder (Kafka & Hennen, 2002).

FORENSIC ISSUES

Little information is available on the relationship between criminality and fetishism, although it has been suggested that many crimes that appear to be nonsexual (e.g., burglary) may be sexually motivated (Krafft-Ebing, 1886/1965; Revitch, 1978). For instance, Wise (1985) proposed a link between fetishism and kleptomania (i.e., a disorder in which there is a compulsive urge to steal objects that are not needed for their personal use or for their monetary value). Schlesinger and Revitch (1999) identified two types of sexual burglaries: (1) "fetishistic" burglaries with overt sexual dynamics, and (2) "voyeuristic" burglaries, which may involve more subtle dynamics (i.e., voyeuristic impulses stimulate the act, such as looking around, inspecting drawers, or attempting to see a naked female). In a sample of 52 individuals who had committed sexual homicide, approximately 42%

(n = 22) had a history of burglary, with seven offenders having committed fetishistic burglaries. Schlesinger and Revitch suggest that the sexual dynamics of certain offenders often go unrecognized, and that it is important to explore masturbatory fantasies and feelings of sexual arousal, even in routine assessments of burglars. Regardless of the criminal behavior, legal agencies (i.e., courts, probation offices) represent the second leading source of referrals for mental health evaluations of fetishists (Chalkley & Powell, 1983).

THEORIES OF ETIOLOGY

Human sexuality has long been recognized as "a rich, confusing tangle, in which biological drives, sociocultural meanings, formative individual experiences, and additional unknown factors play powerful roles" (Baumeister, 2000, p. 347). Most of the early explanations of fetishism focused on psychoanalytic theory. However, over the years attention has also been focused on possible biological, sociocultural, and sociobiological factors.

Biological Perspective

A number of authors have considered the relevance of biological factors to fetishism, including normal cerebral function and the development of sexuality, as well as brain injury and neurological abnormalities (Mason, 1997). Mitchell, Falconer, and Hill (1954) described a case study in which a man's fetish for safety pins was eliminated after a temporal lobectomy. Other authors have also addressed the link with temporal lobe abnormalities, but have also commented on the presence of more diffuse pathology (Huws, Shubsachs, & Taylor, 1991).

Several studies have investigated the use of electroencephalography (EEG) to assess sexual arousal/response (Howard, Longmore, & Mason, 1992; Howard, Longmore, Mason, & Martin, 1994). Waismann, Fenwick, Wilson, Hewett, and Lumsden (2003) compared EEG responses to visual erotic stimuli in men with normal and paraphilic interests to investigate whether paraphilia is characterized by an excessive response to paraphilic stimuli or a deficient reaction to *conventional* stimuli. Eighty-two percent (n = 23) of the paraphilic group declared fetishistic interests, 79% reported sadomasochistic interests, and 50% were transvestic. The results indicated that when presented with fantasy-concordant stimuli, control males showed greatest activation in the right parietal region, while the paraphilic men showed most activation in the left frontal region. As well, the paraphilic men were aroused equally by paraphilic and conventional stimuli, while the men in the control group were less interested in the paraphilic stimuli. The authors concluded that these findings could support a "response deficiency" theory of paraphilia.

Psychological Perspectives

Classical Conditioning

Several studies have demonstrated that men can be conditioned to develop erections in response to unusual stimuli under experimental conditions (Bancroft, 1974; Kantorowitz, 1978; McConaghy, 1974; Rachman & Hodgson, 1968). Rachman and Hodgson (1968) found that a photograph of a pair of women's boots could elicit erections in five men when the photo was paired with erotic slides, while McConaghy (1974) demonstrated conditioned erection elicited by colored geometric figures that were paired with erotic videotapes or still pictures. Kantorowitz (1978) presented subjects with still pictures during the plateau, refractory, and resolution stages of masturbation. He found that stimuli paired with the plateau phase produced an increase in penile erection; stimuli paired with the refractory phase produced a reduction in erection; and stimuli paired with the resolution phase had no effect.

Unfortunately, most of these studies were complicated by methodological factors, such as the use of motivated/informed subjects, small sample size, and/or the lack of appropriate control conditions (Lalumiere & Quinsey, 1998; O'Donohue & Plaud, 1994). However, more recent and better-controlled studies continue to find evidence for classical conditioning of male sexual arousal. Lalumiere and Quinsey (1998) found enhanced genital responding to slides of partially nude females when they were paired with videotapes of heterosexual interactions. Plaud and Martini (1999) even demonstrated increases in penile circumference to a slide of *a penny jar* when it was paired with slides of nude or partially nude females!

Citing the lack of generalization of learning, the discriminate reinforcement of certain stimuli and not others, and individual differences (i.e., some individuals develop fetishism, while others do not), several authors argue that a simple conditioning model is not sufficient to explain fetishism (Bancroft, 1989; Wilson, 1987a). For instance, certain conditioned stimuli (CSs) appear more readily associated with certain unconditioned stimuli (Dellarosa Cummins & Cummins, 1999; Mineka & Ohman, 2002). In a group of male fetishists, sexual arousal was primarily associated with pink, black, smooth, silky, and shiny stimuli (Gosselin & Wilson, 1980). McConaghy (1987) proposed that these characteristics may be more sexually arousing because they are similar to properties of the female vulva, suggesting a biological preparedness.

Hoffman, Janssen, and Turner (2004) examined the effects of CS duration (subliminal vs. conscious) and relevance (sexually relevant vs. irrelevant) on the classical conditioning of sexual arousal in males and females. Both women and men showed more evidence of conditioning to the sexually relevant CS (i.e., photo of an abdomen of an individual of the opposite sex) than to the irrelevant CS (i.e., photo of a gun) when the CS was presented subliminally. However, when the consciously perceived CS was utilized, women demonstrated conditioned arousal to the sexually irrelevant CS rather than the sexually relevant CS (the opposite was observed in men). Although the authors suggested that this unexpected result might have been due to increased autonomic arousal associated with the gun in the female subjects, it also suggests the possibility that conditions under which sexual learning occurs may differ for men and women.

Instrumental Learning

Several authors have investigated the role of instrumental conditioning in sexual arousal. Rosen, Shapiro, and Schwartz (1975) demonstrated that men could learn to become sexually aroused in the absence of erotic stimuli when they were provided with feedback and contingent monetary reinforcement. Several studies found that both women and men could suppress or increase sexual arousal (as measured by penile erection or vaginal pulse) when provided with feedback; however, no learning effects were demonstrated across trials (Reynolds, 1980; Zingheim & Sandman, 1978).

Social Learning

Social learning theory incorporates elements of both operant conditioning and social cognition (e.g., interpretation of feedback, expectancies about rewards, etc.). La Torre (1980) demonstrated that men who had been rejected (i.e., informed that the potential girlfriend they had selected did not reciprocate their interest) were more likely to rate pictorial stimuli of women's garments (e.g., underwear) and women's body parts (e.g., feet) as more attractive than pictorial stimuli of a whole woman or an abstract design. Munroe and Gauvain (2001) speculate that the motivational state known as the "Zeigarnik effect" (i.e., interrupted tasks are better recalled than completed tasks) can assist the understanding of paraphilias in terms of their addictive/compulsive quality, the difference in sex ratio, and why paraphilic tendencies are apparently quite rare in traditional societies. Wilson (1987a) suggests that sexual deviance is associated with highly sexually restrictive families while Money (1986) links the genesis of fetishism with restriction of typical childhood sex play.

In an investigation of some of these theories, Weinberg, Williams, and Calhan (1995) found no support for a restrictive family environment, but did find that a slight majority of males with foot fetishes reported having fewer friends than other children their age during adolescence. However, given the lack of control data, as well as the self-selected subjects, it is difficult to draw any definite conclusions from these data.

Ethology

Ethological models focus on sexual instinct and how the sex drive evolved to promote gene survival. The behavioral strategies that serve sexual instincts are thought to be driven by powerful, inflexible emotions that originate deep within ancient parts of the brain (Wilson, 1987a). Wilson (1987a) identified two major instinctual mechanisms involved in sexual desire: (1) innate releasing mechanisms, which result in organisms responding in a sexual manner to the sexual signals of the opposite sex (even if an organism is reared in isolation); and (2) imprinting, whereby experience in early life has a latent effect on subsequent sexual behavior (i.e., the stimuli that elicit sexual arousal later in life are delineated during this critical period of development). Fetishism is thought to occur when the imprinting mechanism leads to an excessively narrow and incorrect specification of the sex object. Upon reviewing the available animal literature on conditioning and sexual behavior, Pfaus, Kippin, and Centeno (2001) suggest the following: "Instinct and hormones appear to 'set the stage' for sexual responding, whereas learning appears to 'write the play,' to determine the kinds of stimuli that animals will respond to and how vigorously such responses will be made" (p. 310).

Sociobiological and Sociocultural Factors

In their examination of evolution and phylogenicity, both Wilson (1987a) and Epstein (1987) considered sociobiological factors. Epstein concluded that fetishism (1) is evident in primates as well as humans; (2) may be based on a reflex component associated within the temporo-limbic region of the brain; (3) is usually inhibited, but can be "released" in several contexts, including brain damage; and (4) may be affected by other forces, including the strong human interest in external objects.

Numerous authors have highlighted the influence of culture and socialization on human sexual desire (Baumeister, 2000). For instance, certain cultures place erotic significance on particular body parts, whereas other cultures show greater tolerance of particular sexual behaviors such as childhood sexual activity (Wise, 1985). Baumeister (2000) proposes that female sexuality is more subject to the influence of sociocultural factors in adulthood than is male sexuality. Several authors (Levy, 1992; Williams, 1994) have suggested the use of the foot as a safe sex alternative to genital intercourse. Giannini, Colapietro, Slaby, Melemis, and Bowman (1998) reviewed the literature from 1965 to 1994 and hypothesized a relationship between epidemics of sexually transmitted disease and an increase in the sexualization of the foot. Preliminary data indicated a rise in the number of foot-oriented photos in mass-circulation pornographic magazines, beginning in the mid-1980s (the height of the AIDS epidemic). They suggest that a decline in the general interest in foot fetishism may be expected once the AIDS epidemic subsides.

Munroe and Gauvain (2001) reviewed cross-cultural data and concluded that paraphilias are almost nonexistent in traditional societies. Examination of 44 ethnographic cases yielded 2 instances of probable paraphilic tendencies, neither of which appeared to involve fetishism. However, these authors acknowledged that due to methodological problems, particularly the overall absence of evidence, "the paucity of data might reflect not a true low incidence but rather the secrecy with which paraphilias may need to be practiced" (p. 50).

The Psychoanalytic Perspective

Most psychoanalytic theorists postulate that fetishism is the result of intrapsychic conflicts stemming from unresolved issues in an individual's personal history (Kaplan, 1979). Typically, these unresolved conflicts were thought to date back to childhood and centered on unresolved Oedipal conflicts or childhood traumatic experiences. In one of his later writings, Freud (1927/1962) developed the concept of "castration anxiety" and suggested that the fetish object represents a penis, protecting the male from his fear of castration.

In addition to castration anxiety, psychoanalytic theorists have attributed fetishism to the following: anxiety associated with separation from the mother (Bak, 1953); early parental humiliation (Stoller, 1979); a desire to overcome low self-esteem/feelings of inadequacy through the use of an inanimate object (Nagler, 1957); use of transitional objects to maintain ego identity (Zavitzianos, 1971); and a need for defense against pure expression of sexuality (Bass, 2001).

Unfortunately, as with much of the work in the field of fetishism, experimental testing of these theories is lacking.

SUMMARY AND FUTURE DIRECTIONS

In the first edition of this chapter, Mason (1997) stated, "Throughout this review, the difficulty of extrapolating from clinical populations, single case reports, and small series of cases has been highlighted" (p. 89). As noted in this chapter, these problems continue to exist today. One of the greatest difficulties is the lack of research specific to fetishism. Many studies draw conclusions about paraphilias in general, rather than differentiating among the various types of paraphilias. Given the considerable overlap among paraphilias, this is not too surprising. However, one wonders whether combining the various paraphilias results in a loss of important information.

Mason (1997) also suggested that given the apparent relaxation in attitudes toward sexual matters, researchers may gain greater access to larger "normal" populations, thereby increasing our understanding of the etiology of fetishism. Although this appears to be the case for research involving other aspects of human sexuality (sexual dysfunction, sexual orientation, etc.), the interest in fetishism has not grown to the same extent. This may be the result of higher priorities (i.e., focusing on paraphilias that have weightier social implications, such as pedophilia), as well as continuing methodological difficulties (e.g., lack of appropriate controls and the issue of self-selection). Regardless, in order to increase our understanding of fetishism, future research will need to focus on large, population-based, representative samples.

REFERENCES

Abel, G. G., Becker, J. V., Mittelman, M., Cunningham-Rathner, J., Rouleau, J. L., & Murphy, W. D. (1988). Multiple paraphilic diagnoses among sex offenders. *Bulletin of the American Academy of Psychiatry and the Law, 16*(2), 153–168.

Abel, G. G., & Osborn, C. (1992). The paraphilias: The extent and nature of sexually deviant and criminal behavior. *Psychiatric Clinics of North America, 15*(3), 675–686.

American Psychiatric Association. (2000). *Diagnostic and statistical manual of mental disorders* (4th ed., text rev.). Washington, DC: Author.

Bak, R. C. (1953). Fetishism. *Bulletin of the American Psychoanalytic Association, 1,* 285–294.

Bancroft, J. (1974). *Deviant sexual behavior: Modification and assessment.* Oxford, UK: Clarendon Press.

Bancroft, J. (1989). *Human sexuality and its problems* (2nd ed.). Edinburgh, UK: Churchill Livingstone.

Bass, A. (2001). *Difference and disavowal: The trauma of eros.* Stanford, CA: Stanford University Press.

Baumeister, R. F. (2000). Gender differences in erotic plasticity: The female sex drive as socially flexible and responsive. *Psychological Bulletin, 126*(3), 347–374.

Chalkley, A. J., & Powell, G. E. (1983). The clinical description of forty-eight cases of sexual fetishism. *British Journal of Psychiatry, 142,* 292–295.

Crepault, C., & Couture, M. (1980). Men's erotic fantasies. *Archives of Sexual Behavior, 9*(5), 565–581.

Curren, D. (1954). Sexual perversion. *Practitioner, 172,* 440–445.

Dellarosa Cummins, D., & Cummins, R. (1999). Biological preparedness and evolutionary explanation. *Cognition, 73,* B37–B53.

Epstein, A. W. (1987). The phylogenetics of fetishism. In G. Wilson (Ed.), *Variant sexuality: Research and theory.* London: Croom Helm.

Flor-Henry, P. (1989). On the cerebral neurophysiology and neurotransmitter determination of sexual deviations. *International Review of Psychiatry, 1,* 83–86.

Freud, S. (1962). Fetishism. In J. Strachey (Ed. & Trans.), *The standard edition of the complete psychological works of Sigmund Freud* (Vol. 3). London: Hogarth Press. (Original work published 1927)

Giannini, A. J., Colapietro, G., Slaby, A. E., Melemis, S. M., & Bowman, R. K. (1998). Sexualization of the female foot as a response to sexually transmitted epidemics: A preliminary study. *Psychological Reports, 83,* 491–498.

Gosselin, C., & Wilson, G. (1980). *Sexual variations.* London: Faber & Faber.

Hoffman, H., Janssen, E., & Turner, S. L. (2004). Classical conditioning of sexual arousal in women and men: Effects of varying awareness and biological relevance of the conditioned stimulus. *Archives of Sexual Behavior, 33*(1), 43–53.

Howard, R. C., Longmore, F. J., & Mason, P. A. (1992). Contingent negative variation as an indicator of sexual object preference: Revisited. *International Journal of Psychophysiology, 13,* 185–188.

Howard, R. C., Longmore, F. J., Mason, P. A., & Martin, J. L. (1994). Contingent negative variation (CNV) and erotic preference in self-declared homosexuals and in child sex offenders. *Biological Psychology, 38,* 169–181.

Huws, R., Shubsachs, A. P. W., & Taylor, P. J. (1991). Hypersexuality, fetishism and multiple sclerosis. *British Journal of Psychiatry, 158,* 280–281.

Kafka, M. P., & Hennen, J. (2002). A DSM-IV Axis I comorbidity study of males with paraphilias and paraphilia-related disorders. *Sexual Abuse: A Journal of Research and Treatment, 14*(4), 349–366.

Kantorowitz, D. A. (1978). An experimental investigation of preorgasmic reconditioning and postorgasmic deconditioning. *Journal of Applied Behavioral Analysis, 11,* 23–34.

Kaplan, H. S. (1979). *Disorders of sexual desire.* New York: Brunner/Mazel.

Kendrick, K. M., Hinton, M. R., Atkins, K., Haupt, M. A., & Skinner, J. D. (1998). Mothers determine sexual preferences. *Nature, 395,* 229–230.

Kinsey, A. C., Pomeroy, W. B., Martin, C. E., & Gebhard, P. H. (1953). *Sexual behavior in the human female.* Philadelphia: Saunders.

Krafft-Ebing, R. von. (1965). *Psychopathia sexualis* (12th ed., F. S. Klaf, Trans.). New York: Stein & Day. (Original work published 1886)

Lalumiere, M. L., & Quinsey, V. L. (1998). Pavlovian conditioning of sexual interests in human males. *Archives of Sexual Behavior, 27,* 241–252.

La Torre, R. (1980). Devaluation of the human love object: Heterosexual rejection as a possible antecedent of fetishism. *Journal of Abnormal Psychology, 89,* 295–298.

Levy, H. S. (1992). *The lotus lovers: The complete history of the curious erotic custom of foot binding.* Buffalo, NY: Prometheus Books.

Lowenstein, L. F. (1997). Fetishes: General and specific. *Psychotherapy in Private Practice, 16*(4), 53–65.

Mason, F. L. (1997). Fetishism: Psychopathology and theory. In D. R. Laws & W. O'Donohue (Eds.), *Sexual deviance: Theory, assessment, and treatment* (pp. 75–91). New York: Guilford Press.

McConaghy, N. (1974). Penile volume responses to moving and still pictures of male and female nudes. *Archives of Sexual Behavior, 3,* 565–570.

McConaghy, N. (1987). A learning approach. In J. Greer & W. T. O'Donohue (Eds.), *Theories of human sexuality* (pp. 287–334). New York: Plenum Press.

McConaghy, N. (1993). *Sexual behavior: Problems and management.* New York: Plenum Press.

Mineka, S., & Ohman, A. (2002). Phobias and preparedness: The selective, automatic, and encapsulated nature of fear. *Biological Psychiatry, 51,* 927–937.

Mitchell, W., Falconer, M., & Hill, D. (1954). Epilepsy with fetishism relieved by temporal lobectomy. *Lancet, ii,* 626–630.

Money, J. (1986). *Love maps.* Buffalo, NY: Prometheus Books.

Money, J. (1990). *Vandalized love maps.* Buffalo, NY: Prometheus Books.

Munroe, R. L., & Gauvain, M. (2001). Why the paraphilias?: Domesticating strange sex. *Cross-Cultural Research, 35*(1), 44–64.

Nagler, S. H. (1957). Fetishism: A review and case study. *Psychiatric Quarterly, 10,* 713–770.

O'Donohue, W., & Plaud, J. J. (1994). The conditioning of human sexual arousal. *Archives of Sexual Behavior, 23,* 321–344.

Pfaus, J. G., Kippin, T. E., & Centeno, S. (2001). Conditioning and sexual behavior: A review. *Hormones and Behavior, 40,* 291–321.

Plaud, J. J., & Martini, R. (1999). The respondent conditioning of male sexual arousal. *Behavior Modification, 23,* 254–268.

Pitcher, D. (1990). Fetishism. In R. Bluglass & P. Bowden (Eds.), *Principles and practice of forensic psychiatry.* Edinburgh, UK: Churchill Livingstone.

Rachman, S., & Hodgson, R. (1968). Experimentally induced "sexual fetishism": Replication and development. *Psychological Record, 18,* 25–27.

Reynolds, B. S. (1980). Biofeedback and facilitation of erection in men with erectile dysfunction. *Archives of Sexual Behavior, 9,* 101–113.

Revitch, E. (1978). Sexually motivated burglaries. *Bulletin of the American Academy of Psychiatry and the Law, 6,* 277–283.

Rosen, R. C., & Kopel, S. A. (1974). Penile plethysmography and bio-feedback in the treatment of a transvestite-exhibitionist. *Journal of Consulting and Clinical Psychology, 45,* 908–916.

Rosen, R. C., Shapiro, D., & Schwartz, G. (1975). Voluntary control of penile tumescence. *Psychosomatic Medicine, 37,* 479–483.

Schlesinger, L. B., & Revitch, E. (1999). Sexual burglaries and sexual homicide: Clinical, forensic, and investigative considerations. *Journal of the American Academy of Psychiatry and the Law, 27*(2), 227–238.

Steele, V. (1996). *Fetish: Fashion, sex and power.* New York: Oxford University Press.

Stoller, R. J. (1979). *Sexual excitement: Dynamics of erotic life.* London: Maresfield Library.

Waismann, R., Fenwick, M. B., Wilson, G. D., Hewett, T. D., & Lumsden, J. (2003). EEG responses to visual erotic stimuli in men with normal and paraphilic interests. *Archives of Sexual Behavior, 32*(2), 135–144.

Weinberg, M. S., Williams, C. J., & Calhan, C. (1994). Homosexual foot fetishism. *Archives of Sexual Behavior, 23*(6), 611–626.

Weinberg, M. S., Williams, C. J., & Calhan, C. (1995). "If the shoe fits . . . ": Exploring male homosexual foot fetishism. *Journal of Sex Research, 32*(1), 17–27.

Wiederman, M. W. (2003). Paraphilia and fetishism. *The Family Journal: Counseling and Therapy for Couples and Families, 11*(3), 315–321.

Williams, R. (1994). Striving to reach new heights. *Leg Action, 12*(10), 3.

Wilson, G. D. (1987a). An ethological approach to sexual deviation. In G. Wilson (Ed.), *Variant sexuality: Research and theory.* London: Croom Helm.

Wilson, G. D. (1987b). Male–female differences in sexual activity, enjoyment and fantasies. *Personality and Individual Differences, 8*(1), 125–127.

Wise, T. N. (1985). Fetishism: Etiology and treatment. A review from multiple perspectives. *Comprehensive Psychiatry, 26*(3), 249–57.

Wise, T. N., & Kalyanam, R. C. (2000). Amputee fetishism and genital mutilation: Case report and literature review. *Journal of Sex and Marital Therapy, 26*(4) 339–344.

World Health Organization. (1992). *International classification of diseases* (10th rev.). Geneva: Author.

Zavitzianos, G. (1971). Fetishism and exhibitionism in the female and their relationship to psychopathology and kleptomania. *International Journal of Psycho-Analysis, 52,* 297–305.

Zingheim, P. K., & Sandman, C. A. (1978). Discriminative control of the vaginal vasomotor response. *Biofeedback and Self-Regulation, 3,* 29–41.

CHAPTER 7

FETISHISM

Assessment and Treatment

SHAUNA DARCANGELO
ALANA HOLLINGS
GABRIELLE PALADINO

Many fetishists have mixed feelings about the assessment and treatment of their fetishism. Many have recognized that their sexual interests and behaviors differ from the norm and have gone to great lengths to conceal them (Wiederman, 2003). Thus exploring their fetishistic behavior in an open and forthright manner can be an uncomfortable and foreign experience. In addition, although some may believe that their lives will be less complicated without their fetishism, their fetish objects also represent great sources of sexual satisfaction and pleasure. The idea of losing this satisfaction/pleasure can be disconcerting to some and unacceptable to others.

Individuals' motivations for pursuing treatment can also influence their receptiveness and responsiveness to the assessment and treatment of their fetishism. Some may be pursuing treatment to alleviate symptoms such as depression or anxiety, or to reduce personal distress such as relationship discord. Thus they may be more forthcoming in the information they are willing to disclose. Others, by contrast, may be experiencing social pressure to pursue treatment after receiving a referral from their general practitioner or after repeated encouragement from family and friends (Crown, 1983). Moreover, an individual's freedom may be at stake if legal agencies (i.e., courts, probation offices) are insisting on treatment to reduce risk. As a result of all these issues, the assessment and treatment of fetishism can be challenging endeavors.

ASSESSMENT

General Assessment

Typically, identifying fetish objects is a fairly straightforward process (i.e., obtaining a detailed account of the objects and behaviors involved in an individual's masturbation routine and/or sexual relationship). As mentioned by Darcangelo in Chapter 6, although any object has the potential to serve as a fetish, certain objects are more likely to be associated with sexual arousal than others (Chalkley & Powell, 1983; Steele, 1996). These objects include clothing (particularly undergarments), rubber, footwear, body parts (e.g., feet and hair), leather, and soft fabrics such as silk. However, other objects/stimuli can also play an important role for the fetishist. For instance, radio static, the smell of urinals, and diapers have been identified as fetish objects for particular individuals (Junginger, 1997). Thus, in order to identify and address all appropriate treatment targets, it is essential that as much information as possible be obtained.

For instance, in addition to obtaining an accurate record of an individual's masturbation routine and/or sexual relationship, it is also important to gather information about conditions/situations in the individual's natural environment that elicit sexual arousal. For example, when asked to record details of the situations that cause at least a minimum level of arousal, an individual may identify triggers that were previously outside his awareness (such as certain smells or sounds). The individual can also be asked to record his response to the stimulus and his perceived level of sexual arousal. The goal is to collect as much information about the individual's pattern of sexual arousal in the natural environment, in the most noninvasive manner possible.

Once a fetish object is identified, additional areas to assess include the degree of significance an individual places on the fetish object, the behaviors associated with the fetish, his reliance on the fetish, and the degree of impairment it has caused in his life. As stated by Weinberg, Williams, and Calhan (1995), fetishism can be seen as a "graduated phenomenon." This means that fetishes present on a continuum from a mild preference to a strong preference, in which a fetish object is required, to the point where the object is substituted for a human partner. The behaviors associated with a fetish object may include fondling/stroking/sucking the object while masturbating or engaging in sexual intercourse; wearing or having a sexual partner wear the fetish object; gazing at the fetish object; inserting the fetish object up the rectum; collecting/hoarding the fetish object; lying on or rolling in the fetish object; and/or being touched or caressed by the fetish object.

As mentioned in Chapter 6, fetishistic behavior alone is not sufficient to warrant a diagnosis of fetishism; clinically significant distress or impairment must also be observed. If an individual is specifically seeking treatment for his fetishism, or if he is being referred by the courts or a general practitioner for the treatment of fetishism, then significant distress or impairment is generally obvious. However, when fetishism is not the primary focus of treatment, the decision to diagnose fetishism and identify it as a treatment target will depend on the degree of distress or impairment observed or reported.

Specific Assessment Measures

Once a general assessment is completed (i.e., gaining a general idea about the objects/situations that elicit sexual arousal and the behaviors associated with these objects/situations), a more specific assessment can be conducted to determine the actual pattern and level of sexual arousal to the fetish objects/situations (Junginger, 1997). A specific assessment might include both self-report measures and more objective or direct measures, such as penile plethysmography (Junginger, 1997). However, it must be emphasized that at this point, there is no consensual, standard assessment protocol for fetishism with adequate psychometrics.

Self-Report Inventories

There are few measures that specifically assess fetishistic behaviors. The Multiphasic Sex Inventory II (MSI II; Nichols & Molinder, 1996) includes a Fetishism Index, which contains item content related to a panty fetish (i.e., stealing and using female underclothing for sexual arousal), but no other fetishes. Items related to urophilia, coprophilia, zoophilia, and necrophilia are also included, but these are not considered fetishes in current classification systems. Research conducted on 1,951 adult male sex offenders and normal adult males found that neither group scored high on the Fetishism Index (Nichols & Molinder, 1996). The Fetishism Index correlated moderately with the MSI II Sex Obsessions scale ($r = .42$), and modestly with the MSI II Rape (.36), Exhibitionism (.34), Voyeurism (.40), Pornography (.33), Bondage/Discipline (.32), Emotional Neediness (.30), and Gender Identity (.36) Indices. The Fetishism Index did not correlate with any Minnesota Multiphasic Personality Inventory scale except for a modest relationship to Scale 8 (.32), and there was no correlation with IQ (.07). Finally, a principal-components factor analysis of the Fetishism Index suggested that it was related to the Masochism, Bondage/Discipline, and Gender Identity Indices.

The Abel Assessment for Sexual Interest (AASI; Abel, Huffman, Warberg, & Holland, 1998) is an assessment tool utilized to determine whether an individual has sexual interest in children. The AASI provides three types of information: subjective ratings of sexual interest; viewing times to various categories of inappropriate sexual stimuli (including fetish objects—specifically, bras and panties); and sex-offender-specific questionnaire results. A section on the questionnaire portion addresses fetishism by asking the individual whether he has "obsessively" been aroused to specific objects such as lingerie or shoes. If the individual acknowledges this, there are follow-up questions that provide more detailed information. However, the Fetishism scale is not normed, and psychometric information is lacking. Thus caution must be taken in using this scale for assessment and treatment purposes.

The Sexual Outlet Inventory (SOI) has been used in several studies investigating paraphilias (Kafka, 1994; Kafka & Hennen, 2003; Kafka & Prentky, 1992). The SOI is a self-report inventory designed to identify problematic or unconventional sexual behaviors and nonproblematic or conventional sexual behaviors. It is divided into two sections; the first section measures the frequency of fantasies, urges, and sexual activities in a designated week, while the second section involves rating the intensity of sexual desires and the average amount of time per day engaged in sexually deviant behaviors. The SOI can be used to gain important details regarding a client's sexual functioning. However, like the AASI, it has not been empirically validated.

Thus, overall, the use of self-report inventories to assist in the assessment of fetishism is limited. The inventories that are currently available lack empirical validation and tend to focus on only a few fetish objects (i.e., female underclothing).

Objective Measures

The phallometric method has been utilized to assess fetishistic arousal and behavior in multiple studies (Freund, Seto, & Kuban, 1996; Junginger, 1988; Kunjukrishnan, Pawlak, & Varan, 1988). As described by Junginger (1997), a typical phallometric assessment of fetishism involves the use of a device to record penile circumference, body movement, and time. Additional considerations include the medium in which the paraphilic stimuli are presented (i.e., videotape, audiotape, slides, or "free fantasy"); instructions provided to the client, which may influence penile response; the client's level of cooperation; methodology (i.e., standardization, habituation); and generalizability. In regard to generalizability, a particular issue is that of "summated" arousal. This refers to the possibility that a conditioned response (CR) elicited by two conditioned stimuli (CSs) presented together will be some additive function of the individual CRs of each CS presented alone. This issue can be particularly important in terms of representing the client's natural environment. As noted by Junginger (p. 99), "a full appreciation of the forces behind some patients' fetish behavior may not be possible unless their response to combinations of fetish stimuli is determined."

However, as noted in a recent article by Marshall (2006), phallometric testing also has its limitations, particularly with sex offenders. These limitations include insufficient evidence regarding the reliability and criterion validity of phallometric testing, as well as the lack of standardization.

TREATMENT

Before treatment begins, it is imperative that the treating clinician confirm with the client what the goal(s) of treatment will be. Treatment goals may include the removal of all deviant interest, a reduction in the reliance of the fetish object for sexual arousal, improvement in intimate relationships, and/or elimination of criminal activity. The treating clinician should work with the client in terms of identifying realistic treatment goals after a consideration of various factors, including the strength of the fetishistic behavior (how often is the client engaging in the deviant act?), length of history of the fetishistic behavior, the extent to which the fetishistic behavior serves as a source of gratification and self-esteem, whether the client has sought treatment due to external pressures, and whether the desire to be rid of the deviant sexual interest is the result of a mood disorder (Hawton, 1983).

Behavioral and Cognitive-Behavioral Approaches

Behavioral treatment is the most commonly utilized approach to manage sexual deviations and has been found to have the most positive outcomes in treating fetishism (DeSilva, 1993). Behavioral interventions focus on either decreasing the deviant sexual interest/behavior, increasing nondeviant sexual interest/behavior, or assisting individuals in adjusting to their deviant sexual interest/behavior (Hawton, 1983).

Many believe that fetishism is a learned behavior in which the fetish object was originally linked to early sexual arousal. As a result, aversion therapy has been commonly used to treat it (DeSilva, 1993; Hawton, 1983; Rachman, 1966; Rachman & Hodgson, 1968; Weinberg et al., 1995). The foundation of aversion therapy involves pairing the fetish object and/or the deviant fantasies of the fetishistic behavior with an aversive unconditioned stimulus (e.g., electric shock), which elicits an unconditioned response that is incompatible with sexual arousal.

Studies by Marks and colleagues (Marks & Gelder, 1967; Marks, Rachman, & Gelder, 1965) found electric shock aversion therapy to be successful in neutralizing the effect of the fetish object and increasing the enjoyment of normal sexual relationships.

Other researchers have shown nausea-inducing drugs to be effective aversive stimuli (Raymond, 1956), as well as noxious odor (Junginger, 1997; Laws, 2001). It is important however, for clients to be informed that no treatment, including aversion therapy, is likely to produce permanent effects on behavior. For the suppression of deviant arousal to last, clients will need to continue with a schedule of self-administered treatment. Finally, although aversion training has been demonstrated to be effective in many cases (Laws, 2001), it remains a controversial technique because of the infliction of pain or noxious stimuli (Krueger & Kaplan, 2002).

Covert sensitization is a form of aversive therapy, but depends entirely upon a client's fantasies and imagination (DeSilva, 1993; Hawton, 1983). Covert sensitization involves mentally pairing the preferred stimulus (i.e., the fetish object) with negative imagery. For instance, a man with a fetish for women's underwear might be instructed to imagine his wife ending their marriage or calling him disgusting names when he begins to fantasize about fondling her underwear. A fetishist who engages in illegal activity might be instructed to imagine himself getting arrested, going through a trial, and being incarcerated. Some of the advantages to covert sensitization are that the client can implement the technique outside the practitioner's office; no physical pain is induced; and electrical aversion has been shown to suppress arousal only over the short term (DeSilva, 1993).

Kunjukrishnan and colleagues (1988) used a covert sensitization program to treat a 27-year-old man who had been charged with indecent assault after he coerced a young girl to suck his tongue and big toe (he had initially asked her if he could smell her feet). Treatment consisted of audiotaped pairings of descriptions of fetish activities (e.g., smelling a woman's feet) with descriptions of aversive consequences (e.g., a vile odor that induced vomiting, along with a look of horror and disgust from the woman whose feet he was smelling). Treatment was conducted in 12 weekly sessions, followed by 8 monthly sessions (sessions 13–20) and a final session 4 months after the 20th session. Phallometric assessment indicated that sexual arousal was "practically eliminated" (p. 822) by the 15th session. This suppression was maintained even after 4 months with no booster sessions. The patient's self-reported urges also decreased with treatment (i.e., after the 15th session, the patient reported having no fetish urges at all).

Verbal satiation and masturbatory satiation have also been used successfully to reduce deviant sexual arousal (Laws, 1995; Marshall & Lippens, 1977). Masturbatory satiation therapy involves the individual continuing to masturbate during the refractory period (i.e., the sexually unresponsive period immediately following orgasm) while engaging in deviant fantasies. Verbal satiation is similar to masturbatory satiation, except that it involves repetitive verbalization of deviant sexual fantasies without the added component of masturbation, and thus is much simpler to carry out. Marshall and Lippens (1977) used masturbatory satiation to treat a patient with a fetish for panty hose. The patient was instructed to masturbate to orgasm while verbalizing his deviant fantasies involving panty hose. Following orgasm, he was required to continue masturbating for the remainder of the 90-minute session while verbally fantasizing about panty hose. The results indicated that after nine sessions, he lost almost all interest in panty hose (as measured by penile response, self-report, and the verbal content of his masturbation fantasies).

Although aversive treatment and satiation therapy both reduce deviant sexual arousal, most clinicians realize that reducing deviant arousal is insufficient to normalize sexual interests in individuals with paraphilias. Thus clinicians and researchers have focused on the ability to enhance interest in, or arousal to, appropriate sexual acts/behaviors/partners. Davidson (1968) and Marquis (1970) described a procedure called "orgasmic reconditioning" to train appropriate sexual arousal. In this procedure, the client uses his deviant fantasies to become aroused, but then changes his fantasy to a more acceptable form prior to orgasm (with the goal of switching the fantasy at earlier and earlier stages of masturbation). In time, other clinicians modified this procedure (Abel, Blanchard, Barlow, & Flanagan, 1975; Maletzky, 1985; VanDeventer & Laws, 1978). Unfortunately, as noted by Laws and Marshall (1991), the evidence advanced in support of orgasmic reconditioning (including all the variants proposed) is weak.

In addition to orgasmic reconditioning, clinicians have attempted to increase normal sexual interests/arousal by focusing on cognitive-behavioral techniques. Cognitive approaches focus on an individual's ability to stop or replace deviant and/or problematic thoughts involving the fetish with appropriate, healthy thoughts. Thus, from a cognitive perspective, it is important for the practitioner to assist the client in identifying the thoughts and behaviors that precipitate the fetishistic behaviors. By identifying the deviant thoughts, the client is more likely to recognize them sooner and less likely to follow through with the deviant behavior (Hawton, 1983). These approaches are commonly described as "self-help" techniques, as clients can practice these techniques without the aid of their practitioners (Lowenstein, 1997).

Additional treatment targets may include the development of skills to establish and maintain appropriate sexual relationships. These interventions are based on the observation that many individuals with paraphilias demonstrate deficits in the normative courtship process (Freund & Blanchard, 1986). Such interventions may include addressing social skills, assertiveness, communication, lack of sexual knowledge, and possible sexual dysfunction (Krueger & Kaplan, 2002).

Multiple studies support the use of a combined treatment approach in treating fetishism (Kunjukrishnan et al., 1988; Lowenstein, 1997; Marshall, 1974). In a study by Lowenstein (1997), "combined directive guidance and behavior modification with cognitive–rational emotive approaches" (p. 61) were used with 76 individuals ranging in age from 15 to 34 years. The fetishes included women's clothing, shoes/feet, and inanimate objects. Unfortunately, Lowenstein also identified cross-dressing, sadomasochism, and aggressive rape as types of fetishes; this obviously complicates the interpretation of these results, as these are not considered fetishes in current classification systems. The treatment approach involved identifying early traumatic events in childhood that provided insight into the sexual deviance; discussing the presentation of the fetishes, as well as the symptoms and concerns that led the clients to pursue treatment; and recognition of the association between the fetishes and their effects on the clients' relationships with sexual partners. Clients were also taught self-help techniques such as thought stopping, consideration of their partners' needs, and substituting more acceptable fantasies for any deviant fantasies involving the fetishes.

The results found that of the 76 clients, 70 had favorable results initially or after one or two relapses. Most who participated in the treatment program reduced their fetishistic behaviors and the harmful effects related to their fetishes. Lowenstein (1997) found that the most critical aspects related to treatment success were the clients' level of motivation for change, the therapeutic relationship, and the improved relationships between the clients and their partners (when applicable).

Pharmacological Approaches

Historically, the pharmacological treatment of sexually deviant behavior has been based on the assumption that suppression of the sexual desire would correspondingly decrease deviant sexual behavior (Bradford, 1995). In addition, there continues to be a strong awareness within the treatment community that paraphilias (including fetishism) may well be part of the obsessive–compulsive disorder spectrum, as the same drugs appear to be effective in the treatment of both types of disorders (Person, 2005). In general, two different classes of pharmacological agents have been recognized to have clinically significant effects upon fetishism. These are (1) the antiandrogens and (2) psychotropic medications of the antipsychotic and selective serotonin reuptake inhibitor (SSRI) classes.

Antiandrogens are agents that act directly to reduce the levels of circulating testosterone in the body. Testosterone is the principal male hormone in mammals, including man. These agents reduce the level of testosterone by various means, as will be individually noted with each agent discussed. The first agent to be investigated for this purpose was medroxyprogesterone acetate (MPA). The first case report utilizing MPA was made by Money (1968), who followed this report with an expanded report involving eight patients treated with MPA (Money, 1970). There have since been numerous studies on MPA, generally consisting of case reports; these have documented reductions in deviant fantasy and arousal, along with a subjective sense of relief.

MPA appears to exert its negative effect upon testosterone through interference with a liver enzyme used in the metabolic pathway of testosterone. Although it is widely available in the United States and reasonable in cost, MPA's side effect profile has nonetheless caused it to be, in effect, a second-line agent. Side effects can be problematic and can include deep vein thrombosis, induction of diabetes, feminization, and weight gain (Gagne, 1981). As is the case with all true antiandrogens, MPA is also capable of causing severe demineralization of the bones.

The antiandrogen most commonly used worldwide is cyproterone acetate (CPA). This agent acts directly on androgen receptors, blocking intracellular metabolism of testosterone (Neumann, 1997). It is unique in that it is the only known antiandrogen available via the oral route. Side effects can include liver dysfunction, bone demineralization, and feminization (Cremonocini, Viginati, & Libroia, 1976). A wide body of literature, including double-blind studies (Cooper, Sandhu, & Losztyn, 1992), has endorsed CPA as highly effective in reducing sexual fantasies and other desired outcome measures. An issue profoundly affecting its use is that CPA is not available in the United States.

Leuprolide acetate and goserelin acetate are two potent antiandrogens currently used in the United States to treat paraphilias. Both of these agents are available as long-acting implants, and leuprolide acetate is also available in an injectable form. No double-blind studies exist for either agent, due to their relatively recent recognition as being helpful in the treatment of paraphilias. However, they have been extensively used at such institutions as Johns Hopkins University Hospital in Baltimore, Maryland, and Atascadero State Hospital in Atascadero, California. Leuprolide acetate and goserelin acetate act through a complex hormonal feedback loop that results in the depletion of serum testosterone. Although their cost is often nearly prohibitive, these two agents have a remarkably clean side effect profile, which can include hot flashes and bone demineralization.

Antipsychotic drugs are also a class of medications known to exert a negative effect upon libido (Bradford, 1995), likely via their direct effects on dopamine receptors. Dopa-

mine, a neurotransmitter, figures quite prominently in the pleasure-seeking and sexual behaviors of mammals, including humans. However, the side effects of antipsychotics,
which can cause involuntary movements in the older agents and the induction of diabetes
in the newer types, are usually too problematic for these agents to be used on a long-term
basis.

The introduction of fluoxetine in 1988 as the first SSRI signaled a new era in the
treatment of fetishism and other paraphilias. SSRIs, as their name implies, work via serotonin, a neurotransmitter known to have an effect on both sexual behavior and aggression. Numerous studies exist (e.g., Greenberg & Bradford, 1997; Greenberg, Bradford,
Curry, & O'Rourke, 1996) that document the efficacy of these agents, whose numbers
have grown throughout the years as new medications enter this class.

The relatively benign side effect profile of SSRIs, their wide availability, and their
oral administration are merits of this class of drugs. A potential drawback is that serum
levels of SSRIs do not reliably correlate with responses reported by users, and therefore
cannot be used as predictable indicators of compliance should they be mandated as part
of a court-ordered treatment program.

Pharmacological agents represent a valuable adjunctive approach to the treatment of
fetishism and other paraphilias. However, it must be recognized that none of these treatment agents represents a cure. Pharmacological agents are often combined with cognitive-
behavioral interventions for maximum effect (Wiederman, 2003).

Psychodynamic Approaches

Multiple case studies have reported treating fetishistic behavior via a psychodynamic approach (Bemporad, Dunton, & Spady, 1976; Fink, 2003; Sawyer, 1996). Psychoananlytic
treatment approaches generally have the individual focus on identifying significant developmental milestones and working through the underlying conflicts or unresolved issues
(Wiederman, 2003). For instance, the client may be asked to utilize memories from his
childhood to assist him in achieving insight regarding how his deviant sexual behaviors
and impulses were shaped by his childhood, particularly traumatic events (Tan & Zhong,
2001). Unfortunately, due to design limitations (i.e., single-case studies), the effectiveness
of these treatment approaches has yet to be determined on a large scale.

Treatment Approaches for Couples

For an individual in an existing committed relationship, the treatment program needs to
be flexible enough to permit the involvement of the partner. The goal of treatment is to
decrease the intrusion of the fetishism into the sexual relationship (DeSilva, 1993;
Lowenstein, 1997). In work with a couple, the general focus is on enrichment of the overall sexual relationship between the partners. Basic concepts and philosophies of sex therapy, including sensate focus exercises and communication training, are used to achieve
this (Wiederman, 1998). Typically, as the sexual relationship begins to improve, the dependence on a fetish object decreases. Maintaining excitement in the sexual relationship
is key, as when the relationship becomes mundane, the man's reliance on the fetish object
is likely to reemerge (DeSilva, 1993).

One approach in decreasing the negative effects of a fetish object is to incorporate
the fetish object in the sexual relationship in a controlled and time-limited way (if this is
acceptable to the partner). The practitioner's goal is to help the individual with the fetish

to reduce his dependence on the fetish object, until only minimal contact is preserved. Another technique is to use a time-tabling technique, in which the individual with the fetishistic behavior consents to use the fetish object in conjunction with sexual activity on specific, mutually agreed-upon days of the week. On the other days, sexual interactions occur without the use of the fetish object. This "give and take" approach has shown to be effective in improving the dynamics of a relationship (DeSilva, 1993).

When a fetish object has strongly affected the sexual relationship (i.e., when the man cannot sustain an erection without contact with a fetish object), a combined approach of sex therapy and behavioral therapy has shown to be effective. Techniques such as orgasmic reconditioning and covert sensitization may be introduced into treatment. These techniques should be implemented during individual sessions, while couple therapy should follow with a focus on improving the overall satisfaction in the relationship. It is important to note that treatment will vary and be affected by the type of fetish, the severity of the fetish, and the partner's attitude and involvement in treatment (DeSilva, 1993).

SUMMARY AND FUTURE DIRECTIONS

In the first edition of this chapter, Junginger (1997) suggested several areas that required further research in order to gain a better understanding of the assessment and treatment of fetishism: (1) the role of summated arousal; (2) whether fetishists have higher absolute levels of sexual arousal, or whether they may possess a greater capacity for conditioned arousal; (3) the role of "blocking" in the development and maintenance of fetishistic arousal (i.e., whether prior conditioning of one stimulus in a compound "blocks" subsequent conditioning of the other stimuli in the compound); (4) recovery from "overshadowing" (i.e., whether the extinction of arousal to dominant fetish stimuli can lead to problematic arousal to other stimuli); (5) the importance of social skills training in the treatment of fetishism; (6) the effectiveness of treatments other than aversive conditioning (particularly those involving exposure and response prevention, which is often the treatment of choice for compulsive-like behavior); and (7) how often fetishism really is a "disorder" that warrants treatment. Unfortunately, little research has been conducted addressing these issues, and they continue to be relevant today.

Much of the research currently available is based on single-case studies of individuals with atypical presentations. There continues to be a lack of research involving randomized controlled trials, as well as good single-subject designs. Moreover, little is known about relapse rates and the factors associated with relapse in fetishists. For instance, as discussed in Chapter 6, Baumeister (2000) suggests that biological interventions may be a more effective treatment option in male fetishists, because male sexuality is less responsive to social and cultural influences during childhood. However, there are no adequate studies comparing pharmacological interventions with cognitive-behavioral interventions for fetishism, and there have been no studies investigating the effectiveness of treatment for female fetishists (not to mention the incidence of fetishism in females).

A particular limitation in the assessment and treatment of fetishism is the lack of a standard assessment protocol with adequate psychometric properties. The assessment tools available tend to focus on a limited number of potential fetish objects (i.e., primarily female underclothing) and have not been empirically validated. A psychometrically sound assessment tool addressing a wider range of potential fetishes, coupled with a standardized questionnaire/interview format, would be invaluable for clinicians and researchers investigating the assessment and treatment of fetishism.

REFERENCES

Abel, G. G., Blanchard, E. B., Barlow, D. H., & Flanagan, B. (1975, December). *A case report of the behavioral treatment of a sadistic rapist.* Paper presented at the 9th Annual Convention of the Association for Advancement of Behavior Therapy, San Francisco.

Abel, G. G., Huffman, J., Warberg, B., & Holland, C. L. (1998). Visual reaction time and plethysmography as measures of sexual interest in child molesters. *Sexual Abuse: A Journal of Research and Treatment, 10*(2), 81–95.

Baumeister, R. F. (2000). Gender differences in erotic plasticity: The female sex drive as socially flexible and responsive. *Psychological Bulletin, 126*(3), 347–374.

Bemporad, J. R., Dunton, H. D., & Spady, F. H. (1976). Case reports: The treatment of a child foot fetishist. *American Journal of Psychotherapy, 30*(2), 303–316.

Bradford, J. M. W. (1995). Pharmacological treatment of the paraphilias. In J. M. Oldham & M. Riba (Eds.), *Review of psychiatry* (Vol. 14, pp. 755–778). Washington, DC: American Psychiatric Press.

Chalkley, A. J., & Powell, G. E. (1983). The clinical description of forty-eight cases of sexual fetishism. *British Journal of Psychiatry, 142,* 292–295.

Cooper, A. J., Sandhu, S., & Losztyn, S. (1992). A double-blind placebo controlled trial of medroxyprogestrone acetate and cyproterone acetate with seven pedophiles. *Canadian Journal of Psychiatry, 37,* 33–39.

Cremoncini, C., Viginati, E., & Libroia, A. (1976). Treatment of hirsutism and acne in women with two combinations of cyproterone acetate and ethinyloestradiol. *Acta Europaea Fertilitatitis, 7,* 299–314.

Crown, S. (1983). Psychotherapy of sexual deviation. *British Journal of Psychiatry, 143*(3), 242–247.

Davidson, G. C. (1968). Elimination of a sadistic fantasy by a client-controlled counterconditioning technique. *Journal of Abnormal Psychology, 73,* 84–90.

DeSilva, P. (1993). Fetishism and sexual dysfunction: Clinical presentation and management. *Sexual and Marital Therapy, 8*(2), 147–155.

Fink, B. (2003). The use of lacanian psychoanalysis in a case of fetishism. *Clinical Case Studies, 2*(1), 50–69.

Freund, K., & Blanchard, R. (1986). The concept of courtship disorder. *Journal of Sex and Marital Therapy, 12,* 79–92.

Freund, K., Seto, M. C., & Kuban, M. (1996). Two types of fetishism. *Behaviour Research and Therapy, 34*(9), 687–694.

Gagne, P. (1981). Treatment of sex offenders with medroxyprogesterone acetate. *American Journal of Psychiatry, 138,* 644–646.

Greenberg, D. M., & Bradford, J. M. (1997). Treatment of the paraphilic disorders: A review of the role of the selective serotonin reuptake inhibitors. *Sexual Abuse, 9,* 349–361.

Greenberg, D. M., Bradford, J. M., Curry, S., & O'Rourke, A. (1996). A comparison of treatment of paraphilias with three serotonin reuptake inhibitors: A retrospective study. *Bulletin of the American Academy of Psychiatry and the Law, 24,* 525–532.

Hawton, K. (1983). Behavioural approaches to the management of sexual deviations. *British Journal of Psychiatry, 143*(3), 248–255.

Junginger, J. (1988). Summation of arousal in partial fetishism. *Journal of Behavior Therapy and Experimental Psychiatry, 19*(4), 297–300.

Junginger, J. (1997). Fetishism: Assessment and treatment. In D. R. Laws & W. O'Donohue (Eds.), *Sexual deviance: Theory, assessment, and treatment* (pp. 92–110). New York: Guilford Press.

Kafka, M. P. (1994). Sertraline pharmacotherapy for paraphilias and paraphilia-related disorders: An open trial. *Annals of Clinical Psychiatry, 6*(3), 189–195.

Kafka, M. P., & Hennen, J. (2003). Hypersexual desire in males: Are males with paraphilias different from males with paraphilia-related disorders. *Sexual Abuse: A Journal of Research and Treatment, 15*(4), 307–321.

Kafka, M. P., & Prentky, R. (1992). Fluoxetine treatment of nonparaphilic sexual addictions and paraphilias in men. *Journal of Clinical Psychiatry, 53*(10), 351–358.

Krueger, R. B., & Kaplan, M. S. (2002). Behavioral and psychopharmacological treatment of the paraphilic and hypersexual disorders. *Journal of Psychiatric Practice, 8*, 21–31.

Kunjukrishnan, R., Pawlak, A., & Varan, L. R. (1988). The clinical and forensic psychiatric issues of retifism. *Canadian Journal of Psychiatry, 33*, 819–825.

Laws, D. R. (1995). Verbal satiation: Notes on procedure with speculations on its mechanism of effect. *Sexual Abuse: A Journal of Research and Treatment, 7*(2), 155–166.

Laws, D. R. (2001). Olfactory aversion: Notes on the procedure, with speculations on its mechanism of effect. *Sexual Abuse: A Journal of Research and Treatment, 13*(4), 275–287.

Laws, D. R., & Marshall, W. L. (1991). Masturbatory reconditioning with sexual deviates: An evaluative review. *Advances in Behaviour Research and Therapy, 13*, 13–25.

Lowenstein, L. F. (1997). Fetishes: General and specific. *Psychotherapy in Private Practice, 16*(4), 53–65.

Maletsky, B. M. (1985). Orgasmic reconditioning. In A. S. Bellack & M. Hersen (Eds.), *Dictionary of behavior therapy techniques* (pp. 157–158). New York: Pergamon Press.

Marks, I. M., & Gelder, M. G. (1967). Transvestism and fetishism: Clinical and psychological changes during faradic aversion. *British Journal of Psychiatry, 113*, 711–729.

Marks, I. M., Rachman, S., & Gelder, M. G. (1965). Methods for assessment of aversion treatment in fetishism with masochism. *Behaviour Research and Therapy, 3*, 253–258.

Marquis, J. N. (1970). Orgasmic reconditioning: Changing sexual object choice through controlling masturbation fantasies. *Journal of Behavior Therapy and Experimental Psychiatry, 1*, 263–271.

Marshall, W. L. (1974). Case report: A combined treatment approach to the reduction of multiple fetish-related behaviors. *Journal of Consulting and Clinical Psychology, 42*(4), 613–616.

Marshall, W. L. (2006). Clinical and research limitations in the use of phallometric testing with sexual offenders. *Sex Offender Treatment, 1*(1), 1–32.

Marshall, W. L., & Lippens, K. (1977). The clinical value of boredom: A procedure for reducing inappropriate sexual interests. *Journal of Nervous and Mental Disease, 165*, 283–287.

Money, J. (1968). Discussion on hormonal inhibition of libido in male sex offenders. In R. Michael (Ed.), *Endocrinology and human behavior* (p. 169). London: Oxford University Press.

Money, J. (1970). Use of androgen-depleting hormone in the treatment of sex offenders. *International Psychiatry Clinics, 8*, 165–174.

Neumann, R. (1997). Pharmacology and potential use of cyproterone acetate. *Hormone and Metabolic Research, 9*, 1–13.

Nichols, H. R., & Molinder, I. (1996). *Multiphasic Sex Inventory II: Clinician's handbook*. Fircrest, WA: Nichols & Molinder Assessments.

Person, E. S. (2005). Paraphilias. In B. M. Sadock & V. A. Sadock (Eds.), *Comprehensive textbook of psychiatry* (8th ed., p. 1977). Philadelphia: Lippincott Williams & Wilkins.

Rachman, S. (1966). Sexual fetishism: An experimental analogue. *Psychological Record, 16*, 293–296.

Rachman, S., & Hodgson, R. J. (1968). Experimentally-induced "sexual fetishism": Replication and development. *Psychological Record, 18*, 25–27.

Raymond, M. (1956). Case of fetishism treated by aversion therapy. *British Medical Journal, ii*, 854–857.

Sawyer, D. (1996). An attempt to repair: The meanings of a fetish in the case of Mr. A. *Issues in Psychoanalytic Psychology, 18*(1), 21–35.

Steele, V. (1996). *Fetish: Fashion, sex and power*. New York: Oxford University Press.

Tan, Y., & Zhong, Y. (2001). Chinese style psychoanalysis—Assessment and treatment of paraphilias: Exhibitionism, frotteurism, voyeurism, and fetishism. *International Journal of Psychotherapy*, 6(3), 297–314.

VanDeventer, A. D., & Laws, D. R. (1978). Orgasmic reconditioning to redirect sexual arousal in pedophiles. *Behavior Therapy*, 9, 748–765.

Weinberg, M. S., Williams, C. J., & Calhan, C. (1995). "If the shoe fits . . . ": Exploring male homosexual foot fetishism. *Journal of Sex Research*, 32(1) 17–27.

Wiederman, M. W. (1998). The state of theory in sex therapy. *Journal of Sex Research*, 35(1), 88–99.

Wiederman, M. W. (2003). Paraphilia and fetishism. *The Family Journal: Counseling and Therapy for Couples and Families*, 11(3), 315–321.

CHAPTER 8

FROTTEURISM

Psychopathology and Theory

PATRICK LUSSIER
LYNE PICHÉ

The scanty scientific literature on frotteurism, much like that on any other form of sexual deviance, has been uneven since its onset. In fact, many of the published papers describing activities of frotteurism are limited to single-case studies (see, e.g., Allen, 1969; Bezeau, Bogod, & Mateer, 2004; Fedoroff, 2003; Horley, 2001; Magnan, 1890; Myers, 1991; Perilstein, Lipper, & Friedman, 1991). In these case studies, acts of "frottage"[1] are usually described as being pathological and opportunistic. Toward the end of the 19th century, Valentin Magnan, a well-known French psychiatrist, made a few observations about three men who committed acts of frottage (Magnan, 1890). Magnan was probably one of the first to depict such acts as symptoms of a pathological condition:

> One of the first cases of frotteurs of which I had to take charge, was a 44-year-old, predisposed, alcoholic, suffering from lead poisoning; for a long time now he had been masturbating which almost completely stopped for 1 year; he often made obscene drawings which he distributed to his companions. Alone in his room, he got dressed twice as a woman. For 2 years, he did not have an erection, no sexual intercourse, but [he] still ejaculated at times. Since, he says, he feels pushed to act in a deviant manner. At night, he goes where the crowd is, at the station where the street entertainers are, he takes place behind a woman, preferably overweight, and then he exposes his penis and rubs himself against her buttocks. It is while he was committing such acts at the station of place Clichy that he was arrested by a police officer. He said he received a 4-month prison sentence for the *frottage*, which is true. (Magnan, 1890, p. 467; original emphasis; translation by Patrick Lussier)

Magnan was hinting at the possibility that various impulsive and obsessive behaviors, including acts of frottage, might have a similar cause. Some of Magnan's earlier observations were noted and popularized by the German psychiatrist Richard von Krafft-Ebing

(1965/1998), who kept the same French terminology used by Magnan to describe the disorder.

DESCRIPTION

According to the scientific literature, frotteurism usually involves the following components. First, it usually occurs in public places, mostly in crowded areas such as public transportation vehicles or at public events (Adams & McAnulty, 1993; Fedoroff, 2003). The perpetrator usually takes advantage of the situational context (i.e., the proximity to the victim afforded by the crowd) to have physical contact with the victim. There are usually no physical injuries suffered by the victim unless verbal or physical resistance occurs (Beller, Garelik, & Cooper, 1980). The victim is usually a stranger—vulnerable, distracted, and unaware of the acts—and the perpetrator usually acts with discretion (Allen, 1969; Myers, 1991). In fact, most acts of frotteurism involve approaches from behind without face-to-face encounters, verbal exchanges, or eye contact (Beller et al., 1980). Finally, the majority of the victims tend to be young adult females (Beller et al., 1980; Freund, 1990). Although these components appear relatively straightforward, there are many disagreements and confusions as to what frotteurism actually is, and there is considerable danger of oversimplifying the complex motivations and manifestations of what might generally be considered furtive, unwanted sexual touching.

DEFINITIONAL ISSUES

Until the exclusive use of "frotteurism" in the *Diagnostic and Statistical Manual of Mental Disorders* (DSM), the terms "frottage" and "frotteurism" were often used interchangeably. For Magnan (1890), "frottage" referred to a man rubbing his penis on the body of a stranger, usually in public places. Ellis (1933) shifted the focus, referring to it as a man's sexual desire to bring his clothed body into close contact with the clothed body of an unknown woman. Contrary to Magnan's account, Ellis specified that activities of frottage need not involve the genitals of the perpetrator. In keeping with Ellis's definition, Allen (1969) first used the term "frotteurism," which was vaguely defined as contact with another person in order to obtain sexual excitement. Both Ellis and Allen broadened the definition of frottage to include sexual urges to touch, and not simply the act of rubbing a victim's body. Similarly, Freund and colleagues (Freund, 1990; Freund, Seto, & Kuban, 1997) defined activities of frotteurism as expressions of a pathological erotic preference for rubbing the penis against an unknown person. They also include more specific acts of "toucherism" (i.e., an erotic preference for touching a female stranger's crotch or breasts) as manifestations of frotteurism. Adams and McAnulty (1993) noted that certain experts in the field distinguish frotteurism from toucherism.[2]

DIAGNOSTIC CRITERIA

Unfortunately, the definitions of frotteurism in the DSM have raised more questions than answers and have done little to clarify vexing definitional problems in the clinical and scientific literature.[3] In part, this may be because it has only been a little over 20 years since frotteurism was first recognized as a specific mental disorder by the DSM-III-R (American Psychiatric Association, 1987). Previously, frotteurism was considered an atypical paraphilia and thus excluded as a specific category, due to the lack of sufficient information at the time, while toucherism was not even mentioned. It is unclear what body of scientific evidence became available in the years after the publication of the DSM-III, but frotteurism was recognized as a specific paraphilia in the revision of DSM-III. The DSM-III-R criteria for the diagnosis of frotteurism were as follows:

1. For a period of at least 6 months, recurrent, intense, sexual urges and sexually arousing fantasies, involving touching and rubbing against a nonconsenting person. It is the touching, not the coercive nature of the act, that is sexually exciting.

2. The person has acted on these urges, or is markedly distressed by them. (American Psychiatric Association, 1987, p. 162)

In the DSM-IV (American Psychiatric Association, 1994), the specification that it is not the coercive nature of the act but the touching that elicits sexual arousal was dropped, thus decreasing some confusion over the diagnosis. On the other hand, more confusion was introduced by changing the second criterion: Specifically, in order to qualify for a diagnosis of frotteurism, the fantasies, sexual urges, or behaviors must "cause clinically significant distress or impairment in social, occupational, or other important areas of functioning" (American Psychiatric Association, 1994, p. 527). Therefore, an individual with recurrent ego-syntonic fantasies of frotteurism could not receive a DSM-IV diagnosis of frotteurism. The same was true for individuals committing repeated acts of frotteurism without experiencing any major life impairment. This issue was addressed in the DSM-IV-TR, where the second criterion was reworded in a manner similar to the DSM-III-R version (i.e., "The person has acted on these sexual urges, or the sexual urges or fantasies cause marked distress or interpersonal difficulty"; American Psychiatric Association, 2000, p. 570).

None of these diagnostic criteria are very informative in regard to the etiology, course, and risk of the disorder. Moreover, many problems surround the current description of the disorder as provided by the DSM-IV-TR. First, it is stated that while committing acts of frotteurism, the person "usually fantasizes [about] an exclusive, caring relationship with the victim (American Psychiatric Association, 2000, p. 570). We are not aware of any piece of scientific evidence to support such a speculative statement. Second, it is mentioned that in order to avoid possible prosecution, the perpetrator "must escape detection" after touching. We are unsure about how this might be relevant to a better understanding of this sexual disorder. Yet another major problem in the definition of frotteurism is the potential conceptual overlap with other paraphilias. For example, if the rubbing or touching involves prepubescent boys or girls, should it be conceived as indicative of frotteurism, pedophilia, or both? As in Magnan's (1890) case example, if the behavior involves exposure of the genitals, should it be conceived as indicative of frotteurism, exhibitionism, or even fetishism? Furthermore, because sexual excitement from fondling and touching one's sexual partner is part of normal sexual activity, it must be kept in mind that a central aspect making frotteurism a paraphilia is the *context* in which the behavior occurs. As Smallbone (2006) puts it, as with other paraphilias such as exhibitionism, pedophilia, voyeurism, and telephone scatalogia, it is not the act itself that is deviant, but the fact that it involves an interpersonal transgression involving a nonconsenting victim. Finally, Abel and colleagues (1987) indirectly questioned the utility of the diagnosis of frotteurism by emphasizing the fact that such activities tend to co-occur frequently with other paraphilias. Such observations would suggest that activities of frotteurism may be manifestations of a larger syndrome. Clearly, the nature of this syndrome is still open to much debate.

EPIDEMIOLOGY

The scarce literature on frotteurism and its relatively recent addition to the DSM as a disorder, combined with the definitional and conceptual problems described above, make it difficult to draw a valid and reliable epidemiological picture of frotteurism. Furthermore, there is no legal label specific to acts of frotteurism, making it difficult to get official data about the trends in this criminal behavior over time.[4] Until recently, social scientists have virtually ignored the presence of acts of frotteurism in their sexual victimization surveys, making it difficult to draw a more complete picture of the prevalence of frotteurism in the general population.

Prevalence

"Prevalence" refers to the proportion of a specific population having perpetrated activities of frotteurism. We can distinguish previous empirical studies as to whether they have investigated the prevalence of activities of frotteurism in youth and in adults, and whether the sample was drawn in a nonclinical (i.e., community) setting or a clinical setting.

Nonclinical Samples of Children

A few empirical studies have looked at the prevalence of frotteurism in a normative sample of children. From the empirical evidence available to date, acts of frotteurism appear to be relatively rare during childhood. There could well be some debate about the sexual nature or intent of such behaviors during childhood. Furthermore, the context and the notion of consent have not been addressed in the previous studies. If we leave such considerations aside, these studies suggest that (1) between 4% and 10% of American children commit activities of frottage, while between 6% and 8% have touched others' sexual parts (Friedrich et al., 1992; Friedrich, Grambsch, Broughton, Kuiper, & Beilke, 1991); (2) there may be cultural differences, more specifically for rates of sexual touching, which can be as high as 25% during early childhood in Swedish boys and girls between the ages of 3 and 6 (Larsson, Svedin, & Friedrich, 1999); and (3) there are some preliminary indications that rates of sexual touching may decrease during the period of childhood, whereas rates of rubbing remain relatively low, suggesting different developmental patterns (Schoentjes, Deboutte, & Friedrich, 1999). Unfortunately, comparative data were not found in the scientific literature for the period of adolescence.

Clinical Samples of Children and Adolescents

Much higher prevalence rates for activities of frotteurism have been reported in clinical samples of youth. Taken together, these preliminary results stemming from a few studies suggest that: (1) 26–46% of samples of children who have been sexually victimized have committed acts of sexual touching, while about 22–34% have committed acts of frottage (Friedrich et al., 1992; Gray, Busconi, Houchens, & Pithers, 1997); (2) a prevalence rate of about 6–19% of juvenile sex offenders have a history of sexual touching or frotteurism against a nonconsenting partner (Awad, Saunders, & Levene, 1984; Becker, Cunningham-Rathner, & Kaplan, 1986; Zolondek, Abel, Northey, & Jordan, 2001); and (3) samples of younger juvenile sex offenders and/or juvenile offenders with a high prevalence of sexual victimization tend to report higher levels of acts of frottage, with prevalence rates as high as 70% (Shaw et al., 1993; Wieckowski, Hartsoe, Mayer, & Shortz, 1998). These results should be considered only tentative at this point, considering the early state of this empirical literature and the methodological limitations of these few studies.

Nonclinical Samples of Adults

In a large, randomly selected sample of female college students (n = 4,446), a lifetime victimization rate of 35% was found for unwanted or uninvited touching of a sexual nature, or threats or attempts of such touching (e.g., forced kissing, touching of private parts, grabbing, fondling, and rubbing in a sexual way) (Fisher, Cullen, & Turner, 2000). The same rate (35%) was found in a sample of undergraduate college students (age 21 on average) who self-reported having committed activities of frottage (i.e., tried touching or rubbing up against a woman in a sexual manner in crowds) (Templeman & Stinnett, 1991). Significantly, while 65% of this latter sample reported at least one account of sexual misbehavior (e.g., child molesting, frottage, coercive sex, "window peeping," exhibitionism, and obscene phone calls), only acts of voyeurism (42%) were more prevalent than acts of frotteurism. Similarly, Freund and colleagues (1997) mentioned that about 32% of a sample composed of university students and "less educated volunteers" reported to either fondling the breast/crotch of, or pressing the penis against the buttocks of, a stranger. The similarity of the results to those reported by Templeman and Stinnett (1991) is impressive. Based on these results, it is safe to say at this point that about 30% of the general population of adult men has committed at least one act that would qualify as an instance of frotteurism.

Clinical Samples of Adults

Whereas studies based on the general population have described the prevalence of *activities* of frotteurism, studies based on clinical samples have focused on the prevalence of the *disorder*. Abel and colleagues (1987) conducted a well-known multisite study with 561 individuals seen in the context of evaluation and treatment in a psychiatric setting. They found that 11% of those individuals qualified for a diagnosis of frottage. Of a sample of 743 male individuals who demonstrated or admitted having an activity paraphilia, Freund and colleagues (1997) found that 22% had a history of activities of toucherism and frotteurism. These numbers may be higher than those reported by Abel and colleagues because of the exclusion by Freund and colleagues of child molesters and rapists with one victim or without any other paraphilic activity. In a sample of 120 outpatient males with paraphilia and paraphilia-related disorders, Kafka and Hennen (2002) found that 9% qualified for a diagnosis of frotteurism; this figure is somewhat closer to Abel and colleagues' number. From the Kafka and Hennen and Abel and colleagues studies, we can conclude that about 10% of those individuals with a history of paraphilias or paraphilia-related behaviors have committed acts of frotteurism. Again, however, it is difficult to draw conclusions regarding the prevalence rates, considering the limited number of studies, the use of different methodological designs, and different definitions of frotteurism. The lack of a standardized definition of a diagnosis of frotteurism prevents researchers from drawing firm conclusions here.

Age of Onset

"Age of onset" refers here to the age at the first occurrence of the deviant behavior. In a sample of male juvenile sex offenders, Zolondek and colleagues (2001) found that the average age of onset for acts of frotteurism/toucherism was 11.7 years. It is important to remember that when juveniles are sampled, an earlier age of onset is expected than in studies based on samples of adults, which allow the inclusion of late-onset cases of the deviant behavior. To date, what is probably the most detailed description of the age of onset for frotteurism comes from the study of Abel, Osborn, and Twigg (1993). Using retrospective data based on a sample of 1,025 patients with paraphilias seen in U.S. outpatient clinics, they found that the average age of onset of acts of frotteurism was 20 years old (n = 87); this was later than the age of onset for paraphilias such as transvestism, fetishism, bestiality, obscene phone calls, and homosexual pedophilia, but earlier than that for rape, public masturbation, and incest. Based on this study alone, we can speculate that, on average, activities of frotteurism tend to start in early adulthood—that is, at a relatively later stage of the development of sexual deviance over time.

Frequency

"Frequency" refers to the number of times an individual has committed a certain activity or activities (in this instance, unwanted sexual touching and rubbing). According to Shaw and colleagues (1993), the 25 juvenile sex offenders included in their study had committed a total of 15 acts of frottage, for a mean number of about 0.6 acts per offender. In the Zolondek and colleagues (2001) study including about 80 frotteurs, the mean number of victims and the mean number of acts were 9 and 15, respectively. These results should be interpreted with caution, considering that these researchers only reported means, which is an inaccurate method of reporting information that is not normally distributed in the population. This inaccuracy is clearly demonstrated by Abel and colleagues (1987), who found that their sample of frotteurs (n = 62) had a mean of 849 acts of frotteurism but a median of only 29. The results regarding the numbers of victims were relatively similar, suggesting that these frotteurs had about one episode of unwanted touching and/or rubbing per victim. Furthermore, the discrepancy observed between the mean and the median seems to indicate the presence of a few chronic frotteurs committing an extremely large number of deviant acts with a large number of victims.[5] Abel and colleagues' findings should be interpreted cautiously, however, considering that Bradford, Boulet, and Pawlak (1992) found that their 58 cases had committed on average about 3 incidents of frotteurism apiece. Therefore, it is difficult at this point to determine the typical number of incidents frotteurs tend to be involved in, because of the wide variance found across studies (0.6–849.0 acts).

Escalation

"Escalation" refers to the qualitative sequence of deviant sexual behaviors over time. A question of great interest in regard to activities of frotteurism is whether such acts tend to be precursors of more serious deviant sexual behaviors, such as sexual aggression (i.e., rape). In the Freund and Seto (1998) study based on a sample of rapists ($n = 127$), 22% reported acts of voyeurism, 22% reported acts of exhibitionism, and 18% reported activities of frotteurism. These results suggest that only a small minority of rapists show a pattern of escalation from frotteurism to rape. On the other hand, 54% of those rapists who also reported exhibitionistic activities (28% of the total sample) were characterized by activities of frotteurism. In other words, for a small proportion of rapists, manifestations of frotteurism tend to co-occur more specifically when exhibitionistic activities have also been committed. Unfortunately, Freund and Seto did not look at the temporal occurrence of those manifestations. Therefore, it is unclear from the data whether these results show a pattern of escalation from exhibitionism to rape, or whether they simply reflect more sexual deviance in those with more paraphilic activities. It is also possible that acts of frotteurism occur in different pathways of sexual deviance, one being characterized by an escalation from acts of exhibitionism to rape. Such a pathway, however, appears to characterize only a small proportion of sexual offenders.

COMORBIDITY AND CORRELATED FACTORS

One of the most documented features regarding frotteurism is its co-occurrence with other sexual disorders, primarily other paraphilias. Of the 163 individual frotteurs included in Freund and colleagues' (1997) study, 69% of the mandated and 85% of the self-referred individuals reported another paraphilia activity (these figures did not include individuals with below borderline intelligence, psychosis, or child molesting). Similarly, of the 62 frotteurs studied by Abel and Rouleau (1990), 79% had more than one other paraphilia activity, while 63% had more than two.

Other Courtship Disorders

Freund (1990) argued that frotteurism, along with voyeurism, exhibitionism, and preferential rape, is best conceptualized under the broader category of "courtship disorders." These manifestations are aberrations of the behavioral interactions that precede and initiate sexual intercourse: (1) the finding phase, consisting of locating and appraising a potential partner (i.e., voyeurism); (2) an affiliative phase, characterized by nonverbal and verbal overtures such as looking at, smiling at, and talking to a potential partner (i.e., exhibitionism); (3) a tactile phase, in which physical contact is made (i.e., frotteurism); and (4) a copulatory phase, in which sexual intercourse occurs (i.e., rape). Of the 144 frotteurs included in Freund and colleagues' (1997) study, 98 of them (68%) were characterized by another courtship activity (see also Bradford et al., 1993). Re-analysis of the data showed that activities of frotteurism tended to co-occur with activities associated with the pretactile phases of courtship disorders (i.e., exhibitionism and voyeurism) more often than with other manifestations such as rape, sadism, and masochism. Similar results were found in a sample of college students (Templeman & Stinett, 1991). An important limitation of such a conceptualization, however, is that frotteurism tends to co-occur with paraphilia activity other than those found under the umbrella of courtship disorders.

Pedophilia

Data on the co-occurrence of frotteurism and pedophilia are somewhat inconsistent across empirical studies. Two studies, one based on a prison population and the other in an outpatient clinic, found that about 3–9% of child molesters were characterized by acts of frottage or a formal diagnosis of frotteurism (Abel & Osborn, 1992; Smallbone & Wortley, 2004). Two other studies based in forensic hospitals found much higher co-occurrence rates, ranging between 16% and 20% (Bradford et al., 1993; Raymond, Coleman, Ohlerking, Christenson, & Miner, 1999). On the other hand, Langevin and colleagues (1985) did not find statistical differences between child molesters and a control group of community men in reported activities of frotteurism. It is hard to draw firm conclusions from these studies because of their diverse methodologies, but it is safe to conclude that some child molesters do commit acts of frottage and that a smaller proportion can be characterized by a diagnosis of frotteurism.

Hypersexuality

Krafft-Ebing (1965/1998) suggested that activities of frotteurism should be understood as masturbatory acts reflecting a hypersexual disorder. Whereas paraphilias are socially deviant expressions of sexual behavior, "hypersexuality" involves a disturbance of socially sanctioned or more conventional sexual behavior to a point where it becomes excessive and compulsive (Krueger & Kaplan, 2001). Kafka and Hennen (2002) reported that close to 74% of their sample with paraphilic diagnoses (9% of this sample had a diagnosis of frotteurism) showed manifestations of hypersexuality, most commonly as compulsive masturbation. Prentky and Knight's (1991) classification model of sexual aggressors against women distinguishes those offenders with an antisocial personality from those showing a high level of sexualization (i.e., acts that are sexually motivated). Offenders in the high-sexualization profile are described as showing low levels of aggression during the course of the offense, which lead to some similarities to the descriptions of frotteurs. The distinction between antisociality and sexualization appears to have some limitations in classifying sex offenders, considering the overlap between the two (Lussier, Leclerc, Cale, & Proulx, in press). Furthermore, Smallbone and Wortley (2004) found a significant positive correlation between the number of convictions for nonsexual crimes and a diagnosis of frotteurism. The comorbidity (covariance) among antisociality, hypersexuality, and frotteurism should definitely warrant more scrutiny in future studies.

RISK FACTORS AND ASSOCIATED DEVELOPMENTAL FEATURES

We know very little about the risk factors of individuals who develop features of frotteurism. In fact, to our knowledge, no empirical study to date has been conducted specifically to investigate the risk factors for this disorder. We found four domains of risk factors associated with behavioral manifestations of frotteurism, usually identified in studies without a control/comparison group. At this stage, considering the state of the empirical literature, these domains should be considered tentative at best.

Sexual and Physical Abuse

Empirical studies have reported that activities of rubbing against people, while relatively uncommon in normative samples of American children, are relatively frequent in clinical samples of American children. Friedrich and colleagues (1992) found that acts of frotteurism and toucherism were almost four times more likely to occur in clinical samples of sexually abused children than in a normative sample. Furthermore, Friedrich and colleagues (2001) found that manifestations of rubbing and touching were significantly higher in a clinical sample of sexually abused children than in a clinical sample of children who had not been sexually abused. It is important to note that the sexually abused sample was showing higher prevalence rates for 36 manifestations of sexual behavior other than rubbing or touching others' genitals. Also, the clinical sample of children without sexual abuse showed higher prevalence rates of certain types of sexual behaviors compared to the normative samples.[6] Finally, Becker, Kaplan, and Tenke (1992) found that juvenile sex offenders who reported a history of abuse (i.e., sexual and/or physical) were more sexually aroused by audiotaped descriptions of various deviant sexual behaviors, including acts of frottage, during a phallometric assessment. Therefore, it appears from these results that sexually victimized children are at greater risk of showing a wide range of sexual behaviors, among them sexual rubbing and touching. It is not clear, however, whether sexual victimization precedes or co-occurs with those early sexual manifestations.

Deviant Sexual Fantasy and Arousal

There have been few attempts to investigate the role of deviant sexual interests and deviant sexual arousal in acts of frotteurism. Templeman and Stinnett (1991) found that those men who reported having committed such acts were also likely to report being more sexually aroused by depictions of acts of frottage in a card sort system. It is unclear whether the fantasies preceded, co-occurred, or followed the deviant behavior. On the other hand, it is possible that frotteurs' deviant sexual interest may not be specific to acts of frotteurism. Seto and Kuban (1996) reported that courtship-disordered men ($n = 31$) were similar to rapists in sexual arousal measured phallometrically to audiotaped stimuli of sexual violence. Interestingly, sexual arousal to audiotaped descriptions of acts of frottage has been shown to be inversely related to age in a sample of juvenile sex offenders (Kaemingk, Koselka, Becker, & Kaplan, 1995). Barbaree, Blanchard, and Langton (2003) also found a strong inverse relationship between sexual arousal and age at testing. That is, younger offenders were those showing more sexual arousal to acts of frottage. This might reflect a greater difficulty among younger offenders in suppressing/controlling their sexual arousal. It is too early to draw any conclusions, but future studies should investigate whether activities of frotteurism reflect a difficulty suppressing/controlling sexual arousal, a sexual preference for rape, or more specifically a sexual preference for acts of frotteurism.

Brain Injury

A retrospective file review of a large sample of adult males and females in an inpatient–outpatient hospital for individuals with traumatic brain injury ($n = 445$), Simpson, Blaszczynski, and Hodgkinson (1999) found that 29 males (6.5%) had committed at least one "sexually aberrant behavior" (i.e., exhibitionism, frotteurism/toucherism, or sexual assault). The most common inappropriate sexual behavior witnessed was frotteurism/toucherism, which accounted for more than 64% of all inappropriate sexual behaviors committed by those patients.[7] Bivariate statistical analyses showed that those having committed a sexually aberrant act had sustained more severe injuries at a younger age. Further analyses (Simpson, Tate, Ferry, Hodgkinson, & Blaszczynski, 2001) showed that failure to return to work, substance abuse, and nonsexual criminal behavior post-injury were correlated with the presence of inappropriate sexual behaviors. Overall, neuro-radiological (type of injury, site of brain injury) and neuropsychological factors did not appear to be strong correlates of aberrant sexual behaviors. This study contrasts with another showing evidence of sexual dysfunction following brain injury (Kreuter, Dahlloef, Gudjonsson, Sullian, & Sioesteen, 1997).

Antisociality

The links between antisociality and frotteurism appear to be manifold. First, Beller and colleagues (1980) reported that some incidents of unwanted sexual touching in public transportation can occur during the commission of nonsexual crimes. Second, Small-bone and Wortley (2004) reported a significant positive correlation between the number of convictions for nonsexual crimes and a diagnosis of frotteurism, controlling for number of convictions for sexual crimes. Third, Beller and colleagues found that 50% of their sample of recidivists (i.e., individuals arrested for a sexual crime in the subway, mostly for acts of exhibitionism and frotteurism) had a history of nonsexual violent crimes. These results resonate with those obtained more recently by Lussier and colleagues (Lussier, 2005; Lussier, LeBlanc, & Proulx, 2005), showing that sex offenders do not restrict themselves to sexual crimes, but engage in a wide range of antisocial behaviors (e.g., oppositional defiant, reckless and risk-taking, aggressive, dishonest and deceitful, etc.) and nonsexual criminal behaviors (e.g., fraud, drug trafficking, robbery). Furthermore, sex offenders, especially those having offended against women, tend to be characterized by a life-course persistent antisocial trajectory where sexually deviant acts appear to be manifestations of their tendency to behave against societal norms (Lussier et al., 2005). Taken together, these results suggest that there may be some communality between behavioral manifestations of nonsexual deviance and sexual deviance, including frotteurism.

THEORETICAL MODELS

Over the years, researchers have proposed two main groups of hypotheses (which are not necessarily contradictory) to explain manifestations of frotteurism.

The Social Incompetence Hypothesis

The first group of hypotheses tends to describe frotteurs as presenting certain psychological disturbances that lead to social incompetence, and thus limit their access to consenting partners (Allen, 1969). Different forms of incompetence have been described, such as shyness and inhibition (Brockman & Bluglass, 1996), uncertainty about virility in the presence of women (Krafft-Ebing, 1965/1998), severe psychological impairment such as

Asperger syndrome, and mental retardation/developmental delay (Fedoroff, 2003). To date, no empirical study has looked at the personality characteristics and mental disorders of frotteurs, making it difficult to draw any inferences. Furthermore, the fact that a substantial proportion of young adults in the general population self-report acts of unwanted sexual touching and rubbing suggests that severe psychological impairment is not a necessary condition for these manifestations to occur. A fruitful approach has been proposed by O'Donohue, Penix, and Oksol (2000). From a rational-choice perspective, they argue that acts of frotteurism can lead to immediate sexual gratification with very little cost and investment. Indeed, the perpetrator can obtain immediate sexual stimulation without taking the time and risk of being rejected by a potential sexual partner. This is especially true for those men with little to offer consenting partners (e.g., high income, housing, personality). As O'Donohue and colleagues (2000) suggest, different strategies may be used by the perpetrator in order to increase the benefit–cost ratio by selecting victims who are least likely to report the crime (e.g., children, adolescents).

The Sex Drive Hypothesis

Others have emphasized strong sexual drive or the inability to control such a drive in explaining frotteurism. As noted above, Krafft-Ebing (1965/1998) first suggested that frotteurs might be hypersexual individuals with difficulties in controlling their masturbatory urges. We have found no evidence, however, supporting such claim. From an evolutionary standpoint, Thornhill and Palmer (2000) have argued that many sexual behaviors are by-products of the intense sexual desire of males and the sexual choosiness of human females. Similarly to O'Donohue and colleagues (2000), they describe acts of frotteurism as giving sexual stimulation to male perpetrators by circumventing female choice. It is not clear, however, whether the tendency to circumvent female choice is attributable to individual traits such as egocentrism, impulsivity, hostile masculinity, or a lack of empathy, for example. Along the same line, Freund and colleagues (1997) have argued that activities of frotteurism may reflect the preference for a virtually instant conversion of sexual arousal into orgasm at the tactile phase of courtship. Such a hypothesis could be interpreted in terms of frotteurism as a manifestation of hypersexuality or a high sexual drive. It is not clear from the account by Freund and colleagues why some individuals would become fixated at one phase of courtship rather than at another, however.

An Integrative Approach to Sexual Deviance

Our review of the literature suggests that a theoretical model attempting to explain frotteurism should address the following observations: (1) It can start very early in childhood, especially when sexual victimization is part of an individual's childhood experiences; (2) activities associated with frotteurism tend to co-occur with a wide range of other sexually inappropriate behaviors in childhood; (3) those youth who are sexually aroused by activities of frotteurism are also aroused by other paraphilic activities as a function of age; (4) there is some preliminary evidence that different paraphilias first occur at different ages, with acts of frotteurism first occurring in early adulthood, on average; (5) a later onset of activities of frotteurism has been noticed after individuals have sustained brain injuries; (6) in adulthood, acts of frotteurism tend to co-occur with more specific paraphilic activity (namely, exhibitionism and voyeurism), as well as with other nonsexual criminal behavior; and (7) a small number of individuals appear to commit a great many acts of frotteurism.

Clearly, a broader approach that takes age and development into account is needed in order to better understand frotteurism. Previous models tend to describe sexual offenders as being characterized by a single developmental pathway, which is somewhat at odds with the heterogeneity found in sexual offenders. A more fruitful approach would be to distinguish those showing a childhood onset of paraphilic activity from those showing an adolescent onset and an adult onset. In fact, the periods of childhood, adolescence, and adulthood are associated with specific developmental tasks leading to sexual maturity (Bancroft, 2005; DeLamater & Friedrich, 2002; Smallbone, 2006). It is thus possible that the emergence of acts of frotteurism in one period or another may reflect various difficulties in successfully completing these developmental tasks: (1) shifting to a more covert expression of sexual activities in childhood as the child grows older and become more aware of parental and cultural norms (Bancroft, 2006); (2) developing internal inhibitors to control sexual urges while experiencing a shift from parental vigilance and influence to peer influence and opportunities in early adolescence (Lussier et al., in press); (3) learning to develop trusting and intimate relationships with peers in middle and late adolescence (Marshall & Barbaree, 1990; Smallbone, 2006); and (4) learning to communicate effectively with an intimate partner in adulthood (DeLamater & Friedrich, 2002). The continuity of the manifestations of frotteurism may be attributable to the persistence of those excess and deficits over time.

FORENSIC ISSUES

A risk assessor must focus on ensuring that an assessment offers a true picture of an offender. An accurate presentation of the offender's sexual deviance and sexual behaviors is the ultimate goal of any risk assessment. Furthermore, suggestions for effective risk management strategies should be incorporated into the risk assessment. In order to achieve these goals, it is crucial for assessors to be familiar with the expected prevalence of frotteurism in clinical samples and hypotheses that underlie frotteurism.

General Guidelines

Though frotteurism is rarely reported in clinical samples, risk assessors should assess for the presence of this behavior, especially if the offender has reported the presence of other paraphilias. These conclusions hold true for both youth and adult assessments. The high reported frequency of crimes committed by frotteurs must also be taken into account in conducting risk assessment interviews as well as in planning risk management strategies. Assessors should be mindful that it is possible that an offender has committed past offenses that have not yet been detected. The studies reviewed in this chapter point to the necessity of inquiring about all paraphilias during a typical risk assessment for frotteurism. Although not all offenders have multiple paraphilias, it is recommended that an assessor assume that there are other deviant sexual activities in an individual's repertoire.[8] The assessor cannot, however, assume that deviant sexual interests pervade the individual's entire range of interpersonal functioning (McAnulty, Dillon, & Adams, 2001). This may be one reason why personality testing is not always indicative of pathology in individuals with paraphilias.

The presence of comorbid disorders may influence the frequency of sexual behaviors. Comorbid disorders and their possible impact on future risk are important and should be included in a risk assessment. If a traumatic brain injury is present, specifically explaining the nature of the brain injury and the possible consequences of that injury for the individual's cognitive functioning and behavior is essential. Several questions should be addressed: Will the individual be able to overcome the impact of the injury? Will it lead to a subsequent change in his behavior? What are the interventions specific to this particular brain injury, and will these interventions modify his risk to the community? Similar sorts of questions should be asked about low-functioning individuals in general. Answering these questions is essential to a complete assessment that can direct future treatment considerations and supervision requirements both while the offender is incarcerated and when he is returned to the community.

Common Practices

Asking specific questions is essential to proper evaluation of an individual's behaviors. The assessor must be comfortable with asking very explicit questions.[9] These questions demonstrate the importance of having a good understanding of the usual practices of frotteurs.[10] The inclusion of questions pertaining to the details of the behavior is the cornerstone of a good assessment. (Specifically, what was being done? When? To whom? Thoughts? Fantasies?) It is important to assess both the quantity and the quality of this behavior. Quantity of the behavior includes such matters as the number of offenses, the number of victims, the frequency of reoffenses with the same victim, the frequency of masturbation to fantasies, and the frequency of offending over various time periods (a day, a week, a month). Quality of the behavior includes location of the offenses, behaviors committed, behavior plan, nature of the fantasies, and level of intrusiveness (use of hands, hips, penis).[11] It is also important to probe past actual or fantasized rape behaviors (attempted rape, date rape, rape fantasies). Having a good knowledge of the offender's chosen location for offending is particularly important. If the offense took place in an area with which an assessor is not familiar, using a map and having discussions about that location (level of activity, culture, type of people frequenting the area, etc.) both with the individual and with collateral informants can provide invaluable details about the extent of planning and the hostile intent surrounding the individual's offending.

As discussed previously, exploring the whole spectrum of paraphilic behavior is important. We emphasize that this exploration needs to be conducted in an engaging way. Various paraphilias are clearly illegal and not supported by social norms. In addition, most risk assessments are conducted within the context of the criminal justice system.[12] Thus the evaluator is encouraged to create a climate of open discussion of sexual behavior prior to specifically addressing various other paraphilias.[13] Discussing sexual history is a good way of engaging the individual, beginning with a focus on normal sexual behavior and then moving to deviant sexual interests. The assessment should include the presence of sexual dysfunctions, sexual attitudes, and past attempts to self-regulate sexual behaviors. If the person has been able to control his behaviors in the past, how did he do this? What led to his eventual repeating of the behavior? If he has not been able to control his behavior or has not made any attempts to do so in the past, this speaks to his future ability to do so. Sexual activity is not always indicative of sexual preference (McAnulty et al., 2001). Being thoughtful about the vocabulary used to describe the offender's actions is essential. Careful consideration of the use of language (i.e., "sexual deviance," "sexual preference," "sexual interest") is important. The extent of the sexual preference can be determined by examining frequency of behavior, fantasies, and masturbation patterns. The label "sexual interest" can be used to describe a situation where it is difficult to conclude that an individual has a definite sexual preference. An individual may have engaged or is believed to have engaged in a behavior, without having a particular sexual preference for that same behavior.

It is also the assessor's responsibility to ask about precursors to the deviant sexual behavior, as well as to explore the presence of an escalation in behavior. The possibility of moving on to more aggressive, contact offenses in future behavior may be evaluated by examining various facets of the case.[14] Assessors may wish to address this possibility, while limiting the scope of their conclusions, as research identifying predictors of escalation is in its infancy.

Verifying differential diagnoses (as per DSM-IV-TR), as well as assessing various other comorbid disorders, is likewise important. Exploring for various mental health difficulties that may have an impact on future offending—such as alcohol abuse, other substance abuse (in particular, stimulants may increase sex drive), conduct disorder, attention-deficit/hyperactivity disorder, anxiety, and depression—is suggested (Kafka & Hennen, 2002). Past treatment attempts are very informative for decision makers and can help the assessor evaluate future adherence to treatment plans, medication regimens, and supervision requirements. Reporting on past medication use to control paraphilias, the individual's adherence to these medications, and their reported effects on fantasies and behaviors is an expected and important part of every risk assessment. Past behaviors will assist in determining the likely difficulties with an individual's current risk management plan.

In conclusion, assessors should concentrate on research-based variables that show a link to paraphilias. The risk assessment must address the behavioral patterns relating to the offending, as well as the client's ability to interrupt those behavioral patterns. It is important to consider that the offender may have committed other offenses. Assessors should also remember that both adults and youth can engage in frotteuristic acts, and frotteurism should thus be assessed in both populations. Finally, care should be taken in the wording of risk assessments, so that the extent of the individual's sexual deviance is as clearly presented as possible.

SUMMARY AND FUTURE DIRECTIONS

The lack of a clear consensus about the behaviors that are classified as frotteurism, its conceptual overlap with other paraphilias, and its relatively recent addition to the DSM have severely limited the development of an empirically based assessment of the construct of frotteurism. Considering these limitations, we should be wary of making firm pronouncements about the prevalence, onset, frequency, and escalation of the behavior over time. A few studies conducted with samples drawn from the general population highlight that the occurrence of this behavior may be underreported in clinical samples of sex offenders. The co-occurrence of frotteurism with other paraphilias and the overlap of the risk factors suggest the need for a more integrated approach to the understanding of frotteurism. More specifically, longitudinal studies investigating the development of sexual behaviors should be conducted to better understand the within-individual changes in manifestations of sexual behavior and the establishment of sexual preferences over the life course.

NOTES

1. The word "frottage" comes from the French verb *frotter*, which has no sexual connotation, referring only to the act of rubbing or putting pressure on someone or something (Larousse, 1995).

2. For example, Lane (1997) used the term "grabbage" as a stand-alone term to designate acts of grabbing the breasts, buttocks, or genitals of a victim.

3. In the clinical literature, there is a marked lack of consensus as to what frottage or frotteurism is or should be. It appears that the term "frottage" is more specific to the act of rubbing the genitals, while "frotteurism" has sometimes been described as including acts of touching other body parts as well. When such acts of touching are included, the concept of frotteurism becomes unclear in relation to other paraphilias. Based on the limited evidence, it is not clear whether the more restricted or the more inclusive definition of frotteurism is more warranted at this point. Furthermore, some authors limit their definition of frottage/frotteurism to acts involving the genitals of the victims, whereas others do not make such a specification. Similarly, some have used the term "frottage" to refer to sexual acts between two consenting partners, whereas "frotteurism" has been characterized as involving an unknown, nonconsenting partner. Moreover, the specification of an unknown person as the target of the behavior (see Ellis, 1933; Freund, 1990) excludes the possibility of acts of frotteurism against acquaintances, relatives, and intimates. More importantly, perhaps, Magnan's, Ellis's, and Freund's definitions of frottage/frotteurism exclude the possibility of females' perpetrating the act or presenting with the disorder.

4. Acts of frotteurism as defined by the DSM-IV-TR (American Psychiatric Association, 2000) are punishable by law in Canada. Although there is no evidence as to how such cases are treated by the courts, activities of frotteurism should generally fall under two broad legal categories: "sexual interference" and "sexual assault." Persons guilty of sexual interference are defined in the criminal code as follows: "Every person who, for a sexual purpose, touches, directly or indirectly, with a part of the body or with an object, any part of the body of a person under the age of fourteen years" (Greenspan, 2006). According to this definition, acts of child molestation and acts of frotteurism would fall into the same legal categories, if the victim's age is under 14. In a case where the victim is 14 or older, acts of frotteurism could fall under the legal term of a level one sexual assault, which refers to circumstances of a sexual nature where the sexual integrity of the victim is violated, but minor or no physical injuries are sustained.

5. Among the other deviant sexual behaviors analyzed by Abel et al. (1987), only acts of public masturbation, obscene phone calling, and exhibitionism had a higher median number of victims reported.

6. Examples included trying to look at pictures of nude or partially dressed people, talking about sexual acts, and knowing more about sex than other children their age.

7. In fact, 44% of the patients who had committed sexually aberrant acts following brain injury had committed acts of toucherism where members of the hospital staff appeared to be the primary targets.

8. For example, if an offender has a history of rape or child sexual abuse, an assessor should specifically address any prior history of engaging in the other paraphilias (including frotteurism). Similarly, if the offender has a history of noncontact offenses such as exhibitionism, a circumspect assessor should not assume that this person has never committed a contact offense without directly inquiring about this with collateral sources and/or with the offender himself.

9. For frotteurs, questions used by Freund and Seto (1998, p. 438) include the following: "Since age 16, have you ever fondled or attempted to fondle the breasts or crotch of an unsuspecting female who was almost or totally a stranger to you? Since age 16, have you ever stood behind an unsuspecting female who was almost or totally a stranger to you, and pressed (intentionally) your penis against her buttocks?"

10. A good example is presented by Myers (1991, p. 114). In his clinical example, he noted that the client would "let the crush of the people on the subway car carry him and his erect penis against her buttocks. He would not move at first, in order to allay any fear or anger the woman

might feel at the presence of his penis against her buttocks. Then, when he felt more secure in her lack of verbal response, he would press closer to her and begin to move his penis against her gluteal region until he had an orgasm."

11. Other topics for questions include victim type and characteristics (including age, gender, physical characteristics, level of vulnerability), time of day, usual precursors, past medication use to control behaviors, past substance use to increase or decrease the behavior, victim reactions, perceived victim thoughts, and leisure and work activities as they apply to facilitating or deterring the offending behavior.

12. Most assessments involve a distinct lack of confidentiality surrounding the information obtained. Although this may appear obvious to most readers, it should not be assumed that the individual being assessed understands the limits of confidentiality. This can be particularly true of individuals with limited intelligence. As such, it is essential to obtain consent for these assessments. Discussion surrounding the possible distribution of the report, as well as the probable use of the report by the criminal justice system, is necessary. Issues surrounding consent should be discussed prior to beginning the assessment. Many individuals will minimize and deny their deviant sexual interests and behaviors during an assessment (McAnulty et al., 2001), but others will report additional offenses. Ensuring that the individual is aware of the standard practice regarding disclosure of additional offenses is important. Although it may be tempting to preserve client engagement by not reporting such disclosures, in all cases these disclosures must be documented and reported as required.

13. As noted by Zolondek et al. (2001), attempts to assess socially desirable responding, minimizing, and denial are all important facets of the assessment.

14. Considering such facets as Psychopathy Checklist—Revised scores, general level of hostility, increased frequency of offenses, victim characteristics (including age and vulnerability), location choice, sadistic themes in fantasy, or other areas of an offender's life can be helpful.

REFERENCES

Abel, G. G., Becker, J. V., Mittelman, M., Cunningham-Rathner, J., Rouleau, J. L., & Murphy, W. D. (1987). Self-reported sex crimes of nonincarcerated paraphiliacs. *Journal of Interpersonal Violence, 2*, 3–25.

Abel, G. G., & Osborn, C. A. (1992). The paraphilias: The extent and nature of sexually deviant and criminal behavior. *Psychiatric Clinics of North America, 15*, 675–687.

Abel, G. G., Osborn, C. A., & Twigg, D. A. (1993). Sexual assault through the life span: Adult offenders with juvenile histories. In H. E. Barbaree, W. L. Marshall, & S. M. Hudson (Eds.), *The juvenile sex offender* (pp. 104–117). New York: Guilford Press.

Abel, G. G., & Rouleau, J.-L. (1990). The nature and extent of sexual assault. In W. L. Marshall, D. L. Laws, & H. E. Barbaree (Eds.), *Handbook of sexual assault: Issues, theories, and treatment of the offender* (pp. 9–21). New York: Plenum Press.

Adams, H. E., & McAnulty, R. D. (1993). Sexual disorders: The paraphilias. In H. E. Adams & P. B. Sutker (Eds.), *Comprehensive handbook of psychopathology*. New York: Plenum Press.

Allen, C. (1969). *A textbook of psychosexual disorders* (2nd ed.). London: Oxford University Press.

American Psychiatric Association. (1987). *Diagnostic and statistical manual of mental disorders* (3rd ed., rev.). Washington, DC: Author.

American Psychiatric Association. (1994). *Diagnostic and statistical manual of mental disorders* (4th ed.). Washington, DC: Author.

American Psychiatric Association. (2000). *Diagnostic and statistical manual of mental disorders* (4th ed., text rev.). Washington, DC: Author.

Awad, G. A., Saunders, E., & Levene, J. (1984). A clinical study of male adolescent sexual offenders. *International Journal of Offender Therapy and Comparative Criminology, 28*, 105–115.

Bancroft, J. (2005). Normal sexual development. In H. E. Barbaree & W. L. Marshall (Eds.), *The juvenile sex offender* (2nd ed., pp. 19–57). New York: Guilford Press.

Barbaree, H. E., Blanchard, R., & Langton, C. M. (2003). The development of sexual aggression through the life span: The effect of age on sexual arousal and recidivism among sex offenders. *Annals of the New York Academy of Sciences, 989,* 59–71.

Becker, J. V., Cunningham-Rathner, J., & Kaplan, M. S. (1986). Adolescent sexual offenders: Demographics, criminal and sexual histories, and recommendations for reducing future offenses. *Journal of Interpersonal Violence, 1,* 431–445.

Becker, J. V., Kaplan, M. S., & Tenke, C. E. (1992). The relationship of abuse history, denial and erectile response profiles of adolescent sexual perpetrators. *Behavior Therapy, 23,* 87–97.

Beller, A., Garelik, S., & Cooper, S. (1980). Sex crimes in the subway. *Criminology, 18,* 35–52.

Bezeau, S. C., Bogod, N. M., & Mateer, C. A. (2004). Sexually intrusive behaviour following brain injury: Approaches to assessment and rehabilitation. *Brain Injury, 18,* 299–313.

Bradford, J. M., Boulet, J., & Pawlak, A. (1992). The paraphilias: A multiplicity of deviant behaviours. *Canadian Journal of Psychiatry, 37,* 104–108.

Brockman, B., & Bluglass, R. S. (1996). A general approach to sexual deviation. In I. Rosen (Ed.), *Sexual deviation* (3rd ed., pp. 1–42). New York: Oxford University Press.

DeLamater, J., & Friedrich, W. N. (2002). Human sexual development. *Journal of Sex Research, 39,* 10–14.

Ellis, H. (1933). *Psychology of sex: A manual for students.* New York: Long & Smith.

Fedoroff, J. P. (2003). The paraphilic world. In S. B. Levine, C. B. Risen, & S. E. Althof (Eds.), *Handbook of clinical sexuality for mental health professionals* (pp. 333–356). New York: Brunner-Routledge.

Fisher, B. S., Cullen, F. T., & Turner, M. G. (2000). *The sexual victimization of college women.* Washington, DC: U.S. Department of Justice, National Institute of Justice.

Freund, K. (1990). Courtship disorders. In W. L. Marshall, D. R. Laws, & H. E. Barbaree (Eds.), *Handbook of sexual assault: Issues, theories, and treatment of the offender* (pp. 195–207). New York: Plenum Press.

Freund, K., & Seto, M. C. (1998). Preferential rape in the theory of courtship disorder. *Archives of Sexual Behavior, 27,* 433–443.

Freund, K., Seto, M. C., & Kuban, M. (1997). Frotteurism: The theory of courtship disorder. In D. R. Laws & W. O'Donohue (Eds.), *Sexual deviance: Theory, assessment, and treatment* (pp. 111–130). New York: Guilford Press.

Friedrich, W. N., Fisher, J. L., Dittner, C. A., Acton, R., Berliner, L., Butler, J., et al. (2001). Child Sexual Behavior Inventory: Normative, psychiatric, and sexual abuse comparisons. *Child Maltreatment, 6,* 37–49.

Friedrich, W. N., Grambsch, P., Broughton, D., Kuiper, J., & Beilke, R. L. (1991). Normative sexual behavior in children. *Pediatrics, 88,* 456–464.

Friedrich, W. N., Grambsch, P., Damon, L., Hewitt, S. K., Koverola, C., Lang, R. A., et al. (1992). Child Sexual Behavior Inventory: Normative and clinical comparisons. *Psychological Assessment, 4,* 303–311.

Gray, A., Busconi, A., Houchens, P., & Pithers, W. D. (1997). Children with sexual behavior problems and their caregivers: Demographics, functioning, and clinical patterns. *Sexual Abuse: A Journal of Research and Treatment, 9,* 267–290.

Greenspan, E. L. (2006). *Martin's Annual Criminal Code.* Aurora, ON: Canada Law Book.

Horley, J. (2001). Frotteurism: A term in search of an underlying disorder? *Journal of Sexual Aggression, 7,* 51–55.

Kaemingk, K. L., Koselka, M., Becker, J. V., & Kaplan, M. S. (1995). Age and adolescent sexual offender arousal. *Sexual Abuse: A Journal of Research and Treatment, 7,* 249–252.

Kafka, M. P., & Hennen, J. (2002). A DSM-IV Axis I comorbidity study of males ($n = 120$) with paraphilias and paraphilia-related disorders. *Sexual Abuse: A Journal of Research and Treatment, 14*(4), 349–366.

Krafft-Ebing, R. von. (1998) *Psychopathia sexualis.* New York: Arcade. (Original work published 1965)

Kreuter, M., Dahlloef, A. G., Gudjonsson, G., Sullian, M., & Sioesteen, A. (1997). Sexual adjustment and its predictors after traumatic brain injury. *Brain Injury, 12,* 349–368.

Krueger, R. B., & Kaplan, M. S. (2001). The paraphilic and hypersexual disorders: An overview. *Journal of Psychiatric Practice, 7,* 391–403.

Lane, S. (1997). Assessment of sexually abusive youth. In G. Ryan & S. Lane (Eds.), *Juvenile sexual offending: Causes, consequences, and correction* (pp. 219–263). San Francisco: Jossey-Bass.

Langevin, R., Hucker, S. J., Handy, L., Hook, H. J., Purins, J. E., & Russon, A. E. (1985). Erotic preferences and aggression in pedophilia: A comparison of heterosexual, homosexual, and bisexual types. In R. Langevin (Ed.), *Erotic preference, gender identity, and aggression in men* (pp. 137–160). Hillsdale, NJ: Erlbaum.

Langevin, R., Paitich, D., & Russon, A. E. (1988). Are rapists sexually anomalous, aggressive, or both? In R. Langevin (Ed.), *Erotic preference, gender identity, and aggression in men: New research studies* (pp. 17–38). Hillsdale, NJ: Erlbaum.

Larousse, P. (1995). *Le petit Larousse illustré.* Paris: Author.

Larsson, I., Svedin, C. G., & Friedrich, W. N. (2000). Differences and similarities in sexual behaviour among pre-schoolers in Sweden and USA. *Nordic Journal of Psychiatry, 54,* 251–257.

Lussier, P. (2005). The criminal activity of sexual offenders in adulthood: Revisiting the specialization debate. *Sexual Abuse: A Journal of Research and Treatment, 17,* 269–292.

Lussier, P., LeBlanc, M., & Proulx, J. (2005). The generality of criminal behavior: A confirmatory factor analysis of the criminal activity of sexual offenders in adulthood. *Journal of Criminal Justice, 33,* 177–189.

Lussier, P., Leclerc, B., Cale, J., & Proulx, J. (in press). Developmental pathways of deviance in sexual aggressors. *Criminal Justice and Behavior.*

Lussier, P., Proulx, J., & LeBlanc, M. (2005). Criminal propensity, deviant sexual interests and criminal activity of sexual aggressors against women: A comparison of alternative explanatory models. *Criminology, 43,* 247–279.

Magnan, V. (1890). Des exhibitionnistes. *Les Archives de l'Anthropologie Criminelle et de Sciences Pénales, 5,* 456–471.

Marshall, W. L., & Barbaree, H. E. (1990). An integrated theory of the etiology of sexual offending. In W. L. Marshall, D. R. Laws, & H. E. Barbaree (Eds.), *Handbook of sexual assault: Issues, theories, and treatment* (pp. 257–278). New York: Plenum Press.

McAnulty, R., Dillon, J., & Adams, H. (2001). Sexual disorders: The paraphilias. In H. E. Adams & P. B. Sutker (Eds.), *Comprehensive handbook of psychopathology* (3rd ed., pp. 749–773). New York: Kluwer/Springer.

Myers, W. A. (1991). A case history of a man who made obscene telephone calls and practiced frotteurism. In G. I. Fogel & W. A. Myers (Eds.), *Perversions and near perversions in clinical practice: New psychoanalytical practice* (pp. 109–123). New Haven, CT: Yale University Press.

O'Donohue, W., Penix, T., & Oksol, E. (2000). Behavioral economics: Understanding sexual behavior, preference and self-control. In D. R. Laws, S. M. Hudson, & T. Ward (Eds.), *Remaking relapse prevention with sex offenders* (pp. 123–139). Thousand Oaks, CA: Sage.

Perilstein, R. D., Lipper, S., & Friedman, L. J. (1991). Three cases of paraphilia responsive to fluoxetine treatment. *Journal of Clinical Psychiatry, 52,* 169–170.

Prentky, R. A., & Knight, R. A. (1991). Identifying critical dimensions for discriminating among rapists. *Journal of Consulting and Clinical Psychology, 59,* 643–661.

Raymond, N. C., Coleman, E., Ohlerking, F., Christenson, G. A., & Miner, M. (1999). Psychiatric comorbidity in pedophilic sex offenders *American Journal of Psychiatry, 156,* 786–788.

Schoentjes, E., Deboutte, D., & Friedrich, W. D. (1999). Child sexual behavior inventory: A Dutch-speaking normative sample. *Pediatrics, 104,* 885–893.

Seto, M. C., & Kuban, M. (1996). Criterion-related validity of a phallometric test for paraphilic rape and sadism. *Behaviour Research and Therapy, 34,* 175–183.

Shaw, J. A., Campo-Bowen, A. E., Applegate, B., Perez, D., Antoine, L. B., Hart, E. L., et al. (1993).

Young boys who commit serious sexual offenses: Demographics, psychometrics, and phenomenology. *Bulletin of the American Academy of Psychiatry and the Law, 21,* 399–408.

Simpson, G., Blaszczynski, A., & Hodgkinson, A. (1999). Sex offending as a psychosocial sequela of traumatic brain injury. *Journal of Head Trauma Rehabilitation, 14,* 567–580.

Simpson, G., Tate, R., Ferry, K., Hodgkinson, A., & Blaszczynski, A. (2001). Social, neuroradiologic, medical, and neuropsychologic correlates of sexually aberrant behavior. *Journal of Head Trauma Rehabilitation.*

Smallbone, S. W. (2006). Social and psychological factors in the development of delinquency and sexual deviance. In H. E. Barbaree & W. L. Marshall (Eds.), *The juvenile sex offender* (2nd ed., pp. 105–127). New York: Guilford Press.

Smallbone, S. W., & Wortley, R. K. (2004). Criminal diversity and paraphilic interests among adult males convicted of sexual offenses against children. *International Journal of Offender Therapy and Comparative Criminology, 48,* 175–188.

Templeman, T. L., & Stinnett, R. D. (1991). Patterns of sexual arousal and history in a "normal" sample of young men. *Archives of Sexual Behavior, 20,* 137–150.

Thornhill, R., & Palmer, C. T. (2000). *A natural history of rape: Biological bases of sexual coercion.* Cambridge, MA: MIT Press.

Wieckowski, E., Hartsoe, P., Mayer, A., & Shortz. (1998). Deviant sexual behavior in children and young adolescents: Frequency and patterns. *Sexual Abuse: Journal of Research and Treatment, 10,* 293–303.

Zolondek, S. C., Abel, G. G., Northey, W. F., Jr., & Jordan, A. (2001). Self-reported behaviors of juvenile sexual offenders. *Journal of Interpersonal Violence, 16,* 73–85.

CHAPTER 9

FROTTEURISM

Assessment and Treatment

RICHARD B. KRUEGER
MEG S. KAPLAN

The first mention of frotteurism in the scientific literature was in Krafft-Ebing's *Psychopathia Sexualis* (1886/1998). He described cases of four frotteurs and wrote: "The simplest explanation seems to be that 'frottage' is a masturbatory act of a hypersexual individual who is uncertain about his virility in the presence of women. This would also explain the motive of the assault being made not anteriorly but posteriorly" (p. 351). The word "frottage" is a French word meaning "rubbing" or "friction," according to the *Oxford English Dictionary* (Burchfield, 1972), which goes on to state that "The special perversion of frottage . . . consists in a desire to bring the clothed body, and usually though not exclusively the genital region, into close contact with the clothed body of a woman" (p. 1168).

Through the years, though, frotteurism has not been a subject of much clinical or scientific interest. A literature search by the Research Library of New York State Psychiatric Institute in October 2006, using *Psychological Abstracts* and examining sources from the 19th century to the present with "frotteurism" as a keyword, returned only 24 references. A second search only brought up 10 references in PubMed, which lists sources from 1966 to the present. Since the chapters on frotteurism in the first edition of *Sexual Deviance* (Freund, Seto, & Kuban, 1997; Krueger & Kaplan, 1997), we have been able to locate only two published articles that focus primarily or exclusively on frotteurism (Krueger & Kaplan, 2000b, 2000c); one of these includes several case reports (Krueger & Kaplan, 2000b).

Reasons for this lack of interest are manifold. Typically, frotteurism is considered a nuisance crime by the legal system, and available resources and penalties are focused more on sexual crimes involving children or sexual crimes of violence, such as rape. When frotteurism is mentioned in case series, it is not among the most prevalent of deviant behaviors. For instance, Abel, Becker, Cunningham-Rathner, Mittelman, and Rouleau

(1988), reporting on a group of 561 nonincarcerated individuals with paraphilias who were recruited through a newspaper advertisement, identified 17 categories of paraphilic behavior and found that frottage was sixth in terms of frequency. In another study of 443 males consecutively admitted to the Sexual Behaviors Clinic at the Royal Ottawa Hospital, 14% of individuals admitted to frotteuristic behavior (Bradford, Boulet, & Pawlak, 1992).

Finally, it is the case that frotteurism is difficult to prosecute. It often occurs under crowded circumstances, where witnesses may be hard to identify and interview; or the frotteuristic act itself may be of such a subtle nature that it is hard for the victim, let alone witnesses, to perceive. For example, the two individuals we treated most recently for this crime, referred by their defense attorneys, dropped out of treatment when their attorneys successfully plea-bargained their cases down to nonsexual offenses (requiring no treatment) because of the weakness of the prosecution's arguments.

Nevertheless, this disorder has recently been identified in case reports as a diagnosis and focus of treatment (Cannas et al., 2006; Perilstein, Lipper, & Friedman, 1991) and as being one of the paraphilic disorders treated in larger case series (Rösler & Witztum, 1998; Saleh, Niel, & Fishman, 2004). Although better epidemiological data are unavailable, frotteurism continues to be a paraphilia that clinicians are quite likely to encounter in addition to other paraphilias.

ASSESSMENT

How is frotteurism diagnosed? First, a history should be obtained, and the current criteria from the *Diagnostic and Statistical Manual of Mental Disorders* (fourth edition, text revision) (DSM-IV-TR; American Psychiatric Association, 2000) should be applied. The DSM-IV-TR diagnostic criteria are as follows:

> A. Over a period of at least 6 months, recurrent, intense sexually arousing fantasies, sexual urges, or behaviors involving touching and rubbing against a nonconsenting person.
> B. The person has acted on these sexual urges, or the sexual urges or fantasies cause marked distress or interpersonal difficulty. (p. 570)

We should note that the DSM-IV Criterion B for frotteurism was changed in DSM-IV-TR. The requirement that for paraphilic behavior involving a victim, sexual urges or fantasies cause clinically significant distress or impairment in social, occupational, or other important areas of functioning was changed to one that contained these elements, but also allowed the criterion to be met if an individual had acted on such urges. This was done to avoid the clinically absurd situation in which an individual who acts on such impulses, but is not distressed by them (because they are ego-syntonic), and who therefore claims no impairment, cannot be diagnosed as having the paraphilia (Hilliard & Spitzer, 2002).

How does a therapist know whether a client has this problem? This is a matter of clinical assessment and involves a decision as to whether the client fulfills the criteria listed above. Such an assessment should involve a comprehensive clinical/psychiatric interview with a focus on the client's sexual history, including illegal or atypical sexual behavior and fantasy. Such an interview requires skill and training and has been described elsewhere (Risen, 1995). If a client has been arrested and presents for assessment before adjudication (we use the generic term "he" to refer to individuals with this disorder, because to our knowledge there are no reports of frotteurism occurring in females in the literature), he should be asked whether he has an attorney and be advised that he should consult or have consulted one prior to the interview. A written release of information should be obtained that informs the patient of the nature and purpose of the interview, as well as the persons to whom the information or report will be given. A consent form detailing the nature and the risks and benefits of any psychological or psychophysiological testing should be obtained. We also routinely make a note that the patient understands this information and is competent to sign such a release or consent.

Prior to any initial diagnostic interview, relevant legal documents (e.g., arrest reports, victim's statements, criminal record, or any other materials that are available) should be reviewed. Typically we like to begin with a general psychiatric and personal history, thus initially establishing rapport while we acquire more neutral information, and then proceed to questions that might be more embarrassing for a client to answer or about which he may be particularly guarded. It is useful to have all written documentation in hand so that a client can be gently or firmly encountered, or inconsistencies presented, with the focus being on trying to establish what the client did and helping or getting him to admit what he did.

How, then, can we be sure that an individual has a diagnosis of frotteurism? Seto, Cantor, and Blanchard (2006) for the diagnosis of another paraphilia, pedophilia, indicate that clinicians rely on three sources of information in determining whether an individual has this diagnosis: self-report, a history of sexual behavior involving children, and psychophysiological assessment. Extending these guidelines to frotteurism, one should obtain a history in order to obtain an individual's self-report.

In the absence of such an acknowledgment, the clinician should discuss the individual's criminal record with him, as well as all victim or witness statements. If an individual still fails to self-report the frotteurism, and if there is sufficient evidence that an individual has so acted or if there is a guilty finding or plea, then we would also make this diagnosis. Multiple arrests and convictions for frotteuristic acts extending over more than a 6-month period would clearly support this diagnosis. If an individual denies such behavior, then—provided that the individual has an attorney and provides consent—one can also suggest polygraphy, although the limitations of this methodology must be kept in mind (Abrams, 1991; Marshall & Serran, 2000; Meyer, 1999). Often when an individual fails a polygraph test, or is in the process of being polygraphed, he will subsequently acknowledge his sexual offending behavior. In our experience, a polygraph is valuable for these reasons. We know of no instance where an individual has been sanctioned by the legal system for failing a polygraph per se. Rather, in our experience, penalties have come about because of admissions made in the course of polygraphy, or failure to take a polygraph test. We would also point out that although a polygraph concluding that no deception is indicated when a patient denies key allegations is not admissible in court, it may have some influence with prosecutors or judges in the preadjudication phase of the case.

Although penile plethysmography could be considered and is widely used to assess other paraphilias, in the United States there is an absence of either auditory or visual stimulus sets whose validation is described or supported by peer-reviewed literature. There is one system marketed by Behavioral Technology, Inc, in Salt Lake City, Utah, with one published study supporting its ability to discriminate between gynephilic and pedophilic sexual offenders (Card & Dibble, 1995). Otherwise, one is left to use available stimuli on a case-by-case basis, where verbal vignettes depicting frotteuristic behavior or other paraphilic behavior along with a variety of other stimuli are presented and an individual's response is measured. This could serve potentially as a good pre–post means of assessment. Some authorities have used such customized stimuli to create an index of arousal, measuring arousal to the individualized stimuli against arousal to stimuli depicting mutually consenting sexual behavior with adult females, and using these measurements to create a foot fetish index, a frotteurism index, or other indices (J. M. W. Bradford, personal communication, 2007). We have used a system provided by Limestone Technologies, of Odessa, Ontario, with a number of narrated vignettes provided by that company, but these have not been normed or validated.

Viewing time could also be considered and is used for other paraphilias. One system, the Abel Assessment of Sexual Interest (AASI), is available (Abel, 1995; Krueger, Bradford, & Glancy, 1998) and contains an item on its AASI z-scored graph for frotteurism against an adult female. However, Abel Screening indicates that this graph cannot be relied upon in determining whether this is a sexual interest pattern for frotteurs or not, and in our experience it has not proved useful with this population.

What diagnoses should be ruled out? First, an extensive literature suggests that individuals with one paraphilia may have progressed through or have had other paraphilias (Abel et al., 1988; Bradford et al., 1992); a clinician should take such a history. We would note, however, that these studies only document a history of other sexually deviant behaviors, and not necessarily diagnoses; the latter require the application of DSM-IV-TR (in particular, the establishment of at least 6 months of intense fantasy, activity, or interest, and the requirement that an individual has acted on such interests or that it has been a source of distress of dysfunction).

In assessing for other paraphilias, plethysmography, viewing time assessment, and polygraphy may be more useful. In particular, the detailed questioning of sexual history and functioning provided by the AASI (Krueger et al., 1998) has been helpful. Other authors (Freund et al., 1997; Freund & Watson, 1990) have suggested that frotteurism is one of a series of behaviors that represent a disturbance in the normal sequence of courtship behavior, and that frotteurism is more closely associated with voyeurism and exhibitionism than with other paraphilias; therefore, these two paraphilias should be especially asked about.

More recently, Kafka and his colleagues (Kafka, 1994; Kafka & Hennen, 2002) have drawn attention to the occurrence of paraphilia-related disorders, such as compulsive masturbation, compulsive use of pornography, or cybersexual behavior, which have been associated with paraphilic disorders. These paraphilia-related disorders can also be referred to as "sexual disorders not otherwise specified," according to the DSM-IV-TR nomenclature, or as "hypersexual disorders" (Stein, Black, & Pienaar, 2000; Stein, Black, Shapira, & Spitzer, 2001). These disorders, unlike paraphilic disorders, involve more conventional types of sexual behavior that some individuals have engaged in to such a degree that they have lost their ability to control such behavior and it has become a source of distress or dysfunction in their lives. We have found such a typology useful in our practice, and patients should be asked about such behaviors.

Neuropsychiatric conditions have been associated with paraphilias (Krueger & Kaplan, 2000a), and an individual should be questioned about any history of head trauma, or, in the review of systems, about any medications, drugs of abuse, or neurological symptoms that might be related to sexually aggressive behavior.

Regarding psychometric considerations, individuals should be questioned in an organized way regarding their sexual history and more general psychological and psychiatric history. In particular, for this population there is a substantial occurrence of comorbid psychiatric conditions, and these are important to identify (Kafka & Hennen, 2002; Raymond, Coleman, & Miner, 2003; Raymond, Coleman, Ohlerking, Christenson, & Miner, 1999). Many different self-administered and clinician-administered measures are available to examine for general psychopathology (Rush et al., 2000), general sexual behavior (Davis, Yarber, Bauserman, Schreer, & Davis, 1998), and deviant sexual behavior (Prentky & Edmunds, 1997).

Generally speaking, individual clinicians should review available instruments and alternatives, and decide for themselves what would be most useful. In recent years we have relied on a sexual Structured Clinical Interview for DSM-IV (SCID), developed with the permission of the original SCID's authors, and have been pilot-testing this, although it has not as yet been validated. We have also used a SCID-I (First, Spitzer, Gibbon, & Williams, 1997) to screen for general psychopathology. Because of the high correlation of psychopathy with recidivism (Hare, 2006) we also routinely complete a Hare Psychopathy Checklist—Revised (Hare, 2003) on all patients. In cases where substance abuse may be an issue, the use of drug testing is important.

Clients are ideally assessed for treatment with an interview and a selection of the above-described instruments. If a client is under a legal mandate, it is important to have contact with the patient's probation or parole officer, so that this officer may be informed and also involved in the patient's treatment, should the need arise. It is important to know the conditions of probation or parole. If a patient is not under legal mandate, then an interview with a significant other or family member is important, as well as consent to maintain contact if questions about a recurrence should arise.

All of the measures described above can be used effectively to assess this disorder. If one were to contrast clinician-administered measures with self-report measures, some literature suggests that self-administered questionnaires regarding sexuality may be more advantageous than a face-to-face interview (Catania, McDermott, & Pollack, 1986; Durant & Carey, 2000). We have used the AASI (Abel, 1995) and the Clarke Sex History Questionnaire for Males (Langevin, Handy, Paitich, & Russon, 1985; Paitich, Langevin, Freeman, Mann, & Handy, 1977).

We have in the past used the Minnesota Multiphasic Personality Inventory–2 (Butcher et al., 2001) and the Millon Clinical Multiaxial Inventory–III (Millon, 1997), but have found that a general clinical interview or the DSM-IV-based versions of the SCID mentioned above offer a more solid basis for the identification of psychiatric syndromes to treat. Depending on the syndrome identified, we would use specific inventories to follow treatment response. For instance, we would recommend random urine or Breathalyzer tests (or have probation or parole do these) to follow an individual's substance abuse problems; or we would use specific inventories to assess treatment outcome for depression, such as the Beck Depression Inventory (Beck, Ward, Mendelson, Mock, & Erbaugh, 1961) or the Hamilton Rating Scale for Depression.

We also regularly use at baseline and then subsequently a number of sexual interest instruments; however, none have been validated or normed on any population of sex offenders. One of these, the Bancroft Sexual Interest and Activity Scale (Bancroft, Tennent, Lougas, & Cass, 1974), is very useful in quantitating how sexually active an individual is. It asks an individual to indicate how many times masturbation or any overt sexual activity has resulted in orgasm in the past 7 days, and asks an individual to identify on a scale from 0 to 5 what the frequency of sexual thoughts has been, from a score of 0 (*no sexual thoughts at all*) to 5 (*sexual thoughts frequent and usually associated with feelings of sex-*

ual excitement). This was used by Rösler and Witztum (1998) to follow the effects of tryptoreline.

Another instrument that is useful for baseline and serial outcome (used mostly in medication studies) is the Clinical Global Impressions (CGI) Scale (Guy, 1976). Originally developed at the National Institute of Mental Health for the study of medication treatment of mood and psychotic disorders, its use has been extended to other hard-to-measure disorders, such as pathological gambling disorder (Kim, Grant, Adson, Shin, & Zaninelli, 2002) and body dysmorphic disorder (Phillips, Albertini, & Rasmussen, 2002). Most recently, it has been used in the assessment of compulsive sexual behavior in a study involving men who have sex with men (Wainberg et al., 2006).

Two other scales that we have found useful for assessing treatment response are the Coleman Compulsive Sexual Behavior Inventory (Coleman, Miner, Ohlerking, & Raymond, 2001), and the Yale–Brown Obsessive Compulsive Scale Modified for Compulsive Sexual Behavior (YBOCS-SB; Wainberg et al., 2006). We have also found it useful to draw a line, identifying one end as representing 0% control over deviant urges and the other end as representing 100% control over deviant urges, and then to ask an individual to mark on the line what percentage of control he currently has over acting on sexual urges or fantasies (Krueger & Kaplan, 2000b, p. 195). We regularly use some combination or all of these measures at baseline to provide some quantitative assessment of how extensive an individual's sexual problem is and how much control an individual reports having over his urges, and then to use these to follow the effects of treatment.

Regarding research priorities in the area of assessment of frotteurs, a paramount one is to develop a validated and standardized set of stimuli for viewing time assessment and plethysmographic assessment that can be used by any researchers in any country. Even though plethysmography is extensively used in the United States and Canada, and such standardization was called for more than 10 years ago (Howes, 1995), there are still no validated stimulus sets that can be used to replicate studies or to perform new ones. A significant issue is that even the excellent work done by groups in Canada cannot be subject to verification or validation in the United States, because such stimulus sets contain images of child pornography. Such images cannot be legally transferred across borders, and, to our knowledge, no specific legal exemption that would allow use of such material by researchers has been obtained. Similar arguments apply to the development of sets of stimuli to use for viewing time assessment. Additional problems are that images used in many of the Canadian studies, to our knowledge, were obtained without proper consent of subjects. Although auditory stimuli are available or could be created, there is again, to our knowledge, no set of validated auditory stimuli available for widespread usage.

A second critical need is for the validation and assessment of the various treatment outcome instruments mentioned above—aside from the Coleman Compulsive Sexual Behavior Inventory, which has been validated in a preliminary fashion (Coleman, Miner, et al., 2001). The Bancroft Scale, the YBOCS-SB, and the CGI have not been studied in a population of sex offenders compared with a control group, and the basic validity of these instruments is unknown.

TREATMENT

At the outset of this section on treatment, we should note that we have found no publications describing treatment for a case series of individuals with frotteurism, but rather only sporadic references to treatment of such individuals in larger series of patients treated for paraphilias or in case reports. In general, the scientific demonstration of treatment efficacy for individuals with paraphilias has an extensive literature with conflicting results; the largest and most recent well-controlled study showed no clear effect of cognitive-behavioral treatment (CBT) compared with a no-treatment control at a 6-year follow-up (Marques, Wiederanders, Day, Nelson, & van Ommeren, 2005). However, recent meta-analytic studies have demonstrated significant effects of CBT (Hanson et al., 2002) and organic and psychological treatment (Lösel & Schmucker, 2005) on recidivism for sexual crimes. These meta-analytic studies do not describe specific components of CBT or organic treatment; nor do they have the requisite design to evaluate specific types of treatment. Accordingly, we present our usual treatment practice, along with information from case reports and other studies. However, this should not be understood as constituting a scientific demonstration that such treatments have been effective for the treatment of frotteurism beyond simply a description of open treatment. We should also note that unless an individual's behavior is extremely out of control, or unless there is some other clear indication for medical treatment, we begin with behavioral and/or verbal psychotherapy, and then proceed to serotonin-specific reuptake inhibitors (SSRIs) and then androgen reduction therapy if the earlier treatments fail to impart control to the patient.

Reviews of CBT and other treatments are available (Abel & Osborn, 1996; Coleman et al., 1996; Coleman, Dwyer, et al., 2001; Krueger & Kaplan, 2002c). Additionally, a description of what might be involved in establishing standards of care (Coleman et al., 1996; Coleman, Dwyer, et al., 2001) has been published, as well as a manual that describes step by step how to do CBT with child molesters (which, many would argue, could be easily extended to individuals with frotteurism) (Abel et al., 1984). For example, a therapist can counter a frotteur's deviant cognitions, such as "She likes it" or "She doesn't know what I am doing." The therapist can also increase empathy from the victim by informing the frotteur how humiliating it is for a woman to be in the subway on the way to work with semen on her skirt, or how she feels when someone is pressing against her back and rubbing her and she is unable to move. Or the therapist can describe the fear that women experience with this activity, especially because of its nonconsensual nature.

Two organizations, the Association for the Treatment of Sexual Abusers (*www.atsa.com*) and the Safer Society Foundation (*www.safersociety.org*), maintain websites that offer various literature, manuals, and referrals to local treatment providers (Krueger & Kaplan, 2002b).

Over the past 10 years, coincident with the identification of "sexual addiction" or "hypersexual behavior," 12-Step programs have been developed for the treatment of compulsive sexual disorders, akin to Alcoholics Anonymous (AA) for alcohol, Overeaters Anonymous for overeating, or Gamblers Anonymous for pathological gambling. Sex Addicts Anonymous (SAA), Sexaholics Anonymous (SA), Sex and Love Addicts Anonymous (SLAA), and Sexual Compulsives Anonymous (SCA) are such organizations, all focusing on the individual with the problem (Krueger & Kaplan, 2002b). For partners and/or family members, there are S-Anon International Family Groups and Codependents of Sex Addicts (COSA); for couples, there is Recovering Couples Anonymous (RCA).

Several self-help texts also exist, akin to AA's *The Big Book* (Carnes, 1983, 1989; Carnes & Adams, 2002; Sbraga & O'Donohue, 2004). As with AA, individuals should be advised to try several different meetings (so as to find some that address their particular style and preference and that they can attend regularly), and also to find a sponsor and home group. Some patients find these groups useful and some do not, and we suggest to certain patients that they try these out and see if they are helpful.

Group treatment, in our experience, has been most effective in treating individuals with frotteurism, inasmuch as a group of peers can be very effective at confronting denial and offering support to a patient. In contrast, individual therapy can often focus more effectively on a particular patient's lifestyle and needs, and can develop specific treatment plans to deal with them. A significant other, such as a spouse, can also be involved by an individual or couple therapist. For instance, a careful review of a frotteur's routine might identify several hours per day that are unaccounted for, and a wife could be enjoined to report on any unexplained absences. Such treatment is aimed at helping the patient gain and maintain control over his sexual urges and behavior.

In our experience, frotteurs will often present with problems of erectile dysfunction or a frank phobia of sexual intercourse, and individual therapy focusing on this sexual dysfunction is indicated. Or broader issues of commitment and intimacy may be encountered, and ongoing insight-oriented psychotherapy may be indicated to address these problems. There are no studies that specifically compare the treatment efficacy of individual therapy versus group therapy in frotteurs, or that specifically identify the most effective type of individual therapy, so the selection of therapies and sequencing of priorities constitute more of an art than a science.

In regard to the medical therapy of frotteurism, a recent case report illustrates the complexity of behaviors that may be encountered and the necessity for a careful evaluation (Cannas et al., 2006). In this case, a 51-year-old male with Parkinson's disease developed hypersexual behavior, frotteurism, and delusional jealousy after being treated with pergolide, a dopamine agonist, for several years; these symptoms remitted after the pergolide was reduced and quetiapine, an atypical neuroleptic, was added.

Open treatment with SSRI drugs has been reported as being effective for individuals with paraphilias and paraphilia-related disorders (Kafka, 2000a, 2000b), and this is the first option we would consider for medication treatment, unless an individual's behavior is extremely out of control. The SSRIs can be particularly useful and may be indicated in any event for individuals who are depressed or who have obsessive–compulsive disorder. However, there is less support for the use of SSRIs in the literature on treatment of paraphilias than for the use of androgen-reducing agents (Gijs & Gooren, 1996; Krueger & Kaplan, 2002a).

A large literature in animals and humans clearly demonstrates that testosterone is important in the motivation of sexual behavior in males, and that its reduction is associated with a diminution in sexually motivated behavior (Bradford, 1985, 2006; Krueger, Wechsler, & Kaplan, in press). A recent article reported on the open treatment with Depo-Provera of 275 men convicted of sexual crimes and given various diagnoses in Oregon, and a positive effect of this medication was observed (Maletzky, Tolan, & McFarland, 2006).

Gonadotropin-releasing hormone (GnRH) agonists have also been reported in larger case series as being effective for the treatment of individuals with paraphilias in general and frotteurism in particular (Rösler & Witztum, 1998; Saleh et al., 2004). Various androgen-reducing agents are available; some professionals believe that GnRH agonists are the most effective and safest (Rösler & Witztum, 2000), although other authors still favor earlier agents, such as cyproterone acetate (CPA—not available in the United States) or Provera (J. M. W. Bradford, personal communication, 2007). Specifically, some authorities (J. M. W. Bradford, personal communication, 2007) use SSRI agents initially before moving to CPA, with roughly a 10:1 ratio favoring SSRI usage over CPA. Beyond this, usage of CPA over GnRH agonists occurs roughly at a ratio of 100:1 in favor of CPA (J. M. W. Bradford, personal communication, 2007). As noted, CPA is not available in the United States and, other authorities have different algorithms for progression of medication therapy.

The main side effects of all androgen reduction therapy in men are osteopenia (a condition of demineralization and thinning of bone) and/or osteoporosis (a more extreme form of osteopenia, where bone mass and structure are more severely weakened and individuals are subject to fractures) (Gallagher & Rapuri, 2003; O'Connell & Seaton, 2005). These effects can be prevented by appropriate treatment with alendronate, calcium, and vitamin D (Smith, 2003). Other side effects of androgen reduction therapy include hyperhydrosis (excessive sweating), decreased muscle mass, weight gain, mild anemia, and azospermia (decreased sperm count), to name the most significant ones (Thomson Healthcare, 2006). It should be emphasized that the medical literature and the Physicians' Desk Reference (Thomson Healthcare, 2006) should be always be consulted before such medications are prescribed.

Additionally, an individual treated with androgen reduction therapy should have a baseline physical examination, laboratory assessment, including testosterone levels, and bone density evaluation, and these should be repeated every 6 or 12 months. We would advise that an internist, family physician, or endocrinologist be involved in the patient's care if androgen reduction therapy is initiated, so that this physician will be aware that the patient has been placed on this medication and will be able to follow the patient medically and arrange for appropriate laboratory and physical assessments. Some psychiatrists do not feel that the involvement of other physicians is necessary, and that psychiatrists with appropriate experience and training with these agents are capable of initiating and following such treatment independently (J. M. W. Bradford, personal communication, 2007).

In regard to the combination of treatments for frotteurism, Rösler and Witztum (1998) reported that all 30 men treated in their study received supportive psychotherapy on a regular basis (from one to four sessions a month), that 7 men in their series continued to receive a maintenance dose of one psychoactive drug, and that 2 men continued receiving two psychoactive agents.

How does one decide on an appropriate course of therapy for a particular client? The cornerstone of therapy is a thorough initial evaluation. One important aspect of this is to establish how much control an individual has over his behavior. Often the process of arrest, which can be quite traumatic for an individual, has a deterrent effect, and we have seen some individuals who report that a single adverse legal sanction has been enough to dissuade them from engaging in this behavior again.

However, some individuals—either after the expiration of probation or parole, or before it but because of poor judgment or exceptional compulsion—*will* engage in such behavior again, and these individuals present treatment challenges. If an individual reports that his behavior is out of control despite a recent arrest, or if he engages in such behavior as part of another psychiatric disorder (such as a bipolar disorder), then psychiatric hospitalization should be considered as an option to ensure that the patient will not harm others or get himself into greater legal difficulty.

We generally approach treatment with the aim of using the least restrictive alternative, and try individual in combination with group therapy first. If an individual is depressed (as frotteurs usually are after an arrest), or if he has been engaging in sexually acting-out behavior as one symptom of depression, then use of an SSRI antidepressant can be considered. If SSRIs have not worked before, or if androgen reduction therapy is indicated, then such therapy may be helpful. We are able to treat most individuals successfully with behavioral and verbal therapy and/or antidepressants, and would note that, particularly in the case of frotteurs, it is unusual to progress to androgen reduction therapy.

It has been our experience that up to 2 months of a trial at therapeutic levels may be needed for antidepressants to exert an effect (this is the usual case with the use of antidepressant agents to treat depression). Clinical experience has shown that there is a considerable reduction of sexual fantasies in the first week, with more than 60% reduction by week 12 (J. M. W. Bradford, personal communication, 2007). Depot or oral Provera works quickly (within a few days), but may take weeks to adjust upward to achieve therapeutic effects and control. GnRH agonists generally work within 2–4 weeks, with testosterone falling to castrate levels; great caution should be used, however, because there is an initial testosterone surge in the first week or two, which is associated with increased arousal and with a risk of sexual acting out. This danger can be dealt with by hospitalizing the patient, by warning him and cautioning him to stay home, or by giving androgen-blocking agents such as flutamide for 1–2 weeks to treat these "flare" effects. These agents, however, have their own side effects, including potentially (though extremely rare) fatal hepatic necrosis (Crownover et al., 1996). Patients will often prefer staying at home or increasing self-surveillance over the use of flutamide.

The effects of nonpharmacological therapy—individual CBT, couple therapy, or group therapy—can take much longer to achieve, on the order of weeks, months, or even years.

SUMMARY AND FUTURE DIRECTIONS

Research priorities for assessment and treatment of frotteurs should involve the identification and treatment of a group or case series of patients with frotteurism, with attention to a careful description of the development of their paraphilias and of their other sexual and general comorbidity. It is only through selecting and treating a larger case series of individuals with frotteurism that a more solid basis for assessment and treatment can be developed.

We should also note that the use of androgen reduction therapy to treat men with paraphilias is unusual in one sense: Most experience with long-term androgen reduction therapy that is described in the literature involves urologists treating individuals with prostate cancer, who have had limited survival. Thus the most nearly comparable population that has been treated over the long term consists of individuals with gender identity disorder. Studies of long-term effects and outcome of androgen reduction therapy in otherwise healthy younger males, such as those treated for paraphilias, are needed.

Finally, it should be noted that research support for studies of the paraphilias, in the United States at least, has been inadequate. The National Institute of Mental Health has tended to avoid studying criminal behaviors and paraphilias, and the National Institute of Justice has expressed to us that it does not have the capability to monitor biological studies. Drug companies, usually eager to enlist clinicians to perform research, typically avoid any project involving deviant sexuality. And state governments, with a few exceptions, have been content to spend vast sums of money incarcerating individuals with paraphilias, and very little or nothing on research into the etiology or management of sexually aggressive behavior. More extensive research will only occur when society and legislators see the increasing costs that sexual disorders are causing for society, and decide that an investment in data collection and research could actually result in cost savings— as we believe it would (Shajnfeld & Krueger, 2006).

REFERENCES

Abel, G. G. (1995). *The Abel Assessment for Sexual Interest.* (Available from Abel Screening, Inc., 1280 West Peachtree Street, Suite 100, Atlanta, GA 30309)

Abel, G. G., Becker, J. V., Cunningham-Rathner, J., Mittelman, M., & Rouleau, J.-L. (1988). Multiple paraphilic diagnoses among sex offenders. *Bulletin of the American Academy of Psychiatry and the Law, 16*(2), 153–168.

Abel, G. G., Becker, J. V., Cunningham-Rathner, J., Rouleau, J. L., Kaplan, M., & Reich, J. (1984). *The treatment of child molesters.* Unpublished manual.

Abel, G. G., & Osborn, C. A. (1996). Behavioural therapy treatment for sex-offenders. In I. Rosen (Ed.), *Sexual deviation* (3rd ed., pp. 382–398). New York: Oxford University Press.

Abrams, S. (1991). The use of polygraphy with sex offenders. *Annals of Sex Research, 4*(4), 239–263.

American Psychiatric Association. (2000). *Diagnostic and statistical manual of mental disorders* (4th ed., text rev.). Washington, DC: Author.

Bancroft, J., Tennent, G., Lougas, K., & Cass, J. (1974). The control of deviant sexual behaviour by drugs: 1. Behavioural changes following oestrogens and anti-androgens. *British Journal of Psychiatry, 125,* 310–315.

Beck, A. T., Ward, C. H., Mendelson, M., Mock, J., & Erbaugh, J. (1961). An inventory for measuring depression. *Archives of General Psychiatry, 4,* 561–571.

Bradford, J. M. W. (1985). Organic treatment for the male sexual offender. *Behavioral Sciences and the Law, 3*(4), 355–375.

Bradford, J. M. W. (2006). On sexual violence. *Current Opinion in Psychiatry, 19,* 527–532.

Bradford, J. M. W., Boulet, J., & Pawlak, A. (1992). The paraphilias: A multiplicity of deviant behaviours. *Canadian Journal of Psychiatry, 37*(2), 104–108.

Burchfield, R. W. (1972). *A supplement to the Oxford English Dictionary.* Oxford, UK: Oxford University Press.

Butcher, J. N., Graham, J. R., Ben-Porath, Y. S., Tellegen, A., Dahlstrom, W. G., & Kaemmer, B. (2001). *Minnesota Multiphasic Personality Inventory–2: Manual for administration, scoring, and interpretation* (rev. ed.). Minneapolis: University of Minnesota Press.

Cannas, A., Solla, P., Floris, G., Tacconi, P., Loi, D., Marcia, E., et al. (2006). Hypersexual behaviour, frotteurism and delusional jealousy in a young parkinsonian patient during dopaminergic therapy with pergolide: A rare case of iatrogenic paraphilia. *Progress in Neuro-Psychopharmacology and Biological Psychiatry, 30,* 1539–1541.

Card, R. D., & Dibble, A. (1995). Predictive value of the Card/Farrall stimuli in discriminating between gynephilic and pedophilic sexual offenders. *Sexual Abuse: A Journal of Research and Treatment, 7*(2), 129–141.

Carnes, P. (1983). *Out of the shadows.* Minneapolis, MN: CompCare.

Carnes, P. (1989). *Contrary to love.* Minneapolis, MN: CompCare.

Carnes, P. J., & Adams, K. M. (Eds.). (2002). *Clinical management of sex addiction.* New York: Brunner-Routledge.

Catania, J. A., McDermott, L. J., & Pollack, L. M. (1986). Questionnaire response bias and face-to-face interview sample bias in sexuality research. *Journal of Sex Research, 22*(1), 52–72.

Coleman, E., Dwyer, S. M., Abel, G., Berner, W., Breiling, J., Eher, R., et al. (2001). Standards of care for the treatment of adult sex offenders. *Journal of Psychology and Human Sexuality, 13*(3–4), 115–121.

Coleman, E., Dwyer, S. M., Abel, G., Berner, W., Breiling, J., Hindman, J., et al. (1996). Standards of care for the treatment of adult sex offenders. In E. Coleman, S. M. Dwyer, & N. J. Pallone (Eds.), *Sex offender treatment* (pp. 5–11). Binghamton, NY: Haworth Press.

Coleman, E., Miner, M., Ohlerking, F., & Raymond, N. (2001). Compulsive sexual behavior inventory: A preliminary study of reliability and validity. *Journal of Sex and Marital Therapy, 27*(4), 325–332.

Crownover, R. L., Holland, J., Chen, A., Krieg, R., Young, B. K., Roach, M., III, et al. (1996). Flutamide-induced liver toxicity including fatal hepatic necrosis. *International Journal of Radiation Oncology, 34*(4), 911–915.

Davis, C. M., Yarber, W. L., Bauserman, R., Schreer, G., & Davis, S. L. (1998). *Handbook of sexuality-related measures* (2nd ed.). Thousand Oaks, CA: Sage.

Durant, L. E., & Carey, M. P. (2000). Self-administered questionnaires versus face-to-face interviews in assessing sexual behavior in young women. *Archives of Sexual Behavior, 29*(4), 309–322.

First, M. B., Spitzer, R. L., Gibbon, M., & Williams, J. B. W. (1997). *Structured Clinical Interview for DSM-IV Axis I Disorders*. Washington, DC: American Psychiatric Press.

Freund, K., Seto, M. C., & Kuban, M. (1997). Frotteurism: The theory of courtship disorder. In D. R. Laws & W. O'Donohue (Eds.), *Sexual deviance: Theory, assessment, and treatment* (pp. 111–130). New York: Guilford Press.

Freund, K., & Watson, R. (1990). Mapping the boundaries of courtship disorder. *Journal of Sex Research, 27*(4), 589–606.

Gallagher, J. C., & Rapuri, P. B. (2003). Osteoporosis: Pathophysiology. In H. L. Henry & A. W. Norman (Eds.), *Encyclopedia of hormones* (Vol. 3, pp. 89–98). San Diego, CA: Academic Press.

Gijs, L., & Gooren, L. (1996). Hormonal and psychopharmacological interventions in the treatment of paraphilias: An update. *Journal of Sex Research, 33*(4), 273–290.

Guy, W. (1976). *ECDEU assessment manual for psychopharmacology*. Rockville, MD: U.S. Department of Health, Education and Welfare, Public Health Service, Alcohol, Drug Abuse, and Mental Health Administration.

Hanson, R. K., Gordon, A., Harris, A. J. R., Marques, J. K., Murphy, W., Quinsey, V. L., et al. (2002). First report of the Collaborative Outcome Data Project on the Effectiveness of Psychological Treatment for Sex Offenders. *Sexual Abuse: A Journal of Research and Treatment, 14*(2), 169–194.

Hare, R. D. (2003). *Hare Psychopathy Checklist—Revised* (2nd ed.). North Tonawanda, NY: Multi-Health Systems.

Hare, R. D. (2006). Psychopathy: A clinical and forensic overview. *Psychiatric Clinics of North America, 29*, 709–724.

Hilliard, R. B., & Spitzer, R. L. (2002). Change in criterion for paraphilias in DSM-IV-TR. *American Journal of Psychiatry, 159*(7), 1249.

Howes, R. J. (1995). A survey of plethysmographic assessment in North America. *Sexual Abuse: A Journal of Research and Treatment, 7*(1), 9–24.

Kafka, M. P. (1994). Paraphilia-related disorders—common, neglected, and misunderstood. *Harvard Review of Psychiatry, 2*, 39–40.

Kafka, M. P. (2000a). The paraphilia-related disorders: Nonparaphilic hypersexuality and sexual compulsivity/addiction. In S. R. Leiblum & R. C. Rosen (Eds.), *Principles and practice of sex therapy* (3rd ed., pp. 471–503). New York: Guilford Press.

Kafka, M. P. (2000b). Psychopharmacologic treatments for nonparaphilic compulsive sexual behaviors. *CNS Spectrums, 5*(1), 49–59.

Kafka, M. P., & Hennen, J. (2002). A DSM-IV Axis I comorbidity study of males ($n = 120$) with paraphilias and paraphilia-related disorders. *Sexual Abuse: A Journal of Research and Treatment, 14*(4), 349–366.

Kim, S. W., Grant, J. E., Adson, D. E., Shin, Y. C., & Zaninelli, R. (2002). A double-blind placebo-controlled study of the efficacy and safety of paroxetine in the treatment of pathological gambling. *Journal of Clinical Psychiatry, 63*(6), 501–507.

Krafft-Ebing, R. von. (1998). *Psychopathia sexualis*. New York: Arcade.

Krueger, R. B., Bradford, J. M. W., & Glancy, G. D. (1998). Report from the Committee on Sex Offenders: The Abel Assessment for Sexual Interest—a brief description. *Journal of the American Academy of Psychiatry and the Law*, 26(2), 277–280.

Krueger, R. B., & Kaplan, M. S. (1997). Frotteurism: Assessment and treatment. In D. R. Laws & W. O'Donohue (Eds.), *Sexual deviance: Theory, assessment, and treatment* (pp. 131–151). New York: Guilford Press.

Krueger, R. B., & Kaplan, M. S. (2000a). Disorders of sexual impulse control in neuropsychiatric conditions. *Seminars in Clinical Neuropsychiatry*, 5(4), 266–274.

Krueger, R. B., & Kaplan, M. S. (2000b). Evaluation and treatment of sexual disorders: Frottage. In L. Vandecreek & T. L. Jackson (Eds.), *Innovations in clinical practice: A source book* (Vol. 18, pp. 185–197). Sarasota, FL: Professional Resource Press.

Krueger, R. B., & Kaplan, M. S. (2000c). The nonviolent serial offender: Exhibitionism, frotteurism, and telephone scatalogia. In L. B. Schlesinger (Ed.), *Serial offenders: Current thought, recent findings* (pp. 103–118). Boca Raton, FL: CRC Press.

Krueger, R. B., & Kaplan, M. S. (2002a). Behavioral and psychopharmacological treatment of the paraphilic and hypersexual disorders. *Journal of Psychiatric Practice*, 8(1), 21–32.

Krueger, R. B., & Kaplan, M. S. (2002b). Treatment resources for the paraphilic and hypersexual disorders. *Journal of Psychiatric Practice*, 8(1), 59–60.

Krueger, R. B., Wechsler, M., & Kaplan, M. (in press). Orchiectomy. In F. Saleh, J. Bradford, A. Grudzinsakas, & D. Brodsky (Eds.), *Sex offenders: Identification, risk assessment, treatment, and legal issues* (pp. 1–49). New York: Oxford University Press.

Langevin, R., Handy, L., Paitich, D., & Russon, A. (1985). Appendix A: A new version of the Clarke Sex History Questionnaire for Males. In R. Langevin (Ed.), *Erotic preference, gender identity, and aggression in men: New research studies* (pp. 287–305). Hillsdale, NJ: Erlbaum.

Lösel, F., & Schmucker, M. (2005). The effectiveness of treatment for sexual offenders: A comprehensive meta-analysis. *Journal of Experimental Criminology*, 1, 117–146.

Maletzky, B. M., Tolan, A., & McFarland, B. (2006). The Oregon Depo-Provera program: A five-year follow-up. *Sexual Abuse: A Journal of Research and Treatment*, 18, 303–316.

Marques, J. K., Wiederanders, M., Day, D. M., Nelson, C., & van Ommeren, A. (2005). Effects of a relapse prevention program on sexual recidivism: Final results from California's Sex Offender Treatment and Evaluation Project (SOTEP). *Sexual Abuse: A Journal of Research and Treatment*, 17(1), 79–107.

Marshall, W. L., & Serran, G. A. (2000). Improving the effectiveness of sexual offender treatment. *Trauma, Violence and Abuse*, 1(3), 203–222.

Meyer, F. R. (1999). Clinical polygraph testing as a tool in the treatment process. *NJATSA*, 1–4.

Millon, T. (1997). *The Millon inventories: Clinical and personality assessment*. New York: Guilford Press.

O'Connell, M. B., & Seaton, T. L. (2005). Osteoporosis and osteomalacia. In J. T. DiPiro, R. L. Talbert, G. C. Yee, G. R. Matzke, B. G. Wells, & L. M. Posey (Eds.), *Pharmacotherapy: A pathophysiologic approach* (6th ed., pp. 1645–1669). New York: McGraw-Hill.

Paitich, D., Langevin, R., Freeman, R., Mann, K., & Handy, L. (1977). The Clarke SHQ: A clinical sex history questionnaire for males. *Archives of Sexual Behavior*, 6(5), 421–436.

Perilstein, R. D., Lipper, S., & Friedman, L. J. (1991). Three cases of paraphilias responsive to fluoxetine treatment. *Journal of Clinical Psychiatry*, 52(4), 169–170.

Phillips, K. A., Albertini, R. S., & Rasmussen, S. A. (2002). A randomized placebo-controlled trial of fluoxetine in body dysmorphic disorder. *Archives of General Psychiatry*, 59, 381–388.

Prentky, R., & Edmunds, S. B. (1997). *Assessing sexual abuse: A resource guide for practitioners*. Brandon, VT: Safer Society Press.

Raymond, N. C., Coleman, E., & Miner, M. H. (2003). Psychiatric comorbidity and compulsive/impulsive traits in compulsive sexual behavior. *Comprehensive Psychiatry*, 44(5), 370–380.

Raymond, N. C., Coleman, E., Ohlerking, F., Christenson, G. A., & Miner, M. (1999). Psychiatric comorbidity in pedophilic sex offenders. *American Journal of Psychiatry*, 156(5), 786–788.

Risen, C. B. (1995). A guide to taking a sexual history. *Clinical Sexuality, 18*(1), 39–53.

Rösler, A., & Witztum, E. (1998). Treatment of men with paraphilia with a long-acting analogue of gonadotropin-releasing hormone. *New England Journal of Medicine, 338*(7), 416–422.

Rösler, A., & Witztum, E. (2000). Pharmacotherapy of paraphilias in the next millennium. *Behavioral Sciences and the Law, 18*(1), 43–56.

Rush, A. J., Jr., Pincus, H. A., First, M. B., Blacker, D., Endicott, J., Keith, S. J., et al. (2000). *Handbook of psychiatric measures*. Washington, DC: American Psychiatric Association.

Saleh, F. M., Niel, T., & Fishman, M. J. (2004). Treatment of paraphilia in young adults with leuprolide acetate: A preliminary case report series. *Journal of Forensic Sciences, 49*(6), 1–6.

Sbraga, T., & O'Donohue, W. (2004). *The sex addiction workbook*. New York: Harbinger.

Seto, M. C., Cantor, J. M., & Blanchard, R. (2006). Child pornography offenses are a valid diagnostic indicator of pedophilia. *Journal of Abnormal Child Psychology, 115*(3), 610–615.

Shajnfeld, A., & Krueger, R. B. (2006). Reforming (purportedly) non-punitive responses to sexual offending. *Developments in Mental Health Law, 25*, 81–99.

Smith, M. R. (2003). Diagnosis and management of treatment-related osteoporosis in men with prostate carcinoma. *Cancer Supplement, 97*(3), 789–795.

Stein, D. J., Black, D. W., & Pienaar, W. (2000). Sexual disorders not otherwise specified: Compulsive, addictive, or impulsive? *CNS Spectrums, 5*(1), 60–64.

Stein, D. J., Black, D. W., Shapira, N. A., & Spitzer, R. L. (2001). Hypersexual disorder and preoccupation with Internet pornography. *American Journal of Psychiatry, 158*(10), 1590–1594.

Thomson Healthcare. (2006). *Physicians' desk reference* (60th ed.). Montvale, NJ: Author.

Wainberg, M. L., Muench, F., Morgenstern, J., Hollander, E., Irwin, T., Parsons, J. T., et al. (2006). Citalopram vs. placebo in the treatment of compulsive sexual behaviors in gay and bisexual men. *Journal of Clinical Psychiatry, 67*, 1968–1973.

CHAPTER 10

PEDOPHILIA

Psychopathology and Theory

MICHAEL C. SETO

DEFINITION

"Pedophilia" is defined as a persistent sexual interest in prepubescent children, manifested in thoughts, fantasies, urges, sexual arousal, or sexual behavior (American Psychiatric Association, 2000; World Health Organization, 1997).[1] Pedophilia is probably the most commonly discussed paraphilia in the clinical and forensic research literatures. In its strongest form, the pedophilic individual has a strong sexual interest in children who show no signs of secondary sexual development and has no sexual interest in sexually mature adults. Some pedophilic individuals are not exclusive, and exhibit sexual interests in both children and adults. There have also been some descriptions of individuals who are specifically sexually interested in infants (Greenberg, Bradford, & Curry, 1995), and others who are specifically interested in pubescent children (Blanchard & Barbaree, 2005). It is not known whether the sexual preference for infants and the sexual preference for pubescent children represent variants of pedophilia or instead represent different paraphilias.

"Pedophilia" is not synonymous with "sexual offending against children," though the terms are often used interchangeably. Some pedophiles are not known to have ever sexually offended against a child, and many sexual offenders against children are not pedophiles (Seto, Cantor, & Blanchard, 2006; Seto & Lalumière, 2001). Having pedophilia is not illegal, whereas an adult having sexual contact with a prepubescent child usually is. "Pedophilia" refers specifically to a sexual preference for prepubescent children. Forensic mental health professionals are primarily involved with the subset of pedophiles who have been detected for committing sexual offenses involving children; a perusal of online support groups for pedophiles (such as GirlChat or BoyChat) would suggest that other pedophiles are not known to the criminal justice system, though they have engaged in sexual contacts with children. Most of what we know about pedophiles comes from clinical or correctional samples of men who have committed sexual offenses against children.

A core element of any definition of pedophilia is the pubertal status of the children of interest (see Seto, 2002, 2008). It is an important motivation for sexual offenses against children, but it is not the only one. The age of the children of interest matters, because sexual contact with postpubertal adolescents up to a legally defined age is prohibited in most jurisdictions; however, these prohibitions are arbitrary in the sense that they vary from country to country (and state to state in the United States; see *www.ageofconsent. com*). Men who seek sexual contacts with postpubertal adolescents under the legally defined age of consent are engaging in criminal behavior, but they are unlikely to be pedophiles. In contrast to the temporal and cultural relativity of legally defined age of consent, puberty and the concomitant development of secondary sexual characteristics are nonarbitrary and objective events that are reproductively relevant. From a Darwinian perspective, sexually preferring nonfertile, prepubescent children over fertile, sexually mature partners would have been maladaptive in the past (because sexual behavior with prepubescent children could not have led to successful reproduction) and probably continues to be maladaptive now, regardless of place or time; this is consistent with Wakefield's (1992) selectionist definition of mental disorder as a harmful dysfunction.[2] Why pedophilia exists is a major biological puzzle (discussed in further detail by Seto, 2004, 2008).

Age of Onset

Pedophilia can be viewed as a sexual preference, akin to heterosexuality or homosexuality, in the sense that it emerges early in life and appears to be stable across the lifespan. Heterosexual or homosexual orientation typically emerges before the onset of puberty and can be described as a process of discovery (McClintock & Herdt, 1996; Quinsey, 2003). Among heterosexual and homosexual men, a developing awareness of sexual interest in females or males, respectively, typically precedes self-identification as heterosexual or homosexual, and also typically precedes engaging in sexual behavior with opposite-sex or same-sex persons (Savin-Williams & Diamond, 2000). Similarly, there is some evidence that pedophiles discover their sexual interest in younger children during adolescence. Abel and colleagues (1987) found that an onset of sexual interest in children before the age of 18 was reported by 50% of offenders against unrelated boys, 40% of offenders against unrelated girls, and 25% of incest offenders. Similar data were reported by Marshall, Barbaree, and Eccles (1991) in a study of 129 sex offenders with child victims: 41% of offenders against unrelated boys, 35% of offenders against unrelated girls, and 10% of incest offenders reported an onset of "deviant" sexual fantasies before age 20. Only a quarter, however, reported the onset of fantasies taking place before their first sexual offense. Some of the offenders may have been concealing an earlier onset of pedophilic sexual interests. Finally, Freund and Kuban (1993) reported that a sample of 76 adult sex offenders with child victims who admitted having some sexual interest in children recalled that they were first aware of a curiosity to see children in the nude as young adolescents.

Freund and Kuban (1993) also surveyed 78 male students in their study, and they found that many of the students recalled being curious about seeing other children in the nude when they were children themselves. The students, however, reported that they had lost this curiosity by the time they reached puberty. It is possible that pedophiles and nonpedophiles share the same curiosity about seeing other children nude when they were children themselves, but that pedophiles remain fixed at this stage and do not develop a sexual attraction to postpubertal individuals as they reach puberty, like most other men. The possible mechanisms for this shift are unknown. As Quinsey and his colleagues have noted in their evolutionarily informed discussion of pedophilia and other atypical sexual interests, we do not know whether most adult men's sexual preference for adult women is due to the expression of a preference that has been dormant until the activating effects of puberty, to the development of inhibition of interest in other categories of people, or to a social learning process (Quinsey, 2003; Quinsey & Lalumière, 1995; Quinsey, Rice, Harris, & Reid, 1993). Whatever the mechanisms involved, adrenarche and puberty are likely to be the critical events in the emergence of sexual preferences, pedophilic or otherwise (Herdt & McClintock, 2000; see also Weinberg, Williams, & Calhan, 1995, on the onset of foot or shoe fetishism among gay men).

Course

There have not been any longitudinal studies describing the course of pedophilia. It has been inferred that pedophilia is stable across the lifespan, because some older pedophiles report being aware of their sexual interests in children from a young age, and some sex offenders with child victims sexually reoffend decades later (Hanson, Steffy, & Gauthier, 1993). Studies of treatment outcome suggest that sexual arousal patterns can be affected by behavioral conditioning techniques, but this probably reflects increased voluntary control over penile responses rather than stable changes in sexual preferences (Lalumière & Earls, 1992; Lalumière & Quinsey, 1998). Longer-term outcome data are needed. In addition, there is some evidence that the likelihood of sexual recidivism is negatively correlated with offender age, such that older offenders are less likely to reoffend sexually than younger offenders; however, this relationship may be better explained by an overall decrease in sexual arousability, sex drive, and aggression than by an age-related change in pedophilic sexual interests (Barbaree, Blanchard, & Langton, 2003).

Only a minority of children with sexual behavior problems involving peers (e.g., coercive sexual behavior such as touching another child's genitals despite resistance) go on to commit sexual offenses as adolescents, and again only a minority of adolescent sex offenders go on to commit sexual offenses as adults (Abel, Osborn, & Twigg, 1993; Burton, 2000; Carpentier, Silovsky, & Chaffin, 2006; Zolondek, Abel, Northey, & Jordan, 2001). In other words, many children with sexual behavior problems and many adolescent sex offenders desist, which may suggest to some that pedophilic sexual interests wane over time. A more likely explanation is that many children with sexual behavior problems and many adolescent sex offenders are motivated by other factors such as sexual precocity or normative play for children, and opportunism and delinquency in the case of adolescents. Juveniles who persist into adulthood are more likely to be pedophilic. Consistent with this idea, a higher proportion of adult sex offenders against children than of adolescent sex offenders against children are pedophilic (Seto & Lalumière, 2001; Seto, Murphy, Page, & Ennis, 2003).

EPIDEMIOLOGY

The incidence and prevalence of pedophilia in the general population are unknown. Epidemiological surveys with the questions that are needed to identify pedophilia—particularly those having to do with persistence and intensity of sexual thoughts, fantasies, urges, arousal, or behavior involving prepubescent children—have not been conducted. Ever having thoughts of sex with a prepubescent child, or even ever having sexual contact with a prepubescent child, would not be sufficient to meet the diagnostic definition of pedophilia, because a central feature is the persistence of the sexual interest in children.

The following anonymous surveys of predominantly young adult men provide upper-limit estimates of the prevalence of pedophilia in the general population, because they do not include questions about persistence or intensity. For example, the finding that 3% of adult men report ever having fantasized about sex with a prepubescent child would indicate that the prevalence of pedophilia is lower than 3%, because only those with persistent fantasies qualify for the diagnosis of pedophilia (this assumes that individuals are willing to be honest in anonymous surveys and will not deny having fantasies about children in this format). Crepault and Couture (1980) surveyed 94 men about specific sexual fantasies during masturbation or intercourse, and found that 3% reported fantasizing about having sex with a young boy. They also found that 62% reported fantasizing about having sex with a young girl (but this figure is clearly an outlier when compared to similar surveys, so it is hard to know what to make of this result). Briere and Runtz (1989) surveyed 193 male university students and found that 9% reported fantasizing about having sex with a young child (age unspecified), 5% reported masturbating to fantasies of sex with children, and 7% reported some likelihood of having sex with a child if they were guaranteed they would not be punished or identified. The proportion who had sexual fantasies about prepubescent children, masturbated to these fantasies, and acted upon these fantasies was not reported. Templeman and Stinnett (1991) surveyed 60 male college students and found that only 5% expressed an interest in having sex with a girl under the age of 12. Fromuth, Burkhart, and Jones (1991) found that 3% of the 582 college men they surveyed reported having a sexual experience with a child when the respondent was age 16 or older (thereby excluding mutual sexual activity among children). The majority of the contacts involved 4 men who admitted committing multiple offenses. Finally, Smith (1994) found that 6 (3%) of her sample of 183 male college students, under condition of anonymity, reported sexual contact with a prepubescent girl age 12 or younger. None reported sexual contact with a prepubescent boy age 12 or younger. Eleven percent reported sexual contact with an adolescent girl between the ages of 12 and 15 after they had reached the age of 18 themselves. Together, these survey results (after exclusion of the outlier result regarding fantasies about girls reported by Crepeault & Couture, 1980) suggest that sexual fantasies about children and sexual contacts with children are uncommon, and thus suggest that pedophilia appears to be rare in the male population, occurring at a frequency less than 3%.

Men are much more likely than women to be sexually interested in children, even after disparities in the rates at which men and women might be reported and prosecuted in the criminal justice system are taken into account (see Finkelhor & Russell, 1984; Smiljanich & Briere, 1996). That said, some women do have pedophilia (e.g., Chow & Choy, 2002). Fromuth and Conn (1997) conducted a survey of 546 female college students regarding their lifetime sexual experiences with children at least 5 years younger than they were. Four percent acknowledged having at least one such experience, and most (92%) involved physical contact, usually touching and kissing rather than genital contact. The average age of the respondent at the time of the sexual contact with a younger child was 12, and the average age of the child was 6. Women who had had sexual contact with a child were more likely to report any sexual attraction or sexual fantasies about children than were women who denied any such contact.

ASSOCIATED FEATURES

Demographic Characteristics

Over 90% of the pedophiles who have been described in the clinical and correctional literatures are male. Other than this large sex difference, there is a great deal of heterogeneity among pedophiles with regard to other demographic characteristics, such as education, socioeconomic status, and ethnicity. Demographic characteristics depend on the sample being studied. For example, new research on child pornography offenders suggests that they are, as a group, more educated and higher in socioeconomic status than sex offenders who have contact with child victims. This may simply reflect the fact that most child pornography offenders nowadays are apprehended for downloading or distributing illegal pornography content over the Internet, and thus are more likely to own and use computers (e.g., Wilson & Andrews, 2004).

Comorbidity

Studies have often found high levels of other psychopathology—such as anxiety, depression, and personality problems—in clinical and correctional samples of pedophilic sex offenders. Kafka (1997) has suggested that this comorbidity reflects an underlying disturbance in serotonergic brain systems, because serotonin is associated with mood, sexual behavior, and aggression. Dysregulation of serotonin could lead to both disturbed mood and sexual offending. Treatment with antidepressant medications that selectively influence serotonin levels can reduce sex drive, and some clinical investigators have gone further and suggested that treatment with such medications may selectively reduce pedophilic sexual arousal (Fedoroff, 1993; Greenberg & Bradford, 1997; Kafka, 1991). The evidence for this idea is weak, however, and consists almost entirely of case studies or open trials without random assignment of placebo conditions.

Alternatively, the high levels of comorbidity found among identified sex offenders could be attributed to a self-selection effect. One would imagine that more disturbed offenders would end up in clinical settings, and that some or all of the observed comorbid psychopathology may be sequelae of being identified as a pedophile or as a sex offender (Galli et al., 1999; Raymond, Coleman, Ohlerking, Christenson, & Miner, 1999). It is possible that nonclinical and noncriminal samples of pedophiles (e.g., anonymous surveys of self-identified pedophiles) would not show high levels of other psychopathology. Research on the timing of psychological distress and psychiatric symptoms is needed to clarify the association between other psychopathology and pedophilia.

Self-selection may also help explain the observation that pedophilia often co-occurs with a variety of social problems, including family conflict, substance misuse, and nonsexual antisocial behavior (see Seto, 2008). Such individuals are more likely to appear in clinical samples because they (or their family members) seek help, and more likely to appear in correctional samples because they come into conflict with the law. Studies of self-identified pedophiles who are not clinically or criminally involved are needed to determine whether these features are in fact associated with pedophilia per se, or are associated with psychological factors such as impulsivity that cause some individuals to have difficulty regulating their sexual behavior.

Pedophiles are more likely to engage in other paraphilic sexual behavior than men randomly selected from the general population; for example, a substantial proportion of pedophiles have also engaged in exhibitionistic or voyeuristic behavior (Abel, Becker, Cunningham-Rathner, Mittelman, & Rouleau, 1988; Bradford, Boulet, & Pawlak, 1992; Freund, Seto, & Kuban, 1997). A particularly worrisome group of men are those who are both pedophilic and sadistic, because they may be the most likely to physically injure children in their sexual offenses (Chaplin, Rice, & Harris, 1995; Hanson & Bussière, 1998). The comorbidity of paraphilic behavior has implications for understanding the etiology of pedophilia, because it suggests that factors that increase the likelihood of one paraphilia increase the likelihood of others.

FORENSIC ISSUES

Risk Assessment

Validated measures of pedophilia are important in the assessment of risk among sex offenders with child victims. Pedophilic sexual interests are significantly related to risk of sexual recidivism (defined as a new criminal charge or conviction for a sexual offense), whether it is assessed in terms of sexual arousal to depictions of children in the laboratory or inferred from someone's sexual offense history (Hanson & Bussière, 1998; Hanson & Morton-Bourgon, 2004; Rice & Harris, 1997; Seto, Harris, Rice, & Barbaree, 2004). Reflecting this well-established finding, validated risk scales used in sex offender risk assessment, such as the Static-99 and Sex Offender Risk Appraisal Guide (SORAG), incorporate variables that reflect pedophilia (and other atypical sexual interests). The Static-99 contains items referring to the number of prior sexual offenses, having a male victim, and having an unrelated victim (Hanson & Thornton, 2000). All of these items are correlates of pedophilic sexual interests, because pedophilic sex offenders are more likely than nonpedophilic sex offenders to have multiple victims, boy victims, and unrelated child victims (Seto & Lalumière, 2001). The SORAG also includes items regarding prior sexual offenses and the age and gender of victims, and has an additional item regarding phallometrically assessed sexual arousal to children or to sexual violence (Quinsey, Harris, Rice, & Cormier, 2006). Though both risk scales were developed in mixed samples of sex offenders, both have been shown to have comparable predictive accuracy among sex offenders distinguished according to the age of their victims (Bartosh, Garby, Lewis, & Gray, 2003; Harris et al., 2003). Given the high predictive accuracy obtained when scoring reliability is excellent and there is no missing information, scales designed specifically for sex offenders with pedophilia may not yield significantly greater accuracy. An empirical question, however, is whether risk scales can be developed for pedophiles who are not known to have committed any sexual offenses.

Risk Management

Unfortunately, there is only weak evidence that treatment can reduce recidivism among sex offenders, whether pedophilic or nonpedophilic (see Camilleri & Quinsey, Chapter

11, this volume). Quantitative reviews find a significant difference in recidivism (new offenses) between treated sex offenders and comparison sex offenders (e.g., men who refuse to participate in treatment), but the methodologically strongest studies (those that use random assignment to treatment and comparison groups) have found no significant differences in recidivism (Hanson et al., 2002). The question of whether treatment has been demonstrated to be efficacious in reducing reoffending is still hotly debated, but the one study to date that has met conventional scientific standards for strong inference—by evaluating a credible treatment program, using random assignment to conditions, and employing multiple measures of outcome—found no significant difference between treated and untreated sex offenders (Marques, Wiederanders, Day, Nelson, & van Ommeren, 2005).

Innovative thinking about new treatment approaches for both pedophilia and pedophilic sex offenders is needed. Until such treatments have been implemented and evaluated, effective risk management strategies are needed in order to improve public safety. A range of options is available for sex offenders, from incapacitation for the highest-risk individuals to supervision in the community and prevention efforts (these options are discussed in more detail in Seto, 2008). Incapacitation can reduce the number of sexual offenses that occur, but it is very expensive, and there are civil rights concerns about false positives (incorrectly identifying persons as likely to reoffend when they will not reoffend). Thus incapacitation is only suitable for the highest-risk pedophilic offenders in any jurisdiction, and high risk is preferably defined by an empirically identified rather than by a legislative threshold. There is some support for community monitoring models such as the Circles of Support and Accountability, but more rigorous evaluations are needed; Wilson, Picheca, and Prinzo (2005) found that offenders who were involved in Circles of Support and Accountability reoffended at a lower rate than a matched comparison group. In contrast, there is no evidence that traditional supervision by probation or parole officers has an impact on recidivism (Andrews et al., 1990).

Finally, there is evidence that school-based sexual abuse prevention programs significantly increase children's knowledge about sexual abuse and protection strategies, both immediately after these programs end and after follow-up (Rispens, Aleman, & Goudena, 1997). The logic of such school-based programs, consistent with that of other crime prevention programs, is that children who learn the knowledge and skills are less susceptible to becoming the victims of a sexual offense or more likely to disclose sexual offending sooner, thereby limiting the extent of their own and possibly others' victimization. One study found that women who had participated in school-based sexual abuse prevention programs as girls were less likely to have been the victims of sexual offenses later in life than those who had not participated in such programs (Gibson & Leitenberg, 2000). Although the women were not randomly assigned to receive the prevention programming, programs were implemented on a schoolwide basis, and it is unlikely that the programs had knowledge of the risk exposure of children in particular schools. Nonetheless, more rigorous evaluations of sexual abuse prevention programs are needed before they can be relied on as part of an overall response to the problem of child sexual abuse.

In addition, some innovative prevention programs targeting men at risk of sexual offending have been implemented but not yet evaluated. Stop It Now!, a nonprofit organization in the United States, uses marketing techniques in efforts to reach individuals who are at risk of committing sexual offenses against children and convince them to seek assistance (*www.stopitnow.com*). Similarly, the Berlin Prevention Project used billboard and television advertising to reach German men who were sexually interested in children and persuade them to participate in their cognitive-behavioral treatment program (Beier, Ahler, Schaefer, & Feelgood, 2006). The logic of these secondary prevention programs is to increase the motivation of at-risk men to refrain from committing sexual offenses, and to give them skills for coping with their sexual attraction to children.

EXPLANATIONS OF PEDOPHILIA

In this section, I review three major explanations of the etiology of pedophilia. I do not cover explanations of sexual offending against children, which often include pedophilia as an important factor. These explanations—which include Finkelhor's (1984) preconditions model, Hall and Hirschman's (1992) quadripartite model, Marshall and Barbaree's (1990) integrated model, and Ward and Siegert's (2002) pathways model—are reviewed and critiqued by Ward, Polaschek, and Beech (2006) and by Seto (2008).

Some of this review covers literature reviewed in other "Psychopathology and Theory" chapters in this volume, because much of the etiological thinking has been concerned with paraphilias in general. At the same time, recent research on the specific roles of sexual abuse history and neurodevelopmental perturbations in the development of pedophilia is highlighted.

Learning

A number of different investigators have proposed that learning, through masturbatory conditioning, plays a role in the development of pedophilia (Laws & Marshall, 1990; McGuire, Carlisle, & Young, 1965). Many people have their initial sexual experiences during childhood with other children, as part of normative sexual play. Some individuals pair the physical cues of their young partners—such as small body size, androgynous shape, and absence of secondary sexual characteristics—with the sexual pleasure elicited by these initial experiences, and eventually learn to associate these cues with the powerful reinforcement of orgasm through repeated masturbation to memories of childhood sexual experiences. Others have the same initial sexual experiences as children, but they continue to have sexual experiences with similar-age peers and do not develop a conditioned response to prepubescent children. Pedophiles are somehow blocked in this shift of age preferences, which suggests that some individuals are predisposed to be affected by this learning process. Candidate predispositions that have been proposed include poor parent–child attachment, experiences of abuse or neglect, high sex drive, and aggressiveness (for a review, see Ward et al., 2006).

Experimental data collected in the laboratory suggest, however, that the conditionability of sexual arousal in humans is not strong. Rachman (1966) and Rachman and Hodgson (1968) reported that normal volunteers showed significantly increased sexual arousal to pictures of boots after repeated pairings with a sexual stimulus, but these studies did not have rigorous control conditions. Both Lalumière and Quinsey (1998) and Hoffmann, Janssen, and Turner (2004) found a significant effect of conditioning on sexual arousal among nonoffending men, while Plaud and Martini (1999) reported mixed results in a conditioning study of nine male volunteers. For example, Lalumière and Quinsey presented 10 nonoffending male volunteers with 11 pairings of a slide of a moderately attractive, partially nude woman with a highly arousing videotaped scene depicting heterosexual intercourse, while another 10 men were exposed to 11 presentations of the slide alone. The men in the paired condition showed a 10% increase in their sexual arousal to the slide; the men in the unpaired condition showed a 11% decrease in their sexual arousal to the slide, which was interpreted by Lalumière and Quinsey as evidence of habituation.

The treatment outcome literature on reconditioning of sexual arousal can also inform our understanding of the role of learning in the etiology of pedophilia. Although this literature does not tell us whether pedophilia develops through learning, it does tell us about the potential impact of conditioning on sexual arousal patterns. Aversive conditioning procedures are typically used to suppress sexual arousal to sexual stimuli depicting children, whereas masturbatory reconditioning procedures are used to enhance sexual arousal to sexual stimuli depicting adults. In aversion procedures, unpleasant stimuli such as ammonia are paired with repeated presentations of sexual stimuli depicting children. Masturbatory reconditioning involves associating sexual arousal and orgasm with stimuli depicting adults; techniques include thematic shift, in which the subject masturbates to a pedophilic sexual fantasy until the point of orgasm, then switches to a sexual fantasy involving an adult.

The efficacy of conditioning approaches for changing sexual arousal patterns is reviewed by Barbaree and Seto (1997), Seto (2008), and Camilleri and Quinsey (Chapter 11, this volume). Overall, this research suggests that behavioral methods can have an effect on the sexual arousal of sex offenders, but it is unclear how long these changes are maintained, what mechanisms mediate the changes in sexual arousal patterns, and whether the changes reflect an actual shift in sexual preference or the learning of greater voluntary control over sexual arousal (Lalumière & Earls, 1992; Mahoney & Strassberg, 1991). Overall, the evidence is weak that conditioning plays an important role in the etiology of pedophilia.

Cycle of Sexual Abuse

There is evidence to suggest that pedophilic sex offenders are more likely to have experienced sexual abuse as a child than other sex offenders (Lalumière, Seto, & Jespersen, 2006). Adult sex offenders who report having been sexually abused are more likely to admit being sexually aroused by children, and adolescent sex offenders who were sexually abused show relatively greater sexual arousal to children than those who were not abused (Becker, Hunter, Stein, & Kaplan, 1989; Becker, Kaplan, & Tenke, 1992; Fedoroff & Pinkus, 1996; Freund, Watson, & Dickey, 1990). In addition, sexual abuse history is correlated with having a boy victim among both adolescent and adult sex offenders (Becker et al., 1992; Hanson & Slater, 1988; Hilliker, 1997; Kaufman, Hilliker, & Daleidin, 1996; Worling, 1995; but not Aylwin, Studer, Reddon, & Clelland, 2003).

The association with childhood sexual abuse seems to be specific to pedophilia (Lee, Jackson, Pattison, & Ward, 2002). Lee et al. compared 64 adult sex offenders with 33 nonviolent offenders, and further distinguished the sex offenders according to the paraphilias they had: pedophilia, biastophilia (a sexual preference for sexual coercion), exhibitionism, and multiple paraphilias. Childhood emotional abuse and childhood behavior problems were common across the paraphilia subgroups, and were more prevalent in all the subgroups than among the nonviolent offenders. Childhood sexual abuse was specifically associated with pedophilia, because it did not distinguish exhibitionists or biastophiles from the combined group of other sex offenders and nonviolent offenders, whereas it did distinguish pedophiles from this combined group. It is not clear whether the association between childhood sexual abuse and pedophilia can be found outside of clinical or correctional samples, however, because Fromuth and colleagues (1991) found no difference in sexual abuse history between male students who admitted to having sexual contact with a child and those who denied such contact.

The large majority of sexually abused children do not go on to offend, so there must be individual differences in one's vulnerability for developing pedophilia. The most obvious vulnerability is being male, because most sex offenders against children are male, while the majority of child victims of sexual offenses are female. It has also been suggested that aspects of the sexual offenses—such as the victim–perpetrator relationship, type of sexual acts, and the duration and timing of the sexual abuse—are relevant to predicting who will go on to sexually offend against children (Burton, 2003; Finkelhor, 1979; Hunter, Figueredo, Malamuth, & Becker, 2003; Knight & Prentky, 1993). Consistent with this view, Burton, Miller, and Tai Shill (2002) found that sexually abused youth were much more likely to later commit sexual offenses themselves if they had both male and female perpetrators, a perpetrator was related to the youth, a perpetrator used violence during the offenses, the abuse took place over several years, and the abuse included sexual penetration.

There is evidence from several different lines of research that there is an association between childhood sexual abuse and later sexual offending. What is not clear, however, is the causality of the relationship. Childhood sexual abuse may affect the sociosexual development of boys so that they are more likely to develop pedophilia, or more likely to engage in antisocial behavior that includes sexual offending against children. Alternatively, childhood sexual abuse and later sexual offending may both be correlated with a third variable; for example, as discussed next, an underlying neurodevelopmental disorder may both increase vulnerability to being the victim of a sexual offense as a child, and the likelihood of committing sexual offenses in adolescence or adulthood. Another possibility is that the association between childhood sexual abuse and later sexual offending is genetically mediated. A large proportion of sexually abused children are victims of their male relatives, so the association may represent familiality of pedophilia or another predisposition to sexual offending against children. There have not been genetically informative studies, however, except for one study on the familiality of paraphilias in a small sample of men (Gaffney, Lurie, & Berlin, 1984).

Neurodevelopmental Disorder

The strongest etiological evidence regarding pedophilia comes from a recent line of neurodevelopmental research. Brain abnormalities have long been suspected as a cause of pedophilia. Late in the 19th century, Krafft-Ebing (1886/1999) observed that an autopsy of a homicidal pedophile's brain showed "morbid changes of the frontal lobes, of the first and second temporal convolutions, and of a part of the occipital convolutions" (p. 86). Other case studies have suggested that brain injuries are associated with pedophilic sexual behaviors, including collection of child pornography and sexual contacts with children (e.g., Burns & Swerdlow, 2003; Casanova, Mannheim, & Kruesi, 2002). The case described by Burns and Swerdlow (2003) is particularly interesting, because the male patient was in his 40s; there was no evidence of a prior sexual interest in children; and his interest in children disappeared upon the removal of a right orbito-frontal tumor. At the same time, the orbito-frontal region is associated with behavioral inhibition, so it is possible that the man had a preexisting sexual interest in children that was never expressed or was successfully concealed until it became apparent as the brain tumor grew.

Estimates of brain functioning, as indices of neurodevelopmental health, can be obtained both directly and indirectly. Indirectly, researchers have compared the scores of sex offenders with child victims with other groups of men on measures of intelligence and other aspects of cognitive functioning. Some studies have found that sex offenders with child victims are significantly lower in intelligence than other offenders (Ellis & Brancale, 1956; Hucker et al., 1986; Langevin, Wortzman, Wright, & Handy, 1989), while other studies have not found differences between these groups on standardized neuropsychological test batteries (Hucker et al., 1986). Much of this research has been limited by small sample sizes and mixed samples of sex offenders and comparison subjects. Cantor, Blanchard, Robichaud, and Christensen (2005) addressed these limitations by conducting a meta-analysis of 236 independent samples of offenders; they found a significant difference between sex offenders and other men, with sex offenders scoring lower on measures of intelligence than other offenders, who in turn scored lower than nonoffending controls. Focusing on the sex offenders, Cantor and colleagues found that intelligence score was related to the proportion of these offenders who were pedophilic: Sex offenders with child victims scored lower than sex offenders without any child victims, and there was a positive relationship between the age cutoff used to define child victims and mean intelligence score. In other words, samples composed of men who offended against younger children tended to produce lower mean IQ scores than samples composed of men who offended against older children.

The same research group demonstrated that men diagnosed as pedophilic on the basis of their sexual histories and phallometric responding scored lower on intelligence tests and on tests of verbal and visual–spatial memory than nonpedophilic men (Cantor et al., 2004). Moreover, the offenders' number of child victims under the age of 12 was significantly and negatively related to total intelligence score, whereas their number of older victims was not significantly (though still negatively) related to this score. In contrast, the number of adult sexual partners reported by the men was positively and significantly correlated with intelligence score, indicating that the relationship between sexual victim history and intelligence score could not be explained by a relationship between overall sexual activity and intelligence.

Pedophilic sex offenders are more likely to report experiencing head injuries before the age of age 13 than other offenders, but do not differ in reports of head injuries experienced after age 13 (Blanchard et al., 2002, 2003). The fact that there was no difference in reports of head injuries after age 13 between pedophilic sex offenders and other offenders argues against the possibility that pedophiles have a retrospective reporting bias in recalling head injuries, because there would be no reason to think that head injuries before the age of 13 are somehow more socially desirable or memorable than head injuries after this age. The fact that there was no difference after age 13 also suggests a critical age window in terms of the impact of head injury on the development of sexual interests. This is an intriguing possibility, because of other work suggesting that childhood and early adolescence is critical in the development of sexual preferences. This speculation assumes that the relationship between head injury and pedophilia is causal. It is possible that a third variable explains both the higher incidence of head injury and pedophilia; for example, prenatal neurodevelopmental perturbations may both increase accident-proneness (resulting in a higher likelihood of experiencing a head injury) and affect the development of sexual preferences.

Given the consistent evidence for neurodevelopmental factors in the etiology of pedophilia, an interesting question is how these differences in cognitive functioning are manifested in the brain. Researchers have attempted to directly assess brain function or structure, especially in the frontal (associated with executive functioning) and temporal (associated with emotional processing and regulation of sexual behavior) regions. Using computerized tomography, Hucker and colleagues (1986) found significant temporal abnormalities in a comparison of 29 pedophilic sex offenders and 12 controls, but this finding was not confirmed by the same research group in subsequent studies with larger samples (Langevin, Wortzman, Dickey, Wright, & Handy, 1988; Langevin et al., 1989). Wright, Nobrega, Langevin, and Wortzman (1990) found that a mixed group of 64 sex offenders (30 with child victims and 34 with adult female victims) had smaller cross-sectional areas in the left frontal and left temporal regions of the brain, compared with 12 nonsexually violent offenders. On the other hand, Cantor and colleagues (2006) compared the magnetic resonance images of 65 pedophilic men and 63 nonpedophilic controls, and found that the two groups did not significantly differ in the brain volumes of either the frontal or temporal regions. Instead, the two groups differed significantly in white matter volume, particularly the association tracts of the superior occipito-frontal fasciculus and right arcuate fasciculus. These tracts connect structures in the frontal and occipital regions of the brain that are implicated in the recognition of visual stimuli as sexual in nature.

There is consistent evidence that pedophilia is a neurodevelopmental disorder, based on neuropsychological testing, educational histories, head injury history, and structural neuroimaging. The deeper questions are what causes the neurodevelopmental perturbations and why the perturbations manifest themselves as pedophilia rather than another paraphilia.

SUMMARY AND FUTURE DIRECTIONS

Some encouraging progress has been made in our understanding of pedophilia, but many unanswered questions remain. Probably because of the importance of pedophilia in the risk assessment of sex offenders, multiple methods of validly assessing pedophilic sexual interests have been developed (see Camilleri & Quinsey, Chapter 11, this volume). Developmentally sensitive assessment methods are needed, however, to study the course of pedophilia over the lifespan—especially to test the hypothesis that this sexual preference emerges around puberty and is stable over time. In addition, we need epidemiological data to determine the incidence and prevalence of pedophilia, which would require assessing pedophilic thoughts, fantasies, urges, arousal, and behavior outside of convenience samples drawn from clinical or correctional settings. Such assessment would require obtaining large representative samples and asking them highly sensitive questions about the frequency and intensity of their sexual thoughts, fantasies, urges, arousal, and behavior involving prepubescent children. Such research would be difficult to conduct but would be invaluable to understanding pedophilia. Anonymous surveys of self-identified pedophiles (e.g., using the Internet) could also shed light on the nature and development of pedophilia, even though such studies are likely to rely on self-report alone and therefore to be vulnerable to socially desirable responding. Of most interest are studies that attempt to replicate findings from research involving pedophilic sex offenders. For example, are self-identified pedophiles more likely to experience head injuries prior to the age of 13, or more likely to fail a grade or be placed in a special education class, when compared to the general population? Anonymous surveys of self-identified pedophiles could also help address the question of whether pedophilia is necessarily comorbid with other psychopathology and interpersonal difficulties.

An interesting theoretical question is whether sexual age preferences can be represented on a continuum, such that most adults are attracted to sexually mature persons, but some individuals are attracted to pubescent children, prepubescent children, or infants in varying degrees. These age preferences may instead represent different "taxa" (plural of "taxon"—i.e., natural group), and it is possible that each taxon involves a different etiological pathway. Thus the causes of pedophilia may differ from the causes of hebephilia (sexual preferences for pubescent children), nepiophilia (sexual preference for infants), or gerontophilia (sexual preference for elderly persons). It is also plausible that there are multiple etiological pathways for atypical age preferences such as pedophilia, including the genetic transmission of predispositions, poor maternal health, fetal exposure to toxins or infections, and early head injuries (see Seto, 2008).

In terms of etiological thinking, research on the link between childhood sexual abuse and pedophilia highlights a major direction for further investigation. There is a specific association for both adolescent and adult sex offenders against children, but the mechanisms underlying this link have not been elucidated (Lalumière et al., 2006; Seto & Lalumière, 2006), and it is not clear whether the relationship exists outside clinical or correctional settings (Fromuth et al., 1991). Future research is needed to determine whether an association exists between childhood sexual abuse and subsequent sexual interest in children (not just sexual offending against children) in nonclinical, noncorrectional samples. Other research is needed to elucidate the mechanisms that might underlie this link. Genetically informative longitudinal studies of individuals who sexually abuse related children, and the children as they grow up, would be particularly valuable. Evidence to support a causal effect of childhood sexual abuse on pedophilia or on sexual offending against children would highlight the importance of child sexual abuse prevention efforts, because such efforts could have both immediate benefits (preventing sexual offenses against the children who participate in primary or secondary prevention programs) and future benefits (preventing future sexual offenses when at-risk children grow up).

Evidence that pedophilia is a neurodevelopmental disorder (as are schizophrenia, autism, and some of the other major mental disorders) is rapidly accumulating, including the study by Cantor and colleagues (2006) demonstrating that pedophilic men have less white matter in the superior occipito-frontal fasciculus and the right arcuate fasciculus. Confirmation of this structural finding, and extension of this work via functional neuroimaging, would contribute to a better understanding of the neural substrates involved in pedophilia. It is possible that the same neural systems are involved in the development and regulation of other paraphilias, and that the specific timing, location, and nature of neurodevelopmental perturbations influence which paraphilias subsequently develop. Once this is better understood, the next major questions are what causes these neurodevelopmental perturbations and how they may be prevented.

NOTES

1. The 1994 DSM-IV diagnostic criteria were criticized by O'Donohue, Regev, and Hagstrom (2000), who noted that the criteria had not been evaluated in field trials, so the reliability and

validity of the diagnosis were not known. Recent research has shown that different assessment methods identify overlapping, but not identical, subsets of sex offenders against children (Kingston, Moulden, & Firestone, 2005). Thus integrating the literature on pedophilia is complicated by the fact that different researchers have used different assessment methods.

2. From this perspective, the central feature of any set of diagnostic criteria for pedophilia is a persistent sexual preference for prepubescent children *when sexually mature partners are potentially available*—whether that interest is reflected in recurrent self-reported thoughts, fantasies, or urges about sexual contact with children; manifested in greater sexual arousal to stimuli depicting prepubescent children than to stimuli depicting adults; or manifested in a pattern of sexual behavior involving children, including possession of child pornography and sexual contacts with children (Seto, Cantor, & Blanchard, 2006; Seto & Lalumière, 2001). Whether the individual is distressed by this sexual interest, or whether the sexual interests causes interpersonal or other difficulties, is not germane.

AUTHOR'S NOTE

Some of the text in this chapter is adapted from a review article I wrote on pedophilia and sexual offending against children (Seto, 2004). In addition, text is adapted with permission from Seto (2008). Copyright 2008 by the American Psychological Association. The use of APA information does not imply endorsement by APA.

REFERENCES

Abel, G. G., Becker, J. V., Cunningham-Rathner, J., Mittelman, M., & Rouleau, J. L. (1988). Multiple paraphilic diagnoses among sex offenders. *Bulletin of the American Academy of Psychiatry and the Law, 16*, 153–168.

Abel, G. G., Becker, J. V., Mittelman, M., Cunningham-Rathner, J., Rouleau, J. L., & Murphy, W. D. (1987). Self-reported sex crimes of nonincarcerated paraphiliacs. *Journal of Interpersonal Violence, 2*, 3–25.

Abel, G. G., Osborn, C. A., & Twigg, D. A. (1993). Sexual assault through the life span: Adult offenders with juvenile histories. In H. E. Barbaree, W. L. Marshall, & S. M. Hudson (Eds.), *The juvenile sex offender* (pp. 104–117). New York: Guilford Press.

American Psychiatric Association. (2000). *Diagnostic and statistical manual of mental disorders* (4th ed., text rev.). Washington, DC: Author.

Andrews, D. A., Zinger, I., Hoge, R. D., Bonta, J., Gendreau, P., & Cullen, F. T. (1990). Does correctional treatment work?: A clinically relevant and psychologically informed meta-analysis. *Criminology, 28*, 369–417.

Aylwin, A. S., Studer, L. H., Reddon, J. R., & Clelland, S. R. (2003). Abuse prevalence and victim gender among adult and adolescent child molesters. *International Journal of Law and Psychiatry, 26*, 179–190.

Barbaree, H. E., Blanchard, R., & Langton, C. M. (2003). The development of sexual aggression through the life span: The effect of age on sexual arousal and recidivism among sex offenders. In R. Prentky, E. Janus, & M. C. Seto (Eds.), *Sexually coercive behavior: Understanding and management* (pp. 59–71). New York: New York Academy of Sciences.

Barbaree, H. E., & Seto, M. C. (1997). Pedophilia: Assessment and treatment. In D. R. Laws & W. T. O'Donohue (Eds.), *Sexual deviance: Theory, assessment, and treatment* (pp. 175–193). New York: Guilford Press.

Bartosh, D. L., Garby, T., Lewis, D., & Gray, S. (2003). Differences in the predictive validity of actuarial risk assessments in relation to sex offender type. *International Journal of Offender Therapy and Comparative Criminology, 47*, 422–438.

Becker, J. V., Hunter, J., Stein, R., & Kaplan, M. S. (1989). Factors associated with erectile response in adolescent sex offenders. *Journal of Psychopathology and Behavioral Assessment, 11*, 353–362.

Becker, J. V., Kaplan, M. S., & Tenke, C. E. (1992). The relationship of abuse history, denial and erectile response profiles of adolescent sexual perpetrators. *Behavior Therapy, 23*, 87–97.

Beier, K. M., Ahlers, C. J., Schaefer, G. A., & Feelgood, S. (2006, September). *The Berlin primary prevention approach: A treatment program for pedophiles.* Paper presented at the 9th Conference of the International Association for the Treatment of Sexual Offenders, Hamburg, Germany.

Blanchard, R., & Barbaree, H. E. (2005). The strength of sexual arousal as a function of the age of the sex offender: Comparisons among pedophiles, hebephiles, and teleiophiles. *Sexual Abuse: A Journal of Research and Treatment, 17*, 441–456.

Blanchard, R., Christensen, B. K., Strong, S. M., Cantor, J. M., Kuban, M. E., Klassen, P., et al. (2002). Retrospective self-reports of childhood accidents causing unconsciousness in phallometrically diagnosed pedophiles. *Archives of Sexual Behavior, 31*, 511–526.

Blanchard, R., Kuban, M. E., Klassen, P., Dickey, R., Christensen, B. K., Cantor, J. M., et al. (2003). Self-reported head injuries before and after age 13 in pedophilic and nonpedophilic men referred for clinical assessment. *Archives of Sexual Behavior, 32*, 573–581.

Bradford, J. M., Boulet, J., & Pawlak, A. (1992). The paraphilias: A multiplicity of deviant behaviours. *Canadian Journal of Psychiatry, 37*, 104–108.

Briere, J., & Runtz, M. (1989). University males' sexual interest in children: Predicting potential indices of "pedophilia" in a non-forensic sample. *Child Abuse and Neglect, 13*, 65–75.

Burns, J. M., & Swerdlow, R. H. (2003). Right orbitofrontal tumor with pedophilia symptom and constructional apraxia sign. *Archives of Neurology, 60*, 437–440.

Burton, D. L. (2003). Male adolescents: Sexual victimization and subsequent sexual abuse. *Child and Adolescent Social Work Journal, 20*, 277–296.

Burton, D. L., Miller, D. L., & Tai Shill, C. (2002). A social learning theory comparison of the sexual victimization of adolescent sexual offenders and nonsexual offending male delinquents. *Child Abuse and Neglect, 26*, 893–907.

Cantor, J. M., Blanchard, R., Christensen, B. K., Dickey, R., Klassen, P. E., Beckstead, A. L., et al. (2004). Intelligence, memory, and handedness in pedophilia. *Neuropsychology, 18*, 3–14.

Cantor, J. M., Blanchard, R., Robichaud, L. K., & Christensen, B. K. (2005). Quantitative reanalysis of aggregate data on IQ in sexual offenders. *Psychological Bulletin, 131*, 555–568.

Cantor, J. M., Kabani, N., Christensen, B. K., Zipursky, R. B., Barbaree, H. E., Dickey, R., et al. (2006). *Cerebral white matter deficiencies in pedophilic men.* Manuscript submitted for publication.

Carpentier, M. Y., Silovsky, J., & Chaffin, M. (2006). Randomized trial of treatment for children with sexual behavior problems: Ten-year follow-up. *Journal of Consulting and Clinical Psychology, 74*, 482–488.

Casanova, M. F., Mannheim, G., & Kruesi, M. (2002). Hippocampal pathology in two mentally ill paraphiliacs. *Psychiatry Research Neuroimaging, 115*, 79–89.

Chaplin, T. C., Rice, M. E., & Harris, G. T. (1995). Salient victim suffering and the sexual responses of child molesters. *Journal of Consulting and Clinical Psychology, 63*, 249–255.

Chow, E. W. C., & Choy, A. L. (2002). Clinical characteristics and treatment response to SSRI in a female pedophile. *Archives of Sexual Behavior, 31*, 211–215.

Crepault, C., & Couture, M. (1980). Men's erotic fantasies. *Archives of Sexual Behavior, 9*, 565–581.

Ellis, A., & Brancale, R. (1956). *The psychology of sex offenders.* Springfield, IL: Thomas.

Fedoroff, J. P. (1993). Serotonergic drug treatment of deviant sexual interests. *Annals of Sex Research, 6*, 105–121.

Fedoroff, J. P., & Pinkus, S. (1996). The genesis of pedophilia: Testing the "abuse to abuser" hypothesis. *Journal of Offender Rehabilitation, 23*, 85–101.

Finkelhor, D. (1979). What's wrong with sex between adults and children?: Ethics and the problem of sexual abuse. *American Journal of Orthopsychiatry, 49*, 692–697.

Finkelhor, D. (Ed.). (1984). *Child sexual abuse: New theory and research.* New York: Free Press.

Finkelhor, D., & Russell, D. (1984). Women as perpetrators: Review of the evidence. In D. Finkelhor (Ed.), *Child sexual abuse: New theory and research* (pp. 171–187). New York: Free Press.

Freund, K., & Kuban, M. (1993). Toward a testable developmental model of pedophilia: The development of erotic age preference. *Child Abuse and Neglect, 17*, 315–324.

Freund, K., Seto, M. C., & Kuban, M. (1997). Frotteurism: The theory of courtship disorder. In D. R. Laws & W. T. O'Donohue (Eds.), *Sexual deviance: Theory, assessment, and treatment* (pp. 111–130). New York: Guilford Press.

Freund, K., Watson, R., & Dickey, R. (1990). Does sexual abuse in childhood cause pedophilia?: An exploratory study. *Archives of Sexual Behavior, 19*, 557–568.

Fromuth, M. E., Burkhart, B. R., & Jones, C. W. (1991). Hidden child molestation: An investigation of adolescent perpetrators in a nonclinical sample. *Journal of Interpersonal Violence, 6*, 376–384.

Fromuth, M. E., & Conn, V. E. (1997). Hidden perpetrators: Sexual molestation in a nonclinical sample of college women. *Journal of Interpersonal Violence, 12*, 456–465.

Gaffney, G. R., Lurie, S. F., & Berlin, F. S. (1984). Is there familial transmission of pedophilia? *Journal of Nervous and Mental Disease, 172*, 546–548.

Galli, V., McElroy, S. L., Soutullo, C. A., Kizer, D., Raute, N., Keck, P. E., Jr., et al. (1999). The psychiatric diagnoses of twenty-two adolescents who have sexually molested other children. *Comprehensive Psychiatry, 40*, 85–88.

Gibson, L. E., & Leitenberg, H. (2000). Child sexual abuse prevention programs: Do they decrease the occurrence of child sexual abuse? *Child Abuse and Neglect, 24*, 1115–1125.

Greenberg, D. M., & Bradford, J. M. W. (1997). Treatment of the paraphilic disorders: A review of the role of selective serotonin reuptake inhibitors. *Sexual Abuse: Journal of Research and Treatment, 9*, 349–361.

Greenberg, D. M., Bradford, J., & Curry, S. (1995). Infantophilia—a new subcategory of pedophilia?: A preliminary study. *Bulletin of the American Academy of Psychiatry and the Law, 23*, 63–71.

Hall, G. C. N., & Hirschman, R. (1992). Sexual aggression against children: A conceptual perspective of etiology. *Criminal Justice and Behavior, 19*, 8–23.

Hanson, R. K., & Bussière, M. T. (1998). Predicting relapse: A meta-analysis of sexual offender recidivism studies. *Journal of Consulting and Clinical Psychology, 66*, 348–362.

Hanson, R. K., Gordon, A., Harris, A. J. R., Marques, J. K., Murphy, W., Quinsey, V. L., et al. (2002). First report of the Collaborative Outcome Data Project on the Effectiveness of Treatment for Sex Offenders. *Sexual Abuse: A Journal of Research and Treatment, 14*, 169–194.

Hanson, R. K., & Morton-Bourgon, K. (2004). *Predictors of sexual recidivism: An updated meta-analysis* (User Report No. 2004-2). Ottawa: Department of the Solicitor General of Canada.

Hanson, R. K., & Slater, S. (1988). Sexual victimization in the history of child molesters: A review. *Annals of Sex Research, 1*, 485–499.

Hanson, R. K., Steffy, R. A., & Gauthier, R. (1993). Long-term recidivism of child molesters. *Journal of Consulting and Clinical Psychology, 61*, 646–652.

Hanson, R. K., & Thornton, D. (2000). Improving risk assessments for sex offenders: A comparison of three actuarial scales. *Law and Human Behavior, 24*, 119–136.

Harris, G. T., Rice, M. E., Quinsey, V. L., Lalumière, M. L., Boer, D., & Lang, C. (2003). A multisite comparison of actuarial risk instruments for sex offenders. *Psychological Assessment, 15*, 413–425.

Herdt, G., & McClintock, M. (2000). The magical age of 10. *Archives of Sexual Behavior, 29*, 587–606.

Hilliker, D. R. (1997). The relationship between childhood sexual abuse and juvenile sexual offending: Victim to victimizer (Doctoral dissertation, Ohio State University, 1997). *Dissertation Abstracts International, 58*(5-B), 2678B. (UMI No. 9731636)

Hoffmann, H., Janssen, E., & Turner, S. L. (2004). Classical conditioning of sexual arousal in women and men: Effects of varying awareness and biological relevance of the conditioned stimulus. *Archives of Sexual Behavior, 33*, 43–53.

Hucker, S., Langevin, R., Wortzman, G., Bain, J., Handy, L., Chambers, J., et al. (1986). Neuropsychological impairment in pedophiles. *Canadian Journal of Behavioural Science, 18*, 440–448.

Hunter, J. A., Jr., Figueredo, A. J., Malamuth, N. M., & Becker, J. V. (2003). Juvenile sex offenders: Toward the development of a typology. *Sexual Abuse: A Journal of Research and Treatment, 15*, 27–48.

Kafka, M. P. (1991). Successful antidepressant treatment of nonparaphilic sexual addictions and paraphilias in men. *Journal of Clinical Psychiatry, 52*, 60–65.

Kafka, M. P. (1997). A monoamine hypothesis for the pathophysiology of paraphilic disorders. *Archives of Sexual Behavior, 26*, 343–358.

Kaufman, K. L., Hilliker, D. R., & Daleiden, E. L. (1996). Subgroup differences in the modus operandi of adolescent sexual offenders. *Child Maltreatment, 1*, 17–24.

Kingston, D., Moulden, H., & Firestone, P. (2005). *A pedophilic interest comparison of child molesters*. Poster presented at the 24th Annual Conference of the Association for the Treatment of Sexual Abusers, Salt Lake City, UT.

Knight, R. A., & Prentky, R. A. (1993). Exploring characteristics for classifying juvenile sex offenders. In H. E. Barbaree, W. L. Marshall, & S. M. Hudson (Eds.), *The juvenile sex offender* (pp. 45–83). New York: Guilford Press.

Krafft-Ebing, R. von. (1999). *Psychopathia sexualis* (12th ed.). Burbank, CA: Bloat. (Original work published 1886)

Lalumière, M. L., & Earls, C. M. (1992). Voluntary control of penile responses as a function of stimulus duration and instructions. *Behavioral Assessment, 14*, 121–132.

Lalumière, M. L., & Quinsey, V. L. (1998). Pavlovian conditioning of sexual interests in human males. *Archives of Sexual Behavior, 27*, 241–252.

Lalumière, M. L., Seto, M. C., & Jespersen, (2006, March). *The link between childhood sexual abuse and sexual offending: A meta-analysis*. Paper presented at the American Psychology–Law Society Conference, St. Petersburg, FL.

Langevin, R., Wortzman, G., Dickey, R., Wright, P., & Handy, L. (1988). Neuropsychological impairment in incest offenders. *Annals of Sex Research, 1*, 401–415.

Langevin, R., Wortzman, G., Wright, P., & Handy, L. (1989). Studies of brain damage and dysfunction in sex offenders. *Annals of Sex Research, 2*, 163–179.

Laws, D. R., & Marshall, W. L. (1990). A conditioning theory of the etiology and maintenance of deviant sexual preference and behavior. In W. L. Marshall, D. R. Laws, & H. E. Barbaree. (Eds.), *Handbook of sexual assault: Issues, theories, and treatment of the offender* (pp. 209–230). New York: Plenum Press.

Lee, J. K. P., Jackson, H. J., Pattison, P., & Ward, T. (2002). Developmental risk factors for sexual offending. *Child Abuse and Neglect, 26*, 73–92.

Mahoney, J. M., & Strassberg, D. S. (1991). Voluntary control of male sexual arousal. *Archives of Sexual Behavior, 20*, 1–16.

Marques, J. K., Wiederanders, M., Day, D. M., Nelson, C., & van Ommeren, A. (2005). Effects of a relapse prevention program on sexual recidivism: Final results from California's Sex Offender Treatment Evaluation Project (SOTEP). *Sexual Abuse: A Journal of Research and Treatment, 17*, 79–107.

Marshall, W. L., & Barbaree, H. E. (1990). An integrated theory of the etiology of sexual offending. In W. L. Marshall, D. R. Laws, & H. E. Barbaree (Eds.), *Handbook of sexual assault: Issues, theories, and treatment of the offender* (pp. 257–275). New York: Plenum Press.

Marshall, W. L., Barbaree, H. E., & Eccles, A. (1991). Early onset and deviant sexuality in child molesters. *Journal of Interpersonal Violence, 6*, 323–336.

McClintock, M. K., & Herdt, G. (1996). Rethinking puberty: The development of sexual attraction. *Current Directions in Psychological Science, 5*, 178–183.

McGuire, R. J., Carlisle, J. M., & Young, B. G. (1965). Sexual deviations as conditioned behaviour: A hypothesis. *Behaviour Research and Therapy, 2*, 185–190.

O'Donohue, W., Regev, L. G., & Hagstrom, A. (2000). Problems with the DSM-IV diagnosis of pedophilia. *Sexual Abuse: A Journal of Research and Treatment, 12,* 95–105.

Plaud, J. J., & Martini, J. R. (1999). The respondent conditioning of male sexual arousal. *Behavior Modification, 23,* 254–268.

Quinsey, V., Harris, G., Rice, M., & Cormier, C. (2006). *Violent offenders: Appraising and managing risk* (2nd ed.). Washington, DC: American Psychological Association.

Quinsey, V. L. (2003). The etiology of anomalous sexual preferences in men. In R. Prentky, E. Janus, & M. C. Seto (Eds.), *Sexually coercive behavior: Understanding and management* (pp. 105–117). New York: New York Academy of Sciences.

Quinsey, V. L., & Lalumière, M. L. (1995). Evolutionary perspectives on sexual offending. *Sexual Abuse: A Journal of Research and Treatment, 7,* 301–315.

Quinsey, V. L., Rice, M. E., Harris, G. T., & Reid, K. S. (1993). The phylogenetic and ontogenetic development of sexual age preferences in males: Conceptual and measurement issues. In H. E. Barbaree, W. L. Marshall, & S. M. Hudson (Eds.), *The juvenile sex offender* (pp. 143–163). New York: Guilford Press.

Rachman, S. (1966). Sexual fetishism: An experimental analogue. *Psychological Record, 16,* 293–296.

Rachman, S., & Hodgson, R. J. (1968). Experimentally-induced "sexual fetishism": Replication and development. *Psychological Record, 18,* 25–27.

Raymond, N. C., Coleman, E., Ohlerking, F., Christenson, G. A., & Miner, M. (1999). Psychiatric comorbidity in pedophilic sex offenders. *American Journal of Psychiatry, 156,* 786–788.

Rice, M. E., & Harris, G. T. (1997). Cross-validation and extension of the Violence Risk Appraisal Guide for child molesters and rapists. *Law and Human Behavior, 21,* 231–241.

Rispens, J., Aleman, A., & Goudena, P. P. (1997). Prevention of child sexual abuse victimization: A meta-analysis of school programs. *Child Abuse and Neglect, 21,* 975–987.

Savin-Williams, R. C., & Diamond, L. M. (2000). Sexual identity trajectories among sexual-minority youths: Gender comparisons. *Archives of Sexual Behavior, 29,* 607–627.

Seto, M. C. (2002). Precisely defining pedophilia. *Archives of Sexual Behavior, 31,* 498–499.

Seto, M. C. (2004). Pedophilia and sexual offenses involving children. *Annual Review of Sex Research, 15,* 321–361.

Seto, M. C. (2008). *Pedophilia and sexual offending against children: Theory, assessment, and intervention.* Washington, DC: American Psychological Association.

Seto, M. C., Cantor, J. M., & Blanchard, R. (2006). Child pornography offenses are a valid diagnostic indicator of pedophilia. *Journal of Abnormal Psychology, 115,* 610–615.

Seto, M. C., Harris, G. T., Rice, M. E., & Barbaree, H. E. (2004). The Screening Scale for Pedophilic Interests and recidivism among adult sex offenders with child victims. *Archives of Sexual Behavior, 33,* 455–466.

Seto, M. C., & Lalumière, M. L. (2001). A brief screening scale to identify pedophilic interests among child molesters. *Sexual Abuse: A Journal of Research and Treatment, 13,* 15–25.

Seto, M. C., & Lalumière, M. L. (2006). *What is so special about juvenile sexual offending?: A review and test of explanations using meta-analysis.* Manuscript submitted for publication.

Seto, M. C., Murphy, W. D., Page, J., & Ennis, L. (2003). Detecting anomalous sexual interests among juvenile sex offenders. In R. Prentky, E. Janus, & M. C. Seto (Eds.), *Sexually coercive behavior: Understanding and management* (pp. 118–130). New York: New York Academy of Sciences.

Smiljanich, K., & Briere, J. (1996). Self-reported sexual interest in children: Sex differences and psychosocial correlates in a university sample. *Violence and Victims, 11,* 39–50.

Smith, T. P. (1994). Effects of the child's relative age appearance and attractiveness on vulnerability to pedosexual interactions (Doctoral dissertation, University of Texas at Austin, 1993). *Dissertation Abstracts International, 54*(12), 6472B. (UMI No. 9413603)

Templeman, T. L., & Stinnett, R. D. (1991). Patterns of sexual arousal and history in a "normal" sample of young men. *Archives of Sexual Behavior, 20,* 137–150.

Wakefield, J. C. (1992). The concept of mental disorder: On the boundary between biological facts and social values. *American Psychologist, 47,* 373–388.

Ward, T., Polaschek, D., & Beech, A. R. (2006). *Theories of sexual offending*. Chichester, UK: Wiley.

Ward, T., & Siegert, R. J. (2002). Toward a comprehensive theory of child sexual abuse: A theory knitting perspective. *Psychology, Crime, and Law, 9*, 197–248.

Weinberg, M. S., Williams, C. J., & Calhan, C. (1995). "If the shoe fits . . . ": Exploring male homosexual foot fetishism. *Journal of Sex Research, 32*, 17–27.

Wilson, D., & Andrews, C. (2004, November). *Internet traders of child pornography and other censorship offenders in New Zealand: Updated statistics*. New Zealand Department of Internal Affairs. Retrieved from *www.dia.govt.nz/pubforms.nsf/URL/profilingupdate.pdf/$file/profiling update.pdf*

Wilson, R. J., Picheca, J. E., & Prinzo, M. (2005). *Circles of Support and Accountability: An evaluation of the pilot project in South-Central Ontario* (Research Report No. R-168). Ottawa: Research Branch, Correctional Service Canada.

World Health Organization. (1997). *The ICD-10 classification of mental and behavioural disorders: Clinical descriptions and diagnostic guidelines*. Geneva: Author.

Worling, J. R. (1995). Sexual abuse histories of adolescent male sex offenders: Differences on the basis of the age and gender of their victims. *Journal of Abnormal Psychology, 104*, 610–613.

Wright, P., Nobrega, J., Langevin, R., & Wortzman, G. (1990). Brain density and symmetry in pedophilic and sexually aggressive offenders. *Annals of Sex Research, 3*, 319–328.

Zolondek, S., Abel, G., Northey, W., & Jordan, A. (2001). The self-reported behaviors of juvenile sexual offenders. *Journal of Interpersonal Violence, 16*, 73–85.

CHAPTER 11

PEDOPHILIA

Assessment and Treatment

JOSEPH A. CAMILLERI
VERNON L. QUINSEY

The literature on the assessment and treatment of pedophilia is sufficiently large that it cannot be reviewed in a single chapter. More comprehensive and detailed reviews of assessment, treatment, and etiology issues can be found in Quinsey and Lalumière (2001), the Safer Society series (*www.safersociety.org*), and Quinsey (2003), respectively. A more general overview is provided by Seto (2008). This chapter focuses on diagnostic and methodological issues specific to assessing sexual preferences for children, the modification of pedophilic preferences, and the outcome literature on the treatment of child molesters.

ASSESSMENT

Diagnosis

One of the earliest set of guidelines used by clinicians to diagnose pedophilia was provided by Richard von Krafft-Ebing (1886/1998) in his book *Psychopathia Sexualis*. He described "paedophilia erotica" as a psychopathology characterized by a primary sexual interest in children that manifests itself in sexual behavior directed toward them. This basic characterization has been retained in all subsequent clinical schemes for diagnosing pedophilia.

According to the *Diagnostic and Statistical Manual of Mental Disorders*, fourth edition, text revision (DSM-IV-TR; American Psychiatric Association, 2000) and the *International Statistical Classification of Diseases and Related Health Problems*, 10th revision (ICD-10; World Health Organization, 1994), a diagnosis of pedophilia requires a person to have recurrent, intense, and sexually arousing fantasies, urges, or behaviors directed toward a prepubescent child over a period of at least 6 months; to have acted on these urges or to be distressed by them; and to be at least 16 years old and at least 5 years older than the child victim. The DSM-IV-TR also requires a clinician to specify whether the person is sexually attracted to males, females, or both; whether the acts or thoughts are limited to incest; and whether the person is exclusively or nonexclusively pedophilic (i.e., attracted only to children, or to children and adults). An individual who is in late adolescence and has an ongoing relationship with a 12- or 13-year-old is to be excluded.

O'Donohue, Regev, and Hagstrom (2000) have criticized the original (1994) DSM-IV approach to diagnosing pedophilia. Their criticisms are that, unlike the criteria for other disorders in DSM-IV, the criteria for pedophilia were not tested for interdiagnostician reliability; there are problems of temporal inconsistency in making the diagnosis; the procedures used to obtain internal consistency in DSM-III were problematic (no such data were collected for DSM-IV); and the validity of the DSM-IV criteria is compromised because they are vague, are arbitrary, and lack adequate operational definitions. It is therefore no surprise that these criteria are rarely used by researchers and clinicians (Marshall, 1997; O'Donohue et al., 2000). However, O'Donohue and colleagues' solution of focusing strictly on behavior, so that a single sexual act with a child would be sufficient evidence for a diagnosis of "pedophilia response disorder," is problematic: It removes the important distinction between individuals who sexually prefer children but have never molested a child, and those who have committed a sexual offense against a child but sexually prefer adults (Cohen & Galynker, 2002).[1]

Not only do the DSM and ICD fail to distinguish between behavior and preference; the attendant confusion between pedophile and child molester categories is found throughout the literature, as noted by Barbaree and Seto (1997). Because pedophilic behavior is used as a sufficient diagnostic criterion, cause and effect are obfuscated. Pedophilia is best understood as a sexual preference for children that may or may not lead to child molestation. Child molestation, on the other hand, involves a sexual offense against a child that may or may not be due to pedophilia.

Pedophiles, child molesters, and pedophilic child molesters should be understood as separate groups, because a diagnosis of pedophilia is a strong predictor of sexual recidivism (Hanson & Bussière, 1998). Using such groups in research and clinical practice allows us to streamline treatments toward targeting those at high risk (see the "Treatment Efficacy and Research Priorities" section of this chapter); to suggest new studies for understanding the link between pedophilia and child molestation by using pedophiles who have not molested children as a control group; and to assess treatment outcomes properly.

The DSM approach to diagnosing pedophilia has also been criticized on the grounds that the victim age criterion is arbitrary (O'Donohue et al., 2000). A solution to this problem comes from a simple yet practical method to understanding psychological disorders: the notion of "harmful dysfunction" (Wakefield, 1992). According to Wakefield, in order for a phenomenon to be classified as a disorder, it must meet two criteria: (1) The mechanism is not functioning in the way it was naturally designed to function; and (2) due to this dysfunction, the person is harmed or is deprived of benefit. This unifying evolutionary approach subsumes the use of biologically relevant diagnostic criteria, such as a preference for sexually immature features, instead of using an arbitrarily selected age (Seto, 1999, 2002). In addition to improvements in diagnostic criteria, approaching sexual behavior as reproductive behavior may help us understand the etiology of pedophilia by focusing on how pedophilic behavior is similar to and different from typical reproductive behaviors (Quinsey, 2002; Quinsey & Lalumière, 1995). A detailed discussion on whether pedophilia is a mental disorder can be found in the *Archives of Sexual Behavior* December 2002 issue.

Comorbidity

Pedophiles and child molesters exhibit psychiatric comorbidity for mood disorders, substance abuse, and impulse control disorders (Galli et al., 1999; McElroy et al., 1999; Raymond, Coleman, Ohlerking, Christenson, & Miner, 1999); other paraphilias (Abel, Becker, Cunningham-Rathner, Mittelman, & Rouleau, 1988; Galli et al., 1999; Raymond et al., 1999); antisociality and psychopathy (Dorr, 1998; Raymond et al., 1999; Seto, Harris, Rice, & Barbaree, 2004; Virkkunen, 1976); and assertiveness deficits (as described in Cohen & Galynker, 2002). Such comorbidity is more likely in adjudicated or hospitalized child molesters than in child molesters assessed from community samples (Quinsey, 1986). A substantial proportion of pedophiles have been found to engage at least once in other types of sexual offenses, such as voyeurism, exhibitionism, and public masturbation (Abel et al., 1988). One of the most important possible concurrent conditions is that of psychopathy. For reasons of public safety, practitioners should assess pedophiles for psychopathy because of its dangerous relationship with sexual deviance: It has been demonstrated that both adult and adolescent psychopathic sex offenders are at a very high risk of both sexual and violent recidivism (e.g., Gretton, McBride, Hare, O'Shaughnessy, & Kumka, 2001; Harris et al., 2003). In addition, actuarial assessments to identify men who are at high risk of sexual and violent recidivism should be routinely used (see Quinsey, Harris, Rice, & Cormier, 2006)—not only to determine the appropriate amount of supervision, but also because treatments appear to be less effective with low-risk men (see "Treatment Efficacy and Research Priorities"; see also Andrews et al., 1990).

Assessment Tools

Generally, the goal of an assessment for pedophilia is to identify the presence or absence of a sexual preference for children. In most cases, these assessments are conducted on men who were either charged or convicted of child molestation. Some referrals, however, come from men who report pedophilic urges and are distressed by them. This section provides a synopsis of ways to assess men in either situation.

Penile Plethysmography

One of the most commonly investigated procedures of assessing pedophilic preferences is the measurement via penile plethysmography (PPG) of changes in penile circumference or volume occasioned by images of persons who vary in age and sex, or audiotaped stories concerning sexual interactions with persons who vary in age and sex. An increase in either penile circumference or volume is assumed to indicate sexual arousal, thereby indicating sexual desire (Kalmus & Beech, 2005; Rempel & Serafini, 1995). Such assumptions have been validated. For example, Harris, Rice, Quinsey, and Chaplin (1996) found a correspondence among phallometric assessment, viewing time (VT), and self-reported attraction to stimulus persons varying in sex and age among nonoffenders[2]; however, and more importantly, they obtained better discrimination between persons who did and did not molest children with phallometric assessment than with the other measures. It has also been demonstrated that PPG can be used to assess pedophilia among adolescent child molesters (Robinson, Rouleau, & Madrigano, 1997; Seto, Lalumière, & Blanchard, 2000). As we discuss in the "Effective Assessment" section, PPG is the best-validated tool for assessing pedophilia.

Phallometric assessment, despite its demonstrable utility in the assessment of deviant sexual preferences, is not without limitations, and these have inhibited its more widespread use. First, the procedure requires psychophysiological equipment (even though this is modest in amount and expense), as well as training of the assessors in gathering and interpreting phallometric data. The procedure can also be viewed as intrusive by clients and lawyers. Lastly, for a variety of reasons, the field has not converged upon a standard procedure with published norms. These limitations have led to various attempts to develop other tools to assess sexual age preferences.

Viewing Time

VT has been an attractive alternative to measuring penile tumescence because it is easier to administer. A number of studies have assessed the validity of VT by comparing it to PPG and by testing how well it can identify offender types. Variability in results has been related to offenders' preference for a particular sex of child victim. Harris and colleagues (1996) found similar patterns between PPG and VT among child molesters who offended against girls. Using VT, Abel, Huffman, Warberg, and Holland (1998) correctly classified 66% of men with an interest in girls and 91% of men with an interest in boys. Letourneau (2002) aimed to replicate Abel's findings and found that both VT and PPG were able to identify offenders against boys, but not offenders against girls. Most recently, Abel and colleagues (2004) significantly discriminated adolescent child molesters from adolescents who presented with other sexual problems with a VT measure.

These mixed findings, though encouraging, are not conclusive enough to warrant the use of VT in clinical practice. We recommend that future studies on VT should incorporate standardized procedures for data manipulation (e.g., z-scores and use of a deviance differential). It should be noted that VT is often used in combination with self-report measures, as, for example, in the popular Abel Assessment for Sexual Interest (AASI; Abel, Jordan, Hand, Holland, & Phipps, 2001). Some researchers have criticized the AASI (Fischer & Smith, 1999; Smith & Fischer, 1999) by outlining concerns about its development, reliability, and validity (see Abel, 2000, for a response).

Behavior

A diagnosis of pedophilia can be inferred from past behavior. For example, Seto and Lalumière (2001) developed the Screening Scale for Pedophilic Interests (SSPI), a four-item scale that assesses characteristics of past child molestation. These characteristics include having at least one male victim, committing offenses against multiple victims, having at least one prepubescent victim, and having an unrelated victim. The SSPI was found to correlate with phallometrically measured pedophilia in both adults and adolescents, and it was also found to predict sexual recidivism among adult sex offenders (Seto et al., 2004; Seto, Murphy, Page, & Ennis, 2003). Seto, Cantor, and Blanchard (2006) provided additional validity for the use of behavior to diagnose pedophilia: They found that men who were charged for possession of child pornography were more likely to have phallometrically measured pedophilic sexual interests. These results suggest that the SSPI is a useful alternative for researchers or clinicians who do not have more sophisticated tools to assess pedophilia.

Implicit Association Test

Cognitive tests have recently been used to assess pedophilia. The popular Implicit Association Test (IAT; Greenwald, McGhee, & Schwartz, 1998) is based on the assumption that a person who holds a favorable view of a topic (e.g., sex with a child) will associate words related to this topic (e.g., "sex" words and "child" words) faster than a person who does not hold such a favorable view, and faster than he will associate words unrelated to this topic (e.g., "sex" words and "adult" words). The potential benefit of this approach is that it can assess the presence of a preference that a person may not want to disclose. Two research groups have used the IAT paradigm to assess sexual preference for children, and found that child molesters provided more positive associations between children and sex than either other offenders or nonoffender controls did (Gray, Brown, MacCulloch, Smith, & Snowden, 2005; Mihailides, Devilly, & Ward, 2004). With further validation, such as identifying the correspondence between IAT scores and phallometric responding or sexual recidivism, this approach may be a very useful alternative for assessing pedophilia.

Scales and Card Sorts

Scales and card sort methods have been developed to identify sexual preference in both forensic and nonforensic populations. Assessing pedophilia in this way is useful for researchers and clinicians who do not have access to a phallometric laboratory. Although such methods should not replace PPG, there is some indication that combining PPG and self-report procedures improves discrimination (Laws, Hanson, Osborn, & Greenbaum, 2000). A list of self-report tools and scales to assess pedophilia, including their psychometric properties, can be found in Quinsey and Lalumière (2001).

Neuroimaging

Neuroimaging and neurophysiological methods have been used to compare child molesters with nonforensic controls on measures of neural activity and composition. Differences between these groups have been demonstrated with various technologies, including computerized axial tomography (Hucker et al., 1986; Wright, Nobrega, Langevin, & Wortzman, 1990), electroencephalography (Flor-Henry, Lang, Koles, & Frenzel, 1991), and most recently magnetic resonance imaging (Cantor et al., 2006). Some studies focusing on pedophiles indicate anomalies in the temporal lobe (Cohen & Galynker, 2002). Bassarath (2001) reviewed the literature on neuroimaging studies of antisocial behavior and found converging evidence for atypical circuitry in the prefrontal cortex. If such findings indicate pathological differences instead of simply differences, they are consistent with pedophilia defined as harmful dysfunction: Atypical circuitry provides some evidence for a dysfunctional psychological mechanism. Neuropsychological measures have the potential for being quite useful, but at this time, due to limited access to equipment and little research on treating anomalies identified from neuroimages, this technology is still in the developmental stage. It should be noted that the neural structural correlates of homosexual preference in men are too small to be identified with current methods of brain imagery used with living participants; the same is likely to be true with pedophilia.

Other Physiological Measures

Other methods used to assess pedophilia include measuring penile temperature, penile surface blood volume, skin conductance responses, and pupillometry. Their ability to discriminate pedophiles from nonpedophiles is poorer than that of PPG, however. Because there is an abundance of research supporting both the discriminative and predictive validity of PPG, and because very little research using these alternative methods have been employed in the last 20 years, PPG remains the most trusted assessment tool (for a detailed review, see Kalmus & Beech, 2005). The following section describes procedures that can be used to maximize PPG capabilities.

Effective Assessment

If we adhere to a definition of pedophilia as a "sexual preference for children," then, after surveying the different methods of assessment, we must conclude that phallometric assessment has emerged as the most reliable and valid procedure to assess this preference. Over the past 30 years, research has addressed concerns over equipment, sensitivity and specificity, and optimal procedures and statistics to optimize discrimination.

Volumetric versus Strain Gauge

Two types of equipment are used to assess sexual preferences phallometrically: an air chamber that measures change in penile volume, and a mercury-in-rubber strain gauge that measures change in penile circumference. An important question is this: Which type of phallometric equipment can better discriminate between pedophiles and nonpedophiles? There has been much discussion in the literature on the equivalence of these apparatuses. In a well-controlled study, where both tools were used simultaneously on a nonforensic sample, Kuban, Barbaree, and Blanchard (1999) found a strong positive correlation between the two methods ($r > .80$) on standardized scores across stimulus categories when they included participants with responses that were 10% greater than a full erection. This relationship disappeared among low responders (mean $r = -.15$). Other researchers found that when they employed deviance differential scores (i.e., difference between highest response to deviant and nondeviant stimuli) and a circumferential device, discriminant validity was not improved by excluding low responders (Harris, Rice, Quinsey, Chaplin, & Earls, 1992). The important questions of which technique more accurately differentiates child molesters from normal individuals, and which more closely correlates with history of victim choice, have yet to be addressed directly.

Sensitivity and Specificity

Three studies have assessed phallometric sensitivity and specificity for diagnosing pedophilia (Blanchard, Klassen, Dickey, Kuban, & Blak, 2001; Freund & Blanchard, 1989; Freund & Watson, 1991). "Sensitivity" is calculated by dividing the number of men identified as pedophiles by the phallometric assessment out of the total number of true pedophiles in the sample. For child molesters who had multiple child victims, sensitivity ranged from 61% to 88.6%. Better sensitivity was found among offenders with male victims. "Specificity" is calculated by dividing the number of men identified as gynephiles (i.e., men who prefer adult women) by the phallometric assessment out of the total number of true gynephiles in the sample. Research has shown specificity to range from 80% to 96.9%. Similar specificity was found among adolescents who sexually offended against children (92%), while sensitivity was lower but still acceptable at 42% (Seto et al., 2000). Of course, these values only apply to the specific stimuli and methods used in these particular demonstrations. In the absence of standardized procedures, clinicians need to determine the psychometric properties of those that they use.

Because sensitivity and specificity are influenced by base rates, we recommend the use of the "receiver operating characteristic" (ROC) statistic, or the "common language effect size" (CLES). Not only are ROC and CLES indices robust to variability in base rates of pedophilia in samples, but they have the added benefit of being easy to interpret. An ROC of .50 tells us that the test performs at chance, whereas an ROC of 1.00 tells us that the test predicts perfectly. Thus an ROC of .75 is exactly between random and perfect prediction. ROCs are now commonly used to assess the predictive accuracy of actuarial assessments (Quinsey et al., 2006). When CLES is applied to the assessment of pedophilia, the value tells us the probability that a randomly selected pedophile scores higher than a randomly selected nonpedophile. Variables that may influence accuracy measured by ROC and CLES include the number and quality of stimuli, instructions, method of measuring penile changes, and so forth. By using these statistics, Chaplin, Rice, and Harris (1995) calculated CLES to be close to 1.00. For a review of using and interpreting these statistics, see Quinsey and colleagues (2006).

Procedures and Statistics

Lalumière and Harris (1998) reviewed the literature to address some common questions on best practices for optimal discrimination using phallometric testing. Some of their recommendations are as follows:

- Use of images best discriminates age and gender preference (e.g., Harris et al., 1996).
- Use of graphic and violent narratives best discriminates preference for coercive sex.
- Use of more than one stimulus per category is optimal. Validity has been established with two to five stimuli per category (e.g., Lalumière & Quinsey, 1994).
- The same duration of stimulus presentation should be used as was used in the validation of the stimulus set (e.g., Quinsey, Chaplin, & Varney, 1981).
- Computation of a "deviance differential"—an index of relative preference between deviant (child or coercive sex) and nondeviant (adult or consenting sex) stimuli—is recommended. The deviance differential is calculated by subtracting the largest mean response of the deviant category from the largest mean response of the nondeviant category (e.g., Harris et al., 1992).
- Use of z-score transformations addresses individual differences in responding (i.e., high vs. low responders), thus improving discriminant validity.
- When auditory stimuli are used, faking can be reduced by including a semantic tracking task to ensure that attention is being paid to the stimuli. For example, subjects can be required to press one button when a description of sex is presented

and another when violence is presented (Proulx, Côté, & Achille, 1993; Quinsey & Chaplin, 1988).

Pedophilia Typologies

Much of the research on pedophilia subcategories has focused on differences in overt behavior and not on differences in sexual preferences per se. We can still draw from this literature to understand possible categories of pedophilic sexual interest. The simplest typologies that account for much of the variability in pedophilia are those of victim sex (i.e., heterosexual–homosexual) and relationship to victim (i.e., intrafamilial–extrafamilial). In order to be useful, other typologies must be able to outperform these distinctions in terms of dealing with treatment issues and predicting recidivism (Quinsey, 1986). Though other typologies have been proposed, such as the one developed by Knight, Carter, and Prentky (1989), none have yet met these criteria.

Heterosexual–Homosexual Typology

A common and important distinction among pedophiles is not just their age preference, but their sexual orientation or gender preference. Although most sex offenses are directed toward females (approximately 67%), a substantial proportion are committed against same-sex victims (estimates range from 12% to 33%) and victims of both sexes (20%; Abel et al., 1988). There is a generally good relationship between a victim's sex and the sex preference found phallometrically (Freund, 1967; Harris et al., 1996). Identifying homosexual pedophiles is important, because homosexual pedophilies are about twice as likely to recidivate as heterosexual child molesters (Quinsey, 1986).

Intrafamilial–Extrafamilial Typology

There is some evidence to support the traditional view that exclusively intrafamilial (i.e., incest) and extrafamilial child molesters are different groups. For example, although victims of incest offending tend to experience a greater frequency of assaults and a greater likelihood of completed intercourse than victims of nonincest offending (Gebhard, Gagnon, Pomeroy, & Christenson, 1965), intrafamilial child molesters are not as sexually deviant, are at lower risk for sexual recidivism, are less psychopathic, are less likely to have intercourse with the victims, are less likely to have male victims, cause less injury, and have lower sexual and violent recidivism rates (Rice & Harris, 2002).

In terms of sexual preference, a clear difference between intrafamilial and extrafamilial sex offenders on phallometric measures of preference has not emerged, even though at least 12 studies have addressed this issue (Abel, Becker, Murphy, & Flanagan, 1981; Barsetti, Earls, Lalumière, & Belanger, 1998; Blanchard et al., 2006; Frenzel & Lang, 1989; Freund, Watson, & Dickey, 1991; Lang, Black, Frenzel, & Checkley, 1988; Langevin & Watson, 1991; Malcolm, Andrews, & Quinsey, 1993; Marshall, Barbaree, & Christophe, 1986; Murphy, Haynes, Stalgaitis, & Flanagan, 1986; Rice & Harris, 2002; Seto, Lalumière, & Kuban, 1999). A consistent finding across these studies is that incest offenders were never more deviant than extrafamilial child molesters, and at least one study found that both intrafamilial and extrafamilial child molesters showed a stronger sexual preference for children than rapists and nonforensic controls did (Seto et al., 1999). In order for these results to be interpretable, however, offenders must be matched on their own age at time of offense, and the age and sex of their victims (see Quinsey, Chaplin, & Carrigan, 1979).

Blanchard and colleagues (2006) found that paternal–nonpaternal groups are better discriminated by PPG scores than intrafamilial–extrafamilial groups. In their study, nonmolesters had the lowest sexual preference for children; nonpaternal molesters (i.e., nonpaternal incest offenders and molesters against unrelated children) had the highest sexual preference for children; and paternal molesters (i.e., biological fathers and stepfathers) were in between. In other words, offenders against extended family members are similar to extrafamilial offenders, and the belief that incest offenders are less likely to be pedophilic appears to be true only for fathers and stepfathers. Implications of these mixed findings suggest that a simple categorization based on relationship to the victim has limited clinical utility (Bickley & Beech, 2001). Seto and colleagues (1999) recommended that incest offenders should not be excluded from phallometric assessments because of the strong relationship between a sexual preference for children and sexual recidivism.

Massachusetts Treatment Center: Child Molester Typology, Version 3

Some researchers have constructed child molester typologies that are guided by traditional psychological theories. A popular typology for child molesters has been advanced by Knight and colleagues (1989). Their typology, the Massachusetts Treatment Center: Child Molester Typology, Version 3 (MTC:CMT3), consists of two axes. Axis I includes fixation (i.e., degree of pedophilic interest—low or high) and social competence (low or high); Axis II includes amount of contact (i.e., actual physical contact with children—low or high), meaning of high contact (i.e., either interpersonal or narcissistic), level of physical injury for low contact, and whether injuries were sadistic or nonsadistic. Child molesters can reliably be assigned to these groups (Knight et al., 1989; Looman, Gauthier, & Boer, 2001), but further research on the MTC:CMT3's predictive validity and treatment relevance is still required.

Assessment Research Priorities

Our evaluation of the research on assessing pedophilia has led us to several methodological and theoretical suggestions. With regard to methodology, there appears to be some evidence that using multiple assessment methods improves the accuracy of identifying pedophilia. Laws and colleagues (2000) found that combining self-report (i.e., card sort), PPG audio, and PPG slides had better diagnostic accuracy for pedophilia than any method alone. Additional research should verify these findings, and clinicians should, if feasible, use such multiple methods to assess a sexual preference for children. When it comes to actuarial assessments of risk, however, it appears as though combining tests is no better than using the best test (Seto, 2005).

Although researchers have identified numerous ways to assign pedophiles into subgroups, we think that more research separating pedophiles, child molesters, and pedophilic child molesters will greatly improve our understanding of the relationship between pedophilic interests and overt behavior. We would also like to see greater use of standardized procedures and stimuli, especially those outlined by Lalumière and Harris (1998). Such standardization not only optimizes discrimination of phallometric assessments, but allows for higher-quality meta-analytic research.

Lastly, we need to find methodologies to assess pedophilia as a dysfunctional mechanism. For example, Quinsey and Lalumière (1995) suggested that pedophilia results from malfunctioning body shape detectors. In the only test of this hypothesis, Rice and Harris (2003b) found that child molesters responded more to visual images of older women than of younger women—a finding that was predicted on the grounds that older women have a waist–hip ratio more like that of prepubertal children than that of sexually mature young women. Additional research using not just VT, but eye-tracking methodology would help us understand which physical aspects of sexual stimuli pedophiles and nonpedophiles attend to. Results would lend support to understanding the etiology of pedophilia, which may be a necessary step in developing treatment programs that properly address pedophilia. We should take cues from research on homosexuality (an area moving much faster on the etiological front), such as using the fraternal birth order effect at the neurohormonal and neural structure level for homosexual pedophilia, and conducting genetic studies of the heritability of pedophilia (see Quinsey, 2003, for a discussion of these issues).

TREATMENT

Treatments for pedophilia emerged as a means to prevent child molestation or as a way to reduce sexual recidivism. That is, pedophilia is treated either when a person wants to remedy his pedophilic tendencies, or when a person has committed a sexual offense against a child and his pedophilic interests are addressed to reduce sexual recidivism. This latter approach combines preference-based treatment with programs designed to manage other criminogenic needs. Both approaches are discussed below.

Before we begin our review of the treatment literature, it may be helpful to describe the optimum state of affairs. In the best of all possible worlds, treatment would change factors known to be related to reoffending. It would be best if these factors were etiologically relevant, although this is not necessary. Improvement in these factors would correlate highly and negatively with recidivism. Progress in treatment technology would be reflected in greater reductions in recidivism over time. Treatment outcome studies using random assignment would show large effect sizes, and better-implemented programs would be more successful. Unfortunately, as we document below, only one of these desired criteria has been met.

Treatment Based on Sexual Preference

Conditioning

We have established that "pedophilia" is a term that describes a sexual preference for prepubescent children, and that PPG is the most effective method for assessing such a preference. PPG is also useful for tracking changes in response patterns across interventions. Several studies have used PPG with treatments that are guided by the principles of conditioning in order to reduce sexual responding to children and to increase sexual responding to adults. These treatments are based on pairing an aversive stimulus with stimuli depicting an individual's sexual preference. Variations on this principle include classical aversive conditioning, classical discriminative conditioning, covert sensitization, satiation, and signaled punishment.

In classical aversive conditioning, an unconditional stimulus (UCS), such as shock, is preceded by a conditional stimulus (CS+; a description of a deviant fantasy or image of a child) in order to reduce interest in the deviant stimulus (Marshall, 1973), whereas classical discriminative conditioning includes a conditional stimulus (CS–; a description of consenting sex with an adult or an image of an adult) that signals the absence of the UCS (Quinsey, Bergersen, & Steinman, 1976). Covert sensitization requires individuals to imagine a situation in which they approach a child but feel nauseous (sometimes they are asked to think of aversive items such as vomit or feces; Barbaree & Seto, 1997) and feel relief when leaving that situation (Barlow, Leitenberg, & Agras, 1969). Satiation can either be verbal or masturbatory; the latter involves a person masturbating to ejaculation while thinking about appropriate sexual acts, then continuing to masturbate after ejaculation while thinking about his inappropriate preference (Marquis, 1970). Signaled punishment involves the use of an indicator such as a red light that goes on when the individual is over a preset penile tumescence criterion in the presence of a deviant stimulus; the red light is associated with a probability per unit time of electric shock to the arm as long as it is on. A green light goes on when the person is over the criterion in the presence of an adult stimulus. An alternative nonconditioning procedure, biofeedback, can be used to determine whether aversive conditioning is actually required for an individual to gain control of his sexual responses in the laboratory. In this procedure, the individual is instructed not to respond in the presence of a deviant stimulus and to respond sexually in the presence of an appropriate stimulus. Penile tumescence changes are signaled to the individual with red and green lights, as in the signaled punishment procedure (Quinsey, Chaplin, & Carrigan, 1980). Several studies have used these methodologies to demonstrate reductions in phallometrically measured arousal to children (e.g., Quinsey et al., 1976, 1980) and in other sexual paraphilias (Abel, Levis, & Clancy, 1970).

More generally, other studies have shown that sexual arousal can be manipulated via conditioning paradigms not just in humans (O'Donohue & Plaud, 1994), but in nonhuman animals as well (Pfaus, Kippin, & Centeno, 2001). Some conditioning procedures appear to be more effective than others. Barbaree and Seto (1997) reported limited evidence for thematic shift, where deviant thoughts while masturbating change to appropriate thoughts during orgasm; limited support for fantasy alternation, where contents of sexual thoughts are changed daily or weekly; and some support for satiation and directed masturbation (i.e., masturbating exclusively to appropriate stimuli). Early conditioning procedures for treating paraphilias used mild electric shocks as the aversive stimuli (e.g., Quinsey et al., 1980). Use of shock has waned in favor of olfactory, visual, and cognitively aversive stimuli.

The greatest problems with conditioning approaches (and other approaches described later) are (1) that changing actual preferences (as opposed to indices that reflect them) has been quite difficult (Furby, Weinrott, & Blackshaw, 1989; Lalumière & Quinsey, 1998); and (2) no studies have shown long-term changes in sexual preference or behavior after treatment (Laws, 2001; Quinsey & Earls, 1990). From a conditioning view, this latter outcome might be explained by extinction: Removal of the contingencies results in reduced frequency of the conditional response. A problematic outcome is the expectation produced by a "honeymoon effect," where patients believe that their deviant preferences are being fixed because of the quick effects of treatment and then fail to acknowledge the possibility of relapsing. Thus practitioners have been advised to inform patients that conditioning procedures does not make permanent changes (Laws, 2001). The difficulty in changing preference and the lack of permanent changes suggest that conditioning procedures do not work by conditioning mechanisms. A plausible explanation for how conditioning works is by training the person to identify and control his responses in order to ease the suppression of sexual responding (also known as "cognitive mediation"; for further discussions of this topic, see Barbaree, Bogaert, & Seto, 1995; Quinsey & Earls, 1990). Training people in this way is easy with signaled punishment, for instance, but the effects of this procedure do not persist or reduce recidivism. The issue of why conditioning and other therapies have had limited success in changing arousal patterns is discussed in the "Treatment Efficacy and Research Priorities" section.

Treatments Designed to Reduce Sexual Recidivism among Child Molesters

As mentioned earlier, many treatment programs have been designed for convicted child molesters in order to address their possible pedophilic tendencies and other criminogenic needs. The ultimate goal of these programs is to reduce sexual recidivism by focusing on different causal factors thought to be related to child molestation. Humanistic and psychodynamic mechanisms are addressed in general psychotherapy; sexual preference, cognitive distortions, and procriminal attitudes are targeted in cognitive-behavioral therapy (CBT); maintaining therapeutic change is the goal of relapse prevention (RP); personal and environmental risk and protective factors are addressed in multisystemic therapy (MST); and inhibiting general sexual arousal is the aim of medical treatments.

General Psychotherapy

General psychotherapies are programs derived from either humanistic or psychodynamic traditions (some of these are atheoretical or eclectic). These programs are not well documented, appear to be unstructured, and have only a few well-controlled outcome evaluations (Lalumière, Harris, Quinsey, & Rice, 2005). Of these studies, none have demonstrated reductions in recidivism, and some evidence even suggests a possible increase in recidivism (e.g., Furby et al., 1989; Romero & Williams, 1983). For all these reasons, we do not describe these programs in any detail.

Cognitive-Behavioral Therapy and Relapse Prevention

CBT and RP are two of the most popular psychotherapeutic treatment approaches used with child molesters. CBT combines behavioral interventions (such as the conditioning techniques described earlier) with cognitive therapies. The behavioral portion focuses on sexual preference, whereas the cognitive portion focuses on the cognitive distortions, attitudes, and thinking errors related to sexual aggression, which are assumed to be the products of social learning (Murphy, 1990). As expected, child molesters appear to have more cognitive distortions associated with child molesting than men who sexually assault adult women have (e.g., Abel et al., 1989; Blumenthal, Gudjonsson, & Burns, 1999). Standard cognitive therapy works to change these aberrant thoughts by (1) teaching offenders how cognitions influence sexually aggressive behaviors, (2) informing them how offending injures victims, (3) training them how to identify their own cognitive distortions, and (4) using various pedagogical tools to help these men understand and work through their distortions (Murphy, 1990).

RP is a separate program module focusing on factors that maintain changes brought by treatment (Rice, Harris, Quinsey, & Cyr, 1990). RP targets three factors in particular: self-efficacy (confidence in coping with high-risk situations), coping skills (skills to cope with high-risk situations), and motivation (increasing desire not to relapse) (Bauml & Quinsey, 1992). Both CBT and RP utilize group and individual modalities, are implemented in inpatient and outpatient settings, and can last anywhere from 4 months to 30 months, with some programs providing booster sessions upon release (Marshall & Barbaree, 1990). Many programs include other modules, such as sex education, anger management, general counseling, empathy training, and social/heterosocial skills training (Rice, Harris, & Quinsey, 2001).

Treatment success has been assessed in terms of both reducing recidivism and achieving more short-term treatment goals. Though rigorous process evaluations of CBT for sex offenders have yet to be established, two studies highlight some early findings. Pithers (1994) found evidence to suggest that CBT programs are capable of reducing cognitive distortions among child molesters, and Eastman (2004) found increases in prosocial attitudes toward sexual behavior among adolescent child molesters after CBT. Unfortunately, the persistence of these improvements is unknown. In a related area, a meta-analysis examining changing rape-supportive attitudes among nonforensic samples, Brecklin and Forde (2001) found that the effects of these interventions did not last; in fact, effects of treatment disappeared just a few months after the intervention. According to Marshall and Laws (2003), lasting change will occur only if the schemas underlying attitudes supportive of sexual aggression are changed. Though there is much research on variables that influence attitude persistence (Petty & Wegener, 1998), we could not locate any study that looked at variables moderating attitude persistence in correctional programs.[3] Also, to our knowledge, no reported studies have demonstrated that a change in either cognitions or attitudes is related to a change in recidivism among sex offenders; one study found no relationship between either therapist ratings of treatment progress or pre–post improvements in self-report attitudinal measures and recidivism (Quinsey, Khanna, & Malcolm, 1998).

Some studies have used alternative measures of treatment success to predict variability in recidivism. Marques, Wiederanders, Day, Nelson, and van Ommeren (2005) measured how well participants learned RP concepts, and found that men at high risk who learned the concepts recidivated less than high-risk men who did not (no differences were found for low- and medium-risk men); however, the program did not reduce recidivism overall. When Rice, Quinsey, and Harris (1991) looked at pre- and posttreatment phallometric scores, the former predicted recidivism better than the latter. Although it is difficult to draw conclusions about the success of CBT from the few properly designed studies conducted to date, the results so far are not encouraging.

The best-designed treatment program using CBT and RP methods was developed by Marques and colleagues (2005). Rice and colleagues (2001) outlined three major advantages of Marques and colleagues' design: clinical sophistication (i.e., the study targeted criminogenic needs and changes throughout treatment); random assignment; and the use of "hard" outcome data (i.e., official records of violent, sexual, and general recidivism). Such a design allowed researchers to properly assess the relationship among specific treatment components, therapeutic change, and recidivism. Unfortunately, after much investment in planning and implementation, and after these men were followed up for at least 5 years, there was no effect of treatment on sexual or violent recidivism. Men who were treated with this program had a sexual recidivism rate of 22%, whereas 20% of the volunteer controls (i.e., men who volunteered for treatment but were randomly selected for no treatment) and 19% of the nonvolunteer controls (i.e., those who refused treatment) had sexually recidivated.

Meta-analyses that included incidental control groups showed modest effects of treatment when the data were collapsed across all sex offenders (Hanson et al., 2002; Hanson & Bussière, 1998) and when the data for child molesters were examined more specifically (R. K. Hanson, personal communication, August 3, 2006), but Hanson and colleagues' conclusions are tempered by the quality of the studies included in their meta-analyses. At the very least, an interesting question is whether treatment programs have shown improvement in their ability to treat offenders over time. In order to answer this question, we looked at the relationship between effect sizes of treatment on recidivism and time of study publication, with the assumption that a correlation should exist if improvements have been made in treatment programs over time. The general finding is that no such relationship exists (Box 11.1). A similar finding has been made within the same program over time. Quinsey, Khanna, and Malcolm (1998) compared sex offenders treated in a single program before and after 1986. Survival curve analysis—a statistic that compares change in recidivism rates over time—yielded no differences between the two groups, though a trend emerged where people treated later in the program reoffended more frequently than men who participated earlier in the program.

Many of these points can be understood as concerns about effectiveness and efficacy (Rice & Harris, 2003a; Streiner, 2002). "Efficacy" refers to whether treatment *can* work under ideal circumstances (i.e., a randomized control design), whereas "effectiveness" refers to whether treatment *does* work in the real world. Across all types of interventions, including psychotherapies and medical interventions, most studies are best classified as effectiveness studies. Streiner (2002) has stated that if treatment is not shown to work under ideal circumstances, there is no chance that it can work under suboptimal circumstances. Based on this line of reasoning, Rice and Harris (2003a) found that references to outcome studies had easily accepted positive treatment effects without considering their methodological limitations. They continued to say that any conclusion must be based on studies using at least minimally informative criteria. In order for a study to be minimally informative, it needs to (1) use official records of recidivism; and (2) use random assignment to treatment and control groups, or match comparison groups on jurisdiction, volunteering for treatment, and established predictors of recidivism (Quinsey et al., 1993; Rice & Harris, 2003a). Studies that fail to meet these criteria have no probative value.

These unfortunate results also need to be understood not simply as a failure of the treatment programs alone, but as a failure to assess exactly what has led to ineffective psychological interventions. A successful intervention requires not just the right intervention, but proper implementation and design, in order for treatment effectiveness to be properly assessed. The literature on program evaluation refers to this as a "process evaluation," and it is considered an essential component of any program evaluation (Rossi, Lipsey, & Freeman, 2004). Because CBT is often implemented alongside other programs unrelated to cognitive or behavioral principles, it is difficult to assess separately, as noted by Rice and colleagues (2001). Moreover, though many clinicians record treatment progress on a daily basis, few studies report the relationship of such progress (or lack thereof) to longer-term outcome measures. Of the studies that were able to demonstrate changes in a variety of theoretically relevant measures involving attitudes, knowledge, and sexual

BOX 11.1. Assessing Treatment Progress over Time

It has sometimes been assumed that considerable advances in the treatment of sexual offenders have occurred over the past 30 years. The unresolved question is whether these advances have made practical improvements in reducing subsequent sexual offenses. If these advances have allowed for better treatment programs, we should expect the effects of treatment on recidivism to improve over time. To test this question, we looked at the relationship between the year of publication and treatment effect size from the 44 studies used in Hanson and colleagues' (2002) meta-analysis on sex offender treatment effectiveness. Year of publication ranged from 1977 to 2000. Although effect sizes increased (as indicated by smaller odds ratios), there was no significant relationship between the year of publication and treatment effect size for sexual recidivism, $r(35) = -.14$, $p = .43$, or any recidivism, $r(27) = -.30$, $p = .12$.

This analysis includes a number of limitations: (1) There was variability in the time gap between when studies were actually conducted and when they were published (information about this could not be obtained); (2) relationship between improvements may depend on either the study design (i.e., efficacy vs. effectiveness) or the type of intervention. There are too few studies using optimal designs in order to assess their change over time, and so we are unable to separate analyses based on methodology quality.

These results can be understood in two ways. First, all results are in the expected direction, but are not significant. Even though the programs are not getting worse over time, a problem with this conclusion is that no significant relationships were found, and the one result that approached significance was found for any recidivism, not the intended outcome of changing sexual recidivism. A second interpretation is that no obvious improvement in the treatment of sex offenders occurred over the last 30 years. This conclusion is supported by two recent evaluations of CBT programs for sex offenders: the Twin Rivers Sex Offender Treatment Program in Washington State (Barnoski, 2006) and the Western Australian Sex Offender Treatment Unit (SOTU) Program (Greenberg, DaSilva, & Lob, 2002).

The Greenberg and colleagues (2002) report illustrates a result and a conclusion typical of much of the treatment literature. The investigators studied the records of 2,165 convicted male sex offenders referred to the SOTU between 1987 and October 2000. There were no significant differences associated with treatment in survival analyses, including those that controlled for risk. In the Executive Summary, the investigators observe:

> Examination of the treated and untreated recidivism rates reveal there to be no significant effect of treatment. Despite this however it cannot be said with certainty that treatment is ineffective. Whilst it is clear that a strong treatment effect would have been apparent in the study results, it must be noted that there are methodological limitations of this evaluation, such as missing and incomplete data sets, which may have rendered it insensitive to smaller treatment effects. (p. viii)

(continued)

BOX 11.1. (continued)

They conclude:

> Despite the lack of a strong treatment effect, it is the opinion of the reviewers that sex offender treatment is essential and necessary. The programs detailed in the SOTU manuals are fitting with international standards and with the addition of psycho-pharmacological treatment options and improved community based post release follow-up, are likely to have a long term beneficial effects [sic] on sex offender recidivism, thus providing improved safety for our community. (p. ix)

We must conclude that these are indeed docile data.

The ultimate goal of sex offender treatment programs is to reduce sexual recidivism, and so there appears to have been no improvement in the ability to do so since publishing outcome studies began. Unfortunately, either conclusion depends on studies that allow us to assess true effect sizes of treatment. Considering that the bulk of studies used weaker designs, even if there had been an improvement over time, we would not be able to assess it properly. This unfortunate situation again highlights the importance of either conducting more efficacy studies (see "Treatment Efficacy and Research Priorities") or, more likely, admitting that different approaches must be tried.

preference, most have not shown that pre–post shifts were related to recidivism (Quinsey et al., 1998; Rice et al., 1991).

Marshall (2006) has argued that the effects of treating sex offenders are comparable to the effects of treating individuals with physical and mental health disorders. Although interventions with small (but statistically significant) effect sizes can be important, that importance is qualified by the cost of the intervention and the clinical significance of the effect. It is clear that the effects of treatment on recidivism pale in comparison to the effects of static risk factors (i.e., factors that do not change, such as criminal history). Meta-analyses on treating sex offenders show treatment effect sizes (using Cohen's d) that range from 0.10 to 0.47, whereas actuarial assessments provide effect sizes that range from 0.64 to 0.76, with some studies showing effect sizes between 1.00 and 2.40 (Hanson, Morton, & Harris, 2003). Though some researchers have suggested that treatment and other dynamic risk factors add to the accuracy of actuarial assessments, as described earlier, none have demonstrated that changes in dynamic risk factors relate to changes in long-term recidivism among sex offenders (for further discussion of this topic, see Rice, Harris, & Quinsey, 2002). Any dynamic risk factor either must be able to predict recidivism outcome after actuarial scores are controlled, or must significantly add to actuarial models. Thus far, there is no evidence that dynamic risk factors add to the long-term predictive accuracy of actuarial instruments using static risk factors among sex offenders. In other words, we can still predict who will recidivate, regardless of whether they receive treatment or not.

In order to have legitimate expectations of CBT treatment success, we first need to identify whether there is a true link among cognitions, attitudes, and subsequent sexually aggressive behaviors. Second, we need to know whether treatment can reliably change these cognitions and attitudes. Third, the effects of treatment on sustaining changes in cognitions and attitudes need to be established, especially when child molesters are released to the community. Fourth, researchers need to demonstrate that a change in treatment is related to a change in recidivism. Lastly, we need to show that changes from treatment predict recidivism over and above actuarial assessments. The first two points have received some support, but for the last three the evidence is negative or lacking.

Multisystemic Therapy

MST addresses general adolescent antisociality. Developed in the late 1970s, MST has become more popular in recent times for dealing with high-risk juvenile offenders. This approach is unique because it is a community-based treatment that targets multiple risk and protective factors, such as aspects of the individual, family, peers, school, neighborhood, and community. Borduin, Henggeler, Blaske, and Stein (1990) reported a random assignment study of MST with adolescent sex offenders. Though their results were highly encouraging (12.5% recidivism for treated offenders vs. 75% for untreated offenders at a 3-year follow-up), there were only 16 participants. Borduin and Schaeffer (2001) referred to an unpublished paper that reported similar results (12.5% vs. 41.7%) with a larger sample ($N = 48$). These sexual recidivism rates are far above those reported in other follow-up studies of adolescent sex offenders (e.g., Prentky, Harris, Frizzell, & Righthand, 2000, found 4% over a 12-month period) and children with sexual behavior problems (Carpentier, Silovsky, & Chaffin, 2006), leading us to wonder about the nature of the samples involved in the MST studies. Finally, MST is a less feasible approach to treating adults because of difficulties in involving an adult's family, peers, and social network during community reintegration.

Medical Treatments

Medical procedures are used to reduce general sexual arousal by targeting sex hormones and regions of the brain related to sexual functioning. It is assumed that reducing general sexual arousal eases the management of any paraphilic thoughts and behavior (Berlin & Meinecke, 1981). Similar to other treatments for pedophilia, most medical interventions target sex offenders—not pedophiles per se— with the intended outcome of reducing recidivism. Historically, this form of treatment involved either surgical castration to reduce testosterone levels or surgical lesioning of brain regions related to sexual activity. These methods have become virtually obsolete because of the emergence of alternative procedures that are similarly effective in adjusting testosterone levels, but are less invasive and not irreversible (Hill, Briken, Kraus, Strohm, & Berner, 2003).

Medical treatments currently in use target either neural activity or hormonal regulation related to sexual arousal. One method uses selective serotonin reuptake inhibitors (SSRIs) to block the reuptake of serotonin, a neurotransmitter associated with sexual function. Fluoxetine and sertraline are the most common types of SSRIs used in this manner (Bradford, 2001). Although SSRIs have been successful in reducing sexual arousal (Meston & Frohlich, 2000), and this reduction may be sufficient for reducing sexual interest in children, there is no evidence of serotonin dysfunction in the paraphilias (Hill et al., 2003). The second method regulates sex hormone levels in one of three ways: (1) using medroxyprogesterone acetate (MPA) to inhibit gonadotropic secretions and reducing testosterone; (2) using an antiandrogen, such as cyproterone acetate (CPA), in order to block androgen receptors throughout the body; or (3) overstimulating the hypothalamus by using a luteinizing hormone-releasing hormone (LHRH) agonist to reduce testosterone to levels usually attained by castration (Bradford, 2001; Briken, Nika, & Berner, 2001). There is evidence supporting the intended effects of medical treatment to reduce sexual arousal and paraphilic desire. For example, Bradford and Pawlak (1993) used a double-blind placebo crossover procedure with CPA to treat a group of paraphilic men. As expected, CPA had the intended effects on hormonal levels, sexual fantasies, and self-reported sexual arousal. Although the relationship between these targets and sexual thoughts and behavior are well established, we could not locate a paper that found aberrant levels of either serotonin or hormones to be diagnostic of pedophilia (or any other paraphilia).

Despite the strong relationship between neurobiological variables in sexual behavior and treatment, reducing general arousal does not alter sexual preference. Researchers found that men with phallometrically measured deviant sexual interests had the same preferences after hormonal treatment (Bancroft, Tennent, Loucas, & Cass, 1974; Cooper, Sandhu, Losztyn, & Cernovsky, 1992). Also, in Bradford and Pawlak's (1993) study described earlier, treatment using CPA showed no changes in PPG-measured arousal throughout treatment, only changes from self-report arousal; this leads us to suspect that demand characteristics may account for this discrepancy (i.e., child molesters are more likely to self-report a change in treatment even if no change actually occurred). It appears as though treatment for paraphilias works by decreasing sexual interest in general, suggesting that medical treatments do not "cure" the sexual preference but mask it by reducing sexual desire.[4] Still, these interventions could be useful and effective among forensic groups if a change in general sexual interest results in a change in sexual recidivism.

To date, there have been no randomized assignment studies relating medical treatment to recidivism among pedophiles. Hanson and Harris (2000) unexpectedly found that men who started antiandrogen treatment were more likely to recidivate than men who did not start treatment, presumably because only high-risk men received antiandrogen treatment. Despite their finding, a meta-analysis showed a moderately lower recidivism rate among those treated medically than men who did not receive medical treatment (Hall, 1995), but this latter finding must be understood in light of the methodological quality of the relevant studies. Hall noted considerable heterogeneity across samples: Follow-up times, source of recidivism data, and recidivism base rates all differed across studies. These and other medical studies also lacked placebo groups and provided treatment on a voluntary basis, using a treatment-refusers-as-controls design (Rice et al., 2001). Also, almost all medical papers specifically addressing pedophilia have been case studies (e.g., Bourgeois & Martina, 1996; Varela & Black, 2002); medical studies with larger samples have collapsed their data across paraphilia subtypes (e.g., Bradford & Pawlak, 1993; Hall, 1995; McConaghy, Blaszczynski, & Kidson, 1988), making it difficult to draw conclusions about treatment effectiveness specific to pedophilia. In view of the many possible confounding factors, the results of these treatment studies should be interpreted with caution.

Drawbacks unique to medical treatments for pedophilia include side effects and noncompliance. Commonly cited side effects include hypertension, hyperglycemia, feminization, depression, and headaches (Hill et al., 2003; Saleh & Guidry, 2003). These adverse effects are likely to cause the low compliance rates with medical treatments. Hucker, Langevin, and Bain (1988) found that of the 100 men eligible for treatment, only 18 began treatment, and just 11 completed the 3-month intervention. Across the literature, Barbaree and Seto (1997) found noncompliance rates to range from 30% to 100%, though Langevin and colleagues (1979) were able to increase compliance by providing assertiveness training. Because a possible consequence of noncompliance is an elevated risk of recidivism (Hanson et al., 2002), dealing with dropouts should receive greater attention.

Combining Treatment Approaches

Most programs include treatment "modules" that are separate interventions targeting known or assumed criminogenic needs. Typical treatment programs for sex offenders include heterosocial skills training, RP, modification of paraphilic arousal, and sex education, with an emphasis on attitudes and values. There has been little research on how such combinations of modules interact to reduce recidivism (Palmer, 1995). Others have provided a rationale for particular combinations of treatments, such as Bradford's (2000, 2001) algorithm to treat paraphilias. Bradford suggested that treatment should first categorize paraphilias into one of four levels of severity—mild, moderate, severe, or catastrophic—and then use these categorizations to determine the level of treatment. For example, CBT and RP are provided for all levels, but full antiandrogen or hormonal treatments are reserved for all severe and catastrophic cases. Other treatment algorithms for paraphilias have been described in the literature (e.g., Hill et al., 2003). Though some evidence suggests that a combination of medical and CBT treatments will provide optimal outcomes (e.g., Bradford & Greenberg, 1996), the utility of specific treatment algorithms still needs empirical support.

Treatment Efficacy and Research Priorities

The research described in this chapter provides a somber view of the effectiveness of treatment for pedophilia. Meta-analyses have shown either weak or no effects of treatment on sexual recidivism (Hanson et al., 2002; R. Lieb, personal communication, August 8, 2006).[5] These meta-analyses are bedeviled by the methodological quality of the studies evaluated—especially the limited use of randomized control designs, and the difficulty of distinguishing treatment dropouts and refusers from completers when control groups include men who would have dropped out or refused treatment if they had been given the opportunity (this procedure artificially decreases the recidivism rate of the treatment group; see Rice & Harris, 2003a). With these considerations in mind, along with efficacy studies showing no effect of treatment (Marques et al., 2005), is there anything at this point that clinicians can do to treat pedophilia? Apart from designing new studies based on a better understanding of the theoretical links between treatment targets and behavior, some recommendations for the design of interventions to reduce recidivism do emerge from the correctional "what works" literature.

These recommendations are best understood from Andrews and colleagues' (1990) principles of risk, need, and responsivity for effective correctional intervention. In their meta-analysis, correctional programs had greater reductions in recidivism when they targeted (1) offenders at high risk of recidivism; (2) criminogenic needs (i.e., aspects of individuals that are empirically linked to criminal behavior); and (3) responsivity to treatment (i.e., adapting programs to learning styles of offenders). Despite such an important finding, a review of the literature 9 years later identified only 10% of outcome studies reporting recidivism rates for higher- and lower-risk groups (Andrews, Dowden, & Gendreau, 1999). Of these studies, Andrews and Dowden (2006) found moderate support for the risk principle: The correlation between presence (vs. absence) of primary treatment and recidivism was .03 for low-risk and .10 for high-risk offenders. Andrews and Dowden also discovered that the risk principle interacted with the criminogenic needs principle; that is, the risk principle was supported only when programs targeted criminogenic needs. Unfortunately, these quantitative reviews collapsed data across all types of offenders, so we are not sure whether these effects would be different for sexual versus violent offenders. We suggest that if resources are scarce, clinicians should utilize these potentially useful principles of correctional intervention, especially by focusing on high-risk offenders[6] (for a discussion of how to identify high-risk offenders, see Quinsey et al., 2006).

We can also use Andrews and colleagues' (1990) principles of correctional intervention to help us understand some reasons why treatments for sex offenders are not successful. If pedophilia is a major path to child molesting, a possible explanation for why sexual preferences have been difficult to change might be that treatment programs do not actually address the neurohormonal or psychological mechanisms controlling sexual preferences. In other words, programs have not been able to treat a central criminogenic need. By drawing from the biological literature on sexual behavior, we can get a better understanding of how these mechanisms work. One of the most important periods for sexual preference development occurs prenatally, when hormones have neural organizational effects (Ellis & Ames, 1987; Meyer-Bahlburg, Ehrhardt, Rosen, & Gruen, 1995). As expected, evidence for an environmental influence on homosexuality occurs prenatally. Blanchard and Bogaert (1996; Bogaert, 2006) found that with every older brother a male has, the chances of being homosexual increase by 33%; this is known as the "fraternal birth order effect." It has been theorized that the fraternal birth order effect occurs because with each male fetus, the maternal immune system becomes more sensitized to some aspect of the male fetus, perhaps the male fetus's H-Y antigens (Y-chromosome-linked histocompatibility antigens found on fetal cells). Quicker and stronger responding of the maternal immune system impedes masculinization of the brain. It has been theorized that among pedophiles, similar neurodevelopmental incidents may alter not just gender preferences, but age preferences as well (Quinsey, 2003). Supporting this view, Lalumière, Harris, Rice, and Quinsey (1998) found that a fraternal birth order effect was related to PPG indices of sexual deviance (i.e., a preference for children or coercive sex), though no such birth order effect was found among heterosexual pedophiles in another study (Blanchard et al., 2000).

Two further comments on the child molester treatment literature are relevant here. The first is that very few sexologists believe that modifying homosexual orientation via current technologies is possible (this is not to argue that such a goal is desirable). It is more than a little surprising that no one applies this central conclusion from the literature on the treatment of homosexuality (now moribund) to the treatment of pedophilia; pedophilia is doubtless a different condition, but nevertheless also an anomaly of sexual preference.

Second, we are a very long way from determining the effective ingredients of treatment programs for child molesters. In much of the psychotherapy literature, treatment gains are easily demonstrated (at least in the short term), and researchers focus their attention on trying to disentangle the effects of specific treatment procedures and related factors from placebo and expectancy effects. In the treatment of pedophilia, investigators remain divided over whether there is *any* overall treatment effect.

After reviewing each treatment approach, we can highlight the central reasons why they have not worked in treating pedophilia:

1. Conditioning/behavioral: Sexual preferences are neither developed nor maintained by conditioning processes.
2. General psychotherapy: Treatments are unrelated to sexual preferences or criminogenic needs.
3. Cognitive: CBT addresses cognitions and attitudes correlated with antisociality, but these have no theoretical link to causing or maintaining atypical sexual preferences.
4. RP: This approach is based on a theory of maintenance, not etiology.
5. Medical: Hormones are used to reduce general sexual arousal, but this does not address pedophilic interests because in adulthood, hormones have motivational rather than organizational effects. If in fact pedophilia results from neurodevelopmental incidents, a better understanding of the psychological and neural processes affected by such incidents is needed to guide the development of novel treatment programs.

SUMMARY AND FUTURE DIRECTIONS

The etiology of pedophilia remains obscure, although (mostly indirect) evidence points to the importance of perturbations of neurohormones during early brain development. Recent advances in brain imaging (Cantor et al., 2006) promise to provide more direct clues to the etiology of this sexual anomaly, although behavior genetic investigations should also receive high priority. Phallometry remains the best-developed method of identifying anomalies in male sexual preference, but direct measurements of brain activity are likely to supersede these methods soon.

Treatment methods for child molesters appear to have produced quite limited reductions in recidivism, despite the ability of some programs to effect proximal improvements in variables assumed to cause child molestation. In our view, these dismal results stem from the failure to develop a method that can durably alter the central criminogenic need factor in pedophilia—sexual preference for children. More etiologically oriented research will be required to remedy this deficiency. It is possible that preventative interventions will prove to be more easily developed than cures for the condition once it is established.

On the other hand, there is hope that CBT approaches developed for offenders more generally can be profitably applied to reducing the recidivism of child molesters who are not pedophilic. There remains grave doubt, however, about the applicability of these methods for the most antisocial of these men. Fortunately, these psychopathic individuals are relatively rare.

ACKNOWLEDGMENTS

We would like to thank R. Karl Hanson for reanalyzing his meta-analysis using only child molesters, and Grant Harris, Martin Lalumière, and Michael Seto for their helpful comments.

NOTES

1. Another criticism of the DSM-IV diagnostic criteria is the use of clinical criteria. A result of using clinical criteria, such as distress, is the exclusion of men with pedophilic sexual interest who do not experience affective symptoms (see Spitzer & Wakefield, 1999). Revisions to DSM-IV-TR have corrected this issue by including clinical criteria as a sufficient, not necessary condition for diagnosis.
2. Among child molesters, a correspondence between sexual attractiveness ratings and penile tumescence responses for adolescents and children was not found; self-reports suggested a preference for adult females, whereas phallometric assessment suggested a preference for children (cf. Quinsey, Steinman, Bergersen, & Holmes, 1975). Such a result, however, is probably due to biased reporting (consider the legal implications of divulging a sexual preference for children).
3. Some have even argued that the relationship between attitudes and behavior is weak (Eckes & Six, 1994).
4. Medications used to treat paraphilias are better recognized by their brand names, such as Prozac (fluoxetine), Zoloft (sertraline), and Depo-Provera (MPA). These drugs were initially designed to treat other illnesses, such as cancer and depression; because reduced interest in sex was a side effect of these treatments, secondary uses emerged.
5. Though Aos, Miller, and Drake (2006) initially found an effect of treatment on sexual recidivism, a recent update found nonsignificant results (R. Lieb, personal communication, August 8, 2006).
6. The risk principle applies in the sense that management and intervention priorities should be directed at those at risk of causing greatest harm to society. The claim that treatments targeting high-risk men result in greater reductions in recidivism is challenged by research demonstrating that men at highest risk (i.e., psychopaths, especially sexually deviant psychopaths) still have extremely high recidivism rates even after treatment (Gretton et al., 2001; Hildebrand, de Ruiter, & de Vogel, 2004; Rice & Harris, 1997; Rice, Harris, & Cormier, 1992; Serin, Mailloux, & Malcolm, 2001; Seto, 2005).

REFERENCES

Abel, G. G. (2000). The importance of meeting research standards: A reply to Fischer and Smith's articles on the Abel Assessment for Sexual Interest. *Sexual Abuse: A Journal of Research and Treatment*, *12*(2), 155–161.

Abel, G. G., Becker, J. V., Cunningham-Rathner, J., Mittelman, M., & Rouleau, J. L. (1988). Multiple paraphilic diagnoses among sex offenders. *Bulletin of the American Academy of Psychiatry and the Law*, *16*(2), 153–168.

Abel, G. G., Becker, J. V., Murphy, W. D., & Flanagan, B. (1981). Identifying dangerous child molesters. In R. B. Stuart (Ed.), *Violent behavior: Social learning approaches to prediction, management, and treatment* (pp. 116–137). New York: Brunner/Mazel.

Abel, G. G., Gore, D. K., Holland, C. L., Camps, N., Becker, J. V., & Rathner, J. (1989). The measurement of the cognitive distortions of child molesters. *Sexual Abuse: A Journal of Research and Treatment*, *2*(2), 135–152.

Abel, G. G., Huffman, J., Warberg, B., & Holland, C. L. (1998). Visual reaction time and plethysmography as measures of sexual interest in child molesters. *Sexual Abuse: A Journal of Research and Treatment*, *10*(2), 81–95.

Abel, G. G., Jordan, A., Hand, C. G., Holland, L. A., & Phipps, A. (2001). Classification models of child molesters utilizing the Abel Assessment for Sexual Interest. *Child Abuse and Neglect*, *25*, 705–718.

Abel, G. G., Jordan, A., Rouleau, J. L., Emerick, R., Barboza-Whitehead, S., & Osborn, C. (2004). Use of visual reaction time to assess male adolescents who molest children. *Sexual Abuse: A Journal of Research and Treatment*, *16*(3), 255–265.

Abel, G. G., Levis, D. J., & Clancy, J. (1970). Aversion therapy applied to taped sequences of deviant behavior in exhibitionism and other sexual deviations: A preliminary report. *Journal of Behavior Therapy and Experimental Psychiatry, 1,* 58–66.

American Psychiatric Association. (2000). *Diagnostic and statistical manual of mental disorders* (4th ed., text rev.). Washington, DC: Author.

Andrews, D. A., & Dowden, C. (2006). Risk principle of case classification in correctional treatment: A meta-analytic investigation. *International Journal of Offender Therapy and Comparative Criminology, 50*(1), 88–100.

Andrews, D. A., Dowden, C., & Gendreau, P. (1999). *Clinically relevant and psychologically informed approaches to reduced re-offending: A meta-analytic study of human service, risk, need, responsivity, and other concerns in justice contexts.* Ottawa, ON, Canada: Carleton University.

Andrews, D. A., Zinger, I., Hoge, R. D., Bonta, J., Gendreau, P., & Cullen, F. T. (1990). Does correctional treatment work?: A clinically relevant and psychologically informed meta-analysis. *Criminology, 28,* 369–404.

Aos, S., Miller, M., & Drake, E. (2006). *Evidence-based adult corrections programs: What works and what does not* (Report No. 06-01-1201). Olympia: Washington State Institute for Public Policy.

Bancroft, J., Tennent, G., Loucas, K., & Cass, J. (1974). The control of deviant sexual behaviour by drugs. I. Behavioural changes following oestrogens and anti-androgens. *British Journal of Psychiatry, 125,* 310–315.

Barbaree, H. E., Bogaert, A. F., & Seto, M. C. (1995). Sexual reorientation therapy: Practices and controversies. In L. Diamant & R. D. McAnulty (Eds.), *The psychology of sexual orientation, behavior, and identity: A handbook* (pp. 357–353). Westport, CT: Greenwood Press.

Barbaree, H. E., & Seto, M. C. (1997). Pedophilia: Assessment and treatment. In D. R. Laws & W. O'Donohue (Eds.), *Sexual deviance: Theory, assessment, and treatment* (pp. 175–193). New York: Guilford Press.

Barlow, D. H., Leitenberg, H., & Agras, W. S. (1969). Experimental control of sexual deviation through manipulation of the noxious scene in covert sensitization. *Journal of Abnormal Psychology, 74*(5), 597–601.

Barnoski, R. (2006). *Sex offender sentencing in Washington State: Does the prison treatment program reduce recidivism?* (Report No. 06-06-1205). Olympia: Washington State Institute for Public Policy.

Barsetti, I., Earls, C. M., Lalumière, M. L., & Belanger, N. (1998). The differentiation of intrafamilial and extrafamilial heterosexual child molesters. *Journal of Interpersonal Violence, 13*(2), 275–287.

Bassarath, L. (2001). Neuroimaging studies of antisocial behaviour. *Canadian Journal of Psychiatry, 46*(8), 728–732.

Bauml, C. M., & Quinsey, V. L. (1992). *Relapse prevention treatment module.* Kingston, ON, Canada: Kingston Psychiatric Hospital.

Berlin, F. S., & Meinecke, C. F. (1981). Treatment of sex offenders with antiandrogenic medication: Conceptualization, review of treatment modalities, and preliminary findings. *American Journal of Psychiatry, 138,* 601–607.

Bickley, J., & Beech, A. R. (2001). Classifying child abusers: Its relevance to theory and clinical practice. *International Journal of Offender Therapy and Comparative Criminology, 45*(1), 51–69.

Blanchard, R., Barbaree, H. E., Bogaert, A. F., Dickey, R., Klassen, P., Kuban, M. E., et al. (2000). Fraternal birth order and sexual orientation in pedophiles. *Archives of Sexual Behavior, 29*(5), 463–478.

Blanchard, R., & Bogaert, A. F. (1996). Homosexuality in men and number of older brothers. *American Journal of Psychiatry, 153,* 27–31.

Blanchard, R., Klassen, P., Dickey, R., Kuban, M. E., & Blak, T. (2001). Sensitivity and specificity of the phallometric test for pedophilia in nonadmitting sex offenders. *Psychological Assessment, 13*(1), 118–126.

Blanchard, R., Kuban, M. E., Blak, T., Cantor, J. M., Klassen, P., & Dickey, R. (2006). Phallometric comparison of pedophilic interest in nonadmitting sexual offenders against stepdaughters, biological daughters, other biologically related girls, and unrelated girls. *Sexual Abuse: A Journal of Research and Treatment, 18*(1), 1–14.

Blumenthal, S., Gudjonsson, G., & Burns, J. (1999). Cognitive distortions and blame attribution in sex offenders against adults and children. *Child Abuse and Neglect, 23*(2), 129–143.

Bogaert, A. F. (2006). Biological versus nonbiological older brothers and men's sexual orientation. *Proceedings of the National Academy of Sciences USA, 103*(28), 10771–10774.

Borduin, C. M., Henggeler, S. W., Blaske, D. M., & Stein, R. J. (1990). Multisystemic treatment of adolescent sexual offenders. *International Journal of Offender Therapy and Comparative Criminology, 34*(2), 105–113.

Borduin, C. M., & Schaeffer, C. M. (2001). Multisystemic treatment of juvenile sex offenders: A progress report. *Journal of Psychology and Human Sexuality, 13*, 25–42.

Bourgeois, J. A., & Martina, K. (1996). Risperidone and fluoxetine in the treatment of pedophilia with comorbid dysthymia. *Journal of Clinical Psychopharmacology, 16*(3), 257–258.

Bradford, J. M. W. (2000). The treatment of sexual deviation using a pharmacological approach. *Journal of Sex Research, 37*, 248–257.

Bradford, J. M. W. (2001). The neurobiology, neuropharmacology, and pharmacological treatment of the paraphilias and compulsive sexual behaviour. *Canadian Journal of Psychiatry, 46*(1), 26–34.

Bradford, J. M. W., & Greenberg, D. M. (1996). Pharmacological treatment of deviant sexual behavior. *Annual Review of Sex Research, 7*, 283–306.

Bradford, J. M. W., & Pawlak, A. (1993). Effects of cyproterone acetate on sexual arousal patterns of pedophiles. *Archives of Sexual Behavior, 22*(6), 629–641.

Brecklin, L. R., & Forde, D. R. (2001). A meta-analysis of rape education programs. *Violence and Victims, 16*(3), 303–321.

Briken, P., Nika, E., & Berner, W. (2001). Treatment of paraphilia with luteinizing hormone-releasing hormone agonists. *Journal of Sex and Marital Therapy, 27*(1), 45–55.

Cantor, J. M., Noor, K., Christenson, B. K., Zipursky, R. B., Barbaree, H. E., Dickey, R., et al. (2006). *MRIs of pedophilic men.* Paper presented at the 25th Annual Conference of the Association for the Treatment of Sexual Abusers, Chicago.

Carpentier, M. Y., Silovsky, J. F., & Chaffin, M. (2006). Randomized trial of treatment for children with sexual behavior problems: Ten-year follow-up. *Journal of Consulting and Clinical Psychology, 74*(3), 482–488.

Chaplin, T. C., Rice, M. E., & Harris, G. T. (1995). Salient victim suffering and the sexual responses of child molesters. *Journal of Consulting and Clinical Psychology, 63*, 249–255.

Cohen, L. J., & Galynker, I. I. (2002). Clinical features of pedophilia and implications for treatment. *Journal of Psychiatric Practice, 8*(5), 276–289.

Cooper, A. J., Sandhu, S., Losztyn, S., & Cernovsky, Z. (1992). A double-blind placebo controlled trial of medroxyprogesterone acetate and cyproterone acetate with seven pedophiles. *Canadian Journal of Psychiatry, 37*(10), 687–693.

Dorr, D. (1998). Psychopathy in pedophiles. In T. Millon, E. Simonsen, M. Birket-Smith, & R. D. Davis (Eds.), *Psychopathy: Antisocial, criminal, and violent behavior* (pp. 304–320). New York: Guilford Press.

Eastman, B. J. (2004). Assessing the efficacy of treatment for adolescent sex offenders: A cross-over longitudinal study. *Prison Journal, 84*(4), 472–485.

Eckes, T., & Six, B. (1994). Fakten und Fiktionen in der Einstellungs-Verhaltens Forschung: Eine Meta-Analyse [Facts and fictions in attitude–behavior research: A meta-analysis]. *Zeitschrift für Sozialpsychologie, 25*, 253–271.

Ellis, L., & Ames, M. A. (1987). Neurohormonal functioning and sexual orientation: A theory of homosexuality–heterosexuality. *Psychological Bulletin, 101*, 233–258.

Fischer, L., & Smith, G. (1999). Statistical adequacy of the Abel Assessment for Interest in Paraphilias. *Sexual Abuse: A Journal of Research and Treatment, 11*(3), 195–205.

Flor-Henry, H. P., Lang, R. A., Koles, Z. J., & Frenzel, R. R. (1991). Quantitative EEG studies of pedophilia. *International Journal of Psychophysiology, 10*(3), 253–258.

Frenzel, R. R., & Lang, R. A. (1989). Identifying sexual preferences in intrafamilial and extrafamilial child abusers. *Annals of Sex Research, 2,* 255–275.

Freund, K. (1967). Diagnosing homo- or heterosexuality and erotic age-preference by means of a psychophysiological test. *Behaviour Research and Therapy, 5*(3), 209–228.

Freund, K., & Blanchard, R. (1989). Phallometric diagnosis of pedophilia. *Journal of Consulting and Clinical Psychology, 57*(1), 100–105.

Freund, K., & Watson, R. J. (1991). Assessment of the sensitivity and specificity of a phallometric test: An update of phallometric diagnosis of pedophilia. *Psychological Assessment, 3*(2), 254–260.

Freund, K., Watson, R., & Dickey, R. (1991). Sex offenses against female children perpetrated by men who are not pedophiles. *Journal of Sex Research, 28,* 409–423.

Furby, L., Weinrott, M. R., & Blackshaw, L. (1989). Sex offender recidivism: A review. *Psychological Bulletin, 105*(1), 3–30.

Galli, V., McElroy, S. L., Soutullo, C. A., Kizer, D., Raute, N., Keck, P. E. J., et al. (1999). The psychiatric diagnoses of twenty-two adolescents who have sexually molested other children. *Comprehensive Psychiatry, 40*(2), 85–88.

Gebhard, P. H., Gagnon, J. H., Pomeroy, W. B., & Christenson, C. V. (1965). *Sex offenders.* New York: Harper & Row.

Gray, N. S., Brown, A. S., MacCulloch, M. J., Smith, J., & Snowden, R. J. (2005). An implicit test of the associations between children and sex in pedophiles. *Journal of Abnormal Psychology, 114*(2), 304–308.

Greenberg, D. M., DaSilva, J. A., & Lob, N. (2002). *Evaluation of the Western Australian Sex Offender Treatment Unit (1987–1999).* Perth: Forensic Research Unit, Department of Psychiatry and Behavioural Sciences, University of Western Australia.

Greenwald, A. G., McGhee, J. L., & Schwartz, J. L. (1998). Measuring individual differences in implicit cognition: The Implicit Association Test. *Journal of Personality and Social Psychology, 74,* 1464–1480.

Gretton, H. M., McBride, M., Hare, R. D., O'Shaughnessy, R., & Kumka, G. (2001). Psychopathy and recidivism among adolescent sex offenders. *Criminal Justice and Behavior, 28*(4), 427–449.

Hall, G. C. N. (1995). Sexual offender recidivism revisited: A meta-analysis of recent treatment studies. *Journal of Consulting and Clinical Psychology, 63*(5), 802–809.

Hanson, R. K., & Bussière, M. T. (1998). Predicting relapse: A meta-analysis of sexual offender recidivism studies. *Journal of Consulting and Clinical Psychology, 66,* 348–362.

Hanson, R. K., Gordon, A., Harris, A. J. R., Marques, J. K., Murphy, W. D., Quinsey, V. L., et al. (2002). First report of the Collaborative Outcome Data Project on the Effectiveness of Psychological Treatment for Sex Offenders. *Sexual Abuse: A Journal of Research and Treatment, 14*(2), 169–194.

Hanson, R. K., & Harris, A. J. R. (2000). Where should we intervene?: Dynamic predictors of sexual offense recidivism. *Criminal Justice and Behavior, 27*(1), 6–35.

Hanson, R. K., Morton, K. E., & Harris, A. J. R. (2003). Sexual offender recidivism risk: What we know and what we need to know. *Annals of the New York Academy of Sciences, 989,* 154–166.

Harris, G. T., Rice, M. E., Quinsey, V. L., & Chaplin, T. C. (1996). Viewing time as a measure of sexual interest among child molesters and normal heterosexual men. *Behaviour Research and Therapy, 34*(4), 389–394.

Harris, G. T., Rice, M. E., Quinsey, V. L., Chaplin, T. C., & Earls, C. (1992). Maximizing the discriminant validity of phallometric assessment data. *Psychological Assessment, 4*(4), 502–511.

Harris, G. T., Rice, M. E., Quinsey, V. L., Lalumière, M. L., Boer, D., & Lang, C. (2003). A multisite comparison of actuarial risk instruments for sex offenders. *Psychological Assessment, 15*(3), 413–425.

Hildebrand, M., de Ruiter, C., & de Vogel, V. (2004). Psychopathy and sexual deviance in treated rapists: Association with sexual and nonsexual recidivism. *Sexual Abuse: A Journal of Research and Treatment, 16*, 1–24.

Hill, A., Briken, P., Kraus, C., Strohm, K., & Berner, W. (2003). Differential pharmacological treatment of paraphilias and sex offenders. *International Journal of Offender Therapy and Comparative Criminology, 47*(4), 407–421.

Hucker, S., Langevin, R., & Bain, J. (1988). A double blind trial of sex drive reducing medication in pedophiles. *Sexual Abuse: A Journal of Research and Treatment, 1*(2), 227–242.

Hucker, S. J., Langevin, R., Wortzman, G., Bain, J., Handy, L., Chambers, J., et al. (1986). Neuropsychological impairment in pedophiles. *Canadian Journal of Behavioural Science, 18*, 440–448.

Kalmus, E., & Beech, A. R. (2005). Forensic assessment of sexual interest: A review. *Aggression and Violent Behavior, 10*, 193–217.

Knight, R. A., Carter, D. L., & Prentky, R. A. (1989). A system for the classification of child molesters: Reliability and application. *Journal of Interpersonal Violence, 4*(1), 3–23.

Krafft-Ebing, R. von. (1998). *Psychopathia sexualis*. New York: Arcade. (Original work published 1886)

Kuban, M., Barbaree, H. E., & Blanchard, R. (1999). A comparison of volume and circumference phallometry: Response magnitude and method agreement. *Archives of Sexual Behavior, 28*(4), 345–359.

Lalumière, M. L., & Harris, G. T. (1998). Common questions regarding the use of phallometric testing with sexual offenders. *Sexual Abuse: A Journal of Research and Treatment, 10*(3), 227–237.

Lalumière, M. L., Harris, G. T., Quinsey, V. L., & Rice, M. E. (1998). Sexual deviance and number of older brothers among sexual offenders. *Sexual Abuse: A Journal of Research and Treatment, 10*(1), 5–15.

Lalumière, M. L., Harris, G. T., Quinsey, V. L., & Rice, M. E. (2005). *The causes of rape: Understanding individual differences in male propensity for sexual aggression*. Washington, DC: American Psychological Association.

Lalumière, M. L., & Quinsey, V. L. (1994). The discriminability of rapists from non-sex offenders using phallometric measures: A meta-analysis. *Criminal Justice and Behavior, 21*, 150–175.

Lalumière, M. L., & Quinsey, V. L. (1998). Pavlovian conditioning of sexual interests in human males. *Archives of Sexual Behavior, 27*(3), 241–252.

Lang, R. A., Black, E. L., Frenzel, R. R., & Checkley, K. L. (1988). Aggression and erotic attraction toward children in incestuous and pedophilic men. *Annals of Sex Research, 1*, 417–441.

Langevin, R., Paitich, D., Hucker, S. J., Newman, S., Ramsay, G., Pope, S., et al. (1979). The effect of assertiveness training, Provera and sex of therapist in the treatment of genital exhibitionism. *Journal of Behavior Therapy and Experimental Psychiatry, 10*, 275–282.

Langevin, R., & Watson, R. (1991). A comparison of incestuous biological and stepfathers. *Annals of Sex Research, 4*, 141–150.

Laws, D. R. (2001). Olfactory aversion: Notes on procedure, with speculations on its mechanism of effect. *Sexual Abuse: A Journal of Research and Treatment, 13*(4), 275–287.

Laws, D. R., Hanson, R. K., Osborn, C., & Greenbaum, P. E. (2000). Classification of child molesters by plethysmographic assessment of sexual arousal and a self-report measure of sexual preference. *Journal of Interpersonal Violence, 15*(12), 1297–1312.

Letourneau, E. J. (2002). A comparison of objective measures of sexual arousal and interest: Visual reaction time and penile plethysmography. *Sexual Abuse: A Journal of Research and Treatment, 14*(3), 207–223.

Looman, J., Gauthier, C., & Boer, D. (2001). Replication of the Massachusetts Treatment Center child molester typology in a Canadian sample. *Journal of Interpersonal Violence, 16*(8), 753–767.

Malcolm, P. B., Andrews, D. A., & Quinsey, V. L. (1993). Discriminant and predictive validity of phallometrically measured sexual age and gender preference. *Journal of Interpersonal Violence, 8*, 486–501.

Marques, J. K., Wiederanders, M., Day, D. M., Nelson, C., & van Ommeren, A. (2005). Effects of a relapse prevention program on sexual recidivism: Final results from California's Sex Offender Treatment and Evaluation Project (SOTEP). *Sexual Abuse: A Journal of Research and Treatment, 17*(1), 79–107.

Marquis, J. N. (1970). Orgasmic reconditioning: Changing sexual object choice through controlling masturbation fantasies. *Journal of Behavior Therapy and Experimental Psychiatry, 1*(4), 263–271.

Marshall, W. L. (1973). The modification of sexual fantasies: A combined treatment approach to the reduction of deviant sexual behavior. *Behaviour Research and Therapy, 11*(4), 557–564.

Marshall, W. L. (1997). Pedophilia: Psychopathology and theory. In D. R. Laws & W. O'Donohue (Eds.), *Sexual deviance: Theory, assessment, and treatment* (pp. 152–174). New York: Guilford Press.

Marshall, W. L. (2006). Appraising treatment outcome with sexual offenders. In W. L. Marshall, Y. M. Fernandez, L. L. Marshall, & G. Serran (Eds.), *Sexual offender treatment: Controversial issues* (pp. 255–273). New York: Wiley.

Marshall, W. L., & Barbaree, H. E. (1990). Outcome of comprehensive cognitive-behavioral treatment programs. In W. L. Marshall, D. R. Laws, & H. E. Barbaree (Eds.), *Handbook of sexual assault: Issues, theories, and treatment of the offender* (pp. 363–385). New York: Plenum Press.

Marshall, W. L., Barbaree, H. E., & Christophe, D. (1986). Sexual offenders against female children: Sexual preferences for age of victims and type of behavior. *Canadian Journal of Behavioural Science, 18*, 424–439.

Marshall, W. L., & Laws, D. R. (2003). A brief history of behavioral and cognitive behavioral approaches to sexual offender treatment: Part 2. The modern era. *Sexual Abuse: Journal of Research and Treatment, 15*(2), 93–120.

McConaghy, N., Blaszczynski, A., & Kidson, W. (1988). Treatment of sex offenders with imaginal desensitization and/or medroxyprogesterone. *Acta Psychiatrica Scandinavica, 77*(2), 199–206.

McElroy, S. L., Soutullo, C. A., Taylor, P. J., Nelson, E. B., Beckman, D. A., Brusman, L. A., et al. (1999). Psychiatric features of 36 men convicted of sexual offenses. *Journal of Clinical Psychiatry, 60*(6), 414–420.

Meston, C. M., & Frohlich, P. F. (2000). The neurobiology of sexual function. *Archives of General Psychiatry, 57*, 1012–1030.

Meyer-Bahlburg, H. F. L., Ehrhardt, A. A., Rosen, L. R., & Gruen, R. S. (1995). Prenatal estrogens and the development of homosexual orientation. *Developmental Psychology, 31*, 12–21.

Mihailides, S., Devilly, G. J., & Ward, T. (2004). Implicit cognitive distortions and sexual offending. *Sexual Abuse: A Journal of Research and Treatment, 16*(4), 333–350.

Murphy, W. D. (1990). Assessment and modification of cognitive distortions in sex offenders. In W. L. Marshall, D. R. Laws, & H. E. Barbaree (Eds.), *Handbook of sexual assault: Issues, theories, and treatment of the offender* (pp. 331–342). New York: Plenum Press.

Murphy, W. D., Haynes, M. R., Stalgaitis, S. J., & Flanagan, B. (1986). Differential sexual responding among four groups of sexual offenders against children. *Journal of Psychopathology and Behavioral Assessment, 8*, 339–353.

O'Donohue, W., & Plaud, J. J. (1994). The conditioning of human sexual arousal. *Archives of Sexual Behavior, 23*(3), 321–344.

O'Donohue, W., Regev, L. G., & Hagstrom, A. (2000). Problems with the DSM-IV diagnosis of pedophilia. *Sexual Abuse: A Journal of Research and Treatment, 12*(2), 95–105.

Palmer, T. (1995). Programmatic and nonprogrammatic aspects of successful intervention: New directions for research. *Crime and Delinquency, 41*(1), 100–131.

Petty, R. E., & Wegener, D. T. (1998). Attitude change: Multiple roles for persuasion variables. In D. T. Gilbert, S. T. Fiske, & G. Lindzey (Eds.), *The handbook of social psychology* (4th ed., Vol. 1, pp. 323–390). New York: McGraw-Hill.

Pfaus, J. G., Kippin, T. E., & Centeno, S. (2001). Conditioning and sexual behavior: A review. *Hormones and Behavior, 40*(2), 291–321.

Pithers, W. D. (1994). Process evaluation of a group therapy component designed to enhance sex offenders' empathy for sexual abuse survivors. *Behaviour Research and Therapy, 32*(5), 565–570.

Prentky, R., Harris, B., Frizzell, K., & Righthand, S. (2000). An actuarial procedure for assessing risk with juvenile sex offenders. *Sexual Abuse: A Journal of Research and Treatment, 12*(2), 71–93.

Proulx, J., Côté, G., & Achille, P. A. (1993). Prevention of voluntary control of penile response in homosexual pedophiles during phallometric testing. *Journal of Sex Research, 30*(2), 140–147.

Quinsey, V. L. (1986). Men who have sex with children. In D. N. Weisstub (Ed.), *Law and mental health: International perspectives* (Vol. 2, pp. 140–172). New York: Pergamon Press.

Quinsey, V. L. (2002). Evolutionary theory and criminal behavior. *Legal and Criminological Psychology, 7*(1), 1–13.

Quinsey, V. L. (2003). The etiology of anomalous sexual preferences in men. *Annals of the New York Academy of Sciences, 989*, 105–117.

Quinsey, V. L., Bergersen, S. G., & Steinman, C. M. (1976). Changes in physiological and verbal responses of child molesters during aversion therapy. *Canadian Journal of Behavioural Science, 8*, 202–212.

Quinsey, V. L., & Chaplin, T. C. (1988). Preventing faking in phallometric assessments of sexual preference. *Annals of the New York Academy of Sciences, 528*, 49–58.

Quinsey, V. L., Chaplin, T. C., & Carrigan, W. F. (1979). Sexual preferences among incestuous and non-incestuous child molesters. *Behavior Therapy, 10*, 562–565.

Quinsey, V. L., Chaplin, T. C., & Carrigan, W. F. (1980). Biofeedback and signaled punishment in the modification of inappropriate sexual age preferences. *Behavior Therapy, 11*(4), 567–576.

Quinsey, V. L., Chaplin, T. C., & Varney, G. (1981). A comparison of rapists and non-sex offenders' sexual preferences for mutually consenting sex, rape, and physical abuse of women. *Behavioural Assessment, 3*, 127–135.

Quinsey, V. L., & Earls, C. M. (1990). The modification of sexual preferences. In W. L. Marshall, D. R. Laws, & H. E. Barbaree (Eds.), *Handbook of sexual assault: Issues, theories, and treatment of the offender* (pp. 279–295). New York: Plenum Press.

Quinsey, V. L., Harris, G. T., Rice, M. E., & Cormier, C. A. (2006). *Violent offenders: Appraising and managing risk* (2nd ed.). Washington, DC: American Psychological Association.

Quinsey, V. L., Harris, G. T., Rice, M. E., & Lalumière, M. L. (1993). Assessing treatment efficacy in outcome studies of sex offenders. *Journal of Interpersonal Violence, 8*(4), 512–523.

Quinsey, V. L., Khanna, A., & Malcolm, P. B. (1998). A retrospective evaluation of the Regional Treatment Centre Sex Offender Treatment Program. *Journal of Interpersonal Violence, 13*(5), 621–644.

Quinsey, V. L., & Lalumière, M. L. (1995). Evolutionary perspectives on sexual offending. *Sexual Abuse: A Journal of Research and Treatment, 7*(4), 301–315.

Quinsey, V. L., & Lalumière, M. L. (2001). *Assessment of sexual offenders against children* (2nd ed.). Thousand Oaks, CA: Sage.

Quinsey, V. L., Steinman, C. M., Bergersen, S. G., & Holmes, T. F. (1975). Penile circumference, skin conductance, and ranking responses of child molesters and "normals" to sexual and nonsexual visual stimuli. *Behavior Therapy, 6*, 213–219.

Raymond, N. C., Coleman, E., Ohlerking, F., Christenson, G. A., & Miner, M. (1999). Psychiatric comorbidity in pedophilic sex offenders. *American Journal of Psychiatry, 156*, 786–788.

Rempel, J. K., & Serafini, T. E. (1995). Factors influencing the activities that people experience as sexually arousing: A theoretical model. *Canadian Journal of Human Sexuality, 4*, 3–14.

Rice, M. E., & Harris, G. T. (1997). Cross validation and extension of the Violence Risk Appraisal Guide for child molesters and rapists. *Law and Human Behavior, 21*, 231–241.

Rice, M. E., & Harris, G. T. (2002). Men who molest their sexually immature daughters: Is a special explanation required? *Journal of Abnormal Psychology, 111*(2), 329–339.

Rice, M. E., & Harris, G. T. (2003a). The size and sign of treatment effects in sex offender therapy. *Annals of the New York Academy of Sciences, 989*, 428–440.

Rice, M. E., & Harris, G. T. (2003b). *What's shape got to do with it?: Age and waist–hip ratio prefer-*

ences among child molesters and normal controls. Paper presented at the 22nd Annual Conference of the Association for the Treatment of Sexual Abusers, St. Louis, MO.

Rice, M. E., Harris, G. T., & Cormier, C. A. (1992). Evaluation of a maximum security therapeutic community for psychopaths and other mentally disordered offenders. *Law and Human Behavior, 16,* 399–412.

Rice, M. E., Harris, G. T., & Quinsey, V. L. (2001). Research on the treatment of adult sex offenders. In J. B. Ashford, B. D. Sales, & W. H. Reid (Eds.), *Treating adult and juvenile offenders with special needs* (pp. 291–312). Washington, DC: American Psychological Association.

Rice, M. E., Harris, G. T., & Quinsey, V. L. (2002). The appraisal of violence risk. *Current Opinion in Psychiatry, 15*(6), 589–593.

Rice, M. E., Harris, G. T., Quinsey, V. L., & Cyr, M. (1990). Planning treatment programs in secure psychiatric facilities. In D. Weisstub (Ed.), *Law and mental health: International perspectives* (Vol. 5, pp. 162–230). New York: Pergamon Press.

Rice, M. E., Quinsey, V. L., & Harris, G. T. (1991). Sexual recidivism among child molesters released from a maximum security psychiatric institution. *Journal of Consulting and Clinical Psychology, 59*(3), 381–386.

Robinson, M. C., Rouleau, J. L., & Madrigano, G. (1997). Validation of penile plethysmography as a psychophysiological measure of the sexual interests of adolescent sex offenders/Validation de la pléthysmographie pénienne comme measure psychophysiologique des intérêts sexuels des agresseurs adolescents. *Revue Québécois de Psychologie, 18,* 111–124.

Romero, J. J., & Williams, L. M. (1983). Group psychotherapy and intensive probation supervision with sex offenders: A comparative study. *Federal Probation, 47*(4), 36–42.

Rossi, P. H., Lipsey, M. W., & Freeman, H. E. (2004). *Evaluation: A systematic approach* (7th ed.). Thousand Oaks, CA: Sage.

Saleh, F. M., & Guidry, L. L. (2003). Psychosocial and biological treatment considerations for the paraphilic and nonparaphilic sex offender. *Journal of the American Academy of Psychiatry and the Law, 31*(4), 486–493.

Serin, R. C., Mailloux, D. L., & Malcolm, P. B. (2001). Psychopathy, deviant sexual arousal and recidivism among sexual offenders: A psycho-culturally determined group offense. *Journal of Interpersonal Violence, 16,* 234–246.

Seto, M. C. (1999). Book review of *Paedophiles and Sexual Offenses against Children. Archives of Sexual Behavior, 28,* 276–279.

Seto, M. C. (2002). Peer commentaries on Green (2002) and Schmidt (2002): Precisely defining pedophilia. *Archives of Sexual Behavior, 31*(6), 498–499.

Seto, M. C. (2005). Is more better?: Combining actuarial risk scales to predict recidivism among adult sex offenders. *Psychological Assessment, 17*(2), 156–167.

Seto, M. C. (2008). *Pedophilia and sexual offending against children: Theory, assessment, and intervention.* Washington, DC: American Psychological Association.

Seto, M. C., Cantor, J. M., & Blanchard, R. (2006). Child pornography offenses are a valid diagnostic indicator of pedophilia. *Journal of Abnormal Psychology, 115*(3), 610–615.

Seto, M. C., Harris, G. T., Rice, M. E., & Barbaree, H. E. (2004). The Screening Scale for Pedophilic Interests predicts recidivism among adult sex offenders with child victims. *Archives of Sexual Behavior, 33*(5), 455–466.

Seto, M. C., & Lalumière, M. L. (2001). A brief screening scale to identify pedophilic interests among child molesters. *Sexual Abuse: A Journal of Research and Treatment, 13*(1), 15–25.

Seto, M. C., Lalumière, M. L., & Blanchard, R. (2000). The discriminative validity of a phallometric test for pedophilic interests among adolescent sex offenders against children. *Psychological Assessment, 12*(3), 319–327.

Seto, M. C., Lalumière, M. L., & Kuban, M. (1999). The sexual preferences of incest offenders. *Journal of Abnormal Psychology, 108*(2), 267–272.

Seto, M. C., Murphy, W. D., Page, J., & Ennis, L. (2003). Detecting anomalous sexual interests in juvenile sex offenders. *Annals of the New York Academy of Sciences, 989,* 118–130.

Smith, D., & Fischer, L. (1999). Assessment of juvenile sexual offenders: Reliability and validity of the Abel Assessment for Interest in Paraphilias. *Sexual Abuse: A Journal of Research and Treatment, 11*(3), 207–216.

Spitzer, R. L., & Wakefield, J. C. (1999). DSM-IV diagnostic criterion for clinical significance: Does it help solve the false positive problem? *American Journal of Psychiatry, 156,* 1856–1864.

Streiner, D. L. (2002). The 2 'Es' of research: Efficacy and effectiveness trials. *Canadian Journal of Psychiatry, 47,* 552–556.

Varela, D., & Black, D. W. (2002). Pedophilia treated with carbamazepine and clonazepam. *American Journal of Psychiatry, 159*(7), 1245–1246.

Virkkunen, M. (1976). The pedophilic offender with antisocial character. *Acta Psychiatrica Scandinavica, 53*(5), 401–405.

Wakefield, J. C. (1992). The concept of mental disorder: On the boundary between biological facts and social values. *American Psychologist, 47*(3), 373–388.

World Health Organization. (1994). *International statistical classification of diseases and related health problems* (10th rev.). Geneva: Author.

Wright, P., Nobrega, J., Langevin, R., & Wortzman, G. (1990). Brain density and symmetry in pedophilic and sexually aggressive offenders. *Sexual Abuse: A Journal of Research and Treatment, 3*(3), 319–328.

CHAPTER 12

SEXUAL SADISM

Psychopathology and Theory

PAMELA M. YATES
STEPHEN J. HUCKER
DREW A. KINGSTON

Since its first appearance in historical writings, sexual sadism has proven to be an elusive concept to define and measure, encompassing a wide array of sexually anomalous behavior. Today, although there is some agreement on the features of sexual sadism—such as the presence of behavior and fantasy related to the infliction of pain, suffering, and humiliation—the psychopathology of the disorder remains uncertain, and a satisfactory, comprehensive theory of the etiology of sexual sadism has not yet been developed and tested. Estimates of the prevalence of sexual sadism vary considerably; the risk for recidivism of sadistic sexual offenders has not been specifically examined; and recent research suggests unreliability in the diagnosis of the disorder (see Kingston & Yates, Chapter 13, this volume). Nonetheless, some commonalities and theories exist that can aid forensic practitioners to identify, understand, and treat these offenders. This chapter examines research and theorizing to date pertaining to the psychopathology and etiology of sexual sadism and its associated features, and provides future directions for work in this area.

DEFINITIONS

Richard von Krafft-Ebing is usually credited with introducing the term "sadism" in his classic text *Psychopathia Sexualis* (Krafft-Ebing, 1886/1892); he derived it from the name of the French author the Marquis de Sade, who described the behavior in his erotic novels. Krafft-Ebing described the essential clinical features of sexual sadism as "the experience of sexual, pleasurable sensations (including orgasm) produced by acts of cruelty, bodily punishment afflicted on one's person or when witnessed by others, be they animals or human beings. It may also consist of an innate desire to humiliate, hurt, wound or even destroy others in order, thereby, to create sexual pleasure in oneself" (p. 109). Schrenck-Notzing (1895/1956) also emphasized the idea that infliction of pain was the central feature of "algolagnia" (literally "pain craving"), which he subdivided into active (sadism) and passive (masochism) forms. Later, Eulenberg (1911) included the notion of psychological pain in the form of humiliation in his conceptualization of sexual sadism.

The concept of sexual sadism expanded under the influence of psychodynamically oriented writers. Karpmann (1954) noted that in the sadist, "the will to power is sexually accentuated . . . he revels in the fear, anger and the humiliation" (p. 10). Pain was viewed as important because it symbolized power and control over the victim. Similarly, Fromm (1977) suggested that the

> core of sadism . . . is the passion to have absolute and unrestricted control over living beings . . . whether an animal, child, a man or a woman. To force someone to endure pain or humiliation without being able to defend himself is one of the manifestations of absolute control, but it is by no means the only one. The person who has complete control over another living being makes this being into his thing, his property, while he becomes the other being's god. (pp. 383–384)

Later descriptions also incorporated the association of such feelings of power and control with sexual pleasure and gratification as an essential feature of sexual sadism (Brittain, 1970; Fromm, 1977; Langevin, 1991; MacCulloch, Snowden, Wood, & Mills, 1983; Myers, Burgess, Burgess, & Douglas, 1999), while other theorists have focused on sadistic and violent sexual fantasy as an essential element in sadism (Brittain, 1970; East, 1949; Ellis, 1936; MacCulloch, Gray, & Watt, 2000; Prentky et al., 1989; Sturup, 1968).

Current official classification systems adopt a more limited view of sexual sadism. The *International Classification of Diseases*, 10th revision (ICD-10; World Health Organization, 1992) defines sadism as the "preference for sexual activity that involves bondage or the infliction of pain or humiliation" (p. 220), and the *Diagnostic and Statistical Manual of Mental Disorders*, fourth edition, text revision (DSM-IV-TR; American Psychiatric Association, 2000) requires "psychological or physical suffering (including humiliation)" (p. 574) of the victim to cause sexual excitement in the sadist. However, as described by Kingston and Yates (Chapter 13, this volume), research has shown that these definitions have proven difficult to apply in practice, with the result that even experienced clinicians appear to employ "official" criteria inconsistently in diagnosing sexual sadism.

TYPES OF SEXUAL SADISM

Krafft-Ebing (1886/1892) described no fewer than eight subtypes of sexually sadistic behavior, including lust murder (in which sexual arousal is intimately linked to the act of killing); necrophilia; injury of women by stabbing or flagellation; defilement of women; other types of assaults on women, such as cutting off their hair; whipping of boys; sadism toward animals; and sadistic fantasies without the occurrence of any actual sadistic acts. Later, Hirschfeld (1956) made a simple distinction between "major" sadism (including lust murder, necrophilia, and stabbing) and "minor" sadism (the rest of Krafft-Ebing's categories, as well as humiliation of a consenting partner via bondage, mild flagellation, submission, or degrading acts). Another major sadistic behavior is "piqeurism," where the attacker stabs a female victim, usually in the buttocks or breasts, and then runs off (Bondeson, 2001; De River, 1958). Still another is the rare phenomenon of vampirism, involving the letting of blood by cutting or biting (and sometimes drinking it), which is accompanied by sexual arousal (Jaffe & DiCataldo, 1994); such individuals will take their own blood for this purpose, but, more importantly in the present context, vampirism is closely related to necrophilia and lust murder.

It has been noted that consenting sadomasochism appears relatively common among nonoffenders, as evidenced by the existence of "S/M" groups and by common themes in pornographic materials (Grubin, 1994b). Sexual sadism has also been linked to masochistic behavior. Individuals who participate in voluntary, consenting acts of minor sadism, as either recipients or perpetrators, often refer to the activity as "bondage and discipline," "dominance and submission," or "sadomasochism"; some do not consider their behaviors deviant at all, but simply as mild variants of the norm (Gosselin, 1987; Weinberg, 1987).

Necrophilia and Sadism

The term "necrophilia" appears to describe a fairly clear-cut sexual anomaly; however, like "sexual sadism," it has been used in a number of different ways by different authors, including some cases in which there have been only fantasies of sexual contact with corpses (Calef & Weinshel, 1972). Krafft-Ebing (1886/1892) regarded necrophilia as a manifestation of sadism. Others observed that infliction of pain is not necessarily a feature of necrophilia (Ellis, 1936; Moll, 1912) and suggested the presence of a strong fetishistic element in these cases (Ellis, 1936). Like Krafft-Ebing, Hirschfeld (1956) divided necrophilia into violation of a person who was already dead and sexual abuse of a person an individual had first murdered, "to possess and destroy her beyond death" (p. 425).

Rosman and Resnick (1989) discriminated between "genuine necrophilia," which fulfilled DSM-III-R (American Psychiatric Association, 1987) criteria, and "pseudonecrophilia." They defined as genuine necrophilia those cases in which during the preceding 6 months an individual had reported recurrent, intense urges and sexually arousing fantasies involving corpses, which the individual had either acted upon or found markedly distressing. By contrast, pseudonecrophilia included "incidental" cases in which the subject engaged in sexual activity with the body without having had any preexisting fantasies of doing so. Rosman and Resnick (1989) also referred to "necrophilic homicide," in which the murderer killed to obtain a body with which to engage in sexual activity, and "necrophilic fantasy," in which the individual engaged in fantasy regarding corpses without engaging in any actual sexual activity with them.

Lust Murder and Sadistic Murder

Homicide in which the killer derives sexual pleasure from the act of killing is termed "erotophonophilia" or "lust murder" (Bartholomew, Milte, & Galbally, 1975), and sexual sadism is hypothesized to underlie this phenomenon (Brittain, 1970; Dietz, Hazelwood, & Warren, 1990; Ressler, Burgess, & Douglas, 1988). These murders are distinguished from "vindictive murder" or "displaced anger murder," in which offenders are not thought to derive sexual pleasure from killing (Myers et al., 1999; Rada, 1978). Much of what is known about sexual sadism has been derived from work on sexual murderers. Although some studies have been conducted specifically to compare diagnosed sadists with nonsadists, the majority of information is descriptive and as such should be interpreted with caution, since not all sexual murderers are sadists (Grubin, 1994b). Furthermore, offense and offender characteristics arising from these descriptions are not necessarily exclusive to sexual sadists, but are also evident in other groups, such as nonsadistic rapists and other sexual offenders (Crepault & Couture, 1980; Gray, Watt, Hassan, & MacCulloch, 2003; Grubin, 1994b).

Perhaps the most influential works on lust murder are those of Brittain (1970) and the U.S. Federal Bureau of Investigation (FBI; e.g., Dietz et al., 1990). Brittain described the typical lust murderer as overcontrolled, introverted, timid, sexually inexperienced, and deeply deviant, holding vivid and violent sadistic fantasies. However, there are multiple contradictions in Brittain's conceptualization of these individuals. For example, some were described as collectors of pornography, whereas others did not collect these materials and were described as prudish and sanctimonious. They were simultaneously described as vain and egocentric, but also as having low self-esteem. Because of these significant contradictions, Brittain's profile of the sadistic murderer and his anecdotal clinical descriptions have not been consistently supported or validated by research (Grubin, 1994a; Langevin, 2003). Although Brittain's work has stimulated additional research and theorizing, as noted by Grubin (1994a), this work should be regarded more as literature than as science, because it represents a composite picture based on clinical impressions rather than the results of systematic research.

In their often-cited study, Dietz and colleagues (1990) examined the characteristics of 30 sexual sadists, the majority of whom were sexual murderers. There was no comparison group of nonsadists, so the findings described below, while descriptive of sadists, do not allow for comparison with nonsadists with respect to the prevalence of these features. They found that the majority of offenders were white males who were employed (75%) and married (50%) at the time of their offenses. Forty-three percent had a history of homosexual experience, 20% cross-dressed, and 20% had a history of other sexually anomalous behavior. Approximately half had parents with a history of marital infidelity or divorce, 23% reported childhood physical abuse, and 20% reported childhood sexual abuse. The majority had no previous criminal record. Fifty percent had a history of drug abuse other than alcohol. Most (93%) had carefully planned their offenses, which they committed predominantly against unknown victims (83%). They usually abducted their victims and held them captive for more than 24 hours, binding, blindfolding, and gagging them. Typical activities included sexual bondage, rape, and forced fellatio, although vaginal intercourse and insertion of foreign objects also occurred. All the victims were tortured. The offenders recorded their crimes in more than half of cases (53%) in diaries, audio- and videotapes, photographs, and drawings, and 40% kept souvenirs of the victims.

Also using FBI data, Warren, Hazelwood, and Dietz (1996) and Burgess, Hartman, Ressler, Douglas, and McCormack (1986) reported similar findings to those of Dietz and colleagues (1990). Warren and colleagues (1996) found that of 20 sexually sadistic serial murderers, all were male, most (95%) were white, 75% were steadily employed, 75% collected violent material, 95% planned their offenses, 80% had offended against unknown victims, and in all cases there was physical evidence of torture. In Burgess and colleagues' study, 36 sexual murderers were found to be predominantly male (92%); of average or higher intelligence; and from families with criminal (50%), psychiatric (53%), alcohol (69%), drug (33%), and sexual (46%) problems in their histories, as well as absent parents and residential instability in a significant number of cases (43% and 68%, respectively). Physical abuse (42%), psychological abuse (74%), and sexual abuse (43%) were confirmed in the childhood histories of these offenders, and 69% had had a psychiatric assessment or confinement as a child or adolescent. Burgess and colleagues also examined a variety of behavioral indicators among sexual murderers in childhood, adolescence, and adulthood. Numerous problems thought to be predictive of sadistic fantasy, such as daydreaming, compulsive isolation, chronic lying, destruction of property, firesetting, and cruelty to children, were found in more than 50% of participants. It is important to note that there were limitations to this study. Specifically, the sexual murderers were not diagnosed as sexual sadists; there was no comparison group; and the checklist from which indicators were derived was not standardized, and its psychometric properties are unknown. As such, these features, while evident among sexual murderers, were not specifically associated with sexual sadism; nor does this research differentiate between sadists and nonsadists on these features. It is likely that these represent overlapping but separate groups with possibly different etiologies, treatments, and prognoses.

Gratzer and Bradford (1995) compared results from the Dietz and colleagues (1990) study with sadistic (N = 28) and nonsadistic (N = 29) sexual offenders, including sexual murderers and other sexual offenders housed in a forensic psychiatric facility, who were diagnosed using DSM-III-R (American Psychiatric Association, 1987) criteria. Although they found some results similar to those of Dietz and colleagues, such as high rates of offense planning (82%), torture (78%), and physical abuse during childhood (43%), there were also significant differences between the two samples on factors such as greater use of bondage, anal rape, and collection of souvenirs from the victims among the sadists as compared to nonsadists.

In examining the characteristics of sexual homicides, Meloy (2000) suggests that crime scenes that reflect organized, rather than disorganized, murder are suggestive of sexual sadism. Organized murders, according to the FBI research, are characterized by such features as planning, targeting unknown victims, the absence of weapons but the use of restraints in the commission of offenses, and elements of control and submission in offense features (Ressler et al., 1988). Meloy has hypothesized that obsessive–compulsive disorder or obsessive–compulsive personality disorder characterizes both organized sexual murderers and sexual sadists. He suggests that the observations of sexual sadists made by Krafft-Ebing, Brittain, and others support this hypothesis, in that their descriptions of sadists clearly demonstrate such characteristics as obsessive–compulsive traits, behavior, and obsessional or intrusive thoughts. It should be noted, however, that the existence of such traits among sexual sadists has not been explicitly assessed; nor have sadists and nonsadists been compared on these characteristics to determine whether such features are exclusive to sexual sadism.

In addition to the differences found between the FBI sample and that of Gratzer and Bradford (1995), it is important to note that the FBI studies concluded (Dietz et al., 1900; Warren et al., 1996) that sexual sadists exhibited psychopathy and narcissism, based on clinical assessments using the then-current DSM-III criteria. However, these have not been assessed with more recently established criteria, and this finding has not been consistently reported. For example, in one study in which psychopathy was assessed with the Psychopathy Checklist—Revised (PCL-R; Hare, 1991), no relationship was found between sexual sadism and psychopathy (Holt, Meloy, & Strack, 1999). Thus it has been suggested that the FBI samples may not be representative of sexual sadists in general, and that the offenders in these studies may represent a particularly extreme group (Beauregard & Proulx, 2002; Hucker, 1997; Marshall & Kennedy, 2003).

Grubin (1994b) compared 21 men who killed during a sexual attack with 121 rapists who did not kill their victims. There were several significant differences between the two groups, with sexual murderers characterized by higher rates of social isolation and difficulties with sexual relationships. The sexual murders were also more likely to have had a previous conviction for rape than rapists who did not kill their victims. Grubin also found that some of the characteristics noted were inconsistent with those of others, such as Brittain (1970) and Dietz and colleagues (1990). For example, sexual murderers and rapists did not differ significantly in their use of pornography and deviant sexual fantasy, and appeared to have comparatively stable familial histories.

Proulx, Blais, and Beauregard (2005) found that sadists (N = 43) were more likely than nonsadistic sexual offenders (N = 98) to have planned their offenses; to kidnap their victims; to use bondage and weapons; to engage in expressive violence, humiliation, and torture of victims; to insert objects into the victims' vaginas; to strangle their victims; and to engage in postmortem intercourse and mutilation. In the 48 hours preceding their offenses, they were also significantly more likely to have had a specific conflict with a woman, to be angry and sexually excited, and to report deviant sexual fantasies prior to their offenses. Finally, Proulx, Blais, and Beauregard (2006) also found that sadists scored higher on the Schizoid, Avoidant, Histrionic, and Schizotypal subscales of the Millon Clinical Multiaxial Inventory (MCMI; Millon, 1983) than nonsadists did.

Sadistic Rape

Comparatively little research has been conducted on the existence of sexual sadism among rapists, and estimates of the disorder among this group of offenders vary widely. Most researchers report that only 5–10% of their samples of rapists fulfill DSM criteria for sexual sadism (e.g., Abel, Becker, Cunningham-Rathner, Mittelman, & Rouleau, 1988), although some have reported rates as high as 45% (Fedora et al., 1992; Hucker, Langevin, & Bain, 1988; Langevin et al., 1985; Langevin & Lang, 1987; Yarvis, 1995).

Rape is a multidetermined phenomenon, and rapists constitute a heterogeneous group (Marshall & Barbaree, 1990). Rape per se is differentiated from sexual sadism predominantly on the basis of the arousal pattern evident within the individual. That is, the former consists of preferential interest toward nonconsenting and resistant victims but not necessarily suffering victims, whereas the latter consists of sexual arousal specifically to the physical suffering and/or humiliation of a particular victim. It has been suggested (Abel, 1989) that rapists differ from sexual sadists in the object of sexual arousal during the commission of the offense. Specifically, rapists are thought to be sexually aroused to sexually aggressive stimuli and forced sexual activity, whereas sexual sadists are sexually aroused to violence and the use of gratuitous violence (Abel, 1989). Within this conceptualization, rapists are not thought to use greater force in offending than is required to gain the compliance of the victim. While it can be difficult to differentiate between these two diagnoses, it has been suggested that sexual arousal that accompanies such behavioral indicators as mutilating the victim, deliberately injuring the victim or causing death, inserting inanimate objects into the victim's orifices, or taking souvenirs can be suggestive of a diagnosis of sexual sadism (Doren, 2002).

As indicated above, sexual sadists are hypothesized to be aroused by the use of gratuitous violence (Abel, 1989), while preferential rapists are believed to use force as necessary to gain the victim's compliance. However, assessment of sexual arousal, primarily conducted using physiological measures of arousal or sexual interest (see Kingston & Yates, Chapter 13, this volume), has yielded inconclusive results with respect to the relationship between arousal and degree of violence in the commission of offenses, victim injury, and dangerousness; arousal patterns to depictions varying in degree of consent, humiliation, degradation, sexual violence, or physical violence; or differences between rapists and other groups (Abel, 1989; Abel, Barlow, Blanchard, & Guild, 1977; Avery-Clark & Laws, 1984; Barbaree, Marshall, & Lanthier, 1979; Eccles, Marshall, & Barbaree, 1994; Quinsey & Chaplin, 1982; Quinsey, Chaplin, & Upfold, 1984; Quinsey, Lalumière, & Seto, 1994; Rice, Chaplin, Harris, & Coutts, 1994; Seto & Barbaree, 1993; Seto & Kuban, 1996). Furthermore, these measures suffer from methodological problems, such as lack of reliability and validity, as well as inability to discriminate sexual offenders from other males (Barbaree, Baxter, & Marshall, 1989; Eccles et al., 1994; Marshall, 1996; Marshall & Fernandez, 2000). Furthermore, some characteristics of preferential rapists overlap with those of sexual sadists (Dietz et al., 1990), such as coercing a victim to perform fellatio or to submit to anal intercourse; offending against strangers; and the existence of other paraphilias such as voyeurism, telephone scatalogia, or exhibitionism (Warren et al., 1996). As such, although sexual arousal to sadistic and/or violent themes is viewed as an essential feature of sexual sadism, research clearly does not provide clinicians with definitive information that could be used to differentiate sadists from rapists and other offenders.

Attempts to understand sadistic rape, as inferred from studies of rapists with varying characteristics, have been inconclusive and provide mixed support for the existence of characteristics presumed to be important to the diagnosis of sexual sadism, such as offense violence and the influence of deviant sexual fantasy. Studies of rape are further complicated by research conducted on "normal" (i.e., noncriminal) men, various proportions of whom admit to sexual fantasies of raping or tying up a woman (30% of subjects; Crepault & Couture, 1980), arousal to sadomasochistic narratives (16–20% of subjects; Malamuth, Haber, & Feshbach, 1980), fantasies involving pain on the part of the victim (Malamuth & Check, 1983), and fantasies depicting women bound and in distress (Heilbrun & Leif, 1988). Furthermore, numerous studies have found that male college students indicate that they would rape a woman if they were assured of not being caught (Koss, Gidycz, & Wisniewski, 1987; Malamuth, 1981; Malamuth, Heim, & Feshbach, 1980; Yates, 1996). Common though these themes may be in fantasy, however, such studies do not provide information on how frequently truly sadistic fantasies are acted upon—or, more importantly, whether these themes represent the preferred method of sexual expression.

PREVALENCE AND COMORBIDITY

It is estimated that the prevalence of sexual sadism among sexual offenders is low, representing approximately 2–5% of offenses (Quinsey, Chaplin, & Varney, 1981). However, estimates can vary significantly as a result of the diagnostic criteria used, with broader criteria, such as those of Krafft-Ebing, yielding estimates as high as 50% (Langevin, 2003).

Given problems with diagnostic consistency, accuracy of assessment methods, and samples used in research to date, data pertaining to the prevalence of sexual sadism are variable and must be viewed with caution (Marshall & Kennedy, 2003). For example, the reliability of diagnoses of paraphilias in general (Levenson, 2004) and of sexual sadism in particular (Levenson, 2004; Marshall, Kennedy, Yates, & Serran, 2002) has been found to be unacceptably low, although these findings may result from the specific statistical procedures employed, which may underestimate reliability (Packard & Levenson, 2006).

Further complicating estimates of the prevalence of sexual sadism is the view by some (e.g., Karpmann, 1954) that sadism and masochism are complementary anomalies or separate poles of the same disorder. Supporting this notion are findings that individuals who report masochistic fantasies are likely to report sadistic ones as well (Arndt, Foehl, & Good, 1985); that self-identified sadomasochists alternate between these two roles (Spengler, 1977); and that there is an association between asphyxiophilia (an expression of extreme masochism) and sadistic murder (Hucker & Blanchard, 1992). In addition, sadism and masochism have been found to be relatively common among the general population. For example, Kinsey, Pomeroy, Martin, and Gebhard (1953) reported that between 3% and 12% of women and between 10% and 20% of men admitted to responding sexually to sadomasochistic narratives. Crepault and Couture (1980) found that approximately 15% of men in a sample from the general population reported fantasies of humiliating a woman, and approximately 11% of assaulting a woman. Furthermore, as noted above, it has also been found that sadomasochistic and sadistic themes are common in general, such as in mainstream pornographic magazines (Dietz & Evans, 1982; Donnelly & Fraser, 1998; Grubin, 1994a).

In addition to the difficulty in estimating prevalence rates are findings of comorbidity of paraphilias among sexual offenders in general and among sexual sadists in particular. For example, Abel and colleagues (1988) found that 18% of sadists were also masochistic, 46% had raped, 21% had exposed themselves, 25% had engaged in voyeurism and frottage, and 33% had molested children. Similarly, other authors have noted an overlap among sadism, masochism, fetishism, and transvestism (Gosselin & Wilson, 1980). Among self-identified sadomasochists and among serious sadistic offenders, transvestism and fetishism have also been noted (Dietz et al., 1990; Prentky, Cohen, & Seghorn, 1985).

ETIOLOGICAL THEORIES

Although early conceptualizations of sexual sadism did not propose hypotheses about its etiology, these ideas, along with the research described above, continue to be reflected today—including within the diagnostic classification systems, ICD-10 (World Health Organization, 1992) and DSM-IV-TR (American Psychiatric Association, 2000), and in theories of the etiology of sexual sadism. Theories of the etiology of sexual sadism were initially proposed via the development of theoretical formulations based on collections of case studies, such as those compiled by Krafft-Ebing (1886/1892) and Brittain (1970), and later via descriptive and comparative studies of the similarities and differences between individuals presumed or assessed to be sexually sadistic and those with other paraphilias.

Various explanations of the etiology of sexual sadism have been proposed and revised over the years, although little new theorizing has been evident in recent years. Theories have been advanced from psychodynamic, behavioral, cognitive-behavioral, and physiological perspectives, but little research has validated or confirmed these theories. Most research on sexual sadism involves describing and profiling characteristics of known offenders who have been convicted for single and serial sexual murder, and extrapolates offender and offense characteristics assumed to be relevant to sexual sadism and its diagnosis from these descriptions. As our earlier discussion has indicated, little research has systematically or directly assessed or compared known groups of sadists and nonsadists on diagnostic criteria or other characteristics pertinent to the diagnosis of sexual sadism. Therefore, etiological theories of sexual sadism are based either on applications of various theoretical perspectives to the phenomenon; on descriptive reports from case studies of individuals who may or may not meet diagnostic criteria for sexual sadism, or who may or may not have committed sexually sadistic offenses; or on research that has been, to date, inconclusive. Although it has been suggested that most sexual murderers can be diagnosed as sadists (Langevin, 2003), the majority of descriptions and studies do not explicitly assess sexual sadism among this group, and others have noted that not all sexual murderers are sadists (Grubin, 1994b). In addition, although there are some similarities between sexual murderers and sexual sadists, the two groups have also been found to be significantly different on a number of important features and characteristics (Langevin, 2003). This suggests that these groups may differ, that results may not be fully generalizable to sexual sadists, and therefore that inferences about sexual sadism and its etiology should be drawn with caution.

Psychodynamic Theories

Psychodynamic theorists have proposed various motivations for sexual sadism. Freud (1961) variously regarded sexual sadism as resulting from fixation at the oral–aggressive stage of development in infancy, from the development of "mental impulses" based on the association of sexuality with aggression, from the child coming to regard parental intercourse as representing subjugation or maltreatment, or from the death instinct (rather than from the pleasure instinct, as he had earlier proposed). Later psychodynamic theorizing proposed that sexual sadism developed during toilet training or parental teaching with respect to masturbation, during which sexual pleasure was both supported and denied (Sadger, 1926), or from the teething (oral) stage (Friedenberg, 1956), as well as from fixation at the oral–aggressive stage (as originally proposed by Freud). More recent psychodynamic theorizing suggests that sexual murders represent "displaced matricides" (Meloy, 2000, p. 14; Revitch & Schlesinger, 1989). According to this hypothesis, rage against the mother results from a lack of differentiation between the mother and the perpetrator as a boy, arising from such maternal behaviors as aggression, dominance, control, manipulation, and sexualized behavior toward the child (Meloy, 2000). In combination with the physical or emotional absence of a masculine/father figure, the child develops feelings of hostility, mistrust, rage, inadequacy, and fear of being engulfed by adult women, which are ultimately expressed in sexual murder. It is hypothesized that these early developments—in conjunction with other factors later in adulthood, such as thought disorders, chronic anger, impaired reality testing and interpretation of perceptual materials, emotional dysregulation, and feelings of entitlement and grandiosity—provide a comprehensive account of the etiology of sexual homicide (Meloy, 2000).

Psychodynamic theories have not been subjected to or supported by empirical research, and have done little to advance our understanding of the etiology of sexual sadism.

Physiological Theories

Physiological explanations have also been proposed as pertinent to the etiology of sexual sadism, based on research examining chromosomal, endocrine, hormonal, and neurological abnormalities among sexual sadists and/or sexual or serial murderers (Bain, Langevin, Dickey, & Ben-Aron, 1987; Graber, Hartmann, Coffman, Huey, & Golden, 1982; Gratzer & Bradford, 1995; Hucker, Langevin, Wortzman, et al., 1988; Kolarsky, Freund, Machek, & Polak, 1967; Langevin, 1990, 1991, 2003; Langevin, Ben-Aron, Wright, Marchese, & Handy, 1988; Money, 1990). In general, this research is based on small samples or case studies, and is therefore not conclusive. Some studies have found differences between sexual sadists and control subjects, or associations between sexual sadism and abnormalities; others have reported no abnormalities or differences. At present, it is suggested that subtle abnormalities may exist, but that additional research using different measurement methodology is needed (Hucker, 1997). It is most likely that psychobiological features interact with social-psychological features in the development of sexual sadism.

Behavioral and Cognitive-Behavioral Theories

Early behavioral theories of the etiology of sexual sadism proposed that sexual sadism originates in early developmental pairings of sexual urges, excitation, or arousal with aggressive stimuli, which are later reinforced and maintained via sexual fantasy and masturbation (e.g., McGuire, Carlisle, & Young, 1965). MacCulloch and colleagues (1983) proposed a learning model of sexual sadism based on classical and operant conditioning. Based on a small number of cases of murderers with sadistic features, they proposed that such conditioning results in the development of links between sexuality and aggression, including fantasy, in interaction with personality features and sexual failures that result in feelings of inadequacy and lack of assertiveness. As escalation in the sadistic content of fantasies increases over time, it is hypothesized that individuals then begin to try out fantasies through real acts. Similarly, Prentky and colleagues (1989) noted that behavioral principles suggest that stronger conditioned associations among arousal, fantasy, and masturbation develop over time and via reinforcement. Integrating the influence of modeling and behavioral disinhibition, Prentky and colleagues proposed that when behavioral disinhibition is no longer present, the individual begins to act out sadistic sexual fantasies through a series of "trial runs" (p. 890) or behavioral tryouts in order to act on fantasies.

More recently, MacCulloch and colleagues (2000) noted that behavioral explanations of the development of sadistic sexual fantasy, while potentially applicable to the maintenance and escalation of sadistic sexual fantasy and behavior, do not adequately explain the initial development of sadistic sexual fantasy. Drawing from research on early childhood abuse and animal models of conditioning, they have proposed a model attempting to explain the initial development of sexual sadism. They have posited that sadistic fantasies result from a combination of early childhood abuse (which alone is insufficient to account for the occurrence of sexual sadism) with classical (Mackintosh, 1974; Pavlov, 1927) and operant (Skinner, 1938) conditioning processes. MacCulloch and colleagues further propose that sadistic fantasies have functional significance for individuals, resulting either in direct benefits through instrumental gain, or in indirect benefits via reducing negative consequences and negative affect (negative reinforcement). According to this model, sadistic fantasy develops initially from "sensory preconditioning" (Brogden, 1939), the process by which unrelated representations of stimuli that are concurrently active in cognition become associated with one another. These representations are then reinforced via classical and operant reinforcement (MacCulloch et al., 2000). Abuse results in fear, anxiety, and physiological and behavioral reactions to the stress induced by abuse; in MacCulloch and colleagues' model, it also results in atypical responses, such as sexual arousal following abuse. Thus aggression and sexual fantasy co-occur during abuse, and with repeated abuse there are multiple pairings of these two stimulus representations. This results in the development of an association between sex and aggression, and in the formation (sensory preconditioning) of a representation of sexual arousal that also includes aggression. When the individual later experiences aggression, sexual arousal is activated, and vice versa, providing the conditions necessary for the reinforcement of sexually aggressive behavior via classical and operant conditioning. MacCulloch and colleagues further suggest that because sensory preconditioning does not in itself result in strong conditioned associations between stimulus representations, and because multiple repeated pairings of representations of sexual and aggressive ideation (via the experience of abuse during childhood) are necessary for the development of sadistic sexual fantasies, this explanation is consistent with the observation that sexual sadism is a relatively rare phenomenon.

One relatively recent theory of the etiology of sexual sadism is the motivational model (Burgess et al., 1986; Ressler et al., 1988). This model, developed from interviews with sexual murderers, includes five phases accounting for the development of sadistic sexual fantasy and cognitive structures that support sexually murderous behavior. The first phase involves an ineffective social environment in which the individual is not provided with nurture, protection, and consistent discipline. In the second phase, formative events, such as experiencing or witnessing abuse, result in the emergence of aggressive fantasies designed to achieve control in an environment in which the child is otherwise helpless. In addition (similar to MacCulloch et al.'s [2000] theorizing), this abuse is hypothesized to be influential in general social development and to result in physiological arousal in response to the abuse, which alters the child's perceptions and patterns in interpersonal relationships (Burgess et al., 1986). It is also proposed that these traumatic events result in insecure attachment to caregivers, and that these conditions are exacerbated by a lack of adequate role modeling. In the third phase of the model, Burgess and colleagues (1986) propose that individuals develop negative personal traits impairing the formation of interpersonal relationships; the results are social isolation, a reliance on fantasy that contains elements of sex and aggression as a substitute for social contact and emotional arousal, and a failure to develop prosocial values. The individual at this stage also develops cognitive structures and schemas in which information processing is aimed at self-preservation and the reduction of negative affect associated with helplessness and pervasive anxiety, as well as a sense of entitlement and antisocial values and beliefs. Burgess and colleagues further suggest that the individual develops a sense of control and dominance over others rather than a sense of internal mastery in the development of cognitive style, and that these fantasies result in stress, which is reduced by physiological responses resulting in relief and pleasure. In the fourth stage of the model, it is proposed that early violent acts, such as abuse of animals or persons and other antisocial behaviors, are reinforced both via their positive effects and the absence of sanctions in the child's ineffective social environment. The individual additionally does not develop empathy, impulse control, or the ability to resolve conflict. In the final phase of the model, defined as a feedback filter (Burgess et al., 1986), the individual evaluates his actions and determines future actions, with a sexual murderer experiencing arousal to sexual fantasy; increased feelings of power, control, and dominance; and increased ability over time to avoid detection and sanctions.

As indicated previously, violent or sadistic sexual fantasy has long been proposed as playing a central role in sexual sadism and sexual murder (Brittain, 1970; MacCulloch et al., 1983; Meloy, 2000; Reinhardt, 1957), and some recent research appears to support the existence of sexual fantasy in some sexual murderers and/or sadists. However, the etiology, the precise role, and the mechanism of action of such fantasy in the manifestation of sexually sadistic behavior have not yet been consistently explained. Hazelwood and Warren (1995) proposed that sexual fantasy among sexual murderers includes five components: relational, paraphilic, situational, self-perceptual, and demographic. These variously shape the choice of victim (Meloy, 1988, 2000; Money, 1986), provide positive reinforcement, sustain pleasure when paired with masturbation, stimulate grandiosity and omnipotence, reduce behavioral inhibition, increase physiological arousal, and allow for practice of sexually murderous behavior (Meloy, 2000). However, the precise mechanisms and conditions under which such fantasy manifests itself in sexually sadistic behavior remain largely unexplained. It has been hypothesized that such factors as stress, various emotional states, and situational cues and their interpretation result in acting out behaviorally on sexually violent fantasies when the opportunity to offend presents itself (Meloy, 2000; Prentky et al., 1989; Ressler et al., 1988). In addition, it is hypothesized that the likelihood of acting out on violent sexual fantasy increases with a decrease in the intensity and gratification of masturbatory activity to fantasies, resulting in an increased desire to act on such fantasies (Gacono & Meloy, 1994; Hull, 1952).

Building on the work of Burgess and colleagues (1986) and on Hickey's (1997) similar trauma control model, Arrigo and Purcell (2001) suggested that some individuals are predisposed biologically, psychologically, and/or sociologically to commit "lust murder,"—via processes similar to those described by Burgess and colleagues, although stress and behaviors such as substance use and pornography use are also thought to contribute to the development and maintenance of sexually sadistic fantasy and behavior.

As with other theories of sexual sadism, it is important to note that none of these models have been examined or empirically validated, and represent hypotheses of the development of sexual sadism that remain untested. Taken together, the confluence of theory and research suggest an interplay among biological, psychological, learning, and social/environmental factors in the development and maintenance of sexual sadism, although additional research is required to validate these models and hypothesized mechanisms.

FORENSIC ISSUES

In forensic settings, professionals are called upon to make assessments of risk and diagnosis that influence decisions such as sentencing, imprisonment, hospitalization, treatment, and civil commitment, and that have a significant influence on the offender's life and liberty. Murder (whether of a sexual nature or not) and sexually sadistic offenses garner much attention and necessarily much concern about recidivism, since reoffending by these individuals is likely to result in significant harm to victims. However, as can be seen from our review, research has not conclusively established the characteristics of sexual sadists, particularly those features that differentiate these individuals from nonsadistic offenders. In much of the research that has been used to determine the relevant characteristics of sexual sadism, the existence of sexual sadism has not been explicitly assessed or diagnosed among subjects. As indicated above, many of these studies have been conducted on sexual murderers—not all of whom are expected to meet established criteria for a diagnosis of sexual sadism—and this has limited the applicability of findings. Research efforts differentiating sexual sadists and nonsadistic rapists have been similarly inconclusive, as have studies of the existence and influence of deviant sexual arousal and fantasy in sexual sadism, although such arousal and fantasy are considered essential to the diagnosis. Research using behavioral and other indicators to infer the existence of diagnostic criteria also yields inconsistent results, as well as problems in the application of criteria in making a diagnosis.

In addition to these problems with definitional and diagnostic issues, although some authors assume that sexual sadists are at high risk of reoffending (Marshall & Hucker, 2006), this assumption is not supported by research. In fact, the research on the characteristics of sexual sadists and sexual murderers suggests that these offenders actually possess numerous characteristics of lower-risk offenders when risk factors used in actuarial schemes are considered. In the one study we found utilizing actuarial risk assessments in cases of sexual murder and attempted sexual murder, Langevin (2006), using either the Violence Risk Appraisal Guide (VRAG; Webster, Harris, Rice, Cormier, & Quinsey, 1994) or the Sex Offender Risk Appraisal Guide (SORAG; Quinsey, Harris, Rice, & Cormier, 1998), found that only 32% of offenders ($N = 38$) would have been assessed as at high risk of committing their offenses. To date, the validity and utility of actuarial risk assessment instruments with this subpopulation of sexual offenders have not been established, and their unique characteristics and low prevalence rates suggest that such measures may not be appropriate for this group (Doren, 2002).

SUMMARY AND FUTURE DIRECTIONS

In 1986, Busch and Cavanagh stated that most of the work in this area consisted of unfounded statements unsupported by data, unevaluated case reports lacking rigorous evaluation of other contributory factors, and scientific case reports of individuals or small groups. Regrettably, the same can be said today, over 20 years later. Recent research has provided some insight into the probable features of sexual sadism; however, these indicators need to be operationalized so that sadists and nonsadists may be compared and that these indicators may be replicated and validated across studies. Recently, in reviewing research on diagnostic inaccuracy (Marshall, Kennedy, & Yates, 2002; Marshall & Yates, 2004), Marshall and Hucker (2006) have suggested that sexually sadistic behaviors may still provide a useful basis for more accurate and reliable identification of these problematic offenders; they have developed a rating scale for such behaviors that is undergoing validation. Should the psychometric integrity of this scale be established, it might assist in determining whether individuals meet diagnostic criteria in existing schemes, and hence increase diagnostic accuracy. Until such a scheme is validated, it is incumbent upon professionals to be cognizant of the shortcomings of research to date, and of sexual sadism's various and complicated interrelationships with other paraphilias and with nonparaphilic behavior, as described in this chapter.

REFERENCES

Abel, G. G. (1989). Paraphilias. In H. I. Kaplan & B. J. Sadock (Eds.), *Comprehensive textbook of psychiatry* (5th ed., Vol. 1, pp. 1069–1085). Baltimore: Williams & Wilkins.

Abel, G. G., Barlow, D. H., Blanchard, E. B., & Guild, D. (1977). The components of rapists' sexual arousal. *Archives of General Psychiatry, 34,* 895–903.

Abel, G. G., Becker, J., Cunningham-Rathner, J., Mittelman, M., & Rouleau, J. (1988). Multiple paraphilic diagnoses among sex offenders. *Bulletin of the American Academy of Psychiatry and the Law, 16,* 153–168.

American Psychiatric Association. (1987). *Diagnostic and statistical manual of mental disorders* (3rd ed., rev.). Washington, DC: Author.

American Psychiatric Association. (2000). *Diagnostic and statistical manual of mental disorders* (4th ed., text rev.). Washington, DC: Author.

Arndt, W., Foehl, J., & Good, F. (1985). Specific sexual fantasy themes: A multidimensional study. *Journal of Personality and Social Psychology, 48,* 472–480.

Arrigo, B. A., & Purcell, C. E. (2001). Explaining paraphilias and lust murder: Toward an integrated model. *International Journal of Offender Therapy and Comparative Criminology, 45,* 6–31.

Avery-Clark, C. A., & Laws, D. R. (1984). Differential erection response patterns of sexual child abusers to stimuli describing activities with children. *Behavior Therapy, 15,* 71–83.

Bain, J., Langevin, R., Dickey, R., & Ben-Aron, M. (1987). Sex hormones in murderers and assaulters. *Behavioral Sciences and the Law, 5,* 95–101.

Barbaree, H. E., Baxter, D. J., & Marshall, W. L. (1989). Brief research report: The reliability of the rape index in a sample of rapists and nonrapists. *Violence and Victims, 4,* 399–306.

Barbaree, H. E., Marshall, W. L., & Lanthier, R. D. (1979). Deviant sexual arousal in rapists. *Behavior Research and Therapy, 17,* 215–222.

Bartholomew, A., Milte, K., & Galbally, A. (1975). Sexual murder: Psychopathology and psychiatric jurisprudential considerations. *Australian and New Zealand Journal of Criminology, 8,* 152–163.

Beauregard, E., & Proulx, J. (2002). Profiles in the offending process of nonserial sexual murderers. *International Journal of Offender Therapy and Comparative Criminology, 46,* 386–399.

Bondeson, J. (2001). *The London Monster: A sanguinary tale.* Philadelphia: University of Pennsylvania Press.

Brittain, R. (1970). The sadistic murderer. *Medicine, Science, and the Law, 10,* 198–207.

Brogden, W. J. (1939). Sensory pre-conditioning. *Journal of Experimental Psychology, 25,* 55–58.

Burgess, A. W., Hartmann, C. R., Ressler, R. K., Douglas, J. E., & McCormack, A. (1986). Sexual homicide, a motivational model. *Journal of Interpersonal Violence, 1,* 251–272.

Busch, K. A., & Cavanagh, J. R. (1986). The study of multiple murder: Preliminary examination of the interface between epistemology and methodology. *Journal of Interpersonal Violence, 1,* 5–23.

Calef, V., & Weinshel, E. M. (1972). On certain neurotic equivalents of necrophilia. *International Journal of Psycho-Analysis, 53,* 67–75.

Crepault, E., & Couture, M. (1980). Men's erotic fantasies. *Archives of Sexual Behavior, 9,* 565–581.

De River, P. (1958). *Crime and the sexual psychopath.* Springfield, IL: Thomas.

Dietz, P. E., & Evans, B. (1982). Pornographic imagery and prevalence of paraphilia. *American Journal of Psychiatry, 139,* 1493–1495.

Dietz, P. E., Hazelwood, R. R., & Warren, J. (1990). The sexually sadistic criminal and his offenses. *Bulletin of the American Academy of Psychiatry and the Law, 18,* 163–178.

Donnelly, D., & Fraser, J. (1998). Gender differences in sado-masochistic arousal among college students. *Sex Roles, 39,* 391–407.

Doren, D. M. (2002). *Evaluating sex offenders: A manual for civil commitments and beyond.* Thousand Oaks, CA: Sage.

East, N. (1949). *Society and the criminal.* London: His Majesty's Stationery Office.

Eccles, A., Marshall, W. L., & Barbaree, H. E. (1994). Differentiating rapists and non-offenders using the rape index. *Behaviour Research and Therapy, 32*, 539–546.

Ellis, H. (1936). *Studies in the psychology of sex* (Vol. 1). New York: Random House.

Eulenberg, A. (1911). *Sadism and masochism.* New York: Bell.

Fedora, O., Reddon, J. R., Morrison, J. W., Fedora, S. K., Pascoe, H., & Yeudall, L. (1992). Sadism and other paraphilias in normal controls and aggressive and nonaggressive sex offenders. *Archives of Sexual Behavior, 21*, 1–15.

Freud, S. (1961). The economic problem of masochism. In J. Strachey (Ed. & Trans.), *The standard edition of the complete psychological works of Sigmund Freud* (Vol. 19). London: Hogarth Press.

Friedenberg, F. S. (1956). A contribution to the problem of sadomasochism. *Psychoanalytic Review, 43*, 91–96.

Fromm, E. (1977). *The anatomy of human destructiveness.* New York: Holt.

Gacono, C. B. & Meloy, J. R. (1994). *The Rorschach assessment of aggressive and psychopathic personalities.* Hillsdale, NJ: Erlbaum.

Gosselin, C. C. (1987). The sado-masochistic contract. In G.D. Wilson (Ed.), *Variant sexuality: Research and theory* (pp. 229–257). Baltimore: Johns Hopkins University Press.

Gosselin, C. C., & Wilson, G. D. (1980). *Sexual variations.* London: Faber & Faber.

Graber, B., Hartmann, K., Coffman, J., Huey, C., & Golden, C. (1982). Brain damage among mentally disordered sex offenders. *Journal of Forensic Science, 27*, 127–134.

Gratzer, T., & Bradford, J. M. (1995). Offender and offense characteristics of sexual sadists: A comparative study. *Journal of Forensic Sciences, 40*, 450–455.

Gray, N. S., Watt, A., Hassan, S., & MacCulloch, M. J. (2003). Behavioral indicators of sadistic sexual murder predict the presence of sadistic sexual fantasy in a normative sample. *Journal of Interpersonal Violence, 18*, 1018–1034.

Grubin, D. (1994a). Editorial: Sexual sadism. *Criminal Behavior and Mental Health, 4*, 3–9.

Grubin, D. (1994b). Sexual murder. *British Journal of Psychiatry, 165*, 624–629.

Hare, R. D. (1991). *Manual for the Hare Psychopathy Checklist—Revised.* Toronto: Multi-Health Systems.

Hazelwood, R., & Warren, J. (1995). The relevance of fantasy in serial sexual crime investigation. In R. Hazelwood & A. W. Burgess (Eds.), *Practical aspects of rape investigation* (pp. 127–128). New York: CRC Press.

Heilbrun, A., & Leif, D. (1988). Autoerotic value of female distress in sexually explicit photographs. *Journal of Sex Research, 24*, 47–57.

Hickey, E. (1997). *Serial murders and their victims* (2nd ed.). Belmont, CA: Wadsworth.

Hirschfeld, M. (1956). *Sexual anomalies.* New York: Emerson.

Holt, S., Meloy, J. R., & Strack, S. (1999). Sadism and psychopathy in violent and sexually violent offenders. *Journal of the American Academy of Psychiatry and the Law, 27*, 23–32.

Hucker, S. J. (1997). Sexual sadism: Psychopathology and theory. In D. R. Laws & W. O'Donohue (Eds.), *Sexual deviance: Theory, assessment, and treatment* (pp. 194–209). New York: Guilford Press.

Hucker, S. J., & Blanchard, R. (1992). Death scene characteristics in 118 fatal cases of autoerotic asphyxia compared with suicidal asphyxia. *Behavioral Sciences and the Law, 10*, 509–523.

Hucker, S. J., Langevin, R., & Bain, J. (1988). A double-blind trial of sex drive reducing medication in pedophiles. *Annals of Sex Research, 1*, 227–242.

Hucker, S. J., Langevin, R., Wortzman, G., Dickey, R., Bain, J., Handy, L., et al. (1988). Cerebral damage and dysfunction in sexually aggressive men. *Annals of Sex Research, 1*, 33–47.

Hull, C. (1952). *A behavior system.* New Haven, CT: Yale University Press.

Jaffe, P., & DiCataldo, F. (1994). Clinical vampirism: Blending myth and reality. *Bulletin of the American Academy of Psychiatry and the Law, 22*, 533–544.

Karpmann, B. (1954). *The sex offender and his offenses.* New York: Julian Press.

Kinsey, A., Pomeroy, W. B., Martin, C. E., & Gebhard, P. H. (1953). *Sexual behavior in the human female.* Philadelphia: Saunders.

Kolarsky, A., Freund, K., Machek, J., & Polak, O. (1967). Male sexual deviation: Association with early temporal lobe damage. *Archives of General Psychiatry, 17,* 735–743.

Koss, M. P., Gidycz, C., & Wisniewski, N. (1987). The scope of rape: Incidence and prevalence of sexual aggression in a national sample of higher education students. *Journal of Consulting and Clinical Psychology, 55,* 162–170.

Krafft-Ebing, R. von (1892). *Psychopathia sexualis.* Philadelphia: Davis. (Original work published 1886)

Langevin, R. (1990). Sexual anomalies and the brain. In W. L. Marshall, D. R. Laws, & H. E. Barbaree (Eds.), *Handbook of sexual assault: Issues, theories, and treatment of the offender* (pp. 103–113). New York: Plenum Press.

Langevin, R. (1991). The sex killer. In A.W. Burgess (Ed.), *Rape and sexual assault* (pp. 235–256). New York: Garland Press.

Langevin, R. (2003). A study of the psychosexual characteristics of sex killers: Can we identify them before it is too late? *International Journal of Offender Therapy and Comparative Criminology, 47,* 366–382.

Langevin, R. (2006). An actuarial study of recidivism risk among sex killers of adults and children: Could we have identified them before it was too late? *Journal of Forensic Psychology Practice, 6,* 29–49.

Langevin, R., Bain, J., Ben-Aron, M. H., Coulthard, R., Day, D., Roper, V., et al. (1985). Sexual aggression: Constructing a predictive equation: A controlled pilot study. In R. Langevin (Ed.), *Erotic preference, gender identity, and aggression in men: New research studies* (pp. 39–76). Hillsdale, NJ: Erlbaum.

Langevin, R., Ben-Aron, M. H., Wright, P., Marchese, V., & Handy, L. (1988). The sex killer. *Annals of Sex Research, 1,* 263–301.

Langevin, R., & Lang, R. A. (1987). The courtship disorders. In G. D. Wilson (Ed.), *Variant sexuality: Research and theory* (pp. 202–228). Baltimore: Johns Hopkins University Press.

Levenson, J. S. (2004). Reliability of sexually violent predator civil commitment criteria. *Law and Human Behavior, 28,* 357–368.

MacCulloch, M., Gray, N., & Watt, A. (2000). Brittain's sadist murderer syndrome reconsidered: An associative account of the aetiology of sadistic sexual fantasy. *Journal of Forensic Psychiatry, 11,* 401–418.

MacCulloch, M., Snowden, P., Wood, P., & Mills, H. (1983). Sadistic fantasy, sadistic behavior, and offending. *British Journal of Psychiatry, 143,* 20–29.

Mackintosh, N. J. (1974). *The psychology of animal learning.* New York: Academic Press.

Malamuth, N. M. (1981). Rape proclivity among males. *Journal of Social Issues, 37,* 138–157.

Malamuth, N. M., & Check, J. V. P. (1983). Sexual arousal to rape depictions: Individual differences. *Journal of Abnormal Psychology, 92,* 55–67.

Malamuth, N. M., Haber, S., & Feshbach, S. (1980). Testing hypotheses regarding rape: Exposure to sexual violence, sex differences and the normality of rapists. *Journal of Research in Personality, 14,* 121–137.

Malamuth, N. M., Heim, M., & Feshbach, S. (1980). Sexual responsiveness of college students to rape depictions: Inhibitory and disinhibitory effects. *Journal of Personality and Social Psychology, 38,* 399–408.

Marshall, W. L. (1996). Assessment, treatment, and theorizing about sexual offenders: Developments over the past 20 years and future directions. *Criminal Justice and Behavior, 23,* 162–199.

Marshall, W. L., & Barbaree, H. (1990). An integrated theory of the etiology of sex offending. In W. L. Marshall, D. R. Laws, & H. Barbaree (Eds.) *Handbook of sexual assault: Issues, theories, and treatment of the offender* (pp. 257–275). New York: Plenum Press.

Marshall, W. L., & Fernandez, Y. M. (2000). Phallometric testing with sexual offenders: Limits to its value. *Clinical Psychology Review, 20,* 807–822.

Marshall, W. L., & Hucker, S. J. (2006). Issues in the diagnosis of sexual sadism. *Sexual Offender Treatment, 1.* Retrieved from *sexual-offender-treatment.org*

Marshall, W. L., & Kennedy, P. (2003). Sexual sadism in sexual offenders: An elusive diagnosis. *Aggression and Violent Behavior*, 8, 1–22.

Marshall, W. L., Kennedy, P., & Yates, P. M. (2002). Issues concerning the reliability and validity of the diagnosis of sexual sadism applied in prison settings. *Sexual Abuse: A Journal of Research and Treatment*, 14, 310–311.

Marshall, W. L., Kennedy, P., Yates, P. M., & Serran, G. A. (2002). Diagnosing sexual sadism in sexual offenders: Reliability across diagnosticians. *International Journal of Offender Therapy and Comparative Criminology*, 46, 668–676.

Marshall, W. L., & Yates, P. M. (2004). Diagnostic issues in sexual sadism among sexual offenders. *Journal of Sexual Aggression*, 10, 21–27.

McGuire, R. J., Carlisle, J. M., & Young, B. G. (1965). Sexual deviation as a conditioned behaviour: A hypothesis. *Behaviour Research and Therapy*, 2, 185–190.

Meloy, J. R. (1988). *The psychopathic mind: Origins, dynamics and treatment*. Northvale, NJ: Aronson.

Meloy, J. R. (2000). The nature and dynamics of sexual homicide: An integrative review. *Aggression and Violent Behavior*, 5, 1–22.

Millon, T. (1983). *Millon Clinical Multiaxial Inventory manual*. Minneapolis, MN: Interpretive Scoring Systems.

Moll, A. (1912). *Handbuch de Sexual wissenshaften*. Leipzig: Vogel.

Money, J. (1986). *Lovemaps*. New York: Irvington.

Money, J. (1990). Forensic sexology: Paraphilic serial rape (biastophilia) and lust murder (erotophonophilia). *American Journal of Psychotherapy*, 44, 26–36.

Myers, W. C., Burgess, A. W., Burgess, A. G., & Douglas, J. E. (1999). Serial murder and sexual homicide. In V. van Hasselt & M. Hersen (Eds.), *Handbook of psychological approaches with violent offenders* (pp. 153–172). New York: Kluwer Academic/Plenum Press.

Packard, R. L., & Levenson, J. S. (2006). *Revisiting the reliability of diagnostic decisions in sex offender civil commitment*. Manuscript submitted for publication.

Pavlov, I. P. (1927). *Conditioned reflexes* (G. V. Anrep, Trans.). London: Oxford University Press.

Prentky, R. A., Burgess, A. W., Rokous, F., Lee, A., Hartman, C. R., Ressler, R. K., et al. (1989). The presumptive role of fantasy in serial sexual homicide. *American Journal of Psychiatry*, 146, 887–891.

Prentky, R. A., Cohen, M. L., & Seghorn, T. K. (1985). Identifying critical dimensions for discriminating among rapists. *Journal of Consulting and Clinical Psychology*, 59, 643–661.

Proulx, J., Blais, E., & Beauregard, E. (2005). Sadistic sexual offenders. In J. Proulx, E. Blais, & E. Beauregard, *Sexual murderers: A comparative analysis and new perspectives* (pp. 107–122). Chichester, UK: Wiley.

Proulx, J., Blais, E., & Beauregard, E. (2006). Sadistic sexual aggressors. In W. L. Marshall, Y. M. Fernandez, L. E. Marshall, & G. A. Serran (Eds.), *Sexual offender treatment: Controversial issues* (pp. 61–77). Chichester, UK: Wiley.

Quinsey, V. L., & Chaplin, T. C. (1982). Penile responses to nonsexual violence among rapists. *Criminal Justice and Behavior*, 9, 372–381.

Quinsey, V. L., Chaplin, T. C., & Upfold, D. (1984). Sexual arousal to nonsexual violence and sadomasochistic themes among rapists and non-sex offenders. *Journal of Consulting and Clinical Psychology*, 52, 651–657.

Quinsey, V. L., Chaplin, T. C., & Varney, G. (1981). A comparison of rapists' and non-sex offenders' sexual preference for mutually consenting sex, rape, and physical abuse of women. *Behavioural Assessment*, 3, 127–135.

Quinsey, V. L., Harris, G. T., Rice, M. E., & Cormier, C. (1998). *Violent offenders: Appraising and managing risk*. Washington, DC: American Psychological Association.

Quinsey, V. L., Lalumière, M., & Seto, M. C. (1994). The current status of phallometric assessment. *Violence Update*, 4, 1–2.

Rada, R. T. (1978). *Clinical aspects of the rapist*. New York: Grune & Stratton.

Reinhardt, R. (1957). *Sex perversion and sex crimes: A psychocultural examination of the causes, nature and criminal manifestations of sex perversions.* Springfield, IL: Thomas.

Ressler, R. K., Burgess, A. W., & Douglas, J. E. (1988). *Sexual homicide: Patterns and motives.* New York: Free Press.

Revitch, E., & Schlesinger, L. B. (1989). *Sex murder and sex aggression.* Springfield, IL: Thomas.

Rice, M. E., Chaplin, T. C., Harris, G. T., & Coutts, J. (1994). Empathy for the victim and sexual arousal among rapists and nonrapists. *Journal of Interpersonal Violence, 9,* 435–449.

Rosman, J., & Resnick, P. (1989). Necrophilia: An analysis of 122 cases involving necrophilic acts and fantasies. *Bulletin of the American Academy of Psychiatry and the Law, 17,* 153–163.

Sadger, J. (1926). A contribution to the understanding of sadomasochism. *International Journal of Psycho-Analysis, 7,* 484–491.

Schrenck-Notzing, A. von. (1956). *The use of hypnosis in psychopathia sexualis.* New York: Julian Press. (Original work published 1895)

Seto, M. C., & Barbaree, H. E. (1993). Victim blame and sexual arousal to rape cues in rapists and nonoffenders. *Annals of Sex Research, 6,* 167–183.

Seto, M. C., & Kuban, M. (1996). Criterion-related validity of a phallometric test for paraphilic rape and sadism. *Behaviour Research and Therapy, 34,* 175–183.

Skinner, B. F. (1938). *The behavior of organisms.* New York: Appleton-Century-Crofts.

Spengler, A. (1977). Manifest sadomasochism of males: Results of an empirical study. *Archives of Sexual Behavior, 6,* 441–456.

Sturup, G. K. (1968). Treatment of sexual offenders in Herstedvester, Denmark: The rapists. *Acta Psychiatrica Scandinavica, 44*(Suppl. 204), 1–62.

Warren, J., Hazelwood, R., & Dietz, P. (1996). The sexually sadistic serial killer. *Journal of Forensic Sciences, 41,* 970–974.

Webster, C. D., Harris, G. T., Rice, M. E., Cormier, C., & Quinsey, V. L. (1994). *The violence prediction scheme: Assessing dangerousness in High risk men.* Toronto: University of Toronto, Centre of Criminology.

Weinberg, T. S. (1987). Sadism and masochism in the United States: A review of recent sociological literature. *Journal of Sex Research, 23,* 50–69.

World Health Organization. (1992). *International statistical classification of diseases and related health problems* (10th rev.). Geneva: Author.

Yarvis, R. (1995). Diagnostic patterns among three violent offender types. *Bulletin of the American Academy of Psychiatry and the Law, 23,* 411–419.

Yates, P. M. (1996). *An investigation of factors associated with definitions and perceptions of rape, propensity to commit rape, and rape prevention.* Unpublished doctoral dissertation, Carleton University, Ottawa,

CHAPTER 13

SEXUAL SADISM

Assessment and Treatment

DREW A. KINGSTON
PAMELA M. YATES

Sexual sadism is a paraphilia evident most often in males and consists of deriving sexual pleasure from inflicting pain or humiliation on others. It is generally accepted that the incidence of sexual sadism is likely to be low, representing approximately 2–5% of sexual offenders (Quinsey, Chaplin, & Varney, 1981). However, prevalence rates and estimates vary significantly across studies, ranging from 5% (Hunt, 1974) to 80% (MacCulloch, Snowden, Wood, & Mills, 1983). This variability results from problems associated with the definition and diagnosis of sexual sadism, as well as from differences across studies in samples and in assessment and diagnostic methodology. Given these problems, it is not surprising that there is a lack of agreement on the assessment of sexual sadism, and that limited information is available with respect to appropriate treatment for these offenders. This chapter reviews current assessment methodologies and treatment methods used with this population of sexual offenders.

ASSESSMENT

Diagnostic Assessment

The early assessment of sexual sadism relied on indicators drawn from descriptions of case studies (e.g., Brittain, 1970; Krafft-Ebing, 1886/1892). Later evaluations used indicators derived primarily from profiling studies of sexual and/or serial murderers and crime scene data, such as the research conducted by the U.S. Federal Bureau of Investigation (FBI; e.g., Dietz, Hazelwood, & Warren, 1990). As we and Hucker have noted (Yates, Hucker, & Kingston, Chapter 12, this volume), this research has been used to hypothesize important features for assessment and to formulate etiological theories of the disorder. However, its applicability to the assessment of sexual sadism is questionable, since this research has been conducted on individuals who have not necessarily been diagnosed as sexual sadists, but who have engaged in behaviors during the commission of their crimes that are assumed to represent sadistic motivation. This is an important distinction, because research indicates that not all sexual murders are committed by sexual sadists (Grubin, 1994b), and that not all serial murderers have necessarily committed sexual murder (Ressler, Burgess, & Douglas, 1988). In most of the FBI studies and other research, sexual sadism has not been diagnosed according to established criteria. As a whole, research has not yielded consistent results with respect to features of the disorder that can be reliably used for assessment, although there appears to be some agreement on essential features of the disorder that should be included in assessment (Marshall & Hucker, 2006; Marshall & Kennedy, 2003; Marshall & Yates, 2004).

Currently, there are two classification systems for diagnosing sexual sadism: those of the *International Classification of Diseases*, 10th revision (ICD-10; World Health Organization, 1992) and the *Diagnostic and Statistical Manual of Mental Disorders*, fourth edition, text revision (DSM-IV-TR; American Psychiatric Association, 2000). The ICD-10 defines sexual sadism as "a preference for sexual activity that involves bondage or the infliction of pain or humiliation. If the subject prefers to be the recipient of such stimulation this is called masochism; if the provider, sadism. Often an individual obtains sexual excitement from both sadistic and masochistic activities" (p. 220). As indicated by this definition, the ICD-10 takes a dimensional approach to classification, combining both submissive (masochism) and dominant (sadism) elements. Moreover, the ICD-10 describes the disorder on a continuum, implying that some milder forms of sadomasochistic behavior are conventional (Berner, Berger, & Hill, 2003). The dimensional approach employed by the ICD-10 has been viewed by some (e.g., Marshall & Hucker, 2006; Marshall, Kennedy, & Yates, 2002) as having advantages over categorical approaches (e.g., that of DSM-IV-TR). For example, given that sadistic sexual fantasy and arousal have been found in college samples (e.g., Crepault & Couture, 1980; Straus with Donnelly, 1994), and that pornography with sadistic themes is relatively common (Donnelly & Fraser, 1998; Grubin, 1994b), there would appear to be some support for a dimensional approach to the conceptualization of sexual sadism. Currently it is unclear whether sadistic sexual offenders and sadistic nonoffenders are qualitatively different from each other, or whether they demonstrate the same phenomenon in differing degrees of severity (Grubin, 1994b). It has been suggested that this difference is qualitative rather than substantive (e.g., Grubin, 1994a), and that differences between those who act on sadistic sexual fantasy and those who do not lie in early developmental experiences, such as experiences of child abuse (MacCulloch, Gray, & Watt, 2000), inadequate early social and familial environments (Burgess, Hartmann, Ressler, Douglas, & McCormack, 1986; Ressler et al., 1988), a confluence of factors that lead the individual to act out on sadistic fantasies through "behavioral tryouts" (MacCulloch et al., 1983), and the existence of various personality disorders. Such theories, however, have not been tested.

In contrast to the ICD-10, the DSM-IV-TR focuses solely on the dominance element of sadism. It specifies two criteria necessary for the diagnosis, taking a categorical rather than a dimensional approach:

A. Over a period of at least 6 months, recurrent, intense sexually arousing fantasies, sexual urges, or behaviors involving acts (real, not simulated) in which the psychological or physical suffering (including humiliation) of the victim is sexually exciting to the person.

   B. The person must have acted on these sexual urges with a nonconsenting person, or
      the sexual urges or fantasies cause marked distress or interpersonal difficulty.
      (p. 574)

   At this time, the DSM-IV-TR is the most commonly used method in North America
for assessing sexual sadism. However, despite attempts to revise the criteria from previous
versions to allow for evaluation using behavioral indicators, the DSM categorization suffers from problems of definition, operationalization of terms, and measurement. For example, it has been criticized for the ambiguous nature of the terms "recurrent" and "intense" within Criterion A, and the clinical inference required to assess these features
possibly contributes to reduced reliability (Doren, 2002; O'Donohue, Regev, & Hagstrom, 2000). Moreover, the reliance on clinical inference regarding behavior, urges, and
fantasy is potentially problematic, given that clinical judgment has often performed
poorly in evaluative circumstances (Marshall, 2006; Meehl, 1996). Indeed, recent criticisms have been directed at the use of nosological procedures for the paraphilias in general (Kingston, Firestone, Moulden, & Bradford, 2007; Levenson, 2004; Moser, 2002;
Moulden, Firestone, Kingston, & Bradford, 2006). In these studies, diagnoses failed to
identify homogeneous subgroups of offenders, and did not provide sufficient predictive
utility or reliability—all of which are fundamental to an adequate diagnostic system.
   Recent research also suggests that in addition to the concerns identified above, there
are problems in the application of criteria in formulating a diagnosis of sexual sadism. In
their review, Marshall and Kennedy (2003) found that although most authors specified
the use of ICD or DSM criteria in diagnosis, these criteria were not in fact systematically
applied, and that additional idiosyncratic criteria were used to diagnose study participants. In a follow-up study, Marshall, Kennedy, and Yates (2002) found that despite the
application of DSM criteria, sadists and nonsadists were not reliably differentiated on
features identified as important to diagnosis (e.g., use of threats, sexually violent fantasies, deviant arousal to rape), and in fact that nonsadists were more deviant than those diagnosed with sadism on several variables (e.g., use of torture in the offense). This study
also found a lack of agreement across diagnosticians in criteria considered relevant to the
diagnosis of sexual sadism, as well as a lack of consistency in the application of criteria
for diagnosis. In a third study, Marshall, Kennedy, Yates, and Serran (2002) provided forensic psychiatrists with case information on random samples of offenders diagnosed in
the Marshall, Kennedy, and Yates study. Results indicated that the reliability of diagnosis
among 15 respondents was unacceptably low (kappa = .14). Inadequate reliability was
also demonstrated by Levenson (2004) for the paraphilias in general (kappa = .47) and
for sexual sadism in particular (kappa = .30), although it is noted that that these findings
may underestimate the reliability of diagnosis as a result of the statistical procedures employed in these studies (Packard & Levenson, 2006).

Risk Assessment

In addition to diagnostic assessment, sexual offenders are evaluated in many jurisdictions
for their risk of reoffending. In such evaluations, diagnostic schemes such as the DSM
and ICD, as well as actuarial risk assessment instruments such as the Static-99 (Hanson
& Thornton, 1999), are frequently used in order to assist in sentencing, civil commitment, and treatment and management decisions. However, the use of the latter measures
with sexual sadists is questionable. For example, although sexual sadists, by definition of

the disorder, are typically predisposed to commit offenses that meet various statutory requirements for civil commitment, they also typically present with numerous low-risk characteristics commonly assessed by actuarial assessment measures (Doren, 2002). Furthermore, the rarity of the disorder indicates that the use of current actuarial schemes to predict future sadistic offending may be difficult, given the problems associated with predicting low-base-rate behavior (Doren, 2002; Quinsey, Rice, & Harris, 1995). Thus the assessment of sexual sadists with existing actuarial measures may not be appropriate until further research establishes the validity of these schemes with this population.

Assessment for Treatment

As indicated above, the general lack of agreement on the essential features of sexual sadism has rendered assessment for both diagnosis and treatment problematic. There does, however, appear to be agreement that sexual arousal to violence and/or humiliation, sadistic sexual fantasy, and the desire to exercise power and control over the victim are essential features of the disorder (Hollin, 1997; Marshall & Kennedy, 2003; Marshall & Yates, 2004); therefore, these features may be appropriate targets for treatment. However, these constructs remain difficult to measure, due to the need for reliance on self-report information provided by the offender, as well as to methodological difficulties associated with assessment of these features. Although attempts have been made to infer the existence of these characteristics from crime scene evidence and from behavioral and experiential indicators, reliable measurement remains to be demonstrated. Similarly, various methods of assessing the existence and nature of deviant sexual arousal and fantasy have yielded mixed results, calling into question their use in assessment for treatment planning.

Assessment of Sexual Sadism from Crime Scene Data

In some research, characteristics of the offense have been used to infer the existence of sexual sadism. For example, studies examining crime scene data in cases of serial or sexual murder utilize such offense features as evidence of intercourse, sexual positioning of the victim's body, the degree of organization in the commission of the crime, indicators of torture, or evidence of ritualistic elements in inferring the existence of sexual sadism (Holmes & Holmes, 1994; Michaud & Hazelwood, 1999; Myers, Burgess, Burgess, & Douglas, 1999; Prentky ct al., 1989; Ressler et al., 1988; Ressler, Burgess, Douglas, Hartman, & D'Agostino, 1986). As noted earlier, however, not all serial or sexual murderers are sexual sadists, and participants in these studies were not diagnosed according to DSM or ICD criteria. Furthermore, the absence of comparison groups in these studies creates problems in drawing firm conclusions about the motivation underlying such behavioral indicators and their utility in assessing sadistic fantasy, or the existence of power and control as a motivation for offending. Furthermore, the exclusivity of such indicators to sadistic offenders has been questioned (Barbaree, Hudson, & Seto, 1993; Grubin, 1994b). Excessive violence and aggression in offending, for example, have been demonstrated by a variety of sexual offenders, some of whom would not meet criteria for sexual sadism (Dietz et al., 1990; Marshall, Kennedy, & Yates, 2002; Williams & Finkelhor, 1990). Indeed, a variety of motivations, such as overcoming victim resistance, accidental death, or sexual excitation, may result in the use of excessive violence in the offense (Dietz et al., 1990; Doren, 2002; Grubin, 1994b); however, only in the third case would a diagnosis of sadism be suggested. The fundamental problem for clinicians and researchers in such cases is to determine the motivations underlying violence and other offense characteristics in order to diagnose sexual sadism accurately.

Relevant offense characteristics should be established on the basis of their distinct relationship to sexual sadism. However, it has proved difficult to determine precisely those features on which assessors should focus. Marshall and Kennedy (2003) found that common features evident in sexually sadistic crime scenes included such indicators as torture, use of a weapon, humiliation, victim confinement, bondage, postdeath mutilation, and object insertion. However, there was considerable variability in these indicators across studies, and few have compared known groups of sadists with nonsadists on these indicators. Among studies comparing these two groups, however, some consistency in results has been obtained. Recently, Proulx, Blais, and Beauregard (2003, as cited in Proulx, Blais, & Beauregard, 2006) compared a sample of sadistic (N = 43) and nonsadistic (N = 98) sexual offenders, classified via the two sadism scales from the Massachusetts Treatment Center typology (MTC:R3; Knight & Prentky, 1990), on a variety of offender and offense characteristics. Results indicated that sadists displayed more offence planning, victim confinement, bondage, weapon use, expressive violence, humiliation, physical and sexual mutilation, and insertion of foreign objects into the vagina than did nonsadists. These features were also consistent with other studies comparing sadists and nonsadists on similar offense characteristics (e.g., Beauregard & Proulx, 2002; Gratzer & Bradford, 1995).

Based on earlier reviews of the fundamental characteristics of sexual sadism (Marshall & Kennedy, 2003; Marshall, Kennedy, & Yates, 2002; Marshall, Kennedy, Yates, et al., 2002; Marshall & Yates, 2004), Marshall and Hucker (2006) developed the 17-item Sadism Scale. The scale is intended to assist evaluators in diagnosing sexual sadism by using predominantly official criminal record data, and thereby minimizing the emphasis on professional inference (Marshall & Hucker, 2006). The scale assesses common features of sexual sadism described previously, with items differentially weighted on the basis of their perceived importance to the diagnosis. Given the problems identified above with nosological procedures in determining paraphilic interest (Kingston et al., 2007; Levenson, 2004; Moser, 2002), this scale is promising. However, no published research is currently available on its psychometric properties, although an analysis is currently underway (Marshall & Hucker, 2006).

Self-Report Assessment of Sadistic Sexual Fantasy

Sadistic sexual fantasy, regarded as a common feature of sexual sadism (Marshall & Yates, 2004), has been defined as the use of visual imagery pertaining to domination/control themes for sexual gratification (Hollin, 1997); it is necessarily assessed via the self-report of the offender. If an individual readily admits to such fantasies, the accuracy is usually not in question (Marshall & Kennedy, 2003). However, given the tendency toward impression management in offender populations (Marshall, Anderson, & Fernandez, 1999; Nugent & Kroner, 1996), accurate assessment of thoughts and feelings poses a considerable challenge to clinicians (Hollin, 1997). Moreover, the exclusivity of sadistic fantasy to sexual sadists has not been demonstrated. Specifically, research has found that sadistic fantasy is evident to varying degrees among sexual murderers, rapists who do not kill their victims, and nonoffender control samples (Crepault & Couture, 1980; Gray, Watt, Hassan, & MacCulloch, 2003; Grubin, 1994b).

In assessing deviant sexual fantasy, clinicians should focus on the specific content of fantasy, which can be ascertained through various assessment modalities (see below). In evaluating the content of fantasy to inform diagnosis, there must be differentiation between fantasy regarding a suffering victim (i.e., sadism) and preferential interest in nonconsenting victims. The latter arousal pattern has been referred to as "biastophilia" (Lalumière, Quinsey, Harris, Rice, & Trautrimas, 2003); according to DSM-IV-TR criteria, it would be considered a paraphilia not otherwise specified, rather than sexual sadism. Evidence for this differentiation can be facilitated by examining various offense characteristics (e.g., victim mutilation) in conjunction with fantasy content (Doren, 2002).

Physiological Assessment

In addition to assessment of sadistic fantasy, sexual sadism can be inferred from physiological assessment of deviant sexual arousal to various images. The most widely used method is phallometric assessment (O'Donohue & Letourneau, 1992; Seto & Kuban, 1996), which involves the measurement of volumetric or circumferential erectile changes in response to various sexual stimuli (Blanchard et al., 2006; Konopasky & Konopasky, 2000).

Evaluation of the ability of phallometric assessment to discriminate between sexual sadists and nonsadists has yielded mixed results. For example, whereas some research has found that preferential interest in sadistic stimuli differentiates between groups (Barbaree, Seto, Serin, Amos, & Preston, 1994; Fedora et al., 1992; Proulx et al., 2003), others have found no difference in preferential responding between sadistic and nonsadistic sexual aggressors (Langevin, Bain, et al., 1985; Seto & Kuban, 1996), or have actually observed that nonsadists displayed greater deviant arousal than did sadists (Marshall, Kennedy, & Yates, 2002).

It is also important to note that numerous studies have demonstrated that a significant proportion of offenders are able to suppress penile responses during phallometric assessment (Howes, 1998; Kalmus & Beech, 2005; Marshall & Fernandez, 2000); that the procedure yields low response rates (O'Donohue & Letourneau, 1992) and often fails to differentiate between offenders and nonoffenders (Lalumière & Quinsey, 1994); and that the reliability and validity of the procedure have not been consistently supported (Barbaree, Baxter, & Marshall, 1989; Hall, Proctor, & Nelson, 1988). Such findings have led some researchers (e.g., Marshall, 2006; Marshall & Fernandez, 2000) to question the utility of this procedure in making valid evaluations of sexual offenders in general—a question that is equally applicable to the specific use of phallometric assessment with sexual sadists.

The Abel Assessment for Interest in Paraphilias (Abel Screen; Abel, 1995) was developed as an alternative to phallometric assessment, based on research indicating that viewing time is indicative of sexual interest (Abel, Lawry, Karlstrom, Osborn, & Gillespie, 1994; Harris, Rice, Quinsey, & Chaplin, 1996; Rosenweig, 1942; Ware, Brown, Amoroso, Pilkey, & Preusse, 1972). The measure assesses the time spent viewing a series of slides depicting sexually suggestive stimuli (using clothed models). The stimuli include 22 categories of children and adults, and six paraphilias (frotteurism, exhibitionism, fetishism, voyeurism against females, and sadomasochism against males and females). With regard to the depictions of sadism specifically, Letourneau (2002) found sufficient internal consistency for depictions of female victims (alpha = .91) and male victims (alpha = .87). However, in general, numerous problems have been noted with regard to this scale's psychometric properties, such as a lack of internal consistency, temporal stability, and predictive utility (Fischer, 2000; Fischer & Smith, 1999); in addition, research on the child molester version of the VRT conducted by the scale's developers has been criticized as being unrepresentative, due to the statistical procedures employed (Fischer & Smith, 1999). Furthermore, while Abel, Phipps, Hand, and Jordan (1999) presented reliability statistics for the instrument pertaining to sexual interest in children, information regarding the individual paraphilias was missing. The reliability and validity of the VRT overall have yet to be established, and its utility in assessment has not been demonstrated.

Psychological Tests, Questionnaires, and Inventories

Various self-report and psychological inventories have been designed to assess sexual fantasy and aggressive behavior (Hollin, 1997; Knight et al., 1994). Examples include the Sex Inventory (Thorne, 1966), the Sexual Arousability Inventory (Chambless & Lifshitz, 1984), the Aggressive Sexual Behavior Inventory (Mosher & Anderson, 1986), the Coercive Sexual Fantasies Questionnaire for Males (Greendlinger & Byrne, 1987), and the Clarke Sex History Questionnaire (Langevin, Handy, Paitich, & Russon, 1985). With respect to sexual sadism, following a review of extant inventories (including those mentioned above), Knight and colleagues (1994) developed the Multidimensional Assessment of Sex and Aggression (MASA) to assess sexually aggressive fantasies and behaviors, including sexual sadism specifically. The measure consists of 403 items associated with the MTC:R3 (Knight & Prentky, 1990) classification domains and includes a global Sadism scale and three factor-analytically derived subscales (Bondage, Synergism between Aggression and Sexual Arousal, and Sadistic Fantasy). Initial psychometric evaluations on the global Sadism scale produced good internal consistency (alpha = .95), test–retest reliability (r = .75), and moderate concurrent validity (r = .30); however, the individual subscales performed less well than the global scale. Following revisions to the scale (Knight, 1999; Knight & Cerce, 1999), the global Sadism scale has shown adequate internal consistency (alpha = .79) and test–retest reliability (r = .81; Knight & Cerce, 1999). The most recent clinical version of the instrument, the Multidimensional Inventory of Development, Sex and Aggression (MIDSA), includes over 4,000 items resulting in 55 scales (including Sadism) and is currently undergoing testing (R. A. Knight, personal communication, August 7, 2006).

Two other self-report questionnaires pertaining to sexual sadism are the Sexual Deviance Card Sort (Laws, 1986; Laws, Hanson, Osborn, & Greenbaum, 2000) and the Sexual Interest Card Sort (Abel & Becker, 1979). The Sexual Deviance Card Sort contains 13 scales, one of which pertains to sexual sadism and requires the individual to rate the attractiveness of various descriptions of paraphilic sexual interest (Laws, 1986). The measure has produced results comparable to those of physiologically based assessments (i.e., phallometric assessment [PPG]; Laws et al., 2000), and is markedly less invasive than PPG. However, there is no research to date validating this measure with sexual sadists. The Sexual Interest Card Sort contains 75 items representing 15 discrete categories of sexual interest, including sexual sadism. The items pertaining to sexual sadism have demonstrated excellent reliability (alpha = .91) and validity in psychometric evaluations (Holland, Zolondek, Abel, Jordan, & Becker, 2000).

TREATMENT

The ultimate goal of sexual offender treatment is protecting the public through preventing recurrences of sexually aggressive behavior. To achieve this, various treatment models have been posited over the years, with psychopharmacological and cognitive-behavioral interventions demonstrating the greatest promise (Hanson et al., 2002; Laws & Marshall, 2003; Yates, 2002). Treatment programs, whether medically, behaviorally, or cognitively based, target those factors that, when changed, reduce the possibility of future offending. With the paraphilias in general and sexual sadism in particular, deviant sexual fantasy, urges, and behaviors must be targeted, and these goals are fundamental to each treatment approach described below.

Pharmacological Treatment

The early medical treatment of the paraphilias, specifically sadism and pedophilia, involved surgical castration (Bradford, 1997; Sturup, 1972). These studies, despite some methodological problems, demonstrated that lowering plasma testosterone levels reduced recidivism rates in offenders (Bradford, 2000, 2001). However, given the irreversible nature of the procedure, castration is rarely used today (Rösler & Witztum, 2000; Yates, 2002). Current medical treatment consists of either pharmacological treatments designed to reduce overall levels of testosterone (Bradford, 1997; Gijs & Gooren, 1996) or various antidepressant medications, particularly selective serotonin reuptake inhibitors (SSRIs—Fedoroff, 1993; Greenberg & Bradford, 1997).

The principal androgen related to sexual development and activity is testosterone, and its relationship to sexual aggression (Bancroft, 1989; Bradford, 2000) and to sexual fantasy/desire (e.g., Bradford, 2001; Rösler & Witztum, 2000) is well established. Given the negative correlation between hypoandrogenism and sexual urges, fantasies, and behaviors, several antiandrogen medications have been successfully used with the paraphilias (Bradford, 2000; Gijs & Gooren, 1996). The primary antiandrogens are cyproterone acetate (CPA) and medroxyprogesterone acetate (MPA). CPA was initially employed in the early 1970s (Laschet & Laschet, 1971, 1975) and can be used as a chemical castration agent or, at lower doses, a means of reducing deviant sexual fantasies (Bradford, 1997; Rösler & Witztum, 2000). The use of CPA has been shown to reduce sexual interest, fantasies, and behaviors in a variety of paraphilias, including sexual sadism (Bradford & Pawlak, 1993; Rösler & Witztum, 2000). Similarly, MPA has demonstrated the ability to control paraphilic manifestations. However, the side effects of both medications are considerable; they include diabetes mellitus, dyskinetic and feminization effects, and increased blood pressure (Meyer, Cole, & Emory, 1992).

In addition to CPA and MPA, luteinizing hormone-releasing hormone (LHRH) agonists have been posited as a relatively new treatment option for the paraphilias (Briken, Hill, & Berner, 2003; Dickey, 1992), and have been demonstrated to reduce or alleviate sexual fantasy, urges, and behaviors (Rösler & Witztum, 1998; Thibaut, Cordier, & Kuhn, 1993). Briken, Nika, and Berner (2001) treated 11 patients diagnosed with sadism, pedophilia, or impulse control disorder (based on ICD-10 criteria) for a 3-month period, using an LHRH agonist. Results indicated a reduction in paraphilic activities; decreased sexual desire; and reduced frequency of erections, masturbation, and deviant fantasy. Although no serious side effects were indicated in this study, some patients reported experiencing depression and weight gain.

Another recent development in the medical treatment/management of the paraphilias is the use of SSRIs (Bradford, 2000; Rösler & Witztum, 2000). Despite the fact that most results have come from clinical case reports (e.g., Fedoroff, 1993), some have concluded that these medications have the ability to reduce deviant sexual interest for a variety of paraphilias (see Bradford, 1997, for a review; see also Greenberg, Bradford, Curry, & O'Rourke, 1996; Kafka & Coleman, 1991). However, other studies have failed to demonstrate promising results for the SSRIs with the paraphilias (e.g., Stein et al., 1992), which has led some to be more cautious about the utility of psychotropic interventions (Gijs & Gooren, 1996; Rösler & Witztum, 2000).

Behavioral Treatment

Based on the assumption that arousal patterns develop as a result of early conditioning (Laws & Marshall, 1990, 2003), behavioral therapies have concentrated on altering established sexual preferences via procedures based on operant and classical conditioning (Fernandez, Shingler, & Marshall, 2006). With sexual sadists, the goal of these techniques is to replace deviant fantasies involving pain and humiliation with a preference for appropriate sexual content.

Early behavioral approaches focused on using various aversive procedures to eliminate deviant sexual preference (Marshall & Laws, 2003). Specifically, overt methods paired the deviant stimulus (e.g., sadistic sexual scenes) with noxious consequences such as electric shock (Marshall, 1973) or offensive odors (Laws, Meyer, & Holmen, 1978), whereas covert methods combined the deviant stimulus with internal representations of various negative consequences (e.g., getting caught while engaged in sadistic acts—Fernandez et al., 2006; Hollin, 1997). There was some early support for these procedures in the treatment of sexual sadism; however, these predominantly involved single-case study designs (Hayes, Brownell, & Barlow, 1978; Laws et al., 1978). Overall, there is limited evidence that either aversive procedure is effective in reducing or changing deviant sexual fantasy across the paraphilias (Quinsey & Marshall, 1983; Seto, 1997), and overt procedures have particularly been discouraged by some authors (e.g., Fernandez et al., 2006) because of their potential for evoking aggression within an individual.

Another behavioral method, satiation therapy (Laws & Marshall, 1990; Marshall & Laws, 2003), is designed to eliminate deviant sexual preference by having an individual masturbate to deviant sexual content (e.g., sadistic themes) after previously reaching orgasm, with the aim of developing an association between deviant fantasy and boredom/lack of arousal. Despite some positive support for this method, the evidence for enduring change and for utility with unmotivated clients is weak (Fernandez et al., 2006; Seto, 1997).

In addition to the methods described above, clinicians have attempted to replace deviant fantasy with more appropriate sexual themes, via such procedures as orgasmic reconditioning (directed masturbation to suitable sexual content; Hollin, 1997; Maletzky, 1985). However, once again, the evidence for this procedure is not promising (Marshall & Laws, 2003).

Cognitive-Behavioral Treatment

Cognitive-behavioral treatment (CBT) emphasizes the role of and interrelationships among cognition, affect, and behavior, and is the most common therapeutic approach currently employed with sexual offenders (Hanson et al., 2002; Yates, 2002, 2003; Yates et al., 2000). Treatment using the CBT approach typically combines the risk/needs model of offender rehabilitation (Andrews & Bonta, 1998) with relapse prevention (RP— Marlatt, 1982; Pithers, 1990). Detailed reviews of these models have been provided elsewhere (Andrews & Bonta, 1998; Ward, Melser, & Yates, 2007; Yates, 2002, 2003, in press; Yates & Kingston, 2005; Yates & Ward, 2007). In brief, the risk/needs model suggests that treatment success (i.e., reduced likelihood of recidivism) is most likely when the intensity of treatment and supervision are matched to the risk level posed by an offender and when criminogenic needs are explicitly targeted; research supports this approach to treatment (Andrews & Bonta, 1998; Dowden & Andrews, 1999, 2000). RP was originally developed as a maintenance program for addictive behaviors (Marlatt, 1982; Marlatt & Gordon, 1985), but was reconceptualized and applied to sexual offenders (Pithers, 1990; Pithers, Kashima, Cumming, & Beal, 1988; Pithers, Marques, Gibat, & Marlatt, 1983). The purpose of RP is to assist individuals in identifying and anticipating problems associated with sexual offending, and in developing skills to avoid and to cope with such circumstances. Research to date has not supported the effectiveness of this approach in the treatment of sexual offenders (Hanson, 1996, 2000; Laws, 2003; Marques, Wiederanders, Day, Nelson, & van Ommeren, 2005; Yates, 2003; Yates & Kingston, 2005; Yates & Ward, 2007).

Within CBT interventions, specific treatment targets include such dynamic risk factors as intimacy deficits, cognitive distortions, offense-supportive attitudes, deviant sexual arousal and fantasy, emotion regulation, and empathy deficits (Marshall et al., 1999; Yates et al., 2000). While the majority of these treatment targets would appear to be appropriate for sexual sadists, a focus on empathy deficits may be contraindicated with this group. Although some authors (e.g., Marshall, Marshall, Serran, & Fernandez, 2006) regard sadism as a type of empathy deficit, others (e.g., Ward, Polaschek, & Beech, 2006; Yates et al., 2000) suggest that the features and behavior of sexual sadists clearly demonstrate not only that they are able to take the perspective of the victim during the commission of the offense, but that they may gain pleasure from this perception. As such, enhancement of this ability during treatment could result in a sexual sadist learning how to perceive and respond more accurately to cues indicating pain and suffering on the part of the victim, so that he may actually refine his offense strategies. To prevent this problem, it has been suggested that empathy development during treatment use examples of individuals with whom the sadist has a close relationship, in order to personalize a victim and to develop empathy in the context of an important relationship with a loved one in the individual's life (Marshall et al., 2006). Another suggestion is that empathy deficits be targeted only with those sexual sadists who do not concurrently demonstrate psychopathic features (D. Thornton, personal communication, August 28, 2006). Given that empathy has not been found to be predictive of recidivism, that little research to date supports the development of empathy as an important treatment target, and that a focus on empathy has the potential to increase accurate perceptions of victim suffering in the individual (Yates, 2003; Yates et al., 2000), we do not recommend that empathy training be implemented with sexual sadists.

Within the CBT model of treatment, recent work posits the self-regulation model as an alternative to the RP approach (Ward et al., 2004; Ward & Hudson, 1998, 2000; Ward, Yates, & Long, 2006; Yates, 2006, in press; Yates & Kingston, 2005, 2006; Yates & Ward, in press). Of relevance to the treatment of sexual sadism are the four pathways to offending described within this model, which vary based on the individual's self-regulatory abilities and goals with respect to offending. One pathway within this scheme, the approach-explicit pathway, is characterized by intact self-regulation; the absence of deficits in ability to regulate behavior, affect, and cognition; antisocial goals; and explicit offense planning. As indicated by our earlier review of the features associated with sexual sadism, it would appear that sexual sadists may be likely to follow this pathway to offending, although this has not been empirically tested. Treatment within this model explicitly targets goals, attitudes, cognition, and behaviors that are supportive of offending, and places less emphasis on the development of coping skills, because such deficits are not typically present in these individuals (Ward, Yates, et al., 2006; Yates, 2006). This particular mode of treatment may be appropriate to CBT sexual sadists.

SUMMARY AND FUTURE DIRECTIONS

Sexual sadists are characterized by violent sexual fantasy and a desire for power and control, with various behavioral indicators typically evident during the commission of the offense. As indicated above, assessment of sexual sadism is fraught with problems related to definitions of the disorder, application of diagnostic criteria, reliability of the diagnosis, and the applicability of common actuarial assessment methods. Since a diagnosis of sexual sadism is likely to have significant consequences for the criminal justice system's processing of the offender (Doren, 2002; Marshall & Yates, 2004), it is essential that consistent and reliable methods of assessment and diagnosis be developed. Such methods are also essential to assessment for treatment and for determination of appropriate treatment interventions for these individuals. The predominant approach to classification (the DSM-IV-TR), at least in its current form, holds limited promise for diagnosis and treatment purposes.

To date, no single measure of the features of sexual sadism has been consistently supported by research. The review provided herein indicates that in assessing sexual sadism, clinicians must be cognizant of the overlap between sexual sadism and other behaviors (both including paraphilic and nonparaphilic), and must be diligent in the application of criteria in order to ensure that the appropriate diagnosis is made. Although there are some promising measures of sexual sadism, such as the Sexual Interest Card Sort, the Abel Assessment for Sexual Interest, and the more recent MIDSA and Sadism Scale (Abel, 1995; Abel & Becker, 1979; Knight & Cerce, 1999; Marshall & Hucker, 2006), sufficient research has not yet been conducted to validate these measures with this group of offenders. Similarly, measures such as the Stroop task (Smith & Waterman, 2004) and the Implicit Association Test (Mihailides, Devilly, & Ward, 2004; Nunes, Firestone, & Baldwin, 2007)—which are designed to assess various internal cognitive representations, and which are less susceptible to socially desirable responding and voluntary control than other measures—are potentially promising in identifying sadistic sexual fantasies, but their relationship with sadism in particular has been unexplored, at least to our knowledge. It is recommended that clinicians base diagnosis on a confluence of findings from multiple sources (including offense and crime scene information, diagnostic schemes, and objective and/or self-report measures), keeping in mind the limitations of each. Clinicians also need to be cognizant that similar behaviors may represent disorders other than sexual sadism, and to evaluate behavioral and offense indicators in light of this.

Given the problems associated with the assessment of sexual sadism, it is difficult to state conclusively which treatment interventions are most likely to reduce reoffending.

Antiandrogens such as CPA and MPA have demonstrated positive effects on reducing deviant sexual fantasy; however, their side effects are considerable. Moreover, the use of psychotropic drugs (i.e., SSRIs) has yielded mixed results (Bradford, 1997; Rösler & Witztum, 2000). Among the most promising agents with the fewest side effects seem to be LHRH agonists, as these appear highly effective in reducing features common to sexual sadism. Nevertheless, there is an absence of controlled research examining efficacy, both in general and with sexual sadists specifically; methodologically sound, double-blind controlled studies that examine specific paraphilic populations are needed. There has been limited support to date for the utility of behavioral arousal reconditioning procedures in altering deviant sexual arousal, an essential feature of sexual sadism. Similarly, although the most commonly used intervention with sexual offenders (i.e., CBT) has demonstrated a positive effect in reducing recidivism (Hanson et al., 2002), its impact on sexual sadists specifically is unknown, and CBT may require some modification with this group of offenders. The recently proposed self-regulation model may be more applicable to the treatment of sexual sadists than traditional treatment methods, given its capacity for explicitly targeting the pathway to offending that seems likely to characterize individuals presenting with sexually sadistic features.

REFERENCES

Abel, G. G. (1995). *New technology: The Abel Assessment for Interest in Paraphilias*. Atlanta, GA: Abel Screening.

Abel, G. G., & Becker, J. V. (1979). *The Sexual Interest Card Sort*. Unpublished manuscript.

Abel, G. G., Lawry, S. S., Karlstrom, E., Osborn, C., & Gillespie, C. F. (1994). Screening tests for pedophilia. *Criminal Justice and Behavior, 21,* 115–131.

Abel, G. G., Phipps, A., Hand, C., & Jordan, A. (1999, September). *The reliability and validity of visual reaction time as a measure of sexual interest in children.* Paper presented at the 18th Annual Meeting of the Association for the Treatment of Sexual Abusers, Orlando, FL.

American Psychiatric Association. (2000). *Diagnostic and statistical manual of mental disorders* (4th ed., text rev.). Washington, DC: Author.

Andrews, D. A., & Bonta, J. (1998). *The psychology of criminal conduct*. Cincinnati, OH: Anderson.

Bancroft, J. (1989). *Human sexuality and its problems*. Edinburgh, UK: Churchill Livingstone.

Barbaree, H. E., Baxter, D. J., & Marshall, W. L. (1989). Brief research report: The reliability of the rape index in a sample of rapists and nonrapists. *Violence and Victims, 4,* 399–306.

Barbaree, H. E., Hudson, S. M., & Seto, M. C. (1993). Sexual assault in society: The role of the juvenile offender. In H. E. Barbaree, W. L. Marshall, & S. M. Hudson (Eds.), *The juvenile sex offender* (pp. 1–24). New York: Guilford Press.

Barbaree, H. E., Seto, M. C., Serin, R. C., Amos, N. L., & Preston, D. L. (1994). Comparisons between sexual and non-sexual rapist subtypes: Sexual arousal to rape, offence precursors and offence characteristics. *Criminal Justice and Behavior, 21,* 95–114.

Beauregard, E., & Proulx, J. (2002). Profiles in the offending process of nonserial sexual murderers. *International Journal of Offender Therapy and Comparative Criminology, 46,* 386–399.

Berner, W., Berger, P., & Hill, A. (2003) Sexual sadism. *International Journal of Offender Therapy and Comparative Criminology, 47,* 383–395.

Blanchard, R., Kuban, M. E., Blak, T., Cantor, J. M., Klassen, P., & Dickey, R. (2006). Phallometric comparison of pedophilic interest in nonadmitting sexual offenders against stepdaughters, biological daughters, other biologically related girls, and unrelated girls. *Sexual Abuse: A Journal of Research and Treatment, 18,* 1–14.

Bradford, J. M. (1997). Medical interventions in sexual deviance. In D. R. Laws & W. O'Donohue

(Eds.), *Sexual deviance: Theory, assessment, and treatment* (pp. 449–464). New York: Guilford Press.

Bradford, J. M. (2000). The treatment of sexual deviation using a pharmacological approach. *Journal of Sex Research, 37,* 248–257.

Bradford, J. M. (2001). The neurobiology, neuropharmacology, and pharmacological treatment of paraphilias and compulsive sexual behaviour. *Canadian Journal of Psychiatry, 46,* 26–34.

Bradford, J. M., & Pawlak, A. (1993). A double-blind placebo cross-over study of cyproterone acetate in the treatment of the paraphilias. *Archives of Sexual Behavior, 22,* 383–402.

Briken, P., Hill, A., & Berner, W. (2003). Pharmacotherapy of paraphilias with long-acting agonists of luteinizing hormone-releasing hormone: A systematic review. *Journal of Clinical Psychiatry, 64,* 890–897.

Briken, P., Nika, E., & Berner, W. (2001). Treatment of paraphilia with luteinizing hormone-releasing hormone agonists. *Journal of Sex and Marital Therapy, 27,* 45–55.

Brittain, R. (1970). The sadistic murderer. *Medicine, Science, and the Law, 10,* 198–207.

Burgess, A. W., Hartmann, C. R., Ressler, R. K., Douglas, J. E., & McCormack, A. (1986). Sexual homicide: A motivational model. *Journal of Interpersonal Violence, 1,* 251–272.

Chambless, D., & Lifshitz, J. L. (1984). Self-reported sexual anxiety and arousal: The expanded Sexual Arousability Inventory. *Journal of Sex Research, 20,* 241–254.

Crepault, E., & Couture, M. (1980). Men's erotic fantasies. *Archives of Sexual Behavior, 9,* 565–581.

Dickey, R. (1992). The management of a case of treatment-resistant paraphilia with a long-acting LHRH agonist. *Canadian Journal of Psychiatry, 37,* 567–569.

Dietz, P. E., Hazelwood, R. R., & Warren, J. (1990). The sexually sadistic criminal and his offenses. *Bulletin of the American Academy of Psychiatry and the Law, 18,* 163–178.

Donnelly, D., & Fraser, J. (1998). Gender differences in sado-masochistic arousal among college students. *Sex Roles, 39,* 391–407.

Doren, D. M. (2002). *Evaluating sex offenders: A manual for civil commitments and beyond.* Thousand Oaks, CA: Sage.

Dowden, C., & Andrews, D. A. (1999). What works for female offenders: a meta-analytic review. *Crime and Delinquency, 45,* 438–452.

Dowden, C., & Andrews, D. A. (2000). Effective correctional treatment and violent reoffending: A meta-analysis. *Canadian Journal of Criminology and Criminal Justice, 42,* 449–467.

Fedora, O., Reddon, J. R., Morrison, J. W., Fedora, S. K., Pascoe, H., & Yeudall, L. (1992). Sadism and other paraphilias in normal controls and aggressive and nonaggressive sex offenders. *Archives of Sexual Behavior, 21,* 1–15.

Fedoroff, J. P. (1993). Serotenergic drug treatment of deviant sexual interests. *Annals of Sex Research, 6,* 105–121.

Fernandez, Y. M., Shingler, J., & Marshall, W. L. (2006). Putting "behavior" back into the cognitive-behavioral treatment of sexual offenders. In W. L. Marshall, Y. M. Fernandez, L. E. Marshall, & G. A. Serran (Eds.), *Sexual offender treatment: Controversial issues* (pp. 211–224). Chichester, UK: Wiley.

Fischer, L. (2000). The Abel Screen: A nonintrusive alternative? In D. R. Laws, S. M. Hudson, & T. Ward (Eds.), *Remaking relapse prevention with sex offenders: A sourcebook* (pp. 303–318). Thousand Oaks, CA: Sage.

Fischer, L., & Smith, G. M. (1999). Statistical adequacy of the Abel Assessment for Interest in Paraphilias. *Sexual Abuse: A Journal of Research and Treatment, 11,* 195–206.

Gijs, L., & Gooren, L. (1996). Hormonal and psychopharmacological interventions in the treatment of paraphilias: An update. *Journal of Sex Research, 33,* 273–290.

Gratzer, T., & Bradford, J. M. (1995). Offender and offense characteristics of sexual sadists: A comparative study. *Journal of Forensic Sciences, 40,* 450–455.

Gray, N. S., Watt, A., Hassan, S., & MacCulloch, M. J. (2003). Behavioral indicators of sadistic sexual murder predict the presence of sadistic sexual fantasy in a normative sample. *Journal of Interpersonal Violence, 18,* 1018–1034.

Greenberg, D. M., & Bradford, J. M. (1997). Treatment of the paraphilic disorders: A review of the role of the selective serotonin reuptake inhibitors. *Sexual Abuse: A Journal of Research and Treatment, 9,* 349–360.

Greenberg, D. M., Bradford, J. M., Curry, S., & O'Rourke, A. (1996). A comparison of treatment of paraphilias with three serotonin reuptake inhibitors: A retrospective study. *Bulletin of the American Academy of Psychiatry and the Law, 24,* 525–532.

Greendlinger, V., & Byrne, D. (1987). Coercive sexual fantasies of college men as predictors of self-reported likelihood to rape and overt sexual aggression. *Journal of Sex Research, 23,* 1–11.

Grubin, D. (1994a). Editorial: Sexual sadism. *Criminal Behavior and Mental Health, 4,* 3–9.

Grubin, D. (1994b). Sexual murder. *British Journal of Psychiatry, 165,* 624–629.

Hall, G. C. N., Proctor, W. C., & Nelson, G. M. (1988). Validity of physiological measures of pedophilic sexual arousal in a sexual offender population. *Journal of Consulting and Clinical Psychology, 56,* 118–122.

Hanson, R. K. (1996). Evaluating the contribution of relapse prevention theory to the treatment of sexual offenders. *Sexual Abuse: A Journal of Research and Treatment, 8,* 201–208.

Hanson, R. K. (2000). What is so special about relapse prevention? In D. R. Laws, S. M. Hudson, & T. Ward (Eds.), *Remaking relapse prevention with sex offenders: A sourcebook* (pp. 27–38). Thousand Oaks, CA: Sage.

Hanson, R. K., Gordon, A., Harris, A. J. R., Marques, J. K., Murphy, W., Quinsey, V. L., et al. (2002). First report of the Collaborative Outcome Data Project on the Effectiveness of Psychological Treatment for Sex Offenders. *Sexual Abuse: A Journal of Research and Treatment, 14,* 169–194.

Hanson, R. K., & Thornton, D. (1999). *Static-99: Improving actuarial risk assessments for sex offenders* (User Report No. 99-02). Ottawa: Department of the Solicitor General of Canada.

Harris, G. T., Rice, M. E., Quinsey, V. L., & Chaplin, T. C. (1996). Viewing time as a measure of sexual interest among child molesters and normal heterosexual men. *Behaviour Research and Therapy, 34,* 389–394.

Hayes, S., Brownell, K., & Barlow, D. (1978). The use of self-administered covert sensitization in the treatment of exhibitionism and sadism. *Behavior Therapy, 9,* 283–289.

Holland, L. A., Zolondek, S. C., Abel, G. G., Jordan, A. D., & Becker, J. V. (2000). Psychometric analysis of the Sexual Interest Card Sort questionnaire. *Sexual Abuse: A Journal of Research and Treatment, 12,* 107–122.

Hollin, C. R. (1997). Sexual sadism: Assessment and treatment. In D. R. Laws & W. O'Donohue (Eds.), *Sexual deviance: Theory, assessment, and treatment* (pp. 210–224). New York: Guilford Press.

Holmes, R. M., & Holmes, S. T. (1994). *Murder in America.* Thousand Oaks, CA: Sage.

Howes, R. J. (1998). Plethysmographic assessment of incarcerated nonsexual offenders: A comparison with rapists. *Sexual Abuse: A Journal of Research and Treatment, 10,* 183–194.

Hunt, M. (1974). *Sexual behavior in the 1970's.* New York: Playboy Press.

Kafka, M., & Coleman, E. (1991). Serotonin and paraphilias: The convergence of mood, impulse and compulsive disorders. *Journal of Clinical Psychopharmacology, 11,* 223–224.

Kalmus, E., & Beech, A. R. (2005). Forensic assessment of sexual interest: A review. *Aggression and Violent Behavior, 10,* 193–217.

Kingston, D. A., Firestone, P., Moulden, H. M., & Bradford, J. M. (2007). The utility of the diagnosis of pedophilia: A comparison of various classification procedures. *Archives of Sexual Behavior, 36,* 423–436.

Knight, R. A. (1999). Validation of a typology for rapists. *Journal of Interpersonal Violence, 14,* 303–330.

Knight, R. A., & Cerce, D. D. (1999). Validation and revision of the Multidimensional Assessment of Sex and Aggression. *Psychologica Belgica, 39,* 187–213.

Knight, R. A., & Prentky, R. A. (1990). Classifying sexual offenders: The development and corroboration of taxonomic models. In W. L. Marshall, D. R. Laws, & H. E. Barbaree (Eds.), *Handbook of sexual assault: Issues, theories, and treatment of the offender* (pp. 23–52). New York: Plenum Press.

Knight, R. A., Prentky, R. A., & Cerce, D. (1994). The development, reliability, and validity of an inventory for the multidimensional assessment of sex and aggression. *Criminal Justice and Behavior, 21*, 72–94.

Konopasky, R. J., & Konopasky, A. W. B. (2000). Remaking penile plethysmography. In D. R. Laws, S. M. Hudson, & T. Ward (Eds.), *Remaking relapse prevention with sex offenders: A sourcebook* (pp. 257–284). Thousand Oaks, CA: Sage.

Krafft-Ebing, R. von. (1892). *Psychopathia sexualis*. Philadelphia: Davis. (Original work published 1886)

Lalumière, M. L., & Quinsey, V. L. (1994). The discriminability of rapists from non-sex offenders using phallometric measures: A meta-analysis. *Criminal Justice and Behavior, 21*, 150–175.

Lalumière, M. L., Quinsey, V. L., Harris, G. T., Rice, M. E., & Trautrimas, C. (2003). Are rapists differentially aroused by coercive sex in phallometric assessments? *New York Academy of Sciences, 989*, 211–224.

Langevin, R., Bain, J., Ben-Aron, M. H., Coulthard, R., Day, D., Roper, V., et al. (1985). Sexual aggression: Constructing a predictive equation: A controlled pilot study. In R. Langevin (Ed.), *Erotic preference, gender identity, and aggression in men: New research studies* (pp. 39–76). Hillsdale, NJ: Erlbaum.

Langevin, R., Handy, L., Paitich, D., & Russon, A. (1985). A new version of the Clarke Sex History Questionnaire for Males. In R. Langevin (Ed.), *Erotic preference, gender identity, and aggression in men: New research studies* (pp. 287–305). Hillsdale, NJ: Erlbaum.

Laschet, U., & Laschet, L. (1971). Psychopharmacotherapy of sex offenders with cyproterone acetate. *Pharmakopsychiatrie Neuropsychopharmakologic, 4*, 99–104.

Laschet, U., & Laschet, L. (1975). Antiandrogens in the treatment of sexual deviations of men. *Journal of Steroid Biochemistry, 6*, 821–826.

Laws, D. R. (1986). *Sexual Deviance Card Sort*. Unpublished manuscript, Florida Mental Health Institute, Tampa.

Laws, D. R. (2003). The rise and fall of relapse prevention. *Australian Psychologist, 38*, 22–30.

Laws, D. R., Hanson, R. K., Osborn, C. A., & Greenbaum, P. E. (2000). Classification of child molesters by plethysmographic assessment of sexual arousal and a self-report measure of sexual preference. *Journal of Interpersonal Violence, 15*, 1297–1312.

Laws, D. R., & Marshall, W. L. (1990). A conditioning theory of the etiology and maintenance of deviant sexual preferences and behavior. In W. L. Marshall, D. R. Laws, & H. E. Barbaree (Eds.), *Handbook of sexual assault: Issues, theories, and treatment of the offender* (pp. 209–229). New York: Plenum Press.

Laws, D. R., & Marshall, W. L. (2003). A brief history of behavioral and cognitive-behavioral approaches to sexual offenders: Part 1. Early developments. *Sexual Abuse: A Journal of Research and Treatment, 15*, 75–92.

Laws, D. R., Meyer, J., & Holmen, M. L. (1978). Reduction of sadistic arousal by olfactory aversion: A case study. *Behaviour Research and Therapy, 16*, 281–285.

Letourneau, E. J. (2002). A comparison of objective measures of sexual arousal and interest: Visual reaction time and penile plethysmography. *Sexual Abuse: A Journal of Research and Treatment, 14*, 207–223.

Levenson, J. S. (2004). Reliability of sexually violent predator civil commitment criteria. *Law and Human Behavior, 28*, 357–368.

MacCulloch, M., Gray, N., & Watt, A. (2000). Brittain's sadist murderer syndrome reconsidered: An associative account of the aetiology of sadistic sexual fantasy. *Journal of Forensic Psychiatry, 11*, 401–418.

MacCulloch, M., Snowden, P., Wood, P., & Mills, H. (1983). Sadistic fantasy, sadistic behavior, and offending. *British Journal of Psychiatry, 143*, 20–29.

Maletzky, B. M. (1985). Orgasmic reconditioning. In A. S. Bellack & M. Hersen (Eds.), *Dictionary of behavior therapy techniques* (pp. 157–158). New York: Pergamon Press.

Marlatt, G. A. (1982). Relapse prevention: A self-control program for the treatment of addictive be-
    haviors. In R. B. Stuart (Ed.), *Adherence, compliance and generalization in behavioral medicine*
    (pp. 329–378). New York: Brunner/Mazel.

Marlatt, G. A., & Gordon, J. R. (Eds.). (1985). *Relapse prevention: Maintenance strategies in the
    treatment of addictive behaviors*. New York: Guilford Press.

Marques, J. K., Wiederanders, M., Day, D. M., Nelson, C., & van Ommeren, A. (2005). Effects of a
    relapse prevention program on sexual recidivism: Final results from California's Sex Offender
    Treatment and Evaluation Project (SOTEP). *Sexual Abuse: A Journal of Research and Treat-
    ment, 17*, 79–107.

Marshall, W. L. (1973). The modification of sexual fantasies: A combined treatment approach
    to the reduction of deviant sexual behaviour. *Behaviour Research and Therapy, 11*, 557–
    564.

Marshall, W. L. (2006). Diagnostic problems with sexual offenders. In W. L. Marshall, Y. M.
    Fernandez, L. E. Marshall, & G. A. Serran (Eds.), *Sexual offender treatment: Controversial is-
    sues* (pp. 33–43). Chichester, UK: Wiley.

Marshall, W. L., Anderson, D., & Fernandez, Y. M. (1999). *Cognitive behavioural treatment of sexual
    offenders*. Chichester, UK: Wiley.

Marshall, W. L., & Fernandez, Y. M. (2000). Phallometric testing with sexual offenders: Limits to its
    value. *Clinical Psychology Review, 20*, 807–822.

Marshall, W. L., & Hucker, S. J. (2006). Issues in the diagnosis of sexual sadism. *Sexual Offender
    Treatment, 1*. Retrieved from *sexual-offender-treatment.org*

Marshall, W. L., & Kennedy, P. (2003). Sexual sadism in sexual offenders: An elusive diagnosis. *Ag-
    gression and Violent Behavior, 8*, 1–22.

Marshall, W. L., Kennedy, P., & Yates, P. M. (2002). Issues concerning the reliability and validity of the
    diagnosis of sexual sadism applied in prison settings. *Sexual Abuse: A Journal of Research and
    Treatment, 14*, 310–311.

Marshall, W. L., Kennedy, P., Yates, P. M., & Serran, G. A. (2002). Diagnosing sexual sadism in sexual
    offenders: Rehability across diagnosticians. *International Journal of Offender Therapy and
    Comparative Criminology, 46*, 668–676.

Marshall, W. L., & Laws, D. R. (2003). A brief history of behavioral and cognitive-behavioral ap-
    proaches to sexual offender treatment: Part 2. The modern era. *Sexual Abuse: A Journal of Re-
    search and Treatment, 15*, 93–120.

Marshall, W. L., Marshall, L. E., Serran, G. A., & Fernandez, Y. M. (2006). *Treating sexual offenders:
    An integrated approach*. New York: Routledge.

Marshall, W. L., & Yates, P. M. (2004). Diagnostic issues in sexual sadism among sexual offenders.
    Journal of Sexual Aggression, 10, 21–27.

Meehl, P. E. (1996). *Clinical versus statistical prediction: A theoretical analysis and a review of the lit-
    erature*. Northvale, NJ: Aronson.

Meyer, W. J., Cole, C., & Emory, E. (1992). Depo-Provera treatment for sex offending behavior: An
    evaluation of outcome. *Bulletin of the American Academy of Psychiatry and the Law, 20*, 249–
    259.

Michaud, S. G., & Hazelwood, R. R. (1999). *The evil that men do*. New York: St. Martin's Press.

Mihailides, G. J., Devilly, S., & Ward, T. (2004). Implicit cognitive distortions and sexual offending.
    Sexual Abuse: A Journal of Research and Treatment, 16, 333–350.

Moser, C. (2002). Are any of the paraphilias in DSM mental disorders? *Archives of Sexual Behavior,
    31*, 490–491.

Mosher, D. L., & Anderson, R. D. (1986). Macho personality, sexual aggression, and reactions to
    guided imagery of realistic rape. *Journal of Research in Personality, 20*, 77–94.

Moulden, H. M., Firestone, P., Kingston, D. A., & Bradford, J. M. (2006). *Recidivism in pedophiles:
    An investigation using different methods of defining pedophilia*. Manuscript in preparation.

Myers, W. C., Burgess, A. W., Burgess, A. G., & Douglas, J. E. (1999). Serial murder and sexual homicide. In V. van Hasselt & M. Hersen (Eds.), *Handbook of psychological approaches with violent offenders* (pp. 153–172). New York: Kluwer Academic/Plenum.

Nugent, P. M., & Kroner, D. G. (1996). Denial, response styles, and admittance of offenses among child molesters and rapists. *Journal of Interpersonal Violence, 11,* 475–486.

Nunes, K. L., Firestone, P., & Baldwin, M. W. (2007). Indirect assessment of cognitions of child sexual abusers with the Implicit Association Test. *Criminal Justice and Behavior, 34,* 454–475.

O'Donohue, W., & Letourneau, E. (1992). The psychometric properties of the penile tumescence measures with incarcerated rapists. *Journal of Psychopathology and Behavioral Assessment, 14,* 123–174.

O'Donohue, W., Regev, L. G., & Hagstrom, A. (2000). Problems with the DSM-IV diagnosis of pedophilia. *Sexual Abuse: A Journal of Research and Treatment, 12,* 95–105.

Packard, R. L., & Levenson, J. S. (2006). Revisiting the reliability of diagnostic decisions in sex offender civil commitment. *Sex Offender Treatment, 1,* 3.

Pithers, W. D. (1990). Relapse prevention with sexual aggressors: A method for maintaining therapeutic gain and enhancing external supervision. In W. L. Marshall, D. R. Laws, & H. E. Barbaree (Eds.), *Handbook of sexual assault: Issues, theories, and treatment of the offender* (pp. 343–361). New York: Plenum Press.

Pithers, W. D., Kashima, K. M., Cumming, G. F., & Beal, L. S. (1988). Relapse prevention: A method of enhancing maintenance of change in sex offenders. In A. C. Salter (Ed.), *Treating child sex offenders and victims: A practical guide* (pp. 131–170). Newbury Park, CA: Sage.

Pithers, W. D., Marques, J. K., Gibat, C. C., & Marlatt, G. A. (1983). Relapse prevention: A self-control model of treatment and maintenance of change for sexual aggressives. In J. Greer & I. Stuart (Eds.), *The sexual aggressor: Current perspectives on treatment* (pp. 214–239). New York: Van Nostrand Reinhold.

Prentky, R. A., Burgess, A. W., Rokous, F., Lee, A., Hartman, C. R., Ressler, R. K., et al. (1989). The presumptive role of fantasy in serial sexual homicide. *American Journal of Psychiatry, 146,* 887–891.

Proulx, J., Blais, E., & Beauregard, E. (2003). *Le sadisme sexuel.* Manuscript in preparation.

Proulx, J., Blais, E., & Beauregard, E. (2006). Sadistic sexual aggressors. In W. L. Marshall, Y. M. Fernandez, L. E. Marshall, & G. A. Serran (Eds.), *Sexual offender treatment: Controversial issues* (pp. 61–77). Chichester, UK: Wiley.

Quinsey, V. L., Chaplin, T. C., & Varney, G. (1981). A comparison of rapists' and non-sex offenders' sexual preference for mutually consenting sex, rape, and physical abuse of women. *Behavioural Assessment, 3,* 127–135.

Quinsey, V. L., & Marshall, W. L. (1983). Procedures for reducing inappropriate sexual arousal: An evaluative review. In J. G. Greer & I. R. Stuart (Eds.), *The sexual aggressor: Current perspectives on treatment* (pp. 267–289). New York: Van Nostrand Reinhold.

Quinsey, V. L., Rice, M. E., & Harris, G. T. (1995). Actuarial prediction of sexual recidivism. *Journal of Interpersonal Violence, 10,* 85–105.

Ressler, R. K., Burgess, A. W., & Douglas, J. E. (1988). *Sexual homicide: Patterns and motives.* New York: Free Press.

Ressler, R. K., Burgess, A. W., Douglas, J. E., Hartman, C. R., & D'Agostino, R. B. (1986). Sexual killers and their victims: Identifying patterns through crime scene analysis. *Journal of Interpersonal Violence, 1,* 288–308.

Rosenweig, S. (1942). The photoscope as an objective device for evaluating sexual interest. *Psychosomatic Medicine, 4,* 150–158.

Rösler, A., & Witztum, E. (1998). Treatment of men with paraphilia with a long-acting analogue of gonadotropin-releasing hormone. *Journal of Urology, 160,* 628–629.

Rösler, A., & Witztum, E. (2000). Pharmacotherapy of paraphilias in the next millennium. *Behavioral Sciences and the Law, 18,* 43–56.

Seto, M. C. (1997). Pedophilia: Assessment and treatment. In D. R. Laws & W. O'Donohue (Eds.), *Sexual deviance: Theory, assessment, and treatment* (pp. 175–193). New York: Guilford Press.

Seto, M. C., & Kuban, M. (1996). Criterion-related validity of a phallometric test for paraphilic rape and sadism. *Behaviour Research and Therapy, 34*, 175–183.

Smith, P., & Waterman, M. (2004). Processing bias for sexual material: The emotional stroop and sexual offenders. *Sexual Abuse: A Journal of Research and Treatment, 16*, 163–171.

Stein, D. J., Hollander, E., Anthony, D. T., Schneider, F. R., Fallon, B. A., & Liebowitz, M. R. (1992). Serotonergic medications for sexual obsessions, sexual addictions, and paraphilias. *Journal of Clinical Psychiatry, 53*, 267–271.

Straus, M. A., with Donnelly, D. (1994). *Beating the devil out of them: Corporal punishment in American families.* New York: Lexington Books.

Sturup, G. K. (1972). Castration: The total treatment. In H. L. P. Resnick & M. E. Wolfgang (Eds.), *Sexual behavior: Social, clinical and legal aspects* (pp. 361–382). Boston: Little, Brown.

Thibaut, F., Cordier, B., & Kuhn, J. M. (1993). Effect of a long-acting gonadotrophin hormone-releasing hormone agonist in six cases of severe male paraphilia. *Acta Psychiatrica Scandinavica, 87*, 445–450.

Thorne, F. C. (1966). The Sex Inventory. *Journal of Clinical Psychology, 22*, 367–374.

Ward, T., & Hudson, S. M. (1998). The construction and development of theory in the sexual offending area: A meta-theoretical framework. *Sexual Abuse: A Journal of Research and Treatment, 10*, 47–63.

Ward, T., & Hudson, S. M. (2000). A self-regulation model of relapse prevention. In D. R. Laws, S. M. Hudson, & T. Ward (Eds.), *Remaking relapse prevention with sex offenders: A sourcebook* (pp. 79–101). Thousand Oaks, CA: Sage.

Ward, T., Melser, J., & Yates, P. M. (2007). Reconstructing the risk need responsivity model: A theoretical elaboration and evaluation. *Aggression and Violent Behavior, 12*, 208–228.

Ward, T., Polaschek, D. L. L., & Beech, A. R. (2006). *Theories of sexual offending.* Hoboken, NJ: Wiley.

Ward, T., Yates, P. M., & Long, C. A. (2006). *The self-regulation model of the offence and relapse process: Vol. 2. Treatment.* Victoria, BC, Canada: Pacific Psychological Assessment Corporation.

Ware, E. E., Brown, M., Amoroso, D. M., Pilkey, D. W., & Pruesse, M. (1972). The semantic meaning of pornographic stimuli for college males. *Canadian Journal of Behavioural Science, 4*, 204–209.

Williams, L. M., & Finkelhor, D. (1990). The characteristics of incestuous fathers: A review of recent studies. In W. L. Marshall, D. R. Laws, & H. E. Barbaree (Eds.), *Handbook of sexual assault: Issues, theories, and treatment of the offender* (pp. 231–275). New York: Plenum Press.

World Health Organization. (1992). *International statistical classification of diseases and related health problems* (10th rev.). Geneva: Author.

Yates, P. M. (2002). What works: Effective intervention with sex offenders. In H. E. Allen (Ed.), *What works: Risk reduction: Interventions for special needs offenders.* Lanham, MD: American Correctional Association.

Yates, P. M. (2003). Treatment of adult sexual offenders: A therapeutic cognitive-behavioral model of intervention. *Journal of Child Sexual Abuse, 12*, 195–232.

Yates, P. M. (2006, September). *The self-regulation model of offending: From theory to practice.* Paper presented at the 25th Annual Convention of the Association for the Treatment of Sexual Abusers, Chicago.

Yates, P. M. (in press). Taking the leap: Abandoning relapse prevention and applying the self-regulation model to the treatment of sexual offenders. In D. Prescott (Ed.), *Applying knowledge to practice: The treatment and supervision of sexual abusers.* Oklahoma City, OK: Wood 'N' Barnes.

Yates, P. M., Goguen, B. C., Nicholaichuk, T. P., Williams, S. M., Long, C. A., Jeglic, E. et al. (2000). *National sex offender programs (moderate, low, and maintenance intensity levels).* Ottawa: Correctional Service Canada.

Yates, P. M., & Kingston, D. A. (2005). Pathways to sexual offending. In B. K. Schwartz & H. R. Cellini (Eds.), *The sex offender* (Vol. 5, pp. 3:1–3:15). Kingston, NJ: Civic Research Institute.

Yates, P. M., & Kingston, D. A. (2006). Pathways to sexual offending: Relationship to static and dynamic risk among treated sexual offenders. *Sexual Abuse: A Journal of Research and Treatment, 18,* 259–270.

Yates, P. M., & Ward, T. (2007). Treatment of sexual offenders: Relapse prevention and beyond. In K. Witkiewitz & G. A. Marlatt (Eds.), *Therapists' guide to evidence-based relapse prevention* (pp. 215–234). Burlington, MA: Elsevier.

CHAPTER 14

SEXUAL MASOCHISM
Psychopathology and Theory

STEPHEN J. HUCKER

HISTORICAL INTRODUCTION

The pioneering sexologist and forensic psychiatrist Richard von Krafft-Ebing (1886/1999) coined the term "masochism" from the name of the 19th-century writer Leopold von Sacher-Masoch, whose novel *Venus in Furs* depicts an individual's pursuit of humiliation and suffering at the hands of a dominant woman—a theme reflecting the novelist's own life (Cleugh, 1952). There were also historical, though nonmedical, accounts of such behavior during the 18th century; these included the novels of the Marquis de Sade and the writings of the French philosopher Jean-Jacques Rousseau, who lamented his masochism in his *Confessions* (Rousseau, 1781/1953). However, it was Krafft-Ebing who first brought sexual masochism, as well as other sexual anomalies, out from the purview of sin and made it a subject of medical and scientific enquiry. He also was the first to provide a detailed clinical description of the behavior. He indicated that what he meant by the term was "the idea of being completely and unconditionally subject to the will of a person . . . of being treated by this person as by a master, humiliated and abused" (p. 119), adding that this idea is "coloured by lustful feeling." He was aware that a wide range of activities can be subsumed under the general category. He also noted that, unlike most paraphilias, masochism is found in women, though he did not appear to appreciate that it can occur in homosexuals.

Schrenck-Notzing (1895/1956) used the term "algolagnia," a craving for pain, for both sadism and masochism; however, the term has not found widespread favor. Freud (1938) broadened the concept, noting that "he who experiences pleasure by causing pain to others in sexual relations is also capable of experiencing pain in sexual relations as pleasure" (p. 558), and introducing the term "sadomasochism." (Sadomasochism is often referred to as "S/M" or "S & M"; I use the full term and "S/M" alternatively in this chapter and the next.) Freud also elaborated the notion of "moral masochism," which pertained to a personality type in which the individual seemingly makes repeated wrong personal decisions that cause them distress and suffering. This has led to much confusion in the literature, where the term "masochism" is often used to refer to this behavior in which there are no overt sexual manifestations (Breslow, 1989).

DEFINITIONS AND CLASSIFICATIONS

Worldwide, the definition contained in the *International Classification of Diseases*, 10th revision (ICD-10; World Health Organization, 1992) prevails. The ICD-10 uses the combined term "sadomasochism," which is described as "a preference for sexual activity that involves bondage or the infliction of pain or humiliation. If the individual prefers to be the recipient of such stimulation this is called masochism; if the provider, sadism. Often an individual obtains sexual excitement from both sadistic and masochistic activities" (p. 220).

The alternative and also widely influential classification system—the *Diagnostic and Statistical Manual of Mental Disorders*, fourth edition, text revision (DSM-IV-TR; American Psychiatric Association, 2000)—separates sexual masochism and sexual sadism, while acknowledging that there is commonly an overlap between the two. The DSM-IV-TR defines masochism in the following way. First, "over a period of at least 6 months" the individual experiences "recurrent, intense sexually arousing fantasies, sexual urges, or behaviors involving the act (real, not simulated) of being humiliated, beaten, bound, or otherwise made to suffer" (p. 573). Second, these "fantasies, sexual urges, or behaviors cause clinically significant distress or impairment in social, occupational, or other important areas of functioning" (p. 573). The DSM-IV-TR includes under the rubric of sexual masochism the phenomenon of "hypoxyphilia," which is the induction of sexual arousal by means of oxygen deprivation and is described further below. The ICD-10, on the other hand, places this practice within a separate category of "other disorders of sexual preference," though it notes in that section that other rare erotic practices may also be "part of the behavioural repertoire of sadomasochism" (World Health Organization, 1992, p. 220).

PREVALENCE

Alfred Kinsey and his colleagues reported that 26% of both sexes experienced a definite or frequent response, or both, to being bitten during intense sexual arousal (Kinsey, Pomeroy, Martin, & Gebhard, 1953), though a slightly later survey found rather lower frequencies, with only 3% of men and 5% of women indicating such a response (Hunt, 1974). Among a sample of college students, about 3–4% reported having been bound or sexually degraded during sexual interactions, and 1% reported having recently whipped, spanked, or beaten a consenting partner (Person, Trestman, Myers, Goldberg, & Salvadori, 1989).

Masochistic themes are not uncommon in the erotic fantasies of normal men during sexual activity (Crépault & Couture, 1980). Thus 46% reported having sexual fantasies of being kidnapped and raped by a woman; almost 12% had fantasies of being humiliated; 36% fantasized about being tied up and sexually stimulated by a woman; 17% had fantasies of experiencing aggressiveness; and 5% imagined being beaten up.

SEX DIFFERENCES

Early sexologists noted that masochism could occur in women (Ellis, 1913/1936; Krafft-Ebing, 1886/1999); indeed, some regarded it as based on a biologically based female tendency to general submissiveness (Hirschfeld, 1938). Both Kinsey and colleagues (1953) and Hunt (1974) provided data suggesting that a number of women are interested in S/M, and a later study found that about 30% of females fantasized about being enslaved by a man (Arndt, Foehl, & Good, 1985). However, others (Gebhard, 1969; Spengler, 1977) have found S/M to be rare in women. Spengler (1977) pointed out that his own study surveyed individuals (all of whom were men) who either placed advertisements seeking S/M partners or were members of S/M clubs. He argued that almost all women who offer sexual services to masochistic men are prostitutes who have no personal preference for the activity. He regarded genuine sadism among such women as a "fiction" created by masochistic men. However, more recent studies on both sides of the Atlantic (Alison, Santtila, Sandnabba, & Nordling, 2001; Breslow, Evans, & Langley, 1985; Moser & Levitt, 1987) have revealed a substantial minority of females among S/M practitioners. Breslow and colleagues (1985) found 52 females in their sample of 182 sadomasochists; Moser and Levitt (1987) were able to identify 47 women in their study of 225 sadomasochists; and Santtila, Sandnabba, Alison, and Nordling (2002) found 22 women and 164 men among members of two S/M clubs. Overall, between 13% and 30% of the subjects in these studies were women, few of whom were prostitutes. The women were more often bisexual than the men, most of whom were heterosexual. The women appeared to be more able to adopt submissive roles, but less likely to require S/M activity to achieve a satisfactory sexual response.

MASOCHISTIC AND ASSOCIATED BEHAVIORS

Among the substantial (mostly psychoanalytic) literature on the topic of masochism, most publications are devoted to etiological speculations. Also, as already noted, many often in fact describe a personality type, with few detailed clinical descriptions of the sexual anomaly (Breslow, 1989).

Studies of sexual masochists have included either those who have presented to psychiatrists and other mental health professionals or those who have been identified in some other manner as having an interest in masochistic behavior. The latter have been found via surveys and questionnaires (Alison et al., 2001; Breslow et al., 1985; Donnelly & Fraser, 1998; Levitt, Moser, & Jamison, 1994; Moser & Levitt, 1987; Sandnabba, Santtila, & Nordling, 1999; Spengler, 1977), analysis of the content of S/M publications and graffiti (Baumeister, 1988), or analysis of material obtained from the Internet (Ernulf & Innala, 1995).

Surveys of Sadomasochistic Practitioners

Several surveys of S/M practitioners have been carried out in Europe and North America, and these have provided rather similar results. Most recently, a research group from Finland studied total of 164 men and 24 women who were members of two clubs catering to masochistic sexual interests; one of these clubs was a gay male organization interested in "leathersex" and sadomasochism, while the other consisted of men and women with a variety of esoteric sexual interests. The first Finnish study (Sandnabba et al., 1999) involved only the sadomasochistic males. The researchers found that their subjects first became aware of their sadomasochistic interests between the ages of 18 and 20—a little later than those in the surveys by Moser and Levitt (1987), Breslow and colleagues (1985), and Spengler (1977). More than twice as many men as women (50% vs. 21%) were aware of their S/M interests by age 14. The earlier study by Spengler (1977) had found that 16% of his sample had an exclusive preference for sadomasochistic sex, whereas over a quarter of the Finnish subjects reported that only sadomasochistic sex could satisfy them (Sandnabba et al., 1999).

Earlier studies such as those of Spengler (1977) and Breslow and colleagues (1985) documented the types of behaviors in which self-identified sadomasochists engaged. As noted above, Spengler (1977) stated that there were almost no women among those who advertised for S/M partners or joined S/M clubs, so he limited his study to a group of 245 males. The sexual orientations of the sample broke down into approximately equal subgroups: 30% were exclusively heterosexual, 31% were bisexual, and 38% were exclusively homosexual (these percentages do not total 100% because of rounding). The most common practices among the group included caning (60%), whipping (66%), bondage (60%), anal manipulation (26%), and use of "torture" apparatus (27%). More extreme and potentially dangerous techniques involving needles, glowing objects, knives, and razor blades accounted for fewer than 10% of preferred activities. Fetishistic preferences were also found in about one-third, with leather and boots accounting for 50% of these.

In the study by Breslow and colleagues (1985) of 182 sadomasochists (130 men, 52 women), 33% of the men were usually dominant, 41% were usually submissive, and 26% were versatile; among the women, the proportions were similar. About 60% of both genders were heterosexual, and 1.7% of men (vs. 2.6% of women) were usually or exclusively homosexual. Bisexuality was commoner in the women (31.6% vs. 13.6%). The most preferred sexual activities for both sexes were spanking and involvement in master–slave relationships, but there were some slight differences between the sexes in some other activities. Bondage and restraint were more preferred by women than by men (88% vs. 67% and 83% vs. 60%, respectively), whereas pain and whipping were commoner among men (51% vs. 34% and 47% vs. 39%, respectively). Transvestism was commoner in men (28% vs. 20%), as were the use of enemas (33% vs. 22%) and toilet-related activities (19% vs. 12%). Interest in urination was commoner in women (37% vs. 30%), as were fetishes for erotic lingerie (88% vs. 63%), fetishes for boots and shoes (49% vs. 40%), and suffering verbal abuse (51% vs. 40%).

In the study by Moser and Levitt (1987), 178 men and 47 women were surveyed by questionnaire after being solicited from readers of an S/M magazine or after an S/M support group meeting. Among this sample, the commonest S/M behaviors were flagellation (spanking and whipping) and bondage (rope, chains, handcuffs, gags); the rates at which these were reported ranged from about 50% to more than 80%. Painful activities (using ice or hot wax, biting, and face slapping) were reported by 37–41% of the sample, though more dangerous painful activities (burning, branding, tattooing, piercing, insertion of pins) had been tried much less often (6.8–18.1% of the sample). Nonetheless, 30% of the whole sample feared that their behavior would escalate to a "truly dangerous extent." A large number of the sample (67%) had tried humiliation, and role-playing activities (master–slave, teacher–student, and similar combinations) were also noted in many cases.

A more recent Finnish study (Alison, Santtila, Sandnabba, & Nordling, 2001) reported fairly similar findings. Again, flagellation and bondage were among the most popular activities, with a relative infrequency of activities involving greater likelihood of harm ("fist fucking," piercing, hypoxyphilia, electric shocks, use of knives or razor blades, etc.). These researchers also explored the variations in activities between heterosexual and homosexual practitioners. Anal intercourse, "rimming," leather outfits, "cock binding," wrestling, and use of dildos or other special equipment were more commonly represented among the gay practitioners. These researchers were able to confirm that there are several distinct themes within what is broadly referred to as "sadomasochistic behavior." In a multivariate statistical analysis, the group was able to identify four subgroups, based on the co-occurrence of various sexual behaviors among S/M practitioners. These groups were defined as follows: (1) hypermasculinity ("rimming," use of a dildo, "cock binding," being urinated upon, being subjected to an enema, "fisting," interest in feces and defecation, and enduring insertion of a catheter); (2) administration of pain (clothespin torture, spanking, caning, use of weights/hot wax/electricity, skin branding); (3) humiliation (flagellation, verbal humiliation, use of gags, face slapping, use of knives); and (4) physical restriction (bondage, use of handcuffs/chains/slings, wrestling, use of ice, straightjacketing, hypoxyphilia, and mummifying) (Alison et al., 2001; Santtila et al., 2002). Gay practitioners were found to engage more often than heterosexuals in the hypermasculinity group of behaviors, whereas the heterosexuals had a preference for a larger number of activities in the humiliation group. This is in contrast to the common stereotype that attributes effeminacy to gay men (Deaux & Lewis, 1984). Moreover, gay male sadomasochists reported a greater preference for sadistic roles than straight male sadomasochists did. However, the authors noted that these were group differences and that there was considerable overlap between the humiliation and hypermasculinity groups. Also, it appeared that gay practitioners were better educated than the straight men and had higher incomes. Gay S/M practitioners were found to become aware of their preferences somewhat later than straight men, possibly after they had resolved any problems relating to their homosexuality.

Studies of Clinical Cases

In contrast to the methods used in the foregoing studies, Freund, Seto, and Kuban (1995) studied the clinical files of 54 masochistic heterosexual male patients. These researchers employed DSM-IV criteria (American Psychiatric Association, 1994) to identify their study group within a larger sample of sexually anomalous patients. An obvious limitation of this study is that it was necessarily based on self-reports, which are notoriously unreliable in other paraphilias, as the individuals rarely come to attention unless prompted by external forces (legal charges, threats of relationship breakdown, etc.). Although these factors are less likely to have been influential in this group of patients, other biases may have been introduced in the form of retrospective distortion of the patients' memories. Moreover, this sample was smaller than those in most of the surveys of nonpatients described above, and formal statistical analyses were therefore not considered appropriate.

Freund and colleagues (1995) identified six components of masochistic behavior: (1) erotic arousal to suffering or submission to someone else; (2) the identity of the person involved in executing a masochist's fantasies or preferred practices; (3) the identification of the patient (e.g., with a woman or child); (4) accompanying fetishes; (5) association with other paraphilias; and (6) the age of onset and developmental course of the symptoms.

more then

are

pharaphilia

.

l your notes to further identify
he particular device you want to

about outside sources before you use

10/1/2010

Within the first of these components, patients could be subdivided into those who preferred submission and those who preferred suffering. Submission involved a patient being emotionally powerless (e.g., pretending to be the slave or servant of a powerful person), being physically powerless (e.g., being tied up or gagged), or having an erotic interest in being humiliated or mocked. Suffering, on the other hand, involved an erotic interest in experiencing moderate pain (being whipped, spanked, beaten, burned with cigarettes, etc.), being frightened or feeling as if one's life was threatened (including hypoxyphilia), or undergoing severe levels of pain (e.g., being cut or having very large objects inserted into one's rectum). Of the 54 cases, 17 (31%) were interested primarily in submission and 12 (22%) were interested primarily in suffering, although 39 (72%) expressed an interest in both. Some of the submission–suffering subcomponents were quite common: 30 patients (56%) showed erotic interest in moderate pain, 26 (48%) were interested in being physically powerless, and 23 patients (43%) were interested in being humilitated or mocked. Among the 39 who were interested in powerlessness, 29 (74%) were interested in only one form (physical or emotional), while 10 (26%) were interested in both forms. Other subcomponents were relatively uncommon: 10 patients (19%) were interested in experiencing severe pain, and 8 (15%) were excited by frightening or life-threatening situations, including hypoxyphilia.

In examining the results for their other five components of masochistic behavior (identity of executor, identification of patient, accompanying fetishes, other paraphilias, and age of onset/course), Freund and colleagues (1995) discovered the following. For 47 patients (87%) the executor was female, exclusively so in 37 of these cases; of the remaining 10, 2 had children, 7 had men (a male dog in 2 cases), and 5 had the patients themselves as coexecutors. Two patients fused male and female executor roles into a dominant transvestite. Eight of the patients (15%) showed identification with someone other than themselves in their masochistic scenarios (alloidentification). Three patients identified with a female child or adolescent, four with a male child or adolescent, and one alternated between the two. Twenty (37%) were fetishistic transvestites, 14 (26%) were preoccupied with their own anal/rectal regions, and 18 (33%) were preoccupied with urination and defecation. There was a relatively low rate of association with other paraphilias, though 7 patients sometimes exchanged roles with their executors. This suggested to Freund and his colleagues that a valid distinction can be drawn between sadomasochism and sexual masochism "proper." They also noted that only a small number of patients also showed interest in exhibitionism or troilism ("threesomes" or sexual interest in watching one's partner have sex with someone else), suggesting that masochism and Freund's "courtship disorders" (Freund, Scher, & Hucker, 1983) are separate entities. Thirty patients (56%) reported the onset of their masochistic practices or fantasies at about puberty (10–13 years of age). Sixteen (30%) either dated their onset to childhood or included elements from their childhood experiences in their fantasies.

Freund and colleagues (1995) concluded that masochistic behaviors are an expression of a single basic anomaly or a small number of such anomalies, and that other idiosyncratic features are derived from these. The main general theme is of suffering or submission. Masochism also exhibits a relatively close relationship with fetishism (urine and feces fetishes in particular) and with transvestitic fetishism, as also noted by Krafft-Ebing (1886/1999). The authors also concluded that the rare components of submission–suffering (such as erotic interest in intense pain or frightening/life-threatening situations, including hypoxyphilia) are idiosyncratic manifestations, as are alloidentification and inclusion of children and males as executors or coexecutors.

Studies Based on Material Written by or for Sadomasochists

Studies based on sources such as magazines, letters, graffiti, and Internet postings have provided another means of gaining access to the fantasies and activities of sadomasochists, though this method is limited by the fact that these sources were produced for reasons other than the research of interest and are therefore not comprehensive. Also, the coding of information from such sources may reflect the researchers' perspectives rather than the subjects.' They are therefore best viewed as supplements to survey data (Weinberg, 2006).

In a study of 514 messages derived from an Internet discussion group on sexual bondage (Ernulf & Innala, 1995), it was found that 81% of the messages reflected a heterosexual orientation, 18% homosexual, and 1% bisexual. In regard to the motivations for bondage, 12% mentioned the play aspect of their bondage activities, 4% viewed it in terms of a power dimension, 3% claimed that it intensified sexual enjoyment, and 2.5% mentioned enhanced tactile stimulation and bodily sensations. Ernulf and Innala (1995) also noted differences between homosexual and heterosexual participants, with the latter being more likely to prefer the dominant role; this was the reverse of the findings from the Finnish survey (Sandnabba et al., 1999).

HYPOXYPHILIA

The DSM-IV-TR, though not the ICD-10, includes "hypoxyphilia" (also known as "asphyxiophilia," "autoerotic asphyxia," or "sexual asphyxia") under the rubric of sexual masochism. The commonest method used is self-hanging, though some form of suffocation is often used, especially in nonfatal cases. More esoteric variations include inhalation of volatile chemicals or gases, compression of the chest or abdomen, or submersion under water (Money, Wainwright, & Hingsburger, 1991).

The association of hypoxyphilia with other elements of masochism has been noted in several of the studies reviewed above (Alison et al., 2001; Freund et al., 1995; Santtila et al., 2002). However, most of what is known about the phenomenon comes from studies of fatalities (Hazelwood, Dietz, & Burgess, 1983; Blanchard & Hucker, 1991b; Hucker & Blanchard, 1992) and of a very few individuals who have presented to mental health professionals for treatment (Hucker, 1990, 2004). Studies of survivors of the practice, rare as they are, indicate that nearly all these individuals fantasize about masochistic scenarios as they perform their erotic asphyxiation (Hucker, 2006b). The small number of cases in which the practitioners died as a result of their activities suggest that the practice is rare; based on several studies, it appears that they occur with a frequency of between 1 and 2 deaths per 1 million of the population per year (American Psychiatric Association, 2000). On the other hand, in an Internet-based survey I conducted, over 100 cases identified themselves in the course of a year (Hucker, 2006a).

The death scene in a fatal case may reveal considerable amount about the decedent's sexual interests and practices (Hazelwood et al., 1984). Binding of the body is a common finding. In a recently completed study that expanded on previously published studies of a slightly smaller sample (Blanchard & Hucker, 1991; Hucker & Blanchard, 1992) of 171 autoerotic fatalities in Ontario, Canada, superfluous physical constraints (i.e., not part of the asphyxiating mechanism) were noted in 65 cases; hoods and blindfolds were present in 19 and gags in 15; the genitals were bound or ligated in 20 cases. Other suggestions of masochistic interests included cigarette burns, clamps on parts of the body, and evidence of self-flagellation (6 cases) and of anal stimulation with dildos and the like (18 cases). Specifically sadomasochistic pornography was found at the scene in 5 cases and among the deceased's possessions in another 8.

Among a sample of living practitioners accessed and surveyed over the Internet, 71% reported various masochistic activities, and 31% also took sadistic roles. Sixty-six percent reported using bondage, 44% used clamps on themselves, 14% used electrical stimulation, and 37% self-flagellated (Hucker, 2006a). On a Likert-type scale, the highest level of arousal was reported to be to obstruction of breathing, but loss of control and even loss of consciousness were also important to these individuals' arousal; the lowest arousal ratings were to humiliation and pain. Most individuals who engage in this practice do so in private and alone (Hazelwood et al., 1984), although among the Internet-derived cases I studied, 41% did so with a partner (Hucker, 2006a).

ETIOLOGICAL THEORIES

Theories of sadism and masochism have tended to come from psychoanalysts, and several alternative hypotheses have been presented (Sack & Miller, 1975). Freud (1938) regarded sadism and masochism as complementary and suggested that masochism derives from sadistic impulses. In classical Freudian terms, masochists fear incest, castration, or both, and their behavior represents an implicit appeal to the feared parental figure. It is thus seen as a reenactment of childhood traumatic experiences; reliving the trauma removes the castration fear and the threat. In another formulation, masochists relieve themselves of guilt by allowing their sexual partners to control or abuse them, thereby relieving the masochists of responsibility and allowing them to gain pleasure from the sexual activity. A further hypothesis, based on psychoanalytic view of passive sex as "feminine," has been that masochism represents a wish for sex with the father figure. Freud later revised his theory in the light of his development of his ideas about a "death instinct," of which he viewed masochism as a manifestation. However, all these theories are undermined by research showing that guilt does not typically invoke a desire for punishment (Baumeister, Stillwell, & Heatherton, 2006), and there is little evidence that masochists suffer any degree of underlying guilt at all (Baumeister, 1989). More recent modifications to the psychodynamic theory propose that masochists have experienced a narcissistic injury, and that their behavior is a mechanism for increasing their self-esteem despite the abuse they have to endure by becoming the center of attention in sexual situations (Stolorow, Atwood, & Brandchaft, 1988; Stolorow & Lachmann, 1980), although it is difficult to reconcile this with the observation that masochists willingly surrender control to the other party.

Learning theories, like the theories derived from psychoanalysis, place the developmental origin of all paraphilias in childhood. The person associates pleasure with pain, and the traumas thereby experienced become sexualized in adult life as a means of regaining a sense of control and power (Langevin, 1983). Individual masochists often report aversive situations in their own childhoods, but there is little evidence that masochists as a group suffer from such experiences any more than nonmasochists do. However, the Finnish researchers described earlier have explored the notion that sexual abuse in childhood is a precursor of adult masochism in their sample of self-identified sadomasochists (Sandnabba, Santtila, Alison, & Nordling, 2002; Santtila, Sandnabba, & Nordling,

2000). Such a history was found in 8% of male and 23% of female S/M practitioners. Those who were abused experienced more psychological distress; 39% had attempted suicide (vs. 4% among the nonabused); 33% of those abused had been psychiatric inpatients (vs. 5% among the nonabused). Moreover, those who were abused were more likely to seek medical help for injuries received during S/M activities (11%, vs. 2% among the nonabused).

Social-psychological theories (Baumeister, 1988) view masochistic practices as "an escape from self," meaning that in the submissive role masochists can absolve themselves of responsibility for their own behavior while acting at the demands of their dominant partners. The masochists then do not view their behavior as a reflection of their true selves, and they can behave in ways they would not normally contemplate.

A systematic attempt to assess the psychoanalytic, psychopathological/medical, "escape from self," and radical feminist theories of masochism (the radical feminist theory views S/M as essentially indicative of patriarchal dogma and its notions of dominance and submission) was carried out on a sample of 93 subjects obtained by postings on S/M-related Internet newsgroups; those who volunteered for the study were followed up by email (Cross & Matheson, 2006). Twenty-seven identified themselves as sadists (21 males, 6 females), 34 as masochists (26 males, 8 females), and 32 as "switches" (22 males, 10 females). A control group of non-S/M practitioners was drawn from non-S/M-related Internet newsgroups (46 males, 15 females). A package of questionnaires and other measures was sent to each participant after the email contact was made. No support was found for any of the theories. Based on subsequent studies of online encounters between sadomasochistic practitioners, these researchers suggest that power rather than pain is the central element in sadomasochism.

MEDICAL–LEGAL ISSUES

It might be presumed that acts conducted in private by consenting adults would be unlikely to raise legal issues. However, a recent survey has indicated that in the United States, court cases and other legal matters in relation to sadomasochistic practices have involved such topics as rights to privacy and sexual freedom, child custody, domestic violence, and employment discrimination (Ridinger, 2006; Wright, 2006).

Whereas the infliction of pain or injury on an unwilling victim is, from a legal perspective, always and clearly an assault, the issue remains whether it is possible to consent to be injured by someone else, and thus whether charges can be brought against a person who injures someone else in the course of sexual activity. These questions were being asked as far back as the late 19th century (Krafft-Ebing, 1886/1999).

In the *Spanner* case in Britain (so called after the police investigation, which was dubbed "Operation Spanner"), the consensual activities of a group of adult homosexual sadomasochists were discovered by police during investigations into other matters (Thompson, 1994). Although no one had complained, charges were laid under the Offences against the Person Act of 1861; because the initial trial judge ruled as inadmissible the argument that the parties had consented, they were convicted and sentenced to prison. Their appeal to the Court of Appeal was rejected, and that decision was upheld by the House of Lords. The majority in the latter concluded that the defense of consent may be available only if the accused caused the injury while performing a limited group of lawful activities such as surgery or sports. The majority, as a matter of policy, was not "prepared to invent a defense of consent for sadomasochistic encounters which breed and glorify cruelty," and which the judges viewed as "an evil thing" (Ormerod, 1994). The case was brought before the European Court of Human Rights, but there too the judges were not inclined to approve of such cases, stating that state interference with privacy may be necessary for "protecting health" in a democratic society (Ridinger, 2006).

In 2003, the Sexual Offences Act became law in Britain. Although it contains no reference to sadomasochism, it does include a definition of consent and details evidentiary and other presumptions of consent. However, it does not go so far as to include sadomasochistic acts, as some action groups were hoping (White, 2006).

A similar case in the United States was *Commonwealth of Massachusetts v. Appleby*, in which the defendant, Appleby, was charged with battery for beating his homosexual partner during sadomasochistic activities. In a ruling similar to that in the *Spanner* case, the court held that "because assault is a general intent crime, the only intent required is an intent to do the act causing the injury; a showing of hostile purpose or motive is not required" (Paclebar, Furtado, & McDonald-Witt, 2006, p. 223).

There have also been cases in which an individual has been charged with the murder of another (usually, but not necessarily, a woman) and claimed that the two of them were engaged in sadomasochistic sex during which strangulation was desired by the deceased, who then "went limp" as the act proceeded. Because there are no other witnesses, in such circumstances it is often very difficult to differentiate manslaughter from willful homicide (Koutselinis, 1988; Michalodimitrakis, Frangoulis, & Koutselinis, 1986).

Another area in which sadomasochism has involved the courts is that of child custody disputes. Marital breakdown typically evokes strong emotions, and when children are involved, one partner may try to find reasons to limit the amount of contact the other will have with their offspring. In such contexts the partner's "fitness" as a parent may be questioned by raising the issue of past sexual behavior, especially when atypical sexual propensities are exposed and the question becomes whether or not any harm will befall the children. Even when children have had no exposure to a parent's sadomasochistic behavior, courts have sometimes denied that parent access to the children or limited that parent's visitation arrangements (Klein & Moser, 2006; Ridinger, 2006).

The more outspoken practitioners of sadomasochistic activities assert that society as a whole needs to accept their lifestyle and become more aware that it involves consensual sexual "play" (as they see it). However, the current legal mainstream clearly sees the potential for serious physical harm to occur in sadomasochistic situations; hence the perceived need to override or limit the usual freedoms of sexual expression and right to privacy. The law tends to evolve slowly in response to changing social attitudes.

SUMMARY AND FUTURE DIRECTIONS

Because sexual masochism does not generally result in any criminal charges, and potentially harms only those who voluntarily engage in it, there is perhaps less interest in researching the issues related to it than in the case of, for example, pedophilia or sexual assault. However, the facts that masochists are typically not pressured by others into seeing mental health professionals, and have no reason to lie about their preferences, mean that their self-reports are likely to be more accurate than those of individuals with some other paraphilias. They can therefore teach us a great deal about the nature of paraphilias in general.

Surveys have become more sophisticated in recent years, and the use of the Internet as a means of communicating anonymously with large numbers of individuals has some distinct advantages that have yet to be tapped fully (see Quayle, Chapter 24, and Delmonico & Griffin, Chapter 25, this volume). Still, these approaches are no substitute for direct contact with subjects, and there have been relatively few investigations of that type.

Sadism and masochism are complex phenomena, and their etiology remains poorly understood. At present they are widely viewed as pathological conditions and are encoded in the official classifications of both the World Health Organization (the ICD-10) and the American Psychiatric Association (the DSM-IV-TR). Most earlier writings on the subject focused on individual psychopathology as described in psychiatric case histories. Over time many researchers have also come to view sadomasochism as a form of social interaction, with underlying issues such as dominance–submission, aggressiveness–passivity, and masculinity–femininity being interwoven with the sexual element. The view that the paraphilias, including sadomasochism, should no longer be considered disorders or included in the DSM or ICD has been advocated (Moser & Kleinplatz, 2006; Reiersol & Skeid, 2006). It has been pointed out that most of those studied in surveys of sadomasochists have shown evidence of excellent psychological and social functioning (if their higher educational level, income, and occupational status are used as indicators), compared to the general population (Breslow et al., 1985; Moser & Levitt, 1987; Sandnabba et al., 1999; Spengler, 1977). However, Santtila and colleagues (2000) and Sandnabba and colleagues (2002) found a clear relationship between childhood sexual abuse and adverse psychological effects in some S/M practitioners, thereby undermining the argument that these individuals do not suffer from psychological or social problems apart from their sexual interests.

Freund and colleagues (1995) suggested that their findings could indicate there is a "valid distinction between sadomasochism and sexual masochism proper" (p. 321). There is a great difference between the consensual, play-oriented, and carefully controlled activities of the majority of members of S/M clubs, and the more dangerous and potentially fatal practices of a small minority. The practices are justifiably included in the category of disorders if they can cause physical impairment or death. Moser and Kleinplatz (2006) have been vigorously critical of the current DSM-IV-TR criteria for paraphilias and recommend removing the paraphilias from the sphere of mental disorders. Whereas the DSM-IV-TR notes that sadistic and masochistic behaviors can lead to injuries "ranging in extent from minor to life threatening" (American Psychiatric Association, 2000, p. 567), Moser and Kleinplatz argue that there is no evidence that these individuals more often need emergency services "than practitioners of other sexual behaviours" (p. 106). Again, however, this claim is undermined by evidence from the study by the Finnish group (Santtila et al., 2000).

Similarly, Baumeister and Butler (1997) have emphasized the evidence that sadomasochism does not appear to be a symptom of deeper psychological problems and does not generally "involve wish for injury, punishment for sexual guilt, or self-destructive impulses" (p. 237); like Moser and Kleinplatz (2006), they stress the consensual and game-playing aspects that are evident from surveys of S/M behaviors. On the other hand, the fact that a minority of sadomasochists do present with serious injuries or die during their activities (Agnew, 1986; Hucker, 1985) should make us consider seriously whether removing these behaviors from the domain of mental disorders is wise at the present time, especially as there is much room for more research on the topic. Kurt Freund (1976) applied the term "dangerous" to the more extreme forms of sadism and masochism, and it would seem prudent at this stage in our knowledge to continue to refer to these more extreme cases by such a term, thereby distinguishing them from the more benign manifestations ("mild" masochism or erotic submissiveness) of what may well be a continuum of behaviors that merges with "normal" sexual expression.

REFERENCE

Agnew, J. (1986). Hazards associated with anal erotic activity. *Archives of Sexual Behavior, 15*, 307–314.

Alison, L., Santtila, P., Sandnabba, N. K., & Nordling, N. (2001). Sadomasochistically oriented behavior: Diversity in practice and meaning. *Archives of Sexual Behavior, 30*, 1–12.

American Psychiatric Association. (1994). *Diagnostic and statistical manual of mental disorders* (4th ed.). Washington, DC: Author.

American Psychiatric Association. (2000). *Diagnostic and statistical manual of mental disorders* (4th ed., text rev.). Washington, DC: Author.

Arndt, W. B., Foehl, J. C., & Good, F. E. (1985). Specific sexual fantasy themes: A multidimensional study. *Journal of Personality and Social Psychology, 48*, 480.

Baumeister, R. F. (1988). Masochism as escape from self. *Journal of Sex Research, 25*, 28–59.

Baumeister, R. F. (1989). *Masochism and the self*. Hillsdale, NJ: Erlbaum.

Baumeister, R. F., & Butler, J. L. (1997). Sexual masochism: Deviance without pathology. In D. R. Laws & W. O'Donohue (Eds.), *Sexual deviance: Theory, assessment, and treatment* (pp. 225–239). New York: Guilford Press.

Blanchard, R., & Hucker, S. J. (1991b). Age, transvestism, bondage, and concurrent paraphilic activities in 117 fatal cases of autoerotic asphyxia. *British Journal of Psychiatry, 159*, 377.

Breslow, N. (1989). Sources of confusion in the study and treatment of sadomasochism. *Journal of Social Behavior and Personality, 4*, 263–274.

Breslow, N., Evans, L., & Langley, J. (1985). On the prevalence of roles of females in the sadomasochistic subculture: Report of an empirical study. *Archives of Sexual Behavior, 14*, 303–317.

Cleugh, J. (1952). *The marquis and the chevalier*. Boston: Little, Brown.

Crépault, C., & Couture, M. (1980). Men's erotic fantasies. *Archives of Sexual Behavior, 9*, 565–576.

Cross, P. A., & Matheson, K. (2006). Understanding sadomasochism: An empirical examination of four perspectives. *Journal of Homosexuality, 50*, 133–166.

Deaux, K., & Lewis, L. L. (1984). Structure of gender stereotypes: Interrelationships among components and gender label. *Journal of Personality and Social Psychology, 46*, 991–1004.

Donnelly, D., & Fraser, J. (1998). Gender differences in sado-masochistic arousal among college students. *Sex Roles, 39*, 391–407.

Ellis, H. (1936). Love and pain. In H. Ellis, *Studies in the psychology of sex* (Vol. 1, pp. 66–105). New York: Random House. (Original work published 1913)

Ernulf, K., & Innala, S. (1995). Sexual bondage: A review and unobtrusive investigation. *Archives of Sexual Behavior, 24*, 631–654.

Freud, S. (1938). *The basic writings of Sigmund Freud*. New York: Modern Library.

Freund, K. (1976). Diagnosis and treatment of forensically significant erotic preferences. *Canadian Journal of Criminology and Corrections, 18*, 181–189.

Freund, K., Scher, H., & Hucker, S. J. (1983). The courtship disorders. *Archives of Sexual Behavior, 12*, 369–379.

Freund, K., Seto, M. C., & Kuban, M. (1995). Masochism: A multiple case study. *Sexuologie, 4*, 313–324.

Gebhard, P. H. (1969). Fetishism and sadomasochism. *Science and Psychoanalysis, 15*, 71–80.

Hazelwood, R. R., Dietz, P. E., & Burgess, A. W. (1984). *Autoerotic fatalities.* Toronto: D. C. Heath.

Hirschfeld, M. (1938). *Sexual anomalies and perversions.* London: Encyclopaedic Press.

Hucker, S. J. (1985). Self-harmful sexual behavior. *Psychiatric Clinics of North America, 8,* 323–337.

Hucker, S. J. (1990). Sexual asphyxia. In R. Bluglass & P. Bowden (Eds.), *Principles and practice of forensic psychiatry* (pp. 717–721). London: Churchill Livingstone.

Hucker, S. J. (2004). Hypoxyphilia. *Newsletter of the Association for the Treatment of Sexual Abusers, 16,* 1–2.

Hucker, S. J. (2006a). *An Internet study of hypoxyphilia.* Manuscript submitted for publication.

Hucker, S. J. (2006b). *Living practitioners of auto-erotic asphyxia.* Manuscript submitted for publication.

Hucker, S. J., & Blanchard, R. (1992). Death scene characteristics in 118 fatal cases of autoerotic asphyxia compared with suicidal asphyxia. *Behavioral Sciences and the Law, 10,* 509–523.

Hunt, M. (1974). *Sexual behavior in the 1970's.* New York: Playboy Press.

Kinsey, A. C., Pomeroy, W. B., Martin, C. E., & Gebhard, P. H. (1953). *Sexual behavior in the human female.* Philadelphia: Saunders.

Klein, M., & Moser, C. (2006). SM (sadomasochistic) interests as an issue in a child custody proceeding. *Journal of Homosexuality, 50,* 233–242.

Koutselinis, A. (1988). Accidental sexual strangulation (author's reply). *American Journal of Forensic Medicine and Pathology, 9,* 92.

Krafft-Ebing, R. von. (1999). *Psychopathia sexualis* (12th ed., F. J. Rebman, Trans.). Burbank, CA: Bloat. (Original work published 1886)

Langevin, R. (1983). *Sexual strands.* Hillsdale, NJ: Erlbaum.

Levitt, E. E., Moser, C., & Jamison, K. V. (1994). The prevalence and some attributes of females in sadomasochistic subculture: A second report. *Archives of Sexual Behavior, 23,* 465–473.

Michalodimitrakis, M., Frangoulis, M., & Koutselinis, A. (1986). Accidental sexual strangulation. *American Journal of Forensic Medicine and Pathology, 7,* 74–75.

Money, J., Wainwright, G., & Hingsburger, D. (1991). *The breathless orgasm: The lovemap biography of asphyxiophilia.* Buffalo, NY: Prometheus Books.

Moser, C., & Kleinplatz, P. J. (2006). DSM-IV-TR and the paraphilias: An argument for removal. *Journal of Psychology and Human Sexuality, 17,* 91–109.

Moser, C., & Levitt, E. E. (1987). An exploratory descriptive study of a sadomasochistically oriented sample. *Journal of Sex Research, 23,* 322–337.

Ormerod, D. (1994). Sado-masochism. *Journal of Forensic Psychiatry, 5,* 123–136.

Paclebar, A. M., Furtado, C., & McDonald-Witt, M. (2006). Sadomasochism: Practices, behaviors, and culture in American society. In E. W. Hickey (Ed.), *Sex crimes and paraphilia* (pp. 215–227). Upper Saddle River, NJ: Pearson Education.

Person, E. S., Terestman, E. S., Myers, W. A., Goldberg, E. L., & Salvadori, C. (1989). Gender differences in sexual behaviors and fantasies in a college population. *Journal of Sex and Marital Therapy, 15,* 187–198.

Reiersol, O., & Skeid, S. (2006). The ICD diagnoses of fetishism and sadomasochism. *Journal of Homosexuality, 50,* 243–262.

Ridinger, R. B. (2006). Negotiating limits: The legal status of SM in the United States. *Journal of Homosexuality, 50,* 189–216.

Rousseau, J.-J. (1953). *The confessions.* Harmondsworth, UK: Penguin Books. (Original work published 1781)

Sack, R. L., & Miller, W. (1975). Masochism: A clinical and theoretical overview. *Psychiatry, 38,* 244–257.

Sandnabba, N. K., Santtila, P., Alison, L., & Nordling, N. (2002). Demographics, sexual behaviour, family background and abuse experiences of practitioners of sadomasochistic sex: A review of recent research. *Sexual and Relationship Therapy, 17,* 39–55.

Sandnabba, N. K., Santtila, P., & Nordling, N. (1999). Sexual behavior and social adaptation among sadomasochistically oriented males. *Journal of Sex Research*, 36, 273–282.

Santtila, P., Sandnabba, N. K., Alison, L., & Nordling, N. (2002). Investigating the underlying structure in sadomasochistically oriented behavior. *Archives of Sexual Behavior*, 31, 185–196.

Santtila, P., Sandnabba, N. K., & Nordling, N. (2000). Retrospective perceptions of family interaction in childhood as correlates of current sexual adaptation among sadomasochistic males. *Journal of Psychology and Human Sexuality*, 12, 69–87.

Schrenk-Notzing, A. von. (1956). *The use of hypnosis in psychopathia sexualis*. New York: Julian Press. (Original work published 1895)

Spengler, A. (1977). Manifest sadomasochism of males: Results of an empirical study. *Archives of Sexual Behavior*, 6, 441–456.

Stolorow, R., Atwood, G., & Brandchaft, B. (1988). Masochism and its treatment. *Bulletin of the Menninger Clinic*, 52, 504–509.

Stolorow, R., & Lachmann, F. (1980). *Psychoanalysis of developmental arrests*. New York: International Universities Press.

Thompson, B. (1994). *Sadomasochism*. London: Cassell.

Weinberg, T. S. (2006). Sadomasochism and the social sciences: A review of the sociological and social psychological literature. *Journal of Homosexuality*, 50, 17–40.

White, C. (2006). The Spanner trials and the changing law on sadomasochism in the UK. *Journal of Homosexuality*, 50, 167–187.

World Health Organization. (1992). *The ICD-10 classification of mental and behavioural disorders*. Geneva: Author.

Wright, S. (2006). Discrimination of SM-identified individuals. *Journal of Homosexuality*, 50, 217–231.

CHAPTER 15

SEXUAL MASOCHISM

Assessment and Treatment

STEPHEN J. HUCKER

Despite extensive theoretical deliberations and clinical descriptions, there has been confusion about the meaning of the term "masochism" in the literature (Breslow, 1989). This chapter examines assessment and treatment options that should be considered in dealing with patients who justify a diagnosis of sexual masochism as currently defined by the *Diagnostic and Statistical Manual of Mental Disorders*, fourth edition, text revision (DSM-IV-TR; American Psychiatric Association, 2000), which reflects the conceptualization first elaborated by Krafft-Ebing (1886/1999). This is necessary, because some descriptions of treatment options for "masochists" deal with cases in which sexual deviance is not an obvious component (Fisch, 1989; Shore, Zelin, Clifton, & Myerson, 1971; Stolorow, Atwood, & Brandchaft, 1988). Hence, the chapter does not explore treatments for those with a diagnosis of masochistic or self-defeating personality disorder, which was introduced in DSM-III-R (American Psychiatric Association, 1987) but later dropped, or dependent personality disorder, which is included in DSM-IV-TR and has many of the features of the abandoned terms.

Individuals who manifest features of sexual masochism tend not to present themselves for assessment and treatment by mental health professionals (Hucker, 1985). This is perhaps partly because the behavior is not inherently criminal, but also because, like many individuals with paraphilias, many masochists do not regard themselves as having a sexual problem (Nichols, 2006). A number of masochistic individuals come to light in a general hospital setting, as, for example, when emergency room staff are required to remove various objects (rings, bottles, etc.) from rectal orifices (Allen, 1962). Some may describe activities that involve other medically dangerous practices (e.g., incising arteries or inserting needles into major body organs), or present with unconventional and inappropriate requests such as "Do you have nurses here who will step in your face?" Other individuals have injured themselves when applying electrical currents to themselves for sexual stimulation (Cairns, 1981), and still others may present with a history of self-asphyxiation or hypoxyphilia (Haydn-Smith, Marks, Buchaya, & Repper, 1987). These and other dangerous and potentially life-threatening practices are in contrast to the assertions of many in the sadomasochistic or S/M subculture and their advocates, who claim that their behavior is playful and indeed life-enhancing (Nichols, 2006).

ASSESSMENT

Assessment will to a large extent be determined by the context. There is evidence that sexual masochism occurs with some frequency among sex offender populations, though this paraphilia is not typically the presenting problem. For example, Abel, Becker, Cunningham-Rathner, Mittelman, and Rouleau (1988) found 17 masochists in their sample of 1,170 sex offenders (1.5%), most of whom were pedophiles, exhibitionists, and rapists. Drawing upon several of their previous studies, Thornton and Mann (1997) noted that sex offenders who manifested masochistic interests shared many of the characteristics of sex offenders in general, such as cognitive distortions, a wide range of other sexually deviant interests (including sadism), sensation seeking, and emotional loneliness. This picture of the extent of the deviance in a sample of offender masochists differs markedly from the description that emerges from surveys of masochists in the community, who have (presumably) little or no criminal background, as I have noted in Chapter 14. Thornton and Mann suggested an assessment approach similar to that used for sex offenders in general. So, whether a masochistic individual is an offender or a law-abiding member of the community, a nonjudgmental, supportive, and knowledgeable approach during a clinical interview is more likely to yield results than the converse attitude. Some sexually anomalous individuals will incorporate the interviewer into their fantasies, and the assessor needs to bear this possibility in mind while assessing the account given.

Various formal questionnaires are available that include items assessing sexual masochism, along with most other types of abnormal sexual interests (from commonplace to rare). Perhaps the best-known examples are the Clarke Sex History Questionnaire for Males—Revised (SHQ-R; Langevin & Paitich, 2006) and the Multiphasic Sex Inventory II (MS II; Nichols & Molinder, 2000). Also available is the Wilson Sexual Fantasy Questionnaire (Wilson, 1981), which, though shorter than either the SHQ-R and MSI II, does include a number of items that are less obviously deviant and covers masochistic interests well. In addition, the masochism subscales of other questionnaires may be useful (O'Donohue, Letourneau, & Dowling, 1997).

Finally, mention must be made of psychophysiological measures, including penile plethysmography (PPG or phallometry), though the validity and reliability of these assessments have been called into question in recent years (Laws, 2003; Marshall & Fernandez, 2000; Marshall, Serran, & Cortoni, 2000), and stimuli relevant to sexual masochism are not included in many assessment protocols. There has been recent interest in alternatives to PPG, including viewing time measures (e.g., Abel, Huffman, Warberg, & Holland, 1998), though the evidence so far suggests that this approach also has shortcomings as well as advantages (Letourneau, 2002). Clearly, there is still need for a reliable and valid means of assessing individuals with paraphilic sexual interests that do not depend on the subjects' self-reports. Further exploration of the utility of PPG and viewing time methods may be helpful in the future.

TREATMENT

There is a substantial psychoanalytic literature on masochism, but, as I have already pointed out in this chapter and Chapter 14, much of this relates to the broader concept of "moral masochism" (Freud, 1938) rather than the paraphilia. Though Freud himself was somewhat pessimistic that his method could assist a masochistic patient because of resistance (Freud, 1981), his successors have continued to face the challenge. There are, however, few accounts of treatment specifics, though the basis of it is that the patient and analyst reenact a sadomasochistic relationship in which the aim of therapy is to resolve the patient's transference resistance (Brenner, 1959). There have a been a few reports of psychoanalytic treatment of patients whose problems included apparently masochistic behavior and in which success is claimed (Lihn, 1971; Panken, 1973); however, such claims are difficult to substantiate (Langevin, 1983).

Art psychotherapy has been used in a variety of conditions (Malchiodi, 2003), and its use in a case of autoerotic asphyxia has been documented in detail (Innes, 1997). The patient appeared to gain subjective benefit, though the author indicates that her patient's compulsion would reemerge "during times of intense anxiety at home," raising the obvious question as to how effective this technique had really been.

The recent literature includes some helpful articles intended to assist therapists in dealing with sadomasochistic clients (Kleinplatz, 2006; Kleinplatz & Moser, 2004; Kolmes, Stock, & Moser, 2006; Nichols, 2006). Although Kolmes and her colleagues (2006) believe that S/M interactions are essentially nonpathological, they recognize that the behavior can become nonconsensual and therefore abusive. Having discussed the treatment of sexual dysfunctions in two of her S/M clients, Kleinplatz (2006) suggests that rather than viewing clients' sexual behavior as pathological, a therapist can help them use it as a means of enhancing erotic potential and intimacy—a strategy that can also be used for couples without primarily S/M interests.

In her account of issues commonly encountered in treating S/M clients, Nichols (2006) adopts an "affirming" approach as opposed to viewing the behavior as "evidence of pathology" (p. 282). As already noted here and in Chapter 14, however, there is research undermining some of her basic assertions, such as that S/M is not self-destructive (Hucker, 1985) or stems from child abuse (Sandnabba, Santtila, Alison, & Nordling, 2002). Nevertheless, many of Nichols's suggestions are helpful, no matter what a therapist's own view of the phenomenon may be. Among the issues she discusses is countertransference: A therapist may develop negative feelings and attitudes toward an S/M client, such as disgust or fear, or anxiety that the therapist may have S/M inclinations him- or herself. Indeed, some therapists may experience actual sexual arousal to the behaviors that S/M clients describe. Other S/M clients or patients do not disclose their practices to their therapists, and Nichols notes that the therapist's office may convey negative attitudes nonverbally and thus inhibit such disclosure. She suggests that nonexplicit but supportive literature, books, and pictures in the office may set the appropriate tone. Also, suggesting to clients that, for example, many S/M practitioners have good communication skills may give the clients "permission" to discuss their own sexual interests. She believes this to be important, as many S/M clients will come to therapy for issues not related to their sexual interests, and encouraging them to disclose will be counterproductive.

On the other hand, some issues do appear to have a basis in S/M practices—for example, instances when the dominance and submission elements spill over into everyday life or have the potential to interfere in the therapeutic relationship. Individuals new to the S/M subculture may also have difficulties in overcoming shame, fear, guilt, or self-loathing. Nichols (2006) states that in these cases "providing acceptance and modeling positive attitudes [are] crucial and [have] intense therapeutic power" (p. 290); she suggests that not commenting on the subculture will be viewed as criticism. Supportive and encouraging though the therapist may be, however, it seems important to ensure that a client understands that the activity is intended to be consensual and pleasurable, not abusive.

Some clients may request a "cure" for their S/M interests, creating a conflict for some therapists. Nichols (2006) clearly believes that such requests constitute a phase of "coming out" and occur similarly in many homosexuals, who at one time were considered to qualify for a psychiatric diagnosis by mainstream mental health professionals, and who may still go through a period of regarding their homosexuality as "ego-dystonic." Another area of concern to therapists treating S/M clients who may not have disclosed their interest to their non-S/M partners is the need and ways to involve such partners in the therapy. Many S/M practitioners also engage in conventional sex to varying degrees, but Nichols notes that a non-S/M partner may experience grief for the loss of the previous relationship and may need to work through this before deciding on the future of the relationship, which may include separation or divorce.

Finally, Nichols (2006) acknowledges that the S/M community has been at pains (as it were) to recognize the potential for abusive situations to develop in S/M relationships as in more conventional partnerships, and notes that it is important for therapists to consider a number of questions in evaluating whether a particular relationship is abusive. These include whether the client is worried about the behavior, whether it is interfering in the client's everyday life, whether the behavior is compulsive or the client feels a loss of control over the impulses, whether "genuinely risky behaviors" are occurring, whether substance abuse is impairing the client's judgment, or whether the behavior is making the client feel worse rather than better.

Behavioral therapies have been described in cases of sexual masochism. Positive results for aversion therapy have been reported in several case studies (Marks, Gelder, & Bancroft, 1970; Marks, Rachman, & Gelder, 1965; McGuire & Carlisle, 1965; Pinard & Lamontagne, 1976). However, it has also been reported that electric shocks (or the anticipation of them), which have been used in this method, may cause rather than inhibit arousal. This technique should be used cautiously for sexual masochists (Bancroft, 1974), and olfactory aversion may be preferable (Laws, 2001).

Orgasmic reconditioning and covert sensitization have also been used to treat sexual masochism (Brownell, Hayes, & Barlow, 1977; Carr, 1974; Langevin, 1983; Marques, 1970); however, the follow-up periods are either not given or very brief. In a case study describing "life-threatening masochistic asphyxiation," covert sensitization and teaching coping strategies were used with good results, but the follow-up period was only 6 months (Haydn-Smith et al., 1987). Another study reported the use of covert sensitization followed by psychotherapy that incorporated "cognitive-behavioural techniques and interpersonal therapy techniques" to alleviate depression and social withdrawal (Martz, 2003, p. 368), but the follow-up period was not mentioned.

A sizable literature exists on the medical approaches to the treatment of paraphilias. These are reviewed in detail by Grubin (Chapter 31, this volume), but here a general overview is given with a focus on the applicability of these interventions to sexual masochists.

Drugs have been used to treat sexually anomalous individuals since the middle of the 20th century (Neumann & Kalmus, 1991), though the vast majority of such individuals have been pedophiles, rapists, and others whose sexual behavior has been criminal (e.g., sadists). Only rarely is a diagnosis of sexual masochism been mentioned in such studies (Kafka, 1994).

A case has been reported involving a 38-year-old single man who presented with extensive burns (Shiwach & Prosser, 1998). He gave a long history of sexual fantasies of being burned or crushed, and frequently exposed himself to dangerous situations. The presenting incident was among his recent escapades in which he had set refuse Dumpsters on fire for sexual arousal. He would then masturbate before getting out. His burns had occurred when a plastic Dumpster melted and turned over. His first sexual experience at age 15 had occurred when he curled himself up in an oven and ejaculated—an adventure that had been prompted by having been threatened as a child with being roasted "like a pig" as a punishment. A social isolate, he enjoyed watching videos and reading about people being burned at the stake or crushed. He had also attempted autoerotic asphyxia, but relinquished this as "too dangerous." Treatment on a number of fronts was systematically attempted. These included psychodynamic psychotherapy, aversion therapy (covert sensitization and olfactory aversion), a selective serotonin reuptake inhibitor (SSRI—i.e., fluoxetine), and an antiandrogen (leuprolide acetate). None of these effected a lasting solution, though antiandrogenic therapy and aversion therapy appeared to benefit the patient in the short term. Shiwach and Prosser (1998) recommended considering these two methods in cases where there is a clear risk to the patient. In their case, improving the patient's underlying social isolation might have been helpful in the longer term. Other authors have made stronger claims for the benefits of SSRI antidepressants in the management of sexual masochism, as well as other DSM-IV-TR paraphilias (Kafka, 1991, 1994, 1996; Kafka & Prentky, 1992)

Lithium carbonate, used primarily for the prophylaxis of bipolar disorders, has also been used to treat a case of asphyxiophilia (Cesnik & Coleman, 1989). This patient also had diagnoses of dysthymia and avoidant personality disorder secondary to earlier verbal, physical, and sexual abuse. The authors' treatment of their patient with lithium rather than an antiandrogen was justified on the basis that the patient experienced "cyclical mood disturbances" (p. 281). Good response was claimed for what was described as a previously "extremely difficult case" (p. 284), though with a short follow-up of only 5 months.

SUMMARY AND FUTURE DIRECTIONS

Although it has been argued that S/M practitioners should no longer be deemed pathological, and therefore that sadomasochism should be removed from the official classifications of mental disorders (Moser & Kleinplatz, 2006; Reiersol & Skeid, 2006), there are certainly cases in which masochistic behavior has caused serious physical harm and even been clearly life-threatening (Hucker, 1985). Although the majority of S/M practitioners are said to be otherwise psychologically healthy (Breslow, Evans, & Langley, 1985; Moser & Levitt, 1987; Spengler, 1977), and should therefore (one would think) be infrequent clients of mental health professionals, guidelines for the use of therapists who do cater to such a clientele have been proposed (Nichols, 2006). In cases where there is obvious risk of serious physical harm, then clearly more intensive types of treatment need to be considered.

Of the psychological treatment options available, various forms of behavior therapy have been described, though their long-term efficacy has not been reported. Pharmacological treatment with either SSRIs or antiandrogens has also been described with increasing frequency and has been used for other paraphilias with apparent success. It should be noted that the authors of several accounts in the literature comment on the frequency of mood disorders in their case histories. The importance of considering comorbid psychiatric disorders in the treatment of both paraphilic and nonparaphilic sexual disorders is now well recognized (Kafka & Hennen, 2002).

On the basis of what is currently known, it seems reasonable to recommend a combined approach to the treatment of sexual masochists whose behavior could lead them to suffer serious injury or death. A psychotherapeutic approach should always be a part of any intervention strategy, but more specific behavioral methods have been described for these patients. Similarly, drug treatments (including SSRIs and antiandrogens) need to be given careful consideration. Treatment algorithms have been recommended for paraphilic behaviors of other types, depending on their seriousness (Bradford, 2001; Briken, Hill, & Berner, 2003).

Sexual masochism and sadomasochism are complex phenomena, and much still remains to be learned about their nature, etiology, and management. Some cases appear to be variants of "normal" sexual behavior, while others, because of their potential for serious harm, reasonably justify continued therapeutic concern. The behavior also represents a challenge for sex educators (Saunders, 1989).

REFERENCE

Abel, G. G., Becker, J. V., Cunningham-Rathner, J., Mittelman, M., & Rouleau, J. (1988). Multiple paraphilic diagnoses among sex offenders. *Bulletin of the American Academy of Psychiatry and the Law, 16*, 153–168.

Abel, G. G., Huffman, J., Warberg, B., & Holland, C. L. (1998). Visual reaction time and plethysmography as measures of sexual interest in child molesters. *Sexual Abuse: A Journal of Research and Treatment, 10*, 81–95.

Allen, C. (1962). *Textbook of psychosexual disorders.* Oxford, UK: Oxford University Press.

American Psychiatric Association. (1987). *Diagnostic and statistical manual of mental disorders* (3rd ed., rev.). Washington, DC: Author.

American Psychiatric Association. (2000). *Diagnostic and statistical manual of mental disorders* (4th ed., text rev.). Washington, DC: Author.

Bancroft, J. (1974). *Deviant sexual behaviour.* London: Oxford University Press.

Bradford, J. M. W. (2001). The neurobiology, neuropharmacology, and pharmacological treatment of the paraphilias and compulsive sexual behaviour. *Canadian Journal of Psychiatry, 46*, 26–34.

Brenner, C. (1959). The masochistic character: Genesis and treatment. *Journal of the American Psychoanalytic Association, 7*, 197–226.

Breslow, N. (1989). Sources of confusion in the study and treatment of sadomasochism. *Journal of Social Behavior and Personality, 4*, 263–274.

Breslow, N., Evans, L., & Langley, J. (1985). On the prevalence of roles of females in the sadomasochistic subculture: Report of an empirical study. *Archives of Sexual Behavior, 14*, 303–317.

Briken, P., Hill, A., & Berner, W. (2003). Pharmacotherapy of paraphilias with long-acting agonists of luteinizing hormone-releasing hormone: A systematic review. *Journal of Clinical Psychiatry, 64*, 890–897.

Brownell, K. D., Hayes, S. C., & Barlow, D. H. (1977). Patterns of appropriate and deviant sexual arousal: The behavioral treatment of multiple sexual deviations. *Journal of Consulting and Clinical Psychology, 45*, 1144–1155.

Cairns, F. J. (1981). Death from electrocution during auto-erotic procedures. *New Zealand Medical Journal, 94*, 259–260.

Carr, E. G. (1974). Behavior therapy in a case of multiple sexual disorders. *Journal of Behavior Therapy and Experimental Psychiatry, 5*, 171–174.

Cesnik, J. A., & Coleman, E. (1989). Use of lithium carbonate in the treatment of autoerotic asphyxia. *American Journal of Psychotherapy, 43*, 277–286.

Fisch, R. Z. (1989). Masochistic patients: How to help the person who finds "joy in pain." *Postgraduate Medicine, 85*, 157–160.

Freud, S. (1938). *The basic writings of Sigmund Freud.* New York: Modern Library.

Freud, S. (1981). *Penguin Freud library: Vol. 7. On sexuality.* London: Penguin Books.

Haydn-Smith, P., Marks, I., Buchaya, H., & Repper, D. (1987). Behavioural treatment of life-threatening masochistic asphyxiation: A case study. *British Journal of Psychiatry, 150*, 518–519.

Hucker, S. J. (1985). Self-harmful sexual behavior. *Psychiatric Clinics of North America, 8*, 323–337.

Innes, R. (1997). Auto-erotic asphyxia and art psychotherapy. In E. V. Welldon & C. Van Velso (Eds.), *A practical guide to forensic psychotherapy* (pp. 172–181). London: Jessica Kingsley.

Kafka, M. P. (1991). Successful antidepressant treatment of non-paraphiliac sexual addictions and paraphilias in men. *Journal of Clinical Psychiatry, 52*, 60–65.

Kafka, M. P. (1994). Sertraline pharmacotherapy for paraphilias and paraphilia-related disorders: An open trial. *Annals of Clinical Psychiatry, 6*, 189–195.

Kafka, M. P. (1996). Therapy for sexual impulsivity: The paraphilias and paraphilia-related disorders. *Psychiatric Times, 13*(6), 1–6.

Kafka, M. P., & Hennen, J. (2002). A DSM-IV Axis I comorbidity study of males (*n* = 120) with paraphilias and paraphilia-related disorders. *Sexual Abuse: A Journal of Research and Treatment, 14*(4), 349–356.

Kafka, M. P., & Prentky, R. (1992). Fluoxetine treatment of nonparaphilic sexual addictions and paraphilias in men. *Journal of Clinical Psychiatry, 53*, 351–358.

Kleinplatz, P. J. (2006). Learning from extraordinary lovers. *Journal of Homosexuality, 50*, 325–348.

Kleinplatz, P. J., & Moser, C. (2004). Towards clinical guidelines for working with BDSM clients. *Contemporary Sexuality, 38*, 1–4.

Kolmes, K., Stock, W., & Moser, C. (2006). Investigating bias in psychotherapy with BDSM clients. *Journal of Homosexuality, 50*, 301–324.

Krafft-Ebing, R. von. (1999). *Psychopathia sexualis* (12th ed., F. J. Rebman, Trans.). Burbank, CA: Bloat. (Original work published 1886)

Langevin, R. (1983). *Sexual strands.* Hillsdale, NJ: Erlbaum.

Langevin, R., & Paitich, D. (2006). *Clarke Sex History Questionnaire for Males—Revised.* Toronto: Multi-Health Systems.

Laws, D. R. (2001). Olfactory aversion: Notes on procedure, with speculations on its mechanism of effect. *Sexual Abuse: A Journal of Research and Treatment, 13*, 275–287.

Laws, D. R. (2003). Penile plethysmography: Will we ever get it right? In T. Ward, D. R. Laws, & S. M. Hudson (Eds.), *Sexual deviance: Issues and controversies* (pp. 82–102). Thousand Oaks, CA: Sage.

Letourneau, E. J. (2002). A comparison of objective measures of sexual arousal and interest: visual reaction time and penile plethysmography. *Sexual Abuse, 14*, 207–203.

Lihn, H. (1971). Sexual masochism: A case report. *International Journal of Psycho-Analysis, 52*, 469–478.

Malchiodi, C. A. (2003). *Handbook of art therapy.* New York: Guilford Press.

Marks, I. N., Gelder, M., & Bancroft, J. (1970). Sexual deviants two years after electric aversion. *British Journal of Psychiatry, 117*, 173–185.

Marks, I. N., Rachman, S., & Gelder, M. (1965). Methods for the assessment of aversion treatment in fetishism and masochism. *Behaviour Research and Therapy, 3*, 253–258.

Marques, J. (1970). Orgasmic reconditioning: Changing sexual object choices through controlling masturbation fantasies. *Journal of Behavior Therapy and Experimental Psychiatry, 1*, 263–271.

Marshall, W. L., & Fernandez, Y. M. (2000). Phallometric testing with sex offenders: Limits to its value. *Clinical Psychology Review, 20,* 807–822.

Marshall, W. L., Serran, G. A., & Cortoni, F. A. (2000). Childhood attachments, sexual abuse, and their relationship to adult coping in child molesters. *Sexual Abuse: A Journal of Research and Treatment, 12,* 17–26.

Martz, D. (2003). Behavioural treatment for a female engaging in autoerotic asphyxiation. *Clinical Case Studies, 2,* 236–242.

McGuire, R. J., & Carlisle, J. M. (1965). Sexual deviations as conditioned behaviour. *Behaviour Research and Therapy, 2,* 185–190.

Moser, C., & Kleinplatz, P. J. (2006). DSM-IV-TR and the paraphilias: An argument for removal. *Journal of Psychology and Human Sexuality, 17,* 91–109.

Moser, C., & Levitt, E. E. (1987). An exploratory descriptive study of a sadomasochistically oriented sample. *Journal of Sex Research, 23,* 322–337.

Neumann, F., & Kalmus, J. (1991). *Hormonal treatment of sexual deviations.* Berlin: Diesbach-Verlag.

Nichols, H. R., & Molinder, I. (2000). *Multiphasic Sex Inventory II* (rev. ed.). Fircrest, WA: Nichols & Molinder Assessments.

Nichols, M. (2006). Psychotherapeutic issues with "kinky" clients: Clinical problems, yours and theirs. *Journal of Homosexuality, 50,* 281–300.

O'Donohue, W., Letourneau, E. J., & Dowling, H. (1997). Development and preliminary validation of a paraphilic sexual fantasy questionnaire. *Sexual Abuse: A Journal of Research and Treatment, 9,* 167–178.

Panken, S. (1973). *The joy of suffering: Psychoanalytic theory and therapy of masochism.* New York: Aronson.

Pinard, G., & Lamontagne, Y. (1976). Electrical aversion, aversion relief and sexual retraining in treatment of fetishism with masochism. *Journal of Behavior Therapy and Experimental Psychiatry, 7,* 71–74.

Reiersol, O., & Skeid, S. (2006). The ICD diagnoses of fetishism and sadomasochism. *Journal of Homosexuality, 50,* 243–262.

Sandnabba, N. K., Santtila, P., Alison, L., & Nordling, N. (2002). Demographics, sexual behaviour, family background and abuse experiences of practitioners of sadomasochistic sex: A review of recent research. *Sexual and Relationship Therapy, 17,* 39–55.

Saunders, E. (1989). Life threatening autoerotic behavior: A challenge for sex educators and therapists. *Journal of Sex Education and Therapy, 15,* 82–91.

Shiwach, R. S., & Prosser, J. (1998). Treatment of an unusual case of masochism. *Journal of Sex and Marital Therapy, 24,* 303–307.

Shore, M. F., Zelin, M., Clifton, A., & Myerson, P. G. (1971). Patterns of masochism: An empirical study. *British Journal of Medical Psychology, 44,* 59–65.

Spengler, A. (1977). Manifest sadomasochism of males: Results of an empirical study. *Archives of Sexual Behavior, 6,* 441–456.

Stolorow, R., Atwood, G., & Brandchaft, B. (1988). Masochism and its treatment. *Bulletin of the Menninger Clinic, 52,* 504–509.

Thornton, D., & Mann, R. (1997). Sexual masochism: Assessment and treatment. In D. R. Laws & W. O'Donohue (Eds.), *Sexual deviance: Theory, assessment, and treatment* (pp. 240–252). New York: Guilford Press.

Wilson, G. D. (1981). Sexual deviations. *British Journal of Hospital Medicine, 26,* 8–14.

CHAPTER 16

TRANSVESTIC FETISHISM
Psychopathology and Theory

JENNIFER WHEELER
KIRK A. B. NEWRING
CRISSA DRAPER

TERMINOLOGY AND DIAGNOSIS

At first glance, the term "transvestic fetishism" seems sufficiently behaviorally descriptive: "Transvestic" describes the cross-dressing component of the behavior, and "fetishism" describes the sexual component. Yet there have long been some inconsistencies in the literature as to what is meant by such terms as "transvestism" and "transvestic fetishism," and whether these terms are synonyms or variations of one another (see Zucker & Blanchard, 1997, for a review). These semantic inconsistencies are probably due to the fact that the observable behavior of transvestism (dressing in clothing that is typically reserved for the opposite sex) is not always motivated by sexual desire or urges (a requisite motivation for a behavior to be a fetish). In fact, transvestic behavior may occur under circumstances that are normative (e.g., a man in a kilt, dressing for a costume party or cultural event; a woman in a pantsuit) or psychologically adaptive (e.g., attempting to synchronize one's internal gender identity with one's external appearance), and not necessarily associated with sexual arousal.

In this way, transvestic fetishism is unlike many of the other sexually deviant behaviors described in this text. Unlike zoophilia or pedophilia, for example, the observable behavior of cross-dressing may occur for reasons that are not necessarily sexually motivated, or even necessarily "deviant" or "disordered" (see Adshead, 1997). To distinguish transvestic fetishism from other variants of cross-dressing behavior, it is necessary to understand the function of the transvestic activity. Because of the importance of this motivational criterion to transvestic fetishism, and because of the long-standing semantic confusion surrounding the term "transvestism," we begin this chapter with a clarification of these and other related terms.

"Transvestite/Transvestism"

When the term "transvestite" was coined nearly a century ago, it referred to a person who dressed in the clothing of the opposite sex (see Zucker & Blanchard, 1997, for a brief review of historical literature on the use of this term). Since then, "transvestism" has been used to describe a variety of cross-dressing behaviors, regardless of the purpose—or function—of such behavior. For example, the following are descriptions of persons who engage in cross-dressing behavior for many reasons and to whom the term "transvestite" was once applied:

- "Transsexual": A person who is dissatisfied with his or her biological sex (e.g., a man whose own genitals and other male features are ego-dystonic), and who wishes to live permanently as and be perceived by others as a person of the opposite sex.
- "Transgendered": A person who is satisfied with his or her biological sex (e.g., a man whose own genitals and male features are ego-syntonic), but some or all of the time prefers to occupy social roles and manifest behavioral traits that are typically associated with the other gender (e.g., typical masculine social roles or behaviors are ego-dystonic).
- "Androgynous": A person whose biological sex and gender role are both ego-syntonic, but who derives social or psychological satisfaction from some degree of cross-gender expression (e.g., an otherwise "feminine" female who does not wear skirts or dresses; an otherwise "masculine" male who wears earrings and a "utility kilt").
- "Gender mimic": A person whose biological sex and gender role are ego-syntonic, but who mimics or spoofs traits of the opposite sex for entertainment or occupational purposes (e.g., a man who is a "drag queen").
- "Effeminate homosexuals" (Person & Ovesey, 1978; Stiller, 1971): Homosexual males who may put on women's clothing for very brief periods (minutes or hours), and for whom this behavior is not accompanied by sexual excitement or by any desire to live as or be perceived by others as female. Bailey (2003) has discussed the role of male femininity in his popular science book *The Man Who Would Be Queen*. This work touched off a bit of controversy by highlighting the diversity of thought and opinion surrounding issues of gender, sex, sexuality, and culture.[1]

Although the observable behavior is similar in each of these examples (a person of one sex wears the clothing or accessories of the opposite sex), each is distinguished from the other by function and degree. Also note that, in the examples above, "transvestism" has historically been used to describe cross-dressing behavior that is typically *not* motivated by sexual urges or desires. This is the central distinction between transvestic behavior (i.e., cross-dressing) and "transvestic fetishism" (also referred to as "fetishistic cross-dressing" by Stoller, 1971; see Adshead, 1997, for a review).

It should also be noted that there are some males who identify themselves as cross-dressers, but who deny that this activity is sexually arousing or fetishistic in nature (e.g., Buhrich & McConaghy, 1977; Black, Kehrberg, Flumerfelt, & Schlosser, 1997; Croughan, Saghir, Cohen, & Robins, 1981). However, other data suggest that even these "deniers" demonstrate transvestic sexual arousal on objective measures (e.g., penile plethysmography; Blanchard, Racansky, & Steiner, 1986). Another group of people who may cross-dress without sexual arousal are those who cross-dress as a result of "biologically induced" conditions (e.g., hypogonadism, temporal lobe disease; see Stoller, 1971, for a discussion).

More recently, the term "transvestism" has been defined more narrowly, as "describing biological males who cross-dress in women's clothing which is accompanied, at least at times, by sexual arousal" (e.g., Blanchard et al., 1986; Ovesey & Person, 1973; Stoller, 1971; see Zucker & Blanchard, 1997, p. 253). This narrower definition combines the observable behavior of cross-dressing with the unobservable motivation of sexual gratification, and is consistent with the current definition of "transvestite" found in the online version of the Merriam-Webster Dictionary: "a person and especially a male who adopts the dress and often the behavior typical of the opposite sex especially for purposes of emotional or sexual gratification" (*www.m-w.com*). This narrower definition of "transvestism" is also synonymous with the clinical construct of "transvestic fetishism," as defined by each of the two major clinical diagnostic manuals: the *Diagnostic and Statistical Manual of Psychiatric Disorders*, fourth edition, text revision[2] (DSM-IV-TR; American Psychiatric Association, 2000), and the *International Statistical Classification of Diseases and Related Health Problems*, 10th revision (ICD-10; World Health Organization, 1992).

"Transvestic Fetishism"

According to the DSM-IV-TR (American Psychiatric Association, 2000), "transvestic fetishism" refers to "recurrent, intense sexually arousing fantasies, sexual urges, or behaviors involving cross-dressing" (p. 575). This is similar to the definition of "fetishistic transvestism" found in the ICD-10 (World Health Organization, 1992), which is "the wearing of clothes of the opposite sex principally to obtain sexual excitement and to create the appearance of a person of the opposite sex." Each of these manuals uses the same two basic definitional features: (1) the observable behavior (cross-dressing), and (2) the unobservable motivation for that behavior (to gratify sexual urges or arousal).

Beyond these two shared features, the ICD-10 and the DSM-IV-TR do not agree on how to define transvestic fetishism. For example, the ICD-10 explicitly distinguishes transvestic fetishism from other types of cross-dressing behaviors, which the DSM-IV-TR does not: "Fetishistic transvestism is distinguished from transsexual transvestism by its clear association with sexual arousal and the strong desire to remove the clothing once orgasm occurs and sexual arousal declines" (World Health Organization, 1992). The DSM-IV-TR, on the other hand, not only fails to explicitly differentiate transvestic fetishism from cross-dressing that occurs in the context of a transgender or transsexual identity, but it confuses the matter by adding a specifier to transvestic fetishism when it is accompanied by gender dysphoria. The text further complicates this distinction by excluding a diagnosis of transvestic fetishism when it occurs exclusively in the context of "gender identity disorder" (GID, described below); yet it notes that for some individuals, transvestic fetishism with gender dysphoria may be associated with a transsexual identity (e.g., in males, the desire to live and dress permanently as female). This diagnostic complication is further addressed later in this chapter.

Another notable difference between current ICD-10 and DSM-IV-TR descriptions for transvestic fetishism is that the DSM-IV-TR requires three specific features that the ICD-10 does not: a 6-month duration, status as a heterosexual male, and a distress component. The diagnostic utility of these three features is not well established. First, although a duration criterion may increase diagnostic specificity (i.e., it may reduce false-positive diagnoses among persons who have "experimented" sexually with cross-dressing activity but for whom the behavior did not persist), the duration of 6 months is an arbitrary one; it may be too long or not long enough to permit a differential diagnosis of transvestic fetishism versus other cross-dressing behaviors. Second, although status as a heterosexual male is the modal status for transvestic fetishists (Docter & Prince, 1997; Långström & Zucker, 2005),[3] there is also evidence to suggest that a small but notable percentage of transvestic fetishist men describe themselves as ambisexual, homosexual, or asexual (Långström & Zucker, 2005). Finally, while a distress component may be useful for diagnosing transvestic fetishism as a "disorder" (to be defined in a later section), there is evidence to suggest that a substantial proportion of men who engage in transvestic fetishism are not distressed by this behavior (Långström & Zucker, 2005).

In our view, the descriptive features of transvestic fetishism that are shared by the ICD-10 and the DSM-IV-TR—that is, cross-dressing activity that is sexually motivated—are the ones that provide the most useful clinical information for discussing this behavior. Therefore, they constitute the basis for our use of the term "transvestic fetishism" (hereafter abbreviated as TVF) in the remainder of this chapter. This behavior can range from occasionally wearing female undergarments under otherwise male clothing, to dressing fully in female clothing and makeup out in public. Notice, however, that when TVF is defined this way, the term applies to *all* sexually motivated cross-dressing behaviors, regardless of whether this behavior causes the individual clinically significant distress or impairment (i.e., DSM-IV-TR Criterion B). This issue is discussed further in a later section.

Some clinical research has indicated that there are two subgroups of men exhibiting TVF (Blanchard et al., 1986; Buhrich & McConaghy, 1977; Docter & Prince, 1997). The first group, termed "periodic transvestites" (see Buhrich & Beaumont, 1981; Långström & Zucker, 2005) describe this group as "nuclear transvestites"), are psychologically satisfied with their gender and sexual identity as male. They are sexually and psychologically satisfied with the activity of cross-dressing activity only, and do not feel a need to pursue other forms of feminization. The second group, termed "marginal transvestites" (see Långström & Zucker, 2005), are dissatisfied with their gender and sexual identity as male. They report lower sexual arousal to the cross-dressing activity itself, and desire additional means of feminization, such as hair removal, hormone treatment, or surgical reconstruction (Docter & Prince, 1997). The latter group may include persons who identify themselves as transgendered or transsexual, and who therefore engage in cross-dressing behavior for more than one purpose (i.e., for sexual gratification as well as gender synchrony). If DSM-IV-TR criteria are used, this group will receive the diagnostic specifier "with gender dysphoria." If this co-occurring gender dysphoria is of sufficient severity as to cause clinically significant distress or impairment, then individuals in this group may also meet DSM-IV-TR diagnostic criteria for GID (a "strong and persistent . . . desire to be, or insistence that he or she is, the other sex" and "persistent discomfort with his or her sex or sense of inappropriateness in the gender role of that sex"; American Psychiatric Association, 2000, p. 581). However, if the TVF behavior occurs only in the course of GID, then only a diagnosis of GID is given.

"Deviance" and "Disorder"

Perhaps more than any other topic in this text, TVF requires thoughtful consideration of the application of such terms as "disorder" and "deviance." As stated previously, cross-dressing includes a broad continuum of behaviors that range from the nondeviant and nonsexual (e.g., men's wearing utility kilts) to the sexually deviant and criminally disordered (e.g., men's stealing women's clothing and achieving sexual gratification from these items). Whether or not any particular act of cross-dressing is regarded as "deviant" (i.e., non-normative) may vary across time (e.g., recall that less than 100 years ago women did not typically wear pants) and across cultures (e.g., consider the difference between a man wearing a kilt in Scotland and a man wearing a kilt in rural Montana). When relevant contextual and motivational factors are considered, it is evident that not all acts of cross-dressing are "deviant" (non-normative) or reflective of an underlying "disorder." Furthermore, even those acts of cross-dressing that might be regarded as non-normative (e.g., individuals occasionally cross-dressing for entertainment or professional purposes) are not necessarily motivated by sexual interest and therefore would be excluded from the designation "sexually deviant."

Similarly, many individuals cross-dress in an effort to promote greater psychological synchrony between their internal gender identity and their external appearance (i.e., individuals who are transgendered or transsexual). Although such persons may have psychological problems that arise from being transgendered individuals in our culture (e.g., depression or anxiety resulting from interpersonal isolation or social rejection), the act of cross-dressing under these circumstances might be regarded as relatively adaptive, in that it functions to improve their overall psychological well-being. Accordingly, cross-dressing under these circumstances should not necessarily be conceptualized as a "disorder."

As stated previously, we consider all individuals who cross-dress privately or with consenting partners for the purpose of obtaining sexual gratification to be participating in TVF, even if the behavior is not associated with subjective distress or significant impairments to their interpersonal, occupational, social, or other functioning. In the absence of such negative sequelae, an individual is unlikely to present for treatment or to be detained in a correctional setting. Researchers and clinicians are more likely to see those individuals who *do* experience subjective distress or functional impairment associated with sexually motivated cross-dressing behavior, or whose behavior victimizes others—that is, individuals who are experiencing a behavioral "disorder" (see Zucker & Blanchard, 1997, for further theoretical discussion of when a behavior should be designated as a "disorder").

To differentiate transvestic fetishists who do experience subjective distress or functional impairment associated with sexually motivated cross-dressing (or whose behavior victimizes others) from those who do not, we refer to the latter type of behavior as TVF and consider the former behavior a subtype of TVF, which we refer to from here on as "transvestic fetishism disorder" (TVFD). We feel that this distinction provides some degree of resolution to the question of whether or not TVF is categorically considered a "mental disorder" (Zucker & Blanchard, 1997) by recognizing that cross-dressing for sexual gratification *is* appropriately classified as a "disorder" when the behavior is associated with negative outcomes for oneself or for others (see Moser & Kleinplatz, 2002). Unfortunately, and as noted by previous authors (Långström & Zucker, 2005), many researchers have failed to consider the disorder or impairment criterion when investigating TVF, so this distinction is not typically made in the professional and academic literature.

Another issue to consider is the fact that the diagnosis of transvestic fetishism is traditionally reserved for males (see DSM-IV-TR; American Psychiatric Association, 2000). One interpretation of such a sex-based diagnosis is that, at least in Western cultures, it is "deviant" for males to dress in traditionally female clothing, while it is "normative" for females to dress in traditionally male clothing. This means that females in Western cultures have more socially acceptable outlets for cross-gender expression than do males. In fact, such cross-gender expression seems to have become so subtly integrated into female fashion that it is no longer explicitly considered cross-gendered expression at all (e.g., women's business suits). One hypothesis for such a sex-based difference in cross-gender expression is that—despite significant advances in women's rights and social status throughout the last several decades—there continues to be a gender bias in our culture that favors "maleness" over "femaleness." In other words, it is generally accepted that a woman would want to express (culturally desirable) "male" attributes (e.g., via clothing, career interests), but it is less readily accepted that a man would want to express (less culturally desirable) "female" attributes. Such a hypothesis would help explain why it is considered "deviant" in our culture for men to express "femaleness" by dressing in women's clothing, while the reverse is not true for women.

Another hypothesis to explain the sex-based difference in the "deviance" of cross-gender expression is related to the design of female versus male clothing in our culture. Over a century ago, an important design element in women's clothing was emphasizing certain aspects of the female body (e.g., narrowing the waist, which was regarded as highly feminine), while deemphasizing other aspects of the female form (e.g., covering ankles, which were regarded as too erotic to be exposed). Although trends in women's fashions have changed considerably in the last century, such fashions still emphasize the shape and sensuality of women's bodies (consider corsets, miniskirts, pantyhose, and high-heeled shoes) and the value of form over function. Unlike women's clothing, men's clothing is not typically designed to be "sexy," but rather to serve a particular function (e.g., work, leisure, or sports attire). In other words, men's fashions have long differed from women's fashions in the emphasis on function over form (e.g., men's pants typically have pockets, whereas women's pants often do not). It is no surprise that the increase in women's rights over the last several decades has been accompanied by an increase in women's clothing options. Today's "liberated" woman can wear clothing that is much more like men's clothing, in that it emphasizes comfort, practicality, and function (e.g., pants, flat shoes, socks). But unlike men, women continue to have the option of wearing more traditionally "female" clothing, which is specifically designed to emphasize the sensual and erotic nature of the female body. Therefore, one hypothesis for why female clothing assumes such erotic value for some men is that this is exactly what traditionally "female" clothing was designed to do—elicit erotic attention. It is notable that the prototypical garments desired by men with TVF (women's underwear, high-heeled shoes, skirts, dresses) tend to be the "sexier" (i.e., more feminine) articles of female clothing, as opposed to blue jeans or running shoes, for example. Thus another explanation for sex-based differences in the "deviant" nature of cross-dressing is that women's clothing is by its very design sensual and erotic, whereas men's clothing has traditionally lacked such an erotic emphasis.

ONSET AND DEVELOPMENTAL COURSE

The limited available empirical data suggest that most adults who exhibit TVF report the onset of "secret" cross-dressing behavior prior to or during puberty (Buhrich & Beaumont, 1981; Buhrich & McConaghy, 1977; Croughan et al., 1981; Docter & Prince,

1997; Person & Ovesey, 1978; Zucker & Bradley, 1995). At this early stage, children may experience cross-dressing activity as pleasurable and exciting in a more generalized way than in a sexualized way. For example, an article of clothing that belongs to a young boy's mother or sister may trigger pleasurable sensory experiences (e.g., smells, textures, visual cues) and feelings of comfort and familiarity, thus functioning similarly to a transitional attachment object (see Sullivan, Bradley, & Zucker, 1995). Or he may associate articles of female clothing with certain traits or roles traditionally assigned to females (e.g., nurturing, graceful), and by donning a female costume he is acting a fantasy of possessing these feminine traits (see Buckner, 1970, for a discussion). Additionally, young males may play "dress-up" games—initially at the behest of an older sister, aunt, or grandparent, but later doing so of their own initiative. It has also been suggested that masculinity serves as an "irritant" to some males, who act out against this proscribed role by cross-dressing (Stoller, 1971). In each of these situations, the function of cross-dressing is to elicit positive emotions associated with the clothing itself or to facilitate positive social relationships with family members, or to alleviate negative psychological states associated with being masculine. Eventually, these boys may turn to female articles of clothing during periods of distress, wearing them in an effort to cope with negative emotional states (i.e., to self-soothe), but still not necessarily to obtain sexual gratification. Other than cross-dressing, this population does not typically demonstrate other cross-gender interests or behaviors in childhood.[4]

With the onset of puberty, cross-dressing activities become increasingly paired with the physically pleasurable penile sensations of tumescence, orgasm, and ejaculation. Furthermore, cross-dressing activities are increasingly accompanied by fantasies of actually being female, such as being dressed in women's clothing in public, or engaged in sexual activity (i.e., "heterosexual" sex with another male, "lesbian" sex with a female). Blanchard (1989) used the term "autogynephila" to refer to this broad range of sexually arousing fantasies and behaviors associated with cross-gender wishes and activities. As the autogynephilic fantasy content becomes more elaborated, the erotic value of the clothing itself diminishes, and the primary purpose of the clothing is simply to trigger fantasized images of the self as female.

Some have hypothesized that autogynephila in general, including TVF, interfere or compete with normative heterosexual attraction (e.g., Blanchard, 1991, 1992). Although the mechanism for such interference is as yet unspecified, there is some evidence that psychological factors may be involved in such a process, such as the devaluation of females or hostile relationships with females (see LaTorre, 1980; Zucker & Bradley, 1995). Other clinical observations suggest that some young men with TVF may have exaggerated notions of the requirements of masculinity—which, combined with exaggerated fears of failure, poor performance in traditionally masculine tasks (e.g., sports), and a "blockage" of homosexual outlets, result in low self-esteem as heterosexuals and a return to more comfortable TVF behavior (see Buckner, 1970).

Whereas childhood and adolescent cross-dressing behavior is typically conducted in secret, during late adolescence or young adulthood these males may begin wearing female clothing in public. With the onset of intimate sexual partnerships, the young men may spontaneously discontinue TVF behavior, but they are likely to resume it eventually (either in secrecy with the knowledge and consent of their sexual partners). The majority of transvestites are married and have children (e.g., Docter & Prince, 1997; Långström & Zucker, 2005). TVF may or may not interact with the sexual interests and activities a man enjoys with his partner, although TVF-related fantasies may be required for him to achieve orgasm and ejaculation during partner sex (e.g., Croughan et al., 1981).

For many adult men, the erotic or sexual value of cross-dressing behavior further diminishes with age, although the desire to cross-dress may remain (e.g., Buhrich, 1978). Similar to cross-dressing activity in childhood, such activity in later life assumes a more self-soothing, comforting function than a sexual one. It is not clear whether this shift away from sexual gratification is specific to the developmental course of TVF itself, or whether it is simply related to the overall diminished sexual drive that is typically associated with aging (see Blanchard et al., 1986).

EPIDEMIOLOGICAL FACTORS

Prevalence

Until 2005, no formal epidemiological research had ever been conducted to study the incidence or prevalence of TVF. In that year, Långström and Zucker published a study of 2,450 randomly sampled adults in Sweden, which included an investigation of TVF behaviors[5] in both males and females. Because it is the first study of its kind and includes numerous epidemiological, demographic, and psychological data, this study is reviewed here at length.

In this sample, 2.8% of males (n = 36) and 0.4% of females (n = 5) reported ever having experienced sexual arousal from cross-dressing behavior. TVF occurred primarily in heterosexual males (85.7%, n = 35), and exclusively in men who reported a primary sexual attraction to and experience with females; that is, none of the men reporting TVF had a primary or exclusive sexual interest in or experience with males. This is similar to earlier research indicating that 75–89% of TVF males identified themselves as heterosexual (Docter & Prince, 1997).

With regard to rates of interest in TVF among non-TVF men, one study found that 3% of males who denied having any paraphilia demonstrated arousal to cross-dressing (Fedora et al., 1992). Note the similarity of this rate to the 2.8% prevalence rate for TVF among males in Långström and Zucker's sample (2005).

Incidence

There are currently no empirical data available regarding the incidence of TVF.

Degree of Impairment

In Långström and Zucker's (2005) sample, of those men who endorsed TVF (women were excluded from subsequent analyses due to the small sample size), about 47% reported that the sexual arousal to cross-dressing was acceptable to them (accordingly, nearly 47% of the sample might not meet DSM-IV-TR Criterion B, required for a diagnosis of transvestic fetishism). This suggests that about half of the sample did not find their TVF behavior acceptable, and thus might be regarded as experiencing TVFD.

In their study of 70 TVF males, Croughan and colleagues (1981) reported that over 95% of their sample had experienced at least one adverse consequence from cross-dressing behavior (e.g., had been arrested, divorced, or had suffered negative thoughts or significant impairment in their education or employment or in their social relationships). Participants who had sought treatment for their cross-dressing behavior reported more adverse consequences than those who had not sought treatment.

Other Demographic Characteristics

In the Långström and Zucker (2005) sample, the "modal" man with TVF was in his mid-30s, had at least one sibling, was in a current stable relationship, and had at least one child. There were no significant differences in this sample between TVF and non-TVF men in their sample with regard to age, family size, socioeconomic status, status as a parent, or status in a current stable relationship. However, TVF men were more likely than non-TVF men to live in a major city.

Similarly, in their sample of 1,032 cross-dressers, Docter and Prince (1997) found that most were married (nearly two-thirds); had obtained at least a college degree; and represented numerous professions, including both skilled and unskilled workers.

A study of 70 TVF males reported that 95% of the total sample was white and that most were middle-aged, with higher than average educational levels and incomes (Croughan et al., 1981). Other studies have reported the average age of their samples as the middle to late 30s (e.g., Buhrich & Beaumont, 1981; Buhrich & McConahgy, 1977).

CONCOMITANT PROBLEMS AND COMORBIDITY

In the Långström and Zucker (2005) sample, there were no significant differences between TVF men and non-TVF men with regard to psychological health, physical health, recent alcohol intoxication behavior, and overall life satisfaction. There did appear to be a significant association between TVF and illegal drug use, and TVF men were more likely than non-TVF men to have been separated from one of their parents during childhood. However, two other studies have indicated that cross-dressers are not more likely to come from "distressed families" (Docter & Prince, 1997; Schott, 1995).

With regard to sexual histories and behavior examined in this study (Långström & Zucker, 2005), there were no differences between TVF and non-TVF men in age of onset of sexual activity, current sexual relationship, frequency of intercourse in the month, or promiscuity. However, compared to non-TVF men, TVF men reported being more easily sexually aroused than others, higher rate of pornography use, higher frequency of masturbation, and lower satisfaction with their sex lives. TVF men were more likely than non-TVF men to report having had any same-sex sexual experience; this finding is consistent with a previous study in which 30% of cross-dressers reported same-sex sexual experiences (Docter & Prince, 1997). The Långström and Zucker (2005) study also reported a nonsignificant trend that TVF men were more likely than non-TVF men to report a history of childhood sexual victimization.

With regard to the co-occurrence of other sexual behavior disorders in the Långström and Zucker survey, TVF men were more likely than non-TVF men to report sexual arousal that involved pain (sexual sadism and/or masochism), spying on other people having sex (voyeurism), or exposing their genitals to a stranger (exhibitionism). Similarly, Buhrich and Beaumont (1981) reported high rates of bondage fantasies in their sample of 222 TVF males, typically involving being bound while cross-dressing.

In their study of 70 TVF males, Croughan and colleagues (1981) reported elevated rates of depression, alcoholism, drug use, and antisocial personality compared to general population prevalences.

ETIOLOGY

Biological Theory

There is currently no biological research that has addressed possible genetic transmission of TVF behavior. However, a possible link between familial cross-dressing and GID has been discussed. As previously observed by Zucker and Blanchard (1997), the strong correlation between TVF and status as a heterosexual male suggests that men with TVF would share more biological traits and behavioral markers with non-TVF heterosexual men than with women or with homosexual men. To date, this hypothesis has not been empirically tested. With regard to any family history of TVF, one study of 70 TVF men found that 1% of fathers and 2% of brothers engaged in cross-dressing behavior (Croughan et al., 1981). Given that this rate is slightly lower than the base rate of TVF that has been reported more recently (approximately 3%; Långström & Zucker, 2005), these data do not support a genetic transmission of TVF. Over the past 30 years, several case reports have reported on the use of pharmacotherapy for the treatment of TVF, with varied success. For a discussion of the implicit biological theory supporting the use of pharmacotherapy in the assessment and treatment of TVF, please refer to the next chapter (Newring, Wheeler, & Draper, Chapter 17, this volume).

Behavioral and Reinforcement Theories

There has never been a controlled study comparing the learning experiences of men with TVF to those of men without TVF. Some have hypothesized that the behavior develops after an accidental exposure to female clothing or view of a female disrobing (e.g., Strzyzewsky & Zierhoffer, 1967); this contact is thought to be positively reinforced by the psychologically comforting properties of the clothing, and, later, by the pleasurable sensations associated with sexual arousal. In this analysis, the reinforcing properties function in a respondent manner, akin to Pavlovian classical conditioning. Alternatively, or perhaps in addition to this theory, transvestic behavior may be negatively reinforced when it is used as a means of self-soothing or coping during times of distress by alleviating negative emotional states. In this analysis, the reinforcing properties function in an operant manner. When these theories are taken together, a combination of classical and operant conditioning is believed to influence the acquisition and maintenance of the behaviors. Such an analysis is also the most popular theory to explain the maintenance of psychosexual disorders.

Family-of-Origin Considerations

As indicated previously, the limited available data indicate that there is a low rate of TVF in fathers and brothers of men with TVF (Croughan et al., 1981), suggesting that intrafamilial modeling is an unlikely means of "transmission" for TVF.

Some research indicates that parents of men with TVF are less "sex-typed" and more "sex-reversed" with regard to traits such as dependence and affiliation (Newcomb, 1985). These data might support a hypothesis that TVF men are more likely to have parents with less rigid expectations of gender stereotypes or higher rates of sex role reversal, but they do not support the notion that TVF was learned from these environments.

A more recent study found no differences in the reports of TVF men versus non-TVF men regarding their own parents' attitudes about sex (Långström & Zucker, 1995), suggesting that neither sexually open nor sexually repressive family environments are associated with the development of TVF activity.

Two studies have reported a high rate of parental separation during childhood among TVF males (Långström & Zucker, 2005; Zucker & Blanchard, 1995). One study reported that over 50% of adolescent males in their sample had periods of separation from their mothers—a higher rate than those for samples of gender-dysphoric and homosexual adolescent males (Zucker & Blanchard, 1995). More recently, Långström and Zucker (2005) found that TVF males were more likely than non-TVF males to report having been separated from their parents during childhood. Such maternal or parental separation might further explain the need for or value of a transitional object, which is thought to be the initial function of women's clothing for many young boys who eventually develop TVF (see Sullivan et al., 1995).

Psychoanalytic Theory

It should be noted that transvestism and virtually all sexual fetishes were once believed to have been caused by the Freudian concept of "castration anxiety," or the individual's belief that he is already castrated (see Storr, 1957, for a discussion). According to this theory, a man with TVF feels inadequate as a male and requires female clothing in order to feel "potent." Although not necessarily conducive to empirical testing, a psychoanalytic theory of TVF may be not be wholly incompatible with other, more contemporary theories. For example, negative reinforcement principles would explain how TVF behaviors would be maintained as a response to castration (or any other) anxiety. Furthermore, the negative psychological sequelae that would be expected from maternal separation would not be incompatible with Oedipal fears of losing one's mother to a more masculine figure (the father).

SUMMARY AND FUTURE DIRECTIONS

As with many psychosexual behaviors, it is difficult, if not impossible, to identify a single theory that explains the etiology of TVF in every individual who exhibits it. Human nature is complicated in and of itself, let alone when we are considering such complicated psychological and social constructs as sexual interest, gender identity, and sexual orientation. TVF is no exception, and its etiology has yet to be universally and definitively established.

Perhaps more important than understanding how the behavior started is understanding how it is maintained, since this provides us with critical clinical data for developing intervention and treatment strategies. The most promising of these theories appear to be classical and operant conditioning theories that posit that TVF behavior is acquired and maintained via both positive reinforcement (pleasurable psychological and physical sensations) and negative reinforcement (amelioration of negative emotional states).

Further research is needed to develop our understanding of the development of TVF and its course over the lifespan. Rather than reliance on retrospective data to understand the developmental course of TVF, a longitudinal study is needed to identify children who engage in TVF activities and who maintain these into adulthood, and to distinguish these children from those who do not engage in TVF activities or do not maintain them into adulthood. Research is also needed to better understand what appears to be a trend in the course of TVF, in which the function of the behavior changes from self-soothing, to sexual gratification, to generation of fantasies, and back to self-soothing. Whether this course is actually inherent to TVF, or merely a by-product of male sexual development in general, has yet to be determined. Furthermore, as fewer than half of those who engage in transvestic behavior report distress (Långström & Zucker, 2005), a keen analysis of the etiology of this distress will help guide treatment research. Finally, further research is needed to continue to develop our understanding of the relationship between TVF and gender dysphoria, as well as the difference between TVF males who find their behavior acceptable and those who do not.

NOTES

1. For a detailed discussion of this text and the controversy, please refer to Bailey's website, *www.psych.northwestern.edu/psych/people/faculty/bailey/controversy/htm*.
2. For a thorough history of changes in DSM diagnostic criteria from the DSM-III to the DSM-IV, the reader is referred to a chapter in the previous edition of this text (Zucker & Blanchard, 1997).
3. Accordingly, unless otherwise noted, the current chapter describes transvestic fetishism as it occurs in heterosexual males, since transvestic fetishism occurs primarily in this group (e.g., Docter & Prince, 1997; Långström & Zucker, 2005).
4. Note that because most of these males eventually identify as heterosexual, this behavior is in and of itself a predictor of adult sexual orientation; see Bailey and Zucker (1995) for further consideration of sex-typed behavior as a predictor of adult sexual orientation.
5. In this study, "transvestic fetishism" was defined as positive endorsement of the item "Have you ever dressed in clothes pertaining to the opposite sex and become sexually aroused by this?" Unlike DSM-IV-TR, this study did not require the 6-month duration, heterosexual male status, and "distress" criteria (Långström & Zucker, 2005).

REFERENCES

Adshead, G. (1997). Transvestic fetishism: Assessment and treatment. In D. R. Laws & W. T. O'Donohue (Eds.), *Sexual deviance: Theory, assessment, and treatment* (pp. 253–279). New York: Guilford Press.

American Psychiatric Association. (2000). *Diagnostic and statistical manual of mental disorders* (4th ed., text rev.). Washington, DC: Author.

Bailey, J. B., & Zucker, K. J. (1995). Childhood sex-typed behavior and sexual orientation: A conceptual analysis and quantitative review. *Developmental Psychology, 31*(1), 43–55.

Bailey, J. M. (2003). *The man who would be queen: The science and psychology of gender bending and transsexualism*. New York: Joseph Henry Press.

Black, D. W., Kehrberg, L. D., Flumerfelt, D. L., & Schlosser, S. S. (1997). Characteristics of 36 subjects reporting compulsive sexual behavior. *American Journal of Psychiatry, 154*(2), 243–249.

Blanchard, R. (1989). The concept of autogynephilia and the typology of male gender dysphoria. *Journal of Nervous and Mental Disease, 177*, 616–623.

Blanchard, R. (1991). Clinical observations and systematic studies of autogynephilia. *Journal of Sex and Marital Therapy, 17*(4), 235–251.

Blanchard, R., (1992). Nonmonotonic relation of autogynephilia and heterosexual attraction. *Journal of Abnormal Psychology, 101*(2), 271–276.

Blanchard, R., Racansky, I. G., & Steiner, B. W. (1986). Phallometric detection of fetishistic arousal in heterosexual male cross-dressers. *Journal of Sex Research, 22,* 452–462.

Buckner, H. T. (1970). The transvestic career path. *Psychiatry, 33*(3), 381–389.

Buhrich, N. (1978). Motivation for cross-dressing in heterosexual transvestism. *Acta Psychiatrica Scandinavica, 57,* 145–152.

Buhrich, N., & Beaumont, T. (1981). Comparison of transvestism in Australia and America. *Archives of Sexual Behavior, 26,* 589–605.

Buhrich, N., & McConaghy, N. (1977). The clinical syndromes of femmiphilic transvestism. *Archives of Sexual Behavior, 6,* 397–412.

Croughan, J. L., Saghir, M., Cohen, R., & Robins, E. (1981). A comparison of treated and untreated male cross-dressers. *Archives of Sexual Behavior, 10,* 515–528.

Docter, R. F., & Prince, V. (1997). Transvestism: A survey of 1032 cross-dressers. *Archives of Sexual Behavior, 26,* 589–605.

Fedora, O., Reddon, J. R., Morrison, J. W., Fedora, S. K., Pascoe, H., & Yeudall, L. T. (1992). Sadism and other paraphilias in normal controls and aggressive and nonaggressive sexual offenders. *Archives of Sexual Behavior, 21,* 1–15.

LaTorre, R. A. (1980). Devaluation of the human love object: Heterosexual rejection as a possible antecedent to fetishism. *Journal of Abnormal Psychology, 89,* 295–298.

Långström, N., & Zucker, K. J. (2005). Transvestic fetishism in the general population: Prevalence and correlates. *Journal of Sex and Marital Therapy, 31,* 87–95.

Moser, V., & Kleinplatz, P. J. (2002). Transvestic fetishism: Psychopathology or iatrogenic effect? *New Jersey Psychologist, 52*(2), 16–17.

Newcomb, M. D. (1985). The role of perceived relative parent personality in the development of heterosexuals, homosexuals, and transvestites. *Archives of Sexual Behavior, 14,* 147–164.

Ovesey, L., & Person, E. (1973). Gender identity and sexual psychopathology in men: A psychodynamic analysis of homosexuality, transsexualism, and transvestism. *Journal of the American Academy of Psychoanalysis, 1,* 52–72.

Person, E., & Ovesey, L. (1978). Transvestism: New perspectives. *Journal of the American Academy of Psychoanalysis, 6,* 301–323.

Schott, R. L. (1995). The childhood family dynamics of transvestites. *Archives of Sexual Behavior, 24,* 309–327.

Stoller, R. J. (1971). The term, "transvestism." *Archives of General Psychiatry, 24,* 230–237.

Storr, A. (1957). The psychopathology of fetishism and transvestism. *Journal of Analytical Psychology, 2,* 153–166.

Strzyzewsky, J., & Zierhoffer, Z. (1967). Aversion therapy in a case of fetishism with transvestic component. *Journal of Sex Research, 3,* 163–167.

Sullivan, C. B. L., Bradley, S. J., & Zucker, K. J. (1995). Gender identity disorder (transsexualism) and transvestic fetishism. In V. B. Van Hasselt & M. Hersen (Eds.), *Handbook of adolescent psychopathology: A guide to diagnosis and treatment* (pp. 525–558). New York: Lexington Books.

World Health Organization. (1992). *International statistical classification of diseases and related health problems* (10th rev.). Geneva: Author. Available at *www.who.int*

Zucker, K. J., & Blanchard, R. (1997). Transvestic fetishism: Psychopathology and theory. In D. R. Laws & W. T. O'Donohue (Eds.), *Sexual deviance: Theory, assessment, and treatment* (pp. 253–279). New York: Guilford Press.

Zucker, K. J., & Bradley, S. J. (1995). *Gender identity disorder and psychosexual problems in children and adolescents.* New York: Guilford Press.

CHAPTER 17

TRANSVESTIC FETISHISM

Assessment and Treatment

KIRK A. B. NEWRING
JENNIFER WHEELER
CRISSA DRAPER

Recent writings about transvestic fetishism suggest a conceptualization of it not as a variation of sexual behavior, but as a form of coping behavior. It is quite possible that the third edition of this text will not include chapters on transvestic fetishism as a sexual *deviance*, but rather as a sexual *variance*. The *Diagnostic and Statistical Manual of Mental Disorders*, fourth edition, text revision (DSM-IV-TR; American Psychiatric Association, 2000) notes that transvestic fetishism may actually have a calming effect for some affected individuals. Although for some individuals transvestic behavior may indeed be associated with psychological distress, for others the behavior is satisfying and not associated with psychological or other harm. In this way, transvestic fetishism is comparable to the endless number of other behaviors in which humans engage to ameliorate stress—some of which are generally regarded as maladaptive (e.g., alcohol consumption, drug use, self-mutilation, sexual offending), while others are regarded as adaptive (e.g., progressive muscle relaxation, physical exercise, mindfulness skills, meditation). It is from this framework that we approach the assessment and treatment of transvestic fetishism: not as a small sample of human sexual behavior, but as one of the many coping strategies a person might employ. Thus, while the behaviors associated with transvestic fetishism may be statistically unusual (deviant), the lack of harm, lack of dysfunction, and relative acceptance of the behavior indicate that this form of sexual variance may be different from others (e.g., pedophilia). Accordingly, the emphasis in clinical assessment and treatment shifts from establishing whether or not the behavior is "deviant" to evaluating whether it is adaptive or maladaptive for any particular individual.

One of the historical limitations of understanding transvestic fetishism and those who engage in this behavior is the apparent bias inherent in the nature of most research samples. In the previous edition of this chapter, the author noted that "in common with much sexual behavior perceived by contemporary mores as 'abnormal,' it is likely that clinical descriptions have focused only on those individuals with more severe and complex pathology" (Adshead, 1997, p. 281). This criticism holds true today, as studies of transvestic fetishism have typically been either large-sample epidemiological studies assessing the prevalence of the behavior, or single-case studies of persons presenting for clinical treatment (see Wheeler, Newring, & Draper, Chapter 16, this volume). Thus our current knowledge of persons who engage in this behavior is limited to two self-selected samples: those who happen upon and voluntarily complete surveys and admit to the behavior in this format, and those who are so distressed by their own behavior that they seek clinical attention.

Another major limitation with regard to understanding transvestic fetishism and those who engage in it is the long-standing inconsistency in the behavioral criteria used to define it, and to distinguish it from other behaviors with which it sometimes overlaps. Adshead (1997) noted the long history and cultural breadth of transvestic behavior, as well as variability in transvestic behavior, which could include transvestic fetishism. She correctly observed that "assessment is hampered by the lack of information about the etiology and psychopathology of the disorder," and that "early studies of treatment often did not differentiate between transvestic behavior and transvestic fetishism" (p. 281). These caveats still hold, as disagreements remain in the accurate diagnosis of transvestic fetishism. (For further discussion of these issues and controversies related to the diagnosis of transvestic fetishism, please refer to Wheeler et al., Chapter 16, this volume.)

ASSESSMENT

Establishing a Diagnosis

The DSM-IV-TR provides the following diagnostic criteria for transvestic fetishism:

> A. Over a period of at least 6 months, in a heterosexual male, recurrent, intense sexually arousing fantasies, sexual urges, or behaviors involving cross-dressing.
> B. The fantasies, sexual urges, or behaviors cause clinically significant distress or impairment in social, occupational, or other important areas of functioning.
> *Specify* if:
> **With Gender Dysphoria:** if the person has persistent discomfort with the gender role or identity. (p. 575)

The DSM-IV-TR specifies that the disorder is limited to males who dress in female attire. It also notes that in some individuals, sexual arousal is produced by the accompanying thought or image of the person as a female ("autogynephilia"). The authors of the DSM-IV-TR clarify that the women's garments are arousing primarily as symbols of the individual femininity, not as specific fetishes. The manual notes that a favored article may become erotic and may be used in masturbation, and later in intercourse. It further states that the amount of cross-dressing can range from a few items worn privately to a full outfit worn publicly. The DSM-IV-TR states that men meeting criteria for this disorder are typically unremarkably masculine when not cross-dressed, and that they tend to have a predominantly heterosexual orientation with a history of occasional homosexual acts; sexual masochism is observed as a comorbid disorder in some cases. The manual also reports that the disorder usually begins in childhood or early adolescence, and that it is usually kept private until adulthood.

According to the DSM-IV-TR, the transvestic fetishism may serve as "an antidote to anxiety or depression or [contributor] to a sense of peace and calm" (p. 575), as we have noted earlier. For some individuals, gender dysphoria may emerge under situational stress and may eventually lead to a request for sex reassignment surgery. However, the DSM-IV-TR indicates that transvestic fetishism is to be ruled out if the cross-dressing is exclusively a component of gender identity disorder (GID).

It is important to note that the DSM-IV-TR's restriction of the diagnosis to heterosexual males precludes the assignment of this diagnosis to all women, all transgendered people, and all men who cannot be described as heterosexual. However, some recent empirical data do not support the DSM-IV-TR's rather narrow definitional criteria. One of the most recent studies in the area sampled 2,450 Swedes, with 2.8% of males and 0.4% of females indicating that they had engaged in at least one act of transvestic fetishism (Långström & Zucker, 2005). Långström and Zucker (2005) employed World Health Organization criteria, which do not restrict transvestic fetishism "with respect to the gender or sexual orientation of the subject or any requirement of temporal stability" (p. 87). Zucker and Blanchard (1997) discussed the history of and concerns about the changes in DSM diagnostic criteria for transvestism and transvestic fetishism in their chapter in the first edition of this text. Their concerns remain and are echoed in the chapter's revision (Wheeler et al., Chapter 16, this volume) (cf. Bailey, 2003, for more on contraversies in the science of psychology and gender).

Distress or Impairment

The DSM-IV-TR requires the experience of distress or impairment for the assignment of the transvestic fetishism diagnosis. In their 2005 survey, Långström and Zucker excluded this criterion. Thus the DSM-IV-TR appears to have the strictest criteria (distressed or impaired heterosexual males with a 6-month history of symptoms), while Långström and Zucker have employed some of the most lenient criteria (males or females, at least one occurrence, no requirement for distress or impairment). Zucker and Blanchard (1997), discussing the role and contribution of distress and disability in the diagnosis of transvestic fetishism, have noted that not all men who derive sexual pleasure from dressing in women's clothing are distressed. They reiterate early arguments that transvestic fetishism becomes distressing once the behavior becomes socially known (spouse, friends, etc.), or that the distress may be inherent in the conceptualization of transvestic fetishism as an emotion-regulating behavior. Zucker and Blanchard also note that in terms of disability, men engaging in transvestic fetishism may present clinically with relationship problems (e.g., a focus on objects or activities rather than on their partners). However, they also caution that the directionality of such relationship problems is an open empirical question.

O'Donohue, Regev, and Hagstrom (2000) criticized the appropriateness of the inclusion of a distress or disability requirement for the original DSM-IV diagnosis of pedophilia. In their critique, they challenged the need for ego-dystonic sexual attraction to children as requisite for the diagnosis. Such a requirement implied that an individual with ego-syntonic sexual attraction to children could not be diagnosed as pedophilic. They argued against this exclusionary rule, as several (indeed, a majority of) pedophiles may not be distressed by their attraction. Although this problem has been addressed in DSM-IV-TR by inserting "The person has acted on these sexual urges, or . . ." in Criterion B for pedophilia, this critique may still be applicable to several paraphilias, including transvestic fetishism: Just because individuals are not disturbed by their own behavior, this does not categorically exclude it from status as a "disorder." It may behoove future researchers to adopt the approach of Långström and Zucker (2005)—that is, casting a broad net to include those who engage in the behaviors, and then narrowing the scope of the analysis to those who experience distress or disability as a result of transvestic fetishism.

Interestingly, in their 1997 survey, Docter and Prince stated that 45% of the respondents had reported having access to mental health services (compared to 24% in a 1972 survey). They further reported that of those seeking services, 67% had received some benefit, compared to 47% in the earlier survey. Buhrich and Beaumont (1981) reported that 52% of the Americans and 62% of the Australians in their survey of cross-dressers indicated that the frequency of cross-dressing was the same or increased when they were tense, supporting the notion of cross-dressing as having an emotion-regulating facet.

Differential Diagnosis

Another complication in the accurate diagnosis of transvestic fetishism is its topographical similarity to other behaviors, as well as its (apparent) co-occurrence with other psychological phenomena. Specifically, cross-dressing behavior may occur in the context of an identity disturbance, another paraphilia, or both.

Gender Identity Disorder

The DSM-IV-TR precludes the diagnosis of transvestic fetishism in the presence of GID. Adshead (1997) argued that some transvestic fetishists could progress to "full-blown GID and transsexualism" (p. 281). It is likely that a person with GID may concurrently cross-dress, have a fetish, and engage in sexual behavior. Attempting to distinguish these behaviors from one another may lead to more diagnostic confusion than clarity in the assessment of an individual with gender, transvestic, and fetishistic concerns.

Blanchard and Clemmensen (1988) tested the DSM-III-R's implicit assumption that gender dysphoria and fetishistic (transvestic) arousal are mutually exclusive. They concluded that "heterosexual male cross-dresser who report high levels of gender dysphoria tend to report low levels of fetishistic arousal, and vice versa. As we predicted, however, this negative correlation is far from perfect, and heterosexual cross-dressers who simultaneously report gender dysphoria and fetishistic arousal are relatively common" (p. 430). They also noted that some cross-dressers found their fetishistic arousal to be an "unwanted and bothersome by-product of cross-dressing" (p. 431). These men tended to report higher levels of gender dysphoria as well.

Blanchard, Racansky, and Steiner (1986) included phallometric assessment in a comparison of heterosexual male cross-dressers with heterosexual controls. These researchers reported that even though their sample of male cross-dressers denied being aroused to cross-dressing, they tended to demonstrate penile tumescent responses to cross-dressing narratives. Blanchard et al. also provided cautions that are consistent with avoiding the use of arousal data for exclusionary purposes in the differential diagnosis of GID and transvestic fetishism.

In their case study of an adolescent male meeting criteria for GID, Arcelus and Bouman (2000) noted a family history (two maternal uncles) of cross-dressing. Although they were precluded from interviewing the cross-dressing uncles, Arcelus and Bouman suggested a possible link between transvestic fetishism and GID. However, they also noted many other determinants in the genotypic and phenotypic expression of human sexuality (see also Schott, 1995; Wheeler et al., Chapter 16, this volume).

Sexual Masochism

The DSM-IV-TR notes that some men meeting criteria for transvestic fetishism will also meet criteria for sexual masochism. In their sample of Swedish adults, Långström and Zucker (2005) reported that transvestic fetishism was "strongly related to experiences of sexual arousal from using pain, spying on others having sex, and exposing one's genitals to a stranger. Sexual arousal from cross-dressing being acceptable to oneself was the strongest correlate to an actual experience of this practice" (p. 92). Adshead (1997) reviewed several studies connecting sexual masochism and transvestic fetishism, concurring with earlier authors that there "appears to be considerable overlap between sadomasochistic behavior, general fetishism, and transvestic fetishism" (p. 282). For extended discussions of the psychopathology, theory, assessment, and treatment of these paraphilias, please refer to those specific chapters in this volume.

Components of a Comprehensive Assessment

As mentioned earlier, individuals who present for psychotherapy are likely to represent a subpopulation of those individuals who engage in some type of transvestic fetishism. Specifically, this "clinical" sample is likely to represent the most distressed individuals who engage in this behavior, and those for whom the behavior is associated with other problems and/or co-occurring disorders. These clients may seek treatment for family or relationship concerns, conflicts at work, legal problems, subjective distress, or a combination of these issues; the issue of transvestic behavior may be immaterial in regard to such a client's motivation to seek treatment. However, understanding the client's motivation for seeking treatment can inform subsequent assessment approaches, diagnosis, and treatment planning. Any assessment of a paraphilia should be comprehensive—including the assessment of many dimensions of functioning, as well as a variety of assessment methods (e.g., document review, self-report, clinical interview, testing). A comprehensive intake assessment would include the following:

- Demographic information
- Reason for referral
- A thorough history, including these aspects:
  - Family-of-origin and developmental history (including early sexual identity and gender role development)
  - Psychosexual history (erotic interests and sexual behaviors)
  - Educational history
  - Occupational/vocational history
  - Social and relationship history
  - Substance use and treatment history
  - Criminal/legal history (including adjudicated and nonadjudicated offense behaviors)
  - Relevant medical history
  - Mental health diagnosis and treatment history

- Psychological testing and assessments (intelligence, achievement, and personality tests as necessary)
- Physiological assessment (e.g., plethysmography, biofeedback)
- Collateral interviews

We discuss a selection of these components below.

Psychosexual and Developmental History

As with any clinical assessment, the purpose of taking a comprehensive clinical history is to obtain an overview of the client's social learning history, long-standing behavioral patterns and associated outcomes, and a clear perspective of the context in which the presenting problems were developed and maintained. In addition, for clients who present with co-occurring sexual offending or other criminal behavior, taking a thorough history may elicit useful data regarding static and dynamic risk factors for recidivism (see Wheeler, George, & Stephens, 2005, for a review of structured approaches to dynamic risk assessment). These data may be gathered from a variety of sources, including clinical interview, document review, collateral sources, and questionnaires. The clinician need not limit him- or herself to information that is specifically related to transvestic fetishism or sexual behavior; rather, the clinician should attend to clarifying the context in which the client's transvestic fetishism was developed, was reinforced, and continues to be maintained. This includes an understanding of the client's social learning history. Furthermore, it has been our experience that taking a comprehensive history may require several sessions, and the client may provide additional information over the course of therapy. A full intake interview will include a review of the client's sexual identity (male–female) and gender role (masculine–feminine), as well as erotic interests, fantasies, and practices (including sexual orientation).

Although the ultimate focus of treatment planning should be on the client's current behavior and future goals, it is important to understand the client's early developmental and family-of-origin history, given that evidence of cross-sex and cross-gender identity may be present as early as age 2 or 3. This may include the onset of cross-dressing behavior, as well as other expressions of transgender interests (e.g., gravitation toward toys or activities typically associated with the other sex). Furthermore, early social learning patterns may be useful in understanding how this and other behavioral and relationships patterns were initially developed and have been subsequently maintained. In addition, clients may present with a history of intersex conditions that were present at birth (e.g., Kleinfelter syndrome), which have probably influenced their sexual and gender identity development. When assessing a client's developmental history, a clinician should differentiate between the client's sexual identity development (i.e., the subjective sense of being "male" or "female") and gender role development (i.e., conformity to familial or social constrictions for "masculine" or feminine" behavior).

In addition to understanding the client's early sexual identity and gender role development, it is critical for the clinician to have a detailed understanding of the client's erotic interests and sexual behaviors, beginning as early as any such interests or behaviors were evident. Such interests and behaviors would include, but not be limited to, the client's earliest sexual fantasies, nocturnal emissions, masturbatory activities, eroticized cross-dressing or other fetishistic experiences, and any illegal sexual activities (adjudicated or not). As emphasized by Adshead (1997), fantasy often plays an important role in the development and maintenance of transvestic fetishism, so the nature and history of sexual fantasies should be fully assessed in work with this population.

Other Aspects of History

By reviewing other areas in the client's life that are not directly related to sexual behaviors (e.g., educational, occupational/vocational, social/relational, substance use, criminal/legal), the clinician as well as the client may begin to detect behavioral similarities and differences that occur within and across various life domains. For example, cross-dressing activities may be associated with patterns of social or occupational impairment at different times of the client's life, or with increased with substance use or illegal activity. Furthermore, for clients who present with co-occurring sexual offending behavior, these domains are likely to include data relevant to dynamic risk assessment (e.g., lack of intimate relationships, sexually deviant interests, general lifestyle instability, substance abuse/dependence; see Wheeler, George, & Stephens, 2005).

A client's medical history should also be reviewed, because prior medical conditions or injuries may be relevant to the presenting problem(s) and to subsequent treatment. For example, as noted above, a client may have a congenital intersex condition that has affected sexual identity development (e.g., Kleinfelter syndrome); a head injury may have impaired a client's impulse control; or certain medications may have an impact on sexual interest, arousal, or behavior (e.g., selective serotonin reuptake inhibitors [SSRIs], antihypertensive medication).

The client's mental health history (including diagnosis and treatment) should be assessed for several reasons. First, paraphilias have often been noted to be comorbid with other mental disorders (Adshead, 1997). As noted earlier, transvestic fetishism appears to have a connection to distress and distress management, and the DSM-IV-TR notes the possible occurrence of transvestic fetishism as a mechanism to manage anxiety or depression. Mood disorders may be the most likely to be comorbid conditions, given their relative frequency over other mental disorders in the general population (American Psychiatric Association, 2000). Other comorbid Axis I disorders, and comorbid Axis II disorders, should be assessed as well; these may complicate the effective delivery of treatment (i.e., responsivity needs; see Wheeler, George, & Stephens, 2005, for suggestions for assessing responsivity needs in the context of a psychosexual evaluation). Comorbid disorders may also demand treatment before transvestic fetishism can be addressed (e.g., if a client is reporting suicidality, self-harm behaviors, violence, or sexual offense behavior).

Another reason for assessing the client's mental health treatment history is to obtain useful clinical data about the client's responses to previous treatment attempts, including effective and ineffective treatment strategies and the client's history of complying with treatment recommendations. The clinician should determine how long the client has considered the transvestic fetishism a problem, including any variations in severity. The clinician should also attend to formal and informal efforts the client has made to manage this concern. These could include substance use, informal peer support, formal support groups, individual or group counseling, pharmacotherapy, abstinence, pastoral counseling, and any combination of these or other strategies. This will inform the clinician about what has been previously attempted and why, and the outcomes of these earlier efforts.

Finally, we have discussed the importance of GID as a potential differential diagnosis for clients presenting with concerns related to transvestic fetishism. Likewise, we have also presented concerns about the possible presence of sexual masochism or other paraphilias. When assessing a client for the presence of transvestic fetishism, a clinician should attend to this possibility of additional paraphilias, even though these issues may not be of concern to the client.

Psychological Testing

Although there are no specific measures for the assessment of transvestic fetishism, several self-report questionnaires may be clinically useful for the purposes of diagnosis and treatment planning. Specifically, psychological testing may be useful to obtain information about co-occurring Axis I and Axis II disorders; as noted above, these may be relevant to understanding the client's responsivity needs, including possible cognitive limitations. Furthermore, for clients who present with co-occurring sexual offense behavior, psychological testing may be useful for gathering information about the client's dynamic risk needs (see Wheeler, George, & Stephens, 2005, for recommended approaches to assess the dynamic risk and responsivity needs of sexual offenders).

Examples of potentially useful psychological assessments include the following:

- Personality Assessment Inventory (Morey, 1991)
- Minnesota Multiphasic Personality Inventory–2 (MMPI-2; Hathaway & McKinley, 1983)
- Millon Clinical Multiaxial Inventory–III (Millon, 2004)
- Symptom Checklist–90 (Derogatis, 1983)
- Beck Depression Inventory–II (Beck, Steer, & Brown, 1996)

Psychological testing might also include an assessment of the client's intellectual, functional, and cognitive abilities, since assessment and treatment may be limited if the client's ability to recall historical data or verbally process new information is impaired (e.g., by mental retardation, developmental delay, organic injury, etc.). In such cases, there may be other media through which assessment and treatment can occur, though the effectiveness of alternative approaches has not been thoroughly evaluated. Bowler and Collacott (1993) described some of the concerns about working with clients with learning disabilities and transvestic fetishism. More recently, Coleman and Haaven (1998) have described a treatment program for cognitively impaired sexual offenders. Although transvestic fetishism is not synonymous with sexual offending, the treatment approaches described by Coleman and Haaven may provide a starting point for the clinician assisting a client with a developmental disability who experiences transvestic fetishism. Examples of potentially useful intellectual/cognitive assessments are as follows:

- Shipley Institute of Living Scale (Zachary, 1996)
- Wechsler Adult Intelligence Scale–III (Wechsler, 1997)
- Raven's Progressive Matrices (Raven, Court, & Raven, 1976)

Although some general psychological assessments have been used in the context of assessing a client's gender identity (e.g., the MMPI *Mf* scale), this practice is not advised. Rather, clinicians may obtain more valid and reliable information with scales that were specifically developed for this purpose, such as the Bem Sex Role Inventory (Bem, 1974) or the Gender Identity Scale (Freund, Langevin, Sakterberg, & Steiner, 1977; see Adshead, 1997, for a discussion).

Finally, information specific to a client's sexual thoughts, feelings, and behaviors may be obtained from psychological assessments; however, it is important to note that many of these instruments were developed specifically for clients who present with a history of sexual offending and may not be appropriate for clients who do not have a history of acting out sexually against others. Potentially useful instruments include the following:

- Multiphasic Sex Inventory II (MSI II; Nichols & Molinder, 1996)
- Clarke Sex History Questionnaire for Males—Revised (SHQ-R; Langevin & Paitich, 2003)
- Abel and Becker Sexual Interest Card Sort (Holland, Zolondek, Abel, Jordan, & Becker, 2000)

Physiological Assessment

As mentioned earlier, Blanchard and colleagues (1986) included phallometric assessment in a comparison of heterosexual male cross-dressers with heterosexual controls, although they advised against the use of arousal data for exclusionary purposes in the differential diagnosis of GID and transvestic fetishism. However, physiological assessment can inform a clinician about the breadth and reactivity of a client's penile responding to stimuli. For a recent review of sexual measurement and instruments, please refer to Newring, Draper, and O'Donohue (2006).

Interviews with Collateral Sources

With the client's permission, information obtained from persons in the client's external environment can provide valuable information that may not be available from the client's self-report alone. Examples of useful collateral sources include spouses, romantic partners, friends, family members, coworkers, and previous treatment providers.

As will be discussed later in this chapter, whereas some spouses are supportive of their partners' transvestic fetishism, some men perceive their spouses as being openly antagonistic toward the transvestic fetishism. In some cases, the client, spouse, or both may have misperceptions about the expression and perception of transvestic fetishism. Likewise, the client's parents, siblings, aunts, uncles, grandparents, and children may have information (or misinformation) about the client's experience of transvestic fetishism. Adshead (1997) reviewed the controversies related to spouses of men living with transvestic fetishism; she noted that some authors have recommended considering spouses of transvestic fetishists for therapy, or, at a minimum, including them in treatment planning and posttreatment follow-up.

In addition to providing information about the client's experience and perceptions of transvestic fetishism, collateral interviews will allow the clinician to gain insights into the client's aftercare support network. If the client has a limited social support network, enhancing this network would be a legitimate treatment target.

Other Types of Assessments

Functional Assessment

Following an initial intake assessment, and throughout the course of treatment, the clinician may conduct a "functional assessment" of the transvestic behavior. A functional assessment involves reviewing the client's experience of transvestic fetishism for both intended and unintended outcomes, as well as obvious and subtle outcomes. The rationale behind functional assessment is that people do things because they work, or work in similar situations, or worked previously in the same or similar situations. Functional assessment then becomes an analysis of what works for the client. There are experimental methods for functional assessment (sometimes called "functional analysis"; see Iwata, Kahng, Wallace, & Lindberg, 2000, for further discussion), in which the experimenter removes one possible consequence and evaluates the stability of the behavior (e.g., when parents are taught not to give in when a child has a tantrum, does the tantrum eventually cease?). In many situations this is not possible, as from the therapy room a clinician may not be able to directly influence the contingencies at play in a client's life. Our experience is that clients can be of assistance in this endeavor, because they are often aware of the outcomes of their behavior, though they often lack insight into alternatives.

It is important for the client and clinician to be oriented toward this perspective. While a detailed historical analysis may yield long-standing patterns of misandry, coupled with poor modeling, enabling, and/or strained attachments, there is often something in the current environment that evokes and maintains the client's transvestic fetishism. Some common motivations are escape and avoidance of unpleasant affect, attempts at expressing emotion, and sexual gratification. For a lengthier discussion of the theory and research on the etiology of transvestic fetishism, please refer to the companion chapter (Wheeler et al., Chapter 16, this volume).

In some cases, clients engage in similar behaviors; however, the motivations behind them can be quite different, and functional analysis can help to clarify these differences. Some clients may engage in transvestic fetishism to "let off steam," to self-soothe, to enhance sexual gratification, or a combination of these and perhaps other motivators. Although the topography of transvestic fetishism may be identical from case to case, the function of each instance can be quite different, both within and across individuals.

It will be helpful to orient clients toward this form of analysis, as they may see other areas of their lives where their needs are being unmet because of difficulties similar to those expressed in relation to their transvestic fetishism. The clients may be struggling with issues such as peer rejection, intimacy, or sexual identity issues, to name a few. By assessing the function of their coping strategies, the clients may identify the needs that they are attempting to meet.

At the same time clinicians explore the problem issues, they will begin to ask the clients to do things differently. The clients will be swimming in uncharted waters, without their usual safety nets (for some, fishnets!). When clinicians ask clients to abandon their defenses, the clients experience a sense of vulnerability that is often accompanied by flight, threats, fear, or many other forms of angst-laden acting out. Struggles are to be expected for both clients and clinicians, and it is important for both to have the requisite and helpful support through this process.

Risk Assessment, Legal Issues, Dangerousness

Although nonsexualized cross-dressing is not a loading item on the more popular actuarial measures for the prediction of sexually violent reoffense per se, assessment of transvestic fetishism may be relevant in such assessments. Adshead (1997), among others, has described the "typical" transvestic fetishist as a relatively mild older man who enjoys dressing up on the weekends, with no intent or history of harming others. However, she added that in cases of serial sexual homicide, several authors have noted a history of transvestic fetishism in these offenders. In such cases, the transvestic fetishism is likely to be only one spoke in the broad paraphilic wheel of these offenders. In fact, in a recent meta-analysis of risk factors for sexual recidivism, the presence of any paraphilic interest or behavior—including cross-dressing behavior—was a significant predictor of sexual reoffense risk among detected sexual offenders (Hanson & Morton-Bourgon, 2004). Thus, for those transvestic fetishistic clients who present with co-occurring sexual offense behavior, an assessment of sexual recidivism risk may be indicated (for a review of structured approaches to assess dynamic risk in the context of delivering sexual offender treatment, see Wheeler, George, & Stephens, 2005).

Transvestic fetishism may be associated with "dangerousness" when it occurs in the context of other potentially dangerous sexual practices, such as autoerotic asphyxia, bondage, object insertion, and perhaps some other aspects of masochistic sexual practices. Adshead (1997) noted that in several cases of fatal autoerotic asphyxia, the decedents were cross-dressed at the time of their death. Adshead concluded:

> These findings suggest that assessment of any transvestic fetishist should include questions about sadomasochistic practices, autoerotic asphyxiation practices, and rape fantasies. Clearly, clinicians must do this sensitively, and it raises issues of confidentiality in the nonoffender subject. Suspicion should be heightened if the patient is young, exhibits other paraphilias, or has a record of violence to others, even if nonsexual. Such variations are more likely to be found in more disordered individuals (such as those with personality disorders or substance abuse), or those who exhibit other risk factors for criminal behavior, such as previous criminal convictions. (pp. 287–288)

TREATMENT

As discussed previously, clients who are not distressed by their own behavior—or for whom the behavior is not affecting other domains of their lives—are unlikely to seek treatment. There are rarely legal mandates for treatments related to this specific disorder, although clients may be participating in mandated treatment for another behavioral disorder (e.g., sexual offending) when the presence of co-occurring transvestic fetishism is first detected. However, even in such samples (e.g., prison- or community-based treatment groups), transvestic fetishism itself is rarely the focus of empirical research. Thus our knowledge of treatment effectiveness and efficacy is limited to the available case reports of individuals who are distressed to the point of seeking therapy. For those who do present at a clinician's office, our experience has been that the motivation for treatment has varied with the individual.

Psychotherapeutic Approaches

The psychotherapeutic strategies adopted by the clinician are determined by the clinician's conceptualization of the client's experience of transvestic fetishism. Some clients present with distress related to being "caught"; others have concerns about how to explain their history to, or integrate their behavior into a relationship with, a new partner; still others wish to "stop" or "quit." If the presenting problem is focused on the client's desire to eliminate or reduce the frequency or expression of transvestic fetishism, an approach based on relapse prevention may be ideal (see Brunswig, Penix, & O'Donohue, 2002; Brunswig, Sbraga, & Harris, 2003; O'Donohue, Brunswig, & Sbraga; 2005; see also Laws, 1989; Laws, Hudson, & Ward, 2000; Marlatt & Donovan, 2005). Other possible avenues of treatment that may be applicable are harm reduction (Laws, 1996, 1999) and the "good lives" approach (Marshall, 2005; Marshall et al., 2005).

Harm reduction recognizes the likely recurrence of the undesired target behavior and directs intervention toward reducing the frequency, severity, and adverse impact of the targeted behavior, should it occur. The good lives approach, consistent with the original relapse prevention model (which emphasized increasing lifestyle balance and adaptive functioning), focuses on increasing the frequency, saliency, and positive impact of healthy and approach-goal-oriented behavior. In this sense, clients are directed to focus on doing what they value (e.g., enhancing adult relationships, practicing distress tolerance skills), rather than on avoiding prohibited behaviors (not going to lingerie shops, not going to the shopping mall when distressed, etc.).

If clients present with concerns about their *distress* related to transvestic practices, an acceptance-based approach such as acceptance and commitment therapy (ACT; Hayes, Strosahl, & Wilson, 2003) can be used to clarify their values, and to help them work toward acceptance of their distress in aspiring to their valued lives. Earlier, we have discussed the role of positive and negative reinforcement in the establishment and maintenance of sexualized coping (Wheeler et al., Chapter 16, this volume; see also Sbraga & Brunswig, 2003). In an ACT conceptualization, the transvestic fetishistic behavior is seen as functionally similar to the use of a substance not for the "high" it yields, but for the reduction in suffering fostered by the behavior. The first cup of coffee in the morning might be analogous; it is often consumed not for the flavor, but rather for the alleviation of withdrawal symptoms (headaches, edginess, etc.). In the ACT conceptualization, sexualized cross-dressing may alleviate distress and provide some sense of solace and comfort in an otherwise unpleasant day. An ACT approach fosters a client's ability to live with the distress without engaging in the ameliorating (and unwanted) response. The goal is not necessarily to reduce the frequency of transvestic fetishism, although such a reduction may be a consequence of living *with* the distress, rather than living *in response to* the distress.

The DSM-IV-TR has emphasized the role of transvestic fetishism in the management of emotions. Linehan's dialectical behavior therapy (DBT; Linehan, 1993a, 1993b) includes an emphasis on emotion regulation as a pillar of treatment. Although DBT was initially developed for the treatment of parasuicidal individuals, the approach has been extended to include treatment for people meeting criteria for borderline personality disorder, those experiencing interpersonal chaos and emotional dysregulation, or both. Since its initial development, DBT has been increasingly applied to various behavioral and personality disorders and in a variety of clinical and forensic settings (e.g., Marra, 2005). The application of DBT to target specific thoughts, feelings, and behaviors associated with sexual offending has been suggested (e.g., Wheeler, George, & Stoner, 2005).

Like ACT, DBT concerns itself with a client's emotional distress and the client's reactions and responses to that distress. Whereas ACT assists the client in breaking the bond between distress and maladaptive coping, DBT places an emphasis on increased awareness of the ties between distress and behavior (mindfulness) and developing more adaptive responses to that distress. Specifically, DBT aims to assist the client in generating skillful cognitive, emotional, and behavioral responses in the moment of experiencing distress. Thus a successful outcome in DBT may be a client's demonstrating increased awareness of emotional vulnerabilities in general and the internal and external environmental precursors to sexualized cross-dressing in particular, and also demonstrating an ability to identify and implement an adaptive alternative coping strategy in response to distress.

We also recommend that the clinician consider functional analytic psychotherapy (FAP; Kohlenberg & Tsai, 1991). FAP had its beginnings in the treatment of a person who was using sexualized coping in an effort to manage aspects of his world. FAP often focuses on the interpersonal nature of a client's life, and makes use of the therapeutic context to address the client's interpersonal strengths and weaknesses. If the client's experience of transvestic fetishism appears rooted in interpersonal deficits, conflicts, or struggles, a FAP-based approach may prove useful.

FAP, much like DBT, is intensely interpersonal. FAP uses the therapeutic relationship as the context in which meaningful consequences are contingently delivered in the service of shaping valued behaviors. For a client with a diagnosis of transvestic fetishism, a FAP therapist would look to issues that motivate the client to engage in sexualized cross-dressing, and then attempt to occasion similar situations in the therapy room. Once the client is in contact with that distressing motivator, the FAP therapist would assist in shaping an alternative interpersonal response that would be consistent with the client's values and be generalizable to the client's larger world.

Self-Help and Support Societies

Although there are no self-help books specifically for transvestic fetishism, there are books that may be useful for clients seeking bibliotherapy. The client's and clinician's conceptualization of the "problem" (e.g., sexualized cross-dressing, guilt, distress, relationship difficulties, etc.) would influence the nature and use of bibliotherapy. Hayes (2005) describes a self-directed approach consistent with the ACT approach described above. With each of these books, it is essential to emphasis the client's values and the function of the behavior (e.g., how it works) over its form (e.g., what it looks like—sexual addiction vs. transvestic fetishism). Recently, Sbraga and O'Donohue (2004) published a data-driven book designed as a self-help book for problems of sexual self-control. Although this text gives examples such as excessive pornography use, the functional elements are applicable for a client with problems related to maladaptive sexualized coping. We also recommend the client consider a book on mindfulness. As discussed above, through training in mindfulness, the client may come into contact with a better understanding of the motivations of their behaviors, without feeling the same pull to engage in them.

The largest support group for cross-dressers and their families has been of assistance to researchers in enhancing the knowledge base of cross-dressing. This group, the Society for the Second Self (Tri-Ess), is not a support group for transvestic fetishists per se; it is a support group for people who cross-dress, as well as their families.

> is an international, nonprofit, volunteer organization that provides accurate informational and educational resources about Crossdressing and Crossdressers for the purpose of promoting understanding, acceptance, tolerance and a constructive public and self-image. The Society seeks to identify and meet the needs of both the Crossdresser, most often a heterosexual male, and 'her' wife or other female partner in a committed relationship with the Crossdresser. Our informational and support activities extend to the parents, children,

other family members and friends of the Crossdresser. The Society has a long history of working with other transgender community support organizations toward common goals.

Tri-Ess focuses on the classical, garden-variety crossdresser. While some cross-dressers exhibit a fetishistic component early on, and discussion of sexual issues is certainly appropriate in Tri-Ess, our Society is not the place for fetishistic exhibitionism, fantasy dressing, etc. We are more oriented toward expressing and developing our crossgender potentials, integrating them into our whole personalities, and building marriage and family relationships in the context of crossdressing . . . (J. E. Fairfax, personal communication, August 21, 2006)

Contact information for Tri-Ess is as follows:

Tri-Ess
P.O. Box 980638
Houston, TX 77098-0638
Phone: 713-349-8969
E-mail: *triessinfo@aol.com*
Website: *www.tri-ess.org*

Effective Therapist-Based Treatments

Currently, there are no controlled outcome studies for the treatment of transvestic fetishism. While there are several case reports in the literature, the data are few and far between. We have already discussed psychotherapeutic approaches that may be efficacious, and we recommend that clinicians take data regularly and compile their data with those of others working in this area.

Pharmacological Treatments

Adshead (1997) reviewed the sparse data, often limited to case studies, regarding the pharmacological treatment of transvestic fetishism; current studies in this area are summarized in Table 17.1. Anxiolytics and SSRIs appear to be the most frequently described medications in published case reports. Note that in most of these studies transvestic fetishism was not the only presenting problem (Brantley & Wise, 1985; Clayton, 1993; Jorgenson, 1990). Instead, in most of these studies it was reported as co-occurring with other psychological or behavioral problems, such as a mood disturbance (Massand, 1993; Ward, 1975), an anxiety disorder (Federoff, 1988; Fishbain, 1989), or other problematic sexual thoughts or behaviors (Federoff, 1992; Kruesi, Fine, Valladares, Phillips, & Rapaport, 1992; Lorefice, 1991; Riley, 2002). These limited data suggest that certain pharmacological interventions (antiandrogen therapy, fluoxetine, and buspirone) may be effective at reducing unwanted sexual thoughts, urges, and behaviors. However, due to the methodological limitations of these designs, it is difficult to extrapolate what impact (if any) these interventions had on the specific behavior of transvestic fetishism.

If we approach transvestic fetishism via a therapeutic model in which the behavior is considered problematic only when it is associated with adverse consequences (i.e., transvestic fetishism disorder [TVFD]; see Wheeler et al., Chapter 16, this volume), then pharmacological interventions may be well suited to address the problems accompanying TVFD. For example, anxiolytics and antidepressants may be effective at targeting anxiety

TABLE 17.1. Studies of the Pharmacological Treatment of Transvestic Fetishism

Authors (year)	Substance	Presenting problem	Conclusion(s)
Riley (2002)	Selegiline	Transvestic fetishism secondary to initiation of selegiline treatment; sexual advances toward housekeepers	Transvestic fetishism ceased with cessation of selegiline therapy.
Clayton (1993)	Clomipramine	Transvestic fetishism	Transvestic and fetishist behavior ceased with clomipramine use.
Massand (1993)	Fluoxetine	Sexual masochism and transvestic fetishism associated with depression	Ego-dystonic compulsive urges were resolved or reduced. In both cases, symptoms returned during drug holidays, and remitted when fluoxetine was restarted.
Federoff (1992)	Buspirone	Transvestic fetishism with atypical paraphilia (fantasies involving the client "breaking his sister's neck, arms, and legs")	Prescription may have helped reduced frequency of fantasy, but due to case study design and placebo effects, impact on transvestism is unclear.
Kruesi, Fine, Valladares, Phillips, and Rapaport (1992)	Clomipramine, desipramine	Paraphilias	Both drugs helped reduce paraphilic behavior compared to baseline and placebo, but the two drugs did not create effects statistically different from each other.
Lorefice (1991)	Fluoxetine	Fetish	Successfully decreased interest in fetishistic behavior
Fishbain (1989)	Alprazolam	Response to Federoff (below)	Alprazolam might have been effective if maintained at therapeutic levels.
Fedoroff (1988)	Buspirone	Transvestic fetishism and generalized anxiety disorder	Buspirone, and not alprazolam, led to a reduction in frequency of cross-dressing.
Brantley and Wise (1985)	Antiandrogen therapy	Transvestic fetishism	Successfully decreased interest in deviant behavior.
Ward (1975)	Lithium	Transvestism with manic–depression	Lithium proved useful in treating transvestic symptoms.

and depression associated with TVFD, while not necessarily reducing the frequency of the transvestic behavior. Implicit in this approach is an understanding of the relationship between mood (or other) disorders and transvestic behavior. From the prescriber perspective, if the client is neither depressed nor anxious, the motivation for engaging in transvestic behavior should be controlled. In this way, medications may prove more effective for treating TVFD than for eliminating or reducing the occurrence of cross-dressing behavior. However, this approach can also take advantage of libidinal reduction as a side effect of SSRIs that may decrease sexual thoughts or behaviors in general. Although this rationale has not been explicitly explored in a large trial, the available case studies provide some support for an overall benefit of some pharmacological treatments for ameliorating distress associated with transvestic behavior. Furthermore, there are few data describing the benefits and limitations of combining or integrating therapeutic approaches (e.g., cognitive-behavioral therapy and pharmacotherapy). Again, we encourage clinicians working in this area to collect data, collaborate with colleagues, and publish findings on their treatment approaches, successes, and failures with clients presenting with concerns in this domain.

General Treatment Issues

We recommend that a clinician work collaboratively with a client to generate a workable case conceptualization as a basis for intervention. Several areas of concern may have an impact on this collaborative approach. First, if third-party payment is involved, the relationship between a client's transvestic fetishism and "billable" disorder will need to be clarified, as far as possible, at the outset of therapy. Second, a client might not want to abandon the transvestic behavior, so an abstinence model may not be an achievable goal. Third, a review of empirically supported treatments will not reveal a manualized treatment for transvestic fetishism. This leaves the clinician with a theoretical base, coupled with the relevant literature in the area, for ethical and appropriate work with the client. As we have discussed earlier, the current trend in the treatment of human sexual misbehavior involves an analysis of the development and maintenance of aberrant human sexual expression as based in both positive and negative reinforcement. We have discussed how the third-wave behavior therapies (ACT, DBT, and FAP) can be used for a client presenting with concerns about the experience of transvestic fetishism; we recommend that clinicians consider adopting these approaches when working with these clients. Furthermore, as there have been reported treatment successes with the use of anxiolytic and antidepressant medications, clinicians may consider such approaches for clients for whom a pharmacological intervention may be useful (e.g., those with comorbid depression).

Spouses/Partners

Adshead (1997) and others have discussed the challenges faced by the spouses and romantic partners of transvestic fetishists. Consistent in these discussions are the challenges these partners face, and the psychopathology that they may add to their dyads or families. The data in this area are limited and occasionally speculative. However, Docter and Prince (1997) included spousal surveys as part of their larger study. They concluded that the "wives of transvestites have complained that the solitary sexual satisfaction of a cross-dresser husband can often be detrimental to marital sexual fulfillment" (p. 603). They reported that 19% of the wives were described by their husbands as "completely antagonistic" to their husbands' cross-dressing, whereas 28% were described as being completely accepting. Doctor and Prince noted that, similar to their early survey, 83% of the partners were aware of their husbands' cross-dressing, but only one-third had been informed of the cross-dressing prior to marriage. For clinicians working with clients with transvestic fetishism, we recommend directing clinical attention toward the clients' experience of their partners' support, and an exploration of the need for conjoint or family therapy.

SUMMARY AND FUTURE DIRECTIONS

Before we can treat "it," we need to know what "it" is, or whether "it" is worth a diagnostic label. The current diagnostic manuals are inconsistent in regard to transvestic fetishism, and researchers are free to deviate from those criteria. Consistent with our concerns discussed in the companion chapter (Wheeler et al., Chapter 16, this volume), we recommend that research energies be directed toward clarification of, and greater consistency in, the definition and diagnosis of transvestic fetishism. From this, we can then begin more extensive research on the prevalence and nature of the experience of the "disorder" for those clients meeting criteria for a diagnosis. We would recommend that such a definition extend beyond heterosexual males and remove the distress requirement. We would then be able to learn more about those who do and do not experience distress related to their transvestic fetishism. This research could be directed toward the variables that led to the development and maintenance of the client's presentation of the "disorder." Other research priorities include a greater understanding of what leads some to seek therapy while others do not, with the next step being further analysis of their therapeutic experiences.

REFERENCES

Adshead, G. (1997). Transvestic fetishism: Assessment and treatment. In D. R. Laws & W. T. O'Donohue (Eds.), *Sexual deviance: Theory, assessment, and treatment* (pp. 253–279). New York: Guilford Press.

American Psychiatric Association. (2000). *Diagnostic and statistical manual of mental disorders* (4th ed., text rev.). Washington, DC: Author.

Arcelus, J., & Bouman, W. P. (2000). Gender identity disorder in a child with a family history of cross-dressing. *Sexual and Relationship Therapy, 15*(4), 407–411.

Bailey, J. M. (2003). *The man who would be queen: The science and psychology of gender bending and transsexualism.* New York: Joseph Henry Press.

Beck, A. T., Steer, R. A., & Brown, G. K. (1996). *Beck Depression Inventory–II (BDI-II) manual.* San Antonio, TX: Psychological Corporation.

Bem, S. (1974). The measurement of psychological androgyny. *Journal of Consulting and Clinical Psychology, 42*, 155–162.

Blanchard, R., & Clemmensen, L. H. (1988). A test of the DSM-III-R's implicit assumption that fetishistic arousal and gender dysphoria are mutually exclusive. *Journal of Sex Research, 25*(3), 426–432.

Blanchard, R., Racansky, I. G., & Steiner, B. W. (1986). Phallometric detection of fetishistic arousal in heterosexual male cross-dressers. *Journal of Sex Research, 22*, 452–462.

Bowler, C. C., & Collacott, R. A. (1993). Cross-dressing in men with learning disabilities. *British Journal of Psychiatry, 162,* 556–558.

Brantley, J. T., & Wise, T. N. (1985). Antiandrogenic treatment of a gender-dysphoric transvestite. *Journal of Sex and Marital Therapy, 11*(2), 109–112.

Brunswig, K. A., Penix, T. M., & O'Donohue, W. (2002). Relapse prevention. In M. Hersen & W. Sledge (Eds.), *Encyclopedia of psychotherapy* (pp. 499–505). New York: Academic Press.

Brunswig, K. A., Sbraga, T. P., & Harris, C. D. (2003). Relapse prevention. In W. O'Donohue, J. E. Fisher, & S. C. Hayes (Eds.), *Cognitive behavior therapy: Applying empirically supported techniques in your practice* (pp. 321–329). New York: Wiley.

Buhrich, N., & Beaumont, T. (1981). Comparison of transvestism in Australia and America. *Archives of Sexual Behavior, 26,* 589–605.

Clayton, A. H. (1993). Fetishism and clomipramine. *American Journal of Psychiatry, 150*(4), 673–674.

Coleman, E., & Haaven, J. (1998). Adult intellectually disabled sexual offenders: Program considerations. In W. L. Marshall, Y. M. Fernandez, S. M. Hudson, & T. Ward (Eds.), *Sourcebook of treatment programs for sexual offenders* (pp. 273–285). New York: Plenum Press.

Derogatis, L. R. (1983). *SCL-90R: Administration, scoring, and procedures manual* (2nd ed.). New York: Clinical Psychometric Research.

Docter, R. F., & Prince, V. (1997). Transvestism: A survey of 1032 cross-dressers. *Archives of Sexual Behavior, 26,* 589–605.

Federoff, J. P. (1988). Buspirone hydrochloride in the treatment of transvestic fetishism. *Journal of Clinical Psychiatry, 49*(10), 408–409.

Federoff, J. P. (1992). Buspirone Hydrochloride in the treatment of an atypical paraphilia. *Archives of Sexual Behavior, 21*(4), 401–406.

Fishbain, D. A. (1989). Buspirone and transvestic fetishism. *Journal of Clinical Psychiatry, 50*(11), 436–437.

Freund, K., Langevin, R., Sakterberg, J., & Steiner, B. (1977). Extension of the Gender Identity Scale for males. *Archives of Sexual Behavior, 6,* 507–519.

Hanson, R. K., & Morton-Bourgon, K. (2004). *Predictors of sexual recidivism: An updated meta-analysis* (User Report No. 2004-02). Ottawa: Department of the Solicitor General of Canada.

Hathaway, S. R., & McKinley, J. C. (1983). *The Minnesota Multiphasic Personality Inventory manual.* New York: Psychological Corporation.

Hayes, S. (2005). *Get out of your mind and into your life: The new acceptance and commitment therapy.* Oakland, CA: New Harbinger.

Hayes, S., Strosahl, K. D., & Wilson, K. G. (2003). *Acceptance and commitment therapy: An experiential approach to behavior change.* New York: Guilford Press.

Holland, L. A., Zolondek, S. C., Abel, G. G., Jordan, A. D., & Becker, V. B. (2000). Psychometric analysis of the Sexual Interest Card Sort questionnaire. *Sexual Abuse: A Journal of Research and Treatment, 12*(2), 107–122.

Iwata, B. A., Kahng, S. W., Wallace, M. D., & Lindberg, J. S. (2000). The functional analysis model of behavioral assessment. In J. Austin & J. E. Carr (Eds.), *Handbook of applied behavior analysis* (pp. 61–90). Reno, NV: Context Press.

Jorgenson, V. T. (1990). Cross-dressing successfully treated with fluoxetine. *New York State Journal of Medicine, 90*(11), 566–567.

Kohlenberg, R. J., & Tsai, M. (1991). *Functional analytic psychotherapy: Creating intense and curative therapeutic relationships.* New York: Plenum Press.

Kruesi, M. J., Fine, S., Valladares, L., Phillips, & Rapaport. (1992). Paraphilias: A double-blind crossover comparison of clomipramine versus desipramine. *Archives of Sexual Behavior, 21*(6), 587–593.

Langevin, R., & Paitich, D. (2003). *Clarke Sex History Questionnaire for Males—Revised.* North Tonawanda, NY: Multi-Health Systems.

Långström, N., & Zucker, K. J. (2005). Transvestic fetishism in the general population: Prevalence and correlates. *Journal of Sex and Marital Therapy, 31*, 87–95.

Laws, D. R. (Ed.). (1989). *Relapse prevention with sex offenders.* New York: Guilford Press.

Laws, D. R. (1996). Relapse prevention or harm reduction? *Sexual Abuse: Journal of Research and Treatment, 8*(3), 243–247.

Laws, D. R. (1999). Relapse prevention: The state of the art. *Journal of Interpersonal Violence, 14*(3), 285–302.

Laws, D. R., Hudson, S. M., & Ward, T. (Eds.). (2000). *Remaking relapse prevention with sex offenders: A sourcebook.* Thousand Oaks, CA: Sage.

Linehan, M. M. (1993a). *Cognitive-behavioral treatment of borderline personality disorder.* New York: Guilford Press.

Linehan, M. M. (1993b). *Skills training manual for treating borderline personality disorder.* New York: Guilford Press.

Lorefice, L. S. (1991) Fluoxetine treatment of a fetish. *Journal of Clinical Psychiatry, 52*(1), 41.

Mann, R. E., Webster, S. D., Schofield, C., & Marshall, W. L. (2004). Approach versus avoidance goals in relapse prevention with sexual offenders. *Sexual Abuse: A Journal of Research and Treatment, 16*, 65–75.

Marlatt, G. A., & Donovan, D. M. (Eds.). (2005). *Relapse prevention* (2nd ed.). New York: Guilford Press.

Marra, T. (2005). *Dialectical behavior therapy in private practice.* Oakland, CA: New Harbinger.

Marshall, W. L. (2005). Therapist style in sexual offender treatment: Influence on indices of change. *Sexual Abuse: A Journal of Research and Treatment, 17*(2), 109–116.

Marshall, W. L., Ward, T., Mann, R. E., Moulden, H., Fernandez, Y. M., Serran, G., et al. (2005). Working positively with sexual offenders. *Journal of Interpersonal Violence, 20*(9), 1096–1114.

Massand, P. S. (1993). Successful treatment of sexual masochism and transvestic fetishism associated with depression with fluoxetine hydrochloride. *Depression, 1*(1), 50–52.

Millon, T. (2004). *Millon Clinical Multiaxial Inventory–III.* Bloomington, MN: NCS/Pearson Assessments.

Morey, L. C. (1991). *Personality Assessment Inventory.* Point Huron, MI: Sigma.

Newring, K. A. B., Draper, C., & O'Donohue, W. (2006). Sexual Instrumentation. In J. G. Webster (Ed.), *Encyclopedia of medical devices and instrumentation* (2nd ed., Vol. 6, pp. 149–163). Hoboken, NJ: Wiley.

Nichols, H. R., & Molinder, I. (1996). *Multiphasic Sex Inventory II manual.* Fircrest, WA: Nichols & Molinder Assessments.

O'Donohue, W., Brunswig, K. A., & Sbraga, T. P. (2005). Relapse prevention. In M. Hersen & J. Rosqvist (Eds.), *Encyclopedia of behavior modification and cognitive behavior therapy: Vol. I. Adult clinical applications* (pp. 476–483). Thousand Oaks, CA: Sage.

O'Donohue, W., Regev, L. G., & Hagstrom, A. (2000). Problems with the DSM-IV diagnosis of pedophilia. *Sexual Abuse: A Journal of Research and Treatment, 12*(2), 95–105.

Raven, J. C., Court, J. H., & Raven, J. (1976). *Manual for Raven's Progressive Matrices.* London: H. K. Lewis.

Riley, D. E. (2002). Reversible transvestic fetishism in a man with Parkinson's disease treated with selegiline. *Clinical Neuropharmacology, 25*(4), 234–237.

Sbraga, T. P., & Brunswig, K. A. (2003). *The functions of sexual coping responses: Taxonomic, research and treatment implications.* Paper presented at the 29th Annual Meeting of the Association for Behavior Analysis, San Francisco.

Sbraga, T. P., & O'Donohue, W. T. (2004). *The sex addiction workbook: Proven strategies to help you regain control of your life.* Oakland, CA: New Harbinger.

Schott, R. L. (1995). The childhood family dynamics of transvestites. *Archives of Sexual Behavior, 24*, 309–327.

Ward, N. (1975). Successful lithium treatment of transvestism associated with manic–depression. *Journal of Nervous and Mental Disease, 161*(3), 204–206.

Wechsler, D. (1997). *Wechsler Adult Intelligence Scale—Third Edition*. San Antonio, TX: Psychological Corporation.

Wheeler, J. G., George, W. H., & Stephens, K. (2005). Assessment of sexual offenders: A model for integrating dynamic risk assessment and relapse prevention approaches. In D. M. Donovan & G. A. Marlatt (Eds.), *Assessment of addictive behaviors* (2nd ed., pp. 392–424). New York: Guilford Press.

Wheeler, J. G., George, W. H., & Stoner, S. A. (2005). Enhancing the relapse prevention model for sex offenders: Adding recidivism risk reduction therapy (3RT) to target offenders' dynamic risk needs. In G. A. Marlatt & D. M. Donovan (Eds.), *Relapse prevention* (2nd ed., pp. 333–362). New York: Guilford Press.

Zachary, R. A. (1996). *Shipley Institute of Living Scale: Revised manual*. Los Angeles: Western Psychological Services.

Zucker, K. J., & Blanchard, R. (1997). Transvestic fetishism: Psychopathology and theory. In D. R. Laws & W. T. O'Donohue (Eds.), *Sexual deviance: Theory, assessment, and treatment* (pp. 253–279). New York: Guilford Press.

CHAPTER 18

VOYEURISM

Psychopathology and Theory

MICHAEL LAVIN

HISTORICAL ILLUSTRATION

The Bible (2 Samuel 11–12) tells the story of King David's peeping and its consequences. While David's army waged war on the Ammonites, David remained in Jerusalem. One afternoon, he left the comfort of his couch to amble up to his house's roof. From there, he spotted Bathsheba bathing. He did not avert his eyes; instead, he feasted them on her naked beauty, and this led him to inquire after her. He learned her to be the wife of Uriah, one of his deployed soldiers. David's desire for Bathsheba led him to have her fetched to him by his servants. He had sex with her. Their union resulted in a child, who was stillborn. To continue to enjoy Bathsheba without Uriah's interference, David ordered Uriah to be placed in the thick of fighting, and then to be abandoned to die. David's order doomed Uriah. He died alone, in close combat, as David desired.

David's misdeeds did not escape notice. They drew the attention of the prophet Nathan, who rebuked David. Stung by Nathan's rebuke, David acknowledged that he had sinned against God, but in a grotesque and numbing display of bogus piety, he made no mention of having wronged either Uriah or Bathsheba.

The stark realism of the narrative in 2 Samuel does not indicate any approval of, or optimism about the results of, the sexual hygiene of David's court. Although Bathsheba eventually gave birth to Solomon, David's other children fared less well in life than Solomon. David's daughter, Tamar, was raped by her brother Amnon. One of Tamar's other brothers, Absalom, avenged her by killing Amnon. Absalom himself came to a fatal end by hanging when a collision with a tree's limb knocked him from his mule. Sexually suspect behavior continued in David during his senescence. When David lost his vigor (1 Kings 1), his servants sought to warm him by getting a pretty girl to sleep with him, though David was by then too debilitated by age to have intercourse with her.

The remorseless Biblical narrative of David's peeping and his debauched family life perhaps comes as no surprise to therapists working with men who have committed sexual offenses. The family dynamics of these men are often chaotic. In particular, sexually deviant behaviors tend to cluster, so a man who has exhibited one such behavior is at increased risk of exhibiting others. The children of sexual deviants, or so common clinical lore has it, are also at greater risk of turning out poorly than children born into luckier circumstances.

Furthermore, the story of David identifies clinical difficulties in the assessment of voyeurism that are built into the *Diagnostic and Statistical Manual of Mental Disorders*, fourth edition, text revision (DSM-IV-TR; American Psychiatric Association, 2000) criteria for diagnosing voyeurism. It is important to keep in mind that DSM-IV-TR voyeurism may or may not capture what is ordinarily thought of as voyeurism or defined as such in alternative diagnostic systems, including DSMs both past and future. One feature of the DSM diagnostic system is that it requires inferences and information that make it impossible to diagnose voyeurism—or, just as telling, to distinguish the average peeper from the individual described in an arrest report or from King David in the Biblical narrative.

AGE OF ONSET AND COURSE

The authors of the DSM-IV-TR section on voyeurism assert that peeping usually begins prior to the age of 15; however, peeping itself, by DSM's own account, is insufficient to establish a diagnosis of voyeurism. Moreover, the DSM account of the onset of voyeuristic behavior is at odds with the work of Abel and Rouleau (1990). Abel and Rouleau studied a sample that was not random, but drawn from teenage offenders; they found that only 50% of this sample had an interest in peeping prior to the age of 15.

DSM-IV-TR also declares that the course of voyeurism tends to be chronic and lifelong. It is difficult to know what to make of this unconfirmed hypothesis. After all, it is part of human sexuality that the intensity of sexual desire waxes and wanes, and that sexual desire erodes as human beings age. Consequently, clinicians should at least remain open to the possibility that for some people voyeurism may be a stage in their sexual development that has passed. For other individuals, it may well be a point of fixation. At present, too little is known about the natural history of voyeurism to permit any confident pronouncements about it.

EPIDEMIOLOGY

The epidemiology of DSM voyeurism is uncharted. And if DSM voyeurism is a mystery, a fortiori, so are alternative conceptualizations of voyeurism. At least two features of voyeurism make its epidemiology mysterious. In the first place, perversions typically lack a phenomenology that includes their being distressful to the pervert. Other persons are the ones who find the pervert's behavior repellent. So there is not a distressing symptom that is likely to drive a pervert to seek professional help in the way that there is for a disorder like gout. Indeed, the social facts favor keeping perversions a personal secret. A second circumstances makes it hard to calculate the prevalence of voyeurism: Proxy variables are not promising. Even when individuals are charged with or convicted of peeping, arrest records, for example, are unsuitable for generating proxy figures for estimating the prevalence of voyeurism.

Nathan's charges against King David no more establish that King David was a voyeur than a modern arrest of a peeper does. There is no requirement for convicting a peeper that he does it habitually, let alone that he is preoccupied with watching unsuspecting persons naked, disrobing, or engaging in sexual activity, as a DSM diagnosis requires. All these observations granted, there is plenty of reason to believe that looking at beautiful people under such conditions, even if they are unsuspecting, is an activity that a large number of people enjoy. David's peeping, for example, whatever one thinks his correct diagnosis might have been, is not behavior whose allure is hard to understand. It is easy to concede that averting one's gaze when an unsuspecting beautiful person is naked is a hard thing for a person with lively appetites to do, even if he does not meet DSM criteria for voyeurism.

GENDER ISSUES

Sex crimes are overwhelmingly committed by men against women and children. For example, in one study, 15% of women over the age of 15 reported having been raped (Brener, McMahon, Warren, & Douglas, 1999). This percentage is consistent with other reports reviewed by Koss (1993) or noted in the National Violence against Women Survey 1995 (National Center for Injury Prevention and Control, 2003). By contrast, a reported lifetime prevalence for rape of males is 1.2% (Tjaden & Thoennes, 2000).

Although women do commit sex crimes, the story of David again is a reminder: People who commit sex offenses are usually men. Women are the exotics of the sex offense world. Women who do commit sex crimes tend to have histories of psychiatric disorders, alcoholism, and sexual victimization. In any case, extant studies of sexually offending women are not studies of female voyeurs. Voyeurism in woman is even less clearly understood, given our current knowledge, than voyeurism in men.

ASSOCIATED FEATURES

As the story of King David and his family may lead one to expect, multiple perversions are far from unusual. Persons with a DSM diagnosis of a paraphilia often have more than one such diagnosis, just as persons with one DSM diagnosis of a personality disorder are at increased risk of having another DSM personality disorder. The situation is apparently another instance of the phenomenon of "positive and negative manifolds." That is, good things tend to cluster with other good things, and bad things likewise tend to go together. A woman who is superb at one field sport is probably good at others. If somebody observes a man who is atrocious at one sport, he is an unlikely candidate for being a master at others, though exceptions are possible. In the field of sexual deviance, multiple paraphilias are common (Bradford, Boulet, & Pawlak, 1992).

ASSOCIATED JUVENILE ISSUES

In their chapter on voyeurism in the first edition of this book, Kaplan and Krueger (1997) devoted considerable discussion to juveniles, despite their own recognition that there was no empirically validated account of how paraphilias develop during adolescence. Instead, they cited Becker and Kaplan (1989), who had argued that individual peculiarities, family factors, social factors, and a young person's environment are possible precursors of a teenager's first deviant sex act. As a matter of logic, the aftermath of the first instance of deviant misbehavior is either no repetition of it or additional misbehavior. Of the teenagers who persist in their sexual misbehavior, some of them may engage in deviant sex as part of a criminal disposition, while others may engage in genuinely paraphilic misbehavior (i.e., behavior aimed at securing sexual pleasure). Becker and Hicks (2003), in their contribution to a volume (Prenky, Janus, & Seto, 2003) that includes a suite of papers on the etiology of paraphilias, offer a behavioral account of possible reasons why this latter group continues to engage in paraphilic behavior. One difficulty with this account is that it is not entirely clear what should be counted as a first deviant act. For example, is it the thinking that precedes a boy's peeping, or is it the peeping itself?

Another source of perplexity in regard to understanding accounts of the etiology of voyeurism in the young is that they do not appear to account for individuals with a late onset of voyeurism. For example, Abel, Osborn, and Twigg (1993) had a sample of 133 voyeurs with an average age of onset of 18; this finding implies that a significant number of subjects developed the behavior after age 18. They also reported that 65% of their subjects showed paraphilic interest prior to age 17, the clear implication of which is that a significant number of people develop paraphilic interests after passing through adolescence. All that said, however, it would be stunning—given the development of human sexuality in adolescence—if adolescence was not the time when most people begin to become aware of and begin to express their sexual tastes (deviant and nondeviant). Moreover, it is beyond dispute that most persons engage in more criminal behavior when they are young than when they begin to age. If one views teenagers as less able to govern themselves well than the adults they will become, it would indeed be striking if they commit fewer sexual offenses as teens than they will as they mature. Of course, a subset of people will confound the common expectation and show more or even deeper criminality as they age.

THEORIES OF ETIOLOGY

Characterizations of clinical phenomena, the paraphilias included, benefit from an organizational framework. A good framework ought to provide clinicians with a way of understanding what they observe in their consulting rooms. A good framework should also enable clinicians to make sense of what researchers and theoreticians have had to say about the clinical phenomena in question. In the case of perversions in general, and voyeurism in particular, I propose to build a framework that owes much to John Money's notion of a "lovemap" (1986) and to work that Fred Berlin (Berlin, 1983; Berlin & Meinecke, 1981) gave a number of years ago in a talk at the Arizona Community Protection and Treatment Center. The rudiments of what is to follow can also be extracted from Freud's *Three Essays on the Theory of Sexuality* (Freud, 1905/1953) and his *Introductory Lectures on Psycho-Analysis* (Freud, 1916–1917/1963).

A Lovemap Framework

Money (1986) offers a florid definition of what he means by a lovemap:

> Lovemap: a developmental representation or template in the mind and in the brain depicting the idealized lover and idealized program of sexuoerotic activity projected in imagery or actually engaged in with that lover. (p. 290)

This is a dense passage, indeed. To make Money's scheme easier to use clinically, let us begin with this enumeration of central elements of a lovemap:

1. The map is drawn in a social context.
2. The map has public and private information (social presentation is at work, as well as conscious and unconscious mechanisms).
3. The information concerns a person's sexual (a) objects, (b) activities, (c) drive, and (d) valences.

What is meant by "objects," "activities," "drive," and "valences"?

A person's sexual objects may include actual and fantasized persons or parts of persons (e.g., feet). Things may also be objects—for example, a shoe or a photograph of a naked woman. Sometimes, as in bestiality, an actual or fantasized animal may be an object. A person's very own body can be an object. There is no clear limit on what a person may use as a sexual object.

Sexual activities, in the present context, are the actions, real or fantasized, a person wishes to engage in with or commit upon a sexual object or have the object commit upon him. So a man might wish to look at the woman he desires. Looking is for many people an important sexual activity, and for voyeurs it can even be the preferred sexual activity. However, possible activities also include such ordinary sexual pastimes as kissing, stroking, licking, the varieties of intercourse, and many more. Further possible activities include fantasies, such as having sex with a movie star, being beaten, or raped. Sexual fantasies may be supplemented by actual activity, as when somebody masturbates to the thought of having sex with a celebrity.

Drive is another clinically important concept. (It also has crucial connections to valences, which will be duly explained below). Drive is the press and motivation a person feels to engage in sexual activity with one of his objects. Drive is susceptible to being misunderstood as merely a physiological phenomenon. Phallometry is an example of this potentially misguided operationalization of drive. For instance, a man whose penis stiffens when he is exposed to descriptions of peeping may be thought to have a drive to peep. A man with a strong erection is judged to be more aroused or driven than when he does not have an erection. Although this is one aspect of drive, it ignores the motivational role of drive (Kenny, 1963). When a woman is said to have a strong sex drive, one does not mean merely that she is easily aroused or is in a state of constant lubricity, but that sex plays a large role in her life and has more influence on what she does than on a person with little drive. The matter is the same as with the emotions: For example, to say that a woman is fearless is not to say *just* that she is does not have the physiological markers of fear that cowards have in the face of danger. A fearless woman is also one whose deliberations, for example, do not routinely put the emphasis on danger that a coward's deliberations do. So a voyeur is not merely a person whose physiological response to peeping is strong, but one whose life is in important ways organized by his desire to observe unsuspecting persons while they are disrobed, disrobing, or engaging in sexual activity. It is what the story of King David did not make apparent; that is, the tale did not make it plain how central looking was to David's lovemap. Finally, unsatisfied drives, if strong, are productive of anxiety and other unpleasant states that may lead a person experiencing them to satisfy the drives in the hope of escaping from these disagreeable states.

A person's attitude toward his sexual objects and activities has a valence. One may think of valences as being positive or negative. In addition, valences vary in their intensity, and they tend to fluctuate in response to shifts in drive. Just as a man may refuse foods he relishes, for instance, a hungry one may value food he disdains when full. If a person's sexual objects and activities have one ordering from most to least preferred in a state of low drive, a different ordering may emerge as drive increases, with even reversals in valence occurring. A pedophile who is not aroused and away from children may sincerely express revulsion at the idea of sex with a child, but in a state of high arousal he may view sex with a child as so appealing that he will endure extraordinary risks to satisfy his desire. After he has sated himself, he may then express sincere shame and remorse for acts he committed on children while in a state of high sexual drive. Of course, he may also lie about his remorse in the interest of managing his social presentation.

A person's lovemap may have characteristic constellations of objects, activities, and valences that are drive-dependent—and, it is crucial to add, also dependent on social circumstances. Hungry people may control an urge to steal food while a shopkeeper watches them. Nevertheless, most of us understand that restraint comes more easily when people have full bellies than when they are starving. Teenagers who forswear sex until marriage are likely to value chastity more when they are at home with their parents than on prom night.

A clinician is interested in a patient's characteristic lovemap and its look in different states of arousal and social contexts. Risk assessment and treatment planning hinge on the therapist's understanding of the patient's lovemap.

A typical voyeur's lovemap might be described as follows. His objects include unsuspecting young naked women or young women in the process of disrobing. His preferred activities include hunting for these women and, when he finds one, observing her, perhaps while masturbating. Alternatively, he may not masturbate at the time, but may later draw from a treasure trove of successful hunts to provide him with fantasies that he relies on while masturbating. His objects and activities may or may not be positively valenced. If peeping has a positive valence for him, he probably either is unreflective about what he does or tells himself a story that assigns his victims responsibility for guarding their privacy while naked. If peeping usually has a negative valence for him, he may well have cycles. That is, when the voyeur satisfies his drive to reduce anxiety, he may find himself experiencing shame as a sequel. While in a state of low drive, the voyeur may inhibit his desire to observe unsuspecting naked women, but as the drive intensifies, disagreeable emotions may begin to reestablish themselves. The appeal of peeping may grow until any negative valencing of his preferred sexual activity is overwhelmed. This clinically driven account has eliminated detail not directly relevant to understanding how the idea of lovemap can organize the clinical understanding of a typical kind of voyeurism.

This lovemap account can be enlisted to help us better understand some traditional theoretical accounts of voyeurism and of the appropriate clinical response to it. Several clinical theories or groups of theories are often mentioned in this regard. There is no hope of enumerating all of them, but they include (1) psychoanalytic theories, (2) social learning theories, (3) Freund's theory of courtship disorders, (4) sociobiological theories, and (5) biological theories. In describing these theories, especially theories as elaborately developed as the psychoanalytic and social learning theories, modesty is in order.

For example, psychoanalytic theories underwent radical revisions during Freud's own lifetime. He moved from id psychology, with its commitment to libidinous drives and a psychic apparatus portioned into unconscious, preconscious, and conscious systems, to a structural theory that included an affiliative drive (Eros), an aggressive drive (Thanatos), and a view of the psychic apparatus as functionally subdivided into the Id,

Ego, and Superego. The three functional subdivisions have both conscious and unconscious portions. The Ego's defense mechanisms are normally held to be unconscious; the mind, in this view, is an arena of perpetual conflict. And newer clinical doctrines, such as the view of anxiety as a signal, take prominence. Given this complexity—and psychoanalysis is used here as a convenient example—the following characterizations of the etiology of perversions in general and voyeurism in particular should be understood as heuristics. They are not presented as adequate representations of how a particular kind of theory is elaborated by any particular author.

One further caution is also in order. None of these theories being discussed are competing paradigms. They are best viewed as theories that have emerged from contending schools of thought or even sects. It is plausible to state that the problem with psychology is that it has no paradigm comparable to the Newtonian paradigm and its Einstein–Bohr successor. In Kuhnian terms (Kuhn, 1996; Buchanan, 2000), these two paradigms created frameworks within which normal science proceeded. Psychology in its present state can be thought of as a discipline where multiple theories at best supplement each other, but none has created a paradigm in the way that Newton did, though Freud hoped to do so.

Psychoanalytic Theories

From a psychoanalytic perspective, voyeurism is a sexual deviation, not a perversion. A sexual perversion in this framework has to do with an anomalous object choice and, in current usage, would be referred to as a paraphilia. Freud accepted that the aim of a healthy person's lovemap is to engage in sexual intercourse with a person of the opposite sex, though this insistence on heterosexual intercourse as the aim of normal activity has ceased to be an official position of the psychoanalytic community (American Psychiatric Association, 1999), just as is the case with other major mental health organizations (e.g., American Psychological Association, 1997).

Voyeurism was viewed by Freud as an anomalous outcome of a normal "scopophilic" instinct that is expressed in ordinary sexual activity. In cases likely to interest therapists, looking becomes a compulsive and pleasurable activity. This view of looking as an activity gives seemingly diverse unity to activities such as looking at pornography or looking at art. Deviant looking may also reach the point of becoming an insatiable need (although there is no evidence in the story of King David, for example, implying that he ever reached that point). Psychoanalysts sometimes view exhibitionism as a reversal of voyeurism. Moreover, the desire to look can also serve as a defense that prevents a person made anxious by engaging in genital contact with others from having do so.

Three factors are viewed as central to the development of voyeurism:

1. A preoccupation (hypercathexis), not well understood, with the visual function. One can see examples of this kind of hypercathexis in people who are not voyeurs. Artists and mathematicians are two classes of people who often have the sort of visual-mindedness that psychoanalysts believe to be common in voyeurs.

2. Postnatal experiences involving early visual exchanges with the mother, as well fear of loss of the mother and her breast. Castration fears ignited by observing adult genitals may lead to peeping as a means of gaining a sense of mastery over what was once a fearful or overstimulating episode.

3. Early trauma during the first or second year of life that cripples the relationship of the mother and child. Such trauma is thought to result in pregenital fixation, sexual

identity problems, and impairment of both the ego and superego. By contrast, simple scopophilia is suspected of involving less serious or later traumas.

The account above relies heavily on sections of *Psychoanalytic Terms and Concepts* (American Psychoanalytic Association, 1990); however, the extracted account fits well within the lovemap framework. It has something to say about a person's objects. It says something about the activity (peeping) and its special characteristics. It references the notion of a drive, though perhaps with some shift in meaning, and it has something to say about valence in its references to anxiety and to superego damage.

Social Learning Theories

Social learning theories have an impressive empirical base in psychological science. Within these theories, voyeurism becomes a behavior that develops as a result of an unfortunate learning history. For example, Laws and Marshall (1990) think of a person's arousal pattern as being the product of classical and operant conditioning, modeling, and differential reinforcement. In principle, the way this mode of sexual expression gets built into a lovemap is no different from the way in which any other behavior is acquired. For example, a boy might happen by a window and see a naked woman. He becomes aroused because he is already predisposed, for whatever reasons, to be aroused by the sight of a naked woman of this general type. Perhaps he masturbates and achieves orgasm. At home when he becomes aroused again, he may return to the memory of this episode and use it to achieve another orgasm. Perhaps he has access to books where stalking plays a role. Perhaps he has friends who also have learned where to see a naked woman in the evening. As time passes, he may fall more and more into the habit of peeping or fantasizing about peeping to achieve arousal or orgasm. If this pattern persists, he learns to be a voyeur. According to this account, King David had taken the first step toward becoming a voyeur, though perhaps his ability to expropriate Bathsheba for himself kept him from becoming one. With the power he possessed, he could gratify his desire for her directly.

This behavioral account is open to supplementation. For example, people do differ in their responsiveness to sexual stimuli. A person who has stronger responses or is more readily aroused than another may be more likely to develop unorthodox responses. And, indeed, young people do have more sexual responsiveness or drive than old ones. Furthermore, boys are typically believed to be more easily aroused than girls, which may explain why boys are more likely to be perverts than girls. This social learning account can rely on the same learning processes to account for a person's valencing of his lovemap. If he has learned a guilt-ridden response in regard to sexual activity or atypical object choices, than guilt-ridden he will be when he has sex with his atypical object.

Freund's Courtship Disorder Theory

Freund (1988, 1990; Freund, Scher, & Hucker, 1983, 1984) has elaborated a theory of voyeurism that relates it to other forms of deviant sexuality. As in the psychoanalytic theory, the aim of sex is viewed as vaginal intercourse, with such supplemental benefits as establishing a closer, more intimate bond between the copulating partners. Freund's account harkens back to one of Freud's chapters in his *Introduction to Psycho-Analysis*. Because voyeurism does not serve the procreative *telos* of sexuality, it is a kind of deviance. When viewed in terms of lovemaps, Freund's view can be understood as one that pays special attention to the interconnections of activities in a "healthy" lovemap. In particular, when in pursuit of his actual objects, a "healthy" man ordinarily first identifies a suitable woman with his eyes. Second, he moves on to nonphysical interactions with the object—for example, talking to her. Third, he becomes involved in touching or being touched by her. Fourth, they have vaginal intercourse. For Freund, a courtship disorder is a fixation or overemphasis on a stage or stages of this process. Voyeurs are people preoccupied or fixated on preoccupied with the first stage of selecting a partner. Exhibitionism, frotteurism, and preferential rape are examples of pathologies at different stages of the courtship process. Freund has also noted that the co-occurrence of courtship disorders is high. In his samples, he found that 20% of voyeurs had also committed sexual assaults or rapes.

Freund's theory, more than the others, makes it clear that the ordering of activities in a lovemap has clinical significance. It is not enough that a man has all the activities for a normal courtship in his lovemap. To avoid legal problems, he must also have the sequence in the correct normative order. Freund also kept sight of a previously mentioned commonplace of clinical work: Good things, and bad things, tend to go together. There are positive and negative manifolds. Just as a person who is highly skilled at one mental task is likely to be good at others, so a person with one strong deviant interest is likely to have others.

All the same, Freund's as well as the psychoanalytic positing of the aim or *telos* of sex as procreative sex is in conflict with one current trend. In particular, neither psychoanalysts nor mainstream psychologists view homosexuality as a perversion. Perhaps a view that makes it easier to identify what is sexual is a view that holds the aim of sex to be arousal or orgasm. However, this view does not readily identify what is perverted. Instead, it requires a theory of what forms of activity aimed at arousal or deviance are to be judged perverted—a manifestly normative inquiry, rather than a scientific one.

Sociobiological Theories

Sociobiological theories strive to explain behaviors with reference to their adaptive roles. In the first edition of this book, Kaplan and Krueger (1997) described Symons's (1979) theory. David Buss (1995, 2004) has also championed this approach. As in much sociobiological writing, the emphasis is on "just so" stories. That is, a human behavior is identified, and a sociobiologist (nowadays likely to be called an evolutionary psychologist) constructs an account that relates it to an evolutionarily advantageous strategy. For instance, natural selection is alleged to favor men with a knack for spotting fecund, "alpha" women. Being aroused when performing these inspections, especially if the man is inspecting a naked woman, is reckoned to place men with good eyes at an evolutionary advantage over men with defective vision. Readers can ponder how this account is supposed to explain voyeurism, especially once they think beyond its reliance on the commonplace that many men like observing naked women, and the predictable corollary that some men will like it enough to make a career of it. Dupré (2003, 2005) has argued robustly against this style of theorizing in psychology and elsewhere.

Biological Theories

Biological theories stress the role of drive, especially in regard to its physiological rather than its motivational aspect. The basic approach is to strive to reduce the patient's ability to move into the higher drive states that occur during periods of hyperarousal (Saleh & Guidry, 2003). Of course, biological theories need not focus exclusively on neurochemistry. In neuropsychology, executive function is often thought of as central to the ability to inhibit the expression of drive. Frontal lobe impairment is often implicated in reduced capacity to moderate appetites—as in the notorious case of Phineas Gage, whose behavior changed radically for the worse after an iron rod blasted through his frontal lobes, making him an enduring celebrity in neuropsychology texts.

In regard to a particular patient's lovemap, one can say that biological interventions such as antiandrogenic medications, or even castration, aim at keeping a patient's drive level at a manageable level in order to prevent the emergence of positively valenced or unruly desires for deviant sexual activity.

UNIVERSAL IMPLICATIONS FOR ASSESSMENT AND TREATMENT

The discussions above indicate the relations of various theories to lovemaps. Clinical theories, when combined with the notion of lovemaps, suggest possible intervention strategies. To be sure, no matter which theory a clinician prefers, the assessment and treatment of any particular voyeur occur in a social context. There are obvious features of the social context that make it harder or easier to get at an individual voyeur's lovemap. He may fear arrest. He may already have been arrested and may fear further charges. He may be embedded in a social context that is often tolerant of his deviance or one that is intolerant of it. He may live in a community where opportunities to peep abound or are rare. Systematic reflection on the social context—something psychodynamic devotees of the intrapsychic factors tend to ignore—is sure to present questions in regard to the current risk of peeping and to the kinds of social measures that authorities may need to impose to reduce its likelihood. Both the social context and the patient's inner world will also influence how revealing the person will be with information that allows others to reconstruct his lovemap. An intolerant social context is a poor surface on which to paint a lovemap.

Assessment Considerations

A patient's presentation of information about his lovemap inevitably raises issues of concealment. One reason for multimodal assessment—including interviews, record review, psychological tests, and physiological measures—is to make a patient's lovemap more accurate and easier to read than it otherwise would be. Advantages of multimodal assessment include its being systematic and comprehensive. It ideally reduces the risk of misunderstanding patients. In a case involving sexual offending, it is as if the assessor evaluates the patient's mouth (interview), his hand (paper–pencil testing), his eyes (Abel Screen), his penis (penile plethysmography), and society (record review, interviews with collaterals, and scores on actuarial risk assessment instruments). Discrepancies may indicate the patient's efforts to manage his self-presentation either consciously or unconsciously, making it more difficult for the patient's lovemap to be a public object available to the therapeutic dyad. Therapists and assessors would do well not to criminalize the patient's inevitable efforts to manage the presentation of his lovemap. Readers are invited to ask their own secret hearts how well their most intimate partners know their own lovemaps, or even how well they know these maps themselves.

Treatment Considerations

As already mentioned, framing therapeutic tasks in terms of lovemaps suggests possible intervention strategies, as well as assessment approaches. For the voyeur, likely objects include unsuspecting persons in a state of undress or engaging in sexual activity; covert looking and stalking of the objects are central activities, and also perhaps masturbating while observing the objects or in reverie after a successful hunt. Drive shifts, and shifts in valencing of activities that accompany drives, are central as well. Dysphoric states that lead to defensive use of the lovemap are also likely targets. Therefore, behavioral strategies that make the social context unfavorable to voyeurism, or that reduce drive and enhance negative valencing of voyeuristic behavior, are coherent interventions. Psychoanalytic efforts often center on enhancing a patient's knowledge of his lovemap and its structure to aid his ego's capacity to manage his lovemap (or so these efforts may be interpreted within this framework).

To date, the treatment of voyeurism has received scant independent discussion. It is instead considered together with other paraphilias or with sexual deviance in general. The lovemap approach has the same potential to be nonspecific with regard to voyeurism. Nevertheless, each component of the lovemap is suggestive of possible interventions. Let us consider each in turn.

Social context is a rich field for possible interventions. Interventions could include curfews and psychoeducation on how other people view peeping, to name just two. Furthermore, the ways in which dysphoric states like anxiety and depression are fended off by reliance on peeping might be explored.

Social presentation of voyeurism is another rich potential area for interventions. Such interventions might include having the patient think about how he employs secrecy. Accurate descriptions that challenge vague descriptions of the patient's sneaking and peeping are also worth considering. In addition, efforts to look at the patient's defenses and the role his unconscious processes play in making it easier for him to hide the intrapsychic functions his peeping serves are worth making explicit in this framework.

Although objects might be targeted, past attempts to change persons' object choices have been discouraging and have led to official skepticism (American Psychiatric Association, 1999; American Psychological Association, 1997). Instead, it may be important to press the patient to substitute innocuous objects when he is seeking to gratify himself sexually. An ominous prognostic marker would be a patient whose *sole* objects are unsuspecting persons disrobing, disrobed, or sexually engaged. In the better cases, voyeurs will have objects other than voyeuristic ones toward whom they can behave sexually.

Interventions aimed at activities are similar to ones aimed at objects. Central efforts might focus on what the patient does and what other legal activities are available to him as substitutes. Attention could also be paid to the functional role of these activities, as well as their meaning to the patient—a strategy that is also available in working with objects.

Drive is a readily available biological target. Some psychopharmacological interventions include making the patient less interested in sex by prescribing a selective serotonin reuptake inhibitor or by having the patient take drugs that lower testosterone level. Of course, drives as motives are suitable for a wide range of interventions. Drive might also be managed by helping the patient identify situations that put him in a state of high drive in conditions favorable to peeping.

Valencing is an equally available target. One common cognitive-behavioral intervention is to assist the patient in discovering what thoughts make him feel entitled to peep. In addition, the therapist might wish to assist the voyeur in noting the state dependence of his valencing in regard to peeping. The voyeur may find it far easier to take a dim view of voyeuring when he is unexcited than when he is aroused.

Clinicians from different schools of psychotherapy will undoubtedly rely on different strategies in using a lovemap therapeutically. A lovemap is a heuristic for intervening. It must not be thought that its description is absolute, or that social context, objects, activities, drive, and valencing exist independently of one another. Instead, the heuristic systematizes nodes for possible intervention. Competing schools of psychotherapy can all conceptualize work in terms of a lovemap, and can even develop contending theories regarding how to elaborate the theoretically oversimplified model of a lovemap that is being offered in this chapter.

FORENSIC ISSUES

Voyeurism is a hands-off offense. As a result, it inevitably draws less attention than offenses committed against the body of a person. For example, the United Kingdom did not make peeping a crime until passage in 2004 of the Sexual Offences Act of 2003. Canada did not include peeping in its criminal code until 2004. The impulse to criminalize sexually motivated peeping seems more defensible if peepers commit other, more violent offenses. Hanson and Harris (1997) endorsed Freund's courtship disorder model of voyeurism and noted a high rate of concomitant paraphilias in studied voyeurs. In other words, according to Hanson and Harris, most voyeurs studied by researchers have at least one other paraphilia, especially exhibitionism or frotteurism. Given the difficulty in estimating the actual prevalence of voyeurism, claims extrapolated from studies of voyeurs should obviously be treated with caution. Nevertheless, the available samples support comprehensive assessments of patients presenting as voyeurs or suspected to be voyeurs.

Hanson and Bussière (1998) linked risk factors for reoffending with familiar predictive variables for sexual and criminal recidivism. These variables have proved effective in developing actuarial instruments for predicting sexual reoffense (Hanson & Thornson, 2000; Quinsey, Harris, Rice, & Cormier, 2006); however, none of the actuarial instruments that are in wide use are designed to predict the likelihood of a voyeur committing additional sexual offenses. They are aimed (typically) at offenders whose offenses involved their laying hands on their victims.

SUMMARY AND FUTURE DIRECTIONS

There is plenty of reason to be skeptical about the future of research, diagnosis, and treatment of voyeurism. As the story of King David illustrates, peeping is one thing, but voyeurism as a diagnosis is something else. Often the working clinician has no method for deciding whether a detected peeper is better described as a full-fledged voyeur or simply a creepy opportunist. Moreover, as noted above, research into sexual deviance has led researchers to conclude that the paraphilias are too often discussed as a group, even though researchers and clinicians recognize that persons meeting DSM diagnostic criteria for paraphilias like voyeurism form heterogeneous classes. One begins to suspect—as the late Paul Meehl (2001, 2004) argued regarding the psychiatric diagnoses in general—that the DSM diagnoses of voyeurism, exhibitionism, frotteurism, fetishism, and even pedophilia are focused too closely on symptoms and not closely enough on a compelling clinical picture. In medicine, though this oversimplifies matters, one might say that a diagnosis has a constellation of symptoms (subjective complaint) and signs (findings that a physician can elicit through observations and tests), which are the by-products of an underlying disease process that is changing the patient's physical function and structure. Moreover, in the best of circumstances, a diagnosed disease has a known natural history. Doctors can predict how a patient is likely to respond to different interventions, including no treatment at all. In the case of voyeurism, there is nothing that remotely approximates this level of knowledge. Meehl (2001, 2004) noted that this is a general problem in the diagnosis of mental illness, and his work on diagnostic taxons was intended as a remedy.

Two general strategies are readily available for the problem of peeping. First, one might treat peeping as a behavior that needs to stop. Accordingly, clinicians ought to work on strategies for bringing the behavior under control, whatever the story of the peeper may be. Inveterate peepers may well prove harder to treat than occasional peepers, but the clinical task is the familiar behavioral one of changing an unwelcome response.

The second strategy is to seek out perspicuous sorting of peepers. Is peeping, for example, a symptom that is linked to a limited set of personality organizations or personal histories—as, for example, the psychoanalytic account seems to imply? Are there ways of understanding the behavior of peeping as a symptom that is related systematically to other symptoms, signs, and underlying psychopathology? The current tendency that has resulted in heterogeneous groups appears to be unhelpful in answering this question. Lovemaps may well provide a method for organizing clinical data.

Past efforts are not encouraging. One might expect that the tendency to persist in current theoretical ruts will make it difficult for anybody to break new ground. If so, the problems discussed in this chapter will remain the riddles they now are.

REFERENCES

Abel, G. G., Osborn, C., & Twigg, D. (1993). Sexual assault through the life span: Adult offenders with juvenile histories. In H. E. Barbaree, W. Marshall, & S. M. Hudson (Eds.), *The juvenile sex offender* (pp. 104–117). New York: Guilford Press.

Abel, G. G., & Rouleau, J. L. (1990). The nature and extent of sexual assault. In W. L. Marshall, D. R. Laws, & H. E. Barbaree (Eds.), *Handbook of sexual assault: Issues, theories, and treatment of the offender* (pp. 9–21). New York: Plenum Press.

American Psychiatric Association. (1999). Position statement on psychiatric treatment and sexual orientation. *American Journal of Psychiatry, 156,* 1131.

American Psychiatric Association. (2000). *Diagnostic and statistical manual of mental disorders* (4th ed., text rev.). Washington, DC: Author.

American Psychoanalytic Association. (1990). *Psychoanalytic terms and concepts* (B. E. Moore & B. D. Fine, Eds.). New Haven, CT: Author and Yale University Press.

American Psychological Association. (1997). *Resolution on appropriate therapeutic responses to sexual orientation.* Washington, DC: Author.

Becker, J. V., & Hicks, S. J. (2003). Juvenile sexual offenders: Characteristics, interventions, and policy issues. *Annals of the New York Academy of Sciences, 989,* 397–410.

Berlin, F. S. (1983). Sex offenders: A biomedical perspective and a status report on biomedical treatment. In J. B. Greer & I. R. Stuart (Eds.), *The sexual aggressor: current perspectives on treatment* (pp. 83–123). New York: Van Nostrand Reinhold.

Berlin, F. S., & Meinecke, C. F. (1981). Treatment of sex offenders with antiandrogenic medication: Conceptualization, review of treatment modalities, and preliminary findings. *American Journal of Psychiatry, 138,* 601–607.

Bradford, J. B., Boulet, J., & Pawlak, A. (1992). The paraphilias: A multiplicity of deviant behaviors. *Canadian Journal of Psychiatry, 29,* 104–108.

Brener, N. D., McMahon, P. M., Warren, C. W., & Douglas, K. A. (1999). Forced sexual intercourse and associated health-risk behaviors among female college students in the United States. *Journal of Consulting and Clinical Psychology, 67*(2), 252–259.

Buchanan, M. (2000). *Ubiquity: Why catastrophes happen.* New York: Three Rivers Press.

Buss, D. (1995). *The evolution of desire: Strategies of human mating.* New York: Basic Books.

Buss, D. (2004). *Evolutionary psychology: The new science of mind* (2nd ed.). Boston: Allyn & Bacon.

Dupré, J. (2003). *Human nature and the limits of science.* New York: Oxford University Press.

Dupré, J. (2005). *Darwin's legacy: What evolution means today.* New York: Oxford University Press.

Freud, S. (1953). Three essays on the theory of sexuality. In J. Strachey (Ed. & Trans.), *The standard edition of the complete psychological works of Sigmund Freud* (Vol. 7, pp. 125–243). London: Hogarth Press. (Original work published 1905)

Freud, S. (1963). Introductory lectures on psycho-analysis. In J. Strachey (Ed. & Trans.), *The standard edition of the complete psychological works of Sigmund Freud* (Vol. 15, pp. 1–240; Vol. 16, pp. 241–496). London: Hogarth Press. (Original work published 1916–1917)

Freund, K. (1988). Courtship disorders: Is this hypothesis valid? *Annals of the New York Academy of Sciences, 528,* 172–182.

Freund, K. (1990). Courtship disorder. In W. L. Marshall, D. R. Laws, & H. E. Barbaree (Eds.), *Handbook of sexual assault: Issues, theories, and treatment of the offender* (pp. 209–227). New York: Plenum Press.

Freund, K., Scher, H., & Hucker, S. J. (1983). The courtship disorders. *Archives of Sexual Behavior, 12,* 769–779.

Freund, K., Scher, H., & Hucker, S. J. (1984). The courtship disorders: A further investigation. *Archives of Sexual Behavior, 13,* 133–139.

Hanson, R. K., & Bussière, M. T. (1998). Predicting relapse: A meta-analysis of sexual offender recidivism studies. *Journal of Consulting and Clinical Psychology, 66*(2), 348–362.

Hanson, R. K., & Harris, A. J. R. (1997). Voyeurism: Assessment and treatment. In D. R. Laws & W. O'Donohue (Eds.), *Sexual deviance: Theory, assessment, and treatment* (pp. 311–331). New York: Guilford Press.

Hanson, R. K., & Thornton, D. (2000). Improving risk assessments for sexual offenders: A comparison of three actuarial scales. *Law and Human Behavior, 24*(1), 119–136.

Kaplan, M. S., & Krueger, R. B. (1997). In D. R. Laws & W. O'Donohue (Eds.), *Sexual deviance: Theory, assessment, and treatment* (pp. 297–310). New York: Guilford Press.

Kenny, A. (1963). *Action, emotion, and will.* New York: Humanities Press.

Koss, M. P. (1993). Detecting the scope of rape: A review of prevalence research methods. *Journal of Interpersonal Violence, 8,* 198–222.

Kuhn, T. (1996). *The structure of scientific revolutions* (3rd ed.). Chicago: University of Chicago Press.

Laws, D. R., & Marshall, W. L. (1990). A conditioning theory of the etiology and maintenance of deviant sexual preference and behavior. In W. L. Marshall, D. R. Laws, & H. E. Barbaree (Eds.), *Handbook of sexual assault: Issues, theories, and treatment of the offender* (pp. 209–227). New York: Plenum Press.

Meehl, P. E. (2001). Comorbidity and taxometrics. *Clinical Psychology: Science and Practice, 8,* 507–519.

Meehl, P. E. (2004). What's in a taxon? *Journal of Abnormal Psychology, 113,* 39–43.

Money, J. (1986). *Lovemaps: Clinical concepts of sexual/erotic health and pathology, paraphilia, and gender transposition in childhood, adolescence, and maturity.* New York: Irvington.

National Center for Injury Prevention and Control. (2003). *Costs of intimate partner violence against women in the United States.* Atlanta, GA: Centers for Disease Control and Prevention.

Prentky, R. A., Janus, E. S., & Seto, M. C. (Eds.). (2003). Sexually coercive behavior: Understanding and management [Entire volume]. *Annals of the New York Academy of Sciences, 989.*

Quinsey, V. L., Harris, G. T., Rice, M. E., & Cormier, C. A. (2006). *Violent offenders: Appraising and managing risk* (2nd ed.). Washington, DC: American Psychological Association.

Saleh, F. M., & Guidry, L. L. (2003). Psychosocial and biological treatment considerations for paraphilic and nonparaphilic sex offenders. *Journal of the American Academy of Psychiatry and the Law, 31*(4), 486–493.

Symons, D. (1979). *The evolution of human sexuality.* New York: Oxford University Press.

Tjaden, G. K., & Thoennes, N. (2000). *Full report of the prevalence, incidence, and consequences of violence against women: Findings from the National Violence against Women Survey.* Washington, DC: U.S. Department of Justice, National Institute of Justice.

CHAPTER 19

VOYEURISM

Assessment and Treatment

RUTH E. MANN
FIONA AINSWORTH
ZAINAB AL-ATTAR
MARGARET DAVIES

Legend has it that about the year 1050, Lady Godiva rode naked through the streets of Coventry, in the West Midlands of England, in order to persuade her husband to remit his oppressive taxation of the city's poor. The townspeople obeyed the order to stay inside their homes, doors closed and shutters down, so as not to observe her nakedness. However, one tailor could not contain his sexual curiosity and drilled a hole in his shutter in order to watch Lady Godiva pass by. According to the legend, the wrath of heaven punished Tom the tailor for this crime by blinding him.

The term "Peeping Tom" or "peeper" is still used today to refer to a person who gains sexual excitement from observing unsuspecting strangers naked. Although technically this paraphilia is termed "voyeurism," the term "peeping" is still sometimes used deliberately to distinguish pathological sexual voyeurism from the far more common obsession with observing the lives of others, including their sexual lives, which now defines Western society. This chapter explores the question of how far we have come, in almost 1,000 years since Lady Godiva's famous ride, in developing more sophisticated treatments than blinding for the disorder of "Peeping Tomism."

It should be noted at the outset of this chapter that the published literature on the assessment and treatment of sexual voyeurism is extremely limited. There have been two earlier reviews of the voyeurism literature (Hanson & Harris, 1997; Smith, 1976), and there have been few additional publications since. We have therefore had to rely to a large extent on reappraisal of previously reviewed literature. Where there are gaps (and there are many), we have made suggestions for assessment and treatment procedures based on our clinical experience of working with voyeurs.

ASSESSMENT

Diagnosis

The usual procedure for making a diagnosis of a paraphilia is to follow the criteria set out in the American Psychiatric Association's *Diagnostic and Statistical Manual of Mental Disorders*, fourth edition, text revision (DSM-IV-TR; American Psychiatric Association, 2000). The DSM-IV-TR diagnostic criteria for voyeurism require two features to be present:

A. Over a period of at least 6 months, recurrent, intense sexually arousing fantasies, sexual urges, or behaviors involving the act of observing an unsuspecting person who is naked, in the process of disrobing, or engaging in sexual activity.

B. The person has acted on these sexual urges, or the sexual urges or fantasies cause marked distress or interpersonal difficulty. (p. 575)

The application of these criteria will in many cases be straightforward. However, some features of voyeurism recorded in the research literature seem to be excluded from the DSM-IV-TR definition. First, a number of clinicians have noted the frequent interest in observing women in the act of urinating or defecating. Observing such behaviors without the observed person's knowledge is seemingly excluded from the DSM criteria for voyeurism. There has also been division over whether the voyeurism must be accompanied by orgasm for it to be considered pathological. DSM-IV-TR states that "orgasm, usually produced by masturbation, may occur during the voyeuristic activity or later in response to the memory of what the person has witnessed" (p. 575). However, Langevin (1983) emphasized that the orgasm should be considered an essential part of voyeurism.

The criminal definition of voyeurism may also be useful for diagnosis. As recently as 30 years ago, it was debated whether voyeurism could be considered a criminal act, because "there is no crime in the looking" (Smith, 1976, p. 606). Voyeurism was introduced as a criminal offense in England and Wales for the first time in May 2004. The legal definition of voyeurism there refers to the observation of another person doing a private act "for the purpose of obtaining sexual gratification" (Sexual Offences Act, 2003; Stationery Office, 2003). The term "private act" in this definition is able to encompass not only undressing and sexual activity, but urination and defecation. The legal definition also incorporates the operation of equipment or the adapting of a structure to enable oneself or another person to watch a third party doing a private act, as well as the recording of people doing a private act with the intention that the recording will be used for sexual gratification. This criminal definition helpfully expands the diagnostic criteria by describing in more detail the kinds of behaviors in which voyeurs may engage. For instance, one of our clients, Mr. A, secretly taped naked female clients attending a massage parlor, with the express purpose of watching the tapes later for sexual gratification.

It is probable that only a minority of sexually voyeuristic behaviors are socially deviant and therefore pathological. The viewing of unknown women as they are undressing or engaging in sexual activity is normalized by the widespread availability of pornography, peep shows, and strip clubs. It is generally assumed that the majority of men and women who chanced upon an opportunity to observe a woman or man undressing would stop and take a look. This is particularly likely with adolescent males, of whom as many as half report having engaged in some form of opportunistic voyeurism (McConaghy, 2005). We may not view such behavior as desirable, respectful, or psychologically healthy, but it is not deviant. Therefore, a diagnosis of voyeurism would require the behavior to be frequent, compulsive, and deliberate (as opposed to opportunistic).

Last, it should be noted that diagnoses of voyeurism are usually applied to men. Some authors have noted that voyeurism in women is extremely rare to the point of being unheard of (Freund, 1990; Yalom, 1960). This is not strictly true, and, as with much paraphilic or sexually abusive behavior, it is possible that female voyeurs simply do not come to the attention of clinicians. We found one case report of a female voyeur who clearly met the diagnostic criteria (Hurlbert, 1992). Furthermore, Friday's (1973, 1975) investigations of female sexual fantasies revealed that "a large portion of women also express voyeuristic interests and have either indulged in such activities or fantasised doing so" (Smith, 1976, p. 593). Therefore, it is our view that the diagnosis of voyeurism is potentially as applicable to women as it is to men.

General Assessment Considerations

No assessment instruments or procedures have been reported that are specifically designed for voyeurs. A few broader sexual history measures screen for voyeurism, and these are described below. However, these tools are not intended to assess factors affecting onset or maintenance for individuals diagnosed with sexual voyeurism. On the basis of our review of the voyeurism literature (such as it is), we therefore suggest areas that should be explored during a clinical interview, to assist in a formulation of the voyeuristic behavior.

A second important consideration is that it appears that sexual voyeurism rarely if ever exists alone. It is likely to be associated with other paraphilias—particularly exhibitionism, but also rape, pedophilia, sadism, and frotteurism (Abel & Rouleau, 1990; Freund & Watson, 1990). Clinical assessment of a patient presenting with sexual voyeurism must not neglect the possibility of coexisting paraphilias.

Assessment Measures

Clinical Interview

We recommend that a clinical interview be conducted with a potential or diagnosed voyeur, in order to generate a formulation of the voyeuristic interest and develop a treatment plan. Based on our review of the sexual voyeurism literature (see also Lavin, Chapter 18, this volume), we suggest that the interview should cover the following areas.

Features of Hypersexuality and Compulsivity of the Voyeuristic Behaviors. Voyeurism is strongly associated with hypersexuality (Långström & Hanson, 2006). This information is particularly useful when a clinician is deciding whether the problem behavior may respond to pharmacological treatment (see "Medical Treatment," below).

Sexual and Emotional Intimacy, Including Attachment Patterns. The courtship disorder theory of sexual voyeurism suggests that voyeurs have a disorder of the "finding phase [of courtship]—locating and appraising a potential partner" (Freund & Seto, 1998, p. 433). It is suggested that they find it difficult or unpleasant to move from the initial attraction to another person through the stages of social and verbal interaction as the normal path of progression to emotional and physical intimacy. For this reason, their courtship practices and skills should be assessed. Furthermore, voyeurs "often fail in intercourse, find it unsatisfactory, or find it pleasurable but still prefer the voyeuristic act" (Smith, 1976, p. 594). Although Langevin, Paitich, and Russon (1985) claimed to have disproved this theory with their finding that voyeurs tended to have had more overall sexual experiences with adult females than controls, they simply measured number of partners, rather than confidence or satisfaction with sexual relationships. Number of partners cannot necessarily be taken to indicate that sexual relationships are successful. Indeed, a higher number of sexual partners may indicate that the sexual act is, as Smith (1976) suggested, experienced as "entirely genital in nature" (p. 594) and therefore rather impersonal. This hypothesis should be examined with respect to each individual patient.

Sexual Fantasy Content. Langevin and colleagues (1985) suggested that although voyeurism seemed unrelated to sexual aggression, it is necessary to examine the content of a voyeur's sexual fantasies in order to identify risk of violence.

Beliefs about the Deviance/Harm of Voyeurism. Many voyeurs believe that their voyeuristic behaviors are of no consequence to the observed party, because the person they are observing is unaware of their presence. As Mr. B said frequently during his treatment with one of us, "As long as they don't know, it's OK." Kaplan and Krueger (1997) listed some other beliefs that voyeurs hold about their behavior, including "Many people leave their shades up because they want to be seen undressing or having sex," and "Watching a woman through a window while she takes a shower will not cause her any harm" (p. 300).

Sexual Self-Esteem and Body Image. Marshall, Anderson, and Fernandez (1999) opined that sexual offenders in general may suffer from specific rather than global self-esteem deficits, and suggested that poor body image may be one such deficit. This hypothesis was supported for voyeurs by Langevin and colleagues' (1985) study. Although voyeurs were less often ashamed to appear in a bathing suit than controls, they wished more often that they were more muscular and stronger, and they were also afraid at some times that there was something wrong with their penis; this latter concern was not found at all in the control sample.

Impact on Relationships and Social Functioning. Obviously, the impact of voyeurism on social functioning and relationships is important to explore, because it forms part of the diagnostic criteria for the disorder. Furthermore, if the voyeur perceives that his life is negatively affected by his voyeurism, he may be more motivated to try to overcome the behavior.

Anxiety and Depression. Several studies have found that voyeurs tend to experience more neurotic symptoms than comparison groups and possibly have a greater frequency of suicide attempts (e.g., Langevin et al., 1985).

Hostility. Using scales derived from the Minnesota Multiphasic Personality Inventory (MMPI), Langevin and colleagues (1985) found that voyeurs scored differently from controls on hostility. They showed more features of "acting-out" and "manifest" hostility, and scored lower on "overcontrolled" hostility. Unfortunately, Langevin and colleagues did not define these terms further and did not discuss the meaning of their findings on hostility, but there seems to be scope for including hostility in a clinical examination until further research is conducted.

Lifestyle and Environmental Factors. Some voyeurs may have chosen their occupations and hobbies because they provide opportunities for voyeurism (Hanson & Harris, 1997). For instance, a university security guard has the unique opportunity to walk around a campus at night observing residences without causing any concern. A recent case reported in the U.K. media concerned a landlord who drilled holes into the walls of the bathrooms in his properties so that he could observe his female tenants in the shower and bath. Caprio (1949) gave a similar account of a mother and son observing residents in the mother's rooming house. Fensterheim's (1974) voyeuristic patient was a motel manager and window cleaner—two occupations offering plentiful chances to observe women voyeuristically.

Self-Report Measures

The following sexual history questionnaires contain subscales that assess the extent to which a patient has experienced sexually voyeuristic urges and/or engaged in sexual voyeurism. Such scales may be useful to clinicians at the diagnostic stage and in assessing the strength of the interest in voyeurism in comparison with other paraphilias.

Erotic Preferences Examination Scheme. The purpose of the Erotic Preferences Examination Scheme (EPES; Freund, Watson, & Rienzo, 1988), according to its authors, is to measure the degree to which a patients admits to his "anomalous erotic preference" (p. 245). This information can then be used alongside other data to assist in the differential diagnosis of voyeurism. Responses to the scale items could also be used as a starting point for an analysis of motives for voyeurism. In addition, the authors suggest that the scale could be used in research to characterize known voyeurs as either "admitters" or "nonadmitters." The EPES is an unpublished 385-item questionnaire, and includes 6 items developed for the purpose of diagnosing voyeurism in "cooperative patients." The items include questions about preferred object of peeping (e.g., one person alone vs. people having intercourse), masturbation during peeping (3 items), amount of time spent trying to observe others, and identification with persons observed. Despite the finding that voyeurs score higher on this scale than nonvoyeurs, we do not particularly recommend this scale. There are too few items, and the wording of each item is complex. As Hanson and Harris (1997) pointed out, the scale does not cover several important aspects of voyeurism, such as compulsivity, social impairment, or frequency of voyeurism. It also does not include urination or defecation in its list of possible preferred activities to observe. Urination is only mentioned in the question about amount of time spent; this seems rather confusing. Finally, the EPES does not investigate the use of equipment or recording devices to observe others engaging in private acts.

Multiphasic Sex Inventory. The Multiphasic Sex Inventory (MSI; Nichols & Molinder, 1984) was designed to measure the sexual characteristics and interests of adult male sex offenders. The original MSI contains 300 true–false questions that generate 20 core scales. The main scales measure interests in child molestation, rape, and exhibitionism, with additional scales assessing other paraphilias, such as fetishes, voyeurism, bondage/ discipline, and sadomasochism. The MSI also measures sexual dysfunction, sex knowledge, and treatment attitudes. There are 9 items in total that measure voyeurism, all of which are static (i.e., refer to historical interests). An example of a voyeurism item is "I have used peeping to find the right set-up and person to rape." Because all of the voyeurism items are static, they provide an assessment of a treatment need in this area, rather than being able to show treatment change. If the score on this scale increases after treatment, this is likely to be an indication of a treatment gain (i.e., becoming more open or more insightful about past sexual behavior). An updated version of the MSI, the MSI II, also exists. As test scoring and interpretation for the MSI II is only available from the test authors, we are not able to comment on whether the MSI II offers any advantage over the original version for the assessment of voyeurism.

Clarke Sex History Questionnaire for Males—Revised. The Clarke Sex History Questionnaire for Males—Revised (SHQ; Langevin & Paitich, 2002) is a 508-item questionnaire that contains items relating to voyeurism. These items cover the observation of men and women having sexual intercourse with or without their knowledge, and the observation of women undressing through windows. In each case, the patient is asked to report whether he masturbated while engaging in voyeurism. Like the EPES and the MSI, the SHQ does not examine consequences of voyeurism (e.g., distress caused or effects on relationships), and it does not investigate interest in observing urination or defecation or in using equipment to observe others. The use of the SHQ in facilitating diagnosis seems to be similar to that of the EPES, with neither questionnaire offering a particular advantage over the other.

Sexual Deviance Card Sort. The Sexual Deviance Card Sort (Laws, 1986; Laws, Hanson, Osborn, & Greenbaum, 2000) is a 130-item questionnaire (with versions for pedophiles and nonpedophiles) where participants rate the attractiveness of each item on a 7-point Likert scale. There are 10 items that measure voyeurism on both questionnaires. Cutoff guidelines are provided for interpreting the composite scores. Because the items are phrased in the present tense (e.g., "You're peering in through a bathroom window. A young boy is sitting on the toilet masturbating while he looks through a magazine"), this measure is potentially able to identify changes over time in someone's sexual interests. This is a particular advantage of the measure. The Sexual Deviance Card Sort is sexually explicit in its language and phrasing, and therefore may cause some resistance in participants. Social desirability concerns may prevent patients from answering honestly or complying at all with the assessment process. As with the other assessments, the Sexual Deviance Card Sort looks mainly at the sexual interest of observing persons who do not know they are being observed (e.g., people who are undressing, playing tennis, masturbating, or naked). It does not examine the consequences of voyeurism, or assess the interest either in observing urination or defecation or in using equipment to observe others.

In addition to facilitating diagnosis or grading level of openness about voyeurism, self-report measures could be used to assess degree of pathology on constructs theoretically related to voyeuristic behavior. This use of self-report measures would assist in treatment planning and the evaluation of treatment effectiveness. For instance, the MSI sexual preoccupations scale could assist in detecting hypersexuality coexisting with voyeurism; the MMPI has been found useful in assessing hostility levels; and so forth.

Psychophysiological and Behavioral Assessment

Phallometric Testing. Hanson and Harris (1997) believed that "it is possible to develop [phallometric] stimuli for the assessment of voyeurs" (p. 321), and suggested that such stimuli be produced and evaluated. A search of the literature since 1997 reveals that no such endeavor has taken place. Theoretically, voyeurs should be likely to respond well to phallometric testing, as the procedure involves what they like best: looking at pictures of unclothed strangers and/or listening to audiotaped accounts of sexual activity. We can only surmise that the lack of development in this area reflects the general lack of interest in studying voyeurism at the present time, as well as a somewhat jaded attitude toward phallometric testing, which has been found wanting in terms of standardization, reliability, and validity (Marshall, 2006).

Diary Keeping. Several of the reported successful behavioral treatments for voyeurism (see below for review) used diary keeping as a method for identifying the baseline frequency of voyeuristic urges and behaviors. Although this methodology is of course open to misreporting by a client, with a motivated client it can provide an invaluable record of progress, as well as allowing for a study of triggers and consequences to voyeuristic behavior.

Research Priorities

Past research into voyeurism either has involved investigating courtship disorder theory, or has been an essentially atheoretical, data-driven enterprise (e.g., Langevin et al., 1985). In our view, the dearth of more recent research suggests something of a tolerance for voyeurism—at least in comparison with contact sexual offending, about which there is a high level of public concern. We believe that this tolerance may be dangerous. What little information there is about voyeurs suggests that voyeurism is rarely found as a pure condition, and that in cases where aggressive fantasy is involved, it may signal risk of more serious sexual offending. We hope that the increasing recognition of voyeurism as a criminal offense will encourage clinicians and researchers alike to pay more attention to this paraphilia. Any systematic, theory-driven, empirical study into the motivational correlates of voyeurism would be welcome, as would any attempt to identify voyeurs who are capable of more aggressive offending from those who are unlikely to cause physical harm to others. Finally, there has been no change since Hanson and Harris (1997) pointed out that we still do not know the recidivism rates for voyeurs.

TREATMENT

Effective Documented Treatments

Langevin (1983) stated clearly that the aim of treating a voyeur must be "to reduce the frequency of voyeurism but maintain or enhance the frequency of . . . heterosexual behavior" (p. 388). (Presumably the word "heterosexual" was used here because voyeurism was assumed to be an exclusively heterosexual disorder.) In their review of the voyeurism treatment literature, Hanson and Harris (1997) concluded that "there is insufficient consistency in the literature to support any particular treatment approach. Consequently, all treatment for voyeurism should be considered experimental" (p. 321). This position still stands. The few additions to the treatment literature since 1997 are new case studies examining the benefits of pharmacological treatment, and some brief descriptions of the sexual addiction approach for this disorder. Because published case studies are likely to report positive outcomes, but equally likely to employ only short-term follow-up periods, it is not possible to identify any one treatment approach that can be confidently recommended. In this section, therefore, we briefly review the main approaches that have been applied to voyeurism: psychoanalytic, behavioral, cognitive-behavioral, sexual addiction, and pharmacological.

Therapist-Based Treatments

A range of treatment approaches to voyeurism has been reported, almost always in the form of single-case studies. The approach of choice at any given time period reflects the dominant therapeutic tradition of the day: reports of psychoanalytic treatment in the 1950s and 1960s, behavioral therapies in the 1970s and early 1980s, and pharmacological treatments in the 1990s and beyond 2000. Perhaps surprisingly, given the popularity of the approach with sexual offenders (Marshall et al., 1999), there are few reports of the application of cognitive-behavioral treatment (CBT) with voyeurs. Most of the case study reports give some simple follow-up information. This usually consists of one or two sentences indicating that at follow-up, the client continued to be free of voyeuristic urges (or in some cases had managed to stay out of prison, which is not quite the same thing). Length of follow-up is usually a matter of months and rarely goes beyond 1 year. It is hard to be confident in the rigor of such follow-up when the length of follow-up is brief, the method of follow-up is not stated, and the information source is apparently only the client's self-report.

Psychoanalytic Treatment

A few psychoanalytic case studies have been reported (e.g., Hamilton, 1973; Karpman, 1960; Malkin, 1991; Socarides, 1974; Vasquez, 1970; Yalom, 1960). It is difficult to draw thematic conclusions from these reports, as the theoretical formulation and the consequent treatment approach vary considerably from case to case. Nevertheless, it must be stated that the psychoanalytic approach to voyeurism is at least as well documented as any other approach.

Behavioral Treatment

Smith (1976) reviewed five case study reports of voyeurism treated with behavior therapy (Gaupp, Stern, & Ratlieff, 1971; Jackson, 1969; McConaghy, 1964; McGuire, Carlisle, & Young, 1965; Stoudenmire, 1973). Hanson and Harris (1997) noted an additional four case studies (Fensterheim, 1974; Konopacki & Oei, 1988; Rangaswamy, 1987; Tollison & Adams, 1979). With the exception of one study (Konopacki & Oei, 1988), follow-up periods for these cases were all less than 12 months. One-third of these behavioral case studies used aversive conditioning with electric shock (Gaupp et al., 1977; Rangaswamy, 1987; Tollison & Adams, 1979). Jackson (1969) used orgasmic reconditioning (Laws & Marshall, 1991; Marquis, 1970), encouraging his patient to masturbate to a *Playboy* centerfold whenever he felt the urge to indulge in voyeurism. Stoudenmire (1973) adopted a similar approach, directing his patient to have intercourse with his wife when he felt a voyeuristic urge (or, if this was not possible, to masturbate). Konopacki and Oei (1988) reported the use of satiation therapy (Marshall, 1979), with an apparent persistence of success at a 4-year follow-up. Fensterheim (1974) used desensitization to confrontation (unsuccessfully), followed by covert sensitization (Cautela, 1967) to voyeurism (using the image of vomiting), but did not evaluate whether success persisted after the latter treatment had ceased.

Sexual Addiction Treatment

Sexual addiction theory proposes that some people use sex as a method for numbing their emotional lives. The disease concept, which underlies sexual addiction theory, involves the assumption that conditions of compulsive sexuality such as voyeurism can be either arrested in progress or cured. This is known as "achieving sobriety." Treatment involves enrollment in a 12-Step support group, such as Sex and Love Addicts Anonymous, alongside psychotherapy (often both individual and group) aimed at reducing denial, improving coping skills, and enhancing self-esteem. Clear ground rules of prohibited behavior are established from the outset. Although there are some publications detailing sexual addiction treatment, with descriptions of cases successfully treated by this approach (e.g., Griffin-Shelley, 1993), at this time there are no peer-reviewed publications and no empirical evaluations of sexual addiction treatment for voyeurism.

Cognitive-Behavioral Treatment

Surprisingly, given the popularity of the cognitive-behavioral model in the treatment of sexual offenders (Marshall et al., 1999), there are no published accounts of a comprehensive CBT approach for voyeurs. Equally, there are no published evaluations of CBT with voyeurs, despite this approach being generally accepted as effective with sexual offenders (e.g., Lösel & Schmucker, 2005). We found no English-language case studies of CBT with voyeurs. We found one case study in Norwegian (Stoyler, 1985) reporting a successful outcome of CBT at a 6-month follow-up. It was not possible to deduce the exact nature of the therapy provided from the English-language abstract. In our literature search, we found some references to treatment approaches, such as assertiveness training (Langevin, 1983; Stoudenmire, 1973), that could be assumed to follow a cognitive-behavioral model. However, we also noted that some studies of pharmacological treatment involved patients who had been treated (some for many years) unsuccessfully with CBT (e.g., Krueger & Kaplan, 2001). From this, it can be concluded that CBT is being offered to voyeurs. However, there is no published evidence that CBT is of value for voyeurs. Indeed, Langevin (1983) reported a notable lack of success for assertiveness training with exhibitionists and voyeurs: " All patients recidivated" (p. 909).

In our own experience, placing voyeurs in relapse-prevention-oriented CBT programs designed for contact sexual offenders has had mixed success. For example, in some cases we have treated, the techniques that clients reported as most successful in changing voyeuristic behavior included cognitive restructuring of the thoughts and attitudes that underlay the offending behavior; social skills training in relationship skills; exploring coping skills and consequential thinking; increasing self-confidence and self-esteem; and increasing empathy for the victim to undermine the arousal and reward of voyeuristic behavior. The patients concerned reported that these techniques were beneficial in reducing their voyeuristic fantasies. In other cases, we had less confidence in the success of a regular CBT intervention. For example, one client believed that his voyeuristic offending behavior was acceptable, because no parent or child was ever aware of his filming (he was never convicted of these acts). He maintained this argument throughout victim empathy work. It was therefore difficult for him to generate self-talk or behavioral strategies for future risk management. Interestingly, this client believed that his voyeuristic behavior was in fact a good risk management strategy, because he reported that when filming children he never committed any contact offenses. Our assessment of this client's treatment needs suggested that it would be of more value to focus on his distrust of adults, his lack of skills in gaining intimacy with adults, his habitual use of sex to cope with his negative feelings about himself and society, and his obsession with addiction to sexual excitement.

We believe that the CBT approach most likely to be effective would combine behavior modification methods with cognitive-behavioral work focused on intimacy, relationships, and the client's beliefs about sex. First, the therapist and client should collaboratively assess the nature of the voyeuristic interest by conducting a review of the client's sexual and attachment experiences—whereby the client is encouraged to look back over his life and describe his sexual development, fantasies, and sexual practices, along with other, more generic developmental factors and learning experiences. This information can then be used as a vehicle to understand his current sexual interests and set other treatment goals. We also recommend that at the commencement of therapy, the client's self-esteem should be evaluated. If his self-esteem is low, defensive, or unstable, it will need to be increased and worked on throughout the therapy, to allow him to engage with the therapy and practice the skills.

Second, if the client exhibits deficits in sexual knowledge, the treatment schedule should provide psychoeducational sessions on male and female anatomy, sex education, and information relating to sexual dysfunction, such as male orgasmic disorder, premature ejaculation, and sexual pain disorder. Within these sessions, sexual myths should also be explored and challenged, because the client may hold unhelpful beliefs about sexual behaviors that contribute to or maintain his voyeuristic offending (such as the beliefs about voyeuristic filming described above). A specific consideration at this stage is the hypothesis that voyeurs are motivated to avoid the low-arousal states of early courtship interactions, preferring to move straight to high-arousal states (Freund, 1990). The therapist may therefore need to focus particularly on encouraging a more positive view of early courtship interactions.

Third, the therapist should conduct an exploration of beliefs about healthy sexuality. This would involve helping the client develop realistic beliefs, attitudes, and expectations regarding sex; skills in how to build intimate relationships; and appropriate coping strategies within these relationships. We recommend that gender and sexual identity be explored, as this may be related to abusive stereotypical attitudes that can allow the sexual objectification of others. Ideas about male entitlement to sex may also be usefully explored here.

Fourth, the therapist should discuss the client's specific sexual interests, in order to formulate a way of managing his future sexual arousal. This would include an exploration of the sexual thoughts that accompany his sexual arousal, to assess whether these need to be modified. In order to help him manage his specific voyeuristic sexual arousal, we recommend mood management, so that he has a better understanding of the moods that act as precursors to his offending and can develop strategies to manage these. We also recommend behavioral strategies for promoting healthy sexual interests. These would include behavior modification strategies for increasing appropriate fantasy and arousal, and methods to decrease or modify offense-related sexual fantasy and arousal. In particular, we recommend ammonia aversion (Earls & Castonguay, 1989; Laws, 2001), modified covert sensitization (Marshall & Eccles, 1996), directed masturbation (Kremsdorf, Holmen, & Laws, 1980, Laws & O'Neil, 1981), and verbal satiation (Laws, 1995; Marshall, 1979). Ammonia aversion involves the client pairing offense-related sexual fantasy with inhaling ammonia salts; this has the effect of interrupting a person's train of thought (in addition, ammonia is mediated by the pain system). Modified covert sensitization involves the participant repeatedly associating unpleasant consequences with his offense-related thoughts in order to reduce the attractiveness, and thereby the frequency, of these thoughts (Marshall & Eccles, 1996). Directed masturbation involves the participant being instructed to masturbate only to nondeviant themes. Finally, verbal satiation asks the participant to verbalize offense-related fantasies repeatedly, so that they become boring and are eventually extinguished.

The final component of treatment could consist of modern relapse prevention techniques, such as goal setting, positive statements about personal change, identification of a support network, plans for dealing with setbacks, reviewing coping strategies, and developing approach-focused relapse prevention plans. It should be ensured that these relapse prevention techniques cover all the risk factors that have been formulated for the client. All techniques should be rehearsed through role play with feedback. The client should then be encouraged to experiment with new skills in all areas of his life. Additional work may be needed to ensure that that he is confident and equipped enough to transfer these skills outside of the therapy room.

Medical Treatment

Four pharmacological approaches have been taken to the treatment of paraphilias such as voyeurism (Bradford, 2000): selective serotonin reuptake inhibitors (e.g., SSRIs; fluoxetine hydrochloride), hormonal agents (e.g., medroxyprogesterone acetate or MPA), luteinizing hormone-releasing hormone (LHRH) agonists (e.g., leuprolide acetate), and antiandrogens (e.g., cyproterone acetate or CPA). All four approaches have been shown to be effective in suppressing sexually deviant behavior. With the exception of the SSRIs, however, side effects can be unpleasant and lead to poor compliance with the treatment.

A recent review of the effect of SSRIs on sexual behavior cautiously concluded that there is evidence suggesting that SSRIs can decrease deviant fantasies, paraphilic sexual behavior, and obsessional or compulsive sexual behavior (Adi et al., 2002). Emmanuel, Lydiard, and Ballenger (1991) and Abouesh and Clayton (1999) have both reported effective treatment of voyeurism with SSRIs (fluoxetine and paroxetine, respectively). Both sets of authors comment on the apparent similarities between voyeurism and obsessive–compulsive disorder, and speculate that this may account for the effectiveness of SSRIs. In both cases the patients reported a decrease in the intensity of their voyeuristic urges, as well as improved impulse control and decreased sexual drive. Emmanuel and colleagues reported that the effect continued beyond the discontinuation of medication, but follow-up was only 4 months. Abouesh and Clayton did not report any follow-up data.

Krueger and Kaplan (2001) reported 12 cases of paraphilias, of which 3 included voyeurism (among other paraphilias), treated with depot-leuprolide acetate. Patient 2 was initially treated with MPA but continued to engage in sexually deviant behavior. After another arrest he was started on leuprolide acetate, on which he remained for 10 months. He reported having more control over all aspects of his deviant sexual behavior, and markedly reduced deviant fantasies and behavior; this control continued throughout 2.5 years of follow-up after the medication had been discontinued. Patient 3 had also previously been treated with MPA and had begun to expose himself after this was discontinued. After 6 months of treatment with leuprolide acetate, he reported much greater control of his sexually deviant impulses than he experienced on MPA. Patient 12 reported loss of all sexual functioning and interest on leuprolide acetate, particularly deviant interest. However, he developed side effects and discontinued the medication. Krueger and Kaplan did not report long-term outcomes for Patients 3 and 12. It is of some interest that the patients described above, and other nonvoyeurs in the same study, had previously found CBT ineffective for their disorder.

Bradford (2000) has recommended that for mild or moderate sexual deviation, such as voyeurism or other hands-off paraphilias, pharmacological treatment should start with SSRIs. Only if SSRIs are not effective, and the voyeur has serious difficulties with controlling his behavior, should a small dose of antiandrogen be added. However, Bradford stressed that CBT and relapse prevention should be tried prior to starting any pharmacological regimen.

Self-Help Treatments

A Web search revealed no useful resources for self-help treatment of voyeurism. A handful of general health websites offer brief descriptions of voyeurism and recommend vague courses of action such as "group therapy." We could find no resource that would meet the needs of someone seeking clear guidance on how to manage voyeurism. However, it will probably not surprise readers to learn that there is a plethora of websites catering for those seeking to indulge their voyeuristic interests. For this reason, we would not particularly recommend the Internet as a source of help for voyeurism sufferers.

Combinations of Treatment Approaches

Both Bradford (2000) and Krueger and Kaplan (2002) have suggested that the treatment of paraphilias should always begin with the least restrictive treatment (e.g., behavioral treatment or CBT) and only progress to more restrictive treatment (e.g., pharmacological) if necessary. From our review of the treatment literature (such as it is), and our own experience of working with voyeurs, we concur that the best approach would probably involve a combination of CBT as described above, which should include specific behavior modification techniques, with pharmacological therapy.

Selecting the Right Treatment

Given that no treatments for voyeurism have been empirically established as effective, it is possible for a client's preference to be considered. The benefits and disadvantages of different procedures can be discussed with the client. For speed of effect, behavior modification and/or pharmacological therapy would be indicated as the best approach, based on current information. However, if the client is also aware of deficiencies in intimate relationships or interactions, CBT would probably be of interest.

Research Priorities

The dearth of published empirical studies of voyeurism means that any research into voyeurism would be welcome. In particular, there is an urgent need for systematic evaluation of documented treatment procedures and combinations of treatment procedures. Those who regularly treat voyeurs within regular sex offender treatment programs are urged to investigate and document the value of this approach with their clients, through individual follow-up at the very least.

SUMMARY AND FUTURE DIRECTIONS

One of the challenges in understanding and responding to voyeurism is the often polarized response to the paraphilia. On the one hand, voyeurism is often discussed as a relatively harmless behavior—"there is no crime in the looking." Voyeurism is not stigmatized or demonized in the same way as other paraphilias (particularly pedophilia).[1] It is likely that this tolerance of sexual voyeurism is partly due to the increasingly widespread normalization of observing others' lives through, for example, reality television and the regular invasions of privacy committed by tabloid newspapers. Furthermore, because sexual voyeurism usually seems to be accompanied by other paraphilias that may be seen as more threatening to others (e.g., exhibitionism, sadism), voyeurism may usually be overlooked in comparison. "Pure" voyeurism, unaccompanied by other paraphilias, may not come to professional attention because the usual lack of a knowing victim means that the behavior is generally not reported to the police.

At the other extreme, there are those who consider voyeurism to be a warning sign of dangerous pathology. For instance, Brenzinger (1988) claimed that voyeuristic behavior is found in the developmental histories of many serious sexual offenders, including sexual killers. In Brenzinger's view, such serious sexual crime could possibly

> be interrupted if proper identification of voyeuristic activities and behaviors are made. It is likely that if the voyeur receives psychological treatment for his inappropriate behaviors that the chances are reduced that he will be a threat to others. . . . We must advance our understanding of the voyeur's behaviors and how they assist in the development of the sexual predator. (p. 32)[2]

Laypeople believe that voyeurism can simply be overcome by willpower (Twohig & Furnham, 1998). The reality is different. Men afflicted with voyeurism often report distress associated with the lack of control they feel over their behavior. Women who are the targets of voyeurism find the invasion of privacy deeply distressing. Voyeurism is a condition that needs to be taken more seriously—by the public, by the media, by criminal justice agencies, by researchers, and by professionals who offer treatment services. At present, a voyeur seeking professional help (or mandated to do so) could be offered any of a range of treatment approaches, none of which have empirical support and which therefore are presumably selected because of the orientation of the therapist rather than on any evidence base. This situation is unacceptable for a condition that has been the subject of at least some social concern for almost 1,000 years.

NOTES

1. In 2002, the British teenage pop band Busted released a hit single entitled "That's What I Go to School For," about an adolescent boy's crush on his teacher. It included the lyrics, "I climb a tree outside her home/to make sure that she's alone/I see her in her underwear/I can't help but stop and stare." It is hard to imagine a pop song being tolerated, let alone received with enthusiasm,

if it feted any other paraphilia. In fairness to Busted, voyeurism was not a criminal offense in the United Kingdom when its members wrote this song.

2. This article is illustrated with a silhouette of a topless woman provocatively posed behind half-raised blinds.

REFERENCES

Abel, G. G., & Rouleau, J. L. (1990). The nature and extent of sexual assault. In W. L. Marshall, D. R. Laws, & H. E. Barbaree (Eds.), *Handbook of sexual assault: Issues, theories, and treatment of the offender* (pp. 9–21). New York: Plenum Press.

Abouesh, A., & Clayton, C. (1999). Compulsive voyeurism and exhibitionism: A clinical response to fluoxetine. *Archives of Sexual Behaviour, 28*, 23–30.

Adi, Y., Ashcroft, D., Browne, K., Beech, A., Fry-Smith, A., & Hyde, C. (2002). Clinical effectiveness and cost-consequences of selective serotonin reuptake inhibitors in the treatment of se offenders. *Health Technology Assessment, 6*(28), 1–66.

American Psychiatric Association. (2000). *Diagnostic and statistical manual of mental disorders* (4th ed., text rev.). Washington, DC: Author.

Bradford, J. M. W. (2000). The treatment of sexual deviation using a pharmacological approach. *Journal of Sex Research, 37*, 248–257.

Brenzinger, M. A. (1988). Voyeurism: A harmless erotic preference or a sexual predator in the making? *Crime and Justice International, 14*, 13–14, 32.

Caprio, F. S. (1949). Scotophilia–exhibitionism: A case report. *Journal of Clinical Psychopathology, 10*, 50–72.

Cautela, J. R. (1967). Covert sensitization. *Psychological Reports, 20*, 459–468.

Earls, C. M., & Castonguay, L. G. (1989). The evaluation of olfactory aversion for a bisexual paedophile with a single case study multiple baseline design. *Behaviour Research and Therapy, 20*, 137–146.

Emmanuel, N. P., Lydiard, R. B., & Ballenger, J. C. (1991). Fluoxetine treatment of voyeurism. *American Journal of Psychiatry, 148*(7), 950.

Fensterheim, H. (1974). Behavior therapy of the sexual variations. *Journal of Sex and Marital Therapy, 1*, 16–28.

Freund, K. (1990). Courtship disorders: Toward a biosocial understanding of voyeurism, exhibitionism, toucherism and the preferential rape pattern. In L. Ellis & H. Hoffman (Eds.), *Crime in biological, social and moral contexts* (pp. 100–114). New York: Praeger.

Freund, K., & Seto, M. (1998). Preferential rape in the theory of courtship disorder. *Archives of Sexual Behavior, 27*, 433–443.

Freund, K., & Watson, R. (1990). Mapping the boundaries of courtship disorder. *Journal of Sex Research, 27*, 589–606.

Freund, K., Watson, R., & Rienzo, D. (1988). The value of self-reports in the study of voyeurism and exhibitionism. *Annals of Sex Research, 1*, 243–262.

Friday, N. (1973). *My secret garden: Women's sexual fantasies.* New York: Simon & Schuster.

Friday, N. (1975). *Forbidden flowers: More women's sexual fantasies.* New York: Simon & Schuster.

Gaupp, L. A., Stern, R. M., & Ratlieff, R. G. (1971). The use of aversion-relief procedures in the treatment of a case of voyeurism. *Behavior Therapy, 2*, 585–588.

Griffin-Shelley, E. (1993). *Outpatient treatment of sex and love addicts.* Westport, CT: Praeger.

Hamilton, J. W. (1973). Voyeurism: Some therapeutic considerations. *International Journal of Psychoanalytic Psychotherapy, 2*, 77–91.

Hanson, R. K., & Harris, A. J. R. (1997). Voyeurism: Assessment and treatment. In D. R. Laws & W. O'Donohue (Eds.), *Sexual deviance: Theory, assessment, and treatment* (pp. 311–331). New York: Guilford Press.

Hurlbert, D. F. (1992). Voyeurism in an adult female with schizoid personality: A case report. *Journal of Sex Education and Therapy, 18*, 17–21.

Jackson, B. T. (1969). A case of voyeurism treated by counter-conditioning. *Behavioural Research and Therapy, 7*, 133–134.

Kaplan, M. S., & Krueger, R. B. (1997). Voyeurism: Psychopathology and theory. In D. R. Laws & W. O'Donohue (Eds.), *Sexual deviance: Theory, assessment, and treatment* (pp. 297–310). New York: Guilford Press.

Karpman, B. (1960). Towards the psychodynamics of voyeurism: A case study. *Archives of Criminal Psychodynamics, 4*, 95–142.

Konopacki, W. P., & Oei, T. P. S. (1988). Interruption in the maintenance of compulsive sexual disorder: Two case studies. *Archives of Sexual Behavior, 17*, 411–419.

Kremsdorf, R., Holmen, M., & Laws, D. R. (1980). Orgasmic reconditioning without deviant imagery: A case report with a paedophile. *Behaviour Research and Therapy, 18*, 203–207.

Krueger, R. B., & Kaplan, M. S. (2001). Depot-leuprolide acetate for treatment of paraphilias: A report of twelve cases. *Archives of Sexual Behavior, 30*, 409.

Krueger, R. B., & Kaplan, M. S. (2002). Behavioral and psychopharmacological treatment of the paraphilic and hypersexual disorders. *Journal of Psychiatric Practice, 8*, 21–32.

Langevin, R. (1983). *Sexual strands: Understanding and treating sexual anomalies in men*. Hillsdale, NJ: Erlbaum.

Langevin, R. (Ed.). (1985). *Erotic preference, gender identity and aggression in men: New research studies*. Hillsdale, NJ: Erlbaum.

Langevin, R., & Paitich, D. (2002). *Clarke Sex History Questionaire for Males—Revised*. Toronto: Multi-Health Systems.

Langevin, R., Paitich, D., & Russon, A. E. (1985). Voyeurism: Does it predict sexual aggression or violence in general? In R. Langevin (Ed.), *Erotic preference, gender identity and aggression in men: New research studies* (pp. 77–98). Hillsdale, NJ: Erlbaum.

Långström, N., & Hanson, R. K. (2006). High rates of sexual behavior in the general population: Correlates and predictors. *Archives of Sexual Behavior, 35*, 37–52.

Laws, D. R. (1986). *Sexual Deviance Card Sort*. Unpublished manuscript, Florida Mental Health Institute, University of South Florida.

Laws, D. R. (1995). Verbal satiation: Notes on procedure with speculation on its mechanism of effect. *Sexual Abuse: A Journal of Research and Treatment, 7*, 155–166.

Laws, D. R. (2001). Olfactory aversion: Notes on procedure, with speculations on its mechanisms of effect. *Sexual Abuse, 13*, 275–287.

Laws, D. R., Hanson, R. K., Osborn, C. A., & Greenbaum, P. E. (2000). Classification of child molesters by plethysmographic assessment of sexual arousal and self-report measure of sexual preference. *Journal of Interpersonal Violence, 15*, 1297–1312.

Laws, D. R., & Marshall, W. L. (1991). Masturbatory reconditioning with sexual deviates: An evaluative review. *Advances in Behavior Research and Therapy, 13*, 13–25.

Laws, D. R., & O'Neil, J. A. (1981). Variations on masturbatory conditioning. *Behavioural Psychotherapy, 9*, 111–136.

Lösel, F., & Schmucker, M. (2005). The effectiveness of treatment for sexual offenders: A comprehensive meta-analysis. *Journal of Experimental Criminology, 1*, 117–146.

Malkin, D. (1991). Individuation in a voyeur recidivist. *Australian Journal of Clinical and Experimental Hypnosis, 19*, 117–131.

Marquis, J. N. (1970). Orgasmic reconditioning: Changing sexual object choice through controlling masturbation fantasies. *Journal of Behavior Therapy and Experimental Psychiatry, 1*, 263–271.

Marshall, W. L. (1979). Satiation therapy: A procedure for reducing deviant sexual arousal. *Journal of Applied Behavior Analysis, 12*, 377–389.

Marshall, W. L. (2006). Clinical and research limitations in the use of phallometric testing with sexual offenders. *Sexual Offender Treatment, 1*. Retrieved from *sexual-offender-treatment.org*

Marshall, W. L., Anderson, D., & Fernandez, Y. M. (1999). *Cognitive-behavioural treatment of sexual offenders*. Chichester, UK: Wiley.

Marshall, W. L., & Eccles, A. (1996). Cognitive behavioral treatment of sex offenders. In V. B. Van Hasselt & M. Hersen (Eds.), *A sourcebook of psychological treatment manuals for adult disorders* (pp. 295–332). New York: Plenum Press.

McConaghy, N. (1964). A year's experience with non-verbal psychotherapy. *Medical Journal of Australia, 1,* 831–837.

McConaghy, N. (2005). Sexual dysfunctions and disorders. In J. E. Maddux & B. A. Winstead (Eds.), *Psychopathology: Foundations for a contemporary understanding* (pp. 255–280). Mahwah, NJ: Erlbaum.

McGuire, R. J., Carlisle, J. M., & Young, B. G. (1965). Sexual deviations as conditioned behaviour: A hypothesis. *Behaviour Research and Therapy, 2,* 185–190.

Nichols, H. R., & Molinder, I. (1984). *Multiphasic Sex Inventory manual*. Fircrest, WA: Nichols and Molinder Assessments. Retrieved from *www.nicholsandmolinder.com*

Rangaswamy, K. (1987). Treatment of voyeurism by behavior therapy. *Child Psychiatry Quarterly, 20,* 73–76.

Smith, R. S. (1976). Voyeurism: A review of the literature. *Archives of Sexual Behavior, 5,* 585–608.

Socarides, C. W. (1974). The demonified mother: A study of voyeurism and sexual sadism. *International Review of Psycho-Analysis, 1,* 187–195.

Stationery Office. (2003). *Sexual Offences Act 2003 c. 42*. Retrieved from *www.opsi.gov.uk*

Stoudenmire, J. (1973). Behavioral treatment of voyeurism and possible symptom substitution. *Psychotherapy, 10,* 328–330.

Stoyler, I. J. (1985). Voyeurism: Treatment by cognitive behavior therapy in a case of scopophilia. *Tidsskrift for Norsk Psykologforening, 22,* 561–564.

Tollison, C. D., & Adams, H. E. (1979). *Sexual disorders: Treatment, theory, and research*. New York: Gardner Press.

Twohig, F., & Furnham, A. (1998). Lay beliefs about overcoming four sexual paraphilias: Fetishism, paedophilia, sexual sadism, and voyeurism. *Personality and Individual Differences, 24,* 267–278.

Vasquez, J. (1970). Voyeurism and photophobia: A clinical case. *Interpretation, 4,* 165–186.

Yalom, I. D. (1960). Aggression and forbiddeness in voyeurs. *Archives of General Psychiatry, 3,* 305–319.

CHAPTER 20

RAPE

Psychopathology and Theory

THERESA A. GANNON
TONY WARD

When Hudson and Ward (1997) presented their overview of "Rape: Psychopathology and Theory" in the first edition of this book, they highlighted the heterogeneity evident in rapists, and the need for researchers to capture and explain this heterogeneity. A decade later, professionals have indeed started to explore this diversity further in classificatory systems, etiological models, and rehabilitation models. Thus, while there is still much work to do, we are pleased to see that progress has been made over the past decade, and it is this progress that we attempt to track.

In this chapter, we review relevant diagnostic criteria, epidemiological factors, associated features, risk assessments, and etiological theories associated with rape; we conclude with some suggestions for future conceptual and research developments. Our main aim is to build upon the work summarized by Hudson and Ward (1997) in the first edition of this book, providing commentary on some of the more recent developments in this rapidly changing field. In keeping with Hudson and Ward's chapter, we discuss only sexual crimes perpetrated against adult women.

DESCRIPTION

We commence our description of rape with reference to the current standard classification system for mental disorders—the *Diagnostic and Statistical Manual of Mental Disorders*, fourth edition, text revision (DSM-IV-TR; American Psychiatric Association, 2000). Notably, rape is omitted from DSM-IV-TR, with no apparent plans to introduce it in DSM-V (planned for release in 2011). Within the latest DSM version, a diagnosis of any paraphilia is dependent upon recurrent, intense sexual urges, fantasies, or behaviors that involve unusual objects, activities, or situations, lasting for a period of at least 6 months and causing significant distress to the individual or impairment in functioning. Although professionals in the field of sexual offending have argued that many sexually abusive men such as pedophiles and exhibitionists are unlikely to meet such criteria (Hudson & Ward, 1997; Marshall, 2007), rapists appear equally unlikely to meet DSM-IV-TR's criteria, making rape's absence from DSM-IV-TR perplexing. Rape is cited as a behavior occurring under the diagnosis of sexual sadism (constituting a mere 5–10% of men who rape; Craissati, 2005), but this is the only fleeting glimpse of rape in DSM-IV-TR. Because rape is largely absent from DSM-IV-TR, Marshall (2007) argues that professionals required to provide clinical diagnoses often place rapists into the paraphilia not otherwise specified (NOS) category. Clearly, such overuse of the NOS category does little to inform clinical assessment or treatment for rapists (Marshall, 2007). Similarly, the latest (10th) revision of the *International Classification of Diseases* (ICD-10; World Health Organization, 1992)—used widely outside North America to diagnose a range of sexual disorders, including pedophilia, voyeurism, and exhibitionism—does not specify rape under behavioral disorders.

Legally, "rape" is typically defined as penetration of the vagina or anus without legitimate consent. The source of penetration (e.g., penile, finger, or object), sexual act conducted (e.g., vaginal, anal, or oral), and definition of consent may vary across jurisdictions. In the United Kingdom, for example, the legislative definition of rape encompasses *penile* penetration of the mouth, anus, or vagina, whereas nonpenile penetration is addressed by the separate offense of "assault by penetration" (Sexual Offences Act, 2003). In Canada, however, rape is subsumed under the general heading of "sexual assault" (see the Criminal Code of Canada, 1985), and although assault is defined as "intentional touching without consent," the sexual component is not addressed in the code.[1] These differing legislative definitions of rape are likely to be reflected in the research and statistics proffered by varying countries.

EPIDEMIOLOGICAL FACTORS

Two main methods are used by researchers to estimate the scope of rape: "prevalence" and "incidence" estimates. Prevalence estimates generally refer to the proportion of women indicating that they have been victimized at least once over a given time period. Incidence estimates typically examine the number of recorded rape cases occurring over a specified time period, usually a year. Both methods should be approached with caution, since they are subject to many limitations that are liable to distort overall estimates and underestimate the true extent of rape.

One of the most comprehensive community studies organized to estimate the prevalence of unwanted sexual experiences for women in San Francisco was conducted by Russell (1984), who reported a figure of 24%. A little later, Koss, Gidycz, and Wisniewski (1987) reported comparable findings (27.5%) from a sample of U.S. university women—a finding also supported in Australasia (see Gavey's [1991] 25.3% figure for New Zealand women). More recently, the Violence against Women Survey funded by the U.S. Department of Justice (Tjaden & Thoennes, 1998) found that 17.6% of 8,000 U.S. women reported being victims of rape or attempted rape during their lifetimes. Similarly, a figure of 20% of women was reported by students completing the National College Risk Health Risk Behavior Survey (Brener, McMahon, Warren, & Douglas, 1999). In

Britain, using data from the 1998 and 2000 British Crime Surveys, Myhill and Allen (2002) found that 4.9% of women reported having been raped since reaching the age of consent. A large proportion of these sexually aggressive incidents were perpetrated by partners, ex-partners, or acquaintances. Differing methodologies and samples may well be accountable for some of the differences in reported prevalence rates.

In terms of incidence, a key U.S. federal source frequently drawn upon is the Federal Bureau of Investigation (FBI) Uniform Crime Reports (UCR) program, which documents complaints to local authorities. The latest figures released by the UCR (FBI, 2004) show that 94,635 rapes were recorded in 2004[2]—a 0.8% increase from the previous year. Canada's UCR system records rape under the category of sexual assault, in line with prevailing legislation; thus it is impossible to make any estimate of rapes per se. However, the latest figures show that the police reported in excess of 23,000 unwanted sexual assaults in 2005 (M. Gannon, 2006).

CHARACTERISTICS OF RAPISTS

Rapists are generally accepted as being similar to nonsexual offenders on a variety of sociodemographic variables. For example, rapists tend to be blue-collar workers of low socioeconomic status, as well as early school leavers (Bard et al., 1987). African Caribbean heritage also appears to be much higher in convicted rapists' backgrounds in the United Kingdom than general population rates would suggest (see Craissati, 2005; Craissati, Webb, & Keen, 2005).

However, rapists appear to show clear differences from child molesters in core adult characteristics. In other words, child molesters are the ones who present more differently from the rest of the offender population. In comparison to child molesters, rapists appear generally younger (Dickey, Nussbaum, Chevolleau, & Davidson, 2002), are less likely to hold passive traits, are more likely to have engaged in an intimate relationship (Christie, Marshall, & Lanthier, 1979), and are more heterosocially competent (Dreznick, 2003). Differences from child molesters in developmental background are not quite so clear-cut. Both child molesters' and rapists' backgrounds tend to be characterized by sexual abuse and adverse familial relations (Dhawan & Marshall, 1996). In relation to attachment style, sexual offenders—like many nonsexual offenders—often report poor childhood attachment experiences (Smallbone & Dadds, 1998; Ward, Hudson, & Marshall, 1996). Relatively few studies, however, partition out rapists for separate examination, or an adequate selection of comparison groups. One such study, conducted by Smallbone and Dadds (1998) compared stranger rapists with other sexual offenders, property offenders, and correctional officers. Whereas intrafamilial child molesters tended to have problematic maternal attachment relationships, rapists—like property offenders—reported adversarial attachments with their fathers. Later studies by Smallbone and Dadds (2000, 2001) have empirically supported the link between adverse childhood attachment and sexually coercive behavior in adult university males, although it is unclear whether the link is explained by paternal, maternal, or both types of attachment difficulties. Nevertheless, such adverse developmental attachment patterns appear to explain rapists' adult intimacy deficits and emotional loneliness (Garlick, Marshall, & Thornton, 1996; Marshall, 1989). Further work, however, is needed to investigate rapists' attachment issues, because the few studies available offer only limited insight into the complexities of rapists' attachment styles and associated difficulties.

ASSOCIATED FEATURES

Many attempts have been made to examine features associated with rape, so as to pinpoint possible etiologies. In regard to comorbidity, there are two main issues: (1) Do rapists display specific psychopathologies that differentiate them from other offender groups? (2) Do rapists commit crimes other than rape?

It is not uncommon for researchers to note the presence of psychopathologies in rapists that clearly fit DSM-IV-TR or ICD-10 criteria (Hillbrand, Foster, & Hirt, 1990; Långström, Sjöstedt, & Grann, 2004). However, although many researchers include rapists in their overall samples, many (as noted earlier) never partition rapists out for separate analysis, making any conclusions about the prevalence of psychopathology in rape especially difficult (e.g., Cochrane, Grisso, & Frederick, 2001; Kafka & Hennen, 2002; Lung & Huang, 2004).

In a recent study, Långström and colleagues (2004) examined retrospective inpatient care ICD psychiatric diagnoses for rapists (N = 535) and child molesters (N = 522) discharged from Swedish prisons between 1993 and 1997. By far the most prevalent diagnosis for rapists was alcohol abuse or dependence (9.3%), followed by drug abuse (3.9%), a personality disorder (2.6%), and psychosis (1.7%). Interestingly, these rates were significantly higher than those found in the child molesters, suggesting that although rapists do not exhibit particularly high levels of diagnosable psychiatric disorders, the rates are higher than those reported for child molesters (see also Craig, Browne, & Stringer, 2004). With reference to specific personality disorders, recent studies report that rapists are significantly more likely to be diagnosed as psychopathic, or to hold psychopathic traits, than child molesters (Abracen, Looman, Di Fazio, Kelly, & Stirpe, 2006; Firestone, Bradford, Greenberg, & Serran, 2000; Vess, Murphy, & Arkowitz, 2004). Since antisocial personality traits have been found to predict both general and sexual recidivism (Hanson & Morton-Bourgon, 2004), it is crucial that professionals carefully consider the role of such issues in the facilitation of both general and sexual offenses.

Another factor that may distinguish rapists from other offender groups is neurological impairment. Långström and colleagues (2004), in the study described above, found that rapists were more likely to have been diagnosed with a traumatic head injury than child molesters were (3.9% vs. 1.7%, respectively). Hucker and colleagues (1988; reviewed by Lalumière, Harris, Quinsey, & Rice, 2005) found that nonsadistic rapists demonstrated more impairment on the Luria–Nebraska Neuropsychological Test Battery than sadistic rapists and nonsexual offenders did. Other studies, however, have shown that *sadistic* rapists show structural abnormalities in the temporal horn (see Aigner et al., 2000; Hucker et al., 1988; reviewed by Lalumière et al., 2005). Neurobiological deficits in the form of faulty serotonin functioning have been implicated in the etiology of sexual aggression (see Beech & Mitchell, 2005, for a review), although this avenue of inquiry concerns offenders generally rather than rapists per se. In summary, then, there appears to be no convincing evidence that rapists are characterized by neurological deficits that distinguish them from other offenders (Lalumière et al., 2005).

The other relevant question is whether rapists limit their criminal activity to rape. Abel, Becker, Cunningham-Rathner, Mittelman, and Rouleau (1988) were some of the first researchers to show empirically that rapists assured of confidentiality would disclose numerous offenses involving children also. Similarly, more recent research has found that the polygraph facilitates rapists' disclosures of previously unknown instances of child sexual abuse (see Gannon, Beech, & Ward, in press; Wilcox, Sosnowski, Warberg, &

Beech, 2005). Rape has also been associated with a whole host of other inappropriate sexual behaviors, especially hands-off offenses like exhibitionism (Simon, 2000; Stermac & Hall, 1989). In terms of the commission of nonsexual crimes, rapists appear to be much more similar to violent offenders than to child molesters. For example, Simon (2000) found that rapists and violent offenders (1) displayed significant diversity in their offense records in comparison to child molesters; and (2) had committed equivalent proportions of drug-related offenses, theft, and burglary. Other studies have also found that a considerable number of rapists are likely to hold convictions for nonsexual crimes (see Stermac & Quinsey, 1986; Weinrott & Saylor, 1991). Taken together, these findings suggest that rapists are significantly more versatile than the general public would have us believe. In support of this, rapists appear more likely to recidivate nonsexually than sexually over a 4- to 5-year follow-up period (22.1 vs. 18.9%, respectively; Hanson & Bussière, 1998).

RISK ASSESSMENT

Current knowledge of the factors associated with risk in rapists is unfortunately meager in comparison to that for child molesters, who appear to dominate the research landscape. Exactly why this is the case is puzzling, but Craissati (2005) has proposed that it may have something to do with a general refusal of rapists to participate in research (which would clearly fit with the antisocial personality issues described earlier), lower numbers of incarcerated rapists, and/or the general political pressure to focus on issues pertaining to child molestation.

Actuarial risk assessments—which tend to focus exclusively on unchangeable, static risk factors, such as previous offense history—are designed to predict risk for sexual offenders *generally*. Examples include the Static-99 (Hanson & Thornton, 2000) and the Risk Matrix 2000 (Thornton et al., 2003), both of which are typically regarded to be fairly good estimators of future risk in comparison to unstructured or guided clinical judgment (Hanson, Morton, & Harris, 2003). However, although such tools are commonly utilized by professionals called upon to assess rapists, the validation samples used to construct such tools are often child-molester-focused (e.g., the Risk Matrix 2000). This may in part explain why some actuarial measures have failed to show impressive rates of violence and sexual recidivism prediction for rapists (see Bartosh, Garby, Lewis, & Gray, 2003).

Because sexual offending is a complex, multifactorial process, researchers have attempted to identify risk factors that may be amenable to treatment intervention, and community management (i.e., dynamic risk factors—Beech, Fisher, & Beckett, 1999; Hanson & Harris, 2001; Thornton, 2000, 2002). Craissati (2005) has picked out five core dynamic risk factors relevant to rapists from the general tools available (see Beech, Friendship, Erikson, & Hanson, 2002; Hanson & Harris, 2001; Thornton, 2002): intimacy deficits, social influences, offense-supportive attitudes, sexual self-regulation, and general self-regulation. In brief, rapists' intimacy deficits may arise from beliefs that women are unknowable and devious (Polaschek & Gannon, 2004; Polaschek & Ward, 2002), from an inability to perceive women's facial affect accurately (Malamuth & Brown, 1994), or from lack of empathy (Marshall & Moulden, 2001). Rapists may also associate with antisocial companions who support their sexual offenses in a variety of ways. In terms of offense-supportive attitudes, Craissati suggests that rapists are likely to hold strong attitudes of entitlement. Finally, sexual self-regulation and general self-regulation refer to sexualized and general impulsivity, respectively; in other words, rapists appear poor at inhibiting strong behavioral urges.

In addition to these *stable* dynamic risk factors, acute dynamic risk factors have been identified for both rapists and child molesters that indicate imminence of reoffending (see the Acute-2000—Hanson & Harris, 2000). These are access to victim, emotional collapse, collapse of social supports, hostility, substance misuse, sexual preoccupations, supervision of rejection, and factors unique to the individual (e.g., the anniversary of a loved one's death). Although these factors are believed to be critical for professionals monitoring offenders' progress in the community, further evidence is needed to validate them (Craissati, 2005).

In summary, several general assessments are available for professionals called upon to make estimations of a rapist's future risk to reoffend. Overall, although static, stable dynamic, and acute dynamic assessments of risk appear generally useful in providing benchmarks with which to assess a variety of sexual offenders, designing instruments that focus entirely on rapists would be a considerable step forward in risk assessment practice and may well highlight previously untested divergences and similarities between rapists and other types of offenders.

THEORY

A task of paramount importance for assessing and treating rapists is the construction of good etiological theories. Several attempts have been made to develop classificatory taxonomies to help clarify important etiological issues and assist in the appropriate assessment and design of treatment. Early psychodynamic approaches (e.g., Groth, Burgess, & Holstrom, 1977; Seghorn & Cohen, 1980) differentiated rapists according to the main factors hypothesized to motivate their actions. For example, Seghorn and Cohen (1980) differentiated among rapists characterized by sexual, aggressive, impulsive, and sexual diffusion motivators, while Groth and colleagues (1977) discriminated mainly between power-motivated and anger-motivated rapists. Other typologies have been developed from empirical data (e.g., Cohen, Seghorn, & Calmas, 1969; Knight & Prentky, 1990; Prentky & Knight, 1991). One notable instance is the work of Knight and Prentky (1990), who subdivided rapists along the following primary motivating categories: opportunistic (further subdivided into high or low social competence), pervasively angry, sadistic (further subdivided into overt or muted aggression), sexual nonsadistic (further subdivided into high or low social competence), and vindictive (further subdivided into high or low social competence). Although these distinctions appear useful for surface evaluations of rape etiology, and are subject to ongoing evaluations, they have not been adopted to aid clinical practice with offenders.

In our view, a much broader theoretical base is needed for comprehensive assessment and treatment of rapists. Such theory construction should be appraised along the major critical dimensions specified by Hooker (1987), Newton-Smith (2002), and Ward, Polaschek, and Beech (2005). Briefly, these factors are (1) empirical adequacy and scope (is the theory empirically supported and able to account for the range of phenomena in question?); (2) internal coherence (does the theory convincingly integrate explanatory material, or are there stark contradictions?); (3) unifying power (does the theory unify previously separate theories in order to explain phenomena?); (4) heuristic value (does the theory generate new knowledge in the form of predictions, or in clinical terms, new treatment interventions?); (5) external consistency (is the theory consistent with other, background theories?); and (6) explanatory depth (does the theory convincingly articulate meaningful mechanisms in its explanation of phenomena)? Etiological theories that are relatively strong along each of these dimensions are critical for both conceptual and practical progression. Thus we use some of these values to guide our appraisal of the key theoretical offerings concerning rape.

Since the previous edition of this chapter was published (Hudson & Ward, 1997), various etiological theories have been proffered for the explanation of rape. Due to space limitations, we cannot cover both single-factor and multifactorial etiological theories of sexual aggression in their entirety here. Thus we focus first on one or two good exemplars of single-factor theories (sociobiological and social-cognitive), and then turn to multivariate theories of rape. Readers interested in single-factor feminist, psychodynamic, or pure behavioral perspectives should refer to Hudson and Ward (1997) or Ward and colleagues (2005).

Sociobiological Theories

Several sociobiological theories have been proffered to explain sexual aggression (Ellis, 1989, 1991; Malamuth & Heilman, 1998; Quinsey & Lalumière, 1995; Thornhill & Palmer, 2000). Here, however, we choose to focus on a particularly influential and recent theoretical development—Thornhill and Palmer's theory. Thornhill and Palmer (2000) hypothesize that the causes of rape lie deep within humans' evolutionary history. In short, Thornhill and Palmer contend that rape is a consequence of mating strategies that maximized ancestral men's reproductive value. In other words, men who were able to maximize their reproductive access ensured that their genes survived to be passed on to future generations. Thornhill and Palmer hypothesize that rape may have been selected for either directly or indirectly. If rape was directly selected for in our evolutionary past, it implies that strategies used to force copulation *directly* increased males' reproductive success. However, if rape was *indirectly* selected for, it seems likely that rape evolved incidentally from another trait directly selected for sexual adaptation—for example, the pursuit of low-commitment sex (Symons, 1979).

Since Thornhill and Palmer (2000) propose that rape is a product of nature, and use evidence of rape phenomena across other animal species to back their hypothesis, their theory appears to hold some level of empirical adequacy, unifying power, explanatory depth, and external consistency. A significant problem with the particular evolutionary perspective endorsed by Thornhill and Palmer, however, is the fact that it tends to portray humans as biologically rigid beings with little capacity for mental development as a product of cultural influences or social learning. Since data clearly support the role of cultural factors in a variety of psychological disciplines, this narrow evolutionary perspective now appears challenged in terms of the very same criteria that appeared so strong on the surface (i.e., empirical adequacy, unifying power, external consistency, and explanatory depth). To illustrate, the theory does not adequately explain the range of variables associated with sexual aggression and supported in various attendant literatures (i.e., biological, social, cultural, and psychological factors).

In our view, a way forward is to adopt a more flexible evolutionary perspective, such as the niche construction model of Odling-Smee, Laland, and Feldman (2003). Briefly, the niche construction model stipulates that there are three sources of cognitive and behavioral strategies involved in human mating behavior: genetic constraints or predispositions, individual learning processes, and cultural resources and processes. Problems in either of these domains can result in sexually aggressive behavior. Readers interested in further exploring Thornhill and Palmer's (2000) theory and the application of evolutionary theory to rape should consult Ward and Siegert (2002) or Ward and colleagues (2005).

Social-Cognitive Theories

Over the past two decades, researchers have become increasingly interested in utilizing social-cognitive theories and methods for understanding rape. "Social cognition," in essence, is the study of social interactions with reference to cognitive theory or using methods that tap fundamental cognitive components (Augoustinos & Walker, 1995; Fiske & Taylor, 1991). In brief, three main questions underlie a social-cognitive understanding of rape (cf. Sherman, Judd, & Park, 1989): (1) What offense-relevant information is stored in long-term memory and how is it organized?, (2) How does this information affect information processing, judgments, and subsequent behavior?, (3) How is the information stored in long-term memory updated, altered, or revised? Below, we briefly review relevant literature approaching rape from the social-cognitive perspective.

Ward (2000b) has developed a theoretical framework for organizing and explaining sexual offenders' offense-supportive statements, which has been applied specifically to rapists (Polaschek & Gannon, 2004; Polaschek & Ward, 2002). In brief, Ward hypothesizes that rapists hold a number of offense-supportive schemas (or "implicit theories") that are used to draw inferences about women's beliefs, desires, and future intentions. Drawing upon questionnaire data and interviews with rapists, Polaschek (Polaschek & Gannon, 2004; Polaschek & Ward, 2002) hypothesizes that rapists are characterized by five sets of implicit theories: women as sexual objects (i.e., beliefs that women are sexually preoccupied and highly receptive to sexual advances); women as dangerous (i.e., beliefs that women are unknowable, deceptive, and malevolent); entitlement (i.e., beliefs centering around male supremacy and control); the world as dangerous (i.e., beliefs that the world is generally a threatening and hostile place); and uncontrollability (beliefs that actions cannot be controlled in the face of strong urges and impulses such as sexual arousal). Since these explanatory theories are hypothesized to have developed in order to explain adverse childhood experiences, they are believed to be highly entrenched and extremely difficult to change, resulting in an individual who consistently misinterprets his surrounding world, and the people in it (usually women) in an offense-supportive manner.

Various self-report studies with rapists have generally supported these implicit theory themes or slight variations of them (e.g., Beech, Fisher, & Ward, 2005; Polaschek & Gannon, 2004; Scully, 1990). For example, Scully (1990) found that—even in the presence of a weapon—rapists believed their victims *wanted* the sexual contact forced upon them. Other studies have also provided evidence that rapists misinterpret crucial social information. Using written scenarios, Lipton, McDonel, and McFall (1987) found that, compared with offender comparison groups, rapists had particular difficulty identifying women's negative affect (especially during ambiguous first-date conditions). Malamuth and Brown (1994) used video clips of a male actor attempting to interact with a woman at a bar, and manipulated the woman's responses. When asked to watch the video and interpret the woman's communications, sexually aggressive males tended to misperceive the woman's rejection as seduction. They also misinterpreted the woman's positive cues as hostility—a finding that led Malamuth and Brown to conclude that sexually aggressive males hold a suspiciousness schema. This finding supports the implicit theory theme of women as dangerous, described above—a theme that is likely to facilitate distrust, hostility, and sexual aggression toward women.

Pryor and Stoller (1994) examined the organization of knowledge structures in males demonstrating a high "likelihood of sexually harassing" (LSH). After presenting men with various word pair combinations (of dominance-, control-, and sex-related content), they found that high-LSH men (in comparison to low-LSH men) held strong links between dominance and sexual knowledge, evidenced through higher-frequency estimates of such word pairings and a higher certainty of recognizing these word pairings. Similar findings have been reported by Bargh, Raymond, Pryor, and Strack (1995) with men demonstrating a high likelihood of rape.

In general, social-cognitive theories of rape appear to be empirically substantiated (empirical adequacy) and to hold both research and clinical heuristic value (as evidenced by the proliferation of research into this topic during the 1990s, and the focus on social cognition in most contemporary cognitive-behavioral therapy for sexual offenders). However, as is the case with most single-factor theories, social-cognitive theories of rape by their very nature fail to incorporate all of the factors believed to be causal in rape (i.e., poor explanatory depth and unifying power). Because of this, multifactorial theories of rape appear more promising as explanations of sexual aggression.

Comprehensive Theories

An early multivariate theory developed to explain rape etiology was outlined by Neil Malamuth and his colleagues (see Malamuth, 1986, 1996; Malamuth, Heavey, & Linz, 1993). In brief, Malamuth adopted an evolutionary stance, distinguishing between "ultimate" causes (i.e., explaining why some mechanisms develop) and "proximate" causes (i.e., explaining how some mechanisms develop). In terms of ultimate causes, Malamuth (1996) hypothesized that evolution favored differing mating for men and women because of differential parental cost. This evolutionary hypothesis was used by Malamuth to explain the existence of two interacting pathways resulting in sexual aggression. The "sexual promiscuity" pathway contends that due to evolutionary influences, men have developed a preference for impersonal sexual encounters, which may be optimized through use of sexual coercion. The "hostile masculinity" pathway holds that when men believe that their copulation efforts are being thwarted, they are likely to become angry, thus promoting the use of coercion in order to maximize reproductive success. In terms of proximate causes, Malamuth and colleagues (1993) made four fundamental proposals: (1) Sexual aggression results from a confluence of risk factors that motivate, disinhibit, and provide the opportunity for sexual aggression to occur; (2) these risk factors tend to be domain-specific; (3) these risk factors account for other adverse behaviors targeted toward women (e.g., general dominance or controlling behavior); and (4) environmental factors such as childhood experience play an important part in either facilitating or inhibiting sexual aggression.

The risk factors Malamuth and colleagues (1993) speak of have been empirically supported and generally fall into six predictive categories: tumescence to rape, dominant motivation, hostility toward women, offense-supportive attitudes (e.g., rape myth acceptance), antisocial personality characteristics, and sexual experience (used to measure opportunity of sexual aggression; see Malamuth, 1986). Other fundamental aspects of the model have also been empirically supported—namely, domain specificity and generalization (Malamuth, 1988)—and the model generally appears to be supported when subjected to both internal and independent evaluation (see Malamuth, Linz, Heavey, Barnes, & Acker, 1995; Wheeler, George, & Dahl, 2002). This is testament to the theory's empirical adequacy. Other strengths include the model's obvious heuristic value, which is demonstrated by the large research base it has created and its potential for treatment utility. Unifying power is also demonstrated through the use of broad feminist theory (in relation to dominance and power issues) and evolutionary theory (to explain how rape may be the product of either source). There are some problems with this model, however. It fails to detail the exact interactions between variables outlined in the model (i.e., a lack of explanatory depth), and, unlike other models and taxonomies, it is unable to incorporate the issue of offense heterogeneity (i.e., a lack of empirical scope and external consistency).

Marshall and Barbaree's integrated theory (Marshall & Barbaree, 1990; Marshall & Marshall, 2000) integrates four sets of empirical factors (biological, developmental, sociocultural, and situational) to explain general sexual offending. In brief, a critical aspect of Marshall and Barbaree's theory revolves around a male adolescent's ability to adequately inhibit aggressive impulses that are instinctively associated with male sexual activity. Adverse experiences during childhood (e.g., physical or sexual abuse, poor attachment to parents) may affect the inhibition process, creating vulnerability and a predisposition to offend sexually. In other words, vulnerabilities in the form of low self-esteem or poor coping skills paired with pubertal male hormonal activity are likely to increase the chances of an individual acting in a sexually aggressive manner. Marshall and Barbaree suggest that vulnerable adolescents who lack self-esteem are likely to adopt "macho," negative sociocultural attitudes (e.g., viewing women as sexual objects) to enhance self-esteem. Such vulnerability factors may then interact with transient situational variables (e.g., affect, sexual arousal, intoxication) to trigger sexual aggression.

Marshall and Barbaree's model has been the subject of several developments (e.g., Marshall & Marshall, 2000), which have elaborated key issues within the model. This further refinement has increased the theory's explanatory depth and unifying power through explicitly outlining the connections between developmental adversity and psychological vulnerabilities. The theory also has significant strengths in terms of empirical adequacy and heuristic value. For example, many of the hypotheses concerning intimacy deficits have been empirically supported (e.g., Smallbone & Dadds, 1998), leading to recognition of intimacy skills as a core target for any sexual offender treatment. There are some weaknesses inherent in the theory, however (see Ward, 2002, and Ward et al., 2005, for detailed critiques). Briefly stated, it is unclear how this theory may explain offenders who begin to display sexually aggressive behaviors during late adulthood—a problem with empirical scope. In addition, the theory places deviant sexual impulses at the top of the list as a contributor toward sexual aggression. This does not fit with recent research illustrating that only a small proportion of sexual offenders exhibit enduring sexual self-regulation deficits (Hudson, Ward, & McCormack, 1999; Yates, Kingston, & Hall, 2003). This problem appears to indicate some lack of external consistency and explanatory depth.

Hall and Hirschman's (1991) quadripartite model of sexual aggression has been specifically developed to explain rape. Four main factors are implicated in the commission of rape: physiological sexual arousal; cognitive distortions; affective dyscontrol; and personality problems stemming from developmental experience. Each one of these motivational factors is hypothesized to characterize a subtype of rapists who are strongly motivated by that particular factor. For example, Hall and Hirschman argue that for some rapists, sexual arousal may not be the critical motivating factor of importance; instead, their cognitions may represent the driving motivational force behind sexual assault. Hall and Hirschman argue that the influence of the primary motivating factor provokes offending behavior by pressing individuals over their "inhibitory threshold." It is hypothesized that various inhibitors restrain men's sexual aggression, and that these may be overcome by the primary factor interacting with, and also intensifying, the other three factors. In other words, if the benefits of rape (e.g., cathartic anger, sexual gratification) outweigh the drawbacks (e.g., punishment, moral condemnation), then an individual is more likely to commit rape. A core strength of this model is its ability to classify rapists into four distinct typologies, each hypothesized to hold a unique set of treatment needs. This careful attention to heterogeneity highlights the model's potential strengths in clinical and research heuristic value. Empirical scope also appears strong, since the model is able to explain why nonoffenders who may hold sexual offending vulnerabilities do not sexually offend (since they are not propelled past the offense threshold). Other strengths revolve around the model's ability to explain how the enduring vulnerabilities of each of the four primary motivators interact with situational factors resulting in sexual aggression (i.e., the model's unifying power). For example, a physiological rapist may be more likely to offend sexually after watching explicit pornographic films. Weaknesses with the model center around its internal coherence and explanatory depth. In short, the theory requires more details concerning exactly how each of the factors interacts with the others to produce sexual offending. Without this, the model lacks the explanatory mechanisms and coherence needed to explain sexual aggression adequately (see Ward et al., 2005, for a detailed critique).

The most recently constructed theory—the integrated theory of sexual offending (ITSO; Ward & Beech, 2006; Ward & Beech, Chapter 2, this volume)—draws together many of the earlier-described theories in an attempt to unify current knowledge of sexual aggression. The ITSO proposes that sexual offending is the result of three sets of causal factors that interact continuously and dynamically, in a variety of ways. These are biological factors (i.e., genetics and brain development); proximal and distal ecological niche factors (i.e., physical, social, cultural, and personal circumstances); and three core neuropsychological factors associated with various brain structures (i.e., the motivational/emotional, action selection/control, and perception/memory systems). In brief, the motivational/emotional system functions to "allow goals and values to influence both perception and action selection rapidly and to adjust motivational state to fit changing environmental circumstances" (Pennington, 2002, p. 79). The action selection/control system enables an individual to plan, execute, and evaluate planned actions; thus behavior and thoughts are regulated in order to obtain valued goals. Finally, the perception/memory system processes incoming stimuli and constructs representations of such stimuli (i.e., objects, social events), so that they are available as input for each of the other systems. According to the ITSO, various combinations of the three sets of causal factors—biological, ecological, and neuropsychological—produce the heterogeneous patterns of clinical symptoms or acute dynamic risk factors believed to facilitate sexually abusive actions (i.e., self-regulation deficits, deviant sexual arousal, social difficulties, and cognitive distortions). For example, for one particular rapist, a primary causal factor may be his high levels of impulsivity (a problem in the action selection/control system), which may be a product of a brain injury sustained as a child (brain development), and may be more likely to be displayed during personally distressing and frustrating scenarios (ecological niche). For another, having experienced extremely adverse social circumstances (e.g., war, death of a loved one) may be the core contributor to the commission of the sexual offense. Unlike the first example, then, the causal factors here appear heavily weighted toward this individual's ecological niche rather than factors within the person.

A clear strength of the ITSO is its unification of a great variety of theories (i.e., Pennington's neuroscientific theory, and previous sexual offending theories) in order to explain sexual offending. In other words, the ITSO appears to possess strong unifying power and external consistency. Additionally, the theory shows promise in its ability to guide treatment, since it acknowledges the great deal of heterogeneity evident in sexual offenders (i.e., heuristic value). However, there are some drawbacks to be noted with this theory; many of which stem from its notable youth. First, although it has been developed from current empirical research, it has yet to be thoroughly empirically tested in its own right (i.e., it lacks empirical adequacy and scope). Second, there is room for the authors to refine their explanations of the mechanisms producing sexual offending. For example, how exactly do the brain structures implicated in sexual offending become impaired? More details of the mechanisms creating this impairment would increase the ITSO's explanatory depth.

Rehabilitation Theories

Perhaps one of the most substantial theoretical developments we have seen over the past decade centers on the concept of relapse prevention (RP). The RP model (Marlatt & Gordon, 1985) was modified for use with sexual offenders by Pithers and his colleagues (Pithers, 1990; Pithers, Marques, Gibat, & Marlatt, 1983). In brief, the RP model focuses on high-risk cognitive, affective, and behavioral factors that threaten offense abstinence, aiming to promote offenders' awareness of such threats and to strengthen their self-regulation skills. Although initially popular with treatment professionals, the RP model has been the recipient of intense criticism (for comprehensive critiques, see Laws, 2003; Laws, Hudson, & Ward, 2002; Polaschek, 2003; Ward, 2000a; Ward & Hudson, 1996). A major concern with the RP model is the promulgation of a single pathway to relapse, characterized by negative affect and self-regulation deficits (as we shall see later, more recent data highlight the RP model's lack of empirical scope). Dissatisfaction with this element of the model has resulted in a growing research base investigating heterogeneous pathways to sexual offending, and in the development of a new relapse-related approach—the self-regulation model (Ward & Hudson, 1998).

The self-regulation model emerged from early empirically grounded offense chain process models showing that sexual offenders are characterized by a variety of planning styles, goals, and offense-related emotions (i.e., Hudson et al., 1999; Ward, Louden, Hudson, & Marshall, 1995). Combining contemporary self-regulation theory (Baumeister & Heatherton, 1996; Carver & Scheier, 1990) with offense process data, Ward and Hudson (1998) proposed that sexual offenders' offense styles are directed toward differing goals (i.e., approach vs. avoidance) and characterized by differing strategies used to accomplish these goals (i.e., active vs. passive). In brief, goals are not always inhibitory (as the RP model suggests), but often involve the facilitation or elicitation of deviant sexual behavior as well. Thus sexual offenders may be characterized by avoidance goals (in which they attempt to inhibit sexual behavior, but fail when experiencing high levels of negative affect) or approach goals (in which they attempt to facilitate deviant sexual behavior, often experiencing strong positive affect in anticipation of the offensive act). The strategy used by sexual offenders to achieve their goals reflects a self-regulatory style that may be engaged either consciously or unconsciously. Passive self-regulators behave in a disinhibited manner because they fail to control their behavior by subjugating their avoidance goal. Active self-regulators tend to plan and monitor their behavior effectively so as to reach their intended goal (which may be either avoidance or approach). Sometimes active regulators will misregulate their behavior, choosing an inappropriate strategy in pursuit of their goal (e.g., masturbating to deviant sexual fantasies to eradicate deviant sexual urges).

Overall, the self-regulation model shows good unifying power through combining previous RP approaches with contemporary self-regulation theory. Since the model is relatively recent, however, evidence of empirical adequacy is only slowly being accumulated in relation to rapists. Many validation studies focus on child molesters (Bickley & Beech, 2002; Proulx, Perreault, & Ouimet, 1999) or on sexual offenders as a general group (Webster, 2005). However, Yates and colleagues (2003) partitioned out rapists (*n* = 33) from other sexual offenders in their validation of the self-regulation model and found that the rapists predominantly followed the approach pathway (approach–automatic, 58%; approach–explicit, 36%).

Although its empirical adequacy is yet to be fully realized, the self-regulation model has facilitated some important offense process investigations (i.e., it has heuristic value; see Hudson et al., 1999; Polaschek & Hudson, 2004; Polaschek, Hudson, Ward, & Siegert, 2001). Rape-specific models have been particularly useful for highlighting the complexity and heterogeneity of rapists, which were previously uncaptured by using traditional RP stances (Polaschek et al., 2001; Polaschek & Hudson, 2004). From these rape-specific investigations, three main pathways appear evident: positive affect (i.e., sex is sought to enhance positive affect); sexual gratification (i.e., sex is sought to alleviate negative affect); and a nonsexual pathway (i.e., goals are nonsexual—e.g., sexual aggression against a woman is used to seek revenge). This model illustrates notable differences from contemporary taxonomic descriptions of rapists (e.g., Prentky & Knight, 1991): (1) nonsexual goals are partitioned out from sexual goals; and (2) offenders' goals are recognized as being fluid and may shift throughout the offense process.

The self-regulation model is currently being used to guide professionals who treat sexual offenders (see Ward et al., 2004, and Ward, Yates, & Long, 2006, for the self-regulation model assessment and treatment manuals available from Pacific Psychological Assessment Corporation); this testifies to the model's strong clinical heuristic value. A preliminary checklist of offense pathways for rapists has now also been developed (Hussain, 2005) and awaits further refinement and validation. Finally, the explanatory depth of the self-regulation model has recently been increased through use of the ITSO (described earlier; Ward & Beech, 2006) and the good-lives model of rehabilitation (Ward & Stewart, 2003) to place currently used self-regulatory treatment practice within meaningful theoretical structures (see Ward & Gannon, 2006).

SUMMARY AND FUTURE DIRECTIONS

Our evaluation of the psychopathology and theory associated with rape has highlighted a number of areas in which the field has progressed since the first edition of this book was published. Most notably, etiological theory has progressed, as demonstrated via attempts to capture the heterogeneity and diversity evident in sexual offenders as a whole and in rapists more specifically (Polaschek et al., 2001; Ward & Beech, 2006). In addition, RP approaches have changed radically over the past decade with the birth of the self-regulation theory (Ward & Hudson, 1998), which attempts to capture the broad range of goals and self-regulatory strategies used by sex offenders and rapists in the commission of their offenses. The next major task that we believe is needed, then, is for independent researchers to set about developing research programs to validate and further refine these recently developed etiological and rehabilitatory theories. Our understanding of rape will only be further improved if researchers work hard to develop valid and meaningful etiological models to guide forensic practice. Future theorists interested in conceptualizing new theories of rape may also find it fruitful to knit together violence and rape theories as explanatory frameworks, because rapists are as flexible in their offending behavior as violent offenders (Simon, 2000). Thus researchers should make sustained efforts to investigate rapists alongside more useful counterparts, such as violent offenders, rather than simply just child molesters in future research programs.

In writing this review, we have also been alerted to a number of areas in which we think progress has slowed somewhat. For example, relatively little work has been conducted on investigating rapists' characteristics in comparison to those of other offender groups, and more work is needed on rapists' attachment styles during both childhood and adulthood. Cognitive experimental studies that focus on rapists also appear to be needed, since the vast majority of such research to date has focused on child molesters.

However, one of the major problems we have observed in our synthesizing of rapist-relevant research is that rapists are tending to take a back seat in research that is paramount for developing adequate assessment and treatment programs. We suspect that the main reason for this is the intense focus on child molestation in the Western world at present. Thus a major task for researchers in sexual offending is to ensure that rapists receive adequate attention. For example, there is a strong tendency for researchers at present to subsume rapists within an overall sexual offender category without ever portioning them out for analysis. Partitioning out rapists wherever possible in future studies will ensure that a valid evidence base concerning rape etiology and management can be attained more quickly. One specific area that we believe needs an increased focus on rapists is risk assessment. Here, we think an important task for the future is developing actuarial and dynamic risk assessment instruments that focus specifically on rapists.

As we have outlined in our review, sexual offending against women is highly prevalent in our society. Thus, if we are to understand this phenomenon and protect the safety of future women, we need to make a sustained and focused attempt to investigate the factors pertinent to rape etiology and, ultimately, to effective treatment for rapists.

NOTES

1. This has been broadly defined by the Supreme Court of Canada as "any assault that violates the sexual integrity of the victim" (*Regina v. Chase*, 1987: 2 S.C.R. 293).
2. Detailed 2005 figures are not yet available at this writing.

REFERENCES

Abel, G. G., Becker, J. V., Cunningham-Rathner, J., Mittelman, M. S., & Rouleau, J. L. (1988). Multiple paraphilic diagnoses among sex offenders. *Bulletin of the American Academy of Psychiatry and the Law, 16,* 153–168.

Abracen, J., Looman, J., Di Fazio, R., Kelly, T., & Stirpe, T. (2006). Patterns of attachment and alcohol abuse in sexual and violent nonsexual offenders. *Journal of Sexual Aggression, 12,* 19–30.

Aigner, M., Eher, R., Fruehwald, S., Frottier, P., Guttierez-Lobos, K., & Dwyer, S. M. (2000). Brain abnormalities and violent behavior. *Journal of Psychology and Human Sexuality, 11,* 57–64.

American Psychiatric Association. (2000). *Diagnostic and statistical manual of mental disorders* (4th ed., text rev.). Washington, DC: Author.

Augoustinos, M., & Walker, I. (1995). *Social cognition: An integrated introduction.* London: Sage.

Bard, L., Carter, D., Cerce, D., Knight, R., Rosenberg, R., & Schneider, B. (1987). A descriptive study of rapists and child molesters: Developmental, clinical and criminal characteristics. *Behavioral Sciences and the Law, 5,* 203–220.

Bargh, J. A., Raymond, P., Pryor, J. B., & Strack, F. (1995). Attractiveness of the underling: An automatic power—sex association and its consequences for sexual harassment and aggression. *Journal of Personality and Social Psychology, 68,* 768–781.

Bartosh, D. L, Garby, T., Lewis, D., & Gray, S. (2003). Differences in the predictive validity of actuarial risk assessments in relation to sex offender type. *International Journal of Offender Therapy and Comparative Criminology, 47,* 422–438.

Baumeister, R. F., & Heatherton, T. F. (1996). Self-regulation failure: An overview. *Psychological Inquiry, 7,* 1–15.

Beech, A., Fisher, D., & Ward, T. (2005). Sexual murderers' implicit theories. *Journal of Interpersonal Violence, 20,* 1366–1389.

Beech, A., Friendship, C., Erikson, M., & Hanson, R. K. (2002). The relationship between static and dynamic risk factors and reconviction in a sample of UK child abusers. *Sexual Abuse: A Journal of Research and Treatment, 14,* 155–167.

Beech, A. R., Fisher, D., & Beckett, R. C. (1999). *An evaluation of the Prison Sex Offender Treatment Programme.* U.K. Home Office occasional report. (Available from Home Office Information Publications Group, Research, Development and Statistics Directorate, 50 St. Anne's Gate, Room 201, London SW1 9AT, United Kingdom; also from *www.homeoffice.gov.uk/rds/pdfs/occ-step3.pdf*)

Beech, A. R., & Mitchell, I. J. (2005). A neurobiological perspective on attachment problems in sexual offenders and the role of selective serotonin re-uptake inhibitors in the treatment of such problems. *Clinical Psychology Review, 25,* 153–182.

Bickley, J., & Beech, A. R. (2002). An empirical investigation of the Ward and Hudson self-regulation model of the sexual offence process with child abusers. *Journal of Interpersonal Violence, 17,* 371–393.

Brener, N. D., McMahon, P. M., Warren, C. W., & Douglas, K. A. (1999). Forced sexual intercourse and associated health-risk behaviors among female college students in the United States. *Journal of Consulting and Clinical Psychology, 67,* 252–259.

Carver, C. S., & Scheier, M. F. (1990). Origins and functions of positive and negative affect: A control process view. *Psychological Review, 997,* 19–35.

Christie, M. M., Marshall, W. L., & Lanthier, R. D. (1979). *A descriptive study of incarcerated rapists and child molesters.* Ottawa: Department of the Solicitor General of Canada.

Cochrane, R., Grisso, T., & Frederick, R. (2001). The relationship between criminal charges, diagnoses, and psycholegal opinions among federal defendants. *Behavioral Sciences and the Law, 19,* 565–582.

Cohen, M. L., Seghorn, T. K., & Calmas, W. (1969). Sociometric study of sex offenders. *Journal of Abnormal Psychology, 74,* 249–255.

Craig, L. A., Browne, K. D., & Stringer, I. (2004). Comparing sex offender risk assessment measures on a UK sample. *International Journal of Offender Therapy and Comparative Criminology, 48,* 7–27.

Craissati, J. (2005). Sexual violence against women: A psychological approach to the assessment and management of rapists in the community. *Probation Journal: The Journal of Community and Criminal Justice, 52,* 401–422.

Craissati, J., Webb, L., & Keen, S. (2005). *Personality disordered sex offenders: Report of research across the London probation area.* London: Oxlea NHS Trust and Home Office.

Criminal Code of Canada. (1985). Retrieved from *www.efc.ca/pages/law/cc/cc.html*

Dhawan, S., & Marshall, W. L. (1996). Sexual abuse histories of sexual offenders. *Sexual Abuse: A Journal of Research and Treatment, 8,* 7–15.

Dickey, R., Nussbaum, D., Chevolleau, K., & Davidson, H. (2002). Age as a differential characteristic of rapists, pedophiles, and sexual sadists. *Journal of Sex and Marital Therapy, 28,* 211–218.

Dreznick, M. T. (2003). Heterosocial competence of rapists and child molesters: A meta-analysis. *Journal of Sex Research, 40,* 170–178.

Ellis, L. (1989). *Theories of rape: Inquiries into the causes of sexual aggression.* New York: Hemisphere.

Ellis, L. (1991). A synthesized (biosocial) theory of rape. *Journal of Consulting and Clinical Psychology, 59,* 631–642.

Federal Bureau of Investigation (FBI). (2004). *Uniform Crime Reports—US.* Retrieved from *www.fbi.gov/ucr/ucr.htm*

Firestone, P., Bradford, J. M., Greenberg, D. M., & Serran, G. A. (2000). The relationship of deviant sexual arousal and psychopathy in incest offenders, extrafamilial child molesters, and rapists. *Journal of the American Academy of Psychiatry and the Law, 28,* 303–308.

Fiske, S. T., & Taylor, S. E. (1991). *Social cognition* (2nd ed.). New York: McGraw-Hill.

Gannon, M. (2006). Crime statistics in Canada, 2005. *Statistics Canada,* Catalogue No. 85-002-XIE, 26(4).

Gannon, T. A., Beech, A. R., & Ward, T. (in press). Polygraph and risk assessment. In D. Grubin & D. Wilcox (Eds.), *Polygraph in a forensic context.* Chichester, UK: Wiley.

Garlick, Y., Marshall, W. L., & Thornton, D. (1996). Intimacy deficits and attribution of blame among sexual offenders. *Legal and Criminological Psychology, 1,* 251–258.

Gavey, N. (1991). Sexual victimization prevalence among New Zealand university students. *Journal of Consulting and Clinical Psychology, 59,* 464–466.

Groth, A. N., Burgess, A. W., & Holstrom, L. L. (1977). Rape: Power, anger, and sexuality. *American Journal of Psychiatry, 134,* 1239–1243.

Hall, G. C. N., & Hirschman, R. (1991). Toward a theory of sexual aggression: A quadripartite model. *Journal of Consulting and Clinical Psychology, 59,* 662–669.

Hanson, R. K., & Bussière, M. T. (1998). Predicting relapse: A meta-analysis of sexual offender recidivism studies. *Journal of Consulting and Clinical Psychology, 66,* 348–362.

Hanson, R. K., & Harris, A. J. R. (2000). *Acute-2000.* Ottawa: Department of the Solicitor General of Canada. (Available from the author, Andrew Harris, at *harrisaj@csc-scc.gc.ca*)

Hanson, R. K., & Harris, A. J. R. (2001). *The Sex Offender Need Assessment Rating (SONAR): A method for measuring change in risk levels.* Retrieved from *www.sgc.gc.ca/epub/corr/e200001a/e200001b/e200001b.htm* (please note that this is an older version of SONAR and should not be used).

Hanson, R. K., & Morton-Bourgon, K. (2004). *Predictors of sexual recidivism: An updated meta-analysis.* (User Report No. 2004-02). Ottawa: Department of the Solicitor General of Canada.

Hanson, R. K., Morton, K. E., & Harris, A. J. R. (2003). Sexual offender recidivism risk: What we know and what we need to know. *Annals of the New York Academy of Sciences, 989,* 154–166.

Hanson, R. K., & Thornton, D. (2000). Improving risk assessments for sex offenders: A comparison of three actuarial scales. *Law and Human Behavior, 24,* 119–136.

Hillbrand, M., Foster, H., & Hirt, M. (1990). Rapists and child molesters: Psychometric comparisons. *Archives of Sexual Behavior, 19,* 65–71.

Hooker, C. A. (1987). *A realistic theory of science.* Albany: State University of New York Press.

Hucker, S. J., Langevin, R., Wortzman, G., Dickey, R., Bain, J., Handy, L., et al. (1988). Cerebral damage and dysfunction in sexually aggressive men. *Annals of Sex Research, 1,* 33–47.

Hudson, S. M., & Ward, T. (1997). Rape: Psychopathology and theory. In D. R. Laws & W. O'Donohue (Eds.), *Sexual deviance: Theory, assessment, and treatment* (pp. 332–355). New York: Guilford Press.

Hudson, S. M., Ward, T., & McCormack, J. (1999). Offense pathways in sexual offenders. *Journal of Interpersonal Violence, 8,* 779–798.

Hussain, Q. (2005). *Checklist of offence pathways for rapists: A clinician's guide to informed intervention.* Unpublished doctoral dissertation, University of Melbourne, Australia.

Kafka, M. P., & Hennen, J. (2002). A *DSM-IV* Axis I comorbidity study of males ($n = 120$) with paraphilias and paraphilia-related disorders. *Sexual Abuse: A Journal of Research and Treatment, 14,* 349–366.

Knight, R. A., & Prentky, R. A. (1990). Classifying sexual offenders: The development and corroboration of taxonomic models. In W. L. Marshall, D. R. Laws, & H. E. Barbaree (Eds.), *Handbook of sexual assault: Issues, theories, and treatment of the offender* (pp. 23–52). New York: Plenum Press.

Koss, M. P., Gidycz, C. A., & Wisniewski, N. (1987). The scope of rape: Incidence and prevalence of sexual aggression and victimization in a national sample of higher education students. *Journal of Consulting and Clinical Psychology, 55,* 162–170.

Lalumière, M. L., Harris, G. T., Quinsey, V. L., & Rice, M. E. (2005). *The causes of rape: Understanding individual differences in male propensity for sexual aggression.* Washington, DC: American Psychological Association.

Långström, N., Sjöstedt, G., & Grann, M. (2004). Psychiatric disorders and recidivism in sexual offenders. *Sexual Abuse: A Journal of Research and Treatment, 16,* 139–150.

Laws, D. R. (2003). The rise and fall of relapse prevention. *Australian Psychologist, 38,* 22–30.

Laws, D. R., Hudson, S. M., & Ward, T. (2002). Remaking relapse prevention with sex offenders: A sourcebook and practice standards and guidelines for members of the Association for the Treatment of Sexual Abusers (ATSA). *Journal of Psychiatry and Law, 30,* 285–292.

Lipton, D. N., McDonel, E. C., & McFall, R. M. (1987). Heterosocial perception in rapists. *Journal of Consulting and Clinical Psychology, 55,* 17–21.

Lung, F.-W., & Huang, S.-F. (2004). Psychosocial characteristics of criminals committing incest and other sex offences: A survey in a Taiwanese prison. *International Journal of Offender Therapy and Comparative Criminology, 48,* 554–560.

Malamuth, N., Linz, D., Heavey, C., Barnes, G., & Acker, M. (1995). Using the confluence model of sexual aggression to predict men's conflict with women: A ten year follow-up study. *Journal of Personality and Social Psychology, 69,* 353–369.

Malamuth, N. M. (1986). Predictors of naturalistic sexual aggression. *Journal of Personality and Social Psychology, 50,* 953–962.

Malamuth, N. M. (1988). Predicting laboratory aggression against female vs. male targets: Implications for research on sexual aggression. *Journal of Research in Personality, 22,* 474–495.

Malamuth, N. M. (1996). The confluence model of sexual aggression: Feminist and evolutionary perspectives. In D. B. Buss & N. M. Malamuth (Eds.), *Sex, power, conflict: Evolutionary and feminist perspectives* (pp. 269–295). New York: Oxford University Press.

Malamuth, N. M., & Brown, L. M. (1994). Sexually aggressive men's perceptions of women's communications: Testing three explanations. *Journal of Personality and Social Psychology, 67,* 699–712.

Malamuth, N. M., Heavey, C. L., & Linz, D. (1993). Predicting men's antisocial behavior against women: The interaction model of sexual aggression. In G. C. N. Hall, R. Hirschman, J. R. Graham, & M. S. Zaragoza (Eds.), *Sexual aggression: Issues in etiology, assessment and treatment* (pp. 63–97). Washington, DC: Taylor & Francis.

Malamuth, N. M., & Heilman, M. F. (1998). Evolutionary psychology and sexual aggression. In C. B.

Crawford & D. L. Krebs (Eds.), *Handbook of evolutionary psychology: Ideas, issues and applications* (pp. 515–542). Mahwah, NJ: Erlbaum.

Marlatt, G. A., & Gordon, J. R. (Eds.). (1985). *Relapse prevention: Maintenance strategies in the treatment of addictive behaviors.* New York: Guilford Press.

Marshall, W. L. (1989). Intimacy, loneliness, and sexual offenders. *Behaviour Research and Therapy,* 27, 491–503.

Marshall, W. L. (2007). Diagnostic issues, multiple paraphilias, and comorbid disorders in sexual offenders: Their incidence and treatment. *Aggression and Violent Behavior,* 12, 16–35.

Marshall, W. L., & Barbaree, H. E. (1990). An integrated theory of sexual offending. In W. L. Marshall, D. R. Laws, & H. E. Barbaree (Eds.), *Handbook of sexual assault: Issues, theories and treatment of the offender* (pp. 363–385). New York: Plenum Press.

Marshall, W. L., & Marshall, L. E. (2000). The origins of sexual offending. *Trauma, Violence and Abuse,* 1, 250–263.

Marshall, W. L., & Moulden, H. (2001). Hostility toward women and victim empathy in rapists. *Sexual Abuse: A Journal of Research and Treatment,* 13, 249–255.

Myhill, A., & Allen, J. (2002). *Rape and sexual assault of women: The extent and nature of the problem: Findings from the British Crime Survey.* London: U.K. Home Office.

Newton-Smith, W. (2002). *A companion to the philosophy of science.* Oxford, UK: Blackwell.

Odling-Smee, F. J., Laland, K. N., & Feldman, M. W. (2003). *Niche construction: The neglected process in evolution.* Princeton, NJ: Princeton University Press.

Pennington, B. F. (2002). *The development of psychopathology: Nature and nurture.* New York: Guilford Press.

Pithers, W. D. (1990). Relapse prevention with sexual aggressors: A method for maintaining therapeutic gains and enhancing external supervision. In W. L. Marshall, D. R. Laws, & H. E. Barbaree (Eds.), *Handbook of sexual assault: Issues, theories, and treatment of the offender* (pp. 343–363). New York: Plenum Press.

Pithers, W. D., Marques, J. K., Gibat, C. C., & Marlatt, G. A. (1983). Relapse prevention with sexual aggressives: A self-control model of treatment and maintenance of change. In J. G. Greer & I. R. Stewart (Eds.), *The sexual aggressor: current perspectives on treatment* (pp. 214–239). New York: Van Nostrand Reinhold.

Polaschek, D. L. L. (2003). Relapse prevention, offence process models, and the treatment of sexual offenders. *Professional Psychology: Research and Practice,* 34, 361–367.

Polaschek, D. L. L., & Gannon, T. A. (2004). The implicit theories of rapists: What convicted offenders tell us. *Sexual Abuse: A Journal of Research and Treatment,* 16, 299–315.

Polaschek, D. L. L., & Hudson, S. M. (2004). Pathways to rape: Preliminary examination of patterns in the offence process of rapists and their rehabilitation implications. *Journal of Sexual Aggression,* 10, 7–20.

Polaschek, D. L. L., Hudson, S. M., Ward, T., & Siegert, R. J. (2001). Rapists' offense processes: A preliminary descriptive model. *Journal of Interpersonal Violence,* 16, 523–544.

Polaschek, D. L. L., & Ward, T. (2002). The implicit theories of potential rapists. What our questionnaires tell us. *Aggression and Violent Behavior,* 7, 385–406.

Prentky, R. A., & Knight, R. A. (1991). Identifying critical dimensions for discriminating among rapists. *Journal of Consulting and Clinical Psychology,* 59, 643–661.

Proulx, J., Perreault, C., & Ouimet, M. (1999). Pathways in the offending process of extrafamilial sexual child molesters. *Sexual Abuse: A Journal of Research and Treatment,* 11, 117–129.

Pryor, J. B., & Stoller, L. M. (1994). Sexual cognition processes in men high in likelihood to sexually harass. *Personality and Social Psychology Bulletin,* 20, 163–169.

Quinsey, V. L., & Lalumière, M. L. (1995). Evolutionary perspectives on sexual offending. *Sexual Abuse: A Journal of Research and Treatment,* 7, 301–315.

Russell, D. E. H. (1984). *Sexual exploitation: Rape, child sexual abuse, and workplace harassment.* Thousand Oaks, CA: Sage.

Scully, D. (1990). *Understanding sexual violence: A study of convicted rapists.* Boston: Unwin.

Seghorn, T., & Cohen, M. (1980). The psychology of the rape assailant. In W. Cerran, A. L. McGarry, & C. Petty (Eds.), *Modern legal medicine, psychiatry, and forensic science* (pp. 533–551). Philadelphia: Davis.

Sexual Offences Act. (2003). Retrieved from *www.opsi.gov.uk/ACTS/acts2003/20030042.htm*

Sherman, S. J., Judd, C. M., & Park, B. (1989). Social cognition. *Annual Review of Psychology, 40,* 281–326.

Simon, L. M. J. (2000). An examination of the assumptions of specialization, mental disorder, and dangerousness in sex offenders. *Behavioral Sciences and the Law, 18,* 275–308.

Smallbone, S. W., & Dadds, M. R. (1998). Childhood attachment and adult attachment in incarcerated adult male sex offenders. *Journal of Interpersonal Violence, 13,* 555–573.

Smallbone, S. W., & Dadds, M. R. (2000). Attachment and coercive sexual behavior. *Sexual Abuse: A Journal of Research and Treatment, 12,* 3–15.

Smallbone, S. W., & Dadds, M. R. (2001). Further evidence for a relationship between attachment insecurity and coercive sexual behavior in nonoffenders. *Journal of Interpersonal Violence, 16,* 22–35.

Stermac, L. E., & Hall, K. (1989). Escalation in sexual offending: Fact or fiction? *Annals of Sex Research, 2,* 153–162.

Stermac, L. E., & Quinsey, V. L. (1986). Social competence among rapists. *Behavioral Assessment, 8,* 171–185.

Symons, D. (1979). *The evolution of human sexuality.* New York: Oxford University Press.

Tjaden, P., & Thoennes, N. (1998). *Prevalence, incidence and consequences of violence against women: Findings from the National Violence against Women Survey.* Washington, DC: U.S. Department of Justice, National Institute of Justice.

Thornhill, R., & Palmer, C. T. (2000). *A natural history of rape: Biological bases of sexual coercion.* Cambridge, MA: MIT Press.

Thornton, D. (2000). *Structured risk assessment.* Paper presented at the Sinclair Seminars Conference on Sex Offender Re-Offense Risk Prediction, Madison, WI. (Videotape available from *www.sinclair seminars.com*)

Thornton, D. (2002). Constructing and testing a framework for dynamic risk assessment. *Sexual Abuse: A Journal of Research and Treatment, 14,* 139–154.

Thornton, D., Mann, R., Webster, S., Blud, L., Travers, R., Friendship, C., et al. (2003). Distinguishing and combining risks for sexual and violent recidivism. *Annals of the New York Academy of Sciences, 989,* 225–235.

Vess, J., Murphy, C., & Arkowitz, S. (2004). Clinical and demographic differences between sexually violent predators and other commitment types in a state forensic hospital. *Journal of Forensic Psychiatry and Psychology, 15,* 669–681.

Ward, T. (2000a). Relapse prevention: Critique and reformulation. *Journal of Sexual Aggression, 5,* 118–133.

Ward, T. (2000b). Sexual offenders' cognitive distortions as implicit theories. *Aggression and Violent Behavior, 5,* 491–507.

Ward, T. (2002). Marshall and Barbaree's integrated theory of child sexual abuse: A critique. *Psychology, Crime, and Law, 8,* 209–228.

Ward, T., & Beech, T. (2006). An integrated theory of sexual offending. *Aggression and Violent Behavior, 11,* 44–63.

Ward, T., Bickley, J., Webster, S. D., Fisher, D., Beech, A., & Eldridge, H. (2004). *The self-regulation model of the offense and relapse process: A manual. Vol. 1. Assessment.* Victoria, BC, Canada: Pacific Psychological Assessment Corporation.

Ward, T., & Gannon, T. (2006). Rehabilitation, etiology, and self-regulation: The good lives model of sexual offender treatment. *Aggression and Violent Behavior, 11,* 77–94.

Ward, T., & Hudson, S. M. (1996). Relapse prevention: A critical analysis. *Sexual Abuse: A Journal of Research and Treatment, 8,* 177–200.

Ward, T., & Hudson, S. M. (1998). A model of the relapse process in sexual offenders. *Journal of Interpersonal Violence, 13*, 700–725.

Ward, T., Hudson, S. M., & Marshall, W. L. (1996). Attachment style in sex offenders: A preliminary study. *Journal of Sex Research, 33*, 17–36.

Ward, T., Louden, K., Hudson, S. M., & Marshall, W. L. (1995). A description of the offense chain for child molesters. *Journal of Interpersonal Violence, 10*, 452–472.

Ward, T., Polaschek, D. L. L., & Beech, A. R. (2005). *Theories of sexual offending.* Chichester, UK: Wiley.

Ward, T., & Siegert, R. (2002). Rape and evolutionary psychology: A critique of Thornhill and Palmer's theory. *Aggression and Violent Behavior, 7*, 145–168.

Ward, T., & Stewart, C. A. (2003). The treatment of sex offenders: Risk management and good lives. *Professional Psychology: Research and Practice, 34*, 353–360.

Ward, T., Yates, P., & Long, C. (2006). *The self-regulation model of the offense and relapse process: Vol. 2. Treatment.* Victoria, BC, Canada: Pacific Psychological Assessment Corporation.

Webster, S. D. (2005). Pathways to sexual offense recidivism following treatment: An examination of the Ward and Hudson self-regulation model of relapse. *Journal of Interpersonal Violence, 20*, 1175–1196.

Weinrott, M. R., & Saylor, M. (1991). Self-report of crimes committed by sex offenders. *Journal of Interpersonal Violence, 6*, 286–300.

Wheeler, J. G., George, W. H., & Dahl, B. J. (2002). Sexually aggressive college males: Empathy as a moderator in the "confluence model" of sexual aggression. *Personality and Individual Differences, 33*, 759–777.

Wilcox, D. T., Sosnowski, D., Warberg, B., & Beech, A. R. (2005). Sexual history disclosure using the polygraph in a sample of British sex offenders. *Polygraph Journal, 34*, 171–183.

World Health Organization. (1992). *The ICD-10 classification of mental and behavioural disorders: Clinical descriptions and diagnostic guidelines* (10th rev.). Geneva: Author.

Yates, P. M., Kingston, D., & Hall, K. (2003, October). *Pathways to sexual offending: Validity of Hudson and Ward's (1998) self-regulation model and relationship to static and dynamic risk among treated high risk sexual offenders.* Paper presented at the 22nd Annual Research and Treatment Conference of the Association for the Treatment of Sexual Abusers (ATSA), St. Louis, MO.

CHAPTER 21

RAPE

Assessment and Treatment

JO THAKKER
RACHAEL M. COLLIE
THERESA A. GANNON
TONY WARD

The assessment and treatment of individuals who commit rape are important foci of practitioners working in forensic mental health and correctional services. Research has shown that rapists, or at least subgroups of convicted rapists, present with distinct clinical pictures and high risks of sexual and violent recidivism compared with other sex offenders. However, as noted by Gannon and Ward in Chapter 20 of this book, rapists are a heterogeneous group, making it difficult for theorists to account fully for rape. Also, the terms "rape" and "rapist" present nosological difficulties; rape is not a paraphilia in either of the two major diagnostic systems. The reality is that rapists present for assessment and treatment following conviction for rape, and thus to a large extent those described as rapists (and nonrapists) are defined as such by the legal system. Complicating the picture further is the fact that some rapists commit sexual offenses against both children and adults.

In this chapter, we review the key issues in the assessment and treatment of rapists. Our review primarily addresses the assessment and treatment of rape of adult women—although, as stated above, we recognize that some convicted rapists present with patterns of child sexual abuse and other violence that require assessment and treatment attention also. In the "Assessment" section, we outline various strategies for optimizing the assessment process, review the major assessment domains, and summarize the most widely used assessment methods and measures specific to rape. In the "Treatment" section, we discuss the primary treatment models, review current evidence on the effectiveness of contemporary treatment approaches, and highlight key developments in treatment that are required in light of current rehabilitation theory. The chapter concludes with suggestions for future research.

ASSESSMENT

Assessment is the starting point of effective rehabilitation and risk management. In this regard, assessment is typically concerned with (1) determining an offender's likelihood of future sexual offending and other serious crimes; (2) determining the offender's rehabilitation needs, amenability for treatment, and other issues related to risk management; and (3) monitoring and evaluating rehabilitation and management progress. In addition, assessment may be requested to help courts or paralegal bodies (e.g., parole authorities) determine whether offenders meet criteria for application of specific civil commitment or criminal sentences. To a large extent, these assessment purposes all require a comprehensive psychosexual evaluation covering a range of domains and using multiple assessment methods, including a risk assessment.

Assessment of rapists is often challenging, for several reasons: the heterogeneity of rapist samples; the limited research base available on rapists (especially compared with child molesters); and the interpersonal features of rapists themselves. There is the potential for a clinician to gather large amounts of information without developing a clear understanding of a case or recognizing particularly salient issues. A thorough knowledge of the relevant etiological and offense process theories of rape will help a clinician determine where to focus assessment efforts, how to organize information into meaningful chunks, and when to continue and cease gathering information. In essence, assessment ought to reflect a contemporary understanding of the causes of the sexually aggressive behavior and its associated phenomenology.

Other important aspects requiring assessment and formulation are the offender's treatment readiness and amenability. While a good initial formulation of why and how an offender commits rape is an essential outcome of assessment, treatment and risk management planning also requires an understanding of the offender's strengths and barriers to engaging in treatment and responding constructively to management strategies. Although theories do not replace the need for clinical reasoning, assessment practices that are tightly linked to relevant theories on rape, offender rehabilitation, and risk management help guard against idiosyncratic assessment and theorizing about the causes and treatment needs of individuals who have offended.

Clinicians attempting to understand and successfully treat rapists will need to assess a number of areas. Many areas covered are similar to those included in any psychological assessment (e.g., current mental state), and also in work with any type of offender (e.g., educational and vocational achievement, peer group influences, and indicators of imminent threat to self or others). Preference should be given to assessment tools that are well structured and psychometrically sound. In addition, assessment should draw upon multiple sources of information including collateral information (e.g., court and police documents, reports from other professionals who have assessed the offender, and interviews with family members). In the remainder of this section, we outline key assessment domains and assessment methods. In the interest of brevity, we restrict our focus to issues and research salient to assessment of rape and rapists.

Optimizing the Assessment Interview

The clinical interview is an important part of assessment and remains a significant source of information. Factors important for effective interviews with sexual offenders are similar to those considered important in general clinical settings (Towl & Crighton, 1996). A good level of rapport should be established—something that can be a challenge in interviews with sexual offenders. For example, an offender may be reluctant to discuss his offending because he is embarrassed about the nature of his offense, or he may fear potential legal repercussions if he provides particular detail about his offense history. Clearly explaining the assessment purpose and process from the outset, including the limits of confidentiality, helps offenders know exactly what they are agreeing to when they provide consent and what the potential consequences of disclosure are (Cowburn, 2005; Towl & Crighton, 1996). Discussing such matters in a careful and considered manner assists in the development of a trusting therapeutic relationship.

Other techniques useful in establishing a therapeutic alliance include reflection, accurate interpretation, and encouraging and supporting the expression of emotion; individual qualities such as being flexible, sincere, reliable, friendly, and attentive are advantageous in forging a connection with the client (see Ackerman & Hilsenroth, 2003, for a comprehensive review). Research with sex offenders suggests that therapist expressions of warmth and empathy have measurable therapeutic benefits (Marshall, 2005). Ward, McCormack, Hudson, and Polaschek (1997) also suggest that treating an offender as a whole person through respectful and empathic communication may enhance reliable disclosure and reduce denial. In addition, they suggest framing the interview as an opportunity for unburdening (catharsis) and making a fresh beginning, and asking about known facts related to the offense before asking about the offense proper.

Obviously, a significant proportion of sex offenders (including rapists) approach assessments with a view to depicting a particular impression of themselves; hence clinicians need to be aware of strategies for detecting malingering (for a comprehensive review, see Rogers & Bender, 2003). In addition, offenders' poor insight into their own difficulties, biased perceptions of themselves and others, and state variables (e.g., acute distress) can contribute to their providing significantly distorted accounts of events. One important clue to the presence of malingering is inconsistency in information across multiple sources (Rogers & Bender, 2003; Weiner, 2003). For example, an individual may present very differently on two different psychometric tests that measure similar characteristics, or test results may not match a client's behavioral presentation. Alternatively, an offender's self-report may not align with information gained from other sources, such as family members or other closely involved individuals. Although attempting to verify every piece of assessment data is extremely arduous and probably impossible, including strategies to detect malingering can enhance the reliability of the assessment process and therefore the assessment outcome. Thus it is necessary to use multiple sources of information, including review of collateral information. Our preference is to be explicit about cross-checking offenders' self-reports—usually by telling clients that we routinely check multiple information sources as part of assessment, and that where the clients' self-reports are discrepant with other information, we will discuss this with them and probably comment on this in any report. In addition, several psychometric questionnaires include scales to measure impression management and response bias (e.g., the Millon Clinical Multiaxial Inventory–III [MCMI-III]—Millon, Davis, & Millon, 1997; the Balanced Inventory of Desirable Responding—Paulhus, 1991), and specific measures to test malingering of certain symptoms and syndromes are available (see Rogers & Bender, 2003).

The Offense Process

Gathering a detailed understanding of the sexual offense (or offenses) and the context within which the offense was enacted is a central component of assessment. Investigation of the offense process provides information on and insights into the offender's sexually aggressive behavior(s), motivational and affective states and goals, and psychological and situational characteristics that are linked to his sexually aggressive propensity. The most recent or typical offense is usually selected to interview in detail. However, where an offender has committed offenses over the same time period against multiple victims or has an extensive history of sexual offending, separate interviews can be conducted of different offenses to ensure that a representative sample is selected (Ward et al., 2004; Webster, 2005).

The dominant models used to guide assessment of the offense process have been described by Gannon and Ward (Chapter 20, this volume). To recap briefly, the relapse prevention (RP) model of sex offender recidivism has been the main approach to conceptualizing rehabilitation of rapists over the last 20 years (for reviews, see Laws, Hudson, & Ward, 2000; Polaschek, 2003). According to the RP model, the offense process in all sexual offenders (1) follows a predictable pattern that unfolds over time; (2) may be explained by a number of important concepts and principles; and (3) involves a regulation failure—that is, the offender commits a crime because he is unable to control his impulses. Despite the clinical appeal and subsequent adoption of the RP model, research with sexual offenders suggests that although some offenders recidivate sexually as a result of self-regulatory failure (as depicted in this model), such failure does not account for all pathways to sexual recidivism (Laws et al., 2000; Polaschek & Hudson, 2004; Ward, Louden, Hudson, & Marshall, 1995; Webster, 2005). In fact, a significant proportion of sexual offenders, including rapists (Webster, 2005), sexually reoffend not as a result of self-regulation failure, but through careful and systematic planning.

Ward and Hudson (1998, 2000) developed an alternative approach to conceptualizing sexual recidivism based on self-regulation theory (Baumeister & Heatherton, 1996; Karoly, 1993; Thompson, 1994), to account specifically for the variety of offense pathways evident in sexual offenders and to provide therapists with a more comprehensive treatment model (Ward et al., 2004; Ward, Yates, & Long, 2006). The self-regulation model (SRM) includes four pathways representing different combinations of offense-related goals (i.e., avoidance or approach) and self-regulation styles (i.e., underregulation, misregulation, and effective regulation). The "avoidance–passive" pathway is characterized by the desire to avoid sexual offending, but a lack of coping skills to achieve this goal (i.e., an underregulation style). The "avoidance–active" pathway is also characterized by the desire to avoid sexual offending, but use of ineffective or counterproductive strategies to control deviant thoughts and affective states connected with offending (i.e., a misregulation style). The "approach–automatic" pathway is characterized by the desire to offend sexually, but impulsive and poorly planned behavior (i.e., an underregulation style). Finally, the "approach–explicit" pathway is characterized by the desire to offend sexually and the use of careful planning to achieve the sexual-offense-related goal (i.e., an intact regulation style).

As outlined by Gannon and Ward in Chapter 20, studies validating the SRM of the offense process with rape offending are beginning to emerge (see Webster, 2005; Yates, Kingston, & Hall, 2003). In terms of assessment, careful questioning about the thoughts, feelings, behaviors and events present in each phase of the SRM provides a structured and systematic approach to the offense process interview, and lends itself to identifying and describing the key psychological vulnerabilities and precipitants to an offender's rape (see Ward et al., 2004).

In summary, then, although the RP model of the offense process has proven to be useful in developing both client and clinician understandings of the cycle of decisions and events leading an individual to offend sexually, the SRM arguably allows a more sophisticated evaluation of these phenomena. This is advantageous for assessment, because it facilitates the development of a more accurate and individualized picture of the offense process—one that accounts for the heterogeneity evident among rapists. In turn, a more individualized treatment approach can be devised.

Personal History

It is essential to gain clear and detailed information about a sex offender's personal history (Beech, Fisher, & Thornton, 2003). The gathering of such information is, of course, standard practice in any psychological assessment, and many of the areas that require attention are the same. However, it is also worthwhile to keep in mind the assessment goals in this context, which are to understand and explain the offending in order to ascertain treatment targets. Therefore, when a clinician is assessing an individual who has committed a rape, it is particularly important to gain information about his sexual development (including sexual experiences during childhood) and any incidents in his life that involved violence (as either a victim or a perpetrator). Obtaining detailed information about the offender's general pattern of interacting with others across a range of contexts, such as intimate relationships and wider social circles, also helps identify the distal risk factors and psychological vulnerabilities linked to the offender's rape proclivity.

Insight into the offender's general self-regulatory style (underregulation, misregulation, or intact regulation) can be gained from the psychosocial history as well. Ward and colleagues (2004) state that when particular attention is given to offenders' reactions to various significant transitions (e.g., relationship breakups, job changes), major disappointments, frustrations, or traumatic events, self-regulatory themes become evident. Unstructured or semistructured clinical interviews are usually the main methods for collecting psychosocial histories, although some questionnaires also collect detailed information about specific aspects.

Sexual Preferences and Sexual Behaviors

Obviously, gaining an understanding of sexual preferences and sexual behaviors is essential in the assessment of any type of sexual offense. Such assessment overlaps with obtaining the personal history, insofar as history of sexual behaviors would be covered there also. For example, early intimate relationships should be explored, as well as more proximal relationships. The aims are to determine the offender's pattern of sexual interaction and to discover what motivates his sexual behavior. Although questions about sexual practices and behaviors may be asked via interview, it is generally believed that questionnaires allow offenders to respond more freely to quite personal questions. In addition, use of questionnaires can allow for more efficient gathering of a wide range of detailed information. We outline several commonly used psychometric measures below.

Psychometric Measures

Multiphasic Sex Inventory. The Multiphasic Sex Inventory (MSI; Nichols & Molinder, 1984) is a 300-item true–false self-report test that was developed to measure a wide range of sexual preferences and sexual behaviors. The MSI has 10 scales that cover a range of phenomena related to sexual offending (such as sexual deviance, sexual dysfunction, and offense-related attitudes and beliefs), as well as 4 validity scales. Research suggests that most of the scales in the MSI have adequate to good internal consistency and good construct validity (Kalichman, Henderson, Shealy, & Dwyer, 1992), although Kalichman and colleagues (1992) noted concerns about the MSI's face validity and possible problems with response bias. A modified version called the MSI II (which has over 500 items and assesses a wider range of psychological variables) is available from the authors (Nichols & Molinder, 2000); however, the MSI II has received some mixed reviews (see Arbisi, 2005; Bugaj, 2005).

Sexual Experiences Survey. The Sexual Experiences Survey (SES; Koss & Oros, 1982) was developed to assess levels of unreported rape and other forms of sexual aggression within community samples. Designed primarily as a research tool, it is a short (12-item) self-report questionnaire that asks about the extent to which individuals have used and experienced various forms of aggression in association with sexual activity. Research indicates that the SES is useful in assessment with both victims (Cecil & Matson, 2006) and perpetrators (Lisak & Roth, 1988) of violence.

Attraction to Sexual Aggression Scale. The Attraction to Sexual Aggression Scale (ASA; Malamuth, 1989a, 1989b) is a self-report scale that measures attitudes to and perceptions of sexual aggression. Several scales cover such areas as attraction to deviant sexual practices and accepted sexual practices. Malamuth's research on a sample of over 600 men suggested that the ASA successfully identified sexually aggressive men and also has sound psychometric properties. However, as noted by Ward and colleagues (1997), it remains unclear how useful the ASA will be in clinical settings, given that it was designed to assess a man's predisposition to rape rather than the psychological characteristics of those men who have been convicted for rape. No recent research appears to be available on this measure.

Multidimensional Assessment of Sex and Aggression. The Multidimensional Assessment of Sex and Aggression (MASA; Knight, Prentky, & Cerce, 1994) is a comprehensive self-report measure (with over 400 items) that assesses the association between sexual activity and aggression in both thoughts and behavior. Preliminary evaluation of the psychometric properties of the original version was promising; it had sound reliability, internal consistency, and concurrent validity (Knight et al., 1994). According to the authors, the MASA has been revised four times since its inception, and more recent evaluation using the latest version confirms the robustness of its psychometric properties and its usefulness as an assessment tool (Knight & Cerce, 2001). The key areas of difference between the current and earlier versions are (1) the extended application to juvenile as well as adult rapists, and (2) the inclusion of items to identify deception.

Phallometry

A number of researchers have examined the use of phallometry (also referred to as penile plethysmography) and found that its reliability with rapists is too low for its valid use in assessments (Barbaree, Baxter, & Marshall, 1989; Fernandez & Marshall, 2003). Although earlier small-scale studies found some differences on phallometric measures between rapists and nonrapists (e.g., Abel, Barlow, Blanchard, & Guild, 1977; Barbaree, Marshall, & Lanthier, 1979; Quinsey, Chaplin, & Upfold, 1984), more recent studies found no differences between these groups (e.g., Fernandez & Marshall, 2003; Letourneau, 2002; Looman & Marshall, 2001), and found no association between offense-related variables and sexual arousal in rapists (Looman & Marshall, 2005). Due to these problems in its psychometric properties, as well as variability in administration procedures and a number of other issues, the use of phallometric assessment to determine sexual preferences and deviancy has been severely criticized (Laws, 2003). In fact, Marshall (2006a) has recently concluded that its routine use in evaluations of sex offenders is *not* recommended.

Viewing Time

Efforts to develop less intrusive, but equally "objective," techniques to assess sexual preferences include use of viewing time (see Laws & Gress, 2004). The typical viewing time procedure involves presenting a client with a series of deviant and nondeviant images and inferring sexual preference from differential visual attention to image categories (Gress, 2005; Laws & Gress, 2004). Although the procedure looks promising for the assessment of pedophilic interests (e.g., Gress, 2005; Harris, Rice, Quinsey, & Chaplin, 1996), there is no current evidence that it is useful in the assessment of deviant arousal in rapists (Letourneau, 2002).

Attitudes, Beliefs, and Cognitive Distortions

Attitudes toward, beliefs about, and interpretations of the world are fundamental to the ways in which individuals act. In regard to rape, it is important to determine the range of ideas that may be associated with this type of sexual offense, such as beliefs about sexuality and gender roles. Listed below are some of the key psychometric measures used for this purpose.

Rape Myth Acceptance Scale

The Rape Myth Acceptance Scale (RMA; Burt, 1980) is a widely used, brief (19-item) scale that was designed to measure the attitudes and beliefs associated with rape, such as the ideas that if women wear revealing clothing then they deserve to be raped, and that most women who are raped are promiscuous. Early research supported the use of this measure in differentiating rapists (Burt, 1983) and rape-prone nonoffenders (Malamuth, 1984) from other males, but results from some more recent studies have not encouraged confidence in the use of this psychometric tool with offenders (e.g., Segal & Stermac, 1990).

On the other hand, research using the RMA with student and community samples has produced promising results. An adapted version of the RMA (containing 45 items), called the Illinois Rape Myth Acceptance Scale (Payne, Lonsway, & Fitzgerald, 1999), had robust psychometric properties and identified the presence of rape myths in a college sample (Diem, 2000). Forbes, Adams-Curtis, and White (2004) describe the Illinois version as "psychometrically elegant" and propose that it has superior construct validity. In addition, an adaptation for use in Korea, termed the Korean Rape Myth Acceptance Scale (Oh & Neville, 2004), also identified rape myths in student and community populations. It should be noted that Costin (1985) developed the R Scale, which was also designed to measure rape myth acceptance, as part of a specific research project. It appears that the R Scale has been used for research purposes (e.g., in Bohner, Jarvis, Eyssel, & Siebler, 2005), but not in clinical settings.

Hostility Toward Women Scale

The Hostility Toward Women Scale (HTWS; Check, 1985) is a brief (30-item), true–false, self-report inventory designed to measure feelings of anger and enmity toward women. Using this measure, Lackie and de Man (1997) explored the relationship between sexual aggression and a range of psychological and behavioral variables. They found a slight positive correlation between HTWS scores and sexual aggression, and a strong positive correlation between HTWS scores and general physical aggression. Lackie and de Man's results contrasted with earlier work by the test's author, which indicated a more powerful relationship between HTWS scores and sexual aggression (Check, 1985). Overall, it appears that there are insufficient data available on this test to permit researchers to evaluate its usefulness with rapists.

RAPE Scale

The RAPE Scale (Bumby, 1996) was designed along with a similar scale for use with child molesters. Very little information is available on the RAPE questionnaire; however, Bumby's original research indicated good validity and reliability. Bumby also proposed that the RAPE Scale is free from "social desirability bias," but the test was trialed on a very small sample (N = 25), all of whom were in treatment at the time.

Empathy

The commission of any type of sexual offense implies the presence of problems with empathy, as offending of this nature typically causes a great deal of harm to the victim. Hence it is important to determine whether a lack of empathy is instrumental in the individual's offense behavior. A key question is whether any empathy deficit that is present is generalized or limited to the sexual offending. Below are descriptions of two of the most commonly used scales for assessing empathy. In addition, assessment of psychopathic personality traits provides insight into the specific versus global empathy deficits of offenders.

Rape Empathy Scale

The Rape Empathy Scale (RES; Dietz, Blackwell, Daley, & Bentley, 1982) is a 19-item self-report scale created to measure empathy toward both rapists and victims of rape. Specifically, it targets an individual's attributions of responsibility in regard to those involved in rape situations. Dietz and colleagues (1982) reported that the RES has a high degree of internal consistency, which was confirmed in recent research by Jimenez and Abreu (2003).

Interpersonal Reactivity Index

Developed for use in general populations, the Interpersonal Reactivity Index (IRI; Davis, 1980) is a 28-item self-report questionnaire with four subscales, assessing perspective taking, fantasy, empathic concern, and personal distress. Based on the assumption that empathy is a multidimensional construct, the IRI produces four separate scores that allow each aspect of empathy to be examined independently. Initial validation of the IRI demonstrated reasonable internal consistency (Davis, 1994). Recent research (Beven,

O'Brien-Malone, & Hall, 2004) examined the use of this scale with violent offenders and concluded that while it appears to be "an excellent multidimensional measure of empathy for the general population" (p. 33), it requires alteration for use with offenders. Specifically, they note that test completion requires a high level of reading ability, and they recommend that the "personal distress" subscale not be used due to problems with internal consistency and reliability.

Personality Factors

By their very nature, stable and pervasive personality factors are likely to be associated with sexual offending. Also, given the criteria for a diagnosis of antisocial personality disorder and its base rate in offender populations, it is likely that many rapists can be described as personality-disordered. However, this is not necessarily fruitful from a therapeutic perspective, as it goes without saying that rape is an antisocial behavior. What appears more useful is determining the extent to which an offender's antisocial tendencies are associated with psychopathic personality traits, as their presence may well make treatment more difficult (see Barbaree, Langton, & Peacock, 2006; Hemphill & Hart, 2002; Serin, 1995). The most widely used instruments for measuring psychopathy in offender populations are various versions of the Psychopathy Checklist (see Hare, 1991, 2003; Hart, Cox, & Hare, 1996). Other self-report questionnaires can be useful for assessing additional personality traits (e.g., the MCMI-III; Millon et al., 1997).

Risk of Reoffending

Clinicians are often asked to provide judgments about offenders' likelihood of future sexual or violent offending. The starting point for such evaluations is knowledge of the base rates of such events among the relevant population. Hanson and Bussière's (1998) meta-analysis found that, on average, rapists' sexual offense recidivism rate was 18.9% over a 4- to 5-year follow-up period (vs. 12.7% for child molesters). The same meta-analysis found that rapists' nonsexual violence recidivism rate was 22.1% (vs. 12.2% for child molesters). Harris and Hanson's (2004) recent analysis of 10 large studies from multiple jurisdictions found that rapists' sexual recidivism rates were, on average, 14% within 5 years, 21% within 10 years, and 24% within 15 years. Hanson and Morton-Bourgon's (2005) complementary meta-analysis found that measures of sexual deviancy and antisocial orientation (i.e., antisocial personality, antisocial traits, history of rule violation) were the strongest dynamic predictors of sexual recidivism. The categories of sexual attitudes and intimacy deficits showed smaller but still predictive relationships. Antisocial orientation was the major predictor of nonsexual violent recidivism and any recidivism. However, Hanson and Morton-Bourgon's results were not disaggregated by type of sex offender, making it impossible to identify the relative importance of dynamic risk factors for rapists.

　　A comprehensive assessment of sexual reoffense risk should cover personal traits, historical variables, contextual antecedents, and also clinical factors (Beech et al., 2003) to enable judgments about the likelihood, seriousness, and imminence of sexual harm occurring in the future (Dvorskin & Helibrun, 2001). There are three main assessment approaches that, in combination, cover all these individual variables and enable these judgments: functional assessment, statistical or actuarial methods, and dynamic risk assessment methods (see Beech et al., 2003).

Functional Assessment

A functional assessment should form the underlying basis of any adequate risk assessment (Beech et al., 2003). A competent and comprehensive clinical assessment of a rapist's sexual offense pathway(s) provides insight into the function(s) of rape for the offender and the associated psychological vulnerabilities and precipitants (see the previous description of the SRM). Identifying the proximal events surrounding the offense, and the particular thoughts, feelings, decisions, and behaviors that led to offending, provides insight into the offender's stable and acute dynamic risk factors (Hanson & Harris, 2000). For example, stable dynamic risk factors such as antisocial attitudes and conflict in relationships (intimacy deficits) may be identified from interviewing about general life events occurring prior to offending, or examples of these factors may be directly revealed in the offense process. Acute dynamic risk factors such as anger and substance use are usually clearly evident in the triggering events or psychological states. Careful review of collateral information about the crime also often highlights these factors.

Actuarial Assessment

Actuarial assessment measures the statistical relationship between characteristics of an offender and the probability of reconviction. All actuarial sex offender measures rely extensively on static (historic) risk factors (e.g., number and type of past offenses, victim gender, victim age). These instruments use various coding schemes and produce a final calculation of the offender's risk of sexual recidivism (usually expressed as a simple figure), which can be converted into a categorical risk group, such as low, medium, or high risk. Currently, very few actuarial assessments have been validated with adequate samples of rapists. We outline the most popularly used risk assessment measures and research with rapists where this is available.

Static-99. The Static-99 (Hanson & Thornton, 2000) was developed from two predecessors, the Structured Anchored Clinical Judgment scale (SACJ; Hanson & Thornton, 1999, 2000) and the Rapid Risk Assessment of Sexual Offense Recidivism (RRASOR; Hanson, 1997), and is designed to assess the longer-term likelihood of sexual and violent recidivism in men already convicted of a sexual offense. The Static-99 contains 10 historical items shown to have empirical association with sexual recidivism (prior charges and convictions of a sexual nature, prior sentencing dates, etc.; see Harris, Phenix, Hanson, & Thornton, 2003, for the latest coding information). Items are coded as either present or absent, based predominantly on official information and according to a set of explicit rules; the resulting total score is further classified into a risk category.

Probability estimates for scores and risk categories are provided for both sexual and violent recidivism over 5-, 10-, and 15-year periods. The Static-99 was reported to have moderate predictive accuracy for sexual recidivism (area under the curve [AUC] = .71; see Hanson & Thornton, 1999, 2000). The development samples included over two-thirds child molesters, and results were not disaggregated by sexual offender type. Other studies with larger proportions of rapists have reported similar or slightly better predictive accuracy (e.g., Barbaree, Seto, Langton, & Peacock, 2001; Sjöstedt & Långström, 2001; de Vogel, de Ruiter, van Beck, & Mead, 2004), although this is not universal (see Craig, Beech, & Browne, 2006). Bartosh, Garby, Lewis, and Gray (2003) reported predictive values specifically for a sample of rapists (N = 70); the Static-99 neared conventional levels of significance for prediction of sexual recidivism (AUC = .714, p = .07), and significantly predicted any recidivism (AUC = .623, p = .05), but failed to predict nonsexual violent recidivism. Only 5% of the rapists recidivated sexually during the follow-up period (60–66 months), which is below the base rate reported by others (e.g., Hanson & Bussière, 1998) and suggests that this sample was a lower-risk group of rapists.

Sex Offender Risk Appraisal Guide. The Sex Offender Risk Appraisal Guide (SORAG; Quinsey, Harris, Rice, & Cormier, 1998) is a modification of the Violence Risk Appraisal Guide (Quinsey et al., 1998); it has 14 items including demographic information, criminal history, and psychiatric diagnoses. Like the Static-99, it was designed to predict both violent and sexual recidivism. When compared to the Static-99, it was found to be equally effective in predicting both forms of recidivism (Ducro & Pham, 2006; Nunes, Firestone, Bradford, Greenberg, & Broom, 2002); however, the SORAG has generally been found to predict violent recidivism more accurately than sexual recidivism (Ducro & Pham, 2006). Interestingly, Ducro and Pham (2006) found that the SORAG appeared to be more accurate when used with rapists than with child molesters. However, they note limitations with their study and present this finding cautiously.

Risk Matrix 2000. The Risk Matrix 2000 (RM2000; Thornton et al., 2003) was developed as a revision of the SACJ (Hanson & Thornton, 1999, 2000) and provides risk estimations for sexual recidivism and nonsexual violent recidivism perpetrated by sexual offenders. The instrument is made up of two dimensions: Risk Matrix 2000—Sexual (RM2000-S) and Risk Matrix 2000—Violent (RM2000-V). Both the RM2000-S and RM2000-V consist of three static items (e.g., for the RM2000-S, age at commencement of risk, sexual convictions, and criminal convictions), with points assigned according to the severity of each presenting risk factor. The initial risk category is revised based on the presence of additional aggravating factors (e.g., convictions for a contact sexual offense against a male, lack of long-term age-appropriate relationship). Final risk ratings are *low*, *medium*, *high*, or *very high*.

Thornton and colleagues (2003) reported AUC scores that were favorable and fared well in comparison to those for the Static-99, with results of .77 and .75 noted in the two sexual offender samples (n = 647 and 429, respectively) used both to develop and to cross-validate the instrument (Craissati, 2004). Craig and colleagues (2006) found that the RM2000-V had moderate to high predictive validity with violent, sexual and violent, and any recidivism across 2-, 5-, and 10-year follow-up periods when used with sexual offenders (AUC = .74 to .87). The RM2000-S, however, had low to moderate predictive validity with sexual recidivism in sexual offenders across the follow-up periods (AUC = .59 to .68) and was poorer at predicting sexual recidivism than the RM2000-V.

Minnesota Sex Offender Screening Tool—Revised. The Minnesota Sex Offender Screening Tool—Revised (MnSOST-R; Epperson, Kaul, Huot, Goldman, & Alexander, 2003) was developed for the Minnesota Department of Corrections and contains 16 items examining—among other things—previous conviction history and nature, victim characteristics, and psychosocial information. Although the instrument appears to have good item breadth, it has been criticized for its complex scoring procedure and for the lack of item relevance outside Minnesota (Beech et al., 2003). Bartosh and colleagues (2003) reported that the MnSOST-R did not significantly predict sexual, nonsexual violent, or any recidivism in rapists (AUC = .536, .496, and .617, respectively).

Dynamic Risk Assessment

Actuarial instruments provide a basis for forming longer-term risk predictions that are clearly determined and based on empirical data. However, the instruments currently available are of little use for managing and treating risk, as they predominantly measure risk factors that are historical and unchangeable (Beech et al., 2003; Bonta, 2002; Craig, Browne, & Stringer, 2004; Dvorskin & Heilbrun, 2002; Hanson, 2006). Hence these instruments do not identify the clinical problems that should be targeted in treatment, and are unable to provide a measure of change in risk other than over very significant time frames (e.g., 5 years). Because of such limitations, efforts have recently been made to develop risk instruments that contain changeable factors. These include the Initial Deviance Assessment (Thornton, 2000, 2002), the Sex Offender Need Assessment Rating (SONAR; Hanson & Harris, 2001a), the Sexual Violence Risk–20 (SVR-20; Boer, Hart, Kropp, & Webster, 1997), and the Risk for Sexual Violence Protocol (RSVP; Hart et al., 2003). However, much as in the development of static risk assessment instruments, most of this initial work has been done with samples dominated by child molesters.

Sex Offender Need Assessment Rating. The SONAR (Hanson & Harris, 2001a) is designed to assess both stable dynamic and acute dynamic risk factors in sexual offenders. Stable dynamic factors are psychological and situational characteristics of offenders that, although potentially changeable, are slow to change across time (e.g., intimacy deficits and offense-supportive attitudes and beliefs). Acute dynamic risk factors change rapidly and are proximal signals of imminent offending (e.g., intoxication, being alone with a potential victim). The SONAR also includes case-specific acute risk factors that are personal to the offender and appear to function to elevate risk (e.g., ongoing health problems, victim contact). Subsections are scored to produce stable and acute dynamic risk ratings. Major strengths of the SONAR include its tight link to empirical literature on the dynamic risk factors associated with sexual recidivism, and its ability to assess *change* in risk profiles over time.

Hanson and Harris (2000) found that all items on the SONAR significantly differentiated sexual recidivists from nonrecidivists, and that overall the SONAR showed moderate predictive validity. The development sample had approximately equal numbers of rapists (*n* = 143), girl-victim child molesters, and boy-victim child molesters. Hanson and Harris (2001b) reported that with rare exceptions, the same risk factors were found to be important for all three groups of sexual offenders. The SONAR has since been revised by Hanson and Harris into two separate scales, the Stable-2000 and Acute-2000. Results from a lengthy study investigating these measures are expected in the near future.

Sexual Violence Risk–20. The SVR-20 (Boer et al., 1997) contains structured clinical guidelines designed to predict the risk of sexual recidivism in adult sex offenders. As the name suggests, the SVR-20 has 20 items, which are made up of both static and potentially dynamic predictors of sexual recidivism that span three domains: psychosocial adjustment, sexual offenses, and future plans. The SVR-20 allows for consideration of case-specific factors that are not accounted for among the items and that appear to function to elevate risk; it also includes a recent change score for each item to capture the assessor's judgment about whether items have become more or less salient in a specified period of time. Although the items of the SVR-20 can be summed to provide a total score, the assessor is required to make the judgment of low, moderate, or high risk, depending on consideration of the evidence.

Craig and colleagues (2006) found that the SVR-20 had moderate predictive validity for violent and general recidivism in sexual offenders (AUC = .72 to .74), but not for sexual recidivism over a 2-year follow-up period. de Vogel and colleagues (2004) found that the SVR-20 total score and final risk judgment had high predictive validity for sexual recidivism, while the sexual offenses and future plans domains had moderate predictive validity.

Risk for Sexual Violence Protocol. The RSVP (Hart et al., 2003) is a new set of professional guidelines for assessing risk of sexual violence developed along the lines of the SVR-20 (Boer et al., 1997), but with several improvements (Garret, 2005; Logan, 2005). The RSVP's advantages are that it includes clear specifications of the procedures for obtaining assessment information (including past sexual violence), expanded consideration of risk factors related to management, separate coding of judgments concerning the presence and relevance of risk factors, and scenario-based risk assessment methods (Garret, 2005). The RSVP combines a review of static and dynamic risk factors with extensive case formulation that aids individualized treatment planning and risk management. However, little research investigating the validity of the RSVP is available to date.

Polygraphy

The use of polygraphy since its origins just over 100 years ago has generally been controversial (Branaman & Gallagher, 2005). Its key role in use with offenders is to motivate them to relate the details of their offending honestly, so that a more accurate assessment may be made. Evidence suggests that it is useful in this regard (English, Jones, Pasini-Hill, Patrick, & Cooley-Towell, 2000; Heil, Ahlmeyer, & Simons, 2003). For example, Heil and colleagues (2003) reported that incarcerated sex offenders admitted to many more offenses (than were previously admitted in presentence reports) when questioned under polygraph. However, some researchers have highlighted the ethical issues associated with widespread polygraph use (e.g., Gannon, Ward, & Beech, 2006), such as its tendency to lead to high levels of anxiety and the potential for invasion of privacy. Gannon and colleagues conclude in their comprehensive review that polygraphy should be used with caution when working with sexual offenders, that it should be used alongside other assessment tools, and that it should be embedded within a clear treatment rationale. They also strongly point out the need for further research in the area. This is especially the case for rapists.

TREATMENT

Common Features of Treatment

Sex offender treatment is typically conducted in groups comprising 8–10 offenders with one or two clinicians (Marshall, 2001). Marshall proposes that individual forms of intervention are best avoided, because they are expensive and unproductive. He also contends that a one-on-one situation "lends itself to inadvertent collusion with the offender" (2001, p. 340). Although Marshall does not elaborate, it is obvious why this may occur. Given that a large number of sex offenders deny (or minimize) some or even all aspects of their offending, it is essential for denial to be challenged in treatment. This can be difficult in a one-on-one situation, because it can damage rapport. On the other hand, in a group context the challenge to the offender can come from other group members, which allows the clinician to maintain a good therapeutic relationship more easily while dealing with this difficult issue. Abracen and Looman (2001) discuss the issue of group versus individual therapy at length and report some research findings indicating that these two approaches are equally effective. However, they note that the offenders who received individual therapy were chosen to receive this treatment modality for specific reasons (e.g., because they had a mental illness), and thus may have had atypical risk levels. Abracen and Looman conclude that there may be subgroups of sex offenders who may gain more from individual as opposed to group treatment.

Group treatment is typically manualized, meaning that therapists are provided with clear guidelines for each session (Howitt, 2006). These guidelines include the key learning targets for sessions, along with descriptions of the particular tasks and activities. As noted by Marshall (2006b), this approach has the benefit of maintaining a standard approach to the delivery of treatment across a range of therapists and treatment settings. However, it can also be restrictive and place limits on therapists' ability to deal with process-related issues. According to Marshall, recent research indicates that manuals should be sufficiently flexible to allow therapists to take time to respond to and manage group processes and to employ their skills fully. He ties this suggestion to the growing body of literature that highlights the important role of therapist–client relationships in bringing about lasting treatment gains. This view has been affirmed elsewhere (e.g., Mann, 2004).

Very few treatment programs have been designed especially for rapists; rather, the same intervention approaches are generally used for rapists as for child molesters, and they are often treated alongside one another in the same groups (Lalumière, Harris, Quinsey, & Rice, 2005). Therefore, many of the areas identified as important in treatment for rapists are included in the treatment of sex offenders in general.

Denial, Minimization, and Cognitive Distortions

Research suggests that as a general rule, rapists are less likely than other types of sex offenders to admit to their offending (Ward et al. 1997). It is not uncommon for sex offender treatment programs to exclude individuals who deny that they committed their offenses; however, this precludes a particularly high-risk group from ever receiving treatment (Marshall, 2001). As argued by Marshall (2001, 2006b), there is perhaps a moral obligation, for the sake of public safety, to attempt to treat such individuals. Given that most sex offenders either deny all accountability for their offending or attempt to limit their degree of culpability (Marshall, 2006b), it would seem imperative that denial and minimization are addressed. According to Beech and Fisher (2002), a focus on denial should be central to all approaches to treating sexual offenders.

Two different approaches to treating denial exist. One approach is to design a treatment program specifically for deniers (e.g., Schlank & Shaw, 1996). The other approach is to include a treatment component for denial at the beginning of general treatment (as outlined in Marshall, 2006b). If the latter approach is utilized, it is usual to begin discussing the offender's denial in an individual context (outside of therapy proper), so that he can prepare himself to be challenged within the group (Abracen & Looman, 2001). The group treatment approach appears particularly effective in confronting denial, because offenders can see others who are grappling with the same issues and who have been able to develop insight.

Along with a tendency to deny or minimize their offending, sexual offenders tend to display a range of more general cognitive distortions in regard to their own behavior (Polaschek & Ward, 2002; Ward, 2000). Many treatment approaches address this early in the treatment process also. For example, the Extended Sex Offender Treatment Program (ESOTP) for high-risk sexual offenders in the United Kingdom (Milner, Wakeling, Mann, & Webster, in press) includes the topics of "schema identification" and "schema modification," which focus on changing fundamental dysfunctional beliefs and encouraging "more rational, evidence-based thinking." It is within this type of treatment component that more general cognitive distortions may be addressed.

Deviant Arousal

In recent years deviant arousal has become less prominent in sex offender programs, in part because of an acknowledgment that sexual preferences are not necessarily driving offense behavior (Marshall, 2006b). In regard to rape in particular, it has been frequently argued that rapists are more directly motivated by anger and tendencies toward violence than by specific sexual interests (Lackie & de Man, 1997). Nonetheless, many treatment approaches include a component that targets deviant sexual arousal (Lalumière et al., 2005; Marshall, 2006b), perhaps because some offenders who evidence deviant arousal require assistance in dealing with it directly (Marshall, 2006b). Also, research has shown that the presence of deviant arousal is the most powerful predictor of reoffending (Beech & Fisher, 2002; Hanson & Bussière, 1998; Hanson & Morton-Bourgon, 2005).

As noted by Marshall (2006b), a number of specific techniques have been employed in this regard, such as masturbatory reconditioning (Marquis, 1970), covert sensitization (Cautela, 1967), and satiation therapy (Marshall, 1979); however, there is limited evidence supporting the use of specific approaches. The key aspect of deviant arousal that requires attention in the treatment of rapists is the inclusion of a coercion component in sexual fantasies, although it remains unclear to what extent such sexual fantasies are specific to rapists.

Victim Awareness and Empathy

Many sex offender treatment programs contain a component that aims to increase offenders' understanding of the impact of their offending on their victims (Beech & Fisher, 2002; Lalumière et al., 2005). It is worth noting that research indicates that sexual offenders often have little empathy for their own victims, but do not necessarily have more general empathy deficits (Marshall, 2006b); therefore, the focus in this aspect of treatment is typically offense-specific. Recently Marshall (2006b) has argued that empathy deficits are largely due to cognitive distortions about the nature of harm caused to the victim. For example, an offender may not feel compassion toward his victim because he believes (or at least tells himself) that she dressed provocatively and was therefore subconsciously wanting to be forced to have sex. Marshall proposes, therefore, that it may not be necessary to treat empathy deficits with a specific treatment component, but rather that they may be addressed through targeting cognitive distortions and denial.

When sex offenders do have problems with empathy, these may be related to difficulties in recognizing and understanding emotions. So if an empathy component is included in treatment, emotion recognition and regulation skills should be addressed first (Marshall, 2001). In many treatment programs, the recognition and expression of emotional experience are addressed throughout treatment by encouraging offenders to talk about their feelings and beginning sessions with an invitation for all group members to inform the group of their current mental state and level of well-being. Some general offender programs (e.g., the 100-hour Violence Prevention Program in New Zealand; New Zealand

Department of Corrections, 1999) use prompts for this exercise, in the form of cards with various emotional terms and facial expressions represented on each one. This allows offenders to increase their emotion vocabulary and develop confidence in expressing emotional phenomena.

A recent study investigated the value of offense reenactments via role plays in developing victim empathy (Webster, Bowers, Mann, & Marshall, 2005). Using a matched control design, the researchers found that the inclusion of offence reenactments led to moderately superior treatment gains in some aspects of victim empathy. Interestingly, the researchers concluded that "rapists in particular seemed to benefit from offence reenactment" (p. 63).

Social Skills Training

A growing body of evidence indicates that many sex offenders have difficulties forming consensual intimate relationships with adults, and that they consequently may be inclined to feel lonely and isolated (Mandeville-Norden & Beech, 2004). These authors note also that evidence indicates that some sexual offenders have difficulties behaving in an assertive manner. Hence it is important to address these problems in treatment. Social skills training is a very broad aspect of treatment that may encompass a variety of elements, such as building self-esteem, problem solving, sex education, and assertiveness training (Marshall, 2006b).

The ESOTP for high-risk sexual offenders, including rapists, mentioned above (Milner et al., in press) utilizes a component labeled "intimacy skills," which aims to develop skills in the areas of giving and receiving support, managing jealousy, and resolving conflict. Similarly, the treatment program for sex offenders, including rapists, outlined by Yates and Goguen (2000) (summarized below in Table 21.1) includes a component titled "intimacy, relationships, and social functioning." This covers areas similar to those in the ESOTP, but also includes a focus on sexual behavior. Hence it appears that contemporary treatment in this area is specifically targeted toward individuals' functioning in intimate relationships rather than toward social skills in general.

Emotion Regulation

Evidence suggests that sex offenders may use their offending to escape the experience of negative emotion (Mandeville-Norton & Beech, 2004). Therefore, some researchers argue for the importance of including a treatment component that provides instruction on how to reduce and manage negative emotions in more socially appropriate ways (Beech & Fisher, 2002). However, while there is some research available on the inclusion of this component in the treatment of child sex offenders, there appears to be little such research available for rapists. Perhaps most pertinent is anger management, which is included in some treatment programs for rapists (Lalumière et al., 2005), because it has been proposed that anger may be a key precipitant in rape (Lackie & de Man, 1997). According to Howitt (2006), "Anger control problems have to be seen as an issue with rapists for whom issues of anger are common" (p. 369). However, other researchers have questioned the value of including an anger management component in treatment. For example, a study examining anger levels in a range of offender groups found that rapists and nonrapists had similar anger levels, leading Loza and Loza-Fanous (1999) to question whether targeting anger in the treatment of rapists would reduce recidivism.

   If a sex offender program does include an aspect that targets emotion regulation deficits, it can be tied in part to the empathy component, since both are associated with a focus on emotion identification. The first step in effectively managing one's emotions is to identify the emotions, as only then can they be understood and controlled.

Substance Abuse

Problems with substances in general, and alcohol in particular, are frequently seen in rapists (Marshall, 2001). However, Marshall notes that while a high proportion admit to being intoxicated at the time of their offending, a much lesser number appear to have chronic substance use difficulties, such as substance dependence. Nonetheless, research indicates that substance abuse is often a reflection of general lifestyle problems that are associated with higher rates of recidivism (Looman, Dickie, & Abracen, 2005). It is generally recommended that substance use problems be dealt with in separate specialized treatment programs using complementary treatment models, so that there may be some knowledge integration, especially with respect to RP (Marshall, 2006b).

Treatment Models

Cognitive-Behavioral Therapy

As in the psychological treatment of clients with many other types of offenses or addictions, the type of intervention most commonly used with sexual offenders is cognitive-behavioral therapy (CBT) within an RP framework. Studies show greater support for treatment programs that have CBT as their primary model and include an RP component, rather than the converse (Yates, 2005). This is perhaps because RP alone can involve quite a narrow approach that focuses more on past offending and reducing risk, and may not include such broader aspects of CBT as attending specifically to maladaptive beliefs and attitudes, and increasing the frequency of rewarding experiences in daily life. This issue parallels the discussion that follows, which examines two other models.

The Risk–Need and Good-Lives Models

The most widely used rehabilitation model for sex offender programs is the risk–need model outlined by Andrews and Bonta (1998), which proposes that treatment should (1) be matched to the nature and level of an offender's risk (*risk principle*), (2) target specific criminogenic needs (*need principle*), and (3) be adapted to the offender's learning style (*responsivity principle*). As argued by Ward and colleagues (e.g., Ward, 2002; Ward & Stewart, 2003), this approach is useful—but if it is used alone, it has the disadvantage of casting a negative light on the treatment approach. If the only focus of treatment is avoiding risk, then offenders may simply be taught what *not* to do and may emerge from treatment with a lack of direction and feeling of unworthiness, which could ultimately increase their risk. Ward argues that the risk–need approach may be complemented by the inclusion of a strengths-based approach based on the good-lives model (GLM), which aims to assist sex offenders more directly to rebuild their lives.
   The GLM centers on the idea that all human activity is aimed at fulfilling certain basic needs and their associated goods. When such needs are met in an individual, then it can be said that the individual has a "good life"—that is, a life characterized by funda-

mental benefits such as sexual intimacy, friendship, physical health, autonomy, community connectedness, and creativity. Ward (2002) speaks also about "primary goods" and "secondary goods." The former are actions or conditions that are good in and of themselves (in other words, they are inherently valuable), while the latter are ways and means of acquiring primary goods. For example, if happiness is a primary good, then anything that is instrumental in enhancing one's happiness would be a secondary good.

According to Ward (2002), sexual offenders, like all human beings, need and value these goods, and a GLM approach to rehabilitation seeks to furnish individuals with the internal and external conditions necessary to implement realistic good-lives plans. In this sense, the GLM may be seen as an overarching rehabilitation model that can assist in the identification of individualized treatment goals and provide a more positive framework for treatment than the risk–need model alone. This strength-based approach to rehabilitation has been described by a number of key researchers in the field as "the most important recent innovation" (Mann, 2004, p. 148) and is currently being used in Her Majesty's Prison Service booster program for sexual offenders. Studies of treatment efficacy, however, are yet to emerge.

An Example of a Contemporary Treatment Program

Yates and colleagues (e.g., Hanson & Yates, 2004; Yates, 2003; Yates & Goguen, 2000) have outlined the treatment approach utilized by Correctional Service Canada. It is an empirically robust and comprehensively explained approach that incorporates many (if not all) of the elements currently considered important in sex offender treatment. Like most contemporary approaches, it is founded upon a CBT model and has a number of distinct components. The key components are summarized in Table 21.1. Other aspects of the program that require mentioning are that treatment is offered at three levels of intensity—low, moderate, or high—with assignment to a particular level dependent upon a number of variables, including the offender's level of risk, criminogenic needs, and personal situational factors. Low-intensity programs involve approximately 30–60 hours of treatment, while high-intensity programs involve approximately 360–480 hours. Some specific treatment programs are also available for particular offender groups, such as aboriginal sex offenders and female sex offenders (Hanson & Yates, 2004).

Studies of Treatment Efficacy

Meta-Analyses

Although a large number of studies have assessed treatment efficacy for sexual offenders, there remains a high degree of uncertainty about whether treatment is effective and, if it is, what the key features of successful treatment are (Hanson et al., 2002; Lösel & Schmucker, 2005). Thus we are still finding out what works for sexual offenders generally, and much less emphasis has been given to specifically teasing out treatment effects for rapists.

A meta-analytic review by Hanson and colleagues (2002) examined 43 studies (with a total subject pool of over 9,000 individuals) that investigated recidivism in sexual offenders. In order to be included in their meta-analysis, the studies had to compare rates of general or sexual reoffending in treated sex offenders with rates of reoffending in an untreated comparison group. Another condition of inclusion was that the treated and un-

TABLE 21.1. National Sex Offender Treatment Programme in Canada

Component	Content
Cognitive distortions	Identifies and challenges distorted offense-related attitudes and beliefs, including minimization and justification.
Empathy and victim awareness	Targets the development of an understanding of one's impact on others (the victim in particular). Includes a focus on the offender's own experiences of victimization.
Intimacy, relationships, and social functioning	Attends to specific deficits in social functioning, particularly in the area of intimate relationships. Includes a focus on building self-confidence and self-esteem.
Emotion management	Seeks to develop skills in the areas of the identification of emotion terms and discussion of feelings. Teaches various techniques for managing negative emotional states.
Deviant arousal	Focuses on developing an awareness of the connection between sexual fantasy and arousal, followed by the application of reconditioning techniques.
Self-management	Seeks to instill an understanding of the offense process, including various types of risk factors, in order to prevent relapse. Includes a focus on goal setting and safety plans.
Posttreatment follow-up	Aims to facilitate the generalization and maintenance of treatment gains. Particularly important for those offenders who are treated in prison and need support in generalizing their treatment gains upon release.

Note. Summarized from Hanson and Yates (2003) and Yates and Goguen (2000).

treated groups had to use the same criteria for recidivism and to employ follow-up periods of similar duration. According to Hanson and colleagues, this yielded a total number of usable studies that was significantly larger than the number of studies in any previous meta-analysis with a similar focus.

This meta-analysis found that treatment significantly reduced both sexual and general recidivism. The recidivism rates were 12.3% in the treated group versus 16.8% in the comparison group, for sexual offending, and 27.9% in the treated group versus 39.2% in the comparison group, for general offending. This study found that contemporary treatments such as CBT and systemic therapy (e.g., as explained by Swenson, Henggeler, & Schoenwald, 2001) were associated with reductions in reoffending (of 7.5% for sexual recidivism and 19% for general recidivism). It was found that older modes of treatments (treatments in use prior to 1980) had little effect on rates of recidivism.

A more recent meta-analysis by Lösel and Schmucker (2005) reviewed the results of 69 studies containing a total pool of over 22,000 sexual offenders. As in the Hanson and colleagues (2002) meta-analysis, studies were only included if they utilized a comparison group. Although there was a great deal of variation in the results of the included studies, the researchers found a 6.4% reduction in sexual recidivism, a 5.2% reduction in violent recidivism, and a 11.1% reduction in general recidivism, in treated offenders compared with matched controls. As noted by Lösel and Schmucker, it is likely that the inclusion of medical interventions along with psychological interventions in their meta-analysis contributed to the difference between their results and the results of the analysis by Hanson and colleagues. Lösel and Schmucker found stronger treatment effects for surgical and hormonal modes of treatment. However, as in the Hanson and colleagues study, they also found that CBT was superior to other psychological approaches. It is of interest that unlike Hanson and colleagues, Lösel and Schmucker did not find that more recent modes of treatment had greater efficacy.

Specific Treatment Programs

A number of specific treatment programs have been evaluated, and it is worth looking at these evaluations to better understand the factors that may have an impact on treatment efficacy. Nicholaichuk, Gordon, Gu, and Wong (2000) examined the success of a prison-based Canadian facility that treated high-risk sexual offenders with a CBT approach. Fifty-seven percent of the treated group (total $N = 296$) consisted of rapists, with the remainder being other types of sexual offenders, and the treated group was compared with a matched control group (total $N = 283$). Results showed that significantly fewer treated rapists than untreated controls reoffended sexually (14% vs. 42%, respectively).

McGrath, Cumming, Livingston, and Hoke (2003) presented a similar evaluation, although they did not differentiate between types of sexual offenders. They examined the recidivism rate in sexual offenders who had completed a CBT program at a correctional facility in Vermont. The treatment group was matched with two comparison groups who had similar risk prediction scores on two static measures. During an average follow-up period of 6 years, it was found that 5.4% of the treated group sexually reoffended, compared to 30.6% for a some-treatment group (i.e., individuals who started but did not complete treatment) and 30% for an untreated group.

In contrast, Marques, Wiederanders, Day, Nelson, and van Ommeren (2005) reported on a longitudinal investigation into the efficacy of a California-based sex offender treatment program, and found no significant difference in recidivism between the treated and untreated groups. The treatment approach used was described as "an intensive, cognitive-behavioral inpatient treatment program designed specifically to prevent relapse among sexual offenders" (p. 81). The investigation utilized a rigorous randomized controlled design, in which three groups of subjects were compared over an 8-year follow-up period: an RP group, consisting of imprisoned sex offenders who volunteered to take part in the study and were randomly assigned to treatment in a secure forensic hospital setting ($n = 259$); a "volunteer control group" of inmates who volunteered but were randomly chosen for no treatment ($n = 225$); and a "nonvolunteer control group" of inmates, consisting of individuals who were eligible to participate in the project but declined ($n = 220$). The researchers found no statistically significant differences in reoffending rates among the three groups. Also, when different types of offenders were examined separately, the researchers found no difference in recidivism rates for rapists.

Schweitzer and Dwyer (2003) analyzed the efficacy of an Australian sex offender treatment program and found no evidence of treatment success during a 1-year follow-up period. The prison-based treatment program they assessed was described as "a self paced open ended program based on cognitive behavioral and relapse prevention principles" (p. 1296). The study compared 196 individuals who completed treatment, 85 individuals who began treatment but failed to complete it, and 164 matched controls. The researchers concluded that there were no statistically significant differences among the three groups. This study compared rates of reoffending across various types of sexual offenses and found that while some small and insignificant differences were found for other sexual offenders, there was no difference at all between rapists who had been treated and those who had not. The researchers concluded that participation in this particular intervention did not lead to a quantifiable reduction in recidivism in the 12 months following completion of treatment. They concluded also that regardless of whether offenders engaged in treatment, the most powerful predictor of reoffending was the presence of prior violent and sexual offenses.

Comments

Taken together, this research suggests that treatment for sexual offenders is frequently but not always effective, and that CBT in a group setting is the best form of psychological intervention. Also, researchers have tentatively concluded that psychological treatment is generally less effective for rapists than for child molesters (Marshall, 2001). More recently, Lalumière and colleagues (2005), in their comprehensive review of available research findings, asserted that "the effectiveness of adult sex offender treatment has yet to be demonstrated" (p. 178).

As noted by various researchers, it is difficult to determine the factors that may lead to conflicting results among the research in this area. However, some such factors are differences in length of follow-up (Schweitzer & Dwyer, 2003); differences in the types of offenders who are included in groups—for example, variability in levels of motivation (Marques et al., 2005); and the use of inadequately matched control groups (Nicholaichuk et al., 2000). Another possible influence on program efficacy is the impact of external organizational pressures such as having to meet operational targets, which can result in unmotivated individuals being placed in programs when they are unlikely to benefit.

SUMMARY AND FUTURE DIRECTIONS

As highlighted in this chapter, there is a reasonable body of literature available on the assessment and treatment of rapists, but many unanswered questions remain. It appears that much of the research on sexual offenders has focused on those committing offenses against children, resulting in a dearth of information about the best means to assess and treat rapists. It is perhaps surprising that even the issue of whether rapists are primarily motivated by sexual inclinations or aggression remains uncertain. This underscores the need for tailored assessment and treatment approaches clearly linked with multipathway and multifactorial theories of rape that do not rely on generalizations about the nature of all rapists.

To advance assessment practice, a number of important areas require further investigation. Though assessment areas have been presented herein in a fairly straightforward manner, there is disagreement among researchers about exactly what areas should be covered. The areas we have described are those for which at least some degree of consensus about their inclusion exists. Given the breadth of information required and the time taken to administer many of the psychometric measures, there is a need for greater clarity about what information is important, so that the assessment process is not unnecessarily onerous for either the offender or the clinician. Also, the usefulness of the more intrusive assessment techniques (e.g., phallometry and polygraphy) has yet to be fully demonstrated; therefore, psychologists are obligated to provide clear rationales and evidence for their continued use.

With regard to treatment, there is ongoing debate about exactly what needs to be treated. For example, researchers disagree as to whether the regulation of emotions should be directly targeted and whether empathy deficits should be addressed with a specific treatment component. Perhaps more problematic is the lack of robust evidence that treatment reduces recidivism. Although many studies demonstrate treatment efficacy, the effect sizes are modest, and most of the evidence for treatment success comes from studies dominated by child molesters.

Important and interesting developments in the theoretical underpinnings of treatment have also emerged over the last two decades. There is a trend toward a strength-based approach that emphasizes the positive aspects of offenders and centers on rebuilding their lives, so that they are no longer attracted to the idea of sexually offending. It will be interesting to see what, if any, impact this trend has on treatment approaches in the coming years.

REFERENCES

Abel, G. G., Barlow, D. H., Blanchard, E. B., & Guild, D. (1977). The components of rapists' sexual arousal. *Archives of General Psychiatry, 34,* 895–903.

Abracen, J., & Looman, J. (2001). Issues in the treatment of sexual offenders: Recent developments and directions for future research. *Aggression and Violent Behavior, 1,* 1–19.

Ackerman, S. J., & Hilsenroth, M. J. (2003). A review of therapist characteristics and techniques positively impacting the therapeutic alliance. *Clinical Psychology Review, 23,* 1–33.

Andrews, D. A., & Bonta, J. (1998). *The psychology of criminal conduct* (2nd ed.). Cincinnati, OH: Anderson.

Arbisi, P. A. (2005). Review of the Multiphasic Sex Inventory II. In R. A. Spies & B. S. Plake (Eds.), *The sixteenth mental measurements yearbook* [Online]. Lincoln, NE: Buros Institute of Mental Measurements. Retrieved August 10, 2006, from *www.unl.edu/buros*

Barbaree, H. E., Baxter, D. J., & Marshall, W. L. (1989). The reliability of the rape index in a sample of rapists and nonrapists. *Violence and Victims, 4,* 299–306.

Barbaree, H. E., Langton, C., & Peacock, E. (2006). Sexual offender treatment for psychopaths: Is it harmful? In W. L. Marshall, Y. M., Fernandez, L. E. Marshall, & G. A. Serran (Eds.), *Sexual offender treatment: Controversial issues* (pp. 159–171). Chichester, UK: Wiley.

Barbaree, H. E., Marshall, W. L., & Lanthier, R. D. (1979). Deviant sexual arousal in rapists. *Behaviour Research and Therapy, 14,* 215–222.

Barbaree, H. E., Seto, M. C., Langton, C. M., & Peacock, E. J. (2001). Evaluating the predictive accuracy of six risk assessment instruments for adult sex offenders. *Criminal Justice and Behavior, 28,* 490–521.

Bartosh, D. L., Garby, T., Lewis, D., & Gray, S. (2003). Differences in predictive validity of actuarial risk assessment in relation to sex offender type. *International Journal of Offender Therapy and Comparative Criminology, 47,* 422–438.

Baumeister, R. F., & Heatherton, T. F. (1996). Self-regulation failure: An overview. *Psychological Inquiry, 7,* 1–15.

Beech, A. R., & Fisher, D. D. (2002). The rehabilitation of sex offenders. *Australian Psychologist, 37,* 206–214.

Beech, A. R., Fisher, D., & Thornton, D. (2003). Risk assessment of sex offenders. *Professional Psychology: Research and Practice, 34,* 339–352.

Beven, J. P., O'Brien-Malone, A., & Hall, G. (2004). Using the Interpersonal Reactivity Index to assess empathy in violent offenders. *International Journal of Forensic Psychology, 1,* 33–41.

Boer, D. P., Hart, S. D., Kropp, P. R., & Webster, C. D. (1997). *Manual for the Sexual Violence Risk–20: Professional guidelines for assessing risk of sexual violence.* Vancouver: British Columbia Institute Against Family Violence.

Bohner, G., Jarvis, C. I., Eyssel, F., & Siebler, F. (2005). The causal impact of rape myth acceptance on men's rape productivity: Comparing sexually coercive and noncoercive men. *European Journal of Social Psychology, 35*, 819–828.

Bonta, J. (2002). Offender risk assessment: Guidelines for selection and use. *Criminal Justice and Behavior, 29*, 355–379.

Branaman, T. F., & Gallagher, S. N. (2005). Polygraph testing in sex offender treatment: A review of limitations. *American Journal of Forensic Psychology, 23*, 45–64.

Bugaj, A. (2005). Review of the Multiphasic Sex Inventory II. In R. A. Spies & B. S. Plake. (Eds.), *The sixteenth mental measurements yearbook* [Online]. Lincoln, NE: Buros Institute of Mental Measurements. Retrieved August 10, 2006, at *www.unl.edu/buros*

Bumby, K. M. (1996). Assessing the cognitive distortions of child molesters and rapists: Developments and validation of the MOLEST and RAPE Scales. *Sexual Abuse: A Journal of Research and Treatment, 8*, 37–54.

Burt, M. R. (1980). Cultural myths and supports for rape. *Journal of Personality and Social Psychology, 38*, 217–230.

Burt, M. R. (1983). Justifying personal violence: A comparison of rapists and the general public. *Victimology, 8*, 131–150.

Cautela, J. R. (1967). Covert sensitization. *Psychological Record, 20*, 459–468.

Cecil, H., & Matson, S. C. (2006). Sexual victimization among African American adolescent females: Examination of the reliability and validity of the Sexual Experiences Survey. *Journal of Interpersonal Violence, 21*, 89–104.

Check, J. P. V. (1985). *The Hostility Toward Women Scale.* Unpublished doctoral dissertation, University of Manitoba, Winnipeg, Canada.

Cowburn, M. (2005). Confidentiality and public protection: Ethical dilemmas in qualitative research with adult male sex offenders. *Journal of Sexual Aggression, 11*, 49–63.

Craig, L. A., Beech, A., & Browne, K. D. (2006). Cross-validation of the Risk Matrix 2000 Sexual and Violent scales. *Journal of Interpersonal Violence, 21*, 612–633.

Craig, L. A., Browne, K. D., & Stringer, I. (2004). Comparing sex offender risk assessment measures on a UK sample. *International Journal of Offender Therapy and Comparative Criminology, 48*, 7–27.

Craissati, J. (2004). *Managing high risk offenders in the community: A psychological approach.* Hove, UK: Brunner-Routledge.

Davis, M. H. (1980). A multidimensional approach to individual differences in empathy. *JSAS: Catalogue of Selected Documents in Psychology, 10* (Ms. No. 85).

Davis, M. H. (1994). *Empathy: A social psychological approach.* Madison, WI: Brown & Benchmark.

de Vogel, V., de Ruiter, C., van Beck, D., & Mead, G. (2004). Predictive validity of the SVR-20 and Static-99 in a Dutch sample of treated sex offenders. *Law and Human Behavior, 28*, 235–251.

Diem, T. (2000). A cross validation of the Illinois Rape Myth Acceptance Scale. *Dissertation Abstracts International, 61*, 2812B.

Dietz, S. R., Blackwell, K. T., Daley, P. C., & Bentley, B. J. (1982). Measurement of empathy toward rape victims and rapists. *Journal of Personality and Social Psychology, 43*, 372–384.

Ducro, C., & Pham, T. (2006). Evaluation of the SORAG and the Static-99 on Belgian sex offenders committed to a forensic facility. *Sexual Abuse: A Journal of Research and Treatment, 18*, 15–26.

Dvorskin, J. A., & Heilbrun, K. (2001). Risk assessment and release decision-making: Toward resolving the great debate. *Journal of the American Academy of Psychiatry and the Law, 29*, 6–10.

English, K., Jones, L., Pasini-Hill, D., Patrick, D., & Cooley-Towell, S. (2000). *The value of testing in sex offender management: Research report submitted to the National Institute of Justice.* Denver: Colorado Department of Public Safety, Division of Criminal Justice, Office of Research and Statistics.

Epperson, D. L., Kaul, J. D., Huot, S. J., Goldman, R., & Alexander, W. (2003). *Minnesota Sex Offender Screening Tool—Revised (MnSOST-R): Development, validation, and recommended risk-level cut scores* (Technical paper). St. Paul: Minnesota Department of Corrections.

Fernandez, Y. M., & Marshall, W. L. (2003). Victim empathy, social self-esteem and psychopathology in rapists. *Sexual Abuse: A Journal of Research and Treatment, 15*, 11–26.

Forbes, G. B., Adams-Curtis, L. E., & White, K. B. (2004). First- and second-generation measures of sexism, rape myths and related beliefs, and hostility toward women: Their interrelationships and associations with college students' experiences with dating aggression and sexual coercion. *Violence Against Women, 10*, 236–261.

Gannon, T. A., Ward, T., & Beech, A. R. (2006). *Sex offender risk assessment and the polygraph: A review.* Manuscript submitted for publication.

Garret, T. (2005). Review of the Risk for Sexual Violence Protocol (RSVP)—Structured professional guideline for assessing risk of sexual violence. *Journal of Sexual Aggression, 11*, 321–323.

Gress, C. L. Z. (2005). Viewing time measures and sexual interest: Another piece of the puzzle. *Journal of Sexual Aggression, 11*, 117–125.

Hanson, R. K. (1997). *The development of a brief actuarial risk scale for sexual offense recidivism* (User Report No. 1997-04). Ottawa: Department of the Solicitor General of Canada.

Hanson, R. K. (2006). Stability and change: Dynamic risk factors for sexual offenders. In W. L. Marshall, Y. M. Fernandez, L. E. Marshall, & G. A. Serran (Eds.), *Sexual offender treatment: Controversial issues.* (pp. 17–33). Chichester, UK: Wiley.

Hanson, R. K., & Bussière, M. T. (1998). Predicting relapse: A meta-analysis of sexual offender recidivism studies. *Journal of Consulting and Clinical Psychology, 66*, 348–362.

Hanson, R. K., Gordon, A., Harris, A. J. R., Marques, J. K., Murphy, W., Quinsey, V. L., et al. (2002). First report of the Collaborative Outcome Data Project on the Effectiveness of Psychological Treatment for Sex Offenders. *Sexual Abuse: A Journal of Research and Treatment, 14*, 169–194.

Hanson, R. K., & Harris, A. J. R. (2000). Where should we intervene?: Dynamic predictors of sexual offence recidivism. *Criminal Justice and Behavior, 27*, 6–35.

Hanson, R. K., & Harris, A. J. R. (2001a). *The Sex Offender Need Assessment Rating (SONAR): A method for measuring change in risk levels* (User Report No. 1998-01). Ottawa: Department of the Solicitor General of Canada.

Hanson, R. K., & Harris, A. J. R. (2001b). A structured approach to evaluating change among sex offenders. *Sexual Abuse: A Journal of Research and Treatment, 13*, 105–122.

Hanson, R. K., & Morton-Bourgon, K. (2005). The characteristics of persistent sexual offenders: A meta-analysis of recidivism studies. *Journal of Consulting and Clinical Psychology, 73*, 1154–1163.

Hanson, R. K., & Thornton, D. (1999). *Static-99: Improving actuarial risk assessments for sex offenders* (User Report No. 1999-02). Ottawa: Department of the Solicitor General of Canada.

Hanson, R. K., & Thornton, D. (2000). Improving risk assessments for sex offenders: A comparison of three actuarial scales. *Law and Human Behavior, 24*, 119–136.

Hanson, R. K., & Yates, P. M. (2004). Sexual violence: Risk factors and treatment. In M. Eliasson (Ed.), *Anthology on interventions against violent men* (pp. 151–166). Uppsala, Sweden: Department of Industrial Relations.

Hare, R. D. (1991). *The Hare Psychopathy Checklist—Revised.* Toronto: Multi-Health Systems.

Hare, R. D. (2003). *The Hare Psychopathy Checklist—Revised* (2nd ed.). Toronto: Multi-Health Systems.

Harris, A. J. R., & Hanson, R. K. (2004). *Sex offender recidivism: A simple question* (User Report No. 2004-03). Ottawa: Department of the Solicitor General of Canada.

Harris, A. J. R., Phenix, A., Hanson, R. K., & Thornton, D. (2003). *Static-99 coding rules: Revised—2003.* Ottawa: Department of the Solicitor General of Canada.

Harris, G. T., Rice, M. E., Quinsey, V. L. & Chaplin, T. C. (1996). Viewing time as a measure of sexual interest among child molesters and normal heterosexual men. *Behaviour Research and Therapy, 34*, 389–394.

Hart, S. D., Cox, D. N., & Hare, R. D. (1995). *The Hare Psychopathy Checklist: Screening Version (PCL:SV).* Toronto: Multi-Health Systems.

Hart, S. D., Kropp, P. R., Laws, D. R., Klaver, J., Logan, C., & Watt, K. A. (2003). *The Risk for Sexual Violence Protocol (RSVP): Structured professional guidelines for assessing risk of sexual vio-*

lence. Burnaby, BC, Canada: Mental Health, Law, and Policy Institute, Simon Fraser University; Pacific Psychological Assessment Corporation; and the British Columbia Institute Against Family Violence.

Heil, P., Ahlmeyer, S., & Simons, D. (2003). Crossover sexual offences. *Sexual Abuse: A Journal of Research and Treatment, 15*, 221–236.

Hemphill, J. F., & Hart, S. (2002). Motivating the unmotivated: Psychopathic offenders. In S. Hodgins & R. Muller-Isberner (Eds.), *Violence, crime and mentally disordered offenders* (pp. 87–112). Chichester, UK: Wiley.

Howitt, D. (2006). *Introduction to forensic and criminal psychology*. Harlow, UK: Pearson Education.

Jimenez, J. A., & Abreu, J. M. (2003). Race and sex effects on attitudinal perceptions of acquaintance rape. *Journal of Counselling Psychology, 30*, 252–256.

Kalichman, S. C., Henderson, M. C., Shealy, L. S., & Dwyer, M. (1992). Psychometric properties of the Multiphasic Sex Inventory in assessing sex offenders. *Criminal Justice and Behavior, 19*, 384–396.

Karoly, P. (1993). Mechanisms of self-regulation: A systems view. *Annual Review of Psychology, 44*, 23–52.

Koss, M. P., & Oros, C. J. (1982). Sexual Experiences Survey: A research instrument investigating sexual aggression and victimization. *Journal of Consulting and Clinical Psychology, 50*, 455–457.

Knight, R. A., & Cerce, D. D. (2001). *Validation and revision of the Multidimensional Assessment of Sex and Aggression*. Unpublished research report submitted to the U.S. Department of Justice.

Knight, R. A., Prentky, R. A., & Cerce, D. (1994). The development, reliability, and validity of an inventory for the Multidimensional Assessment of Sex and Aggression. *Criminal Justice and Behavior, 21*, 72–94.

Lackie, L., & de Man, A. F. (1997). Correlates of sexual aggression among male university students. *Sex Roles, 37*, 451–456.

Lalumière, M. L., Harris, G. T., Quinsey, V. L., & Rice, M. E. (2005). *The causes of rape: Understanding individual differences in male propensity for sexual aggression*. Washington, DC: American Psychological Association.

Laws, D. R. (2003). Penile plethysmography: Will we ever get it right? In T. Ward, D. R. Laws, & S. M. Hudson (Eds.), *Sexual deviance: Issues and controversies* (pp. 82–102). Thousand Oaks, CA: Sage.

Laws, D. R., & Gress, C. (2004). Seeing things differently: The viewing time alternative to penile plethysmography. *Legal and Criminological Psychology, 9*, 183–196.

Laws, D. R., Hudson, S. M., & Ward, T. (Eds.). (2000). *Remaking relapse prevention with sex offenders: A sourcebook*. Thousand Oaks, CA: Sage.

Letourneau, E. J. (2002). A comparison of objective measures of sexual arousal and interest: Visual reaction time and penile plesythmography. *Sexual Abuse: A Journal of Treatment and Research, 14*, 207–223.

Lisak, D., & Roth, S. (1988). Motivational factors in non-incarcerated sexually aggressive men. *Journal of Personality and Social Psychology, 5*, 795–802.

Looman, J., Dickie, I., & Abracen, J. (2005). Responsivity issues in the treatment of sexual offenders. *Trauma, Violence and Abuse, 6*, 330–353.

Looman, J., & Marshall, W. L. (2001). Phallometric assessments designed to detect arousal to children: The responses of rapists and child molesters. *Sexual Abuse: A Journal of Research and Treatment, 13*, 3–13.

Looman, J., & Marshall, W. L. (2005). Sexual arousal in rapists. *Criminal Justice and Behavior, 32*, 367–389.

Lösel, F., & Schmucker, M. (2005). The effectiveness of treatment for sexual offenders: A comprehensive meta-analysis. *Journal of Experimental Criminology, 1*, 117–146.

Loza, W., & Loza-Fanous, A. (1999). The fallacy of reducing rape and violent recidivism by treating anger. *International Journal of Offender Therapy and Comparative Criminology, 43*, 492–502.

Malamuth, N. M. (1984). Aggression against women: Cultural and individual causes. In N. M. Malamuth & E. Donnerstein (Eds.), *Pornography and aggression* (pp. 19–52). Orlando, FL: Academic Press.

Malamuth, N. M. (1989a). The Attraction to Sexual Aggression Scale: Part one. *Journal of Sex Research*, *26*, 26–29.

Malamuth, N. M. (1989b). The Attraction to Sexual Aggression Scale: Part two. *Journal of Sex Research*, *26*, 324–354.

Mandeville-Norden, R., & Beech, A. (2004). Community-based treatment of sex offenders. *Journal of Sexual Aggression*, *10*, 193–214.

Mann, R. E. (2004). Innovations in sex offender treatment. *Journal of Sexual Aggression*, *10*, 141–152.

Marques, J. K., Wiederanders, M., Day, D. M., Nelson, C., & van Ommeren, A. (2005). Effects of a relapse prevention program on sexual recidivism: Final results from California's Sex Offender Treatment and Evaluation Project (SOTEP). *Sexual Abuse: Journal of Research and Treatment*, *17*, 79–107.

Marquis, J. (1970). Orgasmic reconditioning: Changing sexual object choice through controlling masturbation fantasies. *Journal of Behavior Therapy and Experimental Psychiatry*, *1*, 263–270.

Marshall, W. L. (1979). Satiation therapy: A procedure for reducing deviant sexual arousal. *Journal of Applied Behavior Analysis*, *12*, 10–22.

Marshall, W. L. (2001). Adult sexual offenders against women. In C. R. Holin (Ed.), *The handbook of offender assessment and treatment* (pp. 333–348). Chichester, UK: Wiley.

Marshall, W. L. (2005). Therapist style in sexual offender treatment: Influence on indices of change. *Sexual Abuse: A Journal of Research and Treatment*, *17*, 109–116.

Marshall, W. L. (2006a). Clinical and research limitations in the use of phallometric testing with sexual offenders. *Sexual Offender Treatment*, *1*. Retrieved from *www.iatso.org/ejournal*

Marshall, W. L. (2006b). Diagnosis and treatment of sexual offenders. In I. B. Weiner & A. K. Hess (Eds.), *The handbook of forensic psychology* (3rd ed., pp. 790–818). Hoboken, NJ: Wiley.

Millon, T., Davis, R., & Millon, C. (1997). *Millon Clinical Multiaxial Inventory–III* (rev. ed.). Minneapolis, MN: National Computer Systems.

Milner, R. J., Wakeling, H. C., Mann, R. E., & Webster, S. D. (in press). Clinical impact of a socioaffective functioning programme for high risk sexual offenders. *Sexual Abuse: A Journal of Research and Treatment*.

McGrath, R. J., Cumming, G., Livingston, J. A., & Hoke, S. E. (2003). Outcome of a treatment program for adult sex offenders. *Journal of Interpersonal Violence*, *18*, 3–17.

New Zealand Department of Corrections. (1999). *Manual for the 100 hour Violence Prevention Program*. Wellington: Author.

Nicholaichuk, T. P., Gordon, A., Gu, D., & Wong, S. (2000). Outcome of an institutional sexual offender treatment program: A comparison between treated and matched untreated offenders. *Sexual Abuse: A Journal of Research and Treatment*, *12*, 139–153.

Nichols, H. R., & Molinder, I. (1984). *Multiphasic Sex Inventory*. Fircrest, WA: Nichols & Molinder Assessments.

Nichols, H. R., & Molinder, I. (2000). *Multiphasic Sex Inventory II* (rev. ed.). Fircrest, WA: Nichols & Molinder Assessments.

Nunes, K. L., Firestone, P., Bradford, J. M., Greenberg, D. M., & Broom, I. (2002). A comparison of modified versions of the Static-99 and the Sex Offender Risk Appraisal Guide. *Sexual Abuse: A Journal of Research and Treatment*, *14*, 253–269.

Oh, E., & Neville, H. (2004). Development and validation of the Korean Rape Myth Acceptance Scale. *Counseling Psychologist*, *32*, 301–331.

Paulhus, D. L. (1991). Measurement and control of response bias. In J. P. Robinson, P. R. Shaver, & L. S. Wrightsman (Eds.), *Measures of personality and social psychological attitudes* (pp. 17–59). San Diego, CA: Academic Press.

Payne, D. L., Lonsway, K. A., & Fitzgerald, L. F. (1999). Rape myth acceptance: The exploration of its structure and its measurement using the Illinois Rape Myth Acceptance Scale. *Journal of Research in Personality, 33,* 27–68.

Polaschek, D. L. L. (2003). Relapse prevention, offence process models, and the treatment of sexual offenders. *Professional Psychology: Research and Practice, 34,* 361–367.

Polaschek, D. L. L., & Hudson, S. M. (2004). Pathways to rape: Preliminary examination of patterns in the offence processes of rapists and their rehabilitation implications. *Journal of Sexual Aggression, 10,* 7–20.

Polaschek, D. D. L., & Ward, T. (2002). The implicit theories of potential rapists: What our questionnaires tell us. *Aggression and Violent Behavior, 7,* 385–406.

Quinsey, V. L., Chaplin, T. C., & Upfold, D. (1984). Sexual arousal to nonsexual violence and sadomasochistic themes among rapists and non-sex-offenders. *Journal of Consulting and Clinical Psychology, 52,* 651–657.

Quinsey, V. L., Harris, G. T., Rice, M. E., & Cormier, C. A. (1998). *Violent offenders: Appraising and managing risk.* Washington, DC: American Psychological Association.

Rogers, R., & Bender, S. D. (2003). Evaluation of malingering and deception. In A. M. Goldstein (Ed.) & I. B. Weiner (Ed.-in-Chief), *Handbook of psychology: Volume 11. Forensic psychology* (pp. 109–129). New York: Wiley.

Schlank, A. M., & Shaw, T. (1996). Treating sex offenders who deny their guilt: A pilot study. *Sexual Abuse: A Journal of Research and Treatment, 8,* 17–23.

Schweitzer, R., & Dwyer, J. (2003). Sex crime recidivism: An evaluation of a sex offender treatment program. *Journal of Interpersonal Violence, 18,* 1292–1310.

Segal, Z. V., & Stermac, L. E. (1990). The role of cognition in sexual assault. In W. L. Marshall, D. R. Laws, & H. E. Barbaree (Eds.), *Handbook of sexual assault: Issues, theories, and treatment of the offender* (pp. 161–174). New York: Plenum Press.

Serin, R. C. (1995). Treatment responsivity in criminal psychopaths. *Forum in Corrections Research, 7,* 23–26.

Sjöstedt, G., & Långström, N. (2001). Actuarial assessment of sex offender recidivism risk: A cross-validation of the RRASOR and the Static-99 in Sweden. *Law and Human Behavior, 25,* 629–645.

Swenson, C. C., Henggeler, S. W., & Schoenwald, S. K. (2001). Family-based treatments. In C. R. Hollin (Ed.), *Handbook of offender assessment and treatment* (pp. 205–220). Chichester, UK: Wiley.

Thompson, R. A. (1994). Emotional regulation: A theme in search of definition. In N. A. Fox (Ed.), The development of emotion regulation: Biological and behavioral considerations. *Monographs of the Society for Research in Child Development, 59*(2–3, Serial No. 240), 25–52.

Thornton, D. (2000). *Structured risk assessment.* Paper presented at the Sinclair Seminars Conference on Sex Offender Re-Offense Risk Prediction, Madison, WI. (Videotape available from *www.sinclairseminars.com*)

Thornton, D. (2002). Constructing and testing a framework for dynamic risk assessment. *Sexual Abuse: A Journal of Research and Treatment, 14,* 139–154.

Thornton, D., Mann, R., Webster, S., Blud, L., Travers, R., Friendship, C., et al. (2003). Distinguishing and combining risks for sexual and violent recidivism. *Annals of the New York Academy of Sciences, 989,* 225–235.

Towl, G. J., & Crighton, D. A. (1996). *The handbook for forensic practitioners.* London: Routledge.

Ward, T. (2000). Sexual offender' cognitive distortions as implicit theories. *Aggression and Violent Behavior, 5,* 491–507.

Ward, T. (2002). Good lives and the rehabilitation of sex offenders: Problems and promises. *Aggression and Violent Behavior, 7,* 1–17.

Ward, T., Bickley, J., Webster, S. D., Fisher, D., Beech, A., & Eldridge, H. (2004). *The self-regulation model of the offense and relapse process: A manual. Vol. 1: Assessment.* Victoria, BC, Canada: Pacific Psychological Assessment Corporation.

Ward, T., & Hudson, S. M. (1998). A model of the relapse process in sexual offenders. *Journal of Interpersonal Violence, 13*, 700–725.

Ward, T., & Hudson, S. M. (2000). A self-regulation model of relapse prevention. In D. R. Laws, S. M. Hudson, & T. Ward (Eds.), *Remaking relapse prevention with sex offenders: A sourcebook* (pp. 79–101). Thousand Oaks, CA: Sage.

Ward, T., Louden, K., Hudson, S. M., & Marshall, W. L. (1995). A descriptive model of the offence chain for child molesters. *Journal of Interpersonal Violence, 10*, 452–472.

Ward, T., McCormack, J., Hudson, S. M., & Polaschek, D. (1997). Rape: Assessment and treatment. In D. R. Laws & W. O'Donohue (Eds.), *Sexual deviance: Theory, assessment, and treatment* (pp. 356–393). New York: Guilford Press.

Ward, T., & Stewart, C. A. (2003). The treatment of sex offenders: Risk management and good lives. *Professional Psychology: Research and Practice, 34*, 353–360.

Ward, T., Yates, P., & Long, C. (2006). *The self-regulation model of the offense and relapse process: Vol. 2: Treatment.* Victoria, BC, Canada: Pacific Psychological Assessment Corporation.

Webster, S. D. (2005). Pathways to sexual offense recidivism following treatment: An examination of the Ward and Hudson self-regulation model of relapse. *Journal of Interpersonal Violence, 20*, 1175–1196.

Webster, S. D., Bowers, L. E., Mann, R. E., & Marshall, W. L. (2005). Developing empathy in sexual offenders: The value of offence re-enactments. *Sexual Abuse: A Journal of Research and Treatment, 17*, 63–77.

Weiner, I. B. (2003). The assessment process. In J. R. Graham & J. A. Naglieri (Eds.) & I. B. Weiner (Ed.-in-Chief), *Handbook of psychology: Vol. 10. Assessment psychology* (pp. 3–25). New York: Wiley.

Yates, P. M. (2003). Treatment of adult sexual offenders: A therapeutic cognitive-behavioral model of intervention. *Journal of Child Sexual Abuse, 12*, 195–232.

Yates, P. M. (2005, Summer). Pathways to the treatment of sexual offenders: Rethinking intervention. *Forum* [Newsletter]. Beaverton OR: Association for the Treatment of Sexual Abusers.

Yates, P. M., & Goguen, B. C. (2000). *National Sex Offender Treatment Programme description.* Ottawa: Correctional Service Canada.

Yates, P. M., Kingston, D., & Hall, K. (2003, October). *Pathways to sexual offending: Validity of Hudson and Ward's (1998) self-regulation model and relationship to static and dynamic risk among treated high risk sexual offenders.* Paper presented at the 22nd Annual Research and Treatment Conference of the Association for the Treatment of Sexual Abusers (ATSA), St. Louis, MO.

CHAPTER 22

PARAPHILIA NOT OTHERWISE SPECIFIED

Psychopathology and Theory

JOEL S. MILNER
CYNTHIA A. DOPKE
JULIE L. CROUCH

The term "paraphilia" (from the Greek, *para*, "beyond, amiss, altered"; *philia*, "love"; Money, 1990a) first appeared in American psychiatry in 1934 (Money & Lamacz, 1989). Paraphilia was first officially used to specify a "subclass" of psychosexual disorders in the third edition of the *Diagnostic and Statistical Manual of Mental Disorders* (DSM-III; American Psychiatric Association, 1980), as a replacement for the legal term "perversion" (Money, 1990a). The category of "paraphilia not otherwise specified" (paraphilia NOS), the current term for residual paraphilias, initially appeared in DSM-III-R (American Psychiatric Association, 1987) and remains in use in the DSM-IV-TR (American Psychiatric Association, 2000).

CLASSIFICATION HISTORY

Prior to the publication of the first DSM (DSM-I; American Psychiatric Association, 1952), paraphilias, including those falling into the current paraphilia NOS category, were classified as cases of "psychopathic personality with pathologic sexuality" (American Psychiatric Association, 1952, p. 39). Continuing this practice, DSM-I included sexual deviation as a subtype of sociopathic personality disturbance within the broad category of personality disorders. The only qualification was that the diagnosis of sexual deviation was "reserved for deviant sexuality which [was] not symptomatic of more extensive syndromes, such as schizophrenic and obsessional reactions" (American Psychiatric Association, 1952, p. 38). In the sexual deviation category, the specific sexual disorder was described using a "supplementary term" (American Psychiatric Association, 1952, p. 7). DSM-I provided examples of supplementary terms or categories: homosexuality, transvestism, pedophilia, fetishism, and sexual sadism (including rape, sexual assault, and mutilation) (American Psychiatric Association, 1952). Thus, for example, in DSM-I the current paraphilia NOS category of urophilia would have been listed as "sociopathic personality disturbance—sexual deviation: urophilia." Because in DSM-I it was possible for any paraphilia to be specified by using a supplementary term, no residual category such as paraphilia NOS was needed.

In DSM-II (American Psychiatric Association, 1968), the term "sexual deviations" continued to be used. Sexual deviations, however, were no longer described as a subtype of sociopathic personality disturbance. Although sexual deviations still appeared under a catch-all category called "personality disorders and certain other nonpsychotic mental disorders," the sexual deviations were listed as a category separate from the personality disorders. The sexual deviations category described individuals whose sexual interests were "directed primarily toward objects other than people of the opposite sex, toward sexual acts not usually associated with coitus, or toward coitus performed under bizarre circumstances as in necrophilia, pedophilia, sexual sadism, and fetishism" (American Psychiatric Association, 1968, p. 44). The deviant sexual behavior was seen as primary, in that the individual was not able to substitute normal sexual behavior for the deviant behavior. In DSM-II, the following types of sexual deviations were listed: sexual orientation disturbance (homosexuality), fetishism, pedophilia, transvestitism (*sic*), exhibitionism, voyeurism, sadism, masochism, and other sexual deviation. Although no definition or examples of other sexual deviation were provided, it is apparent that the "other sexual deviation" category was the forerunner of the current paraphilia NOS category.

When the term "paraphilia" was introduced in DSM-III (American Psychiatric Association, 1980), it was included under the broad category of "psychosexual disorders." In DSM-III, the following types of paraphilias were listed: fetishism, transvestism, zoophilia, pedophilia, exhibitionism, voyeurism, sexual masochism, sexual sadism, and atypical paraphilia. Thus, in DSM-III, the term "other sexual deviation" was replaced with the term "atypical paraphilia." Atypical paraphilia was defined as a residual category for types of paraphilia that did not meet the criteria for any of the listed paraphilias.

In DSM-III-R (American Psychiatric Association, 1987), the paraphilias were included under the broad category of "sexual disorders," which was essentially the psychosexual disorders category from DSM-III renamed, and the following types of paraphilias were listed: exhibitionism, fetishism, frotteurism, pedophilia, sexual masochism, sexual sadism, transvestic fetishism, voyeurism, and paraphilia NOS. In DSM-III-R, the term "atypical paraphilia" (which was used in DSM-III) was replaced with the term "paraphilia NOS." Also in DSM-III-R, frotteurism was added to the list of specific paraphilias, and zoophilia was omitted (which meant that the latter was moved to the paraphilia NOS category). For the first time, examples of paraphilia NOS were provided. The seven listed examples, which were not meant to be exhaustive, were telephone scatalogia, necrophilia, partialism, zoophilia, coprophilia, klismaphilia, and urophilia.

In DSM-IV (American Psychiatric Association, 1994), the paraphilias still were considered sexual disorders, but were included in a broader category entitled "sexual and gender identity disorders." In DSM-IV, with only minor definitional changes, the same categories of paraphilias listed in DSM-III-R appeared again. Similarly, the same seven examples of paraphilia NOS were provided.

DIAGNOSTIC CRITERIA

DSM-IV (American Psychiatric Association, 1994) did not provide individual diagnostic criteria for any of the paraphilia NOS categories, and the same is true of its text revision, DSM-IV-TR. Although DSM-IV and DSM-IV-TR indicate that the paraphilia NOS category is to be used when an individual's behavior does not meet criteria for any of the listed paraphilias, the only definitional information regarding what can be diagnosed as paraphilia NOS is found in the general guidelines used to define the essential features of any paraphilia.

In the American Psychiatric Association's efforts to conceptualize paraphilia in DSM-IV and DSM-IV-TR, the definition has been guided in part by three considerations: the focus (preferred stimulus) of the sexual activity, the role of covert and overt sexual behavior, and the primacy of the preferred stimulus for sexual arousal. In order to provide a conceptual framework for DSM-IV and DSM-IV-TR criteria for paraphilia NOS, the evolution of these three components is first described.

Historically, to make a diagnosis of paraphilia, the individual's sexual focus had to involve stimuli other than an adult of the opposite gender, sexual behavior that was not typically associated with coitus, or coitus performed under bizarre circumstances (DSM-II; American Psychiatric Association, 1968). With the exception of the removal of homosexuality from DSM-III, this general standard has been maintained throughout subsequent editions and has guided the definition of paraphilias in DSM-IV and DSM-IV-TR.

The DSM description of what constitutes paraphilic behavior was expanded across the different DSM editions, so that the DSM-IV definition included covert activities (i.e., "sexually arousing fantasies and sexual urges," American Psychiatric Association, 1994, p. 522), in addition to overt behaviors. In DSM-IV, unlike in DSM-I and II, for an individual to be diagnosed with a paraphilia, the individual no longer had to have acted on the sexual fantasy or urge; the sexual fantasy or urge only had to be present and causing distress or impairment of functioning.

Finally, the requirement related to the primacy of the paraphilic stimuli or imagery for arousal was modified. Originally, in DSM-II, the preferred sexual stimuli or imagery were described as necessary for sexual excitement in individuals diagnosed with a paraphilia. The primacy of the preferred stimuli or imagery was demonstrated by the fact that the individual was not able to substitute normal sexual behavior for the preferred stimuli. In DSM-III-R and DSM-IV, however, the primacy of the stimuli (fantasies, urges, or behaviors) for arousal was no longer included as a necessary diagnostic criterion. Instead, the presence of clinically significant distress or impairment in functioning (resulting from the sexual fantasies, urges, or behaviors) was used to define the presence of a paraphilia. Although the primacy of the stimuli was not required, if the stimuli were obligatory or resulted in sexual dysfunction, these types of problems met the impairment criterion for defining paraphilia (American Psychiatric Association, 1994, p. 525).

As previously mentioned, in DSM-IV, for an individual to be diagnosed as having a paraphilia NOS, it was necessary that the individual meet the general requirements for a paraphilia, which were represented in the specific DSM-IV criteria for paraphilia. These criteria required the individual to display the following: "recurrent, intense sexually arousing fantasies, sexual urges, or behaviors generally involving 1) nonhuman objects, 2) the suffering or humiliation of oneself or one's partner, or 3) children or other nonconsenting persons, that occur over a period of at least 6 months (Criterion A)" (American Psychiatric Association, 1994, pp. 522–523). In addition, the "behavior, sexual urges, or fantasies cause clinically significant distress or impairment in social, occupational, or other important areas of functioning (Criterion B)" (American Psychiatric Association, 1994, p. 523).

In the most recent version of the DSM, DSM-IV-TR (American Psychiatric Association, 2000), the authors indicate that "no substantive changes in the criteria set were considered" in preparation of this revision (American Psychiatric Association, 2000, p. xxix). However, this statement is inaccurate with respect to the paraphilias. DSM-IV-TR contains a substantive change in Criterion B for all paraphilias involving a nonconsenting person. As indicated above, in DSM-IV, Criterion B was not met if the individual displayed the behavior, sexual urges, or fantasies but there was no evidence that these caused clinically significant distress or impairment in social, occupational, or other important areas of functioning. In DSM-IV-TR, however, if the activity involves a nonconsenting person, Criterion B now indicates that "the diagnosis is made if the person has acted on these urges *or* [emphasis added] the urges or sexual fantasies cause marked distress or interpersonal difficulties" (American Psychiatric Association, 2000, p. 566). Thus, when a nonconsenting person is involved, there is no longer a requirement that "marked distress or interpersonal difficulties" be present for a diagnosis to be made. Likewise, if marked distress or interpersonal difficulties are present, the urges or sexual fantasies need not be acted upon for a diagnosis to be made.

CONTROVERSIES SURROUNDING THE CRITERIA

Examination of the literature yields several areas of concern regarding the current diagnostic criteria for paraphilias, including paraphilia NOS. Potential problems include the validity of the expansion of Criterion A to incorporate covert behavior, the limited array of stimulus categories listed in Criterion A, the arbitrary nature of the time period selected to define chronicity, and the nosological overlap between paraphilia NOS categories and the eight individual paraphilias.

As discussed above, the DSM description of what constitutes paraphilic behavior has been expanded across DSM editions, with the DSM-IV and DSM-IV-TR definition of paraphilia including covert activities. Criterion A is written so that overt paraphilic behavior does not have to be present for a paraphilia diagnosis to be made. The presence of covert paraphilic behavior (sexual urges or fantasies) is adequate for a diagnosis of paraphilia, if the duration and impairment criteria are met. However, the rationale for this definitional change is not adequately discussed in the DSM. Since an individual's covert sexual behaviors, particularly fantasies, typically represent a broader range of interests than are present in the individual's overt behaviors, this definitional change substantially increases the number of individuals qualifying for a diagnosis of paraphilia. This may be problematic, because research indicates that the relationship between cognitions, such as fantasies, and behavior is often modest (Gold, Letourneau, & O'Donohue, 1995; Lee, 1992). Thus many people who have fantasies never act on them, and these individuals may be substantially different from those who display the overt behavior. Furthermore, given the wide range of sexual fantasies reported by individuals in the general population (e.g., Allgeier & Allgeier, 1995; O'Donohue, Letourneau, &

Dowling, 1995), the extent to which the presence of sexual fantasies without associated behaviors should be considered a mental disorder is unclear.

Even though Criterion A has been expanded to include covert sexual behavior, a problem with the current definition of paraphilia is that Criterion A is not broad enough to capture all of the paraphilia NOS categories described in the literature. For example, in Table 22.1 we present a comprehensive, albeit not exhaustive, list of paraphilia NOS categories mentioned in the literature. Inspection of these paraphilias reveals a number of categories that do not appear to meet any of the three parts of Criterion A (i.e., focus on nonhuman objects, focus on the suffering or humiliation of oneself or one's partner, or focus on children or other nonconsenting persons). In our view, a substantial number of the paraphilia NOS categories represent what we call an "atypical sexual focus involving human subjects (self and others)" that is not captured by the aforementioned three criteria that define Criterion A.

For example, individuals whose sexual focus is on an elderly partner (gerontophilia), on being observed (autagonistophilia), or on one or more body parts of a sexual partner (morphophilia, partialism) do not clearly meet any of the three parts of Criterion A. These examples of paraphilia NOS often involve a consenting adult partner, which means that they do not meet part 1 (nonhuman focus) or part 3 (children or nonconsenting persons) of Criterion A. Furthermore, given the nature of the sexual foci in these examples, the sexual arousal does not appear to be related primarily to the suffering or humiliation of oneself or one's partner (part 2 of Criterion A).

The limitations in Criterion A could be resolved in several ways. Criterion A could be expanded by adding a fourth part that would allow for an atypical sexual focus involving human subjects (self and others) (which we recommend; see Table 22.1), or the paraphilia NOS categories that do not meet one of the three parts of Criterion A could be removed from the broader diagnostic category of paraphilia NOS. In the latter case, either a new sexual deviation category (such as the old category of "sexual disorders not elsewhere specified" used in DSM-III) would be needed, or sexual behaviors that represent an atypical focus involving human subjects (self and others) could be omitted from the DSM nosology of sexual disorders.

In the general criteria for paraphilia (and the definitions of each of the eight listed paraphilias in DSM-IV and DSM-IV-TR), there is a requirement that the deviant sexual focus must have lasted for 6 months before a diagnosis of paraphilia can be made. Although the literature suggests that most paraphilic urges, fantasies, and behavior are long-standing in nature, we could not find any data indicating that a 6-month duration (or any other specific duration of time) in the individual's sexual focus should be used as a criterion for defining paraphilia NOS.

Another definitional problem is that many of the paraphilia NOS categories included in Table 22.1 are discussed as subtypes of one of the eight major paraphilias listed in DSM-IV and DSM-IV-TR, which suggests they should not be diagnosed as paraphilia NOS. However, the inclusion of many of the categories listed in Table 22.1 as manifestations of one of the major paraphilias is frequently not supported by the literature. For example, in DSM-IV and DSM-IV-TR, hypoxyphilia is included as an example of sexual masochism. However, as discussed in a later section, case data suggest that individuals with hypoxyphilia often do not meet the criteria for sexual masochism, which requires a focus on suffering. Thus, when suffering is not evident, hypoxyphilia qualifies as paraphilia NOS. In the following descriptions of the paraphilia NOS categories, we include discussions of the degree of independence and comorbidity of these categories.

TABLE 22.1. Paraphilia NOS Categories, Erotic Focus, and Possible Overlapping Paraphilia Categories

Paraphilia NOS categories	Erotic focus	Possible overlapping paraphilia categories
	Nonhuman objects	
Zoophilia (zooerasty, zooerastia, bestiality, bestiosexuality)	Animals	
Formicophilia	Small creatures	Zoophilia
Klismaphilia	Enemas	
Olfactophilia (osmolagnia, osphresiolagnia, ozolagnia)	Odors	
Mysophilia	Filth	
Urophilia (urolagnia, urophagia, ondinism, renifleurism, undinism)	Urine	Fetishism, sexual sadism, sexual masochism
Coprophilia (coprolagnia)	Feces	Fetishism
Vampirism	Blood	Sexual sadism, necrophilia
	Suffering or humiliation of oneself or one's partner	
Biastophilia (rape)	Unsuspecting, terrified persons	Sexual sadism, erotophonophilia
Telephone scatophilia (telephone scatalogia, telephonicophilia)	Obscenities over the telephone	Exhibitionism
Narratophilia	Obscene language with partner	Telephone scatophilia
Chrematistophilia	Being charged or forced to pay	
Saliromania	Soiling/damaging clothing/body	Sexual sadism
Vomerophilia (erotic vomiting)	Vomiting	Fetishism
	Children or other nonconsenting persons	
Necrophilia (necrosadism, necrostuprum, necrophagy)	Corpses	
Somnophilia	Sleeping partner	Necrophilia
Symphorophilia	Stage-managed disaster	
	Atypical focus involving human subjects (self and others)	
Hypoxyphilia (asphyxiophilia, sexual asphyxia, autoerotic asphyxia, kotzwarrism)	Reduced oxygen intake	Sexual masochism
Urethral manipulation	Insertion of objects	Sexual masochism
Morphophilia	One or more body characteristics of partner	Partialism
Partialism	A body part	Morphophilia
Stigmatophilia	Partner/self tattooed, scarified, or pierced for jewelry	
Abasiophilia	Lame or crippled condition of partner	Morphophilia, partialism
Autoabasiophilia	Own lame or crippled condition	Sexual masochism
Acrotomophilia	Amputation in partner	Morphophilia, partialism
Apotemnophilia	Own amputation	Sexual masochism
Autonepiophilia (infantilism)	Impersonating or being treated as an infant	Sexual masochism
Adolescentilism (juvenilism)	Impersonating or being treated as an adolescent	Sexual masochism
Gerontophilia	Elderly partner	
Andromimetophilia	Andromimetic partner	
Gynemimetophilia	Gynemimetic partner	
Autogynephilia (automono-sexuality, eonism, sexo-aesthetic inversion)	Image of self as woman	Transvestic fetishism

(*continued*)

TABLE 22.1. (*continued*)

Paraphilia NOS categories	Erotic focus	Possible overlapping paraphilia categories
Gynandromorphophilia	Cross-dressed feminized male	
Scoptophilia (scopophilia, scoptolagnia)	Viewing sexual activity	Voyeurism, mixoscopia
Mixoscopia	Viewing couple having intercourse	Voyeurism, scoptophilia
Troilism	Observing partner having sex with another person	Voyeurism
Pictophilia	Pornographic pictures, movies, or videos	Voyeurism
Autagonistophilia	Being observed/being on stage	
Hybristophilia	Partner who has committed an outrageous act or crime	
Kleptophilia (kleptolagnia)	Stealing	

PARAPHILIA NOS CATEGORIES

In the remainder of this chapter, we define the examples of paraphilia NOS presented in Table 22.1. As previously noted, the list presented in Table 22.1 is representative rather than exhaustive. Indeed, the number of new paraphilia NOS categories has expanded rapidly in recent years. For example, Money (1990a) indicated that there were at least 40 named paraphilias, whereas in our recent review we counted more than 150 named paraphilias in both the professional and general literatures. However, because many of the newly named paraphilias appear to be subtypes of existing paraphilias, how many of these newer paraphilia NOS categories are needed is an open question.

Despite possible overlap, the paraphilia NOS categories described herein are organized using the three-part definitional structure for types of paraphilic focus provided in DSM-IV and DSM-IV-TR (i.e., nonhuman objects, suffering or humiliation of oneself or one's partner, children or other nonconsenting persons) plus the previously proposed fourth component of atypical focus involving human subjects (self and others). The extent to which we discuss each type of paraphilia NOS is highly variable. In some cases, we provide only a brief definition of the paraphilia because of the paucity of information available. In selected cases, when more information exists, we provide a discussion of issues related to definition, epidemiology, associated features, and etiological theories.

Nonhuman Objects

Zoophilia

"Zoophilia" (from the Greek, *zoon*, "animal"; *philia*, "love"—Money, 1986), a term coined by Krafft-Ebing (Traub-Werner, 1986), is defined as sexual fantasies, urges, or behaviors involving nonhuman animals (American Psychiatric Association, 1994, 2000). Other terms used to describe this paraphilia are "zooerasty," "zooerastia," "bestiality," and "bestiosexuality." Zoophilic behaviors include fellatio, cunnilingus, coitus, masturbation of the animal (London & Caprio, 1950), and anal intercourse (Peretti & Rowan, 1983). In addition, a case of zoophilic exhibitionism has been described (McNally & Lukach, 1991). The animal selected is often one to which an individual was in close proximity during childhood, such as a farm animal or pet (American Psychiatric Association, 1980).

Historically, references to sexual contact between humans and animals date back to early civilization. For example, cave paintings created 15,000 to 20,000 years ago depict such behavior (Peretti & Rowan, 1983), and mythological narratives of many cultures contain references to zoophilia. Although some civilizations have sanctioned certain forms of zoophilia (see Traub-Werner, 1986), religious prohibitions against this form of sexual behavior can be found in the Old Testament and Talmud. Currently, in the United States, legal prohibitions exist against sexual contact with animals.

In the past, a distinction was made between covert and overt zoophilic behavior. For example, Krafft-Ebing distinguished between "zoophilia," or lascivious emotion while petting domesticated animals, and "zooerasty," or sexual involvement with animals and concomitant lack of "normal" sexual activity (cited in Rappaport, 1968). However, a distinction between fantasy, urges, and behavior is not maintained in DSM-IV and DSM-IV-TR.

Although zoophilia is considered a rare paraphilia (e.g., American Psychiatric Association, 1994, 2000; Cerrone, 1991), few data are available either to support or to refute this claim. Estimates are available, however, on the rates of sexual contact with animals. In the general population, Kinsey and associates (Kinsey, Pomeroy, & Martin, 1948; Kinsey, Pomeroy, Martin, & Gebhard, 1953) reported these prevalence rates of at least one sexual contact between humans and other animals: 8% for males, and 1.5% (preadolescence) and 3.6% (postadolescence) for females. They found higher frequencies in rural settings, with 40–50% of the rural population engaging in sexual activity with animals. Rates also were higher among individuals with lower educational status. In contrast, Nagaraja (1983) examined sexual contacts with animals among Native American adolescents and reported a 1% prevalence rate. In a study of male sexual fantasies, Crepault and Couture (1980) found that only 5.3% of their sample had fantasized about sexual activity with an animal.

The mean age of onset of zoophilia has been estimated to be 17.4 years (Abel & Osborn, 1992). After the initial preference for animals has appeared, it has been suggested that zoophilia follows a progressive and chronic course (American Psychiatric Association, 1980). Examination of the available data, however, reveals a skewed distribution for the behavior: Most individuals commit only a few acts, whereas a smaller number of individuals engage in a large number of acts. Abel and colleagues (1987) found the median number of zoophilic acts committed by their sample was 2.2, whereas the mean number of acts (distorted by outliers) was 222.4.

Many persons with zoophilia appear to have more than one paraphilia. In a survey of 561 nonincarcerated individuals seeking treatment for paraphilias, Abel, Becker, Cunningham-Rathner, Mittelman, and Rouleau (1988) found that 100% of the zoophilic respondents ($n = 14$) reported more than one paraphilia and 50% had 5 or more paraphilias. In their sample, the mean number of paraphilias present in the zoophilic respondents was 4.8, with comorbid diagnoses of pedophilia, exhibitionism, voyeurism, frotteurism, telephone scatophilia, transvestic fetishism, fetishism, sexual sadism, sexual masochism, urophilia, and/or coprophilia.

The American Psychiatric Association (1994, 2000) suggests that other mental disorders are frequently present in paraphilic individuals. Evidence that this is true for zoophilia has been provided by several authors (e.g., Alvarez & Freinhar, 1991; Duffield, Hassiotis, & Vizard, 1998). For example, Alvarez and Freinhar (1991) found the prevalence of zoophilia (contacts and fantasies) to be higher among psychiatric inpatients (55%) than among other medical inpatients and psychiatric staff (10–15%). Case reports also frequently mention that withdrawal and poor interpersonal skills are associated with zoophilia (e.g., Cerrone, 1991; Chee, 1974; Holden & Sherline, 1973). In contrast, based on three case reports and an anonymous Internet interview, Dittert, Seidl, and Soyka (2005) reported that all the zoophilic individuals in their study were "socially well adapted and displayed good interpersonal skills" (p. 61).

In a study of motivations for zoophilia, Peretti and Rowan (1983) found that zoophilic individuals often cited the ease and flexibility of involvement (e.g., no negotiation required) as contributing to their behavior. In a survey of 93 zoophilic volunteers, Miletski (2000) found that respondents reported engaging in zoophilia because they had a sexual orientation toward animals, had sexual fantasies about animals, or wanted to express love/affection to an animal. In a study of 114 zoophilic individuals surveyed online who were asked about why their sexual interest in animals "began or continued," Williams and Weinberg (2003) found that respondents most often replied that sex with animals was pleasurable and that they desired affection. The reasons that respondents gave *least often* for having sex with animals were that they were drunk or high (99% did not report this), that other people influenced them (89%), that they lived on a farm (85%), and that they felt they were not physically attractive (80%).

Various theories of zoophilia have been put forth. Krafft-Ebing initially distinguished lustful emotion for domesticated animals from the ability to function sexually solely when the behavior involves "unnatural acts" with animals. He considered only the latter pathological (cited in Rappaport, 1968). Another early view considered zoophilia to be initiated by "simpletons—sometimes even imbeciles" or merely as a matter of convenience (e.g., Balint, 1956).

Contrary to earlier speculations, Shenken (1964) argued that zoophilia is neither practiced solely by those of below-average intelligence nor used solely as a substitute for normal relations. He believed that zoophilia is sometimes a form of psychopathology itself and that it is always related to a general clinical problem (i.e., a neurosis or psychosis). Shenken also proposed that zoophilia need not be defined as an exclusive preference for animals (i.e., normal human sexual relations also may be present). He theorized that zoophilic individuals are not able to express emotions appropriately toward humans, so instead feelings are directed toward an animal (which is usually a parent substitute).

In 1968, Rappaport suggested that animals incite envy in children due to their unrestrained exhibition of animal instincts. He suggested that children are interested and aroused by the behavior (including sexual behavior) of animals. Rappaport believed that most often, cases of zoophilia are the result of object substitution or convenience. However, he also speculated that sexual contact with animals might represent a repetition compulsion, with the animal abuse serving as a reenactment of earlier traumatic experiences and as a displacement of rage felt toward the parents onto the animal.

Traub-Werner (1986) conceptualized zoophilia as an old perversion that has been repressed by civilization; he argued that zoophilia manifests itself under either repressive failure or cultural sanction. He also described zoophilia as an inability to differentiate aggressive from sexual drives, a breakdown in integration of the genital body image, and actions against parent symbols. Cerrone (1991) hypothesized that individual, family, and sociocultural factors contribute to the manifestation of zoophilia. He suggested that intercourse with animals permits a release of repressed anger, and that dominance over animals affords a sense of control that is otherwise lacking. Other explanations for zoophilic behavior focus on the role of incestuous desires (London & Caprio, 1950; Schneck, 1974), the relationship with borderline personality disorder with attachment separation dynamics (Meyer, 1980), and the role of heterosexual fearfulness and extreme self-doubt (Kolb & Brodie, 1982). Using a social learning perspective, Nagaraja (1983) proposed that zoophilic individuals become aroused by observing animals copulating. In the absence of a consenting sexual partner, individuals will then satisfy sexual urges with animals.

When the sexual focus is on causing pain and suffering in animals, the label used is "zoosadism." If the sexual focus is on the killing of animals and/or on animal corpses, the behavior is called "necrozoophilia" (also referred to as "necrobestiality"). The extent of overlap between these categories and zoophilia is unknown, although it has been suggested that animal killing and attraction to animal corpses may cooccur with necrophilia, lust murder (erotophonophilia), and biastophilia (especially in cases of serial rapists who kill).

Formicophilia

"Formicophilia" (from the Latin, *formica*, "ant"; Greek, *philia*, "love"—Dewaraja & Money, 1986) has been defined as a subtype of zoophilia where the focus is on small creatures, such as "snails, frogs, ants, or other insects creeping, crawling or nibbling on the body, especially the genitalia, perianal area or nipples" (p. 140). Dewaraja and Money (1986; Dewaraja, 1987) also reported that formicophilia is very rare. In their description of formicophilia, Dewaraja and Money suggested that it arises developmentally during childhood, but just how this occurs is unclear.

Klismaphilia

In "klismaphilia" (from the Greek, *klisma*, "enema"; *philia*, "love"—Money, 1986), the paraphilic focus is on receiving an enema. Historically, erotic enemas were provided in "specialty brothels" and in "enema spas" (Denko, 1976). Klismaphilic behavior is common to both genders. In fact, Kinsey and colleagues' (1948, 1953) survey research mentions females' use of enemas as a masturbatory procedure, but does not mention enema use in the description of male masturbatory practices.

Boglioli, Taff, Stephens, and Money (1991) indicated that many individuals use warm water to clean the lower rectum (anal douching), whereas others have used coffee, yogurt, air, whiskey, wine, beer, and cocaine. de Boer, Moolenaar, de Leede, and Breimer (1982) reviewed the actions of drugs introduced rectally and found that aqueous and alcoholic solutions are absorbed very rapidly. Absorption may be so rapid that it has a "mainlining effect" similar to that of intravenous injection. The use of enemas for erotic stimulation is not without risk. Accidental rectal trauma and the lodging of foreign bodies in the gastrointestinal tract have been reported (e.g., Eckert & Katchis, 1989; Eisele & Reay, 1980; Herrerias, Muniain, Sanchez, & Garrido, 1983).

There is a lack of information on the factors associated with klismaphilia. Because of the paucity of research, Arndt (1991) placed advertisements in sex tabloids in an attempt to obtain data on the practices of erotic enema users. Twenty-two individuals (21 males and 1 female) responded to his ad. The median age of the respondents was 39 years (range = 25–54 years). Approximately 60% were married or had been married. Eighty percent were heterosexual; the remaining 20% were bisexual. The median number of years of enema use was 20 (range = 1–43 years); the median frequency of enema use was twice a week (range = once a day to once a month). Approximately one-half of the respondents reported that their enemas were self-administered, with the other half reporting giving and/or receiving enemas with a partner. Many without partners indicated a desire to find an enema partner. Forty percent of the sample reported accompanying paraphilic interests that included mild spanking and other punishments, suggesting sexual masochism.

Based on a study of 15 cases, Denko (1976) concluded that klismaphilic individuals fall into three groups. In her study, six individuals formed a group that she labeled Type A. These individuals were unhappy with their klismaphilia and viewed it as abnormal. They usually self-administered enemas and dated their behavior to childhood. In the Type A group, one case also involved mild sexual masochism, one case involved coprophilia, and one case involved fetishism. Despite their unhappiness about their behavior, Denko indicated that the Type A individuals "[kept] their condition compartmentalized and it had little effect on their work or social lives (including marriage)" (p. 250). In cases where there was social or occupational impairment, Type A individuals appeared to be those who would be most likely to be diagnosed with paraphilia NOS under DSM-IV criteria or DSM-IV-TR. Type B individuals were similar to Type A individuals, with the exception that they accepted their klismaphilia. These individuals also were more likely to have involved a partner. Type C individuals were viewed as different from Type A and Type B individuals in that they had integrated the klismaphilic activity into their life and relationships. They tended to know others with similar interests and displayed a variety of paraphilias, including transvestic fetishism and sexual masochism. Type B and Type C individuals would be less likely to be diagnosed with DSM-IV(-TR) paraphilia NOS, and Type C individuals were more likely to be diagnosed with another paraphilia.

Agnew (1982) indicated that the enema ritual consists of insertion, filling, and expulsion activities. The insertion of the enema nozzle is experienced as pleasurable, due to the highly sensitive nature of the anal and perineal areas. The filling and distention of the lower rectum causes internal pressure that can affect the prostate and seminal vesicles in the male and the back of the vagina in the female. In both males and females, filling produces stimulation of the rectal stretch receptors. Expulsion stimulates the rectal and perineal areas, as well as producing waves of peristalsis that stimulates adjacent genital structures. In attempting to explain kilsmaphilia, Agnew provided a detailed description of the physiological similarities between rectal stimulation and vaginal intercourse. Although there is little information on the etiology of klismaphilia, it is clear that the physiological sensations produced by encmas are similar to those experienced during masturbation and intercourse, and are therefore very reinforcing. In discussing the etiology of klismaphilia, Denko (1973) suggested the possibility of childhood conditioning of the enema experience.

Olfactophilia

In "olfactophilia" (from the Latin, *olfacere*, "to smell"; Greek, *philia*, "love"—Money, 1986), also referred to as "osmolagnia," "osphresiolagnia," and "ozolagnia," the sexual focus involves smells and odors. Frequently the erotic focus is on body odors of a sexual partner, including odors from the genital area.

Mysophilia

In "mysophilia" (from the Greek, *mysos*, "uncleanness"; *philia*, "love"—Money, 1986), the paraphilic focus is on filth. This focus may involve the "smelling, chewing or otherwise utilizing sweaty or soiled clothing or articles of menstrual hygiene" (Money, 1986, p. 265). Karpman (1948, 1949) provided several psychodynamic speculations on the etiological factors associated with mysophilia. For example, one analytic interpretation was that mysophilic behavior involves a symbolic association of sex with something that is dirty (i.e., bad). The pairing of sex and filth is thought to be functional, because any guilt associated with sexual behavior can be washed away.

Urophilia

"Urophilia" (from the Greek, *ouron*, "urine"; *philia*, "love"—Money, 1986), also called "urolagnia," "urophagia," "ondinisme," "renifleurism," and "undinism" (after Undine, a water nymph, from the Latin, *unda*, "wave"; Money, 1986), refers to a focus on the act of urination or on the urine itself. "Water sports" and "golden showers" are vernacular terms for urophilia. Historically, the terms "urophilia," "urolagnia," "urophagia," and "undinism" have been used to describe any erotic use of the urinary stream, which may or may not involve a partner.

In DSM-IV and DSM-IV-TR, urophilia is listed as an example of paraphilia NOS. In addition, Denson (1982) has described subtypes of urophilia. Denson suggested that "undinism" refers to those cases of urolagnia (urophilia) where urine constitutes a fetish. When the fetishism leads to oral incorporation of the urine, Denson indicated that it should be described as "undinism with urophagia." Denson also contended that urination may serve masochistic (being urinated on) or sadistic (urination on one's partner) purposes, in which cases it should be labeled "uromasochism" or "urosadism." These latter erotic foci suggest that in some cases urophilia would fit more appropriately under part 2 of Criterion A in DSM-IV and DSM-IV-TR, which refers to a focus on suffering and humiliation of oneself or one's partner. In these cases, the diagnosis would more appropriately be sexual masochism or sexual sadism, respectively.

Coprophilia

"Coprophilia" (from the Greek, *kopros*, "dung"; *philia*, "love"—Money, 1986), also called "coprolagnia," represents a specific focus on feces. Although some authors have defined the focus of coprophilia as the act of elimination (McCary, 1967), others have defined it as the act of consumption of excrement (Allen, 1969). To complicate the definition further, it appears that some individuals may have an interest in eliminating on one's partner or in playing with the fecal matter. According to Smith (1976), a common analytic interpretation is that the excrement symbolically represents the penis and that the presence of the fecal matter serves as a defense against castration anxiety.

Vampirism

"Vampirism" refers to sexual arousal attained through blood extraction. Prins (1985) proposed four types of vampirism: complete vampirism (defined as necrosadism, ingestion of blood, and necrophilic activity); vampirism without ingestion of blood (called "necrophilia" by Prins); vampirism without death being involved; and autovampirism (ingestion of one's own blood). As evident in this taxonomy, the definition of vampirism overlaps with that of necrophilia. Nevertheless, Vanden Bergh and Kelly (1964) distinguished between vampirism and necrophilia, since vampirism is sometimes directed toward the living. In addition, Vanden Bergh and Kelly and Prins distinguished vampirism from sexual sadism, because vampirism is not always accompanied by pain and suffering.

Although this issue is not directly addressed in DSM-IV or DSM-IV-TR, it appears that vampirism should be diagnosed as sexual sadism if pain and suffering are involved, but as paraphilia NOS if pain and suffering are not involved and the behavior is separate from necrophilia. This approach is consistent with DSM-IV-TR paraphilia NOS classifications involving other body fluids/substances (other than blood) that also are listed as separate syndromes (urophilia, coprophilia).

Suffering or Humiliation of Oneself or One's Partner

Biastophilia

"Biastophilia" (from the Greek, *biastes*, "to rape"; *philia*, "love"—Money, 1990a) involves a sexual focus on the act of sexually assaulting a nonconsenting and terrified person, who can be a stranger or someone who is known to the biastophile. The sexual attack is unsuspected and physically violent. Biastophilia is used to describe violent serial rape and may overlap with lust murder ("erotophonophilia"). In some cases, if the resistance of the victim lessens, the biastophile may become less aroused or may increase the level of violence to increase the fear displayed by the victim. Biastophilia can be heterosexual or homosexual in nature. The condition where the sexual focus is on being responsive to being raped is referred to as "raptophilia."

Money (1990a) suggested that several factors may contribute to biastophilia. These factors include hereditary predispositions (e.g., predispositions toward impulsiveness and emotional instability), hormonal abnormalities during development, disturbed relationships in the family of origin (including child sexual abuse), and contributions from other syndromes (e.g., bipolar disorders, antisocial personality disorder, dissociative identity disorder).

Telephone Scatophilia

"Telephone scatophilia" (from the Greek, *skopein*, "to view"; *philia*, "love"—Money, 1986), also referred to as "telephone scatalogia" and "telephonicophilia," involves "deception and ruse in luring or threatening a telephone respondent, known or unknown, into listening to, and making personally explicit conversation" (Money, 1986, p. 271) of a sexual nature. The literature indicates that most obscene callers are male (e.g., Matek, 1988).

Despite the statements in DSM-IV and DSM-IV-TR that the individually listed paraphilias occur more frequently than the paraphilia NOS categories (hence the reference to residual paraphilias), Matek (1988) indicated that the frequency of telephone scatalogia is "of a different magnitude" (p. 113) than other paraphilia NOS examples. Supporting this view, Murray (1967) found that 26% of college females reported receiving obscene telephone calls (i.e., calls involving sexual suggestions and propositions). In a replication of the Murray study, Murray and Beran (1968) found that about 28% of female and 11% of male undergraduates had received such calls. However, these data do not reflect prevalence rates for telephone scatophilia, because no information is available on how many calls one individual might make or how many of the obscene callers would meet the criteria for paraphilia NOS.

In a preliminary attempt to develop a typology, Mead (1975) described three types of obscene callers. The first type is the caller who immediately uses profanity and/or makes obscene propositions. Mead indicated that most of these callers are in their preteens or teens. A second type is described as "the ingratiating seducer." These callers are more subtle in their approach, often providing a plausible story about prior introductions, admiration from afar, and/or mutual friends. This initial discussion, however, leads to offensive suggestions. A third type is labeled the "trickster." This individual uses some type of ruse (e.g., taking a survey) in order to discuss personal matters. The discussion invariably leads to offensive suggestions. Matek (1988) discussed a fourth type of caller, which he suggested does not fit into Mead's typology. He indicated that this fourth type uses crisis lines in order to request help (from a female volunteer), discuss sexual material, and masturbate. According to Matek, this type of caller is so common that "it is likely that not a single crisis telephone program anywhere in the U.S.A. has been free from these telephone masturbators" (p. 114).

Some case studies have reported an association between telephone scatophilia and exhibitionism (Kentsmith & Bastani, 1974; Matek, 1988; Nadler, 1968). Matek (1988) described areas of conceptual overlap. For example, Matek suggested that the methods associated with both telephone scatophilia and exhibitionism demonstrate attempts to express aggression, to exhibit power and control, and to gain recognition. Others have suggested that both obscene callers and exhibitionists require the victims to respond with shock or disgust (Hobson, 1983; Mead, 1975).

Although there appears to be some conceptual overlap between telephone scatophilia and exhibitionism, a distinction is that some obscene callers want complete anonymity. In addition, case studies have been reported wherein obscene phone calls were made without evidence of any other paraphilia, including exhibitionism (Dalby, 1988). Although some authors have described the telephone as a fetish (Richards, 1989), case data do not support the view that the erotic focus of the obscene caller is the telephone, instead of the sexually oriented conversation with a victim and/or the associated victim reactions. In an evaluation of case data, Matek (1988) indicated that the most common features of obscene telephone callers are low self-esteem and anger toward women. Matek also indicated that mental retardation, brain damage, psychosis, and intoxication (alcohol or drugs) are infrequently associated with obscene calls.

Freund (Freund & Blanchard, 1986; Freund, Scher, & Hucker, 1984; Freund, Seto, & Kuban, 1997) proposed a "courtship disorder" model that has been used to explain telephone scatophilia. The courtship model contains four stages. Stage 1 involves identification and selection of a partner. Stage 2 involves "pretactile interaction." Stage 3 involves "tactile interaction." Stage 4 involves "genital union." Freund suggested that individuals with telephone scatophilia and exhibitionism have not been able to move out of the pretactile interaction stage. Although stage 2 of Freund's model appears to describe many cases of telephone scatophilia and exhibitionism, some obscene callers have been reported to have adequate courtship behavior (Dalby, 1988).

Narratophilia

"Narratophilia" (from the Latin, *narrare*, "to narrate"; Greek, *philia*, "love"—Money, 1986) involves a focus on the use of dirty and obscene words with a sexual partner. This activity includes the telling of salacious or pornographic stories to a partner. According to Money (1986), narratophilia is also used to describe the reciprocal condition where an individual's sexual focus is on the hearing (or reading) of erotic, obscene, or porno-graphic words or stories. When the criteria for narratophilia are met, the mode of communication can take any form, including telephone sex services, computer-based erotic bulletin boards, and Internet emails. Thus, although a new paraphilia, "chat-scatophilia," has been proposed to describe an erotic focus on sending obscene words over the Internet (Abal, Marin, & Sanchez, 2003), we do not believe that a new category for Internet transmission of obscene messages is warranted. Furthermore, the degree of overlap between the existing paraphilic categories of narratophilia and telephone scato-philia remains to be determined.

Chrematistophilia

In "chrematistophilia" (from the Greek, *chremistes*, "money dealer"; *philia*, "love"—Money, 1986), the paraphilic focus is on being charged money for sexual activities. Also included in chrematistophilia are cases where the erotic focus is on being robbed by one's sexual partner. There is no name for the reciprocal condition where the erotic focus is on charging or robbing one's sexual partner (Money, 1986).

Saliromania

In "saliromania" (from the French, *salia*, "soiling"; Greek, *mainomai*, "mad"), the focus is on the soiling or damaging of a partner's clothing or body (McCary & McCary, 1982). The behavior may involve either symbolic acts directed toward clothing, pictures, and statues of women, or direct assault on a woman; however, it is also known to occur in same-sex relationships. Although saliromania has been described as a category separate from sexual sadism (McCary & McCary, 1982), it would appear that most cases of saliromania would meet the criteria for sexual sadism, as described in DSM-IV-TR. At present, it is unclear whether cases exist in which the saliromanic behavior (e.g., the act of damaging clothing) is distinct from a focus on the suffering and humiliation of the sex-ual partner. The extent of overlap with fetishism, bukkake, mysophilia, urophilia, and coprophilia is unknown.

Vomerophilia

Erotic vomiting, which we have named "vomerophilia" (from the Latin, *vomere*, "vomit"; Greek, *philia*, "love")—also called "Roman showers" when another individual is vomited on—involves a paraphilic focus on the process of regurgitation. Congruent with the DSM-IV(-TR) conceptualization of paraphilias, Stoller (1982) provided case data suggesting that vomerophilia may manifest in a variety of ways: real or imagined, self or others, and facilitative or obligatory. Vomerophilia has been reported in both males and females (Stoller, 1982). If an individual has a sexual attraction to the vomit it-self, and not to the vomiting process, then the diagnosis would be fetishism.

Children or Other Nonconsenting Persons

Necrophilia

"Necrophilia" (from the Greek, *nekros*, "dead"; *philia*, "love"—Money, 1986) is defined in DSM-IV and DSM-IV-TR as sexual fantasies, urges, or behaviors involving human corpses. Dead bodies may be the target of vaginal intercourse; anal intercourse; kissing, sucking, or fondling of breasts; fellatio; and cunnilingus. Necrophilic individuals most commonly gain access to dead bodies through work, homicide, and chance occurrences (Rosman & Resnick, 1989); although some individuals may seek out corpses at mortuaries, funerals, or graveyards (Lancaster, 1978; Rapoport, 1942; Torre & Varetto, 1987), or preserve the bodies of loved ones (Foraker, 1976).

The term "necrophilia" has been used to describe a myriad of behavioral patterns, which is reflected in the nosological debate regarding this paraphilia that has persisted for the past 100-plus years. For example, in 1886, Kraft-Ebing (cited in Burg, 1982) distinguished between individuals who seek sexual contact with dead bodies, and those who engage in murder and mutilation in addition to having sexual experiences with corpses. In 1910, a tripartite categorization of sexual activity with corpses was promulgated by Wulffen (cited in Bartholomew, Milte, & Galbally, 1978). Wulffen described "necrosadism" (lust murder, erotophonophilia), "necrostuprum" (stolen corpses), and "necrophagy" (mutilation and cannibalism) as different manifestations of necrophilia. Later, Jones (1931) distinguished between inhibited necrophilia (extension of love in mourning) and overt necrophilic acts (sexual contact or mutilation and ingestion). Hirschfeld (1948) also discussed two forms of necrophilia: cases that involve murder, and cases that use existing corpses.

Thus, within the category of necrophilia, a distinction has frequently been made between sexual contact with corpses preceded by murder and sexual contact with corpses not preceded by murder. This division is supported by a review of cases reported in the literature (Rosman & Resnick, 1989), which suggests that the two syndromes may overlap but do not always co-occur. DSM-IV and DSM-IV-TR employ this differentiation by separating lust murder, described as a form of sexual sadism, from necrophilia. If an individual meets the criteria for both sexual sadism and necrophilia, then the individual should receive the diagnoses of both sexual sadism and paraphilia NOS (American Psychiatric Association, 1994, 2000). Similarly, although it appears there may be overlap between vampirism (attaining sexual excitement via blood extraction) and necrophilia, Vanden Bergh and Kelly (1964) based their distinction between the two on the observation that vampirism is sometimes directed toward the living.

Necrophilia is often cited as a rare clinical condition (e.g., Baker, 1984; Smith & Braun, 1978; Torre & Varetto, 1987); however, prevalence and incidence rates, as well as other epidemiological data, for the general population are unknown. The only available information is that reported in case studies. Rosman and Resnick (1989) reviewed 122 cases of necrophilia and found that the mean age at the time necrophilia was reported was 34 years (range = 17–59). Of the cases reviewed, 92% were male and 8% were female. Seventy percent were heterosexual, 15% were bisexual, and 15% were homosexual in orientation. The distribution of sexual orientation paralleled the gender choice of corpses obtained. Rosman and Resnick also found a 57% incidence rate of occupational access among necrophilic individuals, with the most common occupations being hospital orderly, cemetery employee, and morgue attendant.

Necrophilia has been associated with sadism and alcohol abuse (Burg, 1982; Hirschfeld, 1948). In the review by Rosman and Resnick (1989), 78% of the necrophilic individuals who murdered to obtain corpses had a history of sadistic behavior, whereas 30% of those who engaged in sexual contact only and 56% of the fantasizers only had a history of sadistic behavior. They also found that 60% of those who murdered their victims had consumed alcohol before the event, whereas 25% of those engaging in sexual contact only had consumed alcohol prior to engaging in the paraphilic behavior.

In the description of associated features, some have suggested that necrophilic individuals are incapable of securing a consenting partner (see Burg, 1982; Klaf & Brown, 1958). However, in the review of cases by Rosman and Resnick (1989), 86% of the individuals had had "normal" intercourse before engaging in necrophilic activities. Sixty percent of all these individuals were single, 26% were married, and 14% were widowed or divorced. Ninety percent of the fantasizers only were single. Although there is evidence that many persons with necrophilia engage in normal forms of sexual behavior, the extent to which these individuals regularly obtain consenting partners is not clear from the available literature.

In an initial attempt to explain necrophilia, Krafft-Ebing (1886, cited in Burg, 1982) suggested that several factors contributed to the manifestation of necrophilia: immorality, heredity, and subjection of another. Krafft-Ebing described the general condition of necrophilia as "perverse," although he also indicated that it is not necessarily pathological unless accompanied by either "neuropathic or psychopathic" conditions or murder or mutilation of the bodies. Other theorists have attributed necrophilia to "mental weakness or a lack of moral sense" (Burg, 1982; Klaf & Brown, 1958). In their review, Rosman and Resnick (1989) reported that although 59% of the cases had diagnoses of personality disorders, only 11% of the sample had psychoses and 14% of the individuals had IQs below 100.

From the 1930s to the present, speculations about the causes of necrophilia have been dominated by psychoanalytic views. For example, Jones (1931) hypothesized that the helpless, faithful, and tireless nature of the partner (corpse) is desired. In addition, he posited that murder and mutilation as part of necrophilic behavior are evidence of a return to primitive oral and anal sadism. Other psychoanalytical theorists attributed necrophilia to weak sexual constitution and mother fixation (e.g., Brill, 1941), object loss (e.g., Rapoport, 1942), and satisfaction of primitive oral and anal drives (e.g., Baker, 1984; Rapoport, 1942). Baker (1984) noted that the corpse offers no resistance or opposition, and therefore there is no chance of rejection or retaliation for the necrophilic individual. He proposed that the individual's sense of being alive is enhanced by projection of annihilation onto the dead body.

Calef and Weinshel (1972) proposed the "Sleeping Beauty" syndrome ("somnophilia"), or the desire to engage sexually with someone who is sleeping, as a neurotic equivalent of necrophilia. As discussed in the next section, Burg (1982) suggested the possibility of a theoretical continuum of erotic focus from the Sleeping Beauty fantasy through necrophilic acts involving murder.

The understanding of necrophilia is limited by the paucity of data available beyond case reports. However, some ideas have received preliminary empirical support. For example, Rosman and Resnick (1989) examined the motives stated or implied by the individuals in the 122 case reports they reviewed. They reported the following motivations were the most common: possessing an unresisting and nonrejecting partner (68%), reunion with a deceased partner (21%), attraction to corpses (15%), gaining comfort or overcoming isolation (15%), and power over a homicide victim (12%).

"Autonecrophilia" is the term given to the condition in which the focus of sexual arousal is on imagining oneself as a corpse. Given the passive nature of this sexual focus, it is possible that the motives of autonecrophiles include not having to take responsibility for initiating or maintaining sexual behaviors.

Somnophilia

"Somnophilia" (from the Latin, *somnus*, "sleep"; Greek, *philia*, "love"—Money, 1986), or the "Sleeping Beauty" syndrome (see above), involves an erotic focus on having sex with a partner who is sleeping. Although little is known about somnophilia, Burg (1982) suggested the possibility of a continuum of erotic focus from the somnophilic fantasy through necrophilic acts. In contrast, Calef and Weinshel (1972) suggested that somnophilia may be a neurotic equivalent of necrophilia. However, Calef and Weinshel concluded that although somnophilia may appear to have some characteristics in common with necrophilia, the two syndromes do not necessarily reflect the same underlying pathology. These authors speculated that the wish to return to the maternal body, Oedipal conflict, pregenital fixations, and castration anxiety contribute to somnophilia.

Symphorophilia

In "symphorophilia" (from the Greek, *symphora*, "disaster"; *philia*, "love"—Money, 1986), the sexual focus involves stage-managing a "disaster, such as a conflagration or traffic accident, and watching for it to happen" (Money, 1986, p. 271).

Atypical Focus Involving Human Subjects (Self and Others)

Hypoxyphilia

"Hypoxyphilia" (from the Greek, *hypo*, "under"; *oxy*, "oxygen"; *philia*, "love") is also known as "asphyxiophilia," "sexual asphyxia," "autoerotic asphyxia," and "kotzwarrism" (after a musician named Kotzwarra, who died in 1791 when a prostitute agreed to hang him briefly as part of a sexual encounter [Hazelwood, Dietz, & Burgess, 1983; Resnik, 1972]). This paraphilia is defined as achievement or enhancement of sexual arousal due to decreased arterial blood flow, which produces oxygen deprivation and an increase in carbon dioxide. In addition to the United States, this method of sexual arousal has been reported in Africa, Europe, and Eastern Asia (Byard & Bramwell, 1988; Garza-Leal & Landron, 1991; Innala & Ernulf, 1989). It has been a topic of interest for several centuries in Western literature. For example, Arndt (1991) pointed out that in the Marquis de Sade's (1791/1966) novel *Justine*, a man has himself hanged in an attempt to experience sexual ecstasy. Innala and Ernulf (1989) reported that historically brothels (e.g., the "Hanged Men's Club") in England provided sexual asphyxia through controlled hanging as a means to enhance sexual pleasure. In addition, there have been reports that men who have been executed by hanging experience orgasm just prior to death (see Resnik, 1972, for a review).

In hypoxyphilia, oxygen deprivation is achieved by a variety of methods, including "chest compression, noose, ligature, plastic bag, mask, or chemical (often a volatile nitrite that produces a temporary decrease in brain oxygenation by peripheral vasodilation)" (American Psychiatric Association, 2000, pp. 572–573). The most frequent method of inducing asphyxia is the use of a ligature around the neck (Sinn, 1993). Some of the chemicals used to increase autoerotic pleasure include dichlorodifluoromethane, nitrous oxide, and isobutyl nitrite (Gowitt & Hanzlick, 1992). It is generally believed that the focus of attention is not on the technique used, but on the asphyxia produced by these methods (Hazelwood et al., 1983).

In DSM-IV and DSM-IV-TR, hypoxyphilia is described as a form of sexual masochism. However, for sexual masochism to be diagnosed, the individual must have "over a period of at least 6 months, recurrent, intense sexually arousing fantasies, sexual urges, or behaviors involving the act (real, not simulated) of being humiliated, beaten, bound, or otherwise made to suffer" (American Psychiatric Association, 2000, p. 573). In many cases, hypoxyphilic individuals do not appear to be interested in suffering per se; rather, they are interested in the enhancement of sexual arousal produced by a manipulation that limits oxygen intake. Innala and Ernulf (1989) also noted that many cases of hypoxyphilia do not appear to meet the criteria for sexual masochism, and Diamond, Innala, and Ernulf (1990) suggested that the presumed association between hypoxyphilia and sexual masochism may not exist. In fact, there is evidence that hypoxyphilic individuals may actively seek to avoid pain and suffering. Case studies reveal that safety devices are often present, and in cases of hanging, padding may be used to avoid injury (e.g., rope burns) and pain (e.g., Diamond et al., 1990).

Estimates of the prevalence and incidence rates for hypoxyphilia are not available. However, estimates of the annual rates of fatalities resulting from the practice of hypoxyphilia have been made, and these numbers have increased across the past three decades. For example, in 1972, Resnik estimated there were 50 deaths annually in the United States; in 1979, Rosenblum and Faber estimated 250 deaths a year. In 1983, Hazelwood and colleagues suggested that between 500 and 1,000 deaths occurred annually (the majority of which were adolescents and young adults). DSM-IV-TR (American Psychiatric Association, 2000) indicates that 1 or 2 cases of hypoxyphilia-related fatalities per 1 million individuals are detected annually. Despite an increased awareness of this paraphilia, it appears that current estimates of hypoxyphilia-related fatalities are underestimates, because careful assessment is required to differentiate cases where death is due to suicide from those where death is an unintended consequence of paraphilic behavior.

Supporting the view that rates of hypoxyphila are underestimated, Sheehan and Garfinkel (1988) found that when all adolescent hanging deaths in two counties (Hennepin and Ramsey Counties in Minnesota) during a 20-year period from 1965 to 1985 were reevaluated, 31% of these deaths were judged to be accidental deaths due to sexual asphyxia and not suicides. If these findings can be replicated, not only would they have implications for understanding adolescent sexual behavior; they also would indicate that adolescent suicide rates by hanging need to be adjusted for accidental deaths due to hypoxyphilia.

Although in the early case descriptions of hypoxyphilia it was indicated that only males engage in these practices (Edmondson, 1972), subsequent case studies have reported hypoxyphilia in females (e.g., Burgess & Hazelwood, 1983; Byard & Bramwell, 1988; Byard, Hucker, & Hazelwood, 1993; Danto, 1980; Sass, 1975). Nevertheless, available data suggest that this paraphilia is infrequent in females. Diamond and colleagues (1990) estimated that females account for only 4% of hypoxyphilia cases, a rate found in a study of 132 asphyxial deaths (Burgess & Hazelwood, 1983). Byard, Hucker, and Hazelwood (1990, 1993) pointed out that one reason the phenomenon is rarely reported in women may be that it has a less obvious presentation. For example, in a review of the literature, Byard and colleagues (1990) found that a majority of women, unlike males, did not use clothing, props, or other devices to augment the sexual asphyxia.

As with prevalence and incidence rates, definitive conclusions about the associated features of hypoxyphilia in the general population cannot be made, because almost all of the reported cases involve those ending in death (e.g., Burgess & Hazelwood, 1983;

Byard & Bramwell, 1988; Diamond et al., 1990; Eriksson, Gezelius, & Bring, 1987; Hazelwood et al., 1983). Even though the data primarily represent cases where fatalities have occurred, investigators have reported that the majority of cases do not contain evidence of sexual masochism. Supporting the conceptualization that hypoxyphilia is a separate paraphilia from sexual masochism, Hazelwood and colleagues (1983) estimated a 12% rate of sexual masochism in cases of hypoxphilia. Indeed, some cases show "no special activities beyond masturbation and self-asphyxiation" (Blanchard & Hucker, 1991, p. 375).

Many case descriptions, however, provide evidence of a variety of paraphilic stimuli. The two most frequently mentioned associated sexual behaviors are cross-dressing and bondage (Blanchard & Hucker, 1991; Hazelwood et al., 1983). Although cross-dressing appears common (e.g., 20.5%; Hazelwood et al., 1983), Diamond and colleagues (1990) stated that it is unclear whether this fetishistic feature indicates fetishism, transvestic fetishism, sexual masochism, or some other phenomenon. Also, cases involving cross-dressing in males may be more easily identified as accidental deaths and therefore may have a higher prevalence rate. Bondage is indicated by case descriptions reporting that the hands, feet, and other body parts are often bound; Hazelwood and colleagues (1983) reported a rate of 51% (males) for bondage. Of course, bondage may be more often associated with fatal cases of hypoxyphilia simply because escape is more difficult. Bondage may or may not be typical of nonfatal hypoxyphilic behavior.

Fatal hypoxyphilia appears to be a solo activity performed by young males (Innala & Ernulf, 1989). These males tend to be partially or totally nude (Diamond et al., 1990), with pornographic material and a mirror present. The use of a mirror is thought by some to be related to the presence of cross-dressing behavior (Blanchard & Hucker, 1991; Boglioli et al., 1991). Fatal cases typically show evidence of penile engorgement or ejaculation. In a study of adolescents who had died by either sexual asphyxia or suicide, Sheehan and Garfinkel (1988) compared the characteristics of the two groups to identify features that differentiated between them. Deaths in the sexual asphyxia group were more likely to have the following associated features: partial or complete nudity, cross-dressing, bondage, obscene or pornographic materials near the body, a mirror for self-observation, and penile engorgement or ejaculation. Other distinguishing features of the adolescents in the sexual asphyxia group were that they were more often white, had more intact parental marriages, had less depression, had fewer conduct disorders, and had fewer previous suicide attempts. In contrast to the notes frequently found in suicide cases, Sheehan and Garfinkel also reported there was an absence of suicide notes in the sexual asphyxia group.

Hazelwood, Burgess, and Groth (1981) and Walsh, Stahl, Unger, Lilienstern, and Stephens (1977) reported that only a few hypoxyphilic accidental deaths are associated with intoxication. For example, Walsh and colleagues studied 21 autoerotic asphyxial fatalities in which toxicological analyses had been conducted. These analyses produced only two significant blood alcohol concentrations and one toxic level of barbiturates. Hazelwood and colleagues reported that in a series of 157 autoerotic fatalities, only 6.3% of the victims had evidence of homosexual orientation. This finding prompted the authors to conclude that autoerotic asphyxia is not associated with homosexuality above base rates.

A review of reported cases of hypoxyphilia reveals that many fatalities appeared to result from errors in the construction of the strangulation device and/or escape mechanisms. In addition, a physiological reflex (carotid sinus reflex) can result from sudden compression or pressure surge associated with sexual asphyxia. This stimulation of the carotid sinus can result in a rapid drop in blood pressure, with sudden cardiac arrest (Diamond et al., 1990; Reay & Eisele, 1982; Resnik, 1972). Diamond and colleagues (1990) pointed out that most individuals who have a focus on sexual asphyxia are probably not aware of this reflex, which increases the risk of death.

Diamond and colleagues (1990) noted that the etiology of hypoxyphilia is unknown. Although there are no well-developed explanatory models of hypoxyphilia, extant paradigms have been used to explain the data found in case studies. Psychoanalytic theorists have advanced several explanations; these usually include the belief that hypoxyphilia represents a form of masochistic behavior (see Resnik, 1972, for a discussion), which is congruent with the DSM-IV(-TR) definition. For example, it has been suggested that sexual and aggressive impulses toward incestuous objects become masochistic (directed against the self because of castration fears) as punishment for the incestuous desires. Other dynamic interpretations suggest that sexual asphyxia is driven by a desire to assume a passive role with the father. Hanging behavior, which involves being suspended by the neck (symbolic castration), is thought to reduce castration fears. It also has been suggested that individuals engaging in hypoxyphilia have eroticized feelings of weakness and helplessness, which are overcome through survival of the asphyxia (Litman & Swearingen, 1972). In another analytic interpretation, asphyxia is viewed as a punishment for masturbation, which reduces superego-derived anxiety (Resnik, 1972).

From a social learning perspective, the experience of strict, punitive parenting is viewed as the basis for an association between punishment (e.g., hanging) and sexuality. The literature, however, provides only modest support for the existence of punitive parents in the childhood histories of hypoxyphilic individuals. For example, Friedrich and Gerber (1984) reported that in a group of five male hypoxyphilic adolescents, there was evidence that each male had experienced a history of choking in conjunction with physical or sexual abuse. However, Rosenblum and Faber (1979) reported that adolescents in only two of four cases of nonfatal hypoxyphilia had controlling and punishing mothers and nonsupportive fathers, and Sheehan and Garfinkel (1988), who studied nine cases of adolescent autoerotic death, reported that only two of the nine adolescents had "strict" parents.

An alternate behavioral model, which we propose, is that the act of producing sexual asphyxia represents an acquired behavior that becomes part of a paraphilic masturbatory ritual because of the positive (reinforcing) effects it produces. In addition to the pleasurable effects of oxygen debt, it is proposed that the act of producing asphyxia enhances orgasm through increased sympathetic arousal. Although the male erection is associated with parasympathetic arousal (a similar assumption is made for the female vulva and vaginal engorgement), the male and female orgasm is believed to be under sympathetic control (McCary & McCary, 1982). Thus the enhancement of orgasm in hypoxyphilic individuals may be due in part to the increased sympathetic arousal that occurs during the process of achieving asphyxia. Indirect support for this hypothesis can be found in reports that a variety of techniques other than asphyxia have been used to increase sympathetic arousal immediately prior to orgasm (e.g., application of an icepack to the scrotum as orgasm approaches) in order to enhance the orgasm experience. If this hypothesis is correct, the asphyxia should be timed to occur after initial sexual arousal has been achieved and as an adjunct to the precipitation of orgasm.

Of course, the question remains as to how a person makes the initial choice to engage in this paraphilic activity. In contrast to complex speculations, it is possible that the discovery is due largely to chance exposure to the technique. For example, some authors have suggested that many participants learn about autoerotic asphyxia from word of mouth, by reading pornographic literature, from the news media, from viewing films, or simply by self-discovery (e.g., Byard et al., 1990; O'Halloran & Lovell, 1988).

Urethral Manipulation

In urethral manipulation, the erotic focus is on stimulation of the urethra, generally by insertion of objects. Wise (1982) noted that this may be accomplished either actively as part of autoerotic activities, or passively via requested medical procedures. Objects used in active manipulation include fingers, pencils, pens, lipstick containers, sticks, straws, candles, pins, wires, cuticle knives, and razors. Dangers associated with this form of sexual behavior include urinary tract damage, urinary tract and bladder infections, lodged objects in the bladder, and blocked urinary tracts due to tissue adhesions formed during wound healing. Because of these secondary effects, these individuals may present more often for medical services than for mental health services (Mitchell, 1968). Urethral manipulation has been reported in both males and females (Mitchell, 1968).

Psychodynamic interpretations have suggested that individuals whose erotic focus is urethral manipulation have underlying problems of fixation or regression and castration anxiety (Mitchell, 1968; Wise, 1982). Wise (1982) proposed that urethral manipulation shares features with both fetishistic and sadomasochistic behavior. However, reviews of case reports (Mitchell, 1968; Wise, 1982) do not indicate a strong association between these behaviors. Furthermore, in urethral manipulation, case data suggest that the focus of arousal is not on the objects employed. Individuals also frequently report a lack of pain during stimulation. At present, without additional data, the extent to which urethral manipulation does or does not share qualities with fetishism and sexual masochism remains unclear.

Morphophilia

"Morphophilia" (from the Greek, *morphe*, "form"; *philia*, "love"—Money, 1986) involves an erotic focus on one or more of the body characteristics of one's sexual partner. Morphophilia appears to include partialism, which is defined as a focus on a single body part (see below). It is unclear from the literature whether these two categories are unique paraphilias or different names for the same paraphilia. Both morphophilia and partialism are differentiated from fetishism, which involves a focus on "the use of nonliving objects" (American Psychiatric Association, 2000, p. 570).

Partialism

In "partialism," the paraphilic focus is on some part of the partner's body, such as the hands, legs, feet, breasts, buttocks, or hair. Partialism appears to overlap with morphophilia (see above), which is defined as a focus on one or more body characteristics of one's sexual partner. As previously mentioned, it is unclear whether these two categories are unique paraphilias or different names for the same paraphilia. Historically, some authors (e.g., Berest, 1971; Wise, 1985) have included partialism as part of the general definition of fetishism, which once included both parts of bodies and nonliving objects (e.g., shoes, underwear, skirts, gloves). Again, however, the DSM-IV-TR criteria for fetishism indicate that the focus must involve the "use of nonliving objects," which eliminates body parts from meeting this criterion.

Stigmatophilia

In "stigmatophilia" (from the Greek, *stigma*, "mark"; *philia*, "love"—Money, 1986), the focus is on a sexual partner who is tattooed or scarred. The focus can include a partner who has had a body part pierced in order to wear jewelry. In some cases the jewelry is worn in the genital area. According to Money (1986), stigmatophilia also refers to the reciprocal condition where the focus is on oneself having tattoos, scars, or pierced areas with jewelry.

Abasiophilia

"Abasiophilia" (from the Greek, *a*, "negating"; *basis*, "step"; *philia*, "love"—Money, 1990b) involves an erotic focus on a partner who is "lame, crippled, or unable to walk" (Money, 1990b, p. 165). Although Money relatively recently coined the term "abasiophilia," case examples have been previously described under other names, such as "orthopedic fetishism" (Fleischl, 1960). Abasiophilia, however, does not appear to qualify as fetishism, because fetishism (as noted above) requires a sexual focus on a nonhuman object. The degree to which a distinction should be made between abasiophilia and other similar paraphilia NOS categories, such as morphophilia and partialism, is less clear. For example, abasiophilia may be a subtype of morphophilia rather than a separate paraphilia. Although predominantly reported in males, abasiophilia also has been reported in females (Money, 1990b). When the focus is on one's own condition of being "lame, crippled, or unable to walk," the label used is "autoabasiophilia" (see below).

Although the etiology of abasiophilia is unknown, psychodynamic interpretations suggest that for a male, the deformed limb of a woman partner represents a female penis (Fleischl, 1960). According to analytic theory, a man may be attracted to a crippled woman because his anxiety and hostility related to "the shock of threatened castration at the sight of the female genital" (Fleischl, 1960, p. 741) are reduced when the deformed limb (representing a penis) is present.

Autoabasiophilia

"Autoabasiophilia" (from the Greek, *autos*, "self"; *a*, "negating"; *basis*, "step"; *philia*, "love"—Money, 1990b) involves a focus on one's own condition of being "lame, crippled, or unable to walk" (Money, 1990b, p. 165). This disorder contrasts with abasiophilia, which involves a focus on a partner who is "lame, crippled, and unable to walk." Although the vast majority of cases appear to involve males, autoabasiophilia has been reported in a female (Money, 1990b).

Acrotomophilia

In "acrotomophilia" (from the Greek, *akron*, "extremity"; *tome*, "a cutting"; and *philia*, "love"—Money & Simcoe, 1984–1986), the sexual focus is the stump of a partner, which has resulted from the amputation of a body part. Typically there is sexual attraction to a partner who already has a stump. There is anecdotal evidence, however, that some individuals have requested that a partner have a limb amputated in order to obtain a stump

(Taylor, 1976). Although the stump of an amputated limb appears to be the most common paraphilic focus, some cases involve a focus on mutilated genitalia (Taylor, 1976). Even though acrotomophilia is presented as a separate category, the extent to which a distinction should be made among acrotomophilia, morphophilia, and partialism remains unclear. As in the case of abasiophilia, acrotomophilia may be a subtype of morphophilia rather than a separate category. Although usually reported in males, acrotomophilia has been reported in females (Money, 1990b).

Apotemnophilia

In "apotemnophilia" (from the Greek, *apo*, "from"; *temnein*, "to cut"; *philia*, "love"—Money, 1986), also called "amputee fetishism" (Wise, 2000), the sexual focus is the stump resulting from one's own amputation. There is case evidence that some individuals have requested amputation (Everaerd, 1983; Money, Jobaris, & Furth, 1977) or engaged in self-mutilation (Taylor, 1976) in order to obtain a stump. The stump of an amputated limb appears to be the most common paraphilic focus. Although evidence indicates that this disorder typically occurs in males, it has been reported in females (Money, 1990b). According to Money and colleagues (1977), apotemnophilia may be conceptually related to sexual masochism, but it is not the same disorder. This view is supported by case data in which pain is not part of the clinical presentation. Although Money and colleagues indicated that the etiology of the disorder is not known, they have suggested that apotemnophilia in males serves to avert or reduce castration anxiety.

Autonepiophilia

In "autonepiophilia" (from the Greek, *autos*, "self"; *nepon*, "infant"; *philia*, "love"—Money, 1986), also referred to as "infantilism," the sexual pleasure is derived from acting and dressing like an infant or from being treated as an infant by one's sexual partner (Money, 1986). Although infantilism is classified as sexual masochism in DSM-IV and DSM-IV-TR, it is questionable whether the criteria for sexual masochism are always met. For example, if the infantile role playing does not involve feelings of humiliation and suffering, then the diagnosis of sexual masochism would not be appropriate and a diagnosis of infantilism as paraphilia NOS is warranted.

Adolescentilism

In "adolescentilism," also called "juvenilism," the sexual pleasure is derived from acting (e.g., sexual ineptness, dependency) and dressing like an adolescent or from being treated as an adolescent by one's sexual partner. Although adolescentilism, like infantilism, might be classified as sexual masochism, it is questionable whether the criteria for sexual masochism are always met. As with infantilism, if the adolescent role playing does not involve feelings of humiliation and suffering, then the diagnosis of sexual masochism is not warranted.

Gerontophilia

In "gerontophilia" (from the Greek, *geras*, "old age"; *philia*, "love"—Money, 1986), the erotic focus involves a sexual partner who is in the age range of an individual's parent or grandparent.

Andromimetophilia

"Andromimetophilia" (from the Greek, *andros*, "man"; *mimos*, "mime"; *philia*, "love"—Money, 1986) involves a person who has an erotic focus on a sexual "partner who is andromimetic or, in some instances, a sex-reassigned, female-to-male transsexual" (Money, 1986, p. 258); "andromimesis" refers to a homosexual female who engages in male impersonation without sex reassignment. In males, the paraphilic equivalent is "gynemimetophilia" (see below).

Gynemimetophilia

"Gynemimetophilia" (from the Greek, *gyne*, "woman"; *mimos*, "mime"; *philia*, "love"—Money, 1986) involves a person who has an erotic focus on "a partner who is a gynemimetic or, in some instances, a sex-reassigned, male-to-female transsexual" (Money, 1986, p. 262); "gynemimesis" refers to a homosexual male who engages in female impersonation without sex reassignment. In females, the paraphilic equivalent is "andromimetophilia" (see above).

Autogynephilia

"Autogynephilia" (from the Greek, *autos*, "self"; *gyne*, "woman"; *philia*, "love"), a term coined by Blanchard (1989, 2005), refers to a focus on sexually arousing cross-gender fantasies and behaviors in males. Alternately, autogynephilia has been referred to as "automonosexuality," "eonism," and "sexo-aesthetic inversion." Four types of autogynephilia with defining features have been proposed by Blanchard (1991): physiological autogynephilia (i.e., a focus on physiological functions, such as pregnancy, lactation, breast feeding, menstruation); behavioral autogynephilia (i.e., a focus on stereotypical behaviors, such as knitting with other women, imagining oneself as a woman in intercourse); anatomic autogynephilia (i.e., a focus on body parts, such as breasts, vulva, hairless legs); and transvestic autogynephilia (i.e., transvestic fetishism). There is evidence that approximately 10% of autogynephilic individuals do not exhibit transvestic fetishism (Blanchard, 1991). Blanchard contends that the broader notion of autogynephilia has been overshadowed by one type, transvestic fetishism, and that the superordinate category is of interest itself and might prove useful in understanding the syndromes of transvestic fetishism and gender dysphoria.

Cases of autogynephilia have been conceptually differentiated from other manifestations of cross-gender behavior. Blanchard (1993b) distinguished between "partial autogynephilia," a subtype of anatomic autogynephilia where the erotic focus is on a mixture of male and female body parts (usually enlarged breasts with male genitalia) (Blanchard, 1993a; Kremer & den Daas, 1990), and "gynemimetics" (Money & Lamacz, 1984), which refers to homosexual men who live as women without sex reassignment. Gynemimetic individuals may obtain breast augmentation, but are not erotically aroused by viewing themselves as females. The term "she-male," which refers to a particular physical status (dressed as a woman with or without breast augmentation with male genitalia), overlaps with both autogynephilia and gynemimesis, depending on whether or not the characteristics are sexually arousing. "Gynandromorphophilia," the attraction to anatomically or cross-dressed feminized men, is the reciprocal paraphilia of autogynephilia.

There is evidence that autogynephilia is associated with fetishism (beyond transvestic fetishism) and gender dysphoria. In one study, 55% of autogynephilic individuals reported some history of fetishism (Blanchard, 1991). It also has been reported that autogynephilic individuals who imagine themselves nude as females are more gender-dysphoric than those who imagine themselves dressed in female clothing or underwear (Blanchard, 1993a). Additionally, autogynephilia appears more in individuals with heterosexual, bisexual, or analloerotic (unattracted to male or female partners) interests than in those with exclusive homosexual interests (Blanchard, 1989). Furthermore, Lawrence (2004) has suggested that autogynephilia underlies "the desire for sex reassignment in some male to female transsexuals" (p. 69).

Gynandromorphophilia

"Gynandromorphophilia" (from the Greek, *gyne*, "woman"; *andros*, "man"; *morphe*, "form"; *philia*, "love") is defined as sexual interest in anatomically or cross-dressed feminized men, including "cross-dressers, transvestites, transsexuals, or she-males" (Blanchard & Collins, 1993). An examination of 119 personal advertisements involving cross-dressing supported the concept of gynandromorphophilia (Blanchard & Collins, 1993). The authors found two groups of individuals displaying an interest in cross-dressers: those with gynandromorphophilia only (desired others to be cross-dressers, but did not identify themselves as such) and those with gynandromorphophilia who were also cross-dressers (desired others to be cross-dressers and identified themselves as cross-dressers).

Scoptophilia

"Scoptophilia" (from the Greek, *skopein*, "to view"; *philia*, "love"—Money, 1986), which is also referred to as "scopophilia" and "scoptolagnia," involves deriving sexual pleasure from viewing sexual activity. A special case of scoptophilia is "mixoscopia," which involves the viewing of a couple having intercourse (see below).

Historically, the terms "scoptophilia" (Karpman, 1954), "scopophilia" (Hirschfeld, 1948), "peeping" (Gebhard, Gagnon, Pomeroy, & Christenson, 1965), "inspectionalism" (Coleman, 1964), and "voyeurism" have been used to describe sexual viewing. Smith (1976) questioned whether certain types of sexual viewing warrant categories of their own. However, as currently defined, scopophilia is differentiated from voyeurism. In voyeurism, the paraphilic focus "involves the act of observing unsuspecting individuals, usually strangers, who are naked, in the process of disrobing, or engaging in sexual activity" (American Psychiatric Association, 2000, p. 575). Since voyeurism criteria require that the observed individuals be unsuspecting, when the sexual viewing involves an individual or individuals who are aware that they are being viewed, a label of scoptophilia (or mixoscopia) and a diagnosis of paraphilia NOS are warranted.

Mixoscopia

"Mixoscopia" (from the Greek, *mixis*, "intercourse"; *skopein*, "to examine"; *philia*, "love"—Money, 1986) refers to a sexual focus on the observation of other individuals engaging in coitus. Mixoscopia is applicable in cases where the individuals being viewed are willing participants, whereas voyeurism is diagnosed in cases involving unsuspecting individuals, as noted above. The reciprocal paraphilia NOS category is "autagonisto-philia."

Troilism

In "troilism" (from the French, *trois*, "three"), also called "threesies," the paraphilic focus is an activity that involves the "sharing of a sexual partner with another person while one looks on, after which the onlooker may or may not share the sexual partner" (Smith, 1976, p. 586). Troilism also has been defined as "observing one's partner on hire or loan to a third person while engaging in sexual activities, including intercourse, with that person" (Money, 1986, p. 272). Allen (1969) has indicated that troilism may describe not only a man who desires his wife to have sex with another partner while he is present, but also a father who arranges to observe "his grown-up daughter" and her partner engage in sexual behavior (p. 179).

Although historically troilism has been conceptualized as a form of voyeurism, DSM-IV-TR criteria again require a paraphilic focus in voyeurism on observing unsuspecting individuals, whereas in cases of troilism the sexual partners are typically aware that they are being observed. However, the literature does not provide information on the possibility that troilism is a special case of scoptophilia; nor is information available on the degree of overlap between troilism and mixoscopia. Although troilism is usually reported to be a male activity (Chesser, 1971; McCary, 1967), female involvement in troilistic activities has been reported (Reinhardt, 1957).

In attempts to explain troilism, authors have speculated about different motivational factors. For example, Allen (1969) suggested that the viewing of another couple is an attempt to reenact the primal scene. Yalom (1960) suggested that there is incestuous identification whereby the observer can have sex vicariously with a mother, sister, or daughter. Coleman (1964) proposed that in males, the motivation is heterosexual identification with the man performing the sexual activity.

Pictophilia

In "pictophilia" (from the Latin, *pictura*, "picture"; *philia*, "love"), the erotic focus involves viewing obscene or pornographic pictures, movies, or videos of sexual activities alone or with a partner (Money, 1986). Pictophilia can be differentiated from voyeurism because, in most cases, it does not involve the observation of unsuspecting individuals; the participants in pornographic pictures and movies are usually aware of the erotic nature of their activities and know that they will be observed (erotically) by others. However, data are lacking on the degree of overlap between pictophilia and voyeurism.

Autagonistophilia

In "autagonistophilia" (from the Greek, *autos*, "self"; *agonistes*, "principal actor"; *philia*, "love"—Money, 1986), the erotic focus involves being observed by an audience. The observation may involve being seen on stage or on camera (Money, 1986). Autagonistophilia is applicable in cases where the viewers are willing participants, whereas exhibitionism is diagnosed in cases involving an "unsuspecting stranger" (American Psychiatric Association, 2000, p. 569). The reciprocal paraphilia NOS category is "mixoscopia."

Hybristophilia

In "hybristophilia" (from the Greek, *hybridzein*, "to commit an outrage against someone"; *philia*, "love"—Money, 1986), the sexual focus is on having a sexual partner who is known to have "committed an outrage or crime, such as rape, murder, or armed robbery" (Money, 1986, p. 263). The sexual partner may have been incarcerated for criminal activity. On some occasions the hybristophilic individual may urge the sexual partner to commit a crime and thus be convicted. Some cases involve women who marry men (including murderers) who are in prison.

Kleptophilia

In "kleptophilia" (from the Greek, *kleptein*, "to steal"; *philia*, "love"—Money, 1986), also known as "kleptolagnia," the sexual focus involves "illicitly entering and stealing from the dwelling of a stranger or potential partner" (Money, 1986, p. 264; Revitch, 1983; Zavitzianos, 1983). If objects (e.g., clothing) are the focus, then fetishism may be the appropriate diagnosis. If the act (e.g., entering or stealing) and not the object taken is the focus, then a label of kleptophilia and a diagnosis of paraphilia NOS are appropriate. In some instances, kleptophilia may be associated with sexual sadism. For example, Boglioli and colleagues (1991) indicated that in some cases a kleptophilic individual may force sexual intercourse (i.e., biastophilia).

SUMMARY AND FUTURE DIRECTIONS

In many of the paraphilia NOS categories, there is disagreement on what constitutes the paraphilias. However, adequate definitions are needed before any progress can be made in our understanding of residual paraphilias (e.g., even the collection of descriptive data requires consensus regarding definitions). Beyond a refinement of definitions, there is the need for additional model development. Models are needed to generate a priori predictions so that research can be hypothesis-driven. Paraphilic models need to move from the single-focus (e.g., psychoanalytic and learning) models to multiple-level (e.g., biological, personality, familial, and cultural), interactional models. Not only should the interrelationships among putative causal variables be examined, but the possibility that the same paraphilic behavior may result from different conditions should be explored. Ideally, to inform intervention efforts properly, models need to contain a series of conditional statements indicating how each disorder develops.

The present literature on the residual paraphilias is plagued by inadequate sampling procedures and a general lack of matched comparison groups. Source- and setting-related biases (data come primarily from mental health and forensic settings, responses to newspaper advertisements, or Internet surveys) limit the representativeness of findings. In addition, setting confounds may produce associated factors that are artifacts of the setting and are not causally related to the residual paraphilias. Extant descriptive and correlational studies are also limited because it is impossible to separate causal variables from marker variables. Finally, there is little information on ethnic and socioeconomic differences in the residual paraphilias, and few data are available on the incidence of female participation.

Admittedly, research problems in the area of residual paraphilias present formidable challenges. For example, the development of discrete definitions of the paraphilia categories is complicated by the fact that the paraphilia categories frequently overlap (e.g., many reported cases of a paraphilia involve more than one type of paraphilia). Although more representative and larger samples are needed, we recognize that sample sizes are affected by a number of factors: Most paraphilic behaviors are low-base-rate phenomena, involve socially and legally sensitive issues, and occur in populations that are difficult to engage in research.

Beyond the definitional, theoretical, and empirical shortcomings in our understanding of the paraphilias, several authors have questioned the inclusion of paraphilias, including the residual paraphilias, in a taxonomy of mental disorders. Some have argued that statistical and ideal behavioral definitions of abnormality, upon which the general category of paraphilias appears to be based, should not apply to sexual behavior (e.g., Silverstein, 1984; Tallent, 1977).

First, there is evidence that people routinely engage in a wide array of sexual fantasies and behaviors, thus bringing into question issues of statistical rarity in some cases of paraphilia. In addition, precisely what constitutes "normal" and "abnormal" sexual behavior varies as a function of culture and time. Tallent (1977) noted that diagnosing sexual deviations is based on dominant cultural values and efforts to produce conformity. In discussing the paraphilias, Davis and Whitten (1987) have written that "by comparison with many other societies, Western cultures appear to be particularly concerned with sexual norms and variation, and have taken extreme measures to enforce normality" (p. 76). Silverstein (1984) suggested that moral reasoning is the principal criterion in the diagnosis of sexual deviations. He argued that such behaviors are labeled pathological in part because they appear "kinky" and are offensive to some. Obfuscating moral values and psychological determinates makes the defining and understanding of paraphilias as mental disorders more difficult.

Second, DSM-IV-TR indicates that for a diagnosis of paraphilia to be made, except when a nonconsenting adult is involved, the individual must suffer distress or impairment. It is often unclear, however, whether the distress associated with paraphilic behavior represents a disturbance due to the paraphilia or merely a conflict with society. In the latter case, DSM-IV-TR states that "Neither deviant behavior (e.g., political, religious, or sexual) nor conflicts that are primarily between the individual and society are mental disorders unless the deviance or conflict is a symptom of a dysfunction in the individual" (American Psychiatric Association, 2000, p. xxxi). Furthermore, much of the research, at least in the paraphilia NOS categories, has focused solely on the behavioral manifestations of individuals (e.g., sexual contact with animals, sexual asphyxia) and has *not* assessed distress or impairment. Thus the research base for these categories provides little information to clarify the relevance of distress or impairment to variations in sexual behavior.

Finally, in line with the removal of homosexuality from the DSM, Tallent (1977) and Silverstein (1984) have proposed that the general category of paraphilias should be eliminated. At the present time, additional consideration of this suggestion appears warranted. Although it is impossible to remove values from a diagnostic system, the bases for inclusion and exclusion of categories from the nosology of mental disorders should be clearly defined and followed. As previously discussed, this has not been the case for the paraphilias. If most or all of the paraphilias, including paraphilia NOS, were removed from the DSM system, the study of sexual variation still would remain a moral, legal, and scientific endeavor, but would generally be separated from the study of psychopathology.

REFERENCES

Abal, Y. N., Marin, J. A. L., & Sanchez, S. R. (2003). Nueva parafilia del siglo XXI: Chat-escatofilia. *Archivos Hispanoamericanos de Sexologia, 9,* 81–104.

Abel, G. G., Becker, J. V., Cunningham-Rathner, J., Mittelman, M., & Rouleau, J. L. (1988). Multiple paraphilic diagnoses among sex offenders. *Bulletin of the American Academy of Psychiatry and the Law, 16,* 153–168.

Abel, G. G., Becker, J. V., Mittelman, M., Cunningham-Rathner, J., Rouleau, J. L., & Murphy, W. D. (1987). Self-reported sex crimes of nonincarcerated paraphiliacs. *Journal of Interpersonal Violence, 2,* 3–25.

Abel, G. G., & Osborn, C. (1992). The paraphilias: The extent and nature of sexually deviant and criminal behavior. *Psychiatric Clinics of North America, 15,* 675–687.

Agnew, J. (1982). Klismaphilia: A physiological perspective. *American Journal of Psychotherapy, 36,* 554–566.

Allen, C. (1969). *A textbook of psychosexual disorders* (2nd ed.). London: Oxford University Press.

Allgeier, A. R., & Allgeier, E. R. (1995). *Sexual interactions* (4th ed.). Lexington, MA: Heath.

Alvarez, W. A., & Freinhar, J. P. (1991). A prevalence study of bestiality (zoophilia) in psychiatric in-patients, medical in-patients, and psychiatric staff. *International Journal of Psychosomatics, 38,* 45–47.

American Psychiatric Association. (1952). *Diagnostic and statistical manual of mental disorders.* Washington, DC: Author.

American Psychiatric Association. (1968). *Diagnostic and statistical manual of mental disorders* (2nd ed.). Washington, DC: Author.

American Psychiatric Association. (1980). *Diagnostic and statistical manual of mental disorders* (3rd ed.). Washington, DC: Author.

American Psychiatric Association. (1987). *Diagnostic and statistical manual of mental disorders* (3rd ed., rev.). Washington, DC: Author.

American Psychiatric Association. (1994). *Diagnostic and statistical manual of mental disorders* (4th ed.). Washington, DC: Author.

American Psychiatric Association. (2000). *Diagnostic and statistical manual of mental disorders* (4th ed., text rev.). Washington, DC: Author.

Arndt, W. B., Jr. (1991). *Gender disorders and the paraphilias.* Madison, CT: International Universities Press.

Baker, R. (1984). Some considerations arising from the treatment of a patient with necrophilic fantasies in late adolescence and young adulthood. *International Journal of Psycho-Analysis, 65,* 283–294.

Balint, M. (1956). Perversions and genitality. In S. Lorand & M. Balint (Eds.), *Perversions: Psychodynamics and therapy* (pp. 16–27). New York: Random House.

Bartholomew, A. A., Milte, K. L., & Galbally, F. (1978). Homosexual necrophilia. *Medical Science and Law, 18,* 29–35.

Berest, J. J. (1971). Fetishism: Three case histories. *Journal of Sex Research, 7,* 237–239.

Blanchard, R. (1989). The classification and labeling of nonhomosexual gender dysphorias. *Archives of Sexual Behavior, 18,* 315–334.

Blanchard, R. (1991). Clinical observations and systematic studies of autogynephilia. *Journal of Sex and Marital Therapy, 17,* 235–251.

Blanchard, R. (1993a). Partial versus complete autogynephilia and gender dysphoria. *Journal of Sex and Marital Therapy, 19,* 301–307.

Blanchard, R. (1993b). The she-male phenomenon and the concept of partial autogynephilia. *Journal of Sex and Marital Therapy, 19,* 69–76.

Blanchard, R. (2005). Early history of the concept of autogynephilia. *Archives of Sexual Behavior, 34,* 439–446.

Blanchard, R., & Collins, P. I. (1993). Men with sexual interest in transvestites, transsexuals, and she-males. *Journal of Nervous and Mental Disease, 181,* 570–575.

Blanchard, R., & Hucker, S. J. (1991). Age, transvestism, bondage, and concurrent paraphilic activities in 117 fatal cases of autoerotic asphyxia. *British Journal of Psychiatry, 159,* 371–377.

Boglioli, L. R., Taff, M. L., Stephens, P. J., & Money, J. (1991). A case of autoerotic asphyxia associated with multiplex paraphilia. *American Journal of Forensic Medicine and Pathology, 12,* 64–73.

Brill, A. A. (1941). Necrophilia. *Journal of Criminal Psychopathology, 2,* 433–443.

Burg, B. R. (1982). The sick and the dead: The development of psychological theory on necrophilia from Krafft-Ebing to the present. *Journal of the History of the Behavioral Sciences, 18,* 242–254.

Burgess, A. W., & Hazelwood, R. R. (1983). Autoerotic asphyxial deaths and social network response. *American Journal of Orthopsychiatry, 53,* 166–170.

Byard, R. W., & Bramwell, N. H. (1988). Autoerotic death in females: An underdiagnosed syndrome? *American Journal of Forensic Medicine and Pathology, 9,* 252–254.

Byard, R. W., Hucker, S. J., & Hazelwood, R. R. (1990). A comparison of typical death scene features in cases of fatal male and female autoerotic asphyxia with a review of the literature. *Forensic Science International, 48,* 113–121.

Byard, R. W., Hucker, S. J., & Hazelwood, R. R. (1993). Fatal and near-fatal autoerotic asphyxial episodes in women: Characteristic features based on a review of nine cases. *American Journal of Forensic Medicine and Pathology, 14,* 70–73.

Calef, V., & Weinshel, E. M. (1972). On certain neurotic equivalents of necrophilia. *International Journal of Psycho-Analysis, 53,* 67–75.

Cerrone, G. H. (1991). Zoophilia in a rural population: Two case studies. *Journal of Rural Community Psychology, 12,* 29–39.

Chee, K. T. (1974). A case of bestiality. *Singapore Medical Journal, 15,* 287–288.

Chesser, E. (1971). *Strange loves: The human aspect of sexual deviation.* New York: Morrow.

Coleman, J. C. (1964). *Abnormal psychology and modern life* (3rd ed.). Glenview, IL: Scott, Foresman.

Crepault, C., & Couture, M. (1980). Men's erotic fantasies. *Archives of Sexual Behavior, 9,* 565–581.

Dalby, J. T. (1988). Is telephone scatalogia a variant of exhibitionism? *International Journal of Offender Therapy and Comparative Criminology, 32,* 45–49.

Danto, B. L. (1980). A case of female autoerotic death. *American Journal of Forensic Medicine and Pathology, 1,* 117–121.

Davis, D. L., & Whitten, R. G. (1987). The cross-cultural study of human sexuality. *Annual Review of Anthropology, 16,* 69–98.

de Boer, A. G., Moolenaar, F., de Leede, L. G. J., & Breimer, D. D. (1982). Rectal drug administration: Clinical pharmacokinetic considerations. *Clinical Pharmacokinetics, 7,* 285–311.

Denko, J. D. (1973). Klismaphilia: Enema as a sexual preference. *American Journal of Psychotherapy, 27,* 232–250.

Denko, J. D. (1976). Klismaphilia: Amplification of the erotic enema deviance. *American Journal of Psychotherapy, 30,* 236–255.

Denson, R. (1982). Undinism: The fetishization of urine. *Canadian Journal of Psychiatry, 27,* 336–338.

de Sade, D. A. F. (1966). *Justine* (H. Weaver, Trans.). New York: Putnam. (Original work published 1791)

Dewaraja, R. (1987). Formicophilia, an unusual paraphilia, treated with counseling and behavior therapy. *American Journal of Psychotherapy, 41,* 593–597.

Dewaraja, R., & Money, J. (1986). Transcultural sexology: Formicophilia, a newly named paraphilia in a young Buddhist male. *Journal of Sex and Marital Therapy, 12*, 139–145.

Diamond, M., Innala, S. M., & Ernulf, K. E. (1990). Asphyxiophilia and autoerotic death. *Hawaii Medical Journal, 49*, 11–12, 14–16, 24.

Dittert, S., Seidl, O., & Soyka, M. (2005). Zoophilie zwischen pathologie und normalitat darstellung dreier kasuistiken und einer Internetbefragung. *Der Hervenarzt, 76*, 61–67.

Duffield, G., Hassiotis, A., & Vizard, E. (1998). Zoophilia in young sexual abusers. *Journal of Forensic Psychiatry, 9*, 294–304.

Eckert, W. G., & Katchis, S. (1989). Anorectal trauma: Medicolegal and forensic aspects. *American Journal of Forensic Medicine and Pathology, 10*, 3–9.

Edmondson, J. S. (1972). A case of sexual asphyxia without fatal termination. *British Journal of Psychiatry, 121*, 437–438.

Eisele, J. W., & Reay, D. T. (1980). Deaths related to coffee enemas. *Journal of the American Medical Association, 244*, 1608–1609

Eriksson, A., Gezelius, C., & Bring, G. (1987). Rolled up to death: An unusual autoerotic fatality. *American Journal of Forensic Medicine and Pathology, 8*, 263–265.

Everaerd, W. (1983). A case of apotemnophilia: A handicap as sexual preference. *American Journal of Psychotherapy, 37*, 285–293.

Fleischl, M. F. (1960). A man's fantasy of a crippled girl. *American Journal of Psychotherapy, 14*, 741–748.

Foraker, A. G. (1976). The romantic necrophiliac of Key West. *Journal of the Florida Medical Association, 63*, 642–645.

Freund, K., & Blanchard, R. (1986). The concept of courtship disorder. *Journal of Sex and Marital Therapy, 12*, 79–92.

Freund, K., Scher, H., & Hucker, S. (1984). The courtship disorders: A further investigation. *Archives of Sexual Behavior, 13*, 133–139.

Freund, K., Seto, H. & Kuban, M. (1997). Frotteurism: The theory of courtship disorder. In D. R. Laws & W. T. O'Donohue (Eds.), *Sexual deviance: Theory, assessment, and treatment* (pp. 111–130). New York: Guilford Press.

Friedrich, W. N., & Gerber, P. N. (1994). Autoerotic asphyxia: The development of paraphilia. *Journal of the American Academy of Child and Adolescent Psychiatry, 33*, 970–974.

Garza-Leal, J. A., & Landron, F. J. (1991). Autoerotic asphyxial death initially misinterpreted as suicide and a review of the literature. *Journal of Forensic Sciences, 36*, 1753–1759.

Gebhard, P. H., Gagnon, J. H., Pomeroy, W. B., & Christenson, C. V. (1965). *Sex offenders: An analysis of types.* New York: Harper & Row.

Gold, S. R., Letourneau, E. J., & O'Donohue, W. (1995). Sexual interaction skills. In W. O'Donohue & L. Krasner (Eds.), *Handbook of psychological skills training: Clinical techniques and applications* (pp. 229–246). Boston: Allyn & Bacon.

Gowitt, G. T., & Hanzlick, R. L. (1992). Atypical autoerotic deaths. *American Journal of Forensic Medicine and Pathology, 13*, 115–119.

Hazelwood, R. R., Burgess, A. W., & Groth, A. N. (1981). Death during dangerous autoerotic practice. *Social Science and Medicine, 15*, 129–133.

Hazelwood, R. R., Dietz, P. E., & Burgess, A. W. (1983). *Autoerotic fatalities.* Lexington, MA: Lexington Books.

Herrerias, J. M., Muniain, M. A., Sanchez, S., & Garrido, M. (1983). Alcohol-induced colitis. *Endoscopy, 15*, 121–122.

Hirschfeld, M. (1948). *Sexual anomalies: The origins, nature, and treatment of sexual disorders.* New York: Emerson.

Hobson, W. F. (1983). Objective of exhibitionists. *Medical Aspects of Human Sexuality, 17*, 91–92.

Holden, T. E., & Sherline, D. M. (1973). Bestiality, with sensitization and anaphylactic reaction. *Obstetrics and Gynecology, 42*, 138–140.

Innala, S. M., & Ernulf, K. E. (1989). Asphyxiophilia in Scandinavia. *Archives of Sexual Behavior, 18*, 181–189.

Jones, E. (1931). *On the nightmare.* London: Hogarth Press.

Karpman, B. (1948). Coprophilia: A collective review. *Psychoanalytic Review, 35*, 253–272.

Karpman, B. (1949). A modern Gulliver: A study in coprophilia. *Psychoanalytic Review, 36*, 260–282.

Karpman, B. (1954). *The sexual offender and his offenses.* New York: Julian Press.

Kentsmith, D. K., & Bastani, J. B. (1974). Obscene telephoning by an exhibitionist during therapy: A case report. *International Journal of Group Psychotherapy, 24*, 352–357.

Kinsey, A. C., Pomeroy, W. B., & Martin, C. E. (1948). *Sexual behavior in the human male.* Philadelphia: Saunders.

Kinsey, A. C., Pomeroy, W. B., Martin, C. E., & Gebhard, P. H. (1953). *Sexual behavior in the human female.* Philadelphia: Saunders.

Klaf, F. S., & Brown, W. (1958). Necrophilia: Brief review and case report. *Psychiatric Quarterly, 32*, 645–652.

Kolb, L. C., & Brodie, H. K. H. (1982). *Modern clinical psychiatry* (10th ed.). Philadelphia: Saunders.

Kremer, J., & den Daas, H. P. (1990). Case report: A man with breast dysphoria. *Archives of Sexual Behavior, 19*, 179–181.

Lancaster, N. P. (1978). Necrophilia, murder and high intelligence: A case report. *British Journal of Psychiatry, 132*, 605–608.

Lawrence, A. A. (2004). Autogynephilia: A paraphilic model of gender identity disorder. *Journal of Gay and Lesbian Psychotherapy, 8*, 69–87.

Lee, C. (1992). On cognitive theories and causation in human behavior. *Journal of Behavior Therapy and Experimental Psychiatry, 23*, 257–268.

Litman, R. E., & Swearingen, C. (1972). Bondage and suicide. *Archives of General Psychiatry, 27*, 80–85.

London, L. S., & Caprio, F. S. (1950). *Sexual deviations.* Washington, DC: Linacre Press.

Matek, O. (1988). Obscene phone callers. *Journal of Social Work and Human Sexuality, 7*, 113–130.

McCary, J. L. (1967). *Human sexuality.* New York: Van Nostrand Reinhold.

McCary, J. L., & McCary, S. P. (1982). *McCary's human sexuality* (4th ed.). Belmont, CA: Wadsworth.

McNally, R. J., & Lukach, B. M. (1991). Behavioral treatment of zoophilic exhibitionism. *Journal of Behavior Therapy and Experimental Psychiatry, 22*, 281–284.

Mead, B. T. (1975). Coping with obscene phone calls. *Medical Aspects of Human Sexuality, 9*, 127–128.

Meyer, J. K. (1980). Paraphilias. In H. I. Kaplan, A. M. Freedman, & B. J. Sadock (Eds.), *Comprehensive textbook of psychiatry* (3rd ed., pp. 1770–1783). Baltimore: Williams & Wilkens.

Miletski, H. (2000). Beastiality/zoophilia: An exploratory study. *Scandinavian Journal of Sexology, 3*, 149–150.

Mitchell, W. M. (1968). Self-insertion of urethral foreign bodies. *Psychiatric Quarterly, 42*, 479–486.

Money, J. (1986). *Lovemaps: Clinical concepts of sexual/erotic health and pathology, paraphilia, and gender transposition in childhood, adolescence, and maturity.* New York: Irvington.

Money, J, (1990a). Forensic sexology: Paraphilic serial rape (biastophilia) and lust murder (erotophonophilia). *American Journal of Psychotherapy, 44*, 26–36.

Money, J. (1990b). Paraphilia in females: Fixation on amputation and lameness; two personal accounts. *Journal of Psychology and Human Sexuality, 3*, 165–172.

Money, J., Jobaris, R., & Furth, G. (1977). Apotemnophilia: Two cases of self-demand amputation as a paraphilia. *Journal of Sex Research, 13*, 115–125.

Money, J., & Lamacz, M. (1984). Gynemimesis and gynemimetophilia: Individual and cross-cultural manifestations of a gender-coping strategy hitherto unnamed. *Comprehensive Psychiatry, 25*, 392–403.

Money, J., & Lamacz, M. (1989). *Vandalized lovemaps: Paraphilic outcomes of seven cases in pediatric sexology.* Buffalo, NY: Prometheus Books.

Money, J., & Simcoe, K. W. (1984–1986). Acrotomophilia, sex and disability: New concepts and case report. *Sexuality and Disability, 7,* 43–50.

Murray, F. S. (1967). A preliminary investigation of anonymous nuisance telephone calls to females. *Psychological Record, 17,* 395–400.

Murray, F. S., & Beran, L. C. (1968). A survey of nuisance telephones calls received by males and females. *Psychological Record, 18,* 107–109.

Nadler, R. P. (1968). Approach to psychodynamics of obscene telephone calls. *New York State Journal of Medicine, 68,* 521–526.

Nagaraja, J. (1983). Sexual problems in adolescence. *Child Psychiatry Quarterly, 16,* 9–18.

O'Donohue, W. T., Letourneau, E., & Dowling, H. (1995). Development and preliminary validation of a paraphilic sexual fantasy questionnaire. *Sexual Abuse: A Journal of Research and Treatment, 9,* 167–178.

O'Halloran, R. L., & Lovell, F. W. (1988). Autoerotic asphyxial death following television broadcast. *Journal of Forensic Sciences, 33,* 1491–1492.

Peretti, P. O., & Rowan, M. (1983). Zoophilia: Factors related to its sustained practice. *Panminerva Medica, 25,* 127–131.

Prins, H. (1985). Vampirism: A clinical condition. *British Journal of Psychiatry, 146,* 666–668.

Rapoport, J. (1942). A case of necrophilia. *Journal of Criminal Psychopathology, 4,* 277–289.

Rappaport, E. A. (1968). Zoophily and zooerasty. *Psychoanalytic Quarterly, 37,* 565–587.

Reay, D. T., & Eisele, J. W. (1982). Death from law enforcement neck holds. *American Journal of Forensic Medicine and Pathology, 3,* 253–258.

Reinhardt, J. M. (1957). *Sex perversions and sex crimes.* Springfield, IL: Thomas.

Resnik, H. L. P. (1972). Erotized repetitive hangings: A form of self-destructive behavior. *American Journal of Psychotherapy, 26,* 4–21.

Revitch, E. (1983). Burglaries with sexual dynamics. In L. B. Schlesinger & E. Revitch (Eds.), *Sexual dynamics of anti-social behavior* (pp. 173–191). Springfield, IL: Thomas.

Richards, A. K. (1989). A romance with pain: A telephone perversion in a woman? *International Journal of Psychoanalysis, 70,* 153–164.

Rosenblum, S., & Faber, M. M. (1979). The adolescent sexual asphyxia syndrome. *Journal of the American Academy of Child Psychiatry, 18,* 546–558.

Rosman, J. P., & Resnick, P. J. (1989). Sexual attraction to corpses: A psychiatric review of necrophilia. *Bulletin of the American Academy of Psychiatry and the Law, 17,* 153–163.

Sass, F. A. (1975). Sexual asphyxia in the female. *Journal of Forensic Sciences, 20,* 181–185.

Schneck, J. M. (1974). Zooerasty and incest fantasy. *International Journal of Clinical Experimental Hypnosis, 22,* 299–302.

Sheehan, W., & Garfinkel, B. D. (1988). Adolescent autoerotic deaths. *Journal of the American Academy of Child and Adolescent Psychiatry, 27,* 367–370.

Shenken, L. I. (1964). Some clinical and psychopathological aspects of bestiality. *Journal of Nervous and Mental Disease, 139,* 137–142.

Silverstein, C. (1984). The ethical and moral implications of sexual classification: A commentary. *Journal of Homosexuality, 9,* 29–38.

Sinn, L. E. (1993). The silver bullet. *American Journal of Forensic Medicine and Pathology, 14,* 145–147.

Smith, R. S. (1976). Voyeurism: A review of the literature. *Archives of Sexual Behavior, 5,* 585–608.

Smith, S. M., & Braun, C. (1978). Necrophilia and lust murder: Report of a rare occurrence. *Bulletin of the American Academy of Psychiatry and the Law, 6,* 259–268.

Stoller, R. J. (1982). Erotic vomiting. *Archives of Sexual Behavior, 11,* 361–365.

Tallent, N. (1977). Sexual deviation as a diagnostic entity: A confused and sinister concept. *Bulletin of the Menninger Clinic, 41,* 40–60.

Taylor, B. (1976). Amputee fetishism: An exclusive journal interview with Dr. John Money of Johns Hopkins. *Maryland State Medical Journal, 25,* 35–39.

Torre, C., & Varetto, L. (1987). An exceptional case of necrophilia. *American Journal of Forensic Medicine and Pathology, 8,* 169–171.

Traub-Werner, D. (1986). The place and value of bestophilia in perversions. *Journal of the American Psychoanalytic Association, 34,* 975–992.

Vanden Bergh, R. L., & Kelly, J. F. (1964). Vampirism: A review with new observations. *Archives of General Psychiatry, 11,* 543–547.

Walsh, F. M., Stahl, C. J., Unger, H. T., Lilienstern, O. C., & Stephens, R. G., III. (1977). Autoerotic asphyxial deaths: A medicolegal analysis of forty-three cases. In C. H. Wecht (Ed.), *Legal medicine annual 1977* (pp. 155–182). New York: Appleton-Century-Crofts.

Williams, C. J., & Weinberg, M. S. (2003). Zoophilia in men: A study of sexual interests in animals. *Archives of Sexual Behavior, 32,* 523–535.

Wise, T. N. (1982). Urethral manipulation: An unusual paraphilia. *Journal of Sex and Marital Therapy, 8,* 222–227.

Wise, T. N. (1985). Fetishism—etiology and treatment: A review from multiple perspectives. *Comprehensive Psychiatry, 26,* 249–257.

Wise, T. N. (2000). Amputee fetishism and genital mutilation: Case report and literature review. *Journal of Sex and Marital Therapy, 26,* 339–344.

Yalom, I. D. (1960). Aggression and forbiddenness in voyeurism. *Archives of General Psychiatry, 3,* 305–319.

Zavitzianos, G. (1983). The kleptomanias and female criminality. In L. B. Schlesinger & E. Revitch (Eds.), *Sexual dynamics of anti-social behavior* (pp. 132–158). Springfield, IL: Thomas.

CHAPTER 23

PARAPHILIA NOT OTHERWISE SPECIFIED

Assessment and Treatment

TAMARA M. PENIX

The variety of paraphilias not known to be prevalent enough to garner a specific paraphilia diagnosis are categorized under the "not otherwise specified" (NOS) designator in the *Diagnostic and Statistical Manual of Mental Disorders* (DSM-IV-TR; American Psychiatric Association, 2000). These may be the most fascinating of the paraphilias because they appear to be uncommon if not rare, and because as a result of their apparently low base rates (or at least low disclosure rates) in the population, little is known about them. No doubt imagination will continue to fill in the gaps with respect to these less understood paraphilias until such time as the field makes a concerted effort to raise public consciousness. Fewer than 20 articles and book chapters have been published on the topic since the first edition of *Sexual Deviance* was published in 1997, and none of these is more empirical than observational in nature. Thus the largely descriptive information that follows should not be viewed as either exact or exhaustive.

ASSESSMENT

Diagnosis

The DSM-IV-TR (American Psychiatric Association, 2000) identifies as paraphilias recurrent, intense, sexually arousing sexual fantasies, urges, and behaviors lasting at least 6 months that involve nonhuman objects, the suffering or humiliation of oneself or one's sexual partner, or nonconsenting persons (Criterion A). A person must have acted upon the sexual fantasies and/or experienced significant distress or impaired functioning to receive the diagnosis. Eight specific types of paraphilias are recognized by the form or object of the non-normative sexual behavior and are discussed elsewhere in this volume. The unusual object or activity associated with sexual desire may be necessary for sexual arousal in some cases, and preferred but not necessary in others (Williams & Weinberg, 2003). Sexual behavior or fantasy that references the object is common in times of stress. The NOS category represents all other behaviors that fulfill Criterion A above, but do not manifest themselves in one of the better-known forms. The more familiar of these subcategories, according to the DSM-IV-TR, are "telephone scatalogia" (achieving sexual arousal by making obscene or erotic telephone calls to nonconsenting people), "necrophilia" (sexual interest in or practice with corpses), "partialism" (sexual focus on one part of the body), "zoophilia" (sexual focus on animals), "coprophilia" (focus on feces), "klismaphilia" (focus on enemas), and "urophilia" (focus on urine). In truth, the multiplicity of forms may be endless, as exemplified by a recent report of "autogynephilia" (sexual focus on oneself as a transgendered individual) in the literature (Lawrence, 2004).

Telephone Scatalogia

Casual, obscene telephone calling is often mistaken for telephone scatalogia. Whereas prank phone calls are a relatively common phenomenon in modern society (Price, Kafka, Commons, Gutheil, & Simpson, 2002), scatalogia, in which the caller becomes sexually aroused by exposing an unsuspecting victim to sexual material and may masturbate during or while remembering the call, is far less widespread. A review of the characteristics of telephone scatologists by Pakhomou (2006) indicates that they are typically heterosexual, discovered in young adulthood, possess an average or elevated sexual drive, do not evidence significant cognitive deficits, have no significant psychopathology, and have typically attempted but failed to maintain a long-term committed relationship (often with children). They also tend to have limited social interactions, criminal histories involving theft, a high school or some college education, and menial jobs (Alford, Webster, & Sanders, 1980; Almansi, 1979; Dalby, 1988; Kentsmith & Dastani, 1974; Price et al., 2002).

Three major types of scatalogical telephone calls were identified by Masters, Johnson, and Kolodny (1982). Most prevalent is the type in which the perpetrator boasts about himself and his sexual organs, and describes his masturbation. Another sort is characterized by sexual and other threats toward the listener, and the final variety attempts to manipulate the respondent into revealing intimate sexual or otherwise intimate information about herself. Characteristic ruses for obtaining private information include posing as another female (Almansi, 1979; Dalby, 1988; Pakhomou, 2006) and acting as a sexual survey researcher (Schewe, 1997; Skinner & Becker, 1985).

Necrophilia

Necrophilia from a diagnostic standpoint must involve persistent sexual arousal when one is fantasizing about or in the presence of a deceased human body. Some people may have an emotional attachment to a corpse or want to be near a corpse for nonsexual reasons. Such persons would not fit the spirit of the paraphilia NOS diagnosis, although they may be accused of the act in the vernacular. There appear to be no reports on the prevalence of transient necrophilic fantasies among people who engage in more normative sexual behavior (Burg, 1982).

The only published study of the characteristics of necrophilic individuals (N = 122) was conducted by Rosman and Resnick (1989). Their sample was mostly heterosexual, male (95%), and unmarried (74%); the majority were discovered to be necrophilic in their mid-30s, and half accessed human remains through their jobs. The authors discovered what they termed "genuine" necrophilia and "pseudonecrophilia" in their sample, discriminated by the existence of a persistent sexual attraction to corpses in the former. They also found that most of their sample used corpses that were already dead; a third of their sample killed the object for the purpose of engaging in necrophilia; and another third only fantasized about defiling a corpse (Rosman & Resnick, 1989).

Zoophilia

As with telephone scatalogia and necrophilia, a difference is seen between casual interest or participation in sexual behavior with animals on the one hand, and intense and ongoing fantasies about, urges toward, and participation in zoophilia on the other. A distinction is sometimes drawn between the bestialist, who engages in the behavior casually out of curiosity or opportunistically (Tollison & Adams, 1979), and the zoophile, who displays a persistent and strong sexual arousal to animals. A dissimilarity in nomenclature and identity exists between the clinical view of the behavior and the participants' view as well: Among many practitioners, zoophiles are persons who truly have a romantic or intimate love for animals, while bestialists are people who use animals for their sexual gratification without regard for the animals' welfare (Williams & Weinberg, 2003). Several studies of the behavior have revealed the following characteristics of zoophiles and bestialists.

The early human sexuality studies of Kinsey and his colleagues (Kinsey, Pomeroy, & Martin, 1948; Kinsey, Pomeroy, Martin, & Gebhard, 1953) revealed that 8% of males and 3.6% of females in their sample had engaged in bestiality. People who had engaged in the behavior with the highest probability were boys raised on farms (40–50%), and they reported engaging in the behavior infrequently. Only 17% of them reported having had an orgasm during the experience (Kinsey et al., 1948). As a result of these data, Kinsey and colleagues (1948) viewed the behavior as opportunistic acts that served as a substitute for heterosexual human sexual relationships. Hunt (1974) concurred with this hypothesis. He found that 5% of males and 2% of females in his sample of 982 men and 1,044 women had engaged in bestiality—a decrease in the behavior he attributed to a general population shift to more urban areas. A study of sex offenders conducted by Gebhard, Gagnon, Pomeroy, and Christenson (1965) found that men who had engaged in sexual activity with animals appeared hypersexual, with a high degree of openness to any kind of sexual activity. Alvarez and Freinhar (1991) found the behavior to be strongly associated with mental illness, but not rare in their nonpsychiatric comparison sample. They found that 55% of their sample of 20 psychiatric inpatients, 15% of the mental health staff, and 10% of their medical inpatient sample had engaged in sexual behavior with animals.

Either the characteristics of people who engage in sexual behavior with animals have changed with time; reporting has changed; or new research methods such as recruiting participants via the Internet have captured samples of practitioners differing from those of the Kinsey and colleagues studies and other early research. Recent investigations by Miletski (2002) and Beetz (2002) have provided greater clarity. Miletski's sample of 82 men and 11 women were in their 30s on average, and half had completed college; nearly half were single, and a third were married. She found that a third of the sample reported being shy. Most (83%) had had heterosexual human sexual contact, while 76.8% had had homosexual contact and 40.5% were bisexual. Dogs and horses were the most common animal conquests, with 87.2 % of the sample attracted to canines and 80% at-tracted to equines. Other species included cows, sheep, and cats. Most of the participants reported being attracted to more than one species and gender of animal. The men en-gaged in both oral and genital contact with the animals, as both contact recipients and providers. Seventeen percent of the men reported having been sexually abused in child-hood. More than two-thirds of the sample lived in a suburban to urban environment. Beetz's sample of 113 men and 3 women was similar. The average age of her participants was 30, with one-third of them college graduates. Seventy-nine percent were single, and 62% reported wanting a human sexual partner. About a quarter of the sample had had no human sexual contact. Seventy percent of this sample reported sexual contact with dogs, while 50% reported sexual practices with horses. Sexual behaviors engaged in (from most to least frequently) were masturbation of the animal, mutual oral–genital contact, oral–oral contact, vaginal or anal penetration of the animal, and vaginal or anal penetration of the person. Other reported species were cows, cats, and dolphins.

Motivations for bestiality have been explored by a number of researchers. Kinsey and many others speculated that the lack of a human sexual outlet is causal in the behav-ior (Alvarez & Freinhar, 1991; Dekkers, 1994), and to some extent this hypothesis has been borne out in more modern samples. Miletski (2002) found that 30% of her partici-pants reported having sex with animals as a substitute for human contact. Other causal factors cited include sexual experimentation (Hunt, 1974), sadomasochism (Beetz, 2002; Miletski, 2002; Trimble, 1969), conditioning (Kinsey et al., 1948), loneliness (Cerrone, 1991), proximity (Kinsey et al., 1948), novelty seeking (Stekel, 1952), boredom (Miletski, 2002), a strong sexual drive (Trimble, 1969), social skills deficits (Beetz, 2002; Cerrone, 1991; Stekel, 1952; Trimble, 1969), and mental illness (Alvarez & Freinhar, 1991; Shenken, 1960). Donofrio (1996) was the first to suggest the existence of a sexual prefer-ence for animals in some bestialists—a hypothesis that appears to be supported by the findings of Miletski (2002), Beetz (2002), and Earls and Lalumière (2002). Miletski (2000) concluded that the 94 participants in her study engaged in zoophilia because they were sexually oriented toward animals, had a desire to express love for animals, and had sexual fantasies about animals. Remarkably, two-thirds of Williams and Weinberg's (2003) sample of 114 zoophiles reported that they would rather have sex with an animal than with a person.

Coprophilia and Urophilia

In coprophilia and urophilia, the focus is on using feces and urine, respectively, to achieve sexual arousal. An individual may be urinated or defecated on, may perform these acts on another person, or may ingest human waste to obtain sexual pleasure (Denson, 1982; Skinner & Becker, 1985). Denson (1982) found in his study of urophiles that the urine fulfilled many different functions, including serving as a fetish object, capturing the spirit of a sexual partner, or being used to humiliate or be humiliated (i.e., through urinating on another person or being urinated upon).

Partialism

Partialism is a specific form of fetish behavior in which sexual arousal is obtained through fantasy about or contact with a particular body part that is not a traditional erogenous zone. One case of oral partialism was found in the literature: a 19-year-old male of borderline intellect who was sexually fixated on ingesting bacteria from ulcerated lesions under his arms, above the pubis, and in the groin area (McGuire, Choon, Nayer, & Sanders, 1998).

Klismaphilia

Very little is known about klismaphilia, which involves giving or receiving enemas. Some authors (Adams & McAnulty, 1993; Schewe, 1997) regard the behavior as possibly linked to a rubber fetish or sadomasochism.

Comorbidity among Paraphilias

A high degree of comorbidity among the paraphilias has been observed in a number of studies (Abel, Becker, Cunningham-Rather, Mittelman, & Rouleau, 1988; Abel & Rouleau, 1990; Bradford, Boulet, & Pawlak, 1992)—a trend that is also evident in the disorders classified as paraphilia NOS. Freund, Watson, and Rienzo (1988) found that exhibitionists made obscene telephone calls at double the rate of sex offenders who were not exhibitionistic (28.7% vs. 13.7%, respectively). Price and colleagues (2002) found significant relationships between telephone scatalogia and voyeurism, compulsive masturbation, and paying for telephone sex, in addition to a trend toward a significant association with exhibitionism. They found no significant association with frotteurism, pedophilia, fetishism, transvestic fetishism, and sadomasochism. Despite these findings, Pakhomou (2006) noted that there is "no conclusive evidence that scatologists are prone to sexual assaults, rape, or sexual homicide, or that they physically pursue their victims" (p. 179). A relationship has been found between bestiality and both sadomasochistic and sexually abusive fantasy/behavior in several studies. Miletski (2002) found that 4% of her sample fantasized about sadomasochistic sex regularly, 9% admitted having forced someone into a nonconsensual sexual experience, and 9% reported fantasizing about sexual relations with children. Beetz (2002) found that 2% of her sample acknowledged an interest in sadism and 4.4% in masochism. Gebhard and colleagues (1965) studied the relationship between bestiality and sexual offending in a sample of 1,000 male sex offenders, 881 nonsexual/nonviolent offenders, and 471 offenders without any criminal conviction beyond a traffic ticket. They defined "bestiality" as sexual penetration of an animal. Results indicated that the controls had engaged in sex with animals at a rate of 8.3%, while 33.3% of female child sex abusers had had sexual contact with animals.

The focus on the form of the sexual behavior seems to create the appearance of separate co-occurring disorders, when it may be the function of the behavior that could be meaningfully linked to a more parsimonious understanding of the problem(s) and efficient treatment. It is not clear that the type of fetish object chosen (e.g., form of human waste) is meaningful in terms of causation, maintenance, or treatment of these behaviors. Therefore, why should we approach the problems as if there were meaning in form? For example, segments of the populations with telephone scatalogia, necrophilia, and zoophilia appear to engage in these behaviors in an effort to connect sexually with another being, in the absence of the social skills generally required to produce a more normative human sexual experience. Presumably treatment of this subtype, which crosses disorders, would involve social communication and intimacy skills training, whereas the causal factors and treatment for other subtypes would relate to entirely different functions of the behavior that would imply different interventions. For example, the urophilic individual who drinks urine to capture the essence of his sexual partner may be more like the necrophilic person who kills his victim in order to somehow experience the victim's soul leaving the body more closely than he does the urophilic person who attempts to alleviate unwanted guilt feelings by being dominated sexually or the necrophilic individual who has a conditioned physiological arousal to the sensation of cold flesh.

Comorbidity with Other Psychological Disorders

Comorbidity of the paraphilias in general and the paraphilia NOS disorders in particular with other mental illnesses is evidenced as well. In a study of 60 outpatient males diagnosed with paraphilias and paraphilia-related disorders (e.g., compulsive masturbation, ego-dystonic protracted promiscuity, and pornography dependence), Kafka and Prentky (1994) found that 76.7% had an elevated lifetime prevalence of mood disorders, 46.7% admitted to psychoactive substance abuse, 40% reported alcohol abuse, and 46.7% had an anxiety disorder (predominantly social phobia—31.6%). Hoyer, Kunst, and Schmidt (2001) examined anxiety as a comorbid condition in sex offenders with either a paraphilia or an impulse control disorder. Their two studies of 72 sex offenders and 30 controls yielded markedly higher scores for social anxiety and social phobia in those with a paraphilia. Kafka and Prentky (1998) examined the comorbidity of attention-deficit/hyperactivity disorder (ADHD) in males with paraphilias ($n = 42$) and paraphilia-related disorders ($n = 18$). They found that the samples had similarly high prevalences of mood disorders, anxiety disorders, substance use disorders, and impulse control disorders; however, they differed significantly in respect to childhood ADHD. Fifty percent of those with paraphilias met the retrospective diagnostic criteria for ADHD, as opposed to only 16.7% of those with paraphilia-related disorders. Both these rates are higher than an ADHD childhood prevalence rate of 6.2% in the general population (Neuman et al., 2005). Alvarez and Freinhar (1991) found that 50% of their small ($n = 20$) psychiatric inpatient sample had engaged in sexual behavior with animals. Another indicator of comorbidity was found by Beetz (2002), who noted that 38% of the male participants in her zoophilic sample had participated in psychotherapy, but that only 7% reported it was related to the zoophilia; the implication was that other psychological or life problems were present. Beetz also found that 12% of her sample had experienced depression and 5% reported social problems.

Assessment Model

There is no standardized model of assessment for the paraphilias in general, or for the rarer paraphilias in particular. Thus this type of assessment should be guided by the general principles of good assessment practice, with the recognition that the enterprise is less standardized because of the lack of psychometrically sound measures normed on the populations of interest. It is therefore more dependent on clinical judgment, which is known to be less accurate than a more stringent actuarial approach (Dawes, Faust, & Meehl, 2002). Any assessment should be guided by the referral question—that is, the expressed purpose of the assessment—as well as by whether the assessment is clinical or forensic in nature. Any criminal records of the behavior should be obtained prior to conducting a thorough clinical interview (see Penix & Suraweera, 2007, for guidelines), and other pertinent institutional records (such as those from medical and school sources) may be collected afterward to corroborate relevant information.

A functional analysis of the behavior may provide useful organizing theory and a framework for understanding the context in which the behavior is embedded. A good functional analysis will identify contextual variables that occasion the behavior and the consequences that maintain it over time. Collateral interviews with individuals who have had access to the behavior may also be useful in gathering data that are essential to understanding how the behavior operates. Valid objective psychological measures that assess these behaviors are few; however, if they are available, they should be part of a comprehensive assessment. Due to the apparently low prevalence rates of these paraphilias and the concomitantly low rates of study and measure development, it is necessary to make conservative inferences about the behaviors by using measures that provide information about correlated variables, such as other types of sexual deviance, sexual fantasies, attraction to sexual violence, and erotic preferences. These data may be supplemented by the physiological data regarding sexual arousal provided by penile plethysmography (see O'Donohue & Letourneau, 1993, for a review). There is no evidence that projective psychological testing is useful in the assessment of any type of paraphilia NOS.

Assessment Instruments

The following objective instruments may be useful in gathering data that may be related to the presence of a paraphilia NOS. None of the following instruments was designed to diagnose or to assess the level of risk with respect to these types of paraphilias. However, they may be useful in cuing a discussion about related behaviors or the behavior of interest.

Clinician-Administered Measures

Psychopathy Checklist—Revised. The Psychopathy Checklist—Revised (PCL-R; Hare, 1991) is a clinician-completed measure that uses a lengthy clinical interview and records review to assess for psychopathic characteristics. These characteristics have been correlated with less successful treatment outcomes for sex offenders (Firestone et al., 1999; Harris & Rice, 1997). Analyses of the psychometric properties of the PCL-R indicate moderate to strong effect sizes in its predictive validity for violent and general recidivism (Salekin, Rogers, & Sewell, 1996). See Hare and Neumann (2006) for additional psychometric information and an updated research agenda for the instrument.

Violence Risk Appraisal Guide. The Violence Risk Appraisal Guide (VRAG; Quinsey, Harris, Rice, & Cormier, 1998) is a 12-item instrument used to predict violence following the release of a mentally disordered offender with a history of violence. One study has demonstrated the utility and validity of the VRAG in a nonforensic patient population (Harris, Rice, & Camilleri, 2004). A study by Loza and Dhaliwal (1997) found good reliability and concurrent validity for the measure.

Self-Report Measures

Clarke Sex History Questionnaire. The Clarke Sex History Questionnaire—Revised (SHQ-R; Langevin & Paitich, 2002) is a self-report measure that is used to assess the variety of expressions of sexual behavior. Its short-answer format may lend itself to clients writing in or discussing unusual related varieties of sexual experience. Twenty-three scales were derived through factor analysis in its initial development and revision. These scales were found to discriminate clinically relevant groups from controls.

Multidimensional Assessment of Sex and Aggression. The Multidimensional Assessment of Sex and Aggression (MASA; Knight, Prentky, & Cerce, 1994) is a self-report measure used to assess the full range of sexual and aggressive behaviors. An adolescent form is available. The administration of the MASA to a sample of 127 offenders, and the repeated administration after 6 months to a subsample of these same offenders, provided evidence of its reliability and concurrent validity. According to Knight and colleagues (1994), "with the exception of generic questions about offense planning and specific questions about adult vandalism and the nature of sadistic fantasies, responses demonstrated cross-temporal stability, and the a priori summative scales that were constructed to assess the major domains required for assigning offenders to MTC:R3 [Massachusetts Treatment Center: Rape 3] types showed high levels of internal consistency" (p. 86).

Multiphasic Sex Inventory. The Multiphasic Sex Inventory (MSI; Nichols & Molinder, 1984) is a self-report measure used to assess the full range of sexual behaviors. It includes questions about less common paraphilic behaviors and interests, such as fetishes and obscene telephone calling, that may be related to the paraphilias of interest in this chapter. A juvenile form is available in addition to an updated measure, the MSI II (Nichols & Molinder, 1996). The MSI II must be submitted to the testing company for scoring at a cost, which makes its use more prohibitive than that of the original. Adequate alphas were reported for the scales most relevant to the paraphilia NOS disorders on Nichols and Molinder's website (*www.nicholsandmolinder.com*). They have not published a full review of their analyses of the instrument. Kalichman, Henderson, Shealy, and Dwyer (1992) reported high internal consistency, convergent validity, and discriminant validity for the original MSI. They identified its face validity and potential for response biases as detriments.

Sexual Fantasy Questionnaire. The Sexual Fantasy Questionnaire (SFQ; O'Donohue, Letourneau, & Dowling, 1997) is a self-report measure that assesses the full range of sexual fantasy content, including zoophilia, necrophilia, and telephone scatalogia. The authors reported adequate test–retest reliability, percentage agreement, internal consistency, and convergent validity.

Attraction to Sexual Aggression Scale. The Attraction to Sexual Aggression Scale (ASA; Malamuth, 1989a, 1989b) is a self-report measure designed to measure the appeal of sexually aggressive behavior. There is some evidence to suggest that some of the rarer paraphilic behaviors may be associated with violence (Gratzer & Bradford, 1995; Masters & Lea, 1963; Ressler, Burgess, Hartmann, Douglas, & McCormack, 1986). Some zoophilic individuals kill animals either during or after sexual activity with them (Beetz, 2002); some necrophilic individuals kill people in order to have access to their lifeless bodies (Rosman & Resnick, 1989); and there is mixed evidence for violence relative to telephone scatalogia (which is primarily verbal violence; Price et al., 2002), coprophilia, and urophilia (primarily the sadistic subtypes; Denson, 1982). The ASA may be useful in identifying the propensity for violence as it relates to the behavior(s) of interest. Malamuth's investigations into the properties of his scale revealed good internal consistency, test–retest reliability, discriminant and construct validity, and predictive validity for risk of sexual coercion.

Erotic Preferences Examination Scheme. The Erotic Preferences Examination Scheme (EPES; Freund et al., 1988) is a self-report measure of a variety of paraphilic interests. It has been shown to discriminate between paraphilic and nonparaphilic individuals on a number of indices, and as such may indicate the presence of an uncharacteristic form of paraphilic behavior, if not the specific form itself. A more informative psychometric profile on this measure has not been reported in the literature.

Behavioral Assessment

Phallometry. Measuring physiological arousal genitally may be useful in the assessment of sexual sadism, which appears to be either an associated feature of or a comorbid disorder with some of the rarer paraphilias, depending on how diagnosis is viewed. A distinctive arousal profile has been identified for sexual sadists (Fedora et al., 1992). However, no distinctive physiological profiles have emerged with respect to the other paraphilias. Despite the scarcity of studies for specific subtypes, a case study of a preferential bestialist by Earls and Lalumière (2005) indicates that the use of specialized stimulus materials for particular paraphilias may warrant further investigation. A useful review of penile plethysmography is found in Kalmus and Beech (2005). Alternative, less intrusive physiological measures of sexual arousal are in development including a viewing time measure (Laws & Gress, 2004), emotional Stroop task (Smith & Waterman, 2005) and others (Abel et al., 2004), but they have not been validated for use in assessing or treating the "other" paraphilias.

Behavior-Specific versus Global Measures of Psychopathology

No one has studied the clinical or forensic utility of a behavior-specific approach versus a global psychopathology approach with respect to the lesser-known paraphilias. Several points support the reasoning that a more global approach may be warranted at this time. First, high comorbidity across the paraphilias may indicate a more fundamental core function or diagnosis, of which the particular form is simply a sign. Similarly, high comorbidity with other types of psychological disorders may indicate a more fundamental pathology, of which the sexual behavior is an unusual symptom. For example, in order to avoid the feeling of anxiety in complex human social relationships, some people who would meet criteria for paraphilia NOS may choose animals or dead human beings as alternative sexual objects. One might also abuse substances in order to reduce feelings of anxiety, a common comorbid condition. The implication is that aiding the client in managing social anxiety may alleviate the secondary but related paraphilic symptoms, as well as other important symptoms. Consequently, identification of the more primary process may be fundamental to efficient and effective treatment outcomes, and more global measures of psychopathology may be helpful in this process. It seems important to note that there are psychometrically sound measures of global pathology as well—a strength that is notably absent from the sexuality-specific paraphilia NOS literature. Although a review of those measures extends beyond the scope of this chapter, a few bear mention.

The Brief Symptom Inventory and the Symptom Checklist 90—Revised (Derogatis & Fitzpatrick, 2004) are useful screening measures, while more specific measures of mood, thought processes, or substance abuse may be employed when information from the clinical interview indicates their appropriateness. There is no particular personality profile derived from Minnesota Multiphasic Personality Inventory–2 (MMPI-2) data that distinguishes people with paraphilic behaviors from others (Marshall & Hall, 1995). However, insight into how an individual has approached the assessment, clinically relevant behaviors and behavioral repertoires, and indicators of special concerns (e.g., gender identity issues and substance abuse) may be discovered with the MMPI-2, and in that sense it may be incredibly useful.

Research Priorities

So little is definitely known about these paraphilias that the research field is essentially wide open. The first priority would seem to be achieving greater funding for sexual deviance research. Grant funding for sexuality research has declined in the United States in recent years, as morality-based arguments have entered into decision making about research funding priorities. Researchers need to become better governmental and private foundation advocates for the public health benefits of their work if this is to change. A second priority is introducing new researchers to, and mentoring them in, the sexual deviance assessment area. Most doctoral students who receive the research training necessary to support the development of good assessment instruments abandon research at the end of their training in order to pursue clinical careers. Of those who continue into a research position, many are not encouraged to prioritize instrument development in their areas, instead opting to use unvalidated or more global instruments in their studies of other aspects of sexual deviance. Others have not learned the requisite skills set for completing such a measure. Thus research and career mentoring seems essential to the growth of this subfield.

A third research priority would be to include paraphilia NOS items on new or revised sexual history, sexual behavior, and violence questionnaires, rather than assuming that such behaviors are rare. These questions would aid in identifying some practitioners of the behaviors and normalizing discussion of the less readily revealed sexual behaviors. Similarly, the inclusion of paraphilia NOS stimulus materials in studies of physiological arousal—including, but not limited to, plethysmography (Earls & Lalumière, 2002)—is warranted. Inventive research methodology is needed in order to access the populations of interest. Steps in this direction have been seen in the use of international websites that cater to groups of people with very specific sexual interests, as well as volunteer referrals of others who engage in these practices; nevertheless, more innovation is needed, in concert with clear ways to protect participants and assure them of their confidentiality. Researchers who want to access these pocket populations may need to think more broadly in their agendas, seeking funding for national and international studies rather than investigating in their own backyards. Finally, means of accessing less technologically inclined portions of the population—in addition to members of the upper class, who are far less likely to volunteer for research—are needed.

TREATMENT

People exhibiting the minor paraphilias do not regularly present for treatment, for a number of reasons. These may include the reviled nature of their behavior, possibly low distress associated with enacting the behaviors, and perhaps a lack of confidence in the possibility of a favorable treatment outcome. As a result, reports of effective treatments for these paraphilias tend toward case studies, although the broader findings from treatment outcome studies of the more prevalent paraphilias would seem to offer a reasonable place to begin with respect to treating the rarer paraphilias.

Case studies indicate that psychodynamic, cognitive-behavioral, behavioral, and psychopharmacological interventions have been useful in treating some of these problems. There are no data indicating successful treatment of necrophilia, coprophilia, or klismaphilia to date.

Treatment Resources

Books and Treatment Manuals

Sexuality-specific interventions are described in detail in the peer-reviewed sexual offender treatment literature, as well as in treatment manuals that are not readily available to the general public. Some of the better-supported therapist-led interventions are described below. Several books describing or providing interventions that may be accessed by therapists and clients are published through the Safer Society Press and New Harbinger Publications. They include *Changing Me* (Card & Steinhauser, 2002), *The Adult Relapse Prevention Workbook* (Steen, 2000), and *The Sex Addiction Workbook* (Sbraga & O'Donohue, 2004). Eldridge (1998) has published a set of therapist and client manuals that includes some of these techniques. Publications with useful descriptions of cognitive-behavioral interventions include classics by Barlow (2002), Beck, Rush, Shaw, and Emery (1979), Ellis (2003), Martell (2003), and Wolpe (1990). Social skills training is well described in McFall (1990). A classic and readable reference on motivational interviewing is Miller and Rollnick (2002). Useful information regarding human sexuality is provided in *Understanding Human Sexuality* (Hyde & DeLamater, 2006). The practice of brief psychodynamic psychotherapy is described in Binder (2004).

Informational Websites

Informational websites offering assistance to both laypeople and professionals who are concerned about paraphilic fantasies and behavior include those of the Association for the Treatment of Sexual Abusers (*www.atsa.com*), the National Center for Sexual Addiction and Compulsivity (*www.ncsac.org*), the Safer Society (*www.safersociety.org*), the National Sexual Violence Resource Center (*www.nsvrc.org*), and an organization devoted to helping those with computer-related sexual problems (*www.cybersexual addiction.com*).

Self-Help Treatments

There is some evidence indicating that bibliotherapy produces results similar to those of therapist-led psychotherapy for the mood disorders and some paraphilias (Marrs, 1995; Sbraga, Pickett, & West, 2005). Considering the low rates of entry into psychotherapy and the high levels of difficulty in discussing aberrant sexual behaviors with therapists and strangers, bibliotherapy may provide an effective and more consumer-acceptable set of interventions for the paraphilias.

The Sex Addiction Workbook (Sbraga & O'Donohue, 2004) addresses compulsive and paraphilic sexual behaviors, using empirically supported techniques to address the treatment needs delineated above. The client works at his or her own pace. There have been reports to its authors that this workbook is being used successfully in sex offender treatment groups as well. It has been evaluated with both nonoffender and incarcerated offender populations; preliminary results indicate effect sizes equivalent to or better than those for traditional therapist-led treatments for both groups in reducing out-of-control sexual behavior (Sbraga et al., 2005).

Effective Therapist-Based Treatments

Group

There are no known effective group treatments for any type of paraphilia NOS.

Individual

Telephone scatalogia has been treated from the behavioral, psychodynamic, and psycho-pharmacological perspectives. Alford and colleagues (1980) discussed the successful treatment of a male with a 1-year history of scatalogia and a 4-year history of exhibitionism with covert sensitization—a cognitive-behavioral intervention that involves imagining the paraphilic situation and introducing a highly aversive thought at the point of highest sexual arousal to the scenario, so that arousal is diminished. Obscene telephone calling was eliminated and exhibitionism reduced through the use of this intervention. Moergen, Merkel, and Brown (1990) also used covert sensitization in combination with social skills training in their treatment of a scatologist. They found reduced arousal to the calls, decreased social anxiety, and improved social behavior that was sustained for a year. Goldberg and Wise (1985), on the other hand, used a psychodynamic approach in twice-weekly treatment sessions over the course of a year. Their focus was on the obscene caller's dependency and masochism. They reported that the calls were eliminated after 1 year, and that the client's depression was diminished as well. According to the authors, there was no other symptom substitution following this intervention (Goldberg & Wise, 1985). Lastly, a scatologist was treated with buspirone and supportive psychotherapy by Pearson, Marshall, Barbaree, and Southmayd (1992). They reported that the client's urges to make calls and expose himself diminished significantly and were maintained at a 30-month follow-up.

McNally and Lukach (1991) treated a man with mild mental retardation who engaged in masturbation behaviors in the presence of dogs. They employed masturbatory satiation, covert sensitization, and contingency management procedures for 6 months. They reported that the client's rated interest in his most exciting scenario dropped from 10 to 0 after 15 sessions of satiation, and that his arousal to nondeviant scenes increased from 5 to 10 after 12 sessions, according to his self-report. Psychoeducation regarding the dangers of ingesting certain substances also made an impact in a case of urophilia and a case of oral partialism (Denson, 1982; McGuire et al., 1998).

Treatment of the paraphilia NOS will benefit from attention to interventions with the greatest empirical support in producing change in the major symptom categories in the better studied paraphilias. These categories include decreasing deviant sexual arousal, increasing more normative sexual arousal and behavior, decreasing associated mental health problems (e.g., mood and cognitive disturbances), changing social skills deficits, improving motivation, and addressing developmental issues in the sexual history. Deviant arousal may be addressed through several interventions, including covert sensitization, aversion therapy, contingency management techniques, verbal and physiological satiation strategies, and cognitive restructuring (Quinsey & Earls, 1990). Interventions with demonstrated efficacy in increasing more normative sexual behavior include various cognitive-behavioral interventions: systematic desensitization for social anxiety about attempting to develop more normative human relationships; cognitive restructuring to decrease distorted, negative, or irrational thoughts that may be affecting social/sexual relationships and to increase useful thoughts; and orgasmic reconditioning (Quinsey & Earls, 1990; Wincze, 1989). All of the interventions mentioned above are described in detail elsewhere in this volume.

Many of the mental health issues that are highly comorbid with the paraphilias, including depression and anxiety, may be effectively addressed through cognitive-behavioral techniques. Examples include exposure therapy for different types of anxiety, cognitive therapy for depression, and behavioral activation for depression. Cognitive-behavioral therapy with a relapse prevention component appears effective in the treatment of associated substance abuse problems as well (Brunswig, Sbraga, & Harris, 2003). Social skills training has demonstrated efficacy in improving normative social relationships for people whose social history has been found lacking (McFall, 1990). Motivational interviewing techniques have been shown to be useful in getting and keeping people into psychotherapy (Miller & Rollnick, 2002). Finally, developmental issues centering around sexuality may be addressed through psychoeducation regarding human sexuality and sexual norms. Psychodynamic techniques have been reported useful in resolving early childhood sexual development issues (Goldberg & Wise, 1985).

Effective Medical Treatments

Medical interventions aimed at decreasing sexual drive have been used for a number of years, with varying results. These have included chemical and surgical castration, neurosurgery, and pharmacological approaches. Surgical castration and neurosurgery aim to reduce the sexual drive and its associated behavioral expressions. Both interventions are currently unpopular—the former because, even though it is precise and essentially eradicates the sex drive, it has tremendous potential to be used to punish people with paraphilic behavior; and the latter because it is imprecise and may destroy useful aspects of human brain functioning (Gijs & Gooren, 1996; Rösler & Witztum, 2000).

Hormone-focused pharmacology and psychotropic medications have also been employed to alter deviant sexual behavior. Early hormonal interventions included the use of antiandrogens, including cyproterone acetate and medroxyprogesterone acetate. These drugs reduce sexual responding; however, they do not have a selective impact on deviant sexual arousal (Rösler & Witztum, 2000). They have also been accompanied by a variety of side effects (including depression, dry mouth, and weight gain), making it unlikely that clients will stay on the drugs for the extended period of time needed to continue to manage the behavior (Bradford, 2000). More recently, another hormonal intervention has been tested with more promising results. Long-acting gonadotropin-releasing hormone (GnRH) agonists have been tested in reducing unwanted sexual behavior. Studies have indicated that GnRH agonists have fewer side effects; that they may be administered effectively via injection every 1–3 months, increasing compliance; and that the effects are reversible (Briken, Nika, & Berner, 2001; Rösler & Witztum, 2000). Rösler and Witztum (2000) suggest that GnRH agonists and psychotherapy may be an effective combination treatment for exhibitionism and voyeurism, two behaviors that have been found to be comorbid with various types of paraphilia NOS. However, Thibaut, Cordier, and Kuhn (1996) caution that the pharmacological intervention may need to be extensive—perhaps a minimum of 4 years in duration.

Another pharmacological approach has capitalized on the sexual side effects of a variety of psychotropic medications, including fluoxetine, sertraline, fluvoxamine, clomipramine, and paroxetine (Clayton, 1993; Greenburg, Bradford, Curry, & O'Rourke, 1996). Along with a presumed direct impact on sexual desire and arousal, it has been hypothesized that they have an impact on sexual behavior as a symptom of obsessive–compulsive disorder (Abouesch & Clayton, 1999). Coleman, Gratzer, Nesvacil, and Raymond (2000) tested this idea with nefazodone and found that the intervention resulted in reduced sexual obsessions and compulsive behaviors, with fewer sexual desire and arousal side effects (which are important to increasing appropriate sexual behavior). Bradford (2000) reviewed the effectiveness of the selective serotonin reuptake inhibitors (SSRIs) in reducing sexual thoughts, urges, and masturbatory behaviors in patients with paraphilia diagnoses. According to Bradford, SSRIs seem to be most effective with sexual behaviors that appear to have core affective bases. Findings regarding the use of the SSRIs in treating paraphilic behaviors should be viewed with caution, however, as these are early days for this vein of investigation. Many studies have not used the double-blind approaches, large sample sizes, placebo controls, and long follow-up periods that would firmly establish their effectiveness and safety (Hill, Briken, Kraus, Strohm, & Berner, 2003).

Treatment Selection

Treatment selection should be linked to demonstrated effectiveness in altering the causal and maintaining factors of the problem(s) for the individual (i.e., the probability that the intervention will work), as well as to consumer acceptability. Toward these ends, it is recommended that the assessor use his or her data to determine these factors and to employ a combination of treatment approaches with the best support in changing the specific components that are relevant for the individual, whether these are physiological, affective, cognitive, behavioral, or contextual. For the rarer paraphilias in particular, the relevant variables seem highly individualistic, requiring an idiographic approach to assessment and treatment.

Research Priorities

In addition to the research priorities described for an assessment agenda for the paraphilia NOS disorders, one further element would advance the treatment literature. The use of single-case design methodology may be of great importance to a subfield of study in which the focal behaviors or constellations of behaviors are presumed to be rare. For example, in the absence of an identifiable group of necrophilic individuals who would participate in a treatment development and outcome study, it becomes imperative to conduct every experimental treatment of such a person from a hypothesis-testing standpoint and to gather data systematically on the interventions and outcomes. Knowledge gleaned from these cases, whether from one clinical scientist or preferably many in succession, could advance the collective knowledge of what works and does not work with these types of problems. This is dependent on there being a venue for sharing single-case information. Many journals have been adverse to publishing such information in the past, citing lack of scientific rigor and utility; only the strongly psychoanalytic and behavioral journals have consistently supported this type of research. However, use of formal single-case design methods across cases would provide strong and useful data for those who find themselves treating these problems. A call for a peer-reviewed single-case design publication pertaining to the lesser-known paraphilias seems appropriate—perhaps in conjunction with a more informal approach, such as a common website or listserv where treatment providers could share and compile results over time.

FUTURE DIRECTIONS

Since the first edition of *Sexual Deviance* was published, several articles have addressed whether or not the paraphilia category is appropriate either at all, or in its current form, in a diagnostic manual for psychopathology (Karasic & Drescher, 2005; Lehne & Money, 2003; Moser & Kleinplatz, 2005). Moser and Kleinplatz (2005) evaluated the paraphilia category according to the DSM-IV-TR definition of a mental disorder (American Psychiatric Association, 2000). The category was reviewed on a number of dimensions, including its logic, its consistency, its clarity, and the facts used to support its claims. The authors concluded that the category did not fulfill the DSM criteria, that the veracity of information included as fact was questionable, and consequently that the category should be removed from the next edition.

A related issue is that of the high comorbidity of paraphilic diagnoses. Lehne and Money (2003) argued that using a parsimonious taxonomy, rather than assigning multiple paraphilic codes, would capture various forms of a true disorder. They observed that the underlying process may present in different ways throughout the lifespan. As a result, they argued for the inclusion of a multiplex paraphilia diagnosis that would be given when multiple paraphilias are present in an individual.

Finally, whether the diagnostic manual is truly capturing the variety of unusual sexual behaviors is an issue addressed by Kafka and Prentky's research (Kafka, 1995; Kafka & Prentky, 1994, 1998) on sexual desire problems and paraphilia-related disorders, which are not currently clearly included in the taxonomy. The current paraphilia category addresses only the form and decline of sexual behavior, ignoring what appear to be non-normative, an above-average frequency, intensity, impulsivity, and novelty seeking in sexual behavior that cannot be categorized clearly as either sexual deviance or sexual dysfunction in the current system.

Understanding the various types of paraphilia NOS better in the coming years will require a broad-ranging research agenda, with one branch firmly entrenched in assessment and treatment utility. These efforts must be supported by a significantly stronger and more cohesive theoretical and taxonomic foundation if they are to make a meaningful impact.

REFERENCES

Abel, G., Becker, J. V., Cunningham-Rathner, J., Mittelman, M., & Rouleau, J. (1988). Multiple paraphilic diagnoses among sex offenders. *Bulletin of the American Academy of Psychiatry and the Law, 16*, 153–168.

Abel, G., Jordan, A., Rouleau, J. L., Emerick, R., Barboza-Whitehead, S., & Osborn, C. (2004). Use of visual reaction time to assess male adolescents who molest children. *Sexual Abuse: A Journal of Research and Treatment, 16,* 255–265.

Abel, G., & Rouleau, J. (1990). The nature and extent of sexual assault. In W. L. Marshall, D. R. Laws, & H. E. Barbaree (Eds.), *Handbook of sexual assault: Issues, theories, and treatment of the offender* (pp. 9–21). New York: Plenum Press.

Abouesch, A., & Clayton, A. (1999). Compulsive voyeurism and exhibitionism: A clinical response to paroxetine. *Archives of Sexual Behavior, 28,* 23–30.

Adams, H. E., & McNulty, R. D. (1993). Sexual disorders. In P. Sutker & H. E. Adams (Eds.), *Comprehensive handbook of psychopathology* (2nd ed., pp. 563–579). New York: Plenum Press.

Alford, G., Webster, J., & Sanders, S. (1980). Covert aversion of two interrelated deviant sexual practices: Obscene telephone calling and exhibitionism. A single case analysis. *Behavior Therapy, 11,* 15–25.

Almansi, R. J. (1979). Scopophilia and object loss. *Psychoanalytic Quarterly, 48,* 601–619.

Alvarez, W. A., & Freinhar, J. P. (1991). A prevalence study of bestiality (zoophilia) in psychiatric in-patients, medical in-patients, and psychiatric staff. *International Journal of Psychosomatics, 38,* 45–47.

American Psychiatric Association. (2000). *Diagnostic and statistical manual of mental disorders* (4th ed., text rev.). Washington, DC: Author.

Barlow, D. H. (2002). *Anxiety and its disorders: The nature and treatment of anxiety and panic* (2nd ed.). New York: Guilford Press.

Beck, A. T., Rush, A. G., Shaw, B. F., & Emery, G. (1979). *Cognitive therapy of depression.* New York: Guilford Press.

Beetz, A. M. (2002). Bestiality/zoophilia: A scarcely investigated phenomenon between crime, paraphilia, and love. *Journal of Forensic Psychology Practice, 4,* 1–36.

Binder, J. L. (2004). *Key competencies in brief dynamic therapy: Clinical practice beyond the manual.* New York: Guilford Press.

Bradford, J., Boulet, J., & Pawlak, A. (1992). The paraphilias: A multiplicity of deviant behaviours. *Canadian Journal of Psychiatry, 37,* 104–108.

Bradford, J. M. W. (2000). The treatment of sexual deviation using a pharmacological approach. *Journal of Sex Research, 37,* 248–257.

Briken, P., Nika, E., & Berner, W. (2001). Treatment of paraphilia with luteinizing hormone-releasing hormone (LHRH): A systematic review. *Journal of Clinical Psychiatry, 27,* 45–55.

Brunswig, K. A., Sbraga, T. P., & Harris, C. D. (2003). Relapse prevention. In W. O'Donohue, J. E. Fisher, & S. C. Hayes (Eds.), *Cognitive behavior therapy: Applying empirically supported techniques in your practice* (pp. 321–329). New York: Wiley.

Burg, B. R. (1982). The sick and the dead: The development of psychological theory on necrophilia from Krafft-Ebing to the present. *Journal of the History of the Behavioral Sciences, 18,* 242–254.

Card, R., & Steinhauser, C. (2002). *Changing me.* Brandon, VT: Safer Society Press.

Cerrone, G. H. (1991). Zoophilia in a rural population: Two case studies. *Journal of Rural Community Psychology, 12,* 29–39.

Clayton, A. H. (1993). Fetishism and clomipramine. *American Journal of Psychiatry, 48,* 730–738.

Coleman, E., Gratzer, T., Nesvacil, L., & Raymond, N. C. (2000). Nefazodone and the treatment of nonparaphilic compulsive sexual behavior: A retrospective study. *Journal of Clinical Psychiatry, 61,* 282–284.

Dalby, J. T. (1988). Is telephone scatalogia a variant of exhibitionism? *International Journal of Offender and Comparative Criminology, 1,* 45–49.

Dawes, R. M., Faust, D., & Meehl, P. E. (2002). Clinical versus actuarial judgment. In T. Gilovich, E. Dale, & D. Kahneman (Eds.), *Heuristics and biases: The psychology of intuitive judgment* (pp. 716–729). New York: Cambridge University Press.

Dekkers, M. (1994). *Dearest pet: On bestiality* (D. Vincent, Trans.). New York: Verso.

Denson, R. (1982). Undinism: The fetishizaton of urine. *Canadian Journal of Psychiatry, 27,* 336–338.

Derogatis, L. R., & Fitzpatrick, M. (2004). The SCL-90-R, the Brief Symptom Inventory (BSI), and the BSI-18. In M. Maruish (Ed.), *The use of psychological testing for treatment planning and outcomes assessment: Vol. 3. Instruments for adults* (3rd ed., pp. 1–41). Mahwah, NJ: Erlbaum.

Donofrio, R. (1996). *Human/animal sexual contact: A descriptive–exploratory study.* Unpublished doctoral dissertation, Institute for the Advanced Study of Human Sexuality, San Francisco.

Earls, C. M., & Lalumière, M. L. (2002). A case study of preferential bestiality (zoophilia). *Sexual Abuse: A Journal of Research and Treatment, 14,* 83–88.

Eldridge, H. (1998). *Maintaining change: A personal relapse prevention manual.* Thousand Oaks, CA: Sage.

Ellis, A. (2003). Cognitive restructuring of the disputing of irrational beliefs. In W. O'Donohue, J. E. Fisher, & S. C. Hayes (Eds.), *Cognitive behavior therapy: Applying empirically supported techniques in your practice* (pp. 79–88). New York: Wiley.

Fedora, O., Reddon, J., Morrison, J., Fedora, S., Pascoe, H., & Yeudall, C. (1992). Sadism and other paraphilias in normal controls and aggressive and non-aggressive sex offenders. *Archives of Sexual Behavior, 21,* 1–15.

Firestone, P., Bradford, J. M., McCoy, M., Greenberg, D. M., Larose, M. R., & Curry, S. (1999). Prediction of recidivism in incest offenders. *Journal of Interpersonal Violence, 14,* 511–531.

Freund, K., Watson, R., & Rienzo, D. (1988). The value of self-reports in the study of voyeurism and exhibitionism. *Annals of Sex Research, 1,* 243–262.

Gebhard, P. H., Gagnon, J. H., Pomeroy, W. B., & Christenson, C. V. (1965). *Sex offenders: An analysis of types.* New York: Harper & Row.

Gijs, L., & Gooren, L. (1996). Hormonal and psychopharmacological interventions in the treatment of paraphilias: An update. *Journal of Sex Research, 33,* 273–290.

Goldberg, R. L., & Wise, T. N. (1985). Psychodynamic treatment for telephone scatalogia. *American Journal of Psychoanalysis, 45,* 291–297.

Gratzer, M. D., & Bradford, J. M. (1995). Offender and offence characteristics of sexual sadists: A comparative study. *Journal of Forensic Sciences, 455,* 450–455.

Greenburg, D. M., Bradford, J. M. W., Curry, S., & O'Rourke, A. B. (1996). A comparison of treatment of the paraphilias with three serotonin reuptake inhibitors: A retrospective study. *Bulletin of the American Academy of Psychiatry and the Law, 24,* 525–532.

Hare, R. D. (1991). *The Hare Psychopathy Checklist—Revised.* Toronto: Multi-Health Systems.

Hare, R. D., & Neumann, C. S. (2006). The PCL-R assessment of psychopathy: Development, structural properties, and new directions. In C. J. Patrick (Ed.), *Handbook of psychopathy* (pp. 58–88). New York: Guilford Press.

Harris, G. T., & Rice, M. E. (1997). Risk appraisal and management of violent behavior. *Psychiatric Services, 48,* 1168–1176.

Harris, G. T., Rice, M. E., & Camilleri, J. A. (2004). Applying a forensic actuarial assessment (the Violence Risk Assessment Guide) to nonforensic patients. *Journal of Interpersonal Violence, 19,* 1063–1074.

Hill, A., Briken, P., Kraus, C., Strohm, K., & Berner, W. (2003). Differential pharmacological treatment of paraphilias and sex offenders. *International Journal of Offender Therapy and Comparative Criminology, 47,* 407–421.

Hoyer, J., Kunst, H., & Schmidt, A. (2001). Social phobia as a comorbid condition in sex offenders with paraphila or impulse control disorder. *Journal of Nervous and Mental Disease, 189,* 463–470.

Hunt, M. (1974). *Sexual behavior in the 1970s.* Chicago: Playboy Press.

Hyde, J. S., & DeLamater, J. D. (2006). *Understanding human sexuality* (9th ed.). Boston: McGraw-Hill.

Kafka, M. P. (1995). Sexual impulsivity. In E. Hollander & D. Stein (Eds.), *Impulsivity and aggression* (pp. 201–228). New York: Wiley.

Kafka, M. P., & Prentky, R. A. (1994). Preliminary observations of DSM-III-R Axis I comorbidity in men with paraphilias and paraphilia-related disorders. *Journal of Clinical Psychiatry, 55*, 481–487.

Kafka, M. P., & Prentky, R. A. (1998). Attention-deficit/hyperactivity disorder in males with paraphilias and paraphilia-related disorders: A comorbidity study. *Journal of Clinical Psychiatry, 59*, 388–396.

Kalichman, S. C., Henderson, M. C., Shealy, L. S., & Dwyer, M. S. (1992). Psychometric properties of the Multiphasic Sex Inventory in assessing sex offenders. *Criminal Justice and Behavior, 19*, 384–396.

Kalmus, E., & Beech, A. R. (2005). Forensic assessment of sexual interest: A review. *Aggression and Violent Behavior, 10*, 193–217.

Karasic, D., & Drescher, J. (2005). Introduction: Sexual and gender diagnoses of the *Diagnostic and Statistical Manual* (DSM): A reevaluation. *Journal of Psychology and Human Sexuality, 17*, 1–5.

Kentsmith, D., & Datsani, J. (1974). Obscene telephone calling by an exhibitionist during therapy: A case report. *International Journal of Group Therapy, 24*, 352–357.

Kinsey, A. C., Pomeroy, W. B., & Martin, C. E. (1948). *Sexual behavior in the human male*. Philadelphia: Saunders.

Kinsey, A. C., Pomeroy, W. B., Martin, C. E., & Gebhard, P. H. (1953). *Sexual behavior in the human female*. Philadelphia: Saunders.

Knight, R., Prentky, R., & Cerce, D. (1994). The development, reliability, and validity of an inventory for the multidimensional assessment of sex and aggression. *Criminal Justice and Behavior, 21*, 72–94.

Langevin, R., & Paitich, D. (2002). *Clarke Sex History Questionnaire for Males—Revised*. Toronto: MHS.

Lawrence, A. A. (2004). Autogynephilia: A Paraphilic model of gender identity disorder. In U. Leli & J. Drescher (Eds.), *Transgender subjectivities: A clinician's guide* (pp. 69–87). New York: Haworth Press.

Laws, D. R., & Gress, C. L. (2004). Seeing things differently: The viewing time alternative to penile plethysmography. *Law and Criminal Psychology, 9*, 183–196.

Lehne, G. K., & Money, J. (2003). Multiplex versus multiple taxonomy of paraphilia: Case example. *Sexual Abuse: A Journal of Research and Treatment, 15*, 61–72.

Loza, W., & Dhaliwal, G. K. (1997). Psychometric evaluation of the Risk Appraisal Guide (RAG): A tool for assessing violent recidivism. *Journal of Interpersonal Violence, 12*, 779–793.

Malamuth, N. M. (1989a). The Attraction to Sexual Aggression Scale: I. *Journal of Sex Research, 26*, 26–49.

Malamuth, N. M. (1989b). The Attraction to Sexual Aggression Scale: II. *Journal of Sex Research, 26*, 324–354.

Marrs, R. (1995). A meta-analysis of bibliotherapy studies. *American Journal of Community Psychology, 23*, 843–870.

Marshall, W. L., & Hall, G. C. N. (1995). The value of the MMPI in deciding forensic issues in accused sex offenders. *Sexual Abuse: A Journal of Research and Treatment, 7*, 205–219.

Martell, C. R. (2003). Behavioral activation treatment for depression. In W. O'Donohue, J. E. Fisher, & S. C. Hayes (Eds.), *Cognitive behavior therapy: Applying empirically supported techniques in your practice* (pp. 28–32). New York: Wiley.

Masters, W., Johnson, V., & Kolodny, R. (1982). *Human sexuality*. Boston: Little, Brown.

Masters, W., & Lea, E. (1963). *Sex crimes in history: Evolving concepts of sadism, lust-murders, and necrophilia from ancient to modern times*. New York: Julian Press.

McFall, R. M. (1990). The enhancement of social skills. In W. L. Marshall, D. R. Laws, & H. E. Barbaree (Eds.), *Handbook of sexual assault: Issues, theories, and treatment of the offender* (pp. 311–330). New York: Plenum Press.

McGuire, B. E., Choon, G. L., Nayer, P., & Sanders, J. (1998). An unusual paraphilia: Case report of oral partialism. *Sexual and Marital Therapy, 13*, 207–210.

McNally, R. J., & Lukach, B. M. (1991). Behavioral treatment of zoophilic exhibitionism. *Journal of Behavior Therapy and Experimental Psychiatry, 22*, 281–284.

Miletski, H. (2000). Bestiality/zoophilia: An exploratory study. *Scandinavian Journal of Sexology, 3*, 149–150.

Miletski, H. (2002). *Understanding bestiality/zoophilia*. Bethesda, MD: Author.

Miller, W. R., & Rollnick, S. (2002). *Motivational interviewing (2nd ed.): Preparing people for change*. New York: Guilford Press.

Moergen, S. A., Merkel, W. T., & Brown, S. (1990). The use of covert sensitization and social skills training in the treatment of an obscene telephone caller. *Journal of Behavior Therapy and Experimental Psychiatry, 21*, 269–275.

Moser, C., & Kleinplatz, P. J. (2005). DSM-IV-TR and the paraphilias: An argument for removal. *Journal of Psychology and Human Sexuality, 17*, 91–109.

Neuman, R. J., Sitdhiraksa, N., Reich, W., Ji, T. H. C., Joyner, C. A., Sun, L., et al. (2005). Estimation of prevalence of DSM-IV and latent class-defined ADHD subtypes in a population-based sample of child and adolescent twins. *Twin Research and Human Genetics, 8*, 392–401.

Nichols, H., & Molinder, I. (1984). *Multiphasic Sex Inventory*. Fircrest, WA: Nichols & Molinder Assessment.

Nichols, H., & Molinder, I. (1996). *Multiphasic Sex Inventory II*. Fircrest, WA: Nichols & Molinder Assessments.

O'Donohue, W., & Letourneau, E. (1993). The psychometric properties of the penile tumescence assessment of child molesters. *Journal of Psychopathology and Behavioral Assessment, 14*, 123–174.

O'Donohue, W., Letourneau, E., & Dowling, H. (1997). The measurement of sexual fantasy. *Sexual Abuse: A Journal of Research and Treatment, 12*, 167–178.

Pakhomou, S. M. (2006). Methodological aspects of telephone scatalogia: A case study. *International Journal of Law and Psychiatry, 29*, 178–185.

Pearson, H. J., Marshall, W. L., Barbaree, H. E., & Southmayd, S. (1992). Treatment of a compulsive paraphiliac with buspirone. *Annals of Sex Research, 5*, 239–246.

Penix, T. M., & Suraweera, D. (2007). Sexual dysfunction and deviation. In M. Hersen & J. C. Thomas (Eds.), *Handbook of clinical interviewing with adults* (pp. 317–339). Thousand Oaks, CA: Sage.

Price, M., Kafka, M., Commons, M. L., Gutheil, T. G., & Simpson, W. (2002). Telephone scatalogia comorbidity with other paraphilias and paraphilia-related disorders. *International Journal of Law and Psychiatry, 25*, 37–49.

Quinsey, V. L., & Earls, C. M. (1990). The modification of sexual preferences. In W. L. Marshall, D. R. Laws, & H. E. Barbaree (Eds.), *Handbook of sexual assault: Issues, theories, and treatment of the offender* (pp. 279–295). New York: Plenum Press.

Quinsey, V. L., Harris, G. T., Rice, M. E., & Cormier, C. A. (1998). *Violent offenders: Appraising and managing risk*. Washington, DC: American Psychological Association.

Ressler, R. K., Burgess, A. W., Hartmann, C. R., Douglas, J. E., & McCormack, A. (1986). Murderers who rape and mutilate. *Journal of Interpersonal Violence, 1*, 273–287.

Rösler, A., & Witztum, E. (2000). Pharmacotherapy of the paraphilias in the next millennium. *Behavioral Sciences and the Law, 18*, 43–56.

Rosman, J., & Resnick, P. (1989). Sexual attraction to corpses: A psychiatric review of necrophilia. *Bulletin of the American Academy of Psychiatry and the Law, 17*, 153–163.

Salekin, R. T., Rogers, R., & Sewell, K. W. (1996). A review and meta-analysis of the Psychopathy Checklist and the Psychopathy Checklist—Revised: Predictive validity of dangerousness. *Clinical Psychology: Science and Practice, 3*, 203–215.

Sbraga, T. P., & O'Donohue, W. (2004). *The sex addiction workbook: Proven strategies to help you regain control of your life*. Oakland, CA: New Harbinger.

Sbraga, T. P., Pickett, L., & West, A. (2005, October). *Cognitive-behavioral bibliotherapy for sex of-*

fenders: Minimalist intervention, maximum impact. Paper presented at the annual meeting of the Association for the Treatment of Sexual Abusers, Salt Lake City, UT.

Schewe, P. A. (1997). Paraphilia NOS: Assessment and treatment. In D. R. Laws & W. O'Donohue (Eds.), *Sexual deviance: Theory, assessment, and treatment* (pp. 424–433). New York: Guilford Press.

Shenken, L. (1960). Psychotherapy in a case of bestiality. *American Journal of Psychotherapy, 14,* 728–740.

Skinner, L. J., & Becker, J. V. (1985). Sexual dysfunctions and deviations. In M. Hersen & S. M. Turner (Eds.), *Diagnostic interviewing* (pp. 211–239). New York: Plenum Press.

Smith, P., & Waterman, M. (2005). Processing bias for sexual material: The emotional Stroop and sex offenders. *Sexual Abuse: A Journal of Research and Treatment, 16,* 163–171.

Steen, C. (2000). *The adult relapse prevention workbook.* Brandon, VT: Safer Society Press.

Stekel, W. (1952) *Patterns of psychosexual infantilism.* New York: Liveright.

Thibaut, F., Cordier, B., & Kuhn, J. (1996). Gonadotropin hormone releasing hormone agonist in a case of severe paraphilia: A lifetime treatment? *Psychoneuroendocrinology, 21,* 411–419.

Tollison, C. D., & Adams, H. E. (1979). *Sexual disorders: Treatment, theory, research.* New York: Gardner Press.

Trimble, J. F. (1969). *Female bestiality.* Torrance, CA: Monogram.

Williams, C. J., & Weinberg, M. S. (2003). Zoophilia in men: A study of sexual interest in animals. *Archives of Sexual Behavior, 32,* 523–536.

Wincze, J. P. (1989). Assessment and treatment of atypical sexual behavior. In S. R. Leiblum & R. C. Rosen (Eds.), *Principles and practice of sex therapy* (2nd ed., pp. 382–404). New York: Guilford Press.

Wolpe, J. (1990). *The practice of behavior therapy* (4th ed.). New York: Pergamon Press.

CHAPTER 24

ONLINE SEX OFFENDING

Psychopathology and Theory

ETHEL QUAYLE

DESCRIPTION

Unlike other paraphilias, online sexual offending does not have a set of agreed-upon diagnostic criteria outlined by the *Diagnostic and Statistical Manual of Mental Disorders* (DSM), or any other categorical model. Instead, we are largely limited by what such offenders are observed to do in relation to the Internet. This includes downloading illegal images from the Internet (which are largely, but not exclusively, pornographic pictures of children[1]); trading or exchanging such images with others; producing images through photographing children or modifying existing images; and engaging in the solicitation or seduction of children.

The use of behaviors as diagnostic categories is not without problems. For example, in relation to downloading images from the Internet, how many images need to be downloaded, displaying what kind of activity and over what period of time, for the behavior to be considered pathological? This is not a trivial question, as it would appear that searching the Internet to find illegal images is increasingly common (e.g., Demetriou & Silke, 2003). This raises the issue as to whether casual searching should be seen as problematic in itself (i.e., as indicative of some aberrant sexual interest in children), or whether alternatively, for example, it should be viewed as resulting from the draw of the taboo (Adler, 2001). Similar definitional problems are also experienced with reference to trading images, as this does not specify volume, duration, or the number of people who have to be involved. In the context of the Internet, trading of images may take place through a small, private channel, or extensively through peer-to-peer networks where the various players remain largely unknown to each other. Even in defining the production of child pornography, how do we categorize images that are not illegal (children in a swimming pool or at a beach), or where images are produced commercially? In this instance, the photographer (or printer), though clearly committing a criminal offense, may have no necessary sexual interest in children and is motivated by money.

What is also problematic is how far our criteria for pathological behavior are intertwined with legal perspectives. This is a particularly difficult issue in relation to the Internet, because the Internet has no geographical boundaries. Of the 184 Interpol member countries, 95 have no legislation at all that specifically addresses child pornography, and 41 countries do not criminalize possession of child pornography, regardless of intent to distribute (International Centre for Missing and Exploited Children [ICMEC], 2006). This means, for example, that the production and distribution of child pornography in Thailand are not illegal (and concomitantly presumably are not seen as pathological), whereas in the United States these activities are illegal and will probably be seen as pathological. Problems like this in relation to legislation are not new. Antipornography laws were repealed in Denmark in 1969 and in Sweden in 1971; this resulted in a booming trade in child pornography, with the appearance of material in the media and in ordinary shops (Schuijer & Rossen, 1992). Such decriminalization of child pornography, and the subsequent ease of both its production and distribution, arguably resulted in the depathologizing of some interests and behaviors—or at least in a decoupling of some assumptions about the relationship between the nature of sexual interest in children and the notion of sexual harm.

DIAGNOSTIC CRITERIA

Internet sex offenders are often called pedophiles (Durkin, 1997); however, the DSM-IV-TR (American Psychiatric Association, 2000) criteria used to diagnose pedophilia have been criticized (Fisher, Ward, & Beech, 2006; Studer & Aylwin, 2006), and it has been argued that the category adds little to our understanding of patients beyond describing their behavior. Studer and Aylwin (2006) suggest that the pedophilia diagnosis actually subsumes a "continuum" of sexual responses rather than dichotomous or exclusive groups, and that it would be better to interpret pedophilia strictly as a behavioral disorder. They conclude that the criteria are too broad to allow for any meaningful discrimination between child molesters and pedophiles, and too narrow in cases where arousal by adult–child sex is ego-syntonic and not acted upon—a more relevant point with the huge increase in child pornography available on the Internet.

It is with these criticisms in mind (see also Roche & Quayle, in press) that we turn our attention to the diagnosis of *online* sexual offending. One factor that distinguishes this form of sexual offending from other forms is that it leaves an evidential trail in the form of text and pictures; in behavioral terms, there is a permanent product. Furthermore, the picture content may reveal a producer's sexual behavior with a child, or it may reflect sexual fantasies through downloading images, with no contact with the child or children in the photographs.

On a cautionary note, the empirical research on Internet offending is sparse and precludes profound conclusions about the long-term course of the behavior(s). Table 24.1 is an attempt to categorize online offending behaviors, although it should be kept in mind that these categories may not be mutually exclusive; they do not include, for example, incitement of others to commit online or offline offenses against children (Gallagher, Fraser, Christmann, & Hodgson, 2006).

TABLE 24.1. Potential Diagnostic Criteria for Online Sexual Offending

A. Downloading child pornography from the Internet
  1. Content of images (i.e., images of people under the age of 18, regardless of the age of sexual consent in the country of origin or the country of access; ICMEC, 2006). Preferential content can be subdivided by predominant gender, predominant age, predominant racial group, and predominant activities.
  2. Intensity of behavior (i.e., confirmation that it is purposeful rather than accidental). This may be assessed by the volume of images, the duration of activity, the frequency of activity, and the duration of sessions.
  3. Number of Internet behaviors/applications used (see Carr, 2004; O'Brien & Webster, in press), which may include email; websites; peer-to-peer networks; newsgroups; Internet relay chat (IRC); Internet chat queue (ICQ); chat rooms; social networking sites; the storage medium used; the nature of image organization and cataloguing; and electronic attempts to hide activities.
  4. Self-report evidence of sexual preoccupation, with reference to the frequency of masturbation to images and text.

B. Trading or exchange of child pornography
  1. Protocols used to effect image exchange, which may include email, websites, peer-to-peer networks, newsgroups, IRC, ICQ, chat rooms, and social networking sites.
  2. Exclusivity of exchange, evidenced through private networks or public fora.
  3. Intensity of behavior, assessed through the volume of images traded, the duration of activity, and the frequency of activity.
  4. Evidence of social engagement, online or offline.

C. Production of child pornography
  1. The content of images (as above).
  2. The nature of the photographer's relationship with child/children in the images: parental role, other family member's role, other position of trust, or stranger.
  3. The level of a child's engagement with the process of image taking (see Taylor & Quayle, 2005): hidden photographs; as part of abuse of child (without child's knowledge of being photographed); as part of abuse of child (with child's knowledge of being photographed); or as part of abuse of child with child's knowledge of being photographed and engagement in activity of production and/or trading.
  4. Intensity of the behavior, assessed through the number of children involved, over what period of time, and the number of images produced.
  5. Number of Internet behaviors/applications (as above).

D. Child seduction/grooming through the Internet
  1. Internet protocols used (as above).
  2. Age(s) of child(ren).
  3. Gender(s) of child(ren).
  4. Intensity of behavior, evidenced by the number of children contacted, the duration of activity, and the frequency of activity.
  5. Relationship with child: parental role, other family member's role, other position of trust, or stranger.
  6. Online activities: befriending/grooming to gain the trust of a child; cybersex with compliant victim restricted to online activity; or aggressive solicitation.
  7. Offline activities: contacting child by phone/texting; writing to child/sending gifts; arranging to meet child without sexual activity taking place; or arranging to meet child with sexual activity taking place.

AGE AT ONSET

Age at onset of Internet offending is almost impossible to quantify, given that the majority of offenders will (like the rest of the population) have acquired access to the Internet and the skills to use it within the last few years. The data from the New Zealand Censorship Compliance Unit (Sullivan, 2005) suggest that online offending activity may start during teenage years, but that access to the Internet can be associated with the onset of offending in any age group. A complicating issue relates to the need to learn typing and computer skills before using the Internet; there may be age-related factors in such skills acquisition.

PREVALENCE AND INCIDENCE

We have no idea of the numbers of people who offend on the Internet. We can examine conviction rates, but these are only available from countries where possession and distribution of child pornography are both illegal and where there are either the resources or inclination to act upon detection. In the United States, Wolak, Mitchell, and Finkelhor (2003) reported that law enforcement agencies made an estimated 2,577 arrests during 12 months (starting July 1, 2000) for Internet sex crimes against minors. These crimes were categorized into three mutually exclusive types: Internet crimes against identified victims (39%); Internet solicitations to undercover law enforcement officers (25%); and possession, distribution, or trading of child pornography with no identified victim (36%). Two-thirds of offenders who committed any of the types of Internet sex crimes against minors possessed child pornography, with 83% of these possessing images of children between the ages of 6 and 12, and 80% having images explicitly showing sexual penetration of minors.

Finkelhor and Ormrod (2004) examined child pornography patterns from the FBI's National Incident-Based Reporting System. The data from 1997 to 2000 on 2,469 crime incidents involving pornography revealed that over these 3 years pornography offenses increased by 68% and juvenile victim/child exploitation pornography offenses increased 200%. But at the time of this report, only a small minority of all pornography offenses known to the police were coded as involving a computer.

However, these statistics reflect only those who are caught. Other data, such as those provided by one leading U.K. Internet service provider, suggested that this provider blocks more than 35,000 attempts per day to access child pornography on the Internet (BBC News, 2006). However, such attempts were easy to block, because the material requested was from known sources. More difficult is material that is produced with a perfectly valid reason, but that is used by others in a problematic way. A good example of this is provided by Lehmann, Cohen, and Kim (2006) in relation to the detection and management of pornography seeking in an online clinical dermatology atlas. During the study period, one-third of the search queries related to anatomical sites, and over half specified children.

Our own unpublished data from CROGA, a self-help website for people experiencing difficulties in relation to child pornography (*www.croga.org*), indicate that there were 8,684 users of the site between June 2004 and April 2006. Similarly, in the United Kingdom, the statistics from the Stop It Now! organization suggested that between 2002 and 2005, 45% of calls to its help line were from people experiencing problems in relation to their own behavior—a significant number of whom were using, or feeling a compulsion to use, the Internet (Stop It Now! UK & Ireland, 2006).

RISK

There is little understanding of what risks online several offenders may pose. Although the discussion that follows is not exhaustive, it may serve to illustrate some of the challenges in this area. Much of what we know is derived from police operations, case studies, and unpublished anecdotal material. Any difficulties are compounded by the different kinds of populations used (e.g., prison vs. community); the time frames for data collection (more recent accounts would suggest a greater current availability of illegal images of children—through, e.g., peer-to-peer networks); the ways in which the data are gathered (telephone interviews, self-report questionnaires, reconviction rates); and the lack of longitudinal data. Research in this area is also confounded by the fact that new technologies constantly evolve, and the arena for offending thus continually changes. A good example of this relates to the emergence of the mobile Internet. However, we might start to conceptualize risk in the following ways.

The Risk of Becoming an Internet Offender

To date, the Internet remains a largely uncontrolled and unmoderated medium, and although a few years ago most practitioners and researchers in the area of sexual offending would have seen child pornography as being effortful to come by, this is not the case today—in spite of increased legislation and a vast investment by law enforcement agencies in policing activity on the Internet.

Can exposure (either purposeful or accidental) to child pornography on the Internet therefore be a catalyst for the appearance of problems? There are a number of clinical case studies (e.g., Quayle, Holland, Linehan, & Taylor, 2000) in which offenders convicted of downloading child pornography appeared to have no prior history of sexual interest, fantasy, or behavior in relation to children. Galbreath, Berlin, and Sawyer (2002) have suggested that clinicians may encounter a number of cases where the presence of the Internet itself seems to have been the primary impetus for paraphilic behaviour. Within a psychoanalytical framework, Wood (2007) has presented a coherent and articulate argument about apparent "new behavior" in relation to the Internet. She suggests that the Internet may "fan the flames" of something that might otherwise have remained smoldering within the psyche.

The concept that accidental or purposive exposure to materials may have an impact on future behavior is of concern in relation not only to adults, but also to young people (Quayle & Taylor, 2006). Other authors have highlighted the accidental exposure of young people to unwanted sexual material on the Internet (e.g., Cameron et al., 2005). Ybarra and Mitchell (2005) have indicated that those young people who report intentional exposure to pornography are also more likely to report delinquent behavior and substance use in the previous year, along with clinical features of depression and lower levels of emotional bonding with caregivers. Similarly, in one of the first studies of adolescent Internet offenders, Moultrie (2006) found that within a sample of seven young people, two had also engaged in contact offenses and five reported sexual arousal to the images of children that they had viewed.

The Risk of Committing a Similar Offense

A later section of this chapter examines some of the theoretical models that have been used in relation to online sexual offending. Possibly the most compelling (at least at face value) of these models lies within the "addiction" framework (e.g., Carnes, Murray, & Charpentier, 2005; Delmonico, 2005); this framework helps to explain why Internet offenders are commonly observed to go back online, sometimes even after they have been caught and are awaiting conviction. However, another explanation may relate to the function that online activity has for a person—in simple terms, what "needs" this activity appears to be meeting. It may seem very obvious that the function is largely a sexual one: People download images of children because they are sexually arousing and because they can masturbate to them. However, it does not explain why they need to go on engaging in risk-taking behavior when they have already secured material that possibly matches their unique sexual scripts and that can be used to fuel fantasy and arousal. In a qualitative analysis of interviews with 13 men who had been convicted of various offenses related to online child pornography, we (Quayle & Taylor, 2002a) suggested that such behavior may in fact have multiple possible functions: as an aid to arousal and masturbation; as a collecting activity; as a way of facilitating social relationships; as a way of avoiding "real life"; and, on occasion, as a form of self-administered "therapy." If the online activity is meeting needs that either cannot be met elsewhere, or can no longer be met as the behavior begins to replace other (offline) activities or social supports, then it is not surprising that there should be a strong compulsion to go back online.

Webb, Craissati, and Keen's (2006) study would appear to add some support to this view. Their comparative study of Internet offenders and child molesters indicated that the former were significantly less likely to fail in the community. Although the numbers of Internet offenders who failed in the community and reoffended were small, the analysis indicated that these individuals fitted into two subgroups that posed a risk of repeated Internet offending, but not necessarily an escalation to contact sex offending.

The Risk of Escalating to a Further Category of Internet Offending

Although there has been very little empirical research in this area, case studies from within a variety of theoretical frameworks do suggest clearly that for some online offenders, their behavior is not static, but shows escalation or movement through a process (Quayle et al., 2000; Sullivan & Beech, 2004; Wood, 2007). We (Quayle & Taylor, 2003) have generated a model of problematic Internet use, which examines the role of cognitions and contextual cues that facilitate offending. We realized in developing the model that such offending is a dynamic rather than a static process, with individuals moving along a range of continua related to satiation of sexual arousal, processes of engagement with both collecting and online communities, and the exploration of different online personas. The process may also include movement through nonoffending activities, such as accessing other, legal forms of pornography. A previous history of contact offenses, personal circumstances, and opportunity also appear to be critical elements. However, on a cautionary note, what is often referred to as "cybersex" (Alapack, Blichfeldt, & Elden, 2005) is a major part of many people's experience of the Internet, and for some this experience may well have problematic qualities, in addition to (or regardless of) any *specifically* child-focused issues.

The Risk of Committing a Contact Offense against a Child

The question of whether online sexual offending increases the risk of contact sexual offending against children is currently posing grave concerns for practitioners working in the area of risk assessment. Yet, again, there is very little to inform judgments about which Internet offenders may also pose a risk to children within an offline environment, and much of the research that has examined the relationship between viewing pornography and committing contact offenses predates the Internet. Marshall (2000) suggested that there is not a causal link between viewing pornography and sexually offending behavior, but that it can accelerate psychological processes, enhancing the cognitive distortions of offenders. Seto, Maric, and Barbaree (2001) also felt that the evidence for a causal link between pornography use and sexual offending remains equivocal, and concluded that people who are already predisposed to offend are the most likely to show an effect of pornography exposure. Men who are not predisposed to offend are unlikely to show an effect, and if there is an effect it is likely to be transient. However, Sullivan (2005) expressed concern that within an Internet sample, the number of offenders who had committed sexual offenses was greater than that found in the general population. In addition, recent research by Seto and Eke (2005) examined the criminal histories and later offending activities of child pornography offenders. Of 201 adult males who were child pornography offenders, those with prior criminal records were significantly more likely to offend again in the same way during the follow-up period, and those who had committed a prior or concurrent sexual offense were the most likely to offend again, either generally or sexually. However, it is not clear from this study how many of the offenders had used the Internet to access child pornography. Finkelhor and Ormrod (2004) found only a modest association of general pornography crimes with child victimization. However, Wolak, Finkelhor, and Mitchell's (2005) study of child pornography possessors arrested in Internet-related crimes indicated that 40% of their sample were "dual offenders" who sexually victimized children and possessed child pornography. Galbreath and colleagues' (2002) data from 39 Internet offenders indicated that 24% had actually attempted to meet a minor for sex.

One of the difficulties in making comparisons between studies relates to the populations themselves. This is aptly illustrated by O'Brien and Webster (in press), who have described the construction, and preliminary validation, of a measure of the attitudes and behaviors of convicted men whose offenses related to online child pornography. The pilot stage of the study involved 40 men who were in prison, whereas phase 2, the validation of an improved version of the scale, included men who were in prison and those whose offense had warranted a community sentence. The data analysis indicated clear demographic differences between the two samples. The men included in phase 1 were likely to be older, were more likely to have been arrested as part of a "ring," and were described as possibly a more "deviant group" than those in phase 2. It may be that as the Internet has become more available to a larger group of people, and has facilitated access to child pornography, we are more likely to see the convictions of people who appear similar to the general population. A recent study by Middleton, Elliot, Mandeville-Norden, and Beech (2006) found that almost half of their sample did not display above-average scores on any of the standard psychometric measures, suggesting a population of offenders who do not exhibit the psychological vulnerabilities typically displayed by other sex offenders.

As previously mentioned, the relationship between online sexual offending and the diagnostic category of pedophilia is a contentious one. An interesting and challenging study by Seto, Cantor, and Blanchard (2006) investigated whether being charged with a child pornography offense was a valid diagnostic indicator of pedophilia, as represented by an index of phallometrically assessed sexual arousal to children. Their results indicated that child pornography offenders had almost three times greater odds of being phallometrically identified as pedophiles than offenders against children had. Seto and colleagues suggested that child pornography offending is a stronger diagnostic indicator of pedophilia than is sexual offending against child victims. However, such a conclusion poses problems for us: How do we make sense of the many thousands of people who seem to be accessing child pornography every day? Do we conclude from this that our understanding of the number of people who may be classified as pedophiles is a gross underestimate of the prevalence within the general population? Another possible, or at least partial, explanation for the results of this important study may lie in the nature of the stimuli themselves. That is, for men who have spent long periods downloading and accessing child pornographic images and masturbating to ejaculation to them, the visual stimuli themselves are highly salient—perhaps more so than for men who use private fantasies or actual children as the focus of their arousal.

OTHER DEMOGRAPHIC CHARACTERISTICS

Although the population of online sexual offenders is largely described as heterogeneous (Taylor & Quayle, 2003), there are some striking demographic consistencies between study samples. The most notable of these relates to gender. Wolak and colleagues (2003, 2005), in their study of Internet crimes against minors, reported that 99% of their sample was male. This is similar to the findings of other studies (Finkelhor & Ormrod, 2004; Seto & Eke, 2005; Sullivan, 2005; Webb et al., 2006). From a different perspective, Mitchell, Becker-Blease, and Finkelhor (2005) conducted a national survey of 1,504 U.S. mental health practitioners on social and psychological problems associated with the Internet; 63% of their clients with such problems were male.

Ethnicity appears to be another common characteristic, with the majority of offenders being of European descent (O'Brien & Webster, in press; Sullivan, 2005; Wolak et al., 2003, 2005). Webb and colleagues (2006) indicated that their 90 Internet offenders were predominantly white—an apparent difference from their child molester sample, which represented a greater mix of ethnicities. This raises an interesting issue about sexually abusive practices and ethnicity, and whether these offender characteristics are the results of sociodemographic patterns of Internet use, or whether they reflect actual differences in ethnicity and pornography use. These ethnic patterns are also reflected in the availability of child pornography by ethnic group. An analysis of the Combating Paedophile Information Networks in Europe (COPINE) archive in 2003 indicated that the majority of images available were of children of European and Asian descent, with very few children of African descent (Taylor & Quayle, 2005). Similarly, Carr's (2004) study, which was one of the few to analyze the images used by offenders, indicated that the vast majority of offenders selected material portraying children of European and Asian descent. It is clearly unknown whether this will change as Internet availability and uptake increase in other countries. Indeed, in 2003, the COPINE archive showed that websites had started advertising specialist sites that included interracial pictures.

A further demographic variable of interest is to age, and here there is less consensus. In Wolak and colleagues' (2003) study, of the 2,577 arrests made for Internet sex crimes against minors, 14% were age 25 years or under, 45% were between 26 and 39 years of age, and 41% were over age 40. Wolak and colleagues' (2005) analysis of those who had possessed child pornography indicated that 45% were age 40 or older. This is similar to other reported samples (Middleton et al., 2006; O'Brien & Webster, in press; Webb et al., 2006), although the age range in these samples was quite wide. However, the data gathered by the New Zealand Censorship Compliance Unit appeared very different (Sullivan, 2005). Of the 201 cases in its most recent analysis, the largest single age group was 15–19 years, which accounted for 24.32% of all offenders. Over half were under the age of 30 at the time of the investigation, with an age range of 14–67 years.

Other demographic factors, such as occupation, level of education, and experience in Internet use, are equally mixed across populations. As would be expected given the age distribution of the New Zealand sample, students were the largest occupational group; two-thirds of these were studying at tertiary level, and 37.5% of the tertiary-level group were studying subjects related to information technology. Within this sample as a whole, the second largest group consisted of those working in information technology. Wolak and colleagues (2005) indicated that 73% of their population was in full-time employment, with the majority (82%) having an income greater than $20,000 (in U.S. dollars). Similarly, in O'Brien and Webster's (in press) sample, just over half had received tertiary-level education, and 75.5% were in full-time occupations. Unlike the New Zealand group, this latter study indicated that 92.6% had not received any formal training in Internet use. Certainly, to date, only gender and ethnicity are common factors across all populations.

COMORBIDITY

There is little information about comorbidity of other disorders with online sexual offending. Webb and colleagues (2006) compared Internet offenders with child molesters from probation caseloads across the greater London (U.K.) area. Over an 8-month period, 210 offenders were assessed (90 of whom were Internet offenders). Both groups had experienced substantial levels of childhood difficulties, although child molesters were more likely to have been physically abused. A significantly higher number of Internet offenders had been in contact with the mental health services as adults, and had had significantly fewer live-in relationships. On the Hare Psychopathy Checklist—Revised, child molesters scored higher than Internet offenders, although the latter were reported as having significantly more problems with "sexual self-regulation" than child molesters. The Millon Clinical Multiaxial Inventory–III was used to examine personality and mental health, and no significant differences were found between child molesters and Internet offenders, although child molesters scored higher on the social desirability scale.

In this study, 65% of Internet offenders had had one life event or more in the 12 months prior to their arrest (related to financial difficulties, social issues, personal health problems, or sexual difficulties). Both groups presented with a more schizoid, avoidant, and dependent profile, which the authors felt was suggestive of either individuals who retreat from interpersonal and social situations (sometimes fearing rejection and cutting themselves off emotionally), or individuals who place excessive reliance on their relationships with others in order to be able to cope.

Webb and colleagues (2006) concluded that there may be different types of Internet offender groups, as suggested by their analysis. These results are interesting, and this study was the first to examine specific personality and mental health variables; however, the population was relatively small in each of the groups, and it will be important to see whether these results hold across a larger and more diverse sample.

ASSOCIATED JUVENILE OR DEVELOPMENTAL ISSUES

Establishing the degree of influence that pornography and related sexual media can have on sexual violence, sexual attitudes, moral values, and sexual activity among children and young people is complex. A study by Emerick and Dutton (1993) indicated that 80% of adolescent sexual offenders acknowledged the use of pornography for stimulation, and that the number of female child victims increased progressively with the severity of the pornography used as a stimulus for masturbation. Similarly, studies by Zolondek, Abel, Northey, and Jordan (2001) and by Ford and Linney (1995) found an elevated use of pornographic materials among young people engaged in sexually abusive behavior. However, other research (O'Reilly et al., 1998) showed no differences in pornography use (magazines, films, and sex phone lines) between youth who engaged in sexually abusive behavior and those who did not.

Burton and Meezan (2005) have recently suggested that pornography may be a medium for learning sexually abusive behavior, and that orgasm resulting from pornography use reinforces cognitive rehearsals of sexual behaviors or aggression generated from memories of sexual victimization. The masturbatory fantasies that are stimulated by pornography thus lead to cognitive distortions about sex, possible sexual partners, or potential partners for sexually aggressive behaviors. Clearly the results obtained by the New Zealand Censorship Compliance Unit would give cause for concern in relation to this, given the large number of students in their sample.

FORENSIC ISSUES

Electronic Evidence

It is important to note that for the majority of Internet offenders, forensic analysis of their computers and software will provide much of the information needed to assist in expert witness testimony (Tanner, 2005). Tanner also emphasizes the importance of what he terms "TRAPS" information (themes, ratio, amount, pace, and sessions), all of which are included in the criteria listed in Table 24.1. Ferraro, Casey, and McGrath (2005) give helpful guidelines about U.S. law and investigation of child exploitation and pornography on the Internet.

Risk Assessment Tools

To date, there are no risk assessment tools that have been designed solely for use with Internet offenders, although Middleton and colleagues (2006) used the Risk Matrix 2000 Schedule with their sample. O'Brien and Webster's (in press) Internet Behaviours and Attitudes Questionnaire (IBAQ) was also able to discriminate between groups of offenders, and was able to associate Internet-related behaviors with deviance.

Objective Measures of Image Content

Outside of high-tech crime units, the majority of people working in the area of Internet offending may never have seen child pornographic images from the Internet (Quayle & Taylor, 2002b). In part, this is because legislation in many countries criminalizes possession of such images. However, this can result in a difficult situation where communication among professionals (e.g., the police, child protection workers, and the judiciary) becomes problematic, and highly subjective terms are used to describe the content of the images held by an individual. To deal with this difficulty, we (Taylor, Holland, & Quayle, 2001) developed a typology of Internet child pornography images for the COPINE organization, based on an analysis of publicly available images obtained from newsgroups and websites. The COPINE scale is presented in Table 24.2.

In 2002, in England and Wales, the Sentencing Advisory Panel (SAP) published its advice to the Court of Appeal on offenses involving child pornography. The SAP believed that the nature of the material should be the key factor in deciding the level of sentence, and condensed the COPINE scale from the 10 levels shown in Table 24.2 to 5 levels. It dropped levels 1 to 3 completely, arguing that nakedness alone is not indicative of indecency. The proposed structure was therefore that COPINE levels 5 to 6 should constitute sentencing level 1, and that COPINE levels from 7 onward should each constitute an individual sentencing stage (Gillespie, 2003). These levels are under revision again at this writing, and it is likely that further minor changes may be made.

The use of such an objective measure increases the likelihood of consistency across sentencing without necessitating that all involved should have had to view the images, and the COPINE scale is increasingly being used in countries outside England and Wales (Cooper, 2006). One difficulty, however, is that while the typology was created as an indicator of how children are victimized through Internet child pornography, it is increasingly being used by the courts as an indicator of the seriousness of the offense, or even the dangerousness of the offender. The latter is problematic, in that there is little evidence to indicate whether, for example, viewing images of children sexually engaged with animals is more likely than viewing images of children who are clothed to increase the risk of a contact offense. However, a meta-analysis of recidivism studies by Hanson and Morton-Bourgon (2005) did suggest that sexual recidivism was associated with two broad factors: deviant sexual interests and antisocial orientation. Deviant sexual interests were indicated through an enduring attraction to sexual acts that are illegal (e.g., sex with children or rape) or highly unusual (e.g., fetishism and autoerotic asphyxia). These factors may be of relevance in relation to Internet offenses, but this has yet to be confirmed.

Internet Protocols and Behaviors

In our description of an online trading network, we (Taylor & Quayle, 2005) suggested that risk might usefully be conceptualized as being at least in part related to the Internet protocols used by an offender. As the individual engages more with the Internet and its deviant social groups, so the risk of engaging in more deviant cognitions, feelings, and behaviors increases. This has been given empirical support by O'Brien and Webster (in press), who analyzed the distribution of Internet behaviors into low- and high-risk groups. Engaging in certain behaviors (e.g., accessing images via less common technologies; the trade of images; and habitual behaviors related to viewing, categorization, and masturbation) was associated with a greater level of Internet-related offense "deviance." In a similar vein, Wolak and colleagues (2005) suggested that those Internet offenders who had organized child pornography collections were more likely to have over 1,000 images, to possess moving images, to have child pornography in noncomputerized formats, to have images of children younger than 6, to have sophisticated computer systems, and to possess methods to store or hide images. They also noted, however, that these people were not more or less likely to have sexually victimized children than were other child

TABLE 24.2. The COPINE Scale

- *Level 1: Indicative*. Nonerotic and nonsexualized pictures showing children in their underwear, swimming costumes, etc., from either commercial sources or family albums; pictures of children playing in normal settings, in which the context or organization of pictures by the collector indicates inappropriateness.
- *Level 2: Nudist*. Pictures of naked or seminaked children in appropriate nudist settings, and from legitimate sources.
- *Level 3: Erotica*. Surreptitiously taken photographs of children in play areas or other safe environments, showing either underwear or varying degrees of nakedness.
- *Level 4: Posing*. Deliberately posed pictures of children fully clothed, partially clothed, or naked (where the amount, context, and organization suggest sexual interest).
- *Level 5: Erotic posing*. Deliberately posed pictures of fully clothed, partially clothed, or naked children in sexualized or provocative poses.
- *Level 6: Explicit erotic posing*. Pictures emphasizing the genital area of a child who is either naked, partially clothed, or fully clothed.
- *Level 7: Explicit sexual activity*. Pictures involving touching, mutual or self-masturbation, oral sex, or intercourse by a child, but not involving an adult.
- *Level 8: Assault*. Pictures of children being subjected to a sexual assault, involving digital touching, and involving an adult.
- *Level 9: Gross assault*. Grossly obscene pictures of sexual assault, involving penetrative sex, masturbation or oral sex, and involving an adult.
- *Level 10: Sadistic/bestiality*. (a) Pictures showing a child being tied, bound, beaten, whipped, or otherwise subjected to something that implies pain; (b) pictures where an animal is involved in some form of sexual behavior with a child.

pornography possessors. A difficulty here is that skill in computer use and the nature and degree of computer access may have been contaminating factors.

Pseudoimages

One final forensic issue of concern relates to "pseudoimages" (digitally altered images). Gillespie (2003) has raised important issues about how greatly an image has to be altered from its original to constitute a pseudoimage, possession of which in England and Wales is likely to attract a lower sentence. In the United States, the constitutionality of virtual child pornography remains a critical issue. In *Ashcroft v. Free Speech Coalition* (2002), a majority of the U.S. Supreme Court struck down portions of the Child Pornography Prevention Act of 1996, stating that criminalization of virtual child pornography created without real or identifiable minors was unconstitutionally overbroad. However, the number of children who have been identified in relation to Internet child pornography remains small. For example, of the thousands of images in the Interpol-managed database, it was estimated in April 2005 that just 320 children have ever been located (Muir, 2005).

THEORY

Hypersexual Disorder

Stein, Black, Shapira, and Spitzer (2001) presented a single clinical case study of a man whose experience of depression was associated with increased use of the Internet. He spent several hours per day searching for particular pornographic images and experiencing feelings of loss of control. This Internet use also reduced his productivity at work. The case history does not describe an Internet offender as such, but it does raise interesting questions about the relationship among pornographic material, excessive masturbation, and depressed mood, as well as the difficulties in diagnosis. Over time, this man's Internet searches became more focused on looking for particular types of pornography. Finding the "right picture" might take several hours, but once he found it, he would masturbate. The authors felt that this was behavior reminiscent of obsessive–compulsive disorder, but there was no evidence of any other anxiety disorder. At follow-up 12 months later, this man was still making excessive use of pornography when work was stressful or when he felt lonely.

Stein and colleagues (2001) proposed the term "hypersexual disorder," supported by the fact that the total sexual outlet (number of sexual behaviors in a week that culminate in orgasm) is relatively high in this group. Also in keeping with DSM, they tentatively generated diagnostic criteria distinguishing hypersexual disorder from behavior that is symptomatic of another disorder, as well as normal behavior. This is where the terms "hypersexual disorder" and "online sexual offending" diverge: They suggested that the former should consist of excessive preoccupation with nonparaphilic sexually arousing fantasies, urges, or excessive sexual behaviors over a notable length of time (e.g., 6 months).

In the context of the Internet, it is becoming more difficult to make assumptions about what the "normal" content and frequency of sexual activity are (Delmonico, 2004). Online sexual activity of any kind, for some people, increases the overall amount of orgasmic activity. If we also look at content, we can see that the Internet has brought with it a change in the nature of pornographic material (more extreme and portraying more nonconsensual sex), as well as in its availability.

Emotional Avoidance

The observation that some people use sexual activity to cope with difficult emotional situations is not a recent one, nor is it confined to Internet sexual behavior (Quayle, Vaughan, & Taylor, 2006; Shepherd & Edelmann, 2005). The literature pertaining to the relationship between affect/emotions and sex offending was reviewed by Howells, Day, and Wright (2004), who found that studies on anger and sexual arousal, offense pathways studies, and sexual fantasy studies provided substantial empirical support for the relationship between affect and offending. However, while Howells and colleagues (2004) have suggested that it is relatively easy to explain why some emotions (such as anger) may result in sexual aggression, it is less clear why other emotions (such as anxiety and sadness) should elicit deviant sexual behavior. One explanation comes from the work of Marshall and Marshall (2000), who examined affective states and coping behavior. These authors proposed that when in a state of negative affect, sex offenders are more likely to use sexual behaviors as a means of coping than are nonoffenders. Sex becomes a way of resolving nonsexual problems, which Howells and colleagues have suggested is reinforced and learned precisely because it is effective in reducing a state of negative affect. LoPiccolo (1994) has suggested that in all such cases, the individual is displacing his emotional distress onto sexually deviant acting out. However, one criticism of using a model that focuses on function, rather than a traditional categorical model, is that emotional avoidance may be one of many functional categories and does not account for all the cases where emotional avoidance is not an issue. More importantly, emotional avoidance may be the functional property of many topographically dissimilar behaviors—but it does not tell us why the use of Internet pornographic images of children should be chosen, as opposed to any other behaviors. One model that has been proposed that may account from this relates to the work of Ward and Siegert (2002) and their pathways model of sexual offending.

Pathways Model

Middleton and colleagues (2006) have examined the applicability of the pathways model of child sexual abuse to online sexual offending. Their version of this model identifies five etiological pathways, each with primary psychological deficits, that interact to create a vulnerability to sexually offending behavior. Ward and Siegert (2002) postulated that these dysfunctional mechanisms are initially caused and then influenced by learning events, as well as by biological and cultural factors—all of which can exert both a proximal and a distal influence on behavior. The original model proposes four core mechanisms that correspond to those suggested in previous theories. These are intimacy and social skill deficits, distorted sexual scripts, emotional dysregulation, and antisocial cognitions. Middleton and colleagues included a final pathway (multiple dysfunctional mechanisms), which describes those who have developed distorted sexual scripts, coinciding with dysfunctions in all of the other primary psychological mechanisms. They predicted that this group was likely to exhibit a multitude of offending behaviors and to constitute "pure pedophiles."

The applicability of this model was tested on 72 cases, drawn from a community sample in England and Wales, via the analysis of primary and associated psychometric indicators of pathway membership. Of those men who could be assigned to the pathways, the majority were in either the intimacy deficits pathway (35%) or the emotional dysregulation pathway (33%). Within the sample, there did not appear to be high levels of cognitive distortions and/or emotional congruence with children. In this respect, these results are different from those of O'Brien and Webster (in press) using the IBAQ.

Middleton and colleagues (2006) concluded that those included in the intimacy deficits pathway may be attracted to the Internet at times of loneliness and dissatisfaction to create a pseudointimacy, due to their low estimates of how effective they would be in initiating and maintaining intimacy in more appropriate adult relationships. Internet child pornography is therefore used as a maladaptive strategy to avoid their perceived likelihood of failure with adult relationships. They hypothesized that their second largest group—those in the emotional dysregulation pathway—may experience strong negative mood states that result in a lack of control, which, in conjunction with sexual desire, can lead those individuals to seek contact with children to meet their sexual needs. Sex is used as a self-soothing strategy, to alleviate negative emotions and to increase feelings of wellbeing. This behavior is externalized as "loss of control," allowing them to conclude that they are not responsible for their offending.

When Ward and Siegert (2002) published their original study, they acknowledged that the model needed "further fleshing out" and was still provisional in nature. Other studies, such as that by Connolly (2004), have also experienced some difficulty in allocating non-Internet-related offenders to the model, and in Middleton and colleagues' (2006) study almost half of the sample could not be assigned to any of the five etiological pathways. Further work is needed in this area, possibly using measures that are more sensitive to the behaviors and distortions shown by this heterogeneous group of offenders. Nonetheless, these results show congruence with the two earlier theoretical models, indicating that a proportion of offenders may be using Internet child pornography to deal with difficult emotions—albeit in an inappropriate way, which at times is associated with subjective loss of control.

Addiction Model

A dominant theory concerning problematic Internet use is that of addiction. Kandell (1998) defined "Internet addiction" as an increasing investment of a person's resources in Internet-related activities; unpleasant feelings (e.g., anxiety, depression, emptiness) when the person is offline; an increasing tolerance to the effects of being online; and denial of the problematic behaviors. Such a perspective characterizes Internet addiction as behavioral and as similar in character to other impulse control disorders. Those who meet the criteria are thought to experience social, psychological, and occupational impairment.

Beard and Wolf (2001) were critical of the term "addiction," and raised questions about what it actually is that people are addicted to: "Is it the computer? Is it the typing? Is it the information gained? Is it the anonymity? Is it the types of activity in which the individual is engaged? All of these factors may play a role in making the Internet reinforcing" (p. 381). Song, LaRose, Eastin, and Lin (2004) have suggested that in fact some online activities may fulfill both process and content gratifications.

Internet addiction has been associated with depressed feelings and work-related stress (Widyanto & McMurran, 2004) and with elevated levels of loneliness, depressed mood, and compulsivity (Delmonico & Miller, 2003). Li and Chung (2006) concluded that a social function was the key function of the Internet within their student sample and led to the most severe Internet addiction. However, students are probably more likely to use the Internet and other new technologies to communicate with each other and to socialize than other population samples. In contrast, Meerkerk, Vanden Eijnden, and Garretsen (2006) have suggested that using the Internet for sexual gratification should be regarded as the most important risk factor for the development of compulsive or problematic Internet use. Chaney and Chang (2005), in the context of men who have sex with men, looked at the relationship among boredom proneness, Internet addiction, and compulsive behavior. They suggested that a constant cycle of experiencing boredom, engaging in online sexual stimulation, and the temporary relief of boredom allows online sexual behavior to be positively reinforced. This is accompanied by online dissociation (a disturbance in consciousness, memory, identity, or perception of one's environment); the use of the Internet to express sexual behavior may possibly increase the likelihood of such dissociative experiences. This suggestion may be of relevence to Internet offending.

Carnes and colleagues (2005) have described sex addiction as part of a larger phenomenon, and discussed the fact that many behaviors can become addictive by drawing on the concept of "flow," a state when people are at their very best. The perversion of flow can happen with any activity that requires focus; almost any activity can become addictive in the sense that instead of being a conscious choice, it becomes a necessity that interferes with other activities, leaving the individual captive of a certain kind of order. Carnes and colleagues present a compelling explanation of replacement, ritualizing, and novelty-seeking behaviors that will have a resonance for those working with Internet offenders. Their argument also aptly illustrates how the very architecture of the Internet affords opportunities for offending activities (see also Taylor & Quayle, 2006).

Psychodynamic Model

Wood (2007) has been critical of the addiction model, arguing that it can be used defensively by patients and clinicians alike to turn a "blind eye" to the meaning of the behaviors, and specifically to their perverse aspects. The addiction model is further criticized because it attributes the omnipotence associated with the Internet to the pornography itself, which is then seen as an irresistible drug. Wood has suggested that the question we really need to ask in the context of Internet offenders is this: What does Internet pornography offer—not only to the conscious mind, but also to the unconscious—that makes it compelling, and what is it about some individuals that makes them so vulnerable to this?

Wood's theory draws on a number of case histories from the Portman Clinic in the United Kingdom and describes the similarities between addictions and perversions from within a psychodynamic framework, including "the manic high," escalation of "dosage," and the illusion of an object relationship. However, she also describes the differences between compulsive use of virtual sex and drug addiction. The first of these relates to the fact that one feature of virtual sexual activity is the creation of a scenario loaded with meaning, which she describes as a "compelling scenario." Wood (2007) suggests that this scenario often seems to encapsulate specific traumatic experiences and key object relationships from childhood and adolescence.

The second major difference described is the equalization of aggression in perversion with virtual sex functioning to express sadistic impulses toward the object. The Internet may appear to invite a disregard for authority because offenders imagine that there are no witnesses to their actions. The breaching of social boundaries and taboos in the use of child pornography may not be just a side effect of specific sexual preferences, but a vital part of the behavior. Pleasure is shown in transgression of social norms and taboos.

Wood's (2007) contribution to the theory of Internet offending is important. Not only does it help us conceptualize a possible etiology of the disorder, but it examines the factors that both allow the emergence of the behavior and enable its maintenance. One difficulty with this model is that it draws heavily on single-case studies. Although the single-case study is a traditional psychoanalytical approach, it is very different from both the research with vast sample sizes found in the addiction literature, and the evidence-based models that are more commonly found in work on sexual offending. For many researchers and practitioners, the language used within this model is at times obscure and difficult, and yet for many working in this area it will resonate with their experiences of such offenders.

SUMMARY AND FUTURE DIRECTIONS

Generating meaningful conceptual and practical structures to help us understand online sexual offending raises a number of complex issues. Perhaps the greatest problem is the lack of empirical information about basic processes. This suggests that a major investment in gathering information about the current situation would provide at least a clearer factual base from which to develop notions of psychopathology, as well as new theories. However, a fundamental complicating factor is the sense in which a presumed psychological state (the offending activity) is in fact identified from an offense. This factor is not of course unique to this area; it is a problem in relationship to all sexual offending. However, it does mean that the pragmatics of social control, local moral and legal perspectives, and even levels of law enforcement funding complicate data collection and conceptual analysis.

Three other factors can be identified that further complicate analysis. First, the skills necessary to engage effectively with the Internet are not necessarily evenly distributed throughout society; they are influenced both by educational level and by social, cultural, and economic factors. When these factors are taken into account, coming to some understanding of the distribution of, incidence/prevalence of, and potential for Internet offending becomes quite complex. In addition, given that opportunity is a significant factor in any crime analysis, the structural variation in opportunity clearly adds to the practical and conceptual problems of analysis. Finally, technological change has an impact on the nature of Internet interactions and on people's capacity to engage with either other people or images. The context in which Internet offending takes place is therefore also dynamic and constantly changing.

NOTE

1. In Europe, the term "abuse image" is increasingly used to describe what, in law, is usually called "child pornography." A decision has been made to use the term "child pornography" throughout this chapter. However, this does not imply that such pornography is consensual; nor does it take away from the harm done to children by its production and use. Because of the vast predominance of child pornography in online sexual offending, moreover, the focus in this chapter is on behavior involving images of children (rather than adult women, animals, etc.).

REFERENCES

Adler, A. (2001). The perverse law of child pornography. *Columbia Law Review, 209,* 1–101.

Alapack, R., Blichfeldt, M. F., & Elden, A. (2005). Flirting on the Internet and the Hickey: A hermeneutic. *CyberPsychology and Behavior, 8,* 52–61.

American Psychiatric Association. (2000). *Diagnostic and statistical manual of mental disorders* (4th ed., text rev.). Washington, DC: Author.

Ashcroft v. Free Speech Coalition, 535 U.S. 224 (2002).

BBC News. (2006). *How net providers stop child porn.* Retrieved from *news.bbc.co.uk/2/hi/technology/4689386.stm*

Beard, K. W., & Wolf, E. M. (2001). Modification of the proposed diagnostic criteria for Internet addiction. *CyberPsychology and Behavior, 4,* 377–383.

Burton, D. L., & Meezan, W. (2005). Revisiting recent research on social learning theory as an etiological proposition for sexually abusive male adolescents. In M. Calder (Ed.), *Children and young people who sexually abuse: New theory, research and practice developments* (pp. 74–96). Lyme Regis, UK: Russell House.

Cameron, K. A., Salazar, L. F., Bernhardt, J. M., Burgess-Whitman, N., Wingood, G. M., & DiClemente, R. J. (2005). Adolescents' experience with sex on the Web: Results from online focus groups. *Journal of Adolescence, 28,* 535–540.

Carnes, P. J., Murray, R. E., & Charpentier, L. (2005). Bargains with chaos: Sex addicts and addiction interaction disorder. *Sexual Addiction and Compulsivity, 12,* 79–120.

Carr, A. (2004). *Internet traders of child pornography and other censorship offenders in New Zealand.* Wellington: New Zealand Department of Internal Affairs.

Chaney, M. P., & Chang, C. Y. (2005). A trio of turmoil for Internet sexually addicted men who have sex with men: Boredom proneness, social connectedness, and dissociation. *Sexual Addiction and Compulsivity, 12,* 3–18.

Connolly, M. (2004). Developmental trajectories and sexual offending: An analysis of the pathways model. *Qualitative Social Work, 3*(1), 39–59.

Cooper, S. (2006). Discussion at the Expert Meeting on Children and Young Persons with Abusive and Violent Experiences Connected to Cyberspace: Challenges for Research, Rehabilitation, Prevention and Protection, Allmannana Barnhuset, Satra Bruk, Sweden.

Delmonico, D. L. (2005). Sexual addiction and compulsivity: Watching the field evolve. *Sexual Addiction and Compulsivity, 12,* 1–2.

Delmonico, D. L., & Miller, J. A. (2003). The Internet Sex Screening Test: C comparison of sexual compulsives versus non-compulsives. *Sexual and Relationship Therapy, 18*(3), 261–276.

Demetriou, C., & Silke, A. (2003). A criminological Internet "sting": Experimental evidence of illegal and deviant visits to a website trap. *British Journal of Criminology, 43,* 213–222.

Durkin, K. F. (1997). Misuse of the Internet by pedophiles: Implications for law enforcement and probation practice. *Federal Probation, 61*(3), 14–18.

Emerick, R. L., & Dutton, W. A. (1993). The effect of polygraphy on the self-report of adolescent sexual offenders: Implications for risk assessment. *Annals of Sex Research, 6,* 83–103.

Ferraro, M. M., Casey, E., & McGrath, M. (2005). *Investigating child exploitation and pornography: The Internet, the law and forensic science.* Boston: Elsevier.

Finkelhor, D., & Ormrod, R. (2004). *Child pornography: Patterns from the NIBRS.* Washington, DC: U.S. Department of Justice, Office of Juvenile Justice and Delinquency Prevention.

Fisher, D., Ward, T., & Beech, A. R. (2006). Pedophilia. In J. E. Fisher & W. T. O'Donohue (Eds.), *Practitioner's guide to evidence based psychotherapy* (pp. 531–540). New York: Springer.

Ford, M. E., & Linney, J. A. (1995). Comparative analysis of juvenile sexual offenders, violent nonsexual offenders, and status offenders. *Journal of Interpersonal Violence, 10,* 56–70.

Galbreath, N. W., Berlin, F. S., & Sawyer, D. (2002). Paraphilias and the Internet. In A. Cooper (Ed.), *Sex and the Internet: A guidebook for clinicians* (pp. 187–205). New York: Brunner-Routledge.

Gallagher, B., Fraser, C., Christmann, K., & Hodgson, B. (2006). *International and Internet child sexual abuse and exploitation.* Huddersfield, UK: University of Huddersfield, Centre for Applied Childhood Studies.

Gillespie, A. A. (2003). Sentences for offences involving child pornography. *Criminal Law Review,* pp. 80–92.

Hanson, R. K., & Morton-Bourgon, K. E. (2005). The characteristics of persistent sexual offenders: A meta-analysis of recidivism studies. *Journal of Consulting and Clinical Psychology, 73*(6), 1154–1163.

Howells, K., Day, A., & Wright, S. (2004). Affect, emotions and sex offending. *Psychology, Crime and Law, 10,* 179–195.

International Centre for Missing and Exploited Children (ICMEC). (2006). *Child pornography: Model legislation and global review.* Retrieved from *www.icmec.org/en_X1/pdf/Model LegislationFINAL.pdf*

Kandell, J. J. (1998). Internet addiction on campus: The vulnerability of college students. *Cyber Psychology and Behavior, 1,* 11–17.

Lehmann, C. U., Cohen, B. A., & Kim, G. R. (2006). Detection and management of pornography-seeking in an online clinical dermatology atlas. *Journal of the American Academy of Dermatology, 54*(6), 1123–1137.

Li, S.-M., & Chung, T.-M. (2006). Internet function and Internet addictive behavior. *Computers in Human Behavior, 22,* 1067–1071.

LoPiccolo, J. (1994). Acceptance and broad spectrum treatment of paraphilias. In S. C. Hayes, N. S. Jacobson, V. M. Follette, & M. J. Dougher (Eds.), *Acceptance and change: Content and context in psychotherapy* (pp. 149–170). Reno, NV: Context Press.

Marshall, W. L. (2000). Revisiting the use of pornography by sexual offenders: Implications for theory and practice. *Journal of Sexual Aggression, 6,* 67–77.

Marshall, W. L., & Marshall, L. E. (2000). The origins of sexual offending. *Trauma, Violence and Abuse, 1*, 250–263.

Meerkerk, G.-J., Vanden Eijnden, R. J. J. M., & Garretsen, H. F. L. (2006). Predicting compulsive Internet use: It's all about sex. *CyberPsychology and Behavior, 9*(1), 95–103.

Middleton, D., Elliot, I. A., Mandeville-Norden, R., & Beech, A. (2006). The pathways model and Internet offenders: An investigation into the applicability of the Ward and Siegert pathways model of child sexual abuse with Internet offenders. *Psychology, Crime and Law, 12*(6), 589–603.

Mitchell, K. J., Becker-Blease, K. A., & Finkelhor, D. (2005). Inventory of problematic Internet experiences encountered in clinical practice. *Professional Psychology: Research and Practice, 36*(5) 498–509.

Moultrie, D. (2006). Young people with harmful sexual behaviours: Adolescents convicted of possession of abuse images of children—a new type of adolescent sex offender? *Journal of Sexual Aggression, 12*(2), 165–174.

Muir, D. (2005). *Violence against children in cyberspace.* Bangkok: ECPAT.

O'Brien, M. D., & Webster, S. D. (in press). The construction and preliminary validation of the Internet Behaviours and Attitudes Questionnaire (IBAQ). *Sexual Abuse: A Journal of Research and Treatment.*

O'Reilly, G., Sheridan, A., Carr, A., Cherry, J., Donohoe, E., McGrath, K., et al. (1998). A descriptive study of adolescent sexual offenders in an Irish community-based treatment programme. *Irish Journal of Psychology, 19*(1), 152–167.

Quayle, E., Holland, G., Linehan, C., & Taylor, M. (2000). The Internet and offending behaviour: A case study. *Journal of Sexual Aggression, 6*(1–2), 78–96.

Quayle, E., & Taylor, M. (2002a). Child pornography and the Internet: Perpetuating a cycle of abuse. *Deviant Behavior, 23*(4), 331–362.

Quayle, E., & Taylor, M. (2002b). Paedophiles, pornography and the Internet: Assessment issues. *British Journal of Social Work, 32*, 863–875.

Quayle, E., & Taylor, M. (2003). Model of problematic Internet use in people with a sexual interest in children. *CyberPsychology and Behavior, 6*(1), 93–106.

Quayle, E., & Taylor, M. (2006). Young people who sexually abuse: The role of the new technologies. In M. Erooga & H. Masson (Eds.), *Children and young people who sexually abuse others* (pp. 115–128). London: Routledge.

Quayle, E., Vaughan, M., & Taylor, M. (2006). Sex offenders, Internet child abuse images and emotional avoidance: The importance of values. *Aggression and Violent Behavior, 11*(1), 1–11.

Roche, B., & Quayle, E. (in press). Sexual disorders. In W. S. Woods & J. R. Kantor (Eds.), *Understanding behavior disorders: A contemporary behavioral perspective.* Reno, NV: Context Press.

Schuijer, J., & Rossen, B. (1992). The trade in child pornography. *IPT Journal, 4.* Retrieved from *www.ipt-forensics.com/journal/volume4/j4_2_1.htm*

Seto, M. C., Cantor, J. M., & Blanchard, R. (2006). Child pornography offenses are a valid diagnostic indicator of pedophilia. *Journal of Abnormal Psychology, 115*, 610–615.

Seto, M. C., & Eke, A. (2005). The criminal histories and later offending of child pornography offenders. *Sexual Abuse: A Journal of Research and Treatment, 17*(2), 201–210.

Seto, M. C., Maric, A., & Barbaree, H. E. (2001). The role of pornography in the etiology of sexual aggression. *Aggression and Violent Behavior, 6*, 35–53.

Shepherd, R.-M., & Edelmann, R. J. (2005). Reasons for Internet use and social anxiety. *Personality and Individual Differences, 39*(5), 949–958.

Song, I., LaRose, R., Eastin, M. S., & Lin, C. A. (2004). Internet gratifications and Internet addiction: On the uses and abuses of the new media. *CyberPsychology and Behavior, 7*(4), 384–394.

Stein, D. J., Black, D. W., Shapira, N. A., & Spitzer, R. L. (2001). Hypersexual disorder and preoccupation with Internet pornography. *American Journal of Psychiatry, 158*, 1590–1594.

Stop It Now! UK & Ireland. (2006). *Helpline report.* Retrieved from *www.stopitnow.org.uk/publications.htm*

Studer, L. H., & Aylwin, A. S. (2006). Pedophilia: The problem with diagnosis and limitations of CBT in treatment. *Medical Hypotheses, 67*(4), 774–781.

Sullivan, C. (2005). *Internet traders of child pornography: Profiling research.* Wellington: New Zealand Censorship Compliance Unit.

Sullivan, J., & Beech, A. (2004). Assessing Internet sex offenders. In M. C. Calder (Ed.), *Child sexual abuse and the Internet: Tackling the new frontier* (pp. 69–83). Lyme Regis, UK: Russell House.

Tanner, J. (2005). *Beyond prosecution: Improving computer management of convicted sex offenders.* Retrieved from *www.kbsolutions.com/beyond.pdf*

Taylor, M., Holland, G., & Quayle, E. (2001). Typology of paedophile picture collections. *Police Journal, 74*(2), 97–107.

Taylor, M., & Quayle, E. (2003). *Child pornography: An Internet crime.* New York: Brunner-Routledge.

Taylor, M., & Quayle, E. (2005). Abusive images of children and the Internet: Research from the COPINE Project. In S. W. Cooper, R. J. Estes, A. P. Giardino, N. D. Kellogg, & V. I. Vieth (Eds.), *Medical, legal and social science aspects of child sexual exploitation* (Vol. 1). St. Louis, MO: GW Medical.

Taylor, M., & Quayle, E. (2006). The Internet and abuse images of children: Search, precriminal situations and opportunity. In R. Wortley & S. Smallbone (Eds.), *Crime prevention studies: Vol. 19. Situational prevention of child sexual abuse* (pp. 169–196). Monsey, NY: Criminal Justice Press/Willan.

Ward, T., & Siegert, R. J. (2002). Toward a comprehensive theory of child sexual abuse: A theory knitting perspective. *Psychology, Crime and Law, 8*, 319–351.

Webb, L., Craissati, J., & Keen, S. (2006). *Characteristics of Internet child pornography offenders: A comparison with child molesters. Version 2: Follow up study.* London: Bracton Centre (Oxleas NHS Trust) and London Probation Area.

Widyanto, L., & McMurran, M. (2004). The psychometric properties of the Internet Addiction Test. *CyberPsychology and Behavior, 7*(4) 443–450.

Wolak, J., Finkelhor, D., & Mitchell, K. J. (2005). *Child-pornography possessors arrested in Internet-related crimes: Findings from the National Juvenile Online Victimization Study.* Alexandria, VA: National Center for Missing and Exploited Children.

Wolak, J., Mitchell, K., & Finkelhor, D. (2003). *Internet sex crimes against minors: The response of law enforcement.* Alexandria, VA: National Center for Missing and Exploited Children.

Wood, H. (2007). Compulsive use of virtual sex and Internet pornography: Addiction or perversion? In D. Morgan & S. Ruszczynski (Eds.), *Lectures on violence, perversion and delinquency.* London: Karnac.

Ybarra, M., & Mitchell, K. Y. J. (2005). Exposure to Internet pornography among children and adolescents: A national survey. *CyberPsychology and Behavior, 8*, 473–487.

Zolondek, S., Abel, G., Northey, W., & Jordan, A. (2001). The self-reported behaviors of juvenile sex offenders. *Journal of Interpersonal Violence, 16*(1), 73–85.

CHAPTER 25

ONLINE SEX OFFENDING

Assessment and Treatment

DAVID L. DELMONICO
ELIZABETH J. GRIFFIN

In the early 1970s, the U.S. Department of Defense constructed an electronic network designed to facilitate communication between the world's top military and research institutions. No one imagined that 30 years later this same network would be used for sexual purposes, including sexual crimes against children. The sexual use of the Internet has increased dramatically over the past decade. An estimated 322 million individuals actively use the Internet (Nielsen//NetRatings, 2006), and an estimated 40 million adults admit to regularly visiting pornographic websites (Family Safe Media, 2006). The pornography industry has seized the opportunity to market sex online. An estimated 4.2 million websites generate a profit of approximately $2.5 billion annually (Family Safe Media, 2006). In addition to general adult pornography, there has been increased interest in the possession and dissemination of child abuse images. It is estimated that there are approximately 1 million pornographic images of children on the Internet (Wellard, 2001). The ages of the children depicted in these child abuse images appear younger than ever before, and the types of abuses more serious and graphic in nature (Quayle, Erooga, Wright, Taylor, & Harbinson, 2006). Not only are child abuse images promulgated online, but children are often approached by adults with sexual intent. Finkelhor, Mitchell, and Wolak (2000) reported that nearly 20% of Internet users between the age of 10 and 17 are sexually solicited online by adults they do not know. Statistics are similar in other developed countries. For example, in the United Kingdom, Livingstone and Bober (2005) found that nearly 33% of Internet users under age 18 reported receiving unwanted sexual solicitations from unknown adults. Such statistics also reveal children's increased awareness of the presence of sexual predators in the online world.

Clinicians who treat sex offenders are continually challenged to keep pace with this ever-changing e-world. Most clinicians are faced with both individuals who commit their sex offenses on the Internet, and offline sex offenders who use the Internet to sustain and promote sexual behaviors that may not be illegal but are counterproductive to the therapeutic process. Dealing with all these issues requires special consideration, knowledge, and approaches.

Many existing sex offender treatment programs have failed to acknowledge the relevance of the Internet in the treatment of sex offenders. Those programs that do recognize the Internet as a relevant factor often apply the same methods and techniques utilized for offline offenders. Although there is overlap between online and offline sex offending, there are unique challenges in the assessment and treatment of the "new age" sex offender who either uses the Internet to commit a sexual offense, or uses it to maintain sexually deviant fantasies and behaviors. The purpose of this chapter is to provide clinicians with assessment and treatment guidelines useful in therapeutic work with sex offenders who have access to the Internet. First, however, some comments about basic Internet psychology are in order.

BASIC INTERNET PSYCHOLOGY

Wallace (1999) discussed the "psychology of the Internet" to explain why individuals may behave differently in an online environment versus "real life." As early as the 1980s, theorists noted that the lack of social cues in computer-mediated communications made individuals more self-oriented and less concerned with the feelings and evaluations of others; in turn, their behaviors became less inhibited. More recently, Suler (2004) has defined and described what is termed the "online disinhibition effect." Suler wrote the following about this effect:

> It's well known that people say and do things in cyberspace that they wouldn't ordinarily say or do in the face-to-face world. They loosen up, feel more uninhibited, express themselves more openly. Researchers call this the "disinhibition effect." It's a double-edged sword. Sometimes people share very personal things about themselves. They reveal secret emotions, fears, wishes, or they show unusual acts of kindness and generosity. On the other hand, the disinhibition effect may not be so benign where individuals explore the dark underworld of the internet, places of pornography and violence, places where they would never visit in the real world.
>
> What causes this online disinhibition? What is it about cyberspace that loosens the psychological barriers? Several factors are at play. For some people, one or two of them produces the lion's share of the disinhibition effect. In most cases, though, these factors interact with each other, supplement each other, resulting in a more complex, amplified effect. (p. 323)

The elements of the online disinhibition effect as described by Suler (2004) are summarized below.

• *You don't know me.* This factor is fueled by the layer of anonymity the Internet offers its users. When individuals feel anonymous, they are more inclined to engage in behaviors they would have otherwise never considered.

• *You can't see me.* Although related to anonymity, this factor refers to the feeling of invisibility that Internet users often experience. Because individuals feel as if they are invisible, they therefore believe that their online behavior can neither cause nor receive consequences. The opportunity to be physically invisible amplifies the disinhibition effect.

- *See you later.* The Internet provides a time delay in which individuals can be more thoughtful about their communication, often leading to a deeper expression of thought and feeling. Although this is not a necessarily a negative effect, it is a disinhibited one nonetheless. Another dimension of the "see you later" concept is the fact that when on-line interactions create discomfort, a person can easily escape such situations by exiting the conversation or deleting the text, almost as if it never existed.

- *It's all in my head.* This concept relates to the idea of projection. In the absence of sensory and nonverbal cues, individuals may assign personal attributes to an unknown virtual partner. The line between projected fantasy and reality is blurred, allowing individuals to say or do things they would not consider saying or doing in the real world. At that moment, reality *is* one's imagination.

- *It's just a game.* Individuals often see the virtual world as one in which the rules and norms of everyday offline living are not applicable. Once they turn off the computer and return to their daily routine, they believe that they can leave their online "games" and game identities behind. Internet users may feel that they should not be held responsible for what happens in this make-believe world, which in their minds has nothing to do with reality.

- *We're equals.* A person's status is unknown to others online and may not have the same impact as it does in the face-to-face world. Everyone, regardless of status, wealth, race, gender, age, or other characteristics, starts off on a level playing field. This lack of hierarchy on the Internet has its advantages; however, hierarchies play an important role in our society—including the division between adults and children, which can be easily downplayed in the online world.

Cooper, Delmonico, and Burg (2000) have explained attraction to the Internet as the "triple-A engine." The three A's are "anonymity," "accessibility," and "affordability." Cooper and colleagues believe that these characteristics of the Internet make it far more attractive than other media.

In addition to the disinhibition effect and the triple-A engine, we (Delmonico, Griffin, & Moriarity, 2001) have developed a model known as the "cyberhex." The cyberhex is a six-sided figure, each side of which represents a different facet of the Internet. When the facets are combined, they create a type of "hex" or trance state. These facets include the following: "interactive," "intoxicating," "isolating," "integral," "inexpensive," and "imposing." The Internet is the only communication medium that brings together so many attractive features, and the synergy created through the interaction of the cyberhex facets makes the Internet more seductive than any other medium. The cyberhex model, the online disinhibition effect, the triple-A engine, and the lure and reinforcement of sexuality all make it clear why the Internet is an ideal venue for problematic sexual behavior.

ASSESSMENT

Non-Internet-Related Assessment

The non-Internet-related assessment involves gathering psychological data that do not directly involve Internet behaviors, but that may be related to problematic use of the Internet. Techniques and tools in this part of the assessment include a comprehensive psychosocial/sexual interview, personality assessments, depression and anxiety inventories, attention deficit screening, and screens for other compulsive or addictive behaviors, including a specific assessment for offline sexually compulsive behavior.

The Psychosocial/Sexual History

The psychosocial/sexual history interview is critical to understanding an individual's underlying issues and will help to determine which type of cybersex user the person is (as discussed later in this chapter). Basic information gathered during the basic interview process includes family/childhood history, abuse/trauma history, sexual history, occupational/education history, and social/relational history. This globally focused interview provides significant data that will be combined with the other assessment information to provide a profile of the individual's problematic online behavior.

Personality Inventories

Personality inventories can be useful in determining whether other pathology is present and may be complicating Internet sex behavior. Many long-term Internet sex users present as stable, functional individuals on the surface; however, a more in-depth examination of personality traits may reveal underlying psychological issues. Various personality inventories may be useful in the assessment process. The two inventories most often used in examining personality are the Minnesota Multiphasic Personality Inventory–2 (MMPI-2; Hathaway, McKinley, & Butcher, 1990) and the Millon Clinical Multiaxial Inventory–III (MCMI-III; Millon, Antoni, Millon, Meagher, & Grossman, 2001). These inventories should be administered and interpreted by qualified clinicians. Although there are no data to support the existence of specific personality profiles for problematic online sex users, the results of the MMPI-2 and MCMI-III are often useful in determining states or traits that may be contributing to online sexually deviant behavior.

Depression and Anxiety Inventories

Other factors to assess include depression and anxiety. The literature has failed to show a causal relationship between depression/anxiety and Internet misuse (or vice versa); however, the research has demonstrated a positive relationship between depression/anxiety and Internet use (Young & Rogers, 1998).

Measures of Attention Deficits

The Internet attracts individuals who struggle with attention-related issues. Various instruments are available for screening attentional issues, but caution should be taken to use instruments specifically designed to assess adults with attention-related problems. The Test of Variables of Attention (Greenberg, Corman, & Kindischi, 1996) is one example of such an instrument. The effectiveness of treatment can be greatly reduced if attention deficit issues are not assessed and treated properly.

Addiction or Compulsion Inventories

Problematic online sexual behaviors often exist in the presence of other addictive/compulsive behaviors (Carnes, Delmonico, Griffin, & Moriarity, 2001). A comprehensive assessment should attempt to address the presence of other compulsive or addictive behaviors. Although it is impossible to screen for all such issues, the clinical interview can indicate possible behaviors that may require additional screening. Common co-occurring addictive or compulsive behaviors include offline sexual behavior, gambling, drug use, and eating. Specific attention should be given to the assessment of offline sexually compulsive behavior. If such behavior is not detected and addressed, it can create a frustrating and difficult treatment situation. Basic screening instruments for sexual compulsivity are available to assist in this portion of the assessment, including the Sexual Addiction Screening Test (SAST; Carnes, 1989) and the Kalichman Sexual Compulsivity Scale (Kalichman & Rompa, 2001).

Measures of Sexual Interest and/or Arousal

The assessment of online sex offenders may include physiological measures to determine the individuals' sexual interest and arousal levels. Clinicians should *always* conduct screens of sexual interest and arousal in cases that involve sex and children—including possessing, creating, or distributing child pornography. Two common physiological measures are the Abel Assessment for Sexual Interest or Abel Screen (Abel, Huffman, Warberg, & Holland, 1998), a viewing time procedure, and penile plethysmographic (phallometric) testing, which measures sexual arousal (e.g., Marshall & Fernandez, 2003). An additional method is the Affinity Measure of Sexual Interest (Glasgow, Osborne, & Croxen, 2003). The Affinity Measure combines reports of individuals' rankings and ratings of sexual attractiveness to prototype images with covertly measured viewing times. These tools have numerous advantages and disadvantages, and many states will not permit these types of measures to be used in court cases. However, the benefits of the information gained from these instruments often outweigh the weaknesses associated with them. For example, it cannot be assumed that simply because individuals view or collect child pornography, they are either interested in or aroused by such material. Internet child pornography may serve many possible functions, and measures such as the Abel Screen or phallometric testing will help to distinguish those with true interest in arousal to such material from those who are motivated by other psychological reasons (Quayle, 2004).

Polygraph Assessments

One physiological measure that may be useful early in the assessment process is polygraphy. Hindman and Peters (2001) outline the basic historical and more recent use of polygraphy in the assessment and treatment process of both adult and juvenile sex offenders. A baseline polygraph can both help establish the extent of the sexual offending and suggest future treatment directions. Based on our experience a separate polygraph should be conducted in regard to cybersex use, and that this should not be combined with general questions regarding sexual behavior.

Global Internet Assessment

The Need for Knowledge about the Internet

Lack of technical knowledge puts many clinicians at a significant disadvantage when conducting evaluations of sex offenders who have access to the Internet. Although such clinicians need not become computer experts, it is imperative for them to become familiar with the ways technology can be used for sexual purposes. A client's technological activity needs to be assessed repeatedly throughout treatment, and unless a clinician learns technology basics, the assessment process is futile (Quayle et al., 2006). The World Wide Web is a widely known and used area of the Internet; however, it is only one aspect of the much larger network known as the Internet. Although it is not possible to go into detail about each of the areas included on the Internet, examples include Internet relay chat (IRC), usenet newsgroups, peer-to-peer filesharing networks, fileservers, and more. Clinicians working with individuals who have problematic online behaviors should become sufficiently familiar with these areas to complete an assessment and formulate treatment goals.

In addition to a basic understanding of technology, clinicians must learn to assess all aspects of an offender's Internet use. The following section proposes various instruments to use in conducting a global Internet assessment.

Instrumentation

Few instruments are available to assess an individual's problematic use of the Internet, including sexual offense behavior. Online sex research relies on self-report surveys to determine who engages in online sexual activity, what they do while online, and the impact of their online behavior on themselves and others. Based on this survey research and anecdotal case examples, various screening instruments have been developed to detect online sexual problems (Weiss, 2000; Young, 2006). These instruments may be useful for initial screening; however, most lack empirical validation. One exception to this is the Internet Sex Screening Test (ISST), which has limited empirical validation (Delmonico & Miller, 2003).

Internet Sex Screening Test. The original ISST (Delmonico, 1999) consists of 25 core items and 9 general offline sexual compulsivity items. Delmonico and Miller (2003) reported that factor analysis yielded eight distinct subscales with low to moderate internal consistency reliability (.51–.86). These subscales are reported and defined below.

- *Online Sexual Compulsivity.* This factor measures indicators of compulsive online sexual behavior, including the continuation of online sex despite its offline consequences; repeated efforts to stop online sexual behavior with little or no success; and excessive time spent preparing for, engaging in, or recovering from online sexual experiences.
- *Online Sexual Behavior: Social.* This factor measures online sexual behaviors that occur in the context of a social relationship or involve interpersonal interactions with others while online (e.g., chat rooms, email).
- *Online Sexual Behavior: Isolated.* This factor measures online sexual behaviors that occur in the absence of a social relationship and involve limited interpersonal interaction. Little interest is given to building or maintaining relationships online; rather, the focus is on attaining sexual images or other media (e.g., surfing websites, downloading pornography).
- *Online Sexual Spending.* This factor examines the extent to which subjects spend money to support their online sexual activities, and the consequences associated with such spending.

- *Interest in Online Sexual Behavior.* This factor examines general interest in online sexual behavior, not necessarily interest in negative forms of such behavior. Scores on this factor are high for most individuals who engage in online sexual activities.

- *Non-Home Use of the Computer.* This factor measures the extent to which individuals use a computer outside of their home (e.g., use at work) for sexual purposes. This information may be useful, since such computer use for sexual activity typically increases the risk level of the behavior.

- *Illegal Sexual Use of the Computer.* This factors examines online sexual behaviors that would be considered illegal or borderline illegal sexual activities, including downloading child pornography or exploiting a child online.

The final factor performs a brief screening for offline sexual compulsivity. Delmonico and Miller (2003) found that offline sexually compulsive behavior is an important consideration in assessing online sexual activities. This factor is named General Sexual Compulsivity. Questions on this factor have been adapted from the SAST (Carnes, 1989).

Since 2003, the ISST has undergone significant revisions. Although the original 34-item instrument can still be used for screening purposes, the more comprehensive 117-item Internet Sex Screening Test—Revised (ISST-R) incorporates additional items into the eight subscales for more accurate assessment, and a deception scale has been added to assist in detecting subject responses that may be deliberately misleading. Psychometric data are currently being collected to assess the reliability and validity of the ISST-R. The original ISST (the screening version) is presented in Figure 25.1 and is available in the public domain for use and reproduction. It may also be found in electronic form at our website (*www.internetbehavior.com/sexualdeviance*).

One significant limitation of most screening tests is their reliance on subject self-report. As such, these tests rely on individuals to have a certain degree of psychological insight and honesty—two traits not always common among those with problematic online sexual behavior. Clinicians should keep this caveat in mind when using any self-report screen.

The Internet Assessment: A Structured Interview. Whereas the ISST and ISST-R use a more standardized, empirical method for gathering and interpreting information about clients, there is also a need for a thorough clinical interview regarding a client's online behavior. One such instrument developed for this purpose is the Internet Assessment (Delmonico & Griffin, 2005a). There are two versions of this instrument: the Internet Assessment Quickscreen (IA-Q) and the standard Internet Assessment (IA) (Delmonico & Griffin, 2005a). The IA-Q should be used as an initial interview to determine whether a more in-depth interview is necessary. If such is the case, the full IA can be used. The IA-Q and IA are divided into two sections: (I) Internet Knowledge and Behavior, and (II) Social, Sexual, and Psychological aspects of Internet behavior. In addition, questions on the full IA are identified as belonging to one of six themes:

- *Arousal.* This subscale examines where an individual may go for sexual material online, as well as the content of the online sexual materials or behaviors. These aspects are important to identify sexual themes and arousal templates.

- *Tech-Savvy.* Tech-savvy individuals know how to access online sexual materials efficiently and how to camouflage their online sexual behavior, both of which may increase the complexities during the treatment process.

FIGURE 25.1. Internet Sex Screening Test (ISST; original 34-item version). Document in the public domain.

Directions: Read each statement carefully. If the statement is mostly TRUE, place a check mark on the blank next to the item number. If the statement is mostly FALSE, skip the item and place nothing next to the item number.

____ 1. I have some sexual sites bookmarked.

____ 2. I spend more than 5 hours per week using my computer for sexual pursuits.

____ 3. I have joined sexual sites to gain access to online sexual material.

____ 4. I have purchased sexual products online.

____ 5. I have searched for sexual material through an Internet search tool.

____ 6. I have spent more money for online sexual material than I planned.

____ 7. Internet sex has sometimes interfered with certain aspects of my life.

____ 8. I have participated in sexually related chats.

____ 9. I have a sexualized username or nickname that I use on the Internet.

____10. I have masturbated while on the Internet.

____11. I have accessed sexual sites from other computers besides my home.

____12. No one knows I use my computer for sexual purposes.

____13. I have tried to hide what is on my computer or monitor so others cannot see it.

____14. I have stayed up after midnight to access sexual material online.

____15. I use the Internet to experiment with different aspects of sexuality (e.g., bondage, homosexuality, anal sex, etc.).

____16. I have my own website, which contains some sexual material.

____17. I have made promises to myself to stop using the Internet for sexual purposes.

____18. I sometimes use cybersex as a reward for accomplishing something. (e.g., finishing a project, stressful day, etc.).

____19. When I am unable to access sexual information online, I feel anxious, angry, or disappointed.

____20. I have increased the risks I take online (give out name and phone number, meet people offline, etc.).

____21. I have punished myself when I use the Internet for sexual purposes (e.g., time out from computer, cancel Internet subscription, etc.).

____22. I have met face to face with someone I met online for romantic purposes.

____23. I use sexual humor and innuendo with others while online.

____24. I have run across illegal sexual material while on the Internet.

____25. I believe I am an Internet sex addict.

____26. I repeatedly attempt to stop certain sexual behaviors and fail.

____27. I continue my sexual behavior despite its having caused me problems.

____28. Before my sexual behavior, I want it, but afterwards I regret it.

____29. I have lied often to conceal my sexual behavior.

____30. I believe I am a sex addict.

____31. I worry about people finding out about my sexual behavior.

____32. I have made an effort to quit a certain type of sexual activity and have failed.

____33. I hide some of my sexual behavior from others.

____34. When I have sex, I feel depressed afterwards.

ISST Scoring Directions

1. Sum the number of check marks placed in items 1 through 25. Use the following scale to interpret the final number. Tell the client:

1 to 8 = You may or may not have a problem with your sexual behavior on the Internet. You are in a low-risk group, but if the Internet is causing problems in your life, seek a professional who can conduct further assessment.

9 to 18 = You are at risk for your sexual behavior to interfere with significant areas of your life. If you are concerned about your sexual behavior online, and you have noticed consequences as a result of your online behavior, it is suggested that you seek a professional who can further assess and help you with your concerns.

19 + = You are at highest risk for your behavior to interfere and jeopardize important areas of your life (social, occupational, educational, etc.). It is suggested that you discuss your online sexual behaviors with a professional who can further assess and assist you.

(continued)

FIGURE 25.1. (*continued*)

2. Items 26 through 34 are an abbreviated version of the Sexual Addiction Screening Test (SAST). These items should be reviewed for general sexual addiction behavior, not specifically for cybersex. Although there is no cutoff scores calculated for these items, a high score on items 1 through 25 paired with a high number of items in 26 through 34 should be seen as an even greater risk for sexual acting-out behavior on the Internet.
** Please note: Items 26 through 34 should not be calculated in the total score for part 1.

Note for clinicians: No item alone should be an indicator of problematic behavior. You are looking for a constellation of behaviors, including other data, that may indicate the client is struggling with Internet sexuality. For example, it would not be unusual to have sexual sites bookmarked, or to have searched for something sexual online—but, paired with other behaviors, it may be problematic.

- *Risk.* Assessing risk can help identify those whose online sexual behavior may be motivated not only by sexual content, but also by the "rush" related to the risk level of the behavior. Individuals who thrive on risky behaviors may continue to increase their level of risk to achieve the same degree of arousal as they reached in previous experiences (i.e., they may develop psychological tolerance).
- *Illegal.* This theme can help identify individuals who may have crossed the line into illegal behaviors.
- *Secrecy.* Excessive secrecy may be used to hide extreme shame-based behaviors, and it may be important to identify these ego-dystonic behaviors early.
- *Compulsive.* Questions in this area are used to identify individuals whose behaviors appear compulsive, need-driven, and ritualistic. Individuals identified as sexually compulsive online can be difficult to manage and treat.

Structured interviews are only as good as the interviewer; therefore, more knowledgeable and skilled clinicians will be able to use the IA or IA-Q more productively to reveal the breadth and depth of the issues involved for a particular client.

As previously mentioned, there are two sections of the IA-Q and IA. The first section is designed to gather information regarding the individual's Internet knowledge and behavior. This includes questions that address the client's methods and venues of Internet use, extent of use, and overall technical skill and knowledge. At the completion of Section I, the examiner will have a great deal of data on how much the individual knows about the Internet and the basic ways the individual uses the Internet for sexual purposes.

In addition to understanding the technological issues involved in online sexual behavior, it is important to addresses the social, psychological, and sexual issues related to such use. The second section of the IA-Q and IA provides the types of interview questions necessary to assess these less quantifiable aspects. Questions in Section II include issues such as how an individual's online behavior has interfered with or jeopardized important aspects of his life, levels of obsessive thinking and compulsive behaviors with online sexuality, and underlying psychological issues. In addition, Section II will assist in determining behaviors related to online sexual activities, arousal patterns, and the negative impact online sexual activity has had on the individual. The IA-Q is presented in Figure 25.2. An electronic copy of the IA-Q can be found at our website (*www.internetbehavior.com/ sexualdeviance*).

Disclosure Forms. Although disclosure forms were originally developed for use by probation and parole departments, they can be useful to clinicians in the assessment pro-

FIGURE 25.2. Internet Assessment Quickscreen (IA-Q): A structured interview for assessing problematic online sexual behavior. Document in the public domain.

Section I: Internet Knowledge and Behavior

1. Over the past 6 months, on average how many hours per week is your computer logged on to the Internet? On average, how many of those online hours do you sit in front of your computer and use the Internet (not necessarily for sexual purposes)?
2. Over the past 6 months, on average how many hours per week have you actively engaged in Internet sex (including downloading images, sexual chats, etc.)?
3. Have you ever posted/traded any sexual material on or through the Internet? This would include self-photos, photos of others, sexual stories, videos, audio clips, sexual blogs, sexual profiles, etc.
4. Have you ever viewed child pornography or images of individuals who appeared to be less than 18 years old?
5. Have you ever tried to conceal yourself or the places you have been online (e.g., by clearing your history or cache, using programs to hide/clean your online tracks, deleting/renaming downloaded files, using anonymous services or stealth surfers, etc.)?
6. Have you ever had offline contacts with individuals (children, teens, or adults) you met online (e.g., phone calls, sending/receiving items through the mail, face-to-face meetings, etc.)?
7. Have you ever had any of the following types of programs installed on any computer you have used: peer-to-peer networks (e.g., Kazaa), Internet relay chat (e.g., Mirc), Newsreader (e.g., FreeAgent), Webcam (e.g., PalTalk)?

Section II: Social, Sexual, and Psychological

8. Has your offline sexuality ever been affected by your online sexual behaviors?
9. Has there ever been a relationship between your masturbation and cybersex behaviors?
10. Have you ever noticed a progression in your sexual risk-taking behavior (either online or offline) as a result of your cybersex behavior?
11. Have you ever experienced consequences, or jeopardized important life areas (e.g., work, family, friends), as a result of your online sexual behaviors?
12. Has your partner ever complained about your Internet sexual behavior?
13. Have you ever become more isolated (physically or emotionally) from family and friends as a result of your online sexual behaviors?
14. Have you ever noticed your Internet sexual behaviors affecting your mood, either positively or negatively?
15. Have you ever wished you could stop using sex on the Internet, but are unable to set limits or stop the behavior?

cess as well. A disclosure form gives an offender the opportunity to disclose specific technology-related information, such as the number of computers owned and used; patterns of daily Internet use; email addresses, screen names, and passwords; and so forth. A sample disclosure form is presented in Figure 25.3 and can also be found at our website (*www.internetbehavior.com/sexualdeviance*). This document is best used early in the assessment to gain insight into the client's technological understanding, use, potential problematic issues, and willingness to disclose. Although there is no scoring for the disclosure form, these data can be combined with the other assessment techniques to form a picture of an individual's problematic use. Questions a clinician might ask when reviewing the form include the following:

"Do you have sexualized screen names or passwords?"
"Do you have a specific email address for sexual purposes?"
"How many computers do you own, and why?"
"Do you engage in sexual use of the computer away from home (e.g., at work)?"

	FIRST	MI	LAST		DOB	
Name:						
	Street	Apt	City	State		ZIP
Address:						
	Home		Work		Mobile	
Phones:						

1.   List all the computers you use or have access to:

	Location	Make	Model	Operating System
1				
2				
3				
4				
5				

List additional computers in item 9 below.

2.   Where do you have access to the Internet?

	Location	ISP	Type (e.g., cable, DSL)
1			
2			
3			
4			
5			

List additional access in item 9 below.

3.   List all email accounts you use.

	Email			Email
1		4		
2		5		
3		6		

List additional accounts in item 9 below.

4. Do you have or use instant messaging (IM)?   Yes   No
List all instant message screen names and services.

	Screen Name	Service (e.g., AOL, Yahoo, MSN)
1		
2		
3		
4		
5		

List additional screen names and services in item 9 below.

(*continued*)

FIGURE 25.3. Computer and Internet disclosure form. Document in the public domain.

FIGURE 25.3. (*continued*)

5. Are you a member of, or do you visit, any chat rooms or Internet groups?   Yes   No
List all screen names, services, and group names.

	Screen Name	Service (e.g., Yahoo)	Group name
1			
2			
3			
4			
5			

List additional screen names, services, or group names in item 9 below.

6. Do you have or use any of the following hardware or equipment?   Yes   No

	Equipment	Make	Model
1	Digital camera Yes No		
2	Video recorder Yes No		
3	Scanner Yes No		
4	MP3 player Yes No		

7. Describe how you use computers.

8. Describe how you use the Internet.

9. Additional information:

I, _____, certify that this is a complete and accurate
accounting of my computer and Internet equipment and usage.

_____   _____
Signature   Date

"Are the chat rooms you visit sexualized? Do you trade pornography in chat rooms?"

"Do you use digital cameras to create pornography?"

When possible, a partner, parent, or other individual who is familiar with the client's Internet behavior should also be asked to complete the disclosure form to help validate the information provided. This form will provide basic self-report information that can be utilized and verified throughout the evaluation process.

The data gathered from the disclosure form, the ISST or ISST-R, and the IA or IA-Q may have considerable repetitiveness and overlap. Although completing all these instruments may seem redundant to the client, it is important to assess consistent patterns across a number of assessment tools and techniques as a way of ensuring as much accuracy and honesty as possible.

At this point in the evaluation, the clinician will have data regarding underlying offline psychological issues; technological knowledge, use, and factors; the online social and psychological issues; and the motivation behind the client's sexual use of the Internet. The various data collected can be useful in and of themselves; however, the data may also be used to determine other important factors to lay the roadmap for treatment of problematic cybersex users. Although the data may be used in a number of ways, two important aspects of utilizing the data collected include determining the client's cybersex user category and establishing the role and function of the client's online sexual behavior.

Utilization of Assessment Data

Cybersex User Categories

We (Delmonico et al., 2001) have proposed a typology of cybersex users, termed the "cybersex user categories." According to this model, cybersex users fall into one of several categories, and breadth and depth of treatment may vary among these categories. A revised version of the original cybersex user category model appears in Figure 25.4. Data collected from the comprehensive evaluation of an individual who engages in cybersex activities, including the global Internet assessment, can be used to assist in determining the appropriate cybersex user category. The categories are described in detail below.

- *Recreational users.* An appropriate recreational user accesses cybersex on the Internet and does not report obsession, compulsion, or consequence as a result of cybersex use. In fact, some individuals use cybersex to enhance their current relationships (e.g., to learn new sexual techniques or positions, etc.). Others use the Internet as an avenue to remain healthy as they recover from an addiction, sexual or otherwise (Putnam & Maheu, 2000). Still others simply use cybersex as a form of entertainment and do not report any difficulties as a result of its use. It is important to note that any form of illegal sexual activity online (e.g., viewing child pornography, enticing children for sexual purposes, etc.) may never be considered recreational; although the consequences may not have been realized, the risk of and potential for significant consequences are always present.
- *Sexual harassers.* These individuals will often use Internet material inappropriately, such as sending or showing sexually explicit materials to unsuspecting adults. They may use sexually explicit backgrounds on their computer screens or screen savers, and often use the material they find online to ignore or cross sexual boundaries with others,

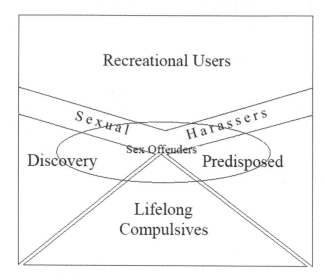

FIGURE 25.4. Cybersex user categories (revised). Copyright 2001 by David L. Delmonico and Elizabeth J. Griffin.

sometimes in an attempt to be humorous. Individuals in this group often border between problematic behavior and recreational behavior, and they warrant further assessment. Their behavior may be symptomatic of other problematic sexual thoughts, feelings, fantasies, urges, or behaviors; however, their behavior may also be related to ignorance or a lack of proper education regarding the sharing of sexual information with others.

• *Discovery users.* This group includes those who never had any problems with sexual fantasy or behavior until they discovered sex on the Internet. Exposure to sex on the Internet triggered a problematic sexual behavior that they might not have otherwise developed. Typically, standard evaluation and assessment procedures and tools do not reveal the presence or history of problematic sexual behavior or mental health issues. For example, personality inventories often show no maladaptive patterns, and measures of sexual interest/arousal typically do not indicate inappropriate sexual thoughts, feelings, fantasies, or urges. If deep-seated issues are present, they are difficult if not impossible to detect in this group of cybersex users. Persons in this group may begin their cybersex use as recreational users; however, over time they move into problematic or illegal online sexual behaviors. Although there is little research to support the existence of this group, it is discussed anecdotally in a wide range of professions (including psychology, law enforcement, and probation/parole circles), and it is beginning to be recognized in the literature. For example, Quayle and colleagues (2006) and Galbreath, Berlin, and Sawyer (2002) indicate that ease of Internet accessibility creates a subset of individuals who might not have engaged in problematic behaviors had it not been for the Internet.

• *Predisposed users.* This group consists of individuals who have had some history of problematic sexual fantasies, but managed to control these urges. A predisposed user has a set of internal and external controls that assists in moderating and preventing thoughts, feelings, or urges from becoming actual behaviors. Use of the Internet causes the individual's "braking system" to deteriorate, and behaviors that were once controlled offline become more out of control online. The Internet fosters the development of an already existing sexual fantasy or urge that might have remained dormant without it.

• *Lifelong sexually compulsive users.* Members of this group have dealt with sexually compulsive behavior throughout their lives, and the Internet facilitates an extension
of an already well-established, existing pattern of inappropriate sexual behaviors. In
some cases the Internet may escalate the thoughts, feelings, fantasies, and behaviors both
online and offline. Individuals in this group may see the Internet as an additional way to
act out their sexual behavior that enhances their already ritualized and compulsive pattern. Others may see it as a "safer" way of acting out their problematic sexual behaviors,
because it may reduce their direct contact with others. In either case, individuals in this
group will engage in problematic sexual behavior even in the absence of the Internet.

• *Sex offenders.* The sex offender oval in the model overlaps all other cybersex user
categories (see Figure 25.4). That is, a sex offender may commit an offline offense, but
use the Internet for sexual purposes that are not necessarily illegal. There is much debate
as to whether sex offenders should have access to any sexual materials or behaviors on
the Internet, but the fact remains that many sex offenders use the Internet for nonillegal
sexual purposes.

Individuals who commit sex offenses online (e.g., downloading child pornography,
luring kids through online venues) are typically assumed to be pedophiles or hebephiles;
however, this is not always the case. Access to real children and child abuse images is
more readily available than ever before in history. This accessibility, combined with other
technological and psychological factors, may tempt individuals to engage in forms of sexual behaviors in which they might not have otherwise participated. According to Quayle
(2004), "it is unclear whether adults with a sexual interest in children use internet abuse
images and pornography more than the general population" (p. 27). For these reasons, a
comprehensive assessment of arousal and interest in children should be completed for any
individual who views or possesses online child abuse images. It is important for a clinician to approach the evaluation objectively, and not to base diagnostic assumptions
about whether an individual is a pedophile on Internet behavior alone.

Role and Function of Online Sexual Behavior

Understanding the role and function of online sexual behavior is a critical use of assessment data (Beech, Fisher, & Thornton, 2003). The function of a behavior is best described as the motive or primary reason for engaging in a behavior. Quayle and colleagues (2006) state that "a functionalist approach de-emphasizes the form that [a]
problem takes and shifts attention to the purposes that the behavior might serve for the
individual" (p. 11). The function focuses on the gains an individual receives from engaging in the process, rather than on the behavior itself. Functions provide the meaning
behind a behavior and are fairly dynamic in nature, particularly on the Internet. An individual may start engaging in a behavior for a specific reason, but as the behavior continues,
the function of the behavior may change. Although there are many ways to conceptualize
the function of a behavior, two models particularly helpful in assessing the function of
Internet sex are the "six principal discourses" and the "pathways model."

Six Principal Discourses. Taylor and Quayle (2003) qualitatively derived six principal discourses related to individuals who view child abuse images (child pornography) on
the Internet. Although these discourses were developed only through interviews with individuals who viewed child pornography online, they can easily be generalized to explain

and understand the function of many online sexual behaviors. These six principal discourses include (1) "aid to sexual arousal," (2) "collectibles" (i.e., the desire to attain and maintain large collections of sexual materials), (3) "facilitation of social relationships," (4) "way to avoid real life," (5) "a form of therapy," and (6) "the Internet" (i.e., the characteristics of the Internet that make it attractive to cybersex users). These six discourses are not mutually exclusive, and individuals may have a variety of reasons why they engage in cybersex behavior; however, some factors are usually more salient than others. The assessment process should begin to determine which of these factors should be focused on during the treatment phase. Once a discourse is identified, certain treatment interventions can be used to modify the discourse to help break the dysfunctional relationship an individual may have with the Internet. Although there is no single way to assess for these discourses, the data gathered during the full assessment should provide a clinician with enough information to make an accurate hypothesis about the discourse.

Pathways Model. Middleton, Beech, and Mandeville-Norton (2005) explored five possible pathways to help explain an individual's Internet sexual misuse: (1) intimacy deficits, (2) distorted sexual scripts, (3) emotional dysregulation, (4) antisocial cognitions, and (5) multiple dysfunctional mechanisms. Middleton and colleagues reported that of these five pathways, two seemed most salient for individuals who viewed child pornography online: intimacy deficits (38%; $n = 43$) and emotional dysregulation (35%; $n = 43$). The remaining 27% of subjects were divided over the three other pathways. Although this study focused specifically on individuals who viewed child pornography online, the pathways model may be applied to all individuals who engage in online sexual activity. Once an individual's dysfunctional pathway is determined, intervention strategies may focus on weakening this pathway, thereby diminishing the need for problematic online sexual behavior.

Concluding the Assessment

The preceding sections have discussed a variety of assessment methods, techniques, and instruments. Data gathered during the assessment process (psychological testing, biological measures, etc.), are critical to the treatment planning process for cybersex users. As the evaluation of a cybersex user concludes, a clinician should have a clear sense of which cybersex user category best describes the offender, as well as the primary function or functions (e.g., discourses and/or pathways) of the online sexual behavior. The recognition and understanding of the user category and the function will determine the depth and breadth of treatment, as outlined in the following section.

TREATMENT

Basic Treatment Assumptions

The assumptions on which treatment should be based, regardless of the problematic online sexual behavior to be addressed, are explained below.

Assumption 1: Online Sex Offenders Should Have Internet Access

It may seem logical to argue if an individual has committed a sexual offense via the Internet, or the Internet has supported inappropriate sexual behaviors, then Internet use should simply be removed as a privilege. However, it is unrealistic to expect that individuals will not access the Internet, whether they do so in their homes, at work, or in other public or private areas. The Internet has become a commonly accepted method for communicating and seeking information. Some district courts have ruled it unconstitutional to remove a person's right to access the Internet. Legal issues aside, allowing individuals to have access to the Internet (in a monitored or restricted way) can assist them in learning healthy ways to use the Internet. It is therapeutically beneficial to permit individuals to struggle with their Internet use while under close supervision and receiving treatment, rather than to set the stage for relapse upon release from such supervision. Moreover, helping such individuals develop healthy ways to use the Internet is not only solid clinical protocol, but a necessary component of sex offender treatment. Cooper and Griffin-Shelley (2002) have stated that "as a communication tool the Internet offers a means of promoting physical and mental health, especially sexual health, through innovative methods" (p. 7). Allowing online sex offenders controlled and/or monitored access to the Internet can provide a number of resources not otherwise available to them, while also providing important feedback data to clinicians about the clients' ability to manage their Internet behavior in order to promote healthy lifelong use of the Internet.

Assumption 2: Lapse and Relapse Should Be Expected for Online Sex Offenders

Prochaska, Norcross, and DiClemente (1995) proposed that one stage *expected* during the "change process" is relapse. Although no clinician would condone an online sex offender engaging in additional sexual offenses, it should be expected that such individuals not only will struggle with their online sexual behaviors, but will be more likely to have lapses during the change process. These lapses (defined as nonoffending but inappropriate online sexual behaviors) should be expected for at least two reasons. First, as previously mentioned, lapses are a normal part of the change process. Second, the Internet has certain inherent characteristics that allows lapses to occur more frequently. These characteristics include the ease of access to Internet sexuality, the level of secrecy afforded Internet users, and online factors that allow individuals to do things online that they may not do offline (see our earlier discussion of online disinhibition). Lapses during the change process can be used to educate clients on appropriate ways to prevent such occurrences in the future.

Assumption 3: Treatment of Online Sex Offenders Depends on Their User Category

As discussed extensively in the "Assessment" section of this chapter, determining an individual's cybersex user category is a critical component of the assessment and treatment process. There are four possible problematic cybersex user categories: "sexual harasser," "discovery user," "predisposed user," and "lifelong sexually compulsive user." Although there is not space in this chapter to discuss all the implications of cybersex user categories and treatment approaches, it is important to note that a client's cybersex user category can influence and direct the course of treatment planning. For example, a discovery user may not require the same level of time and intensity in treatment as a lifelong sexually compulsive individual. The discovery user may benefit most from psychoeducational approaches and relapse prevention strategies more, and earlier, than the predisposed user or lifelong sexually compulsive individual may. At the other end of the spectrum, the lifelong sexually compulsive individual is most likely to require intensive and extensive individual and group therapies, medication management, and a variety of other treatment methods. Again, these are just brief examples of how the cybersex user categories may influence treatment.

Basic Components of Treatment

There are three basic components involved in the treatment of sex offenders online: (1) basic Internet management, (2) electronic management, and (3) medication management.

Basic Internet Management

Several basic Internet management techniques can initially be helpful to the sex offender who uses the Internet (Delmonico & Griffin, 2005b; Delmonico, Griffin, & Carnes, 2002). Although these techniques appear superficial as compared to larger issues, they tend to be overlooked and underutilized in the treatment of problematic cybersex behavior or online sex offending in general. Typically, these basic interventions are most useful for discovery users and least useful for lifelong sexually compulsive individuals. These basic interventions may include the following:

Ensuring that the computer is only used in high-traffic areas.
Limiting the days/times of use (e.g., not using the computer after 11:00 P.M.).
Using the computer only when others are nearby (e.g., not when home alone).
Specifying locations where the Internet can/cannot be used (e.g., not at hotels).
Making sure that the monitor is visible to others (e.g., coworkers).
Placing screen savers/backgrounds within view of important people (e.g., family, partner).

Since each individual will need to establish his own list of techniques for managing cybersex behavior, it is important to discuss what may be useful on a case-by-case basis. One exercise to facilitate this discussion is called the "Internet health plan." This plan allows individuals not only to name unhealthy rituals or behaviors that support their problematic online sexual behaviors, but also encourages individuals to list those behaviors that are healthy and will support a more positive use of the Internet. More details about developing an Internet health plan can be found on our website (*www.internetbehavior. com/sexualdeviance*).

Electronic Management

Just as technology has created a number of new problematic sexual issues, it also offers a number of electronic solutions. There are three basic areas involved in the electronic management of an online sex offender: (1) searching computers for problematic files, (2) employing filtering/blocking methods, and (3) utilizing monitoring methods to track Internet use. Each of these has strengths and weaknesses, and may or may not be appropriate, depending on the individual case.

Searching. Procedures or software can search storage components (e.g., hard drive, CDs, etc.) for inappropriate files. Although illegal images are the target of such searching, these methods can also be used to find movie clips, software, music, or any other type of file that may be problematic or illegal. Searching is only useful for finding files after they are on the computer in question. Searching is typically performed by law enforcement or probation/parole officers, and while clinicians do not usually execute such searches, the data discovered may be useful in the assessment and treatment process.

Filtering/Blocking. Filtering and/or blocking can occur in a number of ways. Software may be installed on a computer that previews all information prior to displaying it on the monitor. If an offending site or keyword is found in the reviewed information, the blocking software will prevent the site from being displayed. Filtering may also occur at the source of the Internet connection—the Internet service provider (ISP). Some ISPs preview material before it is sent over the Internet connection and prevent any objectionable material from being transmitted to the user. Filtering/blocking methods can be effective, but they have their disadvantages. First, they may block out useful areas of the Internet and make it difficult to surf even "safe" areas. Second, they may easily be circumvented by any individual with intermediate-level skills. Filtering methods often focus on specific areas of the Internet (e.g., the World Wide Web, email); however, they may completely ignore other areas (e.g., IRC, peer networks) that can be equally problematic. Filtering and blocking methods create a false sense of security among clinicians and clients, and will be ineffective if used as the only intervention.

Computer Monitoring. Monitoring software may be installed on an individual's computer to track Internet use and provide reports of hours accessed, places visited, and patterns of use. Monitoring software may include blocking/filtering methods, so software can be set to block certain websites or areas of the Internet in addition to the monitoring process. Monitoring typically occurs in "real time," meaning that, if desired, the individual can be monitored at the moment of behavior. Another form of monitoring software allows individuals to have reports emailed directly to an accountability partner or probation/parole officer. This person can then review the information and discuss an individual's usage to support healthy online habits. The accountability partner may be a friend, fellow group member, sponsor, or other responsible individual; however, it should be noted that the accountability partner should never be the spouse or romantic partner of the person in question, due to the negative dynamics that may result in the relationship. A list of resources and suggested searching, filtering, and monitoring tools is available (*www.internetbehavior.com/sexualdeviance*).

Electronic management will vary, depending on the needs of the individual. In general, discovery and predisposed users will often benefit from electronic management techniques, since they have been able to control their behavior in the past. Lifelong sexually compulsive individuals may not benefit as much, since their compulsion generally outweighs their desire to use these electronic management methods.

It is important for clinicians to remember that there are many innovative ways to access the Internet, and that these methods are constantly changing and developing. In the past, the personal computer and laptop have been viewed as the main methods for Internet access; however, cell phones, gaming systems, iPods, and personal data devices must now also be considered. Clinicians working with individuals who are trying to manage or change their Internet behavior should not ignore these "portable Internet devices" in the assessment or treatment process. It is very difficult to use management methods on such devices. For example, not all forms of electronic management previously discussed necessarily apply to these devices. Simply knowing that these devices exist and discussing their appropriate use with clients are important aspects of the assessment and treatment process.

Medication Management

Since many psychological issues often co-occur with inappropriate cybersex use, medication management is an important element in the treatment of cybersex-related issues. Examples include relationships between cybersex use and depression, anxiety, attention deficits, or personality disorders. Medication issues should be carefully considered during the assessment and treatment process. The medication evaluation should be performed by an experienced psychiatrist who understands sexual and addictive disorders. In general, lifelong sexually compulsive individuals are not likely to be responsive to treatment or successful in stopping their compulsive behavior without some medication intervention. Discovery users may benefit from pharmacological interventions, but medications are often used for shorter periods of time and are used to treat symptoms that arise from the cybersex use (e.g., depression, anxiety). Predisposed users may fall somewhere between the discovery and lifelong groups and may have specific medication needs that must be addressed.

Addressing Underlying Issues

As is the case with many problematic sexual behaviors, inappropriate cybersex use is often symptomatic of an underlying constellation of deeper issues. The "iceberg" metaphor is commonly used to explain this concept, since the "tip of the iceberg" is often representative of deeper individual issues. If the "tip" is the only issue addressed, the larger supporting elements of the behavior go untreated and eventually cause new negative behaviors to occur. Although the cybersex behavior may be representing an unlimited number of issues, there are some typical core issues: intimacy, attachment, shame, sexuality, emotional dysregulation, and spirituality. Some of these issues (i.e., intimacy and emotional dysregulation) have research to support their existence in cybersex behavior problems, as discussed by Middleton and colleagues (2005). The others are supported by anecdotal evidence from clinicians who treat inappropriate online sexual behavior. It is important for clinicians to recognize the existence of underlying issues and to address them in the treatment process. Any attempt to treat the cybersex behavior without recognizing these underlying issues will result in short-lived successes, since relapse is likely when these deeper, underlying issues are minimized or ignored.

There are a number of ways to address these underlying issues. The following sections summarize two such methods: cognitive-behavioral approaches and multimedia approaches. Although these methods can be employed in individual therapy, they are often most effective when used in a group therapy setting. Groups that include a number of members who are knowledgeable about online sexual behaviors can increase accountability among all members with regard to problematic Internet use.

Cognitive-Behavioral Approaches

Cognitive-behavioral therapy is often considered the treatment of choice among clinicians who treat sexual offenders. This model is effective at addressing the thoughts, feelings, and behaviors typically found in the sexual offense cycle. The theoretical model is the underpinning for a variety of techniques and approaches in working with sexual offenders. Although the specifics of these approaches may vary, the goals are often the same: healthier cognitions and safe, nonexploitive sexual behavior. Many of the already existing cognitive-behavioral techniques can be modified to treat sex offenders who use the Internet. Two books that illustrate the use of cognitive-behavioral methods in the treatment of cybersex behavior are *Only Pictures: Therapeutic Work with Internet Sex Offenders* (Quayle et al., 2006) and *Cybersex Unhooked* (Delmonico et al., 2001). (A link for the *Cybersex Unhooked* workbook can be found at *www.internetbehavior.com/sexualdeviance*.)

Multimedia Approaches

Clinicians treating problematic cybersex behavior are competing with a very powerful force—multimedia sex. Instant gratification, sexual arousal, and behavioral reinforcement combine to create a tremendous force. Therefore, it is critical for clinicians to find interesting and engaging treatment methods that capture attention and assist individuals in changing their behavior. Describing creative and engaging therapies is difficult, since writing can only be descriptive and not interactive; since these methods rely on interaction with clients, these pages cannot capture the full power of these techniques. Given that limitation, below are descriptions of some of the multimedia methods we have often found to be effective in addressing the underlying issues of cybersex behavior. Each method is explained, and a short example is provided.

Motion Picture Clips. Motion pictures (including television clips) can be a powerful medium to discuss difficult concepts. Movies allow individuals to step back and discuss themselves through the characters in the clips. Clients often come to understand concepts more clearly, and even begin to see the relevance of important psychological issues, in this way. Once concepts are understood at the intellectual level, clinicians may assist the clients in applying the concepts to their own situations.

There is an endless supply of motion picture clips that are relevant to the underlying issues of cybersex. One example is the movie *Hoodwinked: The True Story of Red Riding Hood* (Edwards, Edwards, & Leech, 2005). This movie has various meanings; however, one salient therapeutic interpretation is that there are multiple perspectives in every story or situation. In the movie, all the characters believe their perceptions are the right ones, while the viewer is led to make many assumptions about the characters' roles and responsibilities. The frog enters the story and interviews each character to uncover his or her perceptions of the situation. During the frog's interviewing process, the viewer becomes aware that many of the characters' assumptions are incorrect, but realizes the characters are all being honest, based on their interpretation of their own experiences. The movie can help introduce the client to the purpose of the therapeutic process (via the role of the frog), introduce the importance of being able to see things from another's perspective, and identify that assumptions about a situation are not always accurate. Other movies applicable to the treatment of cybersex issues can be found on our website (*www.internetbehavior.com/sexualdeviance*).

Books and Other Text-Based Materials. Whereas some clients are more visual in their learning style, others enjoy reading and text-based learning. The use of books, poems, and other written text is an excellent way to engage clients and teach concepts relevant to their particular underlying issues. Common wisdom would support the idea that individuals who enjoy chat rooms, emails, or other types of "reading-based" use of the Internet may benefit from this method of intervention; after all, they already exhibit interest in the written word rather than the visual. However, there are no data to support this notion.

One example of such an intervention is the text *Wicked: The Life and Times of the Wicked Witch of the West* (Maguire, 1995). Most individuals know the story of the book and movie *The Wizard of Oz*; however, this book provides the reader with the life story of the Wicked Witch of the West. As the story develops, it becomes clear that the witch, although seemingly wicked in the original book and movie, has a story to help us understand how she came to be so hated and wicked. The reader learns the importance of the ruby slippers and the reason why the witch will stop at nothing to take them from Dorothy. At the conclusion of the book, the context of the witch's "wickedness" helps illustrate a key concept in sex offender treatment—empathy. The text helps demonstrate that each individual has a story, including a sex offender, the victim or victims, and the victims' families. One of the ultimate goals of treatment is to help online sex offenders understand and tell their stories, while also understanding the impact their behavior has had on others' stories. In the end, the sexually inappropriate behavior is not excused; rather, it is put in the context of a story, whose meaning can become the foundation for preventing future relapse.

The Telling of Stories, Legends, and/or Fairy Tales. The question often following a legend, fairy tale, or story is "What is the moral of this story?" Although this is not necessarily the question a clinician would pose to a client, the point is that fairy tales are often aimed at teaching information in a metaphorical manner. There has been much research on the use of narrative and metaphorical techniques in the treatment process. The premise of such techniques is that individuals can relate to characters in the story at a level that makes it safe to discuss the characters' assets and deficits. Appropriately chosen stories allow therapists to guide clients into relating the story to their own lives in a safe, nondefensive manner.

An example of one such story is "The Sleeping Beauty in the Wood," better known to most people as simply "Sleeping Beauty" (Perrault, 1922). In the pre-Disney version of this fairy tale, all the fairies in the land are invited to the christening feast of the daughter of the King and Queen to provide their blessing, except one who is despised by everyone in the kingdom. During the feast, the despised fairy appears and curses Sleeping Beauty to die. A fairy who has not yet given her blessing alters this curse so that Sleeping Beauty will only fall into a deep sleep and be awakened 100 years later by a prince. Although this is a condensed version of the fairy tale, the therapeutic point to be made is that there are many aspects to one's personality—both good and bad. What the fairy tale teaches is that all aspects of the human personality are important to identify and acknowledge, even the darker aspects that are disliked (not unlike the despised fairy). Because the despised fairy is not honored, she arrives at the feast with a vengeance and wreaks havoc on the entire kingdom. Similarly, not honoring the darker aspects of our personalities (including our sexuality) creates a dynamic that allows these disowned aspects to show up and cause significant distress at the most inopportune times. Although many offenders wish to ignore the negative aspects of their personality (the despised fairy), treatment should incorporate ways for clients to acknowledge all aspects of themselves and invite every aspect to the feast. This acknowledgment will help prevent the darker aspects from showing up uncontrollably and unexpectedly in the future.

The Use of Toys as Tools in Treatment. Although toys are most often thought of in relation to play therapy with children, they can also be excellent tools in treating adults. The tactile and visual combination assists in teaching clients various psychological concepts. In addition, therapists often learn a great deal as clients relate their own stories to the toys. Toys can represent various aspects of a client's personality, which are often easier to discuss when they are separated out. Addiction professionals have done this for years with concepts like "King Baby"—a concept that helps explain the narcissistic, selfish, and immature behaviors of people who are actively addicted (to substances, gambling, etc.). Discussing the concept is powerful; however, actually placing a "King Baby" doll or figurine in a client's hands can give more meaning to the concept and allows the client and others to explore ways it fits into their own lives. In addition, this method can be usefully combined with various other media. For example, when clients are discussing a fairy tale or story, having the characters in hand adds a dimension to the story that can increase its power and effectiveness.

Specific examples of the use of toys in the treatment of cybersex offenders include the "attorney" and "core whore." The "attorney" is a well-dressed businessman toy whose role is to appear any time an individual becomes defensive about his behaviors or character flaws. The attorney helps defend the ego at all costs and provides the arguments (i.e., cognitive distortions and thinking errors) that help the cybersex offender avoid taking full responsibility for his behavior. Once an individual understands the importance of the attorney, and it is given a name (and actual toy), it is easier to discuss the concept of accountability and responsibility when the client launches into a series of excuses for any negative behavior or decision. (The toy may also be used to help the client understand the function of a real attorney.) Early recovery may require the use of the ego's attorney to feel safe, but over time the goal is for the attorney's role to diminish and the client to take ownership of his thoughts, feelings, attitudes, and behaviors.

The other example of using a toy in treatment is the "core whore." The core whore is a sexualized lady warrior toy; she is used to represent the sexual behavior that a client would sell his soul for or do anything else to obtain. The critical moment in therapy is when the online sex offender recognizes the core whore, owns her, communicates with her, and (to use the words of the "Sleeping Beauty" fairy tale) invites her to the feast. The toy serves as a physical representation of the dark aspect of sexuality and encourages the exploration of its function and impact. Individuals who cannot (or will not) recognize and take responsibility for their core whore will continue to struggle with relapse and accountability issues. The core whore allows for the exploration of the hidden and forbidden in a safe, nonthreatening manner.

Use of the Internet Itself in Recovery. As noted earlier, most clients will use the Internet again. Researchers and clinicians working with cybersex behavior problems believe that the answer is not to forbid Internet use, but rather to work toward healthy use of this multimedia-rich environment. The same processes that draw individuals into problematic online behavior can engage them in the recovery process. Not only can the Internet be used in healthy ways personally, but the therapeutic environment may also benefit from correctly timed use of the Internet's resources and influence. "It seems likely that while Internet interventions will not replace face to face care, there is little doubt that they will grow in importance as a powerful component of psychological treatment" (Quayle, 2005, p. 135; see also Ritterband et al., 2003). Obviously, the use of the Internet should be incorporated gradually into treatment for those who have committed online sex offenses, and such clients should be carefully monitored for future offenses; however, therapeutic Internet use should not be overlooked as a possible technique that can have lasting impact on a client's thoughts, feelings, and behaviors.

One innovative way of using the Internet to help individuals with their sexual offense behavior is CROGA, a website designed for education, self-exploration, and self-help based on cognitive-behavioral approaches (*www.croga.org*). Specifically, it provides educational and self-awareness exercises for individuals who are interested in sexual images of children.

SUMMARY AND FUTURE DIRECTIONS

The process of understanding, assessing, managing, and treating online sex offenders is a complex one. This chapter has outlined important areas clinicians must recognize in order to effectively assess, manage, and treat such offenders. The most salient of these points are as follows:

1. The Internet is a unique medium with powerful, and seductive characteristics that must be addressed and understood throughout the assessment and treatment process.
2. It is a disservice not to screen/assess all sex offenders for the role technology plays in their lives, regardless of whether they committed their offenses online.
3. All cybersex users are not the same, and the cybersex user categories play a critical role in determining the direction, duration, and depth of treatment.
4. Not all individuals who view or possess child pornography are pedophiles/hebephiles.
5. Once the Internet is determined to be part of an offender's life, a global Internet assessment should be completed to determine the extent, role, and influence of the person's Internet use.
6. Although some traditional sex offender treatment approaches may be applicable, the unique characteristics of problematic cybersex use and the Internet require specific assessment, management, and treatment approaches.
7. Underlying issues (e.g., shame, spirituality, emotional regulation) are important to address for successful long-term treatment and relapse prevention.
8. Because it is unlikely that sex offenders will never use technology in the future, treatment should teach healthy use of the Internet.
9. Creative and engaging methods must be used in treatment to address the underlying issues. Since multiple media play a role for the online sex offender, the use of multimedia methods to address these issues may be appropriate.

It is unclear what the future holds for the interaction between technology and sexuality; however, it is clear that this relationship will remain strong. Indeed, technology will continue to stimulate, intensify, and complicate sexuality as new and innovative ways are developed for individuals to be sexual in an online environment. For example, one such innovation allows an individual to control a cybersex partner's sexual toys (e.g., vibrators, pseudovaginas) remotely over the Internet. On the horizon are virtual reality kits that include live, three-dimensional sexual experiences, which eventually will include brain stimulators aimed at enhancing orgasm during cybersex sessions. The marriage (or, as some may consider it, the unholy alliance!) of sex and technology seems solid, and clinicians must be willing to acknowledge this union and incorporate the implications for such a relationship into treatment.

The field of cybersex is relatively new. Although researchers have shown interest in this area, the amount of literature discussing the impact of technology on sexuality is limited. The majority of professional writings in this area are theory-based, and few data are available about the specifics of online sexual behavior. Research needs to continue, and widespread, well-funded research projects should be aimed at methodically studying the online sexual behaviors of various groups of individuals. Data can be difficult to gather in an online environment, and research is currently underway to determine the best standardized methodology for collecting such data. It is our belief that the field is years away from valid, reliable, data-driven answers to many questions regarding online sex behavior.

The purpose of this chapter has been to review the current literature regarding our understanding of inappropriate online sexual behavior in general and online sexual offending in particular. Additionally, we hope that as clinicians are introduced to assessment, management, and treatment approaches for online sex offenders, traditional sex offender treatment programs will see the relevance of incorporating online sexual behaviors into already existing protocols. It is a rare case when the Internet does not play a role in a sexual offender's thoughts, feelings, fantasies, urges, and behaviors. Even when the actual sexual offense does not occur online, the Internet often has sustained or fueled the offense behavior in some way. It is our belief that until the Internet's role and impact on sexual offense behavior is acknowledged, the system will increasingly fail the offenders, their victims, and the community at large.

REFERENCES

Abel, G. G., Huffman, J., Warberg, B. W., & Holland, C. L. (1998). Visual reaction time and plethysmography as measures of sexual interest in child molesters. *Sexual Abuse, 10*(2), 81–95.

Beech, A. R., Fisher, D. D., & Thornton, D. (2003). Risk assessment of sex offenders. *Professional Psychology: Research and Practice, 34*, 339–352.

Carnes, P. J. (1989). *Contrary to love.* Center City, MN: Hazelden.

Carnes, P. J., Delmonico, D. L., Griffin, E., & Moriarty, J. (2001). *In the shadows of the Net: Breaking free of online compulsive sexual behavior.* Center City, MN: Hazelden.

Cooper, A., Delmonico, D. L., & Burg, R. (2000). Cybersex users, abusers, and compulsives: New findings and implications. *Sexual Addiction and Compulsivity: The Journal of Treatment and Prevention, 7*(1–2), 5–30.

Cooper, A., & Griffin-Shelley, E. (2002). Introduction the Internet: The next sexual revolution. In A. Cooper (Ed.), *Sex and the Internet: A guidebook for clinicians* (pp. 1–16). New York: Brunner-Routledge.

Delmonico, D. L. (1999). *Internet sex screening test.* Retrieved from *www.internetbehavior.com/sexualdeviance*

Delmonico, D. L., & Griffin, E. J. (2005a). *Internet Assessment: A structured interview for assessing online problematic sexual behavior.* Unpublished instrument, Internet Behavior Consulting.

Delmonico, D. L., & Griffin, E. J. (2005b). Sex offenders online: What clinicians need to know. In B.

Schwartz (Ed.), *The sex offender: Issues in assessment, treatment, and supervision of adult and juvenile populations* (Vol. 5, pp. 1–25). Kingston, NJ: Civic Research Institute.

Delmonico, D. L., Griffin, E. J., & Carnes, P. J. (2002). Treating online compulsive sexual behavior: When cybersex is the drug of choice. In A. Cooper (Ed.), *Sex and the Internet: A guidebook for clinicians* (pp. 147–167). New York: Brunner-Routledge.

Delmonico, D. L., Griffin, E. J., & Moriarity, J. (2001). *Cybersex unhooked: A workbook for breaking free of online compulsive sexual behavior.* Center City, MN: Hazelden.

Delmonico, D. L., & Miller, J. A. (2003). The internet sex screening test: A comparison of sexual compulsives versus non-sexual compulsives. *Sexual and Relationship Therapy, 18*(3), 261–276.

Edwards, C., Edwards, T., & Leech, T. [Writers & Directors]. (2005). *Hoodwinked: The true story of Red Riding Hood.* Los Angeles: Weinstein Company/Canbar Entertainment.

Family Safe Media. (2006). *Pornography statistics.* Retrieved *www.familysafemedia.com/pornography_statistics.html*

Finkelhor, D., Mitchell, K. J., & Wolak, J. (2000). *Online victimization: A report on the nation's youth.* Alexandria, VA: National Center for Missing and Exploited Children.

Galbreath, N. W., Berlin, F. S., & Sawyer, D. (2002). Paraphilias and the Internet. In A. Cooper (Ed.), *Sex and the Internet: A guidebook for clinicians* (pp. 187–205). New York: Brunner-Routledge.

Glasgow, D. V., Osborne, A., & Croxen, J. (2003). An assessment tool for investigating paedophile sexual interest using viewing time: An application of single case methodology. *British Journal of Learning Disabilities, 31,* 96–102.

Greenberg, L. M., Corman, C. L., & Kindischi, C. L. (1996). *Test of Variables of Attention* (Version 703). Los Alamos, CA: Universal Attention Disorders.

Hathaway, S., McKinley, J. C., & Butcher, J. M. (1990). *Minnesota Multiphasic Personality Inventory–2.* Minneapolis: University of Minnesota Press.

Hindman, J., & Peters, J. M. (2001). Polygraph testing leads to better understanding adult and juvenile sex offenders. *Federal Probation, 65*(3), 8–15.

Kalichman, S., & Rompa, D. (2001). The Sexual Compulsivity Scale: Further development and use with HIV-positive persons. *Journal of Personality Assessment, 76,* 379–395.

Livingstone, S., & Bober, M. (2005). *UK children go online.* Retrieved from *www.children-go-online.net*

Maguire, G. (1995). *Wicked: The life and times of the Wicked Witch of the West.* New York: Regan Books.

Marshall, W. L., & Fernandez, Y. M. (2003). *Phallometric testing with sexual offenders: Theory, research, and practice.* Brandon, VT: Safer Society Press.

Middleton, D., Beech, A., & Mandeville-Norton, R. (2005). What sort of person could do that?: Psychologocial profiles of Internet pornography users. In E. Quayle & M. Taylor (Eds.), *Viewing child pornography on the Internet: Understanding the offence, managing the offender, helping the victims* (pp. 99–107). Lyme Regis, UK: Russell House.

Millon, T., Antoni, M., Millon, C., Meagher, S., & Grossman, S. (2001). *Millon Behavioral Medicine Diagnostic.* Minnetonka, MN: NCS Assessments.

Nielsen//NetRatings. (2006, August). *Nielsen Netratings resources: Data and rankings.* Retrieved from *www.nielsenne/ratings.com*

Perrault, C. (1922). The sleeping beauty in the wood. In C. Perrault, *Tales of passed times written for children.* London: Selwyn & Blount.

Prochaska, J. O., Norcross, J. C., & DiClemente, C. C. (1995). *Changing for good.* New York: Avon Books.

Putnam, D. E., & Maheu, M. M. (2000). Online sexual addiction and compulsivity: Integrating Web resources and behavioral telehealth in treatment. *Sexual Addiction and Compulsivity: Journal of Treatment and Prevention, 7*(1–2), 91–112.

Quayle, E. (2004). The impact of viewing on offending behavior. In M. Calder (Ed.), *Child sexual abuse and the Internet: Tackling a new frontier* (pp. 25–36). Lyme Regis, UK: Russell House.

Quayle, E. (2005). The Internet as a therapeutic medium. In E. Quayle & M. Taylor (Eds.), *Viewing child pornography on the Internet: Understanding the offence, managing the offender, and helping the victims* (pp. 127–144). Lyme Regis, UK: Russell House.

Quayle, E., Erooga, M., Wright, L., Taylor, M., & Harbinson, D. (2006). *Only pictures?: Therapeutic work with Internet sex offenders*. Lyme Regis, UK: Russell House.

Ritterband, L. M., Gonder-Frederick, L. A., Cox, D. J., Clifton, A. D., West, R. W., & Borowitz, S. M. (2003). Internet interventions: In review, in use, and into the future. *Professional Psychology: Research and Practice, 34*(5), 527–534.

Suler, J. (2004). The online disinhibition effect. *Cyberspsychology and Behavior, 7*, 321–326.

Taylor, M., & Quayle, E. (2003). *Child pornography: An Internet crime*. Hove, UK: Brunner-Routledge.

Wallace, P. (1999). *The psychology of the Internet*. New York: Cambridge University Press.

Weiss, R. (2000). *Cyber-addiction checklist*. Retrieved from *www.sexualrecovery.com/sri_docs/cyber.htm*

Wellard, S. (2001, March). Cause and effect. *Community Care*, pp. 26–27.

Young, K. (2006). *The cybersexual addiction quiz*. Retrieved from *netaddiction.com*

Young, K. S., & Rogers, R. C. (1998). The relationship between depression and Internet addiction. *CyberPsychology and Behavior, 1*(1), 25–28.

CHAPTER 26

SEXUAL DEVIANCE IN FEMALES

Psychopathology and Theory

CAROLINE LOGAN

In the first edition of this volume, Hunter and Mathews (1997) lamented the lack of attention to the subject of sexual deviance in females. In this earlier volume, a single and relatively brief chapter was devoted to the subject. It is a reflection of both the quantity and the quality of research and practice since 1997 that the topic of female sexual deviance now warrants two full chapters in the manner of the other subjects covered in this publication—the present one on psychopathology and theory, and the chapter to follow on assessment and treatment (Ford & Cortoni, Chapter 27).

Why is there more to say about the sexually harmful behavior of women now than there was in 1997? The traditional images of women as nonviolent and as protectors of vulnerable others, particularly children, are increasingly acknowledged as flawed and as constituting a barrier to the recognition of some women's harmful potential (Christiansen & Thyer, 2002; Craissati, 2004; Hislop, 2001). Consequently, information about the types and frequencies of sexually harmful behavior among women, previously difficult to obtain because of incomplete or nonexistent records, is slowly becoming easier to gather in systematic ways (Cortoni & Hanson, 2005; Denov, 2003). There is more clarity now than there has ever been about the kinds of sexual abuse perpetrated by women (Ford, 2006; Vandiver, 2006). There is also more awareness of how and why women abuse young people (Grayston & de Luca, 1999; Nathan & Ward, 2001), and of how the nature of the abuse perpetrated by women differs from that perpetrated by men (Craissati, 2004; Miccio-Fonseca, 2000; Ward & Siegert, 2002).

As a consequence of these important developments in the understanding of women's behavior, there is now more guidance available for practitioners about the assessment and treatment of sexually abusive women (e.g., Ford & Eldridge, 2006) and about the assessment and management of their risks to others (e.g., Craissati, 2004; Hart et al., 2003). This chapter and the one to follow describe some of the most important recent findings and developments in each of these areas.

The present chapter begins with a brief discussion of terminology. "Sexual deviance" is defined and contrasted with "sexual offending" and "sexual abuse" by women—distinctions that are important to make because of their relevance to questions of recognition and prevalence, as well as to the design of intervention programs for this population. There follows a review of recent research examining the clinical and social problems frequently reported by women who are sexually harmful. The general characteristics of the children and young people who are abused by women are then described. Studies of the prevalence of sexual abuse by women (using information derived from a variety of sources and from a variety of countries) are examined next, followed by juvenile and developmental issues. Risk assessment and management practice in relation to women who are sexually harmful is then considered in a section dealing with forensic issues more generally. In the next section of the chapter, progress in the development of theories accounting for the etiology of sexually abusive behavior in women is examined. The chapter finishes with a review of current and future developments in theory and research—developments that have the potential to improve this literature and its practical implications further.

TERMINOLOGY

The subject of this book is "sexual deviance," which is defined in terms of the paraphilias described in the *Diagnostic and Statistical Manual of Mental Disorders*, fourth edition, text revision (DSM-IV-TR; American Psychiatric Association, 2000). The literature on paraphilias in women is very small; the study of paraphilias is largely the study of males (Laws & O'Donohue, 1997). Research on women who are "sexually abusive" or "sexually harmful" is more abundant. Such women either have received convictions for sexual offenses (in which case they are referred to as "sexual offenders") or have self-reported sexually harmful behavior toward others, but no diagnosis of paraphilia has been made or is even assumed to be present. This chapter largely focuses on this latter body of research, although what exists on sexual deviance in women is also discussed. Research on sexually harmful men also features studies of individuals without a formal diagnosis of paraphilia; their abusive behavior (e.g., child molestation, rape) is the identifying characteristic, rather than any single underlying cause (Beech & Ward, 2004). But paraphilias feature prominently in the conduct of sexually abusive men, as well as in the design of interventions and in the assessment and management of risk. The more inclusive nature of the current literature on women who are sexually harmful needs to be borne in mind when comparisons are made between the genders in regard to their behavior, its prevalence, its assessment and management, and the derivation of theories by which it may be explained.

THE SEXUALLY HARMFUL BEHAVIOR OF WOMEN

The majority of sexual assaults perpetrated by women are committed against young people (Grayston & de Luca, 1999), although the abuse of adults has also been the subject of occasional study (e.g., Krahé, Waizenhöfer, & Möller, 2003). Sexually harmful behavior by women encompasses such activities as inappropriate or unwanted kissing, fondling, sexual games, masturbation, oral sex, digital or object penetration, and intercourse

(Christiansen & Thyer, 2002). Such actions may be perpetrated by a woman after a period of grooming, during which the victim's resistance to sexual abuse is reduced and controlled. Alternatively, sexual abuse may involve more physical than psychological coercion, and victims may acquiesce because they fear for their physical safety or for the safety and support of those on whom they depend (e.g., Krahé et al., 2003; Saradjian & Hanks, 1996). Grayston and de Luca (1999) refer to women who perpetrate such forms of sexual abuse as "active" or "direct" perpetrators. Such women may be distinguished from "passive" or "indirect" perpetrators, who (1) observe the occurrence of sexual abuse but do not intervene to stop the abuse from happening; (2) expose children to inappropriate sexual activity, such as sexual intercourse or pornography; or (3) procure potential victims for their male accomplices.

Typologies of women's sexually harmful and abusive behavior have been discussed for a number of years. Saradjian and Hanks (1996) refer to such typologies as "heuristics," or tools to aid in the understanding of complex behavior. Various heuristics have been proposed in which abusers are organized into types on the basis of the involvement of others and the relationship between the perpetrator and the victim. For example, Nathan and Ward (2002), based on the work of Mathews (1987) and Mathews, Matthews, and Speltz (1989), divided female sexual abusers into two groups: the "self-initiated abusers," who actively abuse one or more victims on their own, and "accompanied abusers," who operate actively or passively with coabusers.

In the category of self-initiated abusers, Nathan and Ward (2001) described two subcategories. The first consists of "predisposed abusers," whose often violent sexual abuse of young children may be motivated by anger, emotional loneliness, powerlessness, or sexual urges that are compulsive in nature. Most women in this subcategory have themselves experienced sexual abuse in childhood, in addition to dysfunctional and often chaotic relationships with their caregivers. The second subcategory is that of "teacher/lover" (see also Matthews, Mathews, & Speltz, 1991)—an aptly named subcategory reflecting the belief of an adult woman that her sexual abuse of an adolescent, usually a male, is a romantic affair or a relationship of equals. Motivations for such abusive relationships include the search for an ideal form of intimacy or an idealized loving sexual relationship (Ford, 2006), as well as power and the expression of complex and otherwise poorly expressed feelings of anger and frustration.

In the category of accompanied abusers, Nathan and Ward (2002) describe "male-coerced abusers." Such a woman is compelled or forced into sexual offending, usually against her own children, because of her fear of an abusive male (e.g., partner, family member) on whom she is emotionally dependent. Her motivation in accompanying the male abuser is therefore to limit the likelihood that he will harm or abandon her (Ford, 2006). On occasion, however, sexually harmful conduct by women in this context can become reinforcing. Saradjian and Hanks (1996) and others suggest that for a small number of such coerced women, the sexual abuse of children may be so effective in alleviating feelings of powerlessness and lack of control that they can go on to abuse alone.

Finally, Nathan and Ward (2002) describe "male-accompanied abusers," who usually participate willingly and actively in the abuse of children or young people alongside coabusing males. Such a sexually harmful woman is likely to be motivated by a primary desire for sexual gratification (Atkinson, 2000; Mathews, 1987); she abuses by choice rather than compulsion. However, feelings of anger, rejection, and revenge have also been suggested as possible drivers for sexual abuse by women alongside men. For example, women who accompany male abusers have frequently been thought sufficiently anxious and fearful about rejection by their coabusers that when such emotions are strong, the sexual abuse of children is thought to be more likely (Nathan & Ward, 2002).

Typologies are a valuable way of organizing complex information about female sexual abuse. However, typologies are superficial, in that they give consideration to the characteristics of the observed behaviors—they are descriptive of the encounters—without offering a framework for explaining the origins of or the motivations for these activities. About sexual offending in general, Ward and Siegert (2002) conclude that "simply making sexually abusive behavior the focus of explanatory attempts is too general and runs the risk of masking distinct offence pathways and offence types" (p. 323). The very small but slowly growing literature on theories of sexually harmful behavior by women is considered later in this chapter. Theories of such conduct offer more to practitioners than typologies, in terms of how they can come to understand the interplay of complex processes involved in female sexual abuse, and how they can then respond therapeutically and in terms of risk management.

COMORBIDITY

There remains reluctance on the part of practitioners and researchers to regard women as sex offenders in the same way as men who offend against children (Nathan & Ward, 2001); the gender dichotomy of child abuse was a dominant paradigm (Allen, 1991). Female sexual abuse was regarded as such an intolerable crime, and such a reversal of women's traditional role as carers for children and young people, that a woman found to be sexually harmful was thought very likely to be mentally ill; a mentally well woman could not act in such a way (Abel & Rouleau, 1995; Allen, 1991; Ford, 2006; Viki, Massey, & Masser, 2005). When mentally well women are recognized as sexual offenders against children, they are generally regarded as either "monsters or victims" (Nathan & Ward, 2001, p. 45) and treated accordingly by the criminal justice system, treatment and social services, the media and the public (Viki et al., 2005). What is the evidence of psychological disturbance in sexually harmful women?

Mental health needs are certainly common among women who sexually abuse. However, psychotic disorders—the most severe forms of mental illness—are thought to occur relatively infrequently (Green & Kaplan, 1994; Hislop, 2001). Faller (1987), for example, evaluated a group of female sexual abusers and diagnosed psychosis and gross psychiatric disturbance in 7.5% of the sample. When compared with the findings from a systematic review of 62 studies on mental disorders among women in prison (i.e., 4% of women in prison had a current or recent diagnosis of a psychotic disorder; Fazel & Danesh, 2002), Faller's observation may suggest that the prevalence of severe psychiatric disorders is elevated among female abusers compared to offending women in general, but it is far from high.

More common among sexually harmful women than psychosis are disorders of mood and anxiety (Hunter, Lexier, Goodwin, Browne, & Dennis, 1993; Saradjian & Hanks, 1996), and the often related activities of self-harming and suicidal behavior (Miccio-Fonseca, 2000). In particular, a diagnosis of posttraumatic stress disorder (PTSD) is regarded as prevalent in female sexual abusers (e.g., Green & Kaplan, 1994; Welldon, 1996), in both older (adult) and younger (adolescent) offenders (Mathews, Hunter, & Vuz, 1997). Symptoms of PTSD are generally linked to a woman's or young person's own experience of abuse. Substance abuse and dependence are also common conditions in women who abuse (e.g., Aylward, Christopher, Newell, & Gordon, 2002; Freel, 1995), although substance use and other mood and anxiety problems are also common in women who offend nonsexually (Logan & Blackburn, in press; Singleton, Meltzer, Gatward, Coid, & Deasy, 1998). In general, more severe psychological disturbance has been detected in women who offend alone, as opposed to abusing in the company of a male (Davin, Hislop, & Dunbar, 1999). However, dependency needs, low self-esteem, and social isolation are thought to be particularly evident in women who sexually offend (willingly or otherwise) with usually dysfunctional men (Matthews, 1993).

Personality disorders have been identified in several studies of female sexual abusers (Nathan & Ward, 2002). For example, Green and Kaplan (1994) reported a mean of 3.6 personality disorder diagnoses among female sexual offenders, in comparison to 2.4 comorbid personality disorder diagnoses in a comparison sample of nonsexually offending women. The most frequently occurring personality disorder diagnoses in this study were borderline, avoidant, and dependent disorders. The diagnosis of borderline personality disorder—in which problems with the requirements of personal relationships and the establishment and maintenance of appropriate boundaries are prominent features—is thought to be more common in female than in male sexual abusers (Nathan & Ward, 2001). Studies have also detected a higher than expected prevalence of learning difficulties among women who are sexually harmful (e.g., Mathews et al., 1997; Vandiver, 2006).

As suggested earlier in this chapter, the prevalence of paraphilias as primary motivators or drivers for sexual abuse by women is not thought to be as high as among male perpetrators (Davin et al., 1999); female sexual offending is influenced by a wide range of factors. However, the types of abusers identified by Nathan and Ward (2001, 2002) and others suggest that deviant sexual arousal may be integral to some of the categories identified (Grayston & de Luca, 1999; Saradjian & Hanks, 1996). A major limitation to the establishment of a clearer relationship between deviant sexual interests and sexually harmful conduct by women is the failure to recognize that sexual abuse by women may reflect uncommon and unacceptable sexual preferences (Nathan & Ward, 2001). Another limitation is the measurement of such interests where they may exist; the physiological and psychological measurement of deviant sexual interests in women is problematic and rare (Cooper, Swaminath, Baxter, & Poulin, 1990). Presently, sexual deviance is assumed only in rare cases where women are repeat sexual offenders, where they use violence, and where they demonstrate an escalating pattern of harmful sexual activity over a long criminal career (Ferguson & Meehan, 2005). Otherwise, sexually deviant interests are assumed to be absent (Ford, 2006). This could be a significant problem in the treatment and management of sexually harmful conduct in women; ignorance of primary motivating factors, especially one as important as deviant sexual arousal, may limit the effectiveness of interventions that fail to take them into account.

Cognitive distortions may be more common than deviant arousal among sexually harmful women. That is, such women may view their abuse of children and adolescents as an aspect of normal sexual behavior and/or as an acceptable means of achieving intimacy or affiliation, especially if they have experienced abuse and neglect and been exposed to dysfunctional and chaotic parenting styles (Rowan, Rowan, & Langelier, 1990). Although still aberrant and highly damaging, such distorted thinking and the conduct it underpins fall short of a diagnosis of paraphilia in many instances and may be more likely to respond to treatment when identified.

DEMOGRAPHIC CHARACTERISTICS

Craissati (2004) suggests that female sexual offenders share a number of characteristics with male sexual offenders. On the whole, female offenders tend to be young (between 20 and 30 years old), of low socioeconomic status, poorly educated, and often unemployed. Allen (1991), Grayston and de Luca (1999), and Nathan and Ward (2002) also note the trend toward youth and social disadvantage in women sexual abusers. In addition, Saradjian and Hanks (1996) and others have reported that even when employed, most female sexual offenders perform jobs that are poorly paid and unskilled. Ford (2006) comments that such a host of social disadvantages accentuate feelings of powerlessness in women who abuse. However, Saradjian and Hanks make the point that there are exceptions to this rule; these authors noted in their sample the presence of several abusive women who were socially active and outwardly successful. Consequently, Grayston and de Luca speculate that the stereotype of the socially disadvantaged female sexual offender has arisen simply because women with these common characteristics are most likely to be in contact with services that will observe, report, and act on evidence of sexual abuse.

Saradjian and Hanks (1996) described the poor social skills of the female sexual offenders in their sample; such skill deficits serve to compound feelings of low self-esteem, emotional loneliness, and social isolation. Problems in the adult relationships of sexually harmful women are also notable, and occur at rates higher than those observed in samples of nonsexual female offenders (Lewis & Stanley, 2000). For instance, early marriage and multiple partners are frequent in female sexual offenders, and a small age gap between mothers and children is common (Saradjian & Hanks, 1996). In addition, Miccio-Fonseca (2000) compared sexually offending women with a sample of nonsexual female offenders and observed that the former reported a higher number of pregnancy terminations and sexually transmitted diseases, in addition to poorer sexual knowledge and awareness. As a group, abusive women demonstrate more evidence of irresponsible sexual behavior than nonsexual offenders do, and they appear more likely to seek emotional intimacy through sex, leading to unsatisfactory adult encounters and enduring relationship problems (Marshall, Serran, & Cortoni, 2000).

Finally, women who offend with partners are thought to be more likely to have convictions for nonsexual offenses, demonstrating a higher level of general criminogenic need as well as criminal attitudes and beliefs in women of this type (Vandiver, 2006).

VICTIMS OF SEXUALLY HARMFUL WOMEN

More children and young people than adults are sexually abused by women (Craissati, 2004). Furthermore, the evidence suggests that girls are more at risk than boys from women who sexually abuse (e.g., Aylward et al., 2002; Nathan & Ward, 2002), although a number of studies have observed the opposite (e.g., Denov, 2003). Richardson, Graham, Bhate, and Kelly (1995) have suggested that although the majority of the victims of female sexual abusers are girls, as victim age drops, the number of male victims increases. Variation in findings may be related either to research methodology or to the comparative willingness of boys and girls to acknowledge and report their experiences as abuse (Ford, 2006). Women who have multiple victims tend to demonstrate a gender preference in their choice of victims (Vandiver & Kercher, 2004)—a preference likely to be influenced by a woman's own sexual orientation (Saradjian & Hanks, 1996). Women who have cooffending male partners may be more likely to have multiple victims (Vandiver, 2006).

Women are much more likely to abuse children for whom they have caregiving responsibilities (e.g., their own children, siblings, nieces, nephews, or cousins, or children they care for as babysitters or in their role as educators; Saradjian & Hanks, 1996). In contrast to male sexual offenders, therefore, women who sexually offend against children and young people who are strangers are thought to be very rare.

Early research (e.g., Rudin, Zalewski, & Bodmer-Turner, 1995) suggested that women who abused children alone were more likely to abuse very young children. However, recent research has indicated that the victims of sexually harmful women cover a more extensive age range. For example, 67% of the victims abused by women in the sample described by Aylward and colleagues (2002) were between the ages of 9 and 15 years—a figure comparable to that reported by Nathan and Ward (2002). Ford (2006) proposes that sample selection may play a role in estimations of the mean age of victims. Specifically, Ford posits that older children are more likely than young children to report abuse because a younger child is invariably accompanied by a caregiving female—often the abuser—when speaking to adults in authority, to whom disclosure could otherwise be a possibility. Ford also suggests that very young children may be more reluctant to disclose abuse to an adult because they fear the loss of an abusing carer, on whom they may otherwise be totally dependent. Consequently, the age of victims may appear older on average, but as yet unresolved questions about barriers to disclosure may have a bearing on the accuracy of this finding.

Compared with men who sexually abuse, women generally use less physical violence. However, in cases where a woman is sexually abusive in the company of a man—either because she is coerced into doing so, or because she abuses as an equal partner to a male abuser—the use of physical coercion and aggression is thought to be more likely (e.g., Vandiver, 2006).

PREVALENCE

Denov (2003) suggests that female sexual offending is a rare event. In the United States in 2001, 1.2% of those charged with forcible rape and 8% of those charged with sexual offenses in general were female (Federal Bureau of Investigation, 2002). Data from the Canadian Centre for Justice Statistics (2001) reveal that in 2000, 1.5% of adults convicted of sexual assault in this region were female. And Home Office figures for England and Wales indicate that 2% of adults convicted of sexual offenses in the late 1990s were female (Home Office, 2001). Therefore, across North America and Britain, women make up only a small proportion of all those convicted of sexual offenses. However, official statistics are thought to underestimate the rate of actual offending, due to the various problems inherent in securing a conviction for this kind of offense in women (Nathan & Ward, 2001). Therefore, official statistics alone cannot be used to gauge the prevalence of women who sexually abuse.

Cortoni and Hanson (2005) undertook a systematic review of victimization surveys, as well as official police and court reports in which female perpetrators were counted. Data from the United States, Canada, Britain, Australia, and New Zealand were examined, and unpublished as well as published research was included. Using police and court reports, Cortoni and Hanson noted that the proportion of female sexual offenders ranged from 0.6% (among New Zealand inmates) to 8.3% (among women committing sexual offenses other than rape in the United States). They concluded, therefore, that based on this evidence, the unweighted average proportion of sexual offenders who are women is 3.8%. When they examined the database of victimization studies, the proportion of female sexual offenders ranged from 3.1% (New Zealand, 2001) to 7.0% (Australia, 2002) of all perpetrators. From this type of data, Cortoni and Hanson concluded that the unweighted average proportion of sexual abusers who are female is 4.8%. Therefore, official reports and results from victimization surveys are broadly consistent and, when examined together, suggest that women are responsible for between 4% and 5% of all sexual abuse.

Might this still be a conservative estimate of the prevalence of harmful sexual conduct among women? A recent publication highlights a key problem with the disclosure of sexual abuse by children. In 2005, the U.K. charity Childline published a briefing paper on children disclosing sexual abuse between 2003 and 2004 (Childline, 2005). Where perpetrator gender was known, 46% of boy callers to Childline reported sexual abuse by a female (a further 6% reported abuse by a male and a female together), compared with 5% of girl callers (a further 2% reported abuse by a male in conjunction with a female). Victimization studies generally suggest higher overall rates of sexual abuse by females than are reported through more official criminal justice channels (Cortoni & Hanson, 2005). However, this Childline study may suggest that in the U.K. at least, victimization studies demonstrate a gender bias; boys reported proportionately more sexual abuse by female perpetrators than girls did when given the opportunity to do so anonymously. In studies of victims based on conviction data, more female victims tend to be identified. Do boy victims therefore have more problems accessing formal support structures, or more difficulty understanding and divulging their abusive experiences, than girls do? Are support services less sensitive to the needs of boys when women are perpetrators? Are boys more likely to be disbelieved than girls? The answers to such questions remain unknown for the present.

Finally, another kind of victimization study offers an insight into the question of prevalence. In a retrospective study, Groth (1979) reported that 8.3% of his sample of 348 male sexual offenders described having been sexually abused as a child by a woman. (A further 4.3% of male sexual offenders reported that they had been abused by an older though not yet adult female.) Travin, Cullen, and Protter (1990), Hunter and colleagues (1993), and Johnson (1989) have also commented on the prevalence of sexual abuse by females in the early lives of adult female abusers, reporting estimates of between 23% and 60%.

Together, these findings indicate that the sexual harm of young people—and adults—by women may not be common, but it is far from negligible. It remains the case that most perpetrators of sexual abuse are men. However, according to figures gleaned from a variety of sources and from several countries, *at least* 4% of sexual abusers are female. Official statistics, based on convictions for sexual offenses, are underestimates of the true rate of female sexual offending. Although the true extent of this underestimation is unknown, estimates of the prevalence of female sexual abuse of boys may be less accurate than those of girls. And the experience of abuse by a woman in the early lives of male and female sex offenders is, at the very least, notable. Attitudes supporting the view that women who perpetrate sexual abuse are rare are inaccurate and may limit the recognition of female sexual abuse. Such attitudes ensure that ignorance about female sexual abuse will continue to prevail, leaving victims undetected and ultimately unprotected (Cortoni

& Hanson, 2005). For these reasons, more attention to the questions of identification and detection, as well as prevalence, is warranted.

JUVENILE AND DEVELOPMENTAL ISSUES

Sexually harmful activity in young people and adults must be detected because of its association with prior victimization, the risk of continued victimization and sexually harmful behavior, and the difficult nature of treatment for adult offenders (Cantwell, 1995). Therefore, the experience in childhood of abuse, rejection, and attachment problems is a particularly important consideration in any discussion about the origins and management of sexual offending in females—just as it is in males.

The prevalence of childhood abuse in women who abuse sexually as adults is thought to be very high indeed (e.g., Saradjian & Hanks, 1996; Vandiver, 2006). Lewis and Stanley (2000) reported that over three-quarters of their admittedly small sample of 15 women sexual offenders had been sexually abused as children, with the majority of such abuse involving some form of vaginal or anal penetration. Similarly, Miccio-Fonseca (2000) reported that over half of the women in her sample of young female sexual abusers had been sexually traumatized by the age of 6 years, and over three-quarters by the age of 10 years. Of all the abused women evaluated in Miccio-Fonseca's study, a third were the victims of incest. Similarly, in a sample of young female sexual abusers, Mathews and colleagues (1997) reported that 78% had a history of sexual victimization. Many participants in the study described by Mathews and colleagues also reported drug or alcohol abuse (25%), learning difficulties (23%), suicidal ideation or suicide attempts (44%), and a history of mental health treatment (72%); over a third of their sample had also run away from home.

Physical abuse, emotional neglect, and family dysfunction are also thought to be very common in the backgrounds of women who sexually offend (e.g., Araji, 1997). Mathews and colleagues (1997) reported that 60% of their sample of young female sexual abusers described physical abuse in childhood. Freel (1995) highlighted findings that a high proportion of female sexual abusers had spent time in extrafamilial care as children. Relatedly, Green and Kaplan (1994) described the perceptions of female sexual offenders of their relationships in childhood with primary caregivers as mainly negative and damaging. Miccio-Fonsccca (2000) observed that 50% of her sample of female sexual offenders came from families in which at least one member had attempted suicide, compared to 8% of a comparison group of male sexual offenders.

Young female sexual abusers are thought to differ from young male abusers mainly in terms of their offending characteristics (Vick, McRoy, & Matthews, 2002). Specifically, young females invariably abuse younger victims who are known to them. For example, Fehrenbach and Monastersky (1988) described 28 young female sexual abusers in an outpatient clinic. The average age of perpetrators in this study was 13.9 years, and the mean age of their victims was 5.2 years. A common victim of a young female perpetrator in this study was a family member or child in the care of the perpetrator (e.g., while she was working as a babysitter); only very rarely was her victim a stranger, and only infrequently did she offend in the company of a male offender (Fehrenbach & Monastersky, 1988).

Like adult female abusers, the majority of young female sexual abusers appear to target girls as opposed to boys. Mathews and colleagues (1997) suggested that baby-sitting offenders are largely motivated by sexual curiosity and are less influenced by such factors as psychopathology, family dysfunction, and history of maltreatment than are those who offend against family members. Some studies suggest that a young female sexual abuser tends to be the family scapegoat, has poor peer relations, and possesses poor social skills; as a result, she strikes out at other children, particularly a more favored child (Araji, 1997; Johnson, 1989). Other motivations prevalent among young people include the reduction of anger (Araji, 1997), confusion (Johnson, 1989), anxiety (Johnson, 1989), shame (Araji, 1997; Johnson, 1989), and loneliness (Araji, 1997). Consequently, sexual gratification is thought to be a motive only rarely in young female sexual offenders, although this observation may be an artifact of the more general problem of measuring deviant sexual interests in females.

Vick and colleagues (2002) have suggested three possible categories of young female sexual abusers. First, they describe a "curious adolescent abuser," who is sexually as well as socially anxious and awkward. Second, they describe a "self-initiated abuser," whose abuse of others (generally family members) is a replay of her own experiences of abuse within a highly dysfunctional and harmful family. The third type of abuser described by Vick and colleagues is a "male-coerced abuser," even though this presentation is not thought to be particularly common (e.g., Fehrenbach & Monastersky, 1988). The male-coerced young female sexual abuser is characterized as an older child or adolescent who is dependent and isolated, and has low self-esteem. Further research examining this typology of young female sexual abusers is warranted, both to explore offending characteristics in this group and also to make links between young and adult female abusers. However, such research should only take place when the limitations of typologies are recognized and the more fundamental and desired object of theory development is paramount.

Therefore, young female sexual abusers display a range of behaviors, motivations, experiences, and needs that mirror those observed in adult abusers. The experience of abuse, dysfunctional relationships, and disruption in the care provided by the family of origin appear endemic; as with adult women, deviant sexual interests are thought to be a less common motive than other factors, such as curiosity, confusion, anxiety, and loneliness.

FORENSIC ISSUES

Risk Assessment

Cortoni and Hanson (2005) compared the rates of sexual recidivism among 380 convicted female sexual offenders and large samples of male sexual offenders (Hanson & Bussière, 1998; Hanson & Morton-Bourgon, 2004). A follow-up period of 5 years was examined. The authors reported that 1% of female offenders committed a further sexual offense during the 5-year follow-up period, compared with 13–14% of male sexual offenders. The rate of violent recidivism (including sexual) was higher in both groups: 25% of male sexual offenders reoffended violently over the 5 years, compared with 6% of female sexual offenders. And the rate of general recidivism (including sexual and violent) was higher still, at 37% after 5 years in the male sexual offenders compared with 20% in the females. Male–female differences in recidivism rates reported by Cortoni and Hanson (2005) were statistically significant ($p < .001$). According to official records, therefore, women convicted of sexual offenses reoffend sexually at a far lower rate than that observed in convicted men, although the rate of general recidivism in the women sexual offenders is notably high.

Cortoni and Hanson (2005) also compared the arrest rates for males and females. They found that whereas a third of all recorded allegations of sexual assault by men resulted in police arrest, women were arrested in response to more than half of the allegations of sexual assault made against them. Thus, once sexual assault is reported, police arrest is more likely to follow for female than for male alleged perpetrators. The rate of convictions following charges is unknown; what proportion of charges of sexual assault result in prosecution? How difficult is it to prosecute a woman "successfully" for a sexual assault? How often are charges of sexually motivated offenses carried out by women reduced to lesser charges, thus concealing the true scale of sexual abuse by women? And how often are alternative agencies such as the social services placed in the position of having to (or, indeed, choosing to) detect and manage women who are sexually harmful without recourse to the criminal justice system? Risk assessment and management as practical objectives are underpinned both by a recognition of the scale of the conduct to be prevented and by an understanding of the factors that contribute to its occurrence in the first place. Practices that limit the official recognition of sexual abuse—perhaps because of the problems inherent in securing convictions for sexual offenses in women, or because of a well-intentioned desire to protect damaged but abusive woman and girls from the criminal justice system—undermine risk management, to the detriment of unprotected and unrecognized victims (Denov, 2003). So, on the basis of what we know already, how can we improve our ability to protect those most at risk?

Saradjian and Hanks (1996) outlined a model of risk assessment with sexually harmful women that is comparable to good practice with male abusers. They suggest that attention should be paid to assessment in four areas: (1) an abuser's history, especially if she has experienced severe developmental trauma and disturbed attachments; (2) socioaffective functioning, especially if there is evidence that the abuser's skills in this area are deficient and her history of relationships is characterized by abuse, disrespect, and exploitation; (3) attitudes to relationships, intimacy and sex, and children, especially where there is evidence of problematic or misplaced emotional expression, experience, and congruence, as well as inappropriate sexualization and hostility; and (4) her offending behavior, including her criminal thinking styles, cognitive processing, sexual interests and arousal, capacity for empathy, disinhibitors, and motivation to change. Given the prevalence of mental health needs in women who are sexually harmful, a diagnostic assessment is an obvious fifth area of investigation, given the relevance of such needs to harmful behavior more generally (Monahan et al., 2001).

In regard to the availability of tools to structure the assessment of risk in sexually harmful women, no actuarial guides have demonstrated any real suitability with this group (Craissati, 2004). Approaches that utilize structured professional judgment are recommended, although research is still awaited that demonstrates the broad utility of these instruments with women, and concern has been expressed in some quarters about the transparency of the decision making when such techniques are used (Beech & Ward, 2004). The Risk for Sexual Violence Protocol (RSVP; Hart et al., 2003) has been suggested as a framework for the assessment and management of risk posed by adult female perpetrators. Consistent with the framework presented by Saradjian and Hanks (1996), risk factors requiring particularly close scrutiny with women and covered by the RSVP include problems with their own experience of child abuse; their beliefs about and their management of intimate and nonintimate relationships; their attitudes toward the behavior identified by others as sexually harmful; arousal to sexual contact with children; mental health problems and personality difficulties; substance abuse issues; problems with stress and coping; and self-awareness. In addition, an evaluation of attitudes toward planning and treatment will offer guidance on prospects for remediation and risk management. The advantage of the RSVP over other instruments designed to assess risk is that it provides a framework for risk management planning based on the findings of the assessment and a formulation of the risks posed by the individual abuser. In regard to young female sexual abusers, the Estimate of Risk of Adolescent Sexual Offence Recidivism (ERASOR, Version 2; Worling & Curwen, 2001) has been suggested as a general guide to risk assessment with this group, although users must take into consideration the fact that most research on young sexual offenders has been carried out on young men (J. R. Worling, personal communication, December 15, 2006).

Risk Management Issues

Risk management depends entirely on risk assessment. An understanding of critical individual and situational risk factors, and of how they interact with one another and over time to influence the potential of one individual to harm another, will dictate what is done to prevent that harm from arising again in the future (Risk Management Authority, 2007).

As with male sexual offenders, a comprehensive clinical formulation of sexually aggressive behavior in women requires the consideration of several potentially relevant risk and protective factors. Specifically, attention needs to be given to the interplay among an individual's history, her psychological vulnerabilities and capacity, her current stressors, and the internal and external resources she has to cope with these stressors—as well as to the problem behavior itself, her attitudes and beliefs about its occurrence, and her understanding of the need for change (Ward & Stewart, 2003). The resultant risk formulation is a causal narrative or conceptual model that links the predisposing and precipitating risk factors most relevant to her abusive conduct to those areas of strength and skill—or protective factors—that have the potential to counterbalance risk. This conceptual model then links the assessment findings with the management plan to follow, and is (or should be) the channel through which assessment findings continually update management planning and, ultimately, the prevention of further sexual abuse.

Risk management has at least three components (Hart et al., 2003). The first and most obvious component is treatment. A small number of treatment programs for sexually offending women have been described in the literature in the last 10 or more years. For example, Matthews (1994) describes the Genesis II program, which has many features in common with sex offender treatment programs for men but includes a number of more gender-specific components, such as strategies for managing dependence on dominant males. However, a significant development in the treatment of female sexual abusers has been pioneered by the Lucy Faithfull Foundation in England. Described in detail by Ford (2006) and by Ford and Cortoni (Chapter 27, this volume), this is a manualized program that was pilot-tested in female prisons in England and involves a combination of group treatment and one-to-one therapy. Additional treatments can have relevance for the risk management of sexually harmful women. For example, treatments with medication and psychological therapies may be administered for mental health needs and personality difficulties, and more cognitively based programs may be delivered to remedy aspects of deficient socioaffective functioning and attitudes to offending more generally. More psychotherapeutic interventions may be indicated in cases where traumatic past experiences have generated distorted and problematic core beliefs and schemas. Such treatments can function as risk management strategies if they are likely to have a positive impact on factors directly related to risk of sexual abuse.

A second important component of risk management is supervision. Supervision involves the imposition on sexual offenders of restrictions on activity, movement, association, and communication designed to limit access to possible victims or scenarios that might initiate a sexual offense. For example, an offender who previously accessed victims through her employment as a babysitter could be required to refrain from employment with children, either indefinitely or for the duration of supervision or a term of conditional release. Alternatively, a sexual offender may be required to maintain a minimum distance between herself and a former victim, or between herself and a venue where children congregate (e.g., a school or kindergarten). Restrictions on communication are intended to limit the capacity of a convicted offender to use less direct means to groom or threaten former or potential victims.

A third important component is monitoring. Monitoring involves the identification, either as a part of treatment or in a risk assessment, of the early warning signs of a relapse into sexual abuse or violence. Information about early warning signs is then used by supervisors, treatment providers, support workers, or others involved in the care and management of a convicted sex offender to monitor changes in risk. Such practitioners are obligated, therefore, to respond accordingly when an elevation in risk is indicated by the detection of one or more early warning signs. Ideally, responses to the detection of such indicators should be specified in advance and, more ideally still, discussed and agreed upon with the offender. Involving the offender in risk management planning of this kind creates opportunities to generate more information that is relevant to ongoing risk management, as well as improvements in the rapport between offender and practitioners. If offenders feel involved in a process that will ultimately keep them at liberty in the community as opposed to incarcerated in prison, their motivation to engage could improve, to the benefit of the safety of others.

A possible fourth component of risk management is victim safety planning, which refers to the steps taken or recommended to improve the safety and security of the possible victims of sexual offenders. Such steps might include community notification or the relocation of offenders released from detention to an area far from the home of a former victim. Steps may also include the issue of providing personal alarms and guidance in personal safety to victims. If the targets of female sexual offenders are made harder to victimize, the risk to individual victims may be limited, and efforts at further offending may become more detectable and likely to be reported.

An excellent overall framework for risk management is the good-lives model (GLM; Ward, Polaschek, & Beech, 2006; Ward & Stewart, 2003). For many reasons, the GLM is an inspiring model of care and offender rehabilitation for women as well as men. One important reason why it is a useful framework in the management of the risks posed by women is the fact that it pays as much attention to positive or protective factors as to risk factors. If offending behavior, including sexual offending, is a manifestation of the difficulties sexual abusers have in achieving life goals or "primary goods" (such as mastery, knowledge, and relatedness), then risk management is as much about enhancing learning and skills as it is about reducing undesirable and unacceptable behavior. In a field where so many perpetrators have experienced so much hardship themselves, it is refreshing to behold a model of understanding and management that is not excessively negative or punitive.

Legal Issues

The most significant issue in expert witness testimony is the lack of systematic research on the subject of female sexual abusers, compared to that on men. Practitioners preparing legal reports and giving evidence in court on the harmful sexual behavior of women must exercise caution in describing the findings of empirical research. Such practitioners must make it clear that findings are often based on small sample sizes, are reliant on self-report information, and are often retrospective in design. This does not make this form of information or testimony any less valid, but its influence in the case being discussed will be improved if its limitations are explicitly noted.

In the event that the sexual abuse of a child is reported and the child has been in the care of a male and a female, and the male is the suspected perpetrator, it should not automatically be assumed either that the female is innocent or that any action on her part to support or promote the abuse was inevitably forced by the male. Practitioners assessing family caregiving units should examine family dynamics in general and the role of the female in particular, and should avoid assuming from the start that examination is unnecessary and that her role is inevitably insignificant.

Because children appear to be the most common victims of female sexual abusers, practitioners assessing children and concerned about any form of abuse should try to ensure that they give themselves the opportunity to assess the children separately from their female caregivers. In the event that a child is being abused, such information may remain unreported if an assessment is carried out with the perpetrator present.

Finally, there is a requirement to educate the police, lawyers, judges, and ultimately juries about sexual offending in general and by women in particular. Education for police and court officials, either in the form of direct teaching or in the background information provided in expert witness reports, is necessary to limit the potential for people in a position of power to allow biased or misinformed judgments about women's offending behavior to influence their treatment of a case. Women can and do sexually abuse—children, young people, and adults—and just because a woman does not have a penis, her potential to significantly harm is not reduced (Hislop, 2001).

THEORY

Etiology

Where does female sexual deviance come from? Why do some women sexually assault children or young people? So far, this chapter has examined patterns in female sexual abuse and identified some of the common or shared characteristics among women who offend in this way. This section speculates on the possible origins of sexual abuse in women and on some of the difficulties encountered in trying to establish etiology. Only by understanding the origins of this behavior, what it is, how it develops, and how it changes over time will practitioners and researchers be in a position to reduce the frequency of this social problem (Ward et al., 2006). Treatment programs for sexual offenders are typically based on theoretical assumptions concerning the psychological, biological, and sociocultural causes of sexual abuse (Ward et al., 2006). This section delineates the possible causes of female sexual abuse, based on the literature reviewed earlier; the following section examines the state of the literature on theories of female sexual abuse, based on the interplay among the different causes identified.

A recurrent finding in women who demonstrate sexually harmful behavior is their own experience of abuse in general, not just sexual abuse. Although the literature is not extensive, and the number of empirical studies of female sexual abuse is more limited still, a persistent finding is that harmful women have themselves been harmed as children and young women. The harmful experiences reported range from prolonged sexual abuse through physical and emotional abuse and neglect. The possible causal relevance of abuse experiences to subsequent offending may be characterized in several different ways.

First, abused children are more susceptible to the development of mental health problems and personality difficulties, including personality disorders. Difficulties in problem solving, in relationship management, and in the development of empathy for others may ensue; such children may also develop distorted attitudes and beliefs about others and relationships. All of these problems can contribute to the development and tolerance of sexual abuse. Emotion regulation can be impaired as well in individuals with mental health needs, rendering deficient their understanding of their own emotions and emotional needs as well as those of others, including children.

Second, children who are abused by members of their close social networks are, by virtue of the presence of the abusers, more likely to be exposed to deficient models of relationships and the roles of caregivers such as parents. Young girls and women from disturbed family backgrounds therefore acquire only a limited repertoire of skills and experiences and are subjected to the poor modeling of relationships. Their own intimate relationships and caregiving experiences are rendered deficient as a result. Thus a child's experience of physical, emotional, and sexual abuse, especially if it is long term, potentially handicaps the child in her development of core interpersonal, relationship, and caregiving skills; it also deprives her of the confidence to gain them from other sources. Not only does sexual abuse have long-term effects on children, but it also serves as a contagion that follows the victims into the next generation, with repetitive and cyclical traumatization of others (Warren & Hislop, 2001).

Third, the experience of sexual abuse, especially if it is prolonged and if it occurs in the context of a neglectful and dysfunctional family or caregiving unit, may generate in the growing child distorted sexual scripts or expectations about the role of sexual conduct in relationships. Distorted sexual scripts in the context of poor emotion regulation raise the risk of confusing sexual activity with control or mastery or relatedness.

However, many girls (and boys) are abused, and the majority do not go on to abuse children and young people in their care. What causes harmful sexual conduct in women, in addition to the experience of abuse?

Mental health problems (including learning difficulties) and clinically significant personality patterns (such as traits of dependence or narcissism) may have a bearing on women's sexually harmful behavior, independent of their experience of abuse in childhood. Factors that may be as much biological as social in origin may generate problems with emotion regulation, in which sex comes to have a soothing role. Alternatively, insecure attachments characterized by need or dominance may prevail—in which sex functions to reduce feelings of loneliness, and sex with children or adolescents functions to replace much more threatening age-appropriate adult attachments. A disrupted or neglectful family environment may have exacerbated rather than compensated for these limitations by restricting the development of skills to manage self and relationships more effectively. Therefore, the presence of mental health needs in addition to an environment in which the growing child's needs are neglected may make more likely the development of distorted attitudes and beliefs about children, relationships, intimacy, and the appropriate expression of sexual need.

Two other factors may make a contribution to the etiology of sexual abuse in women. The first is criminal attitudes and beliefs, which support the disregard of social norms, the breaking of rules, and the disrespect of others (i.e., the belief that the needs of the individual can be placed above the needs and wishes of others). Criminal attitudes and beliefs not only serve to condone rule-breaking behavior, but make punishment less threatening and less likely to bring about a lasting change in behavior while these attitudes and beliefs remain unchallenged. Antisocial cognitions may limit a woman's resistance to perpetrating a sexual assault, although other offense types may be just as likely.

The second factor is deviant sexual interests and arousal. This subject has been examined previously in this chapter, and its consideration there has reflected the general belief that women who display sexually harmful conduct are on the whole not sexually deviant; they usually do not warrant a diagnosis of one of the sexual paraphilias considered elsewhere in this volume. However, paraphilias *have* been detected and suspected in a number of studies, and the role of this factor in the etiology of some women's sexual offending—possibly a larger role than has been suspected hitherto—simply cannot be overlooked. In a small number of women, indeed, this factor may be the most influential in causing sexually harmful behavior. In many other cases, it is suspected, deviant sexual arousal will be influenced by the woman's own experience of abuse and the subsequent reinforcement of the abuse of others. In the remainder, perhaps the majority, deviant sexual arousal plays a minimal role beside factors relating to family life, attitudes and beliefs, and mental health.

Do men make women sexually harmful? There is no question that women made vulnerable by disturbed early experiences and relationships are in turn potentially vulnerable to the influence of dominant males, which may include males who are sexually abusive. Such a man may coerce such a woman to sexually offend against her own or other children against her will. In such an event, he can be said to have created the environment in which the woman feels it to be acceptable or desirable to abdicate responsibility for her own behavior. But she is still responsible for putting her own needs—to maintain her dependent relationships with her partner, for example—or the needs of her partner ahead of those of her children. He may make her weak, but she fails to prevent damage that may require a lifetime to repair; and her behavior is thus abusive, albeit indirectly so (Grayston & de Luca, 1999). Men are unquestionably a factor in the sexually harmful conduct of many women, but the causes of such abuse almost always include more than the presence of a complicit male.

Therefore, etiological factors may be clustered as follows: problems with emotional competence and response; problems with attitudes and beliefs as well as cognitions; problems in interpersonal skills and functioning, leading to intimacy deficits; and deviant sexual arousal. A combination of childhood abuse and other childhood experiences, learning history, social and cultural context, and biological factors will account for problems in these areas. Only when professionals in this field go beyond superficial behavior and speculation upon it, and investigate the underlying causes, will theoretical models emerge. Over many years, many models of male sexual offending have been proposed, culminating in wide-ranging and rational models such as the pathways model proposed by Ward and Siegert (2002). This process is just beginning in the literature on women.

The experience of trying to understand the etiology of sexual offending in men should be studied, and the best ideas and models should be adapted as appropriate—not just rejected because of possibly ill-founded assumptions that sexual offending is entirely different for women.

Theory Development

Theory construction enables practitioners and researchers to identify the important clinical phenomena evident in the sexual offending domain and to consider the causal mechanisms that are responsible for their occurrence (Ward & Siegert, 2002). In reviewing the research on men who offend sexually, Ward and Siegert (2002) suggest that a theory of child sexual abuse must include the following desirable features: (1) It must accommodate psychological, biological, cultural, and situational factors; (2) the theory should explicitly identify the clinical phenomena it is attempting to explain; (3) it should postulate mechanisms capable of generating the core clinical phenomena associated with sexual offenders, and detail the interrelationships of these mechanisms; (4) the theory should contain multiple offense pathways or etiological trajectories and allow for different types of sexual offenders (where knowledge permits such distinctions); (5) it should also include both distal and proximal causal factors, thereby providing a framework for understanding why some offenders commit some offenses against victims in certain contexts; (6) the theory should be as detailed as the empirical evidence and understanding will permit; (7) it should explain why different types of developmental adversity may or may not result in later offending; and (8) it should embody the epistemic virtues of comparative simplicity, explanatory depth, scope, theoretical consistency, coherence, and simplicity.

Do we know enough about sexual offending in women to propose one or even more theoretical models demonstrating such features? At the present time, the answer is no. Much research has been carried out into the psychological factors relevant to female sexual abuse, and there is good awareness of the cultural factors relevant to this activity. However, biological factors cannot be divorced from sexual offending, even in women, and these require more consideration before theory development can continue in earnest. Also, while research on typologies has been invaluable for identifying the clinical phenomena of interest, it has been conducted at the expense of developing an understanding of the mechanism of how the most relevant and likely factors interact to produce offending scenarios in some circumstances but not others. Finally, although good attention has been paid in research to predisposing factors in women's sexual offending, the identity of triggers to specific instances of abuse and the definition of offense chains relevant to the social context in which women operate and offend require further work.

Although there have been many calls to avoid the use of models of male sexual offending to explain sexual offending in women, and with good reason, researchers and practitioners working with women may learn much from their colleagues working with men in respect of theory development. The seminal work of Ward and Siegert (2002) on the pathways model would be an excellent place to start.

Research Priorities

There are many areas in which research into female sexual abuse is warranted, and only the most important will be reviewed here. These research priorities may be divided into three areas: (1) epidemiological studies, (2) treatment studies, and (3) research into the development of theories of female sexual offending that will generate debate and underpin invaluable research work in the other two areas.

First, although there is now a substantial body of research on women and girls who are sexually harmful, there is still a need for studies with large sample sizes in which the nature and frequency of female sexual abuse will be explored in depth (Becker, Hall, & Stinson, 2001). Such research will offer the opportunity to clarify definitions of abuse and the nature of the acts involved; identify predisposing factors, and differentiate these from precipitating or proximal factors that act in the short term; and determine inhibitions to offending. More attention has to be paid to biological factors in female sexual offending in studies that will measure physiological responses as well as psychological and social factors. In addition, more research is required to help understand the barriers to disclosure of female sexual abuse, in the context of a study about knowledge and attitudes toward female sexual offending among researchers, practitioners, and the criminal justice system more widely. Such research will require the cooperation of multiple agencies (the courts, the police social services, charities, and private organizations), so that the broadest range of women relevant to a study of this sort will be sampled.

Second, the treatment of sexually abusive women and girls needs far more scrutiny, so that the design and mechanisms of such treatment can be both better understood and applied. Well-planned treatment outcome studies with long-term follow-ups are desperately needed (Becker et al., 2001; Ford, 2006; Vick et al., 2002). Unfortunately, the small numbers of women presenting for treatment, as well as the limited number of practitioners willing, able, and trained to administer the limited number of treatment programs in existence for sexually offending women, are likely to limit this area of development for a while yet. Developments in the recognition of the sexually harmful potential of women and its more open discussion may stimulate research in this area.

Finally, researchers and practitioners need to work toward the development of appropriate and robust theories of women's sexually harmful behavior, bearing in mind the rational recommendations of Ward and Siegert (2002). Theory development must be sensitive to the culture within which it is developed, but it should not be limited by a view that minimizes the harm women cause or excuses it as the fault of others. Theory development will stimulate the field and put female sexual offending in the context of a broader framework of understanding about women and how they try to lead their lives.

SUMMARY AND FUTURE DIRECTIONS

In this chapter, many different issues in the sexually harmful conduct of women have been considered. First, "sexual deviance" in women has been defined and contrasted with other frequently used terms, such as "sexual abuse" and "sexual offending." The ways in which these different terms influence how sexual harm by women is recognized, recorded, and dealt with have been considered. Widely used and discussed typologies of female sexual abuse have been reviewed, and some of the limitations of the typological approach to understanding abuse have been discussed. The characteristics of women who abuse and the children and the young people who are their victims have also been described, as have developmental issues in female sexual abuse and in the identification and management of young female abusers. Risk has been considered, followed by a lengthy discussion about risk assessment and management with women. Finally, the chapter has reviewed the state of the field in terms of its understanding of the possible causes of female sexual abuse, as well as the form of theories that might explain sexual offending in this group and lead to a clearer understanding of what treatment and risk management more generally will require.

The literature on sexually harmful women is quite substantial now; great progress has been made in the years since the first edition of this volume was published. But despite the volume of work completed to date, some parts of the field still require substantial development. Our basic understanding of sexually abusive women is limited by the dearth of good epidemiological studies involving large samples and preferably a longitudinal design. Also, the development of theories of female sexual abuse still awaits acknowledgment by some working in the field that deviant sexual arousal is a relevant factor in the conduct of some women who abuse, and that the source of their abusive behavior is not always the men who harm them. Although much of what has been developed in the field of male sexual offending will not be transferable to women who sexually abuse, the potential for overlap should not be discounted; and more effort is required to integrate the best of the work on men with the best of that on women, in order that improvements can be made in both areas.

Rates of reported female sexual offending are likely to rise as practitioners are guided in what to look for, given encouragement and support to recognize and identify sexually inappropriate conduct by females, and given clear guidance on what to do in response. Although practitioners are showing an increased willingness to recognize the potential of females to sexually abuse others, more remains to be done to improve their awareness of what to assess, their confidence in responding, and the skills to respond appropriately.

REFERENCES

Abel, G. G., & Rouleau, J. L. (1995). Sexual abuses. *Psychiatric Clinics of North America, 18,* 139–153.

Allen, C. M. (1991). *Women and men who sexually abuse children: A comparative analysis.* Orwell, VT: Safer Society Press.

American Psychiatric Association. (2000). *Diagnostic and statistical manual of mental disorders* (4th ed., text rev.). Washington, DC: Author.

Araji, S. (1997). *Sexually aggressive children: Coming to understand them.* Thousand Oaks, CA: Sage.

Atkinson, J. (2000). *Case studies of female sex offenders in the Correctional Service Canada.* Ottawa: Correctional Services Canada.

Aylward, A., Christopher, M., Newell, R. M., & Gordon, A. (2002). *What about women who commit sex offences?* Paper presented at the annual conference of the Association for the Treatment of Sexual Abusers, Montreal.

Becker, J. V., Hall, S. R., & Stinson, J. D. (2001). Female sexual offenders: Clinical, legal and policy issues. *Journal of Forensic Psychology Practice, 1,* 29–50.

Beech, A. R., & Ward, T. (2004). The integration of etiology and risk in sexual offenders: A theoretical framework. *Aggression and Violent Behavior, 10,* 31–63.

Canadian Centre for Justice Statistics. (2001). *Adult criminal court data tables 1999/00.* Ottawa: Author.

Cantwell, H. (1995). Sexually aggressive children and society response. In M. Hunter (Ed.), *Child survivors and perpetrators of sexual abuse* (pp. 79–107). Thousand Oaks, CA: Sage.

Childline. (2005, May). *Young people displaying sexually harmful behavior* (Briefing paper). Retrieved from *www.childline.org.uk*

Christiansen, A. R., & Thyer, B. A. (2002). Female sexual offenders: A review of empirical research. *Journal of Human Behavior in the Social Environment, 6,* 1–16.

Cooper, A., Swaminath, S., Baxter, D., & Poulin, C. (1990). A female sexual offender with multiple paraphilias: A psychologic, physiologic (laboratory sexual arousal) and endocrine study. *Canadian Journal of Psychiatry, 35,* 334–337.

Cortoni, F. A., & Hanson, R. K. (2005). *A review of the recidivism rates of adult female sexual offenders* (Research Report No. R-169). Ottawa: Correctional Service Canada.

Craissati, J. (2004). *Managing high risk sex offenders in the community: A psychological approach.* Hove, UK: Brunner-Routledge.

Davin, P. A., Hislop, J. C. R., & Dunbar, T. (1999). *Female sexual abusers.* Brandon, VT: Safer Society Press.

Denov, M. S. (2003). The myth of innocence: Sexual scripts and the recognition of child sexual abuse by female perpetrators. *Journal of Sex Research, 40,* 303–314.

Faller, K. C. (1987). Women who sexually abuse children. *Violence and Victims, 2,* 263–276.

Fazel, S., & Danesh, J. (2002). Serious mental disorder in 23,000 prisoners: A systematic review of 62 surveys. *Lancet, 359,* 545–550.

Federal Bureau of Investigation. (2002). *Crime in the United States 2001.* Washington, DC: U.S. Department of Justice.

Fehrenbach, P. A., & Monastersky, C. (1988). Characteristics of female adolescent sexual offenders. *American Journal of Orthopsychiatry, 58,* 148–151.

Ferguson, C. J., & Meehan, D. C. (2005). An analysis of females convicted of sex crimes in the state of Florida. *Journal of Child Sexual Abuse, 14,* 75–89.

Ford, H. (2006). *Women who sexually abuse children.* Chichester, UK: Wiley.

Ford, H., & Eldridge, H. (2006). Intervening with female abusers: Treatment needs, methods and outcomes. In H. Ford, *Women who sexually abuse children* (pp. 111–125). Chichester, UK: Wiley.

Freel, M. (1995). *Women who sexually abuse children* (Social Work Monograph No. 135). Norwich, UK: University of East Anglia.

Grayston, A. D., & de Luca, R. V. (1999). Female perpetrators of child sexual abuse: A review of the clinical and empirical literature. *Aggression and Violent Behavior, 4,* 93–106.

Green, A. H., & Kaplan, M. S. (1994). Psychiatric impairment and childhood victimization experiences in female child molesters. *Journal of the American Academy of Child and Adolescent Psychiatry, 33,* 954–961.

Groth, A. N. (1979). Sexual trauma in the life histories of rapists and child molesters. *Victimology, 4,* 10–16.

Hanson, R. K., & Bussière, M. T. (1998). Predicting relapse: A meta-analysis of sexual offender recidivism. *Journal of Consulting and Clinical Psychology, 66,* 348–362.

Hanson, R. K., & Morton-Bourgon, K. (2004). *Predictors of sexual recidivism: An updated meta-analysis* (User Report No. 2004-02). Ottawa: Office of the Solicitor General of Canada.

Hart, S. D., Kropp, P. K., Laws, D. R., Klaver, J., Logan, C., & Watt, K. A. (2003). *The Risk for Sexual Violence Protocol: Structured professional guidelines for assessing risk of sexual violence.* Burnaby, BC, Canada: Simon Fraser University, Mental Health, Law and Policy Institute.

Hislop, J. (2001). *Female sex offenders: What therapists, law enforcement and child protective services need to know.* Ravensdale, WA: Issues Press.

Home Office. (2001). *Statistics on women and the criminal justice system.* London: Her Majesty's Stationery Office.

Hunter, J. A., Lexier, L. J., Goodwin, D. W., Browne, P. A., & Dennis, C. (1993). Psychosexual, attitudinal, and developmental characteristics of juvenile female sexual perpetrators in a residential treatment setting. *Journal of Child and Family Studies, 2,* 317–326.

Hunter, J. A., & Mathews, R. (1997). Sexual deviance in females. In D. R. Laws & W. O'Donohue (Eds.), *Sexual deviance: Theory, assessment, and treatment* (pp. 465–480). New York: Guilford Press.

Johnson, T. C. (1989). Female child perpetrators: Children who molest other children. *Child Abuse and Neglect, 13*, 571–585.

Krahé, B., Waizenhöfer, E., & Möller, I. (2003). Women's sexual aggression against men: Prevalence and predictors. *Sex Roles, 49*, 219–232.

Laws, D. R., & O'Donohue, W. (1997). *Sexual deviance: Theory, assessment, and treatment.* New York: Guilford Press.

Lewis, C. F., & Stanley, C. R. (2000). Women accused of sexual offences. *Behavioral Sciences and the Law, 18*, 73–81.

Logan, C., & Blackburn, R. (in press). Personality disorder, psychopathy, and other mental disorders: Comorbidity among violent women in secure settings. *International Journal of Law and Psychiatry.*

Marshall, W. L., Serran, G. A., & Cortoni, F.A. (2000). Childhood attachments, sexual abuse, and their relationship to adult coping in child molesters. *Sexual Abuse: Journal of Research and Treatment, 12*, 17–26.

Mathews, R. (1987). *Preliminary typology of female sexual offenders.* Unpublished manuscript.

Mathews, R., Hunter, J. A., & Vuz, J. (1997). Juvenile female sexual offender: Clinical characteristics and treatment issues. *Sexual Abuse: A Journal of Research and Treatment, 9*, 187–199.

Mathews, R., Matthews, J. K., & Speltz, K. (1989). *Female sexual offenders: An exploratory study.* Orwell, VT: Safer Society Press.

Matthews, J. K. (1994). Working with female sexual abusers. In M. Elliott (Ed.), *Female sexual abuse of children* (pp. 57–73). New York: Guilford Press.

Matthews, J. K., Mathews, R., & Speltz, K. (1991). Female sexual offenders: A typology. In M. Q. Patton (Ed.), *Family sexual abuse: Frontline research and evaluation* (pp. 199–219). Newbury Park, CA: Sage.

Miccio-Fonseca, L. C. (2000). Adult and adolescent female sexual offenders: Experiences compared to other female and male sex offenders. *Journal of Psychology and Human Sexuality, 11*, 75–88.

Monahan, J., Steadman, H. J., Silver, E., Appelbaum, P. S., Robbins, P. C., Mulvey, E. P., et al. (2001). *Rethinking risk assessment: The MacArthur study of mental disorder and violence.* Oxford, UK: Oxford University Press.

Nathan, P., & Ward, T. (2001). Females who sexually abuse children: Assessment and treatment issues. *Psychiatry, Psychology and Law, 8*, 44–55.

Nathan, P., & Ward, T. (2002). Female sex offenders: Clinical and demographic features. *Journal of Sexual Aggression, 8*, 5–21.

Richardson, G., Graham, F., Bhate, S. R., & Kelly, T. P. (1995). A British sample of sexually abusive adolescents: Abuser and abuse characteristics. *Criminal Behavior and Mental Health, 5*, 187–205.

Risk Management Authority. (2007). *Risk management standards and guidelines: for offenders subject to an Order for Lifelong Restriction.* Paisley, UK: Author. (Available at *www.RMA scotland.gov.uk*)

Rowan, E. L., Rowan, J. B., & Langelier, P. (1990). Women who molest children. *Bulletin of the American Academy of Psychiatry and the Law, 18*, 79–83.

Rudin, M. M., Zalewski, C., & Bodmer-Turner, J. (1995). Characteristics of child sexual abuse victims according to perpetrator gender. *Child Abuse and Neglect, 19*, 963–973.

Saradjian, J., & Hanks, H. (1996). *Women who sexually abuse children: From research to clinical practice.* Chichester, UK: Wiley.

Singleton, N., Meltzer, H., Gatward, R., Coid, J. & Deasy, D. (1998). *Psychiatric morbidity among prisoners in England and Wales.* London: HMSO.

Travin, S., Cullen, K., & Protter, B. (1990). Female sex offenders: Severe victims and victimisers. *Journal of Forensic Sciences, 35*, 140–150.

Vandiver, D. M. (2006). Female sex offenders. In R. D. McAnulty & M. Burnette (Eds.), *Sex and sexuality: Vol. 3: Sexual deviation and sexual offenses* (pp. 47–80). Westport, CT: Greenwood Press.

Vandiver, D. M., & Kercher, G. (2004). Offender and victim characteristics of registered female sex offenders in Texas: A proposed typology of female sexual offenders. *Sexual Abuse: A Journal of Research and Treatment, 16,* 121–137.

Vick, J., McRoy, R., & Matthews, B. M. (2002). Young female sex offenders: Assessment and treatment issues. *Journal of Child Sexual Abuse, 11,* 1–23.

Viki, G. T., Massey, K., & Masser, B. (2005). When chivalry backfires: Benevolent sexism and attitudes towards Myra Hindley. *Legal and Criminological Psychology, 10,* 109–120.

Ward, T., Polaschek, D. L. L., & Beech, A. R. (2006). *Theories of sexual offending.* Chichester, UK: Wiley.

Ward, T., & Siegert, R. J. (2002). Towards a comprehensive theory of child sexual abuse: A theory knitting perspective. *Psychology, Crime and Law, 8,* 319–351.

Ward, T., & Stewart, C. (2003). Criminogenic needs and human needs: A theoretical model. *Psychology, Crime and Law, 9,* 125–143.

Warren, J. I., & Hislop, J. (2001). Female sex offenders: A typological and etiological overview. In R. R. Hazelwood & A. W. Burgess (Eds.), *Practical aspects of rape investigation: A multidisciplinary approach* (3rd ed., pp. 421–434). Boca Raton, FL: CRC Press.

Welldon, E. (1995). Perversions in men and women. *British Journal of Psychotherapy, 12,* 480–486.

Worling, J. R., & Curwen, T. (2001). *Estimate of Risk of Adolescent Sexual Offence Recidivism, Version 2.0.* Toronto: Ontario Ministry of Community and Social Services. (The ERASOR is available free of charge as a PDF at *jworling@ican.net*)

CHAPTER 27

SEXUAL DEVIANCE IN FEMALES

Assessment and Treatment

HANNAH FORD
FRANCA CORTONI

The assessment and treatment of females displaying sexually deviant behavior are relatively new developments, because acknowledgment of females as capable of sexual deviance or sexual offending has only occurred comparatively recently. Although this is now changing, a considerable gap remains between the extant knowledge base for sexually deviant males and that for their female counterparts. Perhaps as a consequence of this, many current assessment and treatment approaches for females broadly follow those devised for males, although the appropriateness of this has been questioned (e.g., Nathan & Ward, 2002; Saradjian, 1996). To highlight some of these issues, this chapter briefly outlines problems in conceptualizing and diagnosing sexually deviant behavior in females; discusses the current assessment and treatment methods and options; highlights where more gender-specific approaches may be preferable; and discusses the form these approaches could take.

ASSESSMENT

Diagnostic Difficulties

The first step in diagnosing sexual deviance among females is acknowledging that they engage in such behavior. Until recently, understanding of sexual deviance in females seemed largely limited to activities such as promiscuity or prostitution; it tended not to extend to behaviors such as child molestation or sexual assault of adult males. This discrepancy in perceptions of male and female sexual behavior is neatly summarized by Mathews, Matthews, and Speltz (1990):

> Few female offenders appear in clinical and research populations for exposing, stealing men's underwear, making obscene phone calls or window peeping. Do females not engage

in these nontouch types of behaviors, or are they not considered offenses when committed by females, or both? (p. 289)

The failure to acknowledge sexual deviance in females has been at least partly sustained through professional discourse. Denov (2001), for example, found that both psychiatrists and the police had "an informal yet well-established way of 'seeing' sexual assault" (p. 314), in which males were perpetrators and females victims; this excluded the possibility of females being sexually abusive. As one police officer stated, "A woman doesn't have the capacity to sexually assault . . . it's not in their nature" (quoted in Denov, 2001, p. 315). Such discourses have been supported by the gendered nature of the law in both the United Kingdom and the United States (Denov, 2003), which, until recent changes in the United Kingdom at least, defined many sexual crimes as perpetrated by males against primarily female victims. Furthermore, gender-specific guidelines for the diagnosis of sexual deviance in females are lacking; the *Diagnostic and Statistical Manual of Mental Disorders*, fourth edition, text revision (DSM-IV-TR; American Psychiatric Association, 2000) may be highlighting either the lack of recognition of such behaviors in females, or the difficulties in diagnosing them, when it states that "except for Sexual Masochism . . . the other Paraphilias are almost never diagnosed in females, although some cases have been reported" (p. 568).

In regard to sexually deviant behaviors such as child molestation, females have been reported to engage in many of the same activities as males (e.g., Kaufman, Wallace, Johnson, & Reeder, 1995); thus, in theory, indicators of sexual deviance in females should not necessarily differ markedly from those for males. However, societal norms and schemas of female roles and behaviors may hamper such recognition. In the case of child sexual abuse, for example, females are typically viewed as the carers and nurturers of children. Therefore, accepting that females may be sexually abusive toward children is not only difficult, but may threaten our view of women (perhaps mothers particularly) and the safety of children. Equally, it is easier for females to disguise abuse as part of routine child care—for example, abusing children while bathing them. Stereotypes may also have an impact on whether certain sexual behaviors by females are labeled as problematic; sexual relations between an older woman and a male adolescent, for example, may be viewed as an acceptable form of sexual "initiation." Moreover, because it can be argued that our society tolerates or even encourages greater nudity among females than males (Minasian & Lewis, 1999), this perhaps influences how acts such as exhibitionism in females are viewed. Hugh-Jones, Gough, and Littlewood (2005) note that early studies of female exhibitionism portrayed the behavior as fundamentally different from exhibitionism by men, and as somewhat less serious. Fehrenbach and Monastersky (1988) suggested that exhibitionism in a teenage female might be labeled as promiscuity, not indecent exposure as it might be in males. Still other researchers have suggested that in keeping with female stereotypes of passivity, masochistic behaviors in women could be viewed as an extension of their socialization to traditional submissive gender roles (Donnelly & Fraser, 1998).

It is perhaps on account of such factors that some have suggested that females entering the judicial system as a result of sexually deviant behaviors may be treated differently from males. The Iowa Commission on the Status of Women (1997) described the "paternal" attitude often shown toward girls in the criminal justice system, and suggested that authorities may be less likely to recognize that females may be as violent or dangerous as males. Viki, Massey, and Masser (2005) similarly report studies suggesting that females may be treated comparatively leniently, perhaps owing to assumptions of their lesser danger. However, others have suggested that this paternalism and leniency disappears if female behavior deviates significantly from female norms (see Ford, 2006); such behavior could include sexual deviance.

Clearly, such factors influence whether sexually deviant behaviors by females are initially recognized as "deviant" and the extent to which they are seen as problematic. The degree to which such behaviors are seen as deviant and problematic influences whether it is felt important to "treat" them. The fact that society has been slower to reach this level of recognition about female sexual deviance has led to very small numbers of women being available for study, making it difficult to outline what is specifically required to diagnose sexual deviance in females and to identify their specific needs.

What Information Is Required?

The purposes of assessment are to determine an individual's likelihood of engaging in further sexually deviant behavior and to identify areas of need that, through intervention, may reduce the risk of further deviant behavior and offer the individual alternative models of thinking and behavior (Denov & Cortoni, 2006). In this respect, then, it is important for the clinician to obtain in-depth information about the behavior in question—including its onset, the context in which it occurs, and its particular meaning for the individual—and to ground this in the information from a full clinical history. There are, however, issues of particular pertinence to females. In the case of females who have sexually abused children, a high proportion of perpetrators report histories of sexual, physical, or psychological abuse, or a combination of these (e.g., Saradjian, 1996; Tardif, Auclair, Jacob, & Carpentier, 2005; Travin, Cullen, & Protter, 1990), and childhood sexual abuse also features significantly in the histories of women who have been sexually aggressive toward men (Krahé, Waizenhöfer, & Möller, 2003). Although it is not suggested that a history of abuse directly causes sexually abusive behavior, it is important to be aware of any abuse history and its potential impact on the development of self-concept, coping patterns, and victim empathy, as well as the therapeutic relationship. A history of abuse may have affected the female's developing sexuality and her experience of sex and relationships. In Saradjian's (1996) study, for example, most women who had sexually abused children had themselves been abused as children. When asked what sex meant to them, all the women reported at least one negative feeling about their sexual experiences with adult partners, and negative feelings were particularly prominent among those who had initially abused young children or been coerced into abuse by others. In general, nonoffending women reported fewer negative feelings and more positive feelings (such as warmth and bonding) about their experience of sex with adults. Russell and Oswald (2001) found that women who sexually coerced others were more likely to adopt what they termed a "Ludic lovestyle"—a pattern of being emotionally uninvolved and manipulative in relationships, and preferring to be in control. It is therefore important to explore a female's sexual experiences and her feelings about these, and the extent to which these may have contributed to the motivation to behave in sexually deviant ways.

Other aspects of relationships and personal supports should also be explored. In women who have abused children, there is evidence that relationships in their families (Green & Kaplan, 1994; Saradjian, 1996) and later with peers or adult partners (Lewis & Stanley, 2000; Saradjian, 1996) have been poor, resulting in social isolation and a lack of supportive networks. This may have influenced the formation of relationships with victims or potentially coercive partners, as well as the ability to deal with stresses. Assessment of coping style is important, particularly given the high levels of difficulty reported in earlier stages of abusive women's lives. Saradjian (1996) noted that it was when women were not abusing children that many showed symptoms of psychological distress such as self-harm, depression, and anxiety. She hypothesized that these women might abuse children as a means of coping, particularly with negative feelings such as anger, fear, or loneliness (Eldridge & Saradjian, 2000).

Related to this is the need to identify any mental health difficulties. Research has yielded mixed findings, with some studies reporting high levels of psychiatric difficulties in female sex offenders (e.g., Green & Kaplan, 1994) and others (e.g., Saradjian, 1996) reporting lower levels. Although it is important not to explain sexual deviance in females solely as a consequence of (or indeed as evidence of) psychiatric disorder, it is clearly necessary to assess whether any such difficulties may have contributed to the behavior committed or are currently limiting a woman's ability to respond effectively to an intervention program.

A full understanding of the nature and context of the behavior committed is of great importance. This is perhaps particularly so in cases of child sexual abuse by females, which has often been reported to occur primarily under the coercion of male partners (e.g., Forbes, 1993; Wolfers, 1992). Such reports remove much responsibility from the females and portray them more as victims, in keeping with the professional discourse described previously. Although there are sufficient reported cases to suggest that this is the reality for some cases of female sexual abuse, Johansson-Love and Fremouw (2006) note that of the 13 studies they reviewed, only 3 reported most female sex offenders as having co-offenders. There are many clinical examples of women abusing without coercion from others: Gallagher (2000) describes a woman who "appeared to be the ring-leader of a group of abusers . . . living in the same town to whose homes she took the children to be abused" (p. 806). Equally, females may coerce adult males into sexual activity (Struckman-Johnson & Struckman-Johnson, 1994) or sexually abuse adult females (Vandiver & Kercher, 2004). It is therefore important not to assume that a woman's sexually deviant behavior is the result of coercion from another.

The assessment should also explore the role of sexual arousal/interests in the behavior committed. Whereas deviant sexual interests have been described as "one of the most distinctive and important problems for child molesters" (Laws, Hanson, Osborn, & Greenbaum, 2000, p. 1297), there appears to have been some reluctance to consider this possibility in sexually deviant behavior by females (Ford, 2006); such behavior is often ascribed to meeting needs for power or emotional intimacy, rather than, in some cases, a possible aim of obtaining sexual gratification (e.g., Kaufman et al., 1995). Although there may be genuine differences between males and females in terms of the importance of sex, such suggestions may also reflect traditional "sexual scripts" about women. These scripts suggest that men are motivated to engage in sexual activity, while women are sexually reluctant and exchange sex for attention or commitment rather than engaging in sex for its own sake (Byers & O'Sullivan, 1998); women are therefore not seen as inherently sexual beings. Although sexual gratification or arousal is unlikely to play a major role in all deviant behaviors committed by females, the possibility that deviant arousal or fantasy motivates or maintains the behavior of some females has been underresearched. Deviant arousal may be more relevant to females acting alone, for example, as they do not have others coercing or otherwise persuading them into the particular behavior. Sexual gratification may also be more important for women abusing adolescents or adults, because they may be more likely to select victims according to their own sexual orientation or to treat them as surrogate partners.

A further important assessment component is the individual's motivation to undertake a treatment program. Sgroi and Sargent (1994) suggested female offenders to be more skeptical than males that sex offenders can change. Allen (1991) also noted this, but found greatest skepticism in women who had not undergone treatment. Such skepticism has implications for treatment; beliefs in one's self-efficacy to deal with high-risk situations without resorting to the problematic behavior is an important variable in the outcome and future success of attempts to change behaviors (Casey, Day, & Howells, 2005). Negative beliefs in this respect may lower motivation, which may be further reduced by the limited resources and supportive social networks of many female offenders. Even if women believe the costs of offending to outweigh the benefits, they may feel that they lack the opportunity or power to respond differently (Kemshall, 2004). Additionally, Maison and Larson (1995) suggest that many female offenders lack motivation for treatment, perhaps because they have numbed the pain of their own abuse. This emphasizes the need to be aware of previous abuse experiences and to assess whether work to build self-belief and motivation for treatment are necessary treatment precursors.

This discussion can offer only a brief summary of some key issues in the assessment of females. Further assessment domains are outlined by Grayston and De Luca (1999) and described more fully by Saradjian (1996). Implications for treatment are discussed later in this chapter.

Aids to Assessment

Work with sexually deviant males has identified a number of areas that may contribute to their behaviors, such as attitudes supporting those behaviors, poor self-esteem, or difficulties in empathizing with others (e.g., Beckett, Beech, Fisher, & Fordham, 1994). The literature offers clinical examples of many of these same difficulties in females (see Saradjian, 1996). Although the clinical interview will give some indication of the extent of any denial and offense-supportive thinking, psychometric assessment of such thinking in females is currently difficult; the typically small sample sizes have hampered the development of robust measures, and most work in this area has been male-focused. Whereas many measures have been developed for male offenders, their validity and reliability with females have not been sufficiently researched, and the results must be treated cautiously. Beckett (2005) describes ongoing work with his colleagues in the United Kingdom, comparing a small group of female abusers with a larger male group on standardized measures. They have found many similarities, including equally high levels of cognitive distortions, similar victim-specific and general empathy deficits, and similarly low levels of self-esteem. Using the same sample, Ring (2005) found that all the abusive women reported emotional loneliness, poor self-esteem, and little perceived control over events in their lives, although those abusing with males showed more difficulties in these respects. Women abusing alone had significantly higher levels of cognitive distortions than women brought into offending by males, and also poorer scores on the victim empathy measure than "high-deviance" male offenders described by the STEP team (Beckett et al., 1994). While interesting, and querying whether women abusing alone differ psychometrically from those initiated by men, these findings are based on measures selected for male offenders and may therefore fail to tap key psychological aspects for women.

Similar difficulties exist in the area of physiological assessment, particularly assessment of sexual interest. Research in this field has focused primarily on penile plethysmography (PPG) in males, although assessment of females with the vaginal photoplethysmograph is possible; it measures vaginal blood volume, vaginal pulse rate, and amplitude and response duration to different sexual stimuli (Cooper, Swaminath, Baxter, & Poulin, 1990). However, a number of concerns have been raised about PPG with males in terms of validity, reliability, and the ethics of stimulus materials involving children (Kalmus & Beech, 2005), and, relatedly, its inappropriate or inconsistent usage (Laws, 2003). These same concerns are likely to apply in using the technique with females, particularly given the small amount of work in that area. Furthermore, there is uncertainty as to whether males and females show the same paraphilic preferences (Nathan & Ward, 2001) and whether male and female sexual arousal follows the same process. According to Chivers and Bailey (2005), a number of studies demonstrate that female genital responses are less informative about women's sexual interests than is the case for men. Their own work found that women showed nonspecific genital arousal to human stimuli, whereas male genital arousal was category-specific, and that women could demonstrate genital arousal without experiencing subjective sexual arousal. The authors conclude that "little can be inferred about a woman's sexual preference on the basis of her genital responses alone" (p. 119); if so, this calls into question the usefulness of such techniques with females. Other ethical concerns have been raised, particularly with women who have been abused, as the technique could be deemed a form of reabuse (H. Eldridge, personal communication, 2003).

New techniques using attentional and information-processing methodologies to measure sexual interest are being developed (Kalmus & Beech, 2005). As Kalmus and Beech (2005) note, however, more research still needs to be done on these new techniques—and, as the development work has been undertaken with males, thought must be given to their applicability with females.

Comparing Sex-Specific Measures and Global Measures of Psychopathology

As the discussion above makes clear, it is difficult to compare these different types of measures, because there are limited (or, in many cases, no) data on female subjects. Where such data exist, they tend to come from small samples—or, particularly in the case of behavior-specific measures, the measures have been designed with males in mind, making their validity with females questionable. Laws and colleagues (2000), for example, suggest that sexual interest card sorts or the Clarke Sex History Questionnaire (Paitich, Langevin, Freeman, Mann, & Handy, 1977) are potentially useful self-report measures for males, but the extent to which this is true for females is not yet known. Some female-specific measures are available, such as the adult female form of the Multiphasic Sex Inventory II (MSI II; Nichols & Molinder, 1994), but little published research looks specifically at this group. Further work in this area is clearly important.

There has been some small-scale work using more global measures of psychopathology. Nathan and Ward (2002), for example, reported Minnesota Multiphasic Personality Inventory (MMPI-2; Hathaway & McKinley, 1989) results for seven female sex offenders. Four women showed elevations on the Psychopathic Deviate scale, suggesting antisocial tendencies; the remaining three showed elevation on the Paranoia scale, which, the authors state, indicates suspicion, resentment, and anger. Smaller numbers of women showed elevations on other scales. Clearly, however, the very small sample size precludes definite conclusions. Mathews and colleagues (1990) also reported elevations on the Psychopathic Deviate scale of the original MMPI, both in women coerced into abuse by males and in those engaging in sexual behavior with teenage boys. However, the profiles also indicated that many female offenders held traditional views of women and that their sense of self was underdeveloped. In summarizing work in this area, Curnoe and Langevin (2002) stated that studies using the MMPI with males have not yielded a particular profile describing male sex offenders as a group; given the heterogeneity of women committing sexually deviant behavior, such a profile is perhaps not likely for females either. However, Curnoe and Langevin identified some profile differences between male offenders according to the presence or absence of deviant sexual fantasies. It remains to be seen whether such differences exist between types of female offenders, and, if so, how this information can be incorporated into assessment of treatment needs.

Assessing Risk

The questionable relevance of using assessment measures designed for males with females holds true in assessing risk of reoffending. Beech, Fisher, and Thornton (2003) reviewed the many different risk assessment tools developed for male offenders and questioned whether they could be applied to other sex offender populations. There has been much work with sexually deviant males to determine the static and dynamic risk factors predicting sexual reoffending, but the relevance of these to females is uncertain. It is not clear, for example, whether risk predictors for males such as previous offending histories have the same utility with females, given that relatively few females have such histories (Nathan & Ward, 2001). Friendship and Thornton (2002) found that among male child abusers, those abusing male victims were at greater risk of being reconvicted for further sexual offenses, and those targeting young male victims presented similar levels of risk to females as those who initially offended against females. It is currently unclear whether females are more likely to sexually abuse male or female children; Denov (2003) has noted that females seem to be abusing male victims at higher rates than female victims, whereas Aylward, Christopher, Newell, and Gordon (2002) found that both male and female offenders abused primarily female victims. Such discrepant findings may make it difficult to ascertain whether a male victim increases a female offender's risk in the way it does for a male offender.

It may be useful to consider factors related to recidivism in female nonsexual offenders. Clark and Howden-Windall (2000) found that variables such as previous offense history, early onset of offending, or previous sentence were significantly related to reconviction—although, as stated previously, comparatively few sexually deviant females may have such histories. However, they also found familial factors such as a problematic childhood home life and lack of continuity in care to be highly predictive of reconviction, and these were exacerbated if combined with few educational qualifications and substance abuse. Other work has suggested that factors such as antisocial attitudes, relationship difficulties, and emotional dyscontrol are related to recidivism in female offenders generally, and that such factors should therefore be considered in any assessment of female sexual recidivism (Denov & Cortoni, 2006).

There may be other factors to consider in assessing the risk of sexually deviant women. At least some female offenders seem to have been coerced into sexual abuse by others or to have co-offended with others. The extent to which these women are able to resist such pressure from others in the future should therefore be examined. Because female offenders may also be the primary caregivers to children, this additionally requires careful assessment (Beech et al., 2003), particularly if family reunification is sought.

Research Priorities

Development of Assessment Measures

Assessing sexual deviance in females is not an easy endeavor. Even if such behavior is recognized as deviant and reported to appropriate agencies, the clinicians assessing this behavior have limited options. They can rely on women's self-reports or on their own clinical judgment (both of which may have drawbacks), or can form conclusions on the basis of assessment measures that, in the main, were not devised for women. Perhaps a key priority, then, is the development of appropriate, gender-specific measures. Simply rewording items for female respondents may not be sufficient. Researchers need to take account of potential differences between males and females—not just in terms of their offending, but in aspects such as their sexual interests, life experiences, and social roles. Similarly, while comparing female offenders' scores with those of males is interesting, it is important to develop appropriate normative data for nondeviant females.

Research on Risk Assessment

The current difficulties in identifying a female's risk of committing further deviant behavior has important implications both in allocating females to treatment and in managing them in the community. In the United Kingdom, a report on multiagency public protection arrangements across England, Wales, and Northern Ireland emphasized that the lack of risk assessment tools for female abusers created difficulties in forming management plans and sometimes resulted in downgrading these women's risk levels (Bunting, 2005). Clearly, then, work is needed to determine whether existing risk assessment tools are appropriate for females, and to develop new tools if they are not.

Identifying risk factors for females depends on information about their rates of reoffending. To date, it appears that the sexual reoffending rates of these women are very low. Cortoni and Hanson (2005) reviewed the recidivism rates of female sexual offenders in Canada, the United Kingdom, the United States, Australia, and New Zealand; they found that after an average of 5 years, only 1% had committed new sexual crimes. In a follow-up of 62 female sexual offenders, Williams and Nicholaichuk (2001) found that only 2 of these women had committed a new sexual offense. In both cases, these women had engaged in the sexually abusive behavior without a co-offender.

Finally, in addition to identifying risk factors for female sexual deviance, we should also consider any protective factors that an individual has or is able to develop (Hamilton & Browne, 2002). Research attention therefore needs to be directed toward identifying these factors in sexually deviant women and identifying means of developing them throughout treatment.

Development of Typologies

A third area for research is the continued study of typologies for sexually abusive women. As the research base has expanded, researchers have begun to develop typologies that highlight different general motivating factors for each offender type. Although an assessment should go beyond simply assigning an individual to a particular typology, these groupings may have clinical utility in helping to understand the differential development of the behavior and identifying areas of treatment need. As Vandiver and Kercher (2004) note, however, much of this work is in its early stages and has been limited by small sample sizes. The most frequently reported typologies for women who sexually abuse children are those reported by Matthews, Mathews, and Speltz (1991) and Saradjian (1996), although the two have similarities. Most recently, Vandiver and Kercher have used a significantly larger sample and identified six categories of female sexual offenders, although this was not specific to offending against children. The different findings suggest that there is still work to be done in this area and that these typologies do not "fit" all female abusers. Saradjian, for example, reported some "atypical" perpetrators in her sample. Nathan and Ward (2001) drew on their clinical experience to suggest several further subtypes, including (1) women who have been rejected sexually by male partners in favor of children, and whose feelings of rejection and anger are precursors to offending; and (2) "compliant victims"—women with strong dependency needs who, through setting up situations that make abuse more likely, indirectly contribute to the abuse of children.

    Although different typologies suggest different general motivating factors, each female will have personal motivations for her behavior, which may be highly idiosyncratic. Eldridge and Saradjian (2000) stress the importance of examining the individual needs that sexually deviant behavior meets for each woman. As they state, "unmet needs are associated with aversive emotional states to which the woman may have responded by sexually abusing" (p. 403). Therefore, these individual needs should be explored in the initial assessment, so they can be further identified and worked on in treatment.

TREATMENT

Extensive research has examined the factors that are related to sexual deviance in males, and the best ways to address these factors in treatment (e.g., Laws, Hudson, & Ward, 2000). As the discussion to this point has indicated, however, the state of knowledge regarding women who engage in sexually deviant behavior continues to be characterized by very small sample sizes and theoretical postulations that await further empirical verification. Consequently, pronouncements about the treatment needs of these women remain tentative. The unusualness of female sexual deviance may lead professionals to focus on the deviance itself, at the expense of other aspects of a woman's life that may be just as important. In fact, albeit limited, the evidence to date suggests that treatment should focus on a range of factors (Eldridge & Saradjian, 2000; Grayston & De Luca, 1999; Mathews et al., 1990; Nathan & Ward, 2002).

Treatment Needs

On the basis of available evidence, women who engage in sexually deviant behavior demonstrate distorted cognitions about their sexual deviance, problematic intimate relationships, and difficulties in emotional regulation; they utilize sex to regulate emotional states or fulfill dependence or intimacy needs (Eldridge & Saradjian, 2000; Grayston & De Luca, 1999; Nathan & Ward, 2002). Furthermore, for at least some of these offenders, a desire for sexual gratification is directly related to the sexual deviance (Nathan & Ward, 2002). A portion of these women demonstrate mental health difficulties, particularly posttraumatic stress syndrome and depression; high levels of substance abuse; personality disorders, including antisocial and borderline personality disorders; severe interpersonal difficulties, particularly in the area of romantic relationships; and general psychosocial deficits (see Grayston & De Luca, 1999, for their excellent review of the literature on these issues). The treatment of women who demonstrate sexual deviance therefore has two intertwined foci: treating the central elements that are directly related to the sexual deviance, and treating the broader additional problematic psychological and psychosocial factors that set the stage for the sexual deviance.

The Treatment of Factors Directly Related to Sexual Deviance

Due to the dearth of clear empirical information to guide the treatment of women who engage in sexually deviant behavior, various authors have proposed their own treatment models, based on limited research combined with their clinical experiences (e.g., Eldridge & Saradjian, 2000; Matthews, 1998; Steen, 2006). All these treatment models are based on a cognitive-behavioral approach and follow a relapse prevention model. There is also recognition that the treatment approach needs to be based on an understanding of women's communication styles and relational issues (Blanchette & Brown, 2006; Young, 1994). After she and her colleagues developed a typology of female sexual offenders (see Mathews et al., 1990), Matthews (1994) proposed that the appropriate treatment targets for these women are anger, shame, low self-esteem, misinterpretation of victims' needs, and misinterpretation of what victims are communicating. Matthews suggested that for these women, shame and anger have become fused with sexuality, leading to the sexual acting out. The goal of treatment is therefore to intervene in the acting-out process.

Eldridge and Saradjian's (2000) model of sexual deviance in women posits that for these women, unmet needs result in aversive emotional states that are alleviated by the sexually deviant behavior. These behaviors in turn become rewarding in themselves, leading to the development or reinforcement of knowledge, beliefs, and attitudes that facilitate further sexually deviant behavior. Drawing from the broader literature on women, and from their knowledge of sexual deviance in females, these authors described a relapse prevention model of treatment designed to help these clients develop a "new life" (Eldridge & Saradjian, 2000). They specified that effective treatment with these women includes identifying sexually deviant patterns, including thoughts, emotions, and behaviors; identifying the needs met by the sexually deviant behavior, and generating non-deviant alternative strategies to meet those needs; addressing the factors that gave rise to those otherwise unmet needs, including victimization histories; challenging distorted abuse-related cognitions; managing negative emotional states; managing sexual fantasies; and developing coping strategies to deal directly with the factors that immediately place the women at risk of sexually acting out. Eldridge and Saradjian particularly noted that their clients tended to have very problematic emotional self-management. Consequently, they incorporated some of Linehan's (1993) therapeutic interventions for borderline personality disorder into their treatment, to help improve these women's ability to manage their negative emotional states. Steen's (2006) treatment targets are virtually identical to those of Eldridge and Saradjian, and her treatment workbook provides specific strategies to address these areas.

Although a history of victimization is common in women who engage in antisocial behaviors, there is evidence that the victimization histories of women who engage in sexual deviance may be particularly severe (Grayston & De Luca, 1999). There is no doubt that for a large number of sexually deviant women, their histories of victimization are related to their current functioning, including their patterns of sexually deviant behaviors, patterns of relating with others, and patterns of coping (Eldridge & Saradjian, 2000); all these factors must be taken into account during treatment. It is important, however, to ensure that treatment for the victimization histories of these women does not take precedence over treatment for their sexually deviant behavior (Denov & Cortoni, 2006). Failing to differentiate between past victimization and current sexual acting out may prevent women in treatment from developing the necessary understanding of the issues that have led to their decision to engage in sexually deviant behavior. In addition, as these women frequently exhibit patterns of denial or minimization of responsibility for their behavior (Grayston & De Luca, 1999), such a failure may also obscure the responsibilities these women have for acknowledging their own behavior and for making necessary changes.

Eldridge and Saradjian (2000) have highlighted the modification of cognitive distortions directly related to sexual deviance as a central feature of treatment. Denov and Cortoni (2006) have added that targeting only these distortions, while important, is insufficient; treatment must also address the broader maladaptive cognitive patterns that influence a woman's life beyond the sexual deviance. Cognitions influence behavior in all areas of life (Alcock, Carment, & Sadava, 1988), and faulty cognitive patterns are a central feature in a variety of pathological conditions, including violence (Beck, 1999). Ellerby, Bedard, and Chartrand (2000) have outlined a model that demonstrates how sexually deviant behavior takes place within the context of a negative life pattern. This negative life cycle consists of emotions, negative styles of thinking, and unproductive or counterproductive coping strategies that eventually lead to the experience of inappropriate sexual thoughts or fantasies. Within this context, the cognitive elements that facilitate the negative life pattern should be examined and altered. A woman's core beliefs that facilitate the sexual deviance (Mann & Beech, 2003), as well as her habitual patterns of thinking, can be identified and examined in terms of their impact on all spheres of the woman's life—with a particular focus on the most common problematic areas, such as relationships and emotion regulation (Denov & Cortoni, 2006).

In keeping with the concept of sexual deviance occurring within a negative life cycle, an examination of the general coping styles of these women is indicated (Cortoni, Anderson, & Bright, 2002). Research shows that people have a preferred or prototypical *manner* or *style* of coping across a wide variety of problematic situations (Endler & Parker, 1999). Eldridge and Saradjian (2000) describe how sexually deviant women need help in developing and practicing coping strategies that are matched to the particular emotional and physical factors related to sexual deviance. Such specific coping strategies, however, do not address the day-to-day stressors related to an overall negative life pattern—a pattern that has probably facilitated the sexual deviance (Cortoni et al., 2002). Treatment should additionally focus on helping these women develop coping patterns that will be effective in all types of problematic situations, not just those specifically linked to those factors found in discrete instances of sexually deviant behavior (Denov & Cortoni, 2006).

In the Correctional Service Canada (CSC), a standardized approach to the assessment and treatment of women convicted of sexual crimes was established in 2001 (CSC, 2001). This approach has involved an accurate identification of cases, a standardized protocol for the assessment of risk and treatment needs, the provision of treatment designed to specifically address the criminogenic needs of these women, and ongoing maintenance during incarceration and subsequent supervision in the community. Integral to this approach have been the ongoing training and consultation services offered to assessors and treatment providers. Therapists are provided with a treatment manual to guide therapy sessions and to ensure consistency of intervention and continuity of services as each woman moves through her incarceration and into the community.

The original treatment program was based on what was known about the treatment of sexually deviant men, and adapted for women on the basis of a literature review indicating that sexually abusive women exhibit characteristics and dynamics somewhat similar to those of male sexual offenders (Grayston & De Luca, 1999). Consequently (and in a way highly similar to the treatment models described above), the program targeted cognitive distortions, victim empathy, sexually deviant arousal, and emotional management. In addition, the program included a special focus on relationships, since many of these women engage in sexually deviant behavior in the company of others, and often as a direct result of these others' influences. Inherent in the program were (1) the development of a behavioral chain to help a woman understand the elements that led her to her sexually deviant behavior, and (2) the development of a self-management plan. Because the numbers of federally incarcerated women in Canada who are known to have engaged in sexual deviance are consistently low (average of 15 per year), and spread over a wide geographical area, the program was designed to be delivered either to an individual or to a group. To date, no group sessions have taken place.

Unfortunately, due to the low numbers of women, the data are still insufficient to permit an examination of this program's effectiveness in resolving issues related to the sexually offending behavior. Furthermore, as most of these women do not reengage in their sexual deviance once they have been detected and sanctioned (Cortoni & Hanson, 2005; Williams & Nicholaichuk, 2001), much more time and much larger numbers will be required before sufficient empirical evidence can be collected to determine whether women who complete this treatment have successfully eliminated sexual deviance from their lives. After 5 years of clinical experience, however, it became clear that the existing program was inadequate to meet the varied needs of these women. Many of the women targeted for treatment exhibited additional difficulties that included cognitive limitations, mental health issues, and/or a very strong antisocial orientation, and these difficulties interfered with treatment. A portion of these women also maintained categorical denial of their offenses. Among this subgroup of women, this denial was frequently linked to their ongoing relationships with their co-offenders, who were also incarcerated. Consequently, it was determined that the treatment of these sexually deviant women needed to offer great flexibility, as well as a broader range of interventions to be tailored to each unique case.

In response to these issues, an updated treatment program is currently under development. The updated treatment refocuses its content on these broad treatment areas: cognitive and emotional processes; intimacy and relationship issues; sexual dynamics; and social functioning. Embedded throughout the treatment are the interrelationships among these factors, and the development of a self-management plan that includes goals for a healthier life. This approach recognizes that sexual deviance cannot be treated in isolation from the rest of a woman's life, and ensures that all areas of functioning are targeted. Furthermore, it allows the treatment to be adapted to each woman's individual treatment needs.

Additional Treatment Issues

As previously discussed, sexually deviant women may also present with mental health difficulties. When severe mental health issues are present, these issues must be addressed and the client's condition sufficiently stabilized before the factors related to the sexual deviance are dealt with. In more pronounced cases, psychiatric treatment, including medication, may be required. Our clinical experience has shown that failure to address these issues virtually eliminates any possibility that a woman will benefit from treatment for her sexual deviance. Furthermore, at least in the CSC, some women have demonstrated such profound mental health problems that treatment for the sexual deviance cannot be attempted. In these cases, the focus has been on stabilizing the women's condition and providing them with psychiatric care and intensive support (both while they are incarcerated and in the community) to help them manage their mental health problems.

Women account for the vast majority of diagnoses of borderline personality disorder (American Psychiatric Association, 2000), and borderline personality features are not uncommon among sexually deviant women (Grayston & De Luca, 1999). Emotional management is a central treatment need of such women. Although Eldridge and Saradjian (2000) incorporated techniques to deal with this issue in treatment, some clients may require intensive intervention specifically designed for this problem, such as dialectical behavior therapy (Linehan, 1993), before treatment for their sexually deviant behavior can begin. Similarly, if a woman has a substance abuse problem, it should be brought under control before other treatment takes place. While substance abuse exacerbates problems in a woman's life, it may simultaneously have become a dysfunctional strategy to help the woman cope with life difficulties (Blanchette & Brown, 2006).

Another possibility often neglected in women who engage in sexually deviant behavior is that they may present with egocentric or antisocial features (Grayston & De Luca, 1999; Nathan & Ward, 2002). Matthews (1998) noted that women with such features were particularly difficult in the context of group treatment, and were eventually discharged for their attempts to sabotage the treatment process. As in any treatment, a thorough assessment of the factors related to the sexually deviant behavior, as well as an assessment of the problematic areas of the client's life—including the presence of mental health problems, personality disorders, or substance abuse—will help determine the treatment priorities and guide how best to deliver treatment. As part of treatment planning, the woman's strengths and resiliency factors should also be identified and capitalized upon during treatment. Too often the focus in treatment is on deficits, while the presence of positive attributes is ignored. By capitalizing on these strengths, treatment concurrently helps a woman develop a better sense of self-efficacy and self-confidence that will serve her well in the future (Eldridge & Saradjian, 2000).

Finally, many women will need additional help to rebuild their lives in a manner that removes the need for sexual deviance. These women may require support to improve their general community functioning, with a particular focus on their ability to develop and maintain a more stable lifestyle with less dependence on others. Consequently, areas such as education and employment, as well as recreational activities, may require particular attention and additional services outside treatment. In contrast to men, women tend to be in more need of extensive and appropriately supportive social networks, as these play an important role in their ability to deal with stress (Rumgay, 2004). Part of treatment, therefore, will involve helping these women develop and access appropriate networks and services.

Measuring Treatment Progress

As previously noted, few psychometric tools have been validated for sexually deviant women. For this reason, the measurement of treatment progress can only be left to clinical judgment at this time. Nevertheless, clinical judgment of progress should still be guided by the available empirical evidence on the factors that should change as a result of treatment. Progress should be assessed by comparing changes through treatment with the pretreatment baseline. Furthermore, as noted by Eldridge and Saradjian (2000), therapists believe in change and may decide that change has occurred simply because clients are saying the right things in treatment. It is very useful to collect collateral information from relevant others in a woman's life to determine whether the changes apparent during treatment sessions are evident in the rest of her life. As Eldridge and Saradjian state, the only real test of treatment progress is whether behavior itself has changed.

Other Issues in Client Management

Eldridge and Saradjian (2000) have discussed the importance of providing an empathic, but noncolluding, therapeutic environment to permit the development of an appropriate therapeutic relationship. Matthews (1998) notes that sexually abusive women tend to resist entering group therapy; this resistance appears to be related to a fear that others will judge and demean them for their behavior, or that their sexually deviant behavior will become openly known. Matthews further notes that once these fears are assuaged, these women usually engage openly in the group process. To deal with resistance, she recommends that individual sessions be first utilized to help a woman become comfortable discussing her sexual deviance in a nonthreatening environment.

Another frequent issue with this particular client population is the need to determine whether family reunification is in order. Women who have sexually abused children also tend to have engaged in other types of child maltreatment (Grayston & De Luca, 1999). A thorough understanding of a woman's attitudes and behaviors that are likely to result in significant harm to a child is required before reunification can be contemplated (Saradjian, 1996). In addition, any reunification effort should only occur when it is clearly established that the children also wish to reunite with their mother. The reunification process should therefore include the involvement of child protection agencies and family therapists skilled in dealing with abused children. The continued involvement of agencies is also crucial to monitor progress, as well as to monitor warning signs that a woman's behavior is deteriorating (Matthews, 1994).

Research Priorities

There is much yet to be learned about the factors that lead women to engage in sexually deviant behavior and how best to treat them. The evidence to date, albeit based on small samples (Grayston & De Luca, 1999; Saradjian, 1996), suggests that many of these women's treatment needs are similar to those of men. The manifestation or the relative importance of these factors, however, may be different. For example, once they acknowledge their sexual deviance, women tend to show much less minimization of their behavior than men do (Matthews, 1994). When the sexually deviant behavior has occurred in the company of others, however, many of these women also wrongly take responsibility for the deviant behavior of their partners (Mathews et al., 1990). They typically show very problematic relationships with significant others (Grayston & De Luca, 1999; Matthews, 1994), including excessive dependence or overreliance on the men in their lives (Eldridge & Saradjian, 2000). Finally, although it is clear that some of these women do engage in deviant sexual fantasies (Grayston & De Luca, 1999; Nathan & Ward, 2002), such fantasies do not appear to be as predominant as with males (Wiegel, Abel, & Jordan, 2003). Many of these issues, however, require further empirical verification.

Given the low numbers of female sexual offenders, concerted efforts should be devoted to developing international research groups that can pool clinical and empirical information and build relevant databases on these women. Cortoni and Hanson (2005) have already started this effort in Canada by pooling available international information on the recidivism rates of women who have engaged in sexually abusive behavior. We and our colleagues are continuing in this endeavor by collecting more detailed clinical information on these women from various jurisdictions, and we hope that others will join us in this important exercise.

SUMMARY AND FUTURE DIRECTIONS

What is clear from this chapter is that although research interest in female sexual deviance has increased considerably in recent years and many clinical developments are underway, our understanding of sexual deviance in females lags behind that for males. Although still few in number, such women are now being recognized as needing assessment and treatment services, and it is important for us to be able to respond with appropriate, specialized programs. Many research, theory, and practice developments in the field of sexual offending use male child sexual abusers as "templates" (Polaschek & Hudson, 2004), and the resulting theories or treatment approaches are often transferred to other offender groups without sufficient consideration of whether this is appropriate. Although the evidence to date suggests that there are some similarities between sexually deviant males and females, there may be differences in the relative importance of these shared factors, as well as areas in which the two genders show little overlap. It is therefore important not to rely solely on measures or treatment models originally developed for males, and instead to begin development of more gender-specific methods.

Although the primary message of this chapter is that much more work is needed, the comparatively small numbers of sexually deviant women entering the criminal justice system or other services render research more difficult. For the same reasons, group treatment provision for females is problematic. This chapter has outlined these difficulties for the CSC, and similar problems have been encountered in the United Kingdom. Treatment programs have to be developed in a way that permits both individual and group treatment. Although individual work perhaps offers the possibility of greater flexibility in approach and tailoring to clients' particular needs, a disadvantage of such work is that women can feel isolated and "bizarre" (Eldridge & Saradjian, 2000), which could have an impact on outcome.

Although treating sexual deviance clearly requires some focus on the deviant behavior and the thinking patterns supporting it, we hope that this chapter has made clear the importance of expanding interventions to include consideration of sexually deviant females' general life situations and the contributions these make to their deviance. Many sexually deviant women have reported feelings of powerlessness, arising from factors such as their experiences of abuse, limited social supports, or employment status

(Saradjian, 1996), but perhaps also partly reflecting the lesser position of women in some aspects of society. It is therefore important that treatment—a situation in which a female again may feel relatively powerless—does not reinforce this powerlessness, but instead helps the woman to enhance her capabilities in order to improve her quality of life and lessen the likelihood of further deviant behavior.

REFERENCES

Alcock, J. E., Carment, D. W., & Sadava, S. W. (1988). *A textbook of social psychology.* Scarborough, Ontario: Prentice-Hall Canada.

Allen, C.M. (1991). *Women and men who sexually abuse children: A comparative analysis.* Orwell, VT: Safer Society Press.

American Psychiatric Association. (2000). *Diagnostic and statistical manual of mental disorders* (4th ed., text rev.). Washington, DC: Author.

Aylward, A., Christopher, M., Newell, R. M., & Gordon, A. (2002, October). *What about women who commit sex offences?* Paper presented at the 22nd Annual Research and Treatment Conference of the Association for the Treatment of Sexual Abusers, Montréal.

Beck, A. T. (1999). *Prisoners of hate: The cognitive basis of anger, hostility, and violence.* New York: HarperCollins.

Beckett, R. C. (2005). What are the characteristics of female sex offenders? *NOTANews, 51,* 6–7.

Beckett, R. C., Beech, A. R., Fisher, D., & Fordham, A. S. (1994). *Community-Based Treatment For Sex Offenders: An Evaluation Of Seven Treatment Programs* (Home Office Occasional Report). (Available from Home Office Publications Unit, 50 Queen Anne's Gate, London SW1 9AT, UK).

Beech, A. R., Fisher, D. D., & Thornton, D. (2003). Risk assessment of sex offenders. *Professional Psychology: Research and Practice, 34,* 339–352.

Blanchette, K., & Brown, S. L. (2006). *The assessment and treatment of women offenders.* Chichester, UK: Wiley.

Bunting, L. (2005). *Executive summary: Females who sexually offend against children: Responses of the child protection and criminal justice systems.* Retrieved from *www.nspcc.org.uk/Inform/Research/Findings/FemalesWhoSexuallyOffend_ifega27751.html*

Byers, E. S., & O'Sullivan, L. F. (1998). Similar but different: men's and women's experiences of sexual coercion. In P. B. Anderson & C. Struckman-Johnson (Eds.), *Sexually aggressive women: Current perspectives and controversies* (pp. 144–168). New York: Guilford Press.

Casey, S., Day, A., & Howells, K. (2005). The application of the transtheoretical model to offender populations: Some critical issues. *Legal and Criminological Psychology, 10,* 157–171.

Chivers, M. L., & Bailey, J. M. (2005). A sex difference in features that elicit genital response. *Biological Psychology, 70,* 115–120.

Clark, D., & Howden-Windall, J. (2000). *A retrospective study of criminogenic factors in the female prison population.* London: Her Majesty's Prison Service.

Cooper, A. J., Swaminath, S., Baxter, D., & Poulin, C. (1990). A female sex offender with multiple paraphilias: A psychologic, physiologic (laboratory sexual arousal) and endocrine case study. *Canadian Journal of Psychiatry, 35,* 334–337.

Correctional Service Canada (CSC). (2001). *Women who sexually offend: A protocol for assessment and treatment.* Ottawa: Author.

Cortoni, F., Anderson, D., & Bright, D. (2002). Locus of control, coping and sexual offenders. In B. A. Schwartz & C. Cellini (Eds.), *The sex offender* (Vol. 4, pp. 5-1–5-17). Kingston, NJ: Civic Research Institute.

Cortoni, F., & Hanson, R. K. (2005). *A review of the recidivism rates of adult female sexual offenders* (Research Report No. R-169). Ottawa: Correctional Service Canada.

Curnoe, S., & Langevin, R. (2002). Personality and deviant sexual fantasies: An examination of the MMPI's of sex offenders. *Journal of Clinical Psychology, 58*(7), 803–815.

Denov, M. S. (2001). A culture of denial: Exploring professional perspectives on female sex offending. *Canadian Journal of Criminology, 43*(3), 303–329.

Denov, M. S. (2003). The myth of innocence: Sexual scripts and the recognition of child sexual abuse by female perpetrators. *Journal of Sex Research, 40*(3), 303–314.

Denov, M. S., & Cortoni, F. (2006). Adult female sexual offenders. In C. Hilarski & J. Wodarski (Eds.), *Comprehensive mental health practices with sex offenders and their families* (pp. 71–99). New York: Haworth Press.

Donnelly, D., & Fraser, J. (1998). Gender differences in sado-masochistic arousal among college students. *Sex Roles, 39*(5–6), 391–407.

Eldridge, H. J., & Saradjian, J. (2000). Replacing the function of abusive behaviors for the offender: Remaking relapse prevention in working with women who sexually abuse children. In D. R. Laws, S. M. Hudson, & T. Ward (Eds.), *Remaking relapse prevention with sex offenders: A sourcebook* (pp. 402–426). Thousand Oaks, CA: Sage.

Ellerby, L., Bedard, J., & Chartrand, S. (2000). Holism, wellness, and spirituality. In D. R. Laws, S. M. Hudson, & T. Ward (Eds.), *Remaking relapse prevention with sex offenders: A sourcebook* (pp. 427–452). Thousand Oaks, CA: Sage.

Endler, N. S., & Parker, J. D. A. (1999). *Coping inventory for stressful situations: Manual* (2nd ed.). Toronto: Multi-Health Systems.

Fehrenbach, P. A., & Monastersky, C. (1988). Characteristics of female adolescent sexual offenders. *American Journal of Orthopsychiatry, 58*(1), 148–151.

Forbes, J. (1993). Female sexual abusers: The contemporary search for equivalence. *Practice, 6*(2), 102–111.

Ford, H. (2006). *Women who sexually abuse children.* Chichester, UK: Wiley.

Friendship, C., & Thornton, D. (2002). Risk assessment for offenders. In K. D. Browne, H. Hanks, P. Stratton, & C. Hamilton (Eds.), *Early prediction and prevention of child abuse: A handbook* (pp. 301–316). Chichester, UK: Wiley.

Gallagher, B. (2000). The extent and nature of known cases of institutional child sexual abuse. *British Journal of Social Work, 30*, 795–817.

Grayston, A. D., & De Luca, R. V. (1999). Female perpetrators of child sexual abuse: A review of the clinical and empirical literature. *Aggression and Violent Behavior, 4*(1), 93–106.

Green, A. H., & Kaplan, M. S. (1994). Psychiatric impairment and childhood victimization experiences in female child molesters. *Journal of the American Academy of Child and Adolescent Psychiatry, 33*(7), 954–961.

Hamilton, C., & Browne, K. (2002). Predicting physical maltreatment. In K. D. Browne, H. Hanks, P. Stratton, & C. Hamilton (Eds.), *Early prediction and prevention of child abuse: A handbook* (pp. 41–55). Chichester, UK: Wiley.

Hathaway, S. R., & McKinley, J. C. (1989). *Minnesota Multiphasic Personality Inventory–2 (MMPI-2): Manual for administration and scoring.* Minneapolis: University of Minnesota Press.

Hugh-Jones, S., Gough, B., & Littlewood, A. (2005). Sexual exhibitionism as 'sexuality and individuality': A critique of psycho-medical discourse from the perspectives of women who exhibit. *Sexualities, 8*(3), 259–281.

Iowa Commission on the Status of Women. (1997). *Female juvenile justice report.* Retrieved from *www.infoiowa.state.ia.us/DHR/PDF/Public%20info/FemaleJuvJustice.pdf*

Johansson-Love, J., & Fremouw, W. (2006). A critique of the female sexual perpetrator research. *Aggression and Violent Behavior, 11*(1), 12–26.

Kalmus, E., & Beech, A. R. (2005). Forensic assessment of sexual interest: A review. *Aggression and Violent Behavior, 10*, 193–217.

Kaufman, K. L., Wallace, A. M., Johnson, C. E., & Reeder, M. L. (1995). Comparing male and female perpetrators' modus operandi: Victims' reports of sexual abuse. *Journal of Interpersonal Violence, 10*, 322–333.

Kemshall, H. (2004). Female sex offenders. In H. Kemshall & G. McIvor (Eds.), *Managing sex offender risk* (pp. 49–64). London: Jessica Kingsley.

Krahé, B., Waizenhöfer, E., & Möller, I. (2003). Women's sexual aggression against men: Prevalence and predictors. *Sex Roles, 49*, 219–232.

Laws, D. R. (2003). Penile plethysmography: Will we ever get it right? In T. Ward, D. R. Laws, & S. M. Hudson (Eds.), *Sexual deviance: Issues and controversies* (pp. 82–102). Thousand Oaks, CA: Sage.

Laws, D. R., Hanson, R. K., Osborn, C. A., & Greenbaum, P. E. (2000). Classification of child molesters by plethysmographic assessment of sexual arousal and a self-report measure of sexual preference. *Journal of Interpersonal Violence, 15*(12), 1297–1312.

Laws, D. R., Hudson, S. M., & Ward, T. (Eds.). (2000). *Remaking relapse prevention with sex offenders: A sourcebook*. Thousand Oaks, CA: Sage.

Lewis, C. F., & Stanley, C. R. (2000). Women accused of sexual offences. *Behavioral Sciences and the Law, 18*, 73–81.

Linehan, M. M. (1993). *Cognitive-behavioral therapy for borderline personality disorder*. New York: Guilford Press.

Maison, S. R., & Larson, N. R. (1995). Psychosexual treatment program for women sex offenders in a prison setting. *Nordisk Sexologi, 13*, 149–162.

Mann, R. E., & Beech, A. R. (2003). Cognitive distortions, schemas, and implicit theories. In T. Ward, D. R. Laws, & S. M. Hudson (Eds.), *Sexual deviance: Issues and controversies* (pp. 135–153). Thousand Oaks, CA: Sage.

Mathews, R., Matthews, J. K., & Speltz, K. (1990). Female sexual offenders. In M. Hunter (Ed.), *The sexually abused male: Vol. 1. Prevalence, impact and treatment* (pp. 275–293). Lexington, MA: Lexington Books.

Matthews, J. K. (1994). Working with female sexual abusers. In M. Elliott (Ed.), *Female sexual abuse of children* (pp. 57–73). New York: Guilford Press.

Matthews, J. K. (1998). An 11-year perspective of working with female sexual offenders. In W. L. Marshall, Y. M. Fernandez, S. M. Hudson, & T. Ward (Eds.), *Sourcebook of treatment programs for sexual offenders* (pp. 259–272). New York: Plenum Press.

Matthews, J. K., Mathews, R., & Speltz, K. (1991). Female sexual offenders: A typology. In M. Q. Patton (Ed.), *Family sexual abuse: Frontline research and evaluation* (pp. 199–219). Newbury Park, CA: Sage.

Minasian, G., & Lewis, A. D. (1999). Female sexual abusers: An unrecognized culture. In A. D. Lewis (Ed.), *Cultural diversity in sexual abuser treatment: Issues and approaches* (pp. 71–82). Brandon, VT: Safer Society Press.

Nathan, P., & Ward, T. (2001). Females who sexually abuse children: Assessment and treatment issues. *Psychiatry, Psychology and Law, 8*(1), 44–55.

Nathan, P., & Ward, T. (2002). Female sex offenders: Clinical and demographic features. *Journal of Sexual Aggression, 8*(1), 5–21.

Nichols, H., & Molinder, I. (1994). *The Multiphasic Sex Inventory II—Adult Female Form*. Fircrest, WA: Nichols & Molinder Assessments.

Paitich, D., Langevin, R., Freeman, R., Mann, K., & Handy, L. (1977). The Clarke SHQ: A clinical sex history questionnaire for males. *Archives of Sexual Behavior, 6*(5), 421–436.

Polaschek, D. L. L., & Hudson, S. M. (2004). Pathways to rape: Preliminary examination of patterns in the offence processes of rapists and their rehabilitation implications. *Journal of Sexual Aggression, 10*(1), 7–20.

Ring, L. (2005). *Psychometric profiles of female sexual abusers: A preliminary analysis into the differences between sexually abusive and non-offending females*. Unpublished master's thesis, University of Birmingham, Edgbaston, Birmingham, UK.

Rumgay, J. (2004). Living with paradox: Community supervision of women offenders. In G. McIvor (Ed.), *Women who offend* (pp. 99–125). London: Jessica Kingsley.

Russell, B. L., & Oswald, D. L. (2001). Strategies and dispositional correlates of sexual coercion perpetrated by women: An exploratory investigation. *Sex Roles, 45*(1–2), 103–115.

Saradjian, J. (1996). *Women who sexually abuse children: From research to clinical practice.* Chichester, UK: Wiley.

Sgroi, S. M., & Sargent, N. M. (1994). Impact and treatment issues for victims of childhood sexual abuse by female perpetrators. In M. Elliott (Ed.), *Female sexual abuse of children* (pp. 14–36). New York: Guilford Press.

Steen, C. (2006). *Choices: A relapse prevention workbook for female offenders.* Thousand Oaks, CA: Sage.

Struckman-Johnson, C., & Struckman-Johnson, D. (1994). Men pressured and forced into sexual experience. *Archives of Sexual Behavior, 23*(1), 93–114.

Tardif, M., Auclair, N., Jacob, M., & Carpentier, J. (2005). Sexual abuse perpetrated by adult and juvenile females: An ultimate attempt to resolve a conflict associated with maternal identity. *Child Abuse and Neglect, 29,* 153–167.

Travin, S., Cullen, K., & Protter, B. (1990). Female sex offenders: severe victims and victimizers. *Journal of Forensic Sciences, 35*(1), 140–150.

Vandiver, D. M., & Kercher, G. (2004). Offender and victim characteristics of registered female sex offenders in Texas: A proposed typology of female sexual offenders. *Sexual Abuse: A Journal of Research and Treatment, 16*(2), 121–137.

Viki, G. T., Massey, K., & Masser, B. (2005). When chivalry backfires: Benevolent sexism and attitudes towards Myra Hindley. *Legal and Criminological Psychology, 10,* 109–120.

Wiegel, M., Abel, G. G., & Jordan, A. (2003, October). *The self-reported behaviors of adult female child abusers.* Paper presented at the 22nd Annual Research and Treatment Conference of the Association for the Treatment of Sexual Abusers, St. Louis, MO.

Williams, S. M., & Nicholaichuk, T. (2001, November). *Assessing static risk factors in adult female sex offenders under federal jurisdiction.* Paper presented at the 20th Research and Treatment Conference of the Association for the Treatment of Sexual Abusers, San Antonio, TX.

Wolfers, O. (1992, March 12). Same abuse, different parent. *Social Work Today,* pp. 13–14.

Young, V. (1994). Women abusers: A feminist perspective. In M. Elliott (Ed.), *Female sexual abuse of children* (pp. 100–114). New York: Guilford Press.

CHAPTER 28

MULTIPLE PARAPHILIAS

Prevalence, Etiology, Assessment, and Treatment

PEGGY HEIL
DOMINIQUE SIMONS

Standardized definitions of paraphilias were first established in the third edition of the *Diagnostic and Statistical Manual of Mental Disorders* (DSM-III; American Psychiatric Association, 1980; see also Milner & Dopke, 1997). Initially, a paraphilia was thought to be a singular deviant sexual interest. There was little recognition that an individual might have multiple paraphilias, or normal sexual interests along with paraphilic interests. In 1988, through the use of a federal certificate of confidentiality, Abel, Becker, Cunningham-Rathner, Mittelman, and Rouleau discovered that few individuals with paraphilias engaged in only one type of paraphilia; their study acknowledged the existence of multiple paraphilias within the sex offender literature. The federal certificate of confidentiality, granted by the Secretary of Health, Education, and Welfare, allowed the researchers to circumvent mandatory child abuse reporting laws and protect the sensitive research data from forced disclosure to an outside entity, thereby permitting the participants to disclose sexual offending behaviors without fear of legal consequences. As a result of this novel research, Abel and colleagues (1988) noted a "wave effect" in some individuals with multiple paraphilias. That is, as preferences changed over time, the intensity of one behavior rose while others subsided, although there was some overlap in the behaviors. This research also indicated that the majority of individuals who engaged in paraphilic behaviors simultaneously engaged in nonparaphilic sexual behaviors.

In response to this research, there have been revisions to the paraphilia classifications over time. The current edition of the DSM, the DSM-IV-TR (American Psychiatric Association, 2000), defines the essential features of a paraphilia as

recurrent, intense sexually arousing fantasies, sexual urges, or behaviors generally involving 1) nonhuman objects, 2) the suffering of humiliation of oneself or one's partner, or 3) children or other nonconsenting persons that occur over a period of at least 6 months (Criterion A). For some individuals, paraphilic fantasies or stimuli are obligatory for erotic arousal and are always included in sexual activity. In other cases, the paraphilic preferences occur only episodically (e.g., perhaps during periods of stress), whereas at other times the person is able to function sexually without paraphilic fantasies or stimuli. For Pedophilia, Voyeurism, Exhibitionism, and Frotteurism, the diagnosis is made if the person has acted on these urges or the urges or sexual fantasies cause marked distress or interpersonal difficulty. For Sexual Sadism, the diagnosis is made if the person has acted on these urges with a nonconsenting person or the urges, sexual fantasies, or behaviors cause marked distress or interpersonal difficulty. For the remaining Paraphilias, the diagnosis is made if the behavior, sexual urges, or fantasies cause clinically significant distress or impairment in social, occupational, or other important areas of functioning (Criterion B). (p. 566)

The DSM-IV-TR also recognizes that it is not uncommon for individuals to have more than one paraphilia. Paraphilia categories include exhibitionism, fetishism, frotteurism, pedophilia, sexual masochism, sexual sadism, transvestic fetishism, voyeurism, and paraphilia not otherwise specified (NOS). However, the DSM-IV-TR paraphilic classifications have limited utility for sex offender treatment providers. Since some of the more common offending behaviors (e.g., rape) do not fit into a specific category, several authors have discussed modifications to the criteria and categories that might make the classifications more useful (Abel & Osborn, 1992; Bradford, Boulet, & Pawlak, 1992; Marshall, 1997). Abel and Rouleau (1990) have characterized rape as a paraphilia because rapists often report recurrent and compulsive urges to commit sexual assault, whereas Bradford and colleagues (1992) support the inclusion of a "coercive paraphilic disorder" as a remedy for this clinical dilemma. Furthermore, researchers contend that classification based on admitted deviant behavior appears more reliable than substantiating criteria based on whether bizarre imagery is present or whether the acts are necessary for sexual excitement.

"Multiple paraphilias" are frequently defined in the literature as three or more paraphilias, one of which has to be pedophilia, rape, or exhibitionism (e.g., Lee, Pattison, Jackson, & Ward, 2001). For purposes of this chapter, an admission or an official record report that an offender has engaged in the behavior is used as a proxy for the diagnosis of a paraphilia. Whether the offender fantasizes or is distressed by these urges, or the length of time that the offender has experienced these urges, is difficult to determine without the offender's honest cooperation. However, the fact that the offender has come to the attention of authorities and is facing legal intervention indicates that the behavior has resulted in interpersonal difficulty and brought the offender into conflict with society. This chapter reviews the growing body of information regarding the prevalence and etiology of multiple paraphilias, and consequently recommends techniques to identify and effectively treat this adult population of sex offenders.

PREVALENCE

Sexual offenses are carried out in secret; the only people with complete information about an offense are the victim and the offender, both of whom may be reluctant to disclose the assault. Subsequently, two factors hinder our knowledge of sex offending. First, sex offenders are unlikely to accurately report the variety, intensity, and duration of their undocumented deviant sexual histories, due to fear of legal consequences and societal disdain. Second, victims fear that others will blame them (Kilpatrick, Edmunds, & Seymour, 1992) and that they will be stigmatized if the offense is revealed, especially in the majority of cases where the victim knows the offender. As a result of these factors, few offenses are reported to authorities.

Underreporting of Offenses

Surveys of nationally representative samples have determined that certain categories of offenses are less likely to be reported. The most current studies indicate the following reporting rates for rape across groups: 19% for adult women and 13% for adult men (Tjaden & Thoennes, 2006), and 14% for adolescents ages 12–17 (Kilpatrick, Saunders, & Smith, 2003). Perhaps the crimes that are least likely to be reported are those committed against children under the age of 12. Research indicates that younger victims and sexual offenses perpetrated by persons the victims know well are less likely to be reported (Hanson, Resnick, Saunders, Kilpatrick, & Best, 1999; Smith et al., 2000), and the majority of females under age 12 are victimized by relatives (Tjaden & Thoennes, 2006).

The underreporting of sexual offenses results in an underidentification of crimes. In the case of adult female rapes, only 8% were prosecuted; 3% were convicted; and 2% resulted in incarceration of the offender (Tjaden & Thoennes, 2006). Therefore, offenders have a 97% chance of avoiding consequences and a 92% chance of avoiding criminal justice documentation of the crime. To judge from the disproportionate rates of reporting, other types of sexual offenses are even more likely to remain hidden.

Prevalence of Multiple Paraphilias

Following Abel and colleagues' influential research in the 1980s, traditional assumptions about sex offenders' committing only one type of sex offense began to be challenged. Since that time, numerous studies employing guaranteed confidentiality (e.g., Weinrott & Saylor, 1991), anonymous surveys (e.g., Freeman-Longo & Blanchard, 1998), or treatment with polygraphy (e.g., Emerick & Dutton, 1993; English, Jones, Patrick, & Pasini-Hill, 2003; Heil, Ahlmeyer, & Simons, 2003; O'Connell, 1998; Simons, Heil, & English, 2004; Wilcox, Sosnowski, Warberg, & Beech, 2005) have confirmed Abel and colleagues' (1988) findings. Taken together, this research indicates that most sex offenders supervised by the criminal justice system have more extensive sex offending histories than their official records indicate. Not only does this research reveal additional prior victims and offenses, but many offenders also engage in a variety of offending behaviors, which suggests that the presence of multiple paraphilias is not uncommon. Because some sexual offenses do not fall into a paraphilic diagnostic category, several researchers have used the term "crossover" in referring to the fact that certain offenders engage in more than one type of sexual offending or victimize individuals from different relationship categories, genders, or age groups (Abel & Osborn, 1992; English, Jones, Pasini-Hill, Patrick, & Cooley-Towell, 2000; Heil et al., 2003; O'Connell, 1998; Wilcox et al., 2005).

Despite differences in location and supervision status of the offenders, similar findings are beginning to emerge from studies using guaranteed confidentiality, anonymous surveys, or treatment with polygraphy. As Table 28.1 indicates, offenders on average admit significantly more victims and offenses than are documented in official records. The mean age of onset of sexual offending is before 18 years, with most studies finding a mean age of onset in early adolescence. These studies also reveal a lengthy time period be-

TABLE 28.1. Results of Research on the Prevalence of Multiple Paraphilias

Sex offender studies	Emerick and Dutton (1993)	Abel et al. (1988); Abel and Osborn (1992)	O'Connell (1998)	Wilcox et al. (2005)	English et al. (2000)	Weinrott and Saylor (1991)	Freeman-Longo and Blanchard (1998)	Simons et al. (2004)
Sample description	76 high-risk adolescents assessed at a hospital treatment facility	561 individuals with paraphilias evaluated in the community	127 adult males evaluated in the community	14 medium- to high-risk adult males in treatment and on probation	180 adults in treatment and on probation or parole[a]	99 adult males civilly committed to a forensic treatment program	53 adult male inmates in a forensic treatment program	35 and 223* adult male inmates in a prison treatment program
Location	Arizona	New York and Tennessee	Washington	United Kingdom	Wisconsin, Oregon, and Texas	Washington	Oregon	Colorado
Data collection technique	Polygraphed self-report	Confidential self-report	Polygraphed self-report	Polygraphed self-report	Polygraphed self-report	Confidential computer-administered interview	Anonymous self-report survey	Polygraphed self-report
Mean age of onset	13 for contact offenses (median)	13 to 26, with the majority prior to age 20	—	13.4	11.2 for incest 12.8 for nonincest	—	18 for rapists 15 for child molesters	12
Mean years from onset to detection	3.5 years	—	—	14 years	10 years (estimated)	—	6 years for rapists 13 years for child molesters	16 years
% with one type of behavior	—	10.4%[b]	9%	—	26%	47%	—	11%
Mean no.of different behaviors	—	3 to 5	4.5 mean 3 to 5 mode	—	—	—	—	4 mean* 3 mode*

(continued)

TABLE 28.1. (continued)

Sample description	76 high-risk adolescents assessed at a hospital treatment facility	561 individuals with paraphilias	127 adult males evaluated in the community	14 medium- to high-risk adult males in treatment and on probation	180 adults in treatment and on probation or parole	99 adult males civilly committed to a forensic treatment program (37 rapists and 67 child molesters)	53 adult male inmates in a forensic treatment program (23 rapists and 30 child molesters)	222 nondeceptive adult male inmates and 223 adult male inmates* in prison treatment program
Age crossover	—	42.3%	—	29%	33%	—	—	73%
Gender crossover	43.3%	20%	—	—	29%	—	—	37%
Relationship crossover	41.7%	—	—	—	—	—	—	87%
Rapists victimizing children	—	49%	64%	60%	53.6%	32%	(23 rapists reported 319 incidents of child SA)	52%*
Incest offenders victimizing nonrelatives	—	65.8%[c]	59%	—	64%	50%	—	64%*
Noncontact offenders committing contact offenses	—	64%	—	44%[d]	80%[e*]	—	—	—

(continued)

531

TABLE 28.1. (continued)

Sex offender studies	Emerick and Dutton (1993)	Abel et al. (1988); Abel and Osborn (1992)	O'Connell (1998)	Wilcox et al. (2005)	English et al. (2000)	Weinrott and Saylor (1991)	Freeman-Longo and Blanchard (1998)	Simons et al. (2004)
Median (mean) offenses at referral/official record	(27.2) contact	—	(22.5) contact; (28.1) offenses	3 (37.2) contact; 3 (26.2) noncontact	—	Rapists: (1.8) contact; child molesters: 2 contact	—	2 (11.3) contact
Median (mean) offenses with clinical interview	(20.7) contact	—	(46.2) contact; (84.6) offenses	—	—	—	—	20.5 (152) contact
Median (mean) offenses with polygraph, confidentiality, or anonymous survey	12 (76.6) contact	Child molesters: 1.4 to 10.1 (23.2 to 281.7, depending on type; rapists: 0.9 (7.2)	(91.2) contact; (220.5) offenses	4 (81.9) contact; 5 (80.8) noncontact	—	Rapists: (11.7) contact; child molesters: (119.4) contact	Rapists: (21.6) contact and (242.9) offenses; child molesters: (203.5) contact and (892.4) offenses	35.5 (218.4) contact
% of self-reported sex offenses in official records	35%	3% contact; 0.7 noncontact	—	45.4% contact; 32.4% noncontact	Three to five times the numbers of victims were disclosed in treatment/polygraph	Rapists: 15.4% contact; child molesters: 1.7%	—	5.6% contact

[a] The sample of probationers and parolees was combined after it was determined that the two groups were not statistically different on the variables of interest, although parolees had more extensive criminal histories.

[b] This percentage represents all paraphilias combined. Based on primary diagnosis, 27% of rapists, 15.2% of those with nonincest female-target pedophilia, 19% of those with nonincest male-target pedophilia, 28.3% of those with incest female-target pedophilia, and 4.5% of those with incest male-target pedophilia admitted only one type of behavior.

[c] This represents the percentage of individuals committing paraphilic behaviors against family members who also committed paraphilic behaviors against nonrelatives.

[d] Percentage of exhibitionists admitting female child molestation.

[e] Percentage of 10 convicted exhibitionists admitting hands-on offenses.

532

tween onset of sexual offending and criminal justice detection. Adult offenders have successfully hidden their offending behaviors for an average range of 6–16 years, dependent upon the study. Very few sex offenders engage in only one type of sexual offending behavior. The majority of studies report a mode of three types of admitted paraphilias or sexual offending behaviors per offender, although a substantial number of offenders have more than three.

Traditional sex offender typologies separate sex offenders into the categories of child sexual abusers and rapists. The findings of these studies challenge notions that sex offenders are either rapists or child molesters. Although the results are inconsistent across studies, age crossover (i.e., victimizing both children and adults) ranges from 29% to 73% in some samples (Simons, Heil, & English, 2004; Wilcox et al., 2005). It is interesting to note that 71% of the sexual history polygraphs were scored deceptive in the study with the lowest rate (Wilcox et al., 2005), whereas the study with the highest rate only included individuals with nondeceptive sexual history polygraphs (Simons et al., 2004). Of further interest is the high percentage of official-record-identified rapists who admit child victimization. Studies range from 32% to 64%, with the majority at 50–60% (Abel & Osborn, 1992; English et al., 2000; Heil et al., 2003; O'Connell, 1998; Wilcox et al., 2005). This finding raises serious questions about the safety of housing rapists with children (Heil et al., 2003; Laws, 1994).

Findings regarding gender crossover (i.e., victimizing both males and females) are relatively consistent across studies and range from 20% to 43%. A further breakdown indicates that the majority of offenders who assault males have also assaulted females, but not the reverse: Offenders who victimize females are less likely to have victimized males (Abel & Osborn, 1992; English et al., 2000; Heil et al., 2003). Researchers found that the following percentages of offenders who victimize females have also victimized males: 22.9% (Abel & Osborn), 30.8% (English et al.), and 37% (Heil et al.). On the other hand, researchers found that the following percentage of offenders who victimize males have also victimized females: 62.6% (Abel & Osborn), 80% (English et al.), and 91.9% (Heil et al.). While these findings indicate a higher presence of multiple paraphilias in the sex offender population, the extent to which versatility in individual offenders is rare or frequent is not apparent. To address this question, we (Simons, Tyler, & Heil, 2005) categorized a sample of 215 offenders into the following: (1) primarily child sexual abusers (who reported at least 80% child victims); (2) primarily rapists (who reported at least 80% adult victims); and (3) indiscriminant offenders (who offended against both adults and children and did not meet the 80% criterion for either group).

As Table 28.2 indicates, indiscriminant offenders had significantly more total victims, and on average had more child victims, than child sexual abusers. High-risk behaviors during treatment with monitoring polygraphs were also analyzed for the three groups. Indiscriminant offenders were more likely to engage in high-risk behaviors with high frequency throughout the course of treatment. In comparison to rapists (32%) and child sexual abusers (44%), indiscriminant offenders (58%) engaged in high-risk behaviors with higher frequency (Simons et al., 2004). These findings support prior research indicating that a history of diverse victim types (Hanson & Harris, 1998) and diverse sex crimes (Hanson & Bussière, 1998) is predictive of recidivism risk.

Researchers using data from official records or offender self-reports during treatment have found less dramatic rates of crossover and multiple paraphilias (Guay, Proulx, Cusson, & Ouimet, 2001; Marshall, Barbaree, & Eccles, 1991; Smallbone & Wortley, 2004). It appears that additional methods are necessary to obtain more complete infor-

TABLE 28.2. Victim Characteristics for Child Sexual Abusers, Rapists, and Indiscriminant Offenders

	Child sexual abusers (n = 81)	Rapists (n = 60)	Indiscriminant offenders (n = 74)
Total victims	10.06 (12.84)	9.17 (6.73)	30.77 (20.73)
Child victims	8.23 (11.21)	1.00 (1.84)	22.62 (16.59)
Adult victims	1.83 (2.91)	8.17 (5.31)	8.15 (4.15)
Bestiality (%)	59	30	81

Note. Means and (standard deviations) are presented. Data from Simons, Tyler, and Heil (2005).

mation on the extent of multiple paraphilias and crossover. Although the reported numbers of offenses are staggering, the information is compatible with victim reporting research. When guaranteed confidentiality, anonymous survey, or treatment with polygraphy is used, the percentage of self-reported crimes in official records ranges from 1% to 45% (Abel et al., 1987; Wilcox et al., 2005). Victim research indicates an 8.3% chance that a rape of an adult female will be documented in an offender's criminal justice record as an arrest (Tjaden & Thoennes, 2006). Criminal justice documentation of other types of sexual crimes is likely to be even lower. Therefore, the findings of these studies appear realistic.

ETIOLOGY

Etiological research has suggested that an interaction of biological and social learning factors influences the development of sexual offending behaviors (see Ward & Beech, Chapter 2, this volume). These researchers explain that genetic factors may predispose an individual to pursue a specific human need (e.g., sex or intimacy), but that environmental experiences provide the methods for which these needs are met—either appropriately through the development of relationships, or inappropriately through the use of violence (Ward & Beech, Chapter 2, this volume). Negative developmental experiences figure prominently in many models of sexual offending behavior. Indeed, a recent meta-analysis has confirmed the association between sexual abuse experience and subsequent sexual offending against children (Lalumière, Seto, & Jespersen, 2006). These findings support the social learning explanations of sexual offending: Some sexually abusive individuals learn from and tend to repeat the characteristics of their own abuse. Yet not all sexual offenders report being sexually victimized during their childhoods. Recent findings illustrate that no one type of abuse may serve as a developmental risk factor for later sexual offending; instead, multiple abusive experiences, or a pathological family environment, may precede offending behaviors (Dube et al., 2001). Recent research has also suggested that different types of maltreatment may be associated with different types of sexual offending behaviors (e.g., Lee, Jackson, Pattison, & Ward, 2002; Simons, Wurtele, & Heil, 2002). Because research characterizes multiple paraphilias as a particularly severe form of sexual psychopathology, this section reviews the current research findings that compare the developmental risk factors and psychiatric features of different offending behaviors (i.e., child sexual abuse, rape, and multiple paraphilias).

Researchers have found that child sexual abusers exhibit childhood histories characterized by heightened sexuality. Meta-analysis results indicated that juvenile sexual offenders were more likely than nonsexual offenders to experience exposure to sexual violence, sexual abuse, emotional abuse, and neglect. Within the adult sex offender population, Simons, Wurtele, and Durham (2004) found that child sexual abusers, as compared to rapists, reported more experiences of child sexual abuse, early exposure to pornography, an earlier onset of masturbation, and sexual activities with animals. From a social learning perspective, offenders commit their first act due to internalized social definitions that support sexual offending obtained from their own abuse experiences, and continue to engage in sexual offending behaviors to resolve trauma (i.e., regain power), or as a result of strict conditioning processes (i.e., ritualistic, reinforcing patterns) related to sexual arousal (Burton, 2003; Marshall & Eccles, 1993; Veneziano, Veneziano, & LeGrand, 2000).

In contrast to the histories of child sexual abusers, rapists' childhood histories appear more indicative of violence. Simons and colleagues (2004) found that rapists, as compared to child sexual abusers, reported more frequent experiences of physical abuse, parental violence, emotional abuse, and cruelty to animals. Researchers contend that physical abuse, parental violence, and emotional abuse result in externalizing behaviors only when they are considered in combination (Lee et al., 2002; McGee, Wolfe, & Wilson, 1997). As an illustration, Beauregard, Lussier, and Proulx (2004) found that physical and verbal abuse during childhood led to antisocial behavior and callous personality traits, both of which led to aggressive sexual fantasies. Likewise, Salter and colleagues (2003) illustrated that the combination of physical violence, domestic violence, emotional abuse, and neglect predicted subsequent sexual offending. Researchers (e.g., Craissati, McClurg, & Browne, 2002a) explain that an individual who has been raised in an emotionally impoverished environment is often unable to identify his emotions accurately, and as a result is likely to become confused when confronted with emotionally charged situations. Due to social learning, these individuals often react to confusing situations with overt aggression.

In studies that have examined the developmental risk factors of offenders with multiple paraphilias (e.g., Ahlmeyer & Simons, 2002; Simons, Tyler, & Heil, 2005), findings indicated that indiscriminant offenders reported childhood histories of both violence and heightened sexuality (see Table 28.3). With respect to heightened sexuality, we (Simons, Tyler, & Heil, 2005) found that indiscriminant offenders were less likely than child sexual abusers to be sexually abused, but they were more likely to report early sexual experiences with peers (before age 10), to witness sexual abuse, and to report more frequent exposure to pornography before age 10. Similar to child sexual abusers (i.e., 62%), 58% of indiscriminant offenders reported an early onset and frequent masturbation (before age 11). The majority of indiscriminant offenders (81%) disclosed engaging in bestiality during childhood, whereas fewer child sexual abusers (59%) and rapists (30%) reported this. With respect to childhood violence, both indiscriminant offenders and rapists described childhood experiences consistent with physical and emotional abuse. However, indiscriminant offenders were exposed to domestic violence significantly more frequently than rapists. Results indicated that parental violence and bestiality were strong predictors of multiple paraphilias. Clinical implications of these findings support the inclusion of trauma treatment for the majority of adult sexual offenders with multiple paraphilias.

According to researchers, childhood adversities may result in the failure to establish secure attachment bonds to parents (Cicchetti & Lynch, 1995). Marshall (1993) contends that the failure of sex offenders to develop secure attachment bonds in childhood results in their failure to develop sufficient social skills and self-esteem to achieve intimacy with

TABLE 28.3. Comparison of Childhood Experiences for Rapists, Child Sexual Abusers, and Indiscriminant Offenders

Childhood experience	Child sexual abusers ($n = 81$)	Rapists ($n = 60$)	Indiscriminant offenders ($n = 74$)
Sexual abuse (%)	65_a	42_b	46_b
Mean (standard deviation)	$18.46\ (18.51)_a$	$2.50\ \ (4.79)_b$	$12.61\ (15.32)_c$
Physical abuse (%)	54_a	68_a	66_a
Mean (standard deviation)	$6.67\ \ (7.81)_a$	$16.32\ (15.62)_b$	$16.42\ (15.54)_b$
Emotional abuse (%)	61_a	72_a	64_a
Mean (standard deviation)	$12.64\ (11.68)_a$	$19.28\ (16.40)_b$	$17.36\ (15.94)_{ab}$
Domestic violence (%)	53_a	77_b	87_c
Mean (standard deviation)	$9.22\ (11.25)_a$	$19.78\ (13.79)_b$	$26.22\ (16.60)_c$
Exposure to pornography (%)	62_a	57_a	64_a
Mean (standard deviation)	$11.14\ (10.22)_a$	$5.15\ \ (5.95)_b$	$15.82\ (15.87)_c$
Early masturbation (%)	62_a	5_b	58_a
Mean (standard deviation)	$26.44\ (11.07)_a$	$11.67\ \ (6.54)_b$	$28.74\ \ (9.94)_a$
Witnessing sexual abuse (%)	21_a	8_b	34_c
Mean (standard deviation)	$2.04\ \ (5.12)_a$	$.63\ \ (2.98)_a$	$5.32\ \ (9.01)_b$
Early sexual experiences with peers (%)	33_a	20_b	54_c
Mean (standard deviation)	$2.33\ \ (4.73)_a$	$1.70\ \ (4.13)_a$	$7.16\ \ (8.05)_b$
Social phobia			
Mean (standard deviation)	$16.28\ (14.03)_a$	$2.30\ \ (6.54)_b$	$7.01\ (11.07)_c$
Major depressive disorder			
Mean (standard deviation)	$14.91\ (11.87)_a$	$2.63\ \ (7.77)_b$	$6.91\ (10.33)_c$
ADHD (combined subtype)			
Mean (standard deviation)	$16.04\ (18.26)_a$	$2.10\ \ (6.35)_b$	$35.28\ (25.18)_c$

Note. Means represent frequency of experiences. Means or percentages in the same row that do not share the same subscript differ at $p < .05$ using the appropriate statistical procedures (i.e., Welch's t test, independent t test, and chi-square test). "Early masturbation" is defined as occurring before age 11. "Early sexual experiences with peers" are defined as occurring before age 10. Data from Simons, Tyler, and Heil (2005).

adults. Recent models of sexual deviance suggest that poor parental bonding enhances the effects of child maltreatment and may subsequently initiate the processes that lead to sexual offending, by creating vulnerability in the child (Marshall & Marshall, 2000), a lack of empathy for others (Craissati, McClurg, & Browne, 2002b), or intimacy deficits (Ward, Hudson, Marshall, & Siegert, 1995). Indeed, studies have shown a relationship between disorganized attachment styles and sexual offending (Burk & Burkhart, 2003). With respect to paraphilic behaviors, Lee and colleagues (2001) found that individuals with multiple paraphilias were more likely than those with only one paraphilia (i.e., rape, pedophilia, or exhibitionism) and nonsexual offenders to exhibit insecure attachment styles. Other studies have illustrated that child sexual abusers exhibit more preoccupied (i.e., anxious) or fearful attachment styles than rapists and violent offenders, who display more dismissive (i.e., avoidant) attachment styles (Simons, Wurtele, & Durham, 2004). Findings from these studies suggest that attachment issues need to be evaluated and addressed in treatment.

Recent studies have also shown that sexual offenders exhibit retrospective diagnoses of Axis I disorders. Specifically, Kafka and Prentky (1998) found a high prevalence of social phobia and depressive disorders among individuals exhibiting clinical hypersexuality (i.e., paraphilias or paraphilia-related disorders). In addition, they reported that individuals with paraphilias were more likely than individuals with compulsive sexual behavior (paraphilia-related disorders) to be retrospectively diagnosed with attention-deficit/hyperactivity disorder (ADHD), to have experienced childhood abuse, and to abuse cocaine. Later studies indicated that the retrospective diagnosis of ADHD (combined subtype) is prevalent among individuals with multiple paraphilias. Kafka and Hennen (2002) reported strong associations among childhood symptoms of ADHD (combined subtype), conduct disorder, and multiple paraphilias. Similarly, Ahlmeyer and Simons (2002) found that an extensive nonsexual criminal history and childhood abuse (both physical and sexual) were strong predictors of indiscriminant sexual offending. In a comparison of childhood histories of sexual offenders, we (Simons, Tyler, & Heil, 2005) found that child sexual abusers affirmed childhood symptoms consistent with major depression and social phobia, which were also significantly related to the experience of sexual abuse during childhood. In contrast to child sexual abusers and rapists, indiscriminant offenders reported symptoms consistent with an ADHD (combined subtype) diagnosis. The retrospective diagnosis of ADHD (combined subtype) was strongly associated with an increase in the number of victims (i.e., both adults and children). These findings support the use of pharmacological treatments for sexual offenders.

Taken together, these findings emphasize the importance of a thorough assessment of the developmental history and comorbid psychiatric disorders of offenders with multiple paraphilias. The complexity of the psychiatric issues indicated by the research necessitates the use of a comprehensive treatment program that consists of containment, cognitive-behavioral treatment, pharmacology, trauma therapy, and attachment interventions.

ASSESSMENT

A diagnosis of multiple paraphilias requires a comprehensive assessment protocol that includes (1) structured clinical interviews addressing paraphilic behaviors, sexual fantasies, urges, and developmental history; (2) risk assessments; (3) polygraph testing; (4) objective measures of sexual interest and/or arousal; and (5) psychiatric and pharmacological evaluations.

Structured Clinical Interview

Abel and colleagues (1988) emphasized the significance of utilizing a thorough sexual history inventory to obtain information regarding the development and the extent of paraphilic interests and behaviors. The interview or questionnaire should require respondents to disclose the age, gender, and relationship of each victim; to quantify the offenses; and to describe the behaviors during the offense. In addition, the clinician or questionnaire should address past consensual sexual experiences, criminal history, paraphilias, substance use, pornography use, prostitution procurement, age of onset of sexual interests and behaviors, and other developmental experiences (including childhood victimization). Several methodological issues should be considered. Abel and Osborn (2000) recommend asking how often an offender engages in a behavior, rather than asking whether he has ever engaged in the behavior. This technique makes it easier to admit paraphilias. In addition, clinicians need to take into account that various data collection methods employing emotionally laden terms such as "abuse" or "assault" influence rates of disclosure. Specifically, such labels have been shown to be related to lower prevalence rates, as many male offenders are either reluctant to disclose abuse histories due to shame or perceive their abuse experience as consensual, especially when the abuser is a female.

For the assessment of attachment, the Adult Attachment Interview (AAI) has demonstrated the strongest psychometric properties and has been empirically validated across populations. The AAI is an in-depth interview that requires adults to describe their relationships to parents during childhood, including responses to separations, illnesses, and traumatic childhood experiences (Main, 1996). The scoring of the AAI is based on how the respondents discuss their parental relationships, rather than the actual experiences. The resulting classifications correspond to the various attachment styles (i.e., secure, avoidant, ambivalent/anxious, and disorganized). Individuals who are classified as securely attached demonstrate the ability to discuss their parental relationships openly and clearly, regardless of abuse experiences (Main, 1996). The AAI may be disadvantageous, however, as it is time-consuming and requires extensive training to administer. There are other attachment questionnaires that are easier to administer and score (e.g., Bartholomew & Horowitz, 1991), but many of these tests appear transparent and therefore may be vulnerable to dissimulation. In addition, these measures do not assess disorganized attachment. To measure this type of attachment, it remains necessary to include items that address traumatic experiences and disassociation (Simons, Wurtele, & Durham, 2004).

Collateral sources of information can also be a rich source of information to assess an offender's treatment and supervision needs. The offender's family of origin, relatives, or past childhood placements can provide information on childhood experiences and behavior that might signal posttraumatic stress disorder (PTSD), mood disorders, or impulse control disorders. The offender's adult sexual partners or family members can provide information on the offender's lifestyle habits, such as leisure activities and work patterns, interest in and access to children, and frequency and variety of sexual behaviors. Clinicians should consider all these factors when recommending treatment and management strategies.

Risk Assessment

Risk evaluation is an important component of assessment and is commonly carried out with actuarial risk instruments. To date, there are no studies evaluating actuarial risk instruments with offenders who admit multiple paraphilias under guaranteed confidentiality or polygraph testing. As a result, the predictive accuracy of these instruments for such offenders is unknown. Since some actuarial instruments such as the Static-99 (Hanson & Thornton, 2000) measure types of victimization that are associated with high rates of crossover (i.e., male victims and noncontact sex offenses), these instruments may accurately reflect the offenders' risk. Future research should determine whether criminal justice data sufficiently predict this population's recidivism risk.

There is plenty of evidence suggesting that persons with multiple paraphilias are at high risk of reoffending. Variety in offending is associated with a higher frequency and duration of offending (see Lussier, 2005). For example, Emerick and Dutton (1993) found that adolescent sex offenders who assaulted victims from more than one relationship type (family, relative, acquaintance, or stranger) had an average of 4.4 victims, as compared to an average of 1.77 victims for offenders with victims from one type of relationship. Similarly, they found that offenders who victimized both genders had an average of 4.19 victims, whereas offenders who only victimized females averaged 1.9 victims, and offenders who only victimized males averaged 1.63 victims. Furthermore, Hanson and Bussière (1998) found strong empirical support for diverse sex crimes as a recidivism risk factor. In a follow-up meta-analysis, Hanson and Morton-Bourgon (2004) found that offenders with interests in deviant sexual activities, which included sexual interest in children and general paraphilias, were the most likely to reoffend. Sexual preoccupations, defined as high rates of sexual interests and activities, were also significantly predictive of risk. These studies highlight the importance of identifying multiple paraphilias and crossover behaviors in sex offenders. Nevertheless, offenders' reluctance to disclose these behaviors makes identification difficult, as does underreporting by victims. When the presence of multiple paraphilias is identified, treatment and supervision strategies should address the increased risk of this specific population.

Polygraph Testing

Polygraph testing is one tool that assists in the identification of multiple paraphilias. Although polygraph testing is not 100% accurate, it does provide one of the stronger methods to validate offender self-admissions and typically results in increased information on the intensity, duration, and variety of offending (Ahlmeyer, Heil, McKee, & English, 2000; English, Jones, Patrick, & Pasini-Hill, 2003; O'Connell, 1998; Wilcox et al., 2005). In fact, Clark and Tift (1966) studied college students and found that polygraph testing resulted in more admissions of criminal behavior than either anonymous surveys or personal interviews did.

Carefully established polygraph procedures (see Colorado Department of Public Safety, 2004b) produce the most beneficial information. As part of the process, offenders typically document their deviant sexual histories in a preestablished format, detailing their age and the age, gender, and relationship of each victim at the time of the offense. Procedures should address informed consent, immunity, and mandatory reporting as they relate to the level of detail collected. Polygraph examiners should be trained and experienced in postconviction sex offender testing. These tests are difficult to conduct and are not typical polygraph exams.

Prior to an exam, a clinician should ensure that the examiner has pertinent offense information from official records and documented sexual history. Generally, only three to four relevant questions can be asked on an exam, so multiple exams may be necessary to obtain comprehensive information. Therefore, the clinician and the polygraph examiner should discuss the focus of the exam ahead of time. Deceptive scores should prompt the clinician to seek further information.

When assessment is conducted before sentencing, polygraph testing can present some dilemmas. If offenders are not in treatment, they may rationalize their offenses and believe that the behaviors are not criminal. As a result, they may achieve nondeceptive scores on sexual history tests, depending on how the questions are constructed. Testing may be more accurate once an offender participates in treatment, understands definitions and sex offense terminology, and has had time to prepare a sexual history. Additionally, offenders may be less reluctant to disclose offenses after they are sentenced. Up until that point, the offenders have every reason to believe that disclosing unknown sexual offenses will have a negative impact on sentencing decisions.

Measures of Sexual Arousal/Interest

Sexual arousal as measured by penile plethysmography (PPG; see Laws, 2003), or sexual interest as measured by visual reaction time, may indicate a deviant sexual interest and possible paraphilia. These measurements cannot provide information on those who show no measurable arousal or interest (Quinsey, Harris, Rice, & Cormier, 1998) but engage in the behavior for other reasons, or who have deviant arousal or interest but do not act on the behavior. When there are PPG findings that differ from known sexual offending behaviors, suspicions of multiple paraphilias should be raised. However, the opposite is not true: A lack of PPG findings should not be used to rule out multiple paraphilias.

When objective measures such as PPG, the Abel Assessment for Sexual Interest (AASI; Abel, Jordan, Hand, Holland, & Phipps, 2001), or polygraph testing are not available, the evaluator should assess whether the offender has any history of behaviors that are frequently associated with multiple paraphilias. For example, Abel and Osborn (2000) studied a sample of 5,873 adult males who were evaluated for inappropriate sexual interests with the AASI, and found that the following behaviors were significantly associated with the presence of additional paraphilias: transvestic fetishism, public masturbation, fetishism, obscene telephone calls, sadism, frotteurism, voyeurism, zoophilia, exhibitionism, coprophilia, masochism, and rape. Thus evaluators should consider whether an offender has multiple paraphilias if any of these behaviors are identified.

In Abel and colleagues' (1988) study conducted under a certificate of confidentiality (described earlier), certain behaviors were always associated with multiple paraphilias. These included fetishism, sadism, masochism, and bestiality. Additionally, Abel and Rouleau (1990) reported that all adult sex offenders who reported an onset of deviant sexual interest prior to age 18 reported more than one paraphilia and an average of 380.2 sex offenses by adulthood, indicating that clinicians should suspect multiple paraphilias in this population. Although adult offenders with an early age of onset have been found to be a high-risk group (Hanson & Bussière, 1998), the reverse cannot be assumed: Not all juveniles with sexual offending behaviors will progress to become adult offenders.

Psychiatric/Medical Considerations

Clinicians should assess indicators of psychiatric disorders, especially mood disorders or impulse control disorders, as these can play a significant role in exacerbating multiple paraphilias. Particular attention should be paid to ADHD, all forms of bipolar disorder, depression, anxiety, impulsiveness, obsessive–compulsive traits, PTSD, and excessive anger (Kafka & Hennen, 2002; Kafka & Prentky, 1998; Lee et al., 2001; Nelson, Soutullo, DelBello, & McElroy, 2002). All of these conditions can interfere with an offender's ability to benefit from cognitive-behavioral treatment and can increase risk if left untreated. If any of these conditions are suspected, the offender should be referred for psychiatric evaluation, preferably to a psychiatrist with expertise in treating sex offenders. However, many areas do not have psychiatrists with this experience. In that situation, the evaluator should find a psychiatrist who is willing to treat sex offenders and assist him or her in developing the expertise.

The extent of hypersexuality in individuals with multiple paraphilias should also be assessed. Kafka (1997) defines "hypersexuality" as seven or more orgasms per week for a period of 6 months or more. Consequently, evaluators should ask offenders about weekly sexual activities, including masturbation. When hypersexuality is identified, offenders should be referred to a psychiatrist for further evaluation.

There are many conditions that contribute to increased risk in multiple paraphiliacs. Accurate identification and treatment of comorbid psychiatric conditions are important elements of effective treatment and risk reduction with this particular sex offender population.

Additional Considerations

The presence of multiple paraphilias may not be detected at initial assessment. The importance of identifying multiple paraphilias speaks to the importance of ongoing assessment and revision of the treatment plan as additional paraphilias are identified.

TREATMENT

As for most sex offenders, evidence-based treatment approaches such as cognitive-behavioral treatment with relapse prevention (RP) should constitute the core component of treatment for offenders with multiple paraphilias (Marshall & Laws, 2003). However, the severity of the problem and heterogeneity of offenders with multiple paraphilias suggest that traditional cognitive-behavioral treatment alone may not be sufficient to prevent reoffense. Instead, effective treatment of these offenders requires a comprehensive program that includes (1) a containment model, (2) RP to address criminogenic needs, (3) individualized treatment planning in collaboration with an offender for treatment engagement and attachment issues, (4) trauma treatment as needed, (5) specific pharmacological interventions as needed to address comorbid disorders and hypersexuality, and (6) community support.

Containment Model

Since offenders with multiple paraphilias pose a high risk of reoffending, treatment should take place within the context of a containment model. The containment model relies on a team approach to managing sex offenders (English, Pullen, & Jones, 1996). Core members of the team include, at a minimum, the supervising officer, the offense-specific treatment provider, and a polygraph examiner. The containment model produces a more comprehensive picture of the offender's problems, needs, strengths, and progress through active communication among treatment, supervision, and polygraph professionals, in addition to collateral sources of information and assessments. While under supervision, offenders are required to participate in offense-specific assessments and treatment and to take periodic polygraph examinations. Under this model, multiple paraphilias are likely to be detected, and a variety of methods can be employed to treat an offender and manage his risk.

Although the containment model (English, 1998, 2004; English et al., 1996; English, Jones, & Patrick, 2003) is a newer approach with limited research, current studies indicate that the approach is effective. An evaluation of 419 probationers supervised by the Maricopa County (Arizona) Adult Probation Department found 2.2% sexual recidivism and a 13.1% general crime recidivism rates, as measured by arrest across an average 36-month follow-up period (Hepburn & Griffin, 2002). In comparison, a meta-analysis by

Hanson and colleagues (2002) reviewed the outcome of current cognitive-behavioral or systemic programs and found an average of 9.9% sexual recidivism and 32% general recidivism rates, as measured by rearrest or reconviction over a median 46-month follow-up period. Although the Hepburn and Griffin study covers a shorter time period, results indicate that the containment approach enhances cognitive-behavioral treatment results.

Other studies have also found promising results with the containment approach. Lowden and colleagues (2003) studied a therapeutic community within the Colorado Department of Corrections. Results indicated that 84% of offenders who participated in treatment versus 52% of untreated sex offenders successfully completed parole. A study of the Jackson County (Oregon) probation and parole containment model program found that offenders who stayed in treatment for at least 1 year were 40% less likely to be convicted of a new felony than those in the comparison group (Aytes, Olsen, Zakrajsek, Murray, & Ireson, 2001).

Multiple paraphilias are difficult to detect, monitor, and treat. The containment model's collaborative team approach and comprehensive strategy produce increased information on offenders' sexual history and current risk factors, thereby facilitating effective treatment of offenders with multiple paraphilias. Within the context of containment, offense-specific treatment should address the assessed treatment needs and social environment necessary to prevent recidivism.

Relapse Prevention

Offenders with multiple paraphilias have structured their lives to gain access to sexual outlets, and consequently they may have developed few other interests and social contacts. Frequently these individuals select employment on the basis of their sexual and/or criminal interests. From witnessing or experiencing abuse, these offenders have developed a mode of thinking and relating to others that permits maladaptive strategies of goal attainment. Without cognitive restructuring and lifestyle changes, such individuals may encounter and succumb to triggers for their prior deviant behavior. Derived from substance abuse treatment models, RP consists of a self-management strategy that instructs offenders in maintaining behavioral change by identifying individual risk factors and by developing effective coping responses. In RP treatment, the therapists assist offenders in the creation of detailed accounts of the events (i.e., cognitive-behavioral chains) that lead to the sexual offending behaviors (Pithers, 1990). Specific treatment interventions are derived from this chain of events to teach the offenders behavioral management strategies to avoid the high-risk situations and to redirect their behavior to a more socially appropriate method of meeting needs.

Overall, meta-analyses and recidivism studies have illustrated that cognitive-behavioral treatment combined with RP components has been effective for reducing reoffense rates (Hanson & Bussière, 1998). However, these studies have shown that there is variability among program outcomes, which suggests that other factors (such as the therapeutic relationship and responsivity issues) may influence treatment efficacy (Serran, Fernandez, Marshall, & Mann, 2003). Likewise, results from a recent longitudinal study of the effectiveness of RP treatment raises concerns about RP. Specifically, these findings indicated that offenders who received RP did not differ from offenders who did not receive treatment with respect to sexual and violent recidivism over an 8-year follow-up period (Marques, Wiederanders, Day, Nelson, & van Ommeren, 2005). However, to maintain comparison groups and reduce treatment dropout, this program did not require a high level of accountability from participants; recent studies have demonstrated that accountability with support is associated with positive treatment outcome (Marshall et al., 2002; Simons, Tyler, & Lins, 2005). Additionally, as polygraph testing was not used, RP plans were based on unverified offender self-reports and official record data; this suggests that the full extent of the offenders' paraphilic behaviors may not have been known. How can RP possibly work when plans are developed to address one small component of an offender's actual risk behaviors? Without this knowledge, clinicians may fail to identify underlying elements of hypersexuality, impulsivity, compulsivity, or trauma. This raises questions about the effectiveness of RP when the intensity, duration, and variety of sexual offending behaviors are unknown. Nonetheless, these findings suggest the need for adjunct therapies in traditional sex offender treatment. Additionally, Marques and colleagues (2005) noted that since offenders were facing high-risk situations shortly after returning to the community, the containment model might have prevented some of the early failures through added surveillance and teamwork.

Another concern regarding RP treatment is that these programs often demonstrate high rates (e.g., 30–50%) of treatment attrition (see Beyko & Wong, 2005). Recidivism studies have demonstrated that premature treatment termination or attrition significantly increases the likelihood of reoffense, whereas treatment completion decreases the likelihood of reoffense (Marques, 1999; Miner & Dwyer, 1995). Preliminary studies have shown that individuals with multiple paraphilias (e.g., Simons, Tyler, & Lins, 2005; Simons & McCullar, 2005), and rapists (e.g., Beyko & Wong; Marques, Day, Nelson, & West, 1994) are more likely than child sexual abusers to quit or be terminated from treatment. Specifically, we (Simons, Tyler, & Lins, 2005) found that as compared to child sexual abusers, indiscriminant offenders displayed more hostile attitudes, were difficult to engage in treatment, were less willing to take responsibility for their offenses, engaged in high-risk behaviors with high frequency, were more likely to fail a monitoring polygraph, and were most likely to quit or be terminated from treatment.

Other researchers note that the strongest limitation of RP is that this risk management model provides skills to offenders that assist them in avoiding high-risk situations, but it fails to assist offenders in learning to live healthy lifestyles (Ward & Brown, 2003). Within this model, individuals are regarded as a bundle of risk factors; they are not perceived as self-directed, goal-oriented human beings (Ward & Stewart, 2003). Indeed, the RP model assumes that individuals attempt to avoid sexual offending, but that they do not have adequate coping skills to abstain from their problem behaviors. Thus the RP model fails to account for the variability among motivations for sexual offending, which has been demonstrated in numerous studies (e.g., Bickley & Beech, 2002; Ward, Louden, Hudson, & Marshall, 1995).

To account for this deficiency of the RP model, the self-regulation model was developed to address the unique treatment needs of sexual offenders. According to the self-regulation model, individuals engage in goal-directed behavior, develop cognitive scripts that direct behavior, and select strategies to achieve their goals based on these scripts (see Ward & Beech, Chapter 2, this volume). This model further proposes that four pathways lead to sexual offending (Ward & Hudson, 1998). Two pathways characterize offenders who attempt to avoid offending (i.e., avoidance-oriented) but do not have adequate strategies (i.e., either underregulation or misregulation) to avoid the undesired behavior; the two remaining pathways characterize the individuals who seek to achieve goals associated with sexual offending (approach-oriented) and experience positive affect as a result. These approach-oriented individuals vary with respect to self-regulation; some individuals exhibit deficient self-regulation (i.e., impulsivity), whereas others display intact self-regulation. Within this model, individualized treatment interventions are based on the offenders' goals and self-regulation abilities (Ward et al., 2004; Yates, 2004). Yates, Kingston, and Hall (2003) demonstrated that pathway membership differentiated types of sexual offenders (e.g., rapists, intrafamilial child abusers, and extrafamilial child abusers); however, further research is needed with respect to the pathway membership of indiscriminant offenders.

Taken together, these findings imply that offenders with multiple paraphilias lack motivation for treatment and demonstrate an increased risk of reoffense, which emphasizes the importance of motivating clients, identifying risk factors, taking into account motivation for offending, and developing plans that are individualized for the offender.

Individualized Treatment Planning

Clinical implications of etiological studies indicate that offenders with multiple paraphilias have been socialized to satisfy human needs through the use of maladaptive means. Specifically, these individuals have observed and experienced violence as a means to attain autonomy, sexual abuse as a form of intimacy, and frequent masturbation as a means of sexual satisfaction. Because they exhibit insecure attachment styles, they lack the internal capabilities to develop healthy relationships with others. In addition, the lack of social support and opportunities for employment may further promote isolation and loneliness. These factors, combined with ineffective coping and poor self-control, may ultimately lead to reoffense. These findings emphasize the importance of individualized treatment planning and the therapeutic relationship, to assist in the development of interpersonal skills and empathy; the inclusion of the offender in the treatment planning, to facilitate understanding of the origins of the sexual offending and to engage the offender in treatment; and the creation of a healthy life plan, which will ensure that the offender acquires the skills and opportunities to lead a life without offending.

The good-lives model (GLM) holds promise as an adjunct therapy to RP, due to its emphasis on self-efficacy, individual strengths, individualized interventions, and the collaborative nature of the therapeutic relationship (Ward & Stewart, 2003). Treatment within this model provides offenders with the skills, values, social supports, and opportunities to meet their needs in a prosocial manner; hence the GLM focuses on achievement of basic needs rather than on risk reduction (Ward & Marshall, 2004). The GLM examines offenders' motivation for sexual assault. Specifically, it is based on the premise that individuals commit sexual offenses as misguided attempts to meet primary needs such as autonomy, relatedness, or sexual satisfaction. It further states that although offenders may have a life plan, they neglect one human need at the expense of another, or they lack the abilities to develop a life plan and adapt to changing circumstances (Ward & Marshall, 2004).

Preliminary studies have provided support for the use of a GLM-type approach to treatment planning. In a study by Mann, Webster, Schofield, and Marshall (2004), the findings indicated that individuals who received approach-oriented (GLM-type) interventions were more likely than individuals who received avoidance-oriented (RP-type) interventions to demonstrate behaviors indicative of treatment engagement. At the end of treatment, these individuals were evaluated by therapists as motivated to live healthy lives without offending. In a similar study (Simons, McCullar, & Tyler, 2006), incarcerated sexual offenders were treated within one of two modalities: RP alone or GLM with RP.

Offenders were evaluated by therapists upon entering treatment and after treatment with respect to motivation and treatment progress (as assessed by time in treatment and by the demonstrated competencies of skills, respectively). After controlling for criminal history and demographics, results indicated that offenders who created a GLM plan demonstrated improved coping skills and problem-solving abilities, appeared more motivated for treatment, and remained in treatment for significantly longer than the offenders who received RP treatment plans.

Offenders' attachment issues may also be addressed within the context of the therapeutic relationship. To facilitate the development of attachment bonds, therapists must disconfirm the clients' maladaptive beliefs associated with relationships. For anxiously attached clients, therapists should maintain appropriate boundaries, be consistent, and be gently challenging to avoid decreasing self-esteem (Ward, Hudson, et al., 1995). For avoidantly attached clients, the strategies include evoking appropriate emotion, acknowledging and rewarding indicators of intimacy, monitoring signs of emotional withdrawal, and using open-ended questions to engage the clients (Ward, Hudson, et al., 1995). Avoidantly attached individuals are sensitive to criticism and expect others to be rejecting; therefore, therapists must not confirm their existing beliefs. The therapeutic challenge in working with disorganized individuals is to provide a secure base while displaying sensitivity and warmth to the clients' abuse and pain. According to Holmes (1997), therapists need to assist such clients in acknowledging the pain of the abuse without denial, in order to work toward a reorganization of the experience into a coherent representation. This requires the flexibility of providing empathy and firm containment with the encouragement of appropriate emotional expression. In working with individuals with attachment issues, therapists should provide opportunities to illustrate the association among emotions, behaviors, and internal working models of attachment relationships (Ward, Hudson, et al., 1995). According to researchers, the comprehension of this relationship will assist the offenders in the creation of behavior chains associated with their interpersonal relationships, which in turn will permit the creation of interventions that will result in more adaptive strategies and perspective-taking abilities.

Trauma Treatment

Because recent findings have illustrated that many offenders with multiple paraphilias have experienced childhood maltreatment, evidence-based trauma interventions remain a critical component of sex offender treatment. Indeed, some researchers (e.g., McMackin, Leisen, Cusack, LaFratta, & Litwin, 2002) have suggested that offenders' abuse experiences may serve as offense triggers. Studies have also demonstrated the neurological consequences of childhood trauma: Severe abuse experiences have been associated with altered brain structure and functioning in various areas, which may limit individuals' capacity to participate and progress within a cognitive-behavioral treatment modality (Bremner, 2002; Creeden, 2004; Perry, 2001; Siegel, 1999; Teicher, Anderson, Polcari, Anderson, & Navalta, 2002). Failure to participate adequately in treatment may also be interpreted as lack of progress and thus may result in premature termination.

Researchers recommend a structured approach to trauma resolution to maximize safety and effectiveness, especially within an institutional setting (e.g., Creeden, 2004). Specifically, a structured approach to trauma resolution uses relaxation training for stabilization (Creeden, 2004), eye movement desensitization and reprocessing (EMDR; Shapiro & Forrest, 1997) for processing the trauma, and cognitive restructuring for integration with offender issues. The use of EMDR and other specialized trauma techniques requires that therapists receive specialized training and maintain criteria for client participation. Specifically, clients with documented histories of PTSD or extensive trauma who have made previous unsuccessful attempts at sex offender treatment and have been assessed using validated instruments for trauma symptomatology should be given high priority to receive trauma treatment.

To maximize safety, clients must be fully informed of the techniques, risks, and benefits of treatment. During the processing phase of treatment, it is advised that clients not participate in sex offender groups that relate to sexual assault cycles, as the content of the discussions may be too sensitive; this may provoke negative emotions that may ultimately trigger offense-related behaviors. In addition, the timing of the processing phase remains critical in sex offender treatment. Offenders must accept responsibility for and learn to control their perpetrating behavior before intensive trauma work is initiated. Offenders may destabilize during trauma treatment and may resort to familiar anxiety-relieving behaviors such as offending. Moreover, some offenders may receive secondary gain from victimization trauma and may not progress in trauma treatment. Offenders who are ineligible for the processing phase may participate in the relaxation component.

Relaxation techniques are taught to clients to prepare them for trauma treatment and to serve as a maintenance strategy during and after the therapy. In addition, these techniques serve to establish rapport, to increase the clients' ability for self-regulation, and to teach coping skills (stabilization phase). The process phase utilizes EMDR, a form of exposure therapy, which has recently been described as an empirically validated treatment for PTSD (see Foa, Keane, & Friedman, 2000). The processing phase consists of deconditioning the trauma and the restructuring of the narrative. To maintain consistency within the sex offender treatment modality, the final phase of trauma treatment uses a group format for integration, to provide clients with ongoing support from peers and the trauma therapist. This appears critical for safety within an institutional environment, as the group provides assistance to clients as they integrate and adopt skills to cope with issues, events, and adversities. Within a group format, clients examine the relationship between their own abuse experiences and subsequent offending behaviors; specifically, they develop new narratives about their abusive behavior that include empathy for their victims and feelings of self-worth without shame. They also learn to establish equitable relationships and obtain a sense of personal empowerment through assisting others with their trauma resolution. Although trauma treatment appears necessary, and clinical reports indicate its usefulness, further research is needed to evaluate its effectiveness as an adjunct therapy.

Pharmacological Interventions

Specific behavioral interventions designed to decrease deviant interests may not be sufficient to address the intense urges and changeable nature of deviant sexual interests in offenders with multiple paraphilias; instead, the use of pharmacological interventions may be necessary to decrease deviant arousal and hypersexuality. Additionally, studies have shown that these offenders exhibit comorbid Axis I disorders (e.g., depressive disorders, anxiety disorders, and ADHD), which further emphasizes the importance of pharmacological interventions (Kafka & Prentky, 1998). Psychiatric evaluations should assist in determining the type of medication that is most likely to assist each offender. Overall, studies have shown the benefits of the inclusion of selective serotonin reuptake inhibitors (SSRIs) and hormonal medications in sex offender treatment.

In recent years, SSRIs have been used to reduce sex offenders' deviant sexual thoughts and fantasies. Serotonin, a neurotransmitter, plays a role in regulating sexual drive, depression, obsessions, compulsions, anxiety, impulsiveness, and anger. SSRIs are antidepressants that are also approved by the U.S. Food and Drug Administration (FDA) for the treatment of obsessive–compulsive disorder and social anxiety. Although double-blind placebo-controlled trials are needed, studies using self-report measures or PPG have found these medications to reduce some repetitive sexually deviant fantasies and/or behaviors (Greenberg & Bradford, 1997; Kafka, 1991, 1994; Kafka & Prentky, 1992; Stein et al., 1992), and to selectively decrease deviant arousal without significantly decreasing appropriate arousal (Bradford, Greenberg, Gojer, Martindale, & Goldberg, 1995; Kafka, 1992; Kafka & Prentky, 1994). Greenberg and Bradford (1997) have hypothesized that paraphilias may result when there is an inability to suppress unconventional sexual appetites. Since serotonin affects sexual appetite, SSRIs may help alter a dysfunctional serotonergic system, thereby allowing suppression of unconventional sexual appetites.

The fact that SSRIs treat depression may also be beneficial to sex offenders. Kafka (1991) speculated that hypersexuality could be considered an atypical symptom of a depressive disorder. Because cognitive distortions are frequently associated with depression, sex offenders who are depressed or anxious may have a difficult time learning cognitive restructuring without these medications (Heil, Ahlmeyer, & English, 2000). Furthermore, SSRIs have been used in the treatment of PTSD. One study found that after a year of SSRI treatment, subjects with PTSD had a 5% increase in hippocampal volume and a 35% increase in memory function (Bremner, 2006). Together, these findings indicate a variety of reasons why SSRIs may be beneficial for offenders with multiple paraphilias.

Before SSRIs are prescribed, clinicians should rule out the possibility of bipolar disorders, since SSRIs have been known to exacerbate these. Some forms of bipolar disorder, such as bipolar II disorder and cyclothymia, have more subtle presentations and may be more difficult to diagnose. Since hypersexuality and impulsiveness are associated with hypomania and mania, accurate diagnosis of and proper medication for bipolar disorders in individuals with multiple paraphilias are critical.

In cases where SSRIs are not sufficient to decrease hyperarousal, other medications should be considered. After finding higher rates of retrospectively diagnosed childhood ADHD in offenders with paraphilias, Kafka and Hennen (2000) found that a combination of methylphenidate (sustained release) and SSRI produced positive results when offenders' symptoms were not adequately treated with SSRIs alone.

When sex offenders continue to have intrusive sexual urges that have not responded to other medications, antiandrogen medications such as medroxyprogesterone acetate (MPA) or leuprolide acetate (Lupron) should be explored. MPA and Lupron decrease testosterone levels, with a resulting reduction in sexual thoughts and fantasies (Hucker, Langevin, & Bain, 1988; Krueger & Kaplan, 2001). Unlike SSRIs, these medications appear to reduce all sex drive equally. These medications are FDA-approved drugs; however, they are not approved for use with sex offenders. As a result, many psychiatrists are uncomfortable using these drugs for this purpose. In addition, MPA has significant side effects, some of which can be life-threatening. Among those who can medically tolerate MPA, long-term compliance can be low because of the side effects. Lupron does not have the steroid effect of MPA, but it increases testosterone and sex drive for approximately 1 month prior to an eventual reduction of the sex drive (Bradford, Abel, & Greenberg, 1996). Therefore, precautionary measures must be taken during the first month of administration.

In summary, the benefits of SSRIs appear superior to those of hormonal treatments with MPA and Lupron. SSRI studies have shown the effectiveness of these drugs for reducing sexual arousal in addition to alleviating symptoms of depression, PTSD, and obsessive–compulsive disorder. In addition, there are less dangerous side effects associated with these medications than with MPA and Lupron. Certain SSRIs have been shown to be safe and effective within the adolescent and geriatric population, which suggests that these medications may be used throughout the duration of sex offender risk (Bradford et al., 1996; Grimsley & Jann, 1992). However, SSRIs are not effective for all offenders, and careful psychiatric evaluation is needed to determine which medication is most likely to assist offenders.

Polygraph Testing

As discussed in the "Assessment" section, polygraph testing helps verify the extent of an offender's past history of paraphilias. Besides clarifying sexual histories, polygraph testing is used to monitor offenders' current behaviors and has been shown to serve as a deterrent to engaging in high-risk or offending behavior (Abrams & Ogard, 1986; Grubin, Madson, Parsons, Sosnowski, & Warberg, 2004; Harrison & Kirkpatrick, 2000). Furthermore, polygraph monitoring results in greater detection of treatment and supervision violations and facilitates prompt responses to high-risk behaviors. The information polygraphy provides can help therapists focus on the offenders' greatest needs and risk factors. Thus pertinent RP strategies can be developed that take into account the broader risk patterns and flexible nature of multiple paraphilias.

Community Support

The environment in which an offender lives can support or compromise treatment. By definition, the presence of multiple paraphilias indicates the malleability of an offender's deviant interests. As such, easy access to vulnerable populations may be particularly risky with this population of offenders. Therefore, comprehensive treatment should include efforts to establish safe environments and positive community support systems for individuals with multiple paraphilias.

Some treatment programs have developed creative options to decrease offenders' risk. Many programs work with the offenders' family members to help them provide informed positive support for the offenders' change efforts. Other programs have housed treatment participants together in shared living arrangements (SLAs). This allows a supervising officer to conduct more frequent home visits. There is also an expectation that offenders will report other cohabitants' violations. A Colorado study determined that high-risk offenders living in SLAs had fewer technical and criminal violations than offenders living with family members, friends, or roommates who refused to cooperate with the criminal justice containment team (Colorado Department of Public Safety, 2004a). An SLA provides an informed positive support system that is aware of each offender's sex offending history, manipulation tactics, and treatment and supervision requirements. In addition, the support system is capable of holding the offender accountable and reporting concerns to the criminal justice supervision team.

Other methods of providing positive support include surveillance teams (Abel & Osborn, 2000) and community Circles of Support and Accountability (COSAs; Wilson, Picheca, & Prinzo, 2005). Abel and Osborn (2000) recommend surveillance teams for offenders with multiple paraphilias that consist of five individuals per offender, including one person from the offender's family, employment, and social environment. Therapists train team members to monitor and report on each offender's high-risk behaviors. COSAs are based on restorative justice concepts (Wilson et al., 2005). Each COSA is composed of five lay volunteers who meet with an offender individually and as a group on a weekly basis as the offender makes the transition back to the community from prison. A survey of offenders participating in COSAs determined that 90% thought they would have had more difficulty adjusting to the community and 67% would have been likely to return to criminal behavior without benefit of the COSAs. In a 4.5-year follow-up study of treated sex offenders, those released with COSA support had reductions in all types of recidivism, in comparison to those released without COSAs: sexual recidivism of 5% versus 16.7%, violent recidivism of 15% versus 35%, and any recidivism of 28.3% versus 43.4% (Wilson et al., 2005).

Sex Addicts Anonymous is another community support program that may be beneficial to some individuals with multiple paraphilias. However, support programs should only be considered an adjunct and not a substitute for comprehensive offense-specific treatment. Clinicians should be familiar with these types of support groups before determining whether these programs will be beneficial for specific offenders.

Although not a traditional focus of treatment, establishing informed community support is an important treatment consideration, particularly for offenders with multiple paraphilias. For most offenders, criminal justice supervision is time-limited. Once supervision ends, offenders may choose to discontinue treatment. An informed community support system will assist offenders to maintain lifestyle changes over the long term.

SUMMARY AND FUTURE DIRECTIONS

Although the presence of multiple paraphilias in a substantial portion of the detected sexual offending population has been identified for over 20 years, there has been some resistance to embracing this knowledge. For years Abel's work was discredited as having a unique sample or unsound research techniques. More recent studies employing polygraphy have also been discredited as causing false admissions by offenders. It is certainly unimaginable how some sex offenders could engage in the number of sex offenses they self-report without the behaviors being detected at an earlier point. It is only through the knowledge of underreporting by victims and the consistency of findings across multiple studies and samples that the information begins to appear credible. We can only speculate that clinicians are concerned about the implications of these findings for fueling public fear and irrational legislative action in response to the perceived risk of sex offenders. In addition, the task of treating offenders with such extensive deviant sexual histories is onerous and may seem hopeless. However, we view the documentation of the extent of multiple paraphilias as a hopeful development. Accurate information on the extent of multiple paraphilias may lead to additional theories about sexual offending, and ultimately to more effective treatment techniques.

Etiological studies have been able to identify risk factors as well as processes that may mediate the translation of risk for multiple paraphilic behaviors. While these studies provide evidence that multiple factors contribute to the development of indiscriminant sexual offending, future studies need to include nonsexual offender comparison groups with similar backgrounds. Nevertheless, selective preventive interventions can be provided to individuals and families with these risk factors. Most importantly, universal preventive interventions can be developed to decrease the prevalence of these factors in the general population as a means to reduce the prevalence of multiple paraphilic behaviors.

ACKNOWLEDGMENT

Special thanks to Kim English, Michael O'Connell, and Michael Seto for sharing their unpublished research findings. We also thank Candice Osborn and Gene Abel for clarifying published data.

REFERENCES

Abel, G. G., Becker, J. V., Cunningham-Rathner, J., Mittelman, M., & Rouleau, J. L. (1988). Multiple paraphilic diagnoses among sex offenders. *Bulletin of the American Academy of Psychiatry and the Law, 16*, 153–168.

Abel, G. G, Becker, J. V., Mittelman, M., Cunningham-Rathner, J., Rouleau, J. L., & Murphy, W. (1987). Self-reported sex crimes of nonincarcerated paraphiliacs. *Journal of Interpersonal Violence, 2*(1), 3–25.

Abel, G. G., Jordan, A., Hand, C. G., Holland, L. A., & Phipps, A. (2001). Classification models of child molesters utilizing the Abel Assessment for Sexual Interest. *Child Abuse and Neglect, 25*, 703–718.

Abel, G. G., & Osborn, C. (1992). The paraphilias: The extent and nature of sexually deviant and criminal behavior. In J. M. W. Bradford (Ed.), *Psychiatric Clinics of North America, 15*, 675–687.

Abel, G. G., & Osborn, C. A. (2000). The paraphilias. In M. G. Gelder, J. J. Lopez-Ibor, Jr., & N. C. Andreasen (Eds.), *Oxford textbook of psychiatry* (Vol. 1., pp. 897–913). New York: Oxford University Press.

Abel, G. G., & Rouleau, J. L. (1990). The nature and extent of sexual assault. In W. L. Marshall, D. R. Laws, & H. E. Barbaree (Eds.), *Handbook of sexual assault: Issues, theories, and treatment of the offender* (pp. 9–21). New York: Plenum Press.

Abrams, S., & Ogard, E. (1986). Polygraph surveillance of probationers. *Polygraph, 15*, 174–182.

Ahlmeyer, S., Heil, P., McKee, B., & English, K. (2000). The impact of polygraphy on admissions of victims and offenses in adult sexual offenders. *Sexual Abuse: A Journal of Research and Treatment, 12*, 123–138.

Ahlmeyer, S., & Simons, D. (2002, October). *Path-analytic models of risk behaviors, age crossover, and sexual victims and offenses.* Poster presented at the 21st Annual Research and Treatment Conference of the Association for the Treatment of Sexual Abusers, Montréal.

American Psychiatric Association. (1980). *Diagnostic and statistical manual of mental disorders* (3rd ed.). Washington, DC: Author.

American Psychiatric Association. (2000). *Diagnostic and statistical manual of mental disorders* (4th ed., text rev.). Washington, DC: Author.

Aytes, K. E., Olsen, S. S., Zakrajsek, T., Murray, P., & Ireson, R. (2001). Cognitive behavioral treatment for sexual offenders: An examination of recidivism. *Sexual Abuse: A Journal of Research and Treatment, 13*, 223–231.

Bartholomew, K., & Horowitz, L. (1991). Attachment styles among adults: A test of a four category model. *Journal of Personality and Social Psychology, 61*, 226–244.

Beauregard, E., Lussier, P., & Proulx, J. (2004). An exploration of developmental factors related to deviant sexual preferences among adult rapists. *Sexual Abuse: A Journal of Research and Treatment, 16,* 151–161.

Beyko, M. J., & Wong, S. C. P. (2005). Predictors of treatment attrition as indicators for program improvement, not offender shortcomings: A study of sex offender treatment attrition. *Sexual Abuse: A Journal of Research and Treatment, 17,* 375–389.

Bickley, J. A., & Beech, A. (2002). An empirical investigation of the Ward and Hudson pathways model of offending in child sexual abusers. *Journal of Interpersonal Violence, 17,* 371–393.

Bradford, J. M. W., Abel, G. G., & Greenberg, D. M. (1996). *Transcript of panel discussion: Understanding assessment and treatment of paraphilias.* (American College of Psychiatrists Psychiatric Update 16, No. 11). New York: Medical Information Systems.

Bradford, J. M. W., Boulet, J., & Pawlak, A. (1992). The paraphilias: A multiplicity of deviant behaviors. *Canadian Journal of Psychiatry, 37,* 104–108.

Bradford, J. M. W., Greenberg, D. M., Gojer, J. J., Martindale, J. J., & Goldberg, M. (1995, May). *Sertraline in the treatment of pedophilia: An open labeled study.* Paper presented at the annual meeting of the American Psychiatric Association, Miami, FL.

Bremner, J. D. (2002). *Does stress damage the brain?* New York: Norton.

Bremner, J. D. (2006). The relationship between cognitive and brain changes in posttraumatic stress disorder. In R. Yehuda (Ed.), *Psychobiology of posttraumatic stress disorder: A decade of progress* (pp. 80–86). Boston: Blackwell, on behalf of the New York Academy of Sciences.

Burk, L. R., & Burkhart, B. R. (2003). Disorganized attachment as a diathesis for sexual deviance: Developmental experience and motivation for sexual offending. *Aggression and Violent Behavior, 8,* 487–511.

Burton, D. L. (2003). Male adolescents: Sexual victimization and subsequent sexual abuse. *Child and Adolescent Social Work Journal, 20,* 277–296.

Cicchetti, D., & Lynch, M. (1995). Failures in the expectable environment and their impact on individual development: The case of child maltreatment. In D. Cicchetti & D. J. Cohen (Eds.), *Developmental psychopathology: Vol. 2. Risk, disorder, and adaptation* (pp. 32–71). New York: Wiley.

Clark, J. P., & Tift, L. L. (1996). Polygraph and interview validation of self-reported deviant behavior. *American Sociological Review, 31,* 516–523.

Colorado Department of Public Safety. (2004a). *Report on safety issues raised by living arrangements for and location of sex offenders in the community.* Denver: Author, Sex Offender Management Board.

Colorado Department of Public Safety. (2004b). Standards for polygraphy. In *Colorado Sex Offender Management Board standards and guidelines for the assessment, evaluation, treatment and behavioral monitoring of adult sex offenders* (pp. 99–102). Denver: Author, Sex Offender Management Board.

Craissati, J., McClurg, G., & Browne, K. (2002a). Characteristics of perpetrators of child sexual abuse who have been sexually victimized as children. *Sexual Abuse: A Journal of Research and Treatment, 14,* 225–239.

Craissati, J., McClurg, G., & Browne, K. (2002b). The parental bonding experiences of sex offenders: A comparison between child molesters and rapists. *Child Abuse and Neglect, 26,* 909–921.

Creeden, K. (2004). The neurodevelopmental impact of early trauma and insecure attachment: Rethinking our understanding and treatment of sexual behavior problems. *Sexual Addiction and Compulsivity, 11,* 223–247.

Dube, S. R., Anda, R. F., Felitti, V. J., Croft, J. B., Edwards, V. J., & Giles, W. H. (2001). Growing up with parental alcohol abuse: Exposure to childhood abuse, neglect, and household dysfunction. *Child Abuse and Neglect, 25,* 1627–1640.

Emerick, R. L., & Dutton, W. A. (1993). The effect of polygraphy on the self-report of adolescent sex offenders: Implications for risk assessment. *Annals of Sex Research, 6,* 83–103.

English, K. (1998). The containment approach: An aggressive strategy for the community management of adult sex offenders. *Psychology, Public Policy, and Law, 4*(1–2), 218–235.

English, K. (2004). The containment approach to managing sex offenders. *Seton Hall Law Review, 34*(4), 1255–1272.

English, K., Jones, L., Pasini-Hill, D., Patrick, D., & Cooley-Towell, S. (2000). *The value of polygraph testing in sex offender management* (Final research report submitted to the National Institute of Justice for Grant No. D97LBVX0034). Denver: Colorado Division of Criminal Justice, Office of Research and Statistics.

English, K., Jones, L., & Patrick, D. (2003). Risk management of adult sex offenders. In B. Winick & J. LaFond (Eds.), *Protecting society from sexually dangerous offenders: Law, justice, and therapy* (pp. 265–280). Washington, DC: American Psychological Association.

English, K., Jones, L., Patrick, D., & Pasini-Hill, D. (2003). Sexual offender containment: Use of the postconviction polygraph. *Annals of the New York Academy of Sciences, 989*, 411–427.

English, K., Pullen, S., & Jones, L. (1996). *Managing adult sex offenders: A containment approach.* Lexington, KY: American Probation and Parole Association.

Foa, E. B., Keene, T. M., & Friedman, M. J. (2000). *Effective treatments for PTSD.* New York: Guilford Press.

Freeman-Longo, R., & Blanchard, G. (1998). *Sexual abuse in America: Epidemic of the 21st century.* Brandon, VT: Safer Society Press.

Greenberg, D. M., & Bradford, J. M. W. (1997). Treatment of paraphilic disorders: A review of the role of selective serotonin reuptake inhibitors. *Sexual Abuse: A Journal of Research and Treatment, 9*, 349–360.

Grimsley, S. R., & Jann, M. W. (1992). Paroxetine, sertraline, and fluvoxamine: New selective serotonin reuptake inhibitors. *Clinical Pharmacy, 11*, 189–199.

Grubin, D., Madsen, L., Parsons, S., Sosnowski, D., & Warberg, B. (2004). A prospective study of the impact of polygraphy on high-risk behaviors in adult sex offenders. *Sexual Abuse: A Journal of Research and Treatment, 16*, 209–222.

Guay, J., Proulx, J., Cusson, M., & Ouimet, M. (2001). Victim-choice polymorphia among serious sex offenders. *Archives of Sexual Behavior, 30* (5), 521–533.

Hanson, R., Resnick, H., Saunders, B., Kilpatrick, D., & Best, C. (1999). Factors related to the reporting of childhood rape. *Child Abuse and Neglect, 23*, 559–569.

Hanson, R. K., & Bussière, M. T. (1998). Predicting relapse: A meta-analysis of sexual offender recidivism studies. *Journal of Consulting and Clinical Psychology, 66*, 348–362.

Hanson, R. K., Gordon, A., Harris, A., Marques, J. K., Murphy, W., Quinsey, V. L., et al. (2002). First report of the Collaborative Outcome Data Project on the Effectiveness of Psychological Treatment for Sex Offenders. *Sexual Abuse: A Journal of Research and Treatment, 14*(2), 169–194.

Hanson, R. K., & Harris, A. (1998). *Dynamic predictors of sexual recidivism.* Ottawa, Department of the Solicitor General of Canada.

Hanson, R. K., & Morton-Bourgon, K. M. (2004). *Predictors of sexual recidivism: An updated meta-analysis* (User Report No. 2004-02). Ottawa: Department of the Solicitor General of Canada.

Hanson, R. K., & Thornton, D. (2000). Improving risk assessment for sex offenders: A comparison of three actuarial scales. *Law and Human Behavior, 24*, 119–136.

Harrison, J. S., & Kirkpatrick, B. (2000). Polygraph testing and behavioral change with sex offenders in an outpatient setting: An exploratory study. *Polygraph, 29*, 20–25.

Heil, P., Ahlmeyer, S., & English, K. (2000). *The impact of selective serotonin reuptake inhibitors on adult sex offender sexual activity: A retrospective pilot study.* Unpublished manuscript.

Heil, P., Ahlmeyer, S., & Simons, D. (2003). Crossover sexual offenses. *Sexual Abuse: A Journal of Research and Treatment, 15*, 221–236.

Hepburn, J., & Griffin, M. (2002). *An analysis of risk factors contributing to the recidivism of sex offenders on probation* (Report submitted to the Maricopa County Adult Probation Department and the National Institute of Justice, Document No. 203905). Phoenix: Arizona State University West.

Holmes, J. (1997). Attachment, autonomy, intimacy: Some clinical implications of attachment theory. *British Journal of Medical Psychology, 70*, 231–248.

Hucker, S. J., Langevin, R., & Bain, J. (1988). A double-blind trial of sex drive reducing medication in pedophiles. *Annals of Sex Research, 1*, 227–247.

Kafka, M. P. (1991). Successful antidepressant treatment of nonparaphilic sexual addictions and paraphilias in men. *Journal of Clinical Psychiatry, 52*, 60–65.

Kafka, M. P. (1994). Sertraline pharmacotherapy for males with paraphilias and paraphilia-related disorders: An open trial. *Annals of Clinical Psychiatry, 6*, 189–195.

Kafka, M. P. (1997). Hypersexual desire in males: An operational definition and clinical implications for males with paraphilias and paraphilia-related disorders. *Archives of Sexual Behavior, 26*, 505–526.

Kafka, M. P., & Hennen, J. (2000). Psychostimulant augmentation during treatment with selective serotonin reuptake inhibitors in men with paraphilias and paraphilia-related disorders: A case series. *Journal of Clinical Psychiatry, 61*, 664–670.

Kafka, M. P., & Hennen, J. (2002). A DSM-IV Axis I comorbidity study of males (*n* = 120) with paraphilias and paraphilia-related disorders. *Sexual Abuse: A Journal of Research and Treatment, 14*, 349–365.

Kafka, M. P., & Prentky, R. A. (1992). Fluoxetine treatment of nonparaphilic sexual addictions and paraphilias in men. *Journal of Clinical Psychiatry, 55*, 351–358.

Kafka, M. P., & Prentky, R. A. (1998). Attention deficit hyperactivity disorder in males with paraphilias and paraphilia-related disorders. *Journal of Clinical Psychiatry, 59*, 388–396.

Kilpatrick, D., Edmunds, C., & Seymour, C. (1992). *Rape in America: A report to the nation.* Charleston: Medical University of South Carolina, National Victim Center and Crime Victims Research and Treatment Center.

Kilpatrick, D., Saunders, B., & Smith, D. (2003). *Youth victimization: Prevalence and implications* (NIJ Research in Brief). Washington, DC: U.S. Department of Justice, National Institute of Justice.

Krueger, R. B., & Kaplan, M. S. (2001). Depot-leuprolide acetate for treatment of paraphilias: Twelve cases. *Archives of Sexual Behavior, 30*, 409–422.

Lalumière, M., Seto, M., & Jesperson, A. (2006, September). *The link between child sexual abuse and sexual offending: A meta-analytical examination.* Poster presented at the 25th Annual Research and Treatment Conference at the Association for the Treatment of Sexual Abusers, Chicago.

Laws, D. R. (1994). How dangerous are rapists to children? *Journal of Sexual Aggression, 1*(1), 1–14.

Laws, D. R. (2003). Penile plethysmography: Will we ever get it right? In T. Ward, D. R. Laws, & S. M. Hudson (Eds.), *Sexual deviance: Issues and controversies* (pp. 82–102). Thousand Oaks, CA: Sage.

Lee, J. K. P., Jackson, H. J., Pattison, P., & Ward, T. (2002). Developmental risk factors for sexual offending. *Child Abuse and Neglect, 26*, 73–92.

Lee, J. K. P., Pattison, P., Jackson, H. J., & Ward, T. (2001). The general, common, and specific features for different types of paraphilias. *Criminal Justice and Behavior, 28*, 227–256.

Lowden, K., Hetz, N., Harrison, L., Patrick, D., English, K., & Pasini-Hill, D. (2003). *Evaluation of Colorado's prison therapeutic community for sex offenders: A report of findings.* Denver: Colorado Division of Criminal Justice, Office of Research and Statistics.

Lussier, P. (2005). The criminal activity of sexual offenders in adulthood: Revisiting the specialization debate. *Sexual Abuse: A Journal of Research and Treatment, 17*, 269–289.

Main, M. (1996). Introduction to the special section on attachment and psychopathology: Overview of the field of attachment. *Journal of Consulting and Clinical Psychology, 64*, 237–243.

Mann, R. E., Webster, S. D., Schofield, C., & Marshall, W. L. (2004). Approach versus avoidance goals in relapse prevention with sexual offenders. *Sexual Abuse: A Journal of Research and Treatment, 16*, 65–75.

Marques, J. (1999). How to answer the question: Does sex offender treatment work? *Journal of Interpersonal Violence, 14*, 437–451.

Marques, J., Day, D., Nelson, C., & West, M. (1994). Effects of cognitive-behavioral treatment on sex offender recidivism. *Criminal Justice and Behavior, 21*, 28–54.

Marques, J. K., Wiederanders, M., Day, D. M., Nelson, C., & van Ommeren, A. (2005). Effects of a relapse prevention program on sexual recidivism: Final results from California's Sex Offender Treatment and Evaluation Project (SOTEP). *Sexual Abuse: A Journal of Research and Treatment, 17*, 79–107.

Marshall, W. L. (1993). The role of attachments, intimacy, and loneliness in the etiology and maintenance of sexual offending. *Sexual and Marital Therapy, 8*, 109–121.

Marshall, W. L. (1997). Pedophilia: Psychopathology and theory. In D. R. Laws & W. O'Donohue (Eds.), *Sexual deviance: Theory, assessment, and treatment* (pp. 152–174). New York: Guilford Press.

Marshall, W. L., Barbaree, H. E., & Eccles, A. (1991). Early onset and deviant sexuality in child molesters. *Journal of Interpersonal Violence, 6*, 323–336.

Marshall, W. L., & Eccles, A. (1993). Pavlovian conditioning processes in adolescent sex offenders. In H. E. Barbaree, W. L. Marshall, & S. M. Hudson (Eds.), *The juvenile sex offender* (pp. 118–142). New York: Guilford Press.

Marshall, W. L., & Laws, D. R. (2003). A brief history of behavioral and cognitive behavioral approaches to sexual offender treatment: Part 2. The modern era. *Sexual Abuse: A Journal of Research and Treatment, 15*, 93–120.

Marshall, W. L., & Marshall, L. E. (2000). The origins of sexual offending. *Trauma, Violence, and Abuse, 1*, 250–263.

Marshall, W. L., Serran, G. A., Moulden, H., Mulloy, R., Fernandez, Y. M., Mann, R. E., et al. (2002). Therapist features in sexual offender treatment: Their reliable identification and influence on behaviour change. *Clinical Psychology and Psychotherapy, 9*, 395–405.

McGee, R. A., Wolfe, D. A., & Wilson, S. K. (1997). Multiple maltreatment experiences and adolescent behavior problems: Adolescents' perspectives. *Development and Psychopathology, 9*, 131–149.

McMackin, R. A., Leisen, M. B., Cusack, J. F., LaFratta, J., & Litwin, P. N. (2002). The relationship of trauma exposure to sex offending behavior among male juvenile offenders. *Journal of Child Sexual Abuse, 11*, 25–40.

Milner, J. S., & Dopke, C. A. (1997). Paraphilia not otherwise specified: Psychopathology and theory. In D. R. Laws & W. O'Donohue (Eds.), *Sexual deviance: Theory, assessment, and treatment* (pp. 394–423). New York: Guilford Press.

Miner, M., & Dwyer, S. (1995). Analysis of dropouts from outpatient sex offender treatment. *Journal of Psychiatry and Human Sexuality, 7*, 77–93.

Nelson, E. B., Soutullo, C. A., DelBello, M. P., & McElroy, S. L. (2002). The psychopharmacological treatment of sex offenders. In B. Schwartz (Ed.), *The sex offender: Current treatment modalities and systems issues* (pp. 13-1–13-23). Kingston, NJ: Civic Research Institute.

O'Connell, M. A. (1998). Using polygraph testing to assess deviant sexual history of sex offenders (Doctoral dissertation, University of Washington, 1998). *Dissertation Abstracts International, 49*, 1–131. (UMI No. 48106)

Perry, B. (2001). The neurodevelopmental impact of violence in childhood. In D. Shetky & E. Benedek (Eds.), *Textbook of child and adolescent forensic psychiatry* (pp. 221–238). Washington, DC: American Psychiatric Press.

Pithers, W. D. (1990). Relapse prevention with sexual aggressors: A method for maintaining therapeutic gain and embracing external supervision. In W. L. Marshall, D. R. Laws, & H. E. Barbaree (Eds.), *Handbook of sexual assault: Issues, theories, and treatment of the offender* (pp. 343–361). New York: Plenum Press.

Quinsey, V. L., Harris, G. T., Rice, M. E., & Cormier, C. A. (1998). *Violent offenders: Appraising and managing risk.* Washington, DC: American Psychological Association.

Salter, D., McMillan, D., Richards, M., Talbot, T., Hodges, J., Bentovim, A., et al. (2003). Development of sexually abusive behavior in sexually victimized males: A longitudinal study. *Lancet*, *361*, 471–476.

Serran, G., Fernandez, Y., Marshall, W. L., & Mann, R. E. (2003). Process issues in treatment: Application to sexual offender programs. *Professional Psychology: Research and Practice, 34*, 368–375.

Shapiro, F., & Forrest, M. S. (1997). *Eye movement desensitization and reprocessing.* New York: Basic Books.

Siegel, D. J. (1999). *The developing mind: Toward a neurobiology of interpersonal experience.* New York: Guilford Press.

Simons, D., Heil, P., & English, K. (2004, October). *Utilizing polygraph as a risk prediction/treatment progress assessment tool.* Paper presented at the 23rd Annual Research and Treatment Conference of the Association for the Treatment of Sexual Abusers, Albuquerque, NM.

Simons, D., & McCullar, B. (2005, November). *Attachment and the therapeutic relationship: Preliminary findings.* Workshop presented at the 24th Research and Treatment Conference of the Annual Association for the Treatment of Sexual Abusers, Salt Lake City, UT.

Simons, D., McCullar, B., & Tyler, C. (2006, September). *Evaluation of the good lives model approach to treatment planning.* Workshop presented at the 25th Annual Research and Treatment Conference of the Association for the Treatment of Sexual Abusers, Chicago.

Simons, D., Tyler, C., & Heil, P. (2005, November). *Childhood risk factors associated with crossover offending.* Poster presented at the 24th Annual Research and Treatment Conference of the Association for the Treatment of Sexual Abusers, Salt Lake City, UT.

Simons, D., Tyler, C., & Lins, R. (2005, November). *The influence of therapist characteristics on treatment progress.* Poster presented at the 24th Annual Research and Treatment Conference of the Association for the Treatment of Sexual Abusers, Salt Lake City, UT.

Simons, D., Wurtele, S. K., & Durham, R. L. (2004, October). *Developmental experiences of child sexual abusers and rapists.* Paper presented at the 23rd Annual Research and Treatment Conference of the Association for the Treatment of Sexual Abusers, Albuquerque, NM.

Simons, D., Wurtele, S. K., & Heil, P. (2002). Childhood victimization and lack of empathy as predictors of sexual offending against women and children. *Journal of Interpersonal Violence, 17*, 1291–1305.

Smallbone, S. W., & Wortley, R. K. (2004). Onset, persistence, and versatility of offending among adult males convicted of sexual offenses against children. *Sexual Abuse: A Journal of Research and Treatment, 16*, 285–298.

Smith, D., Letourneau, E., Saunders, B., Kilpatrick, D., Resnick, H., & Best, C. (2000). Delay in disclosure of childhood rape: Results from a national survey. *Child Abuse and Neglect, 24*, 273–287.

Stein, D. J., Hollander, E., Anthony, D. T., Schneier, F. R., Fallon, B. A., Liebowitz, M. R., et al. (1992). Serotonergic medications for sexual obsessions, sexual addictions, and paraphilias. *Journal of Clinical Psychiatry, 53*, 211–222.

Teicher, M., Anderson, S., Polcari, A., Anderson, C., & Navalta, C. (2002). Developmental neurobiology of childhood stress and trauma. *Psychiatric Clinics of North America, 25*, 397–426.

Tjaden, P., & Thoennes, N. (2006). *Extent, nature, and consequences of rape victimization: Findings from the National Violence Against Women Survey* (No. NCJ 183781). Washington, DC: U.S. Department of Justice, National Institute of Justice.

Veneziano, T., Veneziano, E., & LeGrand, O. (2000). The relationship between adolescent sex offender behaviors and victim characteristics with prior victimization. *Violence and Victims, 15*, 363–374.

Ward, T., Bickley, J., Webster, S. D., Fisher, D., Beech, A., & Eldridge, H. (2004). *The self-regulation model of the offense and relapse process: Assessment.* Victoria, BC, Canada: Pacific Psychological Assessment Corporation.

Ward, T., & Brown, M. (2003). The risk need model of offender rehabilitation: A critical review. In T.

Ward, D. R. Laws, & S. M. Hudson (Eds.), *Sexual deviance: Issues and controversies* (pp. 338–353). Thousand Oaks, CA: Sage.

Ward, T., & Hudson, S. M. (1998). A model of the relapse process in sexual offenders. *Journal of Interpersonal Violence, 13,* 700–715.

Ward, T., Hudson, S. M., Marshall, W. L., & Siegert, R. (1995). Attachment style and intimacy deficits in sexual offenders: A theoretical framework. *Sexual Abuse: A Journal of Research and Treatment, 7,* 317–335.

Ward, T., Louden, K., Hudson, S. M., & Marshall, W. L. (1995). A descriptive model of the offence chain for child molesters. *Journal of Interpersonal Violence, 10,* 452–472.

Ward, T., & Marshall, W. L. (2004). Good lives, aetiology, and the rehabilitation of sex offenders: A bridging theory. *Journal of Sexual Aggression, 10,* 153–169.

Ward, T., & Stewart, C. A. (2003). The treatment of sexual offenders: Risk management and good lives. *Professional Psychology: Research and Practice, 34,* 353–360.

Weinrott, M. R., & Saylor, M. (1991). Self-report of crimes committed by sex offenders. *Journal of Interpersonal Violence, 6,* 286–300.

Wilcox, D., Sosnowski, D., Warberg, B., & Beech, A. (2005). Sexual history disclosure using the polygraph in a sample of British sex offenders in treatment. *Polygraph, 34,* 171–181.

Wilson, R. J., Picheca, J. E., & Prinzo, M. (2005). *Circles of Support and Accountability: An evaluation of the pilot project in south-central Ontario.* Ottawa: Correctional Service Canada.

Yates, P. M. (2004). Treatment of adult sexual offenders: A therapeutic cognitive-behavioural model of intervention. *Journal of Child Sexual Abuse, 12,* 195–232.

Yates, P. M., Kingston, D. A., & Hall, K. (2003, October). *Pathways to sexual offending: Validity of Ward and Hudson's 1998 self-regulation model of and relationship to static and dynamic risk among treated sexual offenders.* Paper presented at the 22nd Annual Research and Treatment Conference of the Association for the Treatment of Sexual Abusers, St. Louis, MO.

CHAPTER 29

SEXUAL DEVIANCE
AND THE LAW

STEPHEN D. HART
P. RANDALL KROPP

As this volume makes clear, sexual deviance is a form of mental disorder that has been the focus of scientific study for more than a century. It also makes clear that people who suffer from sexual deviance sometimes break the law in an effort to gratify their deviant sexual arousal. This makes sexual deviance important in decision making with respect to a variety of clinical, clinical–forensic, and legal issues (e.g., Melton, Petrila, Poythress, & Slobogin, 2007). In civil settings (e.g., private practices, community clinics, inpatient facilities), mental health professionals who assess or treat sexual deviance must consider whether people pose a risk for sexual violence that may trigger their ethical, professional, or legal duties to warn or protect others. In forensic settings, mental health professionals who assess and treat sexual deviance or people accused of sexual offenses may be asked to determine whether people pose a risk for sexual violence as part of decisions regarding community registration and notification of sexual offenders, criminal sentencing, community supervision orders (e.g., criminal peace bonds), or even custody and access evaluations. They may also be requested to conduct specialized psycholegal assessments, such as criminal responsibility or civil commitment (e.g., "sexually violent predator") evaluations.

Most mental health professionals try their best to avoid lawyers and to avoid even thinking about law. They may practice for years without going to court or communicating with lawyers. But those who assess or treat sexual deviance cannot afford to bury their heads in the sand. Even if they are not forensic specialists, there is a reasonable likelihood that they will be asked to present their findings and opinions as part of legal proceedings before courts, tribunals, or review boards; they may even have to defend themselves against complaints of malpractice or negligence. In these contexts, assessments of and opinions about sexual deviance may have a profound impact on people's lives and are often subjected to intense scrutiny and criticism. Knowing this, mental health professionals can take some steps to ensure that they follow appropriate standards of practice and that their forensic adventures—be they planned or accidental—are minimally distressing and disruptive.

We begin this chapter with a very brief overview of the relevance of sexual deviance in Anglo-American law—the adversarial legal system based on English common law that is dominant in many countries, including England and Wales, the United States, Australia, Canada, and New Zealand. We then turn to a discussion of standards of practice with respect to two issues: first, the diagnosis of sexual deviance in forensic settings; and second, the assessment of volitional impairment associated with sexual deviance.

THE FORENSIC RELEVANCE OF SEXUAL DEVIANCE

"Law," most generally defined, is a set of rules and procedures designed to regulate the behavior of people (Melton, 1985). The fundamental goal of the law is to prevent and resolve, in a principled manner, conflicts among people. The law assumes that people think and act in a reasoned, deliberate manner and responds accordingly (Morse, 2004). But people may be treated differently under the law when their behavior is irrational or involuntary—that is, when they suffer from some kind of cognitive or volitional impairment. Mental disorder has been recognized in the law for millennia as a factor that may cause such impairment. Courts, tribunals, and review boards often call on mental health professionals to render opinions concerning the existence and impact of mental disorder, recognizing the special expertise that psychiatrists and psychologists have in evaluating people and understanding human behavior (especially abnormal behavior).

To determine the legal relevance of sexual deviance, we must consider the answer to three questions:

- *Question 1: Does the law recognize sexual deviance as a form of mental disorder?* Although there are many legal definitions of "mental disorder," varying across jurisdictions as well as across statutes within a given jurisdiction, the answer is generally yes. The definition of "mental disorder" in the law is typically narrower than in the mental health professions, including only impairments of psychological functioning that are internal, stable, and involuntary in nature (Verdun-Jones, 1989). But sexual deviance meets even this narrow definition. The law is also influenced by the fact that sexual deviance has been recognized as a form of mental disorder by mental health professionals for the past 100 years or so, and is included in authoritative treatises such as the text revision of the fourth edition of the *Diagnostic and Statistical Manual of Mental Disorders* (DSM-IV-TR; American Psychiatric Association, 2000) and the 10th revision of the *International Classification of Diseases* (ICD-10; World Health Organization, 1992).

- *Question 2: Can sexual deviance cause cognitive impairment?* According to the law, no; sexual deviance does not cause people substantial problems in terms of perceiving the outside world or rationally manipulating information. Although people with sexual deviance often demonstrate distorted thinking (e.g., a person with pedophilia may believe that children naturally desire sexual relations with adults), they have the capacity to understand that it is, according to accepted social norms, both immoral and illegal to engage others in sexual activity without consent or to commit certain sexual acts in public (e.g., Morse, 2004).

- *Question 3: Can sexual deviance cause volitional impairment?* According to the law, yes; sexual deviance as mental disorder affects behavioral motivation or regulation.

What are uncertain, according to the law, are the nature and severity of the volitional impairment. Some forms of sexual deviance may give rise to thoughts, urges, or fantasies involving illegal behavior (e.g., stealing women's underwear, exposing one's genitals in public, having sexual contact with children). Thus some people with sexual deviance have an appetitive drive to commit certain crimes; they find the thought of committing these crimes to be potentially rewarding. Two follow-up questions then arise. First, to what degree has sexual deviance affected such people's ability to control their behavior, either currently or in the past? And second, to what degree has sexual deviance increased the risk that these people will commit sexual violence in the future? The answers to these questions may be used to justify the imposition of harsh punishment or intensive supervision and intervention designed to strengthen or supplement people's internal behavioral controls. There are two rationales for this (e.g., Morse, 2004). One is retributive, and is based on the notion that ascription of blame and imposition of punishment may help to deter people from committing sexual violence in the future. The other is rehabilitative, and is based on the notion that supervision and intervention may help people to avoid committing sexual violence in the future.

Sexual deviance, then, is most often viewed in the law as a form of mental disorder that has the potential to cause at least some degree of volitional, but not cognitive, impairment. (The net result is that sexual deviance—like some other forms of mental disorder, such as personality disorder—typically is not considered a mitigating factor in the law, but may be considered an aggravating factor; Hart, 2001; Morse, 2004.) But a diagnosis of sexual deviance on its own cannot be used to infer the presence of volitional impairment. Although the law accepts that sexual deviance *may* be associated with volitional impairment, it also accepts that this is not always or necessarily true. A diagnosis of sexual deviance is only legally relevant if it can also be demonstrated that (i.e., explained clearly how) the sexual deviance caused volitional impairment of a specific type of degree *in this case*. In this way, the law avoids stereotypical or discriminatory decisions (i.e., all people with mental disorder are incompetent to make important decisions and unable to control their behavior). The link between a diagnosis of sexual deviance and volitional impairment is sometimes referred to as the "causal nexus" (e.g., Janus, 2000).

In the sections that follow, we discuss standards of practice in the mental health professions related to the diagnosis of sexual deviance and the assessment of volitional impairment in forensic settings.

STANDARDS OF PRACTICE

In forensic settings, the mistakes made by mental health professionals may have a profound negative impact on the civil liberties of people with sexual deviance or on public safety. For this reason, mental health professionals who conduct forensic evaluations of sexual deviance—evaluations in which the issue of sexual deviance has been, will be, or is likely to be raised in front of courts, tribunals, or review boards—should use procedures that not only meet but exceed the standards of practice in general clinical settings (Heilbrun, 1992, 2003).

The concept of "standards of practice" is somewhat vague and amorphous, yet critical to good and ethical service delivery. This is in part because standards of practice are established by and embodied in many different documents that reflect the views of disparate groups and individuals, and that change over time. Despite the fact that they are difficult to define, standards of practice are extremely important: As normative statements regarding the "state of the discipline," they serve pedagogical, aspirational, and evaluative functions. They can be used to determine what mental health professionals should do, as well as what they should have done.

Mental health professionals who conduct forensic evaluations of sexual deviance have an ethical duty to familiarize themselves with the standards of practice relevant to forensic mental health in general, as well as those relevant to sexual deviance more specifically. These standards can include authoritative treatises, such as the DSM-IV-TR and ICD-10; the practice guidelines of professional organizations that specialize in forensic mental health (e.g., the American Academy of Forensic Psychology, the American Psychology–Law Society, the American Academy of Psychiatry and the Law) or sexual offenders (e.g., the Association for the Treatment of Sexual Abusers, the International Association for the Treatment of Sexual Offenders); and works by people widely accepted as experts in the field (e.g., this volume; see also Heilbrun, 2003; Marshall, 2006; Prentky, Janus, Barbaree, Schwartz, & Kafka, 2006).

DIAGNOSIS OF SEXUAL DEVIANCE

Although a comprehensive review of standards of practice relevant to the diagnosis of sexual deviance is beyond the scope of this chapter, we will take the opportunity to discuss some important standards and then discuss them in the context of illustrative cases.

Standard 1: Assessments of Sexual Deviance Should Be Comprehensive

There are many different forms of sexual deviance, each of which has diverse symptomatology. Also, paraphilias are frequently comorbid with each other and with other forms of mental disorder (e.g., Kafka & Hennen, 2002). Mental health professions should attempt a direct and comprehensive evaluation of sexual deviance, gathering information about normal and abnormal sexual thoughts, urges, images, fantasies, behavior, and physiological arousal.

An important corollary of this standard is that assessments of sexual deviance should avoid overfocusing on convictions for sexual offenses. Sexual offenses are neither necessary nor sufficient for a diagnosis of sexual deviance. Many people with sexual deviance never act on their thoughts, images, urges, or fantasies; and many of those who act in a manner consistent with their sexual deviance do so in a way that may be perfectly legal (e.g., Marshall, 2006). Also, many—perhaps the majority—of people who commit sexual offenses do not suffer from sexual deviance. Sexual offenses may be the result of many other causal factors, including such things as anger, generalized negative attitudes toward women, poor impulse control, poor heterosocial skills, and inappropriate sexualization of nonsexual needs. Assuming that all sexual offenders have sexual deviance is as illogical as assuming that all thieves have kleptomania or that all arsonists have pyromania.

Standard 2: Assessments of Sexual Deviance Should Evaluate Its Course

Sexual deviance must be persistent to qualify as a mental disorder; transient or isolated symptoms are insufficient grounds for a diagnosis. The DSM-IV-TR, for example, requires a duration of at least 6 months, but the usual presentation is that the sexual deviance has its onset in puberty and persists into late adulthood. As First and Tasman (2004) have pointed out, "Erotic intentions that are *not* longstanding . . . may be problematic in some ways but they are not clearly paraphilic" (p. 1086; emphasis in original). Also, symptoms of all mental disorders, including sexual deviance, fluctuate over time (e.g., Seligman & Hardenburg, 2000). Symptoms may go into partial or even full remission, either spontaneously or as the result of treatment. Thus mental health professionals should evaluate the course of each symptom of sexual deviance that has been present at some point in the person's life.

A corollary of this standard is that assessments of sexual deviance should avoid assuming that, once diagnosed, the disorder is always present. Human sexual functioning, both normal and abnormal, changes across the lifespan; there is a marked decrease in the intensity of sexual appetite and the frequency of sexual behavior that is generally evident by the age of about 60–70 years. Also, sexual appetite and sexual behavior may decline as a result of physical illness or injury. It is possible that age or illness may lead to partial or full remission of sexual deviance (e.g., Barbaree, Blanchard, & Langton, 2003).

Standard 3: Assessments of Sexual Deviance Should Be Multimethod

Because the symptomatology of sexual deviance is complex in its nature and course, mental health professionals should use multiple methods of assessment. These include personal interviews, interviews with collateral informants, polygraphic interviews, record reviews, medical or psychophysiological testing (e.g., penile plethysmography), and behavioral observations (e.g., McConaghy, 2003; Seligman & Hardenburg, 2000).

A corollary of this standard is that assessments should avoid overfocusing on single methods of assessment, such as personal interviews, self-report questionnaires, or reviews of criminal records. Any assessment method that relies on uncorroborated statements made by the person being evaluated (e.g., interviews, self-report questionnaires) is suspect, because people with sexual deviance often minimize or deny symptoms, due to feelings of shame or embarrassment and to their desire to avoid negative consequences for sexual misbehavior. Similarly, for reasons discussed previously, convictions for sexual offenses are weak evidence of sexual deviance. Evidence concerning the presence or absence of symptomatology obtained via personal interview, self-report questionnaires, interviews, or review of criminal records should be corroborated by evidence gathered via other assessment methods, such as polygraphic interviews, penile plethysmography, or behavioral observation (e.g., Heilbrun, 2003; Marshall, 2006).

Standard 4: Assessments of Sexual Deviance Should Reflect Standardized Diagnostic Criteria

The law is inherently conservative, and evidence based on idiosyncratic views and opinions may be viewed as potentially unreliable and accorded little or no weight in forensic settings. When making diagnoses, mental health professionals should adhere as closely as possible to criteria that are generally recognized and accepted in the field, such as those in the DSM-IV-TR or ICD-10. As Prentky and colleagues (2006) have noted in their discussion of the role of diagnosis in sexually violent predator proceedings, "The DSM-IV-TR is almost universally relied on as the authoritative support for expert opinions on mental abnormality or personality disorder. The classification of a syndrome as a mental disorder in the DSM-IV-TR must be regarded as the primary standard for medical validity" (p. 364).

A corollary is that mental health professionals should avoid giving novel or inchoate diagnoses when someone manifests symptoms of personality disorder but does not meet the criteria for one or more specific forms of sexual deviance. It is common practice to diagnose such people as possibly suffering from sexual deviance (e.g., "paraphilia, provisional" or "rule out paraphilia") or as suffering from a rare or unspecified form of sexual deviance (e.g., "Paraphilia not otherwise specified [NOS]"). In civil settings, this practice makes some sense. Alerting others to the possibility that a patient suffers from sexual deviance may help them to plan or deliver treatments more effectively. The costs of false-positive and false-negative diagnoses are relatively small and roughly equal. In forensic settings, though, the routine diagnosis of possible or unspecified sexual deviance can have serious repercussions. Judges, juries, review boards, or tribunals may not realize that such a diagnosis may reflect relatively minor or isolated problems or significant uncertainty on the part of the evaluator. They may also not be aware that diagnostic criteria for the various forms of sexual deviance are sources of considerable controversy, and that their reliability and validity are largely unknown (e.g., Levenson, 2004; Marshall, Kennedy, Yates, & Serran, 2002; Miller, Amenta, & Conroy, 2005; Prentky et al., 2006). Improper diagnoses made by some may lead the legal system to become skeptical of mental health professionals more generally. As Prentky and colleagues (2006) have noted, "The introduction of new mental disorders and the distortion of standard mental disorder categories undercuts the legitimacy of science and limits its ability to provide a sound and objective touchstone in the fight to understand and reduce sexual violence" (p. 361).

ASSESSMENT OF VOLITIONAL IMPAIRMENT

The general legal concept of "volition" refers to people's ability to exercise their agency, intentionality, or instrumentality. It is the capacity to make choices—to form goals and then to develop, implement, evaluate, and revise plans to achieve these goals (e.g., Denno, 2003; Malle & Nelson, 2003; McSherry, 2003; Morse, 2001, 2004). This definition focuses on what people could have done, rather than on they actually did. Isolated instances of failing to exercise agency or make choices do not prove that a person was *incapable* of doing so. Also, it is not necessary that people's choices be rational, reasonable, or sensible according to some external criterion; the definition focuses on the internal consistency or coherence of their goals, plans, and behavior. Some people consider their options, perceive that the potential rewards of criminal conduct outweigh the potential costs, choose to commit a crime, and embark on a systematic course of action consistent with that choice. These people may be irrational (i.e., because their goals, plans, and behavior are based on faulty perceptions of or beliefs about the world) or antisocial (i.e., because their evaluation of potential rewards and benefits defies conventional morality), but they are not volitionally impaired.

The idea that mental health professionals may need to assess volitional impairment is anxiety-provoking. First, the concept of "volitional impairment" is legal and therefore unfamiliar to many of them (e.g., Prentky et al., 2006). Trying to understand the concept requires mental health professionals to read legal statutes and cases and to talk with lawyers. Second, there exist no specialized tests or procedures that mental health professionals can use for this purpose (e.g., Rogers & Jackson, 2005). They must "fly solo," relying on their own judgment or discretion.

It may give mental health professionals some measure of comfort if they recognize that assessments of volitional impairment are routinely done as part of psycholegal evaluations of legal culpability (e.g., with respect to legal defenses such as insanity, diminished capacity, or extreme emotional disturbance). Also, assessments of volitional impairment are similar to clinical formulations or functional analyses of the link (causal nexus) between mental disorder (sexual deviance) and behavior (sexual violence) that are fundamental to assessments of treatability and violence risk, and part of the day-to-day practice of mental health professionals.

We now present some standards of practice relevant to the assessment of volitional impairment.

Standard 5: Assessments of Volitional Impairment Should Address Relevant Legal Issues

Opinions about volitional impairment should adhere to applicable constitutional, statutory, and case law specifying the nature and severity of volitional impairment required for sexual deviance to be relevant in a given case. Depending on the legal issues, the volitional impairment may be relevant only if it is present currently (e.g., for some sex offender registration evaluations); only if it is so severe that people are incapable of conforming their behavior to the requirements of the law (e.g., for some culpability evaluations); only if it puts people at risk for sexual violence targeted at victims with whom a relationship has been established for the sole or primary purposes of committing a sexual offense (e.g., for some sexually violent predator evaluations); or only if it puts people at imminent risk for sexual violence (e.g., for some peace bond evaluations).

An important corollary of this standard is that mental health professionals should be familiar with the laws of the jurisdictions in which they practice. One way to become familiar with the law is to complete professional education and training programs. Another is to request direction from legal experts involved in the matter (e.g., the court that, or counsel who, retained the mental health professional).

Standard 6: Assessments of Volitional Impairment Should Reflect the State of the Discipline

An assessment of volitional impairment is an attempt to develop a theory of the causal nexus between sexual deviance and sexual violence (past, present, or future) in the case at hand. This theory serves dual purposes, being both descriptive and explanatory. If it is a good theory, it may be understood by decision makers and influence many of their decisions about the case. The law recognizes that the theory is conjectural or speculative in nature. Accordingly, the theory is judged not according to its ultimate truth or validity (which is unknown and unknowable), but according to its plausibility, verisimilitude, or consistency vis-à-vis the current scientific and professional literature. Put simply, the theory of volitional impairment developed as part of an evaluation should take into account what is known about sexual deviance and sexual violence in general.

An important corollary is that mental health professionals who assess volitional impairment should have demonstrated expertise with respect to sexual deviance and sexual violence. Some mental health professionals have expertise in the delivery of sex offender treatment, but do not have expertise in sexual deviance. Similarly, some mental health professionals have expertise in the assessment and diagnosis of sexual deviance in general clinical settings, but do not have expertise in sexual violence. Expertise may be developed and demonstrated through a combination of graduate and postgraduate training, supervised practice, work experience, attendance at meetings of scientific and professional associations, and familiarity with the relevant literature.

Standard 7: Assessments of Volitional Impairment Should Be Individualized

To be useful, mental health evaluations must go beyond a consideration of general factors and take into account the totality of circumstances relevant to the person being evaluated. Both in clinical practice and in law, people are treated as individuals, not as interchangeable members of some reference group. In legal proceedings, opinions of mental health professionals that do not reflect the specifics of the case at hand may be accorded little weight or even ignored altogether. Accordingly, the theory of volitional impairment developed as part of an evaluation will be judged vis-à-vis the specific facts and details of the case at hand, as well as vis-à-vis what is known about sexual deviance and sexual violence more generally.

An important corollary is that mental health professionals should avoid making indirect, generalized inferences about volitional impairment. For example, if people suffer from sexual deviance and commit sexual violence, it is illogical to assume that they all commit sexual violence *because of* sexual deviance; similarly, if people suffer from sexual deviance and are at high risk for sexual violence, it is illogical to assume that the elevated risk is *due to* sexual deviance. In both these examples, the existence of a volitional impairment or causal nexus is assumed from a simple conjunction or co-occurrence of sexual deviance with past sexual violence or risk for future sexual violence. This is at best *post hoc ergo propter hoc* reasoning, and at worst a complete tautology. Mental health professionals must attempt to directly evaluate the volitional impairment by scrutinizing how and why the person being evaluated made choices about sexual violence—why he or she decided to commit sexual violence at some times or against some people or for some reasons, but not at other times or against other people or for other reasons (e.g., Hart et al., 2003).

Standard 8: Assessments of Volitional Impairment Should Evaluate Competing Explanations

Sexual violence, like all forms of violence, has no simple cause; it is the result of a complex web of individual and contextual factors, each of which can change in important ways over time, and all of which may interact or transact (e.g., Hart et al., 2003; see also Marshall & Barbaree, 1990; Ward & Beech, 2006). As sexual deviance is only one factor in sexual violence, its causal influence can be determined and judged only in relation to that of other factors. If the evaluator develops a theory of volitional impairment based in part on sexual deviance, its plausibility or verisimilitude must be judged vis-à-vis alternative theories.

An important corollary is that mental health professionals should not ignore the possibility that sexual violence is the result of causal influences other than sexual deviance. Comprehensive evaluations are needed to rule out other factors (e.g., anger toward women, antisocial attitudes, impulsivity, disinhibition due to intoxication), either as primary causes of sexual violence or as important cofactors.

CASE ILLUSTRATIONS

Mr. K

Mr. K was a 38-year-old man referred for presentencing evaluation, following convictions for four counts related to unlawful confinement and impersonation. The first three offenses involved approaching three different young girls about 12 years of age, showing them each a fake badge, telling them he was a police officer, and directing them to get into the back of his car. The offenses all occurred within a period of about 1 hour. The girls all went home and told their parents, who phoned the police. Upon investigation, Mr. K was found leaving the vicinity in his car with a 20-year-old mentally handicapped woman in the back seat. After the vehicle was pulled over, it was discovered that the woman could not exit on her own, as the rear passenger doors were locked from the inside (with childproof locks). A subsequent search of the vehicle located a large kitchen knife under the driver's seat; in the trunk were beer, pornography, handcuffs, rope, a rubber face mask, and lubricant jelly. Mr. K claimed that his actions were merely a prank. At the time these offenses occurred, Mr. K was on probation with an order to participate in sex offender treatment due to previous convictions for sex crimes, but he had failed to attend either the probation office or the treatment program.

According to personal and collateral interviews, as well as past plethysmographic evaluations and available documentary evidence, Mr. K was sexually aroused primarily by consenting relations with adult females. He had had several long-term but unstable intimate relationships. He was very controlling and angry in his relations with women and had committed serious assaults against various partners. His marriage of 5 years had recently ended in divorce following a sexual assault against his ex-wife that involved beating her, binding her, and raping her orally, anally, and vaginally. But Mr. K's sexual appetite was diverse in focus. For one thing, he was sexually aroused by prepubescent girls. Starting in his late adolescence, he had on a dozen or so occasions engaged in noncoercive sexual touching of young girls, most of them strangers whom he had approached in public places. He also had been arrested on two occasions for masturbating in public view while watching young girls play in public parks. During personal interviews covering the previous years, he acknowledged that he had been sexually aroused by girls in the past, but said that this arousal was now much less intense and frequent; to illustrate these changes, he reported that he still frequently "cruised" looking at young girls, but now was better able to control his urges to commit a sexual offense. Mr. K was also sexually aroused by making obscene telephone calls. This behavior had occurred on several occasions over the years, for a month or two each time. According to his phone records, he made several thousand calls per week to random numbers and talked to adult females, pretending to be doing a survey on lingerie preferences.

The mental health professional who conducted the evaluation diagnosed Mr. K as suffering from multiple paraphilias, including pedophilia (nonexclusive type) and paraphilia NOS (telephone scatalogia). The professional acknowledged that at times Mr. K's sexual arousal appeared to involve or be enhanced by the exertion of power and control over victims; however, due to the lack of a clear pattern of deviant thoughts, images, urges, fantasies, or behavior, no diagnosis of biastophilia or sexual sadism was given. The professional made a number of additional observations. First, he noted that although Mr. K was very preoccupied with paraphilic fantasies and had admitted that in the past he often spent many hours per day thinking about deviant sexual acts, he demonstrated good behavioral controls (e.g., he went weeks or even months without engaging in deviant sexual behavior, despite deviant fantasies on a daily basis; he planned his sexual offenses to minimize the chance that he would be detected and arrested). Mr. K sometimes committed sexually deviant acts that had elements of opportunism or impulsivity, but this seemed to be accounted for by symptoms of psychopathic personality disorder and by deliberate disinhibition due to consumption of alcohol. Second, the professional noted that Mr. K's desire to engage in deviant sexual behavior was unambivalent (e.g., he never expressed distress over his sexual deviance; he consistently rejected or participated insincerely in sex offender treatment programs). The professional concluded that Mr. K posed a high risk for future sexual violence, including both coercive and noncoercive sexual contact or communication with a wide range of potential victims, due primarily to sexual deviance and secondarily to personality disorder and substance use. In light of Mr. K's history, the professional expressed his concern that effective management of Mr. K's risk for sexual violence in the community would be very difficult. The professional recommended intensive sex offender treatment programming that included specific treatment for sexual deviance, as well as other correctional treatment for impulsivity and substance use, but also expressed his doubt that Mr. K would attend or complete treatment.

Comment

This case highlights the importance of Standards 1 and 7. Mr. K exhibited a complex pattern of symptoms that varied in nature and severity, reflecting the presence of two specific forms of sexual deviance as well as the possible or partial presence of a third. Also, the professional's opinions regarding the nature and severity of sexual deviance played an important role in the development of clinical formulations of treatability and risk for Mr. K.

Mr. V

Mr. V was an 84-year-old man who was referred for evaluation to determine whether he continued to meet statutory criteria for detention as a sexually violent predator. Mr. V had a history of six sexual offenses that involved sexual touching and oral sex with and by prepubescent boys, ages 10–12. In each instance, Mr. V approached the boys (who were previously unknown to him) in public places and offered them money to engage in sex. The offenses had occurred over an extended period of time: the first offense when Mr. V was about 45 years old, and the most recent offense when he was about 72 years old. Although Mr. V minimized his symptoms in a highly defensive manner, it was clear from available evidence that he had experienced thoughts and urges involving sex with boys, and in fact had masturbated to such thoughts on many occasions. Based on his history, Mr. V had been diagnosed as suffering from pedophilia. At the expiration of the sentence for his most recent offenses, when he was about 80 years old, a jury had found him to be at high risk for future sexual violence on account of his pedophilia and had committed him indefinitely as a sexually violent predator.

During his evaluation, Mr. V claimed that he had started to experience a decline in his sexual appetite at about age 75, and that this decline had accelerated between the ages of 75 and 80. For the past 5 years or so, he had not experienced sexual thoughts, images, or fantasies; had not engaged in masturbation or any other sexual activity, and had experienced no urges to do so; and in fact had been unable to achieve an erection while awake or asleep. His reports were consistent with reports by staff members at the hospital to which he was committed: Mr. V had not been observed masturbating in his room, engaging in sexual talk or sexual activity with other patients, or attempting to acquire or make pornographic materials. Mr. V's reports also were consistent with the results of medical testing (which indicated that he was suffering from heart disease and prostate problems that would be likely to cause erectile difficulties), and with the results of polygraphic interviews (which indicated that he was not lying about his decreased sexual functioning and behavior).

The mental health professional who conducted the evaluation interpreted the evidence to mean that Mr. V had suffered in the past from a paraphilia that had gone into full remission during the past 5 years or so. The professional also noted the existing scientific research indicated that the rate of sexually violent recidivism among people over the age of 70 is very low. Based in part on this evidence, a jury found that Mr. V was no longer suffering from a mental disorder that caused him to be a high risk for sexual violence, and decided to release him from commitment.

Comment

This case highlights the importance of Standards 2, 3, 5, and 6. Mr. V's sexual deviation was unusual with respect to course, but not with respect to nature or severity. By combining information gathered via multiple assessment methods, the professional was able to determine with considerable confidence that Mr. V's sexual deviance first became clinically significant rather late in life, and also went into full remission as he aged. Also, the professional was careful to cite the scientific literature in support of his opinion that age was a very important factor to consider with respect to the risks posed by Mr. V. Finally, the professional's opinion directly focused on two questions (Does Mr. V *currently* suffer from sexual deviation? Is Mr. V *currently* a high risk to commit sexual violence on account of sexual deviation?) that were critical to legal decision making under the relevant statute.

Mr. D

Mr. D was a 35-year-old male referred for evaluation to determine whether he met statutory criteria for initial commitment as a sexually violent predator. Mr. D had committed sexual offenses on three occasions. At age 16, he had had sexual relations, including anal intercourse, with another boy in the residential facility where he was living. The sexual relations occurred on multiple occasions and involved coercion in the form of threats. At age 22, he had had sexual relations, including vaginal intercourse, on several occasions with a girl age 16. At first the sexual relations began with the girl's assent, in the context of a dating relationship; on the last occasion, however, Mr. D physically coerced sex after the girl stated that she did not want to have vaginal intercourse with him. At age 30, Mr. D pursued a sexual relationship with an adult female he met in the course of his employment at a fast-food restaurant. He visited her residence and telephoned her frequently, up to several times daily, over the course of about a month, despite her attempts to convince her that she was not interested in a having a relationship with him. Eventually, he entered her residence without her permission while she was sleeping, and when she awoke she discovered him standing unclothed in her living room. She pushed him out of her residence and phoned the police. At the end of his 5-year sentence for the third offense, the state filed a motion in court to have Mr. D committed on the basis that he suffered from a mental abnormality (i.e., sexual deviance) that made him a high risk for sexual violence, due to impairment of his emotional or volitional functions.

The two mental health professionals reached very different opinions regarding Mr. D. The first diagnosed Mr. D as suffering from paraphilia NOS, nonconsent type, on the basis of his history of sexual offenses.

The second professional did not make any diagnosis of paraphilia, as she did not believe that any evidence indicated a persistent pattern of deviant sexual arousal. Indeed, in her opinion, the victims of his sexual offenses were diverse with respect to age, sex, and acquaintanceship; his sexual behavior during the offenses was also diverse with respect to nature of the contact and the use of coercion. When Mr. D did use physical coercion, it appeared to the second professional that he was sexually aroused *despite* the coercion, not *because* of it. Similarly, she did not observe a pattern in his other thoughts, images, fantasies, urges, or behavior suggestive of sexual deviance. She concluded that Mr. D's sexual offenses were motivated by his distorted attitudes toward sexuality combined with general deficits in social judgment, rather than by mental disorder.

Comment

This case highlights the importance of Standards 4 and 8. The first mental health professional made an idiosyncratic diagnosis of sexual deviance—one that is not generally accepted or recognized in the field. (As Miller et al., 2005, p. 39, have noted, "Numerous evaluators have utilized the diagnosis 'paraphilia not otherwise specified' to apply to rapists. However, the definition of this appellation is so amorphous that no research has ever been conducted to establish its validity."). He also based the diagnosis on isolated sexual offenses rather than on any systematic assessment of symptomatology, and he failed to consider the possibility that Mr. D's sexual violence might be the result of factors other than sexual deviance. Finally, he compounded these errors by failing to acknowledge the potential limitations of his assessment and diagnosis for the benefit of the judge and jury. If he had followed standards of practice, it might have avoided a major disagreement with the other professional, an unwarranted infringement of Mr. D's civil rights in the form of extended pretrial commitment, and the unnecessary time and expense of trial.

CONCLUSION

Sexual deviance is a form of mental disorder that may be relevant to a range of legal issues. Mental health professionals who conduct psycholegal evaluations of sexual deviance, or who know that their evaluations are likely to be considered by a court, tribunal, or review board, should take care to ensure that their opinions are legally relevant and based on accepted standards of practice in the field. Good assessments have the potential to help decision makers strike a balance between the rights and needs of people with sexual deviance on the one hand and public safety on the other hand. Conversely, bad assessments may do more harm than good. We hope this chapter motivates mental health professionals who assess or treat sexual deviance to become more familiar with the law as it relates to their practice.

REFERENCES

American Psychiatric Association. (2000). *Diagnostic and statistical manual of mental disorders* (4th ed., text rev.). Washington, DC: Author.

Barbaree, H. E., Blanchard, R., & Langton, C. (2003) The development of sexual aggression through the lifespan. *Annals of the New York Academy of Sciences, 989,* 59–71.

Denno, D. W. (2003). A mind to blame: New views on involuntary acts. *Behavioral Sciences and the Law, 21,* 601–618.

First, M. B., & Tasman, A. (2004). Sexual disorders. In M. B. First & A. Tasman (Eds.), *DSM-IV-TR mental disorders: Diagnosis, etiology, and treatment* (pp. 1051–1097). New York: Wiley.

Hart, S. D. (2001). Forensic issues. In J. Livesley (Ed.), *Handbook of personality disorders* (pp. 555–569). New York: Guilford Press.

Hart, S. D. (in press). Preventing violence: The role of risk assessment and management. In A. C. Baldry & F. W. Winkel (Eds.), *Intimate partner violence prevention and intervention: The risk assessment and management approach.* Hauppauge, NY: Nova Science.

Hart, S. D., Kropp, P. R., Laws, D. R., Klaver, J., Logan, C., & Watt, K. A. (2003). *The Risk for Sexual Violence Protocol (RSVP): Structured professional guidelines for assessing risk of sexual violence.* Burnaby, BC, Canada: Mental Health, Law, and Policy Institute, Simon Fraser University; Pacific Psychological Assessment Corporation; and British Columbia Institute Against Family Violence.

Heilbrun, K. (1992). The role of psychological testing in forensic assessment. *Law and Human Behavior, 16,* 257–272.

Heilbrun, K. (2003). Principles of forensic mental health assessment: Implications for the forensic assessment of sexual offenders. *Annals of the New York Academy of Sciences, 989,* 167–184.

Janus, E. S. (2000). Sexual predator commitment laws: Lessons for law and the behavioral sciences. *Behavioral Sciences and the Law, 18,* 5–21.

Kafka, M., & Hennen, J. (2002). A DSM-IV Axis I comorbidity study of males (*n* = 120) with paraphilias and paraphilia-related disorders. *Sexual Abuse: A Journal of Research and Treatment, 14,* 349–366.

Levenson, J. (2004). Reliability of sexually violent predator civil commitment criteria in Florida. *Law and Human Behavior, 28,* 357–368.

Malle, B. F., & Nelson, S. E. (2003). Judging *mens rea*: The tension between folk concepts and legal concepts of intentionality. *Behavioral Sciences and the Law, 21,* 563–580.

Marshall, W. L. (2006). Diagnostic problems with sexual offenders. In W. L. Marshall, Y. M. Fernandez, L. E. Marshall, & G. A. Serran (Eds.), *Sexual offender treatment: Controversial issues* (pp. 33–44). Chichester, UK: Wiley.

Marshall, W. L., & Barbaree, H. E. (1990). An integrated theory of the etiology of sexual offending. In W. L. Marshall, D. R. Laws, & H. E. Barbaree (Eds.), *Handbook of sexual assault: Issues, theories, and treatment of the offender* (pp. 257–275). New York: Plenum Press.

Marshall, W. L., Kennedy, P., Yates, P., & Serran, G. (2002). Diagnosing sexual sadism in sexual offenders: Reliability across diagnosticians. *International Journal of Offender Therapy and Comparative Criminology, 46,* 668–677.

McConaghy, N. (2003). Sexual dysfunctions and deviations. In M. Hersen & S. Turner (Eds.), *Diagnostic interviewing* (3rd ed., pp. 239–277). New York: Kluwer Academic/Plenum Press.

McSherry, B. (2003). Voluntariness, intention, and the defence of mental disorder: Toward a rational approach. *Behavioral Sciences and the Law, 21,* 581–599.

Melton, G. B. (Ed.). (1985). *Nebraska Symposium on Motivation: Vol. 33. The law as a behavioral instrument.* Lincoln: University of Nebraska Press.

Melton, G. B., Petrila, J., Poythress, N., & Slobogin, C. (2007). *Psychological evaluations for the courts (3rd ed.): A handbook for mental health professionals and lawyers.* New York: Guilford Press.

Miller, H. A., Amenta, A. E., & Conroy, M. A. (2005). Sexually Violent Predator evaluations: Empirical evidence, strategies for professionals, and research directions. *Law and Human Behavior, 29,* 29–54.

Morse, S. J. (2001). From Sikora to Hendricks: Mental disorder and criminal responsibility. In L. E. Frost & R. J. Bonnie (Eds.), *The evolution of mental health law* (pp. 129–166). Washington, DC: American Psychological Association.

Morse, S. J. (2004). Preventive confinement of dangerous offenders. *Journal of Law, Medicine, and Ethics, 32,* 56–72.

Prentky, R. A., Janus, E., Barbaree, H., Schwartz, B., & Kafka, M. (2006). Sexually violent predators in the courtroom: Science on trial. *Psychology, Public Policy, and Law, 12,* 357–393.

Rogers, R., & Jackson, R. L. (2005). Sexually violent predators: The risky enterprise of risk assessment. *Journal of the American Academy of Psychiatry and the Law, 33,* 523–528.

Seligman, L., & Hardenburg, S. A. (2000). Assessment and treatment of paraphilias. *Journal of Counseling and Development, 78,* 107–113.

Verdun-Jones, S. N. (1989). *Criminal law in Canada: Cases, questions and the Code.* Toronto: Harcourt Brace Jovanovich.

Ward, T., & Beech, A. (2006). An integrated theory of sexual offending. *Aggression and Violent Behavior, 11,* 44–63.

World Health Organization. (1992). *International statistical classification of diseases and related health problems* (10th rev.). Geneva: Author.

CHAPTER 30

NEUROBIOLOGICAL PROCESSES AND COMORBIDITY IN SEXUAL DEVIANCE

MARTIN P. KAFKA

Sexual offending constitutes a diverse group of socially deviant sexual behaviors. Thus it comes as no surprise that studies attempting to define specific sexual offender subtypes conclude that groups such as "child molesters" and "rapists" are heterogeneous (Knight & Prentky, 1987, 1990; Prentky & Burgess, 2000). Despite this heterogeneity, in this chapter I attempt to define certain general attributes that many (perhaps most) sexual offenders share. Within the context of defining these common characteristics, I propose that a neurobiological or brain-based perspective derived from these characteristics can help clinicians as well as researchers to conceptualize sexual offending behaviors more clearly, and then intervene more specifically to reduce such behaviors. Although stating that sexual offenders are heterogeneous and then declaring that they may share common attributes may at first seem like a contradiction, trying to discern the "forest" or "genus" before identifying the "tree" or "species" can help us to proceed from a broader, top-down rather than from a bottom-up typology.

The delineation of biological components associated with sexually disinhibited behavior is not intended to be a reductionistic explanation for sexual aggression. Cultural, historical, and other nonbiological factors are clearly important factors as well. The identification of salient neurobiological factors, however, may help to provide a multidimensional understanding of a specific offender's intentionality and volitional "control," as well as to enhance our understanding of the neurobiological substrate for sexually deviant behaviors. This perspective can also inform us of possible biologically derived treatment interventions, and can affect the social response of blame attribution and punishment for sexual aggression (Elliott, 1996; Miresco & Kirmayer, 2006).

As a central hypothesis, I suggest that the typical sexual offender is male and that his dys-social offending behaviors are in large part sexually motivated. In addition, the self-regulation of his sexual motivation is impaired or disinhibited by brain-based disorders or conditions, and these disorders or conditions can have subtle manifestations. Last, many of these disorders/conditions are currently eluding clinicians during sexual offender assessment.

THE MALE BRAIN AND TESTOSTERONE

It can be definitively stated that sexual offenses are perpetrated nearly exclusively by men. This is certainly true for pedophilia (Marshall, 1997) and rape (Hudson & Ward, 1997), and has been reported in contemporary non-Western cultures as well (Grubin, 1992; Liu, Ng, Zhou, & Haeberle, 1997). Even hands-off offenses (e.g., voyeurism, exhibitionism) are nearly exclusively male-gender-based behaviors. It has been estimated that only 2–5% of sexual offenders are females, and substantial numbers of those women are convicted as accomplices of men (O'Connor, 1987; Song, Lieb, & Donnelly, 1993). What is it about men specifically that makes them so much more likely than women to commit sexual crimes?

The sex hormones—specifically, testosterone in males and estrogen and progesterone in females—are associated with distinct but overlapping patterns of prosexual and mating behaviors in both male and female mammals, including humans (Simerly, 2000). Even *in utero*, the "masculinization" of the fetal human and mammalian brain by testosterone during the first trimester is associated with important and distinct organizational differences between the male and female fetal brains (Arnold & Gorski, 1984; Roselli, Klosterman, & Resko, 2001). At later stages of developmental maturation, specific activational effects of the sex hormones help to evoke sexual motivation, sexual response, and gestational behaviors (Rubinow & Schmidt, 1996; Woodson & Gorski, 2000), as well as contributing significantly to gender differences in physical aggression (Giammanco, Tabacchi, Giammanco, Di Majo, & La Guardia, 2005; Hyde, 2005).

In addition to testosterone's direct physiological effects on sexual motivation and physical aggression, testosterone also reduces the important inhibitory role of the monoamine neuroregulator serotonin (5-hydroxytryptamine) in limbic and hypothalamic nuclei associated with sexual and aggressive behavioral regulation in mammals (Martinez-Conde, Leret, & Diaz, 1985; Sundblad & Ericksson, 1997).

Adult postpubertal males, including adolescents of course, are either blessed or cursed with an amount of physiologically active testosterone 6–10 times greater than that of adult females. In Westernized cultures where data are available, adult males are much more likely than females to endorse interest in casual sexual encounters, to engage in more sexual fantasizing, to utilize a greater diversity of sexual fantasies, to report more lifetime sexual partners, to be more readily visually sexually aroused, to subscribe to beliefs supportive of sexually aggressive behavior, and to masturbate regularly (Baumeister, 2000; Ellis & Symons, 1990; Murnen & Stockton, 1997; Oliver & Hyde, 1993). Adult females have about the same amount of circulating testosterone as a prepubertal male child, but despite this relatively low amount of bioavailable testosterone, levels below this threshold are associated with female sexual dysfunction—specifically, loss of sexual desire (Davis, 1998).

Testosterone's physiological effects on the male forebrain, especially on limbic (e.g., amygdala), thalamic, and hypothalamic nuclei, are associated with male sexual motivation, arousal, and performance (McKenna, 1999). For these reasons, it is highly likely that testosterone's physiological effects play an important and predisposing role in the marked predominance of men as sexual aggressors against women and children. In this regard, it is of significant interest that recent neuroimaging (functional magnetic resonance imaging [fMRI] and positron emission tomography) studies to identify the brain circuitry activated by visually stimulated sexual arousal include the testosterone-sensitized thalamus, hypothalamus, and amygdala in studies of men (Arnow et al., 2002; Beauregard, Levesque, & Bourgouin, 2001; Redoute et al., 2000), but not of women (Gizewski et al., 2006; Hamann, Herman, Nolan, & Wallen, 2004; Karama et al., 2002; Park, Kang, et al., 2001). In addition, neuroimaging studies have revealed that the hypothalamus and amygdala—areas characterized by the highest density of androgen receptors—are larger in human males than in females (Goldstein et al., 2001; Hamann, 2005).

If testosterone is essential in determining a physiological substrate for aspects of male-gender-based behaviors (including sexual motivation, sex "drive," sexual arousal, and a greater propensity for physical aggression), and if circulating testosterone values are substantially higher in men than in women, is testosterone elevated in sex offenders? Although sexual offenders as a group may not have supraphysiological levels of serum testosterone, there are data suggesting that a subpopulation of the most violent and sexually aggressive offenders may have proportionally higher serum testosterone levels (although typically within the "normal" range) than those of less violent sexual offenders (Bradford, 1990; Brooks & Reddon, 1996; Hucker & Bain, 1990; Rada, 1978). This is of interest, because higher levels of serum testosterone are better correlated with irritability, aggression, and violence (Christensen & Knussman, 1987; Khouri, Lukas, Pope, & Oliva, 1995) than specifically with increased sexual motivation (Knussmann, Christiansen, & Couwenbergs, 1986). Studies reporting serum testosterone in males are confounded by recently enacted sexual behavior, however, as such behavior increases circulating serum testosterone (Knussmann et al., 1986; Stoleru, Ennaji, Cournot, & Spira, 1993) . Inasmuch as there are more data (to be discussed below) indicating that male sexual offenders are "hypersexual," studies that did not control for recent sexual behavior (including masturbation) in offender samples may have reported higher testosterone levels on the basis of the complex cause–effect reciprocity between recent sexual behavior and serum testosterone.

Perhaps the clearest indications of the importance of testosterone in maintaining male sexual motivation and influencing the propensity for sexual offending are the historical data on the dramatic effects of surgical castration on sexual offender recidivism (Bremer, 1959; Sturup, 1972; Wille & Beier, 1989). Indeed, these data provided the rationale for some of the major theoretical approaches to the medical treatment of sex offenders over the past 50 years, including the prescriptive use of antiandrogens (medroxyprogesterone acetate and cyproterone acetate), and the gonadotrophin-releasing hormone agonists (leuprolide and triptorelin) (Bradford, 2001; Briken, Hill, & Berner, 2003). Thus, even if we cannot demonstrate that such men have a consistent or specific "abnormality" associated with circulating levels of testosterone, we can substantially diminish sexual motivation, arousal, and behavior in men (and women) by markedly reducing either circulating physiologically active testosterone or the biological signal effect that testosterone has on physical aggression as well as sexual motivation and performance in specific limbic, thalamic, and hypothalamic nuclei.

SEXUAL APPETITE, HYPERSEXUALITY, AND SEXUAL DEVIANCE

In his pioneering studies of male mammals, Frank Beach (1942) suggested that masculine sexual behavior depends on two relatively independent but related neurobiological processes: (1) an appetitive or incentive/motivational mechanism that is responsible for preparatory sexual arousal and behavior prior to copulation; and (2) a consummatory mechanism associated with erection, intromission, ejaculation, and the postejaculatory refractory period. Indeed, physiological studies of male rats (the most common laboratory animal models for mammalian sexual behavior) have confirmed that the appetitive and consummatory aspects of masculine sexual response are mediated by different but interacting neuroanatomical areas of the brain, particularly the hypothalamic nuclei (Everitt, 1995; Mas, 1995; McKenna, 1999). In the human sexuality literature, "sexual desire" refers to the presence of sexual fantasies, urges, or activities and the subjective conscious motivational determination to engage in sexual behavior in response to relevant internal or external cues (American Psychiatric Association, 2000; Kaplan, 1995; Levin, 1994); it is analogous to the appetitive/motivational phase described in other male mammalian species.

In contrast to the sexual dysfunctions, paraphilias are a separate and distinct diagnostic category of sexual and gender identity disorders (American Psychiatric Association, 1994, 2000). They are characterized by socially unconventional or deviant "recurrent, intense sexually arousing urges or behaviors" (American Psychiatric Association, 2000, p. 566) that cause significant personal distress and/or impairment. This definition only implicitly suggests, but does not explicitly designate, that paraphilias are associated with dysregulation of sexual desire/motivation. That is, some appetitive, motivational, or sexual drive/desire-related "intensity" associated with paraphilic diagnostic status impels men to engage repetitively in these sexual behaviors, in spite of the fact that the behaviors are highly stigmatized as socially deviant and can be associated with severe psychosocial consequences. I would contend that this same sexual "intensity" may be associated with criminally motivated rape as well, based on the data to be addressed below.

Recurring, intense sexually arousing urges and behaviors may be associated with both an increased frequency of enacted sexual behaviors and an increased amount of time consumed by sexual fantasies or activities. This combination may then be associated with excessive sexual behavior or hypersexuality. Any operational definition for "hypersexuality" or "excessive sexual behavior" should be derived from large nonclinical community samples, where a normative range of sexual behaviors can first be ascertained. Kinsey, Pomeroy, and Martin (1948, p. 197) reported that only 7.6% of American males (from adolescence to age 30) had a mean total sexual outlet (TSO)/week (i.e., orgasms/week) of seven or more for at least 5 years' duration. In that subsample of males, masturbation was their primary sexual outlet, in preference to sexual intercourse. It is of clinical interest to note that Kinsey and associates included a small ($n = 81$) male "underworld" subsample in their American male survey; in that subgroup, 49% self-reported a persistent TSO/week of seven for a minimum duration of 5 consecutive years.

Atwood and Gagnon (1987) reported that 5% of high school and 3% of college-age white males ($N = 1,077$) masturbated on a daily basis (i.e., had a typical TSO/week of at least seven for at least 1 year). Laumann, Gagnon, Michael, and Michaels (1994), in the most recent sexuality survey of American males and females, reported that only 7.6% of American males ($N = 1,320$; ages 18–59) engaged in partnered sex four or more times/week for at least 1 year. They also reported that only 14.5% masturbated two to six times/week for the past year, 1.9% masturbated daily, and an additional 1.2% masturbated more than once/day during the past year (S. Michaels, personal communication, October 18, 1995). Inasmuch as these investigators were looking at nonclinical samples, they were not able to provide data linking time-consuming sexual fantasies and urges (i.e., sexual preoccupation, if present) with orgasm-associated sexual behaviors (TSO/week).

In an earlier publication (Kafka, 1997b), I proposed an operational definition for "hypersexual desire." Based on data from a clinically derived sample, and on the empirical evidence from the sexuality surveys cited above, I proposed that those adult males who self-reported a persistent TSO/week of seven or more for at least 6 consecutive months after the age of 15 years met one of the suggested criteria for hypersexual desire. In addition, males who were defined as hypersexual had to be currently sexually preoccupied (engaging in non-primary-partner-associated sexual fantasy, urges, or behaviors for more than 1–2 hours/day/week). The most commonly enacted sexual behavior in my clinical sample was masturbation, not partnered sex, as was similarly reported by Kinsey and colleagues (1948, p.197) and Långström and Hanson (2006) (see discussion below).

Långström and Hanson (2006) defined high rates of sexual behavior in a large Swedish community sample ($N = 2,450$ men and women). These researchers provided a definition for "impersonal sex" that included eight factors, including specific behaviors such as masturbation (four or more times/week), frequent pornography use, frequent soliciting of prostitutes, and/or having multiple sexual partners. They utilized a composite of these measures to identify "excessive sex" or hypersexuality. In the group of both men and women who were rated as "high" in indicators of impersonal sex, correlations among such sexual behaviors were statistically significant.

Males who scored in the "high" group on Långström and Hanson's composite measure of hypersexuality ($n = 151$ of 1,244 men ages 18–60; 12.1% of the male sample) were more likely to be younger, to have experienced separation from parents, and to live in major urban areas. They were more likely to start sexual behavior at an earlier age, and in addition to increased frequency of sexual behavior, they reported a greater diversity of sexual experiences. These included same-sex behavior (but not necessarily being homosexual); paying for sex; and exhibitionistic, voyeuristic, and sadomasochistic behavior. The adjusted odds ratios (i.e., statistical strength of the likelihood of co-occurrence) between "high" hypersexuality factors and the three aforementioned paraphilic interests were particularly noted (4.66, 7.12, and 14.16, respectively). Despite acknowledging a higher frequency of sexual behavior, these males were less likely to feel satisfied with their sexual lives, had more relationship-associated problems, had more sexually transmitted diseases, and were more likely to have sought professional help for sexuality-related issues. It is of interest that women defined as hypersexual were quite similar to males on the variables just described, but in addition, women were more likely to report a history of sexual abuse and to have sought psychiatric care in the last year. In a separate report on the same sample, Långström and Zucker (2005) reported similar statistically significant associations in males who acknowledged sexual arousal from fetishistic transvestism, particularly with indicators of impersonal sex/hypersexuality and the three paraphilic behaviors mentioned above.

Any definition of hypersexual desire is merely a "line in the sand" in the continuous frequency distribution curve of male sexual appetitive behavior; hypersexuality itself does not necessarily designate a pathological condition unless some "significant impairment," including help-seeking behavior, is associated with persistent hypersexual behaviors. A longitudinal history of hypersexual desire with sexual preoccupation as defined above, in association with significant adverse psychosocial consequences, was reported by over 66% of males seeking treatment for paraphilias (including sexual offending) and paraphilia-related disorders (Kafka, 1997a; Kafka & Hennen, 2003). In a clinical sample of 220 consecutively evaluated outpatient males seeking treatment (Kafka, 2003b), the subgroup ($n = 50$) with the highest lifetime indicators of hypersexuality were recidivistic sexual offenders with multiple paraphilias, typically exhibitionism, pedophilia, and voyeurism. Additional indices associated with hypersexuality in that group were multiple paraphilia-related disorders, the highest level of current sexual preoccupation (2–4 hours/day), the highest current TSO/week (mean = 10), the highest persistent lifetime hypersexual TSO/week (mean = 14 for a minimum duration of 6 months), and the highest rate of incarceration for a sexual offense (34.6%). It is clinically noteworthy that approximately 20% of these men were no longer hypersexual (as operationally defined above) at the time of evaluation. Either aging or factors associated with seeking clinical evaluation (e.g., being apprehended or discovered) had comparatively diminished their current TSO/week and self-reported sexual preoccupation. In addition, it is important to note that if we established the hypersexual TSO/week boundary at five for a minimum duration of 6 months while maintaining the amount of time consumed by nonintimate partner–related sexual behaviors as at least 1 hour/day, this would indeed capture nearly 90% of the aforementioned clinical samples seeking help for sexual impulsivity disorders.

Additional descriptive accounts of sex offenders have characterized some sex offenders as "hypersexual" (Bradford, 2001; Brotherton, 1974; Cooper, 1981; Davies, 1974; Orford, 1978). Prentky and Burgess (2000), after reviewing empirically derived risk factors associated with predicting recidivism in child molesters and rapists, included the intensity or strength of sex drive among those factors. Hanson and colleagues (Hanson & Harris, 2000; Hanson & Morton-Bourgon, 2004) suggested that sex drive and sexual preoccupation were risk factors specifically associated with sexual offender recidivism. Firestone and colleagues (1999) reported that incestuous sex offenders who recidivated had higher sex drive than nonrecidivists. Knight and colleagues' tripartite model of sexual coercion implicated sexual drive/preoccupation or "sexualization" as one of the core processes associated with the propensity of sexual aggression against women, including rape (Knight & Cerce, 1999; Knight & Sims-Knight, 2003).

Taken together, these data from clinical samples of men with paraphilias and paraphilia-related disorders (Kafka, 1997a, 2003b; Kafka & Hennen, 2003); larger samples, including both community controls and incarcerated sexual offenders (Knight & Cerce, 1999; Knight & Sims-Knight, 2003); and a community-based survey sample (Långström & Hanson, 2006; Långström & Zucker, 2005) suggest that the sexual behavior of "typical" sexual offenders is characterized not only by its apparent social deviance, but in addition by an increased frequency, intensity, and diversity of sexual interests; a propensity for increased sexual fantasizing or "preoccupation"; and the repetitive enactment of sexual behavior that is either primarily masturbatory or includes other expressions of "impersonal sex." This combination of characteristics, when associated with significant psychosocial sequelae, has been also described as "sexual addiction" (Carnes, 1983; Goodman, 1997), "sexual compulsivity" (Coleman, 1987; Raymond, Coleman, & Miner, 2003), "hypersexuality" (Kafka, 2003b; Långström & Hanson, 2006), "sexualization" (Knight & Sims-Knight, 2003), "sexual impulsivity" (Barth & Kinder, 1987) or simply sexual behavior that is "disinhibited" or "out of control" (Bancroft & Vukadinovic, 2004).

HYPERSEXUALITY, SEXUAL OFFENDING, AND BRAIN-BASED DISORDERS

If sexual offending is associated with hypersexuality or sexualization, either currently or longitudinally, what might account for the intensified sexual motivation or sexual disinhibition of offenders? It is clear that certain parts of the human brain and certain brain circuits are more specifically associated with such behaviors as complex moral choice, impulse control, and assessment of behavioral consequences. In contrast to the phylogenetically "old" brain structures of the hypothalamus and limbic amygdala, where testosterone is most physiologically active (Adbelgadir, Roselli, Choate, & Resko, 1999), the frontal and prefrontal cortices constitute the seat of the so-called "executive functions," which make us a distinct and "human" species. Frontal-lobe-associated executive functions include cognitive planning, anticipation, attention, motivation, and reward salience; retaining and organizing information for complex decisions; and integrating and synthesizing complex sensory and affective information provided by other phylogenetically "older" regions of the brain, such as the forebrain and limbic areas (Salloway, Malloy, & Duffy, 2001). For example, the right inferior frontal cortex and the ventral anterior cingulate cortex are immediately adjacent areas of the cerebral cortex associated with the integration of sensory information and motivational states. These areas are also activated by visually evoked sexual arousal in both males (Hagemann et al., 2003; Park, Seo, et al., 2001; Rauch et al., 1999; Stoleru et al., 1999) and females (Karama et al., 2002; Park, Kang, et al., 2001). The orbital prefrontal cortex and ventral anterior cingulate cortex are functionally associated with motivation, reward appraisal, and mediation/inhibition of impulsive aggression (Best, Williams, & Coccaro, 2002; Horn, Dolan, Elliott, Deakin, & Woodruff, 2003; New et al., 2002). Dysregulation in the relationship of these brain circuits with limbic structures (particularly the amygdala) has been detected by fMRI and the neuroimaging procedures, as well as by sophisticated neuropsychological testing, in persons with disorders of impulse control (including substance use disorders and behavioral addictions) (Bechara, 2005; Cavedini, Riboldi, Keller, D'Annucci, & Bellodi, 2002; Volkow & Fowler, 2000). These data suggest that if we can identify or intervene within the neurobiological circuits integrating and facilitating social judgment, motivation, reward salience, and impulse control in the orbito-frontal and ventral anterior cingulate cortex, we will have an additional means with which to understand and treat sexual offending behaviors as well.

AXIS I PSYCHOPATHOLOGY AND SEXUAL DEVIANCE

Axis I neuropsychiatric disorders are generally associated with prefrontal cortical dysfunction, inasmuch as social judgment, impulse control, attention, and insight are commonly affected in these disorders (Lichter & Cummings, 2001). If certain specific Axis I neuropsychiatric disorders could be consistently identified in male sex offenders, and if the treatment of such conditions enhanced frontal and prefrontal cortical function (or mollified limbic overactivation), then such treatments might affect "moral" judgments, enhance the reasoned assessment of reward salience, and ameliorate antisocial impulsivity. In essence, such treatments would be able to restore the primacy of the frontal cortex as the executive decision-making matrix.

Recent studies of sex offenders, men with paraphilias, and men with nonparaphilic expressions of hypersexuality suggest that mood disorders (dysthymic disorder, major depression, and bipolar spectrum disorders), certain anxiety disorders (especially social anxiety disorder and childhood-onset posttraumatic stress disorder [PTSD]), psychoactive substance use disorders (especially alcohol abuse), and attention-deficit/hyperactivity disorder (ADHD) may occur at higher than expected rates in sexually impulsive men, including sexual offenders (Allnut, Bradford, Greenberg, & Curry, 1996; Almeyer, Kleinsasser, Stoner, & Retzlaff, 2003; Black, 1998; Dunsieth et al., 2004; Eher, Neuwirth, Fruehwald, & Frottier, 2003; Fago, 1999; Galli et al., 1999; Grant, 2005; Hoyer, Kunst, & Schmidt, 2001; Kafka & Hennen, 2002; Kafka & Prentky, 1994, 1998; Kavoussi, Kaplan, & Becker, 1988; Långström, Sjöstedt, & Grann, 2004; McElroy et al., 1999; Raymond et al., 2003; Raymond, Coleman, Ohlerking, Christenson, & Miner, 1999; Vaih-Koch & Bosinski, 1999; Weiss, 2004).

For example, my colleagues and I have reported a high prevalence of dysthymic disorder in paraphilic men (60–70%) (Kafka & Hennen, 2002; Kafka & Prentky, 1994, 1998). Raymond and colleagues (1999) reported a high lifetime prevalence of major depression (56%) in pedophiles, and Grant (2005) reported a lifetime prevalence of 40% for major depression (but no dysthymia or bipolar disorders) in a sample of 25 exhibitionists. Galli and colleagues (1999) and Dunseith and colleagues (2004) reported a markedly increased prevalence of lifetime bipolar disorders (35–55%) in sexual offenders, especially in residential settings. Symptoms associated with both mood and anxiety disorders were reported more frequently in a large sample of incarcerated sexual offenders than in incarcerated nonsexual offenders (Almeyer et al., 2003), and more frequently in pedophiles than in rapists.

Social phobia was reported in 20–30% of paraphilic males (Kafka & Hennen, 2002; Kafka & Prentky, 1994, 1998) and 19% of convicted sexual offenders (Dunsieth et al., 2004). Lifetime social anxiety was more common in paraphilic sexual offenders (53%) than in other mentally disordered nonsexual offenders (20%) (Hoyer et al., 2001). In some reports, pedophiles in particular have been noted to be more socially anxious and to have concomitant social skills deficits, in comparison to other offender subtypes. For example, Raymond and colleagues (1999) reported a lifetime prevalence of nearly 38% of social phobia in their sample of pedophilic sexual offenders, and anxious/avoidant personality traits were associated with the "personality impairment" of pedophiles in other reports (Almeyer et al., 2003; Cohen et al., 2002; Fisher, Beech, & Browne, 1999).

The comorbidity between alcohol abuse and sexual offending is more widely acknowledged—not only because of its high prevalence, but also because alcohol intoxication is more readily apparent than chronic mood or anxiety disorders, and therefore more likely to be diagnosed. Consistent with this clinical observation, Långström and colleagues (2004) identified alcohol abuse or dependence in only 8% of hospitalized Swedish sexual offenders, but noted this to be the most common psychiatric diagnosis ascertained in their large sample (N = 1,215). Their methodology to ascertain Axis I psychiatric diagnosis was not uniform, however, as only 11% of their hospitalized sample had been diagnosed with any lifetime psychiatric disorder prior to their index sexual offense. In studies utilizing more uniform methodology, high rates of lifetime psychoactive substance abuse, including alcohol abuse, were reported for both paraphilic (82%) and nonparaphilic (100%) individuals in a sample of 113 male convicted sexual offenders (Dunsieth et al., 2004). In other reports, 28–50% of sexual offenders were diagnosed with alcohol abuse or dependence (Allnut et al., 1996; Galli et al., 1999; Grant, 2005; Kafka & Hennen, 2002; Kafka & Prentky, 1994, 1998; Raymond et al., 1999).

ADHD, especially the combined subtype, has not been systematically studied in many previous studies of sexual offenders; however, when it has been specifically examined, high lifetime prevalences have been reported. Fago (1999) reported that 77% of children and adolescents evaluated for sexually aggressive behavior (N = 35) met diagnostic criteria for ADHD. A similar prevalence rate (71%) was reported by Galli and colleagues (1999) in their sample of adolescent hands-on offenders.

In adult males, the retrospective ascertainment of ADHD is complicated by the diminished reliability of self-report of childhood-onset symptoms, as well as by the diminution of overt motor restless and hyperactivity in adults with clinically significant residual ADHD. In our series of Axis I comorbidity studies, sexual offenders were specifically noted to self-report a high prevalence of ADHD (36–53%) (Kafka & Hennen, 2002; Kafka & Prentky, 1998), in comparison with nonsexual offenders.

Other neuropsychiatric conditions specifically associated with sexual disinhibition and sexual offending include fetal alcohol spectrum disorders (Baumbach, 2002; Mattson, Goodman, Caine, Delis, & Riley, 1999); Tourette syndrome and its comorbidities (Comings, 1994, 2001); autism spectrum disorders (especially Asperger syndrome) (Kumagami, 2006); mental retardation (Cochrane, Grisso, & Frederick, 2001); the schizophrenias; and neurological insults such as head injury (Blanchard et al., 2002; Blanchard, Kuban, Klassen, Dickey, & Christensen, 2003) and neurodegenerative disorders. If the aforementioned neuropsychiatric disorders are more prevalent among sexual offenders, is such lifetime association or comorbidity a specific or nonspecific relationship?

Mood disorders in particular are associated with the dysregulation of biologically mediated drive states or appetitive behaviors, such as sleep (insomnia/hypersomnia and sleep disorders) (American Psychiatric Association, 2000; Kaneita et al., 2006); psychomotor activity (agitation/retardation); and hunger (anorexia/hyperphagia, eating disorders) (Braun, Sunday, & Halmi, 1994; Perez, Joiner, & Lewinsohn, 2004). In contrast to eating disorders, which are markedly and predominantly (90%) female-based disorders, could some mood disorder subtypes be associated with the disinhibition or dysregulation of sexual appetite in men?

It is clinically well established that mania and hypomania may be associated with increased sexual impulsivity (American Psychiatric Association, 2000), and that major depression—a mood disorder characterized in part by prominent neurovegetative symptomatology—is typically associated with diminished sexual interest and hypoactive sexual desire (Schiavi, 1996; Schreiner-Engel & Schiavi, 1986). There is a growing recognition, however, that less severe anxious and depressive mood states (Bancroft, Janssen, Strong, Carnes, et al., 2003; Bancroft, Janssen, Strong, & Vukadinovic, 2003; Mathew, Largen, & Claghorn, 1979; Mathew & Weinman, 1982), including dysthymic disorder (Kafka & Prentky, 1992; Nofzinger et al., 1993) can be associated with increased sexual appetite, including operationally defined hypersexuality (Kafka, 1997a, 2003b) and "out-of-control" sexual behavior (Bancroft & Vukadinovic, 2004). Additional theoretical support for the association of mood disorders with increased sexual appetitive behavior was reported by Mathew and colleagues (1979), who reported increased libido in 21% of depressed patients (n = 51) compared to 0% of controls (n = 51), and Nofzinger and colleagues (1993), who reported increased libido in 30% (n = 12 of 40) in a clinical sample of males treated with cognitive therapy for depressive disorders. More recently, Bancroft and colleagues have studied 919 heterosexual men (Bancroft, Janssen, Strong, Carnes, et al., 2003) and 662 homosexual men (Bancroft, Janssen, Strong, & Vukadinovic, 2003), and reported that a "significant minority" (15–25%) reported increased sexual behavior in response to anxious/depressive affect.

AXIS I PSYCHIATRIC DISORDERS, NEUROBIOLOGY, AND SEXUAL DEVIANCE

The neural circuitry of depressive mood is correlated with diminished metabolic efficacy (Bremner et al., 1997, 2003), volume reduction (Bremner et al., 2002) and diminished serotonergic receptors (Biver et al., 1997) in the orbito-frontal cortex, as well as with metabolic (Phillips, Drevets, Rauch, & Lane, 2003) and structural (Drevets et al., 1997) abnormalities in the ventral anterior cingulate cortex. Analogous findings have also been reported for dysthymic disorder as well—a milder but more chronic depressive disorder in comparison with major depression (Lyoo et al., 2002; Sarikaya, Karasin, Cermik, Abay, & Berkada, 1999). Dysthymic disorder is a comparatively understudied mood disorder in comparison to major depression, but its increased lifetime prevalence among sexually impulsive males has been noted in some studies of Axis I comorbidity (Kafka & Hennen, 2002; Kafka & Prentky, 1994, 1998).

Bipolar disorders are associated with antisocial impulsivity and incarceration (Hirschfeld, Calabrese, & Weissman, 2003), and the more subtle manifestations of hypomania may be undetected without careful direct inquiry (Angst & Cassano, 2005). The bipolar spectrum—including bipolar II disorder, cyclothymic disorder, mixed states, pharmacologically induced hypomania, and bipolar disorder not otherwise specified—are cumulatively more prevalent than the more readily observable manic symptoms associated with bipolar I disorder (previously designated manic–depression). The population prevalence of bipolar I disorder has been estimated at approximately 1% (with equal gender distribution), but the lifetime prevalence of the broader spectrum of bipolar disorders in larger community samples was estimated to be 4–6% (Hirschfeld et al., 2003; Judd & Akiskal, 2003).

The neuropsychological and neurobiological circuitry affected by bipolar disorders is an area of active clinical investigation. Irregularities in neural networks, including limbic (e.g., amygdala), anterior cingulate, and prefrontal regional abnormalities, have been identified in many studies of bipolar subjects (Blumberg et al., 2003; Malhi, Cahill, Ivanovski, & Lagopoulos, 2006; Yurgulin-Todd & Ross, 2006), and it is better appreciated clinically that hypomania and mania are associated with generalized impulsivity, impaired decision making, and sexual disinhibition.

ADHD, especially the combined subtype, is associated with antisocial impulsivity (Biederman, Faraone, et al., 2006; Biederman, Monuteaux, et al., 2006), including sexual offending (Kafka & Hennen, 2002; Vaih-Koch & Bosinski, 1999). In males with childhood-onset conduct disorder, concurrent ADHD predicts a more maladaptive outcome (Abikoff & Klein, 1992; Loeber, Farrington, Stouthamer-Loeber, & Moffitt, 2001; Waschbush, 2002), including adult antisocial personality disorder (ASP) and psychopathy (see below). Multiple anatomical (Shaw et al., 2006), brain imaging (Seidman, Valera, & Makris, 2005), and neuropsychological (Rhodes, Coghill, & Matthews, 2005) studies have implicated several brain areas in ADHD, including the anterior cingulate and prefrontal cortical structures as well as the amygdala (Plessen et al., 2006). ADHD is also found embedded in Tourette syndrome, Asperger syndrome, and early-onset bipolar disorder as well.

The relationship between PTSD and sexual offending is complex. It is well known that childhood-onset verbal, physical, and sexual abuse can have long-lasting effects on both physical and emotional adjustment in adults (Teicher et al., 2003). Such adverse early life experiences as caregiver instability (e.g., family disruption during childhood, multiple caregivers, residential placements) (Prentky et al., 1989); physical abuse (Knight & Prentky, 1987; Knight & Sims-Knight, 2003; Lewin, Beary, Toman, & Sproul-Bolton, 1994; Widom & Ames, 1994); sexual abuse (Abel & Harlow, 2001; Dhawan & Marshall, 1996; Seghorn, Prentky, & Boucher, 1987); and emotional abuse (Knight & Sims-Knight, 2003; Lee, Jackson, Pattison, & Ward, 2002) are commonly reported in the developmental history of hands-on sexual offenders. Although it is unclear whether specific developmental events predispose individuals to commit hands-on sexual crimes against children versus adults, higher rates of childhood sexual abuse have been reported among child molesters than among rapists in some studies (Abel & Harlow, 2001; Lee et al., 2002; Seghorn et al., 1987; Simons, Wurtele, & Heil, 2002). In comparison with hands-on offenders, noncontact offenders were reported to have lower rates of developmental adversity, including physical and sexual abuse (Macpherson, 2003). The delineation of particular developmental antecedents as risk factors for sexual offending is complicated by the co-occurrence of caretaker instability, physical abuse, sexual abuse, and emotional abuse among hands-on offenders (Lee et al., 2002; Prentky et al., 1989; Seghorn et al., 1987), as well as among child (Kaplan, Pelcovitz, & Labruna, 1999) and adult (Dong et al., 2004; Scher, Forde, McQuaid, & Stein, 2004) victims of abuse, in community samples.

Children and adolescents with sexual disinhibition are specifically characterized by a marked increase in the prevalence of complex childhood trauma (Friedrich, Davies, Feher, & Wright, 2003; Knight & Sims-Knight, 2004), and repetitive and severe childhood-onset abuse can affect brain structure and functioning, particularly neuronal loss in the corpus callosum, amygdala, hippocampus, anterior cingulate, and prefrontal cortices (De Bellis & Keshavan, 2003; Teicher et al., 2003). Inasmuch as childhood trauma is longitudinally distant in the history of adult sexual offenders, it is more difficult to determine a direct, immediate, or specific effect for PTSD or complex childhood trauma in most adult sexual offenders.

Antisocial personality disorder (ASP), an Axis II psychiatric diagnosis, is particularly prevalent in incarcerated adult male offender samples (Fazel & Danesh, 2002), including sexual offenders (Abracen & Looman, 2006; Becker, Stinson, Tromp, & Messer, 2003; Janus & Walbek, 2000; Levenson, 2004; Zander, 2005). What might be clinically overlooked in a significant subpopulation of antisocial adults, however, are the comorbid childhood-onset neuropsychiatric disorders that contribute to adult-defined ASP. The co-occurrence of ADHD with other externalizing behavior disorders (including conduct disorder), mood disorders, and psychoactive substance abuse (marijuana and alcohol) has been reported in studies of the adolescent and adult outcomes of children diagnosed prospectively with ADHD (Abikoff & Klein, 1992; Lynam, 1996; Schubiner et al., 2000). In addition, the combination of ADHD with conduct disorder, mood disorders, and psychoactive substance abuse was associated with externalizing behavior disorders (including adult ASP), arrest, and incarceration as sequelae (Biederman, Monuteaux, et al., 2006; Eyestone & Howell, 1994; Loeber et al., 2001). Early-onset bipolar disorders may also be associated with conduct disorder, oppositional defiant disorder, and ASP (Geller, Tillman, Craney, & Bolhofner, 2004; Goldstein & Levitt, 2006; Kovacs & Pollock, 1995; Turley, Bates, Edwards, & Jackson, 1992). Despite the high likelihood that ADHD and bipolar disorders are persistent (but perhaps attenuated) in incarcerated adult sexual offenders, studies reporting diagnoses made in civilly committed sexual offenders rarely include ADHD, bipolar disorders, or dysthymia (Becker et al., 2003; Janus & Walbek, 2000; Levenson, 2004)—although, as previously mentioned, they report a high frequency of ASP as the most common Axis II psychopathology.

Psychopathy, a clinically derived construct that includes diverse antisocial as well as specific characterological deficits associated with interpersonal violence, may be embedded in childhood-onset neuropsychiatric disorders as well, including ADHD, bipolar disorders, Asperger syndrome, and conduct disorder (Johansson, Kerr, & Andershed, 2005; Piatogorsky & Hinshaw, 2004; Soderstrom, Nilsson, Sjodin, Carlstedt, & Forsman, 2005; Soderstrom, Sjodin, Carlstedt, & Forsman, 2004; Lyman, 1998).

THE PROBLEM OF DETECTION AND PROPER ASSESSMENT

The persistence of early-onset but chronic low-grade anxious and depressive symptoms, complex bipolar spectrum disorders, Asperger syndrome, and/or residual ADHD and learning disabilities presents a subtle diagnostic challenge to clinicians evaluating sexual offenders, as these specific diagnoses still elude clinicians (Angst & Cassano, 2005; Hirschfeld & Vornik, 2004; Kessler et al., 2006; Klein & Santiago, 2003). In addition, the spectrum of fetal alcohol syndrome may go undetected if one only examines for the classic and more readily observable facial anomalies associated with it or if an adequate prenatal history of an offender is not available. This can be a particular problem among adopted or foster children removed from parental homes during early postnatal life. Many of the aforementioned specific neuropsychiatric disorders have their onset during childhood or adolescence, as do paraphilias and sexual offending behaviors; it is therefore reasonable to suggest that the presence of these conditions can have an adverse effect on the development of sexuality, as well as of impulse control and social judgment.

The data needed to enhance the specificity of Axis I psychiatric diagnoses are dependent on a subject's self-report as well as external sources of information, including archival data. Although archival data may be available for incarcerated males, specific childhood-onset psychiatric diagnoses may be difficult to ascertain, as many of these disorders were not well characterized or even reified as distinct diagnoses until recent decades. Last, even more recent structured psychiatric diagnostic interviews for adult populations do not typically include validated questions to ascertain childhood ADHD, some bipolar spectrum disorders, lifetime prior episodes of dysthymic disorder, fetal alcohol spectrum disorders, or autism spectrum disorders. From my perspective as a clinician-investigator, these are some of the substantial barriers that prevent the proper assessment and identification of these conditions, and possibly then their amelioration.

There are some reports that the pharmacological treatment of Axis I comorbidity in males with paraphilias, including sexual offenders, ameliorates sexual impulsivity (Greenberg, Bradford, Curry, & O'Rourke, 1996; Kafka & Hennen, 2000). It will thus be clinically salient to establish whether pharmacologically responsive disorders (such as mood disorders, anxiety disorders, and ADHD) can be better identified and successfully treated, especially in incarcerated samples. In particular, in nonbipolar males with anxious/depressive cluster symptoms and/or diagnoses, the selective serotonin reuptake inhibitors (SSRIs) can ameliorate depressive, anxiety, "compulsive," and impulsive disorders by enhancing serotonin neurotransmission in the prefrontal and anterior cingulate cortex while normalizing metabolic changes associated with these conditions (Brody et al., 1999; Saxena et al., 2002). In addition, these same medications, by enhancing serotonin, may directly reduce testosterone's prosexual signal effects in the male hypothalamus as well (Baum & Starr, 1980; Lorrain, Matuszewich, Friedman, & Hull, 1997; Lorrain, Riolo, Matuszewich, & Hull, 1999). These aforementioned observations are associated with a "monoamine hypothesis" for paraphilias, which postulates that serotonin and dopaminergic neuroregulation play a central role in sexual inhibition and disinhibition associated with deviant sexual arousal (Kafka, 1997b, 2003a). Further methodologically sound studies of diagnosis and pharmacological intervention for sexual offenders with Axis I psychiatric disorders are needed.

RESEARCH PRIORITIES

Although the prevalence of the psychiatric disorders discussed in this chapter may be increased in sexual offenders, the specificity of these conditions as predictors of sexual offending remains undetermined. It would be sensible to presume that neuropsychological/psychiatric conditions that affect prefrontal, anterior cingulate, or limbic lobe functional integrity may be associated with multiple or generalized expressions of impulsivity, including (but not necessarily limited to) sexual offending or dysregulation of sexual appetite. A theoretical preposition that particular Axis I psychiatric disorders are cumulatively, comorbidly, or individually associated specifically with sexual offending is limited by the lack of knowledge as to why all males—or, more particularly, what percentage of males meeting criteria for these aforementioned brain disorders—do not become sexual offenders or have any sexual impulsivity disorders. Which particular generalized or individual genetic factors, developmental antecedents, and cultural/social factors shape and cumulatively heighten the risk that a specific male (or female) will offend sexually are still matters for both important research endeavors and clinical speculation.

Every person suffering from a sexual affliction that includes intense, repetitive, highly sexually arousing fantasies, urges, and activities that are socially deviant deserves a thorough psychiatric, sexual, and neuropsychological evaluation, as well as treatments that are specifically tailored to the individual's situation and diagnostic profile. Psychiatric diagnosis and treatments to mitigate Axis I psychiatric illnesses or to diminish serum testosterone need to be more routinely integrated into comprehensive treatment plans that include empirically validated psychosocial and psychotherapeutic interventions. Neurobiological conditions, including neuropsychological abnormalities, are only recently beginning to be more seriously considered in sexual offenders. In fact, this particular type of research with sexually aggressive men is still very limited. Despite the increased attention to delineate the neural circuitry associated with "normal" visual sexual arousal, there are no published reports yet that might illuminate whether these processes are different among sexually aggressive males or men with paraphilic and repetitive noncontact sexual offenses. However, not only would the presence of such abnormalities provide a novel framework for understanding the nature of sexual aggression, but the additional dimension of a biological component associated with sexual offending could help to diminish the harsh social stigmatization currently associated with these behaviors.

Sexual behavior, including sexual offending, is brain-based, and its biological substrates are only slowly being identified. The delineation of the neuroanatomical and neurobiological pathways associated with deviant sexual behavior, however, remains an understudied and underappreciated endeavor.

❧ REFERENCES

Abel, G., & Harlow, N. (2001). The Abel and Harlow Stop Child Molestation study. In G. Abel & N. Harlow, *The stop child molestation book* (pp. 301–324). Philadelphia: Xlibris.

Abikoff, H., & Klein, R. G. (1992). Attention-deficit hyperactivity and conduct disorder: Comorbidity and implications for treatment. *Journal of Consulting and Clinical Psychology, 60*, 881–892.

Abracen, J., & Looman, J. (2006). Evaluation of civil commitment criteria in a high risk sample of sexual offenders. *Journal of Sexual Offender Civil Commitment: Science and the Law, 1*, 124–140.

Adbelgadir, S. E., Roselli, C. E., Choate, J. V., & Resko, J. A. (1999). Androgen receptor messenger ribonucleic acid in brains and pituitaries of male rhesus monkeys: Studies on distribution, hormonal control and relationship to luteinizing hormone. *Biology and Reproduction, 60*, 1251–1256.

Allnut, S. H., Bradford, J. M., Greenberg, D. M., & Curry, S. (1996). Co-morbidity of alcoholism and the paraphilias. *Journal of Forensic Science, 41*, 234–239.

Almeyer, S., Kleinsasser, D., Stoner, J., & Retzlaff, P. (2003). Psychopathology of incarcerated sex offenders. *Journal of Personality Disorders, 17*, 306–318.

American Psychiatric Association. (1994). *Diagnostic and statistical manual of mental disorders* (4th ed., pp. 493–538). Washington, DC: Author.

American Psychiatric Association. (2000). *Diagnostic and statistical manual of mental disorders* (4th ed., text. rev.). Washington, DC: Author.

Angst, J., & Cassano, G. (2005). The mood spectrum: Improving the diagnosis of bipolar disorder. *Bipolar Disorders, 7*(Suppl. 4), 4–12.

Arnold, A. P., & Gorski, R. A. (1984). Gonadal steroid induction of structural sex differences in the central nervous system. *Annual Review of Neuroscience, 7*, 413–442.

Arnow, B. A., Desmond, J. E., Banner, L. L., Glover, G. H., Solomon, A., Polan, M. L., et al. (2002). Brain activation and sexual arousal in healthy, heterosexual males. *Brain, 125*, 1014–1023.

Atwood, J. D., & Gagnon, J. (1987). Masturbatory behavior in college youth. *Journal of Sex Education and Therapy, 13*, 35–42.

Bancroft, J., Janssen, E., Strong, D., Carnes, L., Vukadinovic, Z., & Long, S. L. (2003). The relation between mood and sexuality in heterosexual men. *Archives of Sexual Behavior, 32*, 217–230.

Bancroft, J., Janssen, E., Strong, D., & Vukadinovic, Z. (2003). The relation between mood and sexuality in gay men. *Archives of Sexual Behavior, 32*, 231–242.

Bancroft, J., & Vukadinovic, Z. (2004). Sexual addiction, sexual compulsivity, sexual impulsivity or what?: Toward a theoretical model. *Journal of Sex Research, 41*, 225–234.

Barth, R. J., & Kinder, B. N. (1987). The mislabeling of sexual impulsivity. *Journal of Sex and Marital Therapy, 13*, 15–23.

Baum, M. J., & Starr, M. S. (1980). Inhibition of sexual behavior by dopamine antagonists or serotonin agonist drugs in castrated male rats given estradiol or dihydrotestosterone. *Pharmacology, Biochemistry and Behavior, 13*, 47–67.

Baumbach, J. (2002). Some implications of prenatal alcohol exposure for the treatment of adolescents with sexual offending behaviors. *Sexual Abuse: A Journal of Research and Treatment, 14*, 313–327.

Baumeister, R. F. (2000). Gender differences in erotic plasticity: the female sex drive as socially flexible and responsive. *Psychological Bulletin, 126*, 347–374.

Beach, F. A. (1942). Analysis of factors involved in the arousal, maintenence and manifestation of sexual excitement in male animals. *Psychosomatic Medicine, 4*, 173–198.

Beauregard, M., Levesque, J., & Bourgouin, P. J. (2001). Neural correlates of self-conscious regulation of emotion. *Journal of Neuroscience, 21*, 1–6.

Bechara, A. (2005). Decision making, impulse control and the loss of willpower to resist drugs: A neurocognitive perspective. *Nature Neuroscience.* Retrieved from *www.nature.com/neuro/journal/v8/n11/full/nn1584.html*

Becker, J., Stinson, J., Tromp, S., & Messer, G. (2003). Characteristics of individuals petitioned for civil committment. *International Journal of Offender Therapy and Comparative Criminology, 47,* 185–195.

Best, M., Williams, M., & Coccaro, E. F. (2002). Evidence for a dysfunctional prefrontal circuit in patients with impulsive aggressive disorder. *Proceedings of the National Academy of Sciences USA, 99,* 8448–8453.

Biederman, J., Faraone, S. V., Spencer, T. J., Mick, E., Monuteaux, M. C., & Aleardi, M. (2006). Functional impairments in adults with self-reports of diagnosed ADHD: A controlled study of 1001 adults in the community. *Journal of Clinical Psychiatry, 67,* 524–540.

Biederman, J., Monuteaux, M. C., Mick, E., Spencer, T., Wilens, T., Silva, J. M., et al. (2006). Young adult outcome of attention deficit hyperactivity disorder: A controlled 10 year follow-up study. *Psychological Medicine, 36,* 167–179.

Biver, F., Wikler, D., Lotstra, F., Damhaut, P., Goldman, S., & Mendlewicz, J. (1997). Serotonin 5-HT2 receptor imaging in major depression: Focal changes in orbito-insular cortex. *British Journal of Psychiatry, 171,* 444–448.

Black, D. W. (1998). Compulsive sexual behavior: A review. *Journal of Practical Psychiatry and Behavioral Health, 4,* 217–229.

Blanchard, R., Christensen, B. K., Strong, S. M., Cantor, J. M., Kuban, M. E., Klassen, P., et al. (2002). Retrospective self-reports of childhood accidents causing unconsciousness in phallometrically diagnosed pedophiles. *Archives of Sexual Behavior, 31,* 511–526.

Blanchard, R., Kuban, M. E., Klassen, P., Dickey, R., & Christensen, B. (2003). Self-reported injuries before and after age 13 in pedophilic and non-pedophilic men referred for clinical assessment. *Archives of Sexual Behavior, 32,* 573–581.

Blumberg, H. P., Leung, H. C., Skudlarski, P., Lacadie, C. M., Fredricks, C. A., Harris, B. C., et al. (2003). A functional magnetic resonance imaging study of bipolar disorder: State and trait-related dysfunction in the ventral prefrontal cortices. *Archives of General Psychiatry, 60,* 601–609.

Bradford, J. M. W. (1990). The antiandrogen and hormonal treatment of sex offenders. In W. L. Marshall, D. R. Laws, & H. E. Barbaree (Eds.), *Handbook of sexual assault: Issues, theories, and treatment of the offender* (pp. 297–310). New York: Plenum Press.

Bradford, J. M. W. (2001). The neurobiology, neuropharmacology, and pharmacological treatment of paraphilias and compulsive sexual behaviour. *Canadian Journal of Psychiatry, 46,* 26–33.

Braun, D. L., Sunday, R., & Halmi, K. A. (1994). Psychiatric comorbidity in patients with eating disorders. *Psychological Medicine, 24,* 859–867.

Bremer, J. (1959). *Asexualization: A follow-up study of 244 cases.* New York: Macmillan.

Bremner, J. D., Innis, R. B., Salomon, R. M., Staib, L. H., Ng, C. K., Miller, H. L., et al. (1997). Positron emission tomography measurement of cerebral metabolic correlates of tryptophan depletion-induced depressive relapse. *Archives of General Psychiatry, 54,* 364–374.

Bremner, J. D., Vythilingham, M., Ng, C. K., Vermetten, E., Nazeer, A., Oren, D. A., et al. (2003). Regional brain metabolic correlates of alpha-metaparatyrosine-induced depressive symptoms: Implications for the neural circuitry of depression. *Journal of the American Medical Association, 289,* 3125–3134.

Bremner, J. D., Vythilingham, M., Vermetten, E., Nazeer, A., Adil, J., & Khan, S. (2002). Reduced volume of orbitofrontal cortex in major depression. *Biological Psychiatry, 51,* 273–279.

Briken, P., Hill, A., & Berner, W. (2003). Pharmacotherapy of paraphilias with long-acting agonists of luteinizing hormone-releasing hormone: A systematic review. *Journal of Clinical Psychiatry, 64,* 890–897.

Brody, A. L., Saxena, S., Silverman, D. H., Alborzian, S., Fairbanks, L. A., Phelps, M. E., et al. (1999). Brain metabolic changes in major depressive disorder from pre- to post-treatment with paroxetine. *Psychiatry Research, 91,* 129–139.

Brooks, J. H., & Reddon, J. R. (1996). Serum testosterone in violent and nonviolent young offenders. *Journal of Clinical Psychology, 52,* 475–483.

Brotherton, J. (1974). Effect of oral cyproterone acetate on urinary and serum FSH and LH levels in adult males being treated for hypersexuality. *Journal of Reproduction and Fertility, 36,* 177–187.

Carnes, P. (1983). *Out of the shadows: Understanding sexual addiction.* Minneapolis, MN: CompCare.

Cavedini, P., Riboldi, G., Keller, R., D'Annucci, A., & Bellodi, L. (2002). Frontal lobe dysfunction in pathological gambling patients. *Biological Psychiatry, 51,* 334–341.

Christensen, K., & Knussman, R. (1987). Androgen levels and components of aggressive behavior in men. *Hormones and Behavior, 21,* 170–180.

Cochrane, R. E., Grisso, T., & Frederick, R. I. (2001). The relationship between criminal charges, diagnoses, and psycholegal opinions among federal pretrial defendants. *Behavioral Sciences and the Law, 19,* 565–582.

Cohen, L. J., McGeoch, P. G., Watras-Gans, S., Acker, S., Poznansky, O., Cullen, K., et al. (2002). Personality impairment in pedophiles. *Journal of Clinical Psychiatry, 63,* 912–919.

Coleman, E. (1987). Sexual compulsivity: Definition, etiology, and treatment considerations. *Journal of Chemical Dependency Treatment, 1,* 189–204.

Comings, D. E. (1994). Role of genetic factors in human sexual behavior based on studies of Tourette syndrome and ADHD probands and their relatives. *American Journal of Medical Genetics, 54,* 227–241.

Comings, D. E. (2001). Clinical and molecular genetics of ADHD and Tourette's syndrome. *Annals of the New York Academy of Sciences, 931,* 50–83.

Cooper, A. J. (1981). A placebo-controlled trial of the antiandrogen cyproterone acetate in deviant hypersexuality. *Comprehensive Psychiatry, 22,* 458–465.

Davies, T. S. (1974). Cyproterone acetate for male hypersexuality. *Journal of Internal Medicine Research, 2,* 159–163.

Davis, S. R. (1998). The role of androgens and the menopause in the female sexual response. *International Journal of Impotence Research, 10*(Suppl. 2), s82–83, s98–101.

De Bellis, M., & Keshavan, M. (2003). Sex differences in brain maturation in maltreatment-related pediatric posttraumatic stress disorder. *Neuroscience and Biobehavioral Reviews, 27,* 103–117.

Dhawan, S., & Marshall, W. L. (1996). Sexual abuse histories of sexual offenders. *Sexual Abuse: A Journal of Research and Treatment, 8,* 7–15.

Dong, M., Anda, R. F., Felitti, V. J., Dube, S. R., Williamson, D. F., Thompson, T. J., et al. (2004). The interrelatedness of multiple forms of childhood abuse, neglect and household dysfunction. *Child Abuse and Neglect, 28,* 771–784.

Drevets, W. C., Price, J. L., Simpson, J. R., Todd, R. D., Reich, T., & Vannier, M. (1997). Subgenual prefrontal cortex abnormalities in mood disorders. *Nature, 386,* 824–827.

Dunsieth, N. W., Nelson, E. B., Brusman-Lovins, L. A., Holcomb, J. I.., Beckman, D., Welge, J. A., et al. (2004). Psychiatric and legal features of 113 men convicted of sexual offenses. *Journal of Clinical Psychiatry, 65,* 293–300.

Eher, R., Neuwirth, W., Fruehwald, S., & Frottier, P. (2003). Sexualization and lifetime impulsivity: Clinically valid discriminators in sexual offenders. *International Journal of Offender Therapy and Comparative Criminology, 47,* 452–467.

Elliott, C. (1996). *The rules of insanity: Moral responsibility and the mentally ill offender.* Albany: State University of New York Press.

Ellis, B. J., & Symons, D. (1990). Sex differences in sexual fantasy: An evolutionary psychological approach. *Journal of Sex Research, 27,* 527–555.

Everitt, B. J. (1995). Neuroendocrine mechanisms underlying appetitive and consummatory elements of masculine sexual behavior. In J. Bancroft (Ed.), *The pharmacology of sexual function and dysfunction* (pp. 15–31). Amsterdam: Elsevier Science.

Eyestone, L. L., & Howell, R. J. (1994). An epidemiological study of attention-deficit hyperactivity disorder and major depression in a male prison population. *Journal of the American Academy of Psychiatry and the Law, 22,* 181–193.

Fago, D. P. (1999). Comorbidity of attention deficit hyperactivity disorder in sexually aggressive children and adolescents. In B. Schwartz (Ed.), *The sex offender: Vol. 3. Theoretical advances, treating special populations and legal developments* (pp. 16.11–16.15). Kingston, NJ: Civic Research Institute.

Fazel, S., & Danesh, J. (2002). Serious mental disorder in 23,000 prisoners: A systematic review of 62 surveys. *Lancet, 359,* 545–550.

Firestone, P., Bradford, J. M., McCoy, M., Greenberg, D. M., Larose, M. R., & Curry, S. (1999). Prediction of recidivism in incest offenders. *Journal of Interpersonal Violence, 14,* 511–531.

Fisher, D., Beech, A., & Browne, A. (1999). Comparison of sex offenders to nonoffenders on selected psychological measures. *International Journal of Offender Therapy and Comparative Criminology, 43,* 473–491.

Friedrich, W. N., Davies, W. H., Feher, E., & Wright, J. (2003). Sexual behavior problems in preteen children. *Annals of the New York Academy of Sciences, 989,* 95–104.

Galli, V., McElroy, S. L., Soutello, C. A., Kizer, D., Raute, N., Keck, P. E., et al. (1999). The psychiatric diagnoses of twenty two adolescents who have sexually molested other children. *Comprehensive Psychiatry, 40,* 85–87.

Geller, B., Tillman, R., Craney, J. L., & Bolhofner, K. (2004). Four-year prospective outcome and natural history of mania in children with a prepubertal and early adolescent bipolar disorder phenotype. *Archives of General Psychiatry, 61,* 459–467.

Giammanco, M., Tabacchi, G., Giammanco, S., Di Majo, D., & La Guardia, M. (2005). testosterone and aggressiveness. *Medical Science Monitor, 11,* 136–145.

Gizewski, E. R., Krause, E., Karama, S., Baars, A., Senf, W., & Forsting, M. (2006). There are differences in cerebral activation between females in distinct menstrual phases during viewing of erotic stimuli: An fMRI study. *Experimental Brain Research.* Retrieved from *dx.doi.org/10.1007/s00221-006-0429-3*

Goldstein, B. J., & Levitt, A. J. (2006). Further evidence for a developmental subtype of bipolar disorder defined by age of onset: Results from the National Epidemiological Survey on Alcohol and Related Conditions. *American Journal of Psychiatry, 163,* 1633–1635.

Goldstein, J., Seidman, L. J., Horton, N. J., Makris, N., Kennedy, D. N., Caviness, V. S., Jr., et al. (2001). Normal sexual dimorphism of the adult human brain assessed by *in vivo* magnetic resonance imaging. *Cerebral Cortex, 11,* 490–497.

Goodman, A. (1997). Sexual addiction. In J. H. Lowenson, P. Ruiz, R. B. Millman, & J. G. Langrod (Eds.), *Substance abuse: A comprehensive textbook* (3rd ed., pp. 340–354). Baltimore: Williams & Wilkins.

Grant, J. E. (2005). Clinical characteristics and psychiatric comorbidity in males with exhibitionism. *Journal of Clinical Psychiatry, 66,* 1367–1371.

Greenberg, D. M., Bradford, J. M. W., Curry, S., & O'Rourke, A. (1996). A comparison of treatment of paraphilias with three serotonin reuptake inhibitors: A retrospective study. *Bulletin of the American Academy of Psychiatry and the Law, 24,* 525–532.

Grubin, D. (1992). Sexual offending: A cross-cultural comparison. *Annual Review of Sex Research, 3,* 201–217.

Hagemann, J. H., Berding, G., Bergh, S., Sleep, D. J., Knapp, W. H., Jonas, U., et al. (2003). Effects of visual sexual stimuli and apomorphine SL on cerebral activity in men with erectile dysfunction. *European Urology, 43,* 412–420.

Hamann, S. (2005). Sex differences in the responses of the human amygdala. *Neuroscientist, 11,* 288–293.

Hamann, S., Herman, R. A., Nolan, C. L., & Wallen, K. (2004). Men and women differ in amygdala response to visual sexual stimuli. *Nature Neuroscience.* Retrieved from *www.nature.com/natureneuroscience*

Hanson, R. K., & Harris, A. (2000). Where should we intervene?: Dynamic predictors of sexual offense recidivism. *Criminal Justice and Behavior, 27,* 6–35.

Hanson, R. K., & Morton-Bourgon, K. (2004). *Predictors of sexual recidivism: An updated meta-analysis*. Retrieved from *nicic.org/Library/019553*

Hirschfeld, R. M. A., Calabrese, J. R., & Weissman, M. M. (2003). Screening for bipolar disorder in the community. *Journal of Clinical Psychiatry, 64,* 53–59.

Hirschfeld, R. M. A., & Vornik, L. A. (2004). Recognition and diagnosis of bipolar disorder. *Journal of Clinical Psychiatry, 65*(Suppl. 15), 5–9.

Horn, N. R., Dolan, M., Elliott, R., Deakin, J. F. W., & Woodruff, P. W. R. (2003). Response inhibition and impulsivity: An fMRI study. *Neuropsychologia, 41,* 1959–1955.

Hoyer, J., Kunst, H., & Schmidt, A. (2001). Social phobia as a comorbid condition in sex offenders with paraphilia or impulse control disorder. *Journal of Nervous and Mental Disease, 189,* 463–470.

Hucker, S. J., & Bain, J. (1990). Androgenic hormones and sexual assault. In W. L. Marshall, D. R. Laws, & H. E. Barbaree (Eds.), *Handbook of sexual assault: Issues, theories, and treatment of the offender* (pp. 93–102). New York: Plenum Press.

Hudson, S. M., & Ward, T. (1997). Rape: Psychopathology and theory. In D. R. Laws & W. O'Donohue (Eds.), *Sexual deviance: Theory, assessment, and treatment* (pp. 332–355). New York: Guilford Press.

Hyde, J. S. (2005). The gender similarities hypothesis. *American Psychologist, 60,* 581–592.

Janus, E. S., & Walbek, N. H. (2000). Sex offender commitments in Minnesota: A descriptive study of second generation commitments. *Behavioral Sciences and the Law, 18,* 343–374.

Johansson, P., Kerr, M., & Andershed, H. (2005). Linking adult psychopathy with childhood hyperactivity–impulsivity–attention problems and conduct problems through retrospective self-reports. *Journal of Personality Disorders, 19,* 94–101.

Judd, L. L., & Akiskal, H. S. (2003). The prevalence and disability of bipolar spectrum disorders in the US population: A re-analysis of the ECA database taking into account subthreshold cases. *Journal of Affective Disorders, 73,* 123–131.

Kafka, M. P. (1997a). Hypersexual desire in males: An operational definition and clinical implications for men with paraphilias and paraphilia-related disorders. *Archives of Sexual Behavior, 26,* 505–526.

Kafka, M. P. (1997b). A monoamine hypothesis for the pathophysiology of paraphilic disorders. *Archives of Sexual Behavior, 26,* 337–352.

Kafka, M. P. (2003a). The monoamine hypothesis for the pathophysiology of paraphilic disorders: An update. *Annals of the New York Academy of Sciences, 989,* 86–94.

Kafka, M. P. (2003b). Sex offending and sexual desire: The clinical and theoretical relevance of hypersexual desire. *International Journal of Offender Therapy and Comparative Criminology, 47,* 439–451.

Kafka, M. P., & Hennen, J. (2000). Psychostimulant augmentation during treatment with selective serotonin reuptake inhibitors in males with paraphilias and paraphilia-related disorders: A case series. *Journal of Clinical Psychiatry, 61,* 664–670.

Kafka, M. P., & Hennen, J. (2002). A DSM IV Axis I comorbidity study of males (*n* = 120) with paraphilias and paraphilia-related disorders. *Sexual Abuse: A Journal of Research and Treatment, 14,* 349–366.

Kafka, M. P., & Hennen, J. (2003). Hypersexual desire in males: Are males with paraphilias different from males with paraphilia-related disorders? *Sexual Abuse: A Journal of Research and Treatment, 15,* 307–321.

Kafka, M. P., & Prentky, R. (1992). Fluoxetine treatment of nonparaphilic sexual addictions and paraphilias in men. *Journal of Clinical Psychiatry, 53,* 351–358.

Kafka, M. P., & Prentky, R. A. (1994). Preliminary observations of DSM III-R Axis I comorbidity in men with paraphilias and paraphilia-related disorders. *Journal of Clinical Psychiatry, 55,* 481–487.

Kafka, M. P., & Prentky, R. A. (1998). Attention deficit hyperactivity disorder in males with paraphilias and paraphilia-related disorders: A comorbidity study. *Journal of Clinical Psychiatry, 59,* 388–396.

Kaneita, Y., Ohida, T., Uchiyama, M., Takemura, S., Kawahara, K., Yokoyama, E., et al. (2006). The relationship between depression and sleep disturbances: A Japanese general population survey. *Journal of Clinical Psychiatry, 67,* 196–203.

Kaplan, H. S. (1995). *The sexual desire disorders: Dysfunctional regulation of sexual motivation.* New York: Brunner/Mazel.

Kaplan, S. J., Pelcovitz, D., & Labruna, V. (1999). Child and adolescent abuse and neglect research: A review of the past 10 years. Part 1: Physical and emotional abuse and neglect. *Journal of the American Academy of Child and Adolescent Psychiatry, 38,* 1214–1222.

Karama, S., Lecours, A. R., Leroux, J., Bourgouin, P., Beaudoin, G., Joubert, S., et al. (2002). Areas of brain activation in males and females during viewing of erotic film excerpts. *Human Brain Mapping, 16,* 1–13.

Kavoussi, R. J., Kaplan, M., & Becker, J. V. (1988). Psychiatric diagnoses in adolescent sex offenders. *Journal of the American Academy of Child and Adolescent Psychiatry, 27,* 241–243.

Kessler, R. C., Adler, L., Barkley, R., Biederman, J., Connors, C. K., Demler, O., et al. (2006). The prevalence and correlates of adult ADHD in the United States: Results from the National Comorbidity Survey Replication. *American Journal of Psychiatry, 163,* 716–723.

Khouri, E. M., Lukas, S. E., Pope, H. G. J., & Oliva, P. S. (1995). Increased aggressive responding in male volunteers following the administration of gradually increasing doses of testosterone cypionate. *Drug and Alcohol Dependence, 40,* 73–79.

Kinsey, A. C., Pomeroy, W. B., & Martin, C. E. (1948). *Sexual behavior in the human male.* Philadelphia: Saunders.

Klein, D. N., & Santiago, N. J. (2003). Dysthymia and chronic depression: Introduction, classification, risk factors, and course. *Journal of Clinical Psychology/In Session, 59,* 807–816.

Knight, R. A., & Cerce, D. (1999). Validation and revision of the Multidimensional Assessment of Sex and Aggression. *Psychologica Belgica, 39,* 135–161.

Knight, R. A., & Prentky, R. A. (1987). The developmental antecedents and adult adaptations of rapist subtypes. *Criminal Justice and Behavior, 14,* 403–426.

Knight, R. A., & Prentky, R. A. (1990). Classifying sex offenders: The development and corroboration of taxonomic models. In W. L. Marshall, D. R. Laws, & H. E. Barbaree (Eds.), *Handbook of sexual assault: Issues, theories, and treatment of the offender* (pp. 23–52). New York: Plenum Press.

Knight, R. A., & Sims-Knight, J. E. (2003). The developmental antecedents of sexual coercion against women: Testing alternative hypotheses with structural equation modeling. *Annals of the New York Academy of Sciences, 989,* 72–85.

Knight, R. A., & Sims-Knight, J. E. (2004). Testing an etiological model for male juvenile sexual offending against females. *Journal of Child Sexual Abuse, 13,* 33–55.

Knussmann, R., Christiansen, K., & Couwenbergs, C. (1986). Relations between sex hormone levels and sexual behavior in men. *Archives of Sexual Behavior, 15,* 429–445.

Kovacs, M., & Pollock, M. (1995). Bipolar disorder and comorbid conduct disorder in childhood and adolescence. *Journal of the American Academy of Child and Adolescent Psychiatry, 34,* 715–723.

Kumagami, T. (2006). Characteristics of juvenile court cases with pervasive developmental disorder. *Seishin Shinkeigaku Zasshi, 108,* 327–336.

Långström, N., & Hanson, R. K. (2006). High rates of sexual behavior in the general population: Correlates and predictors. *Archives of Sexual Behavior, 35,* 37–52.

Långström, N., Sjöstedt, G., & Grann, M. (2004). Psychiatric disorders and recidivism in sexual offenders. *Sexual Abuse: A Journal of Research and Treatment, 16,* 139–150.

Långström, N., & Zucker, K. J. (2005). Transvestic fetishism in the general population: Prevalence and correlates. *Journal of Sex and Marital Therapy, 31,* 87–95.

Laumann, E. O., Gagnon, J. H., Michael, R. T., & Michaels, S. (1994). *The social organization of sexuality: Sexual practices in the United States.* Chicago: University of Chicago Press.

Lee, J. K. P., Jackson, H. J., Pattison, P., & Ward, T. (2002). Developmental risk factors for sexual offending. *Child Abuse and Neglect, 26,* 73–92.

Levenson, J. S. (2004). Sexual predator civil commitment: A comparison of selected and released offenders. *International Journal of Offender Therapy and Comparative Criminology, 48,* 638–648.

Levin, R. J. (1994). Human male sexuality: Appetite and arousal, desire and drive. In C. R. Legg & D. Booth (Eds.), *Appetite: Neural and behavioral bases* (pp. 128–164). Oxford, UK: Oxford University Press.

Lewin, J., Beary, M., Toman, G. S., & Sproul-Bolton, R. (1994). A community service for sex offenders. *Journal of Forensic Psychology, 5,* 297–310.

Lichter, D. G., & Cummings, J. L. (Eds.). (2001). *Frontal–subcortical circuits in psychiatric and neurological disorders.* New York: Guilford Press.

Liu, D., Ng, M., Zhou, L. P., & Haeberle, E. (1997). *Sexual behavior in modern China.* New York: Continuum.

Loeber, R., Farrington, D. P., Stouthamer-Loeber, M., & Moffitt, T. E. (2001). Male mental health problems, psychopathy, and personality traits: Key findings from the first 14 years of the Pittsburgh Youth Study. *Clinical Child and Family Psychology Review, 4,* 273–297.

Lorrain, D. S., Matuszewich, L., Friedman, R. D., & Hull, E. M. (1997). Extracellular serotonin in the lateral hypothalamic area is increased during the postejaculatory interval and impairs copulation in male rats. *Journal of Neuroscience, 17,* 9361–9366.

Lorrain, D. S., Riolo, J., Matuszewich, L., & Hull, E. M. (1999). Lateral hypothalamic serotonin inhibits nucleus accumbens dopamine: Implications for sexual satiety. *Journal of Neuroscience, 19,* 7648–7652.

Lynam, D. R. (1996). Early identification of chronic offenders: Who is the fledgling psychopath? *Psychological Bulletin, 120,* 209–234.

Lynam, D. R. (1998). Early identification of the fledgling psychopath: Locating the psychopathic child in the current nomenclature. *Journal of Abnormal Child Psychology, 107,* 566–575.

Lyoo, I. K., Kwon, J. S., Lee, S. J., Han, M. H., Chang, C.-G., Seo, C. S., et al. (2002). Decrease in genu of the corpus callosum in medication-naive, early-onset dysthymia and depressive personality disorder. *Biological Psychiatry, 52,* 1134–1143.

Macpherson, G. J. D. (2003). Predicting escalation in sexually violent recidivism: Use of the SVR-20 and PCL:SV to predict outcome with non-contact recidivists and contact recidivists. *Journal of Forensic Psychiatry and Psychology, 14,* 615–627.

Malhi, G. S., Cahill, C. M., Ivanovski, B., & Lagopoulos, J. (2006). A neuropsychological 'image' of bipolar disorder. *Clinical Approaches to Bipolar Disorders, 5,* 2–13.

Marshall, W. L. (1997). Pedophilia: Psychopathology and theory. In D. R. Laws & W. O'Donohue (Eds.), *Sexual deviance: Theory, assessment, and treatment* (pp. 152–174). New York: Guilford Press.

Martinez-Conde, E., Leret, M. L., & Diaz, S. (1985). The influence of testosterone in the brain of the male rat on levels of serotonin and hydroxyindole-acetic acid (5-HIAA). *Comprehensive Biochemistry and Physiology, 80,* 411–414.

Mas, M. (1995). Neurobiological correlates of masculine sexual behavior. *Neuroscience and Biobehavioral Reviews, 19,* 261–277.

Mathew, R. J., Largen, J. L., & Claghorn, J. L. (1979). Biological symptoms of depression. *Psychosomatic Medicine, 41,* 439–443.

Mathew, R. J., & Weinman, M. L. (1982). Sexual dysfunctions in depression. *Archives of Sexual Behavior, 11,* 323–328.

Mattson, S. N., Goodman, A. M., Caine, C., Delis, D. C., & Riley, E. P. (1999). Executive functioning in children with heavy prenatal alcohol exposure. *Alcoholism: Clinical and Experimental Research, 23,* 1808–1815.

McElroy, S. L., Soutello, C. A., Taylor, P., Nelson, E. B., Beckman, D. A., Brusman, L. A., et al. (1999). Psychiatric features of 36 convicted sexual offenses. *Journal of Clinical Psychiatry, 60,* 414–420.

McKenna, K. (1999). The brain is the master organ in sexual function: Central nervous system control of male and female function. *International Journal of Impotence Research, 11*(Suppl. 1), S48–S55.

Miresco, M. J., & Kirmayer, L. J. (2006). The persistence of mind–brain dualism in psychiatric reasoning about clinical scenarios. *American Journal of Psychiatry, 163,* 913–918.

Murnen, S. K., & Stockton, M. (1997). Gender and self-reported sexual arousal in response to sexual stimuli: A meta-analytic review. *Sex Roles, 37,* 135–153.

New, A. S., Hazlett, E. A., Buchsbaum, M. S., Goodman, M., Reynolds, D., Mitropoulou, V., et al. (2002). Blunted prefrontal cortical fluorodeoxyglucose positron emission tomography response to meta-chlorophenylpiperazine in impulsive aggression. *Archives of General Psychiatry, 59,* 621–629.

Nofzinger, E. A., Thase, M. E., Reynolds, C. F., Frank, E., Jennings, J. R., Garamoni, G. L., et al. (1993). Sexual function in depressed men: Assessment by self-report, behavioral and nocturnal penile tumescence measures before and after treatment with cognitive therapy. *Archives of General Psychiatry, 50,* 24–30.

O'Connor, A. (1987). Female sex offenders. *British Journal of Psychiatry, 150,* 615–620.

Oliver, M. B., & Hyde, J. S. (1993). Gender differences in sexuality: A meta-analysis. *Psychological Bulletin, 114,* 29–51.

Orford, J. (1978). Hypersexuality: Implications for a theory of dependence. *British Journal of Addiction, 73,* 299–310.

Park, K., Kang, H. K., Seo, J. J., Kim, H. J., Ryu, S. B., & Jeong, G. W. (2001). Blood-oxygenation-level-dependent functional magnetic resonance imaging for evaluating cerebral regions of female sexual arousal. *Urology, 57,* 1189–1194.

Park, K., Seo, J. J., Kang, H. K., Ryu, S. B., Kim, H. J., & Jeong, G. W. (2001). A new potential of blood oxygenation level dependent (BOLD) functional MRI for evaluating cerebral centers of penile erection. *International Journal of Impotence Research, 13,* 73–81.

Perez, M., Joiner, T. E., & Lewinsohn, P. M. (2004). Is major depression or dysthymia more strongly associated with bulimia nervosa? *International Journal of Eating Disorders, 36,* 55–61.

Phillips, M. L., Drevets, W. C., Rauch, S. L., & Lane, R. (2003). Neurobiology of emotion perception: II. Implications for major psychiatric disorders. *Biological Psychiatry, 54,* 515–528.

Piatogorsky, A., & Hinshaw, S. P. (2004). Psychopathic traits in boys with and without attention-deficit/hyperactivity disorder: Concurrent and longitudinal correlates. *Journal of Abnormal Child Psychology, 32,* 535–550.

Plessen, K. J., Bansal, R., Zhu, H., Whitemen, R., Amat, J., Quackenbush, G. A., et al. (2006). Hippocampus and amygdala morphology in attention-deficit/hyperactivity disorder. *Archives of General Psychiatry, 63,* 795–807.

Prentky, R. A., & Burgess, A. W. (2000). *Forensic management of sexual offenders.* New York: Kluver Academic/Plenum.

Prentky, R. A., Knight, R. A., Sims-Knight, J. E., Straus, H., Rokous, F., & Cerce, D. (1989). Developmental antecedents of sexual aggression. *Developmental Psychopathology, 1,* 153–169.

Rada, R. T. (1978). Biologic aspects and organic treatment of the rapist. In R. T. Rada (Ed.), *Clinical aspects of the rapist* (pp. 133–160). New York: Grune & Stratton.

Rauch, S. L., Shin, L. M., Dougherty, D. D., Alpert, N. M., Orr, S. P., Lasko, M., et al. (1999). Neural activation during sexual and competitive arousal in healthy men. *Psychiatry Research, 91,* 1–10.

Raymond, N. C., Coleman, E., & Miner, M. H. (2003). Psychiatric comorbidity and compulsive/impulsive traits in compulsive sexual behavior. *Comprehensive Psychiatry, 44,* 370–380.

Raymond, N. C., Coleman, E., Ohlerking, F., Christenson, G. A., & Miner, M. (1999). Psychiatric comorbidity in pedophilic sex offenders. *American Journal of Psychiatry, 156,* 786–788.

Redoute, J., Stoleru, S., Gregiore, M., Costes, N., Cinotti, L., Lavenne, F., et al. (2000). Brain processing of visual sexual stimuli in human males. *Human Brain Mapping, 11,* 162–177.

Rhodes, S. M., Coghill, D. R., & Matthews, K. (2005). Neuropsychological functioning in stimulant naive boys with hyperkinetic disorder. *Psychological Medicine, 35,* 1109–1120.

Roselli, C. E., Klosterman, S., & Resko, J. A. (2001). Anatomic relationships between aromatase and androgen receptor m-RNA expression in the hypothalamus and amygdala of adult male cynomolgus monkeys. *Journal of Comprehensive Neurology, 439*, 208–223.

Rubinow, D. R., & Schmidt, P. J. (1996). Androgens, brain and behavior. *American Journal of Psychiatry, 153*, 974–984.

Salloway, S. P., Malloy, P. F., & Duffy, J. D. (2001). *The frontal lobes and neuropsychiatric illness.* Washington, DC: American Psychiatric Press.

Sarikaya, A., Karasin, E., Cermik, T. F., Abay, E., & Berkada, S. (1999). Evaluation of dysthymic disorder with technicium-99 m hexamethylpropylene amine oxime brain single-photon emission tomography. *European Journal of Nuclear Medicine, 26*, 260–264.

Saxena, S., Brody, A. L., Ho, M. L., Alborzian, S., Maidment, K. M., Zohrabi, N., et al. (2002). Differential cerebral metabolic changes with paroxetine treatment of obsessive–compulsive disorder vs. major depression. *Archives of General Psychiatry, 59*, 250–261.

Scher, C. D., Forde, D. R., McQuaid, J. R., & Stein, M. B. (2004). Prevalence and demographic correlates of childhood maltreatment in an adult community sample. *Child Abuse and Neglect, 28*, 167–180.

Schiavi, R. C. (1996). Sexual disorders. In T. A. Widiger, A. J. Frances, H. A. Pincus, R. Ross, M. B. First, & W. D. Davis (Eds.), *DSM-IV sourcebook* (Vol. 2). Washington, DC: American Psychiatric Publishing.

Schreiner-Engel, P., & Schiavi, R. C. (1986). Lifetime psychopathology in individuals with low sexual desire. *Journal of Nervous and Mental Disease, 174*, 646–651.

Schubiner, H., Tzelepis, A., Milberger, S., Lockhart, N., Kruger, M., Kelley, B. J., et al. (2000). Prevalence of attention deficit/hyperactivity disorder and conduct disorder among substance abusers. *Journal of Clinical Psychiatry, 61*, 244–251.

Seghorn, T. K., Prentky, R. A., & Boucher, R. J. (1987). Childhood sexual abuse in the lives of sexually aggressive offenders. *Journal of the American Academy of Child and Adolescent Psychiatry, 26*, 262–267.

Seidman, L. J., Valera, E. M., & Makris, N. (2005). Structural brain imaging of attention deficit/hyperactivity disorder. *Biological Psychiatry, 57*, 1263–1272.

Shaw, P., Lerch, J., Greenstein, D., Sharp, W., Clasen, L., Evans, A., et al. (2006). Longitudinal mapping of the cortical thickness and clinical outcome in children and adolescents with attention-deficit/hyperactivity disorder. *Archives of General Psychiatry, 63*, 540–549.

Simerly, R. B. (2000). Development of sexually dimorphic forebrain pathways. In A. Matsumoto (Ed.), *Sexual differentiation of the brain* (pp. 175–202). Boca Raton, FL: CRC Press.

Simons, D., Wurtele, S. K., & Heil, P. (2002). Childhood victimization and lack of empathy as predictors of sexual offending against women and children. *Journal of Interpersonal Violence, 17*, 1291–1305.

Soderstrom, H., Nilsson, T., Sjodin, A. K., Carlstedt, A., & Forsman, A. (2005). The childhood-onset neuropsychiatric background to adult psychopathic traits and personality disorders. *Comprehensive Psychiatry, 46*, 111–116.

Soderstrom, H., Sjodin, A. K., Carlstedt, A., & Forsman, A. (2004). Adult psychopathic personality with childhood-onset hyperactivity and conduct disorder: A central problem constellation in forensic psychiatry. *Psychiatry Research, 121*, 271–280.

Song, L., Lieb, R., & Donnelly, S. (1993). *Female sex offenders in Washington State.* Seattle: Washington State Institute for Public Policy.

Stoleru, S., Gregoire, M., Gerard, D., Decety, J., Lafarge, E., Cinotti, L., et al. (1999). Neuroanatomical correlates of visually evoked sexual arousal in human males. *Archives of Sexual Behavior, 28*, 1–22.

Stoleru, S. G., Ennaji, A., Cournot, A., & Spira, A. (1993). LH pulsatile secretion and testosterone blood levels are influenced by sexual arousal in males. *Psychoneuroendocrinology, 18*, 205–218.

Sturup, G. K. (1972). Castration: The total treatment. In H. L. P. Resnik & M. E. Wolfgang (Eds.), *Sexual behaviors: Social, clinical and legal aspects* (pp. 361–382). Boston: Little, Brown.

Sundblad, C., & Ericksson, E. (1997). Reduced extracellular levels on serotonin in the amygdala of androgenized female rats. *European Neuropsychopharmacology, 7*, 253–259.

Teicher, M. H., Andersen, S. L., Polcari, A., Anderson, C. M., Navalta, C. P., & Kim, D. M. (2003). The neurobiological consequences of early stress and childhood maltreatment. *Neuroscience and Biobehavioral Reviews, 27*, 33–44.

Turley, B., Bates, G. W., Edwards, J., & Jackson, H. J. (1992). MCMI-II personality disorders in recent onset bipolar disorders. *Journal of Clinical Psychology, 48*, 320–329.

Vaih-Koch, S. R., & Bosinski, H. A. G. (1999, June). *Childhood attention deficit hyperactivity disorder and conduct disorder in 121 sex offenders*. Paper presented at the 25th Annual Meeting of the International Academy of Sex Research, Stony Brook, NY.

Volkow, N. D., & Fowler, J. S. (2000). Addiction, a disease of compulsion and drive: Involvement of the orbitofrontal cortex. *Cerebral Cortex, 10*, 318–325.

Waschbush, D. A. (2002). A meta-analytic examination of comorbid hyperactive–impulsive–attention problems and conduct problems. *Psychological Bulletin, 128*, 118–150.

Weiss, D. (2004). The prevalence of depression in male sex addicts residing in the United States. *Sexual Addiction and Compulsivity, 11*, 57–69.

Widom, C. P., & Ames, M. A. (1994). Criminal consequences of childhood sexual victimization. *Child Abuse and Neglect, 18*, 303–318.

Wille, R., & Beier, K. M. (1989). Castration in Germany. *Annals of Sex Research, 2*, 103–133.

Woodson, J. C., & Gorski, R. A. (2000). Structural sex differences in the mammalian brain: Reconsidering the male/female dichotomy. In A. Matsumoto (Ed.), *Sexual differentiation of the brain* (pp. 229–255). Boca Raton, FL: CRC Press.

Yurgulin-Todd, D. A., & Ross, A. J. (2006). Functional magnetic resonance imaging studies in bipolar disorder. *CNS Spectrums, 11*, 287–297.

Zander, T. K. (2005). Civil commitment without psychosis: The law's reliance on the weakest link in psychodiagnosis. *Journal of Sexual Offender Civil Commitment: Science and the Law, 1*, 17–82.

CHAPTER 31

MEDICAL MODELS
AND INTERVENTIONS
IN SEXUAL DEVIANCE

DON GRUBIN

Medical doctors in general, and psychiatrists in particular, often express doubts regarding their role in the treatment of sex offenders. There are a number of reasons for this. First, although therapeutic work with sex offenders has its origins in medicine, especially in the work of doctors like Krafft-Ebing and Freud, psychiatrists have taken a battering because of the esoteric, speculative, and ultimately unproductive path down which resulting psychoanalytic approaches have often led them. The focus on theories associated with infantile sexuality, Oedipal concepts, and mothers in the development of "perversion" and offending (see, e.g., Rosen, 1996), and the belief that insight can ameliorate sexual offending behavior, are intellectually interesting but have not met with notable success—at least if measured by a reduction in reoffending.

Second, perhaps in the context of a reaction to the influence of psychoanalysis in psychiatry more generally, the search for more hard-wired, "scientific" causes and cures for sex offending became fashionable (Galski, Thornton, & Shumsky, 1990; Prentky, 1985). The concentration on genes, brain lesions, and hormones, however, has also proved largely unfruitful, ignoring as it often does the obvious significance of psychological contributors to sexual offending. Occasionally but rarely is a clear link made between such offending and an overtly physical cause, and as a number of promising leads in the search for an organic basis to sex offending have fizzled out, so too has the enthusiasm of some doctors.

Third, adherence to a so-called "medical model," which limits psychiatry's role to mental illness and "mental disorder" (Grubin & Mason, 1997), has pushed sexual offending beyond the orbit of psychiatric practice for many psychiatrists and nonpsychiatrists alike. Most sexual offenders, after all, are not mentally ill, and deviant behavior on its own does not amount to mental disorder. In addition, some doctors (and others who work with sex offenders) appear to believe that a medical approach to sex offending somehow lessens offenders' responsibility for their behavior, and therefore should be avoided.

The reluctance of psychiatrists to become involved in the treatment of sex offenders, while perhaps understandable, is unfortunate. Regardless of how "psychological" sexual offending may be, it is dependent on sexual drive and sexual functioning, and is closely associated with biological processes. Not only can a medically based understanding of these factors assist in a better modeling of sexual offending behavior, but it also provides potentially powerful adjuncts to treatment.

SEXUAL OFFENDING, SEXUAL DEVIANCE, AND PARAPHILIAS

In order to understand the issues psychiatrists face in becoming involved in the treatment of sex offenders, and their role when they do become involved, it is important to emphasize that the psychiatrist's duty of care, like that of any doctor, is to his or her patient. Patient welfare, not social control, is the basis of psychiatric practice. Failure to appreciate this can result in confusion and frustration in the discourse between psychiatrists and nonpsychiatrists. For example, in his criticism of the way in which the American Psychiatric Association's *Diagnostic and Statistical Manual of Mental Disorders* (DSM) defines pedophilia, Marshall (1997) states that "most clinicians recognize a need to evaluate and treat all child molesters" (p. 152); however, if he intends to include psychiatrists among "most clinicians" (as he almost certainly does), then he is simply wrong. To understand why, it is necessary to consider briefly the concepts of sexual offending, sexual deviance, and paraphilia.

"Sexual offenses" are behaviors that are defined and proscribed by a society because of the harm they cause its citizens, or because of their impact on public order. What counts as an offense varies over time and place, and can change virtually overnight with the passage or repeal of specific pieces of legislation. Although some who commit sexual offenses may be mentally disordered, most are not, and sexual offenders are dealt with through the criminal justice system rather than the mental health system. There is no direct role for psychiatrists to play in respect to most sex offenders, and many psychiatrists are concerned that by being drawn into sex offender management, they risk becoming agents of social control—carrying out the bidding of lawmakers and politicians, rather than acting in the best interests of their patients.

"Sexual deviance" refers to sexual behaviors that contravene the norms of society, and that may or may not amount to sexual offenses. It also refers to regular, rather than one-time, interests or behaviors. What is recognized as deviance depends on the shared norms of a culture (Bancroft, 1989), although it may reflect a general perception of what *should* be "normal" or "proper" rather than what people really do, as often becomes apparent when the private sexual practices of public figures find their way into the newspapers. Although sexual deviance is sometimes defined in statistical terms, there are many subcultures where "sexually deviant" behavior is the norm, ranging from fetishism to sadomasochism; moreover, what at one time is considered sexually deviant may move into the mainstream, with uncertainty about whether it should be considered deviant or not, as is the case with homosexuality. As Bancroft (1989) has pointed out, however, social rather than medical criteria determine what is considered to be deviant. Sexual deviance is a moral rather than a psychiatric construct, and, as with sexual offending, there is typically no reason for a psychiatrist to become involved.

"Paraphilia" is a technical term used in the DSM for a type of sexual behavior that is considered to be a mental disorder; in the *International Classification of Diseases* (ICD), the diagnostic taxonomy typically used in Europe, the term "disorders of sexual preference" is favored. Both classification systems require symptoms or behaviors to be recurrent and to cause distress to the individual or to interfere with the individual's personal functioning (rather than their impact on others). The two manuals list a number of specific types of "abnormal" sexual preferences in this category, but the reality is that any sexual behavior can meet the bill. Indeed, the ICD-10 (World Health Organization, 1992) acknowledges that "erotic practices are too diverse and many too rare or idiosyncratic to justify a separate term for each" (p. 220). Furthermore, as a number of authors have noted, nondeviant behaviors, if hypersexual in nature, can also cause marked distress or dysfunction, and probably should be included under the paraphilic rubric as "paraphilia-related disorders" (Coleman, 1991; Kafka, 2003b). Although the diagnostic definitions in the DSM and ICD have major shortcomings, they do at least make clear that psychiatric involvement in sexual behavior requires a medical rather than a social or moral basis.

These three categories—sexual offending, sexual deviance, and paraphilia—overlap, but are not identical. Rape, for example, is a sexual offense, but usually it does not amount to either sexual deviance or a paraphilia (although it could). Sadism may be sexually deviant, but it is not in itself a criminal offense; nor is it a paraphilia if it does not involve a nonconsenting other person, distress the individual, or interfere with the individual's interpersonal functioning. And, if the notion of paraphilia-related disorders is correct, compulsive masturbation can be recognized as a psychiatric problem without being either sexual deviance or a sexual offense. Thus, while some nonpsychiatric authorities like Marshall (1997) seem perplexed that a child molester who is not distressed by his arousal is not considered to suffer from a paraphilia (at least not according to DSM-IV criteria, although see comments in other chapters of the present volume on the change in DSM-IV-TR that addresses this point), it makes good sense to the psychiatrist who seeks to deliver treatment on a medical rather than a moral basis. A pedophile is certainly sexually deviant, but this does not necessarily make him mentally disordered. The two perspectives, however, are not really at cross purposes: The child molester who seeks out or agrees to treatment for his deviant arousal is recognizing a problem with his sexuality that brings him into the medical tent. Whether or not the individual has committed an offense is irrelevant.

MEDICAL MODELS

The problems of using either the DSM or ICD concept of paraphilias to make medical diagnoses of sexual disorders are well rehearsed (Laws & O'Donohue, 1997). The main difficulty is that although the DSM and ICD rightly seek to disentangle concepts of deviance (be they sexual or social) from concepts of disorder, they do so in a clumsy manner, with somewhat arbitrary notions of what constitutes a paraphilia. The focus tends to be on describing behavior rather than psychopathology, and as such it can confuse the very concept they try to elucidate—the distinction between deviant behavior and mental disorder.

A more satisfactory medical understanding of paraphilic behavior depends on being able to describe the psychopathology that underlies it. Without such an account, the distinction between deviance and mental disorder becomes blurred. Toward that end, sexually problematic behaviors have been conceptualized as manifestations of a range of other disorders, such as the obsessive–compulsive disorder (OCD) spectrum, mood disorders, attention-deficit/hyperactivity disorder (ADHD), and personality disorders. While none of these other disorders are exact fits, they do provide models that help explain the psychological processes that might be involved, as well as suggesting possibilities for treatment.

The OCD Spectrum

OCD is characterized by ruminations (unwanted ideas, images, or impulses) and compulsions (repetitive, stereotyped mental acts or behaviors) that are unwanted and distressing (sometimes referred to as "ego-dystonic"), and often associated with feelings of guilt. Typically, the individual makes attempts to resist the thoughts or behaviors, which are associated with high levels of anxiety. Other conditions, such as impulse control disorders (e.g., pathological gambling), addictions, and eating disorders, have similar (but not identical) clinical features and are thus sometimes said to form part of the same psychiatric spectrum (Hollander & Allen, 2006).

Because sexual fantasy can have an obsessive quality to it, and some sexual behaviors appear to be compulsive in nature, it has been suggested that paraphilias and some instances of hypersexuality should be included within the OCD spectrum (Bradford, 2001; Hollander et al., 1996), although whether they should be considered as akin to OCD, behavioral addiction, or problems with impulse control is left vague. The finding that selective serotonin reuptake inhibitors (SSRIs)—which are effective treatments in OCD, because they reduce the intensity and frequency of fantasies as well as feelings of compulsion (Fineberg & Gale, 2005)—can have similar effects in some paraphilias suggests the possibility of shared brain networks and a common causal role for the neurotransmitter serotonin.

But while the concept of OCD spectrum disorders may provide an attractive framework for treatment in some cases (Fong, 2006), whether the relationship between abnormal sexual functioning and OCD spectrum disorders is more than a useful analogy remains to be demonstrated convincingly. Although diagnostic instruments exist for so-called sexual "addictions" (Carnes, 1991; Kafka, 1997), these are not well validated. More importantly, the combination of OCD, addictions, and impulse control disorders into a more or less single entity may result in a blurring of boundaries that can obscure rather than define clinical realities. Determining whether the relevant behaviors are the result of ego-dystonic compulsions, ego-syntonic repetitive activities (i.e., behaviors consistent with an individual's beliefs and view of himself), or a failure to control impulses that falls somewhere in between is not a trivial distinction. The model is strongest when it combines the notions of OCD, addiction, and impulse control, but by doing so it departs from the homogeneity inherent in each of the conditions on its own. This may not be a problem in the long term, provided that a well-defined set of symptoms and behaviors can be validated, and a consistent natural history described.

Mood Disorders and ADHD

A number of studies have reported high levels of various Axis I psychiatric disorders among sexual offenders, with depression and dysthymia particularly common (Kafka,

2003a; Långström, Sjöstedt, & Grann, 2004). While mood clearly has an impact on libido/sexual behavior, the claim is that the two are closely linked through common neurological substrates; as with OCD spectrum disorders, the suggestion is that underlying mechanisms are shared between mood disorders and sexual psychopathology. In particular, serotonergic pathways are known to be involved in both sexual arousal and mood (with low serotonergic activity associated with depression), and activity in the hypothalamic–pituitary axis is also related to mood states and sexual behavior. The problem is that both interact with a wide range of functional systems in the brain, and abnormality in one does not necessarily result in dysfunction in another. Much more evidence is needed before it can be accepted that the same brain systems that regulate mood are also directly involved in sexual arousal and behavior.

As an adjunct to models linking mood disorders with abnormalities in sexual behavior, it has also been argued that a history of ADHD is often found in paraphilic individuals, particularly in the presence of a mood disorder (Kafka & Hennen, 2000). The empirical basis for such a claim, however, is limited (even in adolescents); even if it is confirmed, it remains to be shown that this represents a direct relationship between ADHD and paraphilia, rather than a reflection of the poor impulse control that is often part of the legacy of ADHD in adults.

Personality Disorders

Another medical approach to paraphilias and sexual deviance is to concentrate not on the sexual psychopathology itself, but on the personality characteristics that result in its manifestation in behavior. The assumption is that sexual arousal and sexual behavior are distributed normally in the population, but that even at the extremes psychosexuality becomes problematic only in a minority. The issue, then, becomes the personality pathology that colors the behavior, which frequently but not necessarily amounts to a personality disorder. In support of this is the finding that personality disorders are often reported in populations of sex offenders (Black, Kehrberg, Flumerfelt, & Schlosser, 1997; Långström et al., 2004).

In this model, sexual pathology is viewed as just one of a number of dysfunctional behaviors, reflecting perhaps a disregard for social norms, poor impulse control, or a lack of emotional regulation. The attraction of this model is that it simplifies what needs to be targeted in treatment, but by assuming personality pathology it ignores the issues associated with sexual psychopathology in their own right. Although it may be true that sexual offenders have high rates of personality disorders, the reverse is likely to be true in individuals whose sexual difficulties do not result in offending. In addition, because a diagnosis of personality disorder often carries with it a stigma of therapeutic pessimism, it may be a model evoked by some psychiatrists to justify their disengagement from clinical input.

THE NEUROBIOLOGY OF SEXUAL AROUSAL

Regardless of how adequately or otherwise medical models explain sexual psychopathology, it remains the case that sexual arousal and sexual behavior are mediated by biological mechanisms. An understanding of these mechanisms opens the way for medical (primarily pharmacological) interventions with the potential to ameliorate or modify problematic sexual behavior. Unfortunately, our knowledge of the neurobiological basis of sexual arousal is extremely limited. Much of it is based on animal studies that are of uncertain relevance to humans, while research in humans is made difficult by the complex interaction of developmental, social, psychological, and biological elements that underlie sexual arousal and behavior. As animals become more biologically sophisticated, their sexual behavior becomes increasingly influenced by learning and environment. Matters become even more complicated when one considers differences between men and women. For present purposes, the discussion here focuses only on men.

Although many areas of the brain are involved in sexual arousal and the translation of arousal into behavior, with the cortex being particularly important in humans, the hypothalamus and the limbic system are most closely associated with sexual drive and functioning. Their influence arises partly through their role in modulating the hormonal environment of the body, and partly through their influence on biological drives in general and on emotional states. Most is known about the way in which these areas control testosterone production, and the corresponding relationship between testosterone and male sexual arousal.

Testosterone

Testosterone is fundamental to sexual development, sex drive, and sexual functioning in men. This obvious statement, however, masks our marked ignorance of just how this hormone exerts its effects. Indeed, though the relationship between testosterone and male sexual behavior may be obvious now, Bancroft (1989) has pointed out that as recently as 1948 Kinsey, the founder of modern sex research, believed that hormones were redundant in human sexuality, and that any effect they had was simply mediated by their effect on energy and mood.

Testosterone has both organizational and activational effects on the central nervous system (Sisk, 2006; Sisk & Zehr, 2005):

> *Organizational effects* refer to the role of testosterone in "sculpting" the nervous system into its relatively permanent adult state. This is believed to occur at two different stages of development—initially in the perinatal period, and then during adolescence around puberty. The resulting structural design influences the way in which the adult responds to a range of environmental factors, including but not only sexual stimuli; significantly, there is good evidence from animal studies to show that social experience, at least during "adolescence," is an important determinant of subsequent brain organization.
>
> *Activational effects*, on the other hand, are transient. They depend on the actual presence of testosterone, but are a function of the organizational structure that is already in place and on which the hormone acts. Because of this, the impact of hormonal manipulation in the adult is not readily predictable, as it depends to an extent on events that took place some time before.

As a steroid hormone, testosterone is mostly bound to plasma proteins in the blood, with only about 2% in a free, biologically active form (although this is in equilibrium with bound hormone, which in effect acts as a store). The overall level of testosterone in the circulation is substantially higher than what is required to maintain sexual arousal, which suggests that its peripheral actions (i.e., the maintenance of male secondary sexual characteristics) require substantially more hormone than is required for sexual functioning (Bancroft, 1989).

Testosterone Receptors

Testosterone receptors are widespread both in the brain and in other areas of the body. In the male brain testosterone receptors are most dense in the medial preoptic and ventromedial hypothalamic nuclei, the amygdala, the prefrontal cortex, and the temporal cortex. Animal studies suggest that the influence of these parts of the brain on sexual behavior is dependent on the presence of testosterone. For example, intrahypothalamic implants of testosterone restore normal patterns of sexual behavior in castrated rats, while in cats and monkeys bilateral limbic lesions in the piriform cortex result in a marked intensification of sexual activity, including attempts to mount immature females, males, and inanimate objects, but only in the presence of testosterone (Bancroft, 1989). It is of interest, however, that studies using positron emission tomography or functional magnetic resonance imaging demonstrate testosterone effects in brain areas such as the insula and the claustrum, where as yet testosterone receptors have not been found; still, whether this is an indication that testosterone has general effects independent of its direct presence or is simply a reflection of methodological limitations is unclear (Bancroft, 2005).

Testosterone Secretion

Testosterone is produced by the Leydig cells in the testes, where high local concentrations are necessary for spermatogenesis. (Small amounts of testosterone are also produced by the cortex of the adrenal gland.) The synthesis of testosterone by the Leydig cells is stimulated by luteinizing hormone (LH), a peptide hormone that is released from the anterior pituitary gland in a pulsatile manner. The release of LH in turn is controlled by another peptide hormone, luteinizing hormone-releasing hormone (LHRH)—often referred to as gonadotropin hormone-releasing hormone (GnRH), because in addition to LH it stimulates the release of follicle-stimulating hormone (FSH), a second hormone important to gonadal function. GnRH is synthesized in, and secreted by, cells in the periventricular area of the hypothalamus, under the influence of a range of higher centers; in addition to stimulating LH release, GnRH-producing cells also project into the limbic system. A negative feedback loop means that testosterone inhibits LH secretion both by acting directly on the anterior pituitary and by inhibiting the release of GnRH by the hypothalamus (Figure 31.1).

Prolactin

Prolactin is another peptide hormone released by the anterior pituitary. In females, it is known to have important roles in lactation and in respect to ovarian function. In males, its physiological role is unclear; however, abnormally high levels are associated with erectile difficulties and a diminution of libido—an effect that is independent of testosterone levels (Bancroft, 2005). Prolactin is believed to be modulated by the neurotransmitter dopamine, which *inhibits* its release. Consequently, drugs that block dopamine activity (e.g., the major tranquilizers prescribed in schizophrenia) increase plasma prolactin levels, and are thus associated with impotence and loss of libido as common side effects.

The Role of Testosterone in Sexual and Aggressive Behavior

Testosterone is necessary for normal levels of sexual interest and arousal, which are absent in castrated men. It does not, however, have an immediate effect on sexual function-

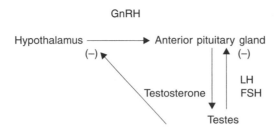

FIGURE 31.1. The control of testosterone secretion.

ing; any changes that are associated with variations in plasma concentration manifest themselves over weeks rather than hours. For example, when testosterone maintenance is withdrawn in hypogonadal men, a reduction in the level of sexual interest does not become apparent for 3–4 weeks, although sexual interest is restored somewhat more quickly, in about 2 weeks; masturbation frequency in these cases is closely associated with levels of sexual interest (Bancroft, 2005).

It is important to recognize that the main effect of testosterone on sexual functioning appears to relate to spontaneous sexual interest and behavior. Sexual functioning itself, including the ability to have erections and engage in sexual intercourse, is maintained even in the absence of testosterone. When testosterone is not present, however, the erectile response becomes strongly stimulus-bound; that is, it depends on immediate sexual cues such as erotic imagery, and is lost once the stimulus is removed (Bancroft, 1989).

Although occasional studies have suggested that testosterone levels are relatively high in violent sex offenders, the results are not consistent. For example, while Rada, Laws, and Kellner (1976) reported that plasma testosterone levels in violent rapists were significantly higher than those of "nonviolent" rapists and child molesters (although still within normal limits), Rada (1981) found higher levels in violent child molesters, with no elevation in the testosterone concentration in violent rapists. Other factors that contribute to aggression further complicate the picture. Perry and colleagues (2003), for instance, reported that aggression was increased in weight lifters who used anabolic steroids, but this was confounded by personality characteristics: The more aggressive individuals also had more antisocial, borderline, and histrionic personality traits. Meta-analyses of the association between testosterone and aggression have described a statistically significant but very modest relationship between the two, with correlation coefficients (r) under .15 (Archer, Birring, & Wu, 1998; Book, Starzyk, & Quinsey, 2001). Furthermore, it may be that dominance status rather than aggression is more closely linked with testosterone concentrations (Mazur & Booth, 1998).

In addition, separating cause from effect is not straightforward. Changes in testosterone levels often follow, rather than precede, relevant behaviors. For instance, testosterone levels are known to be associated with dominance hierarchies in primates (and possibly also in humans, as suggested by Ehrenkranz, Bliss, & Sheard, 1974); however, it has been shown that increases in testosterone levels are most marked *after* a male becomes the dominant member of the group, and decreases in testosterone similarly take place *after* he loses his dominant role (Bernstein, Rose, Gordon, & Grady, 1979; Rose, Bernstein, & Gordon, 1975). In humans, it is known that testosterone levels are higher in the members of winning teams in competitive sports, but the rise occurs after, not before, the competition has finished, and is an effect that appears to be closely associated with mood state (Mazur & Lamb, 1980). This finding is reported even in those who play nonphysical sports or games, such as chess (Mazur, Booth, & Dabbs, 1992), and in spectators who support the winning team (reported in Mazur & Booth, 1998). Even in respect to sexual behavior, plasma testosterone levels in males who have been shown an erotic film peak 60–90 minutes after the film has ended (Pirke, Kockott, & Dittmar, 1974).

When testosterone levels are experimentally manipulated in men with normal baseline levels, changes in sexual arousal and mood are sometimes but not always observed. Anderson, Bancroft, and Wu (1992) gave high doses of exogenous testosterone to young men over a 2-month period, resulting in peak plasma testosterone levels 500% above baseline. Compared with that of men given a placebo, sexual arousal as measured by self-report scales was increased, although, interestingly, sexual activity was not. In contrast, Yates, Perry, MacIndoe, Holman, and Ellingrod (1999) found no effect of exogenous testosterone on either sexual interest or sexual activity, while Buena and colleagues (1993) did not find any change in sexual interest or activity when normal men were first made hypogonadal with medication and then administered various doses of testosterone. Similar studies in older men (over 45), however, have reported a dose–response effect (Gray et al., 2005; Schiavi, Schreiner-Engel, Mandeli, Schanzer, & Cohen, 1990), which may relate to changes in testosterone receptor sensitivity.

Thus, although the importance of testosterone for sexual arousal cannot be disputed, both its mode of action and its precise effects remain to be elucidated. It may, for instance, alter the responsiveness of either general or specific neurological arousal mechanisms; it may have an effect on the processing of sensory stimuli; it may influence motivation and attention; it may do all three; or it may act in entirely different ways. What is clear is that normal levels fluctuate within a wide range, and that only when plasma concentrations fall below a very low threshold (or perhaps rise above a very high one) are overt changes in functioning and behavior observed, albeit over a delayed time period. Testosterone is a necessary component of normal sexual functioning, but it does not act in isolation; it is also likely to have an association with aggression and with dominance, but again as one of many influences.

Dopamine and Serotonin

The neurotransmitter dopamine, which is synthesized in the midbrain, is active in a number of functional systems, including the mesolimbic pathways that are associated with such behaviors as appetite, sleep, and sex; other catecholamines related to dopamine also have relevance to these goal-driven behaviors. Although the mechanisms are unclear, these mesolimbic dopamine pathways are "activating" in nature, facilitating sexual arousal and behavior. In addition to its direct effect on neural systems, dopamine acts indirectly by inhibiting prolactin release from the pituitary gland, thereby suppressing a hormone that acts to dampen sexual functioning. Testosterone enhances dopamine mesolimbic activity, facilitating dopamine release and perhaps increasing receptor sensitivity (Hull, Muschamp, & Sato, 2004).

The neurotransmitter serotonin (5-hydroxytryptamine or 5-HT), on the other hand, is primarily inhibitory in respect to appetitive behaviors, although the situation is complicated by the large number of different 5-HT receptors that are found in the brain, with some having conflicting effects (to date, 7 main receptor types and 15 receptor subtypes have been described). As with dopamine, the basis of 5-HT's activity is uncertain, although in addition to its direct effects on neural systems it has been shown, at least in animal experiments, to inhibit mesolimbic dopamine release (Hull et al., 2004), and to modulate the activity of some 5-HT receptor types (Simon, Cologer-Clifford, Lu, McKenna, & Hu, 1998). Low levels of 5-HT have been implicated in mood disorders, OCD, panic attacks, and impulsive aggression (Coccaro, Siever, & Klar, 1989; Kafka, 2003a; Saleh & Berlin, 2003).

Most of the evidence regarding the role of these two monoaminergic neurotransmitters in sexual behavior either comes from animal studies, or is inferred from the effects that medications known to have an impact on these systems have in humans. For example, in male rats dopamine and dopamine agonists, particularly when active in the hypothalamus, are known to be associated with sexual approach and mating behaviors, while 5-HT inhibits sexual behavior. Similar effects have been shown in primates (reviewed in Bancroft, 1989; Kafka, 2003a; Pomerantz, 1995; Saleh & Berlin, 2003). In human males, the SSRIs, drugs used in the treatment of depression that act by increasing the levels of 5-HT available at receptor sites, are known to have a negative impact on many aspects of sexual functioning; these effects include loss of libido, impaired arousal, erectile dysfunction, and impaired ejaculation (Balon, 2006). Although some researchers have also suggested that impaired serotonergic activity may be associated with abnormalities in the direction of drive, specifically in pedophilia, the evidence for this is weak (Maes et al., 2001).

Although dopamine and 5-HT almost certainly play central roles in sexual arousal and functioning, it should be emphasized that we are well short of understanding the details of how they act, or how they interact with other neurotransmitters and with testosterone. In the case of 5-HT in particular, the multitude of receptor types and the lack of specific receptor agonists and antagonists make teasing out the various effects of this neurotransmitter difficult (Greenberg & Bradford, 1997). Bancroft (1999) has hypothesized that 5-HT-induced inhibition of sexual activity may have had evolutionary importance in reducing sexual behavior at times of higher risk or environmental stress, when attention needs to be focused on other matters. Regardless of whether this is true, what we do know about the relationship between monoamines and sexual activity, limited as it is, can be used to suggest pharmacological approaches to the management of problematic sexual behavior. The limitations in our knowledge, however, mean that any progress is mainly the result of trial and error.

MEDICAL INTERVENTIONS

Although psychological approaches are generally the preferred options in sex offender treatment, pharmacological reduction of arousal may be of benefit in cases where high levels of sexual arousal make psychological techniques difficult. In addition, because psychological treatments are not always successful, complementing such therapy with medical treatments may reduce the risk of reoffending. Indeed, the authors of a large meta-analysis of treatment outcome noted that while pharmacological treatments had a higher effect size on recidivism than did psychological treatments on their own, the pharmacological studies typically also included a cognitive-behavioral component, and this had an independent treatment effect (Lösel & Schmucker, 2005).

From the discussion of the neurobiology of sexual arousal above, it would seem that the two most likely methods for arousal reduction would be either reducing the activity of testosterone or increasing the activity of 5-HT. Toward that end, a large number of studies have examined the effect of manipulating these two biological substrates. The most stark are follow-up studies of sex offenders who were compulsorily castrated in European countries in the early and middle 20th century.

After removal of the testes, plasma testosterone levels fall to prepubertal levels, with some hormone synthesis continuing in the adrenal gland. Although castration was said to be reserved for highly recidivistic and dangerous offenders, this was not in fact the case for many of those who were castrated, who included significant numbers of first-time offenders, homosexuals, persons with mental retardation or mental illness, indecent exposers, and incest offenders; in some countries, women (although the physical basis of this is not made clear), and boys as young as 13, were castrated (Heim & Hursch, 1979; Sturup, 1968). In any case, although beset by substantial methodological problems, follow-up of these offenders reported extremely low recidivism rates—typically below 5% over lengthy time periods. However, while sexual functioning was markedly reduced, many individuals still engaged in low levels of sexual activity. Side effects such as osteoporosis, cardiovascular disease, gynecomastia, redistribution of fat, loss of muscle tone, and "menopausal" symptoms (e.g., hot flashes) were common.

It is not surprising that castration should have a profound impact on sexual reoffending, if we bear in mind that the primary influence of testosterone is on sexual interest and spontaneous sexual activity. Although it is still carried out on a voluntary basis on small numbers of men with sexually problematic behavior, it is an unattractive option for a number of reasons. It is relatively irreversible (although its effects can be countered by exogenous testosterone, taken either surreptitiously or for medical reasons); it cannot be titrated to account for any impact of psychological treatment, age, or the development of healthy relationships; and many surgeons are reluctant to carry out a surgical procedure that is not without risk to meet a social rather than a medical need.

Antiandrogen Medications

Effects similar to those of castration can be achieved by the use of medications intended to reduce the biological activity of testosterone. Specifically, these medications can reduce testosterone synthesis, block its access to receptors in its target cells, or increase its metabolism and removal from the body. Doctors have gained experience with these types of drugs, as they are often prescribed in the treatment of prostate cancer.

Medications containing estrogen (the female hormone) were among the earliest drugs to be used in this way, and were first prescribed in the 1940s. Bancroft, Tennent, Loucas, and Cass (1974) demonstrated that ethinyl estradiol reduced sexual interest and masturbatory activity to levels found in hypogonadal men; they found that while total plasma testosterone actually increased, so too did the proportion bound to plasma proteins, thereby lowering free (i.e., biologically active) hormone. Estrogens were commonly prescribed in North America up to the 1960s to treat sexually aggressive men, but their marked side effects, particularly nausea, cardiovascular complications, and feminization, made their use problematic (Prentky, 1997).

Since the 1960s, two antiandrogens with different modes of action began to be commonly used: in Europe and Canada, cyproterone acetate (CPA); and in the United States and to a lesser extent Canada, medroxyprogesterone acetate (MPA), a synthetic hormone better known for its role as a contraceptive (for patent reasons, CPA is not available in the United States). More recently, GnRH agonists such as leuprolide, tryptorelin, and goserelin—which overstimulate the pituitary, resulting in a depletion of LH and consequently a marked reduction in testosterone synthesis—have been increasingly prescribed.

Although they have similar effects, MPA and CPA have different modes of action. MPA primarily stimulates the breakdown of testosterone in the liver, although it also inhibits the secretion of LH by the pituitary (Saleh & Berlin, 2003). CPA blocks testosterone receptors, although in addition it reduces GnRH secretion by the hypothalamic nuclei and LH secretion from the pituitary. The net result in both cases is to reduce testosterone activity to that seen following physical castration. The doses of both, however, can be titrated so that sexual arousal is reduced but not eliminated.

A number of studies involving the use of these agents have been reported in the literature (for reviews, see Bradford, 1997; Maletzky, Tolan, & McFarland, 2006; Ortmann, 1980; Prentky, 1997; Saleh & Berlin, 2003). They typically show low recidivism rates, usually below 5% (the same rates as described in the follow-up of physically castrated offenders); markedly reduced sexual interest, fantasy, and sexual behavior; and low serum testosterone levels. With some exceptions, however, most involve small numbers of subjects; they often fail to take into account subjects who drop out of treatment; and they are reliant on self-report measures of sexual activity. In addition, double-blind randomized control trials are rare, although one such study involving CPA and placebo demonstrated a significant effect of medication in reducing sexual activity, consistent with the relationship between testosterone and sexual interest (Bradford & Pawlak, 1993).

Although study authors tend to play them down, most of these studies demonstrate that in addition to their efficacy in reducing sexual arousal, antilibidinal medications are also associated with a high level of side effects—in particular, feminization, depression, weight gain, and gynecomastia. Serious side effects, however, appear to be uncommon; this is reassuring, given the potential for negative impact on cardiovascular, hepatic, and endocrine systems.

As referred to above, the use of GnRH agonists is becoming more widespread. These drugs appear to have a more potent impact on testosterone levels than the traditional antilibidinals, as well as a greater effect on sexual arousal and activity—the latter possibly because of their action on GnRH neurons that project to brain areas beyond the pituitary, particularly the amygdala (Rösler & Witztum, 2000). A review of the small literature relating to case reports and studies involving the use of these drugs in sex offenders found very low reoffending rates, with apparently better outcomes for subjects who had previously been prescribed MPA or CPA (Briken, Hill, & Berner, 2003); Rösler and Witztum (1998), for example, reported that in men who remained on tryptorelin for a year, the number of sexual fantasies and urges disappeared completely, and masturbation frequency dropped to at most twice a fortnight. Again, however, sample sizes were small, comparison groups absent, and outcome highly dependent on self-report.

The GnRH agonists are thus apparently more potent and seem to carry with them fewer side effects than the traditional antilibidinals, although hot flashes and osteoporosis are both problematic. Another issue to be taken into account in respect to these agents is their cost, as they are markedly more expensive than either MPA or CPA.

Selective Serotonin Reuptake Inhibitors

Because of the role of 5-HT in sexual arousal, and the efficacy of SSRIs in treating OCD spectrum and mood disorders that bear similarities to the phenomenology found in some individuals with problematic sexual behaviors (Kafka & Prentky, 1994), the use of SSRIs was proposed for the treatment of paraphilias and paraphilia-related disorders. Since the early 1990s, there have been over 200 case reports and open studies reported in the literature (Kafka, 2003a), with most reporting success in reducing the frequency and intensity of sexual fantasy, urges, and arousal, often without negative effects on normal sexual behavior (Greenberg & Bradford, 1997). Fluoxetine, sertraline, and fluvoxamine appear to be the SSRIs most commonly prescribed, and though in theory there should be little difference among them in terms of efficacy, Kafka (1994) found that subjects who did not respond to sertraline improved when switched to fluoxetine. The advantage of SSRIs over the antilibidinals is that they are associated with a much milder side effect profile; gastrointestinal symptoms such as nausea and changes in bowel habits are the most common.

As with the antilibidinals, the evidence concerning the use of SSRIs for paraphilias is supportive, but not robust. Most of the reports involve small numbers of patients and short follow-up periods; there is a heavy reliance on self-report; and there is a dearth of double-blind control studies. A systematic review up to 2001 (Adi et al., 2002) found very few trials that were considered to be of reasonable methodological quality, and none that included cost-effectiveness analyses. Nevertheless, outcomes were positive, and it was concluded that the use of SSRI medications for sex offenders (who were the focus of the review) was warranted.

Major Tranquilizers

Major tranquilizers such as benperidol and fluphenazine, which are used to treat psychotic disorders, are sometimes prescribed to reduce sexual arousal, and in a controlled trial the former was shown to be more effective than placebo in reducing sexual interest (Tennent, Bancroft, & Cass, 1974). They act by blocking dopamine receptors (although some also act at 5-HT receptor sites), and hence give rise to a range of side effects associated with this blockage, particularly movement disorders. Loss of libido and erectile difficulties are also common occurrences (although whether these are the results of direct inhibition of dopaminergic mechanisms or are caused by a secondary rise in prolactin secretion is unclear), but these drugs do not have an effect on testosterone levels. Regardless, the reduction in sexual arousal produced by them is unreliable and unpredictable, and their use is best reserved for cases where a more general reduction in arousal is also sought, or where symptoms of relevant mental illness are present.

PRESCRIBING PROTOCOLS

Although the empirical basis for the efficacy and cost-effectiveness of medication in the treatment of paraphilias and other problematic sexual behaviors is imperfect, antilibidinal and SSRI medications appear to be clinically effective. There are good theoretical reasons for their use, and the limited research evidence is largely supportive, even if its pedigree could be stronger.

Because this is not an area in which large numbers of doctors have an interest, guidance on the use of medication is limited. Bradford (2000, 2001) has suggested an algorithm for the treatment of paraphilias, based on four levels of severity borrowed from DSM-III-R criteria: mild (paraphilic urges that have not been acted on), moderate (urges that have been acted on occasionally), severe (urges that have been acted on repeatedly), and catastrophic (in effect, sexual sadism). Based on these categories, he describes six levels of treatment:

Level 1: Cognitive-behavioral treatment in all cases.
Level 2: SSRIs in all cases of mild paraphilias.
Level 3: A small dose of an antiandrogen if SSRIs are not effective.
Level 4: Full doses of oral antiandrogen treatment in moderate and some severe cases.
Level 5: Intramuscular antiandrogen treatment in severe and some catastrophic cases.
Level 6: Complete suppression of androgens (high doses of GnRH agonists) in some severe and most catastrophic cases.

A similar protocol is outlined by Briken and colleagues (2003).

These approaches, although sensible, run the risk of prescribing for social control rather than medical indications if adhered to slavishly, and it is important to obtain a good clinical understanding of the underlying phenomenology in each case if treatment is to be most effective. It may be, for example, that even a so-called level 3 case would benefit from a GnRH agonist, while in some instances SSRI medication may be more appropriate for an individual who falls at level 5. This was recognized, for example, when determining which offenders should be included in a mandated medication program with Depo-Provera, with clinical as well as risk issues being considered (Maletzky et al., 2006).

CONCLUSION

Sexual behavior in human beings, whether "normal" or not, is more than simply a manifestation of testosterone interacting with monoaminergic neurotransmitter systems in the central nervous system. It is influenced by a complex array of personality characteristics, learning experiences, social factors, and the environment. But medications influencing testosterone functioning and activity in the central nervous system can assist individuals in controlling what is in effect a strong biological drive. However, when an individual's problematic behavior not only affects himself, but can also cause harm to others, there can be confusion about whether the individual or his potential victims are driving treatment. Given the choice between long-term incarceration and taking medication in the community, most such individuals would probably opt for the latter, even at the risk of serious adverse effects caused by the medication; their doctors, however, will need to determine whether the prescription of medication is clinically indicated, or whether it is really only a means of social control. Doctors, of course, are also citizens, and the distinction will not always be an easy one.

REFERENCES

Adi, Y., Ashcroft, D., Browne, K., Beech, A., Fry-Smith, A., & Hyde, C. (2002). *Clinical effectiveness and cost–consequences of selective serotonin reuptake inhibitors in the treatment of sex offenders* (Health Technology Assessment, 6, No. 28). London: Her Majesty's Stationery Office.

Anderson, R. A., Bancroft, J., & Wu, F. C. (1992). The effects of exogenous testosterone on sexuality and mood of normal men. *Journal of Endocrinology and Metabolism, 75*, 1503–1507.

Archer, J., Birring, S. S., & Wu, F. C. W. (1998). The association between testosterone and aggression among young men: Empirical findings and a meta-analysis. *Aggressive Behavior, 24*, 411–420.

Balon, R. (2006). SSRI-associated sexual dysfunction. *American Journal of Psychiatry, 163*, 1504–1509.

Bancroft, J. (1989). *Human sexuality and its problems.* Edinburgh: Churchill Livingstone.

Bancroft, J. (1999). Central inhibition of sexual response in the male: A theoretical perspective. *Neuroscience and Biobehavioral Reviews, 23*, 763–784.

Bancroft, J. (2005). The endocrinology of sexual arousal. *Journal of Endocrinology, 10*, 411–427.

Bancroft, J., Tennent, G., Loucas, K., & Cass, J. (1974). The control of deviant sexual behaviour by drugs: 1. Behavioural changes following oestrogens and anti-androgens. *British Journal of Psychiatry, 125*, 310–315.

Bernstein, I. S., Rose, R. M., Gordon, T. P., & Grady, C. L. (1979). Agonistic rank, aggression, social context, and testosterone in male pigtail monkeys. *Aggressive Behavior, 5*, 329–339.

Black, D. W., Kehrberg, L. L., Flumerfelt, D. L., & Schlosser, S. S. (1997). Characteristics of 36 subjects reporting compulsive sexual behavior. *American Journal of Psychiatry, 154*, 243–249.

Book, A. S., Starzyk, K. B., & Quinsey, V. L. (2001). The relationship between testosterone and aggression: A meta-analysis. *Aggression and Violent Behavior, 6*, 579–599.

Bradford, J. (1997). Medical interventions in sexual deviance. In D. R. Laws & W. O'Donohue (Eds.), *Sexual deviance: Theory, assessment, and treatment* (pp. 449–464). New York: Guilford Press.

Bradford, J. M. W. (2000). The treatment of sexual deviation using a pharmacological approach. *Journal of Sex Research, 37*, 248–257.

Bradford, J. M. W. (2001). The neurobiology, neuropharmacology, and pharmacological treatment of the paraphilias and compulsive sexual behaviour. *Canadian Journal of Psychiatry, 46*, 26–34.

Bradford, J. M. W., & Pawlak, M. A. (1993). Double-blind placebo crossover study of cyproterone acetate in the treatment of the paraphilias. *Archives of Sexual Behavior, 22*, 383–402.

Briken, P., Hill, A., & Berner, W. (2003). Pharmacotherapy of paraphilias with long-acting agonists of luteinising hormone-releasing hormone: A systematic review. *Journal of Clinical Psychiatry, 64*, 890–897.

Buena, F., Swerdloff, R. S., Lutchmansingh, P., Peterson, M. A., Pandian, M. R., Galmarini, M., et al. (1993). Sexual function does not change when serum testosterone levels are pharmacologically varied within the normal male range. *Fertility and Sterility, 59*, 1118–1123.

Carnes, P. (1991). Sexual Addiction Screening Test. *Tennessee Nursing, 54*, 28–29.

Coccaro, E. F., Siever, L. J., & Klar, H. M. (1989). Serotonergic studies in patients with affective and personality disorders. *Archives of General Psychiatry, 46*, 587–599.

Coleman, E. (1991). Compulsive sexual behaviour: New concepts and treatments. *Journal of Psychology and Human Sexuality, 4*, 37–52.

Ehrenkranz, J., Bliss, E., & Sheard, M. H. (1974). Plasma testosterone: Correlation with aggressive behaviour and social dominance in man. *Psychosomatic Medicine, 16*, 469–475.

Fineberg, N. A., & Gale, T. M. (2005). Evidence-based pharmacotherapy of obsessive–compulsive disorder. *International Journal of Neuropsychopharmacology, 8*, 107–129.

Fong, T. W. (2006). Understanding and managing compulsive sexual behaviors. *Psychiatry, 3*, 51–58.

Galski, T., Thornton, K. E., & Shumsky, D. (1990). Brain dysfunction in sex offenders. *Journal of Offender Rehabilitation, 16*, 65–80.

Gray, P. B., Singh, A. B., Woodhouse, L. J., Storer, T. W., Casaburi, R., Dzekov, J., et al. (2005). Dose-dependent effects of testosterone on sexual function, mood, and visuospatial cognition in older men. *Journal of Endocrinology and Metabolism, 90*, 3838–3846.

Greenberg, D. M., & Bradford, J. M. W. (1997). Treatment of the paraphilic disorders: A review of the role of the selective serotonin reuptake inhibitors. *Sexual Abuse: A Journal of Research and Treatment, 9*, 349–360.

Grubin, D., & Mason, D. (1997). Medical models of sexual deviance. In D. R. Laws & W. O'Donohue (Eds.), *Sexual deviance: Theory, assessment, and treatment* (pp. 434–448). New York: Guilford Press.

Heim, N., & Hursch, C. J. (1979). Castration for sex offenders: Treatment or punishment? A review and critique of recent European literature. *Archives of Sexual Behavior, 8*, 281–304.

Hollander, E., & Allen, A. (2006). Is compulsive buying a real disorder, and is it really compulsive? *American Journal of Psychiatry, 163*, 1670–1672.

Hollander, E., Kwon, J. H., Stein, D. J., Broatch, J., Rowland, C. T., & Himelein, C. A. (1996). Obsessive–compulsive and spectrum disorder: Overview and quality of life issues. *Journal of Clinical Psychiatry, 57*(Suppl. 8), 3–6.

Hull, E. M., Muschamp, J. W., & Sato, S. (2004). Dopoamine and serotonin: Influences on male sexual behaviour. *Physiology and Behavior, 83*, 291–307.

Kafka, M. P. (1994). Sertraline pharmacotherapy for paraphilias and paraphilia-related disorders: An open trial. *Annals of Clinical Psychiatry, 6*, 189–195.

Kafka, M. P. (1997). Hypersexual desire in males: An operational definition and clinical implications for males with paraphilias and paraphilia-related disorders. *Archives of Sexual Behavior, 25*, 505–526.

Kafka, M. P. (2003a). The monoamine hypothesis for the pathophysiology of paraphilic disorders: An update. *Annals of the New York Academy of Sciences, 989*, 86–94.

Kafka, M. P. (2003b). Sex offending and sexual appetite: The clinical and theoretical relevance of hypersexual desire. *International Journal of Offender Therapy and Comparative Criminology, 47*, 439–451.

Kafka, M. P., & Hennen, J. (2000). Psychostimulant augmentation during treatment with selective serotonin reuptake inhibitors in men with paraphilias and paraphilia-related disorders: A case series. *Journal of Clinical Psychiatry, 61*, 664–670.

Kafka, M. P., & Prentky, R. A. (1994). Preliminary observations of DSM-III-R Axis I co-morbidity in men with paraphilias and paraphilia-related disorders. *Journal of Clinical Psychiatry, 55*, 481–487.

Långström, N., Sjöstedt, G., & Grann, M. (2004). Psychiatric disorders and recidivism in sexual offenders. *Sexual Abuse: A Journal of Research and Treatment, 16*, 139–150.

Laws, D. R., & O'Donohue, W. (1997). Introduction: Fundamental issues in sexual deviance. In D. R. Laws & W. O'Donohue (Eds.), *Sexual deviance: Theory, assessment, and treatment* (pp. 1–21). New York: Guilford Press.

Lösel, F., & Schmucker, M. (2005). The effectiveness of treatment for sexual offenders: A comprehensive meta-analysis. *Journal of Experimental Criminology, 1*, 1–29.

Maes, M., de Vos, N., van Hunsel, F., van West, D., Westenberg, H., Cosyns, P., et al. (2001). Pedophilia is accompanied by increased plasma concentrations of catecholamines, in particular epinephrine. *Psychiatry Research, 103*, 43–49.

Maletzky, B. M., Tolan, A., & McFarland, B. (2006). The Oregun Depo-Provera Program: A five year follow-up. *Sexual Abuse: A Journal of Research and Treatment, 18*, 303–316.

Marshall, W. L. (1997). Pedophilia: Psychopathology and theory. In D. R. Laws & W. O'Donohue (Eds.), *Sexual deviance: Theory, assessment, and treatment* (pp. 152–174). New York: Guilford Press.

Mazur, A., & Booth, A. (1998). Testosterone and dominance in men. *Behavioral and Brain Sciences, 21*, 353–363.

Mazur, A., & Lamb, T. (1980). Testosterone, status, and mood in human males. *Hormones and Behavior, 14*, 236–246.

Mazur, A., Booth, A., & Dabbs, J. (1992). Testosterone and chess competition. *Social Psychology Quarterly, 55*, 70–77.

Ortmann, J. (1980). The treatment of sexual offenders: Castration and antihormone therapy. *International Journal of Law and Psychiatry, 3*, 443–451.

Perry, P. J., Kutscher, E. C., Lund, B. C., Yates, W. R., Holman, T. L., & Demers, L. (2003). Measures of aggression and mood changes in male weightlifters with and without androgenic anabolic steroid use. *Journal of Forensic Sciences, 48*, 646–651.

Pirke, K. M., Kockott, G., & Dittmar, F. (1974). Psychosexual stimulation and plasma testosterone in men. *Archives of Sexual Behavior, 3,* 577–584.

Pomerantz, S. M. (1995). Monoamine influences in male sexual behaviour of nonhuman primates. In J. Bancroft (Ed.), *The pharmacology of sexual function and dysfunction.* Amsterdam: Elsevier Science.

Prentky, R. A. (1985). The neurochemistry and neuroendocrinology of sexual aggression. In D. P. Farrington & J. Gunn (Eds.), *Aggression and dangerousness.* Chichester, UK: Wiley.

Prentky, R. A. (1997). Arousal reduction in sexual offenders: A review of antiandrogen interventions. *Sexual Abuse: A Journal of Research and Treatment, 9,* 335–347.

Rada, R. T. (1981). Plasma androgens and the sex offender. *Bulletin of the American Academy of Psychiatry and the Law, 8,* 456–464.

Rada, R. T., Laws, D. R., & Kellner, R. (1976). Plasma testosterone levels in the rapist. *Psychosomatic Medicine, 38,* 257–268.

Rose, R. M., Bernstein, I. S., & Gordon, T. P. (1975). Consequences of social conflict on plasma testosterone levels in rhesus monkeys. *Psychosomatic Medicine, 37,* 5–61.

Rosen, I. (1996). The general psychoanalytical theory of perversion. In I. Rosen (Ed.), *Sexual deviation* (3rd ed.). Oxford, UK: Oxford University Press.

Rösler, A., & Witztum, E. (1998). Treatment of men with paraphilia with a long-acting analogue of gonadotropin-releasing hormone. *New England Journal of Medicine, 338,* 416–422.

Rösler, A., & Witztum, E. (2000). Pharmacotherapy of the paraphilias in the next millennium. *Behavioral Sciences and the Law, 18,* 43–56.

Saleh, F. M., & Berlin, F. S. (2003). Sexual deviancy: Diagnostic and neurobiological considerations. *Journal of Child Sexual Abuse, 12,* 53–76.

Schiavi, R. C., Schreiner-Engel, P., Mandeli, J., Schanzer, H., & Cohen, E. (1990). Healthy aging and male sexual function. *American Journal of Psychiatry, 147,* 766–771.

Simon, N. G., Cologer-Clifford, A., Lu, S. F., McKenna, S. E., & Hu, S. (1998). Testosterone and its metabolites modulate 5HT1A and 5HT1B agonist effects on intermale aggression. *Neuroscience and Biobehavioral Reviews, 23,* 325–336.

Sisk, C. L. (2006). New insights into the neurobiology of sexual maturation. *Sexual and Relationship Therapy, 21,* 5–14.

Sisk, C. L., & Zehr, J. L. (2005). Pubertal hormones organize the adolescent brain and behaviour. *Frontiers in Neuroendrocrinology, 26,* 163–174.

Sturup, G. K. (1968). Treatment of sexual offenders in Herstedvester, Denmark. *Acta Psychiatrica Scandinavica, 44*(Suppl. 204), 1–64.

Tennent, G., Bancroft, J., & Cass, J. (1974). The control of deviant sexual behavior by drugs: A double-blind controlled study of benperidol, chlorpromazine and placebo. *Archives of Sexual Behavior, 3,* 261–271.

World Health Organization. (1992). *The ICD-10 classification of mental and behavioural disorders: Clinical descriptions and diagnostic guidelines.* Geneva: Author.

Yates, W. R., Perry, P. J., MacIndoe, J., Holman, T., & Ellingrod, V. (1999). Psychosexual effects of three doses of testosterone cycling in normal men. *Biological Psychiatry, 45,* 254–260.

CHAPTER 32

THE PUBLIC
HEALTH APPROACH

A Way Forward?

D. RICHARD LAWS

Elsewhere, I have argued that the concept of "harm reduction" is a public health approach to serious social problems (Laws, 1996, 1999). The underlying principles (see Marlatt, 1998, pp. 49–57) are that harm reduction (1) is a public health alternative to moral, criminal, or disease models of social misbehavior; (2) recognizes abstinence from deviant behavior as an ideal, but accepts reduced harm as an alternative; (3) promotes client advocacy; (4) promotes low-threshold access to treatment services; and (5) is based on a philosophy of compassionate pragmatism. Harm reduction uses what works. Although this is not the language of public health, these goals are clearly within the general mission of public health efforts. The purpose of this chapter is to examine what the general public health approach involves, how it may be applied in the management of sex offenders, and whether it can be effective.

Looking at the problem of sexual deviance from a general public health point of view, Mercy (1999) has described the problem vividly:

> Imagine a childhood disease that affects one in five girls and one in seven boys before they reach 18 . . . : a disease that can cause dramatic mood swings, erratic behavior, and even severe conduct disorders among those exposed; a disease that breeds distrust of adults and undermines the possibility of experiencing normal sexual relationships; a disease that can have profound implications for an individual's future health by increasing the risk of problems such as substance abuse, sexually transmitted diseases, and suicidal behavior . . . ; a disease that replicates itself by causing some of its victims to expose future generations to its debilitating effects.
>
> Imagine what we, as a society, would do if such a disease existed. We would spare no expense. We would invest heavily in basic and applied research. We would devise systems to identify those affected and provide services to treat them. We would develop and broadly implement prevention campaigns to protect our children. Wouldn't we? (p. 317)

Two observations follow from this quotation. First, Mercy (1999) is speaking of child sexual abuse, but much of what he says applies equally well to all forms of sexually abusive behavior. His remarks exquisitely capture the pervasiveness and insidious nature of the problem. Second, the final paragraph of Mercy's remarks describes a classical public health approach to the problem. This approach has worked very well against small-pox, tuberculosis, and polio, and to a lesser extent against drunk driving, smoking, and HIV/AIDS. It has not worked in the area of sexual offending because, for the most part, it has not been tried.

LEVELS OF PREVENTION IN PUBLIC HEALTH

The general public health approach identifies three levels of prevention: (1) "primary," (2) "secondary," and (3) "tertiary" (Henry, 1996; Laws, 2000; McMahon, 1997, 2000). Elsewhere (Laws, 2000, pp. 31–32), I have described how this approach may be applied to sexual deviance.

The primary level of prevention is the classic public health approach. The goal is to prevent deviant behavior from ever starting. As McMahon (1997, 2000) has noted, the public health approach to sexual violence focuses on primary prevention rather than treatment. Many people believe that this approach is exemplified in so-called "Just Say No" programs that teach potential victims—children or adults—how to avoid being victimized. Although such programs constitute primary prevention of a sort, they put the onus of prevention upon actual or potential victims rather than upon perpetrators. Using public health methods for primary prevention would mean educating adults generally about sexual abuse, its magnitude, individuals at risk for abusing and being abused, and ways to intervene or confront abusers if necessary. The best, although minimal, evidence that we have for primary prevention in sexual abuse comes from the Stop It Now! program (see below; Chasan-Taber & Tabachnick, 1999).

The secondary level of prevention is an intervention approach. Here the concern is with persons who have begun to engage in deviant sexual behavior. It is devoted to early identification and intervention. The secondary level would target children, adolescents, and adults. For example, adults would be made aware of signs of unusual sexual interest or activity in children. These may include inappropriate sexual talk, exhibitionism, masturbation, use of pornography, sexual precocity, antisocial attitudes or beliefs, or outright sexual aggression. Such signs should be viewed as deviant sexual behaviors that require intervention. Similarly, adolescent sexual behaviors that exceed accepted social boundaries should be viewed with some alarm, and intervention should be attempted. Situational (incestuous) or opportunistic offenders would fit into this level. At the secondary level of prevention, it is acknowledged that some form of deviant sexual behavior has occurred. A further and very important assumption is that the behavioral patterns are not stable or chronic and that individuals may be amenable to treatment. It is difficult to know how intervention has succeeded with young children at the secondary level. All too often, sexual behavior between children is dismissed as simply play or a stage that a child is passing through. Certainly there is evidence for successful early intervention with adolescents.

The tertiary level of prevention is the criminal justice approach. Here we are dealing with chronic offenders who probably have deeply entrenched patterns of deviant sexual behavior and who have been offending for many years. These are the persons most often seen in medium- and maximum-security prisons, in mental hospitals, and in the community after their release. The word "prevention" is used at this level in the sense of preventing offending from occurring again, or at least of greatly reducing its frequency and intensity. McMahon (2000) has said that "one limitation of this approach is that there is no direct attempt to alter the conditions or attitudes that led the abuser to the point of abuse" (p. 28). A considerable body of clinicians working with clients at this level would disagree with that evaluation.

Persons seen at the tertiary level would usually be candidates for intensive cognitive-behavioral treatment (CBT), behavior therapy to modify fantasies and deviant sexual arousal, and/or antiandrogenic treatments. The goal at this level is always to stop the behavior now and keep it stopped, or at least minimized. Evidence exists to support the efficacy of treatment at the tertiary level (see, e.g., McGrath, Cumming, Livingston, & Hoke, 2003; Yates et al., 2000).

Figure 32.1 summarizes the situation graphically. Although this figure is reprinted from the alcohol abuse literature (Larimer et al., 1998), the message is equally applicable to sexual abuse. The triangle represents a spectrum of possible interventions. The area from the base of the triangle (at left) to the dotted line below "Mild" would represent no known sexual offending. The focus here would be exclusively on primary prevention. The area from "Mild" to the dotted line below "Substantial" would represent the secondary level. Identification and brief intervention would be applied here. From "Substantial" to the apex of the triangle would be the area of tertiary intervention. Several things are noteworthy in this figure. First, primary and secondary intervention never stop. Second, fewer and fewer people are involved as the triangle narrows. Third, specialized treatment, which is most often provided at the tertiary level, is serving the smallest number of clients displaying the most serious (perhaps intractable) problems.

I have elsewhere summarized current efforts to prevent or alter sexual abuse in a classic public health model:

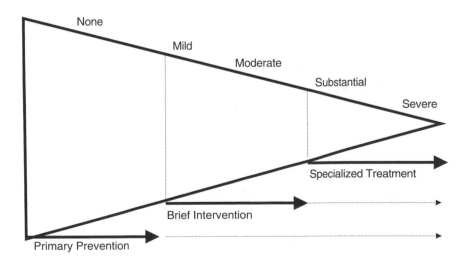

FIGURE 32.1. A spectrum of public health responses to alcohol abuse, which can be applied to sexual abuse. From Larimer et al. (1998, p. 86). Copyright 1998 by The Guilford Press. Reprinted by permission.

In considering sexual violence in a public health perspective it would certainly be ideal if we could focus most of our efforts on primary prevention. While there is much room to exert effort at this level and effort is being exerted, it is far from adequate and much that could be done is simply ignored or put off as not urgent. Most of our efforts are applied at the secondary or tertiary level where [they are] least likely to succeed. (Laws, 2000, p. 32)

THE PUBLIC HEALTH APPROACH TO SEXUAL VIOLENCE

There are four major steps in the general public health approach (McMahon, 1997, 2000; Mercy, Rosenberg, Powell, Broome, & Roper, 1993), which may be equally applicable to the problem of sexual violence (Laws, 2000). McMahon (2000, p. 30) has described these steps (the direct quotes below are from McMahon; the comments in italics on steps 1 and 2 are mine):

1. *Public health surveillance.* This is defined as "the ongoing, systematic collection, analysis, and interpretation of health data." Surveillance involves the tracking of trends in a public health problem. The data are then provided to policymakers who are in a position to do something about the problem. *The sensitivity of a surveillance procedure (i.e., the ability to identify the breadth of the problem) cannot be expected to be very good, given that the majority of sex offenses are not reported. The specificity of the procedure (i.e., the ability to classify supposed offenders accurately once they are identified) would be even worse, particularly if conducted by nonspecialists.*

2. *Risk factor research.* This step focuses on "which factors place an individual at higher risk for an unhealthy consequence." Identification of a risk factor does not mean that all persons exposed to it will develop the consequence. It does say that the unhealthy consequence is more likely if a person is exposed to a specific factor. *These statements are accurate. However, the status of sexual offense risk assessment, in my judgment, is not as good as its proponents profess. Actuarial risk assessments, using static risk factors, are the procedures most often employed (see below). They offer statements of the probability that an offense might occur at specified intervals in the future. This is not useful if intervention is urgent.*

3. *Development and evaluation of programs.* "The likelihood of having effective prevention programs . . . is increased if development of such programs is based on knowledge about modifiable risk factors identified in step two . . . and if the programs are evaluated and modified as suggested by the evaluation results."

4. *Dissemination of information on what works.* The public health approach requires wide dissemination of information. This includes "conferences, journal publications, and networks and can be accompanied by direct consultation and technical assistance."

Let us examine how these steps have thus far been applied toward the goal of controlling deviant sexual behavior.

Surveillance

The dimensions and magnitude of the problem of sexual abuse are not well understood. Such information as we have does not neatly conform to the model presented by

McMahon (2000). Instead, the information is scattered and comes from many diverse sources. Following are some typical examples:

1. Macrolevel estimates, such as those in the Federal Bureau of Investigation (FBI) Uniform Crime Reports, are based on crimes known to the police—but most sexual crimes are never reported.
2. Abel and his colleagues (Abel et al., 1987; Abel & Rouleau, 1990) have described individual sex offenders as having an enormous number of distinct paraphilias; these data were based on a highly deviant and unrepresentative sample, however.
3. Marshall and Barbaree (1988) examined unofficial sources such as complaints, police reports not resulting in charges, and social service investigations to assess the likelihood that a known offender might have committed a crime for which he was never charged; they improved on the official record by a factor of 2.7.
4. Stop It Now! (2000a) has reported that one in five girls and one in seven boys have been sexually abused before the age of 18, and that 90% of these victims knew their abusers (fathers, mothers, siblings, relatives, or other caretakers).
5. The Centers for Disease Control and Prevention (CDC, 2001) conducts the biennial Youth Risk Behavior Survey to assess the prevalence of health risk behaviors in high school students. In the 2001 survey, none of the questions regarding sexual behavior dealt with sexual abuse.
6. The CDC (2000) also publishes the Rape Fact Sheet, based in part on the National Crime Victimization Survey, National Women's Study, and the FBI Uniform Crime Reports. This report provides some limited information on prevalence and incidence, risk factors, and consequences.

These are not extreme examples, but rather common ones in the literature. The message is quite clear: There is a huge problem of sexual abuse, but even reasonably accurate estimates of incidence and prevalence are simply unavailable. The preceding examples should be considered to be snapshots of the problem.

Risk Factor Research

In the sexual abuse field, quite apart from public health issues, risk factor research has developed considerable momentum in recent years. First, the identification of risk factors is a main feature of CBT for sex offenders (Andrews & Bonta, 1998; Hanson, 2006; Hanson & Bussière, 1998; Hanson & Morton-Bourgon, 2004). Generally speaking, CBT seeks to identify the main risk factors threatening an individual in treatment, and then proposes self-management strategies to deal with them. This approach represents a fairly clear application of a secondary or tertiary level of prevention. Second, there has been a movement to develop risk assessment procedures to predict sexual offense recidivism (e.g., Hanson & Bussière, 1998; Hanson & Morton-Bourgon, 2004). There are two types of procedures: actuarial risk assessments, and structured professional guidelines to assess risk. Actuarial risk assessments are based solely on static (unchangeable) risk factors (prior offenses, age, victim gender, substance abuse, etc.). They attempt to predict the exact probability that an individual bearing certain risk factors will reoffend in a given time period (usually 5, 10, or 15 years). This approach is well exemplified in the work of Quinsey, Harris, Rice, and Cormier (1998) and Hanson and Thornton (1999). Structured professional guidelines, on the other hand, combine static and dynamic (changeable) risk factors. This approach, like the Psychopathy Checklist—Revised (PCL-R; Hare, 1991), uses highly specific descriptors and instructions for scoring scale items. Instead of a probability statement, this approach produces a judgment that a person bearing the risk factor(s) is at low, moderate, or high risk for reoffense. The use of structured professional judgment is exemplified in the work of Boer, Hart, Kropp, and Webster (1997) and, more recently, in that of Hart and colleagues (2003). Although closely related, risk factor research is a separate endeavor. For example, Hanson and Bussière (1998) performed a meta-analysis on a large number of sex offender recidivism studies and outlined a series of reoffense risk factors that has had a major impact on treatment design. This analysis was followed up and largely supported by that of Hanson and Morton-Bourgon (2004). In other related work, Andrews and Bonta (1998) have been highly instrumental in tying risk factors to treatment goals. Although widely accepted, their approach has been subject to stringent review and analysis (Ward, Melser, & Yates, 2007; Ward & Stewart, 2003).

The meta-analyses suggest that guarded optimism about the success of treatment may be warranted. However, they are very nonspecific. Saying that CBT is the best model to adopt is very different from saying that CBT including A, B, C, and D components is the best option. The Andrews and Bonta (1998) model based on risk, need, and responsivity fares much better in terms of specificity, because there is a direct effort to match the offender to the intervention.

Development and Evaluation of Treatment Programs

Although things have improved in recent years, the useful yield of clinical information in this area has been appallingly low in general. From the mid-1970s to the late 1980s, the National Institute of Mental Health (NIMH) rather lavishly funded a number of treatment demonstration projects. After 15 years it became apparent that the information gained did not justify the expense, and NIMH abandoned funding for large-scale projects of this type.

This situation was not helped by the publication of a crucial and quite critical review of sex offender treatment (Furby, Weinrott, & Blackshaw, 1989). The review reported that early efforts at treatment were unsuccessful due to poor methodology and outcome evaluation. These results were taken by many to indicate that sex offender treatment did not work. In fact, Furby and colleagues (1989) offered specific suggestions for improving clinical intervention and outcome evaluation, and many of these have been adopted in the ensuing years.

The advent of meta-analysis has been a blessing for the evaluation of treatment outcome studies. The previously mentioned meta-analyses by Hanson and Bussière (1998) and by Hanson and Morton-Bourgon (2004) have been highly instrumental in identifying dynamic risk factors to guide treatment development. The Association for the Treatment of Sexual Abusers (ATSA) has established the Collaborative Outcome Data Project to examine treatment outcome from multiple sites. In the first two reports from this project, Hanson and colleagues (2000, 2001) performed a meta-analysis of data from 43 studies (combined $N = 9,454$). The average follow-up periods ranged from 12 months to 16 years, with a median of 46 months for both treatment and comparison groups. Averaged across all studies, the sexual offense recidivism rate was 12.3% for the treated groups and 16.8% for the comparison groups (38 studies, unweighted average). For general criminal recidivism, the rates were considerably higher (treatment = 27.9%, comparison = 39.2%; 30 studies). CBT (k = 13) and systemic treatment (k = 2) showed the greatest reductions in both sexual recidivism (from 17.4% to 9.9%) and general recidivism (from 51% to 32%). Forms of treatment operating before 1980 had little effect (a finding that supports the data of Furby et al., 1989).

A much larger analysis by Lösel and Schmucker (2005) examined both published and unpublished outcome studies that used biological as well as psychological treatment. They examined 69 studies (combined N = 22,181). One-third of these were published after 2000, and one-third appeared outside of North America. Lösel and Schmucker defined "recidivism" very broadly, from incarceration to lapses in sexual behavior. They found a 11% recidivism rate for treated offenders and a 17.5% rate in comparison groups. The average follow-up period was 5 years (treated M = 63.54 months, SD = 42.09; comparison M = 62.41 months, SD = 42.37). They concluded that treatment provided a 37% reduction in recidivism, and, like Hanson and colleagues (2001), they found that CBT had the greatest impact on sexual recidivism.

The preceding meta-analyses provide brief and encouraging looks at contemporary developments in treatment outcome evaluation. However, these are insufficient. There is as yet no coordinated national or international effort to fund this type of research. That is what will be required for a true public health approach to this problem.

Dissemination of Information on What Works

There has also thus far been no large-scale effort in the sexual abuse field to collate and disseminate information on exactly which assessment and treatment strategies appear to be most effective in maintaining treatment gains and reducing recidivism. Two excellent recent books with a clinical emphasis can be generally helpful (Marshall, Anderson, & Fernandez, 1999; Marshall, Fernandez, Marshall, & Serran, 2006); these highly experienced clinicians help to point the way for program developers and evaluators. In addition, the persuasive meta-analyses of treatment outcome described above (Hanson et al., 2001; Lösel & Schmucker, 2005) and the identification of dynamic risk factors (Hanson & Bussière, 1998; Hanson & Morton-Bourgon, 2004) tell us something about some things that work.

A controversy regarding what works and what does not has been raging in criminology for over 30 years. Gendreau (1996) cited the famous "nothing works" review by Martinson (1974) as kicking off the battle. He stated that Martinson's paper was highly influential in justifying "abandoning rehabilitation and redirecting American correctional philosophy and practice to a new era of deterrence and 'doing justice' " (p. 145). In Gendreau's view, severe deterrence policies (e.g., "three-strikes" laws) have come to dominate U.S. correctional policy. On the other hand, he said, during this same period an impressive number of studies demonstrated effective treatment services in corrections. Gendreau cited in particular the meta-analysis by Lipsey (1992) as a review of all treatment studies that had control group comparisons. This was a review of 443 treatment programs; 64% of the studies reported reductions in recidivism in favor of the treatment group. Gendreau summarized Lipsey's findings:

> The average reduction in recidivism was 10%. . . . [W]hen the results were categorized by the general type of program . . . reductions in recidivism were as high as 18%. . . . However,

one must sort out those characteristics that differentiate between programs that reduced recidivism and those that did not. When that was done the results became even more impressive. Reductions in recidivism routinely ranged from 25% to 60%, with the greatest reductions found for community-based rather than prison programs. (pp. 148–149)

Gendreau, of course, was talking about treatment programs for general criminal offenders. Let us now examine the "what works" argument applied to sex offenders (Hanson, 2006). Influenced by the work of Andrews and Bonta (1998), Hanson (2006) stated that that there are three essential elements in effective correctional interventions: (1) "risk" (treating only offenders who are likely to reoffend [moderate or higher risk]); (2) "need" (targeting criminogenic needs); and (3) "responsivity" (matching treatment to offenders' learning style and culture). In the general Andrews and Bonta model, "criminogenic needs" are identified as follows:

1. Antisocial personality (impulsive, adventurous, pleasure-seeking, restlessly aggressive, callously disregarding others).
2. Grievance/hostility.
3. Antisocial associates.
4. Antisocial cognitions.
5. Low attachment to family or lovers.
6. Low engagement in school or work.
7. Aimless use of leisure time.
8. Substance abuse.

"Noncriminogenic needs" that should not be targeted in treatment are identified as these:

1. Personal distress.
2. Major mental disorder.
3. Low self-esteem.
4. Low physical activity.
5. Poor physical living conditions.
6. Low conventional ambition.
7. Insufficient fear of official punishment.

When this model is applied to sex offenders, criminogenic needs include the following:

1. Deviant sexual interests (paraphilias).
2. Sexual preoccupations.
3. Antisocial orientation (lifestyle instability, rule violation, antisocial personality disorder).
4. Attitudes tolerant of sexual assault.
5. Intimacy deficits (emotional identification with children, lack of stable love relationships).

Factors unrelated to sexual recidivism include these:

1. Victim empathy.
2. Denial/minimization of sexual offenses.

3. Lack of motivation for treatment.
4. Internalizing psychological problems (anxiety, depression, low self-esteem).
5. Sexual abuse in childhood.

There is clearly considerable overlap of criminogenic needs between general criminal offenders and sex offenders.

Hanson (2006) did not make specific recommendations regarding the *content* of treatment programs; he focused instead on the factors that make programs work effectively. For recommendations on program content, I would recommend consulting the books by Marshall and colleagues (1999, 2006). For a newer approach to treatment structure, interested readers might consult Ward and colleagues (2004) and Ward, Yates, and Long (2006). Hanson suggested that the following are some keys to effective treatment implementation:

1. Select staff members for relationship skills.
2. Print or record treatment manuals.
3. Train staff intensively.
4. Start small.

Characteristics of effective therapists, according to Hanson, include the following:

1. Ability to form meaningful (warm, accurately empathic, rewarding) relationships with offenders.
2. Provision of prosocial direction (emphasizing skills, problem solving, values).

And these are some ways things can go wrong:

1. Misuse of risk principle:
   a. Same program for all offenders, regardless of risk/need.
   b. Low-risk offenders introduced to high-risk offenders.
   c. High-risk cases excluded from the program.
2. Focus on noncriminogenic needs.
3. Offenders feeling judged or rejected.
4. Rewarding criminal thinking:
   a. Blind acceptance of alternative subcultures.
   b. Rewarding candor.
   c. Procriminal attitudes of staff members.
5. Punishing prosocial acts.

Hanson's (2006) recommendations are obviously highly influenced by the work of Andrews and Bonta (1998), who have developed a criminological theory based on the above-mentioned three factors: risk, need, and responsivity. "Risk" in this sense refers to identifying those factors that are highly predictive of recidivism. These high-risk offenders are the ones believed to profit most from intensive treatment. Treatment, they say, must target "criminogenic needs" (i.e., those factors most likely to generate criminal behavior) as listed above. The notion of criminogenic needs has filtered into the sexual abuse field through the meta-analyses identifying specific risk factors (e.g., Hanson & Bussière, 1998; Hanson & Morton-Bourgon, 2004) and through the development of actuarial risk predictors (Hanson & Thornton, 1999; Quinsey et al., 1998) and structured professional guidelines for assessing risk (e.g., Boer et al., 1997; Hart et al., 2003). "Responsivity" refers to the principle that the treatment delivered must be relevant and responsive to the needs and capabilities of the offenders.

Ward and Stewart (2003) and Ward and colleagues (2007) have subjected the Andrews and Bonta (1998) theory to a stringent critical analysis. They claim that the concepts of risk and need are confounded, and that the theory delivers considerably less overall than it promises. These authors are distressed that treatment goals consistently focus on criminogenic risk factors and simply ignore noncriminogenic needs, such as low self-esteem, anxiety, and personal distress. They contend that sex offenders are, after all, human beings who may desire and have a right to fulfilling personal lives. Ward and Stewart argue:

> [W]hen offenders enter a rehabilitation programme they are implicitly asking therapists: "How can I live my life differently?" This requires clinicians to offer concrete possibilities for living [a] good or worthwhile life that takes into account each individual's abilities, circumstances, interests, and opportunities. Ethical questions involve clinicians in the consideration of what constitutes a worthwhile life and are not exhausted by issues related to their conduct. There is no discretion here[;] every therapeutic intervention is buttressed by assumptions about what constitutes a desirable outcome, and therefore points to [a] vision of human well being and fulfillment. The rehabilitation of offenders should be driven by an enhancement model. (p. 27)

Although the preceding sounds like a retreat to the old psychodynamic methods, I do not agree. Ward is a powerful cognitive-behaviorist voice in the sexual abuse field, and he is calling for a broadening of treatment goals—not restriction, and certainly not retreat.

So where does this end? An aggressive public health model would agree with Ward and Stewart's (2003) recommendations. That model would urge the maximum effort to make offenders' lives better and more fulfilling, while not removing the focus on risk factors associated with interpersonal violence, abuse, and recidivism. However, until such time as what works is conceptualized, tested, and marketed on a far broader scale than anything imaginable today, we will remain right where we are—not stuck, but moving forward piecemeal, and ever so slowly.

SEXUAL ABUSE AS A PUBLIC HEALTH ISSUE

McMahon and Puett (1999), speaking of child sexual abuse, stated that although violence per se is seen as a major public health issue, the abuse of children (or, for that matter, any sexual abuse) has not received attention as a public health issue. They noted (as I have above) that independent studies have provided some information on the epidemiology of the problem, have discovered risk factors for abuse, and have developed some promising treatment programs. However, there has been no systematic effort to target sexual abuse as a primary prevention goal.

In 1997, McMahon and Puett (1999) reported, the CDC assembled a panel to advise the agency on developing a national response to child sexual abuse. This broadly based group represented federal and state agencies concerned with health issues, clinicians, former abusers, and victims of abuse. Their charge was to determine how to raise awareness of child sexual abuse as a public health problem, and to suggest how the federal government might respond to it. Three work groups were formed, to cover these issues: (1) research, surveillance, and evaluation; (2) public awareness and education; and (3) public policy. In what follows, I summarize the major findings of this panel (McMahon & Puett, 1999, pp. 260–265). The issues raised by this panel apply equally well to sexual violence of all kinds; my phrasing of several recommendations reflects this. Not all of the recommendations are included here.

Research, Surveillance, and Evaluation

The first work group recommended the following:

1. Develop a standardized surveillance system that reports to state agencies. The goal is to capture both reported and unreported cases of abuse. Using the health care delivery sector as a source of surveillance information on unreported cases should be considered.
2. Identify risk factors for perpetration of sexual abuse. This could be accomplished through prospective studies comparing persons who become abusers with those who do not. Define treatment modalities and match these with abuser type.
3. Conduct research to determine the parameters of normative sexual behaviors and fantasies at various developmental stages.
4. Encourage universities to offer courses on sexual abuse.

Public Education and Awareness

The second work group recommended the following:

1. Quickly disseminate research findings to the public and policymakers. What are the most promising practices for early intervention? Outcome studies are needed to determine treatment effectiveness. Cost–benefit issues must be examined.
2. Create a public health agency that deals only with sexual abuse.
3. Develop powerful, person-oriented messages about sexual abuse that will allow people to understand it, free of defensiveness and denial.
4. Create a framework for the media to address sexual abuse frankly. The media's focus on sensational cases leads many middle-class people to believe that sexual abuse is not their problem.
5. Develop a consensus among experts on how to prevent and intervene in cases of sexual abuse. This should be framed as a community issue involving experts from various disciplines. These experts need to provide a consistent message to persons not involved in the abuse on how to recognize, respond, and intervene.
6. Target educational efforts toward medical and mental health professionals, the public, and the media.

Public Policy Issues

To some extent, many of these recommendations overlap with the preceding ones. The third work group recommended the following:

1. Elevate the position of sexual abuse on the national public health agenda. The CDC should encourage public health departments at the state and federal levels to address the issue. States should hold annual research and training meetings, and should disseminate information on promising programs. The main problem here is not only to address the issue, but to fund research, treatment programs, and educational programs.
2. Fund a nationwide study of the problem by the prestigious National Academy of Sciences.
3. Encourage collaboration among agencies dealing with sexual abuse.
4. Encourage foundations to support prevention and research activities.
5. Increase federal funding for research and evaluation. Given the history of recent decades, this seems unlikely to happen.
6. Increase career development incentives in the sexual abuse area. These would be career development grants for clinicians-researchers working in this area.
7. Develop a strategy to increase political activism among adult survivors of sexual violence and their families.

In examining these recommendations, one can easily see that this is an enormous task that would require determined involvement of the U.S. federal government. McMahon and Puett (1999, p. 264) stated that there are many barriers to the realization of these recommendations. There is no common reporting system across states, so there is no surveillance system. There is currently no spokesperson in public health to become the voice for this issue. Foundations do not typically support sexual abuse prevention. The media cover the sensational cases, not the everyday abuse that is the norm. The sociolegal attitude toward sex offenders assures them that if they step forward and ask for treatment, highly punitive sanctions are likely to await them. A final barrier, I might add, is the negative, denying attitude of the public in general. To the ordinary citizen, sexual abuse is something that is happening to someone else, on another street, in another town—anywhere but in his or her own backyard.

STOP IT NOW!: THE CAMPAIGN TO PREVENT CHILD SEXUAL ABUSE

Stop It Now! (2000a) is a community-based public health organization that broadly considers all three levels of prevention. It is not a treatment program, but is able to make appropriate referrals. Their position is that adults, not children or other victims of sexual abuse, are responsible for stopping sexual violence. Their goals are to increase awareness and knowledge about sexual abuse in both offenders and the general public. They encourage abusers to come forward, report their abuse, and make themselves accountable so they may be referred for treatment. In addition, they work with families, peers, and friends of abusers, helping them learn to confront the perpetrators. The main goal is to bring sexual abuse out of the shadows and make it a central object of community concern.

Stop It Now! conducts media campaigns to educate the general public and to change governmental policy regarding sexual abuse. The organization is aware that there is a large and growing social science literature on sexual abuse. It notes, however, that very little of that literature addresses sexual abuse from a public health point of view. Therefore, it conducts its own research through correspondence with recovering sex offenders, through Internet-based questionnaires, and through focus groups. The organization's contacts with social scientists working in the sexual abuse area ensure that its public health messages are received by professionals.

Chasan-Taber and Tabachnick (1999; see also "Evaluation of a Child Sexual Abuse Prevention Program," 2001) have reported on a pilot program that Stop It Now! conducted in Vermont. The purpose of the pilot program was to make an "assessment of public attitudes and beliefs . . . in Vermont to identify facilitators and barriers to adult-targeted child sexual abuse prevention" (Chasan-Taber & Tabachnick, 1999, p. 280). The research was conducted by a market research group, using what these authors called a "social marketing campaign."

Information was initially gathered by a telephone survey in 1995, then followed up in a second survey in 1997. Using random-digit dialing, the Stop It Now! researchers generated a representative sample of 200 Vermont residents; 67.3% agreed to participate. The researchers then asked the participants whether they were familiar with the term "child sexual abuse," what they thought it was, and whether they could identify characteristics or warning signs of sexually abusive behavior. The results indicated that most adults were familiar with the term; however, only about half could define it. Two-thirds of the respondents believed that sex offenders lived in their communities, but were unsure of what signs might indicate who was an abuser. Slightly fewer than half believed that abusers could stop their behavior.

The researchers also formed two small focus groups for each of the three target audiences: adult male abusers, friends and families of adult abusers, and parents of adolescent abusers. This approach was conducted within treatment groups and support groups, and was supplemented by interviews and questionnaires. The work with the focus groups was based on a public health research procedure enabling researchers to organize information into a framework that will guide the choice of intervention strategies. Chasan-Taber and Tabachnick (1999) describe the structure:

> This framework suggests the assessment of predisposing, enabling, and reinforcing factors. *Predisposing factors* deal with a person's knowledge, attitudes, beliefs, values, and perceptions. These are the social and psychological forces that may motivate or inhibit an individual or group to participate in child sexual abuse prevention programs. . . . *Enabling factors* refer to the availability and accessibility of specific resources or skills and policies and procedures that enhance or inhibit appropriate preventive action. . . . *Reinforcing factors* are those elements that appear subsequent to the behavior and provide continuing incentives for the behavior to become persistent. (pp. 282–283; emphasis added)

Stop It Now! then began its social marketing campaign. The goals were to (1) increase adults' awareness and knowledge about sexual abuse, and (2) to have an impact on abusive behavior. The organization blanketed the media—providing information on radio, cable television, and network television; editorials and stories in newspapers; advertising in buses; an interactive website; and advertising banners. All of this was directed toward the three targeted audiences. The program's staffers established one-to-one outreach through treatment providers and other professionals, parent groups, victim advocacy groups, public agencies, and nonprofit organizations. They also set up workshops, conferences, and training, and provided informational materials. A toll-free help line was established to enable offenders to report themselves, as well as to receive information and, if necessary, a referral to treatment providers. Each abuser was given a confidential

ID number. Using this number, the abuser could telephone a clinician and be evaluated without being reported to the police or child protective organizations.

The success of the first 2 years of the program was evaluated in 1997. This included a second telephone survey, interviews with a number of "key decision makers and leaders" in Vermont, and an analysis of the effectiveness of the telephone help line. The telephone survey revealed a 20% increase in recognition of the term "child sexual abuse." There was a 10% increase in the belief that sex offenders probably live in one's community. People were still uncertain that offenders could stop their behavior, but thought that treatment might be effective. Interviewees were less certain of what to do if confronted with a situation of sexual abuse. The community leaders could accurately describe the nature of the Stop It Now! program. They identified an increase in public awareness, getting abusers into treatment programs, and advancing the concept that abusers are human as the main contributions of the program. By late autumn 1997, the help line had received 241 calls; 23% were from abusers, and half were from persons who were aware of specific cases of abuse. The rest of the calls were primarily requests for information.

In 2000, Stop It Now! (2000b) reported on a 1999 follow-up of the social marketing program. The results of this second follow-up could be summarized under four major headings:

1. *Abusers will call for help*. In the first 4 years, there were 657 calls to the help line; 15% of these calls came from abusers, and 50% from persons who were acquainted with an abuser or a victim. About 25% had heard of the help line through the media, 29% from the Stop It Now! website, and 25% from professionals or other help lines or agencies.

2. *There was an increase in adults who could talk about sexual abuse*. The number of citizens who could explain what child abuse is almost doubled in 4 years. Overall awareness of the problem was high.

3. *Adults need better skills to stop abuse*. By 1999, 38% of citizens could name at least one warning sign of sexual abuse. Eighty-eight percent said that they would take direct action if they "definitely" were aware of sexual abuse. However, this fell to 66% if abuse was merely "suspected." Sixty-six percent of respondents said that they had never reported their own abuse. Only 54% of respondents knew where to refer a sexual abuser, compared with 77% who knew where to refer someone with a drinking problem. Only 19% agreed that abusers could stop if they wanted to, but 69% agree that they could stop with appropriate treatment. When presented with descriptive behavioral scenarios, 43% of respondents did not know whether the cases were sexual abuse or "might be" abuse. The organization stated (Stop It Now!, 2000b), "Adults do not seem aware of their potential role in preventing . . . abuse: identifying emerging problems, confronting difficult situations, reporting suspicions of sexual abuse, or referring someone to a qualified treatment provider" (p. 4).

4. *Abusers can stop the abuse*. The program identified 118 people who voluntarily sought assistance for sexual behavior problems (20 adults, 98 adolescents). Through state attorneys and victim advocates, the program identified 15 adults and 10 adolescents who turned themselves in to the legal system.

The two evaluations of the Stop It Now! pilot program in Vermont tell us several things. First, they show that a community-based grassroots effort can succeed in promoting a general public health effort aimed at an extremely serious social problem. In a very real sense, Stop It Now! has done what the U.S. government, with its vast array of resources, has not had the courage to undertake. Second, considering the amount of effort and the high skill level that went into the social marketing campaign, the results are quite encouraging—but, in their overall impact, they will be disappointing to some. However, this began as a pilot program, and the evaluations report results from only the first 4 years. If Stop It Now! keeps the pressure on, the data should improve over time. Third, and perhaps the most important message, is that Vermont is one of the smallest of the U.S. states. If, in 4 years of intensive campaigning, it was difficult to get Stop It Now!'s message across, imagine how difficult it would be to get it across in the remaining 49 states.

SUMMARY AND FUTURE DIRECTIONS

As clinicians and researchers in the area of sexual abuse, we like to pride ourselves on the fact that, unlike most people, we have voluntarily undertaken the fight against a pervasive social menace. And so we should. It is too often forgotten that in reality we are holding our fingers in the dike, struggling to hold back the inexorable tide of sexual abuse. This is admirable, to be sure, but it is a battle that we are not winning. As I have attempted to show in the brief discussion of Figure 32.1, most of our therapeutic efforts are focused at the tertiary level and, to a lesser extent, at the secondary level. This is perfectly understandable, because here reside the identified offenders who are available to us. If we are ever to have a major impact upon the problem of sexual abuse, however, we must focus intense effort on primary prevention—stopping the behavior before it ever gets started.

We cannot wait for any nation's central government to wake up and do something about this problem. That may or may not happen, and it seems unlikely. Governments may acknowledge that sexual abuse is indeed a public health problem, but given the intensely negative social climate concerning sexual offending, they are far more likely to leave it up to the police, the courts, and the correctional system to address the problem. That this approach has not been successful is manifestly evident.

If we are to do what needs to be done—if we are to make a difference that really matters—I suggest that we adopt a model such as that pioneered by Stop It Now! This organization has already done much of the research on how to make social marketing work, and its staff is willing to share that information with anyone. If enough centers undertook this public health model and reported their results to a central organization such as Stop It Now!, ATSA, or the American Professional Society on Abuse of Children (APSAC), an enormous database could be compiled within a very few years. Armed with this information, we could confidently approach federal and state/provincial governments and demand an endorsement of a public health approach to sexual abuse. It will only be when we commit ourselves to a primary prevention approach that we will be able to say confidently that we have done what needs to be done.

I am impressed by the public health model, and I wish to remain optimistic about it. However, a careful reading of this chapter shows that, despite its somewhat messianic tone, the model as described is full of holes. Much of the necessary scientific information on sexual abuse is missing. We need a national (and international) will to carry out this task, which has the properties of a crusade. It does not appear that we have that will at present. As a society, we are willing to devote hundreds of millions of dollars to crimes that we say we care about (property offenses, interpersonal violence, terrorism), but almost nothing to sexual abuse. Given this disgraceful discrepancy, what can we say? We do not seem to value preventing sexual abuse (other than verbally), but we clearly value attempting to prevent more ordinary sorts of crimes. Preventing or stopping sexual abuse to the best of our ability is extremely costly in terms of focus, time, and money to set up a system and then monitor, evaluate, and maintain it. A system like this at a national level may cost even more hundreds of millions of dollars. It can be done, however. If we actually care about this problem, we must put our money where our mouths are. If we do not, that says more about us than we want to know.

ACKNOWLEDGMENT

An earlier version of this chapter appeared as Laws (2003). Copyright 2003 by Sage Publications. Reprinted by permission.

REFERENCES

Abel, G. G., Becker, J. V., Mittelman, M. S., Cunningham-Rathner, J., Rouleau, J. L., & Murphy, W. D. (1987). Self-reported sex crimes of nonincarcerated paraphiliacs. *Journal of Interpersonal Violence, 2*, 3–25.

Abel, G. G., & Rouleau, J. L. (1990). The nature and extent of sexual assault. In W. L. Marshall, D. R. Laws, & H. E. Barbaree (Eds.), *Handbook of sexual assault: Issues, theories, and treatment of the offender* (pp. 9–21). New York: Plenum Press.

Andrews, D. A., & Bonta, J. (1998). *The psychology of criminal conduct* (2nd ed.). Cincinnati, OH: Anderson.

Boer, D. P., Hart, S. D., Kropp, P. R., & Webster, C. D. (1997). *Manual for the Sexual Violence Risk–20.* Vancouver: British Columbia Institute Against Family Violence.

Centers for Disease Control and Prevention (CDC). (2000). *Rape fact sheet: Prevalence and incidence.* Retrieved from *www.cdc.gov/ncipc/factsheets/rape.htm*

Centers for Disease Control and Prevention (CDC). (2001). *Fact sheet: Youth risk behavior trends.* Retrieved from *www.cdc.gov/nccdphp/dash/yrbs/trend.htm*

Chasan-Taber, L., & Tabachnick, J. (1999). Evaluation of a child sexual abuse program. *Sexual Abuse: A Journal of Research and Treatment, 11*, 279–292.

Evaluation of a child sexual abuse prevention program—Vermont, 1995–1997. (2001, March 7). *Journal of the American Medical Association, 285*, 1147–1148. (Original work published in *Morbidity and Mortality Weekly Report*, 2001)

Furby, L., Weinrott, M. R., & Blackshaw, L. (1989). Sex offender recidivism: A review. *Psychological Bulletin, 105*, 3–30.

Gendreau, P. (1996). Offender rehabilitation: What we know and what needs to be done. *Criminal Justice and Behavior, 23*, 144–161.

Hanson, R. K. (2006, September). *What works: The principles of effective interventions with offenders.* Plenary presentation at the meeting of the Association for the Treatment of Sexual Abusers, Chicago.

Hanson, R. K., & Bussière, M. T. (1998). Predicting relapse: A meta-analysis of sexual offender recidivism studies. *Journal of Consulting and Clinical Psychology, 66*, 348–362.

Hanson, R. K., Gordon, A., Harris, A. J. R., Marques, J. K., Murphy, W., Quinsey, V. L., et al. (2000, November). *The effectiveness of treatment for sexual offenders: Report of the Association for the Treatment of Sexual Abusers Collaborative Data Research Committee.* Plenary presentation at the meeting of the Association for the Treatment of Sexual Abusers, San Diego, CA.

Hanson, R. K., Gordon, A., Harris, A. J. R., Marques, J. K., Murphy, W., Quinsey, V. L., et al. (2001). First report of the Collaborative Outcome Data Project on the Effectiveness of Psychological Treatment of Sexual Offenders. *Sexual Abuse: A Journal of Research and Treatment, 14,* 169–194.

Hanson, R. K., & Morton-Bourgon, K. (2004). *Prediction of sexual recidivism: An updated meta-analysis* (User Report No. 2004-02). Ottawa: Department of the Solicitor General of Canada.

Hanson, R. K., & Thornton, D. (1999). *Static-99: Improving actuarial risk Assessment for sexual offenders* (User Report No. 1999-02). Ottawa: Department of the Solicitor General of Canada.

Hare, R. D. (1991). *Manual for the Psychopathy Checklist—Revised.* Toronto: Multi-Health Systems.

Hart, S. D., Kropp, P. R., Laws, D. R., Klaver, J., Logan, C., & Watt, K. A. (2003). *The Risk for Sexual Violence Protocol (RSVP): Structured Professional Guidelines for Assessing Risk of Sexual Violence.* Burnaby, BC, Canada: Simon Fraser University, Mental Health Law and Policy Institute.

Henry, F. (1996, November). *Creating public policy through innovative prevention strategies.* Plenary presentation at the meeting of the Association for the Treatment of Sexual Abusers, Chicago

Larimer, M. E., Marlatt, G. A., Baer, J. S., Quigley, L. A., Blume, A. W., & Hawkins, E. H. (1998). Harm reduction for alcohol problems: Expanding access to and acceptability of prevention and treatment services. In G. A. Marlatt (Ed.), *Harm reduction: Pragmatic strategies for managing high-risk behaviors* (pp. 69–121). New York: Guilford Press.

Laws, D. R. (1996). Relapse prevention or harm reduction? *Sexual Abuse: A Journal of Research and Treatment, 8,* 243–247.

Laws, D. R. (1999). Harm reduction or harm facilitation?: A reply to Maletzky. *Sexual Abuse: A Journal of Research and Treatment, 11,* 233–240.

Laws, D. R. (2000). Sexual offending as a public health problem: A North American perspective. *Journal of Sexual Aggression, 5,* 30–44.

Laws, D. R. (2003). Sexual offending is a public health problem: Are we doing enough? In T. Ward, D. R. Laws, & S. M. Hudson (Eds.), *Sexual deviance: Issues and controversies* (pp. 297–316). Thousand Oaks, CA: Sage.

Lipsey, M. W. (1992). Juvenile delinquency treatment: A meta-analytic inquiry into the variability of effects. In T. D. Cook, H. Cooper, D. S. Cordray, H. Hartmann, L. V. Hedges, R. J. Light, et al. (Eds.), *Meta-analysis for explanation* (pp. 83–127). New York: Russell Sage Foundation.

Lösel, F., & Schmucker, M. (2005). The effectiveness of treatment for sexual offenders: A comprehensive meta-analysis. *Journal of Experimental Criminology, 1,* 117–146.

Marlatt, G. A. (1998). Basic principles and strategies of harm reduction. In G. A. Marlatt (Ed.), *Harm reduction: Pragmatic strategies for managing high-risk behaviors* (pp. 49–68). New York: Guilford Press.

Marshall, W. L., Anderson, D., & Fernandez, Y. (1999). *Cognitive behavioural treatment of sexual offenders.* Chichester, UK: Wiley.

Marshall, W. L., & Barbaree, H. E. (1988). The long-term evaluation of a behavioural treatment program. *Behaviour Research and Therapy, 26,* 499–511.

Marshall, W. L., Fernandez, Y. M., Marshall, L. E., & Serran, G. A. (Eds.). (2006). *Sexual offender treatment: Controversial issues.* Chichester, UK: Wiley.

Martinson, R. (1974). What works?: Questions and answers about prison reform. *The Public Interest, 35,* 22–54.

McGrath, R. J., Cumming, G., Livingston, J. A., & Hoke, S. E. (2003). Outcome of a treatment program for adult sex offenders: From prison to community. *Journal of Interpersonal Violence, 18,* 3–17.

McMahon, P. M. (1997, October). *The public health approach to the prevention of sexual violence.* Plenary presentation at the meeting of the Association for the Treatment of Sexual Abusers, Arlington, VA.

McMahon, P. M. (2000). The public health approach to the prevention of sexual violence. *Sexual Abuse: A Journal of Research and Treatment, 12,* 27–36.

McMahon, P. M., & Puett, R. C. (1999). Child sexual abuse as a public health issue: Recommendations of an expert panel. *Sexual Abuse: A Journal of Research and Treatment, 11,* 257–266.

Mercy, J. A. (1999). Having new eyes: Viewing child sexual abuse as a public health problem. *Sexual Abuse: A Journal of Research and Treatment, 11,* 317–321.

Mercy, J. A., Rosenberg, M. L., Powell, K. E., Broome, C. V., & Roper, W. L. (1993). Public health policy for preventing violence. *Health Affairs, 12,* 7–29.

Quinsey, V. L., Harris, G. T., Rice, M. E., & Cormier, C. A. (1998). *Violent offenders: Appraising and managing risk.* Washington, DC: American Psychological Association.

Stop It Now! (2000a). *About Stop It Now!* Retrieved from *www.stopitnow.com/about.htm*

Stop It Now! (2000b). *Four year evaluation: Findings reveal success of Stop It Now! Vermont* (Report No. 5). Haydenville, MA: Author.

Ward, T., Bickley, J., Webster, S. D., Fisher, D., Beech, A., & Eldridge, H. (2004). *The self-regulation model of the offense and relapse process: Vol. 1. Assessment.* Victoria, BC, Canada: Pacific Psychological Assessment Corporation.

Ward, T., Melser, J., & Yates, P. M. (2007). Reconstructing the risk–need–responsivity model: A theoretical elaboration and evaluation. *Aggression and Violent Behavior, 12*(2), 208–228.

Ward, T., & Stewart, C. (2003). Criminogenic needs and human needs: A theoretical model. *Psychology, Crime, and Law, 9,* 125–143.

Ward, T., Yates, P. M., & Long, C. A. (2006). *The self-regulation model of the offense and relapse process: Vol. 2. Treatment.* Victoria, BC, Canada: Pacific Psychological Assessment Corporation.

Yates, P. M., Goguen, B. C., Nicholaichuk, T. P., Williams, S. M., Long, C. A., Jeglic, E., et al. (2000). *National sex offender programs (moderate, low, and maintenance intensity levels).* Ottawa: Correctional Service Canada.

INDEX

Page numbers followed by *f* indicate figure, *n* indicate note, and *t* indicate table.